BRITISH AUTHORS
BEFORE 1800

THE AUTHORS SERIES

Edited by Stanley J. Kunitz and Howard Haycraft

AMERICAN AUTHORS: 1600-1900
BRITISH AUTHORS BEFORE 1800
BRITISH AUTHORS OF THE NINETEENTH CENTURY
THE JUNIOR BOOK OF AUTHORS
TWENTIETH CENTURY AUTHORS

Edited by Stanley J. Kunitz

TWENTIETH CENTURY AUTHORS: FIRST SUPPLEMENT

Edited by Muriel Fuller

MORE JUNIOR AUTHORS

BRITISH AUTHORS
BEFORE 1800

A Biographical Dictionary

Edited by

STANLEY J. KUNITZ

and

HOWARD HAYCRAFT

COMPLETE IN ONE VOLUME WITH
650 BIOGRAPHIES AND
220 PORTRAITS

NEW YORK
THE H. W. WILSON COMPANY
NINETEEN HUNDRED FIFTY-TWO

Preface

THIS volume is intended as a companion to four earlier reference works produced by the same editors and publisher: *American Authors: 1600-1900, British Authors of the Nineteenth Century, The Junior Book of Authors,* and *Twentieth Century Authors.* Like them, its purpose is to bring together in one place, in concise and convenient form, pertinent biographical and critical information about the literary figures of the period defined.

In all, the volume contains biographies of some 650 authors, of both major and minor significance, from the dawn of English literature to Cowper and Burns. (Later authors are, of course, found in *British Authors of the Nineteenth Century* and in *Twentieth Century Authors.*) As in the other volumes of the series, the biographies are arranged alphabetically, with cross-references from variant name forms. The sketches range in length from approximately 300 to 1500 words, roughly proportionate to the importance of the subjects. Following each sketch is a list of the principal works of the author in question, with dates of original publication as generally accepted. Selected source material about each author is also listed as a suggestion for further study.

In the preparation of the volume the editors have had the pleasure of working with a small but unusually capable staff of research specialists, whose contributions are hereby gratefully acknowledged:

Miriam Allen deFord, Eleanor Evans Kunitz, Vivian Mercier, Jessie M. Rella, and Earle F. Walbridge.

In selecting the portraits which illustrate 220 of the longer biographies, a special effort was made to discover authentic and representative portrayals of the subjects. Dates of portraits and names of artists have been indicated wherever known; absence of such attribution, however, should not be taken as casting doubt on any portrait. To the best of our belief all the likenesses included were originally obtained from life, and clearly fanciful or imaginary depictions were shunned, even when this meant foregoing a portrait entirely. We are happy to acknowledge our indebtedness to Mr. Kneeland McNulty for his painstaking work in tracing and establishing the portraits; to the staff and resources of the New York Public Library; and to the British Information Service for the use of 60 portrait reproductions copyright by the National Portrait Gallery, as follows:

Joseph Addison, Christopher Anstey, Francis Bacon, Sir William Blackstone, Viscount Bolingbroke, James Boswell, John Bunyan, Edmund Burke, Robert Burns, Samuel Butler, Geoffrey Chaucer, the Earl of Chesterfield, Colley Cibber, the Earl of Clarendon, William Congreve, James Cook, William Cowper, Thomas Cranmer, John Donne, Michael Drayton, William Drummond, John Dryden, John Evelyn, John Fletcher, David Garrick, Edward Gibbon, Mary Godwin, Oliver Goldsmith, Thomas Gray, William Harvey, Thomas Hobbes, James I, Samuel Johnson, William Laud, John Locke, Andrew Marvell, John Milton, Sir Thomas More, Sir Isaac Newton, Samuel Pepys, Alexander Pope, Joseph Priestley, Matthew Prior, Sir Walter Raleigh, Samuel Richardson, William Shakespeare, Richard Brinsley Sheridan, Sir Philip Sidney, Adam Smith, Tobias Smollett, Sir Richard Steele, Laurence Sterne, Sir John Suckling, Jonathan Swift, Sir William Temple, William Tyndale, Izaak Walton, Horace Walpole, John Wesley, John Wilkes.

In a work of this scope it is inevitable, despite the most scrupulous care, that some errors should occur. We should appreciate having any such brought to our attention so that they may be corrected in future printings.

THE EDITORS

BRITISH AUTHORS
BEFORE 1800

British Authors Before 1800

ADDISON, JOSEPH (May 1, 1672-June 17, 1719), essayist and journalist, was the eldest son of Lancelot Addison, who became Dean of Lichfield when the boy was nine, and of his first wife, Jane Gulston, sister of the Bishop of Bristol. The mother died when her son was fourteen.

Addison was born in Milston, near Amesbury, Wiltshire, and sent to school in Amesbury, Salisbury, and Lichfield before going to the Charterhouse. Then he proceeded to his father's college, Queen's College, Oxford, but his prowess in Latin poetry earned him a demyship at Magdalen after two years. He received his M.A. in 1693, but remained at Oxford as a fellow until 1699, when a royal pension of £300 a year enabled him to have four years of travel in France, Italy, and Germany. His fellowship he did not resign until 1711. The pension ceased with the death of William III, and the consequent fall of Addison's Whig friends who had secured it for him. In spite of statements to the contrary, Addison was never really poverty-stricken, though it was necessary for him in youth to be frugal.

He returned to England to be made momentarily famous by his poem, *The Campaign*, written in honor of Marlborough's victory at Blenheim. His reward was a sinecure office in the excise, which he held all his life, throughout his tenure of other posts. These came in quick succession—undersecretary of state to Lord Sunderland, secretary to Lord Halifax on a mission to Hanover, chief secretary to Lord Wharton, Lord Lieutenant of Ireland, and a seat in Parliament from 1708 to his death. He sat as a Whig for two constituencies, but so far as has been recorded never opened his mouth in the House of Commons.

The fall of the Whig government arrested Addison's political career, but gave him leisure for a far more important one. He had already attracted attention as a writer, not only by his Latin poems and *The Campaign*, but also by a book on Italy, a literary essay, and the editorship of the *Whig Examiner*. Now he renewed an old friendship with his former schoolmate, Richard Steele,*qv* who in 1709 had started *The*

JOSEPH ADDISON   M. Dahl

Tatler. Addison, then in Dublin, began to contribute to it; in all, in its two years of life, he fathered 42 of the 271 numbers (it was a tri-weekly), and was co-author of 36 others. He was now ready to blossom out as probably the finest essayist in the English language. In 1711 he and Steele started *The Spectator*, which was published daily for twenty-one months, and subsequently was continued for a while under other hands.

Two hundred and seventy-four of the *Spectator* papers are by Addison—nearly all of those relating to "Sir Roger de Coverley" are his. He also contributed twenty-four essays to the later reincarnation of *The Spectator* under Budgell, and fifty-one to Steele's later periodical, the *Guardian*. It is on the *Spectator* essays that Addison's preeminent position as an essayist rests, though perhaps in his own time he was better known as the author of the tragedy, *Cato*, which was hailed as "greater than Shakespeare" (it was the period of Shakespeare's eclipse), and which, says Leslie Stephen, "marks the nearest approach in the English theatre to unreserved acceptance of the French canons."

It is impossible, however, to overestimate the impact of *The Spectator* on early eight-

1

eenth century England. It had lightness and grace, and yet it was a mentor. It portrayed a middle way between Puritan asceticism and Restoration rowdiness. Its ridicule does not wound, it reforms without cant; as Macaulay said, it "reconciles wit and virtue." And all this is done in a style unsurpassed for ease, simplicity, and clarity. Even Dr. Johnson, the arch-Tory, paid ungrudging homage to Addison's style. He was not an original thinker, but he was a genuine scholar who possessed "that eloquence of form which turns human utterance into literature."

With the death of Queen Anne in 1714 and the return of the Whigs to power, Addison resumed his political career. He was appointed secretary to the Lords Justices, then once again chief secretary of Ireland, one of the commissioners for trade and the colonies, and finally, in 1717, one of the Secretaries of State during Lord Sunderland's premiership. This was the period of Addison's greatest fame, wealth, and power, but it was also the least happy portion of his life. He had been in failing health for some years, and finally was obliged to drop all active offices in 1718. In 1716 he had married Charlotte, Dowager Countess of Warwick, whom he had known for many years and whose son had been his protegé and almost his pupil. The marriage was probably not very happy, though not so unhappy as gossip reported. Addison was a reticent, shy man, not given to displaying his emotions. The heavy formality of his wife's milieu doubtless often did weigh on his spirits, but he was forty-four at his marriage (almost past middle age by eighteenth century standards), and could hardly have expected an idyll of romantic passion. The couple had one daughter, who lived to extreme old age, but seems to have been mentally deficient.

How much the rupture of his almost life-long friendship for Steele saddened Addison cannot be known; certainly it made Steele most unhappy. Steele, lovable, improvident, ebullient, was a counterfoil to the taciturn and rather stiff Addison; Addison took to treating him almost as if he were a wayward son who needed harsh correction, and Steele was badly hurt. Finally politics embroiled

them in a war of pamphlets, and though Steele made gestures of reconciliation, it was too late. They were still at outs with each other when Addison died in London at only forty-seven, of asthma and dropsy.

Because Addison was so much less appealing a figure than Steele, there is a tendency to disparage him in favor of his more extroverted colleague. He had besides plenty of enemies, both political and literary. Pope quarreled with him, but then Pope quarreled with everybody. Swift liked him, and Swift did not like many people. He has even been arraigned for intemperance, in an age when every gentleman was a hard drinker; the truth seems to be that it took a few drinks to make him endure social give-and-take. Chiefly he was accused of coldness and arrogance, but these seem to have been mere masks of shyness, behind which there existed both modesty and sensitiveness of spirit. No one was very close to him, unless it was Steele; and Steele, in spite of their unfortunate rift, loved and admired him to the end.

He could write more warmly than he could speak or act. As Harold Routh remarks in *The Cambridge History of English Literature*, "when Steele and Addison ceased to collaborate, both became authors of secondary importance. . . . In a sense, they collaborated with their age. Without any deep fund of ideas or sympathy, they raised . . . the essay to a degree of perfection never since surpassed." Steele himself, in his preface to *The Drummer* (produced anonymously), said the last word on his friend as a writer—though it applied to his essays rather than to his frigid and artificial dramas—when he praised his "eloquence, purity, and correctness." If to these attributes be added ease and grace, plus fancy rather than imagination, and great classical learning, we have a true description of Addison's essays. Despite their conventionality of thought and their limitation to the interests of their day, they are supreme in their field.

As a poet, Addison scarcely exists today, except for the still well-known hymn, "The Spacious Firmament on High" ("Creation" music by Haydn). As a dramatist, in a sense he never did exist—*pace* the contemporary admirers of *Cato*. As an essayist, he will live while English is read.

PRINCIPAL WORKS: The Campaign, A Poem, 1704; Remarks on Several Parts of Italy, 1705; The Spectator, 1711-12; Cato, A Tragedy, 1713; The Drummer, or The Haunted House, 1716; Dialogues Upon the Usefulness of Ancient Medals, 1721; Of the Christian Religion, 1721; Works (T. Tickell, ed.) 1721; A Collection of the Psalms, 1756; Miscellaneous Works, 1914; Letters (W. Graham, ed.) 1941.

ABOUT: Aikin, L. Life of Addison; Courthope, W. J. Addison; Dobrée, B. Essays in Biography; Dobson, A. Introductory Essay, Spectator (ed. of 1897-98); Fraser, J. G. Sir Roger de Coverley and Other Literary Pieces; Johnson, S. Lives of the Poets; Macaulay, T. B. Essay on Addison's Life and Writings; Oliphant, M. Historical Sketches of the Reign of Queen Anne; Phillips, R. Addisoniana; Stephen, L. Hours in a Library; Thackeray, W. M. English Humorists of the Eighteenth Century.

AELFRED. See ALFRED

AELFRIC, called **GRAMMATICUS** (955?-1020?), Anglo-Saxon religious writer, was unfortunately the possessor of so common a name of his era that he has frequently been confused with other writers of the time. It seems certain, however, that the author of the *English Homilies* was the Aelfric who was Abbot of Ensham. Very little is known of his personal life. He was educated at the Benedictine monastery at Winchester, though he may already have been a monk at Abingdon, whence Ethelwold, Bishop of Winchester, imported some of the more intellectually inclined brothers to study and then to teach.

In any event, Ethelwold, who with his father Ethelward was Aelfric's great patron, in 987 sent him as novice-master to Cernel (Cerne Abbas), Dorsetshire, and by that time he had been ordained a priest. It was there he wrote the two series of *Homilies*, dedicated in Latin prefaces to Sigeric, Bishop of Canterbury. In 1005 Aelfric became the first Abbot of Ensham (Eynsham), Oxfordshire. All that is known of him beyond this is that he left a will dated in 1020.

P. G. Thomas has remarked that "Aelfric was not only the greatest prose writer, he was also the most distinguished English theologian, in his own time, and for five centuries afterwards. In no sense was he an original thinker, but he kept the lamps alight." It must be remembered that all his writing, in Latin or in the vernacular, was for his pupils, to enable them to teach religion to the laity. He had a great scorn for the ignorance of the secular clergy of his day, and strove mightily to increase the learning of the monasteries. His master in style was King Alfred, though he outdoes the king in grace and ease; Old English had by Aelfric's time become a literary language.

In none of his work does Aelfric claim originality; it is derived from many sources —St. Gregory, St. Augustine, St. Jerome, Bede, Alcuin, Priscian, Donatus. Theologically he was a child of his time; later, the reformers tried to adduce him as evidence that in the tenth century the English church disbelieved in transubstantiation and in the immaculate conception of the Virgin. One thing that colors all his writing is the universal belief (until after the date had passed) that the world would come to an end in 1000. In the *Homilies* he explained that he was translating church history and doctrine into English for the benefit of the unlearned, to prepare them for Judgment Day. He was a skilled teacher, who understood the importance of clarity and simplicity, and who believed thoroughly that the way to maintain religion was to encourage learning.

Some of Aelfric's writing, especially the *Lives of the Saints*, is highly alliterative and rhythmic, falling naturally into a four-beat meter—a heritage from early Anglo-Saxon poetry. If there is confusion in understanding some of the doctrines he taught, it is a confusion of language, not of thought. His own attitude toward his writing is evidenced by his reluctance to translate the Old Testament (at the request of Ethelward); he considered much of it "not suitable for simple minds." His Latin grammar and glossary, with the *Colloquium* written later, were designed as textbooks for the abbey schools. He was primarily a teacher, but a natural gift turned his texts and homilies into literature.

There was, of course, no "publication" in his own day, and his works remained in manuscript until publication in later centuries.

PRINCIPAL WORKS: Canons of the Old and New Testament (W. L'Isle, ed.) 1623; Latin Grammer and Glossary (W. Somner, ed.) 1659; Heptateuchus (E. Thwaites, ed.) 1699; De Temporibus Anni (T. Wright, ed.) 1841; English Homilies (B. Thorpe, ed.) 1844-46; Lives, or Passions of the Saints (W. W. Skeat, ed.) 1881-1900.

ABOUT: Anglo-Saxon Chronicle; Skeat, W. W. Memoir *in* Lives, or Passions of the Saints; Ten Brink, E. Early English Literature; White, C. L. Aelfric, a New Study of His Life and Writings.

AKENSIDE, MARK (November 9, 1721-June 23, 1770), poet, essayist, physician, was a self-made—or a friend-made—man. His father was a butcher in Newcastle-on-Tyne, and indeed Akenside was lame all his life from a childhood accident when a cleaver fell on his leg. The family were Presbyterians and it was partly by church aid that he was sent to Edinburgh to study for the Presbyterian ministry. Instead, that center of medical research of the period deflected his ambitions—though it is noted that he repaid the money which had been advanced him for another purpose. From Edinburgh he went to Leyden, where he became a Doctor of Physic in 1744. The degree must have been bestowed *in absentia*, for he had come to London permanently the year before.

His first interest at the time was not medicine, but literature. His most famous poem, *Pleasures of the Imagination*, had been begun when he was only seventeen, and was now sold to the publisher Dodsley for the asking price of £120—a remarkable payment even today, but paid by Dodsley on the advice of Pope, who said Akenside was "no everyday writer."

Akenside was one of those men who are born lucky. His next luck came in the form of a wealthy and admiring friend, Jeremiah Dyson, who set up the fledgling physician first in Hampstead and then in Bloomsbury, providing him with a lifelong allowance which enabled him to live in comfort and even in luxury. His medical practice at this time brought him in little; he neglected it for literary pursuits, and what patients he acquired he antagonized by his arrogance and egotism. He began contributing to Dodsley's magazine, the *Museum*, and in 1746 became its editor, meanwhile continuing to write and publish poetry.

When once he did turn his attention to his first profession, however, his advancement was rapid, since despite his personal traits he was a skilled and able physician. In 1753 Cambridge bestowed a doctorate on him and he became a Fellow of the Royal Society. The following year he was made a Fellow of the College of Physicians. In 1759 he was appointed first assistant and then chief physician to Christ's Hospital, but his reputation there was marred by his brutality to the charity patients—which must have been harsh indeed to evoke censure in that callous age. Worse damage was done to his name when, on the accession of George III in 1760, he who had been suspected of republicanism suddenly announced himself as a Tory and was immediately thereafter rewarded by appointment as physician to the queen. The only thing Akenside did not change was his religion, which had been a mild sort of deism since his Edinburgh days. He died at forty-eight, of what was then described as a "putrid fever."

Akenside's best-known and once celebrated poem, the *Pleasures of the Imagination*, is now forgotten, though as late as 1858 George Gilfillan could ask: "Who now cares for Akenside as a philosopher, however much we may admire him as a poet?" The poem, incidentally, is much better as he originally wrote it than as he revised it in later years. His poetry has dignity and sonority, and Dr. Johnson admired his rolling blank verse, but it is all either "occasional" poetry, felicitous but superficial, or didactic poetry of a lofty and rather empty sort.

PRINCIPAL WORKS: The Pleasures of the Imagination, 1744; Epistle to the Reverend Mr. Warburton, 1744; Ode to the Earl of Huntington, 1748; The Remonstrance of Shakespeare, 1749; Ode to the City Gentlemen of England, 1758; Call

After A. Pond

MARK AKENSIDE

to Aristippus, 1758; Ode to the Late Thomas Edwards, 1766; Poems (J. Dyson, ed.) 1772.

ABOUT: Bucke, C. Life, Writings, and Genius of Akenside; Dyce, A. Memoir of Akenside; Johnson, S. Lives of the Poets.

ALBINUS. See ALCUIN

ALCUIN or **ALBINUS** (English name Ealhwine) (735-May 19, 804), theologian and man of letters, was born at Eboracum, the modern York. His name was also sometimes spelt Alchuine, and at the court of Charlemagne he was known as Albinus Flaccus—perhaps in a sort of complimentary reference to the poet Horace. His own writings—all in Latin—were less important than his position as right hand of Charlemagne in the latter's patronage of the revival of learning in Western Europe. (England in that period of the Dark Ages was immensely superior culturally to the Continent.)

Alcuin himself was educated at the cathedral school of York, and accompanied his teacher, Ethelbert, to Rome to search for lost Latin manuscripts. In 766 Ethelbert was appointed Bishop of York, and Alcuin then succeeded him as head of the school. At Parma in 781, on a return journey from Rome, he met Charlemagne, who persuaded him to leave England and become attached to his court; his living the emperor provided for by bestowing on him the abbeys of Ferrières and St. Loup. Alcuin remained in the Frankish court from 781 to 790, teaching the emperor's sons and the young priests attached to the chapel of the palace; he constituted practically the entire faculty of the palace academy, and founded its library.

In 790 Alcuin returned to England, but after two years Charlemagne called him back, and his only subsequent return was for a brief period in 794. To retain his counsel and services permanently, the emperor gave him the great abbey of St. Martin, in Tours, and there he lived for the rest of his life and there he died. The abbey school under Alcuin became a mecca for the scholars of Europe. One of its enterprises was the copying of manuscripts—the sole means by which the classics were preserved during the Dark Ages—and the manuscripts from St. Martin were renowned for their beautiful calligraphy.

A great part of Alcuin's extant writings consists of letters, most of them written to Charlemagne; 312 of them are still preserved. Besides textbooks on rhetoric and grammar (many of them written in the form of dialogues—e.g., the *Dialogue of Pepin and Alcuin*), he wrote sermons and theological treatises, poems and poetic epistles, and a history of the church in York, in verse. He was strictly orthodox in his religious views, and in 794 at the Council of Frankfort, where he was an important figure, he secured the condemnation of the leader of the Adoptionist heresy—a political as well as a theological victory for his royal patron. It is, however, as a cultural enzyme, not as an author in his own right, that Alcuin was chiefly famous in his own day, and that his name has survived. He was, after Charlemagne himself, the life and soul of the Carolingian Renaissance from 781 to his death twenty-three years later, and the impress of his thought remained on Western European culture long after that time. As an authentic figure in English literature he scarcely exists, since he wrote nothing in Saxon and very little of his Latin writing has been translated into English.

PRINCIPAL WORKS: Works (Alcuini Opera) 1617; Letters and Poems *in* Bibliotheca Rerum Germanicorum, 1873; Rhetoric (W. S. Howell, ed. and tr.) 1941.

ABOUT: Duckett, E. S. Alcuin: Friend of Charlemagne; Gaskoin, C. J. B. Alcuin: His Life and His Work; Monod, G. Études critiques sur les sources de l'histoire Carolingienne; Mullinger, J. B. The Schools of Charles the Great and the Restoration of Learning in the Ninth Century; Werner, K. Alkuin und sein Jahrhundert; West, A. F. Alcuin and the Rise of the Christian Schools.

ALDHELM, St. (640?-May 25, 709), theologian, man of letters, belonged by birth to the royal house of Wessex; his father, Kenten or Centwine, may even have been the king. Certainly Aldhelm all his life had great influence with King Ine, who was some sort of kinsman.

Aldhelm's first education came from the Scotsman, Maildulf, who settled in Malmesbury and established a religious community there. Later he became the pupil of Hadrian, an African sent to England by Pope Vitalian as a teacher, who became abbot of Canterbury. Though he later spoke of Hadrian as having been "preceptor of his rude childhood," actually Aldhelm was a man grown when he first went to Canterbury to study Greek, Roman law, astronomy (and astrology), prosody, and arithmetic—which he found "very hard." He went back to Malmesbury to teach, later returning to Canterbury for more study, and finally leaving only because of poor health. When Maildulf died, in 675, Aldhelm became his successor, the community becoming an abbey and he the abbot. Later he also became abbot of two more new monasteries, at Frome and Bradford-on-Avon. About 695 he visited Rome, at the behest of Pope Sergius I. In 705 he was made first Bishop of Sherborne, retaining his abbacies also at the request of the monks, though he had wished to resign them. He wore himself out with his constant pastoral and preaching tours on foot, finally dying at Doulton on one of his diocesan journeys. He was buried in Malmesbury. May 25th, the day of his death, is his "day" as a saint.

In his own time Aldhelm was most widely known for his songs and poems in the vernacular, which Alfred so loved. He was a trained singer, and would stand in the market place singing to his harp until he had a crowd, to which he would then deliver a sermon. None of these English songs is extant. He did, however, write a good deal of Latin poetry, some of which has survived, including the hundred riddles in his *Letter to Acircius on the Number Seven and on Meters*. (The introduction reveals a double acrostic giving Aldhelm's name.) He is supposed to have been the first Englishman to write in Latin verse, and Montague R. James called him "the first considerable literary figure among English writers of Latin." His learning, says James, was "really very great for his day." Though he probably did not know Hebrew, as his contemporaries claimed, and his Greek was small, he was familiar with Virgil, Ovid, Cicero, Pliny, and Sallust, besides a vast number of Christian authors. He was a great builder of churches, and one of the many he erected—St. Lawrence, Bradford—still stands.

Aldhelm could, and did, write simply on occasion; but his chosen style was very ornate and elaborate, often with more devotion to sound than to sense. Still, grandiloquence is, as James remarked, a fault of youth, and Adhelm has freshness and vigor as well as affectation. In his own time the most popular of his Latin writings, after the riddles, were his prose treatise in praise of virginity, and the poetic version which he himself wrote later. Aside from the major works, first collected in 1844, Aldhelm's surviving writings consist mainly of letters on theological topics (chiefly one to the Britons of Cornwall and Devon) and occasional poems.

PRINCIPAL WORKS: Collected Works (in Patres Ecclesiastici Anglici, J. A. Giles, ed.) 1844.

ABOUT: Capgrave, J. Legenda Nova; Duckett, E. S. Anglo-Saxon Saints and Scholars; Faritius, Vita S. Aldhelmi; William of Malmesbury, Gesta Pontificum.

ALEXANDER, Sir WILLIAM, Earl of Stirling (1567?-September 12, 1640), poet, was born at Menstrie, or Menstry, Scotland, probably in 1567 (his most recent biographer argues for 1577), the son of Alexander Alexander and Marion (Couttie) Alexander. On the death of his father in 1580-81 he went to live with a paternal great-uncle, James Alexander of Stirling. He probably attended grammar school there, and may have attended the universities of Glasgow and of Leyden. Alexander accompanied the young seventh Earl of Argyle on the "grand tour" of France, Spain and Italy, during which he probably wrote his love sonnets, *Aurora*. On their return, the Earl introduced him to court, where he was perhaps appointed tutor to young Prince Henry, son of James VI of Scotland (James I of England). To that learned and eccentric monarch Alexander dedicated his *Tragedie of Darius* (1603), and it was probably in hope of retaining the King's favor that he wrote as variously and copiously as he did. His Senecan tragedies on Darius, Croesus, Alexander and Caesar are said to have been based on French models introduced into England by the Countess of Pembroke. Elders of the Scottish Church denounced his metrical translation of the Psalms as "heathenish poeticall conceats."

In 1612 Alexander received a fantastic grant of all Canada, including Nova Scotia—to which he sent an ill-fated expedition—and Newfoundland. Charles II confirmed the grant in 1625. He became Secretary of State for Scotland in 1626; was made Lord Alexander of Tullibody and Viscount Stirling in 1630, Earl of Stirling and Viscount of Canada in 1633; and Earl of Dovan six years later. Alexander died in London, harassed and insolvent, and was buried in the High Church at Stirling.

A few of Alexander's poems survive in anthologies. As for the rest, a recent biographer, Thomas McGrail, writes: "The long Senecan tragedies, the cycle of sonnets, the interminable didactic vapourings in verse—all that dead load of metrical effort that antiquarian zeal has preserved for the present day—are indicative of a mind furnished forth with education and intellectual background, but entirely lacking the imagination, the sensitiveness, the sympathy, the humor, and the inspiration of one who would sing of what the world will be when the years have passed away."

PRINCIPAL WORKS: Aurora, Containing the First Fancies of the Author's Youth, 1604; The Monarchick Tragedies, 1607; Doomesday, 1614; An Encouragement to Colonies, 1624 (as The Mapp and Description of New-England, 1630); Recreations With the Muses, 1637; The Poetical Works of Sir William Alexander (L. E. Kastner and H. B. Charlton, eds.) 1921-1929.

ABOUT: Beumelburg, H. Sir William Alexander als dramatischer Dichter; McGrail, T. H. Sir William Alexander, First Earl of Stirling: a Biographical Study; Modern Language Review, 1908.

ALFRED (AELFRED) (849-October 28, 901), king of the West Saxons, literary historian, translator, man of letters, usually known as Alfred the Great, was the fifth son of King Ethelwulf by his first wife, Osburh, and was born in Wantage, Berkshire. (Ethelwulf later maried the daughter of Emperor Charles the Bald.)

Alfred had no immediate expectation of the throne, but he was nevertheless reared with the frequent royal hazards of that era in mind. There is evidence that he was a charming and precocious child, who grew into one of the most attractive characters of history, and he was apparently a favorite of his father, who had him sent to Rome at the age of five to be hallowed as king by Pope Leo IV, and may himself have taken the child to Rome for a year in 855, though this has been disputed. Alfred did not, however, receive more than the barest education; he knew little Latin until he learned it from Asser,[qv] friend and later biographer.

The father and the older brothers who succeeded him one by one died or were killed in battle, and by the time he was twenty Alfred was the heir presumptive, and involved in the long struggle to save Wessex from the Danish invaders. In 868 he had married Ealhswith, and they had five children.

It was 897 before final victory came in the fight to the death between Saxons and Danes. By the end of 870 the full fury of the Danes burst upon Wessex, and 871 is appropriately known as "Alfred's year of battles." In April of that year King Ethelred, his next older brother, died, and Alfred became king. For five years thereafter an uneasy peace obtained. In 877 the Danes seized Exeter, and the following January they invaded Chippenham, which was Alfred's headquarters. He retreated to Athelney. (It is to this period that the apocryphal "story of the cakes" belongs.) In May 878 Alfred gained a major victory, at Ethandun (probably Edington), clearing both Wessex and Mercia of the Danes. In 885 the Northmen again landed in Kent, only to lose London itself to Alfred the following year. A peace treaty was signed and another lull ensued, ending with the last Danish incursion in 893. The attempt to occupy and conquer Wessex ended at last in 897; the Danes retreated to Northumbria and East Anglia, and the remainder of Alfred's reign—nearly all of which had been consumed by war—was spent in peace.

It is the more remarkable, therefore, that he is remembered, not only as the king who finally swept back the Danes, but primarily as a scholar and as the reviver of learning. As an inscription on a modern monument to him reads: "He found learning dead, and he restored it; education neglected, and he revived it."

The troubled times had all but ruined Saxon culture and scholarship, to which Western Europe had once gone to school. Alfred set himself to remedy this disaster, and in imitation of Charlemagne a century earlier he imported foreign scholars and established a court school, in which he himself was the foremost pupil. He sponsored the *Saxon Chronicle*, and he either had translated, or himself translated, Gregory's *Dialogues* and *Pastoral Care*, Bede's *Ecclesiastical History*, Orosius' *History of the World*, and Boethius' *Consolation of Phi-*

losophy—probably in that order. His other books were his *Handbook* (now lost), a *Code of Laws*, and a translation or adaptation of Augustine's *Soliloquies*. For the translation of the *Pastoral Care* he wrote a preface which has been called "the first important piece of prose in English." He put teachers in all the monasteries, and in effect transferred the center of learning in England from Northumbria to Wessex.

P. G. Thomas, who called Alfred "military leader, lawgiver, scholar, and saint," remarked that "he never lost sight of the importance of keeping his kingdom in organic relation with European civilization." But, he added, "the prominence given to the vernacular during his reign made it possible for English literature to develop on its own lines." Asser, the Welsh scholar whom Alfred brought to teach in his school, as Charlemagne brought Alcuin, said of his patron: "Every minute that he can spare is devoted to the improvement of his mind." He praised the king's "intense desire for learning" and "naturally quick intelligence." Alfred himself wrote that he sought the means "virtuously and fittingly to control the power entrusted to me." Noble in nature and great in mind, he was indeed the Scholar King of whom Plato dreamed.

PRINCIPAL WORKS: (Modern editions in Saxon): Orosius (H. Sweet, ed.) 1883; Proverbs (H. P. Smith, ed.) 1931; Paris Psalter (G. P. Krapp, ed.) 1932. (Translations into English): Whole Works of King Alfred the Great (J. A. Giles, tr.) 1858; Gregory's Pastoral Care (H. Sweet, tr.) 1871-72; Boethius, De Consolatio Philosophiae (W. J. Sedgefield, tr.) 1900; King Alfred's Books (G. F. Browne, tr.) 1920.

ABOUT: Asser (L. C. Jane, tr.); Besant, W. Story of King Alfred; Bowker, A. Alfred the Great; Hayward, F. H. Alfred the Great; Hughes, T. Life of Alfred the Great; Lees, B. A. Alfred the Great; Plummer, C. Life and Times of Alfred the Great; Saxon Chronicle.

AMORY, THOMAS (1691?-1788), fiction writer, was apparently not born in Ireland, although, according to his son Robert, Amory's father went with William III to that country and became Secretary of the Forfeited Estates. The family was said to be connected with the de Monforts, Pettys, and Fitzmaurices. As a boy, Thomas Amory went to a school near Dublin kept by a Dr. Sheridan, who on Swift's authority "shone in his proper element" as a headmaster. The curriculum was unconventional and of high educational value. Amory went up to Trinity College, Dublin, at sixteen, and spent five years there, lodging with Edmund Curll, a bookseller, and studying five subjects of which Divinity was one. About 1787 Amory was living in Westminster, and his one surviving letter proves that he was in Yorkshire in 1773. Part of his old age was spent in Wakefield, where his son was a physician. No clue to the name or character of his wife exists, but in spite of John Buncle's many "charmers," it is safe to assume that he had only one. Amory lived to an advanced age, and was described by his son as "a man of very peculiar look and aspect, though at the same time he bore quite the appearance of a gentleman. He read much, and scarce ever stirred but like a bat in the dusk of evening."

At Trinity, Amory seems to have greatly admired a Mrs. Constantia Grierson, a young bluestocking who edited Terence and Tacitus, was a friend of Swift, and may have inspired Amory's fictitious heroines, those "many accomplished ladies, always young, always attractive, and always ready to discuss divinity, fluxions, the meaning of Hebrew phrases and clauses." His first book was designed to include memoirs of twenty ladies, but boiled down to only one. *The Life and Opinions of John Buncle*, a sort of sequel, called by Leigh Hunt "The Picaresque in Search of the Picturesque," is a rhapsodic "Unitarian romance" which praised the Lake Country twenty years before Gray, attacked Popery and the Athanasian Creed, and showed (according to Katharine Esdaile) "a singular acquaintance with art, literature, and the Fathers [and] a prodigious gust for life." Its total lack of humor rather vitiates Hazlitt's description of Amory as "the English Rabelais."

PRINCIPAL WORKS: Memoirs of Several Ladies of Great Britain, 1755; The Life and Opinions of John Buncle, Esquire, 1765-1766.

ABOUT: Amory, J. The Life and Opinions of John Buncle, Esquire (1904 ed., see Introduction by Ernest A. Baker); Fyvie, J. Some Literary Eccentrics; Pearson, E. L. Books in Black or Red; Essays and Studies by Members of the English Association, 1941.

ANDREWES, LANCELOT (1555-September 25, 1626), theologian, was the son of Thomas Andrewes, master of Trinity House, and was born in London. From the Merchant Taylors' School he went to Pembroke Hall, Cambridge, becoming a fellow of his

LANCELOT ANDREWES

college in 1576 and taking orders in 1580. He was successively vicar of St. Giles', Cripplegate, and prebendary of St. Paul's and then of Southwell. Here he remained for twenty years, from 1589 to 1609, but while retaining this post he advanced rapidly to others of more importance, becoming dean of Westminster in 1601, Bishop of Chichester in 1605, then of Ely in 1609, and finally of Winchester in 1619. This was his final preferment, and he is usually known as Bishop of Winchester.

Andrewes was one of the illustrious group chosen by James I which translated the Bible into English and produced that monument of English prose, the Authorized Version. Indeed, he was a key figure in that group of fifty-four; he was not only a remarkable linguist, familiar with Hebrew, Syriac, Chaldee, Greek, Latin, and some ten other languages, but he was besides a genuine scholar, whose intellectual interests, as Ottley remarked, were "broader, perhaps, than those of any Englishman of his day." He was also a foremost representative of Anglican orthodoxy, steering the tenets of the still young Church of England equally away from Puritanism and from Roman Catholicism.

Personally, Andrewes was an austere and consecrated man who, though frequently called into counsel by Elizabeth, James I, and (in the last year of the Bishop's life) by Charles I, took little part in worldly af-

fairs, but devoted himself primarily to his religious concerns and duties. His sermons were noted for their "passionate and vivid energy" and their scholarly content.

His writings were all theological in nature, many of them purely technical and ecclesiastical. However, his published sermons and his *Manual of Private Devotions*, have real literary interest, besides reflecting the author's unquestioning piety and ascetic saintliness. Just how much of the final version of the King James Bible was from his pen cannot be known, since the revisers were divided into six companies of nine each, and each company worked as a unit. But there can be no doubt that the imprint of his learning and his literary skill remains lastingly on its pages.

T. S. Eliot, who believes that Andrewes' sermons "rank with the finest English prose of any time" (though he grants they are hard reading), has remarked: "Andrewes will never have many readers in any one generation, and his will never be the immortality of anthologies. Yet his prose is not inferior to that of any sermons in the language, unless it be some of Newman's."

PRINCIPAL WORKS: Tortura Torti, 1609; Responsio ad Apologiam Card. Bellarmini, 1610; Articles of Visitation for the Diocese of Winchester, 1625; Two Answers to Cardinal Perron, 1629; 96 Sermons, 1629; A Manual of Private Devotions (R. Drake, ed.) 1648; A Discourse on Second Marriage after Divorce, 1654; Form for the Consecration of a Church or Chapel, 1659; Judgement of the Lambeth Articles, 1660; Notes on the Book of Common Prayer, 1710; Form for Consecrating Church Plate, 1854.

ABOUT: Eliot, T. S. For Lancelot Andrewes; Higham, F. Lancelot Andrewes; Isaacson, H. Lancelot Andrewes; Ottley, R. L. Lancelot Andrewes; Russell, A. T. Lancelot Andrewes.

ANEURIN or **ANEIRIN** (fl. 600?), Welsh poet, is believed to have existed, on the strength of the *Genealogia* annexed to Nennius, *Historia Britonum* (eighth century). According to one theory, he was the son of Caw ab Geraint, chief of the Otadini, who inhabited the seacoast south of the Firth of Forth. Thomas Stephens, who translated his epic poem *Gododin* in 1855, set up a case that Aneurin was a son of Gildas, one of the ten or twenty-one sons of Caw. He seems to have been educated at St. Cadoc's College, Llancarvan, and to have been present at the battle of Cattraeth both as priest and as bard. This battle, depicted in *Godo-*

din, relates the defeat of the Britons of Strathclyde (already partially overcome by drinking too much mead) by the Saxons. *Gododin* is more a series of detached lays or stanzas than a connected poem. The arguments of Edward Davies and Algernon Herbert that the battle described was the massacre of the Britons by Hengist at Stonehenge (472) need not be taken seriously. Stephens identifies the fight with the battle of Degstan, fought in 603, according to the *Saxon Chronicle.*

Aneurin states in the poem that he was taken prisoner, suffered hardships in captivity, and returned to Wales when released. He became friendly with the famous Welsh bard Taliesen; the two poets commemorated the friendship in verse. As an old man he lived with a brother, Nwython, and is supposed to have met his death at the hands of a murderer, one Eldyn ab Einygan.

Gododin, a poem of about 900 lines, is contained in a thirteenth century manuscript, *The Book of Aneirin,* the second oldest extant Welsh manuscript. It is cloudy, confused, and so involved as to make it difficult to obtain a clear picture of whatever battle may have been fought. The poem still fascinates Welsh scholars and commentators.

PRINCIPAL WORK: Gododin.

ABOUT: Jones, T. G. Catraeth [extracts from Gododin] and Hirlas Owain, a Study; Skene, W. F. The Four Ancient Books of Wales Containing the Cymric Poems Attributed to the Bards of the Sixth Century.

ANSTEY, CHRISTOPHER (October 31, 1724-August 3, 1805), poet and satirist, was born in Brinkley, Cambridgeshire, the son of the Reverend Christopher Anstey. He was educated at Bury St. Edmunds, Eton, and King's College; Cambridge, of which he was a fellow. He received his B.A. in 1746, but was refused his M.A. because of his opposition to some changes in the college regulations. Nevertheless, he retained his fellowship until 1754, living at Cambridge most of this time. In that year his mother died and he succeeded to his father's estate. In 1756 he married Ann Calvert, and they had several children, of whom one son, John, also became a minor versifier. For the remainder of his life Anstey lived in leisure— not always as a country gentleman, since from 1770 he resided in Bath, but as a squire and sportsman when he was in Cambridge-

W. Hoare

CHRISTOPHER ANSTEY

shire and as a Member of Parliament. He died in Bath at nearly eighty-one. There is a monument to him in the Poets' Corner of Westminster Abbey.

Noted for his Latin poems while at college, Anstey's contemporary fame rested on a volume of "poetic epistles" which he called *The New Bath Guide, or Memoirs of the B—r—d [Blunderhead] Family.* This was greeted with the utmost enthusiasm; Horace Walpole said that "so much humor, fun, and poetry, so much originality, never met together before." Modern readers are more inclined to agree with Austin Dobson that "by this time the originality has grown somewhat ancient." Anstey's satire was good-humored and forthright, and his verse—in the anapestic meter so much favored by Thomas Moore later—had vigor; but even during his lifetime, though he wrote a great deal more, he remained "a man of one book." Smollett drew on him for some of the material in *Humphrey Clinker,* and as fine a poet as Thomas Gray (whose *Elegy* Anstey translated into Latin verse) admired him; but today he is practically—and deservedly—forgotten. Yet, as George Saintsbury pointed out, we are "indebted to him for patterns of light anapestic verse," and he did have a keen ear for poetic rhythm, though not, as Walpole claimed, a "better ear than Dryden or Handel." Essentially, as Saintsbury said, he was a carry-over from the satiric social verse of Swift and Gay, though far more amiable than either.

Nearly all Anstey's later poems are couched in the same verse "epistles" which proved so successful with *The New Bath Guide*. His versification is not true poetry, but broad humor in rhyme and meter, vivid, outspoken, and too facile. To the puritanical readers of the age immediately succeeding his, he was scandalously "free" in his language, but actually he has none of the outright vulgarity which was characteristic of Swift or even of Gay. There was in his time a whole congeries of satirical versifiers, of whom he was then the most outstanding, though now, with the rest of them, he is unread except by students of the period. One possible influence of Anstey's verse that has not been noted is on Thackeray's *Book of Snobs*, some of which, though of course in prose, has a distinct flavor of *The New Bath Guide*.

PRINCIPAL WORKS: The New Bath Guide, 1766; The Patriot, 1767; An Election Ball, 1776; Envy, 1778; Poetical Works, 1808.

ABOUT: Anstey, J. Account of Life and Writings of C. Anstey, Esq., *in* Poetical Works.

ARBUTHNOT, JOHN (1667-February 27, 1735), pamphleteer, medical writer, was born at Arbuthnot, Kincardineshire, the son of an Episcopal clergyman. He may have studied at Aberdeen, but certainly received his doctor's degree from St. Andrews in 1696. When the revolution deprived his father of his preferment, John and his brothers left home, he coming to London, where he lived six miles from town with William Pate, a woolen draper and journalist. At thirty Arbuthnot published *An Examination of Dr. Woodward's Account of the Deluge, &c*, and in 1704 he was elected a Fellow of the Royal Society. Having the luck to be the only doctor within reach when Prince George of Denmark fell ill at Epsom, Arbuthnot prescribed for the Prince so successfully that he was appointed physician extraordinary to Queen Anne in 1705. In 1710 he was made a Fellow of the Royal College of Physicians, was censor in 1723, and gave the Harveian oration in 1727.

Swift wrote his Stella in 1711 that he had met at Court "a certain Arbuthnot, a Scottish doctor"—the beginning of a friendship so close that Swift once exclaimed,

JOHN ARBUTHNOT

"Oh! If the world but had a dozen Arbuthnots in it, I would burn my *Travels!*" Émile Legouis, who called Arbuthnot "a supple, alert, original, seed-sowing intelligence," believed that he influenced Swift more than he was influenced by him. Arbuthnot's reputation rests chiefly on five pamphlets published at intervals, March-July 1712, which Macaulay called "the most ingenious and humorous political satire extant in our language." The most famous is *Law Is a Bottomless-Pit; or the History of John Bull*. In this satire on the Whigs, Nicholas Frog (the Dutch) and John Bull (ever since the accepted symbol of England or Great Britain) bring a lawsuit (war) against Philip Baboon (Duke of Anjou). Humphrey Hocus represents the Duke of Marlborough. John Bull may not have been an original creation of Arbuthnot's, but he perfected the character, "ruddy and plump, with a pair of cheeks like a trumpeter." American imitations include Jeremy Belknap's *The Foresters* (1792) and James K. Paulding's *The Diverting History of John Bull and Brother Jonathan* (1812).

In the famous Scriblerus Club, organized in 1714 though founded two years before as the Brothers Society, Swift and Arbuthnot joined forces with Pope, Gay, and Parnell to satirize "the abuses of human learning in every branch." The resultant anti-pedantic *Memoirs of Martin Scriblerus* is all or near-

11

ly all his handiwork, although first published in the quarto edition of Pope's works in 1741. Containing some of Arbuthnot's best and most characteristic writing, it influenced Sterne's *Tristram Shandy* and Swift's *Gulliver's Travels*. A reversal of Arbuthnot's fortunes came with the death of Queen Anne in 1714. He lost his place at court and moved to Chelsea, subsequently to Dover, where he kept up a small practice. He died at sixty-eight of disorders partially brought on by habitual overeating.

Dr. Johnson told Boswell that Arbuthnot "was the most unusual genius, being an excellent physician, a man of deep learning, and a man of much humour." Pope addressed a famous *Epistle* to him. Careless of fame, he permitted his children to make kites of his manuscripts and much of the credit for his wit and *bon mots* has gone to Pope, Swift, and Gay. As a writer on medicine, he was often far in advance of his time. He was married, and had two sons and two daughters. The maiden name of his wife is unknown.

PRINCIPAL WORKS: Of the Laws of Chance, 1692; An Examination of Dr. Woodward's Account of the Deluge, &c., 1697; An Argument for Divine Providence, 1710; Law Is a Bottomless-Pit, 1712; John Bull in His Senses, 1712; John Bull Still in His Senses, 1712; An Appendix to John Bull Still in His Senses, 1712; Lewis Baboon Turned Honest, and John Bull Politician, 1712; History of John Bull, 1712; Three Hours After Marriage (play, with A. Pope and J. Gay) 1717; Oratio Anniversaria Harvaeana, 1727; An Essay Concerning the Nature of Aliments, 1731; Know Yourself, a Poem, 1734; Memoirs of the Extraordinary Life, Works, and Discoveries of Martinus Scriblerus, 1741.

ABOUT: Aitken, G. A. The Life and Works of John Arbuthnot; Beattie, L. M. John Arbuthnot, Mathematician and Satirist; Kippis, Andrew. Biographia Britannica; Teerink, H. The History of John Bull; American Literature March 1929; Athenaeum June 17, 1893; London Mercury November 1928; Publications of Modern Language Association March 1930; Virginia Quarterly Review October 1927.

ARMSTRONG, JOHN (1709-September 7, 1779),

poet and physician, was Scottish by birth, a native of Castleton, Roxburghshire, where his father was a clergyman. He was sent to the University of Edinburgh, where he received his M.D. degree in 1732, and settled in London to practice medicine. In 1746 he was appointed physician to the Hospital for Lame and Sick Soldiers, in Buckinghamshire; and in 1760, during the Seven Years' War, he was physician to the army in Germany. He returned to London on half-pay in 1763 and resumed his practice, dying finally as the result of infection following a carriage accident.

Armstrong's was a peculiar character; both as physician and as poet he was injured by inherent indolence and an almost pathological shyness. As he grew older he became increasingly melancholic, and alienated his friends by continued complaint of neglect, or if his work was noticed complained instead of the attacks it provoked. In a coarse age he was rebuked for his coarseness, he was condemned for his love of luxury and pomp, and at the same time accused of misanthropy. To all these seeming contradictions we may add the fact that a few people found him sweet-tempered, whimsical, and full of a shy, unhappy humor. For many years John Wilkes was his greatest friend; then suddenly Armstrong turned on him and attacked him in his poem, *A Day*. Next he attached himself to the painter Henry Fuseli, who though he was thirty-three years Armstrong's junior had much in common with him temperamentally; but in the end he quarreled with Fuseli also.

He was all his life an unhappy man, and his unhappiness is reflected in his poetry, which yet contains passages full of vigor and energy. In his lifetime he was most celebrated as the author of the didactic *Art of*

After S. Shelley

JOHN ARMSTRONG

Preserving Health, which went into many editions. His non-medical essays were also popular for their frank and energetic style. The same people who condemned them for "irreverence" read them with shocked pleasure.

Unorthodox in all else—he went beyond deism in his religious views—Armstrong was an extreme conservative where the English language was concerned. He was a bitter enemy of all new spellings and all neologisms, and detested any coinages of words or any changes in classical eighteenth century rhetoric—even though his own writing, both in prose and in verse, was noted for its freedom and simplicity. *The Art of Preserving Health*, though it owes as much to the physician as to the poet, nevertheless is didactic poetry of a high order—and some of its precepts might well be followed today.

PRINCIPAL WORKS: *Poetry*—The Economy of Love, 1738 (revised ed. 1768); Art of Preserving Health, 1744; Benevolence, 1751; Taste, an Epistle to a Young Critic, 1753; A Day, 1761; Poetical Works (G. Gilfillan, ed.) 1858. *Prose*—An Essay for Abridging the Study of Physic, 1735; The History and Cure of Venereal Disease, 1737; Sketches and Essays on Various Subjects (as Lancelot Temple) 1770.

ABOUT: Gilfillan, G. Memoirs of Armstrong (*in* Poetical Works).

ASCHAM, ROGER (1515-December 30, 1568), educator and essayist, was born at Kirby Wicke, near Northallerton, Yorkshire. Though his father, John Ascham, was house-steward to Lord Scrope of Bolton, both he and the mother came from very old Yorkshire families, and seem to have been generally regarded as "gentry." Ascham's first teacher was his father, whom he always held in the utmost admiration and reverence and whose death in the same year with that of his mother was one of the great griefs of his troubled life. He was next sent to the household of Sir Anthony Wingfield, who had other boys tutored with his own children, and at fifteen (not an unheard-of age in the sixteenth century) he entered St. John's College, Cambridge. There, though he studied also mathematics, music, and penmanship (!), his passion—retained throughout his life—was for Greek and Latin. Already he was an ardent bowman, Sir Anthony having been his first instructor in the ancient English art of archery.

He secured his B.A. in 1533 and his M.A. in 1537, being then a fellow of St. John's and, says W. H. Woodward, already "perhaps the ablest Greek scholar in England." In 1538 he was appointed Greek reader at St. John's, and in 1540 became the first Regius Professor of Greek at Cambridge. In 1546 he was made also the university's public orator, and in that capacity wrote its official letters, his beautiful penmanship being a valued factor. In 1548 he was appointed tutor to Elizabeth, then a girl of sixteen, but two years later he quarreled with her steward and returned to Cambridge, where he still retained his posts. Next he was made secretary to Sir Richard Morysin (Morrison), ambassador to the court of Emperor Charles V, and spent two years in Germany, Belgium, and Italy, meanwhile teaching Greek to his chief. Though he was an open Protestant, his diplomacy, humility, and shrewdness combined to keep him from trouble on that account, and he was even Latin secretary to Queen Mary. Elizabeth kept him on as her Greek tutor. In 1554 he married Margaret Howe, and resigned his fellowship and his public oratorship. They had three sons, of whom one died in childhood.

Though Ascham had temporary pensions from Henry VIII and Edward VI, he was always hard up and always in search of a patron or a permanent pension. He has been accused of gambling away his money, but except for cockfighting and archery he does not seem to have deserved the imputation. Throughout his life he was a semi-invalid, frequently obliged to take long leaves for illness. His pensions, though limited in tenure, were generous for the time; he was enabled to lease a farm at Walthamstowe very cheaply, and in 1559 Elizabeth gave him, though he was a layman, the prebend and canonry of Wetwang, in York Cathedral. A law-suit, however, delayed his receiving any emoluments from this until 1566. His long illness—which may have been tuberculosis—came to an end with a chill received while sitting up to write a New Year's poem for the queen; he died just as the new year came in.

Affectionate, gentle except for some scholarly acerbity and irritability, humane, and modest, Ascham's was an attractive personality. His literary style was the mirror of the author. It was easy, fluent, yet simple and straightforward. Best known of his books is *The Scholemaster*, which, however, is not intended for schools, but as a manual in Latin instruction for private tutors. Ascham died before it was finished, and his widow published it as he had left it. His other well-known book is the dialogue on archery he called *Toxophilus*. In both these works three themes appear—Ascham's humaneness and hatred of cruelty, his passion for the classic tongues, and at the same time his sturdy defense of the writing of serious books in English. It is only English prose, however, that he defends; when it came to English poetry he was blind, and counseled an imitation of classical models. Saintsbury speaks also of his "curious confusion of the aesthetic and the critical"—i.e., to him a work of art was good only if its author was virtuous! He was, nevertheless, a great pioneer of education, many of whose views were several centuries ahead of his time.

PRINCIPAL WORKS: Toxophilus, 1545; Report and Discourse of the Affairs of Germany, 1553; The Scholemaster, a Plaine and Perfite Way of Teachyng Children to Understand, Write, and Speake in Latin Tong, 1570; Familiarum Epistolarum libri tres (E. Grant, ed.) 1576; Rogeri Aschami Epistolarum libri quattuor (W. Elstob, ed.) 1703; Collected Works (J. Bennet, ed.) 1771; The Whole Works of Roger Ascham (J. A. Giles, ed.) 1864-65; English Works (W. A. Wright, ed.) 1904.

ABOUT: Coleridge, H. Worthies of Yorkshire and Lancashire; Giles, J. A. Life *in* Whole Works; Grant, E. Oratio de Vita et Obitu Rogeri Aschami; Johnson, S. Life *in* Collected Works; Quick, R. H. Essays on Educational Reformers; Tannenbaum, S. A. and D. Roger Ascham: A Concise Bibliography.

ASSER (d. 909?), biographer, historian, also known as Asserius Menevensis, was born in Wales, a relative of Nobis, Bishop of St. David's, Menevia, and was "nurtured, taught, tonsured, and ordained" (according to his own account in *Annales Rerum Gestarum Alfredi Magni*, his famous life of King Alfred) in the western part of that country. He already had a reputation for learning when he began correspondence with Alfred regarding the defense of his monastery against the depredations of Hemeid, King of South Wales. A meeting was arranged between Alfred and the priest at Dene, near Chichester, as a result of which Alfred invited him to join his household, which Asser did about 885. The original understanding was that he was to spend half the year in England and the remainder in Wales, but his first stay extended to eight months, and the arrangement was probably not strictly followed. Asser helped Alfred with the study of Latin and assisted in his educational schemes, the king showing his appreciation by bestowing on the priest the monasteries of Amesbury and Banwell, a grant of Exeter, and the bishopric of Sherborne—the latter about 900. Asser died in 909, according to Stubb's *Registrum Anglicanum*; in 910, if the entry in the *Anglo-Saxon Chronicle* is to be believed.

Asser's *Life of Alfred*, the earliest biography of an English layman, combines a first-hand account of the king's career down to 887, and a chronicle of English history from 849 to that date. It is written in a highly rhetorical and parenthetical style, the verbiage sometimes obscuring the meaning. Asser's first editor, Archbishop Parker, did not help matters by his interpolations in his 1574 edition of the *Life*, printed from a manuscript which was lost in the Cottonian Library fire in 1713. Some of this extraneous material was derived from the *Annals of Saint Neot*. The famous legend of the burned cakes, for instance, occurs nowhere in Asser. The *Life* is valuable, nevertheless. "As long as the memory of the king is treasured," remarks L. C. Jane, "the name of his biographer should at least be remembered."

PRINCIPAL WORK: The Life of King Alfred, 894 (?).

ABOUT: Asser's Life of King Alfred, ed. by W. H. Stevenson, 1904; ed. by L. C. Jane, 1924; Giles, J. A. Six Old English Chronicles.

ATTERBURY, FRANCIS (March 6, 1662-February 15, 1732), preacher, political writer, was born at Milton or Middleton Keynes, near Bedford, Buckinghamshire, the son of Lewis Atterbury, rector of the parish. He was educated at Westminster School, London, and at Christ Church, Oxford University, staying there after graduation as tutor. He married Katherine Osborn while at Oxford. His first published work (1682) was a translation into Latin verse of Dryden's *Absalom and Achitophel*; the first of his many polemic works was a reply (1687) to Obadiah Walker, Master of University College, who, as "Abraham Woodhead," had attacked the Reformation. Atterbury's mistaken defense of the genuineness of the *Epistles of Phalaris* was signed by his pupil, Charles Boyle. (In *The Battle of the Books*, Swift pictured Atterbury as Apollo, directing this fight against Richard Bentley.)

Receiving holy orders in 1687, Atterbury soon rose to fame and preferment as a preacher in London. He was appointed lecturer of St. Bride's by the Bishop of London in 1691; preacher at Bridewell Hospital; and chaplain to William and Mary. After the latter's death, he was retained by Queen Anne as her chaplain in ordinary. By 1704 Atterbury was dean of Carlisle; in 1709 preacher at the Rolls Chapel; and in 1711-12 he was appointed to the deanery of Christ Church. He became Bishop of Rochester in 1713, the post carrying with it the deanship of Westminster. These important posts in the Church of England were rewards for Atterbury's persistent and eloquent struggles against protestantism, latitudinarianism, and Erastianism, or state supremacy in ecclesiastical affairs. He lost favor after the accession of George I, when his Jacobite sympathies were suspected, and he published several anonymous pamphlets directed against the Hanoverians. In 1721 he was implicated in a plot to restore the Stuarts—a small spotted dog named Harlequin, the gift of the Earl of Mar, oddly enough helping to convict him—and the following August he was imprisoned in the Tower. Stripped of his ecclesiastical dignities and banished for life, Atterbury went into exile in Brussels and Paris. He died at seventy and was given private burial in Westminster Abbey. Endowed with an attractive personality, Atterbury was regarded as the most striking preacher of his day. His printed sermons show eloquence and genuine emotion, and his polemic writings are marked by logic and biting wit.

PRINCIPAL WORKS: A Letter to a Convocation Man, 1697; A Discourse Occasion'd by the Death of Lady Cutts, 1698; The Rights, Powers, and Privileges of an English Convocation Stated and Vindicated, 1700; Epistolary Correspondence, Visitation Charges, Speeches and Miscellanies, 1783-1790.

ABOUT: Beeching, H. C. Francis Atterbury; Nichols, J., ed. Letters of Pope to Atterbury When in the Tower of London; Williams, F. Memoirs and Correspondence of Francis Atterbury.

AUBREY, JOHN (March 12, 1626-June 1697), antiquary, biographer, miscellaneous writer, was born at Kington, Wiltshire, the son of Richard Aubrey, a wealthy landowner. A frail child, he was tutored at home, and later entered Blandford Grammar School. In 1642 he was enrolled in Trinity College, Oxford, but the next year the civil war and a smallpox epidemic drove him back to the country. In 1646 he became a student at the Middle Temple, but was never called to the bar; instead, he returned at frequently intervals to Oxford, though he never received a degree. During his periods at home he became keenly interested in antiquities of his home county, and in 1649 was the discoverer of the famed megalithic remains at Avebury.

In 1652 Aubrey's father died and he inherited the estate. He soon dissipated it and came to poverty—partly by his lack of business sense and his extravagance, and partly by a series of law suits in which he became involved. One of these at least seems to have been what he called a "love suit"—a suit for breach of promise to marry. The remainder of his life was spent as a guest in the country houses of his friends, for by 1670 he had had to sell all his land, and by 1677 even his books. He has been compared to "Will Wimble" in the *Sir Roger de Coverley Papers*, but this comparison is scarcely fair; he was, to be sure, amiable, cheerful, and obliging, like "Wimble," but he was a serious antiquary

JOHN AUBREY

and an extremely industrious one. Indeed, in 1663 he was made a Fellow of the Royal Society, and in 1671 secured a royal patent to make antiquarian surveys.

His most celebrated work, the *Brief Lives*, was really a series of "minutes of lives," notes compiled for the use of Anthony Wood in his *Athenae Oxonienses*. Later Wood, who quarreled with everybody, quarreled with Aubrey, and left a very ill-natured estimate of him. Actually Aubrey published only one book during his lifetime, the *Miscellanies*, a collection of dream and ghost stories. He died at Oxford at seventy-one.

Richard Garnett called Aubrey "a kind of immature Boswell." He himself said that his *Lives* were written "tumultuarily," without order. Nevertheless, though they were frank and sometimes indiscreet, they were on the whole accurate. What gives them their lasting fame is their intimacy, vividness, and lifelikeness. Aubrey was haphazard in his order and erratic in his manner of writing, but he was a shrewd judge of character and had a keen eye for the revealing detail. He was credulous about ghosts, but not about men and women.

This genial, kindly, improvident man was, as Garnett said, "no man's enemy but his own." Thomas Hobbes was glad to be his friend, and that philosopher did not suffer fools gladly. He was a pleasing and pathetic figure, and though he had no great literary style he knew how to write so that people would want to keep on reading him.

PRINCIPAL WORKS: Miscellanies upon Various Subjects, 1696; Perambulation of Surrey (in Natural History and Antiquities of Surrey, R. Rawlinson, ed.) 1719; Minutes for Lives, 1813 (as Brief Lives Chiefly of Contemporaries, A. Clark, ed., 1898); Natural History of Wiltshire, 1847 (complete ed. 1862).

ABOUT: Britton, J. Memoir of John Aubrey; Collier, J. The Scandal and Credulities of John Aubrey; Powell, A. John Aubrey and His Friends; Strachey, G. L. Biographical Essays.

AUNGERVILLE, RICHARD

AUNGERVILLE, RICHARD (January 24, 1281?-April 14, 1345), commonly known as Richard de Bury, was born near Bury St. Edmunds, Suffolk, the son of Sir Richard Aungerville. When he was a child his father died and he was brought up by an uncle. Educated at Oxford, where he distinguished himself as a scholar, he entered the Benedictine monastery at Durham while still a young man.

On the basis of his reputation for learning, he was appointed tutor to Prince Edward of Windsor. Allying himself with Queen Isabella and her son in the intrigues against King Edward II, he risked both his position and his safety, but was amply rewarded after the deposition of Edward II. Edward III, out of gratitude to his former tutor, made him cofferer to the king, treasurer of the wardrobe and, later, clerk of the privy seal. Twice he was sent abroad as ambassador to the papal court (then in exile at Avignon). On one of these visits, he became friendly with Petrarch, who later wrote of him as "not ignorant of literature and from his youth up curious beyond belief of hidden things." In 1333 he was made dean of Wells and later in the same year, by special papal provision, he became Bishop of Durham, overruling the choice the monks themselves had made. His whole career, in fact, was starred with these marks of special favor from the king. A year after he became a bishop, he was made lord treasurer and lord chancellor, resigning both positions a short while after to serve on diplomatic missions.

All this is of interest in that it gave him greater freedom to exercise his ruling passion—the love of books. "No dearness of price ought to hinder a man from the buying of books, if he has the money demanded for them," says the good bishop practically enough. By virtue both of his increasing prosperity and his position, Bishop Richard was able to scout widely for manuscripts, rescuing many treasures from the hands of ignorant or negligent monks. Nor was this collecting a selfish passion. In the truest sense, Richard de Bury was a patron of learning who collected books in order that men might come to know them. Accordingly, he planned and founded a library in connection with the Durham Benedictines at Oxford, and his one literary work was a kind of dedication for this library In *Philobiblon*, a treatise in praise of learning, Richard recorded his passion for books, himself less a scholar than a man who devoted himself to the nurture of scholarship. *Philobiblon* was completed on his birthday in the year 1345. Three months later he died in penurious circumstances, having invested all the wealth he had in his library.

Today even the catalog of the library has vanished and only two of its volumes are known to be in existence. According to the traditional account, the books of the Benedictine library were divided among other famous libraries when the monastaries were dissolved under Henry VIII, but it seems more probable that the collection was dispersed shortly after Richard's death. His monument remains then the *Philobiblon*, as the Oxford printer, Joseph Barnes called it, "the first book on the love of books."

PRINCIPAL WORKS: Philobiblon: Tractatus pulcherrimus de amore librorum, 1473 (E. C. Thomas, tr. and ed., 1888).

ABOUT: de Chambre, W. Life, *in* Wharton's Anglia Sacra; Thomas, E. C. Biographical introduction to 1888 ed. Philobiblon.

AYTON or **AYTOUN, Sir ROBERT** (1570-February 28, 1638), poet, was born in the castle of Kinaldie, parish of Cameron, near St. Andrews, Fifeshire, the son of Andrew Ayton or Aytoun. He was incorporated a student of St. Leonard's College, St. Andrews, with his eldest brother John, in 1584, receiving his M.A. in 1588. After receiving his patrimony on the death of his father, Ayton traveled on the Continent, studied civil law at the University of Paris, and composed verses in Greek, French, and Latin, of which only the latter have been preserved. On the accession of James VI of Scotland to the English throne, Ayton addressed a Latin panegyric to the monarch, which appeared in Paris in ten quarto leaves, with a prose dedication to the king. In consequence, Ayton soon found himself a Groom of His Majesty's Privy Chamber at a stipend of £20 a year, and was knighted at Ryccott, Oxfordshire, August 30, 1612. He was later made Gentleman of the Bedchamber and private secretary to the Queen, and in 1619 was granted £500 a year to continue thirty-one years. The next July the King made this a life pension. Ayton failed, however, to obtain the Provostship of Eton, the post falling to Sir Henry Wotton, another literary courtier. After James' death, Ayton continued as secretary to Charles' queen, Henrietta; in 1636 was Master of the Royal Hospital of St. Katherine, a sinecure paying £200 a year; and was nominated Privy Councillor. Ayton died at about sixty-seven and was buried in Westminster Abbey. There is, an "elegant monument," with bust, over his grave in the southern aisle of the choir, at the corner of the chapel of Henry VII.

The poem which first gained Ayton some fame was described by Charles Rogers as abounding "in classical phraseology, and abundantly panegyrical." He continued to use classical allusions in his poems, which were lyrical, smooth and graceful in expression. His sonnets have been called terse and epigrammatic. Dryden said that his work comprised some of the best verses of his age. They lacked the extravagant conceits of his friend and fellow-poet, Sir William Alexander. He also kept his eye well on the main chance, with the result that he owned lands in Lincolnshire and the Carse of Gowrie in addition to holding his numerous posts of honor at court.

PRINCIPAL WORKS: The Poems of Sir Robert Ayton (C. Rogers, ed.) 1844.

ABOUT: Memoir, *in* 1871 ed. of Poems (C. Rogers, ed.); Royal Historical Society (London) Transactions 1872.

BACON, Sir FRANCIS (January 22, 1561-April 9, 1626), essayist, philosopher, was the youngest child of Sir Nicholas Bacon, Elizabeth's Lord Keeper of the Great Seal, by his second wife, Anne Cooke. Lady Bacon's sister had married Lord Burghley, thus bringing the great Cecil family directly into the family connection, though they did little to help their relative later on.

Born in London, the boy went up to Trinity College, Cambridge, when he was less than thirteen—not at all unheard of in the sixteenth century. He remained there only two years, and then was entered at Gray's Inn to study for the bar. The next year his father had him sent as part of the entourage of Sir Amias Paulet, ambassador to France. It was taken for granted that his career would be in politics, not in the law. But in 1579 his father died suddenly, on the eve of settling an estate on him, and in consequence he received so small a legacy that he had no choice except to be called to the bar, in 1582, when he was twenty-one. From 1584 until he himself became Lord Keeper, he served in Parliament—rather to his detriment as it turned out, since early in his career he managed to offend Elizabeth badly by opposing her request for double subsidies, and the queen never forgot. His

P. Van Somer

SIR FRANCIS BACON

advancement was very slow until James I came to the throne. He was, to be sure, knighted in 1603, but with so many others that he considered it no honor.

In 1601, at the treason trial of the Earl of Essex, Bacon, who had been his friend and beneficiary, had an important part in securing the disgraced favorite's conviction, an act which earned him many lifelong enemies and played its part in his own fall twenty years later. But by 1607 he was solicitor general, in 1613 attorney general, in 1616 he was privy councillor, the next year Lord Keeper, and finally, in the same year, he became Lord Chancellor. In 1606 he had married Alice Barnham; they had no children. In 1618 he became Lord Verulam, and in 1621 Viscount St. Albans. (Incidentally—though even some of his biographers ignore it—it is entirely incorrect to speak of him as "Lord Bacon.")

A few weeks after Bacon had reached the apogee of prestige and honor, as a wealthy peer who was also already famous as writer, philosopher, and scientist, came his downfall. He was accused of bribery and corruption in Chancery suits, sentenced to imprisonment in the Tower, to a £40,000 fine, and to permanent disbarment from public office, Parliament, or access to the court. The imprisonment was soon over, the fine was put in trust for his own use, and eventually he was allowed to come

within the verge of the court; but his public career was ended.

The question of Bacon's guilt has been hotly discussed, though he himself confessed it in writing—according to some biographers, at the order of the king. The fact seems to be that "presents from suitors" were considered quite proper, though not acceptance when their suits were pending—which was what Bacon had done. It must be noted, however, that he never let these bribes influence his judgment, and frequently decided against those who had bribed him.

Painful as the experience was, and lastingly derogatory to Bacon's prestige, it had its brighter aspects, as it freed him to give all his time to the work for which he remains famous. He retired to his father's estate at Gorhambury, and for the remainder of his life devoted himself to scientific experiments and philosophical (i.e., scientific) writing. Long ago he had said of himself, that though the welfare of his country and the reform of religion were objectives toward which he strove, "I found that I was fitted for nothing so well as for the study of Truth."

It was in direct pursuit of "the study of Truth" that he met his death. One cold winter day he left his carriage to obtain snow with which to stuff a fowl, in order to study the retarding effect of cold on putrefaction. In consequence he incurred bronchitis, of which he died two weeks later, at sixty-five. His grand project, the *Instauratio Magna*, was thus left unfinished, but he had written and published enough to make him immortal as "the first modern mind" and "the father of inductive reasoning."

Pope's gibe, "the wisest, brightest, meanest of mankind," is unfair. There was no meanness in Bacon in the modern sense, and if Pope meant that he was stingy, that is also untrue, as he lived always on a grand scale, frequently beyond even his ample means. It must be acknowledged, however, that Bacon's was not a sympathetic personality. As W. R. Sorley has remarked, "He was capable of high enthusiasm for ideas and for causes, . . . but, on the side of pure sentiment, his nature seems to have been not easily stirred to love and hate." He had no warmth for any human being, including himself. The devious ways of politics were attractive to him, and he sincerely admired Machiavelli—"diplomacy" and manipulation often overcame the demands of abstract truthfulness.

Bacon the philosopher is infinitely greater than Bacon the man. Here too he had his weaknesses—largely the weaknesses of a pioneer. He did not have sufficient knowledge even of what had been accomplished in science by his own day, and this was an obvious flaw in the work of a great synthesist, who by his own assertion had "taken all knowledge to be my province."

Yet he remains the founder of experimental science. His object was "to restore the empire of man over nature," and he emphasized that "true knowledge is knowledge by causes." Inductive science as he conceived it differed from the old induction both by its exhaustion of "instances," and its procedure by gradual stages of increasing generality. He believed that behind all the individual sciences there was "one universal science," which he called Primitive or Summary Philosophy.

A mere glance at his outline for the proposed Great Instauratio, or Renewal of the Sciences, shows the grandeur of his philosophical conceptions. The completed work was to consist of six volumes: Division of the Sciences (The Advancement of Learning); The New Organon, or Directions Concerning the Interpretation of Nature (these two parts he finished); The Phenomena of the Universe; The Ladder of the Intellect; The Forerunners, or Anticipations of the New Philosophy; and The New Philosophy, or Active Science. Most of these he left in fragmentary form, some with no more done on them than their prefaces; and the last he had no intention of writing, believing that, with the foundation he hoped to furnish, that would be the work of his successors.

Incomplete as his philosophical or scientific work was, it is the bible of modern science. He was too far in advance of his age to secure contemporary disciples, but later men built on his foundations. He contributed no new actual scientific discovery; but he laid out the lines and rules whereby the great discoveries of the future might be made.

William Harvey, the great physiologist, was actually Bacon's physician—yet Bacon remained as completely unaware of Harvey's work in experimental science as he was an agnostic to the new Copernican picture of the universe. As for Harvey, he said shrewdly that Bacon "wrote philosophy like a Lord Chancellor." This may perhaps explain why it is in philosophy proper—what Aristotle called metaphysics—that Bacon's influence has been greatest. He was in a sense the godfather of both the Royal Society and the French Encyclopedia. As Dr. Charles Singer, the medical historian, has pointed out, Locke's *Essay on the Human Understanding* is already implicit in the *Novum Organum*. Bacon was not so much a great scientist or even a great philosopher as he was a great fructifier of men's minds, a great indicator of general principles and methods.

Outside of Bacon's philosophical and legal writings, his fame rests on his essays. Fowler called him "the British Socrates," and said nothing could exceed "the grandeur and solemnity of tone, the majesty of diction" of his style. Probably no English writer but Shakespeare has been so extensively quoted, often by people who had no idea of the source of the phrases they used. Quotations from him take up five full pages in Bartlett's *Familiar Quotations*. Most of them are from the essays, which, brief, pithy, highly condensed, are among the most brilliant ever written in any tongue.

He was, says Singer, "the father alike of English psychological speculation and of the empirical method in the department of ethics." Whatever his personal failings, and whatever the limitations of his specialized knowledge, his was one of the world's mightiest intellects, and the legacy left by that intellect to civilization is immortal.

It is, unfortunately, impossible to conclude any sketch of Francis Bacon without alluding to his strange posthumous career as surrogate for Shakespeare. Without going into the intricacies of the "ciphers," or the arguments of the Baconians, it must be said that there exists a huge body of print devoted to the thesis that Bacon, not having had enough to do in his political, legal, scientific, and literary careers, also wrote the plays and poems attributed to William Shakespeare. Some of the Baconians have gone to fantastic lengths in their "discoveries" about their hero—even to making him the son of Queen Elizabeth! The whole controversy is one of the major eccentricities of literary history, and one can imagine no one who would have been more horrified by the imputation that he was a writer of common stage-plays than Francis Bacon.

PRINCIPAL WORKS: Essayes, 1597 (completed ed., 1625); The Advancement of Learning, 1605; Novum Organum, 1620; The Historie of the Raigne of Kinge Henry the Seventh, 1622; Historia Ventorum, 1622; Historia Vitae et Mortis, 1623; De Augmentio Scientiarum, 1623; Apothegmes, New and Olde, 1625; The New Atlantis, 1627; Certaine Miscellaneous Workes (W. Rawley, ed.) 1629; Maxims of the Law, 1630; Letters and Remains (R. Stephens, ed.) 1734; Works (R. L. Ellis; J. Spedding; D. D. Heath, eds.) 1857-74.

ABOUT: Abbott, E. A. Bacon, an Account of His Life and Works; Church, R. W. Bacon; Dixon, W. H. Personal History of Lord Bacon; Dodd, A. The Martyrdom of Francis Bacon; Farrington, B. Francis Bacon: Philosopher of Industrial Science; Fischer, K. Francis Bacon of Verulam; Fowler, T. Bacon; Green, A. W. Sir Francis Bacon: His Life and Works; Hallam, H. Introduction to the Literature of Europe; Lee, S. Great Englishmen of the Sixteenth Century; Levine, I. Francis Bacon; Macaulay, T. B. Bacon; Nichol, J. Francis Bacon, His Life and Philosophy; Singer, C. Studies in the History and Method of Science; Spedding, J. Life and Letters of Lord Bacon; Steegmuller, F. Sir Francis Bacon, The First Modern Mind; Whewell, W. History of Discovery; Williams, C. Bacon.

BACON, ROGER (1214?-1294), philosopher, whom Diderot called "one of the most surprising geniuses that nature ever produced, and one of the most unfortunate of men," known to the scholars of the Renaissance as *doctor mirabilis,* was probably born in Ilchester, Somerset. (An alternative choice is Bixley, Gloucestershire.) Very little is known of his forebears or his early life. By about 1230 he was certainly at Oxford, and in 1233 he received the M.A. degree, then equivalent to ordination. Soon after he went to Paris for further study, again received an M.A., and remained as a teacher. By 1250 he was again at Oxford. Just when he joined the Franciscan Order is unknown—probably some time between 1245 and 1250. It must have been near the latter date, since later he said that he had spent twenty years and £2000 of his own money in scientific research, and this would have been impossible to a Franciscan friar.

In any event, he was certainly sent to Paris again in 1257 by the Order, under conditions of rather mild restraint and seclusion, and he remained there, a virtual prisoner so far as independent scholarly activities were concerned, until 1267, when Pope Clement IV, who as Guy de Foulques had known of Bacon's work, requested him, "regardless of Franciscan rules," to send him an account of his researches.

Bacon, who had previously produced only a few tentative studies, largely in the form of letters, immediately set to work on his great projected encyclopedia or *Organon* which he called *Communia Naturalium,* a compendium of all knowledge of his day. Manifestly, this was a life-task, and in fact the *Communia Naturalium* was never finished. However, in eighteen months Bacon did finish his three greatest books, the *Opus Maius, Opus Minus,* and *Opus Tertium.* It is not known whether these ever reached the Pope, who died soon after. But so much at least of Bacon's writing had definitely reached the limited public to whom it was addressed.

In 1277 real disaster struck him. Jerome de Ascoli, Minister-General of the Franciscans, condemned Bacon for "certain suspected novelties," and this time his silencing was complete. He was deprived of all writing materials and limited to a bread and water diet. This lasted until 1292, when de Ascoli died. Bacon returned to England then, and himself died two years later (or possibly even earlier). He was buried at Friars Minor, but no stone marks his grave.

Dr. Dorothea E. Sharpe contends that "it is foolish to regard him as . . . a rebel against the whole spirit of scholasticism, or an assertor of the freedom of thought. He is essentially the product of his day." It is true, moreover, that Bacon's imperious and quarrelsome disposition, and the invective he heaped on his most revered contemporaries, contributed largely to his persecution. He was, furthermore, a close follower of his great teacher, Robert Grosseteste— an elucidator rather than an innovator.

Nevertheless, when all this is granted, Roger Bacon stands as the precursor of modern scientific thought, a man of the Renaissance born too early. In logic, grammar, mathematics, physics (particularly optics), and above all in experiment as a method of science, his was the first modern voice raised in Europe. Under the conditions of his own time (he was, of course, firmly convinced of the validity of both astrology and alchemy), his approach was that of modern science—of his great successor and namesake (though no relative), Francis Bacon. His Greek was learned from contemporary speakers of the debased modern language, but it enabled him to read Aristotle in the original. He even compiled a Hebrew grammar, most of which is lost. He described the magnifying lens and the magnet, he knew about gunpowder, he even guessed shrewdly that light is not a phenomenon of particles, but of movement in space. Lynn Thorndike, in his *History of Magic and Experimental Science*, points out that Bacon's chief interest was in testing the applications of his speculative theories rather than in actual induction from observed phenomena. But who else in the thirteenth century even envisaged the circumnavigation of the globe, or foresaw motor-driven ships and airplanes?

Bacon left no disciples, though he was not so completely forgotten or neglected as has sometimes been supposed. His work was curious; the ignorant of his day transformed him into a wizard, manufacturer of a "brazen head" that prophesied and did his will, protagonist of Robert Greene's *Friar Bacon and Friar Bungay*. Fortunately, his reputation was rehabilitated in later centuries.

PRINCIPAL WORKS: Opus Maius, Opus Minus, Opus Tertium, 1267; Compendium Studii Philosophiae, 1271-72; Compendium Studii Theologicae, 1292; Opera Quaedam Hactena Inedita (J. S. Brewer, ed.) 1859. (Translations into English): Greek Grammar and a Fragment of Hebrew Grammar (E. S. Nolan and S. A. Hirsch, trs.) 1902; Opus Maius (R. B. Burke, tr.) 1928.

ABOUT: Bridges, J. H. Life and Works of Roger Bacon; Jones, H. G. Life and Works of Roger Bacon; Little, A. G. and Sandys, J. E. Roger Bacon Commemoration Essays (1914, Oxford); Woodruff, F. W. Roger Bacon: A Biography.

BADONICUS. See GILDAS

BAEDA. See BEDA

BAGE, ROBERT (February 29, 1728-September 1, 1801), novelist, was born in a leap year, and as William Hutton facetiously pointed out, "Though he lived to the age of seventy-three, he could not celebrate more than eighteen birthdays." He was born at Darley, a hamlet on the river Derwent, adjoining the town of Derby, the son of a paper manufacturer and the first Mrs. Bage,

who died shortly after his birth. He attended a common school at Derby, where he became proficient in Latin and "the Manual Exercise."

Bage was married at twenty-three, his wife bringing him a sufficient dowry so that he set up a paper mill of his own at Elford, four miles from Tamworth, a business which he conducted all his life. The mill prospered and Bage employed his leisure time in learning Italian and French, as is evident in his novel *The Fair Syrian*, and went once a week to Birmingham to receive instruction from a Thomas Hanson in higher mathematics. In 1765 he ventured into the manufacture of iron with three partners, of whom Dr. Erasmus Darwin was one, but after fourteen years the business failed, leaving Bage with a loss of £1500. For consolation, he turned to writing. As Sir Walter Scott, who could well sympathize with him, put it: "The man of letters committed his cause to a better champion—literary occupation—the tried solace of misfortune, want and imprisonment."

Mount Henneth (1781), Bage's first book, described a Welsh Utopia. He sold it to Lowndes for £30. Its success encouraged him to continue writing novels, usually told in letter form and extending to two or more volumes. The most notable, *Man As He Is* (1792), and *Hermsprong, or Man As He Is Not* (1796), filled four and three volumes respectively. Several were translated into French and German, and Scott included three of them in his Ballantyne's "Novelists' Library." Hutton, Bage's friend, testified to his amiability of disposition, and his kindness to his servants and work animals. He may have been brought up in the Quaker faith, though this has been disputed. Two of his three sons became successful business men.

Bage was an advocate of "the natural man" (like Hermsprong, who, reared among the Indians of North America, came to Europe to finish his education in France and England, and to advocate the equality of man and the emancipation of women). *The Fair Syrian* traces the conversion of a young French aristocrat to democracy in Revolutionary America. He had a vigorous, easy, and frequently rather coarse style.

PRINCIPAL WORKS: Mount Henneth, 1781; Barham Downs, 1784; The Fair Syrian, 1788; James

Wallace, 1788; Man As He Is, 1792; Hermsprong, or Man As He Is Not, 1796.

ABOUT: Fairchild, H. N. The Noble Savage; Fletcher, T. T. F. Robert Bage: a Representative Revolutionary Novelist; Gregory, A. The French Revolution and the English Novel; Hutton, W. Life of William Hutton; Scott, W. The Lives of the Novelists; Mid-West Quarterly April 1918.

BAILEY, NATHAN or NATHANIEL

(d. 1742), lexicographer, was the most popular of dictionary makers preceding Samuel Johnson, but, since he had no Boswell of any kind, the known facts about his life are scanty. A student of his *Dictionary*, writing in 1940, had no new biographical data to offer concerning Bailey. On November 6, 1691, he seems to have been admitted to membership in the Seventh-Day Baptists at the Mill Yard Church in Whitechapel, where he was buried a half-century later. His *An Universal Etymological English Dictionary*—Bailey admitted that he found most of the etymologies in other books— was originally issued in 1721, in a six-shilling octavo volume. In that form it went through many editions, till two small folio editions were issued in 1730 and 1736. A volume of the 1730 edition was interleaved by Johnson as a "guide and repository" for the notes for his own dictionary. Another folio edition of Bailey's dictionary was issued more than a decade after his death, in the same year as Johnson's *Dictionary* (1755). Since it had no more than a nominal connection with the 1730 and 1736 editions, it was in all likelihood prepared for the sole purpose of holding the field against Johnson, from whom numerous definitions were plagiarized. (Johnson's *Dictionary* was published April 15; the publishers of the new edition of Bailey employed a staff of copyists, and had proposals and a specimen ready to show prospective purchasers by the first week in June.)

Bailey was a schoolmaster for a time; that is, if he received any replies to the following advertisement in the first edition of his *Dictionary*: "Youth boarded and Taught the Hebrew, Greek, and Latin languages, in a Method more Easy and Expeditious than is common; also other School-Learning by the *Author* of this *Dictionary*, to be heard of at Mr. *Bailey's*, Bookseller, at the Sign of the Dove in *Paternoster Row*, etc." The inclusion of proverbs made the dictionary more generally popular (the Yale University Press published a decorated volume of them as recently as 1927). William Pitt owned a copy; Lord Chatham was said to have read it twice; and Thomas Chatterton derived so many archaic words from it for his literary forgeries that Skeat, in his essay in the Aldine edition of Chatterton, calls the dictionary the key to the Rowley poems. In *Dictionarium Britannicum* (1730), as the folio edition of that year was called, Bailey had the assistance of two other editors. Though "studded with words of fearful length and cacophony," Bailey's *Dictionary* retained its popularity until after 1800.

PRINCIPAL WORKS: An Universal Etymological English Dictionary, 1721; The Antiquities of London and Westminster, 1726; All the Familiar Colloquies of Erasmus Translated, 1733.

ABOUT: English Dialect Society Publications No. 41; Oxford Bibliographical Society Proceedings and Papers, 1940; Gentleman's Magazine, Vol. 12.

BAILLIE, Lady GRIZEL (GRISEL or GRISELL)

(December 25, 1665-December 6, 1746), poet, was born on Christmas Day in the old castle of Redbraes, Berwickshire, the eldest daughter of Sir Patrick Hume, 8th baron of Polwarth who was a stout friend of the Covenanters. Grizel as a girl of twelve was a go-between for her father and the imprisoned patriot, Robert Baillie of Jerviswood. In this way she met her future husband, the prisoner's son George, to whom she was married in 1692. She was called upon also to smuggle food to her father when the Castle was occupied by troopers and he went into hiding in the vaults of the parish church at Polwarth. Hume eventually made his way to Utrecht, Holland, where he presented himself to the Prince of Orange, and posed for the next three years as Dr. Wallace, a Scotch surgeon. His family joined him, and Grizel, as manager of the household, began to acquire the experience which later went into her exhaustive *Household Book*.

After the Restoration in 1688, Lady Grizel was offered a post as maid of honor to the Princess of Orange, but returned to Scotland to marry Baillie and raise a son and two daughters, one of whom was married to a jealous husband, Charles, Lord Binning, and another who wrote an excellent memoir of her mother, first published in book form in

1822. From 1731 to 1733 Lady Grizel visited Holland, Naples, and other parts of Europe. Since early girlhood she had written prose and verse. Unfortunately, her manuscript book of songs was lost, and only two have been preserved, one a fragment. The most poignant, "Werena my heart licht" was applied by Robert Burns to himself at Dumfries. During the rent riots of 1745, Lady Grizel's estate was for a time in the hands of the Highlanders. George Baillie died at Oxford in 1738, and his widow, who died when nearly eighty-one, was buried beside him at Mellerstein, Berwickshire.

When much younger, Lady Grizel was described as not tall, but handsome, well-made, quick and graceful, with red cheeks, red lips (which she attributed to a diet of porridge and milk), chestnut hair, and "a light and sweetness in her eyes very uncommon."

PRINCIPAL WORKS: Poems (in Allan Ramsey's Tea-Table Miscellany and other anthologies); The Household Book of Lady Grisell Baillie 1692-1733, 1911.

ABOUT: Cairns, C. C. Noble Women; Murray, Grisell, Lady. Memoirs of the Lives and Characters of George Baillie of Jerviswood, and of Lady Grisell Baillie.

BAILLIE, ROBERT (April 30, 1602-August 1662), diarist, was born in Glasgow in 1602, according to a note in his college notebooks; the date has usually been assigned to 1599. His father was Thomas Baillie, a merchant. He attended the Glasgow High School under Robert Blair, entered Glasgow University in March 1617, and took his M.A. with honors in 1620. After studying theology under Byrd, Cameron, and Strang, Baillie was admitted May 25, 1631, to the ministry, by Archbishop Law of Glasgow. The Earl of Eglinton gave him the parish of Kilwinning, Ayrshire, whose "kirk" was part of a ruinous abbey. Baillie married Lilias Fleming, and intended to live and die in Kilwinning but was soon absorbed, in public affairs. His journals, which Carlyle called "a true, rather opulent, but very confused quarry" for students of the time, were begun January 2, 1637. (Masson, in his *Life of Milton*, commented that Baillie's "faculty of narration in his pithy native Scotch is nothing short of genius.")

When Baillie disavowed "Laud's Liturgy" (the Archbishop's new Canon and Service-Book) he was sent by the covenanting lords to London, where he drew up a "Charge of the Scottish Commissioners Against Laud." Baillie was admitted in November 1643 to the University of Glasgow faculty as "doctor et professor theologiae." There he taught Controversies, Oriental languages, and Chronology. When Cromwell advanced against the city, Baillie fled to Cumbrae. His wife died June 7, 1653 after bearing him six children. In 1656 he married Helen Strang. After the Restoration he refused a bishopric, and was appointed as Principal of the University where once he was "regent of the Bajouns" (first-year students). His health began to fail; he complained of "the worme" (Scottish for toothache) and, for the last two years of his life, of a "universall weakness, especially of my stomack." The day of his death is not definitely known.

Henry Martyn Beckwith Reid, who contradicts many of the statements in the article on Baillie in the *Dictionary of National Biography*, writes that Baillie had "a fluency of style, a richness of popular illustration, and a command of Church controversies unequalled in his day in Scotland." A short, eager, temperamental, pushing and excitable man, he was well equipped to write interesting diaries.

PRINCIPAL WORKS: The Letters and Journals of Robert Baillie MDCXXXVII-MDCLXII, 1841-1842.

ABOUT: Carlyle, T. Critical and Miscellaneous Essays; Reid, H.M.B. The Divinity Professors in the University of Glasgow, 1640-1903.

BALE, JOHN (November 21, 1495-November 1563), dramatist, historian, and religious reformer, was born of poor parents at Cove, Suffolk. Somehow, however, he was enabled to secure a good education, first at the Carmelite convent in Norwich and then at Jesus College, Cambridge, where he received a B.D. degree in 1529. At first an ardent Roman Catholic, he came under the influence of the first Baron Wentworth, and emerged as one of the most active of the reform, or Protestant, advocates. He renounced his vows and married, his wife's name being given only as Dorothy. Thomas Cromwell, who had become his patron, secured for him the living of Thornden, Suffolk in spite of his heresy; but was not, however, able to save Bale from being called before the Archbishop of York in 1534 for preaching "an anti-Romish sermon," and when Cromwell fell, in 1540, Bale thought it advisable to flee with his wife and children to Germany.

On the accession of Edward VI, in 1547, he returned to England, and was made rector of Bishopstoke, Hampshire, with the vicarage of Swaffham, Norfolk, added in 1551. The next year Edward made him Bishop of Ossory, in Ireland. He refused to be ordained as bishop by the Roman ritual, and his ordination was delayed until the beginning of 1553. It was at Ossory that he had boys perform his morality plays outdoors on Sunday afternoons.

When Edward died, Bale made the tactical mistake of supporting Lady Jane Grey instead of Mary for the throne. Once more he fled, this time to Holland and thence to Basel, Switzerland. Three times en route he was arrested, and the last time was tried for high treason and (strange penalty) fined £300. He did not come home again until the accession of Elizabeth, in 1558. She made him prebendary of Canterbury, where he died at sixty-eight.

It was Bale's morality plays that had first attracted Cromwell's attention to him. They are important principally because in one of them, *Kynge Johan*, there may clearly be

seen the transition between the medieval miracle plays and the historical dramas which culminated in Shakespeare's. As literature they are not remarkable; they are frankly doggerel, and are besides vituperative and frequently indecent. Bale, in spite of his powerful friends, probably had more enemies than any man of his period. He was justly known as "Bilious Bale," being coarse, bitter, and indiscreet, hewing about him in a vigorous polemic style more noted for energy than for taste.

Nevertheless, he was also an extremely learned man, and his greatest work is not a play but his encyclopedia or compendium of English, Scottish, and Welsh authors of his time, an invaluable source-book. (This, it may be noted, was written in Latin, not in English as were his plays.) This *Summarium* was first published in 1548, and then revised and reissued as a *Catalogus* in 1557-59. It also is marred by personal invective, but it is a scholarly and inclusive work which (rare for his era) gives the sources of its information.

PRINCIPAL WORKS: The Thre Lawes of Nature, Moses and Christ, A Tragedy or Enterlude Manyfesting the Chief Promyses of God unto Man, The Temptacyon of our Lorde, A Brefe Comedy or Enterlude of Johan Baptystes Preaching in the Wildernesse, 1538; Yet a Course at the Romysh Foxe, 1543; Brief Chronicle of the Examination and Death of Sir Johan Oldcastle, 1544; A Mysterye of Iniquyte, 1545; The Actes of Englyshe Votaryes, 1546; The Examinations of Lord Cobham, William Thorpe and Anne Askew, 1547; Illustrium Maioris Britanniae Scriptorum, 1548 (as Scriptorum Illustrium Britanniae Catalogus, 1557-59); Kynge Johan, 1548; The Apologye of Johan Bale Agaynste a Ranke Papyst, 1550; The Image of Bothe Churches, 1550: Select Works of John Bale (H. Christmas, ed.) 1849.

ABOUT: Christmas, H. Biographical Notice *in* Select Works; Smith-Dampier, J. L. East Anglian Worthies.

BARBOUR, JOHN (1325?-March 13, 1395), Scottish poet, is also the first Scottish historian and the first great exponent of vernacular Scottish poetry, but the facts of his life have to be guessed at from safe-conduct permits, pension rolls, and the like. He was born two years after the Battle of Bannockburn, one of the stirring episodes celebrated in his poem *The Bruce*, which stands in relation to Scotland as the *Chanson de Roland* does to France and *The Cid* to Spain. In 1357, he applied to Edward III for a safe-conduct to Oxford for himself and three

JOHN BALE

scholars, and it was granted to him at the request of "David de Bruys," king of Scotland, who was Edward's prisoner. Other safe-conducts were granted to Barbour in 1364; in 1365, when he went to St. Denis in France; and in 1368, when he went again to France as a student. In 1372 he was clerk of the audit of the king's household, and next year one of the auditors of the exchequer, as he was again in 1382 and 1384. *The Bruce*, dealing with the war of independence and the mighty deeds of King Robert and James Douglas, was composed between 1375 and 1378. Consisting of thirteen thousand octosyllabic lines, *The Bruce* is romance rather than history, its most startling, but probably intentional, error being the confusion of Robert the Bruce with his grandfather.

After the completion of the poem, Barbour received a life-pension of twenty shillings sterling from the king (now Robert II). In 1380 he made over the pension to the cathedral of Aberdeen, with instructions that the deans and canons should say a yearly mass for him and his parents. In 1388 the pension was increased "for his faithful service" to ten pounds, to be paid half-yearly at the Scottish terms of Whitsunday and Martinmas. Besides *The Bruce*, translations of Guido da Colonna's *Historia Destructionis Troiae* and of the *Legenda Aurea* have been ascribed to Barbour.

The Bruce was written in a dialect much like that used in Northumbria, but shows the influence of French versifying chroniclers; the political alliance between Edinburgh and Paris helps explain this. Often prosaic and commonplace, the poem rises at times to eloquence, as in the famous passage on liberty, or to near-lyricism, when Barbour describes the season of spring. Robert the Bruce himself is depicted, as would be expected, as a knight *sans peur et sans reproche*. The English enemy, however, does not come in for opprobrium or unfair treatment. As George Eyre-Todd, writing in 1891, puts it: "John Barbour remains not only the first but the most famous of the poet-chroniclers of Scotland. But for his pen and passion the patriotism which gave Scotland a soul for four hundred years might have died with Douglas and Bruce, and but for him the living heroes of the Scottish wars of succession and independence might have come down to us little more than empty names."

ABOUT: Brown, J. T. T. The Wallace and the Bruce Restudied; Eyre-Todd, G. Early Scottish Poetry; Miller, J. H. Early History of Scotland; Neilson, G. John Barbour, Poet and Translator; Tytler, P. F. Lives of Scottish Worthies.

BARCLAY, ALEXANDER (1475?-June 1552), poet, scholar, divine, was probably a Scotsman by birth, on the testimony of Dr. William Bulleyn, who knew him in youth. Since his great patron, the Duke of Norfolk, was the victor at Flodden Field, it was natural for Barclay tactfully to conceal his Scottish origin. Much of his life remains in doubt. He was probably a graduate of Oriel College, Oxford, and may have attended Cambridge as well. He seems to have traveled on the Continent in his younger days (which, incidentally, he himself said were "full of foly"), and was thoroughly conversant with French and of course with Latin, but had only a slight knowledge of Greek. It may be added that probably he knew little German and that his free rendering of Sebastian Brant's satirical allegory, *The Ship of Fools*, was made from a Latin translation.

By appointment of Bishop Cornish, provost of Oriel, Barclay became chaplain of the College of Ottery St. Mary, in Devonshire. It was here that *The Shyp of Folys of the World* was written. He next became a Benedictine monk at Ely, where his *Eclogues* were written. He was in Ely in 1520, when "Maistre Barkleye, the Blacke Monke and Poete" was asked to contribute "histoires" for the famous meeting at the Field of the Cloth of Gold between Henry VIII and François I. Subsequently he joined the stricter order of the Franciscans, at Canterbury. Just what Barclay did when Henry VIII established the Church of England is not known; he may have been the Alexander Barclay who was a refugee in Germany in 1528. Certainly he conformed with the change, for he kept under Edward VI the two posts he had held since 1539 and 1546 respectively, the livings of Great Baddow (Much Badew), Essex, and St. Matthew the Apostle, Wokey, Somerset. Moreover, in 1552 he received also the living of All Hallows, in London. He died soon after at Croydon, where he seems also to have spent part of his early life.

25

Barclay's were the first pastoral poems in English. Rough and prosy as much of his poetry is, it nevertheless reveals him as (to quote T. H. Jamieson) "a social reformer of the broadest type." He was a firm advocate of the countryman against the townsman, the poor against the rich. His other most celebrated work is the English version—rather than translation—of Brant's satiric *Narrenschiff.* What Barclay did was to give an "English coloring" to the German work, adding many personal and patriotic portions of his own. As a more orthodox translator, Barclay also published English versions of Sallust's *Jugurthan War* and of Wynkyn de Worde, and he wrote an early textbook to teach French to English students.

The *Eclogues,* which Barclay subtitled *Miseryes of Courtiers and Courtes of All Princes in General,* and which derived in part from Aeneas Sylvius and Manutianus (John Baptist Spagnuoli), had a curious history; written in Barclay's youth, they were mislaid for many years, finally rediscovered by their author, revised, and published.

As a poet, Barclay was didactic and wordy; he wrote deliberately for the common reader, and occasionally displayed genuine humor—as well as a strong anti-monastic trend, doubtless based on his own experiences. His private detestation was John Skelton,[qv] and he never missed an opportunity to attack him. Arthur Koelbing says of him: "As a scholar he represents Mediaeval rather than Renaissance ideals; as a man, he was modest and grateful, . . . a kind-hearted friend of the poor."

PRINCIPAL WORKS: The Castell of Laboure (Wynkyn de Worde, tr.) 1503; The Shyp of Folys of the World, 1509; Certayne Ecloges, 1513; Cronycle Compiled in Latyn by the Renowned Sallust, 1520; Introductory to Write and Pronounce Frenche, 1521; The Myrrour of Good Maners (Mancinus, tr.) 1523; The Lyfe of the Glorious Martyr and Saynt George, 1530?; The Lyfe of Saynte Thomas, n.d.; The Lyfe of Saynt Thomas of Canterbury, n.d.; The Lyves of Saynt Catharine, Saynt Margaret, Saynt Ethelreda, n.d.

ABOUT: Jamieson, T. H. Memoir *in* Ship of Fools, 1874 ed.

BARCLAY, JOHN (January 28, 1582-August 12, 1621), historical novelist, was born at Pont-à-Mousson, France, the son of William Barclay (a partisan of Mary Stuart, who had migrated to France in 1571 at the invitation of Charles I, Duke of Lorraine)

and Anne de Malleviller, a French noblewoman. John Barclay, one of twins (the other boy died young), studied at his father's college, where William Barclay was principal of the school of Civil Law, and at Leyden under Justus Lipsius. He rapidly became a proficient Latin scholar—all his subsequent novels and other works were written in Latin—and at nineteen published a commentary on the *Thebais* of Statius. At the succession of James VI of Scotland to the throne of England, Barclay joined the throng of young poets who commemorated the occasion in verse, writing a *Carmen Gratulatorium* in 1603. He is supposed to have published the first part of his *Satyricon* in London in the same year, under the name *Euphormio Lusininus,* but no copy exists. Returning to France, he married Louise Debonnaire, daughter of a paymaster in the French army, and had two sons and a daughter.

The amended and first extant edition of the *Satyricon,* a picaresque novel modeled on Petronius, appeared in Paris in 1605, and was regarded as an attack on the Jesuits; Barclay published an *Apologia* in 1610, denying this. James is said to have sent him on diplomatic missions to Emperor Rudolph, Matthew of Hungary, and Emmanuel Philibert of Savoy. In 1614 he published *Icon Animorum,* considered the fourth part of the *Satyricon,* though it has no real relation to it. In 1616 Barclay was in Rome at the invitation of Pope Paul V, even though his books were prohibited there. At thirty-nine he was stricken with fever—though poison has been suspected—and, at his request, was buried near the grave of Tasso in the graveyard of Saint Onofrio. According to Winkelmann, Barclay had a "graceful person, mild brow, soft gray eyes, dark hair, and a cheerful expression."

Argenis, Barclay's best novel, and one of the earliest *romans à clef,* licensed by Pope Gregory XV and dedicated to Louis XIII, was published posthumously. A direct descendant of the Greek novel, it is well constructed, clearly and pithily written, and had some influence on the pseudo-historical romances of the middle seventeenth century. Also a political novel, it presents Queen Elizabeth in the character of Hyanisbe, Philip the Second as Radirobanes, and

Henry IV as Poliarchus. An English translation (unpublished) was made by Ben Jonson.

PRINCIPAL WORKS: Euphormionis Lusinini Satyricon, 1603; Pars Secunda, 1607; Apologia Pro Se, 1610; Johannis Barclaii Pietas, 1612; Icon Animorum, 1614; Poemata, 1615; Joannis Barclaii Argenis, 1621.

ABOUT: Coleridge, S. T. Literary Remains; Colville, K. N. Fame's Twilight: Studies of Nine Men of Letters; Dalrymple, Sir David (Lord Halles) Sketch of the Life of John Barclay; Dukas, J. Étude Bibliographique et Littéraire sur le Satyricon de Jean Barclay.

BARNARD, Lady ANNE (LINDSAY)

(1750-1825), author of the ballad *Auld Robin Gray*, was the daughter of James Lindsay, fifth Earl of Balcarres. Her childhood and youth were spent at the family home in Fifeshire, where the great literary figures of Scotland were frequent visitors.

Lady Anne, determined not to marry, established a home in London with her widowed younger sister. Here she met and married Andrew Barnard, son of the Bishop of Limerick, and went with him to the Cape of Good Hope in 1793. She described the next fourteen years of colonial life in her illustrated *Journal and Notes*. Upon the death of her husband, she returned to her sister's home in London, where such prominent men as Burke, Sheridan, and the Prince of Wales, a life-long admirer of Lady Anne's, were habitués of their Berkeley Square salon. When her sister remarried, Lady Anne lived on alone, carrying on lively friendships and correspondences until her death in her seventy-fourth year.

When she was twenty-one, she had first heard and loved an English-Scotch ballad tune, but disapproved of what she considered the "improper" words. In order to preserve the tune with more suitable verses, she wrote *Auld Robin Gray*. The words were published anonymously, and their authorship was claimed by several people. It was not until she was seventy-two that Lady Anne, in a letter to Sir Walter Scott, acknowledged writing the verses and described the circumstances of their composition.

PRINCIPAL WORK: Auld Robin Gray, 1771.
ABOUT: Anderson, W. Scottish Nation.

BARNES, BARNABE (1569?-December 1609), poet, was the younger son of Dr.

Richard Barnes, Suffragan Bishop of Nottingham and Chancellor of York Minster, and was baptized at St. Michael le Belfrey in the city of York. Barnes matriculated from his father's Oxford college, Brasenose, July 8, 1586, but left the university without a degree. In 1591 he went with the Earl of Essex on the latter's expedition against the Prince of Parma in Normandy. By this time he had probably written much of the verse which appears in *Parthenophil and Parthenophe* (1593), the most extensive collection of love poetry to have appeared up to that time. It included madrigals, sestinas, canzones, elegies, and odes in many meters, including asclepiads and anacreontics. Barnes' appearance in London created some amusement, Thomas Nashe referring to him as "a smattring pert Boy, whose buttocks were not yet coole since he came from the grammar," and who swaggered through London "in a strange payre of *Babilonian* britches." He was also satirized by Campion, Marston, and Sir John Harington (as "Lynus"), and Shakespeare may have had him in mind when he created Parolles, liar and braggart, in *All's Well That Ends Well*.

In the spring of 1598 Barnes became involved in an alleged attempt to poison John Browne, the Recorder of Berwick, by putting mercury sublimate in his claret and sugar, and fled into the North to escape arrest. He was caught and brought back, but broke prison in July. In his later years Barnes probably lived with his brother John, a Clerk of the Peace, who preserved the manuscript of *Parthenophil*. After Barnes' death, supposedly at forty, he was buried in the parish of St. Mary-le-Bow in Durham, between the Cathedral and the Castle. Besides his poems, Barnes wrote an anti-Popish tragedy, *The Divils Charter*, concerning the life and death of Pope Alexander VI, which contains some powerful passages.

Much of Barnes' love poetry is marked by charm and delicacy, although Émile Legouis calls him "a frenzied poet," and states that there is "a curious mixture of factitious delirium, obscure indecency and true verbal vigour in his collection. . . . The best lines occur in the madrigals which follow the sonnets and are of more worth than they."

PRINCIPAL WORKS: Parthenophil and Parthenophe, Sonnettes, Madrigals, Elegies, and Odes, 1593; A Divine Centurie of Spiritual Sonnets, 1595; The Divils Charter, 1607.

ABOUT: Gosse, Edmund. Seventeenth Century Studies; Scott, J. G. Les Sonnets Elisabéthains; Sisson, C. J. (ed.) Thomas Lodge and Other Elizabethans; Academy September 2, 1876; Athenaeum August 20, 1904; Notes and Queries April 12, 1924.

BARNFIELD, RICHARD (June 1574-March 1627), poet, was born in Norbury, Shropshire, the oldest child of Richard Barnfield, "gentleman," and Maria Skrimsher. His mother died in childbirth when he was six, and he was reared by his maternal aunt, Elizabeth Skrimsher. He received his B.A. degree at Brasenose College, Oxford, in 1592, his college days being interrupted by a year of rustication, for what offense is not known. His poems all belong to his youth, when he was the devoted friend of Michael Drayton [qv] and of the poet Thomas Watson, the admirer of Spenser, and in all probability an acquaintance of Shakespeare. He neither published nor wrote anything after the age of twenty-five, but settled down to the life of a prosperous country gentleman at Darlaston, Staffordshire, where he died at only fifty-three. In all probability he was married and left children, but no record exists.

Barnfield's poetry was to him "the elegant amusement of a young scholar." It is highly affected, full of conceits and far-fetched images, slightly unwholesome in its exaggerated expressions of affection for his friends—so much so that it was looked at askance even in an age when this was the accepted poetic pose. As Sidney Lee has remarked, Barnfield had "a true power of fervid expression, . . . but his habit of mind was parasitic." He imitated what he admired. Under different circumstances he might have become a far better poet, for he has not only picturesqueness but genuine melody and limpidity as well.

His few little volumes soon became excessively rare, and he might have been completely forgotten were it not for a curious literary error. In the edition of Shakespeare's *Passionate Pilgrim* in 1599, there appeared a poem, attributed to Shakespeare,

that actually was Barnfield's—the *Address to the Nightingale*, beginning

As it fell upon a day
In the merry month of May.

In this same poem occur the celebrated lines,

He that is thy friend indeed,
He will help thee in thy need.

It is true that several other of the poems included in the *Passionate Pilgrim*, though Shakespeare was named as their author, were certainly not from Shakespeare's pen. Yet a young man in his early twenties who could write a poem which could for some time be accepted without question as having been written by Shakespeare had no inconsiderable talent. It is unfortunate that Barnfield apparently felt the writing of poetry was a recreation suited only to his college days, and unworthy the dignity of a respected landowner.

It should be noted that *The Affectionate Shepherd* is avowedly not an original work, but a "variation" on the Second Eclogue of Virgil. It should also be noted that the "Cynthia" of Barnfield's second volume was Queen Elizabeth.

PRINCIPAL WORKS: The Affectionate Shepherd, 1594; Cynthia, with Certain Sonnets, and the Legend of Cassandra, 1594; The Encomion of Lady Pecunia and Poems in Divers Humours, 1598; The Complaint of Poetrie for the Death of Liberalitie, 1598; Complete Poems, 1882.

ABOUT: Arber, E. Memoir in Complete Poems.

BARRI, GIRALDUS DE. See GIRALDUS CAMBRENSIS

BARROW, ISAAC (October 1630-May 4, 1677), mathematician and religious writer, was born in London, the son of Thomas Barrow, linen-draper to the king and "almost a gentleman," and Anne Buggin. His mother died when he was four, and he was reared by a stepmother. He attended Charterhouse and then Felstead School, but his father (like himself) was an ardent royalist, and lost all his property during the civil war. The boy was made "little tutor" to the young Viscount Fairfax when he was only eleven, then for a while became a "begging scholar." Finally Henry Hammond maintained him at Trinity College, Cambridge for half a year, and at last his father was enabled to come to his rescue. He received his B.A. in 1648, and took an

ISAAC BARROW   C. Lefebvre

M.A. degree from both Trinity and Oxford in 1652 and 1653. In spite of his royalist sympathies, he became a Fellow of Trinity, but an indiscreet speech earned him such unpopularity that he secured three years' leave, which he spent in Paris and in the Near East, particularly Constantinople (his trip including a fight with pirates en route to Smyrna), returning in 1659.

Immediately thereafter he was ordained, and soon after became Regius Professor of Greek. In 1662 he was named also as professor of geometry at Gresham College, London, though he continued to reside in Cambridge. The next year he was made a charter Fellow of the Royal Society. In 1663 he was also appointed first Lucasian Professor of Mathematics at Cambridge, and resigned the Gresham post. Seven years later he resigned that chair also, in favor of his great pupil, Isaac Newton. A Doctor of Divinity in 1670, he received two small livings but remained at Cambridge as College Preacher until 1672, when he became Master of Trinity. In 1675 he was named as Vice Chancellor of the University. Barrow was chiefly responsible for the establishment of the great Trinity library. He died in London at forty-seven and was buried in Westminster Abbey.

Barrow in his own day was considered a mathematician second only to Newton. He was also an anatomist (he had once wanted to study medicine), a botanist, and a classical scholar, who wrote almost entirely in Latin (including some minor poetry). As a teacher he was not a success, and attracted few students; as a preacher he was chiefly remarkable for his long-windedness. But he was a man of great intellectual power and of most attractive personality. A spoiled child, he grew into a small but wiry, athletically inclined man, whom John Evelyn called "that excellent, pious, and most learned divine, mathematician, poet, preacher, and most humble person." He was noted in his own day not only for his eccentricities —his slovenly dress and excessive smoking, among others—but for his wit, his modesty, and his saintly character as well.

As a writer, J. B. Mullinger remarked on his "completeness, coherence, and consecutiveness" and his "mingled strength and richness." His work gave an appearance almost of extemporaneousness, but was actually the product of long and laborious writing. Charles II, who was no fool, called Barrow "the best scholar in Europe."

He never married, and he died intestate, with nothing to leave but his books.

PRINCIPAL WORKS: Lectiones Geometricae, 1664-66 (as Geometrical Lectures, J. M. Child, tr., 1916); Lectiones Opticae, 1669; Exposition of the Creed, Decalogue, and Sacraments, 1669; Treatise on the Pope's Supremacy, 1680; Theological Works (A. Napier, ed.) 1859.

ABOUT: Hill, A. Memoir of Isaac Barrow; Osmond, P. H. Isaac Barrow, His Life and Times; Ward, J. Lives of the Professors of Gresham College.

BAXTER, RICHARD (November 12, 1615-December 8, 1691), religious writer, and one of the most important of the Nonconformist theologians, was born in Rowton, Shropshire, the son of Richard Baxter, a landowner who had dissipated his fortune, and Beatrice Adeny. The parents were separated at his birth, but soon after they were reunited and the child was reared in his father's home, Eaton-Constantine, nearby. Moreover, the wastrel father suddenly reformed, and was a great influence for piety and sobriety in his son's life. Nevertheless, his early education was atrocious, under a series of ignorant and drunken tutors; all his life he regretted his lack of learning and his inability to attend a university. He did have some schooling at the Free School in Wroxeter, but then, in 1632,

RICHARD BAXTER

made the mistake of going to Ludlow Castle as the only pupil of its chaplain, Richard Wickstead. All Wickstead gave him was a temporary change of direction—he had always wanted to be a clergyman, but Wickstead persuaded him to go to London instead, in the hope of court patronage. One month of that disgusted him, and he used his mother's illness as an excuse to return home. After a short period of teaching in his own school, he began to read divinity in earnest. He was ordained in 1638, and after teaching at the Grammar School in Dudley, became assistant minister at Bridgnorth.

Baxter's religious views, which altered during his lifetime, were Nonconformist but not orthodox Puritan; he did not fit well into the Puritan discipline, and though classed as a Presbyterian he would actually, in less disturbed times, have functioned happily as a Low Church Episcopalian. In 1641 he became minister of Kidderminster, Worcestershire, but the following year, with the outbreak of the civil war, he was obliged to leave Kidderminster. He went first to Gloucester, then to Coventry, and later became a chaplain in Cromwell's army. In 1647 he went back to Kidderminster, and until 1660 (the Restoration) carried on a notable career there as a reformer both of the clergy and the laity. Actually his con-

nection with the Puritan forces was as much to counteract some of their doctrines as to express his solidarity with their cause, and he was one of those who helped bring back Charles II. Indeed in 1660 and 1661 he was king's chaplain in London, and was offered and refused the bishopric of Hereford.

But he refused also to sign the agreements exacted by the Act of Uniformity, was forbidden to preach, and from 1662 to 1687 was constantly under persecution because he would not obey. Several times he was arrested for "keeping a conventicle," his goods were distrained, and finally he was tried before the notorious Sir George Jeffreys, in 1685, for "libeling the church," was brutally treated, and imprisoned for eighteen months. It must be remembered that he was then seventy, had suffered all his life from tuberculosis, and was in an extremely frail and perilous state of health.

The one great happiness of Baxter's life was his marriage to Margaret Charlton, in 1662. But she died in 1681. From 1687 to his death in London four years later, he lived in peace and honor, though in loneliness and sorrow. He had much to do with the deposition of James II, and lived to see the Toleration Act under William and Mary.

Archbishop Trent called Baxter "the creator of popular Christian literature." However that may be, he had an enormous influence on his time. A voluminous writer (his religious works alone number more than a hundred), his style is one of "robust and masculine eloquence." It is also discursive and loquacious—which loquacity was the principal reason for Cromwell's personal dislike of him. A life-long semi-invalid, he wrote most voluminously when he was in poorest health and under the most severe persecution. He was persuaded that everyone was open to reason, and that the answer to the Established Church and the Dissenters and "Levellers" alike was reasonable argument. He hated all fanaticism, but on this point he himself was a fanatic.

Baxter's best known work is *The Saints' Everlasting Rest*. His brief life of his wife is touching in its tenderness. His mind was scholarly, but religion to him was everything, and he subordinated to it all secular learning.

PRINCIPAL WORKS: Aphorisms of Justification, 1649; Saints' Everlasting Rest, 1650; Breviate of the Life of Mrs. Margaret Baxter, 1681; Paraphrase of the New Testament, 1685; Reliquae Baxterianae: Mr. Richard Baxter's Narrative of the Most Memorable Passages of his Life and Times (M. Sylvester, ed.) 1696; Practical Works, 1830.

ABOUT: Baxter, R. Reliquae Baxterianae; Grosart, A. B. Representative Nonconformists; Kemp, C. F. Pastoral Triumph: The Story of Richard Baxter and His Ministry at Kidderminster; Morgan, I. Nonconformity of Richard Baxter; Orme, W. Life and Times of Richard Baxter; Powicke, F. J. A Life of the Rev. Richard Baxter; Stephen, J. Essays in Ecclesiastical Biography; Tulloch, J. English Puritanism and Its Leaders; Wilkinson, J. Richard Baxter and Margaret Charlton.

BEATTIE, JAMES (October 25, 1735-1803), poet and essayist, was famous in his day on both counts, but is now practically forgotten. He was born in Laurencekirk, Kincardine, Scotland, the son of a poor shopkeeper and small farmer. His father died when James was seven, and he was reared by his eldest brother, who managed to send him to Marischal College, Aberdeen in 1749. There in the true Scottish tradition of brilliant boys of poor families, he soon secured a bursarship and thenceforward financed his own college career.

He took his M.A. in 1753, and since he could not afford to remain for further study of divinity, as he had wished, he became schoolmaster and parish clerk in a village near his home. He began at the same time publishing poems in the *Scots Magazine* which brought him to the attention of people of influence. He was, after a few years, enabled to return to Marischal to take a course in divinity, but abandoned it when he was appointed a master at the Aberdeen Grammar School. He was still in this post when, in 1760, to his own astonishment, he was, through the influence of a friend, made professor of moral philosophy and logic at his old college.

For the remainder of his life, until in 1797 the first of several strokes made it impossible for him to continue, he held this chair. However, he was able to make frequent long stays in London, where he became a member of the circle around Dr. Johnson, a friend of Burke, Gray, and Reynolds. He was brought to the attention of

After Sir J. Reynolds
JAMES BEATTIE

George III, who was an immense admirer of Beattie's philosophical works, and in 1775 he was put on the Civil List for £200 a year. Reynolds painted him as the "conqueror" of Hume and Voltaire and the other "infidel" philosophers, and Mrs. Thrale declared that if ever she remarried, Beattie would be her choice!

Beattie needed these consolations and flatteries. His personal life was most unhappy. In 1767 he married Mary Dunn, who after the birth of their two sons became hopelessly insane. In a few years she grew so violent that she had to be kept in confinement. Beattie devoted himself to the rearing of his sons, and the elder particularly, James Hay Beattie, became his pride. At twenty the boy was a published poet and his father's assistant at Marischal, with promise of the chair on the older Beattie's retirement. At twenty-one James Hay Beattie died. The other son died six years later. The old man never recovered from the double shock. In 1799 he became completely invalided, and four years later he died in London.

Beattie's fame in his lifetime rested on two works—his long poem, *The Minstrel*, and his *Essay on the Nature and Immutability of the Truth*. Unfortunately, neither has stood the test of time. His poetry, though it influenced many of the Romantics, and particularly Byron, is, as George Saints-

31

bury put it, "watered-out sepia." He was a pioneer of Romanticism, and he was the first to write considerably in the Spenserian stanza, but his manner was static and inanimate, and his matter (to quote Saintsbury again) "silly rubbish." His feeling for the beauty of nature was real—it is said that he often spent whole nights, in his youth, lying out-of-doors gazing at the stars—and he had some ability as a musician; but when he came to describing nature his words were commonplace, and there was little music in his verse.

As for his philosophical essay, which so entranced George III ("The only book I ever stole was yours, which I stole from Hereford to give to the queen"), W. R. Sorley called it "a vigorous polemic, but with no originality or distinction." It, with his other philosophic works, was written to confute Hume, and intended for the reading of non-professionals in philosophy. Its arguments are shallow and its style is flat. Hume's only comment was that he had not been treated in a very gentlemanly manner.

Beattie was, however, sufficiently a scholar to have been chosen to edit Addison's works, and to have been offered a professorship at the University of Edinburgh, which he declined. (He also declined a proferred living in the Church of England.) He was not in general ill-natured; his bitter *Verses on the Death of [Charles] Churchill*, published in 1765, he himself suppressed immediately after their publication. His friends thought so highly of him that when he sent them his *Essay* and they were not able to find a publisher to accept it, they themselves had it printed and sent him fifty guineas on the pretence that this was the publisher's payment!

"The Minstrel," "Retirement," and the "Pastorals" are no longer read except by students of the period. But the fact remains that Beattie as a poet was a pioneer of the Romantic Movement, and in that capacity he deserves to be commemorated.

PRINCIPAL WORKS: *Verse*—Original Poems and Translations, 1761; The Judgment of Paris, 1765; The Minstrel, 1771-74. *Prose*—Essay on the Nature and Immutability of the Truth, 1770 (with three other Essays, 1776); Dissertations Moral and Critical, 1783; Evidences of the Christian Religion, 1786; Elements of Moral Science, 1790; Essays and Fragments in Prose and Verse, 1794; Poetical Works, 1866.

ABOUT: Beattie, J. Autobiographical Sketch *in* Essays and Fragments; Beattie, J. James Beattie's London Diary; Forbes, M. Beattie and His Friends; Forbes, W. An Account of the Life and Writings of James Beattie; Mackie, A. James Beattie, "The Minstrel."

BEAUMONT, FRANCIS (1584-March 6, 1616), dramatist, was born in Grace-Dieu, his ancestral estate in Leicestershire, the third son of Francis Beaumont, a judge of common pleas, and Anne Pierrepoint. The family was an old and distinguished one, and all the sons and the one daughter were gifted. The three boys together were entered at Broadgates Hall (now Pembroke), Oxford, in 1596, when Francis was only twelve. Two years later their father died suddenly, and they all left the university without a degree, though it is possible that the youngest stayed until 1600. In that year, in any event, he was enrolled in the Inner Temple.

He was never called to the bar; instead, he became an integral part of the brilliant, Bohemian crowd of dramatists and poets who centered about the Mermaid Tavern. Ben Jonson and Michael Drayton became his close friends, and he was certainly well acquainted with Shakespeare. Just when he met John Fletcher,[qv] with whom he lived and who was to become his close collaborator, is not known, but it was somewhere around 1605. These two young men were in a different category, in a way, from those like Shakespeare, Marlowe, Jonson, and Webster, who wrote plays for a living; they had private means and it was of little concern to them whether their plays were successful or not. Nevertheless, they became wholly one with the star-cluster that lighted the skies of Elizabethan drama.

Beaumont's earliest work had been in non-dramatic verse, partly in the form of prologues to poems by his older brother. His first play, *The Woman-Hater*, formerly attributed to Fletcher alone, is now known to have been solely his own work. Together with Fletcher he wrote ten more plays, the most outstanding of which were the romantic tragicomedy, *Philaster*, and the broad burlesque, *The Knight of the Burning Pestle*, and then in swift succession he married, left the happy-go-lucky bachelor life with Fletcher in Southwark, and three years later was dead, before he was thirty-two. According to contemporary opinion, he died of fever induced by the fervor of his imagination; actually his family was markedly short-lived, and his constitution had always been frail. Beaumont married Ursula Isley in 1613, and they had two daughters, one born posthumously. He was buried in the Poets' Corner of Westminster Abbey. He died only six weeks before Shakespeare.

The question of exactly how much of Beaumont and Fletcher's joint work belonged to each can never be settled. It is significant that after Beaumont's death, Fletcher, though he produced a good deal, never again achieved first rank. Undoubtedly Beaumont was the better poet, and in some ways the better dramatist. He had a keenly critical mind, and Dryden said that Jonson, who was eleven years his senior, submitted all his plays for Beaumont's censorship before offering them in the theater. Certainly he did a great deal to tone down Fletcher's exuberance and taste for melodrama and for coarseness. As Swinburne has remarked, if Beaumont and Fletcher may be compared to Castor and Pollux, Beaumont was "the twin of heavenlier birth." Charles A. Gayley deprecated the universal habit of considering the two dramatists as "an indivisible pair of Siamese twins." He felt that Beaumont, in his own right, was "the most essentially poetic dramatist of the age next to Shakespeare," with his "joyous irony" and his "refreshingly unhackneyed" style.

FRANCIS BEAUMONT

Émile Legouis, though he too praised Beaumont's "harmonious verse and graceful language" and the "undeniable skill" with which he and Fletcher "make the real unreal," yet has pointed out that Beaumont's and Fletcher's plays mark the apotheosis— and the beginning of decline—of Elizabethan drama. Had it not been for Beaumont— whose "main business," according to John Aubrey, "was to correct the overflowings of Mr. Fletcher's wit"—the decline might have been more apparent than the apotheosis. Undoubtedly his was "the firmer hand and statelier manner; his diction was more solid; there was richer music in his verse."

Though Beaumont's was an attractive personality—thoughtful, gentle, gay—there attaches to him little of the pathos which usually clings around poets who die young. Essentially his writing is the writing of youth, and even if his health had not failed and his death come early, he would in all probability soon have abandoned playwriting for the more usual concerns of a man of good family and private property at a time when connection with the stage had a inescapably raffish aura. He would undoubtedly have gone on writing, as his brother, Sir John Beaumont, did; but the poet would in all likelihood have triumphed over the dramatist. There were signs of this already, markedly in the *Masque of the Inner Temple*, which he wrote in 1613.

Swinburne himself, in his classic critique of "this passionate and fiery genius," made this same point: "There is the glory and grace of youth in all they have left us; . . . we cannot conceive of them grown gray in the dignity of years. . . . In perfect bloom and flower of song-writing, they equal all compeers whom they do not excel; [and there remains] witness enough for the younger brother [Beaumont] of a lyric power as pure and rare as his elder's."

It must, however, be noted that Beaumont did sometimes write in prose, and that Fletcher did so very seldom. He was a subtler poet than Fletcher, but also shared his collaborator's "rich vein of burlesque" and his delight in the droll and broadly comic. He shared with Fletcher a first-hand knowledge of the stage which came from their close association with actors as well as with playwrights in the days when they shared Bohemian quarters near the Globe Theatre. He too has adroitness and flexibility, raciness and dexterity. But in the serious plays of the two authors, one may detect often the hand of Beaumont, moderating, subtilizing, softening. Fletcher too was a poet of great talent, but he lacked the classical, almost Puritan vein which Beaumont possessed. The stately serenity and gravity of Beaumont's portraits were the outward aspects of a nature quieter and less vivid, yet more thoughtful and more sensitive, than his friend's. Their coming together as co-authors was one of the happiest accidents of English literature.

PRINCIPAL WORKS: *Plays* (dates of publication)—The Woman-Hater, 1607 (not with Fletcher); The Scornful Lady, 1610; The Maid's Tragedy, 1611; The Knight of the Burning Pestle, 1613; Cupid's Revenge, 1615; The Triumph of Honor and the Triumph of Love (Beaumont's share in Four Plays) 1617; A King and No King, 1619; Philaster, or Love Lies Bleeding, 1620; The Coxcomb, 1647; The Captain, 1647; Comedies and Tragedies Written by Francis Beaumont and John Fletcher, Gentlemen, 1647. *Non-Dramatic Poems* —Salmacis and Hermaphroditus, 1602; Masque of the Inner Temple, 1613; Poems (with others) 1640 and 1648.

ABOUT: Gayley, C. M. Beaumont, the Dramatist; Macaulay, G. C. Francis Beaumont, A Critical Study; Maxwell, B. Studies in Beaumont, Fletcher, and Massinger; Oliphant, E. H. C. The Plays of Beaumont and Fletcher; Sprague, A. C. Beaumont and Fletcher on the Restoration Stage; Strachey, J. S. Sketch, *in* Plays by Beaumont and Fletcher, 1893 ed.; Swinburne, A. C. Contemporaries of Shakespeare; Wallis, L. B. Fletcher, Beaumont, and Company, Entertainers to the Jacobean Gentry; Wilson, J. H. The Influence of Beaumont and Fletcher on Restoration Drama.

BEDA, BEDE or **BAEDA** (673-May 26, 735), historian, scholar, religious writer, was born, according to the autobiographical account which prefaces his great work the *Ecclesiastical History*, near Wearmouth and Jarrow (now the county of Durham) where he was destined to spend his life in the monastery of St. Peter and St. Paul founded by Benedict Biscop in 674. Apparently (again, according to his own account), he lost his parents before he was seven years old and was given into the care of the Abbot Benedict by relatives. Educated by the Abbots Benedict and Coelfrid, Beda was ordained a deacon at the age of nineteen and a priest at thirty.

His life was without any dramatic event, cloistered by monastery walls; yet so powerful was the strength and dignity of his spirit, so wide his learning, so lucid his power of expression that he is remembered as one of the great figures of Anglo-Saxon history, a man who left an indelible signature on the literature of succeeding centuries. "I have spent the whole of my life within that monastery," he writes, "devoting all my pains to the study of the scriptures; and amid the observance of monastic discipline and the daily charge of singing in the church, it has ever been my delight to learn or teach or write." In his works then, we must look for the personality, as well as the accomplishment, of the gentle scholar-priest.

These works, which in their entirety (according to the Reverend Charles Plummer, most authoritative of his modern editors) sum up all the learning of western Europe in his time, fall into three main categories: the theological writings; the scientific works, including treatises on natural phenomena (*De Natura Rerum*), on chronology and the calendar (*De Temporibus, De Temporum Ratione*), on grammar; and, most important, the historical works culminating in the magnificent *Ecclesiastical History of the English Nation (Historia Ecclesiastica*), of which King Alfred was the first translator, and which gives Beda legitimate claim to the title, Father of English History.

Both in scholarship and in literary skill, the *History* is a valuable and beautiful work. With a conscientiousness rare among medieval scholars, Beda chose his sources carefully, striving always to differentiate between fact and tradition and, what is even more rare, giving full credit to his authorities. He writes, moreover, with a striking lack of prejudice remarkable in one whose life and point of view were so inevitably circumscribed, and with a sheer narrative power which reveals him as a true artist.

It was a fortunate circumstance for Beda that the monastery where he received his education housed one of the finest libraries of the time. The Abbot Benedict Biscop who built the monastery at Wearmouth and seven years later the addition at Jarrow seems to have been anything but provincial. He travelled widely on the continent, collecting manuscripts and establishing relations with other ecclesiastical institutions. The monastery buildings were designed after the

Roman style with pictorial glass windows and a splendid library. Beda knew Latin and Greek, probably Hebrew, and had read widely in the ancient writers. This continental orientation enabled him not only to draw on all the learning of Europe, but later made it possible to disseminate the knowledge contained in his works throughout the western world. Although he wrote almost exclusively in Latin, the scholar's language, Beda still stands as one of the heroic figures in the history of English literature.

Because he was known as the "Venerable Beda," it has been falsely supposed that he lived to a great age. That this is quite untrue seems conclusively proven by a contemporary letter which gives an account of his death. According to the date of this letter, written by one of his pupils, Cuthbert (later an abbot), Beda must have been sixty-two or sixty-three at the time of his death. Characteristically, his last days were spent in teaching and devotion. He seems to have been engaged in dictating a translation of the Gospel of St. John into the Anglo-Saxon vernacular (unfortunately, this work has not survived), and the story of his death as told by Cuthbert is extremely moving. "His young scribe said, "There is yet one more sentence, dear master, to write out.' He answered, 'Write quickly.' After awhile the boy said, 'Now it is finished.' 'Well,' he said, 'thou hast spoken truly. It is finished.' And chanting the Gloria Patri, he died."

PRINCIPAL WORKS: Opera (J. A. Giles, ed.) 12 vols., 1843-44; Bedae Opera Historica, including Historia Ecclesiastica (C. Plummer, ed.) 2 vols., 1896.

ABOUT: Bright, W. Chapters of Early English Church History; Browne, G. F. The Venerable Bede; Carroll, T. A. Venerable Bede: His Spiritual Techniques; Duckett, E. S. Anglo-Saxon Saints and Scholars; Plummer, C. Preface to Historia Ecclesiastica; Thompson, A. H. Bede. His Life, Times and Writings.

BEHN, Mrs. APHRA (AMIS) July, 1640-April 16, 1689), dramatist, novelist, poet, and the first woman in England to earn her own living as a writer, was born at Wye, Kent. Her parents, previously described as John and Amy Johnson, were actually John and Amy Amis, and her brother Peter may have been a twin. Moreover, it is known now that her father was not a barber, but

After M. Beale
MRS. APHRA BEHN

had a much higher standing—in fact, that she may have been correct in saying that when she was sixteen her father was appointed lieutenant governor of Surinam, and that the whole family traveled with him to South America. It is true, as Gwendolyn Bridges Needham has remarked, that Mrs. Behn's "autobiographical data were written to sell, not for later historians to take seriously"; nevertheless it seems likely that she did spend some years in Surinam, whether or not her father died at sea en route and the mother and children were given a house and lived there until the Dutch took over Surinam in 1658. At all events, at some time near that date she married in London a merchant of Netherlands descent named Behn. For a while she seems to have been wealthy and more or less in society; then in 1665 her husband died and she became completely poverty-stricken, though why he left her nothing has never been determined.

A staunch royalist, she turned for succor to the court of Charles II, and was sent to the Low Countries as a secret agent, her Dutch name being of value in that connection. For a year she lived in Antwerp, sending in useful information under the code name of Astrea, which later became her nickname in literary circles. The government treated her very shabbily; she was not paid for her services and was obliged to return to London, where she even underwent a term in a debtors' prison before the money due her was forthcoming.

Thenceforth she set to work to become self-supporting by her pen. She became, as V. Sackville-West puts it, "an inhabitant of Grub Street with the best of them, . . . a phenomenon never seen and . . . furiously resented." She was, as Felix Schelling said, "a very gifted woman, compelled to write for bread in an age in which literature . . . catered habitually to the lowest and most depraved of human inclinations. Her success depended on her ability to write like a man."

Mrs. Behn thought of herself primarily as a poet, and she had a graceful lyric gift; but the way to make money was to write plays, so write plays she did. With the emergence of the novel as a popular form she wrote novels as well. She had little success until the appearance of *The Rover*, in 1677, but thereafter her comedies (*Abdelazar* was her only tragedy) appeared one on the heels of its predecessor. She was never able to stop writing, or to take long enough over her work to permit her to do the kind of writing of which she was capable. She was a model of industry, a hard-working hack writer, not the dissipated debauchee described by her shocked contemporaries. That does not mean that her plays were not frequently very broad and completely bawdy —they were; or that her life was conventional—it was not. She was, as Edmund Gosse remarked, "the George Sand of the Restoration," and she lived the Bohemian life in London in the seventeenth century as George Sand lived it in Paris in the nineteenth. How many lovers she had, no one knows, and it does not matter; the only one whose name has come down to us is John Hoyle, the rake and wit who broke her heart, and to whom she wrote the touching *Love Letters to a Gentleman*.

"Gay, tragic, generous, smutty, rich of nature and big of heart," as V. Sackville-West has phrased it, Aphra Behn's was truly an "abused and wasted genius." She is often spoken of as a forerunner of Defoe and Rousseau in *Oroonoko* (a story of Surinam Indians); the latter ascription is true, the former is not. She had it in her to be a great realist, she had the material, and the ability to deal with it, but she had to write what would bring in money, and risqué comedies packed full of action were what would bring it in. She plagiarized freely, as did most dramatists of her time, taking her plots from here, there, and everywhere; and if dirt was what would make a play popular, then Mrs. Behn could pour it out and outdo the men at their own game. But she had a mind inventive for situation if not for plot, a genius for racy, vivid dialogue, and a fine, free, rapid style. Her novels are nearer to genuine literature than are her plays, but they all came at the end of her life, and she never had time to develop what was undoubtedly her greatest talent.

What if plays and novels alike are unreadable today, what if she romanced about her own career and hid its more sordid spots in colorful fancies? She was her own worst enemy, a warm-hearted, outgoing creature who gave away most of what she made, a woman who loved deeply and suffered much, whom even the prim Gosse called "not degraded, though unconventional." And she was a pioneer of feminism, a woman who did not merely claim the right to live her own life and earn her own living by the gifts nature had given her, but quietly went ahead and did it, in the face of almost insuperable obstacles. She was a fine human being, and in a better age she would have been a fine writer. She died before she reached fifty, worn out, killed by arthritis and her doctor's mistakes; and she is not the worst person to be buried in the Poets' Corner of Westminster Abbey.

PRINCIPAL WORKS: *Plays* (dates of production)—The Forced Marriage, 1670; The Amorous Prince, 1671; Abdelazar, 1671; The Dutch Lover, 1673; The Rover, 1677 (second part, 1681); The Debauchee, 1677; The Town-Fop, 1677; Sir Patient Fancy, 1678; The Feigned Courtesans, 1679; The Round-Heads, 1682; The City Heiress, 1682; The False Count, 1682; The Young King (verse) 1683; The Lucky Chance, 1686; Emperor of the Moon, 1687; The Widow Ranter, 1690; The Younger Brother, 1696; The Plays of Mrs. Aphra Behn, 1702. *Novels*—The Unfortunate Happy Lady, 1685; The Adventures of the Black Lady, 1686; The Unfortunate Bride, 1687; The Dumb Virgin, 1687; The Wandering Beauty, 1687; Oroonoko, or The Royal Slave, 1688; Lycidus, 1688; The History of the Nun, 1688; The Fair Jilt, 1688; Agnes de Castro, 1688; The Court of the King of Bantam, 1696; The Plays, Histories, and Novels of the Ingenious Mrs. Aphra Behn, 1698. *Miscellaneous* — Poems upon Several Occasions, 1684; Le Montre, or the Lover's Watch, 1686; Love Letters to a Gentleman, 1696; Poetical Remains, 1698; Works (M. Summers, ed.) 1915.

ABOUT: Blashfield, E. Portraits and Backgrounds; Canby, H. S. The Short Story in English; Hudson, W. H. Idle Hours in a Library; Jerrold, W. and C. Five Queer Women; Sackville-West, V. Aphra Behn, the Incomparable Astrea; Schelling, F. The Restoration Drama; Summers, M. Memoir in Works; Woodcock, G. Incomparable Aphra.

BENLOWES, EDWARD (1603?-December 18, 1676),

poet, was born on the Brent Hall, Essex, estate which he later inherited from his father. Following graduation from Cambridge and the customary grand tour of the continent, he became a well-known and often-satirized figure in fashionable literary circles of England.

What made him conspicuous in his own time was his lavish patronage of poor students, struggling poets, friends, and flatterers. He published ten or twelve works, all but one of them short and insignificant. His over-generous gifts to friends, sycophants, and a favorite niece (whose affection he estranged when he was converted from Catholicism to Protestantism) consumed his fortune; and his death at Oxford, where he spent his final years, was probably hastened by extreme poverty. His burial in St. Mary's Church was paid for by means of a collection among the scholars.

Benlowes' only work of any importance was a long poem, *Theophilia, or Love's Sacrifice*, which was well received upon its publication in 1652. Primarily intended as a theological expression, its succession of mystical concepts and worldly satires on vice is so ineptly arranged that the meaning is sometimes unclear. The poet's sincerely devout intention often produced passages which evoke true religious atmosphere, just as his subtle and dexterous use of imagery occasionally produced a beautiful poetic phrase. More often, his juxtaposition of psychological and theological details made for confusion, and his unbridled imagination resulted in preposterous conceits.

So extravagant were some of his images, so immoderate his use of puns, word-plays, and elaborately ridiculous metaphors, that there seems almost to be a wilful determination to be as extraordinary as possible. This impression is heightened by his use throughout the long poem of a peculiarly monotonous rhyming triplet.

Benlowes' poetry and his overweening generosity were lampooned by Samuel Butler and Pope, and by many of his fellows among the minor Caroline poets.

PRINCIPAL WORKS: Sphinx Theologia seu Musica Templi, 1626; Lusus Poeticus Poetis, 1635; A Buckler Against the Feare of Death, 1640; Honorifica Armorum Cessatio Sive Pacis et Fidei Associatio, 1643; Theophilia, or Love's Sacrifice, 1652; The Summary of Divine Wisdome, 1657; Threno-Thriambeuticon, 1660.

ABOUT: Corser, T. Collectanea Anglo-Poetica; Hazlitt, W. Handbook; Hazlitt, W. Collections and Notes; Wood, A. à, Fasti.

BENTLEY, RICHARD (January 27, 1662-July 14, 1742),

scholar, critic, was the son of Thomas Bentley and Sarah Willie, his second wife; the family on both sides came of the yeoman class. He was born at Oulton, Yorkshire, and educated first at Wakefield Grammar School. His father dying when the boy was thirteen, his maternal grandfather had him entered at St. John's Cambridge, the same year. He received his B.A. in 1680. After a period as master at Spalding School, he became tutor to the son of Dean Stillingfleet of St. Paul's, later Bishop of Worcester. Stillingfleet had a notable library, and Bentley absorbed it with indefatigable appetite. He said later he would be willing to die at eighty (strangely enough, he did!), because by then he would have read all the books worth reading.

In 1689 he became the first Boyle's lecturer at Oxford, delivering his famous lectures, against Hobbes, on the confutation of Atheism. In 1692 he was appointed to a prebendary at Worcester, doubtless by Stillingfleet's influence, and two years later he became keeper of the royal libraries, with an apartment in St. James's Palace, where he entertained his closest friends — Sir Isaac Newton, John Evelyn, John Locke, and Christopher Wren. This post he retained throughout his life, in spite of other commitments. In 1695 he became also chaplain in ordinary to William III.

Bentley was already used to controversy when the long drawn out great battle of his life began at Trinity College, Cambridge. The fight over the authenticity of alleged writings of Phalaris, the Sicilian tyrant, had raged since 1692, earning Bentley the undying enmity of Sir William Temple, Francis Atterbury, Charles Boyle, and above all

Sir J. Thornhill, 1710

RICHARD BENTLEY

Alexander Pope. But this was nothing to what followed. In 1700 he was made master of Trinity. The fellows of the college were soon at war with his despotism, arrogance, and invasion of their rights. Twice he was removed from office, once he was deprived temporarily of his degrees, and it is doubtful whether when he died he was legally master; but through it all he clung to his office with unremitting pertinacity, every trick of the law, and what James Duff Duff can call only "sordid rapacity."

Yet throughout these years, Bentley remained still primarily the great scholar, one of the greatest known to history. Even his unfortunate editing and "revision" of Milton's *Paradise Lost* cannot take away from his glory in his own fields of classical learning. His writing was all hasty, all polemic; it is not as a writer that he lives, but as the founder of historical philology. As Duff says, "no greater intellect than his has ever been devoted to the study and elucidation of ancient literature." Nor was his relation to Trinity entirely bad; he reformed its discipline and greatly encouraged learning there even in studies entirely outside of his own interests.

Although his public manner was proud and overbearing, in private he was affectionate and magnanimous, despite his pomposity. In 1701 he married Joanna Bernard, and

they had two sons and two daughters. He was an eccentric, who never left Trinity except to go to London to the royal libraries, who took no exercise but a walk in his garden and accepted no social engagements outside his own house. At seventy he became a heavy smoker, which may have contributed to his death from pleurisy ten years later.

Bentley must not be judged by Pope's denunciations of him in *The Dunciad*. He was as far from a dunce as any man could be. His editions of Terence, Cicero, Phaedrus, Manilius, Lucan, and even Horace (the least admirable) are landmarks in the history of classical scholarship. He lacked completely the poetic sense, and should have let poets, Latin as well as English, strictly alone. As Louis Cazamian put it, he possessed "an instinctive sense of method, a strong critical shrewdness, and above all the divine gift for truth." Though his books were all written as direct outgrowths of his various embroilments, his style (to quote Cazamian again) was "compact, cogent, and at the same time racy, and capable of irony, concrete vigor, and eloquence."

The truth seems to be that nature had formed Bentley for the cloistered life of the scholar, and that his temperament was quite unfitted for public office or responsibility. He would certainly have been far happier had he spent his years sequestered in the royal libraries, and the world of learning would have benefited by the increased productivity such a sequestered life would have made possible. He planned many things that his constant disputes and trials prevented him from finishing or even undertaking—e.g., a revised edition of the Greek New Testament. To Pope and Swift he was an obstinate fool (the Phalaris controversy inspired Swift's *Battle of the Books*, Swift being then in the employ of Sir William Temple); but to such men as Newton and Locke he was an object of admiration, their equal in intellect, their superior in erudition. He was not a likable person, but he was a great critic and a mighty scholar.

PRINCIPAL WORKS: Epistola ad Millium, 1671; Sermons on the Confutation of Atheism, 1699 (as separate parts, 1692); Dissertation upon the Epistles of Phalaris, etc., 1699; A Sermon upon Popery, 1715; The Present State of Trinity College in Cambridge, 1719; Proposals to Print a New Edition of the Greek Testament, 1721; Works (A. Dyce, ed.) 1836-38; The Correspondence of Richard Bentley (C. Wordsworth, ed.) 1842.

ABOUT: Bartholomew, A. T. and Clarke, J. W. Bibliography of Bentley; DeQuincey, T. Essay on Bentley; Jebb, R. C. Bentley; Mähly, J. Richard Bentley; Monk, J. H. Life of Richard Bentley; Nicoll, H. J. Great Scholars; Sandys, J. E. History of Classical Scholarship.

BERKELEY, GEORGE (March 12, 1685-January 14, 1753), philosopher, was the son of William Berkeley, a kinsman of the noble family of that name, and a customs officer in Ireland. Berkeley always spoke and thought of himself as an Englishman, though he was born in Kilkenny, Ireland. He went to Kilkenny School, and then to Trinity College, Dublin, in 1700. There he remained, as scholar, fellow, and tutor, until 1713. His first publications were two anonymous pamphlets on mathematics. In 1713 he obtained leave of absence, and was abroad, mostly in France and Italy, until 1721, acting as chaplain and then as private tutor to support himself. This was for Berkeley a period of meditation; already, in his *Common Place Book*, and in two later volumes, he had expounded the beginnings of his famous "principles of human knowledge," but now he wrote little and actually lost the few manuscripts he did manage to produce.

Returning to Trinity in 1721, he took his B.D. and D.D. degrees, and in 1722 was nominated Dean of Dromore. A lawsuit prevented his assuming the deanery, and he continued to act as Hebrew lecturer and senior proctor at Trinity. Then in 1724 he received the much more lucrative deanship of Derry. His private fortune had also been enlarged by a strange legacy—Swift's Vanessa, Hester Vanhomrigh, left him half her fortune (in anger at Swift), though he had met her only once. As her executor, he suppressed for some time the famous correspondence between her and Swift.

For ten years after this, most of Berkeley's energies went into his scheme for the establishment of a college in America, specifically in Bermuda, for the encouragement of learning among the English settlers and conversion of the Indians. He labored ceaselessly, by writing and by personal appeal, and finally secured a grant from Parliament, which opponents of the scheme had no intention of ever allowing to be paid. Nevertheless, Berkeley, who had married Anne Forster in 1728, sailed immediately with his bride, not for Bermuda, but for Newport, Rhode Island, where he lived until 1731, when it became obvious that the money never would be forthcoming. In America he wrote his *Alciphron*, established a philosophical society in Rhode Island, became a close friend of the American Dr. Samuel Johnson (president of King's College [Columbia]), and became a strong influence on the mind and work of Jonathan Edwards. Curiously enough, he owned and justified the owning of slaves!

Returning from America, disheartened as to his educational scheme and ready to resume advocacy of his other great interest, his new system of philosophy, Berkeley lived in London from 1732 to 1734, when he was made Bishop of Cloyne, Ireland. There he remained until 1752, when he asked to be allowed to resign and to spend his remaining years in Oxford. The king told him he might live anywhere he pleased, but would not be allowed to give up his bishopric. He was by this time sixty-seven, deeply engrossed both in his philosophical writings and in a new project, the advocacy of tar water as a panacea for practically all diseases of man and beast. He was besides going through a period of deep melancholy, caused by the deaths of his favorite son (he had four sons

J. Smibert, 1728
GEORGE BERKELEY

and three daughters, of whom three sons and one daughter grew up) and of his lifelong friend Thomas Prior. He moved to Oxford in the summer of 1752, and five months later he was dead.

His name was chosen for Berkeley, California, the seat of the University of California—3000 miles from the America he knew—because of the famous line, "Westward the course of Empire takes its way," from his poem, *Verses on the Prospect of Planting Arts and Learning in America.* Personally he has been called "an almost perfect man," kindly, generous, highminded, devoted to truth as he saw it, willing to be derided as a faddist, if necessary, rather than to refrain from advocating what he believed. (This comment refers, of course, to such matters as the American college and the use of tar water, not to his philosophy, which is in a different category altogether.) He died as he had lived, quietly listening to his wife as she read aloud to him.

The keynote of Berkeley's philosophy is the "immaterial hypothesis"—the contention that "only persons exist; all other things are not so much existences as the manners of the existence of persons." In other words, the world has no being except as we conceive it to exist. Gradually the influence of Locke on this idealistic system of philosophy gave way to a closer approximation to the Platonic "ideas"; with Plato, he believed that "ideas are things." Though his system remained fragmentary, and was never worked out to its logical conclusions, as a philosopher Berkeley ranks with Locke and Hume. The essential kernel of his philosophy came to him in early youth, and though it grew in amplitude and underwent some modification, it remained intrinsically the same to his latest expositions of his theory. As W. R. Sorley said, he remained all his life "loyal to the vision of truth" which had come to him in his early twenties. Plato's "ideas" to Berkeley were divine archetypes, existing in the mind of God; physical things are produced by God's will, and man's experience of sensation is his realization, in his finite mind, of these archetypes. The object of science is to decipher and interpret these divine ideas, and the universe is orderly and comprehensible only because mind—first divine mind, then human mind in its limited sphere—is the mainspring of being.

None of this is set down by Berkeley in dry technicalities. "His very intelligence is impassioned," said Louis Cazamian, "and the character of the man is all lit up with the warm radiance of a sentimental and humanitarian zeal." The nature of the philosopher inspired the style of his writing; it is clear and brilliant—so far as clarity is possible in so abstruse a subject—and his prose has the utmost ease and simplicity. Even when he engaged in polemics—as in his attacks on the higher mathematics as leading to Atheism (shades of the pious Sir Isaac Newton)—he was never arrogant or acidulous. Almost as much as Spinoza, Berkeley was "a God-intoxicated man," but unlike Spinoza, unlike most other philosophers, he was a lover of his kind, ardent to improve the lot of humanity, eager for social as well as for religious reform.

Time has not dealt kindly with Berkeley's philosophy; the progress of material science has invalidated many of its theses. Nevertheless, it remains not only a landmark in philosophical history, but also to some extent a living influence even today. The metaphysical physicists—men like Eddington, Jeans, and Millikan—owe more than perhaps they realize to the central thesis of the Bishop of Cloyne. Baldly stated—the assertion, for example, that the chair in which you sit would have no existence if you were not aware of it—"the immaterial hypothesis" can be made to sound ridiculous. But such men as Hume, Diderot, and Kant—to name only his immediate successors—did not consider it so; it is an integral part of any consideration of the development of philosophic ideas in modern times.

PRINCIPAL WORKS: Essay Towards a New Theory of Vision, 1709; Treatise Concerning the Principles of Human Knowledge, 1710; Three Dialogues Between Hylas and Philonous, 1713; De Motu, 1721; Essay Towards Preventing the Ruin of Great Britain, 1721; A Proposal for . . . a College . . . in Bermuda, 1725; Alciphron, or the Minute Philosopher, 1732; Theory of Vision, or Visual Language . . . Vindicated and Explained, 1733; The Analyst, 1734; The Querist, 1735 (revised, 1750); Siris, A Chain of Philosophical Reflexions, 1744; Collected Works (F. A. Campbell, ed.) (first publication of Common Place Book) 1871.

ABOUT: Balfour, A. J. Biographical Introduction, 1897 ed.; Fraser, A. C. Berkeley and Spiritual

Idealism; Huxley, T. Critiques and Addresses; Luce, A. A. Life of George Berkeley: Bishop of Cloyne; Mill, J. S. Three Essays on Religion; Rand, B. Berkeley and Percival; Sampson, G., ed. in Works; Sidgwick, H. History of Ethics; Tyler, M. C. Three Men of Letters; Weber, A. History of Philosophy.

BERNERS, JOHN BOURCHIER, Second Baron (1467-March 16, 1533), statesman, translator, historian, was born just four years before his father, Humphrey Bourchier, lost his life at the battle of Barnet, fighting for Edward IV. His mother, Elizabeth, was the daughter of Sir Frederick Tilney and the widow of Sir Thomas Howard. A companion of his boyhood was the young Henry who became King Henry VIII. Both by birth and by circumstance then, he was well fitted to play an important role in the pageant of Tudor history.

Little is known of his early life, but there is evidence that he studied at Balliol College, Oxford, and became almost immediately involved in the affairs of the court. As early as 1484, he is known to have taken part in a premature attempt to put Henry, Duke of Richmond (Henry VII), on the throne, as a consequence of which he was forced to flee to Brittany. He returned to England after the accession of Henry VII and won high favor at court, a position of privilege which not surprisingly carried over into the reign of Henry VIII.

Berners' place in English history depends as much on his literary contribution as on his statesmanship, although it was not until 1520 that he found time to pursue his interest in writing. Before this date, his career follows closely on the will of his sovereign. With his wife, Catherine Howard, daughter of the Duke of Norfolk, he attended Henry at Calais and was present at the capture of Terouenne. The next year he was sent to France as chamberlain to the king's sister, Mary, on the occasion of her marriage to Louis XII. In 1516 he was made lord chancellor and in 1518, ambassador to Madrid. He came back to England the following year and accompanied Henry VIII at the famous meeting between Henry and Francis I of France, the "Field of the Cloth of Gold."

In spite of favor at court, Berners was harassed by money troubles. His letters from Spain to the king and to Wolsey are full of complaints about his straitened circumstances quite as vivid as his descriptions of the bullfights. There is record that he borrowed £350 from the king in 1511 and additional amounts at later dates, none of which sums he repaid. Henry made him deputy of Calais in 1520, with £100 annual salary and £104 as "spyall money," but this does not seem to have solved his financial difficulties. He died at sixty-six, all his personal effects under impoundment, bequeathing little more than his reputation to a daughter, Jane, and three illegitimate sons.

During the thirteen years Berners lived at Calais, he devoted his leisure to translations of history and chivalric romance from the French and Spanish. The famous translation of Froissart's *Chronicles*, which he had undertaken at the request of Henry VIII, was first published in 1523. This work became both a source-book and a model to later historians such as Fabian, Hall, Holinshed, and in its clear, vivid idiom, one of the foundation stones of later sixteenth century style. Another work, *The Golden Book of Marcus Aurelius*, translated from a French version of the Spanish Guevera's *El Relox de Principes*, gives Berners, along with Sir Thomas North, claim to be called a forefather of Euphuism. *The Golden Book* appealed to and helped to form the taste of the period, running into fourteen editions during the next fifty years. Yet Berners was more than a translator. Both as historian and as prose stylist, he played a part of enormous importance in the history of English literature. Along with William Caxton and Sir Thomas Malory, he may be considered one of the founders of Tudor prose.

PRINCIPAL WORKS: Syr Johan Froyssart of the Cronycles of England, France, Spayne, Portyugale, Scotland, Bretayne, Flaunders, 1523, 1525; The Golden Boke of Marcus Aurelius, 1534; The Boke of Duke Huon of Burdeux (printed probably by Wynkyn de Worde, 1534, reissued, 1601); The Castell of Love, 1540; The Hystory of the Moost Noble and Valyaunt Knight Arthur of Lytell Brytayne (E. V. Utterson, ed.) 1814.

ABOUT: Ker, W. P. Introductory Critical Note to Froissart's Chronicles, Tudor Translations; Lee, S. Introduction to Huon of Burdeux, Early English Text Society; Utterson, E. V. Memoir in Froissart's Chronicles.

BETTERTON, THOMAS (1635?-April 28, 1710), actor and dramatist, was born in London, son of an undercook in the household of Charles I. Apprenticed to a book-seller who became publisher for the celebrated theatre manager Davenant, young Betterton's first stage appearance was in Davenant's company at the Drury Lane Theatre in 1660. Quickly acknowledged to be the leading actor of the day, he held that preeminence until his retirement and death in 1710. In 1662 he married an actress, Mary Saunderson, and their lives, private and public, were remarkable for their respectability in that licentious age.

A fairly stout, unprepossessing man in appearance, Betterton nevertheless claimed the respect and admiration of audiences for fifty years. Pepys called him "the best actor in the world." His most celebrated role was Hamlet, in which he was coached by Davenant, Shakespeare's godson, who had studied the performance of Taylor, who in turn had been trained for the part by Burbage and by Shakespeare himself.

In addition to his acting, Betterton made two significant contributions to the theatre. Sent to France by Charles II to study that country's production methods, particularly the theatre of Molière, he returned with several innovations, notably the use of movable sets. For Rowe's edition of Shakespeare in 1709, Betterton supplied information on the methods and traditions of Shakespeare's own productions.

To the literature of the theatre he contributed only a few briefly popular adaptations. In two of these, taken from the two parts of *Henry IV*, Betterton played Falstaff, one of his most successful roles. His literary style was markedly influenced by Molière.

He lost his fortune in a business venture in 1692. He made his farewell appearance in a benefit performance of *The Maid's Tragedy*, on April 13, 1710, died two weeks later, and was buried in Westminster Abbey.

PRINCIPAL WORKS: The Roman Virgin, or The Unjust Judge (adaptation of Webster's Appius and Virginia) 1679; King Henry IV, with the Humours of Sir John Falstaff (from Shakespeare) 1700; The Amorous Widow, or The Wanton Wife (from Georges Dandin) 1706; Sequel of Henry IV, c. 1719; The Bondman, or Love and Liberty (from Massinger) 1719.

ABOUT: Downes, J. Roscius Anglicanus (M. Summers, ed.); Gildon, C. The Life of Mr. Thomas Betterton; Halliwell-Phillipps, J. O. Dictionary of Old English Plays; Lowe, R. W. Thomas Betterton; Odell, G. C. D. Shakespeare from Betterton to Irving.

BICKERSTAFFE, ISAAC (1735?-1812?), Irish dramatist, is sometimes confused with an actor of the same name and with "Isaac Bickerstaff," used as a pseudonym by Steele. He was born in Ireland, where at eleven he was a page of Lord Chesterfield, then Lord-Lieutenant. At twenty-one he published a tragic opera, *Leucothoe*, which, however, was never produced. The first of his numerous and successful comic operas, *Love in a Village*, was produced at Covent Garden in 1762 and published the next year. The plot, as was often the case with Bickerstaffe's dramas, was derivative, put together from Charles Johnson's *Village Opera*, Wycherley's *Dancing Master*, and Marivaux's *Le Jeu de l'Amour et du Hasard*. The even more popular *Maid of the Mill* (1765) was based on Richardson's *Pamela*, and *The Sultan, or a Peep into the Seraglio* of ten years later was a paraphrase, sometimes almost a literal translation, of Favart's *Trois Sultanes*. His talent for writing sparkling dialogue and song lyrics in, as Ethel Macmillan says, "the mannered simplicity and artlessness characteristic of the eighteenth century" was not unlike Gay's. *Lionel and Clarissa* (1768), a version of Cibber's *Non-Juror* and later re-titled *A School for Fathers*, was a Covent Garden success, and also, like several others of his comedies, a favorite in America. Charles Dibden, the playwright, wrote music for several of them.

In 1772 Bickerstaffe fled to France to escape trial for some unnamed but "capital" crime. Though once an intimate of Dr. Johnson, Sir Joshua Reynolds, Goldsmith, and Garrick, with all of whom Boswell states that he dined on October 16, 1769, he forfeited their friendship and was also dishonorably discharged from his post as an officer of marines. In a libellous satire, *Love in the Suds, a Town Eclogue*, written by one Dr. Kenrick soon after the flight of Bickerstaffe, the latter's name was discreditably associated with Garrick's. In June he addressed a pitiable letter to Garrick, who found that "he could not answer it." Bickerstaffe's wretched and uncomfortable exile lasted for forty years, during which, like Oscar Wilde a century and a quarter later, he lived part of the time under an assumed name.

PRINCIPAL WORKS: Thomas and Sally, or, The Sailor's Return, 1761; Love in a Village, 1763; The Maid of the Mill, 1765; Daphne and Amintor, 1765; Love in the City, 1767; Lionel and Clarissa, 1768; The Absent Man, 1768; The Padlock, 1768; The Captive, 1769; The Ephesian Matron, 1769; The Recruiting Serjeant, 1770; The Sultan, 1775; The Spoiled Child (doubtful) 1790.

ABOUT: Bell's British Theatre, vol. 8; Biographica Dramatica; Modern Language Notes January 1923; Philological Quarterly January 1926; Spectator December 29, 1923.

BLACKMORE, Sir RICHARD (1650?-October 9, 1729), physician, poet, was born in Corsham, Wiltshire, and educated at Westminster School and St. Edmund's Hall, Oxford, where he received his B.A. in 1674 and his M.A. in 1676. For a while he was a schoolmaster, then went to the Continent to study medicine, taking his M.D. degree at the University of Padua. He returned to England, and for a time seems to have practiced medicine in London without much success. However, he became a fellow of the Royal College of Physicians in 1687, and thenceforward became increasingly prominent. In 1697 he was knighted, and the same year was appointed physician in ordinary to William III; later he held the same post with Queen Anne. (He had been active in the bloodless revolution which deposed James II and brought William and Mary to the throne.) In 1716 he became censor of the Royal College of Physicians, and from 1716 to 1722 was its elector. In the latter year he retired from practice and went to live in Boxted, Essex, where he died. He was married, but nothing is known of his wife or children, except that the former's given name was Mary.

Blackmore said that his poems were written "in scant leisure," chiefly in coffee-houses. It is said that he submitted them first to the "wits" who frequented these resorts for their criticism before offering them for publication. If his leisure was scant, then he was one of the most compulsion-driven writers who ever lived, for his writing was voluminous. Besides poems and essays, he published a number of medical treatises and tracts bearing on theology. His poems all appeared in numerous "books" and each poem constituted a long volume.

After J. Vanderbank
SIR RICHARD BLACKMORE

When one tries to read Blackmore now, it is difficult to see why (except perhaps for political reasons) such men as Johnson and Locke were his admirers and defenders, and why even Addison (though with tongue in his cheek) had kind words to say of him. He is one of Pope's victims in *The Dunciad* who seems really to belong there. Dryden ridiculed his early poems, and Swift, who called him sarcastically "England's Arch-Poet," called him also an "insipid scoundrel."

Yet he was famous in his own day, most of all for *Creation*, which he intended as a poetic treatment of Locke's philosophy and incidentally an "answer" to Lucretius. Its full title is "a philosophical poem demonstrating the existence and providence of God." Johnson felt Blackmore had been badly treated by the attacks on this poem; but, as George Saintsbury remarked dryly, the only thing to be said for it is that his others were still worse! Saintsbury conceded that it "displays some argumentative power, and the verse is not entirely devoid of vigor." But, he added, "the whole is a flat expanse of bare didactic," full of "positive absurdities."

Blackmore was in the habit of describing his successive books of poetry as "philosophic," "heroic," "epic," even "divine." They were all didactic in purpose and deadly dull in content. His translation of the *Psalms* managed to flatten even their magnificent poetry. The secret of his celebrity, and of the praise showered on him in his lifetime, followed by complete forgetfulness of his work, may be found in the fact that he was one of the earliest writers to express what Louis Cazamian called "the moralizing preoccupations" of the newly emerging middle class, which acted to "weigh down and damp the flight of poetic imagination." "What is the moral? Is it sound?" was the first literary concern of this growing group of new readers; and with Blackmore the moral was always there and it was always sound. He is to be considered, indeed, less as a part of the history of poetry than as a part of the history of social thought.

Yet there is something touching in the spectacle of the worthy physician, spending every spare minute when he was not bleeding or dosing his patients, scribbling away indefatigably in coffee-houses and producing volume after volume of pedestrian verse. He was at least not bent on self-aggrandizement; he sought no personal publicity, and not even his date of birth and his parents' names are known, or any detail of his private life. He seems never to have attempted any reply to the cruel satire of Pope or any of the others, but he did not let it crush him; he just went on writing. To be sure, *The Dunciad* did not come out until the year before Blackmore's death, and by that time he had ceased to write verse and was deep in theological exposition.

Blackmore was about as minor as a writer can be, and be a writer at all; he is of interest to the student merely as a link in the chain of history and as the object of the attention, favorable or unfavorable, of the really good writers of his day. But his virtues, if dull, were still virtues; and in his own time he gave pleasure to a number of good people who would have been left either cold or outraged by the reading of genuine poetry. "Insipid" he certainly was, but in no real sense of the word could he ever have been rightly called a "scoundrel."

PRINCIPAL WORKS: *Poetry*—Prince Arthur, 1695; King Arthur, 1697; A Satire Against Wit, 1700; Eliza, 1705; The Nature of Man, 1711; Creation, 1712; Poems on Several Subjects, 1716; Redemption, 1722; Alfred, 1723. *Prose*—A Short History of the Last Parliament, 1699; Essays on Several Subjects, 1716; History of the Conspiracy Against William III, 1723; Natural Theology, 1728; The Accomplished Preacher, 1731.

ABOUT: Cibber, T. The Lives of the Poets of Great Britain and Ireland; Johnson, S. Lives of the English Poets; Saintsbury, G. Collected Essays.

BLACKSTONE, Sir WILLIAM (July 10, 1723-February 14, 1780), writer on law, was born in London, the posthumous son of Charles Blackstone, a merchant. His mother died when he was twelve, and he was reared by an older brother, a surgeon. He was educated at Charterhouse, where he led the school and won a gold medal for some verses on Milton, and at Pembroke Hall, Oxford. In 1741, he entered himself in the Middle Temple, became a B.C.L. in 1745, and the next year was admitted to the bar. Meanwhile, in 1744, he had been made a fellow of All Souls, Oxford. His early career in the law was far from successful; though he became recorder of Wallingford in 1749, his name appeared in only two cases in court between 1746 and 1760. He spent most of these years in Oxford, as bursar of Pembroke and reader in law. In 1758 he became the university's first Vinerian Professor of English Law. As a pleader, a teacher, and a Member of Parliament (for two constituencies, from 1761 to 1769), Blackstone displayed the same defects—he was no orator, and, as Jeremy Bentham (who was his pupil) put it, he was "formal, precise, affected, cold, and wary." In 1761—the year he married Sarah Clitherow—he was made King's Counsel, and also appointed principal of New Inn Hall, Oxford. Two years later he was a bencher of the Middle Temple and solicitor-general to the Queen. In 1766 he resigned both as professor and as principal, and in 1770 was named a justice in the court of common pleas. As a judge he was satisfactory, but undistinguished.

Extremely obese, indolent, and lethargic, he grew old prematurely, and died at Wallingford, an old man at fifty-six, leaving his wife and nine children. His fame rests entirely on his *Commentaries*, but it is of interest to note that before he was twenty he wrote a book on the elements of architecture (never published), and that all his life he wrote verse, which he collected carefully but which never was gathered into a volume. One poem of his which did achieve

Sir J. Reynolds

SIR WILLIAM BLACKSTONE

PRINCIPAL WORKS: An Analysis of the Laws of England, 1754; Commentaries on the Laws of England, 1762; Tracts Chiefly Relating to the Antiquities and Laws of England, 1771; Reports of Cases Determined in the Several Courts of Westminster Hall, from 1746 to 1779 (J. Clitherow, ed.) 1781.

ABOUT: Bentham, J. A Comment on the Commentaries; Boorstin, D. J. The Mysterious Science of the Law; Clitherow, J. Life (in Reports of Cases); Lockmiller, D. A. Sir William Blackstone; Roscoe, H. Lives of Eminent British Lawyers; Warden, L. C. The Life of Blackstone.

publication was written on his entering the Middle Temple—"The Lawyer's Farewell to His Muse." As G. P. McDonnell has remarked, the world has lost little by not knowing Blackstone as a poet, for his verses were "strained and stilted."

The famous *Commentaries* are a landmark in English jurisprudence, though—despite Jefferson's objections—they have had far more influence on American than on English law. As Daniel Boorstin phrased it, Blackstone, "employing eighteenth century ideas of science, religion, history, aesthetics, and philosophy, made of the law at once a conservative and a mysterious science." He made, to quote Francis Sherwood, "a uniform logical system" of the law. With his typically eighteenth century love of order and regularity, he turned legal complexity into a coherent, comprehensive whole by ignoring its intricacies and contradictions. Even Bentham, who was his great antagonist, conceded the lucidity and elegance of his style, and said: "He it is who, first of all institutional writers, has taught jurisprudence to speak the language of the scholar and the gentleman." He was not an original thinker, he was "conservative almost to rigidity," and according to Jefferson he "perverted legal science to degeneracy," but even Jefferson granted that the *Commentaries* were "the most eloquent and best digested" of their kind.

BLAIR, HUGH (April 7, 1718-December 27, 1800), Scottish divine, rhetorician, was born in Edinburgh, the son of John Blair, a merchant, whose grandfather, Robert Blair, was chaplain to Charles I. Entering Edinburgh University in 1730, he received his M.A. in 1739 and published a thesis, "De Fundamentis et Obligatione Legis Naturae." Licensed to preach in 1741 by the presbytery, he was ordained minister of Colossie, Fife, the next September, through favor of his patron, Lord Leven. In July 1743 he returned to Edinburgh and to other churches, finally receiving the desirable life tenure at the High Church on June 15, 1758. The town council made him professor of rhetoric at the university in August 1780, appointing him Regius Professor of Rhetoric and Belles-Lettres when the foundation was created by the crown, at a stipend of £70 a year. Here he delivered the lectures which, with his sermons, made him one of the most popular of didactic writers. The lectures, published in 1783, when he resigned the professorship, acknowledged Blair's debt to Adam Smith's lectures on rhetoric delivered in Scotland in 1748-1751. Like his sermons, they were considered to be exemplary for their finish of style. ("Although reason is still indispensable with Blair," writes Émile Legouis, "it performs only a secondary part; [he believed] all artistic effects are derived from imagination and feeling.") He felt that some forms of prose are more poetical than verse, hence his fervent advocacy of the Ossianic poems which he encouraged James Macpherson to produce. Blair's first volume of sermons (1777) received general acclaim, substantiated by the bestowal of a pension of £200 a year by George III in 1780.

Socially, Blair was also a success. His fellow members at the Poker Club included Alexander Carlyle, Adam Smith, William

Robertson and David Hume, with whom he was especially friendly. Blair married his cousin, Katharine Bannatyne, in April 1748, and they had a son and daughter. Blair was described by his biographers as an amiable, rather vain, and slightly diffident man, precise in dress and deportment.

PRINCIPAL WORKS: A Critical Dissertation on the Poems of Ossian, 1763; Sermons, 1777-1801; Lectures on Rhetoric and Belles Lettres, 1783.

ABOUT: Finlayson, Life of Hugh Blair; Hall, J. Account of the Life and Writings of Hugh Blair; Howard, A., ed. The Beauties of Blair; Schmitz, R. M. Hugh Blair; Philological Quarterly July 1927.

BLAIR, ROBERT (1699-February 4, 1746), poet, was born in Edinburgh. His father, David Blair, was a Presbyterian minister and a chaplain to the king; his mother was Euphemia Nisbet. His father died when the boy was eleven. He was educated at the University of Edinburgh, but took his degree, not there, but at some unnamed university in Holland, the year also being unknown. In any event, he was living in Edinburgh as an "unemployed probationer" from 1718 to 1730, and was not licensed to preach until 1720. During this period he was active in the Athenian Society, and is supposed to have contributed to the *Edinburgh Miscellany* which the society published in 1720, though Blair's contributions are merely matters of conjecture.

In 1731 he was made minister of Athelstaneford, East Lothian, and there he spent the remainder of his life. He married Isabella Law, in 1738, the sister of Blair's old friend, William Law, professor of philosophy at Edinburgh. They had a daughter and five sons, one of whom became a well-known judge. Blair possessed a small private fortune, and outside of his clerical duties he led the life which most appealed to him—quiet, domestic, devoted to his family, his home, his books, and his garden. Considering that he became the father of English mortuary poetry, it is interesting to learn that his was a markedly cheerful nature. He died of a fever at forty-seven.

Many men are "poets of one poem," but seldom so by choice. Blair is. Outside of a poem in memory of William Law, and the possible contributions to the *Edinburgh Miscellany*, *The Grave* is his only published work. It made an immense success, and he

was solicited for more, but he wrote nothing further, and left no literary remains. Perhaps his experiences in getting that one poem published had discouraged him: he had entrusted its placement to his friend, Dr. Isaac Watts, who after several efforts returned the manuscript, saying that the publishers "expressed doubt whether any person living three hundred miles from town could write so as to be acceptable to the fashionable and the polite." The next year Blair himself succeeded in interesting an adventurous bookseller.

The Grave was the first of a whole series of mortuary poems. The first part of Young's *Night Thoughts* appeared in 1742, but as we have seen, Blair's poem was then already going the rounds. There seems to be no doubt that the two poems were written independently and without awareness by either author of the other's work. It was *The Grave* which had the greater influence, though the *Night Thoughts* lived longer.

Blair was a very uneven poet, and his ideas were commonplace; but he had a gift for vigorous expression and what Saintsbury called "almost rugged massiveness." Some portions of his long poem (particularly the section on suicide) have much power. He was given, however, to repetition and redundancy for the sake of dramatic emphasis, and his less happy passages are dull and labored. He did something to bring English blank verse back to life, and his verse at its best has a simple gravity that is the expression of the man himself—good, kindly, orthodox, and peaceable. One never forgets that one is reading a poem by a Presbyterian minister who lived in the eighteenth century; but very frequently also one is aware that this is a genuine poem, and not a mere collection of didactic remarks in meter.

The Grave had its influence not only on poetry but on another art; it inspired William Blake to do a fine set of twelve illustrative drawings in 1808. In fact, Blair had a perceptible influence on Blake the poet as well as on Blake the painter.

A few well-known quotations have come out of *The Grave*—"like those [visits] of angels, few and far between"; "whistling aloud to bear his courage up"; " 'tis long since Death had the majority." On the whole, however, there are few modern readers except students of the period who have any interest in a poem which was once a *sine qua non* for every educated reader of English. The increasing interest in religious and ethical questions of the rising middle class, and the morbid fascination of everything relating to death which (fostered by a high mortality rate and a low life-expectancy) came to a culmination in Victorian times, account for much of the furore created by Blair's poem in its own day. The vogue set up by it may have been the germinal suggestion which, seven years later, blossomed in Gray's *Elegy in a Country Churchyard.* If that be so, then the minister of Athlestaneford, though he did not live to read the great *Elegy,* may indeed have builded better than he ever dreamed.

PRINCIPAL WORKS: Poem Dedicated to the Memory of William Law, 1728; The Grave, 1743.

ABOUT: Anderson, R. Biography *in* Poets of Great Britain; Gilfillan, G. The Poetical Works of Beattie, Blair, and Falconer.

BLIND HARRY. See HENRY THE MINSTREL

BLOUNT, CHARLES (April 27, 1654-August 1693), deist, author of religious and political writings, was born in Upper Holloway, the youngest son of Sir Henry Blount, called "the Socrates of the Age," and author of *A Voyage to the Levant.* His father married him off at eighteen to Eleanora Shotover and endowed the couple with a profitable estate. Charles Blount's first, and anonymous, publication was a defense of Dryden's *Conquest of Granada* entitled *Mr. Dreyden Vindicated*; Dryden repaid the compliment in a translation of Lucian in which Blount shared and which appeared after his death. The first of Blount's free-thinking books, in which he was probably assisted by his father, was *Anima Mundi,* a copy of which he sent to the philosopher Hobbes, whom he much admired. Its rather skeptical discussion of the illusion of immortality displeased the Bishop of London, who caused it to be suppressed, though later permitting it to be reprinted. *Great Is Diana of the Ephesians, or the Original of Idolatry* (1680) also ruffled the clergy, as did Blount's best-known work, *The Two First Books of Philostratus, Concerning the Life of Apol-*

lonius Tyaneus, published the same year. This contained voluminous "philological notes upon each chapter" which were later said to have been derived chiefly from a manuscript of Lord Herbert of Cherbury, whose "five points" he had accepted. These notes or "illustrations" of Blount's were construed as attacks on Christian miracles and on the doctrine of the divinity of Christ.

Besides his adventures as free-thinker, Blount became a defender of the press in two pamphlets, *A Just Vindication of Learning* (signed Philopatris) and *Reasons Humbly Offered for the Liberty of Unlicensed Printing* (1693), which were largely composed of passages from Milton's *Areopagitica.* He was baffled, however, when he came up against the solid British prejudice against marriage with a deceased wife's sister, and finally mortally wounded himself by shooting or stabbing (accounts differ). Blount lingered some time, refusing to accept food from any one but his sister-in-law, and died at thirty-nine, leaving several children. Not an original writer, and often heavily pedantic, Blount was sometimes capable of witty repartee. As a deistic writer, he was influential.

PRINCIPAL WORKS: Mr. Dreyden Vindicated, 1673; Anima Mundi, 1679; A Just Vindication of Learning, or an Humble Address to Parliament in Behalf of the Freedom of the Press, by Philopatris, 1679; Great is Diana of the Ephesians, 1680; The Two First Books of Philostratus, Concerning the Life of Apollonius Tyaneus, 1680; The Oracles of Reason, 1693; Reasons Humbly Offered for the Liberty of Unlicensed Printing, 1693; Miscellaneous Works, 1695.

ABOUT: Blount, C. Miscellaneous Works (see preface by Charles Gildon); Bradlaugh, A. C. Biographies of Ancient and Modern Celebrated Freethinkers; "Mysticus," Charles Blount, Gent.: His Life and Opinions.

BOECE, BOYCE, or **BOËTHIUS, HECTOR** (1465?-1536), Scottish historian, was probably the son of Alexander Boyis, a burgess of Dundee. He studied at the College of Montaigu, University of Paris, and was a professor of philosophy there, probably from 1492 to 1498.

William Elphinstone, Bishop of Aberdeen, who had served in foreign embassies and had become imbued with the new spirit of intellectual activity which was stirring in Europe, determined to establish the first Scottish university at Aberdeen. Recognizing the University of Paris as one of the centers of the revival of learning, he invited Boece to come from Paris to be his chief advisor in the founding of the University of Aberdeen. Boece became principal of the new college, which, while it was organized on a modest scale financially, had extremely high standards of scholarship.

Although history was not taught as a subject on the medieval curriculum, both Elphinstone and Boece were deeply interested in it. Besides discharging his duties as principal and reading lectures to the college on divinity, Boece wrote the first history of Scotland to be printed and widely circulated.

His first essay into historical writing was the *Lives of the Bishops of Mortlach and Aberdeen*, which was printed on the famous press of Iodocus Badius in Paris in 1522. Written simply and accurately, the sections dealing with his own activities, the life of Elphinstone, and the foundation of the university have especial value.

In 1527 Badius printed Boece's *History of Scotland*, from earliest times to the accession of James III. Disdaining the colorless style of the earlier chroniclers, he took Livy as his stylistic mentor. He claimed as authority for his facts certain manuscript histories sequestered at the monastery of Icolmkill, to which he alone had access. In an eloquent narrative style, he recounted fact and fable with equal credence. His history

was accepted as authentic by his contemporaries, being attacked only by rival Irish, Welsh, and English historians who bitterly resented the greater antiquity he claimed for Scotland.

Later critics charged him with inventing both his authorities and his history, but it is more probable that his patriotic zeal, a naïve credulousness, and some medieval chronicler's romances misled him.

The history was translated into French by Nicolas d'Arfeville and widely circulated in Europe. In 1536, James V commissioned a translation into Scots. This work, expertly translated by Bellenden, Archdeacon of Moray, is the earliest book in Scottish prose to survive. Much of its contents was borrowed by Holinshed, through whom the story of Macbeth passed from Boece to Shakespeare.

In recognition of his historical work, Boece was given a doctor's degree from the University of Aberdeen in 1528. From the town of Aberdeen he received "a tun of wine or £20 Scots to help him buy bonnets." He was given a royal pension for the rest of his life, and was made a canon of Aberdeen, vicar of Tullynessle, and finally rector of Tiree, where he remained until his death.

His close friend Erasmus said of him, "He was a man of an extraordinary happy genius, and of great eloquence."

PRINCIPAL WORKS: Episcoporum Murthlacensium et Aberdonensium (Lives of the Bishops of Mortlach and Aberdeen) 1522; Scotorum Historiae (History of Scotland) 1527.

ABOUT: Irving, D. Lives of Scottish Writers; Maitland, T. Biographical Introduction, Boece's History of Scotland (ed. 1821).

BOLINGBROKE, HENRY ST. JOHN, First Viscount

(1678-December 12, 1751), statesman, political and philosophical writer, was baptized at Battersea, October 10, 1678, the son of Sir Henry St. John and Lady Mary Rich, daughter of the second Earl of Warwick. He was brought up under stern Presbyterian influence (complaining to Swift in later years of having been so bored in infancy by the sermons of distinguished Presbyterian divines that he was ready to be a high churchman), and received his education at Eton. Like a Congreve hero, he was devoted to hard drinking and many mistresses, one of whom, a Miss Gumley, was called by

HECTOR BOECE

Goldsmith "the most expensive demirep of the kingdom." After two years of travel, the young St. John married Frances Winchcombe in 1700, but matrimony does not seem to have curbed his dissipations.

For the next forty years Bolingbroke's career was deeply enmeshed in political intrigue. By education and background a Tory, he entered Parliament at the age of twenty-three and attached himself immediately to Robert Harley, then speaker in the House of Commons, winning a position of considerable influence. With Harley, he shared the leadership of the Tory government in 1710, serving as Secretary of State, and in 1712, newly created Viscount Bolingbroke, he was sent to France where he succeeded in negotiating the Treaty of Utrecht, for which he was bitterly attacked by the Whigs. Shortly thereafter the friendship between Harley and Bolingbroke began to weaken under the strains of jealous rivalry. When Harley was made Earl of Oxford and Lord Treasurer, Bolingbroke set himself to seize the reins of Tory leadership, finally bringing about the resignation of Oxford in 1714.

Another thread in the skein of his tangled political fortunes led to the Pretender, James III, whose ambitions for the throne Bolingbroke encouraged in secret negotiations, attempting to persuade him to give up his Catholicism in return for which the Tories would turn Jacobite. Before plans for a new ministry which would repeal the Act of Settlement could be carried out, Queen Anne died and the privy council proclaimed George I king. One of the first acts of the new king was to dismiss Bolingbroke from office.

Warned of impending impeachment proceedings in Parliament, Bolingbroke fled to Paris where he openly identified himself with the cause of the Pretender and became Secretary of State in his mock court. Here too jealousy and intrigue defeated his plans. After the unsuccessful Jacobite expedition to Scotland in 1715, Bolingbroke fell from favor and declared his abandonment of the Pretender. Remaining in France, he turned his interest to more personal matters including the wooing of Marie Claire Deschamps de Marcilly, a forty-two year old widow, and the study of philosophy. The lady he mar-

"French School"

HENRY ST. JOHN, 1ST VISCOUNT
BOLINGBROKE

ried two years later, after the death of the first Lady Bolingbroke; the philosophy led him into a career of letters as much in the limelight as was his political career.

Bolingbroke was pardoned and returned to England after eight years abroad, but Walpole, now minister, remained antagonistic and successfully kept him out of the House of Lords. Retiring to his estate at Dawley, he wrote a series of blistering letters to *The Craftsman*, attacking Walpole, and the outlines of a religious philosophy versified by Pope in his *Essay on Man*. Never content to remain long aloof from the world of politics, he continued his literary war against Walpole and the Whigs until he succeeded in winning an audience with the king (reputedly, by paying a large sum, about £11,000, to the king's mistress). Just as it seemed that Walpole faced certain defeat, the king died and once again Bolingbroke's scheming came to naught.

Thereafter his role in public affairs dwindled and he gave most of his time to writing and to the cultivation of his friendship with Pope, Swift and Voltaire. Only once did he attain anything like his former influence, when he became the adviser of Frederick, Prince of Wales, to whom he is supposed to have addressed his essay *The Idea of a Patriot King*. In 1744 after another period of residence abroad, he settled

49

permanently at Battersea, his father's estate, where he died seven years later.

There is nothing particularly original in Bolingbroke's philosophy, but in his political writings he did attempt a genuine synthesis. His Toryism, associated with the deeper theme of patriotism, is a plea for a revitalized and modernized monarchy. His "patriot king" is at once the ear and the voice of the people. Paradoxically, the reactionary element in his point of view actually becomes the progressive in a historical sense—a kind of democratic conception of monarchy, peculiarly British, which leads through a long Tory tradition to the enlightened conservatism of Disraeli in the nineteenth century.

In much of his work the thread of political expedience is so interwoven with more individual qualities that it is difficult to make a purely literary estimate of its value. His language is far too ornate for the modern taste, yet it remains a brilliant example of classical prose. His argument is that of an orator rather than a philosopher. From the perspective of two centuries, it seems fair to say that both his writings and his career were more impressive to his contemporaries than to any later judge.

PRINCIPAL WORKS: A Dissertation Upon Parties, 1735; The Idea of a Patriot King, 1749; Reflections on Exile, 1752; Of the True Use of Retirement and Study, 1752; Letters on the Study and Use of History, 1752; Some Reflections on the State of the Nation, 1752; A Letter to Sir W. Wyndham, 1753; Collected Works (D. Mallet, ed.) 1754; Letters and Correspondence, Public and Private of Henry St. John Viscount Bolingbroke (G. Clarke, ed.) 1798.

ABOUT: Collins, J. C. Bolingbroke, a Historical Study; Cooke, G. W. Memoirs of Bolingbroke; Harrop, R. Bolingbroke; Hassall, A. The Life of Viscount Bolingbroke; James, D. G. Life of Reason: Hobbes, Locke, Bolingbroke; Macknight, T. The Life of Henry St. John, Viscount Bolingbroke; Merrill, W. M. From Statesman to Philosopher: A Study in Bolingbroke's Deism; Sichel, W. Bolingbroke and His Times.

BOSWELL, JAMES (October 29, 1740-May 19, 1795), biographer, diarist, was born in Edinburgh, the oldest son of Alexander Boswell by his first wife, Euphemia Erskine. (The older Boswell, on becoming a judge, took the title of Lord Auchinleck.) He was educated at Edinburgh High School, the University of Edinburgh, the University of Glasgow (where he studied under Adam Smith), and the University of Utrecht, where at his father's insistence he reluctantly studied law. He was admitted to the Scottish bar in 1766. But his heart was never either in Scotland or in the law; it was in the company of the great wherever he could find them, and most of all in London, which he first visited in 1760. Volatile, hopeful, absurd, "Bozzy" was always, as his father put it, "pinning himself to the tail of somebody or other." Successively he attached himself to Hume, Voltaire, Rousseau, Wilkes, the Corsican patriot Paoli, Lord Chatham, and finally and forever to Samuel Johnson, with whom his famous first meeting, in the back of a bookseller's shop, occurred on May 16, 1763. It was ten years before he was admitted to the celebrated Club of which Johnson was the leader, and to which Burke, Garrick, Reynolds, and Goldsmith belonged.

Boswell, who had once wanted to be a Roman Catholic priest (although he was a Presbyterian) and then an army officer, and whose first great literary interest was the theatre, found it necessary to keep on practising law. He was admitted to the English bar and tried his hand at politics after his father died in 1782, but he was defeated when he stood for Parliament (as a Whig), and the best he could achieve was the recordership of Carlisle, which he resigned in 1790. He was always in debt, always hard up, and during the latter part of his life his fortunes were not helped by increasing addiction to liquor. In and out of love all his life, before his marriage and after, he yet had a great fondness for his cousin, Margaret Montgomerie, who stopped being the confidante of his other affairs and married him herself in 1769—on the same day his father took another of their cousins as his second wife. They had two surviving sons and three daughters, besides two sons who died in infancy. Mrs. Boswell died in 1789, before her husband, who was in London, could reach her bedside; her death was a real grief, yet he was full of new matrimonial schemes for the six years he outlived her.

All this sounds rather unattractive, yet actually Boswell was one of the most appealing of men. His good humor, his frank acceptance of his own shortcomings, his gaiety, and his friendliness more than offset his vanity and weakness. Hume spoke of him as "very good humored, very agreeable, and very mad." Mad he was not; he was far from the "idiot" Macaulay called him. As David Nichol Smith said, "The very freedom from self-consciousness which was no help in his career was a great part of the secret of his skill in description." Boswell is much more than the mere satellite to Johnson that he has been thought to be. It is true that Johnson was his idol, but he treated him much as savages treat their idols, and condemned him when he did not answer his prayers properly. He was shrewd as well as adoring, and though he was a worshipper he was no sycophant. He told the truth when he said that his great biography was "more of a Life than any that has yet appeared." It is besides a marvelous picture of the world around Johnson, of the eighteenth century literary scene.

Though he was not a great stylist, Boswell was a conscious and conscientious author. He wrote easily, simply, flexibly, and is one of the most enjoyable writers in history. The very clarity of his style hides the careful work which went into it. Actually he was primarily a great journalist, with a genius for interviewing, and for extracting and correlating salient facts. Born too early for the profession to which he rightly belonged, he was fortunate in finding the nearest analogy to it. In this respect he belongs in the company of Pepys and Defoe, but in their common metier he outdid them both.

Sir J. Reynolds

JAMES BOSWELL

Though most of Boswell's books aside from the biography of Johnson are of little merit, the *Account of Corsica* and the *Journal of a Tour to the Hebrides* have the typical Boswellian verve, bounce, and candor. His verse was negligible, his political tracts were dull. But that does not matter: he produced one of the world's masterpieces. As Smith put it, "Johnson owes much to Boswell, but it was Johnson who gave us Boswell." Johnson himself would not stand so high in the world's knowledge or estimation today if it were not for the little Scottish advocate he snubbed and bullied and loved. It was easy to laugh at Boswell, even easier to be annoyed by him; he was pushing, inquisitive, opinionated, often a bore. He quarreled with his father and neglected his wife; he was frequently the worse for drink, and often within hailing distance of the debtors' prison. But he had one indispensable virtue for a biographer: he and his pencil were always *there*; he had a keen appreciation of what he saw and heard, he knew how to winnow the wheat from the chaff, and he had a gift for setting it all down so that the man himself comes to life in his pages. He created a new word in the English language: to Boswellize. And to Boswellize does not mean merely to note everything just as it comes and present it in an uncoordinated mass; it means to get under the skin of one's subject, to supplement the multitude of impressions by sound research, and then to weld the whole into a portrait in words by which the subject comes alive and stays alive forever.

The discovery of a great mass of Boswell's unpublished diaries and papers at Malahide Castle, Ireland, in the 1920's and 1930's constitutes one of the great literary detective stories of modern times. After a prolonged and involved legal tangle, publication of the Malahide "find" finally began in 1950, with the *London Journal* for the years 1762-63; it was expected that the full series would require a score of volumes and a decade or more to bring to press.

PRINCIPAL WORKS: An Elegy on the Death of an Amiable Young Lady (verse) 1761; An Ode to Tragedy (verse) 1761; The Cub at Newmarket, 1762; Dorando, a Spanish Tale, 1767; Essence of the Douglas Cause, 1767; An Account of Corsica . . . and Memoirs of Paoli, 1768; British Essays in Favor of the Brave Corsicans,

1769; A Letter to the People of Scotland on the Present State of the Nation, 1783; Journal of a Tour to the Hebrides with Samuel Johnson, LL.D., 1785; The Life of Samuel Johnson, LL.D., 1791 (complete edition, E. Malone, ed., 1799); No Abolition of Slavery: or the Universal Empire of Love (verse) 1791; Letters of James Boswell, Addressed to the Rev. W. J. Temple, 1857; The Letters of James Boswell (C. B. Tinker, ed.) 1924; On the Profession of a Player: Three Essays (1770) 1929; Yale Editions of the Private Papers of James Boswell (Malahide Papers), 1950—.

ABOUT: Bronson, B. H. Johnson and Boswell; Carlyle, T. Essays; Fitzgerald, P. H. Boswell's Autobiography; Henley, W. E. Views and Reviews; Johnson, L. Post Luminium; Leask, W. K. James Boswell; Lewis, D. B. W. The Hooded Hawk; or, The Case of Mr. Boswell; Macaulay, T. B. Essays; Mallory, G. Boswell, the Biographer; Pottle, F. A. The Literary Career of James Boswell, Esq.; Quennell, P. Four Portraits; Rogers, C. Boswelliana; Salpeter, H. Dr. Johnson and Mr. Boswell; Tinker, C. B. Young Boswell; Vulliamy, C. E. James Boswell.

BOURCHIER, JOHN. See BERNERS, JOHN BOURCHIER, Second Baron

BOWDLER, THOMAS

BOWDLER, THOMAS (July 11, 1754-February 24, 1825), editor of expurgated classics, was born in prosperous circumstances at Ashley, near Bath, on July 11, 1754, the younger son of Thomas and Elizabeth Stuart Bowdler. Deciding he would like to be a doctor, young Thomas attended St. Andrews University and took his M.D. at Edinburgh in 1776. Apparently, however, his interest in medicine diminished considerably and after four years of European travel, he returned to England in poor health, determined to find a more sympathetic profession. Settling in London, he attached himself to a literary group the center of which was Mrs. Elizabeth Montagu, a leader in Blue Stocking circles. Here he devoted his days to charity, prison reform and the suppression of vice; his evenings to the pursuit of literature; and after several years of further wandering abroad, he succeeded in publishing a biography and several miscellaneous travel pieces.

It is doubtful whether the pious Dr. Bowdler would even be remembered today if the combination of his inveterate "do-goodism" with his literary preoccupation had not led him to a career which gave a new word to the English language—the verb, "to bowdlerize." Entertaining the notion that great writers frequently included expressions unsuitable to the ears of the young and the pure, Bowdler devoted the remaining years of his life to erasing such words from the classics. In 1818 he published his ten-volume *Family Shakespeare*, "in which nothing is added to the original text; but those words and expressions are omitted which cannot with propriety be read aloud in a family." The set was enormously popular: it appeared in four editions before 1824 and was reissued in 1831, 1853, and 1861.

His next task was the purification of Gibbon's *Decline and Fall of the Roman Empire* in six volumes, which he finished only a short time before his death at Rhyddings, South Wales, on February 24, 1825, and which was published posthumously by a nephew.

Although both books were popular in the nineteenth century, they were also the target of merciless criticism. It is perhaps ironic that the word "bowdlerize," first used in print by General Perronet Thompson in 1836 and coined in a spirit of ridicule, should survive to insure the fame of Thomas Bowdler.

PRINCIPAL WORKS: Letters Written in Holland, 1788; Life of Villettes, 1815; Observations on Emigration to France, 1815; The Family Shakespeare (ed.) 1818; Gibbon's History of the Decline and Fall of the Roman Empire (ed.) 1826.

ABOUT: Bowdler, T. Memoir *in* Annual Biography and Obituary (1826); Bowdler, T. Preface to The Family Shakespeare (4th ed.).

BOWYER, WILLIAM

BOWYER, WILLIAM (December 19, 1699-November 18, 1777), printer, scholar, was born at Dogwell Court, Whitefriars, London, the only son of William Bowyer the elder, and his second wife, Dorothy (Dawks) Bowyer. The boy was literally born to his trade, since his father had started his printer's shop only a few months before. His first tutor was Ambrose Bonwicke the elder. At seventeen Bowyer entered St. John's College, Cambridge University, where he was kept on rather short commons by his father, but won a scholarship (Roper's exhibition) in 1719. He stayed till 1722 without taking a degree, and at the end of that year went into partnership with his father, who assigned him the proofreading of learned works. On October 9, 1728, Bowyer married his cousin, Anne Prudom, who died three years later, leaving him a son Thomas. (Eighteen years later Bowyer married his housekeeper, Mrs. Elizabeth Bill.) In 1729 he was appointed printer to the House of Commons, holding the post for nearly fifty years in spite of occasional objections that he was a non-juror.

Bowyer's *Remarks on Mr. Bowman's Visitation Sermon on the Traditions of the Clergy* (1731) severely criticized the writer's deficiencies in the classics and ecclesiastical history, and attracted considerable attention. A long series of translations, periodical contributions, and annotated and critical editions by Bowyer followed, chief among them the first translation of Rousseau's *Paradoxical Orations on Arts and Sciences,* the 13th and 14th volumes of Swift's *Works* (1762), and a notable edition of the Greek Testament in two volumes (1763), to which Bowyer added "Conjectural Emendations" by other commentators. In May 1736 he was appointed printer to the Society of Antiquaries; in 1761, printer for the Royal Society, retaining the post till his death; and in 1767, printer to the House of Lords. He had taken John Nichols into partnership the year before, and now removed his printing office from Whitefriars to Red Lion Passage, a move which cost him a stroke of paralysis. Bowyer died at nearly seventy-eight, leaving behind his edition of Dr. Bentley's *Dissertation on the Epistles of Phalaris,* and, in press, two imposing folios of the *Domesday Book.* A small, cheerful, charitable man, Bowyer was known as "the Learned Printer."

PRINCIPAL WORKS: Remarks on Mr. Bowman's Visitation Sermon on the Traditions of the Clergy, 1731; The Present State of Europe, 1744; Verses on the Coronation of Their Late Majesties King George II and Queen Caroline, 1761; Conjectural Emendations (ed.) 1763; The Origin of Printing, in Two Essays, 1774.

ABOUT: Nichols, J. Literary Anecdotes of the Eighteenth Century.

BOYCE, HECTOR. See BOECE, HECTOR

BOYER, ABEL (June 24, 1667-November 16, 1729), publisher of political periodicals and historian, was born at Castres, Upper Languedoc, and was christened Pierre Abel de Boyer. His father was a consul or chief magistrate, who was later killed during the Huguenot persecutions, and his mother was Catherine (Campdomerius) de Boyer. Disturbed conditions compelled young Boyer to leave the academy at Puylaurens with a preacher uncle for Friesland, where he studied at Franeker. Boyer went to England in 1689 and put his excellent classical education to use as tutor to Allen Bathurst, through whose father, treasurer of the household of Princess, later Queen Anne, he was appointed French teacher to her son William, Duke of Gloucester. Boyer compiled *The Complete French Master* (1694) for his pupil's use, and in 1702 had expanded this into the *Dictionnaire Royal Français et Anglais, Divisé en Deux Parties,* published at The Hague, which eclipsed all previous French dictionaries and served as model for many subsequent ones.

Boyer's literary ambitions—he also translated and produced a few plays—soon led him far from tutoring. In the same year that his dictionary appeared he published (in English) his *History of William III,* which included the reign of James II. The next year, 1703, saw the first appearance of his annual *History of Queen Anne Digested into Annals,* which, with its brief obituaries, has proved useful to modern historians of the period. *The Political State of Great Britain,* his monthly periodical in the form of letters to a friend in Holland, extended to thirty-eight volumes covering the years 1711-1729, and included valuable reports of parliamentary debates. From 1705 to 1709 he also edited *The Post-boy,* a newssheet published three times a week in London. Boyer's zeal as a Whig sometimes outran his discretion. He ran afoul of Swift, whom he had attacked in a pamphlet, and who denounced him in the *Journal to Stella* as "a French dog," and of Pope, who put him in *The Dunciad.* Boyer died at sixty-two, in a house he had built for himself at Chelsea. Eighteen years after his death a continuation of his history to the death of George I was published, testifying to the value of his lucid and thorough annalistic writing.

PRINCIPAL WORKS: Dictionnaire Royal, Français et Anglais, 1702; The History of King William III, 1702-03; The History of the Reign of Queen Anne Digested into Annals, 1703-1713; The Political State of Great Britain (60 vol.) 1711-40; Memoirs of the Life and Negotiations of Sir W. Temple, 1714; The History of the Life and Reign of Queen Anne, 1722; The Great Theater of Honour and Nobility (in French and English) 1729.

ABOUT: Haag, E. La France Protestante; Phillips, A. E. Monsieur Boyer: French Huguenot Who Became an English Man of Letters.

BOYLE, ROGER, Baron Broghill, First Earl of Orrery (April 25, 1621-October 26, 1679), historical romancer, dramatist, miscellaneous writer, was the third son of Richard Boyle, First Earl of Cork. Educated at Trinity College, Dublin and Oxford, he was taken for a grand tour of the continent at the age of fourteen by an older brother. He returned to England four years later, married Lady Margaret Howard, and went with her to Ireland, arriving on the day the great rebellion broke out.

A royalist by sentiment, Boyle commanded a troop of cavalry against the revolutionists. When the revolution was accomplished, however, he accepted a commission from Parliament to continue his command of the same troop under the new regime. Upon the execution of the king he resigned and returned to England, living in retirement until he became involved in a restoration plot. Cromwell personally informed him that all details of the plot were known, and that only Cromwell's intervention had saved Boyle from arrest for treason. They struck a bargain by which Boyle was made a general in the Parliamentary army, no oaths or obligations which would offend his loyalty to the crown being required of him. The two men liked and respected each other, and Boyle served Cromwell faithfully, as an effective warrior and a confidant. After Cromwell's success in Ireland, Boyle, who had been given Blarney Castle, served as member of Parliament for Cork and Edinburgh, and as Lord President of the Council. He was on Cromwell's private council, urged Cromwell to become king, and proposed a marriage between Cromwell's daughter and Charles II.

Convinced after Cromwell's death that the latter's son, Richard, could not succeed his father, Boyle secured Ireland for the king just before the restoration. He served in the Irish Parliament in 1661, but refused the office of Lord High Chancellor because of ill health. He died of gout in 1679, leaving seven children.

Boyle was on intimate terms with many writers, including Cowley, Dryden and Davenant. He wrote many unpublished poems, eight plays, a long, tedious novel entitled *Parthenissa*, and a detailed treatise on *The Art of War* which was used by Cromwell's army. His plays, in rhymed heroic verse, were intended for the diversion of his own court in Dublin, but were later produced with varying success at the Duke of York's Theatre, in London.

PRINCIPAL WORKS: Henry V, 1664; Parthenissa, 1665; Mustapha, 1665; The Black Prince, 1667; Tryphon, 1668; Guzman, 1669; A Poem on the Death of Abraham Cowley, 1677; Poems on Most of the Festivals of the Church, 1681; Herod the Great (pub. posthumously) 1694.

ABOUT: Clarendon, W. History of the Rebellion; Genest, J. History of the Stage; Walpole, H. Royal and Noble Writers; Ware, Sir J. Writers of Ireland.

BRACTON, BRATTON, or BRETTON, HENRY DE (d. 1268), author of a treatise on English law and customs, probably was named Bratton (Sir Frederick Maitland states definitely that he was), since the form Bracton appears only after his death. The name seems to have been derived from the Devonshire villages Bratton Fleming or Bratton Clovelly. Apparently Bracton entered the King's service as clerk under the patronage of William Raleigh, a royal justice who was Bishop of Winchester when he died in 1250. Dugdale speaks of Bracton as a justice itinerant in Nottinghamshire and Derbyshire in 1245, and mentions him frequently from 1260 to 1267 as a justice of assize in the southwestern counties, especially Somerset, Devon, and Cornwall. Bracton was also a judge in the King's central court, later distinguished as the King's bench, but was retired or dismissed shortly before the meeting of the "Mad Parliament," which assembled at Oxford in 1258 in open rebellion against Henry III and confirmed the Magna Charta. At this time he was obliged to surrender some judicial records he had been using in the preparation of his famous work, *De Legibus et Consuetudinibus Angliae*, the first attempt at a systematic and practical treatment of English law, and, according to Sir Frederick Maitland, "incomparably the best work produced by any English lawyer in the Middle Ages."

Bracton was appointed archdeacon of Barnstaple in 1263-64, resigning in May when elected Chancellor of the Cathedral of Exeter, and also held a prebend in the collegiate church at Bosham. In 1267 he was a member of a commission of prelates, barons, and judges appointed to hear complaints of the disinherited patrons of Simon de Montfort. He died in 1268, probably in the summer or early autumn; was buried in the nave of Exeter Cathedral before an altar dedicated to the Virgin; and a daily mass was said for him for three centuries after his death. On April 5, 1923, a stone inscribed to his memory was placed on the site of his altar, the gift of numerous lawyers. A four-volume edition of his *magnum opus* was published by the Yale University Press between 1915 and 1942.

PRINCIPAL WORKS: De Legibus et Consuetudinibus Angliae, 1569; Note-Book, 1887.

ABOUT: Bracton, H. de, Note-Book (F. W. Maitland, ed.); Holdsworth, Sir W. S. Some Makers of English Law; Selden Society, Bracton and Azo; Law Times 1923.

BRETON, NICHOLAS (1545?-1626?), miscellaneous writer in prose and verse, was born in London, the son of William Breton, a descendant of an old Essex family who made a fortune in trade, and of Elizabeth Bacon. Very little is known of his life, the dates of both his birth and his death being in doubt. He may have been born as early as 1542, or as late as 1555, and the date given for his death is merely the last date on which he published a book. His father died when Nicholas was a boy, and his mother remarried the poet George Gascoigne. He is supposed to have been a graduate of Oxford, perhaps of Oriel College, and seems to have traveled abroad, since he knew Italian well. In 1592 he married Ann Sutton, and they had two sons and two daughters, at least one of the sons dying in infancy. He had some connection with Sir Philip Sidney and with Sidney's sister the Countess of Pembroke, who was Breton's patroness until 1601. His name, which was spelled in a half dozen different ways during the sixteenth and seventeenth centuries, was pronounced "Britton."

Aside from these meager facts and conjectures, Breton is known only as a writer. He was prolific, too much so for his own reputation. His prose is inferior to his verse, his satire labored and his religious works undistinguished. As a poet he harks back to Wyatt and Surrey—even farther back so far as prosody is concerned, since he was fond of the old "poulter's measure" and the four-

teen-syllable line. His literary affiliations, though he was a conscious admirer and imitator of Spenser, were really medieval rather than Renaissance; for example, he reveled in allegory, in plays upon words, in mystical subtleties. The best of his work is in his pastoral poems. Here he has genuine gaiety and pathos, sprightly freshness of feeling, and an engaging flow of fancy.

Breton poured out pastorals and other poems, social satires under the pseudonym of "Pasquil," religious meditations, and even a book on angling (*Wits Trenchmour*), which if he had not deserted his subject toward the end might have been a predecessor of Izaak Walton's *Compleat Angler*. His books were all excessively rare until A. B. Grosart collected most of them in 1879; contemporary copies are still collectors' items and most of them which survive are safely ensconced in the great libraries. He was not an important poet, but a versatile, fertile writer who at his best was pleasing and at his worst could be puerile.

His verse frequently appeared in the anthologies popular in the period, and he himself sometimes edited volumes, not always containing entirely his own verse. One book, *Brittons Bowre of Delights*, he specifically disclaimed as his; but it appears that it really was his own work, and the disclaimer was merely because of a quarrel with the publisher.

PRINCIPAL WORKS: *Poetry*—A Floorish upon Fancie, 1577; Brittons Bowre of Delights, 1591; The Pilgrimage to Paradise, Joyned with The Countess of Pembroke's Love, 1592; The Phoenix Nest, 1593; The Arbor of Amorous Devices, 1597; Englands Helicon, 1600; A Divine Poem, 1601; The Passionate Shepheard, 1604; The Honour of Valour, 1605; Works in Verse and Prose of Nicholas Breton (A.B. Grosart, ed.) 1879. *Prose*—The Workes of the Young Wit, 1577; Wits Trenchmour, 1597; The Wil of Wit, 1599; Melancholike Humours, 1600; Wonders Worth a Hearing, 1602; Grimello's Fortunes, 1604; I Would and I Would Not, 1614; Characters upon Essaies, 1615; Pasquils Mad-Cappe, 1625; Fantasticks, 1626.

ABOUT: Bullen, A. H. Elizabethans; Grosart, A. B. Introduction to Works in Verse and Prose; Tannenbaum, S. A. and D. Nicholas Breton: A Concise Bibliography.

BRETTON, HENRY de. See BRACTON, HENRY de

BRISTOL, GEORGE DIGBY, Second Earl of (October 1612-March 20, 1677) dramatist, translator, was born in Madrid where his father, John Digby, first Earl of Bristol, served as ambassador to Spain. The boy showed brilliant promise when he appeared before the House of Commons at the age of twelve with a petition in defense of his father, who had been committed to the Tower through the machinations of the Duke of Buckingham. Two years later he entered Magdalen College, Oxford, taking his M.A. degree in 1636.

Digby's career was full of cross currents which can only be charted in reference to the religious and political tides of seventeenth century England. As Horace Walpole wrote of him later, he was "a singular person, whose life was one contradiction. He wrote against popery and embraced it; he was a zealous opposer of the court and a sacrifice for it." When he was a young man he wrote a series of letters to Sir Kenelm Digby *qv* attacking Catholicism—yet at the height of his political career when he was in his forties, he became a Roman Catholic and was forced to resign public office because of his religion. First elected to Parliament when he was twenty-eight, he had made himself so unpopular as a close adviser to the first Charles that he was threatened with impeachment and forced to flee to Holland. A prominent figure during the civil war, he fought gallantly in the king's forces and then threw down his commission after a quarrel with Prince Rupert. Exiled in France, he allied himself with the fortunes of Louis XIV until he fell from favor and was expelled from the country in 1656. Returning to England at the time of the Restoration, he was at first excluded from office and then after the fall of Lord Clarendon, long his enemy, was again welcomed at court and a year before his death in 1677 served once more in the House of Lords.

Besides his letters and speeches, many of which are extremely eloquent, Digby wrote or adapted from the Spanish several plays, the most important of which is *Elvira: or, The Worst Not Always True*. The original of *Elvira* was probably Calderón's *No Siempre lo Pior es Cierto*. Digby's version is not distinguished as a translation, stiff, formal, and interminably protracted in action— yet it remains an interesting example of the comedy of cloak and sword which the English stage took over from the Spanish dramas of Lope de Vega and Calderón. According to Walpole, Digby also translated the first three books of *Cassandra* from the French and wrote a number of verses, few of which have survived.

PRINCIPAL WORKS: Letters Between the Ld. George Digby and Sir Kenelm Digby, Kt., concerning Religion, 1651; Elvira: or, The Worst Not Always True, 1667 (included in A Select Collection of Old Plays, R. Dodsley, ed. 1744; W. C. Hazlitt, ed. 1876).

ABOUT: Townshend, D. George Digby, Second Earl of Bristol; Walpole, H. A Catalogue of the Royal and Noble Authors of England.

BROME, RICHARD (d. 1652?), dramatist, was first the servant, then the friend and "son," of Ben Jonson. Very little is known of his life. He was not related either to Alexander Brome, who edited his plays, or to Henry Brome, who published some of them, but he seems to have had a brother whose name was Stephen. Apparently he had had some education, for he read Latin and probably Italian and French. He came into Jonson's service about 1614, and he was certainly dead by 1653, as evidenced by a memorial poem of that date. He appears to have been taken into friendship, on terms of equality, by most of Jonson's friends, including Dekker and Heywood, with whom he collaborated. He was also the object of envy and enmity on the part of some others, who tried unsuccessfully to alienate Jonson from him.

Brome's first play was produced in 1623; it was a collaboration with Jonson's son Benjamin, called *A Fault in Friendship*. His own plays were performed mostly between 1632 and 1642, when a play by Brome was the last to be performed in London before the Puritan Parliament closed the theatres. Following the Restoration his comedies were revived, and *A Jovial Crew*, the best of them, was even transformed into an "opera," as late as 1731. In addition to his published plays, and *The Late Lancashire Witches*, written with Thomas Heywood and produced in 1641, Brome wrote the following comedies (dates give are of first performances): *Christianetta*, 1640; *The Jewish Gentleman*, 1640; *The Love-Sick Maid*, 1653; *The Life and Death of Sir Martin Skink*, 1654, and *The Apprentice's Prize*, 1654.

RICHARD BROME

Brome was modest about his own work, and content to call himself, not a dramatist, but a "playmaker," and "a man of no account." However, though for the most part he was a close imitator of Jonson (as Ronald Baynes remarked, he "patiently and even skilfully follows the manner of Jonson"), he had a real feeling for the theatre, a keenly observant eye, and a vigorous pen. His plays alternated between romantic comedy (e.g., *The Northern Lass*, his greatest success) and comedy of manners (e.g., *A Jovial Crew*, with its real beggars, brought to genuine life). They are not free of grossness and coarseness, and they are often prosy, but they are always "good theatre." Besides the lyrics interspersed in his plays, Brome wrote a few other occasional poems, commonplace verse without distinction. He had a true dramatic talent, and would have developed it better had he been "more ambitious and less humble." In spite of his self-consciousness and excessive humility, amounting almost to servility, he must have had sterling qualities to arouse the obvious affection and admiration felt for him by Ben Jonson and his friends.

PRINCIPAL WORKS: The Northern Lass, 1632; The Antipodes, 1640; The Sparagus Garden, 1640; A Jovial Crew, 1652; Five New Plays (A. Brome, ed.): A Mad Couple Well Matched, Novella, The Court Beggar, The City Wit, The Damoiselle, 1653; Five New Plays: The English Moor, The Love-Sick Court, Covent Garden Weeded, The New Academy, The Queen and Concubine, 1654;

The Queen's Exchange, 1657; Dramatic Works, 1873.

ABOUT: Faust, E. K. R. Richard Brome (in German) ; Ward, A. History of English Dramatic Literature.

BROOKE, HENRY (1703?-October 10, 1783), novelist, poet, was the elder son of the Reverend William Brooke, an Irish Protestant clergyman, and his wife, Lettice Digby. Little information is available on his childhood, but the boy was supposedly educated by Swift's schoolmaster friend, Thomas Sheridan, and entered Trinity College, Dublin, in his seventeenth year. He went to London to study law and on his return to Ireland married Catherine Meares, a young cousin of whom he was guardian.

In many ways, Brooke appears to have been a charming personality, original, kind-hearted, overflowing with feeling. Living part of the time in London and part in Ireland, he made friends in many different walks of life and became deeply engaged in both the political and religious movements of his day. During the Jacobite rebellion of 1745, he published a series of "Farmer's Letters" warning Irish Protestants against Jacobite tendencies. As a result of this successful pamphleteering, Lord Chesterfield awarded him the post of barrack-master at Mullingar, a position which paid him £400 a year. In 1761 he wrote a pamphlet pleading for the modification of drastic laws directed against Catholics. At the same time, he was strongly influenced by Methodism, to such an extent that his novel, *The Fool of Quality*, first published in 1765, was highly praised by John Wesley, who edited an abridged edition especially for Methodists some fifteen years after the original publication. Politically, he supported Frederick, then Prince of Wales (to whom he had been introduced by William Pitt, the elder), against George II, a position so dangerous that he finally yielded to the pleading of his wife and left England to live permanently in Ireland.

Brooke's first published work was a long philosophical poem, *Universal Beauty*, which appeared in 1735, and which is said to have been revised by Pope, friend and adviser to the young writer during his London residence. Many critics believe this work to have been the source for Darwin's *Botanic Garden*, and an early philosophical expression of the theory of physical evolution. A play,

57

After H. Brooke
HENRY BROOKE

Gustavus Vasa, written about 1739, was banned after rehearsing for five weeks at the Drury Lane because of the supposed resemblance of one of the characters to Sir Robert Walpole. Published by subscription, it was widely read and later found production in Dublin under the title, *The Patriot.* Most interesting of all his literary works, however, is *The Fool of Quality,* which George Saintsbury has called a "strange compound of genius and dullness." This picaresque novel, breathing the spirit of both Sterne and Rousseau, combines pranks, adventures, ethical dialogues, mystical philosophy and dissertations on political economy.

In both his life and his work, Henry Brooke was passionately a man of his time, concerned at the deepest level with righting the wrongs of the social system. Yet in spite of the vitality and range of his activities, his personal life moved toward a tragic climax. Harried by ill health and financial worries after his wife's death, he succumbed to a serious mental depression during which he was cared for by his daughter, Charlotte, the only surviving child in a family of twenty-two. At eighty, immured from the world by his mental incapacity, he died in Dublin.

PRINCIPAL WORKS: Universal Beauty, 1735; Gustavus Vasa, the Deliverer of His Country, 1739; Farmer's Six Letters to the Protestants of Ireland, 1746; Jack the Giant Queller, 1748; The Fool of Quality, or the History of Henry Earl of Moreland, 1765-70 (E. A. Baker, ed. 1906); Juliet Grenville, or the History of the Human Heart, 1773; The Poetical Works of Henry Brooke (published by Charlotte Brooke) 1792.

ABOUT: Baker, E. A. Biographical Preface to The Fool of Quality; D'Olier, I. Memoirs of the Life of the Late Excellent and Pious Mr. Henry Brooke; Scurr, H. M. Henry Brooke; Wilson, C. H. Brookiana, Anecdotes of Henry Brooke.

BROOKE, LORD. See GREVILLE, Sir FULKE

BROWN, JOHN (November 5, 1715-September 23, 1766), essayist, dramatist, poet, was the son of a Northumberland vicar. He received his B.A. with distinction at St. John's College, Cambridge, and took holy orders. In 1745 he served as a volunteer in the defense of Carlisle, and in recognition of this and of his sound Whig principles, he was appointed a chaplain by the Bishop of Carlisle.

An *Essay Upon Satire,* written after Pope's death and printed in Pope's collected works, brought Brown to the attention of William Warburton, Pope's literary executor. At Warburton's suggestion, Brown carried out several projects left unfulfilled by Pope, including an essay on Shaftesbury's *Characteristics* which won wide recognition and which contains an excellent exposition of the utilitarian theory. Brown wrote two plays in which Garrick appeared. One achieved minor success, but neither has much literary merit.

Through a friend of Warburton, Brown became rector of Great Horkesley in 1756, and here he wrote his most popular work, *An Estimate of the Manners and Principles of the Times.* A bitter satire on luxury and foppishness, it was critically both applauded and censured, but a nation depressed by war welcomed it warmly. As Cowper said:

The inestimable estimate of Brown
Rose like a paper kite and charmed the town.

In 1761 Brown received the living of St. Nicholas in Newcastle. Appealed to by a Russian educator, he proposed vast plans for the civilization of Russia which pleased the Empress. Catherine sent funds for his journey to Russia, but after preparations were completed, Brown, suffering from gout and rheumatism was dissuaded by his friends from taking the trip. Possibly his deep disappointment over the failure of this project was a contributing cause of his suicide in 1766. A letter from an acquaintance says that he had been subject to "fits of frenzy" for years, and that only the solicitude of friends had prevented his self-destruction long before.

PRINCIPAL WORKS: Honour, a Poem, 1743; Essay upon Satire; Essay on the "Characteristics" of Lord Shaftesbury, 1751; Barbarossa, a Play, 1755; Athelstane, a Play, 1756; Estimate of the Manners and Principles of the Times, 1757-58; Dialogues of the Dead, 1760; Dissertation on Poetry and Music, 1763.

ABOUT: Davies, T. Memoirs of David Garrick; Kippis, A. Biographia Britannica.

BROWN, THOMAS (1663-June 16, 1704), satirist, miscellaneous writer, was born a farmer's son at Shifnal in Shropshire and received his early education at the Newport School. In 1678 he entered Christ Church, Oxford, where he displayed a brilliant facility in the classics along with a talent for wild escapades which brought him to the attention of Dr. Fell, the dean of Christ Church. An anecdote of this period, perhaps apocryphal, tells of his threatened expulsion and assigns to him the famous lines, "I do not love thee, Dr. Fell." Whatever the truth of this story, he left the university without a degree and went to London, the city which was to become his literary *mise en scène*.

After three years of school teaching (a profession for which he had no love), he devoted all his time to writing, producing a remarkably voluminous series of translations, poems, letters, dialogues, lampoons and comedies. Nearly all his work was written topically in a broad satirical style, more notable for coarseness than wit, and the violence of his attack on various public and literary figures resulted at least once, and probably twice, in a prison term. Tom Brown belonged both to Grub Street and to his age. With all his learning, he preferred the life of the street, and the tavern to the study. He belonged, to quote Charles Whibley, to "a strange underworld of letters, an inferno inhabited by lettered vagabonds, who matched in scholarship and scurrility, the heroes of Petronius." Yet out of this tavern literature came at least one notable piece of work, his *Amusements Serious and Comical,* a kind of chapbook which gives us a picture of seventeenth century London so vividly

THOMAS BROWN

human it stands quite independent of its literary period.

Tom Brown "of facetious memory," as Addison wrote after his death, achieved something more like notoriety than fame. He wrote with such lively satire and became so well known as a London figure that many works of similar nature were wrongly attributed to him. In a death-bed letter, appended to his *Collected Dialogues* published in 1704, he repented his literary sins and protested against being responsible for works which, he said, he was much too lazy to have written. That he had justification for such a protest is rather grimly borne out by a curious literary error in the inscription on his tombstone in Westminster Abbey, which attributes the authorship of *The London Spy* to him instead of to Ned Ward, a contemporary writer and alehouse keeper, who was actually the author.

Brown's best work was journalism raised to a scholarly level. Certainly in his own day he was both overpraised and overcensured, but with all his weaknesses, he was truly a man of letters who, if he had not been "too lazy in his temper to write much would have builded himself a better monument."

PRINCIPAL WORKS: A Collection of Miscellany Poems, Letters, &c, by Mr. Brown, &c, 1699; Amusements Serious and Comical, Calculated for the Meridian of London, 1700 (A. L. Haywood, ed. 1927); Letters from the Dead to the Living,

1702; Collected Works (J. Drake, ed.) 1707-08; The Beauties of Tom Brown (C. H. Wilson, ed.) 1808.

ABOUT: Cibber, C. in Lives of the Poets; Drake, J. Memoir in Collected Works; Wilson, C. H. Biographical Preface to The Beauties of Tom Brown.

BROWNE, Sir THOMAS (October 19, 1605-October 19, 1682), physician, miscellaneous writer, was born in London, the son of a mercer who came of a Cheshire family. His father died early and his mother remarried into somewhat higher social station, so that the boy was sent to Winchester, and in 1623 to Broadgates Hall, Oxford, which during his own residence became Pembroke College. He received his B.A. in 1626, and his M.A. in 1629. Then, after a stay in Ireland with his stepfather, who had a government position there, he studied medicine at Montpellier, Padua, and Leyden, where apparently he received his M.D. In 1633 he returned to England, and settled first in Yorkshire, near Halifax, but in 1637 he moved to Norwich, his home thenceforth. In the same year he received another doctorate from Oxford. In 1641 he married Dorothy Mileham; they had ten or twelve children, the exact number being unknown. Throughout the civil war he remained a staunch Royalist, but he took no active part and was left undisturbed in his practice. In 1664, the year he became a fellow of the College of Physicians, he appeared before Sir Matthew Hales as judge and by his testimony secured the execution of two women accused of witchcraft: this, which to modern judgment is a blot on his character, was in the eyes of his contemporaries a public service. He was never a member of the Royal Society, though he contributed some fossil bones to it—the antiquities of Norwich being one of his great interests.

In 1671, when Charles II visited Norwich, he wished to knight some local celebrity; the mayor having refused the honor, Browne became Sir Thomas by default. He died (of "colic") on his seventy-seventh birthday, and was buried in Norwich. In 1840 his coffin was accidentally broken open, and the bones being found well preserved, his skull was taken out and is now in the museum of Norwich Hospital.

Browne's first book, the *Religio Medici*, was written for his own spiritual use about 1635; he had not intended to publish it until a pirated edition appeared in 1642, whereupon he issued an authorized edition the next year. As he became known—primarily as an antiquarian—his correspondence increased, until he was resorted to as a sort of library by scholars and writers. One of his most indefatigable correspondents was the diarist John Evelyn.[qv] It was the discovery of a number of prehistoric mortuary urns in Norfolk that inspired the writing of *Urn Burial*. His antiquarian interests constantly warred with his medical ones. But implicit in all his writings was his profoundly mystical nature; he was himself the battleground between the scientific inclinations of the physician and a natural bent toward religion and even toward superstition. The *Religio Medici* was "an attempt to combine skepticism with belief," and an unsuccessful attempt it was. Translated into Latin by John Merryweather, it spread throughout Europe, and from its pages readers deduced that its author was everything from a Roman Catholic to a Quaker or a deist. Actually, however, he remained an Anglican, and his book was even put on the Papal *Index Librorum Prohibitorum*. The fact seems to be that Browne was fundamentally not a thinker, but an artist, and that in spite of the immense and varied learning displayed in his books it was his emotions rather than his mind that spoke through them. He was indeed less of a scholar in any real sense than a desultory but immensely wide reader.

He was besides a man in love with language, who adorned his beloved splendidly. His Greek and Latin neologisms, his sonorous periods, the cadenced rise and fall of his sentences, bear evidence of the mingled student and poet. His poetic feeling was intense, though he wrote no verse; his musical feeling was strong, though he knew no music. When all this is mingled with a nature primarily anti-rational, openly eccentric, perversely credulous, sometimes fanatical and yet always drawn back reluctantly to the reason his intellect acknowledged and his heart detested, the literary result cannot help being remarkable. Add a love for elaboration and color, and a certain dry humor married to a deep congenital melancholy, and one gets what George Saintsbury called "the mixture of shaded sunlight and half-illumi-

SIR THOMAS BROWNE

bury rightly termed "absolutely sublime rhetoric": such rhetoric as had not been heard since Sir Walter Raleigh also wrote of death.

It is the language of Sir Thomas Browne that makes him immortal. His philosophical and religious beliefs are of merely historical interest. It does not matter in the least to a modern reader that Browne was an anti-Copernican, who thought the sun went round a fixed earth; that he was passionately convinced of the reality of witchcraft, and believed in the philosopher's stone and the control of human destiny by the stars. What does matter is that he could write about these and all his other beliefs and observations with a "unique and splendid" magnificence. Browne antagonizes readers who are cold to the grand style; those who warm to it he fascinates.

One of these latter, of course, was Charles Lamb, and Browne was another of the authors he rescued from neglect. Browne will never be a popular writer, but he will remain always one of the glories of English literature. He himself ceased publishing any of his writings after 1658, but he had the intention of collecting his manuscripts and putting them in shape for a definitive edition before he died. His professional duties and then the disabilities of age prevented this, but it was done for him by others after his death. We probably have all that he wrote which was worth preserving, even to his notes on the natural history of his own neighborhood. The accounts are all in, and by virtue of two great books Sir Thomas Browne's name is secure. He was not an author of the first rank, but in his own narrow field he was supreme. If all else he wrote should disappear, he could stand forever on the last chapter of the *Urn Burial*, which for richness, majesty, and melody has no equal in the whole of English prose.

PRINCIPAL WORKS: Religio Medici, 1642 (authorized edition 1643); Vulgar Errors (Pseudodoxia Epidemica) 1646; Urn Burial (Hydriotaphia) together with The Garden of Cyrus, 1658; Certain Miscellany Tracts, 1684; Works, 1686; A Letter to a Friend, 1690; Posthumous Works, 1712; Christian Morals (J. Jeffrey, ed.) 1716; Notes and Letters on the Natural History of Norfolk (T. Southwell, ed.) 1902; Works (G. L. Keynes, ed.) 1928-31.

ABOUT: Anderton, B. Sketches from a Library Window; Dowden, E. Puritan and Anglican; Dunn, W. P. Sir Thomas Browne, a Study in Religious Philosophy; Gosse, E. Sir Thomas Browne; Hazlitt, W. Lectures on the Age of Eliza-

nated gloom which makes the charm of his style." It was Saintsbury also who spoke of "the mild but potent acid of his peculiar skepticism," the ingredient which continually rescues Browne from medievalism.

The man himself appears in his homely, familiar letters, particularly to his favorite son, a sailor in the navy. His friends knew him as equitable, charitable, modest (he was noted for the ease with which he blushed, even in old age), with none of the self-esteem and self-praise which occasionally creep into his books. This was the Browne his own circle, and doubtless his patients, knew. The Browne of his four best-known books was a very different person. Everything in them is magnified and larger than life, both the language and the subject matter. The most fantastic is *The Garden of Cyrus*, devoted to the quincunx ∴: and the mystic symbolism of the number five. As Coleridge remarked, Browne managed to find quincunxes in everything. The *Vulgar Errors*, which he wrote to confute unsound beliefs of the commonalty, actually contains more than it disproves. But it is in the *Religio Medici*, and still more in the *Urn Burial*, that the quintessential Browne emerges. The great bronze clangor of the Elizabethans sounds in them, not yet sharpened to the silver of the Restoration or the Augustans; for in style Browne harks back to the men who translated the Bible for James I. The homily on death which concludes the *Religio* Saints-

beth; Keynes, G. L. Bibliography of Sir Thomas Browne; Lamb, C. Essays; Nevinson, H. W. Books and Personalities; Sencourt, R. Outflying Philosophy; Stephen, L. Hours in a Library; Wilkin, S. Life, *in* Works, including Correspondence (1835-36); Williams, C. A Bibliography of the Religio Medici.

BROWNE, WILLIAM (1591-March, 1643?), poet, often known as William Browne of Tavistock, was born in the Devonshire town of that name, the son of Thomas Browne. He entered Exeter College, Oxford, in 1603, but left without taking a degree, and was entered in the Inner Temple in 1611. The little that is known of his life is confused because of the commonness of his name. He seems to have been married twice, and to have had two sons who both died in infancy— probably by his first wife. After her death, and following thirteen years of courtship, he married, in 1628, Tymothye Eversfield. Previous to this date, in 1624, he had reentered Exeter, where he acted as tutor of the future Earl of Carnarvon, and finally himself secured his M.A. in October of that year. He was a protegé of the powerful Herbert family, and lived with them for some time in Wilton. By 1640 he seems to have been living in Dorking. A William Browne died in Tavistock in March 1643, and this may have been the poet; or he may be the William Browne who died near by in December 1645.

Browne was a close friend of Michael Drayton [qv] and had other literary connections. From the mentions of him by his friends, he appears to have been a gentle, affectionate man, and much beloved; Drayton spoke of him as having a great mind in a little body, which may or may not have been a reference to his physical height.

He was purely a pastoral poet, an admirer and imitator of Spenser and Sidney. His influence on later and greater poets was more important than anything he himself wrote; a volume of his poems exists annotated by Milton, who certainly got some hints for *Lycidas* from Browne, and Keats also was a close student of his work. He has been called the "classical representative" of pastoral poetry in English. Frequently his verse is heavy, flat, and pompous, yet he has many pleasing and graceful passages. His greatest virtue as a writer is his love for his native Devonshire, which he knew

intimately and celebrated enthusiastically. There is throughout his writing a feeling of youthful verve, of cheerfulness, of poetry that is written because the poet enjoyed writing it. His "quaint simplicity" sometimes became little more than boring tediousness, and he is guilty of a good deal of bald, prosy exposition; on the other hand, he was capable of grace, pathos, and wit. It is in the stock poetic tales he narrates that he is poorest, in his loving admiration for the countryside of his childhood that he is at his best. He was a poet who would be the better for culling; a quiet, retiring, peace-loving man who wrote for his own pleasure and who was gifted without having the least touch of genius. His best pastoral is *The Shepherd's Pipe* (though not all the poems in the volume are his); but the fullest revelation of Browne the man is in the charming couplet:

> There is no season such delight can bring
> As summer, autumn, winter, and the spring.

PRINCIPAL WORKS: Two Elegies on Henry, Prince of Wales (one by Christopher Brooke) 1613; Britannia's Pastorals: Part I 1613, Part II 1616, Parts I and II 1625, Part III 1852; The Shepherd's Pipe (with others) 1614; The Inner Temple Masque, 1614; Collected Works, 1772; Original Poems of William Browne, Never Before Published (S. E. Brydges, ed.) 1815; Whole Works (W. C. Hazlitt, ed.) 1868; Poems (G. Goodwin, ed.) 1894.

ABOUT: Bullen, A. H. Introduction, 1894 edition of Poems; Gosse, E. The Jacobean Poets; Hazlitt, W. C. Memoir, *in* 1868 edition; Moorman, F. W. William Browne; Prince, J. The Worthies of Devon.

BRUCE, JAMES (December 14, 1730-April 27, 1794), explorer and travel writer, was born at Kinnaird House, Stirlingshire, the son of David Bruce, a Scottish laird. Educated at Harrow and Edinburgh University, he began the study of law out of respect for his father's wishes, but gave it up to marry a wine merchant's daughter, Adriana Allen. When Adriana died within nine months of their marriage, the young widower went abroad and began the travels which were to bring him fame.

Bruce seems to have been perfectly equipped by nature for a career of high adventure—over six feet tall (Fanny Burney later described him as "the tallest man you ever saw gratis!"), athletic, daring and with a passion for the picturesque. Indeed, after reading the highly colored story of his travels, one is tempted to call him an eight-eenth-century Richard Halliburton.

After traveling in Spain and Portugal, where he studied Arabic, Bruce was sent to Algiers as British Consul with a special com-mission to examine ancient ruins. This post he resigned after two years. For the three years following, he traveled widely in Afri-ca, experiencing famine and pestilence, plunder and shipwreck, until at last he con-ceived a final goal for his explorations. Bruce was determined to discover the source of the river Nile, which he believed to be in Abys-sinia. Arriving at Alexandria, he disguised himself as a Turkish sailor and embarked on another series of fabulous adventures which took him deep into the interior of Abyssinia. For two years he lived in this unknown country, previously unexplored by any Euro-pean, where he not only made friends with Princess Ozoro Esther, the most beautiful woman in Abyssinia, but actually reached the source of the Blue Nile in 1770. He was quite mistaken, however, in claiming this to be the source of the White Nile and the river of the ancients.

On his return to civilization, Bruce was hailed as a great explorer by the French, but Londoners received the romantic account of his travels with stubborn incredulity. Deeply wounded, Bruce retired to his Kin-naird estate where he let fifteen years elapse before he dictated the five-volume story of his travels, published in 1790 as *Travels to Discover the Source of the Nile*. The book continued to be popular for half a century and while Bruce was most certainly neither a scholar, nor a judicious critic, he proved himself a vivid narrator of exotic adventure.

PRINCIPAL WORKS: Travels to Discover the Source of the Nile, 1790 (A. Murray, ed., 3rd ed. 1813).

ABOUT: Head, F. Life of Bruce; Murray, A. Biography, *in* Travels to Discover the Source of the Nile, 1813 ed.

BUCHANAN, GEORGE (February, 1506-September 28, 1582), classicist, poet, was Scotland's greatest humanist, and the activa-ting reason why in Scotland since his time religion has always been closely associated with learning. He was born in Killearn, Stirlingshire, the son of Thomas Buchanan, a "poor laird," and of Agnes Heriot. His father died early, and his maternal uncle sent him about 1520 to the University of

1581

GEORGE BUCHANAN

Paris. He was there for about two years, then was with Albany's French troops in Scotland, and about 1525 was the student of John Mair (Major) at St. Andrews. He returned to Paris (France was always his second country) a year later, and remained for some ten years, gaining his B.A. degree in 1526, his M.A. in 1527. Back in Scotland, James V encouraged him to write more strongly satiric poems against the Francis-cans, then gave him no protection, but let him be imprisoned by Cardinal Beaton, his greatest enemy. He escaped from prison to Bordeaux, where for three years he taught Latin at the Collège de Guyenne, Montaigne being one of his pupils. It was there he wrote his Latin plays for the boys to perform. The years between 1543 and 1548 are obscure; he was certainly very ill during a large part of this time, and his health was always precarious. He was then appointed head of a college in Coimbra, Portugal, only to find himself accused before the Inquisition. He was sequestered in a monastery for two years, and occupied the time in writing his fine Latin poetic version of the Psalms.

On his release he returned to France, arriving in Scotland once more about 1560. By this time his sympathies, increasingly Protestant, had become crystallized and he was avowedly a Calvinist. Nevertheless, he was Queen Mary's tutor, and it was not

BUNYAN

until the murder of Darnley (who incidentally was head of his own clan) that he became her deadliest enemy. He was a member of the General Assembly in 1563, and its moderator in 1567. When the famous case of the Casket Letters caused Mary's trial for treason in England, Buchanan took an active part in the prosecution. He was accused of having forged the letters; this is unlikely, but there is no doubt that his hatred blinded him to any legal fairness in the trial. Against her pleas, he was made tutor of the young James VI (later James I of England), and his later offices included those of Director of Chancery and Lord Privy Seal, in which capacity he was a member of Parliament to 1579. The great works of his later years were his *History of Scotland* and his *De Jure Regni apud Scotos* ("concerning the law of the kingdom in Scotland"), a book with democratic tendencies that caused it to be condemned by Parliament and burned by Oxford.

Except for two tracts and a few letters in the vernacular, Buchanan wrote entirely in Latin, which was his own tongue as it has seldom been that of anyone since classical times. His *History* has been compared not unjustly to the work of Livy and of Caesar. His Greek was self-taught; it was Latin that he urged as the universal literary language, and made inseparable from Scottish scholarship. As P. Hume Brown has said, "his poetic gifts and his command of Latin were unrivaled." His plays, particularly *Jephthes,* have "moral intensity and elevation of thought," and his paraphrase of the Psalms is poetry in its own right. Yet he also wrote scores of amatory Latin poems.

He himself was a strange mixture: "humane and vindictive, mirthful and morose, cultured and coarse, fond of truth but full of prejudices." He spoke of himself as "a poor wandering exile, tossed about on land and sea"—which for his earlier years he truly was. But, to quote Archbishop John Spottiswoode, "no man did better merit of his nation for learning, nor thereby did bring it to more glory."

PRINCIPAL WORKS: *Latin*—Somnium, 1534?; Franciscanus et Fratres, 1538?; Baptistes (tragedy) 1544; Jephthes (tragedy) 1544 (A. G. Mitchell, tr., 1903); De Jure Regni apud Scotos, 1579; Rerum Scotiarum Historia, 1582 (J. Aikman, tr., 1827-28); Works, 1715, 1725. *English (Scots vernacular)*—The Chameleon, or the Crafty States-

man (written 1570) 1710; An Admonition Direct to the Trew Lordis (with Detectio; Ane Detectioun of the Duinges of Marie Queen of Scottes) 1571; Vernacular Writings (P. H. Brown, ed.) 1892.

ABOUT: Brown, P. H. George Buchanan, Humanist and Reformer; Henriquez, J. C. George Buchanan in the Lisbon Inquisition; Irving, D. Memoirs of the Life and Writings of George Buchanan; Macmillan, D. George Buchanan, a Biography; Millar, D. (ed.) George Buchanan, a Memorial; Murray, D. A Catalogue of Printed Books, Manuscripts, and Other Documents Relating to George Buchanan.

BUCKINGHAM, Duke of. See VILLIERS, GEORGE, Second Duke of Buckingham

BUCKINGHAM and NORMANDY, Duke of. See SHEFFIELD, JOHN

BUNYAN, JOHN (November 1628-August 31, 1688), religious writer, allegorist, was the son of Thomas Bunyan, a "brasier" or tinker, by his second wife, Margaret Bentley. He was born at Elston, near Bedford. Contrary to some statements, the Bunyans had long been settled in Bedfordshire, and there was no gypsy blood in the family. The boy received the barest possible elementary education, and at sixteen was drafted into the Parliamentary army, being on duty at Newport Pagnell from 1643 to 1647. It is interesting to note that his commanding officer was the Sir Samuel Luke who afterwards was lampooned by Samuel Butler as "Sir Hudibras."

At twenty he was married (he never mentions his wife's maiden name), and became the father of two sons and two daughters, one blind from birth. Two books of piety which were his wife's dowry caused his mind first to turn to religion. We must not be deceived by Bunyan's account in *Grace Abounding* of the period of religious agony, amounting to melancholia, he now went through. By any standards but the Puritan ones, he was already a blameless youth, whose worst fault was harmless profanity. The first effect of religious fervor on him was to transform him into a thorough Pharisee—what he himself calls "a poor painted hypocrite." It was not until 1653, when he joined a Baptist church in Bedford, and eventually became its preacher, that he gained perspective and was able to consolidate and objectify his religious views. Meanwhile he was supporting his growing family by working at his father's trade.

His first published writing was the result of a controversy with a Quaker named Edward Burrough; Bunyan's concrete mind rejected violently the mysticism of the Quakers. But it took a stronger stimulus to make a great author out of the half-literate Puritan preacher.

In 1655 his wife died, and he soon remarried. His second wife, Elizabeth, was a true mother to his children (later she had a son and daughter of her own), and his loyal helper and defender in the trial which was soon to come upon him. With the Restoration, and the reestablishment of the Anglican Church, the independent preachers were doomed. Bunyan sturdily refused to stop preaching, and in consequence he spent the long years from 1660 to 1672 in prison. Once he was let out for a few months, but was soon rearrested. His prison life was brutally hard, and his heart was wrung by the plight of his family, left to starve. Unable to support them by his trade, he learned to make tag-laces which his wife sold. In vain she intervened for him at all the courts, even before the House of Lords. His only consolation was to preach to his fellow prisoners.

It was under these conditions that John Bunyan became a writer. His writing was

T. Sadler, 1684

JOHN BUNYAN

for himself, with no thought of readers, let alone of publication. His "reference library" consisted of the Bible and Foxe's *Book of Martyrs*. It is not strange that he wrote in their very language. This book was *Grace Abounding*, "one of the great books of the world on religious experience," which, says John Brown, reads in some passages "as if written with a pen of fire." The author of tracts and doggerel devotional verse had found his theme. Like Milton ("that one talent which is death to hide"), Bunyan believed his gift came from God and its use was holy.

In 1672, Charles II, to cover his alleged plan to return England to the Roman Catholic Church, removed restrictions on dissenting ministers as well as on Catholic priests. Bunyan was released from prison, and licensed. He became pastor of his old church in Bedford. In 1675 the king was forced to withdraw the declaration of indulgence, and Bunyan was again thrown into prison, for six months. It was at this time that he wrote *Pilgrim's Progress*, or the first part of it at least. "I did it mine own self to gratifie," he wrote, insisting that "manner and matter, too, was all mine own." Some of his Puritan brethren condemned it as "a vain story," but their view did not prevail. *Pilgrim's Progress* immediately became one of the most widely read books in English, as it has remained. For the Puritans, it served as a substitute for the novels and plays they were not permitted to read or see. It was only slowly (though Johnson and Swift praised it) that the non-Puritan world came to realize its greatness as literature.

"Most perfect and complex of fairy tales" (Henry Hallam), this supreme English allegory of the search of the soul for salvation is far more than that. One must go back to Chaucer to find another such compelling narrative, with such concreteness of image and vividness of personal portraiture. The language is the language of the King James Bible, but the dramatic unity, the effortless simplicity, the creative genius, are all Bunyan's own. The two later allegories, *The Holy War* and *The Life and Death of Mr. Badman*, are inferior only by comparison with *Pilgrim's Progress* itself. (Macaulay even preferred *The Holy War*.) *Mr. Badman* is notable as giving Bunyan's picture of "worldly wickedness" among the lower classes as he had known it, as soldier and tinker.

Following his release from his second imprisonment, Bunyan returned to preaching, often at considerable danger, particularly around 1685, the year of Monmouth's rebellion. Sometimes he was in hiding; once he is said to have disguised himself as a wagoner. He journeyed constantly about Bedfordshire, and the Baptists dubbed him "Bishop Bunyan." When James II came to the throne, he took note of Bunyan's enormous influence, and had him approached with offers which Bunyan unhesitatingly rejected as bribes. He died in direct consequence of his labors as a minister; going to reconcile a father and son, he was caught in a snowstorm, developed a "fever," and died at sixty, apparently of pneumonia.

To the end he had no suspicion, as Macaulay says, that he had produced a masterpiece—a book that has aptly been called "the lay Bible." He continued to write tracts, verses, and controversial pamphlets— these last sometimes against his fellow Baptists, for he had a broad tolerance for other dissenting sects, and refused to join in attacking Presbyterians or Independents. Of his own personality we know little except what can be gleaned from his writings; for in a sense he had no private life. We know he was a devoted and affectionate husband and father, with a particular love for the blind daughter who died young. After the period in youth when he was going through the excruciating torments of conversion, he was notably well balanced: stubborn and intransigent, but not a fanatic. All his life, however, he retained the self-depreciation, undue modesty, and excessive remorse for trifles which served to give those who knew him only through his own statements a false idea of his character. Physically, he was a tall, well set-up man, with ruddy skin and reddish hair and mustache.

It is interesting to speculate on what Bunyan's career might have been had he been born in a later century. There seems little doubt that he had the makings of a great novelist or dramatist. His mind turned naturally to the depiction of character and the weaving of plot. In a sense his allegories are *sui generis;* he was not a professional writer at all. As J. R. Green says, "Bunyan's English is the simplest and homeliest English

that has ever been used by any great English writer." He wrote because he could not help writing; his is the natural eloquence of a child, though the mind behind it was powerful as well as clear and simple. *Pilgrim's Progress* cannot be compared with any other great book in any language. Its readers could not evaluate it, but they could value it; ninety-two editions were published in the first hundred years after its appearance. Yet, though Bunyan was, as it were, a writer by inner necessity, he was no unconscious child of nature; the changes and improvements in the first three editions show how painstakingly he strove to make even stronger and clearer what he thought of as an evangelical message to the unsaved world.

PRINCIPAL WORKS: Some Gospel Truths Opened, 1656; A Vindication of Gospel Truths, 1657; Sighs from Hell, or the Groans of a Damned Soul, 1658; The Holy City, or the New Jerusalem, 1665; Grace Abounding to the Chief of Sinners, 1666; A Confession of My Faith, and a Reason of My Practice, 1671; Pilgrim's Progress from This World to the World Which Is to Come, 1678, second part 1684; The Life and Death of Mr. Badman, 1680; The Holy War Made by Shaddai upon Diabolus, 1682; A Book for Boys and Girls, or Country Rhymes for Children (originally Divine Emblems, or Temporal Things Spiritualized) 1686; The Works of the Eminent Servant of Christ, Mr. John Bunyan, 1692; The Heavenly Footman, or a Description of the Man Who Gets to Heaven, 1698.

ABOUT: Brown, J. Bunyan, His Life, Times, and Work; Coats, R. H. John Bunyan; Coleridge, S. T. Literary Remains; Dowden, E. Puritan and Anglican; Froude, J. A. Bunyan; Gilfillan, G. Literary Portraits; Griffith, G. O. John Bunyan; Harrison, F. M. A Bibliography of the Works of John Bunyan; Harrison, G. B. John Bunyan: A Study in Personality; Lang, A. Essays in Little; Lindsay, J. John Bunyan, Maker of Myths; Macaulay, T. B. Essays; Southey, R. Life of John Bunyan; Tindall, W. Y. John Bunyan, Mechanick Preacher; Tulloch, J. English Puritanism and Its Leaders; Venables, E. Life of John Bunyan; White, W. H. Life of Bunyan; Willcocks, M. P. Bunyan Calling: A Voice from the Seventeenth Century; Woodberry, G. E. Makers of Literature.

BURGOYNE, JOHN (1722-June 4, 1792), British general, playwright, was the only son of Captain John Burgoyne, army officer and man of fashion. He was educated at the Westminster School where he became a close friend of Lord Strange, the eldest son of the Earl of Derby. After three years of army service, Burgoyne, a twenty-one year old lieutenant, eloped with Lord Strange's sister. Lord Derby vigorously disapproved the marriage, but Lady Charlotte and her gallant officer husband seem to have lived a very pleasant life in London, Burgoyne having purchased a captaincy (presumably out of money presented to his bride as a wedding gift). After three years, an accumulation of debts forced him to sell his commission and live abroad in extremely modest circumstances.

Lord Derby appears to have relented after the marriage had lasted some ten years, for it was by his influence that Burgoyne was reinstated in the army at the outbreak of the Seven Years' War to take up his career as officer and gentleman-statesman. In the next fifteen years he rose to the rank of Major General and was twice elected to Parliament, but his personal interests were more and more concerned with the world of art and fashion. Friend of Sir Joshua Reynolds, amateur actor, clubman and gambler, he turned now to playwriting and saw his first play, *The Maid of the Oaks,* produced by Garrick in 1775.

General Burgoyne is probably best known as the British commander who captured Ticonderoga in the second year of the American Revolution, who was defeated at the Battle of Bennington and surrendered at Saratoga. That he was held to account by Parliament and the British people for mistakes not entirely his, is perhaps not so well known. In any case, popular opinion turned against him; he was deprived of his offices, retaining only the title of "General," and after further political skirmishing, he withdrew from public life, his career as dramatist coming now to full flower. A brilliantly successful comedy, *The Heiress,* was both produced and published in 1786, achieving enormous popularity. Some contemporary critics even preferred it to *The School for Scandal,* and although in perspective there can be no doubt that Burgoyne's work is inferior both in construction and dialogue to Sheridan's masterpiece, at the time it exercised a wider influence.

After the death of Lady Charlotte, Burgoyne formed a liaison with a singer, Susan Caulfield, and fathered several children, all of whom were brought up by Lord Derby. In his seventieth year, two life-sized careers behind him, Burgoyne died suddenly the day after he had attended the opening of a play at the Haymarket Theatre.

PRINCIPAL WORKS: The Maid of the Oaks, 1774; The Lord of the Manor, 1781; The Heiress, 1786; The Dramatic and Poetical Works of the Late Lieutenant-General John Burgoyne, 1808.

ABOUT: Fonblanque, E. B. de. Political and Military Episodes Derived from the Life and Correspondence of Burgoyne; Huddleston, F. J. Gentleman Johnny Burgoyne.

BURKE, EDMUND (January 12?, 1729-July 9, 1797), political writer, orator, was born in Dublin, the son of Richard Burke, a solicitor, who was a Protestant, and of a Roman Catholic mother whose maiden name was Nagle. His sister was reared as a Catholic, but the attacks on Burke on the the ground that he was one also (at that time Roman Catholics had no vote) were false.

He was educated at Balliton, under a Quaker schoolmaster, and in 1743 went to Trinity College, Dublin, where he received his B.A. in 1748. From 1750 to 1759 he was entered in the Middle Temple, but was never called to the bar. His first interest, indeed, was in poetry, and he was never a great or even a very good lawyer. The nine years he spent in London are very obscure; there is no proof for any of the romantic stories told of him in this period. The facts seem to be that he was poor, living on a small allowance from his father, earning some money by hack writing (his father withdrew his allowance when the son declared for literature rather than the law), and leading the shabby Bohemian life of any poor student. His great friend of this period was William Burke, who may or may not have been his cousin; William Burke was a speculator, and Edmund Burke seems to have profited at times by his speculations, though in the end William lost everything. One fact we do know about these years is that in 1756, Edmund Burke married Jane Nugent, the daughter of his physician. He was in poor health, and he lived with the doctor and under his care, both before and after his marriage, which resulted in the birth of two sons. Only one survived, a vain dullard whom his father adored and whose early death broke his heart.

Through the influence of friends, Burke in 1759 became private secretary to William Gerard Hamilton, who later, as chief secretary for Ireland, took the young man back to Dublin with him. In 1765 he became secretary to a much better man and better friend, Lord Rockingham, then Prime Minister. The next year he was elected to Parliament from Wendover. His real career had begun.

The great interests of Burke were successively the break with the American colonies, the emancipation of the Irish Catholics, the impeachment of Warren Hastings for' crimes committed in his government of India, and the French Revolution. In the first three of these he took what might be called a liberal stand, in the last, an extremely reactionary one. Yet there is nothing surprising in the fact. Burke throughout his life remained a Whig—though in a sense he was the father of the present English Conservative (Tory) Party. The one thing that must be remembered is that Burke's governing principle was the supremacy of divine law. He was for justice and for liberty, but unalterably opposed to "the tyranny of unprincipled ability divorced from religious awe and all regard for individual liberty and property." Hence the same man whose magnificent speech on conciliation with America is almost part of the historical documents of the United States also conducted a fierce crusade against Jacobinism in France or in England. He was the eternal Girondist. It is a type of mind not unknown in the rather similar world of today. In his really terrible fourteen-year fight against Hastings, comparable only to Cicero's impeachment of Verres (but not meeting with the same tri-

umph), it was the disorder as much as the cruelty and malfeasance that he attacked. Most of Burke's crusades were unsuccessful, or successful only long after his death. But his bitterest enemies, and he had plenty of them, never denied his intense and fiery integrity of spirit, his passionate sincerity.

As an orator Burke was impressive rather than effectual. His tall, ungainly figure, his harsh voice, and his awkward, milling gestures won him no converts. He reads much better than he could have sounded. And it is in the splendor, the eloquence, the really sublime ardor of his style that his greatness subsists. He was, as Herbert Grierson said, "one of the profoundest, most suggestive, most illuminating of political thinkers," but he was more than that. He raised political speech to the status of high art. He had many defects—pomposity, extravagance, rhetorical "purple patches"; but he also had a nervous, vivid style that has never been excelled and seldom equalled in its own field of thought. That style came from what Grierson called "a sensitive, brooding imagination coupled with a restless, speculative intellect." His friend Samuel Johnson spoke truly when he said that the most casual meeting with Burke would convince a stranger that here was an extraordinary man.

It was in 1764 that Burke joined the famous Literary Club and became thenceforth the intimate of such men as Johnson, Goldsmith, Reynolds, and Garrick. That was before his political career began, when he was earning his living by production of the *Annual Register*. Dissident as most of these men were from his political views—at least until the latter days of the French Revolution—they remained his ardent friends and admirers. Their only regret was that his preoccupation with politics kept him from the wider philosophical writing for which they felt he was most gifted. They may have been right, but it is more probable that Burke functioned just where he could function best, and that he needed the impact of outer events to strike sparks from his spirit.

Calumny indeed followed him all his life. There was great wonder as to how, in 1778, the needy and debt-ridden member of Parliament, who never held public office except as paymaster of the army, had bought the great estate in Buckinghamshire,

Sir J. Reynolds

EDMUND BURKE

Beaconsfield, which was thenceforth his home. The answer was simple; Rockingham lent him part of the money, a small legacy from a brother paid more of the price, and the rest of the purchase came from a heavy mortgage which was still unpaid when Burke died. He was indeed always in debt; he had a passion for beauty and for hospitality, he could not breathe except in grandeur. But he owed no part of his existence to corruption, and his heirs if not himself finally paid all his debts. He took a pension from Pitt in 1795, it is true; but he had earned it. He was then a man in his sixties, who had always been frail in health and who had given his entire being to the service of his country, who was broken by the recent death of his adored son, and who was only two years from his own death.

He left Parliament in 1794, refusing a peerage because the son who would have inherited it was dead. He did not stop writing, and his last efforts were directed against the Directory which preceded the Napoleonic Empire in France. When he died, Fox, with whom he had broken in 1791 over the French Revolution, generously moved for his burial in Westminster Abbey; but Burke had already asked that his funeral be private, and that he lie in his own church at Beaconsfield. That was to have been, incidentally, his name as a peer; it was given in the next century to a very different statesman.

Burke, said John Morley, "is among the greatest of those who have wrought marvels in the prose of the English tongue." The causes he espoused are won or lost or forgotten, but the language of his advocacy has outlived them.

The force and loftiness of his mind, the fervor of his feeling, the cadenced eloquence of his prose—owing something, perhaps, to the Irish brogue which he never lost—combine to take his political speeches out of the category of oratory and raise them to that of pure literature. One may disagree violently with any or all of Burke's views and opinions; one may deplore the occasional bombast, the passion which sometimes explodes in an hysterical scream: but no one who thrills to the magnificence of which our rich and flexible tongue is capable can fail to recognize Edmund Burke as one of its mightiest voices.

PRINCIPAL WORKS: A Vindication of Natural Society, 1756; A Philosophical Enquiry into the Origin of Our Ideas of the Sublime and Beautiful, 1757; Observations on the Present State of the Nation, 1769; Thoughts on the Cause of the Present Discontents, 1770; On American Taxation, 1774; On Conciliation with the Colonies, 1775; Letter to the Sheriff of Bristol, 1777; Address to the King, 1777; On the Nabob of Arcot's Private Debts, 1785; Articles of Charge of High Crimes and Misdemeanors Against Warren Hastings, 1786; Reflections on the Revolution in France, 1790; An Appeal from the New to the Old Whigs, 1791; Thoughts on French Affairs, 1791; Remarks on the Policy of the Allies, 1793; Report on the Lord's Journals, 1794; A Letter . . . to a Noble Lord, 1795; Letters . . . on the Proposals for Peace with the Regicide Directory of France, 1795-97; Two Letters on the Conduct of Our Domestic Parties, 1797; Collected Works, 1792-1827; Speeches, 1816; Works and Correspondence, 1852.

ABOUT: Adams, W. H. D. English Party Leaders and English Parties; Baumann, A. A. Burke: the Founder of Conservatism; Bisset, R. The Life of Edmund Burke; Butler, G. G. The Tory Tradition; Cobban, A. Edmund Burke and the Revolt Against the Eighteenth Century; Copeland, T. W. Our Eminent Friend: Edmund Burke; MacCunn, J. The Political Philosophy of Burke; Magnus, P. M. Edmund Burke, a Life; McCormick, C. Memoirs of E. Burke; Morley, J. Burke; Murray, R. H. Edmund Burke, a Biography; Newman, B. Edmund Burke; O'Brien, W. Edmund Burke as an Irishman; Oliver, R. T. Four Who Spoke Out; Osborn, A. M. Rousseau and Burke; Pillans, T. D. Edmund Burke: Apostle of Justice and Liberty; Prior, J. Memoir of the Life and Character of the Right Honorable Edmund Burke.

BURNET, GILBERT (September 15, 1643-March 17, 1715), bishop, historian, biographer, was born at Edinburgh, the youngest son of Robert Burnet, afterwards Lord Crimond. Both his father and his mother, a sister of Lord Warristoun, were deeply involved in the religious and political struggles that raged between Scotland and England during the reign of Charles I. This early background appears to have been the mold which shaped Burnet's adult career. Educated at Marischal College, Aberdeen, he visited Oxford and Cambridge and later traveled abroad. In Holland he made friends with John Maitland, Duke of Lauderdale, who was at that time sympathetic with the Scottish Covenanters. A few years later Lauderdale swung his favor against the dissident group and came into opposition with Burnet, who was then in Scotland attempting to effect a compromise between episcopacy and presbyterianism.

During the whole of his mature life, Burnet's fortunes rose and fell dramatically with the tide of political events, for al-

GILBERT BURNET

though the main task of his life was the writing of history, it was history based on the living struggles of his own time. When Lauderdale denounced him to Charles II as a center of Scottish discontent, Burnet resigned the chair of divinity at the University of Glasgow, which he had occupied for more than eight years, and went to England where he served as chaplain to Rolls Chapel. Although popular as a preacher, when James II came to the throne, he was deprived of his appointments by order of the court and fled to Paris under the threat of prosecution for high treason. While living abroad, Burnet became a confidential adviser to William and Mary, Prince and Princess of Orange, and at the time of the revolution, he made a triumphant return to England as the trusted friend of the new monarchs. In 1689, as a reward, he was consecrated Bishop of Salisbury.

Through these uneasy years, he wrote voluminously. In 1679 he published the first part of his great historical work, the *History of the Reformation in England,* which had been prepared from original sources even though he was denied access to much of the material he needed by political enemies. A second major work, the *History of His Own Time,* was begun in 1685, but by his instruction remained unpublished until after his death. He was also the author of numerous biographies, treatises and sermons.

Burnet was married three times. His first wife was an heiress, Lady Margaret Kennedy (incidentally, a cousin of Lauderdale). His second wife, whom he married shortly after the death of Lady Margaret, was Mary Scott, a Dutch woman of Scottish descent, by whom he had seven children. When he was fifty-three, again a widower, he married Elizabeth Berkeley, author of *A Method of Devotion.* Both in his personal relations and in his writings, Burnet reveals a shrewd, penetrating knowledge of character. Essentially a practical moralist, he was able to persuade both friends and readers, drawing on his own deep fund of psychological experience.

The pervading purpose of all his work was a vindication of freedom under the law as the guiding principle of ecclesiastical and political life. This aim gives his writing a genuine vitality, even though he was often awkward in style and guilty of historical inaccuracies. Violently criticized in his own time, particularly by Swift, he remains a pioneer in the scientific treatment of history, basing narrative on personal investigation of original documents.

PRINCIPAL WORKS: The Memoirs of the Lives and Actions of James and William Dukes of Hamilton and Castleherald, 1677; The History of the Reformation of the Church of England (three parts) 1679, 1681, 1715 (N. Pocock, ed.) 1865); Some Passages of the Life and Death of John Earl of Rochester, 1680; The Life and Death of Sir Matthew Hale, 1682; The Life of William Bedell, Bishop of Kilmore in Ireland, 1685; A Discourse of the Pastoral Care, 1692; An Essay on the Memory of the Late Queen, 1695; An Exposition of the Thirty-Nine Articles of the Church of England, 1699; Bishop Burnet's History of His Own Time (two parts) 1724, 1734 (M. J. Routh, ed. 1823); Thoughts on Education, 1761.

ABOUT: Burnet, G. Rough Draft of My Own Life (H. C. Foxcroft, ed.) *in* Supplement to Burnet's History; Burnet, Sir T. Life *in* History of His Own Time, 1823 ed.; Clarke, T. E. S. and Foxcroft, H. C. A Life of Gilbert Burnet.

BURNET, THOMAS (1635?-September 27, 1715), English divine, author of an imaginative cosmogony, the *Sacred Theory of the Earth,* was born at Croft in Yorkshire about 1635. Little is known of his early years, but it is on record that he was educated at the free school of Northallerton, where his master pointed him out as a model to later pupils. In 1651 he entered Clare Hall, Cambridge, where he studied with John Tillotson, later Archbishop of

Canterbury, and Ralph Cudworth, a leader in the Cambridge group of idealist philosophers. Three years later he followed Cudworth to Christ's College, where he was elected a fellow and received his M.A. degree in 1658. After his Cambridge years, Burnet traveled abroad with two young noblemen, one a grandson of the Duke of Ormonde, and it was apparently through the influence of the latter that he was appointed master of the Charterhouse in 1685.

Burnet's life was entirely unspectacular but his writings aroused violent controversy. The *Telluris Theoria Sacra,* published first in Latin and then in English, found many admirers and no fewer critics. Addison addressed a Latin ode to Burnet on the basis of this newly published work and Steele wrote an enthusiastic review in the *Spectator.* On the other hand, a number of scientists and philosophers of the period ridiculed Burnet's theory. Actually, his speculation as to the nature and origin of the earth was entirely fanciful and made no use of the scientific knowledge then available. Burnet held that the earth was like a gigantic egg and at the time of the deluge, the interior waters had burst through the shell to form the oceans while the shell fragments formed the continents. Fantastic as this conception may appear, it was presented with considerable eloquence by a master of style and as such, won many adherents. When, however, Burnet published a second work which professed to reconcile his theory with the creation story in Genesis, he was roundly condemned for treating the whole account as allegory.

After the storm subsided, Burnet lived out his life quietly in the Charterhouse, publishing a series of "Remarks" in criticism of the philosophy of John Locke and writing two religious works of a controversial nature, of which he printed only a few copies for his close friends.

PRINCIPAL WORKS: Telluris Theoria Sacra, 1681-89 (English tr. 1684-89) ; Archaeologiae Philosophicae, 1692; Remarks upon an Essay Concerning Human Understanding, 1697.
ABOUT: Heathcote, R. Life of Burnet *in* 1759 edition of Sacred Theory of the Earth.

BURNS, ROBERT (January 25, 1759-July 21, 1796), Scottish poet—the greatest of Scottish poets—known during his lifetime as "the Ayrshire ploughman," was born

in a little cottage in Alloway in that shire, where his father, William Burness or Burnes, leased a small farm. Robert was the oldest of seven children of Burness and his wife, who had been Agnes Brown. The father had a great influence on his son; he was an upright, devout man, somewhat dour, but intellectual, a man who from his scanty earnings bought books, when he could not borrow them, for his children. He also prevailed on a youth named John Murdoch to establish a little school for his own and the neighbors' sons.

These two or three years under Murdoch constituted most of Robert Burns' formal schooling, though later he had a few more weeks under the same teacher, and a short stay at Dalrymple to learn geometry. His real teacher was the traditional songs and ballads of his country, countless numbers of which he knew by heart. (The family by this time was living at Lochlea, Tarbolton, and Robert had written his first poem, "Handsome Nell.") At thirteen he was at work on the farm, at fifteen a full-time farm laborer. His father wanted something better for him, and sent him to Ballochneil to a maternal uncle, to learn surveying. Overwork and nervous strain had already taken their toll of his naturally robust, tall body, and he was forced to abandon this plan and return to Lochlea. In 1781 he tried again to escape from farming by going to relatives at Irvine to learn the flax-dressing business. During a New Year's Eve carouse the shop burned down, and there was nothing to do but return again to the farm, which was already proving a failure. In the interstices of labor, Burns pondered and wrote his songs (he could not sing them, for he was totally tone deaf!), formed a debating society, joined the Masons, and got himself in trouble with the girls. In 1784 his father died, fearing to the last for the well being of his oldest son.

Robert with his brother Gilbert took a farm at Mossgiel, near Mauchlin. He was beginning to have a local reputation as a poet—and as a controversialist in the rivalry between the bigoted Auld Licht faction of the Presbyterians and the more progressive New Lichts—though his satiric poems circulated only in manuscript. The long ambivalent relation with Jean Armour had begun. Jean was the daughter of a master mason, who thought poorly of the young ploughman who already had a bad reputation and an illegitimate daughter by a local girl. Nevertheless when it became apparent that Jean also was going to become a mother by Burns, they were "married" by the simple Scottish process of a paper signed by both. The Armours ordered their daughter to leave Burns and she obeyed; Burns, outraged, destroyed the paper and imagined he had destroyed the marriage also. In the deepest melancholy, he decided to transform his whole life by emigration to Jamaica, where he had been offered a job as overseer. It was at this period that he met and wooed Mary Campbell, "Hieland Mary," who promised to go with him to Jamaica, but died instead. To obtain money for the passage, he arranged for the publication of *Poems Chiefly in the Scottish Dialect*. The success of the poems was so immediate that he gave up the emigration project and journeyed to Edinburgh, where for several months in 1786 and 1787 he found himself rather a bewildered lion. His head was not turned; he retained his sturdy self-respect and independence, his rustic though not cloddish manners. It was at this time that young Walter Scott met him and noted his glowing dark eyes—"I never saw such another eye in any human head."

The Edinburgh experience did, unfortunately, turn Burns to the writing of verse in polite English. He is supremely the poet of the Scottish dialect; his English poems are merely diluted eighteenth century verse. Here also he met "Clarinda," Mrs. McLehose, with whom he conducted a long sentimental correspondence. (The image of Burns, the peasant, the natural revolutionist, the utterly straightforward, uninhibited man, trying to keep up with the lady's prudery, piety, and sentimentality, is one for tears and laughter.) On his return from Edinburgh he had become re-entangled with Jean. She had borne twins, one of whom had died; Burns visited her, was disgusted by the mixed servility and truculence of the Armours and with her herself, but nevertheless resumed relations with her, and again she became pregnant.

Meanwhile, in Edinburgh again (where for some weeks he was laid up by a carriage accident), Burns had met James Johnson, who had the idea of collecting the Scottish

A. Nasmyth

ROBERT BURNS

traditional songs into a volume. For Johnson Burns traveled throughout Scotland, much as a collector of mountaineer folk ballads would do today in the American South. He refused to take any pay for this work; his services were inspired by pure patriotism and love of this elemental genuine poetry. Later he did the same thing in the same way for Thomson's collection. Unfortunately, the farm, with which his brother was still struggling, was not bringing in money enough to live on, and was about to fail completely.

To Johnson's collection Burns contributed some two hundred songs, to Thomson's over a hundred. But these lyrics were not in the crude form in which he had found them. He added, subtracted, amended as he thought best; and from their slag-bound ore he minted pure gold. Most of Burns' lyric poems in the Scottish dialect have some base in the traditional ballads; sometimes entire stanzas are given as they were originally sung; but in any real sense they are his, as he was theirs.

The struggle for existence went on. It became still more complicated, when in 1788, after a series of quarrels, separations, and reconciliations, Burns acknowledged Jean Armour as his legal wife. He probably could not have had a better one, if he must have any; though Jean was weak-willed and far from sharing his intellectual interests, she was sweet-tempered, patient, and loyal. She even reared his illegitimate daughter by another woman (there were three of these daughters in all, all named Elizabeth). She had five sons of her own, the last one born posthumously during his father's funeral. Clarinda was outraged by the marriage, but by that time Burns could not really have cared much what she thought.

Hard as he labored, the brute facts of economics made it apparent that as a farmer Burns would never be able to support his family decently. He applied for and secured a position as gauger for the excise—he who had once consorted with smugglers. At the same time he leased another farm, at Ellisland (now a national museum) and endeavored to combine the two occupations. It helped economically, but it was very bad for Burns. Liquor had always been his worst temptation, after women, and now it was fatally easy to yield to it. He was no common drunkard, but he did indeed drink far too much for his own health and his reputation. More than once he alienated friends by some drunken rudeness which no remorse could repair.

Ellendale was taken in 1788, in 1789 Burns began his journeys as a gauger, and in 1791 he was appointed exciseman in Dumfries, near by. He had hoped to be made supervisor, but instead he came near to losing his position altogether. Just as once he had offended by a harmless boyish Jacobitism and a slur at George III, so now he made no secret of his sympathy with the French Revolution. But with the threats against England from France, he (who had visited England only once and briefly) discovered a patriotic ardor that cooled his sympathies toward the revolutionists; this reversal saved his job, but promotion was still not to be thought of.

Burns' death at only thirty-seven may be attributed to his insobriety; caught in a storm while intoxicated, he developed rheumatic fever, and his heart, weakened by over-strain, gave way. His last days were unhappy; his wife was at Ellisland, about to bear another child, he lay ill in Dumfries, there was no money, he was obliged to write letters pleading for loans. This fact of poverty must never be forgotten in judging Burns. All his life lack of money made him work physically beyond his strength; it sent

him to the bottle for false help and surcease; it could not keep him from writing, but it cut his life in half and deprived the world of much beauty that would have been his heritage. As it was, all the world gave him was a mausoleum in Dumfries erected by public subscription.

Burns cannot be compared justly with any other poet. He distilled from his country's balladry the purest and finest of poetry, which yet reads as if it were the folk music of a nation of geniuses. He was a peasant, of long peasant stock, and he is a peasant poet, as well as a great world poet. With tenderness, with understanding, with simplicity, he depicts the life he knew. His satirical poems have the rough strength and directness of that life; his great lyrics have its utter ease and sweetness. As Leslie Stephen says, he "always wrote at white heat." He owed much to Allan Ramsay and Robert Fergusson, but he far surpassed them. He was, as he himself put it, "an Aeolian harp strung to every wind of heaven." His fame grew from Scotland to England and then to the world, but it is Scotland which rightly claims him first: "He has made every chord in our northern life to vibrate," says John Nichol. Many of his poems were uncollected until the first edition of his *Works* in 1800; they may be found scattered in song books, tracts and pamphlets (most of all in those issued by Stewart and Meikle from 1796 to 1799). As T. F. Henderson says, he "defies classification," yet inherently he was the soul of Scotland—in his fierce independence and love of liberty and justice, in the "living reality" of his verse, in his heart that he said was "completely tinder," even in his weaknesses and occasional crudities. He tried in vain to change himself into an English poet; it was impossible. His greatest work flowed spontaneously from him when he was closest to the life to which he had been born; after 1787 almost his only notable poem is *Tam o' Shanter*. It is as a lyrist that he is supreme, and his lyricism "derived entirely from the Scottish ballads." There is no corner of the English-speaking earth where the songs of this Scottish peasant have not become an integral part of the hearts and minds of their readers and lovers.

PRINCIPAL WORKS: Poems Chiefly in the Scottish Dialect, 1786; The Scots Musical Museum (with others) (J. Johnson, ed.) 1787-1803; A Selected Collection of Original Scottish Airs (with others) (G. Thomson, ed.) 1793-1811; Works of Robert Burns (J. Currie, ed.) 1800; Letters to Clarinda, 1802; Notes on Scottish Song (J. C. Dick, ed.) 1908; Letters (R. B. Johnson, ed. 1928; R. W. McKenna, ed. 1928; J. D. Ferguson, ed. 1931).

ABOUT: Blackie, J. S. Life of Robert Burns; Carlyle, T. Essays; Carswell, C. The Life of Robert Burns; Dakers, A. Robert Burns, His Life and Genius; Ferguson, J. D. Pride and Passion: Robert Burns; Fitzhugh, R. T. Robert Burns, His Associates and Contemporaries; Hecht, H. (J. Lymburn, tr.) Robert Burns, the Man and His Work; Henderson, K. Burns—by Himself; Henley, W. E. Burns: Life, Genius, Achievement; Hughes, J. L. The Real Robert Burns; Lockhart, J. G. Life of Robert Burns; Muriel, J S. ("John Lindsay") The Ranting Dog: the Life of Robert Burns (in America, Immortal Memory: the Real Robert Burns); Shairp, J. C. Burns; Snyder, J. C. Robert Burns, His Personality, His Reputation, and His Art; Stevenson, R. L. Familiar Studies of Men and Books.

BURTON, ROBERT (February 8, 1577-January 25, 1640), author of *The Anatomy of Melancholy,* was born in Lindley, Leicestershire, the son of Ralph Burton. He was educated at schools at Sutton Coldfield and Nuneaton, and in 1593 entered Brasenose College, Oxford. He never left Oxford again. In 1599 he became a student at Christ Church, and received his B.D. degree in 1614. Two years later he became vicar of St. Thomas's, Oxford, and in 1630 rector of Segrave, Leicestershire, but though he held the latter living he remained at his college.

It was natural that anecdotes and legends should gather around this man of one book, and that book so remarkable a production. According to some commentators, Burton wrote *The Anatomy of Melancholy* by way of conjuring away his own gloomy spirit: as he himself said, "I write of melancholy by being busy to avoid melancholy." According to others, he was himself a cheerful person merely interested in so prevalent an affliction. Actually the truth seems to lie somewhere in between; Burton was above all a bookish man, a quiet country clergyman supremely interested in almost everything that came under his magpie eye, something of a pedant, who poured all his gleanings into one book which he kept on polishing to the end of his life—there were eight editions in his lifetime, each one revised by himself and each one promising that this would be the last. He was keeper of the college library; and of himself he said: "I have little,

I want nothing; all my treasure is in Minerva's tower."

Burton himself would far rather have written in Latin than to "prostitute my prose to English," but the "mercenary booksellers" made the "prostitution" necessary. He wrote an anti-Catholic Latin comedy named *Philosophaster,* which was acted at Christ Church in 1617; he wrote occasional Latin verse which appeared in Oxford collections; but the great work of his life was the *Anatomy.* Nothing in it was his own to begin with, but all—even the occasional misquotations and errors of ascription—became peculiarly his own. Everything was wheat to this gleaner—social reform (he describes his own industrious Utopia in the introduction), science, medicine, history, literature, curious learning of all kinds. The book has been pillaged by every author from Milton to Byron: Swift, Johnson, Coleridge, Southey, Keats, drew on it; Sterne practically gutted it. It was Charles Lamb, who called Burton "the fantastic great old man," who brought the *Anatomy* back into public notice after it was beginning to be forgotten. Burton is an author's author, but he is the author also of all who are delighted by the strange, the odd, the imaginative.

Yet it must be remembered that this is no mere desultory hodgepodge of learning, but, as Sir William Osler said, "a great medical treatise, orderly in arrangement, serious in purpose." The full title tells this: "The Anatomy of Melancholy. What it is. With all the Kindes, Causes, Symptoms, Prognostickes, and Severall Cures of it. . . . Philosophically, Medicinally, Historically, Opened and Cut Up. By Democritus, Junior." Part I treats of causes and symptoms and ends with a famous passage on suicide. Part II covers cures, Part III deals with love—melancholy and religious melancholy, with illustrations from history. And the melancholy of which Burton writes is no gentle sorrow, but that "black distemper" which is a real disease, and which we today call melancholia.

Burton, being of his own time, believed in witchcraft, in alchemy, and in astrology. He is said to have cast his horoscope and foretold the day of his death, though the story that, not dying as the day advanced, he hanged himself, is a pure canard. It is quite possible, however, that his implicit

ROBERT BURTON

faith in the stars caused his death on the appointed day by autosuggestion. He had no fortune to leave, but he willed his books to the Bodleian library, and his elder brother, an antiquary, erected a monument in Oxford to his honor.

He loved words; he was like Sir Thomas Browne, a great Latinizer, who since he could not write in Latin turned English into a sort of semi-Latin. His brain was "soaked in literature"; he had a passion for writing, and, as he said, wrote "with as small deliberation as I do usually speak." He had a dry humor and he was capable of passages of natural eloquence and of grave pathos. His natural bent was toward a broad conservatism, a tolerance made up in equal parts of sympathy and irony. He has been compared with Erasmus, with Sebastian Brant, with Montaigne; actually he was himself only, and his book was unique. The nearest thing to it in English is Sir Thomas Browne's *Religio Medici*, but Burton has not Browne's passion or music—nor has he Browne's occasional fanaticism or his struggle between science and superstition. It is the difference between a busy physician who was half a mystic, and who incidentally was born a great writer, and a secluded, scholarly clergyman with an omnivorous mind. Where Browne is superb, Burton is curious; where Browne is grandiloquent, Burton is quaint. But Burton left to the world a great treasure

in his one book—a treasure rifled over and over, yet still full of riches. It is a book, moreover, from which those peculiarly attracted to it by their own melancholic temperaments can gather much more than the "inventive wit and scattered learning" for which it has been praised. There is much dross in it, there are outmoded jewels no longer valuable or never really so: but there are gems too which, like the fabled amethyst, will sober the giddy and hearten the wretched.

PRINCIPAL WORKS: The Anatomy of Melancholy, 1621; Philosophaster (Latin, W. E. Buckley, ed.) 1862 (English: P. Jordan-Smith, tr. 1931).

ABOUT: Fuller, T. Worthies of England; Jordan-Smith, P. Bibliographa Burtoniana; Lamb, C. Detached Thoughts on Books and Reading; Madan, F. Robert Burton and the Anatomy of Melancholy; Mead, G. F. C. and Clift, R. C. Burton, the Anatomist; Whibley, C. Literary Portraits.

BURY, RICHARD de. See AUNGERVILLE, RICHARD

BUTLER, JOSEPH (May 18, 1692-June 16, 1752), English divine and theological writer, the youngest son of a retired draper of considerable means, was born at Wantage, Berkshire. His father, a staunch Presbyterian, intended Joseph for the ministry and sent him accordingly to the dissenting academy of Samuel Jones at Gloucester and later Tewkesbury. When, however, the boy showed a strong preference for the Church of England, his father allowed him to enter Oriel College, Oxford, where he took his B.A. degree in 1718 and a B.C.L. three years later. Ordained deacon and priest, Butler began to preach at the Chapel of Rolls Court, publishing his famous *Fifteen Sermons* in 1726.

Although he was made prebendary of Salisbury by Bishop Talbot in 1721, and later given the living of Houghton-le-Skerne, Butler was anything but prosperous until he became rector of Stanhope, the so-called "golden rectory." For the next twenty-five years, until he became Bishop of Durham in 1750, his ecclesiastical career followed a steady line of ascent. Successively he served as chaplain to Lord Chancellor Talbot, prebend at Rochester, clerk of the closet to Queen Caroline, Bishop of Bristol (to this appointment Butler expressed dignified resentment in a letter to Walpole, since it was the poorest see in the kingdom), and Dean of

St. Paul's. Queen Caroline, who was interested in philosophy, studied his theological works and did much to further his career. After her death, he was appointed clerk of the closet to the king and was even offered the primacy on the death of Archbishop Potter in 1747, an honor which he refused. Bishop of Durham for only two years, he died at Bath in his sixtieth year and was buried at Bristol cathedral. According to his own instructions, all his manuscripts were burned immediately after his death.

Butler's reputation, and it is by far the greatest in the theological thought of the mid-eighteenth century, stands on his two published works, the *Fifteen Sermons* and *The Analogy of Religion, Natural and Revealed, to the Constitution and Course of Nature.* The *Analogy,* while essentially a work of its period, exerted an extraordinary influence in the eighteenth and even the nineteenth century, as a kind of final pronouncement in the long deist controversy. While Butler never attacked the deists directly, his whole system of thought was a critique on deistical speculations in regard to Christian doctrine. In both the *Analogy* and the *Sermons,* Butler takes what W. R. Sorley, professor of moral philosophy, calls a teleological view. "Human nature is a system or constitution; the same is true of the world at large: and both point to an end or purpose." His ethical system, as de-veloped in a number of the sermons, is primarily psychological—in some respects, surprisingly modern, as is his famous dictum, "Probability is the guide of life."

Exhaustive, thorough and somewhat sombre, Butler's prose has a massive force. To some authorities, moreover, the · arguments embodied in these two works place him among the most profound apologists of Christian theology. It is interesting to note that among those who studied his work and have admitted his influence, were two such widely separated thinkers as David Hume and Cardinal Newman.

PRINCIPAL WORKS: Fifteen Sermons preached at the Chapel of the Rolls Court, 1726 (W. R. Matthews, ed. 1914); The Analogy of Religion, Natural and Revealed, to the Constitution and Course of Nature, 1736 (R. Bayne, ed. Everyman's Library, 1906); Works (S. Halifax, ed. 1849; W. E. Gladstone, ed. 1896; J. H. Bernard, ed. 1900).

ABOUT: Baker, A. E. Bishop Butler; Bartlett, T. Memoirs of Butler; Eaton, J. R. J. Bishop Butler and His Critics; Egglestone, W. M. Stanhope Memorials of Bishop Butler; Mossner, E. C. Bishop Butler and the Age of Reason; Napier, Sir J. Lectures on Butler's Analogy; Steere, E. Some Remains of Bishop Butler.

BUTLER, SAMUEL (February 8, 1612-September 25, 1680), poet, satirist, author of *Hudibras,* was born at Strensham, Worcestershire. His father, also Samuel Butler, was a prosperous farmer and church-warden, who sent his son to the cathedral school. He seems to have lived in Cambridge in 1627, but never to have been a student at the university. Instead, he became clerk or secretary to various county magistrates or justices of the peace, the most noted of whom (thanks to Butler himself) was Sir Samuel Luke, a former general in the Parliamentary army, who was to win undying and unwelcome fame as "Sir Hudibras."

Butler's most important employment from the viewpoint of his own welfare was as attendant or secretary of the Countess of Kent, from 1626 to 1628. Here he did a great deal of reading in the large library, and enjoyed the instruction of a well-known lawyer, John Selden, who spent his vacations at the countess' home in Wrest, Bedfordshire. He also studied painting, and is said to have painted a number of portraits which the owners of the house in the next century used to stop up broken windows!

JOSEPH BUTLER

At some time during this period he appears also to have traveled in France and Holland.

In 1660 he became secretary to Richard Vaughan, who as Earl of Carbery was made Lord President of Wales. He gave the post of steward of Ludlow Castle to Butler who held the position only one year, 1661-62. The following year the first part of *Hudibras* appeared. Nothing could have been more timely: the Restoration was new, and the restored royalists hailed with joy a thorough raking-over of their foes the Puritans. Charles II so loved the book that he said he went nowhere, to dinner or bed or anywhere else, without it. The only concrete evidence of his admiration, however, was a gift of £300.

Butler, the poor clerk turned literary celebrity, moved to London and before long had "married money." His wife is variously said to have been a spinster named Herbert and a wealthy widow named Morgan; these may have been her maiden and first married names. In any event, within a few years the two of them had run through her entire fortune, not so much by extravagant living as by rash speculation. The remainder of Butler's life was spent in poverty and bitterness. On the monument to him in Westminster Abbey which was erected in 1721 appear the lines:

The Poet's Fate is here in emblem show'n:
He asked for Bread and he receiv'd a Stone.

This, however, is not entirely just, though undoubtedly Butler himself would have concurred in the sentiment. It is true that he tried in vain to secure some grant or sinecure post or pension in recognition of what the government itself considered his valuable services, and it is also true that lesser writers were far better rewarded. But there is reason to believe that more than once Butler did receive private benefactions which he did not acknowledge; and when the book first appeared he was a wealthy man.

The truth is that Butler's was an unamiable character. He had few friends, for he alienated people by his bluntness and his sarcastic habit of speech. He hated the Puritans, he hated the lawyers, he hated the scientists of the Royal Society, and before he got through he seems to have hated most of mankind. Moreover, he had a ready gift for expressing his hatreds in searing words.

He was a self-taught man of great erudition, with all the touchiness and suspicion of a sensitive ego. Those who neglected him are not to be excused; but he could not have been an easy man to befriend.

The last years of his life were rendered still harder by gout, though he actually died of tuberculosis. He was plagued by spurious versions of *Hudibras* and by inability to make into a publishable book the "Characters" and notes on which he labored for years. Even after his death, the so-called "Posthumous Works" published in his name were completely spurious. He died in the same poverty in which he had lived for so long; his one close friend, William Longueville, tried in vain to have him buried in Westminster Abbey, and failing that, himself paid for his grave in St. Paul's. It was to Longueville that he left his manuscripts, his only property.

Although he never stopped writing, and everything he left has sooner or later appeared in print, Butler was actually a writer of one book. That book, a merciless and brilliant satire against the Puritans, has a queer immortality of its own—queer because, though it is rarely read today, everybody knows (without knowing the source, perhaps) many of the epigrams which stud it rather too thickly. "Look a gift horse in the mouth," "Devil take the hindmost," "Make the fur fly," "Spare the rod and spoil

E. Lutterel
SAMUEL BUTLER

the child," "He that complies against his will// Is of the same opinion still," "Compound for sins they are inclined to, // By damning those they have no mind to"—they are all from *Hudibras.* Indeed, the constant glitter of wit makes the poem difficult to read except in snatches.

The main theme of *Hudibras* is, of course, taken from *Don Quixote,* with trimmings from *The Faery Queen.* Sir Hudibras is the Puritan knight, with Ralpho as his Sancho Panza. Disgruntled classicists have called the poem "a poor imitation of Cervantes," but actually it is not an imitation at all, but a variation on a theme. Its author was, as William Francis Smith has said, a "rare but erratic genius." This high colored man with "sorrel" hair had many of the characteristics which are traditionally associated with redheads. He and his work alike were truculent, violent, brilliant, and notably short tempered. But *Hudibras* is no mere "blaze of wit"; in the end it became a general criticism of society. More than that, it is a genuine poem; its octosyllabic verse is handled by a master. His satire is not the obverse of a wounded passion for justice and love of humanity, as is Swift's; it is more superficial but more robust. He does not scold; he jeers. *Hudibras* is a mock-heroic poem, almost a burlesque, but it is also an extraordinary piece of poetic invective; Butler's burning contempt is implicit in every line.

The remainder of his work, some of it not published until the present century, is of great interest, but of the interest which attaches to promising and unfinished writing. The "Characters" were undoubtedly fashioned after Aubrey's. They do not have the same quaint charm, largely because Butler liked few people and could not observe other men with humor or tolerance; his violent prejudices and his wounded self-esteem stood in his way. His strength is in attack, not in objectivity. His miscellaneous poems have none of the bite and vigor of his satire. He was supremely fashioned to do just one thing, and he did it so thoroughly that to this day our conception of Puritanism and the Puritans is largely colored by Samuel Butler's envenomed view of his former employer. It is a good joke on Sir Samuel Luke, but not quite so good a joke on the Puritans. Perhaps to get an all-round view

of what they were really like, one should add to a reading of *Hudibras* the reading of the works of a common soldier under Sir Samuel Luke in the days before Samuel Butler became his clerk—a Puritan preacher named John Bunyan.

PRINCIPAL WORKS: Hudibras, 1st Part, 1663, 2nd part, 1664, 3rd part, 1678; To the Memory of the Most Renowned DuVall (poem) 1671; Two Letters (prose) 1672; The Genuine Remains in Verse and Prose of Samuel Butler (R. Thyer, ed.) 1759; Characters, Observations, and Reflexions from the Notebooks (A. R. Waller, ed.) 1908; Satires and Miscellaneous Poetry and Prose (R. Lamar, ed.) 1928.

ABOUT: Garnett, R. The Age of Dryden; Hazlitt, W. Lectures on the English Comic Writers; Previté-Orton, C. W. Political Satire in English Poetry; Richards, E. A. Hudibras in the Burlesque Tradition; Shafer, R. (ed.) Seventeenth Century Studies; Taine, H. A. History of English Literature; Veldkamp, J. Samuel Butler, the Author of Hudibras; Wendell, B. The Temper of the Seventeenth Century.

BYRD, WILLIAM (1538?-July 4, 1623), song writer and one of the foremost of the early English composers, was born in or near Lincolnshire, probably the son of Thomas Byrd, a gentleman of that county, although there is no conclusive evidence as to his parentage or the exact year of his birth. According to a contemporary account, he was "bred up to musick under Thomas Tallis" and in 1563 took the post of organist at Lincoln Cathedral. Tallis remained the young man's friend and collaborator, sharing with him the post of honorary organist when Byrd was made a gentleman of the Chapel Royal in 1570, and publishing with him a collection of Latin songs. Five years later the two composers were given an exclusive license to print and sell music, a favor granted them by Queen Elizabeth. Apparently, however, their monopoly was never a source of great profit and Byrd seems to have been harried by financial worries.

As a writer of songs, Byrd was enormously industrious, publishing three voluminous collections, the earliest of which, *Psalmes, Sonets and Songs of Sadnes and Pietie,* appeared in 1588. He was the composer of the first English madrigal, contributed to Nicolas Yonge's *Musica Transalpina,* and was also the author of songs for a Latin play of the period, Thomas Legge's *Ricardus Tertius.* Many of the poems which he set to music were anonymous, some adapted from the Italian, some drawn from English poetry of the previous century, but he has also given musical form to the works of such poets as Sir Edward Dyer, Thomas Watson and the Earl of Oxford.

Musically, Byrd is remembered as the composer of three fine masses as well as a great amount of manuscript material, but his contribution to English literature rests on his song collections. In the Elizabethan age, to quote Emile Legouis, "the song was everywhere, sung in halls and parlors, trolled along the roads. England, destitute of the plastic arts, became the impassioned lover of song." Byrd himself wrote, "There is not any music of instruments whatsoever comparable to that which is made of the voices of men," and it is with the songs he wrote that Byrd speaks in the lyric idiom of his time.

Byrd was in his eighties when he died, survived by his wife, Julian (also called Ellen), and five of their six children. His reputation has outlived him by three centuries and his name can still be read in the *Cheque Book* of the Chapel Royal as a "father of musicke."

PRINCIPAL WORKS: Psalmes, Sonets, & Songs of Sadnes & Pietie, 1588; Songs of Sundrie Natures, Some of Gravitie, and Others of Myrth, 1589 (G. E. P. Arkwright, ed. 1892-93); Psalmes, Songs & Sonets; Some Solemne, Others Joyfull, 1611; Collected Madrigals (E. H. Fellowes, ed.) 1920.

ABOUT: Fellowes, E. H. English Madrigal Composers; Fellowes, E. H. William Byrd; Grew, S. William Byrd (*in* Musical Times, Oct. 1922); Howes, F. William Byrd.

BYROM, JOHN (February 29, 1692-September 26, 1763), poet, diarist, teacher of shorthand, was the seventh of nine children born to Edward Byrom and Sarah Allen at Kersall Cell near Manchester. He attended Trinity College, Cambridge, taking his B.A. in 1712 and his M.A. three years later. While still an undergraduate, he began his writing career, contributing two papers on dreams and a pastoral, *Colin to Phoebe,* to the *Spectator.* In addition to literary pursuits, he was interested in medicine and studied for a time in France. Although he never took his degree and never practiced, for the rest of his life many of his friends liked to call him "Doctor."

Byrom seems to have been a lovable personality, not without his foibles, but gifted, versatile, and capable of great devotion.

JOHN BYROM

When his father died in 1711, the estate went to an elder brother and young Byrom was forced to augment his income by teaching shorthand. While still at Cambridge, he had invented a system of his own, the key of which was jealously guarded from rival teachers. His pupils, among them such illustrious men of the time as Horace Walpole, Gibbon (father of the historian) and Lord Chesterfield, paid Byrom five guineas and were required to take an oath of secrecy as to the master's method. Quite in the spirit of the thing, his pupils formed a secret society of which Byrom was made the grand master. He liked to address the society formally on the history and usefulness of shorthand and, so far as one can judge, not only did he succeed in making many distinguished friends through his teaching but at the same time managed to enjoy the whole business enormously. As for the actual method, which remained unpublished until four years after his death in 1763, *The Universal English Shorthand* proved to be an ingenious system without sufficient speed to be useful in professional stenography. There is no doubt, however, that Byrom's system did influence later and more practical systems.

When he was twenty-nine, Byrom married his first cousin, Elizabeth. After some twenty years of marriage, he inherited property from his wife's family which enabled him to give up teaching and retire to Manchester. Known to have Jacobite leanings (as a fellow of the Royal Society, he had been accused of Jacobitism in a bitter feud with Sir Hans Sloane, a fellow member), Byrom was in Manchester at the time of the Pretender's entry, but seems to have avoided any ultimate commitment in the struggle.

Neither teaching nor politics occupied Byrom to the exclusion of his major interests which were primarily religious and literary. After reading *A Serious Call*, by William Law, religious writer and mystic, Byrom went to call on the master and became one of his most loyal friends and disciples. The relationship between the two men has been compared to that of Boswell and Johnson. Not only did Byrom versify Law's most important writings, hoping they would thereby reach a wider audience, but he kept a detailed record of his meetings and his conversations with Law. The loving account in Byrom's diary remains one of the most important sources of information on the life of the English mystic who had so profound an influence on the religious thought of his time. This journal, later published by the Chetham Society, forms a lively narrative of Byrom's meetings with many distinguished contemporaries and has been called by Caroline Spurgeon an "entirely delightful and too little known book." Byrom also wrote a good deal of verse, first collected in 1773, but as a poet he is distinctly minor, facile in rhyme and weak in imagination.

PRINCIPAL WORKS: An Epistle to a Gentleman of the Temple, 1749; Enthusiasm: a Poetical Essay, 1751; The Universal English Shorthand, 1767; Miscellaneous Poems, 1773; The Private Journal and Literary Remains of John Byrom (R. Parkinson, ed.) 1854-57; The Poems of John Byrom (A. W. Ward, ed.) 1894-95.

ABOUT: Chalmers, A. Biography *in* English Poets; Parkinson, R. Preface to The Private Journal and Literary Remains of John Byrom; Stephen, Sir L. Studies of a Bibliographer.

CAEDMON (corruptly **Cedmon**) (fl. 670), author of hymns and scriptural verse, was (if he ever lived) the earliest English Christian poet. All that we know of him comes from a famous passage in Bede's *Ecclesiastical History*. In it he tells how Caedmon, a herdsman "of advanced age," was wont to leave the feasts when singing to the harp began, because he had "never learnt any poetry." On one occasion, retiring thus to the stables, where he was in charge of the horses, he fell

asleep, and in a dream he heard a voice bidding him sing. When he answered that he could not, the voice commanded him to sing "of the beginning of all things," whereupon he did divinely produce a hymn of Creation. On waking, he remembered the words, and added more. He told his dream to the bailiff of the farm where he worked, who took him to Abbess Hild of the monastery of Streonshalh (Whitby, in Northumbria). There again he sang his hymn, and so impressed her that she persuaded him to become a monk, and delegated other monks to tell him the Bible stories, from which he made poetry.

The other glimpse we have of Caedmon is also from Bede. He was ill with what was thought to be a slight malady when he asked to be moved to a room kept for the dying. There he jested with his friends till midnight, when he asked for the Eucharist. Then he foretold that he would die at the hour of morning prayers, and did so in his sleep.

Caedmon is sometimes called Saint Caedmon, but he was never canonized. If he existed as an individual at all (similar stories are told of an Icelandic poet), he entered the monastery somewhere between 658 and 680, which is the period when Hild was abbess. He died certainly not later than 680.

One thing is certain, and that is that most of the so-called Caedmonic poems are not Caedmon's, though lines from his poems may be incorporated in them; they are by imitators and admirers in later times. The only fairly authentic work by him we have is the nine lines of the hymn translated (into Latin prose) by Bede. In the seventeenth century Francis Junius published a manuscript of about 1000 A.D., supposedly containing Caedmon's poems. If any of these are his, decidedly there are interpolations by other hands. The chief bone of contention is a very fine poetic interpolation in the *Genesis*: to some critics this alone of the *Genesis* is Caedmon's; to others this alone is not his, but is the work of a poet who knew Latin. (Caedmon, it must be remembered, was totally illiterate in any language.) Another work attributed to him (on the basis of misreading of the runes on a monument) is *The Dream of the Rood*, a beautiful poem which has also been attributed to Cynewulf, though it is undoubtedly before his time. The objection that the Junius manuscripts cannot be Caedmon's because they were written in the dialect of the West Saxons means nothing, since most Northumbrian manuscripts were thus translated. Finally, the fanciful idea that the real Caedmon took his name from the Hebrew and had traveled in Palestine has no foundation; the name is Celtic, the present Welsh Cadfan. But Sir Francis Palgrave, for one, thought the whole story a myth.

Caedmon indeed may have been of Celtic (British) descent, though Saxons sometimes were given British names. However, his poems—or the poems ascribed to him—show marked traces of old Saxon poetry, in their alliteration and parallelism of structure. The difference is that, as M. Bentinck Smith said, "subjectivity begins with Christian poetry." Even the martial *Exodus* has not the broad objectivity of—say—*Beowulf*. It is told of Caedmon that he wrote nothing except for the glory of God and the salvation of man; his poetry was a divine gift and held to sacred uses. In Bede's quaint words, "as innocent beasts of the world ruminate, so he turned [everything that was taught to him] into melodious song."

The Caedmonian manuscripts are for the most part in the Bodleian Library in Oxford. They have seldom been printed except in technical works for scholars. One of the interests attaching to them is the claim (probably baseless) that Milton used passages from them in *Paradise Lost*.

PRINCIPAL WORKS: Genesis, Exodus, Daniel, Lamentations of the Fallen Angels, The Harrowing of Hell, Fragment on the Temptation (F. Junius, ed.) 1655; The Exeter Book (B. Thorpe, ed.) 1843.

ABOUT: Bede. Ecclesiastical History; Malmesbury, W. of, Gesta Pontificorum.

CAMDEN, WILLIAM (May 2, 1551-November 9, 1623), antiquary, historian, was born in London where his father, Sampson Camden, was a member of the guild of painter-stainers. His mother, Elizabeth Curwen, came of an ancient Cumberland family. He received his early education at Christ's Hospital and St. Paul's School, entering Magdalen College, Oxford, when he was fifteen, probably as a servitor or chorister. Later he moved on to Broadgates Hall (Pembroke College) and to Christ Church, where the canon, Dr. Thomas Thornton, offered him financial support. When he was

not yet twenty-one, he began his antiquarian travels, collecting materials for a monumental work on England which was published fifteen years later.

Through the kindness of a patron, Dr. Gabriel Goodman, dean of Westminster, Camden was appointed second master at Westminster school, a post which enabled him to study and continue his travels during vacation periods. For the *Britannia* he did enormous research, learning both Welsh and Anglo-Saxon and studying innumerable local histories and public records. In 1586 his great work, a topographical and antiquarian survey of rich historic value, was published under the ponderous Latin title, *Britannia, sive florentissimorum regnorum Angliae, Scotiae, Hiberniae et insularum adjacentium ex intima antiquitate chorographica Descriptio.*

On the basis of his growing reputation, Camden was made prebend of Ilfracombe in 1589, a preferment which he held for life, and eight years later was appointed to the office of Clarenceux king-of-arms. Released from the necessity of earning a living, he resigned from the Westminster school where he had served as headmaster since 1593. His appointment as king-of-arms apparently led to ill feeling on the part of Ralph Brooke, York herald, who had also aspired to the post. Whatever the motive, Brooke led an

M. Gheeraedts, 1609
WILLIAM CAMDEN

81

attack on the genealogical accuracy of Camden's *Britannia* and accused its author of plagiarism, an ill-founded allegation to which Camden replied in an appendix to the fifth edition, published in 1600.

Camden now set to work on a history of the reign of Queen Elizabeth, his second major opus, published in two parts under the title, *Annales Rerum Anglicarum, et Hibernicarum Regnante Elizabetha.* This book also inspired attack, but was highly praised by John Selden who considered the *Annales* and Bacon's *History of Henry VII* the only two serious works of English history up to his day. In 1609 Camden retired to Chislehurst, where he continued to write and study although fighting constant ill health. In 1622 he founded a chair at Oxford, the Camden professorship of ancient history, of which the first occupant was his friend, Degory Wheare. A year later, at the age of seventy-two, he died.

All of Camden's important work was written in Latin, but the *Britannia* was translated into English during his lifetime by Philemon Holland, apparently under Camden's own direction. Of the *Annales* he wrote, "I do not desire that they should be set forth in English until after my death, knowing how unjust carpers the unlearned readers are." This was the book which Charles Whibley calls "by far the best example of its kind." Writing in the *Cambridge History*, Whibley goes on to say, "Old-fashioned in design alone, the work is a genuine piece of modern history. With William Camden the chronicle reached its zenith."

PRINCIPAL WORKS: Britannia sive florentissimorum regnorum . . . etc., 1586-87 (English: P. Holland, tr. 1610); Remains Concerning Britain, 1604 (J. R. Smith, ed. 1870); Annales Rerum Anglicarum, et Hibernicarum Regnante Elizabetha, 1615 (T. Hearne, ed. 1717); Vita Gulielmi Camdeni et Illustrium virorum ad G. Camdenum Epistolae (Dr. T. Smith, ed.) 1691.

ABOUT: Bayle, P. Life, *in* Bayle's Dictionary; Camden, W. Memorabilia de Seipso *in* Smith ed. of Vita Gulielmi Camdeni; Wood, A. a, Athenae Oxonienses.

CAMPION, THOMAS (February 12, 1567-March 1, 1619), poet, author of song lyrics, was born in London, the son of John Campion, a clerk in the Chancery Court, and Lucy Searles, whose father was a sergeant-at-arms of the queen. (A former statement that Campion was the son of Thomas Campion and Anastace Spitty, and born at Withan, Kent, has been proved incorrect.) When he was nine, his father died, and his mother married Augustine Steward, herself dying when the boy was thirteen. Steward then married a widow, acquiring another stepson, Thomas Sisley, and the two boys were reared together. They both went as gentlemen pensioners to Peterhouse College, Cambridge, in 1581, both remained four years, and neither took a degree. Campion in 1586 was entered at Grey's Inn, but though he retained his connection there for some time, he was never called to the bar.

His first poems appeared, anonymously, in *Songs of Divers Noblemen and Gentlemen,* in 1591. In the same year he accompanied the Earl of Essex in an expedition to France on behalf of Henry IV, and participated in the siege of Rouen. Where he studied medicine is not known, probably in some Continental university, but from 1602 on he styled himself "doctor in physic." He did not, apparently, practice very much, but when Sir Thomas Monson was imprisoned for the Overbury murder, it was Campion, as his physician, who was allowed to visit him in the Tower.

Campion's real and greatest interest was in music; he called his lyrics "superfluous blossoms of his deeper studies." He himself wrote the music for the songs in the first part of the *Book of Ayres,* and he published a volume on a "new way" of "making four parts in counterpoint," which was nothing but a rule for harmonization given the bass and the first chord. He was also interested in metrics, and he who was a born lyrist inveighed against the "childish titillation" and "vulgar and unartificial custom" of rhymed verse—a theory which was hotly opposed by Samuel Daniel. He was also a writer of masques, but not a markedly successful one, for the ones he produced were too complicated to hold the observers' interest.

Campion thought of himself as a classicist, in both music and poetry (his first published volume of poems was in Latin), a critic, and a musician, and this was his contemporary reputation as well. Actually, he was a born lyrical poet, melodious, fresh, and spontaneous, with a charm and grace that brought him often near to great poetry—

as witness the well known "Cherry Ripe." An arch-experimentalist in metrics, his rhythms shifted even from line to line, with subtle effects. His songs were meant really to be sung, and he was primarily a poet who used words as music. His Latin epigrams, though clever, are marred by vituperation and obscenity—as were their classic models.

In religion, Campion was a nominal Protestant who was often suspected of being a Roman Catholic, chiefly because many of his friends were of this persuasion. (The Jesuit martyr, Edmund Campion, was a distant relative.) In truth he was more or less indifferent to the religious controversies which so agitated his time. In the history of literature, he constitutes a link between Elizabethan and Jacobean poetry, between Sidney and Donne. It is unfortunate that he had so many and such warring interests, and thought so little of the one thing he could do supremely well.

He never married, and at his death (which is variously given as 1619 and 1620) he left his entire estate to his lifelong friend, Philip Rosseter, a musician and theatrical producer.

PRINCIPAL WORKS: Thomae Campioni Poemata . . . Epigrammatum, 1595; A Booke of Ayres, 1601; Observations on the Art of English Poesie, 1602; The Description of a Maske . . . in Honour of the Lord Hayes and His Bride, 1607; Songs of Mourning, 1613; Two Bookes of Ayres, 1613; The Description of a Maske . . . at the Marriage of the Earle of Somerset, 1617; The Third and Fourth Booke of Ayres, 1617; A New Way of Making Four Partes in Counter-point, 1617; Ayres that Were Sung and Played at Brougham Castle, 1618; Thomae Campioni Epigrammatum . . . Libri II, 1619; The Works of Dr. Thomas Campion (A.H. Bullen, ed.) 1889.

ABOUT: Kastendieck, M. M. England's Musical Poet, Thomas Campion; Vivian, S. P. Thomas Campion.

CAPGRAVE, JOHN (April 21, 1393-August 12, 1464), historian, religious writer, was a native of Lynn in Norfolk where he entered the order of Augustine Friars, probably while still a child. He was college-trained, although it is not definitely known whether he attended Cambridge or Oxford. There is some evidence that he received a D.D. degree from the latter university. About 1417 he was ordained a priest in the Friary at Lynn and shortly after was made a provincial of his order in England.

In his own time, Capgrave came to be widely known both in Britain and on the continent as a man of letters and the most learned of the Augustinian scholars. Under the patronage of Humphrey, Duke of Gloucester (whose life he wrote and to whom he dedicated many of his works), Capgrave devoted himself to history and theology, traveling at least once to Rome, but spending the greater part of his time at Lynn where he died in his seventy-first year.

He wrote for the most part in Latin, then the language of the learned, leaving a great mass of manuscripts which include Biblical commentaries, sermons, several lives of the saints, and historical works. Of the Latin writings, the most notable are his *Liber de Illustribus Henricis,* a collection of the lives of German emperors, English kings and other famous Henries in various parts of the world; and the *Nova Legenda Angliae,* or Catalogues of the English Saints, actually a revision of the *Sanctilogium* of an earlier chronicler, John of Tinmouth. In English he wrote *The Life of St. Gilbert of Sempringham,* a metrical *Life of St. Katharine,* and his greatest work, *A Chronicle of England from the Creation to A.D. 1417.* The *Chronicle* is a compilation from a number of sources with occasional observations by the writer, or as Capgrave himself described it, "a schort remembrauns of elde stories, that whanne I loke upon hem and have a schort touch of the writing I can sone dilate the circumstances." This remains a valuable historical work, notable for its terseness of style, yet graphic in detail, particularly in the latter sections dealing with the learned friar's own time. Unfortunately, many of Capgrave's writings have been lost, but the major works named above are still in existence either in manuscript or in later printed editions.

PRINCIPAL WORKS: Nova Legenda Angliae (printed by Wynkyn de Worde) 1516; The Chronicle of England (F. C. Hingeston, ed. Rolls series) 1858; Liber de Illustribus Henricis (F. C. Hingeston, ed. Rolls series) 1858; The Life of St. Katharine (C. Horstmann, ed.) 1893; The Lives of St. Augustine and St. Gilbert of Sempringham (J. Munro, ed.) 1910.

ABOUT: Hingeston, F. C. Biography in Rolls editions of the Chronicle and Liber de Illustribus Henricis; Leland, J. Commentarii de Scriptoribus Britannicis (A. Hall, ed.); Tanner, T. Bibliotheca Britannico-Hibernica.

CAREW, RICHARD (July 17, 1555-November 6, 1620), antiquary, poet, translator, was the eldest son of one of the leading families of Cornwall—his father, Thomas Carew of Antony House, his mother, Elizabeth Edgecombe. When he was only eleven years old, he entered Christ Church, Oxford, and three years later was chosen to represent his college in an extempore debate with Sir Philip Sidney before an audience of notables. From Oxford he went to Middle Temple where he studied for three years, after which he traveled abroad as befitted a young gentleman of his position. In 1577 he returned to England and married Juliana, the eldest daughter of John Arundel of Trerice.

From the beginning, his career helped to equip him for his later task of antiquary and historian of his native county. When he was thirty-nine he entered Parliament and two years later was appointed high-sheriff of Cornwall, where he also served as deputy-lieutenant and treasurer under Sir Walter Raleigh. Carew was extremely well thought of both for his zeal in carrying out the duties of an English country gentleman and for the scholarly works which flowered from his leisure. A student of Latin, Greek, Italian, German, French and Spanish, he made a verse translation of the first five cantos of Tasso's *Gerusalemme Liberata,* published under the title, *Godfrey of Bulloigne or the Recouverie of Hierusalem,* and of an Italian version of the Spanish John Huarte's *Examen de Ingenios.*

Becoming a member of the Society of Antiquaries, he set to work on what was to be his greatest undertaking, the *Survey of Cornwall,* first published in 1602 and twice reprinted. As an historical survey of his own county, this remains an extraordinarily entertaining work, lively and detailed in its picture of the life of a country gentleman in Elizabethan times. Of his original poetry there is little trace except for one poem, *A Herrings Tayle,* sometimes attributed to him. His verse translations are certainly accurate but the Tasso, in particular, suffers from an attempt to render the original literally line by line. Another work, *The Excellencie of the English Tongue,* in which he points out the merits of the language as "significancy, easiness to be learnt, copiousness and sweetness," is of interest as one of the few critical essays surviving from the Elizabethan period.

Carew died when he was nearly sixty-five "as he was at his private prayers in his study at fower in the afternoon" and was buried at Antony Church in Cornwall.

PRINCIPAL WORKS: Godfrey of Bulloigne or the Recouverie of Hierusalem, An Heroicall poeme (tr.), 1594 (A. B. Grosart, ed. 1881); Examen de Ingenios, The Examination of mens Wits (tr.), 1594; The Survey of Cornwall, 1602 (de Dunstanville and T. Tonkin, ed. 1811); The Excellencie of the English Tongue, 1614 (G. G. Smith, ed. *in* Elizabethan Critical Essays, 1904).

ABOUT: Carew, R. The Survey of Cornwall; Wood, A. à, Athenae Oxonienses.

CAREW, THOMAS (1598?-1639?), poet, song-writer, was born in West Wickham, Kent, the son of Sir Matthew Carew, master in Chancery, and of Alice Ingpenny Rivers, widow of a Lord Mayor of London. Many details of his life are obscure; he may have been born as early as 1595, and have died as late as 1645. The volume of his poems published in 1640 contained several that seem to have been written just previously, and the Earl of Clarendon spoke of him as having lived fifty years. Equally obscure is the college he attended at Oxford; it may have been either Corpus Christi or Merton, but it is certain he took no degree. In 1614 he was entered at the Middle Temple, but he never was called to the bar. His father, who seems to have lost his fortune, complained bitterly of

After Sir A. Van Dyck

THOMAS CAREW

him as "wandering idly without employment," and used his influence to send his son with Sir Dudley Carleton when he was made ambassador to Venice. In 1616 Carew was with Carleton at the Hague, but he quarreled with his employer and came home again. We next hear of him at the French court with Lord Herbert of Cherbury.

Soon after, he found the environment which exactly fitted him and which he never abandoned. He became a great favorite of Charles I, who made him his server (taster) in ordinary and a gentleman of the privy chamber, and gave him the royal estate of Sunninghill, a part of Windsor Forest. Thenceforth Carew and Whitehall were inseparable; he had all the wit, the courtliness, and the licentiousness which characterized the king and his circle. Carew is said to have died in "maudlin repentance" of his life of dissipation, but if so it was purely a deathbed conversion; the clergyman he sent for is reported to have refused to come.

Carew was the first of the Cavalier poets, spoken of as the "unofficial poet laureate of the court" (Ben Jonson was the official one), a friend of Suckling and Davenant, and generally considered, as a lyrist, to be second only to Herrick. Indeed the posthumous volume of his poems includes some of Herrick's which were ascribed to Carew.

Debauched as his life may have been, Carew's poetry for the most part is almost austere. The only exception is that highly sensuous—and sensual—poem, "The Rapture." And that is also the only one (except the elegy to Donne) which displays any personal feeling. Donne, whom he admired greatly, had rather an unhappy effect on Carew's style; he imitated the gnomic harshness without achieving the greater poet's intensity of emotion. But though Carew is cold and often artificial and conventional, with the hyperbole and affectation which was the current fashion, he has a fine feeling for shapely structure, a directness of approach, and a poetic taste which make his best very good indeed. He had a liking for the sonnet form and for the two-stanza poem in which the second stanza balances the first, with the effect of a prolonged epigram. He himself, not unjustly, called his poems "a mine of rich and pregnant fancy." In some of the poems to Celia, he not only justified Anthony à Wood's ascription to him of "delicacy of wit and poetic fancy," but produced almost perfect lyrics of their slight and specialized kind.

He seems not to have married, and is supposed to have died suddenly—though this may be only a euphemism for his disappearance from the public scene around 1638. Whatever happened to him, whether he even fell out of favor with Charles, and when and where that repentant deathbed occurred, are completely unknown.

PRINCIPAL WORKS: Coelum Britannicum, a Masque, 1633; Poems, 1640; Poems, with a Maske, 1671; Poems (T. Maitland, ed.) 1824.

ABOUT: Ebsworth, J. W. Memoir, in Poems and Masques of Thomas Carew; Hazlitt, W. C. Biography in 1890 edition of Poems; Quiller-Couch, A. T. Adventures in Criticism; Wood, A. à, Athenae Oxonienses.

CAREY, HENRY (d. October 4, 1743), song-writer, burlesque dramatist, is supposed to have been the illegitimate son of George Savile, Marquis of Halifax. From a reference in one of his early poems, it has further been supposed that his mother was a school mistress. Nothing is actually known of the date, the place, or the circumstances of his birth. In a preface to his first volume of poems in 1713, he wrote that he was then a very young man and that he had devoted his early years to the study of music.

Two years later he suddenly appeared in the fashionable bohemian world of London as the author of a successful farce, *The Contrivances: or More Ways Than One*, produced at the Drury Lane. Gossip had it that he received a pension from the Savile family, but whatever the truth of the matter, he spent money freely and made himself the gayest and liveliest of companions, in and out of innumerable scrapes, and popular with everyone. A recognized poet and song-writer as well as a dramatist, he quite naturally became a member of the group known as "Addison's little senate" and was overjoyed when the "divine Addison" praised one of his poems. Among the successful musical plays and burlesques which he wrote and produced during the next twenty years were *Hanging and Marriage: or the Dead Man's Wedding; Chrononhotonthologos*, burlesquing the bombast of the continental stage; *A Wonder: or the Honest Yorkshireman*, a ballad opera; and the *Dragon of Wantley*, a

HENRY CAREY

thologos, of many quaint names and some actual lines of verse which have stuck in literary memory; inventor of Ambrose Philips' nickname [i.e.Namby Pamby] and of a rare set of skittish verses attached to it; musician, playwright and (it would seem, almost as much in gaiety of heart as on any other occasion in his life) suicide—Henry Carey will live forever, if not in any of the above capacities, as author of the delightful words, and the almost more delightful music of *Sally in Our Alley."*

PRINCIPAL WORKS: *Plays:* The Contrivances: or More Ways Than One, 1715; Hanging and Marriage: or the Dead Man's Wedding, 1722; Chrononhotonthologos, 1734; A Wonder: or the Honest Yorkshireman, 1735; Dragon of Wantley, 1737; The Dramatick Works of Henry Carey, 1743. *Poems and Songs:* Poems on Several Occasions, 1713; The Musical Century, *in* One Hundred English Ballads, 1737; Songs and Poems by Henry Carey (M. Gibbings, ed.) 1924; The Poems of Henry Carey (F. T. Wood, ed.) 1930.

ABOUT: Bateson, F. W. English Comic Drama, 1700-1750; Hudson, W. H. A Quiet Corner in a Library; Wood, F. T. Introduction to The Poems of Henry Carey.

burlesque opera. None of these plays, with the possible exception of *Chrononhotonthologos,* is of any permanent literary interest, although they display a genuine gift of playful fancy. Carey can be best remembered for his songs, in particular, *Sally in Our Alley,* which he wrote after following a shoemaker's apprentice and his sweetheart on a holiday. It has also been claimed that he wrote *God Save the King,* first published anonymously in 1742, but this is extremely doubtful.

At the height of a successful career and while still a comparatively young man, Carey died suddenly. Contemporary records say only that "he rose in good health and was soon after found dead," but most of his biographers agree that his death was by suicide. He left a widow and four small children for whom a benefit performance was arranged by his friends at the Drury Lane. It is interesting to note that one of his sons became the grandfather of Edmund Kean, the great tragedian.

George Saintsbury makes a brilliant summary of this curiously paradoxical career, writing of Carey as one who, "little as is positively known about him, accumulates an unusual assemblage of interesting details round his personality and work. Reputed son of the great Marquis of Halifax; ancestor, it seems, of Edmund Kean; creator in the farce-burlesque of *Chrononhoton-*

CARLELL, LODOWICK (1602-1675),

dramatist, is credited with the dates above by the *Cambridge Bibliography of English Literature.* Other sources say that he "flourished" from 1629 to 1664. In any case, not much is known about his life aside from his career as courtier under Charles the First and Second, for the first of whom he was "gentleman of the Bows" as well as groom of the king's and queen's privy chamber, and, eventually, keeper of the forest in Richmond. He was a Scot, and may have been an ancestor of Thomas Carlyle. Carlell is credited with nine plays, of which all but one survive. All were derivative, being taken chiefly from French and Spanish romances, and are characterized by unreal, sentimental, and highflown characters and language which were decidedly to the taste of Queen Henrietta Maria. Frederick G. Fleay, the historian of English drama, says that Carlell's plays "show what rubbish was palatable to Charles and Henrietta," and that the blank verse (which is often so poor that it seems likely that the lines were originally written in prose) is "a riot of hybrid iambic." *Heraclius,* a translation from Pierre Corneille, which was considered to be "an excellent play" by Samuel Pepys, is written in rhymed verse. The missing play is *The*

Spartan Ladies, a comedy entered in the books of the Stationers' Company September 14, 1646, no copy of which has been found. *The Deserving Favourite* (1629) was played at Whitehall before Charles I, later at the private theatre in Blackfriars. *The Passionate Lover* (1655) was produced at Somerset House and Blackfriars, and *Arviragus and Philicia* (1639) was revived in 1672 with a preface written by Dryden.

PRINCIPAL WORKS: The Deserving Favourite, 1629; Arviragus and Philicia, 1639; The Passionate Lover, 1655; The Fool Would Be a Favourite, or The Discreet Lover, 1657; Osmond, the Great Turk, or the Noble Servant, 1657; Heraclius, Emperor of the East, 1664; The Spartan Ladies, 1646.

ABOUT: Genest, J. Some Account of the English Stage; Legouis, E. H. A History of English Literature.

CARLISLE, FREDERICK HOWARD, Fifth Earl of (1748-1825), statesman, dramatist, poet, was the only son of the fourth Earl of Carlisle. His mother, Isabella, was the daughter of the fourth Lord Byron. Educated at Eton and Cambridge, he then made the traditional continental tour with his school friend from Eton, Charles James Fox, who became one of England's most celebrated and eloquent parliamentarians.

Returning home in 1769, he took his seat in the House of Lords, and, with Fox, became a leader of the fast young fashionable set of London. His own and Fox's gambling debts so depleted his fortune that he was soon forced to retire to Castle Howard for a couple of years to recoup.

In 1777 he was appointed to the first of several political offices, and began to take his position as a statesman more seriously. The following year he led a commission sent to negotiate a peace treaty with the American colonies. He succeeded in so provoking Lafayette that the latter challenged him to a duel. Carlisle declined the honor, and returned home without a treaty.

He spent two years as Lord Lieutenant of Ireland, advocating home rule for that country and receiving a vote of thanks when he resigned from the Irish House of Commons when he resigned. He retired from public life in 1815.

A patron of the arts, Carlisle numbered many writers among his friends, and wrote numerous letters, a volume of poems, and two poetic tragedies. Samuel Johnson and Horace Walpole, among his contemporaries,

praised his work. He was the cousin and guardian of Lord Byron, who made three literary allusions to his relative. Byron dedicated the second edition of *Hours of Idleness* to Carlisle, but became offended by an imagined slight and insulted him in *English Bards and Scotch Reviewers;* later he publicly acknowledged, in a line in *Childe Harold,* that he owed Carlisle an apology.

Carlisle died at Castle Howard at the age of seventy-eight, the year after his wife's death. Four sons and three daughters survived him.

PRINCIPAL WORKS: Poems, 1773; The Father's Revenge, a Tragedy, 1783; The Stepmother, a Tragedy, 1800.

ABOUT: Boswell, J. Life of Johnson; Lecky, W. E. H. History of England in the 18th Century; Trevelyan, Sir G. O. Early History of Charles James Fox; Walpole, H. Letters.

CARTER, ELIZABETH (December 16, 1717-February 19, 1806), miscellaneous writer, was born at Deal, Kent, the eldest daughter of the Reverend Nicholas Carter, D.D., perpetual curate of Deal Chapter, and one of the six preachers of Canterbury Cathedral, and his first wife, Margaret (Swayne) Carter, who died when Elizabeth was ten. The girl's education was undertaken by her father, who instructed her in Greek, Latin, and Hebrew. At first a rather dull pupil, she applied herself so diligently, with the aid of green tea to keep awake, that she became thoroughly grounded in these and other languages, even including Arabic and Portuguese, as well as laying the foundation for the chronic headaches which tormented her the rest of her life. For diversion she danced, took long walks, and played the German flute—"that 18th century corrective to melancholy."

The Gentleman's Magazine for February 1738 published a riddle by Elizabeth Carter. Other contributions followed, signed "Eliza." Cave, the magazine's publisher, and a friend of her father, that year published a 24-page quarto pamphlet of her work entitled *Poems upon Particular Occasions.* Cave also introduced her to Samuel Johnson, who published some of her essays in *The Rambler,* and remained her friend for fifty years. He once remarked that "My old friend Mrs. Carter [she never married, however] could make a pudding as well as translate Epictetus from the Greek, and work a handkerchief as well as compose a poem." The translation from Epictetus was made at the instigation of her friends Catherine Talbot, grand-daughter of the Bishop of Durham, and Dr. Secker, Bishop of Oxford and later Archbishop of Canterbury, and was printed by Samuel Richardson, the printer-novelist, in 1758. This "conscientious piece of craggy hard work, pursued with adequate equipment," as Austin Dobson described it, established her reputation and made her a modest fortune, with which she bought tenements at Deal, consolidating them into the house where she lived out her long life, with yearly trips to her London rooms in Clarges Street, Piccadilly. She died in London at eighty-eight.

Fanny Burney said that Elizabeth Carter's talk was "all instruction," and there was more of the bluestocking than the creative writer about her. Her epitaph in the Grosvenor Chapel burial ground notes her "deep learning and extensive knowledge." She was rather stout, and dressed plainly.

PRINCIPAL WORKS: Poems upon Particular Occasions, 1738; Sir Isaac Newton's Philosophy Explain'd for the Use of Ladies, translated from the Italian of Sig. Algarotti, 1739; All the Works of Epictetus Which Are Now Extant, tr. from the original Greek, 1758; Poems on Several Occasions, 1762; A Series of Letters Between Mrs. Elizabeth Carter and Miss Catherine Talbot, from 1741 to 1770, 1809.

ABOUT: Dobson, A. Later Essays; Gaussen, A. C. C. A Woman of Wit and Wisdom: a Memoir of Elizabeth Carter; Pennington, M. Memoirs of the Life of Mrs. Elizabeth Carter.

CARYLL, JOHN (1625-1711), diplomatist, poet, dramatist, was born into a family with deep Catholic roots and strong royalist leanings. He inherited a comfortable estate, lived the first part of his life as a "man of fashion and fortune," and wrote several minor poems and a few plays. His wife, who died in 1656, was Margaret, daughter of Sir Maurice Drummond. In 1669 he was jailed on suspicion of implication in a "popish plot," but was soon released.

With the ascension of James II in 1685, Caryll became closely connected with the royal house. His first assignment was as agent to the court of Rome, a post he filled adequately until his recall in 1686. He then became secretary to the Queen, Mary of Modena, and remained in the King's household until his death. He accompanied James into exile, being appointed secretary of state

of the exiled government in 1695-96. At James' especial request, Caryll's estates had not been confiscated following the revolution. When, however, it was discovered that he had furnished funds to a royalist group involved in an assassination plot, he was declared a traitor and his estates were seized. Upon James' death, the Pretender reappointed Caryll secretary of state and he was created Baron Caryll of Dumford. He died at the age of eighty-six, while still in exile, and was buried in the church of the English Dominicans in Paris.

Two of Caryll's plays are recorded. One, a tragedy, produced in 1666, received a favorable notice from Pepys. The other was an imitation of Molière's comedy, École des Femmes. In 1700 he published anonymously a poetic version of the Psalms. There is evidence that before his death he was working on memoirs of the life of King James, but this work has been lost. His epitaph was written by Pope, who was a close friend of his nephew.

PRINCIPAL WORKS: The English Princess, or, The Death of Richard III, a Tragedy, 1666; Sir Salomon, or The Cautious Coxcomb, a Comedy, 1671.

CAVENDISH, GEORGE (1500-1561?), biographer of Cardinal Wolsey, was the elder son of Thomas Cavendish, clerk of the pipe in the Exchequer, whose wife was the daughter of John Smith of Padbrook Hall in Suffolk. The elder Cavendish died in 1524. George Cavendish married Margery Kemp of Spains Hall, Essex, a niece of Sir Thomas More. At twenty-six he abandoned "country, wife, and children, his own house and family, his rest and quietness," in Wolsey's own words, to become gentleman usher and, soon, a close confidant of the cardinal, whom he accompanied on his embassy to France. Cavendish stayed with Wolsey till his death at Leicester in 1530, stripped of his honours and under accusation of high treason by Henry VIII. At London, Cavendish was questioned by the privy council about Wolsey's last words, but was aided by the Duke of Norfolk and given six of Wolsey's best cart-horses and thirty pounds by the King himself. Retiring to his home at Glemsford in Sussex, Cavendish, who clung to his old faith, bided his time till the reign of Mary, when he began to write his Life of Wolsey, probably in 1557. The accession of Elizabeth made publication impossible, but the manuscript was secretly passed from hand to hand, including (probably) Shakespeare's. In 1558 Cavendish granted his manor of Cavendish Overhill to his son William, a London mercer, for £40 a year. He died in 1561 or 1562.

The Life of Wolsey was not published until 1641, when it appeared in a garbled text as *The Negotiations of Thomas Wolsey*. The genuine text was published in 1810, and the authorship, sometimes ascribed to Cavendish's brother, was proved by the Reverend Joseph Hunter of Bath in 1814. "To George Cavendish, a simple gentleman of the cardinal's household," says Charles Whibley, "belongs the glory of having given to English literature the first specimen of artistic biography. . . . Consciously or unconsciously, Cavendish was an artist. His theme is the theme of many a Greek tragedy, and he handles it with Greek austerity." Henry Morley believed that the direct suggestion to Shakespeare of his play of *King Henry VIII* may have come from his reading of Cavendish's work.

PRINCIPAL WORKS: The Life of Cardinal Wolsey, 1641; Metrical Visions (*in* Life, S. W. Singer, ed. 1825).

ABOUT: Bickley, F. The Cavendish Family; Britt, A. Great Biographers; Cavendish, G. The Life of Cardinal Wolsey (see preface by H. Morley in the Universal Library Series).

CAVENDISH, MARGARET, Duchess of Newcastle

(1624?-January 1674), biographer, author of essays, poems, and plays, was born at St. John's near Colchester, Essex. Her father was Sir Thomas Lucas, a gentleman of large estates, who died when she was an infant. Her mother, Elizabeth Leighton, was known in court circles as a great beauty, and when Margaret expressed a desire to be maid of honor to the queen she received every encouragement. Life at court, however, soon proved disappointing. For her shyness and prudery, as well as her already apparent eccentricity, Margaret was regarded as a "natural fool," and when on a visit to Paris in attendance to Henrietta-Maria, she met and married William Cavendish, Marquis and later Duke of Newcastle, she became almost entirely estranged from her former associations.

Cavendish, as a royalist commander who played an important part in the civil war, was known up until the time of the Restoration as "the greatest traitor of England," and with him Margaret lived abroad in virtual exile under extremely trying financial circumstances. She made one unsuccessful trip to England to try to raise money for her husband, after which she returned to France and devoted all her time to writing.

With the Restoration the Duke and his Duchess returned to England. Margaret, who liked to appear in theatrical costume and who seems to have been both a pedant and a prig, was considered quite mad in the court of Charles II, although she was the recipient of fulsome praise in certain intellectual circles. Pepys called her "a mad, conceited, ridiculous woman," whereas Charles Lamb wrote a century later of "that princely woman, the thrice noble Margaret Newcastle."

The Duchess wrote plays, poems, and philosophical essays in great profusion, but her most important work was a biography of her husband, *The Life of William Cavendish*. Along with her lightly sketched autobiography, the *Life* has become a minor classic of English biographical literature. Although her writing suffered from a lack of training, she had genuine wit and considerable charm of portraiture. She is at her worst in the plays, pretentious and overburdened with philosophy, but her poems, lighted by fancy and full of quaint conceits, have something of the originality and eccentric wit which marked her whole personality.

PRINCIPAL WORKS: Philosophical Fancies, 1653; Poems and Fancies, 1653; Philosophical and Physical Opinions, 1655; Nature's Pictures Drawn by Fancie's Pencil (including her autobiography) 1656; Plays Written by the Lady Marchioness of Newcastle, 1662; The Life of William Cavendish, Duke of Newcastle, 1667 (C. H. Firth, ed. with Life of Margaret, Duchess of Newcastle, 1906); Plays Never Before Printed, 1668.

ABOUT: Life of Margaret, Duchess of Newcastle (autobiography); Perry, H. J. E. The First Duchess of Newcastle and Her Husband as Figures in Literary History.

CAVENDISH, WILLIAM, First Duke of Newcastle

(1592-December 25, 1676), dramatist, poet, patron, writer on horsemanship, was the grandson of Sir William Cavendish, a Privy Councillor and Treasurer of the Chamber to Henry VIII, Edward VI, and Mary Tudor. Educated at St. John's College, Cambridge, where he took no degree, he traveled on the Continent with Sir Henry Wotton, and married soon after his return to England. His lavish entertainment of James I induced that monarch to make him successively Viscount Mansfield and Earl of Newcastle. Later he entertained Charles I twice on an even more lavish scale; Ben Jonson wrote masques for these two entertainments and was well paid, as he had been previously for other compliments to the Cavendish family.

In 1638 Cavendish received *his* reward, being made a Privy Councillor and governor of Prince Charles, later Charles II. During the civil war he raised men and money for the king on his usual grand scale; he was not utterly unsuccessful as a general, but left England for the Continent after the Royalist defeat at Marston Moor (1644). In Paris he met and married his second wife, the literary and eccentric Margaret; Elizabeth, his first, had died in 1643.

Cavendish returned to England with Charles II in 1660. He was made a Duke and given the Order of the Garter, but did not frequent the Court much, being busy rehabilitating his estates, training his horses and writing his plays.

The best one can say of the Duke's comedies is that he sometimes found excellent collaborators—Shirley for *The Country Captain*, Dryden for *Sir Martin Mar-all*. The latter is now included in Dryden's works. The Duke's poetry was no better than his plays, but he was generous with his wealth and influence to many poets and dramatists, good and bad. Besides those already mentioned, he patronized Davenant, Shadwell, and the hapless Flecknoe; also the philosopher Hobbes, and perhaps Descartes.

Like many another English gentleman, the Duke was an amateur in literature, politics, philosophy, and generalship, but a downright professional in fencing and horsemanship. He will always be remembered for his two books on the training of horses, and for the adulatory biography of him written by his second wife. "Of His Outward Shape and Behaviour" she wrote: "His shape is neat and exactly proportioned; his stature of middle size, and his complexion sanguine. His behaviour is such that it might be a pattern for all gentlemen." What more could one ask of a Duke?

PRINCIPAL WORKS: The Country Captain and The Variety, Two Comedies, 1649; La Méthode Nouvelle et Invention Extraordinaire de Dresser les Chevaux, 1658; A New Method and Extraordinary Invention to Dress Horses [not a translation of the preceding] 1667; Sir Martin Mar-all, 1668; The Humorous Lovers, A Comedy, 1677; The Triumphant Widow, A Comedy, 1677.

ABOUT: Cavendish, Margaret, Duchess of Newcastle, The Life of the (1st) Duke of Newcastle; Perry, H. T. E. The First Duchess of Newcastle and her Husband as Figures in Literary History.

CAXTON, WILLIAM (1422?-1491), printer, translator, was born in Tenterden, Kent. The date may have been anywhere from 1412 to 1428. The great industry of Kent was clothmaking (thanks to the Flemish clothmakers introduced by Edward III), and in 1438 Caxton was apprenticed to Robert Large, a wealthy London mercer, to learn the trade. When Large died in 1441, Caxton was sent (apparently by the Mercers' Company) to Bruges, where he completed his apprenticeship, became a freeman of the Mercers' Company, and set up in business for himself in 1446. He remained in the Low Countries for thirty years, but he did not cease to be an Englishman; the Merchant Adventurers, or English Nation, of which he became governor in 1463, was a quasi-diplomatic, quasi-commercial English colony.

In 1469 Caxton became commercial advisor to the Duchess of Burgundy, sister of Edward IV of England. He tells us that he had received from his parents "a good education," though how or where we do not know, and now, with more leisure and the duchess' encouragement, he began to translate and write. His first translation was of the French *Recueil [collection] of the Histories of Troy.*

In 1471, in Cologne, he saw a printing press for the first time, and immediately learned how to use it. Returning to Bruges, he set up a press of his own, with Colard Mansion as his illuminator. The *Recueil* became the first book to be printed in English (1475). The next year he himself went back to England, and set up as a printer in the precincts of Westminster Abbey, at the Sign of the Red Pale. The first book to be printed on English soil was an *Indulgence*, in December 1476. Wynkyn de Worde, who became his successor, was his chief assistant.

Caxton's enterprise was commercial as well as literary; he published all sorts of pamphlets and tracts. However, he edited all the books he printed, and himself translated about a third of them. (Anthony Woodville, Earl Rivers, was translator of the *Dictes and Sayings of the Philosophers,* the first *dated* book to be issued in England —1477.) Besides this, Caxton wrote prologues and epilogues to many of the works he published, displaying a working knowledge of French and Latin, a turn for straightforward, idiomatic prose, and a quiet sense of humor. As a translator he was mediocre and far from literal, but he brought many otherwise unavailable books to the attention of the English public. In all, he translated twenty-one books from French, besides *Reynard the Fox* from Dutch. (He printed ninety-six separate books or editions.) His most important translation was probably that of *The Golden Legend* (1483). He added an eighth book to Ralph Higden's *Polychronicon,* and edited Ovid's *Metamorphoses,* Malory's *Morte d'Arthur,* and most of the works of Chaucer. He was an ardent admirer of Chaucer, and paid for the memorial tablet to the poet in Westminster Abbey. An indefatigable worker, whose good nature could be ruffled only by the sight of idleness, he was at work on a translation of *Lives of the Fathers* on the very day of his death.

During his last fifteen years in England, Caxton flourished mightily. He was a favorite of Edward IV and Richard III, and was patronized and enriched by numerous nobles and wealthy mercers. About 1469 he was married—his wife may have been the Maud Caxton who died in 1490. They had at least one daughter, for a separation suit from her husband is on record which involved her father's will.

Caxton as a printer and typographer does not belong here, but it must be said that he is the father of English printing and that his work could still hold its own with that of the finest printers of today. It is as a fructifier of literature that he is most important; but though he himself deprecated his style, derived from the "broad and rude" English of his provincial birthplace, actually his prefaces reveal him as a first-class working author, who aimed at "clerks and gentlemen" and modestly set himself only the goal of intelligibility.

The name Caxton in his time was pronounced "Cauxton."

PRINCIPAL WORKS: Fifteenth Century Verse and Prose (with others) (A. W. Pollard, ed.) 1903; Prefaces and Prologues to Famous Books (with others) (C. W. Eliot, ed.) 1910. *Translations—* Recuell of the Histories of Troy, 1475; The Game and Play of Chesse, 1476; Boke of Histories of Jason, 1477; Morale Proverbs of Christine de Pisan, 1478; The Hystorye of Reynart the Foxe, 1481; Godfrey of Bolyne, 1481; The Golden Legend, 1483; The Lyf of Charles the Grete, 1485; The Four Sonnes of Aymon, 1489; Blanchardyn and Eglantine, 1489.

ABOUT: Blades, R. H. Who Was Caxton? Blades, W. The Life and Typography of William Caxton; Duff, E. G. William Caxton; Lewis, J. Life of Caxton; Plomer, H. R. William Caxton.

CEDMON. See CAEDMON

CENTLIVRE, SUSANNAH (1667?-December 1, 1723), dramatist, was, with Aphra Behn, one of the earliest women in England to earn her living as a writer. Very little that is dependable is known of her early life; apparently it contained episodes which a later generation thought it unwise to recount. She may very possibly have been an Irishwoman, though of English descent. Her maiden name may have been Freeman or Rawkins; she may have been left an orphan early, or have lost her mother and acquired an unkind stepmother. In any event, she seems to have run away from her home, wherever it was, at sixteen or so, and it is fairly sure that she did not go alone. She was either married to or had an affair with a nephew of Sir Stephen Fox, and seemingly several other brief adventures followed. She may or may not have been married to one Carroll, who was killed in a duel; her earliest plays, when not anonymous, are signed S. Carroll. Somewhere she acquired an education; as a contemporary writer of her obituary put it, she was "of mean parentage and education, but improved her natural genius by reading and good conversation."

She was an actress as well as a playwright, but apparently not a very good one; she traveled with strolling companies of players and never appeared in London. She was acting in Bath, in 1706, in her own *Love at a Venture,* when she met and married Joseph Centlivre, principal cook to Queen Anne and King George I. She lived with him till her death, and continued to write plays. Pope, with customary ill nature, re-

After D. Fermin

MRS. SUSANNAH CENTLIVRE

cluded in an anthology of *Verses upon the Sickness and Recovery of the Right Honourable Robert Walpole.* A supposed volume of her *Letters of Wit, Politics, and Morality,* alleged to have appeared in 1702, is entirely lost if it ever existed.

PRINCIPAL WORKS: (dates of publication) The Perjur'd Husband, 1700; The Beau's Duel, 1702; The Stolen Heiress, 1703; Love's Contrivance, 1703; The Gamester, 1705; The Basset-Table, 1706; Love at a Venture, 1706; The Platonick Lady, 1707; The Busie Body, 1709; The Man's Bewitch'd, 1710? (as The Ghost, 1767); A Bickerstaff's Burying, 1710?; The Marplot: Second Part of The Busie Body, 1711 (as The Marplot in Lisbon, 1760); The Perlex'd Lovers, 1712; The Wonder: A Woman Keeps a Secret!, 1714; A Wife Well Manag'd, 1715 (as The Disappointment [opera], 1732); The Cruel Gift, 1717; A Bold Stroke for a Wife, 1718; The Gotham Election, 1718 (as The Humours of Elections, 1737); The Artifice, 1723; The Dramatic Works of the Celebrated Mrs. Centlivre, 1760-61.

ABOUT: Anon. Account of Life, *in* Dramatic Works; Jerrold, W. and C. Five Queer Women; Seibt, R. Die Komödien der Mrs. Centlivre.

ferred to her in *The Dunciad* as "the cook's wife in Buckingham Court." She was a keen politician and an ardent Whig, and her friends and correspondents included such celebrities as Farquhar, Rowe, and Steele and his group; Steele, in *The Tatler,* paid her the compliment of saying she possessed "that subtlety of spirit which is peculiar to females of wit."

Mrs. Centlivre's plays, with the exception of *A Bold Stroke for a Wife,* were all admittedly derived from Molière or from Spanish sources, but she transformed them into her own image. Her forte was farcical comedy; her blank verse tragedy, *The Perjur'd Husband,* was her poorest play. Though she did not suffer the notoriety that pursued Mrs. Behn, her work was just as crudely frank and licentious, with a fifth act repentance of the sinners to make all right. But she had a gift for comic intrigue, for racy dialogue, and for solid dramatic structure, and her plays are genuinely funny. She had little creative power but a great deal of facility in adaptation from her originals. The part of the jealous husband in *A Bold Stroke for a Wife* was one of Garrick's favorite roles.

Besides her plays, Mrs. Centlivre published two long poems—one "A Poem to King George . . . upon his Accession to the Throne," the other "An Ode to Hygeia," in-

CHALKHILL, JOHN (fl. 1600), poet, is known as a person chiefly by the editorial notes of Izaak Walton, who edited Chalkhill's *Thealma and Clearchus; a Pastoral History* (1683), and in his *Compleat Angler* (1653) included two songs, "O, the Sweet Contentment" and "O, the Gallant Fisher's Life," signed by Ion Chalkhill. As George Saintsbury says, some commentators have thought he was a "mere mask" for Walton himself, but a contributor to the *Gentleman's Magazine* in 1860 quoted extracts from Middlesex County records to show that an Ivon or Ion Chalkhill, Gent., was one of the coroners of that county towards the end of Queen Elizabeth's reign, and that he signed his name in either of these two forms, as the songs in *The Compleat Angler* were signed. Another clue to his identity is the fact that the second wife of Thomas Ken, Walton's father-in-law, was Martha Chalkhill, second daughter of John Chalkhill of Kingsbury in Middlesex. Walton, in his preface to *Thealma and Clearchus* (which was written "In Smooth and Easie Verse"), declared that he was "in his time a man generally known and as well beloved; for he was humble and obliging in his behaviour, a gentleman, a scholar, very innocent and prudent: and indeed his whole life was useful, quiet, and virtuous." The poem, he said, was written "long since" by a poet who was "an acquaintant and friend of Edmund Spenser"—who died in 1599.

Thealma and Clearchus is a romantic narrative or heroic-pastoral poem in the same style as the *Pharonnida* (1659) of William Chamberlayne. George Saintsbury, who reproduced the poem in his *Caroline Poets,* Vol. II (1906), remarks that it "indulges in a complication of disguises, mistakes of persons and the like, which even Chamberlayne never permitted himself, and which, probably, had something to do with the relinquishment of a recklessly and hopelessly embroiled enterprise" and that it has "some extremely pretty passages."

PRINCIPAL WORKS: Thealmus and Clearchus, 1683.

ABOUT: Saintsbury, G. Caroline Poets; Walton, I. The Compleat Angler (1851 ed.); Gentleman's Magazine 1860.

CHAMBERLAYNE, EDWARD (1616-1703),

social and political writer, was born at Oddington, Gloucestershire the grandson of Sir Thomas Chamberlayne, ex-ambassador to the Low Countries. Educated in the Gloucestershire schools and at St. Edmund Hall, Oxford, he went abroad following his graduation, spending the years of the civil wars traveling in France, Spain, Italy, Hungary, Bohemia, Sweden and the Low Countries. In 1658 he married Susannah Clifford. Returning to England following the Restoration, he became secretary to Charles Howard, Earl of Carlisle.

Chamberlayne had written and translated several historical tracts, and in 1669 he produced a book which remained a standard reference work for the next hundred years. Patterned after a similar work published in France, *The Present State of England* was a handbook of political and social information, including current statistics and lists of office-holders. The first edition was published anonymously. After Chamberlayne's authorship became known, he was accorded scholastic honors, and became one of the first members of the Royal Society. *The Present State,* revised from time to time, went through twenty editions in his own lifetime, the thirty-sixth and final edition appearing in 1755.

In 1679 Chamberlayne became tutor to Henry Fitzroy, Duke of Grafton, the illegitimate son of Charles II, and he later taught English to Prince George of Denmark. He died at Chelsea, where he had spent the last several years of his life, and was buried in the Chelsea churchyard. At his own direction, copies of his books enclosed in wax were buried with him, for the enlightenment of posterity.

PRINCIPAL WORKS: The Present War Paralleled, or a Brief Relation of the Five Years' Civil Wars of Henry III, 1647; England's Wants, 1667; The Converted Presbyterian, or The Church of England Justified in Some Practices, 1668; The Present State of England, 1669; A Dialogue Between an Englishman and a Dutchman, 1672.

ABOUT: Biographia Britannica; Faulkner, T. History of Chelsea; Wood, A. à, Athenae Oxonienses.

CHAMBERLAYNE, WILLIAM (1619-1689),

physician, dramatist and poet, lived and died at Shaftsbury in Dorsetshire. Little is known of his life except that he was a practicing physician, and that he fought on the royalist side in the civil wars. His reputation as one of the most talented of the school known as the lesser Carolinian poets rests on three published works: a play, a long narrative poem, and a poem celebrating the Restoration.

The play, *Love's Victory,* which he described as a tragi-comedy, has elements of beauty of style and of nobility of idea, but they are combined with other elements of much less merit. Twenty years after its first publication a revised version was produced at the Theater Royale, under the title *Wits Led by the Nose, or a Poet's Revenge.*

Upon the return of Charles II to the throne, Chamberlayne wrote *England's Jubilee,* a vigorous expression of his royalist sentiments. His third work, *Pharonnida,* a long, rambling, romantic story told in heroic verse, contains evidence of a poetic talent so undisciplined that the result, in spite of passages of great beauty and an interesting plot, is almost impossible to read. The story, which has been called a precursor of the unhistorical novel, is confused and diffuse, sometimes to the point of incoherence. The style is a mixture of real poetic imagery, and of over-elaborate figures, loose construction, and bewildering complexities. Southey, who admired Chamberlayne, called him ". . . a poet who has told an interesting story in uncouth rhymes, and mingles sublimity of thought with the quaintest conceits and most awkward inversions."

A novel based on *Pharonnida*, whose authorship is unknown, was published in 1683 under the title of *Eromena, or The Noble Stranger.*

PRINCIPAL WORKS: Love's Victory, a tragicomedy 1658; Pharonnida, 1659; England's Jubilee, 1660.

ABOUT: Parsons, A. E. Forgotten Poet: William Chamberlayne and Pharonnida, Modern Language Review, July 1950; Retrospective Review, 1920; Saintsbury, G. Preface, Minor Poets of the Caroline Period.

CHAMBERS, EPHRAIM (d. May 15, 1740),

encyclopedist, was a farmer's son who, fired by the desire for greater knowledge than his own education had given him, produced a work which gave rise to the great achievement of the French encyclopedists. He was apprenticed, at the conclusion of his grammar school education in his native town of Kendal, to a London cartographer named Senex, who encouraged the young man in his independent studies. Filled with the idea of producing an encyclopedic survey of knowledge, Chambers soon left Senex and devoted several years to the work.

In 1728, he published his *Cyclopedia, or An Universal Dictionary of Arts and Sciences*. Although it was published on a subscription basis at a rather high price, its value was recognized immediately. Chambers was elected a member of the Royal Society, and a French translation of the *Cyclopedia* gave form to the work of D'Alembert and Diderot in their *Encyclopédie*.

Determined to recast the form of the *Cyclopedia* for a second edition and to revise the elaborate prefatory classification of all knowledge, Chambers wrote an outline of these plans in a work titled *Considerations*. The revision was never made because of a change in publishing regulations and no copy of *Considerations* survives, but Boswell quotes Samuel Johnson as saying that he had formed his style partly upon Chambers' proposal for his dictionary. Five partially revised editions were published in the next eighteen years, and the work was finally expanded into Rees' *Encyclopedia*.

Chambers edited a literary magazine, made some scholarly translations from the French, and wrote an account of his travels in France which was never published. He died at about the age of sixty, and was buried in Westminster Abbey.

PRINCIPAL WORKS: Cyclopedia, 1728; Practice of Perspective (tr. from French of Jean Dubreuil); Philosophical History and Memoirs of the Royal Academy of Sciences at Paris (tr. from French with John Martyn).

ABOUT: Biographia Britannica; Chalmers A. Biographies; Nichols, J. Literary Anecdotes.

CHAPMAN, GEORGE (1559?-May 12, 1634),

classical scholar and translator, dramatist, poet, was born near Hitchin, Hertfordshire, but relatively little is known of his life. He may have attended both Oxford and Cambridge, or neither; certainly he had no degree, yet he had a sound classical learning which enabled him to translate Homer and Hesiod. He may have served in the Netherlands, but this also is uncertain. Certain it is that Essex was his first patron, and that after the earl's execution he became server in ordinary to Prince Henry of Wales. Henry died in 1612, and no further provision was made for Chapman: "Homer no patron found, nor Chapman friend." He was in and out of trouble frequently; he served a brief term in the Tower for slurring references to the Scots in *Eastward Ho*, which he wrote with Ben Jonson and John Marston; he was threatened with imprisonment for remarks about the queen of France; and he was in hot water over *Andromeda Liberata*, which celebrated the marriage of the Earl of Somerset with the notorious Frances Howard, divorced wife of Essex. In his lifetime he had more reputation than wealth, and he died poor; his friend Inigo Jones erected and paid for Chapman's monument in the churchyard of St. Giles-in-the-Fields.

Chapman responded, as is not surprising, by bitterness. He admired and copied Marlowe, and he was on cordial terms with Jonson and Marston and a few others of the dramatists of his day, but on the whole he had more enemies than friends. He especially resented Shakespeare, who is suspected of having reacted by depicting Chapman as Holofernes in *Love's Labour Lost*. He may have done more: Acheson and some other critics believe that Chapman was the "rival poet" of Shakespeare's sonnets. ("The proud full sail of his great verse" may well have described some of Chapman's highly romantic writing—but was he "by spirits taught to write," and who was "that affable familiar ghost"—unless it were Homer?)

Robertson in turn thinks that Chapman, not Shakespeare, wrote *Timon of Athens* and *A Lover's Complaint*. In all probability the the question will never be settled; the Elizabethan dramatists and their plays are inextricably confused.

As a matter of fact, Chapman was not primarily a dramatist, though he had a gift for highflown romantic tragedy and for broad comedy as well. He wrote plays as aspiring authors today write novels—because that was the most popular and most accessible form of literature. Lamb is right in saying that though Chapman "approaches nearest to Shakespeare" it is in "passages which are less purely dramatic"; and Swinburne pointed out the fact that Chapman is far better in isolated passages than taken as a whole. John Webster praised Chapman's "full and heightened style" (the words might still better apply to Webster himself), and Jonson thought no one could write masques acceptably but Fletcher, Chapman, and himself (Chapman's best known masque was performed at court in 1613); yet as a dramatist Chapman seems always on the verge of true emotional insight and never quite able to attain it. He himself preferred his tragedies to his comedies, but the comedies are better.

At heart he knew where his real forte lay. "The work which I was born to do was done," he wrote when he had finished his translation of Homer. Homer was his god. Though full of inaccuracies and long superseded, the translation of the *Iliad* and the *Odyssey* is indeed a monument "more lasting than bronze" to Chapman's devotion and skill. If for no other reason, we must be grateful to him for that translation, since two hundred years later it inspired young Keats to write his deathless sonnet "On First Looking into Chapman's Homer."

In his non-dramatic poems, Chapman belongs by right to the "metaphysical school." They are gnomic and didactic; they frequently have exaltation, but they are cerebral, they possess neither feeling nor music. Inigo Jones sensed that when on his monument he described Chapman as a "Christian Philosophical and Homericall Poett." In his own time, and ever since, he has been more admired and praised than he has been read. His plays suffered severe neglect in the next

GEORGE CHAPMAN

century; the Augustans could not understand and disliked the grandiloquent. With so many other Elizabethans, he was rescued from forgetfulness by Charles Lamb.

He is a hard man to evaluate. He had great distinction of mind, he had learning, he had superb self-confidence; but he writes always as if he himself felt out of place. He is the eternal onlooker, never entering into the life of humanity either of his own time or of the times of which he treats. "The multitude I hate," he said; yet for his creative writing he chose a medium which more than any other must appeal to the multitude or fail. He does not seem, either, ever to have felt at home in the Bohemianism of his then raffish craft; Anthony à Wood significantly calls him "religious and temperate"— two adjectives that could never have been applied to most of the Elizabethan playwrights. He had all the literary virtues and all the literary faults of that magnificent period, but they were never quite synthesized. Nevertheless, when all is said and done, Chapman is a distinguished dramatist; many of his contemporaries would have rated him far above Shakespeare. Where he failed was as a poet, which is where Shakespeare was most triumphantly successful. Chapman often gives the effect of shouting to cover the fact that he has nothing important to say; he has no lyric gift and his verse is at once brassy and arid. But it does

95

have the lift of sheer magniloquence, and the periods when Chapman's reputation has been and will be highest are those of admiration for the full-sounding line and heightened rhetoric. Given a station and fortune which would have enabled him to live without what in reality was super-hack writing and a series of literary *tours de force*, Chapman would probably have devoted his entire attention to scholarship and classical humanism.

PRINCIPAL WORKS: *Plays*—(dates of publication) The Blind Begger of Alexandria, 1598; A Humorous Days Myrth, 1599; Eastward Ho (with Ben Jonson and John Marston) 1605; All Fools (produced as The World Runs on Wheels) 1605; Monsier d'Olive, 1606; The Gentleman Usher, 1606; Bussy d'Ambois, 1607; The Conspiracy and the Tragedy of Charles, Duke of Biron, 1608; May Day, 1611; The Widow's Tears, 1612; The Revenge of Bussy d'Ambois, 1614; The Wars of Caesar and Pompey, 1631; The Tragedy of Chabot, Admiral of France (with James Shirley) 1639; Alphonsus, Emperor of Germany, 1654; Revenge for Honour, 1654. *Poems*—The Shadow of Night, 1594; Ovid's Banquet of Sauce, 1595; Continuation of Marlowe's Hero and Leander, 1598; The Tears of Peace, 1609; Andromeda Liberata, 1614. *Translations*—Homer's Iliad, 1598, 1609, 1611; Homer's Odyssey, 1614, 1615; Homer Complete, 1616; Hesiod's Works and Days, 1618.

ABOUT: Acheson, A. Shakespeare and the Rival Poet; Arnold, M. Lectures on Translating Homer; Coleridge, S. T. Literary Remains; Lamb, C. Specimens of the Dramatic Poets; Langbaine, G. Dramatic Poets; Robertson, J. M. Shakespeare and Chapman; Swinburne, A. C. Essay on the Poetical and Dramatic Works of George Chapman; Wieler, J. W. George Chapman: The Effect of Stoicism on His Tragedies; Wood, A. à, Athenae Oxonienses.

CHAPONE, HESTER (October 27, 1727-December 25, 1801), essayist, was born at Twywell in Northamptonshire. The family consisted of her father, Thomas Mulso, a gentleman farmer, several brothers, and a remarkably beautiful mother who was so jealous of her clever daughter that when the little girl, at the age of nine, produced a novel entitled *The Loves of Amoret and Melissa*, her mother suppressed all further literary activity.

Upon her mother's death, Hester took over the management of the household and came into her own as a precociously intelligent and charming girl. Her father allowed her to pursue her studies in many fields. A spirited, impulsive girl with a lovely voice, a talent for drawing, and a lively, good-humored determination to express her ideas, she became a favorite of her father's friends

and of many of the literary figures of the day.

This was the period when the little group of intellectual feminists known as the blue-stockings foregathered, usually at North End, the home of Samuel Richardson. Through Mrs. Elizabeth Carter, one of the leaders of this group, Hester was introduced into this society, quickly becoming a close friend of Richardson, who called her "the little spitfire." She probably served as the prototype of some of the novelist's feminine characters.

It was through Richardson that she met the young attorney, John Chapone, with whom she fell in love. Her father strongly opposed the marriage, but she finally obtained his consent and was married only a short year before the death of her husband in 1761. Recovering from overwhelming grief, she lived quietly for the rest of her long life on the small income left her by her husband and her father, a constant and welcome member of the bluestocking group, occasionally publishing collections of essays, and appearing in *The Gentleman's Magazine*. Her last few years were greatly saddened by the deaths of nearly all her close family.

In 1772 she published her best known work, *Letters on the Improvement of the Mind*, a dissertation on the education of women written for the edification of a favorite niece. The death of this niece was a final sorrow, and Mrs. Chapone herself died a year later, at the age of seventy-four.

PRINCIPAL WORKS: Letters on the Improvement of the Mind, 1772; Miscellanies, 1775; Letter to a New Married Lady, 1777.

ABOUT: Chapone, H. Biographical Prefix to Works, ed. 1807; Chambers, R. Cyclopedia of English Literature; Richardson, S. Correspondence.

CHATTERTON, THOMAS (November 20, 1752-August 24, 1770), poet, is undoubtedly the youngest person whose name appears in this volume. But it is here not because he was a "marvellous boy," as Wordsworth called him, but because he was a genuine and almost a great poet. He was born in Bristol, the posthumous child and namesake of a teacher of a free school for the poor, and of Sarah Young, who after her husband's death opened a dame's school and took in sewing to provide for her children. The office of sexton of the church of

St. Mary Redcliffe was hereditary in his father's family, and from infancy he played in the muniment room, where old manuscripts rested in coffers. Accounted stupid as a small child because he was already lost in dreams, Chatterton was sent at nine to Colston's Hospital (a "blue-coat" school), where his brilliance at once manifested itself. At fifteen he was taken from school and apprenticed to an attorney, John Lambert. Here he slaved from 7 A.M. to 8 P.M., with one hour at home allowed daily, was set to the drudgery of copying documents, and was in general treated like a servant. Sometimes he wrote poetry instead of copying documents, but Lambert discovered it and burned the manuscripts.

Chatterton had been writing poetry from the age of eleven. The attic in his home became his private retreat, where he wrote, painted heraldic designs, and drew up glossaries of medieval words for use in his poems. By the time he was twelve he had created the mythical Thomas Rowley, supposedly a priest of St. Mary's Redcliffe in the fifteenth century, and the alleged author of poems allegedly found in "Canynge's coffer." It must be remembered that this was (at first at least) no conscious deception, but a fantasy world like the Kingdoms of Angria and Verdopolis of the little Brontës. Even the mulcting of five shillings from a worthy

N. Branwhite after Morris
THOMAS CHATTERTON

pewterer for a "discovered" coat of arms and a proud pedigree was little more than a schoolboy prank. For Chatterton, though highly introverted and from childhood an obvious neurotic, was also sufficiently normal to enjoy like any other boy fooling the dull and pompous. He was a highly religious boy, too, whose first poem was "On the Last Epiphany," and who thought of himself as almost a part of the church. He had even learned to read from a black-letter Bible.

Already, when he entered on his apprenticeship, he was beginning to have the Rowley poems and other "fifteenth century manuscripts" published, first in local periodicals, then in national magazines, usually under the name of "Dunelmus Bristoliensis." They were printed in good faith as medieval writings, though more than once Chatterton confessed his authorship of them to friends.

His service to Lambert was growing unbearable. In April 1770 he wrote a half-satirical, half-tragic suicide note, which was intended to frighten the lawyer into releasing him, and had the desired effect. Chatterton at seventeen set out for London to make his living as an author.

This was not so unlikely a hope as it may have seemed. Chatterton, who was able to write brilliantly in the style of almost any author, had published in London, besides his poems, a number of political letters in the mode of the popular "Junius," which he signed "Decimus." He had other justified hopes and expectations, and being an exceedingly abstemious youth, he felt he could live on almost no money. Failing everything else, he wanted to study medicine. So far he had had only one great setback; he had sent Horace Walpole one of his "finds"—*The Ryse of Peyncting in Englande*, "written by T. Rowleie 1469 for Mestre Canynge," and Walpole, after first swallowing the hook, took advice, reconsidered the matter (especially after a letter from Chatterton at which he hinted that as a poor apprentice he needed financial aid to become a writer), and wrote the boy cruelly: "When you have made your fortune you may unbend in your favorite studies." He also refused for a long time to return the manuscript. When Chatterton was dead, and it was too late, Walpole said, "I do not believe there ever existed so masterly a genius."

At first Chatterton lodged in London with relatives, sharing a room; soon he moved so that he could have privacy. His success seemed immediate; the magazines took his work with avidity—both the alleged medieval poems and his own modern prose and verse. Only—they paid on publication, and they delayed publishing. Soon Chatterton's money was gone, and pay absolutely promised him was postponed indefinitely. Nearly all the money he actually received in four months was five guineas for a comic opera, or "burletta," called *Revenge*. Desperately he tried to get an appointment as surgeon's assistant on an African trader, but in vain. He had said of himself: "Nineteen-twentieths of my composition is pride." When his landlady suspected that the boy was not eating, and tried to inveigle him into sharing meals with her, he answered curtly that he had plenty of food and wanted nothing.

So at seventeen years and nine months Thomas Chatterton, alone in his attic room, destroyed all the manuscripts in his possession and took arsenic. He was found dead the next morning, and shoveled into a pauper's grave.

This tall youth with the brilliant grey eyes was perhaps an impostor—though his imposture had become half reality to him—but he was also a poet. Samuel Johnson called him "the most extraordinary young man that has encountered my knowledge"; Wordsworth, Coleridge, Shelley, Rossetti wrote in his praise; Keats dedicated *Endymion* to his memory. The medieval poems were not all ascribed to "Rowley"; they were written in the style of twelve distinct poets. *The Song of Ælla* is a masterpiece whoever wrote it. Others, such as *The Bristowe Tragedie* and *Elinoure and Juga* are scarcely less. Though the authenticity of the spelling and some of the naive archaisms put the poems under suspicion from almost the beginning among medieval scholars, a long controversy raged for years after Chatterton's death, with many critics holding obstinately to the reality of the "ancient" manuscripts. Partly this was due to the keen interest in the Middle Ages during his time, aroused by the Gothic romances of Walpole, Mrs. Radcliffe, and others; partly it was because it was hard for orthodox critics to believe that such poems issued from a half-educated apprentice in his teens. There is not the slightest doubt that they did. Neither is there the slightest doubt that the youth who wrote them would, if he had lived, have gone far beyond them. There was the true spark of genius in Thomas Chatterton. Hardly exaggerated are Rossetti's words: "With Shakespeare's manhood in a boy's wild heart."

PRINCIPAL WORKS: An Elegy on the Much Lamented Death of William Beckford, Esq., 1770; The Execution of Sir Charles Bawdin (T. Eagles, ed.) 1772; Poems Supposed to Have been Written at Bristol by Thomas Rowley and Others in the 15th Century (T. Tyrwhitt, ed.) 1777; Miscellanies in Prose and Verse (J. Broughton, ed.) 1778-84; The Revenge, a Burletta, 1795; Works (R. Southey, and J. Cottle, eds.) 1803.

ABOUT: Ashton, W. ("Clemence Dane") and R. Addinsell, Come of Age (play); Britton, J. The Life, Character, and Writings of Chatterton; Croft, H. Love and Madness; Davis, J. The Life and Letters of Thomas Chatterton; Dixon, W. M. Chatterton; Ellinger, E. P. Thomas Chatterton, the Marvellous Boy; Gregory, G. The Life of Thomas Chatterton; Ingram, J. H. The True Chatterton; Masson, D. Chatterton: A Biography; Meyerstein, E. H. W. A Life of Chatterton; Nevill, J. C. Thomas Chatterton; Richter, H. Thomas Chatterton (in German); Russell, C. E. Chatterton; Southey, R. Life, in Works; Vigny, A. de Chatterton (play); Wilson, D. Chatterton: A Biographical Study.

CHAUCER, GEOFFREY

(1340?-October 25, 1400), the first great English poet, may have been born anywhere between 1328 and 1346; 1340 is usually taken as the most probable date. Everything we know about his life comes from mention of him in official documents, and we must always remember that the Geoffrey Chaucer named in these may not have been the poet—the name was rather common in the fourteenth century. The reasonable assumption, however, is that they are one and the same, from references made by Chaucer himself to episodes in his public career, and from his close acquaintances with so many phases of English life and of French and Italian literature.

His father was John Chaucer, a London vintner, with some sort of connection with the court of Edward III; his mother was Agnes (surname unknown), a second wife. The father died about 1366, and the mother married another Chaucer, probably a cousin of her husband's. Just where the boy got his schooling is not known; he may have been at either Oxford or Cambridge, or neither, and the latter guess is more likely. The first glimpse of him is in 1357, as a page in the household of the Duke of Clarence and his wife. Two years later he was with the English army during the invasion of France, was taken prisoner, and was ransomed in 1360, the king paying part of his ransom. For all the rest of his life he was in the public service in one way or another, and was also the recipient of various pensions from Edward III and later from Richard II. In 1367 he was mentioned as an esquire, having formerly been a "yeoman of the bedchamber." In 1372 he was in Genoa on a commercial mission; in 1374 he was made controller of the great customs (wool and leather) for the port of London; in 1376 and 1377 he was on secret diplomatic missions in Flanders and France, and in 1378 and 1379 he was in France and Italy. In 1382 his customs position was enlarged by taking in the petty customs also, and in 1386 he sat in Parliament as knight of the shire for Kent.

Then came a period of eclipse, coinciding with the absence in Spain of his great patron, John of Gaunt, Duke of Lancaster, and the ascendancy of the Duke of Gloucester. He lost both his controllerships, and for a while was reduced to living on his annuity from Edward III and his pensions; apparently he was hard up and was obliged to ask for constant advances. In 1388 John of Gaunt returned to power and Chaucer prospered with him. The next year he was made clerk of the works to the king (an office he held only until 1391), and in 1390 was named commissioner of roads between Greenwich and Woolwich. This position, which he held by deputy, was his until his death—even though on one unfortunate day he was twice robbed by the same highwaymen of a considerable sum of public money. He was also made forester of North Petherton Park, in Somerset, and new pensions were given him. It is not surprising that he wrote little during the last years of his life; even though he delegated much of his work, there was enough to occupy most of his time.

The house he had leased in Aldgate in 1374 he had lost in 1386, but with his new prosperity he leased another, in 1399, in the Lady Chapel of Westminster. There he died a few months later, and was the first to be buried in what is now the Poet's Corner of

GEOFFREY CHAUCER

the Abbey. The present tomb was built by Nicholas Brigham in 1555, but before that William Caxton *qv* had placed a memorial tablet to him over his grave.

Chaucer was married about 1366 to a "damsel of the queen's bedchamber" whose given name was Philippa. (If she was, as is probable, Philippa Roet, then John of Gaunt's patronage is easily understood, for her sister would be the Katherine Swynford who was long his mistress and finally became his third wife.) It is not certain whether there were children by this marriage, but a Thomas Chaucer inherited the post of forester of North Petherton Park, and an Elizabeth Chaucer became a nun, and in both cases the dates make it likely that they were Geoffrey Chaucer's children. There remains "little Lewis," for whom Chaucer wrote the *Treatise on the Astrolabe* in 1391, when the boy was ten years old. It is more than possible that this was his son, not by his wife, but by a certain Cecelia Chaumpagne, who in 1380 gave him a quit claim on payment of a stated sum in recompense for an abduction. This may have been a case of kidnaping an heiress to marry her to somebody else, a common practice in that time (Chaucer's own father narrowly escaped a similar abduction)—or it may not. The indications are that Chaucer's married life was not happy, that he was cynical about marriage, and that he was much in love with another woman.

99

The only really acid passage in all his writing is an invective against scolding, nagging wives. Philippa in any case died aboout 1387, and Chaucer never married again.

This is about all we know of Geoffrey Chaucer personally, aside from a few portraits which may or may not be authentic. We can gather a few things more from his writings: that he was not a very good administrator, that he was far from thrifty, and that he was a lovable man with many friends—the contemporary poets Gower, Occleve, and Lydgate *qqv* among them. We know his sunny humor, his subtle irony, his touching pathos. And we know above all that he had the searching and seeing eye, that he had an unquenchable curiosity about people and remembered almost everything he had seen and heard. Perhaps it should be added that the word "Dan" sometimes prefixed to his name has nothing to do with Daniel, but is a fourteenth century term of respect, like "master" or "sir"—as in Spenser's famous lines:

Old Dan Geoffrey, in whose gentle spright [spirit]
The pure wellhead of poetry did dwell.

It did indeed. Chaucer is not only the first great poet to write in English, but he is still one of the greatest. Southey remarked that he was "next to Shakespeare the most various of English writers." In narrative he was supreme; T.R. Lounsbury called *The Knight's Tale* "the most perfect narrative poem in our tongue." To his contemporary Occleve he was "the firste finder [poet] of our fair language," and to the modern A. W. Pollard he was "one of the great technical masters of poetry." More than this, he very largely helped to make the language in which he wrote. It is not true that Chaucer unaided created literary English out of Saxon plus Norman French; Wycliffe, Langland, Gower, and others all did their part in fixing a Gallicized dialect as the English norm. He did, however, nationalize in English prosody both the rime royal (decasyllabic seven-line stanzas with the rhyme-scheme ababbcc) and the heroic couplet, ending forever the exclusive rule of the old Saxon octosyllabic line. His prose, it may be added, is adequate but undistinguished; he is great exclusively as a poet.

No satisfactory dates can be affixed to any of Chaucer's poems. In fact, it has taken nearly six hundred years to establish the Chaucer canon—to say definitely which poems are his, and which ones ascribed to him were written by others. The best that can be done is to divide his literary life into three episodes—the first of French influence, the second Italian, the third purely English. Of course none of his work was printed in his lifetime, for the very good reason that the first book printed in England was in 1476. To the first period belong *The Book of the Duchess (The Death of Blanche)*, written on the death of John of Gaunt's first wife; and the translation of *The Romaunt of the Rose*, the most famous European poem of the era (if indeed the version we have is Chaucer's; we know he did one, but not whether this—or all of it—is his). To the second—when perhaps he met Petrarch personally in Italy—belong *The Hous of Fame* and *The Legende of Good Women (The Booke of the Twenty-Five Ladies)*, both left unfinished for the probable reason that their author grew bored with them; *The (Booke of St. Valentine's Day of the) Parlement of Foules* [birds]; and *Troylus and Criseyde*, next to *The Canterbury Tales* the greatest of Chaucer's poems. To the third belong the great *Tales* themselves. The minor poems which are undoubtedly Chaucer's (besides several later incorporated into *The Canterbury Tales*) include *An A B C* (a religious poem), the unfinished *Anelida and Arcite*, and a number of "complaints" and "envoys" (poetic epistles). His prose works are the *Treatise on the Astrolabe* and a translation of Boethius' *Consolation of Philosophy*.

The Canterbury Tales is, of course, Chaucer's masterpiece, and one of the finest English poems in existence, even in its incomplete and unfinished form. The prologue is pure poetry in its opening lines, high narrative as it proceeds. In some of the stories told by the Canterbury pilgrims at the Tabard Inn, and in some of the prologues to these stories (notably the long, vivid, and bawdy prologue to *The Wife of Bath's Tale*) we have the very essence of narrative genius. It has been suggested that in the sixteenth or seventeenth century Chaucer would have been a dramatist, in the nineteenth a novelist. His lively character studies, his sly sidelights on personality, his crisp descriptions, are inimitable. The language may at first seem formidable, but with a glossary Chaucer can be read with little difficulty, and he is one of the most rewarding of authors. As Legouis has said, he not only "reflects his century," but "penetrates to the everlasting springs of human action." Tolerant, light-hearted, sane, master of fire and sweetness alike, he is an unendingly rich mine of delight. To the stiff, formal Addison he may have been "an antiquated buffoon, sometimes coarsely amusing" (George Saintsbury); to warmer natures he will always be the beloved poet of England's springtime. He has his defects, naturally—he is often garrulous and sometimes disorderly in construction; like all the writers of his time he played the "hermit crab," taking what he needed where he found it and transforming it into his own; he wrote primarily for the court circle, to whom the idea of English as a literary language was new and startling, and hence he paraded a bit his knowledge of foreign tongues and literature; and he left far too much unfinished. But he had a remarkably wide knowledge of the world of his time, the power to make that world real to his readers, a broadness of view which we conceitedly think of as "modern," and a command of blended humor and pathos that justifies the epithet "gentle."

Geoffrey Chaucer was not a poetic phenomenon of interest merely because he lived and wrote six hundred years ago; he was and is an everlasting glory to the literature of his country. With him indeed the English literary "sumer is icumen in," and such a summer was not seen again in English letters until the advent of the still greater genius of William Shakespeare.

The generally accepted Chaucer portrait (see above) shows him as an old man. It appears in a copy of Thomas Occleve's *De Regimine Principium* in the Harleian manuscript 4866 and is considered authentic by the National Portrait Gallery.

PRINCIPAL WORKS: (dates of publication) Canterbury Tales, 1482?; Troylus and Criseyde, 1482?; The Hous of Fame, 1486?; The Workes of Geoffrey Chaucer (W. Thynne, ed.) 1532; The Workes of Our Ancient and Lerned English Poet, Geoffrey Chaucer, 1561; Complete Works (W. W. Skeat, ed.) 1897.

ABOUT: Austin, A. Chaucer; Brusendorff, A. The Chaucer Tradition; Chesterton, G. K. Chaucer; Chute, M. Geoffrey Chaucer of England; Coulton, G. G. Chaucer and His England; Cowling, G. H. Chaucer; French, R. D. A Chaucer Handbook; Godwin, W. Life of Geoffrey Chaucer, the Early English Poet; Hadow, G. E. Chaucer and His Times; Kittredge, G. L. Chaucer and His Poetry; Legouis, E. H. (L. Lailavoix, tr.) Geoffrey Chaucer; Lounsbury, T. R. Studies in Chaucer; Lowell, J. R. My Study Windows; Lowes, G. L. Geoffrey Chaucer and the Development of His Genius; Manly, J. M. Some New Light on Chaucer; Masefield, J. Chaucer; Murry, J. M. Heroes of Thought; Patch, H. R. On Rereading Chaucer; Pollard, A. W. Chaucer; Saintsbury, G. Collected Essays; Sedgwick, H. D. Dan Chaucer; Shelly, P. Van D. The Living Chaucer; Skeat, W. W. The Chaucer Canon; Tatlock, J. S. P. and Kennedy, A. G. A Concordance to the Complete Works of Geoffrey Chaucer; Ward, A. W. Chaucer.

CHEKE, Sir JOHN (June 16, 1514-September 13, 1557), scholar, classicist, translator, was born in Cambridge, the son of Peter Cheke, "esquire beadle" of the university, to which his son was sent at the age of twelve. He became a fellow of St. John's in 1529, received his B.A. in 1530, and his M.A. in 1533. He was never in orders, though he often held positions usually open only to clergymen. He began lecturing in Greek in the 1530's, without salary, and was appointed the first Regius Professor of Greek in 1540. Roger Ascham, one of his pupils, says that he "laid the very foundations of learning in his college," and indeed Greek had been very little known in England before this. Though he introduced his pupils to Euripides, Sophocles, Herodotus, Xenophon, and Aristotle's *Ethics*, to his contemporaries he was chiefly known for the long controversy over the new ("Erasmian") as against old ("Reuchlinian") pronunciation of Greek vowels—a battle which Cheke lost temporarily but won permanently. In 1539 and 1540 he was Cambridge's last "Master of Glomery," which seems to have meant head of the grammar school. In 1542 he was appointed public orator of the university.

Though he held his professorship until 1547, he left Cambridge in 1542 to tutor the future Edward VI. He was already a Reformer (Anglican), and had no hesitation in accepting the prince's gifts of confiscated church and conventual lands. For a short time he was made canon (though not a divine) of King's College, Oxford; the college (later Christ Church) was dissolved in 1545

SIR JOHN CHEKE

of his writings were Latin translations from the Greek, including Josephus, Plutarch, and Demosthenes. He also wrote a number of Latin tracts on theological controversies, and a book in English against Ket's rebellion. Most of his writings are still in manuscript, and many have been lost altogether. He had a scheme for making English a phonetic language, which won no followers. His great importance was as a humanist and the teacher who brought Greek learning to England.

PRINCIPAL WORKS: The Hurt of Sedition, 1549; The Gospel according to St. Matthew (translated) 1550 (with Seven Original Letters, J. Goodwin, ed. 1843); Carmen Heroicum, 1551; De pronuntiatione Graecae...linguae, 1555.

ABOUT: Ascham, R. The Scholemaster; Langbaine, G. Life, in 1641 ed. The Hurt of Sedition; Strype, J. Life of Sir John Cheke.

and he accepted a pension instead. During this period he was in high favor at court; he sat in Parliament for Bletchingly in 1547 and again in 1552 and 1553; his sister had married William Cecil, Lord Burghley; in 1551 he was knighted, and given large estates to uphold his rank. In 1547 he had married Mary Hill, and they had three sons. In 1548 he was made provost of King's College, Cambridge; in 1553 he was one of the secretaries of state and hence a member of the Privy Council.

But in that year Edward died and Cheke made the mistake of siding with Lady Jane Grey against Mary. He spent ten months in the Tower in consequence, and all his property was confiscated. On his release he was permitted to travel, and he taught Greek in Padua and Strassburg. In 1556 he was lured to Brussels to see his wife, and was arrested by order of Philip II of Spain (Queen Mary's husband) and returned to England, on the ostensible charge of having outstayed his license to travel. The real reason was his religious views. In the Tower again, under threat of torture and burning, he abjured Protestantism, and was forced to undergo the humiliation of two public recantations. The wretched man did not long survive this ordeal; he died the following year.

Cheke was a good Hellenist, with a "single-eyed devotion to scholarship." Most

CHESTERFIELD, PHILIP DORMER STANHOPE, Fourth Earl

(September 22, 1694-March 24, 1773), statesman, diplomat, man of letters, was the oldest son of the third Earl, Philip Stanhope, and of Elizabeth Savile, daughter of the Marquis of Halifax, and was born in London. His parents paid little attention to him, and he was reared by his maternal grandmother. After private tutoring, he entered Trinity Hall, Cambridge, in 1714, but left after a year, by which time, in his own words, he had become "an absolute pedant." A grand tour of the Continent followed, though most of his time was spent in Flanders. In 1715 he was made a gentleman of the bedchamber to the Prince of Wales, later George II. As a Whig, he sat in Parliament for St. Germains, Cornwall, when he was not yet old enough to vote, and began almost immediately to make a name for himself as an orator. With the diplomacy which was one of his salient characteristics, when dissension arose between the king and the prince, Stanhope (as he then was) removed himself to Paris for nearly two years. In 1722, back in England, he was elected to Parliament again for Lostwithiel, was defeated in 1723, and never again sat in the House of Commons.

From 1723 to 1725 he was captain of the gentleman-pensioners; then his long quarrel with Sir Robert Walpole, the prime minister, came to a head, and he was summarily dropped. The next year his father died and he succeeded to the earldom and to a seat in the House of Lords. In 1727 George I died and George II succeeded. For a while Chesterfield was on the best of terms with the king, though he had made a powerful enemy by siding with the king's mistress instead of with the queen. In 1728 he was privy councillor, in 1729 ambassador to The Hague, and in 1730 Lord Steward of the royal household, and was made a Knight of the Garter. He was sent back to The Hague, where in 1731 he signed the second treaty of Vienna. He resigned the ambassadorship in 1732 because of ill health, and the next year Walpole succeeded in having him dismissed as Lord Steward and in bringing about a final break between Chesterfield and the king. Chesterfield became leader of the opposition to Walpole and his group in the House of Lords, though it took him to 1742 to accomplish his enemy's downfall. The death of Queen Caroline helped to accomplish this, but George was still on bad terms with him.

In 1733 Chesterfield had married Petronilla von der Schulenberg, Countess of Walsingham, the illegitimate daughter of George I by the Duchess of Kendal—another cause of offense. It was purely a marriage of convenience; they lived next door to each other, and Lady Frances Shirley was openly Chesterfield's mistress. When the Duchess died and left £20,000 to her daughter (and hence to her son-in-law), the king prevented Chesterfield from receiving it. Nevertheless George was forced by practical politics in 1744 to appoint Chesterfield Lord Lieutenant of Ireland. After a brief return to The Hague, where he persuaded Holland to join the War of the Austrian Succession, he went to Dublin in 1745. He was there only eight months, but he fell in love with Ireland and was an extremely good governor; he fought for the poor and for the persecuted Irish Catholics, and kept Ireland untouched by the Scottish Rebellion. In 1746, though in very bad health, he was obliged to exchange the Lord Lieutenancy for office as Secretary of State for the Northern Department, a reconciliation with the king having finally been effected. Two years later, completely broken in health, he resigned. Increasing deafness was added to his other ailments; his last speech in the House of Lords was in 1755, his last politi-

A. Ramsay, 1765
PHILIP DORMER STANHOPE, 4TH EARL OF CHESTERFIELD

cal act the reconciliation of Pitt and Newcastle in 1757. Thereafter, very deaf and growing blind, he gave all of what strength he had left to literary pursuits and correspondence. Unfailingly cheerful, he remarked that he had been dead for two years but did not "choose to have it known"; and, unfailingly polite, his actual last words were an order to give a chair to a visiting friend.

The son to whom Chesterfield's famous letters were written was Philip Stanhope, his illegitimate child by a Mlle. du Bouchet, in Flanders. His godson, also Philip Stanhope, was a distant cousin whom he made his heir. Unfortunately neither boy ever developed the *savoir faire* and social grace which he enjoined on them, and his son grieved him by dying young and leaving a widow and two children of whom nobody had ever heard.

Chesterfield was far from the cynical monster he has been accused of being. Sir John Chester in Dickens' *Barnaby Rudge* is an unfair caricature, and even the famous letter by Samuel Johnson seems to have stemmed more from over-sensitivity on Johnson's part than from any deliberate offense. Actually, Chesterfield was affectionate and sincere in his private relationships, and he hated arrogance and insolence. But he was above all a man of the world, with a high regard for social success. It must be remembered that the letters both to his son and his godson were private, and not intended for publication. In personality he was more French than English, and his style has the clarity, precision, and lack of sentimentality of French prose. He was a connoisseur of art and an excellent critic, and nothing could exceed the ease, frankness, and wit of his celebrated letters, which have made "Chesterfieldian" a common adjective to describe polished manners.

PRINCIPAL WORKS: Letters to His Son on the Fine Art of Becoming a Man of the World and a Gentleman, 1774; Miscellaneous Works, 1777; Characters, 1778; Letters to his Godson (Earl of Carnarvon, ed.) 1890; Letters to Lord Huntingdon (A. F. Steuart, ed.) 1923; Private Correspondence of Chesterfield and Newcastle (R. Lodge, ed.) 1930; Some Unpublished Letters (S. L. Gulick, ed.) 1937.

ABOUT: Carnarvon, Earl of. Life in Letters to His Godson; Connely, W. The True Chesterfield; Coxon, R. Chesterfield and His Critics; Craig, W. H. Life of Lord Chesterfield; Ernst-Browning, W. Memoirs of the Life of Philip Dormer Stanhope, Fourth Earl of Chesterfield; Jaeger, M. Adventures in Living; More, P. E. Shelburne Essays; Sainte-Beuve, C. A. Profils Anglais; Shellabarger, S. Lord Chesterfield.

CHETTLE, HENRY (1560?-1607?), dramatist, miscellaneous writer, was the son of a London dyer, Robert Chettle. Very little is known of him beyond the few of his plays which have survived and a number of entries in the diary of Philip Henslowe, director of an Elizabethan theatrical company. These scant clues lead to, but never solve, the puzzle of Chettle's life and talent.

He is known to have worked as apprentice to a printer and stationer in 1577, and eleven years later he became a partner with William Haskins and John Danter in a printing firm. His name first appears as editor of Robert Greene's *Groatsworth of Wit*, a posthumous tract containing a supposed allusion to Shakespeare. In a later work of his own, *Kind Hart's Dream*, Chettle made an apology to persons Greene had attacked. It is not known when Chettle began to write for the theatre, but in 1598, Francis Meres, writing of the dramatists of his time, refers to him as "one of the best for comedy." Unfortunately, his comedies (except for one, *The Pleasant Comodie of Patient Grissill*, written in collaboration with Thomas Dekker and William Haughton) have not survived.

If it were not for the lucky chance which preserved Henslowe's diary, in which he recorded his payments to dramatists and listed their plays, we would know very little about the body of Chettle's work. Henslowe attributes some fifty plays to him, of which all but about twelve seem to have been collaborations. It is noted that he collaborated twice with Ben Jonson and frequently with Anthony Munday, with Dekker, Michael Drayton, John Day, and others. Of the plays attributed solely to him, only one was printed and survives in a badly mutilated text, *The Tragedy of Hoffmann; or a Revenge for a Father*.

Henslowe's diary gives also a few glimpses into Chettle's daily life, which probably was much of a pattern with that of the whole group of minor Elizabethan dramatists maintained in Henslowe's theatrical "stable." He was frequently in debt, depending on small advances from Henslowe, with an occasional extraordinary advance such as one listed to pay his expenses in Marshalsea prison, another to get his current play out of pawn. He seems frequently to have acted in the capacity of "play-doctor" (collaborator is the more polite term), as when he received ten shillings for "mending" the first part of a play by Anthony Munday.

Under the circumstances, it is extremely difficult to evaluate the work of Henry Chettle, and one can only wonder whether his true capacity may not be inadequately represented in the surviving work. The single tragedy, *Hoffmann*, demonstrates an intense power of creating tragic atmosphere along with an emotional and imaginative vehemence which make it at the very least a striking melodrama. Certainly the prose and verse pamphlet, *Englande's Mourning Garment*, written after the death of Elizabeth, displays a literary capacity deeper than that of any hack.

We do not know the exact date of Chettle's death, but in Dekker's *Knight's Conjuring*, written in 1607, he is portrayed as joining the poets in Elysium—Chaucer, Spenser, Marlowe and the rest—then "in comes Chettle sweating and blowing by reason of his fatness." Both by the company to which Dekker assigns him and by the humorous physical description, this tells as much perhaps of Chettle's talent and Chettle's person as anything else we know.

PRINCIPAL WORKS: *Plays*: The Death of Robert, Earle of Huntington (with Munday) 1601 (J. P. Collier, ed. Five Old Plays, 1828); The Pleasant Comodie of Patient Grissill (with T. Dekker, and W. Haughton) 1603 (J. P. Collier, ed. Shakespeare Society, 1841); The Tragedy of Hoffmann: or a Revenge for a Father, 1631 (R. Ackermann, ed. 1894); The Blind Begger of Bednal-Green (with J. Day) 1659 (W. Bang, ed. 1902). *Miscellaneous*: Kind Hart's Dreame, 1593 (C. M. Ingleby, ed. 1874); Piers Plainnes Seaven Yeres Prentisship, 1595; Englande's Mourning Garment: in Memorie of Elizabeth, 1603 (C. M. Ingleby, ed. 1874).

ABOUT: Henslowe, P. Henslowe's Diary; Ingleby, C. M. Shakespeare Allusion-books; Jenkins, H. The Life and Work of Henry Chettle.

CHILLINGWORTH, WILLIAM (1602-1644), theologian, has been called the most "conspicuous controversialist" of his age. One of the strongest influences of his youth was the friendship of his godfather, Laud, the zealous Archbishop of Canterbury.

Following his graduation from Trinity College, Oxford, Chillingworth entered into a series of debates, defending Protestantism against the arguments of a Jesuit, John Fisher. A man of little worldly knowledge but of incorruptible intellectual honesty, Chillingworth was convinced during the debates that his search for infallible authority could be satisfied by the Catholic dogma, and in 1630 he announced his conversion. Knowing the value of such a distinguished convert, but misjudging the maturity of his convictions, the Catholic Church sent him to the College of Douay to write an account of his conversion. The self-examination necessary to such a project, plus some persuasive letters from his godfather, caused him to change his mind once more. In 1634 he published a book detailing the steps which led to his re-conversion to Protestantism.

Although he did not rejoin the Anglican Church, and was attacked by Protestant extremists as well as by Catholics, Chillingworth wrote one of the most widely known defenses of Protestantism of his age. *The Religion of Protestants a Safe Way of Salvation* was written as a result of a public controversy between Edward Knott, a Jesuit, and Dr. Christopher Potter of Oxford. The complicated polemics and an undistinguished style did not prevent the work from having wide-spread influence long after Chillingworth's death. His thesis, the necessity of personal conviction and the right of free inquiry in religious matters, while attacked by the Puritans of his own day, was carried over into other fields of speculation; the eleventh edition of *The Religion of Protestants* was published as late as 1742, and the collected works almost a century later.

Chillingworth joined the Royalist army, became ill, was taken prisoner, and died in captivity in 1644. His death was probably hastened by the treatment accorded him by a Puritan clergyman at the prison.

PRINCIPAL WORKS: The Religion of Protestants a Safe Way of Salvation, 1637; Works (3 vols.) 1820, 1838.

ABOUT: Biographia Britannica; Tulloch, J. Rational Theology; Wood, A. à, Athenae Oxonienses.

CHURCHILL, CHARLES (February 1731-November 4, 1764), poet, author of political and social satires, was born at Westminster where his father was curate and lecturer for the parish of St. John's. He was educated for the ministry, attending the Westminster School, but entrance to Cambridge was denied him when the authorities (and, incidentally, his father) discovered he had acquired a wife at the age of eighteen. Although it was already apparent that young Churchill was temperamentally unsuited to the ministry, he followed the wishes of his father and was ordained in 1756, succeeding to the curateship of St. John's after his father's death. Unhappily married, with two small sons to support, he was now condemned "to pray and starve on £40 a year."

Success came to him very suddenly with the publication of a verse satire, the *Rosciad*, in 1761. This work, a merciless criticism of leading actors and actresses of the London stage, was published anonymously by the author to sell for one shilling a copy. Not only did it set the fashionable London world agog; it brought him no less than £1000 with which he was able to pay his debts and settle an allowance on his wife from whom he had already separated. At the height of the furore, Churchill advertised his authorship (which had been attributed by gossip to his friend, Robert Lloyd) and overnight became a literary figure to be reckoned with. Another pamphlet, the *Apology*, continued the attack and brought a conciliatory letter from David Garrick.

At this stage of his career, the theatre and the ale-house undoubtedly saw more of him than did his parishioners. He went about town in a blue coat bedecked with metal buttons and gold lace, and became the constant companion of several of the most notorious rakes of London. It seems hardly strange then that protest from his parishioners forced him to resign as curate of St. John's. To his credit, let it be said that Churchill never misjudged his own talents; as a clergyman he had always known his limitations.

In December 1761 he published a poem, "Night," addressed to his friend, Robert Lloyd, in which he defended his way of life. Smollett's *Critical Review* remarked of it, "This Night, like many others at this time of year, is very cold, long, dark and dirty." It was through this poem, however, that he met John Wilkes, the political agitator and reformer, who became his friend and idol. Like Churchill, Wilkes was a thoroughgoing rake, and the two of them, together with Sir Francis Dashwood and others, engaged in a series of scandalous escapades, most of them connected with a blasphemous secret fraternity known as the Hell Fire Club or the Medmenham Monks.

More seriously, his association with Wilkes turned his gift for satire to political ends. He became Wilkes' ally in the publication of the *North Briton*, a furious political sheet directed against the Tories, of which Churchill probably wrote at least half. Most of his sharpest political satire was published in the *North Briton*. When Wilkes was arrested under a general warrant issued over the famous "No. 45" copy of the paper, Churchill was enabled to escape arrest by a quick-witted warning from his friend. Wilkes was driven out of England and it was on a visit to Boulogne where Wilkes lived for a time in exile that Churchill died of a fever when he was only thirty-three.

Churchill's unfailing loyalty to his friends, Lloyd and Wilkes, is one of his most likable characteristics. When Lloyd was beggared and in prison, Churchill supported him. When Hogarth printed a wicked caricature of Wilkes, Churchill retaliated with a savage satire, "The Epistle to William Hogarth." It was Hogarth, by the way, who dubbed Churchill with a name which goes far to describe him—"The Bruiser"— elephantine in size and a fighter who recognized no holds as barred.

His work, so powerful in his own time, has undergone almost a total eclipse largely because of its topical character. There is no doubt, however, that truculent and loud as Churchill often could be, a genuine satiric gift, together with an enormous talent for invective, found full expression in his verse. Even his critics, among them Dr. Samuel Johnson, had to admire his force and the fertility of his mind. "To be sure," says the acid Dr. Johnson, "he is a tree that cannot produce good fruit, he only bears crabs. But, Sir, a tree that produces a great many crabs is better than a tree which produces only a few."

PRINCIPAL WORKS: The Rosciad, 1761; The Apology, 1761 (R. W. Lowe, ed. with The Rosciad, 1891); Night, an Epistle to Robert Lloyd, 1761; The Ghost, 1762-63; The Conference, 1763; The Author, 1763; An Epistle to William Hogarth, 1763; The Prophecy of Famine, a Scots Pastoral, 1763; The Duellist, 1764; The Candidate, 1764; Gotham, 1764; Independence, 1764; The Times, 1764; The Farewell, 1764; Collected Poems, 1763-65; The Poetical Works of Charles Churchill with an Authentic Account of his Life by W. Tooke, 1804; Poems (E. J. Laver, ed.) 1933.

ABOUT: Chancellor, R. B. The Hell Fire Club; Fitzgerald, P. The Life and Times of John Wilkes; Hannay, J. Satire and Satirists; Sargent, A. J. English Satirical Writers since 1500; Tooke, W. Memoir, *in* Works (1804 ed.); Walker, H. English Satire and Satirists.

J. S. C. Schaak

CHARLES CHURCHILL

CHURCHYARD, THOMAS (1520?-April 1604), poet, miscellaneous writer, was born near Shrewsbury, the son of a farmer. He became a professional soldier about 1541, and served, for part of the time under Emperor Charles V, in Scotland (where he was imprisoned), Ireland, the Netherlands, and France (where again he was taken prisoner and apparently escaped by breaking his parole). He was more or less attached to the household of Henry Howard, Earl of Surrey, and with this influence returned to England to try in vain to secure some sort of court position. The best he got was an opportunity to write pageants for Elizabeth's tours in 1574 and 1578—and then a passage in *Churchyard's Choise*, published that year, so offended the queen that he thought it wise to retire to Scotland for three years. Finally, in 1593, when he was over seventy, Elizabeth awarded him a small pension.

Though the exact date of his birth is not known, Churchyard certainly lived, and continued to write, to a good old age. Spenser, in *Colin Clout's Come Home Again*, spoke of him as "old Palaemon that had sung so long until quite hoarse he grew." His writing career extended from the reign of Edward VI, who ascended the throne in 1547, to that of James I, who ascended in 1603. His style did not change, so that finally he became a sort of leftover from the school of Wyatt and Surrey^{qqv}. Yet Nashe^{qv}, who was his close friend in spite of one serious quarrel, was able sincerely to speak of "Churchyard's aged Muse that may well be grandmother to our grandiloquentist poets at this present."

Churchyard's books are rare, and some of the earlier ones (e.g., the first edition of *The Myrrour of Man*) entirely lost. Most of what we know about him comes from his own autobiographical passages, which are full of complaints of his ill fortune. From them we learn that he was married to "a sober wife from countrie soile," but no more about his private history. Though his education is obscure (he may possibly have spent some time at Oxford), he knew enough Latin to translate three books of Ovid's *Tristia* and to contemplate, but not finish, a translation of Pliny. He was the author as well of many tracts and broadsides, and much of his work appeared in Tottell's *Miscellany* (1557). His principal prose work (though interspersed with verse) is *The Worthiness of Wales,* an anticipation of Drayton ^{qv} as an antiquarian survey of that country.

As a poet, Churchyard was an extreme eccentric, in spelling and punctuation as well as in verse style, given to forced alliteration and exaggerated figures of speech, with a sort of specious glitter concealing the basic poverty of his talent. At his best he was an accomplished versifier, and he had a gift for narrative displayed in the accounts of his own military experiences. Probably the best of his work is the tragedy, *Shore's Wife,* which first appeared in the 1563 edition of *A Mirror for Magistrates.*

PRINCIPAL WORKS: Shore's Wife, 1653; Churchyardes Chippes, 1575; A Lamentable and Pitifull Description of the Wofull Warres in Flaunders, 1578; Churchyard's Choise (Generall Rehearsal of Warres) 1578; The Miserie of Flaunders, 1579; A Light Bondell of Livly Discourses Called Churchyardes Charge, 1580; The Worthines of Wales, 1587; A Sparke of Friendship and Warme Goodwill...to Sir Walter Raleigh, 1588; A Handeful of Gladsome Verses, 1592; Churchyardes Challenge, 1593; The Myrrour of Man, and Manners of Men, 1594; A Praise of Poetrie, 1595; A Musicall Consort of Heavenly Harmonie...Called Churchyard's Charitie, 1595; The Fortunate Farewel to...the Earle of Essex, 1599; Churchyards Good Will, 1604; The Tragedy of Wolsey (H. Morley, ed.) 1885.

ABOUT: Adnitt, H. W. Thomas Churchyard; Churchyard, T. Churchyardes Chippes (Tragicall Discourse of the Unhappy Man's Life); Cranstoun, J. Satirical Poems of the Time of the Reformation; Wood, A. à, Athenae Oxonienses.

CIBBER, COLLEY (November 16, 1671-December 12, 1757), actor, playwright, poet laureate, was born in London, the son of Caius Gabriel Cibber or Cibert, a Danish sculptor, and of Jane Colley, his second wife, an Englishwoman. He was educated at the Free School, Grantham, Lincolnshire, from 1682 to 1687. Failing to secure entrance to Winchester, he joined his father at Nottingham, where he became a volunteer under the Earl of Devonshire at the time of the landing in England of William of Orange and the deposition of James II. In the hope of patronage from the Earl, the boy went back to London. There without waiting for a post he haunted the Theatre Royal (Drury Lane) until he was taken on (as "Master Colley")—without a salary for six months. (His father made him a small allowance.)

L. F. Roubillac (?)

COLLEY CIBBER

He met with no success until 1692, since he essayed heroic parts unsuited to his weedy blondness and his shrill voice. In 1695 the great actor Betterton opened the "new theatre" in Lincoln's Inn Fields and took Cibber with his company. Here he wrote his first play, chiefly for himself to act in. Gradually he became famous for his acting in eccentric character parts.

He was, however, extremely hard up, since in 1694 he had married (a Miss Shore) and children came yearly, most of them to die in infancy. In 1706 he joined the Haymarket company, which was combined with Drury Lane two years later; Cibber became part owner. Financial difficulties led to closing of the theatre the next year, but Cibber as manager pulled it out of the red. One of the licensees was Sir Richard Steele, and after his death a lawsuit again threatened the theatre, but was won by Cibber and his associates. Steele, Swift, and Walpole were Cibber's friends; Dr. Johnson, Fielding, and above all Pope were his enemies. His chief cause of offense was *The Non Juror*, which insulted Catholics and Jacobites alike—Cibber was a stout Whig and Hanoverian.

His political reward came in gifts from the king and in appointment as poet laureate in 1730. It was a ridiculous choice; Cibber was a clever playwright and something of

a comic genius, but a most indifferent poet. Pope substituted his name for Theobald's as "hero" of *The Dunciad*, thus defeating his own purpose, since whatever else Cibber was he was never dull.

Two indignant letters to Pope were published by Cibber, but the great result of the feud was the invaluable *Apology* which is one of the finest works of dramatic history and criticism in English.

The best of Cibber's plays is *She Would and She Would Not*. All of his comedies, as Congreve remarked, give the impression of wit without actually being witty. What they are is brisk and smart. He was a born actor, with an innate sense of "good theatre," and his plays were meant to be acted, not read. He had no scruples in "altering" Shakespeare for his purposes—in fact, his "alteration" of *Richard III* was the regular acting version to 1821. Impudent, vain, and brassily self-confident, Cibber nevertheless was a likable creature, good humored, without envy or jealousy of others, and completely frank about himself.

Of his "dozen or so" children—he himself never seems to be sure of the number —one son became an actor and playwright, and married a celebrated actress; one daughter was herself an actress and a minor novelist. Cibber left the stage in 1733, but reappeared occasionally, the last time in 1754, at the age of seventy-four. He died suddenly of heart disease at eighty-six, and is buried in the British and Foreign Sailors' Church in London, for which his father (also buried there) had done the sculptural decorations.

PRINCIPAL WORKS: Love's Last Shift, 1696; Woman's Wit, 1697; Xerxes (tragedy) 1699; Love Makes a Man, 1701; She Would and She Would Not, 1702; The Careless Husband, 1704; Perolla and Izadora (tragedy) 1706; The Lady's Last Stake, 1708; The Rival Fools, 1709; The Non Juror (adaptation of Molière's Tartuffe) 1718; Ximena (tragedy) 1719; Dramatic Works, 1721; The Refusal, 1721; The Rival Queens (burlesque on play of same name by Nathaniel Lee) 1729; Love in a Riddle (pastoral) 1729; The School-Boy, 1730?; Venus and Adonis and Myrtillo, 1736; An Apology for the Life of Mr. Colley Cibber, Comedian,...With an Historical View of the Theater during His Own Time, 1740; The Temple of Dullness (opera) 1745; The Lady's Lecture, 1748; Complete Dramatic Works, 1760.

ABOUT: Barker, R. H. Mr. Cibber of Drury Lane; Cibber, C. Apology; D'Israeli, I. The Calamities and Quarrels of Authors; Lowe, R. H. Bibliographical Account of English Theatrical Literature.

CLARENDON, Lord EDWARD HYDE (February 18, 1609-December 9, 1674), historian, autobiographer, was born in Dinton, Wiltshire, the son of Henry Hyde and Mary Langford. In 1622 he entered Magdalen Hall, Oxford (B.A. 1626) and in 1625 was entered in the Middle Temple, being called to the bar in 1633—though he had spent a good part of his time in the literary circle of Ben Jonson. In 1629 he married Anne Ayliffe, who died in six months, and in 1634 Frances Aylesbury, by whom he had three sons and a daughter. (The daughter married the Duke of York and thus became the grandmother of Queen Mary II and Queen Anne.) Both his wives had powerful family connections, and Hyde, as he then was, rose rapidly in his profession. In 1634 he became keeper of the writs and rolls of common pleas, and in 1640 was a Member of the Short Parliament for Wootton Bassett, and of the following Long Parliament for Saltash.

An adherent of the popular party until 1641, when its Puritanism alienated him, Clarendon throughout was a strong influence on Charles I for legality and constitutionalism, but when his advice went unheeded and the civil war broke out, he remained loyal to the king. He was expelled from Parliament in 1642, and spent the next three years in Oxford to be near Charles. In 1643 he was knighted, and became Chancellor of the Exchequer and a privy councillor. He accompanied the Prince of Wales to Bristol, Scilly, and Jersey (where he lived until 1648), then joined the king on the Continent until the Restoration. For a year he was Charles' "ambassador" in Spain, and was named Lord Chancellor in 1658.

In 1660 he was made Baron Hyde of Hyndon, in 1661 Viscount Cornbury and first Earl of Clarendon. He was still Lord High Chancellor and became Chancellor of Oxford University and speaker of the House of Lords. He was one of the eight Lords Proprietor of Carolina, and was concerned also with the settling of New England.

In the course of his career Clarendon had made bitter enemies on all sides—Roman Catholics, Puritans, the queen, the king's mistresses—and Charles himself, always fickle, grew tired of Clarendon's "fixed legal mind" and unwelcome advice, and threw him to the dogs. In 1667 he was accused of treason and banished. He spent the last seven years of his life in exile in France, deprived of citizenship and estates, forbidden for much of the time to see his family, physically attacked on one occasion, and receiving not even answers to his pleas to the king. He had begun his *History of the Rebellion* in Jersey; now, without his notes or papers, he finished the work and combined it with an autobiography and vindication of his life. The result is a kind of patchwork of history in the grand style and acute and vivid narrative. The "characters" incorporated in the history are among the best of their kind. The work was published piecemeal, which adds to its confusion. Clarendon meant it primarily as a source book, and in that capacity it is extremely valuable. With all its defects, it is the work of a great historical writer, who was a part of all of which he wrote, and who possessed (together with indiscretion and lack of tact) political ability, a broad and lucid view of world affairs, and a fine mastery of English prose. He was often wrong-headed, but he was certainly no traitor.

Clarendon died in exile in Rouen, of gout —he was an enormously obese man. His

G. Soest

EDWARD HYDE, 1ST EARL OF CLARENDON

body was brought back to England and buried in Westminster Abbey.

PRINCIPAL WORKS: A Full Answer to an Infamous and Traitorous Pamphlet, 1648; Essays Divine and Moral, 1668; A Brief View of the Errors in Mr. Hobbes' "Leviathan," 1676; The History of the Rebellion and Civil Wars in England, together with an Historical View of the Affairs of Ireland, 1702-04; The Lord Clarendon's History Compleated, 1717; An Appendix to the History, 1724; The History of the Rebellion in Ireland, 1719; Miscellaneous Works (Contemplations and Reflections upon the Psalms of David, A Vindication of Myself from the Charge of High Treason, etc.) 1751; The Life of Edward, Earl of Clarendon, being a Continuation of the History of the Rebellion, 1759; State Papers Collected by Edward Earl of Clarendon, 1767-86; Essays Moral and Entertaining on the Various Passions and Faculties of the Human Mind, 1815.

ABOUT: Boyle, G. D. Characters and Episodes of the Great Rebellion; Clarendon, E. H. Life; Craik, H. The Life of Edward, Earl of Clarendon, Lord High Chancellor of England; Firth, C. H. Edward, Earl of Clarendon, as Statesman, Historian, and Chancellor of the University; Kaye, P. L. English Colonial Administration under Lord Clarendon; Lister, T. H. Life and Administration of Edward, the Earl of Clarendon; Stephen, J. F. Horae Sabbataci; Wormald, B. H. G. Clarendon: Politics, History and Religion, 1640-1660.

CLARKE, SAMUEL (October 11, 1675-May 17, 1729), metaphysical writer, was educated at Caius College, Cambridge. Recognizing the value of Newton's theories before they were current, he translated a French work to replace the Cartesian textbooks being used in the college, so annotating and editing the new book that it served as an introduction to the works of Newton. Clarke took holy orders, and served successively as chaplain to the Bishop of Norwich, rector of Drayton, chaplain to Queen Anne, and rector of St. James, Westminster. He married and had seven children.

He was considered England's foremost metaphysician following the death of Locke, and engaged in innumerable philosophical controversies. Deists accused him of vestigial orthodoxies of phrase and idea; orthodox clerics accused him of hidden deism. His most notable work, a treatise on the trinity, brought formal charges of Arianism from the Convocation, which were eventually dropped. His Boyle Lectures on *The Being and Attributes of God* were, however, generally accepted as an admirably clear and forceful, if not original, work.

Caroline, the Princess of Wales, held a weekly interview with Clarke to which other distinguished philosophers and scientists were often invited, including Berkeley when he visited London. At Caroline's request, Clarke carried on an extensive discussion by correspondence with Leibnitz, which was published after Leibnitz' death. Clarke was a close friend of Newton.

His ethical doctrine, his most original and important contribution, was based on a concept of moral values and relations as immutable and objective as the physical relations of the Newtonian universe. These were known by the application of reason, recognized by their "fitness and suitability." This vagueness of definition led to radically different interpretations of his ideas by his followers.

In addition to his theological and philosophical writings, Clarke wrote a paraphrase of the Gospels, edited Caesar's *Commentaries* and Homer's *Iliad*, and published several scientific theses, the last one being *On the Proportion of Force to Velocity in Bodies in Motion*.

An exceedingly polite and dignified man in public, Clarke liked to relax when he was with his children and friends, who knew him as affable and playful, and fond of cards and other games.

PRINCIPAL WORKS: A Discourse Concerning the Being and Attributes of God; Three Practical Essays on Baptism, Confirmation and Repentance, 1699; Paraphrase of the Gospels, 1701; Caesar's Commentaries, 1712; The Scripture Doctrine of the Trinity, 1712; Homer's Iliad, 1729.

ABOUT: Biographia Britannica; Hoadley, B. Works; Nichols, J. Literary Anecdoes; Smith-Dampier, J. L. East Anglian Worthies.

CLEVELAND, JOHN (June 1613-April 29, 1658), poet, satirist, was born at Loughborough, Leicestershire. His father, a curate of very modest means, was Thomas Cleveland (originally spelt Cleiveland from the former residence of the family in Yorkshire). Although he was educated under the Puritan, Richard Vynes, at Hinckley School, he seems to have been Royalist in his sympathies from the time he entered Christ's College, Cambridge, where he took a B.A. degree in 1631. Elected to a fellowship at St. John's, he lived at Cambridge for nine years, "the delight and ornament of St. John's society." Cleveland became known as one of the group of Cavalier poets including Thomas Carewe, Sir John Suckling, Richard Lovelace and others, but he was

from the beginning unlike the other Royalist poets in that his gift was primarily satiric. Saintsbury has said of him, "he was a journalist of the acutest type in verse—a political leader-writer."

An oration addressed to Charles I on the occasion of a visit to Cambridge pleased the king, and when the victory of the Puritan party in 1643 forced Cleveland to leave Oxford, he was well received by Charles, then at the head of the Royalist army in Newark. Formally deprived of his Cambridge fellowship because of Royalist loyalties, he was made judge-advocate in the garrison and played his part in the defense of the town until 1646 when Charles ordered a surrender. Described as high-spirited, inexhaustible in jests and playful sarcasms, Cleveland became enormously popular with his fellows in the Royalist army. That his loyalty ran as deep as his wit is proven by his most famous poem, *The Rebel Scot*, which he wrote when the Scots surrendered the king to Parliament.

The remaining years of the poet's life were spent in wandering over the countryside, depending on the hospitality of impoverished cavaliers for his bread and lodging, writing when and where he could. In 1655 he was imprisoned as a royalist and spent three months in the Yarmouth gaol, winning his release by a dignified petition to Cromwell whom he had opposed as a candidate for Parliament at Cambridge thirteen years before. His last two years are shadowed in obscurity. He is known only to have lived in London, spending much of his time with Samuel Butler (the author of *Hudibras*) at Gray's Inn, where he died before he was forty-five.

In spite of the fact that there is little detail known of his life, he was a celebrated poet of his period, as evidenced by the numerous editions of his works. Unfortunately, there exists a good deal of confusion in the bibliography of his poems and the work which may be surely attributed to him does not exceed two or three thousand lines. In this comparatively small body of verse, we find him an imperfect poet of extraordinary gifts. To a modern reader, the extravagant metaphysical conceit, the packed allusions, and the rapid comment on contemporary issues make Cleveland's poems difficult to follow, although the invective energy of his satire is, to a limited extent, still perceptible. George Saintsbury has written, "The force and fire are still admirable when realized, but the smoke of the explosion has solidified itself, as it were, and obscures both."

PRINCIPAL WORKS: The Character of a London Diurnal with Severall Select Poems, 1647; The Character of a Moderate Intelligencer, with Some Select Poems, by J. C., 1647; Poems by J. C. with additions, 1651; J. Cleaveland Revived: Poems, Orations, Epistles, and Other of His Genuine Incomparable Pieces, 1659; Clievelandi Vindiciae; or, Clieveland's Genuine Poems, Orations, Epistles, &c. Purged from the Many False & Spurious Ones, 1677; The Poems of John Cleveland (J. M. Berdan, ed.) 1903.

ABOUT: Berdan, J. M. Biographical introduction *in* Poems (1903 ed.); Percy, T. Life, *in* Biographia Britannica (A. Kippis, ed.).

COCKBURN, Mrs. ALICIA or ALISON

(October 8, 1713-November 22, 1794), poet, achieved fame solely as the author of one short ballad, although she wrote poetry throughout her long life.

She was born in Fairnalee, Selkirkshire, Scotland, daughter of Robert Rutherford. The romantically mournful words of "I've seen the smiling of Fortune beguiling" were actually written on the occasion of a depression which bankrupted a number of the gentry of Selkirkshire. The words are set to the music of "Flowers of the Forest," one of the loveliest of ancient Scottish border ballads. The legend is that Mrs. Cock-

After I. Fuller

JOHN CLEVELAND

burn learned the melody from a gentleman who had heard it played on a shepherd's pipe in a lonely glen. Her words, not published until 1765, were written before 1731. A later version, by Jean Elliot, has rivalled the earlier one in popularity.

In 1731 Alison Rutherford married Patrick Cockburn, an advocate, and moved to Edinburgh, where she became a leader of the social life of the city. Her wit and charm attracted many of the leading literary figures of Scotland to her salon, among them David Hume, John Horne and Lord Monboddo. She knew Robert Burns, who expressed admiration for her ballad.

An intimate friend and relative of the mother of Sir Walter Scott, she was a favorite with the author from his childhood. He has written of her talent for conversation, her extensive and lively correspondence, and her long-lived beauty, and adds that she reminded him rather of the French intellectual woman than the English. She was said to resemble Queen Elizabeth in appearance, and had original ideas of dress which did not conform to the prevailing fashions.

Scott, who, at the age of six, liked her "because she is a virtuoso, like myself," wrote that up to her death at over eighty she retained her auburn hair, her wit, and her circle of admiring friends. She was predeceased by her husband, in 1753, and by her only son in 1780.

PRINCIPAL WORKS: "I've seen the smiling," *in* The Lark, 1765; three letters in "Letters of Eminent Persons addressed to David Hume" (J. H. Burton, ed.) 1849; Letters and Memorials with notes by T. C. Brown, 1900.

ABOUT: Johnson, J. Scots Musical Museum; Lockhart, J. G. Life of Scott; Scott, Sir W. Minstrelsy of the Scottish Border.

COCKER, EDWARD (1631-1675), teacher and author of a treatise on arithmetic, was probably born in Northamptonshire. He taught calligraphy and arithmetic, establishing a school of his own in Northamptonshire during the middle sixties, and later one in Southwerk. He was an extremely erudite scholar, amassing an extensive collection of books and manuscripts in many languages. Pepys mentions him as an ingenious and well-read man, and a pleasant companion.

Of his sudden death at the age of forty-four a street ballad current a few years later, entitled *Cocker's Farewell to Brandy,* says,

> Here lies one dead, by Brandy's mighty power,
> Who the last quarter of the last flown hour
> As to his health and strength, was sound and well.

Cocker's closest friend, John Hawkins, took over the school at Southwerk after his friend's untimely death, and also took on the stewardship of Cocker's writings. A few poems, numerous works on calligraphy, and several arithmetic textbooks had been published during Cocker's lifetime, but his most important work, *Cocker's Arithmetic,* was published posthumously in 1678 by Hawkins. Its authenticity has been questioned, but an address included in the first edition by John Collins, one of the most famous mathematicians of the time, attests to Cocker's authorship. The number of its English, Scottish and Irish editions probably reached 112.

Both Cocker and Hawkins are buried in St. George's Church, Southwerk, near the site of their school.

PRINCIPAL WORK: Arithmetic, 1678.

ABOUT: Evelyn, J. Sculptura; Pepys, S. Diary; Massey, W. Origin of Letters.

COKE, Sir EDWARD (February 1, 1552- September 3, 1634), writer on law, was born in Mileham, Norfolk, the only son in a family of eight. His father was a "gentleman of Lincoln's Inn." He was educated at Norwich Grammar School and was an M.A. of Trinity College, Cambridge. In 1572 he was entered at the Inner Temple, and called to the bar in 1578. Not only was this an unusually short period, but the next year he became Reader of Lyon's Inn, a post usually reserved for barristers of at least ten years' experience. In 1582 he married Bridget Paston, an heiress, who died in 1598, leaving several children.

In 1589 Coke was Member of Parliament for Aldeburgh, in 1592 Speaker of the House of Commons, solicitor general, and recorder of London, in 1593 and 1594 attorney general. It was in the course of this professional progress that he first crossed paths with his greatest enemy, Francis Bacon. In 1598 a seal was set to their enmity by his marriage to Lady Elizabeth Hatton, whom Bacon had also courted. The marriage, being private, was considered irregular and he was prosecuted but absolved;

C. Janssen Van Ceulen, 1608
SIR EDWARD COKE

it also turned out to be most unhappy, and his wife was the nemesis of his later career.

In 1606 Coke became Chief Justice of Common Pleas; his prosecution of Essex and Raleigh was notorious for its rancor and brutality. Coke was a just judge, but a savage one. By Bacon's connivance, in order to get him out of the way to a more dignified but less lucrative and powerful office, in 1613 Coke was named chief justice of the King's Bench—he was the first to call himself Lord Chief Justice. By this time he had made plenty of enemies besides Bacon, among them James I, who was angered by Coke's rigid legalism and insistence on the supremacy of the common law. In 1616 charges were brought against him of interference with the chancellory and disrespect to the king, and he was removed from office. But by 1617 he was again a privy councillor, was back in Parliament in 1620, and was among the prosecutors when Bacon's downfall came. In 1622 Coke was again in trouble with James, and even spent nine months in the Tower, but he was acquitted and returned to Parliament. There, affiliating himself with the popular party, he harassed Charles I and his doctrine of absolute monarchy, but he was too formidable and too well entrenched for the king to suppress—though of course his days of public office were over. He retired finally and spent his last years at his famous estate in Stoke

Pogis, where he died. After his death the king seized his papers and kept them for seven years; his will was permanently lost.

Coke was the greatest advocate of the common law of England, the champion of civil as against equity law. He was far from accurate historically, and he was not above twisting fact to suit his views, but he adapted the medieval common law to the uses of the modern state and recast it in intelligible form. His work is the very basis of English and American law today. Together with his own commentaries on Sir Thomas Littleton, and Blackstone's *Commentaries*, his *Institutes* are the Bible of Anglo-Saxon legal procedure. Primarily he was not so much a legal historian as a legal antiquary. Overbearing, narrow, bitter-tongued, obstinate, he was not an amiable person, but he was an utterly single-minded advocate of the people's rights in the courts.

His name was pronounced "Cook."

PRINCIPAL WORKS: Reports, 1600-15; A Book of Entries, 1614; Commentaries on Littleton, 1628; Institutes, 1628-44; The Compleat Copyholder, 1630; A Little Treatise of Bail and Mainprize, 1635 .

ABOUT: James, C. W. Chief Justice Coke; Johnson, C. W. Life of Sir Edward Coke; Lyon, W. H. Edward Coke, Oracle of the Law; Smith-Dampier, J. L. East Anglian Worthies; Woolrych, H. W. The Life of Sir Edward Coke.

COLLINS, WILLIAM (December 25, 1721-June 12, 1759), poet, was born in Chichester, the son of a prosperous hatter who had been once been mayor of the town. In 1733 he entered Winchester College, a precocious boy who was already writing poetry. The next year his father died. In that same year the boy published his first volume, *The Royal Nuptials*, no copy of which remains. In 1740 he proceeded to Queen's College, Oxford, but the next year won a demyship at Magdalene College. A rebellious and undisciplined student, he yet secured his B.A. in 1743. Already he was in debt and had some name for dissipation. His mother died and he inherited a small estate, but it was soon lost. An uncle, an army colonel, decided he was "too indolent" for the army, and suggested the Church. He was promised the reversion of a curacy, but he did not take holy orders. Instead, he went to London, where he soon became part of the literary life; he met Dr. Johnson and the man who became his close friend, James Thomson,

J. Flaxman

WILLIAM COLLINS

and Joseph Warton, a friend from Winchester days. His *Persian Eclogues*, which later became extremely popular, sold badly, and Collins burnt the unsold copies. He spent his days persuading booksellers to advance him money on literary projects that were never undertaken—a translation of Aristotle's *Poetics*, a history of the revival of learning. He lived with duns and bailiffs at his door. Then Colonel Martin died in 1749 and left him £2000; he repaid all the advances and all his debts and returned to Chichester.

That his supposed "indolence" and his indecision and irresponsibility had deep roots soon became apparent. His mind began to fail. He grew not so much insane as prematurely senile. In a vain effort to cure himself he traveled in France; for a while he was in a madhouse in Oxford. Soon he was almost forgotten and his former friends thought him dead, if they thought of him at all, though Goldsmith in 1759 reported that Collins was "still alive, happy if insensible of our neglect." Soon after that he was really dead.

Yet until his mind gave way completely —his last, posthumously published ode was written in 1750—William Collins was writing poetry of grave lyric beauty, sharing with Thomas Gray *qv* the distinction of being the greatest English lyrist of the eighteenth century. His contemporaries admired his Ori-

ental fantasies, which were written in the fashionable style of the time; they thought little of his *Odes*, the best of which—*To Evening, To Music, To Liberty, The Passions, Ode Written in 1746* ("How sleep the brave")—are immortal.

It is not strange that Collins was a very uneven writer, ranging from the status of a poetaster to that of a true poet. What was imitatively of his age was bad, what came from his own spirit was good. In a greater age he would have been a greater poet, in the little time allowed him. At his best he has quiet distinction and great beauty. Though he wrote often in heroic couplets, he represented the Romantic revolt from Pope and the Classicists. Gray said of him that he had "little invention, very poetical choice of expression, a good ear." He was no mean scholar, and had a gift for languages, being fluent in French, Spanish, and Italian, as well as in Latin and Greek. He was a sweet-natured, amiable, charming man with an inherent weakness of will and energy, doomed to early mental decay. The portrait which appears here is from a tablet by Flaxman erected to Collins' memory in the cathedral at Chichester in 1795.

PRINCIPAL WORKS: Persian Eclogues and Odes, 1742 (as Oriental Eclogues, 1757); Verses to Sir Thomas Hanmer on His Edition of Shakespeare, 1743; Odes on Several Descriptive and Allegorical Subjects, 1747; An Ode Occasioned by the Death of Mr. Thomson, 1749; Poetical Works (J. Langhorne, ed.) 1765; An Ode on the Popular Superstitions of the Highlands Considered as the Subject of Poetry, 1788.

ABOUT: Brydges, E. and Nicolas, H. Memoirs, in 1830 ed. Poetical Works; Garrod, H. W. The Poetry of Collins; Johnson, S. Lives of the Poets; Langhorne, J. Memoir, in 1765 ed. Poetical Works; Thomas, M. Life of William Collins; Williams, I. A. Seven 18th Century Bibliographies.

COLMAN, GEORGE ("the Elder") (April 1732-August 14, 1794), dramatist, was born in Florence where his father, Francis Colman, was an envoy at the court of the Grand Duke of Tuscany. His mother was Mary Gumley, the sister of Mrs. Pulteney, afterwards Lady Bath. On the death of his father, the boy was educated by William Pulteney (Lord Bath), who sent him first to Westminster School and later to Christ Church, Oxford. At Oxford he began to write poetry and miscellaneous pieces and with his friend, Bonnell Thornton, the parodist, founded a newspaper, *The Connoisseur*.

Taking his B.A. degree in 1755 and an M.A. three years later, young Colman was prepared to enter a law career following the wishes of Lord Bath, but his interests were already exclusively literary.

Becoming acquainted with David Garrick, Colman turned to the dramatic medium and in 1760 his first play was produced, *Polly Honeycomb,* a comedy mocking the sentimental novel of the period. A year later he achieved fame with *The Jealous Wife,* founded in part on Fielding's *Tom Jones,* and one of the earliest examples of the successful dramatization of a novel. This play, midst the prevailing sentimentality of the period, maintained something of an earlier and more genuine comic spirit, foreshadowing Sheridan's masterpieces. It became one of the most popular comedies of the time and brought its author independent means, further augmented by an inheritance from Lord Bath three years later. A third play, *The Clandestine Marriage,* was written in collaboration with Garrick and for ingenuity and full comic brilliance is perhaps the best of all his plays.

Paralleling his career as author and producer of popular plays, Colman achieved a reputation in a more scholarly field with his metrical translation of Terence and of Horace's *Art of Poetry.* Meanwhile he had bought a share in the Covent Garden Theatre, of which he was acting manager for

seven years, producing many plays of his own, several adaptations of Shakespeare, and the first plays of Oliver Goldsmith. Through his theatrical associations he made a connection with an actress, Miss Ford, whom he later married and who was the mother of George Colman, "the Younger," also a dramatist.

In 1774 he sold his share in the Covent Garden Theatre and bought the old Haymarket where he continued to produce both original plays and his many adaptations from the works of other dramatists. In 1785 he suffered a stroke which affected his mind, and four years later was confined at Paddington, where he died at the age of sixty-two.

A complete collection of Colman's plays has never been made and many of those produced were never printed. That he was a considerable figure in the literary and theatrical world of the later eighteenth century is not to be doubted; that he was overestimated in his own time is certainly to be suspected. One of his admirers, Lord Byron, wrote in his memoirs, "Let me begin the evening with Sheridan and finish it with Colman"—an order that might better be reversed.

PRINTIPAL WORKS: *Original Plays* (dates of production): Polly Honeycomb. A Dramatick Novel, 1760; The Jealous Wife, 1761; The Musical Lady, 1762; The Deuce is in Him, 1763; The Clandestine Marriage (with David Garrick) 1766; The English Merchant, 1767; The Man of Business, 1774; New Brooms!, 1776; The Dramatick Works of George Colman (published) 1777; Ut Pictura Poesis! or The Enraged Musician, 1789. *Miscellaneous:* Critical Reflections on the Old English Dramatick Writers, 1761; The Comedies of Terence Translated into Familiar Blank Verse, 1765; The Works of Beaumont and Fletcher (ed.) 1778; Q. Horatii Flacci Epistola de Arte Poetica, 1783; Prose on Several Occasions: Accompanied by Some Pieces in Verse, 1787.

ABOUT: Page, E. R. George Colman the Elder, 1732-1794; Peake, R. B. Memoirs of the Colman Family; Posthumous Letters addressed to Francis Colman and George Colman, the elder (G. Colman, [the younger] ed.).

After Sir J. Reynolds

GEORGE COLMAN

CONGREVE, WILLIAM (February 1670-January 19, 1729), dramatist, was born at Bardsley, near Leeds, the son of William Congreve, an army officer, who was soon after stationed in Ireland. The boy went to school in Kilkenny, where he formed a lifelong friendship with Swift, and then went to Trinity College, Dublin. He was entered at the Middle Temple in 1691, but soon aban-

115

doned the law for literature, producing a very jejune novel. He was catapulted into fame at twenty-three with his first comedy, *The Old Bachelor,* which was an immediate hit. Betterton and Mrs. Bracegirdle acted the principal parts, and Dryden praised it enthusiastically—the first example of the almost abject admiration felt for Congreve by the older writer.

Compared to Shakespeare, Jonson, and Fletcher, among others, Congreve might well have had his head immediately and completely turned. Instead, he went on from triumph to triumph (even his fustian tragedy, *The Mourning Bride,* was a great success on the stage) until he reached his masterpiece, *The Way of the World*—which was so coolly received that the author is said to have appeared "in front" to rebuke the audience! Soon after, he stopped writing for the theatre altogether. Partly, this may have been due to his anger at the reception of what he must have known to be in every way his greatest play, partly to his frail health. But the real reason seems to have been that Congreve was more interested in social life than he was in writing. He was petted and admired by the great, he had a large income from his plays and from various sinecure offices bestowed upon him, and he had always had an affinity for "high life." When Voltaire called upon him he disgusted the French philosopher by desiring to be con-

sidered as a "gentleman," not a playwright. "If that were so," said Voltaire, "I would not have bothered to call."

He did help Vanbrugh manage his theatre in 1705, and he wrote occasional poems and an opera for which Handel composed the music. He spent most of his time in the country homes of his friends and in the great houses of London. He never married; Mrs. Bracegirdle was apparently his mistress for many years, but when he died he left her £200 and left the bulk of his considerable fortune to the Duchess of Marlborough. She bought a diamond necklace with it, and had a little ivory figure made, representing Congreve, which thereafter graced her dinners.

All this makes Congreve sound like a most unpleasant person. He was not. Mrs. Bracegirdle was not in poverty. The duchess had been his very good friend. He was a gallant, a man of tact, discretion, and diplomacy, a gay, and rather dissipated, natural aristocrat. He was personally kindly, and courageous in the face of a lifetime of illness. He had no particular interest in politics, and managed to keep his various offices (commissioner for the licensing of hackney coaches and of wines, secretary for Jamaica, posts in the paper office, the pipe office, the customs—in none of which, of course, he did any practical service) from 1695 to his death, though occasionally some of his friends had to intervene in his behalf when governments changed. He was amiable, a witty conversationalist when he wanted to be, and a man of the world and about town who saw no particular reason why he should keep on writing when he no longer needed to do so. Writing from the beginning had been for him an elegant accomplishment, a diversion from illness, and a means of making a living when he had no other recourse.

Toward the end of his life he was crippled by gout, and blind from cataracts. He died as the result of a carriage accident. He was buried in Westminster Abbey.

As a man, Congreve was an easily recognizable eighteenth century type. As a dramatist, he superseded the limitations of his temperament. He is the nearest thing to Molière which England possesses. He created a whole new world of comedy—a world glittering, artificial, cynical, deliberately false and affected, and unfailingly, overwhelm-

Sir G. Kneller
WILLIAM CONGREVE

ingly brilliant. *The Way of the World* enjoys constant revivals to this day, and *Love for Love* might well follow it. His plays were immoral—or, rather, amoral—but they had none of the brutal coarseness of those of many of his contemporaries. As Charles Lamb said, Congreve created "a Utopia of gallantry, whose pleasure is duty." At their best, his plays have eloquence, power, and nobility; Swinburne called them "comedy in its purest and highest form."

And they are written in a concise and pointed style which has no equal in English drama, though Wilde comes nearest to it. His speeches have a cadence that raises them from dramatic verse to almost the grandeur of real poetry. (His non-dramatic poems, it must be confessed, are pompous and platitudinous.) In a sense, all Congreve's writing is a magnificent *tour de force*—which is successfully accomplished. His world is made up of rigidly selected types in as rigidly selected relationships; it is never alive, but it is brilliantly lifelike. Even his sombre, grandiloquent tragedy furnishes forth a few gems—"music hath powers to charm the savage breast"—"nor hell a fury like a woman scorned." Dryden, Swift, Steele, Pope (who dedicated to Congreve his translation of *The Iliad*) were good critics, all of them; and they were all Congreve's devoted admirers as well as his enthusiastic friends.

His stagecraft came by instinct, his wit was an inborn aptitude. His irony and cynicism were purposeful, and his coruscating style was almost austere in its selection of the inevitable word. His plays were meant to be *spoken;* Millamant in *The Way of the World* is a challenge to any actress of any time. He just lacked the warmth, the universality, of Molière; but he was midwife to the comedy of manners in England, and that is glory enough for any man.

PRINCIPAL WORKS: *Plays*—The Old Bachelor, 1693; The Double Dealer, 1694; Love for Love, 1695; The Mourning Bride, 1697; The Way of the World, 1700; Semele (opera) (D. D. Arundell, ed.) 1925. *Poetry*—A Pindaric Ode . . . to the King, 1695; The Mourning Muse of Alexis, 1695; The Birth of the Muse, 1698; The Judgment of Paris (masque) 1701; A Hymn to Harmony, 1703; A Pindaric Ode . . . to the Queen, with a Discourse on the Pindaric Ode, 1704; Poems, 1781; A Sheaf of Poetical Scraps (D. Protopopescu, ed.) 1923. *Miscellaneous*—Incognito (novel) 1692; The Justice of the Peace, 1697; Amendments upon Mr. Collier's False and Imperfect Citations, 1698; The Works of Mr. William Congreve, 1710.

ABOUT: Bennewitz, A. Congreve and Moliere; Berkeley, M. Literary Relics; Gosse, E. The Life of William Congreve; Hunt, L. Introduction to the Dramatic Works of Wycherley and Congreve; Johnson, S. Lives of the Poets; Lamb, C. Essays of Elia; Lynch, K. M. A Congreve Gallery; Macaulay, T. B. Critical and Miscellaneous Essays; Meredith, G. An Essay upon Comedy and the Uses of the Comic Spirit; Protopopescu, D. Un Classique Moderne, William Congreve; Thackeray, W. M. English Humorists of the Eighteenth Century; Voltaire, F. A. Lettres sur les Anglais.

CONSTABLE, HENRY (1562-October 9, 1613), poet, was the son of Sir Robert Constable and his wife, Christiana Dabridgecourt. Educated at St. John's College, Cambridge, he graduated when he was eighteen and went abroad. For some years he lived in Paris where, as a convert to the Roman Catholic faith, he found an environment more congenial than that of his own country. There he began to write poetry which was circulated in manuscript among his friends in England, establishing an early reputation as a sonneteer. *Diana,* a volume of twenty-three sonnets, was published in 1592.

Almost nothing is known of his life at this period, but there is some evidence that he served a term in the secret service of the English government while still in his twenties. In 1598 he was sent to Scotland on a papal mission to discuss with James VI the terms for Catholic support to his claims to the English throne. After his return to Paris, Constable seems to have become almost completely estranged from his homeland, establishing close relations with the French court. When he was over forty, having lived abroad most of his adult life, he finally dared to make a visit to England after the death of Elizabeth and the accession of James I. Taken almost immediately into custody, he returned to exile and nine years later died at Liège.

Cut off from his friends, uprooted from the rich soil of Elizabethan poetry, it is perhaps curious that Henry Constable should have an important place in the early development of the English sonnet. Yet certainly he belongs to that group of English lyric poets who during the final decade of the sixteenth century penned more sonnets than in any other ten-year period of English history. In spite of physical separation, he seems to have had a kind of spiritual kinship with such men as Sir Philip Sidney and Sir John Harington, and the melody of his verse has

117

the true Elizabethan ring. Unfortunately, echoes from the French and the Italian sometimes sang louder than his own muse, and many of his later sonnets are almost literal translations from the French of Desportes.

It is not easy to identify all of Constable's writings. A volume published in 1594, which reprinted *Diana* with the addition of some seventy other poems purporting to be the work of Constable, contains at least eight sonnets by Sir Philip Sidney and quite possibly the work of several other men of the period. Constable's talent, like his life, can be judged only as a brightly colored fragment in a larger mosaic.

PRINCIPAL WORKS: Sonnet: Prefixed to King James' Poetical Exercises, 1591; Diana, 1592; Diana, Augmented with Divers Quatorzains of Honourable and Learned Personages, 1594; Four Sonnets to Sir P. Sidney's Soul, 1595; England's Helicon (includes four pastoral poems by Constable) 1600; The Harleian Miscellany (T. Park, ed.) 1812; Spiritual Sonnets (T. Park, ed. *in* Heliconia) 1815; Diana, the Sonnets and Poems of H. Constable (W. C. Hazlitt, ed.) 1859.

ABOUT: Corser, T. Collectanea Anglo-Poetica; Kastner, L. E. Elizabethan Sonneteers and the French Poets (Modern Language Review 1908); Lee, S. Introduction to Elizabethan Sonnets; Ritson, J. Bibliographia Poetica.

COOK, JAMES (October 28, 1728-February 14, 1779), voyager, explorer, author of travel journals, was the son of a farm laborer, born at Marton, Cleveland, in Yorkshire. When he was twelve the boy went to work for a shopkeeper and a little later for a firm of shipowners in Whitby, sailing in the Norway, Baltic, and Newcastle trades. Such was the unspectacular apprenticeship of the man who became the greatest of all British maritime explorers.

James Cook was twenty-five when he joined the Royal Navy. In the ten years following, he taught himself mathematics, astronomy, and practical navigation, and as master of a small vessel, the "Mercury," sailed to Canada where he sounded and surveyed the St. Lawrence River. In 1763 he was appointed by Sir Hugh Palliser "marine surveyor of the coast of Newfoundland and Labrador." Five years later, having achieved something of a reputation by his observation of a solar eclipse during a routine voyage, he was chosen to head an expedition to the South Pacific for observation of the transit of Venus. This was the first of Cook's three

J. Webber

JAMES COOK

globe-scouring voyages, recorded in the famous journals.

Commissioned as a lieutenant, he sailed in the "Endeavor" for Tahiti, accompanied by a shipload of scientists. From Tahiti, where his passengers observed the transit of Venus, Cook sailed into the unknown areas of the southern ocean in search of the great continent which was supposed to exist there. He found no new continent, but he explored and charted numerous island groups; circumnavigated New Zealand, charting its coastline for the first time; sailed to Australia, surveying the whole of the unknown east coast and taking possession in the name of Great Britain; sailed on to Batavia, around the Cape of Good Hope, and returned to England after three years at sea.

Raised to the rank of commander, Cook undertook his second round-the-world voyage with two ships, the "Resolution" and the "Adventure," to search again for the mysterious southern continent referred to in all the geographies of the period. In more than a thousand days of sailing, he forever disproved the existence of any such continent and established the main outlines of the whole southern part of the globe much as they are known today. Of no less importance were the practical measures he developed to conquer scurvy, in three years losing only one man out of a hundred and eighteen. On his return to England in 1775, he was promoted to a captaincy and elected to the Royal Society where a paper on his precautions against scurvy won him the Copley gold medal.

The third and last voyage of Captain Cook, undertaken to settle the question of a northwest passage, ended in tragedy. Again in the "Resolution" he sailed across the Pacific to the west coast of America, which he surveyed as far north as the Bering Straits, then back to the Hawaiian Islands where, on an unmapped shore, he met his death at the hands of hostile natives. It is difficult to judge Cook's journals solely on a literary basis—they are so much the blood and bone of a great saga of discovery. Often they read as uneventfully as a domestic diary, yet here in this plain and modest record, the boundaries of man's knowledge are pushed outward. Cook's achievement was never adequately recognized in his own lifetime, but his true and lasting monument still stands in the map of the Pacific.

PRINCIPAL WORKS: An Account of a Voyage Round the World (first ptd. in John Hawkesworth's Voyages) 1773 (W. J. L. Wharton, ed. 1893); A Voyage towards the South Pole and Round the World, 1777; A Voyage to the Pacific Ocean, 1784; Voyages, with Life by M. B. Synge, 1897.

ABOUT: Hodgson, E. S. Captain Cook's Voyages; Kippis, A. Narrative of the Voyages round the World performed by Captain James Cook; Kitson, A. Captain James Cook, the Circumnavigator; Rowe, Y. G. Captain Cook, Explorer and Navigator; Synge, M. B. Life in Voyages (1897 ed.); Williamson, J. A. Cook and the Opening of the Pacific.

COOPER, ANTHONY ASHLEY. See SHAFTESBURY, Third Earl of

CORYATE, THOMAS (1577?-December 1617), traveler, author of travel narratives, was born in Odcombe, Somersetshire, the son of George Coryate, rector of Odcombe and prebendary of York Cathedral. He was educated at Westminster School and Gloucester Hall, Oxford, though he left without a degree. A few of his Latin poems were published in various anthologies.

From this point Coryate's career deviates entirely from the normal one of an educated man of his time. He became attached to the household of Henry, Prince of Wales (the oldest son, who died early, of James I), and there he was a sort of privileged buffoon and unofficial court fool. His appearance was grotesque, his head misshaped, and he let

After W. Hole (?)

THOMAS CORYATE

himself be made the butt of every kind of practical joke and gibe. In turn, he was allowed to play tricks on the courtiers. He was undoubtedly an eccentric, but he was not insane as were most of the genuine court fools, and his private opinion of his situation may be revealed by his departure in 1608 on a walking tour of the Continent. He returned long enough to publish his books and to hang up in Odcombe Church the shoes in which he had walked all the way from Venice, then set out in 1612 on an overland tour to Greece, Persia, Palestine, and India. He sent letters back to his friends telling of his experiences, which included a claim that he had spent but three pounds between Aleppo and Agra, and often got by "competently" on a penny a day. (The difference in purchasing power between then and now must of course be taken into account.) He died of dysentery in Surat, India, and was buried there.

The fact that Coryate was one of the wits who gathered at the Mermaid Inn is sufficient evidence that his oddities were deliberate. He was a good scholar with a remarkable memory and a gift for pungent speech. Perhaps to conceal his chagrin, he joined in the sallies against himself—"Coryate doth in his self-praise indite." His books are certainly queer and extravagant, mere hodgepodges (the *Crudities* included some posthumous poems by his father, who had died in 1608, probably leaving him the money for his travels), but they are full of sharply observed pictures of places and people. Some fragments of his notes were included in *Purchas His Pilgrimes* (1625). The *Cramb* is made up mostly of verses in mock praise of the *Crudities*, written at the king's behest by Jonson, Donne, Drayton, Chapman, and others, and of flamboyant addresses to the great on behalf of the earlier book. In the course of his journeys he learned Persian, Turkish, and Hindustani, and there is no doubt that he went everywhere he said he went, and saw everything he said he saw.

PRINCIPAL WORKS: Coryats Crudities, Hastillie Gobbled Up in Five Moneths Travells in France, Savoy, Italy, Rhetia, Helvetia, and the Netherlands, 1611; Coryats Cramb, or His Colwort Twice Sodden, . . . as the Second Course to His Crudities, 1611; The Odcombian Banquet, 1611; Letters from Asmere, the Court of the Great Mogul, 1616; T. Coriate, Traveller for the English Wits: Greeting, 1616.

ABOUT: Fuller, T. Worthies of Somersetshire; Hazlitt, W. C. Handbook of Early English Literature; Wood, A. à, Athenae Oxonienses.

COTTON, CHARLES (April 28, 1630-February 16, 1687), poet, was born in Beresford, Staffordshire, the only child of Charles Cotton, a landowner whose estate had been much reduced by lawsuits, and of Olive Stanhope. The father, a man of literary interests, was the friend of such writers as Herrick, Donne, and Jonson.*qqv* The boy was tutored by a former Oxford fellow, and may possibly have gone on to Cambridge, though probably he had no university education. He seems certainly to have traveled in France and Italy, and was completely familiar with the French language and its literature. For a brief time he served as an army captain in Ireland. He had no profession, but spent his life in an unsuccessful effort to keep his dwindling estate from utter bankruptcy, often being reduced to hack writing to make both ends meet. He was a Royalist, but met with no persecution or difficulties during the civil war; everybody seems to have liked him, and he was notoriously a good-natured, improvident fellow, whose heart was in fishing and horticulture, and who was fairly helpless in a sharper world. In 1656 he married his cousin, Isabella Hutchinson (sister of the Puritan Colonel Hutchinson), who died about 1670, leaving three sons and five daughters.

About 1675 he married again, his second wife being Mary Russell, the dowager Countess of Ardglass. What fortune she brought him was soon dissipated, and he finally lost his home altogether, dying in London at not quite fifty-seven.

One of his friends was Lovelace *qv* who, while Cotton had any money, was his pensioner; but characteristically, his closest friend was Izaak Walton, who was a quarter-century his senior but long out-lived him. The fishing shack Cotton built for their joint use had their initials intertwined on its door, and his happiest verses were addressed to Walton. Meanwhile he tried every variety of writing to bring in money—burlesques on the classics (anachronistic and rather gross), a book on gaming and the section on fly-fishing in Walton's *Compleat Angler*, a technical work on horticulture, and, above all, translations from the French. He translated Corneille's *Horace*, the *Commentaries* of Blaise de Montluc (actually his best translation), and others, but the one which made him his reputation was his translation of Montaigne, which superseded Florio's as the standard English version for many years. His aim as a translator was to give the effect of an original work, and unlike many of his colleagues, he was an honest translator, sticking closely to his source.

His poems for the most part were unpublished until after his death, being circulated

After Sir P. Lely

CHARLES COTTON

in manuscript among his friends. As a poet, he was long winded and not very distinguished, but he had a certain simplicity and homely charm. Lamb said of him that he "smacked of the rough magnanimity of the old English vein." Wordsworth and Coleridge both admired his rural poems, which had some influence on the famous joint volume of *Lyrical Ballads*. Coleridge particularly felt that Cotton was "replete with every excellence of thought, images, and passions which we expect or desire in the poetry of the milder muse." This well-meaning, thriftless, cheerful, handsome man, loyal to his friends, generous with little, devoted to his family, and unobtrusively devout, is an attractive figure, and as in his modesty he made small claim to poetic excellence, Coleridge's tribute to his "milder muse" would doubtless have seemed to him full recompense for all his efforts.

PRINCIPAL WORKS: Scarronides, or the First Book of Virgil Travestie (anon.) 1664 (with the Fourth Book, 1670); A Voyage to Ireland in Burlesque (verse) 1670?; The Planters Manual, 1673; The Compleat Gamester (2d and 3d parts, anon.) 1674; Burlesque upon Burlesque (burlesque on Lucian, anon.) 1675; Compleat Angler, 2d part, 1678 (original date of Compleat Angler 1653); The Wonders of the Peak (verse) 1685; Poems on Several Occasions, 1689 (J. Beresford, ed. 1923); The Genuine Works of Charles Cotton, 1715.

ABOUT: Beresford, J. Introduction, Poems. 1923 ed.; Coleridge, S. T. Biographia Literaria; Lamb, C. Essays; Oldys, W. Memoir *in* 2d part Compleat Angler, 1760.

COTTON, NATHANIEL (1705-August 2, 1788),

physician, poet, was born in London, the youngest son of Samuel Cotton, a merchant. It seems probable that his family came originally from Northamptonshire, but nothing definite is known of his background or early education. He studied medicine at Leyden under the Dutch physician and chemist, Boerhaave, and about 1740 settled at St. Albans.

Although Nathaniel Cotton was a poet widely read in his own day, it is doubtful whether his name would even be remembered were it not for a rather odd association with the more distinguished poet, William Cowper. As a physician, Cotton was the proprietor of a private madhouse, pompously named the "Collegium Insanorum," where Cowper was confined after his attempted suicide. Cotton seems to have offered his brother-poet friendliness and excellent care, both of which un-

doubtedly contributed to a recovery. Of the good doctor Cowper later wrote, "I was not only treated with kindness by him while I was ill, and attended with the utmost diligence, but when my reason was restored to me, and I had so much need of a religious friend to converse with, to whom I could open my mind upon the subject without reserve, I could hardly have found a fitter person for the purpose."

Cotton wrote a good deal of verse, pious and didactic in nature, a single volume of which was published anonymously in 1751, under the title, *Visions in Verse, for the Entertainment and Instruction of Younger Minds*. This was largely an attempt to moralize the fables of John Gay for the edification of children. None of his poetry is of any lasting merit, although a few of the short pieces have been frequently anthologized. Cotton's collected works were published three years after his death by his eldest son.

It is not strange that the shadow of obscurity fell so soon across the life and work of Dr. Cotton. Indeed, it seems almost as though he and his family had preferred obscurity to fame. Cotton never signed his name to any of his published writings. His tombstone carries neither date nor significant inscription. His son, in publishing the collected works, included no biography of the author. Possibly Cotton himself knew that he was a good doctor and a poor poet.

PRINCIPAL WORKS: Visions in Verse for the Entertainment and Instruction of Younger Minds, 1751; Various Pieces in Verse and Prose. Many of Which Were Never Before Published, 1791 (N. Cotton, [the younger] ed.); Poems, with the Author's Life, 1800.

ABOUT: Gentleman's Magazine 1807; Life, included in Poems, ed. 1800.

COVERDALE, MILES (1488-February 1568),

bishop, religious writer and translator of the first complete English text of the Bible, was born of Yorkshire parentage, probably in Coverdale, North Riding. A scholar from his youth, he studied philosophy and theology at Cambridge and was ordained a priest at Norwich in 1514. Entering the convent of Austin friars at Cambridge, he became one of a group of religious reformers under the influence of the prior, Robert Barnes, and after a few years left the convent to take up evangelical preaching as a secular priest.

Coverdale's great work, his translation of the Bible, was completed in 1535 and published abroad, apparently by Jacob van Meteren in Zurich. The second edition appeared two years later, the first complete Bible printed in England. Although Coverdale made no claims to original scholarship, drawing on the Tyndale translation of the New Testament and the Zurich Bible rather than on the original Greek and Hebrew texts, his version of the Bible had considerable literary merit and made its influence felt in the later authorized version. He was asked by Thomas Cromwell to work on the Great Bible of 1539, to be placed in all English churches, but the religious reaction of 1540 and the execution of Cromwell forced him into exile. His Bible was banned and for the next seven or eight years he lived and preached in Germany.

Coverdale married Elizabeth Macheson in effective protest against the celibacy of priesthood, and continued to oppose such "popish" institutions as the confession and the veneration of images. After the death of Henry VIII he was able to return to England, where he came into favor as a highly eloquent preacher and was appointed bishop of Exeter. The vigorous protestantism in the west of England during Elizabeth's reign may well have been due to his influence. He also published numerous religious works, most of them translations, and is known to have collaborated on the First Book of Common Prayer with Thomas Cranmer and others.

After the accession of Mary to the throne, Coverdale was deprived of his bishopric, and spent the rest of his life, as determined by the religious weather, in Denmark, Germany, and his native England, where he died at the age of eighty-one.

PRINCIPAL WORKS: Biblia. The Byble: That Is the Holy Scripture of the Olde and New Testament Faythfully Translated into Englyshe, 1535; Goostly Psalmes and Spirituall Songes, 1539?; Christen State of Matrymonye, Wherein Housbandes and Wyfes May Lerne to Kepe House Together with Love (tr.) 1541; A Shorte Recapitulacion of Erasmus Enchiridion, 1545; Certain Most Godly Letters of Such True Saintes as Gave Their Lyves, 1564; Writings and Translations of Myles Coverdale (G. Pearson, ed.) 1844; Remains of Myles Coverdale (G. Pearson, ed.) 1846.

ABOUT: Dixon, R. W. Church History; Hagstotz, G. D. and H. B. Heroes of the Reformation; Kippis, A. Biographia Britannica; Pearson, G. Biography *in* Remains of Myles Coverdale; Sheppard, L. A. The Printers of the Coverdale Bible.

COWLEY, ABRAHAM (1618-July 28, 1667), was born on Fleet Street, London, the seventh and posthumous child of Thomas Cowley, a stationer. He was a very precocious boy, who wrote poetry from the age of ten, and actually published two slim volumes while he was still in Winchester School. From there he went in 1637 to Trinity College, Cambridge, as a scholar; he secured his B.A. in 1630, and his M.A. in 1642. He became a fellow of the college, but was ejected by the Parliamentarians as a Royalist in 1643. He then took refuge in St. John's College, Oxford. He came to the attention of the royal family there, and when Charles I was imprisoned and the queen had fled to France he followed her and acted as her secretary, ciphering and deciphering all her letters to and from the king until the cipher was discovered.

On behalf of the Royalists he made a number of trips to Flanders, Holland, Scotland, and Jersey, and finally in 1656, very reluctantly, returned to England as a Royalist spy. There he was arrested in mistake for another person, and narrowly escaped imprisonment. As a blind, he set himself up as a physician, and seems actually to have wangled an M.D. degree from Oxford in 1657. This and other circumstances apparently aroused some jealousy and even suspicion of his loyalty among the Royalists, though he soon returned to France and stayed there till the Restoration.

In any event, when on his return he applied for the post of master of the Savoy Theatre, he was turned down; and his play, *The Cutter of Coleman-Street* (revised from *The Guardian*) was a rank failure. He had, however, powerful friends, among them Lord St. Albans, who obtained for him an estate near Chertsey, to which he retired for the remainder of his life. He was greatly interested in science, and was one of the first members of the Royal Society. Cowley, famous in his own time for his amatory poems, never married; he is said to have been in love only once in his life (with a lady who later married the brother of his first editor, Thomas Sprat, later Bishop of

M. Beale

ABRAHAM COWLEY

position in the history of prosody. He cleared the way for Dryden's use of the Alexandrine as a narrative vehicle. He himself had some narrative power, but Spenser and the followers of Spenser colored all his earlier verse, Donne all his later, so that Cowley himself seldom emerges from these greater shadows. He was fluent and ingenious, but self-consciously mannered. Yet Dr. Johnson said of him not unjustly that he had "a mind replete with learning . . . the first who imparted to English numbers the enthusiasm of the greater ode and the gaiety of the less, . . . equally qualified for spritely sallies and for lofty flights."

His prose, oddly enough, is superior to his verse; it has beauty and delicacy, and reveals the true nature of "the melancholy Cowley" (as he called himself)—a nature sensitive, introverted, and scholarly. Dryden admired him greatly, saying "his authority is almost sacred to me"; Addison thought that his only fault was "wit in its excess"; and Pope wrote rather touchingly of him:

> Who now reads Cowley? If he pleases yet,
> His moral pleases, not his pointed wit;
> Forgot his epic, nay Pindaric art,
> But still I love the language of his heart.

This is acute criticism as well as a tribute to the man. If Cowley's heart had spoken oftener, he would have been a better poet, and one better known today. Unfortunately his precocious childhood gave him a lasting spirit of emulation, and he is best known to modern readers by his unhappily frank expression of his soaring ambition:

> What shall I do to be for ever known,
> And make the coming age my own?

A word must be said for his Latin poems on botany, which was the chief preoccupation of his retirement in Chertsey. As poetry they are not particularly distinguished, but they are very good botany and display a pleasing side of a man who never quite dared be himself either in literature or in life. His diatribe against Cromwell, written primarily to dispel hints of his suspected disloyalty to the Stuart cause, is vigorous and biting enough. The truth probably is that Cowley was completely loyal to the Royalists, but temperamentally unfitted for the rough and dangerous work his adherence thrust him into. He was not a good partisan—for example, his affection for Crashaw never

Rochester), and then to have been too timid to ask for her hand! His last years were spent among his books, almost in solitude; his greatest friend, Richard Crashaw *qv*, had died in exile in 1649. He was buried in Westminster Abbey.

Cowley suffers from the fact that he was enormously admired during his lifetime for what is actually his worst work. His poem, *The Mistresse,* was almost required reading in his day, and is now unreadable. He was almost the last of the writers of artificial, affected love poems, full of far-fetched conceits and extravagant similes. The same disabilities apply to his Pindaric odes. On the few occasions when he forgot himself and wrote unaffectedly, his verse was simple, natural, and graceful; but his avowed aim was astonishment at his cleverness and brilliance, and he had an unfortunate passion for long digressions to display his learning. He belongs among the so-called metaphysical poets, and was an ardent admirer of their chief, Donne *qv*; but he aped Donne's idiosyncrasies of style without ever achieving his passion or possessing his genius. His contemporaries compared him to Virgil, about as inept a comparison as can well be imagined.

The fact that he was one of the first English poets to write regularly in Alexandrines (iambic hexameters) gives Cowley a certain

wavered, though as an Anglican he deplored his friend's conversion to Roman Catholicism, and even semi-apologized for still being his friend in his noble elegy, one of his best poems. He was one of the too many poets born at just the wrong moment of history for their peculiar talents and personalities.

PRINCIPAL WORKS: Poeticall Blossoms, 1633; Silva, 1636; Loves Riddle (pastoral) 1638; Naufragium Joculare (comedy) 1638; A Satyre: The Puritan and the Papist (anon.) 1643; The Mistresse, 1647; The Guardian (comedy) 1650 (as The Cutter of Coleman-Street, 1663); Poems (Miscellanies, The Mistresse, Pindarique Odes, The Davideis) 1656; Ode upon the . . . Restoration, 1660; A Proposition for the Advancement of Experimental Philosophy (prose) 1660; A Discourse . . . concerning the Government of Oliver Cromwell (prose) 1661; Plantarum libri duo, 1662 (as Poemata Latina, libri sex. 1668); Verses Lately Written upon Several Occasions, 1663; The Works of Mr. Abraham Cowley (T. Sprat, ed.) 1668; A Poem on the Late Civil War, 1679; Complete Works (A. B. Grosart, ed.) 1876; Essays, Plays, and Sundry Verses (A. R. Waller, ed.) 1906; Essays (J. R. Lumbey and A. Tilley, eds.) 1923.

ABOUT: Cowley, A. Of My Self (essay); Johnson, S. Lives of the Poets; Nethercot, A. H. Abraham Cowley, the Muses' Hannibal; Sprat, T. Life and Writings, in Works.

COWLEY, Mrs. HANNAH (1743-1809), playwright and poet, was born at Tiverton, Devonshire, the daughter of Philip Parkhouse, an erudite bookseller whose mother was a cousin of the poet Gay.

She married at twenty-five. Eight years later, attending a dull play with her husband, she declared, "I could write as well." Within two weeks she had finished writing *The Runaway*, a sentimental comedy, which was produced by Garrick at Drury Lane Theatre with enormous success. In the next eighteen years she wrote thirteen plays. They were all comedies, varying from light sentiment in the earliest to sturdier humor of line and episode in the later ones. Her characters were vividly drawn, and most of her plots were original, contrary to the "borrowing" practice of her day.

She pretended to be so uninterested in public success that she never attended the first nights of her own plays. However, she kept a sharp eye on the productions, arguing vigorously with the theatre managers over details of their staging. She engaged in a long public controversy with another playwright, Hannah More, charging her with plagiarism.

Mrs. Cowley's greatest success was *The Belle's Strategem*, produced first in 1782 and used in succeeding generations as a vehicle for many celebrated actors, including Ellen Terry and Henry Irving. In 1794 she wrote a play entitled *The Town Before You*, declaring in the preface that her disgust with the decadent taste of London would permit her to write no more plays; and she kept her word.

She wrote several long narrative poems, but her chief poetic activity was a correspondence carried on in the press, under the name of "Anna Matilda," with the poet Robert Merry who wrote as "Della Crusca." The quality of this verse was such that "Anna Matilda" became a synonym for a foolishly sentimental style of writing.

PRINCIPAL WORKS: The Runaway, 1776; Maid of Aragon, 1780; The Belle's Strategem, 1782; Bold Stroke for a Husband, 1783; The Scottish Village, 1787; The Poetry of Anna Matilda, 1788; Edwina, 1794; The Town Before You, 1794; The Siege of Acre, 1801.

ABOUT: Baker, D. E. Biographia Dramatica; Genest, J. Account of the Stage; Gifford, W. The Baviad, and The Maeviad.

COWPER, WILLIAM (November 15, 1731-April 25, 1800), poet, hymn-writer, was born in Great Berkhamsted, Hertfordshire, where his father, John Cowper, was rector. His mother, Anne Donne, who died in childbirth when William was six, was related to the poet Donne.[qv] The boy was sent first to a school in Markyate, where he was bullied and persecuted. A siege of severe trouble with his eyes rescued him, and when he was ten he was sent to Winchester. Though later he wrote critically of the public school system (in the English meaning of the term), actually this was perhaps the happiest time of his unhappy life. At eighteen he was put in a solicitor's office in London for training in the law, and soon after entered at the Middle Temple. Most of his time, however, was spent in a quiet sort of social life, particularly with an uncle, where his cousin Theodora was the main attraction. Already both Cowper and Theodora showed signs of nervous instability, and the uncle forbade their marriage, on the ostensible grounds of their close relation. It was a severe and lasting blow to the young man, and fatal to Theodora, who spent the remainder of her life in a sort of eccentric spinsterhood, firmly persuaded that Cowper never after had a thought for another woman.

He was called to the bar in 1754, but never practiced. In 1759 he bought chambers in the Inner Temple and was appointed a commissioner in bankruptcy, a post he held till his voluntary resignation in 1764. The first mental crisis of his life came in 1762, when a well-intended nomination for a clerkship in the House of Commons, which involved a public examination, brought about an attack of actual mania and attempted suicide. Obviously his pathological shyness unfitted him for life in the world. A stay at the private hospital of Dr. Nathaniel Cotton in St. Albans brought about a temporary cure, and his brother then settled him in Huntingdon. There he boarded with a clergyman named Unwin, his wife, son, and daughter. Soon after, Unwin was killed by a fall from a horse, but Cowper continued to live with the family; for the rest of his life he was seldom separated from Mrs. Unwin, his beloved Mary. It was she who inspired their move to Olney (the house is now a Cowper Museum), to be near the clergyman John Newton, an ex-slaver who was now a "ranting evangelist." Newton and Cowper became close friends, and nothing could have been more disastrous to the delicately balanced mind of the poet. He was used as a kind of lay curate, forced into public appearances, refused the simple life of exercise and domestic retirement he needed so badly, and constantly stimulated emotionally. The result was a final unsettling of his mind. For recurrent periods thereafter Cowper was the victim of true religious melancholia, with suicidal impulses, and the fixed delusion that he was utterly damned. From 1773 to 1776 he had a series of attacks of acute mania, which ended his engagement to marry Mrs. Unwin. When Newton finally left Olney in 1779, Cowper was able gradually to fight back to temporary sanity, to keep himself from melancholy by his gardening, his carpentering, his country walks and the care of his beloved hares.

A new friendship with Lady Austen inspired the writing of Cowper's most famous long poem, *The Task*, through her suggestion that he write about the simple homely things around him. Unfortunately the two elderly ladies both considered him their property and

L. F. Abbott, 1792
WILLIAM COWPER

care, and Lady Austen was quietly eliminated. In 1786 Cowper was reunited with his cousin Lady Hesketh, Theodora Cowper's sister, who remained his good angel for the rest of his life. She moved him and Mrs. Unwin to a pleasanter home at Westover Underwood, and saw to it that so far as possible he lived the only kind of life in which he could remain free from madness. But even she could not insure him against new invasions of mental illness. In 1787 William Unwin, the son of the family, died, and once more Cowper had a period of violent mania and of nearly successful suicide attempts. Then Mrs. Unwin suffered a series of paralytic strokes, ending with her death in 1796. By that time, though Cowper was still able to work intermittently on his translation of Homer, there was no question of any permanent cure. For the most part he was sunk in a kind of mental stupor, and he finally died (of dropsy) at sixty-eight.

It is quite possible that his medical history would have been the same had he never seen John Newton, but that well-meaning friend undoubtedly gave the final direction to the form of his mania. In his lucid periods William Cowper was a sweet-tempered, lovable, tender-hearted man, narrow in his views but wide in his sympathies, with a fund of quiet gaiety and a vein of Puckish humor which creeps into many of his poems, is the life of the famous ballad, *The Journey of John Gilpin,* and gives flavor to his familiar letters—he was one of the really great letter-writers of all time.

His earlier poems caused little stir, but from the time of publication of *The Task* Cowper was famous; at the end of his life he even enjoyed a royal pension in recognition of his achievement. His is the poetry of nature and of domesticity, simple, natural, direct, and instinct with delicate feeling. Its nearest affinity is to some of the poems of John Greenleaf Whittier, though Whittier lacked Cowper's gentleness and sweetness. There is even a touch of Horace in his homely shrewdness, his precision of style, his affectionate playfulness—for when not clouded by melancholy his mind was clear and exact. The didacticism which is his worst fault was the product of the environment in which he lived. He belongs definitely to the pre-Romantics, for his heroic couplets have none of the rigid classicism of Pope and his school.

Several of the hymns which Cowper wrote for Newton in the early days at Olney (though they were not published until 1779) have survived to this day in the evangelical churches; they include such well-known hymns as "God moves in a mysterious way" and "There is a fountain filled with blood." His translation of Homer was a failure; he was incapable of sharing the spirit of the barbarous age of Greece, and his adoration for Milton made his blank verse version far more Miltonic than Homeric. His translations from the French and Latin—Milton's early French poems, the mystic Mme. de la Mothe Guion, Horace, and others—were far more successful. *Adelphi,* his only prose except for a few articles and reviews, was a memoir of the deathbed conversion to evangelism of his brother, who died in 1770. It must be remembered that Cowper did not start writing poetry until he was nearly fifty, and then merely as a way of diverting his mind from the horrors that encompassed it. Considering his recurring periods of insanity, he left an impressive amount of really good work. In the particular genre which was the only one possible to him, few poets have surpassed him.

PRINCIPAL WORKS: Olney Hymns (with John Newton) 1779; Anti-Thelyphthora, 1781; Poems, 1782-86; The Journey of John Gilpin, 1783; The Task, 1785; Adelphi (prose) 1802; Memoir of Early Life, 1816; Works (J. Newton, ed.) 1817; Private Correspondence (J. Johnson, ed.) 1824; Works (R. Southey, ed.) 1836-37; Unpublished and Uncollected Poems (T. Wright, ed.) 1900; Letters (J. G. Frazer, ed.) 1912; Unpublished and Uncollected Letters (T. Wright, ed.) 1925; Selected Letters (M. Van Doren, ed.) 1951.

ABOUT: Ainger, A. Lectures and Essays; Bagehot, W. Estimates of Some Englishmen and Scotchmen; Brooke, S. A. Theology in the English Poets; Cecil, D. The Stricken Deer; Cowper, W. Memoir of Early Life; Elwin, W. Some 18th Century Men of Letters; Fausset, H. A. William Cowper; Geary, C. Cowper and Mary Unwin; Gilfillan, G. Life, *in* Poetical Works, 1854; Hartley, L. C. William Cowper, Humanitarian; Neave, J. A Concordance to the Poetic Works of William Cowper; Nicholson, N. William Cowper; Sainte Beuve, C. A. Causeries de Lundi; Smith, G. Cowper; Symington, J. A. The Poet of Home Life; Thomas, G. O. William Cowper and the 18th Century; Wright, T. The Life of William Cowper.

CRANMER, THOMAS (July 2, 1489-March 21, 1556), archbishop of Canterbury, principal author of the English liturgy, was the second son of Thomas Cranmer and Anne or Agnes Hatfield, born at Aslacton, Nottinghamshire. Educated by "a marvellous severe and cruel schoolmaster," he was sent to Cambridge at the age of fourteen, taking his B.A. in 1511 and his M.A. four years later. An early marriage deprived him of a fellowship at Jesus College, but when his wife died in childbirth, he was reinstated and ordained.

Cranmer might easily have spent his life as a scholar and a lecturer in divinity had it not been for his chance involvement in the affairs of King Henry VIII. At the time when Henry was seeking a divorce from Catherine of Aragon in order to marry Anne Boleyn, Cranmer made the suggestion that since Catherine had been the widow of Henry's deceased brother, Arthur, the illegalizing of such a marriage—would obviate the need for an appeal to Rome. On hearing of this, Henry immediately sent for him—"I will speak to him. This man, I trow, has got the right sow by the ear"—and the thread of Cranmer's life, picked up in this first meeting with Henry, became curiously interwoven with the whole political and religious tapestry of sixteenth century England.

Henry made him successively archbishop of Taunton, member of an embassy to Rome, ambassador to the German Emperor and archbishop of Canterbury. That Cranmer had never sought the primacy is borne out

G. Flicke, 1546
THOMAS CRANMER

by his marriage to a niece of Osiander in Nuremburg a year before he was consecrated as archbishop in 1533. (So embarrassing was the existence of a wife to the new archbishop that, according to contemporaries, he was forced to carry her about in a chest perforated with holes to let her breathe!) In the highest ecclesiastical office of the land, Cranmer became Henry's agent in setting aside Catherine and putting Anne Boleyn on the throne, in disposing of Anne and arranging the subsequent marriages; he was godfather to the future Queen Elizabeth; he presided at Henry's death and the coronation of Edward VI; he was a member of Edward's regency and lived to bring Lady Jane Grey, the nine-day Queen, to the throne, for which he was sent to the Tower and condemned as a traitor on the accession of Mary.

Parallel to this royal drama ran the greater drama of the Reformation, of which Cranmer to a large degree was the mind and the voice. In the separation of the Church of England from Rome, the Archbishop carried out through two reigns the revision of the creed and liturgy of the church. The King's *Primer*, published in 1545, embodied the present-day English litany, in Cranmer's incomparable rhythmic prose bringing a new beauty of form to the English language. He was responsible for the *First Book of Common Prayer* under Edward VI. He set down the forty-two Articles of Religion (later thirty-nine) which became the code of English protestantism. He revised the codification of the canon law and saw that the English Bible was given to the English people.

Under Queen Mary, a Catholic, it was inevitable that Cranmer should play the role of martyr. That it was a flawed martyrdom makes the final scene of his life even more dramatic. Tried before a high ecclesiastical court, Cranmer was excommunicated by the Pope, degraded from his position as archbishop, and condemned to death at the stake. During his imprisonment he had been led to sign a series of recantations denying the whole substance of the Reformation and with it his own achievement, but in the hour of his death he renounced his previous action and, for a last testimony, thrust his right hand, which had signed the recantations, into the flames.

PRINCIPAL WORKS: Preface to the Bible, 1540; Cathechismus. That Is to Say: a Shorte Instruction into Christian Religion, 1548; Preface to the Book of Common Prayer, 1549; A Defence of the True and Catholike Doctrine of the Sacrament, 1550 (C. H. H. Wright, ed. 1907); An Answer unto a Crafty and Sophistical Cavillation Devised by Stephen Gardiner, 1551; A Confutation of Unwritten Verities, 1558; The Remains of Thomas Cranmer (H. Jenkyns, ed.) 1833; Writings and Disputations of Thomas Cranmer Relative to the Sacrament of the Lord's Supper (J. E. Cox, ed.) 1844; Miscellaneous Writings and Letters of Thomas Cranmer (J. E. Cox, ed.) 1846.

ABOUT: Deane, A. C. Life of Thomas Cranmer; Dixon, R. W. History of the Church of England; Mason, A. J. Thomas Cranmer; Pollard, A. F. Thomas Cranmer and the English Reformation; Smyth, C. H. Cranmer and the Reformation under Edward VI; Strype, J. Memorials of Thomas Cranmer.

CRASHAW, RICHARD (1612?-August 1649), religious poet, was the only child of the Reverend William Crashaw, a divine with Puritanical and violently anti-Papist views, who if he had not died when his son was fourteen would have been outraged by that son's later development. His mother died when he was an infant; his father remarried, and the stepmother was a real mother to him, but she too died when he was seven or eight. He went to Charterhouse School, and then to Pembroke College, Cambridge, in 1631, as a scholar, receiving his B.A. in 1634. In 1636 he became a fellow of Peterhouse College, earning his M.A. two years later, and continued to reside there. It was at the university that he began his lifelong friendship with Abraham Cowley ^{qv}.

Early in his college days he earned a reputation as an ascetic recluse, the unworldly "chaplaine of the Virgine myld," as he himself put it. He came under the influence first of High Church and then of Roman Catholic adherents, but as yet made no open declaration of his change of faith. His life was not all austerity; he loved music, and was talented in drawing and engraving, himself making the decorations for some of his books. He had close friends, and was still able to write gracefully of "that not impossible she" who might be in his future.

With the civil wars he was expelled from Cambridge, and after a brief stay in Oxford went to Paris, where he seems finally to have been confirmed in the Roman Catholic Church. Cowley discovered him there in 1646, living in the utmost poverty and misery, and busied himself at once in finding assistance for him. He interested Queen Henrietta Maria, who was herself a Catholic (Cowley was then in exile with the royal family), and the queen, together with Crashaw's great patroness the Countess of Denbigh, made it possible for him to go to Rome, with letters of introduction which resulted in his employment by Cardinal Palotta as a minor secretary or attendant in his household. The cardinal was a man of rigid morals, but his retinue was lax and profligate, and shocked the ascetic poet to the point where he indiscreetly complained of them to his master. Palotta knew very well that the Englishman's life would be in danger from his revengeful servants when it became known that he had denounced them. Accordingly, he hastily sent Crashaw to his church of Our Lady of Loretto, with appointment as a minor canon (though he was a layman). This was in April 1649; four months later Crashaw was dead. He may have contracted a fatal fever on the journey, or—as has been hinted more than once—the cardinal may not have been quick enough, and Crashaw may have been poisoned. He was buried in Loretto. He had lived to be less than forty years of age.

Classed as one of the "metaphysical poets," Crashaw is chiefly known for his religious poetry, but actually he wrote many secular poems as well, and though they have not the warmth and ardor of his devotional work, they also avoid its faults, and are charming and graceful. He had a gift for languages, knowing Hebrew as well as Greek and Latin, and being very fluent in both Italian and Spanish, from which languages he made many translations. Cowley, in a beautiful elegy, called him "young master of the world's maturitie," and he wielded a mighty influence on the work of later poets as diverse as Milton, Pope, and Coleridge. At his best he is almost Shelleyan, if a devout Shelley can be imagined; but he is one of the most unequal and uneven poets who ever wrote. Passages of sheer felicity and fiery loveliness are interspersed with clumsy, awkward images and pure bathos.

It is in his religious poems, of course, that the essential Crashaw appears, and in them it is possible to understand why he was dubbed "the divine." He himself wrote, in his noble *Hymn to St. Theresa*, "I learnt to know that love is eloquence." His love is often expressed in strangely physical terms for divine ecstasy—but then so was that of the great mystic whom he is celebrating. His faults are those of excess, of crowding imagination, of complete lack of self-evaluation or self-criticism: Swinburne noted his "dazzling intricacy" which often betrays him into meretriciousness of style if not of feeling. His ardor, his passion, are all directed to God and voiced in phrases that seem to have warmth and color of their own. He is capable of ethereal beauty married to gross banality. What he needed above all, and lacked in his exile, was a mentor of good judgment to share his feeling and duly appreciate his genius but prune his excesses.

Crashaw's first volume of "sacred epigrams" in Latin, contains the famous line from the miracle at Cana, "nympha pudica Deum vidit et erubuit" ("the bashful stream hath seen its God and blush'd"). His next volume, really two in one—one devotional, the other secular—was printed in Paris and was full of errors caused by the printers' ignorance of English. Nevertheless, and in spite of the political upheaval of the period, it earned for the poet a lasting reputation in his own country, which was enhanced by the posthumous publication of his final volume of Latin sacred poetry. (This was edited by Crashaw's friend Thomas Carre, confessor to the English nuns in Paris, whose real name was Miles Pinkney.) It was more than two hundred years, however, before a definitive edition of his complete works appeared. He has always been peculiarly the poet of the mystically inclined, and it is interesting to note that many of his biographers are women.

PRINCIPAL WORKS: Epigrammatum Sacrorum Liber, 1634; Steps to the Temple, Sacred Poems, with Other Delights of the Muses, 1646; Carmen Deo Nostro Te Decet Hymnus (T. Carre, ed.) 1652; A Letter from Mr. Crashaw to the Countess of Denbigh, Against Irresolution in Matters of Religion, 1653; Complete Works (A. Grosart, ed.) 1887-88; The Poems, English, Latin, and Greek, of Richard Crashaw (L. C. Martin, ed.) 1927.

ABOUT: Bennett, J. Four Metaphysical Poets; Coleridge, S. T. Literary Recollections; Gilfillan, G. Memoir, in Poetical Works, 1857; Gosse, E. Seventeenth Century Studies; Martin, L. C. Biographical Introduction, Poems, 1927; Wallerstein, R. C. Richard Crashaw, a Study in Style and Poetic Development; White, H. C. The Metaphysical Poets: A Study in Religious Experience; Wiley, B. Richard Crashaw.

CRAWFORD, ROBERT (d. 1733), Scottish song writer, was born at Edinburgh, the second son of Patrick Crawford, a merchant, and his first wife, the daughter of Gordon of Turnberry. Beyond these scant facts nothing is known of Robert Crawford except the few lovely Scotch songs attributed to him on the testimony of Robert Burns.

Crawford's work belongs to the popular lyric revival in Scotland prior to Burns, of which Allan Ramsay, wigmaker and later bookseller and publisher, was an outstanding figure. All of Crawford's songs were contributed to Ramsay's Tea-Table Miscellany, published between 1724 and 1732, and were signed only with the initial "C." Among these the best known are four, The Bush Aboon Traquair, Tweedside, Allan Water and Down the Burn Davie. While intensely Scottish in tone and tenor, many of his songs are, in meter and style, largely modeled on the forms of English verse. T. F. Henderson, writing in the Cambridge History of English Literature, says of Crawford's work, "His Bush Aboon Traquair has one or two excellent lines and semi-stanzas, the best being, probably, that beginning 'That day she smiled and made me glad ; but it evidently owes its repute mainly to its title, and is not

by any means so happy an effort as the more vernacular, and really excellent, Down the Burn Davie; while Allan Water and Tweedside are more or less spoiled by the introduction of the current artificialities of the English eighteenth century muse."

That Burns himself was Crawford's admirer is recorded in the Works where he writes, "the beautiful song of Tweedside does great honour to his poetical talents." Burns says further that he was "a pretty young man and lived in France," but of his personality and the events of his life we have no record. The date of his death is fixed by another reference in Burns who says he was drowned on a voyage from France in 1733. Most of Crawford's songs have been published with music in James Johnson's Scots' Musical Museum, printed in Edinburgh in 1839.

PRINCIPAL WORKS: Songs in The Tea-Table Miscellany (A. Ramsay, ed.) 1724-32 (reprinted, 1871); Songs in Scots Musical Museum (J. Johnson, ed.) 1839.

ABOUT: Burns, R. Comments, in The Works of Robert Burns (World Publishing ed. 1839); Stenhouse, W. Notes to Johnson's Scots' Musical Museum.

CRICHTON, JAMES (1560-1583/5?), poet and orator, was the son of Robert Crichton, at one time Lord Advocate of Scotland. Through his mother he claimed descent from the Scottish royal family. The fabulous career of the youth known as The Admirable Crichton began when he entered St. Andrews College at the age of ten, receiving his B.A. at fourteen and his M.A. at fifteen. From this point on it is difficult to disentangle fact from fable in the story of his brief, spectacular life. He was an exceedingly handsome boy, except for a red birthmark on his right cheek. He mastered eleven languages, had an extraordinary memory, was an expert horseman and an unexcelled fencer.

At seventeen he went abroad, and after two years in the French army went to Genoa, without funds or friends. His fame began to spread when he addressed the Genoa Senate in Latin, and by the time he arrived in Venice he was being followed in the streets by admiring crowds. The Venetian scholar and printer, Aldus Manutius, became his devoted patron, printed his Latin poems, sponsored debates, and published a handbill describing Crichton's attributes in scarcely credible superlatives. Crichton's poems were remarkable for their virtuosity, but possess little poetic value. Only a few are still extant, in the British Museum.

In Padua, in 1581, Crichton challenged the entire University of Padua to a four-day public debate on any subjects they proposed, offering to use either the rules of logic, mathematical demonstration, or extemporaneous Latin verse, depending on the nature of each subject. According to Manutius' eyewitness account, the prodigy's success was complete.

His initial feat in Mantua the following year was to kill a famous swordsman of that city in a duel. The admiring Duke of Mantua thereupon invited him to act as tutor and companion to the Duke's incorrigible son, Vincenzo. Whether the popular account of Crichton's death at twenty-three is authentic or not, it is of a pattern with his fantastic life. Returning from an assignation one dark night, the youth was attacked by a band of street brawlers. He drew his sword to defend himself, but recognized the leader of the band as Vincenzo and knelt before him holding out his sword in surrender. Vincenzo seized the sword and plunged it into young Crichton's heart.

ABOUT: Biographia Britannica; Tytler, P. F. Life of James Crichton of Cluny; Urquhart, Sir T. The Life and Death of The Admirable Crichton.

CROWNE, JOHN (1640?-1703?), dramatist, was the son of William Crowne, who, given a tract of land in Nova Scotia by Cromwell in 1656, lost it after the Restoration. John, deprived of his patrimony, returned to England and embarked on a literary career.

His first effort was an insignificant romance, *Pandion and Amphigenia* published in 1665. His first play, *Juliana*, was produced at the Duke of York's Theatre in 1671. Only in the Restoration theatre, where playgoing was primarily a social event, and where virtuoso acting overshadowed the matter of a play, could Crowne's tragedies have been acclaimed. He considered himself a writer of tragedies, but of the eighteen plays he wrote only a few of his comedies, which were greatly influenced by Molière, have more than passing merit.

His career was sponsored at first by the Earl of Rochester, who, jealous of Dryden's success, used his influence to obtain for Crowne the commission to write a Court Masque which should logically have gone to Dryden as poet laureate. As Crowne's popularity waxed, Rochester's favor waned, and it was as the favorite playwright of Charles II that Crowne achieved his greatest successes.

City Politiques, produced in 1683, was an enormously popular satire in which several prominent Whigs were recognizably caricatured. Disturbed by the political enemies he had made, and averse to the extravagances of court and fashionable life, Crowne asked Charles for appointment to a minor office which would allow him to retire from the theatre. Charles bargained for one more comedy, to be based on a Spanish play by Moreto. The result was Crowne's most successful play, *Sir Courtly Nicely*, which was frequently revived for the next hundred years. Charles died on the last day of rehearsal, his promise of an office unfulfilled.

Crowne wrote several more plays and songs, some of the latter set to music by Purcell. Nothing is known of his last few years, following the production of his last play, *The Married Beau*, in 1694.

PRINCIPAL WORKS: Pandion and Amphigenia, a Romance, 1665; Juliana, or the Princess of Poland, 1671; History of Charles the Eighth, a Tragedy in Rhyme, 1672; Calisto, or the Chaste Nymph, a Court Masque, 1675; The Country Wit, 1675; Destruction of Jerusalem, 1677; City Politiques, 1683; Sir Courtly Nicely, or It Cannot Be, 1685; The English Friar, 1690; The Married Beau, 1694.

ABOUT: Biographia Dramatica; Genest, J. Account of the English Stage; Langbaine, G. English Dramatic Poets.

CRUDEN, ALEXANDER (May 31, 1701-November 1, 1770), compiler of a Biblical concordance, was born in Aberdeen in a house of solid masonry, second of the eleven children of William Cruden, merchant, bailie, and Presbyterian elder, and Isabel (Pyper) Cruden. His upbringing was Calvinistic and severe. At eight he attended the Town Grammar School, where all instruction was given in Latin, and at thirteen went to Marischal College, eventually receiving an M.A. degree, probably when he was nineteen. Cruden fell in love—violently, as he always did—with the daughter of an Aberdeen minister. Rumors, perhaps not unfounded, of her incestuous relations with her brother unsettled his none too stable mind, and he was confined in the Tolbooth for a fortnight, since there was no lunatic asylum in town. In 1722 he sailed for England to become private tutor to the only son of one Coltman, a country squire living at Elm Hall near Southgate, Middlesex, and in 1729 was in the employ of the tenth Earl of Derby as reader in French. Cruden's total ignorance of French pronunciation proved too much for the Earl, who soon discharged him.

In 1732, Cruden opened a bookseller's shop in the Royal Exchange, and in 1735 had the title of Bookseller to Queen Caroline, to whom he dedicated his *Complete Concordance to the Holy Scriptures* (1737). This painstaking work, although not bearing out all Cruden's pretensions to scholarship, held the field for many years. His eccentricity increasing, he was again confined in a private madhouse in Bethnal Green, March 23-May 31, 1737, and described his experiences in the first of many pamphlets. Subsequently Cruden made a reputation as "corrector for the press" (editor and proofreader) for Greek and Latin classics, and gradually felt it incumbent on him to admonish the British on morals in general, assuming the self-styled title of "Alexander the Corrector." He was confined in other asylums, compiled a *Scriptural Dictionary* and possibly an index to Milton, and was found dead at sixty-nine in his Islington lodgings, on his knees in an attitude of prayer. In her excellent biography of Cruden, Edith Olivier states that he had a touch of dignified dandyism, hesitated in his speech, and "saw a snub clearly, but never took one."

PRINCIPAL WORKS: A Complete Concordance to the Holy Scriptures, 1737; A Scriptural Dictionary, 1770; Adventures, 1754.

ABOUT: Chalmers, A. Life (in 1824 edition of Concordance); Olivier, E. The Eccentric Life of Alexander Cruden (U.S. title: Alexander the Corrector).

CUDWORTH, RALPH (1617-June 26, 1688), philosopher, was born in Aller, Somersetshire, the son of Dr. Ralph Cudworth, chaplain to the king, and his wife, who had been nurse to the Prince of Wales. His father died when he was seven, and his mother married a Dr. Stoughton, who educated him at home. At thirteen he entered Emmanuel College, Cambridge, where his father had been a fellow, and received his B.A. in 1635, M.A. 1639 (fellow the same year), B.D. 1646, and D.D. 1651. In 1645, at only twenty-eight, he became master of Clare Hall, and religious professor of Hebrew at Cambridge, remaining in the latter post until his death. In 1672 he became rector of Ashwell, Hertfordshire (non-resident) and in 1678 prebendary of Gloucester.

He married in 1654 (his wife's maiden name is unknown), and the same year, when he was contemplating leaving Cambridge on account of financial stress, he was appointed master of Christ's College. There he remained, though at the Restoration he had some difficulty in having his appointment confirmed, since he had .(though not a Puritan) shown a good deal of sympathy for the Commonwealth, and acted for it on a committee on readmission of Jews to England and in a contemplated revised translation of the Bible.

Cudworth had very little leisure—he was bursar as well as master of Christ's, preached frequently, and gave much time to the study of Hebrew—and he was by nature a slow and deliberate worker. Therefore his indignation when he discovered that Henry More, a fellow of the college, was about to publish a work along the same philosophical lines as that on which he had long been engaged was hardly justified. More waited till 1667, and then published his book—Cudworth's treatise actually did not appear until forty-three years after his death!

Cudworth belonged to what was known as "the Cambridge Platonists." His advocacy of innate moral qualities (opposed to the materialism of Hobbes) was really neo-Platonism; as James Martineau said, he "conceded too much to the pagan philosophers" and placed too little value on either the rites or the dogmas of Christianity to please either Anglicans or Puritans. The principal work published during his lifetime, *The True Intellectual System of the Universe*, antagonized readers of all schools because it was neither scientific nor formally religious; besides this, its Greek quotations were faulty and badly printed, and he read his own sentiments into the philosophers from whom he quoted. But he was a learned, able man of great commonsense, a believer in tolerance and in academic reform; his weaknesses were the obverse of his learning and profundity—unduly long suspension of judgment, over-thoroughness in research, and self-distrust. He believed (with Descartes) that moral laws rise of necessity from the nature of man, and are not man-made; this is the foundation-stone of his philosophy. His reputation was almost entirely posthumous, since his extreme slowness left him with his great central project unfinished and published only in fragments. His manuscripts on free will and ethics are now in the British Museum, many of them still unpublished.

PRINCIPAL WORKS: Discourse Concerning the True Nature of the Lord's Gospel, 1642; The Union of Christ and the Church a Shadow, 1642; Sermon Preached before the House of Commons, 1647; The True Intellectual System of the Universe, 1678 (revised, T. Birch, ed. 1743); A Treatise Regarding Eternal and Immutable Morality (E. Chandler, ed.) 1731; A Treatise of Free Will (J. Allen, ed.) 1838.

ABOUT: Birch, T. Life, in 1743 ed. True Intellectual System; Hallam, H. Literature of Europe; Hunt, J. History of Religious Thought in England; Lowrey, C. E. The Philosophy of R. Cudworth; Martineau, J. Types of Ethical Theory; Maurice, F. D. Modern Philosophy; Passmore, J. A. Ralph Cudworth: An Interpretation; Tulloch, J. Rational Theology and Christian Philosophy in England in the Seventeenth Century.

CULPEPER, NICHOLAS (1616-1654), writer on astrology and medicine, son of a Surrey clergyman, was born in London. His formal education at Cambridge was brief, but he acquired enough knowledge of Latin and Greek to carry on an extensive program of self-education. Apprenticed to an apothecary, he continued his studies of medieval lore and set himself up as physician and astrologer in 1640.

Cheated of his patrimony, responsible for a family of seven children, and remaining in spite of popularity a relatively poor man, Culpeper devoted his life unsparingly to the dissemination of medical knowledge among the people. He gave his time generously to charity patients. Besides his medical practice, during the last five years of his short life, he wrote or translated an almost incredible number of medical works which made available to the general public a vast amount of information hitherto the exclusive property of the College of Physicians.

His first publication, in 1649, was an unauthorized English translation of the *Pharmacopoeia* of the College of Physicians, called *A Physical Directory*, or, in later editions, *The London Dispensatory*. In retaliation, the College viciously attacked both the authenticity of the work and Culpeper's character, labeling him a lecher, a drunkard and an atheist. There seems to have been no justification for these charges, and the College's opposition did not hurt the sale of the book which was enormous, nor Culpeper's popularity as a physician. A series of treatises and translations followed, and in 1653, with Peter Cole, he published *The English Physician*, which again, despite bitter attacks by the organized medical writers, was a sensational success.

The following year, exhausted by his excessive activities, Culpeper contracted tuberculosis and died at the age of thirty-eight. Most of the seventy-nine manuscripts he left were printed posthumously, although a dispute over the publishing rights slightly clouds the authenticity of some. A three-volume collected edition of his work was published in 1802; *The English Physician* has appeared in edition after edition, even being reprinted as a curiosity in the twentieth century.

PRINCIPAL WORKS: A Physical Directory, 1649; An Astronomical Judgement of Diseases, 1651; Directory for Midwives, 1651; Galen's Art of Physic, 1652; The Fall of Monarchy, 1652; Idea Universalis Medica Practica (Amsterdam) 1652; The English Physician, 1653; Anatomy, 1654; A New Method of Physic, 1654; Collected Works, (G. A. Gordon, ed.) 1802.

ABOUT: Chance, B. Annals of Medical History, n.s.1931; Powys, L. Thirteen Worthies; Tyrrell, M. L. Affairs of Nicholas Culpeper: A Novel.

CULVERWEL, NATHANAEL (d. 1651?), philosopher, was born about 1617, in Northamptonshire. Beyond the records of his progress at Emmanuel College, Cambridge, where he received his B.A. in 1636, M.A. in 1640, and a fellowship in 1642, singularly little is known of his life.

His brother Richard, rector of Grundisburg, Suffolk, mentioned in an introduction to one of his brother's published works that Nathanael's health was bad. His self-confident and independent outspokenness seems to have brought criticism from the college authorities toward the end of his short career. Nothing is known of the last five years of his life, from the date of the writing of his one important work, *The Light of Nature*, to his death, probably in 1651, at about the age of thirty-two.

One of the earliest exponents of the school of Cambridge Platonists, Culverwel gave evidence in his few works, which were all college exercises or sermons, of great learning and original thought. He wrote in a forceful, eloquent style. Many of his doctrines were in accord with those of Ralph Cudworth and John Worthington, more celebrated contemporaries at Emmanuel.

In 1646, when he was about twenty-nine years old, he wrote *The Light of Nature*, in which his avowed purpose was "giving to reason the things that are reason's, and unto faith the things which are faith's." Both in this and in a projected later work which was never written, he desired to prove that there is no contradiction between the functions of reason and of faith. Of the two functions, he believed that of faith to be superior.

Light of Nature was first published after the author's death, in 1652, with several other treatises: "the Schism, the Panting Soul, Mount Ebal, the White Stone, Spiritual Optics, the Worth of Souls." For a later edition, in 1857, John Cairns of Berwick wrote a critical essay which placed Culverwel among the foremost of the Cambridge Platonists.

PRINCIPAL WORKS: Spiritual Optics, 1651; An Elegant and Learned Discourse of the Light of Nature, with Several Other Treatises (W. Dillingham, ed. 1652; J. Brown, ed. 1857).

ABOUT: Brown, J. Biographical Preface, Light of Nature, 1857; Hamilton, Sir W. Works of Thomas Reid; Powicke, F. J. The Cambridge Platonists; Tulloch, J. Rational Theology.

CUMBERLAND, RICHARD

CUMBERLAND, RICHARD (February 19, 1732-May 7, 1811), dramatist, novelist, was a great-grandson of the bishop of Peterborough and the son of Dr. Denison Cumberland, bishop of Clonfert and Kilmore. His mother was Joanna Bentley, daughter of the distinguished scholar, Richard Bentley, and supposed to be the heroine of John Byrom's early poem, *Colin and Phoebe*. Richard was born in the master's lodge at Trinity College, Cambridge, and received his education at Westminster school and Trinity, where he took his degree in 1750.

Through his family connections, Cumberland began his career as private secretary to the Earl of Halifax, traveling with him and playing a minor but highly respectable role in government. This allowed him leisure to study and try his hand at poetry and playwriting. His first drama, *The Banishment of Cicero*, was turned down by Garrick but found publication in 1761. A few years later, in need of money, he began a serious writing career, fathering some fifty successful plays before he died at the age of seventy-nine.

Cumberland's happiest vein was sentimental comedy, a form in which he untied domestic tangles by strong dramatic action, pointing the way to later melodramas. He wrote *The Brothers*, a comedy based on *Tom Jones*; *The West Indian*, probably his best play; *The Battle of Hastings*, a tragedy, and adapted a number of works including *Timon of Athens*. He also found time to write two novels, *Henry* and *Arundel*, neither of which had any lasting merit.

Well known in the literary circles of the day, Cumberland met regularly with such men as Foote, Reynolds, Garrick and Goldsmith at the British Coffeehouse. His popularity seems to have given him an enormous self-importance and he became inordinately sensitive to criticism. Garrick called him the "man without a skin." Sheridan satirized him as Sir Fretful Plagiary in *The Critic*, supposedly out of revenge for Cumberland's behavior on the opening night of *The School for Scandal*. The story goes that Cumberland, in a box with his family, reproved his children for laughing; Sheridan retorted, "He ought to have laughed at my comedy for I laughed heartily at his tragedy." Cumberland, however, denies the whole story in his *Memoirs*.

PRINCIPAL WORKS: *Plays* (dates of production)—The Summer's Tale, 1765; Amelia, 1768; The Brothers, 1769; The West Indian, 1771; The Fashionable Lover, 1772; The Choleric Man, 1774; The Battle of Hastings, 1778; The Mysterious Husband, 1783; The Natural Son, 1784; The Imposters, 1789; The School for Widows, 1789; The Jew, 1794; The Wheel of Fortune, 1795; First Love, 1795; False Impressions, 1797; The Eccentric Lover, 1798; The Sailor's Daughter, 1804; A Hint to Husbands, 1806; The Posthumous Dramatick Works of the Late Richard Cumberland, 1813. *Other Works*—Arundel (novel) 1789; Henry (Novel) 1795; Memoirs of Richard Cumberland Written by Himself, 1806-07 (H. Flanders, ed. 1856).

ABOUT: Mumford, W. The Life of Richard Cumberland; Symonds, E. M. Richard Cumberland, *in* Little Memoirs of the Eighteenth Century; Williams, S. T. Richard Cumberland: His Life and Dramatic Works.

CUNNINGHAM, JOHN

CUNNINGHAM, JOHN (1729-September 18, 1773), dramatist, poet, was born in Dublin of Scottish parentage. His father had won a prize in a lottery and invested his winnings in a small wine business but went into bankruptcy while John was still a boy. Educated at Drogheda, young Cunningham when he was twelve years old began to write poems which were published in the Dublin newspapers, and at eighteen wrote a successful farce, *Love in a Mist*. His play was produced at the Crow Street Theatre in Dublin and is said to have been the source for Garrick's comedy *The Lying Valet*.

Attracted by the theatre, Cunningham decided to become an actor. He joined a group of strolling players and traveled widely through Ireland and Scotland, devoting whatever leisure he could find to writing poetry. Although he seems to have had little or no talent as an actor, he was well liked by his associates and enjoyed the easy camaraderie of the theatre. In Edinburgh he became a favorite of a theatrical manager by the name of Digges and his leading lady, Mrs. George Anne Bellamy, and wrote for them a number of dramatic prologues. Between the years 1762 and 1766 he also wrote and published three volumes of poetry: *The Contemplatist, a Night Piece*; *Fortune, an Apologue*, and *Poems, Chiefly Pastoral*. These brought him considerable reputation but little financial return. His most successful poem was the *Elegy on a Pile of Ruins*, published at Edinburgh, which is a pallid imitation of Gray's *Elegy*, but which was widely praised at the time of its appearance. On the strength of this success he was called to London by a firm of booksellers who unfortunately went bankrupt before he could get there.

Cunningham's older brother, a successful "statuary," begged the actor-poet to come live with him in Dublin, but Cunningham continued to prefer the life of a wanderer. When at last his health broke down, he retired to Newcastle where he died at the house of a friend when he was only forty-four. The legend on his tombstone reads, "His works will remain a monument to all ages," but actually both his poetry and his single precocious play have been almost entirely forgotten since the eighteenth century.

PRINCIPAL WORKS: Love in a Mist (a play) 1747; A Poetical Essay in Manner of Elegy on the Lamented Death of his Late Majesty, 1760; An Elegy on a Pile of Ruins, 1761; Day and Other Pastorals, 1761; The Contemplatist, a Night Piece,

1762; Fortune, an Apologue, 1765; Poems Chiefly Pastoral, 1766; The Poetical Works of John Cunningham (J. Bell, ed.) 1781.

ABOUT: Bell, J. Life, *in* Poets of Great Britain; O'Donoghue, D. J. The Poets of Ireland.

CURLL, EDMUND (1675-December 11, 1747), bookseller, pamphleteer, was born of humble parents in the western part of England. As a boy he was apprenticed to a Mr. Smith—probably Richard Smith, the bookseller—becoming himself a bookseller and publisher.

These booksellers of the eighteenth century were a miscellaneous lot, frequently literary men themselves, publishers and businessmen who usually kept a stable of hack writers and were glad to turn a penny at anything from literary forgery to selling patent medicines. If men like Robert Dodsley and Jacob Tonson stood at the zenith in the publishing field, Curll was the nadir. The "unspeakable Curll" had a career which ran from fraud to libel and obscenity, involving him in a remarkable series of personal attacks and legal difficulties.

He first quarreled with Pope over the anonymous publication of *Court Poems* in 1716, which he advertised as containing lines by the eminent translator of Homer. Pope revenged himself in an elaborate practical joke, giving Curll an emetic potion at the Swan Tavern, as recounted in *The Full and True Account of a Horrid and Barbarous Revenge by Poison on the Body of Mr. Edmund Curll, Bookseller*. The quarrel was continued when Curll announced the publication of Pope's literary correspondence and had all his stock seized at Pope's instigation. Pope then added Curll to his gallery of sinners in *The Dunciad* and the publisher retaliated with a heated pamphlet, *The Curliad*, heralded in a series of satiric advertisements.

Twice Curll had to appear before the House of Lords for publishing unauthorized material about its members. A few years later he was convicted and fined for publishing obscene books and the word "Curlicism" became a synonym for literary indecency. At the same time Curll wrote a number of telling pamphlets, edited several books of considerable interest, and published works of antiquarian and biographical value along with fakes and shockers. He had knowledge, a ready pen, courage, impudence, and no scruples.

Amory has described him in the *Life of John Buncle*: "... in person very tall and thin, an ungainly, awkward, white-faced man. His eyes were a light grey, large, projecting, goggle and purblind. He was splay-footed, and baker-kneed." But with justice Amory adds, "He had a good natural understanding and was well acquainted with more than the title pages of books."

PRINCIPAL WORKS: Miscellanies by Dr. Jonathan Swift (ed.) 1711; Some Account of the Life of Dr. Walter Curll, Bishop of Winchester, 1712; Posthumous Works of the late Robert South (ed.) 1717; Mr. Pope's Worms, and a New Ballad on the Masquerade, 1718; Miscellanea (ed.) 1727; The Life of That Eminent Comedian, Robert Wilks, Esq., 1733; Memoirs of the Life and Writings of Matthew Tindal (ed.) 1733; The Curliad, a Hypercritic upon the Dunciad Variorum, 1729.

ABOUT: Straus, R. The Unspeakable Curll; Thomas, W. J. Curll Papers, Stray Notes on the Life and Publications of Edmund Curll.

CYNEWULF (probably a Northumbrian poet of the latter half of the eighth century) is the only Old English vernacular poet whose works of undisputed authorship exist. It is easier to say what is not true about him than what is. Modern research has established the certainty that he was not the Abbot of Peterborough and Bishop of Winchester of about 1000, nor the Bishop of Lindisfarne who died about 781; nor is it likely that he was ever in his youth a wandering ministrel. He may possibly have been a priest of Dunwich who flourished about 800. He may have been a Mercian, but more probably was a Northumbrian; he was definitely not a West Saxon. He certainly lived for a long time near the sea, for which he has a special and intimate feeling; and he lived to be very old (though old age in that era came much sooner than it does now) and felt his years a burden on him. It is probable also that he had been some great lord's scop or thegn, and had known the favor and received the gifts of kings. It is possible, though not likely, that as a young man he wrote secular poems which have now disappeared. He seems to have known Latin, and to have ended, if not begun his career as a priest. He himself said, "I am old and ready to depart, having woven wordcraft and pondered deeply in the darkness of the world. Once I was gay in the hall and received gifts. . . . Yet was I buffeted

with care, fettered by sins, beset with sorrows, until the Lord . . . bestowed on me grace and revealed to me the mystery of the holy cross."

Four poems contain Cynewulf's signature in runes and hence are undoubtedly his. They are the *Crist, Juliana, Fates of the Apostles,* and *Elene.* The first two come from the Exeter Book, the latter two from the Vercelli Book, both eleventh century manuscripts, one now in England, the other in Italy. The other poems in these "books" —*Guthlac, The Phoenix, Physiologus, Riddles, Andreas,* and *Dream of the Rood*—are probably by followers of Cynewulf; he may have written the *Guthlac,* and some of the *Riddles;* it is certain that he did not write *The Dream of the Rood.* His masterpiece is *Elene,* the account of the discovery of the True Cross by the mother of Constantine the Great.

The undisputed poems display a personal religious feeling and the workings of an original mind, which may have taken its material from Latin sources but transmuted it into an expression of the poet's own personality. One of the salient features of his poetry is its prevailing melancholy—what one commentator called its "autumnal grace." The vivid pictures of sea and shore are especially notable. With the exception of *Elene,* however, none of the undoubted poems of Cynewulf is equal to *Andreas* or to *The Dream of the Rood.* His importance is historical rather than literary, in spite of a few passages of great beauty.

PRINCIPAL WORKS: Cynewulf's Crist, a Modern Rendering (I. Gollancz, tr.) 1892; The Poems of Cynewulf, Translated into English Prose (C. W. Kennedy, tr.) 1910.

ABOUT: Brooke, S. A. Early English Literature; Sisam, K. Cynewulf and His Poetry; Smithson, G. A. The Old English Christian Epic; Stevens, W. O. The Cross in the Life and Literature of the Anglo-Saxons; Sweet, H. The Oldest English Texts; Trautmann, M. Kynewulf, der Bischof und Dichter.

DAMPIER, WILLIAM (June 1652-March 1715), privateer, explorer, travel-writer, was born at East Coker, Somersetshire, the son of a tenant farmer. Orphaned when he was still a child, young William was apprenticed to the master of a ship at Weymouth and accompanied him on a voyage to Newfoundland. He served in the Royal Navy under Sir Edward Sprague during the Dutch War in 1673 and the next year retired from the sea to take a job as under-manager of a Jamaica estate. With adventure in his bones, he did not remain long in this position but took to wandering—sailing in the Jamaica coastal trade, cutting logwood in Yucatan, and buccaneering. Much of this early experience is vividly described in his famous travel accounts.

His career as seaman and buccaneer was briefly interrupted when he returned to England and found a wife; but in a year he was on the high seas again. As a member of one or another piratical band, he roamed the western coast of the Americas, sacking, plundering, and burning. In 1683 he was employed by a Captain Cook for a privateering voyage against the Spaniards in the South Seas. Off the Mexican coast Cook died, and with a new captain and a mutinous crew, the vessel proceeded to the Philippines and on to the Nicobars, where Dampier and several companions either deserted or were marooned. Making his way back to England after coming near death in his travels, Dampier apparently decided to seek respectability and set about writing the story of his voyages. *A Voyage Round the World*, published in 1697, was immediately successful, as was a supplementary volume, *Voyages and Descriptions*, published two years later. He also wrote an extremely interesting study on meteorological geography, *A Discourse of Winds*.

On the basis of his newly established reputation, Dampier was chosen by the Admiralty to command two expeditions of exploration, but he was evidently an extremely poor commander, as both voyages were plagued by mutinies, desertion, and disruption and ended in disaster. Dampier underwent a court-martial for his severity towards his subordinates and became, understandably enough, something less than popular with British shipowners. His last voyage was made as a pilot for another famous navigator, Woodes Rogers, sailing again around the world, but he did not live to collect his profits from this highly successful expedition.

Whatever the dubious color of some of his adventures, Dampier's books are first-rate travel accounts, written in clear and virile prose. He had an indisputable gift for observation and he described the seas, coasts, people, plants, and animals that he saw with picturesque fidelity.

PRINCIPAL WORKS: A New Voyage Round the World, 1697 (Gray, Sir A. ed. 1927); Voyages and Descriptions, 1699; A Discourse of Winds, 1699; A Voyage to New Holland, 1703-09; Dampier's Voyages (J. Masefield, ed.) 1906.

ABOUT: Dampier, W. Dampier's Voyages (J. Masefield, ed.)

DANIEL, SAMUEL (1562-1619), poet, dramatist, was born near Taunton, Somersetshire, the son of John Daniel, a music master. His brother John was a well-known writer on music. Samuel Daniel spent three years at Magdalen Hall (now Hertford College), Oxford, but left without a degree. In 1585 he turned up in London, possibly in the service of Lord Stafford, the ambassador to France. His first book, written during this period, was a translation of an Italian work on heraldry. He seems to have spent the year 1586 in Italy, and then he became tutor to the son of the Earl and Countess of Pembroke, William Herbert (later Shakespeare's patron). The countess was the famous sister of Sir Philip Sidney, and she not only encouraged Daniel but, he says, "taught" him to write verse. By 1595 he was tutor to the young daughter of the Countess of Cumberland, and though the latter also became his friend and patroness, he complained of the irksomeness of "associating with children" when he was impatient to be writing. He had by this time published several books, including his best known sonnets, and was beginning his epic poem on the Wars of the Roses.

About 1600 he was introduced at court, probably by Giovanni Florio *qv* who was his brother-in-law. (Florio married Daniel's sister.) Though Ben Johnson said Daniel himself was married ("but had no children"), nothing is known about his wife. He found favor with James I, and in 1603 was appointed inspector of the Children of the Queen's Revels. This was a post he could hold without living in London, and he retired permanently to a farm at Beckington, near Devizes. He held the office for the remainder of his life, writing many masques for the company to play. After Daniel's death his brother inherited the post.

Only once did Daniel himself become involved in the troublous politics of the time.

136

He was called before the authorities because somebody suspected that his tragedy, *Philotas,* concealed a portrait of the Earl of Essex and approval of his treason. Daniel extricated himself with nothing worse than a reprimand from the Earl of Devonshire—whom he had mentioned as approving the play before Essex' downfall—and since he was allowed to remain as one of the grooms of the queen's privy chamber, the king must have believed in his innocence. Nevertheless, Daniel undoubtedly had some sympathy with Essex, whom he had eulogized; like Essex, he was a Protestant but was kindly inclined toward the Roman Catholic cause.

What he was in essence was a *laudator temporis acti,* longing for the golden age of the Tudors, believing firmly in the necessity of a strong and absolute monarchy. He believed also that the poet's function was to instruct and edify, and Drayton[qv] said shrewdly that he was "too much historian in verse. His manner better fitted prose." Ben Jonson, who did not like him much, called him "an honest man, but no poet."

All this may be and is true of Daniel's historical poems, but it does not at all apply to his sonnets. These, written in the form evolved by Wyatt and Surrey,[qqv] with a concluding couplet, have grace, delicacy, and real tenderness though they probably were written, in the style of the day, to no specific "Delia." They were published first without his authority as an appendix to an edition of Sidney, and contained so many errors that Daniel in self-defense brought out the full set of fifty the next year. He was always a slow, careful writer, constantly revising and issuing edition after edition of the same poems with some additions.

The sonnets made him famous; Spenser, in *Colin Clout's Come Home Again,* hailed Daniel as the "new shepherd late upsprong, the which doth all afore him far surpasse," and predicted that "most, me seems, thy accent will excell/In tragick plaints and passionate mischance." Daniel's characteristic mood outside the sonnets is one of heavy gravity. His language had serious dignity and limpid purity—Coleridge called it "quite modern"—but he was a man of fine taste rather than one of fiery genius. His characteristics were "philosophic gravity" and didacticism; he felt keenly the responsibility

SAMUEL DANIEL

of the poet to influence manners and morals, and three hundred years before Matthew Arnold he too had his cult of "sweetness and light." His masques suffered by this deliberate seriousness; there is nothing light or gay about them, and they are fairly pompous and heavy. *Hymen's Triumph* was the best of them.

Daniel himself was modest and unassuming. "Something I shall be," he wrote with simple self-respect, "though not the best." He loved the English language, and he did much to clear from it the conceits and extravagances of the Italianate school. Incidentally, he made a remarkable prophecy, when he foresaw that English would some day be the native tongue of "worlds in the yet unform'd Occident." This was written when the only permanent English settlement in the New World was the newly colonized Jamestown.

It has often been stated that Daniel succeeded Spenser as poet laureate, and then resigned in a few months to make way for Ben Jonson. There is no evidence that he was ever named poet laureate, and in 1599, when Spenser died, he was not even established as yet at court.

Daniel wrote two major prose works, one a history of England, the other his *Defence of Ryme,* written in answer to Campion's[qv] *Observations on the Art of English Poesie.* His robust defense of English as a vehicle for rhymed verse was the final blow to the so-called Latinizers, and totally demolished the arguments of their last champion. He himself was a consistent and accurate rhymer, and he experimented in various forms of prosody. His *Epistle to Lucy, Countess of Bedford* was the first English poem in terza rima.

As a historically minded man, Daniel tended naturally to the epic form. There is little passion or ardor in his poetry, but there is much tenderness and gently mournful reverie; and in his sonnets and epistles at least he is an authentic, though in the eyes of posterity a definitely minor poet.

PRINCIPAL WORKS: Sir PS His Astrophel and Stella (with 27 of Daniel's sonnets), 1591; Delia. Contaynyng certayne Sonnets, 1592; Delia . . . with the complaint of Rosamond, 1592; Delia and Rosamond augmented. Cleopatra, 1594; The Tragedie of Cleopatra, 1594; The first fowre Bookes of the civile wars between the two houses of Lancaster and Yorke, 1595 (eight books, 1607); The Poeticall Essayes of Sam. Danyel (The Civil Wars, Cleopatra, Musophilus, A Letter from Octavia to Marcus Antonius) 1599; The Workes of Samuel Daniel newly augmented (including A Defence of Ryme, A Panegyrike congratulatorie [to James I]) 1603; The Vision of the 12 Goddesses (masque) 1604; Certaine small poems lately printed: with the tragedie of Philotas, 1605; The Queenes Arcadia (masque) 1605; A Funerall Poeme on the Duke of Devonshire, 1606; Tethys Festival (masque) 1610; History of England, 1612 (2d part, 1617); Hymen's Triumph (masque) 1615; The Whole Workes of Samuel Daniel, Esquire, in Poetrie (J. Daniel, ed.) 1623; Complete Works in Verse and Prose (A. B. Grosart, ed.) 1885.

ABOUT: Bullen, A. H. Elizabethans; Coleridge, S. T. Table Talk; Fleay, F. G. A Biographical Chronicle of the English Drama; Quiller-Couch, A. T. Adventures in Criticism; Saintsbury, G. A History of English Prosody; Wood, A. a, Athenae Oxonienses.

DARWIN, ERASMUS (December 12, 1731-April 18, 1802)

DARWIN, ERASMUS (December 12, 1731-April 18, 1802), physician, botanist, evolutionist, poet, was the fourth son of Robert Darwin. His mother's maiden name was Waring, and he was born in her family home at Elston, Nottinghamshire. From Chesterfield School he went in 1750 to St. John's College, Cambridge, on a scholarship. He secured his B.A. in 1754, then went to Edinburgh to study medicine—he received his M.B. degree, however, from Cambridge (in 1755). He started practice in Nottingham, but since no patients arrived, he moved in 1756 to Lichfield (the birthplace of Samuel Johnson), which was his home for twenty-five years. There he established the botanical garden which later was to inspire his verse.

In 1757 he married Mary Howard, who died in 1770, leaving three sons. Charles Darwin, the great evolutionist, was the son of the youngest. In 1781 Erasmus Darwin married a widow, Mrs. Chandos-Pole, with whom he had been in love before her husband's death in 1780. Because she disliked Lichfield they moved to Derby. There he died suddenly at seventy-one of a heart attack. By his second marriage he had four sons and three daughters; one of the daughters became the mother of Sir Francis Galton, the scientist.

Outwardly Darwin was the typical gruff country doctor, testy and imperious, but kind-hearted and generous beneath his shell. He was a crochety man who rode his hobbies —such as temperance—to death. He was famous as a physician, and declined an offer from George III to become the king's personal doctor. A large, heavy man, he was nervous and a stammerer. He had a turn for mechanics and invented many things, including a carriage which involved him in an accident and made him lame thereafter. He was a radical, a freethinker, and a friend of Rousseau; and apparently he was no puritan, for his treatise on "female education" was written on behalf of two illegitimate daughters who ran a girls' school. Nevertheless, even in a small town like Lichfield, and in spite of his irascibility and dictatorial manner, he enjoyed great popularity and received wide acclaim. The biography of him written by Anna Seward must be taken with several grains of salt, since she had hoped to become his second wife, and was disappointed in the hope.

Charles Darwin said that his grandfather "anticipated the views and erroneous grounds of opinions of Lamarck." Samuel Butler (the younger), who was a Lamarckian, was probably his only full disciple. He believed that all warm-blooded animals arose from one living "filament," and were endowed with new propensities achieved by volition. He believed also that plants too have sensation and volition.

His poetry Darwin wrote for the most part while traveling by carriage to visit his patients. *The Loves of the Plants*, his best known verse (one can scarcely call it a poem), appeared anonymously in 1789, two years later reappearing as the second part of *The Botanic Garden*. Horace Walpole

After J. Wright

ERASMUS DARWIN

and William Cowper admired it greatly, but it was killed (and embalmed) by George Canning's wicked parody, *The Loves of the Triangles*. Indeed, *The Loves of the Plants* is its own parody. It is very bad poetry which yet reveals a skillful hand and a powerful mind. Its stilted personifications, its monotonous heroic couplets, its extravagant imagery embodied in rigidly conventional forms, combine to make it quite unreadable. Much the same may be said of Darwin's other verse, while his *Zoonomia* and *Phytologia* are today mere scientific curiosities. He was a "character," an eccentric personality, in many ways a social anticipation and an intellectual pioneer, and a man of strong and original mind born in the wrong period for his peculiar bent; but probably his place in history is most firmly fixed by his providing the ancestral link which insured the birth of his famous grandsons.

PRINCIPAL WORKS: The Botanic Garden: I. The Economy of Vegetation. II. The Loves of the Plants, 1789-91; Zoonomia, or the Laws of Organic Life, 1794-96; A Plan for the Conduct of Female Education in Boarding Schools, 1797; Phytologia, or the Philosophy of Agriculture and Gardening, 1800; The Temple of Nature (verse) 1803; Remembrance, 1812.

ABOUT: Butler, S. Evolution Old and New; Coleridge, S. T. Biographia Literaria; Darwin, C. Life of Erasmus Darwin; Dowson, J. Erasmus Darwin; Krause, E. Life of Erasmus Darwin (W. S. Dallas, tr.); Pearson, H. Dr. Darwin; Seward, A. Memoirs of the Life of Dr. Darwin; Stirling, J. H. Darwinianism: Workmen and Work.

D'AVENANT, Sir WILLIAM (February 1606-April 7, 1668), dramatist, was born in Oxford. His putative father, John D'Avenant or Davenant, kept an inn there. There is some reason to believe that William was really the illegitimate son of Shakespeare, and he never denied it, though he called the great poet his "godfather." For a short time after 1620 he was at Lincoln College, Oxford, but he never took a degree. Instead, he became a page in the family of the Duchess of Richmond, then entered the service of Fulke Greville, Lord Brooke. After Brooke was murdered, in 1628, D'Avenant became a sort of hanger-on at court. He began staging plays for the court about 1630. A great favorite, he was made poet laureate, succeeding Ben Jonson, in 1638. With the beginning of the Revolution, he remained faithful to the royal family, and fought bravely at the siege of Gloucester, in 1643, being knighted by Charles immediately afterward. Several times he was taken prisoner (Milton, his personal friend, is said once to have secured his release), and he acted as a go-between when the king and queen were separated. However, his conversion to Roman Catholicism in 1646 and his consequent ardor in the cause of the Roman Catholic queen, caused some coolness between him and the king. The queen finally sent him to Virginia on a mission in 1650, but he was captured and imprisoned in Cowes Castle, whence he escaped to Paris, where his best-known work, *Gondibert*, was written—but never finished, since he was in fear of his life and could no longer spare energy for anything but "the experiment of dying."

Actually, he survived to return to England, and secured a license to establish a theatre in the Cockpit. Even during the Commonwealth, he had, against Puritan opposition, managed to stage a number of what he called "operas." His post-Restoration plays were among the first to employ scenery and to have women on the stage. D'Avenant's plays and "operas" are mostly "adaptations" of greater works. His place in literature is assured by *Gondibert*, which was founded on the aesthetic theories of Hobbes *qv* and prepared the way for Dryden. His aim was to "represent nature, though not in an affected, yet in an unusual dress,"

SIR WILLIAM D'AVENANT

and he attacked the conceits and affectations of the Elizabethans. Though he succeeded in clearing out a great deal of literary rubbish and restoring much simplicity, he himself was an exceedingly dull and prolix writer. His was the first English epic written in quatrains, and he was one of the pioneers of the heroic couplet. He asserted the moral value of poetry, but he had little poetic gift.

Very handsome in youth, D'Avenant lost his nose through some unnamed disease—a subject for crude jest to his contemporaries. In spite of this disability, he married twice and left a son by his first marriage and "five or six" children by his second. He died in London, and was buried in Westminster Abbey.

PRINCIPAL WORKS: The Tragedy of Alboine, King of the Lombards, 1629; The Wits, 1636; Britannia Triumphans (masque) 1637; Gondibert, 1651; The Siege of Rhodes, 1656; The First Entertainment at Rutland House, 1657; The Cruelty of the Spaniards in Peru, 1658; The History of Sir Francis Drake, 1659; The Rivals, 1668; The Man's the Master, 1669; Works, 1673; Dramatic Works (J. Maidment and W. H. Logan, eds.) 1872-74.

ABOUT: Aubrey, J. Lives of Eminent Men; D'Israeli, I. Quarrels of Authors; Maidment, J. and Logan, W. H. Memoir, in Dramatic Works; Wood, A. à, Athenae Oxonienses.

DAVENPORT, ROBERT (fl. 1623), dramatist, poet, was the author of three plays and two poems of considerable interest, but beyond this nothing is known of him.

Two didactic poems, *A Crowne for a Conqueror* and *Too Late to Call Backe Yesterday*, were printed in 1623 and according to an epistle attached to the poems, they were written at sea. The three plays which survive are *King John and Matilda*, a tragedy, and two comedies, *The City-Nightcap* and *A New Tricke to Cheat the Divell*. The rest of his plays, including two listed in a stationer's register as *Henry I* and *Henry II*, have been lost. It is supposed that they may have been among the manuscripts of Elizabethan plays in the possession of John Warburton, an antiquary, which were inadvertantly burned or put under "pye bottoms" by his cook.

Davenport's tragedy seems to be a careful rewriting of the *Death of Robert, Earle of Huntington*, by Henry Chettle and Anthony Munday, in which the older play is stripped of its crudity and horror. Davenport's version is superior in poetic diction and imagery—yet the original remains more memorable for its atmosphere of gloom and horror. The two comedies were probably also remodelings of older material. The main story of *The City-Nightcap*, which Davenport called a tragi-comedy, is derived from an episode in *Don Quixote*, and there are also echoes of *Measure for Measure* and *Cymbeline*. (It has been supposed that Davenport knew Shakespeare's work well and may have collaborated with him on *Henry II*, one of the lost plays.) *A New Tricke to Cheate the Divell* is an able comedy, more humorous but considerably less ambitious.

A publisher's preface to this latter comedy describes the play as "now an Orphant and wanting the Father which first begot it," but whether Davenport was dead at the time of its publication in 1639, or merely absent from England, has never been made clear. He seems to have been alive in 1640 when laudatory verses written by him were used as a preface to two plays, Rawlin's *Rebellion* and Richards' *Messalina*. Eleven years later we hear of him again in Samuel Sheppard's *Epigrams*. Referring apparently to a then current play, Sheppard addresses "Mr. Davenport on his play called *The Pirate*," saying "Thou rival'st Shakespeare though thy glory's lesse."

PRINCIPAL WORKS: A Pleasant and Witty Comedy: Called, A New Tricke to Cheat the

Divell, 1639; King John and Matilda, A Tragedy, 1655; The City-Nightcap: Or, Crede quod habes, et habes. A Tragi-Comedy, 1661; The Works of Robert Davenport, in Old English Plays, New Series (A. H. Bullen, ed.) 1890.

ABOUT: Bullen, A. H. Preface to Old English Plays, New Series; Retrospective Review Vol. 4.

DAVIDSON, JOHN (1549?-August 1603), Scottish church leader, poet and miscellaneous writer, was born at Dunfermline in Fifeshire. He graduated from St. Leonard's College, St. Andrews, in 1571 and was elected a regent of the college. As a student of theology, he became acquainted with John Knox while still a young man. Knox was said to be a member of the audience for a play by Davidson exposing the evils of Romanism, and it was largely due to the influence of the older religious leader that Davidson dedicated his life to the cause of the Reformation in Scotland.

Unpopular for his religious views, Davidson spent a number of years in exile on the continent, but in 1579 returned to Scotland and became a minister at Liberton near Edinburgh. Three years later he was presented to James VI and began a long contest with the king on religious issues. Critical of the king's desire to restore the prelacy, Davidson was always completely outspoken with his monarch and "would now reprove him for swearing, now hold him by the sleeve to prevent him going away, now remind him that in the church he was not a king but a private citizen." Called "the thunderer" for his earnest style of preaching, Davidson preached a public sermon against the king on the occasion of his marriage to Anne because he had arranged to hold her coronation on a Sunday.

In 1596, after a period of exile in England, Davidson was appointed minister of Prestonpans where he was forced to build a church and a manse at his own expense. At last the king became so outraged by Davidson's unwavering opposition that he refused him permission to go outside the parish of Prestonpans. Davidson lived under this interdict the last years of his life and died in his own parish in August 1603.

This battling reformer wrote a number of poems, religious in nature; a catechism, *Some Helps for Young Schollers in Christ*; a diary, *Memorials of His Time*, which became a source for David Calderwood's religious history of Scotland; and a number of miscellaneous prose pieces. Of particular interest among the latter is *Ane Brief Commendation of Uprichtness*, a eulogistic sketch of the life of John Knox which proved valuable to later biographers. Davidson was an accurate scholar as well as a powerful preacher, and the same boldness of spirit which burned through his long struggle for religious reform characterizes all his writings.

PRINCIPAL WORKS: Ane Dialog Betwixt a Clerk and a Courteour, 1573; Ane Brief Commendation of Uprichtness, 1573; Memorial of Two Worthye Christians, 1595; Some Helps for Young Schollers in Christ, 1602; Mr. John Davidson's Catechism, with Preliminary Discourse by W. Jameson, 1708; Poetical Remains (J. Maidment, ed.) 1829.

ABOUT: Maidment, J. Biography, in Poetical Remains; Rogers, C. Three Scottish Reformers.

DAVIES, JOHN, of Hereford (1565?-July 1618), poet, writing master (not to be confused with Sir John Davies *qv*), was born at Hereford of Welsh parentage. Little is known of his early years, but he was probably educated at Oxford where he later settled as a writing master, winning the reputation of the most skillful penman of the realm. Among his pupils were Henry, Prince of Wales, and many young men of noble family. Nevertheless, Davies seems to have had difficulty in earning a comfortable living and a few years after the turn of the century he moved to London where he began to write voluminously.

Davies' two most important works were the long poems, *Mirum in Modum*, a dissertation on God and the soul, and *Microcosmus*, a vague treatise on physiology and psychology purporting to describe the world of man. The latter was modelled on Joshua Sylvester's translation of Du Bartas' *Semaines*. Religious and philosophical in subject matter, his verse had little imaginative quality but a strongly edifying tone which brought him many admiring readers. He turned out quantities of sacred verse, a book of epigrams addressed to well-known writers of the day (among them, Shakespeare), a book of satires and a book of "amorous" sonnets. His best work is probably contained in the sonnets published as *Witte's Pilgrimage*.

Davies was married three times. His first wife, Mary Croft, died, leaving him a son, Sylvanus. When he was forty-eight he married a widow, Dame Juliana Preston, who died a year or two later. A third wife is mentioned in his will, where he also expressed his desire to be buried at the side of his first wife in the church of St. Dunstan, London. He was buried according to his wishes on July 6, 1618.

Didactic religious poetry was rare in the age of Elizabeth and for this reason Davies' work has some interest. Tedious and prolix, he had little gift for genuine poetry, writing instead long treatises in rhyme modeled on the Spenserian stanza. Davies had neither the imagination nor the intellect to mould his religious feeling into verse of any permanent value, but he is interesting as one of those who first translated the influence of the Huguenot, Du Bartas, into English Christian poetry.

PRINCIPAL WORKS: Mirum in Modum, A Glimpse of God's Glorie and the Soule's Shape, 1602; Microcosmus, The Discovery of the Little World, 1603; Bien Venu, Greate Britaine's Welcome to the Danes, 1606; Summa Totalis, 1607; The Holy Roode, 1609; Humours Heav'n on Earth; with the Civile Warres of Death and Fortune (as also, The Triumph of Death, or, The Picture of the Plague As It Was in 1603) 1609; Witte's Pilgrimage Through a World of Amorous Sonnets, Soule-Passions, and Other Passages, 1610; The Scourge of Folly, 1611; The Muses-Sacrifice, or, Divine Meditations, 1612; The Muses-Teares for the Losse of Henry, Prince of Wales, 1613; A Select Second Husband for Sir Thomas Overburie's Wife, Now a Matchlesse Widow, 1616; Wits Bedlam Where Is Had Whipping-Cheer to Cure the Mad, 1617; A Scourge for Paper-Persecutors, 1625; The Complete Works of John Davies of Hereford (A. B. Grosart, ed.) 1878.

ABOUT: Fuller, T. History of the Worthies of England; Grosart, A. B. Introduction, in Complete Works; Wood, A. à, Athenae Oxonienses.

DAVIES, Sir JOHN (April 1569-December 8, 1626), poet, was born in Tisbury, Wiltshire, the son of John Davies, "gentleman," and Mary Bennett. His father died when he was very young. He was educated at Winchester, and in 1585 entered Queen's College, Oxford, receiving his B.A. in 1590. (He may possibly have attended New College for his first year or two.) He was entered at the Middle Temple in 1588, and called to the bar in 1590. Unfortunately, in 1598, he quarreled with his "very friend" Richard Martin, to whom *Orchestra* had been dedicated, and attacked him with a cudgel in the Inns of Court; for this reason he was disbarred, and retired to Oxford again, where he wrote his philosophical poem, *Nosce Teipsum* (Know Thyself). On making public apology to Martin and to the Templars he was, through the good offices of Lord Ellsmere, reinstated in 1601. Lord Mountjoy, later the Earl of Devonshire, became his patron and advised the dedication of *Nosce Teipsum* to Queen Elizabeth. The queen favored him sufficiently to allow him to write the words of three "entertainments" given her—*A Dialogue between a Gentleman Usher and a Poet, A Contention betwixt a Wife, a Widdow, and a Maide,* and *A Lottery.* In 1601 after his readmittance to the bar, he sat in Parliament for Corfe Castle.

In 1603, James I appointed Davies solicitor-general for Ireland, under Mountjoy, who was Lord Deputy, and who knighted him. Davies was a harsh and rigid anti-Catholic, and an ardent participator in the "pacification" of Ulster. It is from this viewpoint that his later book on Ireland was written. In 1606 he was made attorney general for Ireland and a serjeant-at-law, and in 1613 (by physical unseating of his competitor) he became speaker of the Irish Parliament, in which he sat for Fermanagh. Though he was elected to the House of Commons for Newcastle-under-Lyme in 1614, he remained in Ireland until 1619, when he resigned his offices and took his seat in the House. In 1626 he was appointed Lord Chief Justice, but before he could assume office he died suddenly of an apoplectic stroke.

In 1609 Davies married Eleanor Touchet, daughter of Lord Audley. They had an idiot son, who was drowned in Ireland, and a daughter who later became the celebrated Countess of Huntington. Lady Davies was the author of a number of fanatical books of prophecy. (She claimed to have foretold her husband's death.) Later she married Sir Archibald Douglas, and in 1633 she was imprisoned and fined for witchcraft; she seems to have been not very far from insanity.

Davies is a finer poet than he has generally been given credit for. *Orchestra* is graceful, gay, and brilliant; its hundred and thirty-nine seven-line stanzas (rime royal) were said to have been written in fifteen days. *Hymnes of Astræa* is a true tour-de-force; it consists of a series of acrostics to

"Elizabetha Regina," and in spite of its rigidity of form is unforced and lyrical. *Nosce Teipsum*, though its theme seems unpoetic, displays mastery and force, and the treatment clarifies instead of obscuring its theses. Despite its arid stretches, it is one of the most successful philosophical poems in the language. Davies' legal and historical volumes reflect his interest in antiquities—he was a founder of the Society of Antiquaries. The "French" work on the law was in Davies' own mixture of English and incorrect French. His epigrams, uncollected until 1870, were notorious in his own time for their indecency. He was in fact not a very good exemplar of his philosophical advocacy of self-control—he was grossly obese and noted for his love of good living.

PRINCIPAL WORKS: Orchestra, or a Poem of Dancing, 1596; Nosce Teipsum: I. Of human knowledge. II. Of the soule of man, 1599; Hymnes of Astræa, in acrostick verse, 1599; A Discoverie of the true Causes why Ireland was never entirely subdued . . . until the beginning of his Majesties happy raigne, 1612; Poemes, 1622; England's Independency, 1674; Poetical Works, 1773; Historical Tracts (G. Chalmers, ed.) 1786; Epigrammes, 1870; Complete Poems (A. B. Grosart, ed.) 1876; Poems (C. Howard, ed.) 1941.

ABOUT: Bullen, A. B. Introduction *in* Some Longer Elizabethan Poems; Grosart, A. B. Memorial Introduction *in* Complete Poems; Howard, C. Introduction, Poems; Wood, A. à, Athenae Oxonienses; Woolrych, H. W. Lives of Eminent Serjeants-at-Law.

DAVISON, FRANCIS (fl. 1602), poet, the eldest son of William Davison, Queen Elizabeth's secretary of state, was born about 1575. Not much is known of his life or his early work, although he appears as a member of the Grey's Inn group, contributing to the Grey's Inn Masque in 1594.

For a number of years he traveled abroad in the company of a tutor, Edward Smyth, some of whose letters survive. One written from Venice to Francis' father complained that their allowance of £100 a year for expenses was inadequate and went on to say that his pupil was "not so easily ruled touching expences, about which we have had more brabblements than I will now speak of." There are also letters from Francis to his father and to Anthony Bacon, the brother of Francis Bacon, which indicate that he was writing both poetry and prose. Anthony Bacon wrote young Davison commending a prose piece, *Relation of Saxony*, which unfortunately has disappeared.

Davison returned to England presumably about 1597. The first edition of his major work, a collection of poems edited by him and titled *A Poetical Rapsody*, appeared in 1602. Many of the poems included were his own but there were also a number by his younger brother, Walter, as well as by Sir John Davies, Sir Philip Sidney, Mary, Countess of Pembroke, and a mysterious A. W. who has never been identified. One of these poems, "In Praise of a Beggar's Life," has been made widely familiar through its quotation by Izaak Walton in *The Compleat Angler* as "Frank Davison's song, which he made forty years ago."

Both Francis and Walter Davison were the authors of popular madrigals which appear in song collections of the period, but their work for the most part is merely that of persons of taste and education rather than true poets. Francis Davison also made a metrical translation of the Psalms which is extant in manuscript and which has a good deal of merit.

William Davison died in 1608 and it is probable that his son, Francis, died about eleven years later, for in 1619 many of his manuscripts and his father's papers came into the possession of Ralph Starkey. It is unfortunate that more of Francis Davison's work is not available, but he deserves to be remembered, if not for his own verse, for his collection of poems in *A Poetical Rapsody*, one of the more important Elizabethan anthologies.

PRINCIPAL WORKS: A Poetical Rapsody Containing Diverse Sonnets, Odes, Elegies, Madrigalls, and Other Poesies, Both in Rime, and Measured Verse (editor and contributor) 1602 (Sir H. Nicholas, ed. 1826; A. H. Bullen, ed. 1890).

WORKS: Nicolas, Sir H. Memoirs, *in* Poetical Rapsody (1826 ed.).

DAY, JOHN (1574-1640?), dramatist, miscellaneous writer, was born at Cawston, Norfolk, went to school in Ely, and entered Caius College, Cambridge, in 1592. The next year he was expelled for stealing a book. He drifted to London, where he became one of Philip Henslowe's "stable" of playwrights, who collaborated on plays and adaptations, and occasionally wrote plays of their own. The best known of the group was Dekker.[qv] Many of Day's plays and those on which he collaborated are lost, and it is difficult to know just how much was his in those which survive. He worked hard, and he had a certain aptitude for sprightly repartee, but with one exception he was simply an industrious hack. That exception is *The Parliament of Bees*, published in 1641 but probably written as early as 1607. This is not a play, but a sort of allegory or a series of pastoral eclogues, in which all the characters are bees; it is a charming thing, and justifies Arthur Symons' ascription to Day of "a sense of delicate music in the fall and arrangement of quite common words." Day deprecated the bawdiness of the popular drama of his day, but again and again he yielded to public demand and was as coarse as any of his contemporaries. His gift was for delicate fancy, but his job was to collaborate on comedies for "the Children of the Revels."

Either Henslowe paid his playwrights very badly, or Day was very improvident, for Henslowe's diary is full of notes of advances and loans to Day, sometimes of only a few shillings. Not unnaturally, he was despondent and bitter in his earlier years, but gradually mellowed to a calm serenity, and in his *Peregrinatio Scholastica* rather pathetically presented himself as a scholar, and dared to claim affiliation with the college which had expelled him for theft! There is even some evidence that toward the end of his life he contemplated taking holy orders— just how, it is difficult to conceive—and that this intention was based not merely on a desire for a safe livelihood, but also on genuine religious feeling.

Very little is known about Day's life, even whether he ever married, or the date of his death. It was certainly by 1640, since in that year John Tatham, the "city poet," wrote an elegy on him. His first play is supposed to have been *The Conquest of Spayne by John à Gaunt*, written with William Haughton and Richard Hathaway, and produced in 1601, but lost. However, it is possible that as early as 1593 he collaborated with Marlowe (who died that year) in another lost play, *The Maiden's Holiday*. Under the conditions of Elizabethan playwriting, a minor hack like John Day was too unimportant for any but casual mention to be made of him. It is unfortunate that the author of *The Parliament of Bees* never had an opportunity to do more of the kind of writing for which he was best equipped.

PRINCIPAL WORKS: The Isle of Gulls, 1606; The Travailes of the Three English Brothers (with W. Rowley and G. Wilkinson) 1607; Humour Out of Breath, 1608; Law-Trickes, 1608; Peregrinatio Scholastica, 1640; The Parliament of Bees, 1641; Collected Works (A. H. Bullen, ed.) 1881.

ABOUT: Bullen, A. H. Introduction to Collected Works; Lamb, C. Specimens of the English Dramatic Poets; Swinburne, A. C. The Age of Shakespeare; Symons, A. Introduction to Nero and Other Plays.

DAY, THOMAS (June 22, 1748-September 28, 1789), writer on social and moral reform, didactic juvenile writer, author of *Sandford and Merton,* was born at Wellclose Square, London, where his father was collector of customs. He received his early education at the Charterhouse and entered Corpus Christi College, Oxford, at the age of sixteen. There he immersed himself in the study of philosophy, finding in the works of Rousseau a principle and a point of view which was to govern his life. Although he studied law and was admitted to the bar in 1775, he never practiced but devoted himself to carrying out his own ideas of educational and social reform.

After wooing several ladies, one of them the sister of his friend, Richard Lovell Edgeworth, he decided to take a wife on philosophical principles, and chose accordingly two female orphans about twelve years old— one a blonde, Sabrina, and one a brunette, Lucretia. Lucretia proved "invincibly stupid" and was placed with a milliner, but Sabrina was subjected for two years to a variety of educational experiments before Day judged her wanting in character because she started when he dropped hot sealing wax on her arm and screamed when he fired a pistol at her petticoats. Sabrina was packed off to boarding-school and Day turned his attentions to the Sneyd sisters, Honora and Elizabeth, who later became the second and third wives of his friend, Edgeworth.

Day was just past twenty-five when he settled in London and wrote *The Dying Negro*, a poem which denounced American patriots for maintaining the institution of slavery. This poem was much admired and one of the admirers was Esther Milnes, herself an author, who proved to be the ideal woman for whom Day had searched so long.

After a full rehearsal of virtues, with high-minded pledges on both sides, they were married in 1778. Mr. and Mrs. Day experimented in politics, in farming, and in the cultivation of natural goodness, while Mr. Day converted his findings into saleable prose. His most famous work, *Sandford and Merton,* written to set forth the ideal of manliness, became one of the most widely read children's books of its day. Completely lacking in humor, it invites parody—yet in spite of its old-fashioned didacticism the story still carries a certain amount of interest. Day may too easily be catalogued as a well-meaning crackpot. He was, in spite of his eccentricities, a social critic who lived and wrote and died by his principles. On the theory that kindness would control any animal, he mounted an unbroken colt one autumn day to pay a visit to his mother, was thrown on his head and died before he could revise his assumption.

PRINCIPAL WORKS: The Dying Negro, 1773; The Devoted Legions, 1776; The Desolation of America, 1777; Reflections on the Present State of England and the Independence of America, 1782; History of Sandford and Merton (3 vols.) 1783-89; History of Little Jack, 1788.

ABOUT: Blackman, J. Life and Writings of Thomas Day; Edgeworth, R. L. Memoirs; Keir, J. Account of Life and Writings of Thomas Day.

DEE, Dr. JOHN (July 13, 1527-December 1608), mathematician, astrologer, scholar was born in London, of Welsh descent. His father, Rowland Dee, may have been a vintner, or (more probably) gentleman sewer (server) to Henry VIII; his mother was Johanna Wild. In 1542 he entered St. John's College, Cambridge, receiving his B.A. in 1545, and becoming a foundation fellow in 1546. When Trinity College was founded in this same year, he was one of the original fellows. In 1577 he went to the Low Countries for study, bringing back new astronomical instruments. These he gave to Trinity, which conferred an M.A. on him in 1548. He spent the next two years in Louvain, where he may possibly have gained his doctor's degree. The next year he gave the first public lectures in mathematics at the University of Paris. In 1551 he returned to England and received a pension from Edward VI, which he exchanged for the rectory of Upton-upon-Severn. Accused of conspiring to poison Queen Mary, he was acquitted

DR. JOHN DEE

but transferred to the Bishop of London's prison on charges of heresy, finally being released in 1555 on his own recognizance for good behavior. Elizabeth showed him much if fluctuating favor, studying under his tutelage and sending him to Germany to confer about her medical care.

In 1582 he fell under the influence of the notorious Edward Kelly, who became his "scryer" in the crystal-gazing he conducted at his home in Mortlake and who thoroughly exploited the scholarly but credulous Dee. By this time Dee had a bad reputation as a wizard and a magician—and he himself believed devoutly in astrology, alchemy, and the divine properties of his crystal. A mob assailed and wrecked his house, scattering his books and instruments. Dee and Kelly fled and spent the years from 1583 to 1589 in Poland and Bohemia, under the patronage of Albert Laski, Palatine of Siridez, who soon tired of them and tried in vain to get rid of them. Finally Dee broke with Kelly and returned to England, to find himself ruined financially. In spite of assistance from the queen and others, he remained in deep poverty. In 1594 Elizabeth appointed him warden of Manchester College, but his haughty, arrogant manners kept him in constant hot water with the fellows, and in 1604 he resigned and returned to Mortlake. There he died, very poor, and utterly discredited,

145

since James I had refused to clear him of the charge of conjury.

Though Dee was gullible in the extreme, and his self-confidence and "impudence" made him many enemies, he really was a profound scholar with genuine scientific leanings, particularly in mathematics. Most of his writings were in Latin, and he has no distinction of style in his English works. His place in literary history comes almost solely from his *Private Diary*, which constitutes an invaluable picture of the world in which he lived. His best written work was an unpublished discourse on the need for reformation of the calendar.

Dee was married twice, his first wife dying in 1575. In 1578 he married Jane Fromond, and they had eleven children.

PRINCIPAL WORKS: A Supplication to Queen Mary for the Recovery and Preservation of Ancient Writings and Monuments, 1556; Propaedeumata Aphoristica, 1558; Divers Annotations and Inventions Added to . . . Euclid, 1570; Preface Mathematicall to the English Euclid, 1570; A Fruitfull Preface, Specifying the Chiefe Mathematicall Sciences, 1580; Compendious Rehearsal of John Dee, 1592; A True and Fruitful Relation of What Passed for Many Years between Dr. John Dee . . . and Some Spirits (M. Casaubon, ed.) 1659; Private Diary of Dr. John Dee (J. O. Halliwell-Phillips, ed.) 1842.

ABOUT: Aubrey, J. Lives of Eminent Men; Dee, J. Compendious Rehearsal, Private Diary; Fell-Smith, C. John Dee; Hort, G. M. Three Famous Occultists; Smith, T. Vitae Quorundorum Eruditissimorum et Illustrium Virorum (as The Life of John Dee, W. R. Ayton, tr.); Taylor, E. G. R. Tudor Geography.

DEFOE, DANIEL (1660?-April 26, 1731), political and fiction writer, was born in London, the son of James Foe, a butcher. Daniel added the "de," apparently to make his name sound more aristocratic, and until later years wrote it indifferently as "Foe," "Defoe," and "DeFoe." The family were Presbyterians, and he was sent at fourteen to the famous school at Stoke Newington kept by Charles Morton, where most of the pupils were dissenters. At this time he was intended for the ministry, but after three or four years he gave up this ambition and took to business. In 1684, when he married Mary Tuffley (she survived him with seven children), he was a hosiery factor. Very much of Defoe's life is obscure, mostly because of its very nature. He seems to have been a commission merchant in Spain from 1678 to 1683, and perhaps at this time traveled also in France,

After M. Vandergucht
DANIEL DEFOE

Italy, and southern Germany. He may possibly have been involved in Monmouth's rebellion in 1685 and may have been pardoned because he was a Londoner and hence an innocent "outsider." There is probably no truth in the story that he was ever a Presbyterian minister in Tooting. Certainly he was strongly against James II and in favor of William and Mary (he was a volunteer trooper in William's army), and from the beginning of their reign to the death of Queen Anne (or from 1688 to 1714), he had a close though ambiguous connection with the government.

A satire in verse written in 1691 is Defoe's first known published writing. It was several years later before he became a professional journalist, pamphleteer, and author. In 1692 he went bankrupt, and though his creditors were willing to compromise, he eventually paid back the entire £17,000 for which he failed. This he did as secretary and manager, and later chief owner, of a tile factory near Tilbury. He was also accountant of the commissioners of glass duty from 1695 to 1699. Up to this time, though he was a sharp businessman, and perhaps not always too scrupulous a one, he had made few enemies and had not been the subject of scandal.

What ruined him, in 1703, was a satire that backfired—like Swift's *Modest Proposal.* This was *The Shortest Way with the Dis-*

senters, the irony of which completely deceived the Tories, so that several high churchmen recommended it warmly. When they came to, a warrant was issued for his arrest. It is from this police description that we obtain our only glimpse of Defoe's appearance—"middle-sized," spare, with brown complexion and brown hair, a hooked nose, sharp chin, grey eyes, and a large mole near his mouth.

He was imprisoned in Newgate for fifteen months, fined, and forced to give surety for good behavior for seven years. His business in Tilbury was wrecked. What rankled most, however, and turned him into a bitter, discredited mercenary, willing to serve any cause for money, was his sentence to the pillory. There was not much sympathy for him, for he had already antagonized his fellow Nonconformists by his satires; yet his appearance in the pillory was turned into a triumph. Despite this, the public humiliation soured him permanently.

He became, in plain words, a government spy. First he was Harley's man—Edward Harley, later Earl of Oxford, the Whig prime minister, who had secured his release from prison, for a price. In 1706 and 1707 he was in Scotland as a secret agent against the Jacobites. When Harley fell, he served the Tory government until the return of the Whig. Whigs and Tories alike distrusted and used him. In 1704 he established the thrice-weekly *Review*, a forerunner of the *Tatler* and *Spectator;* this and his other papers—the *Monitor, Weekly Journal, Daily Post, Director, Mercator*, etc., were probably subsidized in part by the government, and were to a certain extent its unofficial organs. From this rather dubious journalism, however, came a great good—the evolution of Daniel Defoe as a novelist.

In 1713 a satire got him into trouble again —the *Reasons Against the Succession of the House of Hanover*. This time, however, his brief imprisonment arose from a charge of contempt of court, because of an allusion to a judge in one of the last numbers of the *Review*. With Queen Anne's death Defoe for a time disappeared from public view, on the specious plea of illness. He turned up again as a Whig secret agent from 1716 to 1726. Perhaps the least defensible portion of his career was his service as

editor of *Mist's Journal*, a Jacobite paper, his underground function being to soften its Jacobitism and report on its activities. Later when Mist discovered Defoe was a spy, and was sent to prison because of it, he went hunting for Defoe.

All this time Defoe was writing voluminously and indefatigably. It is impossible to list all his works—there were more than two hundred volumes, though many of them were mere pamphlets. Nearly all of them were political in nature, though some revealed his shamefaced interest in the supernatural. Apparently as soon as he finished one he started another. The half dozen great books are almost lost in the throng.

There was another brief hiatus in Defoe's public career, and then an enigmatic ending. In 1729 he left the house he had built in Stoke Newington, left his family, and vanished into the depths of London. There have been many surmises as to what happened. Was Mist out of prison and looking for him again? Had he quarreled with a son who had inherited his father's sharp practices and deprived him of his property? Had he lost all his money by speculation, to which he had been addicted in his youth? Or was he mentally ill, and suffering from hallucinations? Evidently there was some rupture between him and his political sponsors; his last works were written anonymously or under the name of "Andrew Moreton." He died alone, of an apoplectic stroke, not far from his birthplace in St. Giles, Cripplegate, and was buried in Bunhill Fields. He left no will, and all his property was found to be assigned and was seized by his creditors.

Not an admirable character, on the whole, though perhaps a victim of the unscrupulous politicians of his time. Yet he was the father of English journalism, the pioneer of the picaresque novel in English, a satirist of almost the calibre of Swift, the master of an effortless, racy, magnificently simple and pithy style. "The greatest of plebeian geniuses," W. P. Trent called him.

All Defoe's novels were half-based on truth; he thought of them rather as what we call today fictionized biographies. Captain Jack, Moll Flanders, Jonathan Wild, Roxana, were all real people, and so was Alexander Selkirk, whose adventures as a castaway were the foundation of *Robinson Crusoe*. To its author, *Robinson Crusoe* was a work not of entertainment but of edification, though the didactic second part is seldom printed in modern editions. What the book has come to mean to the world is the epic of civilized man as a single-handed antagonist of nature. To most readers, Defoe is the author of *Robinson Crusoe* alone. Probably, however, his very greatest work is that marvellous tour-de-force, *A Journal of the Plague Year*. Reading his sober, factual, yet vivid account, it is hard to realize that the "I" of the narrative actually was just six years old when the great plague struck London. This is imaginative reconstruction of the very highest order. Almost in the same class is Defoe's great—and entirely fictitious—ghost story, the "true relation" of the apparition of Mrs. Veal. As his book on Duncan Campbell, the deaf-mute conjuror, and several of his later pamphlets evidence, Defoe was fascinated and almost convinced by psychic phenomena, and this half-conviction gives life to his story, as did Dr. Johnson's to *The Cock Lane Ghost*.

But granting the supremacy of Defoe's "lives" of highwaymen and courtesans, and of his "history" of the great plague, doubtless as long as English is read young people will begin to enter a magic world with the words: "I was born in the year 1632, in the city of York, of a good family." *Robinson Crusoe* is among the dozen immortal books in English. A strange, and yet somehow just, immortality for the shady secret agent!

PRINCIPAL WORKS: An Essay Upon Projects, 1697; The True-Born Englishman (verse) 1700; The Original Powers of the Collective Body of the People of England, 1701; The Shortest Way With the Dissenters, 1702; The Consolidator, or, A Journey to the World in the Moon, 1705; A True Relation of the Apparition of One Mrs. Veal, 1706; History of the Union of Great Britain, 1708-09; Reasons Against the Succession of the House of Hanover, 1713; An Appeal to Honour and Justice, 1715; The Life and Strange Surprizing Adventures of Robinson Crusoe of York, Mariner, 1719; The Further Adventures of Robinson Crusoe, 1719; The Life and Adventures of Mr. Duncan Campbell, 1720; The Life of Captain Singleton, 1720; The Fortunes and Misfortunes of the Famous Moll Flanders, 1722; The History of . . . Colonel Jack, 1722; A Journal of the Plague Year, 1722; The Fortunate Mistress (Roxana), 1724; A Tour Through the Whole Island of Great Britain, 1724-25; The True and Genuine Account of the Life and Actions of the Late Jonathan Wild, 1725; The Political History of the Devil, 1726; The Compleat Tradesman, 1726; An Essay on the History and Reality of Apparitions, 1727; A Plan of English Commerce, 1728; Works (G. H. Maynadier, ed.) 1903; Novels and Selected Writings, 1927-28.

ABOUT: Chadwick, W. The Life and Times of Daniel DeFoe; Chalmers, G. Life of Daniel Defoe; Defoe, D. An Appeal to Honour and Justice; Dotting, P. Daniel DeFoe et ses Romans (The Life and Strange Surprizing Adventures of Daniel Defoe); Forster, J. Historical and Biographical Writings; Lee, W. Daniel Defoe: His Life and Recently Discovered Writings; Minto, W. Daniel Defoe; Oliphant, M. O. W. Historical Sketches of the Reign of Queen Anne; Phelps, W. L. The Advance of the English Novel; Ross, J. H. Swift and Defoe, a Study in Relationship; Sutherland, J. R. Defoe; Trent, W. P. Daniel Defoe, How to Know Him; Wright, T. The Life of Daniel Defoe; Wyatt, E. F. Great Companions.

DEKKER, THOMAS (1570?-1632?), dramatist, miscellaneous writer, was born in London, perhaps in 1570, perhaps in 1572. Nothing is known of his family or his education, and very little of his life. His name was sometimes spelled "Decker," and a Thomas Decker, who may have been the dramatist, died in London on August 25, 1632. If not, he may have lived to as late as 1641. He seems to have been married before 1594, and to have had several children, most of whom died in childhood, but here again some other Dekker or Decker may be concerned.

The one thing certain is that he was one of the large group of playwrights who worked for Philip Henslowe, and that in that capacity he collaborated constantly with all the others, including Ford, Rowley, Webster, and Massinger.*qqv* Henslowe befriended him over and over again, and after an early success he needed befriending, for he lived in the utmost poverty, was imprisoned for debt in 1598, and again lay in the debtors' prison from 1613 to 1616—or possibly even to 1619. It is no wonder that he wrote, "God help the poor, the rich can shift!"

Unpractical, good natured, cheerful, and lovable, Dekker was the prototype of the happy-go-lucky Bohemian. He knew London life from its very dregs, and he mirrored it as it had not been mirrored since Chaucer wrote of a simpler England. Besides being a playwright, he was a great pamphleteer, and in that capacity he was a forerunner of Defoe as a realist. Never idle, he yet was a rapid, careless writer who relied on his light touch, his gift for humorous invention, and paid no attention to loose ends or dropped stitches. Actually, he was that strange mixture, a born journalist and a born lyric poet. In the tangle of plays in which he had a part, it is often possible to know which portion is

Dekker's by the beauty of an interpolated song or the lyrical fall of a poetic passage. As Lamb said of him, he had "poetry enough for anything."

The only serious quarrel of his life was with the testy Ben Jonson, who ridiculed him as "Demetrius Fannius, the dresser of plays," in *The Poetaster*. Dekker retorted with *Satiro-Mastix*, but he had not acerbity enough to keep the quarrel up, whereas Jonson pursued it to the end.

Dekker was a playwright by default; it was the one way for a free lance writer to make a living in his day, and though his work deteriorated with the years, his natural flow of inspiration kept him going. Many of his pamphlets also were hack work, written for a quick monetary return; but they are so full of life, so soundly based on shrewd observation, that he is undoubtedly the most important pamphleteer of the period. The real Dekker is revealed in his religious poems, full of deep feeling and quiet beauty, and in his songs. There is something ludicrous and touching in a man who from a debtors' prison can write with heartfelt sincerity:

> Art thou poor, yet hast thou golden
> slumbers?
> O sweet content!

Scholars have disagreed for three hundred years on the Dekker canon. Some critics believe that the only plays entirely his are *If It Be Not Good, the Divel Is in It* and *Match Mee in London.* Yet most critics think he wrote all, or most, of *The Honest Whore*, and from internal evidence *Satiro-Mastix* must have been his. All one can do is to list the most probable titles, and to say that Dekker apparently had a finger, or in some cases a whole hand, in them.

PRINCIPAL WORKS: *Plays*—The Shoemakers Holiday, 1600; The Pleasant Comedie of Old Fortunatus, 1600; Satiro-Mastix, 1602; The Honest Whore, 1604 (2d part, 1630); The Whore of Babylon, 1607; The Roaring Girle (with T. Middleton, and W. Rowley) 1611; If It Be Not Good, the Divel Is in It, 1612; The Virgin Martir (with P. Massinger) 1622; Match Mee in London, 1631; The Wonder of a Kingdome, 1636; The Witch of Edmonton (with W. Rowley, J. Ford, et al.) 1638; Dramatic Works (R. Shepherd, ed.) 1873. *Masques*—The Magnificent Entertainment Given to King James, 1604; Troja-Nova Triumphans, 1612; Britannia's Honour, 1628; Londons Tempe, 1629; The Sun's Darling (with J. Ford) 1656. *Pamphlets*—The Wonderfull Yeare, 1603; The Seven Deadly Sinnes of London, 1606; Fowre Birds of Noahs Arke, 1609; Worke for Armoroures, 1609; A Strange Horse Race, 1613; Dekker His Dreame, 1620; A Rod for Run-Awayes, 1625; Newes from Hell, 1625; English Villainies, 1637; Non-Dramatic Works (A. B. Grosart, ed.) 1884.

ABOUT: Chambers, E. K. The Elizabethan Stage; Grosart, A. B. Memorial Introduction, Non-Dramatic Works; Hazlitt, W. C. Bibliographical Collections; Lamb, C. Specimens of the English Dramatic Poets; Swinburne, A. C. The Age of Shakespeare.

DELANY, Mrs. MARY (GRANVILLE) PENDARVES (May 14, 1700-April 15, 1788), author of autobiography and letters, was born at Coulston, Wiltshire, the daughter of Bernard Granville. As a child she was sent to live with an aunt, Lady Ann Stanley, who had been maid of honor to Queen Mary, and was brought up to expect a place in Queen Anne's household. When Anne died in 1713, the Granvilles fell out of favor and Bernard Granville was arrested as a Tory. After his release the family retired to the country where Mary fell in love with a young man named Twyford. This match was not considered proper and she was packed off to stay with an uncle, Lord Lansdowne, where she found a new suitor, Alexander Pendarves, a fat and rather unpleasant gentleman nearly sixty years of age. Under family pressure, Mary married Pendarves when she was eighteen and moved to London.

In 1725, two years after the death of her father, Mr. Pendarves died, leaving her a charming widow with many aristocratic friends and not much money. She was courted by many, among them Lord Baltimore, but when after five years of wooing he turned his attentions elsewhere, Mary went to Ireland with a Mrs. Donnellan and became one of the circle of literary ladies who worshipped Swift. She came to know the great man well and was introduced by him to Patrick Delany, an Irish preacher and Swift's faithful friend. After Mary had returned to England, Delany, then a widower, followed to propose marriage. They were married in 1743, in spite of the disapproval of Mary's brother and friends, and lived happily until Delany's death in 1768.

As Mrs. Delany, Mary enjoyed great popularity. She was considered "literary," although she had actually written little, and was famous for her paper flower work which consisted of a mosaic of bits of colored paper cut out and pasted on paper, a sample of which she presented to the queen. George III always called her his "dearest Mrs.

149

Delany," and gave her a pension and a house where the royal family often visited her. A friend and patroness to Fanny Burney, Mrs. Delany took the young novelist into her household and introduced her at court.

This "fairest model of female excellence" wrote six volumes of autobiography and letters full of anecdote about Swift, Pope, and others, lively with social gossip. She was accepted by both aristocrats and Bluestockings. Yet of all her accomplishments, her best claim to remembrance is probably her friendship with Fanny Burney.

PRINCIPAL WORKS: Letters of Mrs. Delany to Mrs. Frances Hamilton, 1820; Autobiography and Correspondence of Mary Granville, Mrs. Delany (Lady Llanover, ed.) 1861-62.

ABOUT: Dobson, A. Dear Mrs. Delany, *in* Sidewalk Studies; Symonds, E. M. (George Paston, pseud.) Mrs. Delany, a Memoir.

DELONEY, THOMAS (1543?-1600?), ballad writer, fiction writer, pamphleteer, was born about 1543, probably in London. A silk weaver by trade, he lived in Norwich where he began to write occasional ballads. This was a period when ballads and broadsides were printed by the hundred, serving much the same function as the special feature section of a Sunday newspaper. "Scarce a cat can look out of a gutter," notes a contemporary writer, "but presently a proper new ballad of a strange sight is indited." Deloney wrote ballads on the happenings of the day, on historical personages, on murders, on current jokes and "tall tales," as well as on more exalted patriotic themes, and although the verse was of no great merit, many of his ballads won wide popularity. Two collections were published after his death, *Strange Histories* and *The Garland of Good Will*, but because of their ephemeral character many of the individual ballads written between 1585 and 1595 have disappeared.

About 1585 the "balleting silke-weaver of Norwich" seems to have given up his looms and moved to London where he could devote all his time to writing. The coming of the Armada in 1588 inspired him to write three broadsides, *The Happy Obtaining of the Great Galleazo*, *The Strange and Cruel Whips Which the Spaniards Had Prepared* and *The Queen's Visiting the Camp at Tilsburie*, which made him famous. A year later, however, an indiscreet reference to the queen in one of his verses forced him into tem-

porary hiding and led him to turn from balladry to prose.

As a prose writer, and more particularly a pioneer in the development of the novel, Deloney has been discovered only recently. In the last decade of his life he wrote three narratives, each concerned with a particular craft: *The Gentle Craft*, in praise of shoemakers; *Thomas of Reading*, in praise of clothiers; and *Jack of Newbury*, in praise of weavers. All of these curious tales are built on a frame of historical or legendary material into which the author has set a series of lively bourgeois scenes and realistic characters drawn from contemporary London life. Full of humor, colorful and robust, they reproduce the daily drama of the craftsman's world to which Deloney belonged. Although these stories have been largely forgotten for three centuries, they were appreciated in their own day and exerted an influence on contemporary writing—Dekker undoubtedly used *The Gentle Craft* as a basis for his *Shoemaker's Holiday* and Thomas Heywood probably also drew from Deloney's material.

Even in Deloney the ballad-maker, the potential novelist is visible, but it is only in the realistic prose fiction of his latter years that his very genuine talent came to full stature. His limitations are those of a pioneer. This was an art as yet unformed and these broadly sketched stories are interesting chiefly as a record of experiment and a reflection of fundamental changes in Elizabethan society.

PRINCIPAL WORKS: *Poetry*—Strange Histories, 1602; The Garland of Good Will, 1631; The Works of Thomas Deloney (F. O. Mann, ed.) 1912. *Prose* —The Gentle Craft. A Most Merry and Pleasant Historie, 1598 (A. F. Lange, ed. 1903); Thomas of Reading, Or the six worthy yeomen of the West, 1612 (W. H. D. Rouse, ed. 1920); The Pleasant Historie of John Winchcombe in His Younger Yeares Called Jack of Newberie, 1619 (W. H. D. Rouse, ed. 1920).

ABOUT: Chevalley, A. Thomas Deloney; Sievers, R. Thomas Deloney.

DENHAM, Sir JOHN (1615-March 1659), poet, dramatist, miscellaneous writer, was born in Dublin, but his father, also Sir John, lord chief justice of the King's Bench in Ireland, was from Essex, and his mother, Eleanor More, was the daughter of Viscount Drogheda. He was reared in London, entered Trinity College, Oxford, in 1631, but left in 1634 without a degree, and was entered in Lincoln's Inn. He was never called to the bar; his father died in 1639 and he succeeded to his ancestral estate at Egham, Surrey, on the Thames, the scene of *Cooper's Hill.* He was a Royalist during the civil war, and transmitted the correspondence between the king and queen; being discovered, he was obliged to flee to France, but returned to England in 1652. As high sheriff of Surrey, he had been appointed governor of Farnham Castle, and was imprisoned for a while in 1642 when it fell. Until the Restoration he was penniless, his estate having been confiscated. The purchaser of his beloved house was the poet Wither [qv]; later, when the tables were turned, he saved Wither's life on the plea that with Wither alive he himself would not be "the worst poet in England!" At the coronation of Charles II he was made a Knight Commander of the Bath, and appointed surveyor general of the royal works, though he was no architect. But if he was in favor with the king he was hated by the courtiers; Samuel Butler, for one, wrote a cruel satire on him. His matrimonial scandal and its aftermath were common subjects for gibes.

In 1634 Denham had married Ann Cotton, who died, leaving a son and two daughters. In 1665, when he was fifty and prematurely aged, he married Margaret Brooke, a beautiful eighteen-year-old girl. Before long she openly flaunted the fact that she was the mistress of the Duke of York. Denham went completely insane, to the point where he called on the king and informed him that he, Denham, was the Holy Ghost! However, he recovered his senses, and though deeply bitter was prepared to make the best of the situation when in 1667 his wife died and rumor, completely false, accused him of poisoning her. Despite this, he did not relapse into insanity; it was, in fact, at this period that he wrote his beautiful elegy on his friend Abraham Cowley.[qv]

An eccentric Denham undoubtedly was; as a youth he troubled his father by his propensity for gambling, and wrote *The Anatomy of Play* as proof of his reformation —after which he kept right on gambling and eventually lost most of his fortune by it. He was very tall, with piercing eyes. His bitter tongue and his excitability made him easy game for the court wits, who had no mercy on the wretched, vulnerable man.

SIR JOHN DENHAM

Yet this betrayed husband and place-hunter at the court where he had been betrayed was also, in happier days, a genuine poet, the first writer of exclusively descriptive poetry in England. *Cooper's Hill,* with its celebration of the Thames and its marrying of natural beauty to moral reflection, anticipates Gray and Pope. Dryden said that Denham "transferred the sweetness of Waller's lyrics to the epic"; Pope and Swift both imitated him. Except for the elegy on Cowley, Denham's serious poetry belongs to his youth—the satirical doggerel he wrote in later years is not worth preserving. Charles I had discouraged him from writing, saying that poetry was an occupation fit only for young men, and Denham, the obedient courtier, wrote little thereafter. His *Destruction of Troy* was a paraphrase rather than a translation of Virgil, his *Cato Major of Old Age* a poetic paraphrase of the very unpoetic Cicero. The studied brevity of his style, and his use of the heroic couplet, are both more characteristic of the eighteenth than of the seventeenth century. But *Cooper's Hill* still has beauties for the lover of quiet descriptive verse.

PRINCIPAL WORKS: The Destruction of Troy, 1636; The Sophy (tragedy) 1642; Cooper's Hill, 1642; The Anatomy of Play (anonymous) 1651; A Relation to a Quaker, 1659; Poems and Translations, 1667-68; Cato Major of Old Age, 1669; A Version of the Psalms of David, 1714.

ABOUT: Aubrey, J. Lives of Eminent Men; Evelyn, J. Diary; Johnson, S. Lives of the Poets; Pepys, S. Diary; Wood, A. à, Athenae Oxonienses.

DENNIS, JOHN (1657-1734), critic, dramatist, was born in London, the son of Francis Dennis, a prosperous tanner. He was educated at Harrow and at Caius College, Cambridge (B.A. 1679), then became a fellow of Trinity College (M.A. 1683). In 1680 he was fined and lost his scholarship for "wounding with a sword" a fellow student. After some travel in France and Italy, he settled in London, where through the patronage of the Duke of Marlborough he was named, in 1705, one of the "royal waiters" in the port of London, a post he sold in 1720. He had inherited some property from his father and from an uncle, a London alderman, but by 1705 his money was gone and he had to earn his living by writing. Fortunately for him, he had espoused the cause of William and Mary against that of James II, and so was in favor with the government. Though his plays were all unsuccessful, his critical writings found a ready public, and he was able for some time to live as a free-lance writer, a member of the group surrounding Dryden, Congreve, and Wycherley.*qv* He does not seem ever to have married. His last years were wretched indeed; he was very poor and became blind. However, Horace Walpole, the Earl of Pembroke, and others befriended him and kept him from utter misery.

Dennis was made the butt of Pope's most savage satire; the quarrel (very partially mended at the end) lasted for years, and both sides indulged in the grossest personalities. He also engaged in a long dispute with Addison, and Swift ridiculed him brutally. Yet, though he was a very bad playwright, who borrowed from everybody and produced a sad patchwork of fustian, he was, in his earlier work at least, a more than competent critic. Later his criticism grew to be pedantic and abusive, and he was boringly insistent on his theory that "every tragedy ought to be a very solemn lecture," that the object of poetry was "to instruct and reform the world," and that its main reason for existence was what he called "poetical justice." Nevertheless, he played a useful part in the long argument with Jeremy Collier, vigorously "vindicating the stage, not its corruptions or abuses."

It must be acknowledged that Dennis laid himself open to ridicule. He believed that the ancient writers excelled the moderns because they mixed religion with their poetry, and said loftily that Shakespeare would have been a good writer if only he had possessed "art and learning." He was the inventor of a new method of simulating thunder on the stage, and on one occasion when it was being employed during a play by someone else he exclaimed angrily, "The villains will play my thunder, but not my plays!"

Outside of his plays and critical essays, Dennis was the author of some poor Pindaric odes. His first play, *A Plot and No Plot* (1697) had a certain interest because of its anti-Jacobitism; *Liberty Asserted* (1704) attacked the French, and when the war ended he was in actual fear that France would demand his extradition and punishment. He complained to Marlborough, who said dryly that he had done even more against the French, and that he was not afraid. Dennis is now pretty well forgotten; he has survived mainly as the antagonist of Pope and Addison.

PRINCIPAL WORKS: Miscellanies in Verse and Prose, 1693: Letters Upon Several Occasions, 1696; Miscellany Poems by Mr. Dennis, 1697; The Advancement . . . and Reformation of Modern Poetry, 1701; A Collection of Divine Hymns and Poems (with others) 1709; Reflections, Critical and Satirical, on a Late Rhapsody Called, An Essay on Criticism, 1711; An Essay on the Genius and Writings of Shakespeare, 1712; Remarks Upon [Addison's] Cato, 1713; Select Works, Consisting of Plays, Poems, etc., to Which Is Added, Coriolanus, a Tragedy, 1718-21; Original Letters, Familiar, Moral, and

JOHN DENNIS

Critical, 1721; The Stage Defended, 1726; Miscellaneous Tracts, 1727; Collected Works (E. N. Hooker, ed.) 1939-43.

ABOUT: D'Israeli, I. Quarrels of Authors, Calamities of Authors; Johnson, S. Lives of the Poets; Paul, H. G. John Dennis: His Life and Criticism.

DIBDIN, CHARLES (1745-July 25, 1814),
dramatist, song writer, was born at Southampton and baptized on March 4, 1745, the twelfth child of a parish clerk named Thomas Dibdin. Whatever musical education he had seems to have been acquired as a boy chorister at Winchester. When he was thirteen or fourteen, his sea-going brother, Thomas, invited him to London where he was engaged to sing at Covent Garden.

Dibdin's first work, *The Shepherd's Artifice*, for which he wrote both words and music, was produced in 1762. During the next ten years he became known as an actor as well as a playwright, working with the Drury Lane company which produced two of his best-known plays, *The Waterman* and *The Quaker*. When a violent quarrel with David Garrick ended this connection, he moved on to other theatres, among them the Royal Circus which he managed, and the Sans Souci where he gave one-man shows, singing his own songs and performing what might be described as an eighteenth century vaudeville turn.

Dibdin was the author of an autobiography which gives a good deal of interesting detail about the theatrical life of the day, although it is on the whole a dreary and egotistical account, notable for its inaccuracies. Both his personal and his domestic relations were apparently snarled by a wandering disposition and a quick temper. He had three children by Harriet Pitt, a dancer at Covent Garden, two of whom—Charles and Thomas John—became popular playwrights. He also had two wives and an extraordinary number of enemies. Handsome and high spirited, he was an excellent entertainer, but neither a good husband, a good friend, nor indeed a good dramatist.

In his songs, however, he reached a higher level. The opera, *Liberty Hall*, produced in 1785, contained three well-known songs, "The Bells of Aberdovey," "The High-Mettled Racer," and "Jock Ratlin." Of the many sea songs he wrote which were extremely popular with the British Navy during the war with France, the most outstanding is the immortal "Tom Bowling," written on the death of his well-loved brother, Captain Thomas Dibdin. During his lifetime Dibdin wrote over fourteen hundred songs and some thirty dramatic pieces. Although he achieved popularity and a fair slice of worldly success, his life was continuously threatened by creditors, embittered by quarrels and ended in lonely poverty.

PRINCIPAL WORKS: *Plays* (dates of publication)—The Shepherd's Artifice, A Dramatic Pastoral, 1765; The Deserter, A New Musical Drama, 1773; The Waterman: or, The First of August, 1774; The Cobbler: or, A Wife of Ten Thousand, 1774; The Quaker, 1777; Poor Vulcan, 1778; The Chelsea Prisoner, 1779; The Harvest-Home, 1788. *Other Works*—The Musical Tour, 1788; The Younger Brother (novel) 1793; A Complete History of the English Stage, 1800; Observations on a Tour Through Scotland and England, 1801-2; The Professional Life of Mr. Dibdin, Written by Himself, Together with the Words of Six Hundred Songs, 1803.

ABOUT: Kitchener, W. A Brief Memoir of Charles Dibdin, With Some Letters and Documents Supplied by His Grand-Daughter.

DIGBY, GEORGE. See BRISTOL, GEORGE DIGBY, Second Earl of

DIGBY, Sir KENELM (June 11, 1603-June 11, 1665), naval commander, miscellaneous writer, was the son of Sir Everard Digby, who was executed for participation in the Gunpowder Plot when the boy was three. He was reared as a Roman Catholic by his mother, Mary Mulsho. His father's estate had been confiscated, but part of it was recovered. Digby spent 1617 and 1618 in Spain with his cousin, Sir John Digby (afterward the Earl of Bristol), the British ambassador. In 1619 he entered Gloucester Hall (now Worcester College), Oxford, but left the next year without a degree. From 1620 to 1623 he was on the Continent; then he returned to England and was knighted by James I, who made him a gentleman of the privy chamber to the future Charles I.

For years Digby had been courting the beautiful and intellectual Venetia Stanley, three years his senior. His mother opposed the marriage and sent him abroad to forget her, and though they were pledged to each other she became the mistress of the Earl of Dorset and bore him several children. On Digby's return he forgave her and renewed his suit, and they were secretly married in

Sir A. Van Dyck

SIR KENELM DIGBY

1625. The earl remained their friend and visitor and gave a pension to the lady. On the birth of the Digby's second son in 1627, when Digby himself was about to leave on a privateering expedition in the Mediterranean, the marriage was made public. It was on this expedition, as naval commander, that he captured a number of French and Venetian ships at Scanderoon, and freed some English captives of the Algerian pirates; he was named commissioner of the navy, but his great victory at Scanderoon was disavowed because of complaints from the Venetian government.

Lady Digby died suddenly in 1633, leaving five children from her unconventional but extremely happy marriage. Her husband was foolishly accused of having caused her death by feeding her boiled vipers to retain her beauty. He was heartbroken, and retired to Gresham College for two years of seclusion, engaging in experiments in chemistry. (He had always been interested in science, and was on the council of the Royal Society when it was founded.) He spent the years from 1635 to 1639 in France.

When the long struggle between king and parliament began, Digby (who had announced himself a Protestant after his wife's death but soon reverted to Roman Catholicism) was accused as a recusant and banished in 1641. He went to Flanders and France, but returned in 1642, and was imprisoned. The queen of France, the English queen's mother, secured his release. He joined Queen Henrietta Maria in France and was made her chancellor, and on her behalf tried to raise money for the Royalists from the Pope—promising, without authorization by Charles, that the king would grant religious toleration to Catholics and independence to Ireland. Even so, his mission was unsuccessful. In 1649 he went back to England and was banished again. But in 1654 he was permitted to return—and became an agent for Cromwell. Since his one aim was the securing of rights for the Catholics, his playing both sides was forgiven when Charles was restored to the throne, though he was forbidden the court in 1661. He died on his sixty-second birthday—also the anniversary of Scanderoon.

Digby is remembered today for his grotesque "powder of sympathy," applied to the sword instead of the wound. He was a brilliant, handsome giant, vastly entertaining as a conversationalist, master of six languages, ebullient and versatile, a noted duelist who killed a man in Paris for traducing Charles. In his own time his treatises on the body and soul were famous, but they are forgotten. His highly allegorical *Private Memoirs*, telling the story of his courtship, is written in a highflown, fantastic style, but his other works are in plain, vigorous English.

PRINCIPAL WORKS: Journal of a Voyage Into The Mediterranean, 1628; A Conference With a Lady About Choice of Religion, 1638; Sir Kenelm Digby's Honour Maintained, 1641; Observations on Spenser's Faery Queene, 1643; A Treatise of the Nature of Bodies, 1644; A Treatise Declaring the Operations and Nature of Man's Soule, 1644; Observations Upon Religio Medici, 1645; A Discourse Concerning Infallibility in Religion, 1652; A Discourse Touching the Cure of Wounds by the Powder of Sympathie, 1658; A Discourse Concerning the Vegetation of Plantes, 1661; The Closet of the Eminent Sir Kenelm Digby Knt. Opened, 1677; Private Memoirs (M. H. Nicolas, ed.) 1827; Poems (G. F. Warner, ed.) 1877.

ABOUT: Bligh, E. W. Sir Kenelm Digby and His Venetia; Digby, K. Private Memoirs, Journal of a Voyage into the Mediterranean, Sir Kenelm Digby's Honour Maintained; Evelyn, J. Diary; Longueville, T. The Life of Sir Kenelm Digby by One of His Descendants.

DILLON, WENTWORTH. See ROSCOMMON, WENTWORTH DILLON, Fourth Earl of

DODD, WILLIAM (May 29, 1729-June 27, 1777), clergyman, miscellaneous writer, executed for forgery, was born at Bourne, Lincolnshire, where his father was vicar. At the age of sixteen he entered Clare Hall, Cambridge, on a sizarship and took his B.A. degree five years later. Having already written a number of facetious poems, he decided, against the wishes of family and friends, to pursue a literary career. Living in London, he published an elegy on the death of Frederick, Prince of Wales, and wrote a comedy for which he received a small advance from a theatrical manager. In the same year he met and married Mary Perkins, a young woman whose reputation seems to have been somewhat doubtful. In view of this new responsibility, his friends were able to persuade him to return the money advanced on his play and resume a clerical career.

Ordained in 1751, he served first as curate at West Ham, Essex and in the next few years enjoyed a series of rapid preferments. As tutor to Philip Stanhope, Earl of Chesterfield, he conceived the notion of devoting all his time to teaching and resigned most of his clerical duties. When his wife received a legacy, however, he invested in a chapel in Pimlico, where he became known as a popular preacher, attracting a large and fashionable congregation. During this period he also wrote and published a number of edifying books and served as editor of the *Christian Magazine*.

His career was first endangered by scandal when he began to write dainty verses to ladies and, as a contemporary account tactfully puts it, "fell into snares." Most certainly he fell heavily into debt, winning himself the nickname of "macaroni parson." When in 1774, his wife wrote an anonymous letter to the wife of the lord chancellor offering a large bribe for the living of St. George's, Hanover Square, Dodd's name was struck off the list of chaplains and he was forced to leave England. Returning home in desperate financial straits, Dodd forged a bond for £4200 on his former pupil, Lord Chesterfield. He was arrested and after months of imprisonment, during which he wrote a long poem, *Thoughts in Prison*, he was executed despite a number of eloquent letters from Samuel Johnson and several petitions, one bearing the signature of 23,000

citizens of London. Dr. Johnson's letters are of greater interest today than the complete works of the unfortunate clergyman.

PRINCIPAL WORKS: *Poems*—Diggon Davy, A Pastoral on the Death of His Last Cow, 1747; The African Prince When in England to Zara at His Father's Court, 1749; Zara at the Court of Annamaboe to the African Prince Now in England, 1749; An Elegy on the Death of HRH the Prince of Wales, 1751; An Epistle to a Lady Concerning Some Important and Necessary Truths in Religion, 1753; Thoughts on the Glorious Epiphany of the Lord Jesus Christ, 1758; Ode to the Marchioness of Granby, 1759; Hymn to Good Nature, 1760; Poems, 1767; Thoughts in Prison, in five parts, 1777. *Other Works*—The Beauties of Shakespeare (ed.) 1752; The Sisters (a novel) 1754; A Familiar Explanation of the Poetical Works of Milton, 1762; A Commentary on the Old and New Testaments, 1770.

ABOUT: Dodd, W. Account of the Author, *in* Thoughts in Prison; Fitzgerald, P. A Famous Forgery; Papers Written by Dr. Johnson and Dr. Dodd in 1777 (R. W. Chapman, ed.).

DODDRIDGE, PHILIP (June 26, 1702-October 26, 1751), Nonconformist divine, hymn writer, author of religious works, was born in London, the twentieth and last child of Daniel Doddridge, a prosperous businessman, and his wife who was the daughter of John Bauman, a Lutheran preacher. Educated at an academy for dissenters at Kibworth, Leicestershire, he became a minister when he was twenty-one, and six years later was chosen by a general meeting of Nonconformist ministers to conduct an academy established at Market Harborough. The academy was later moved to Northampton where Doddridge also served as minister of an independent congregation, combining the duties of schoolmaster, preacher, reformer, and writer.

Tall, slight, extremely nearsighted and always in delicate health, this dissenting preacher seems nevertheless to have been a man of zest and high spirits. His personal letters, of which a good many have been published, are frequently playful, particularly those addressed to female friends. Looking for a wife, Doddridge was jilted by one young woman, refused by another, and at the age of twenty-eight married Miss Mercy Maris with whom he seems to have been deeply in love all the rest of his life.

Doddridge was a man of extraordinarily liberal temper, working in a period when to be liberal was to be unpopular. Both in his writing and his preaching, he did more than any other man of his time to obliterate old party lines and unite Nonconformists on a common religious ground. The work which best illustrates his religious gift is *The Rise and Progress of Religion in the Soul,* published in 1745. In literary as well as spiritual quality, these powerful addresses are outstanding among eighteenth century writings of dissent. He was also the author of many well-known hymns modeled on the work of Isaac Watts. Another work, the *Family Expositor,* a didactic commentary on the New Testament, was extremely popular in its own time but seems today colorless and a trifle pompous.

Doddridge's daughter later said, "The orthodoxy my father taught his children was charity," and, indeed, this seems to have been the guiding principle of his own life. He gave untiringly of his energy and talent until his health broke down and he was sent by friends to Lisbon. There he died at the age of forty-nine.

PRINCIPAL WORKS: Free Thoughts on Reviving the Dissenting Interest, 1730; The Family Expositor, 1739; Of the Evidences of Christianity, 1743; The Rise and Progress of Religion in the Soul, 1745; Hymns (J. Orton, ed.) 1755 (J. D. Humphreys, ed. 1839); Works, 1802; The Correspondence and Diary of Philip Doddridge (J. D. Humphreys, ed.) 1829-31.

ABOUT: Boyd, J. R. Memoir of the Life, Character and Writings of Philip Doddridge; Stanford, C. Philip Doddridge; Stoughton, J. Philip Doddridge, His Life and Labors.

DODSLEY, ROBERT (1703-September 23, 1764), poet, dramatist, publisher, was reputedly born in Mansfield on the border of the Sherwood Forest, where his father, Robert Dodsley, kept a free school. Apprenticed to a stocking weaver, he ran away while he was still a boy and entered domestic service. As footman to a Mrs. Lowther, he began to write verse and finding a number of fashionable lady patrons, was enabled to publish his first poem, *Solitude,* in 1729. Continuing his literary career, he wrote a dramatic satire, *The Toy Shop,* which was acted at Covent Garden with considerable success several years later.

Dodsley appears to have been a man of great charm who won the friendly interest of Defoe, Pope, and Johnson as well as a coterie of fashionable ladies. In 1735 with the assistance of several of these new friends, he opened a bookseller's shop in Pall Mall, the "Tully's Head," which became a favorite meeting place for the literati of the day. He and his brother James published Johnson, Pope, Goldsmith, Gray, Shenstone and others, establishing the firm of Robert and James Dodsley as publishers of sound literary judgment and shrewd business ability. Dodsley published a great deal of the work of Johnson and is said to have suggested the "English Dictionary." Whether or not this is accurate, Johnson was certainly very fond of him, referring to him playfully as "Doddy, my patron."

Dodsley wrote a number of poems and plays, one of which, the tragedy *Cleone,* was very successful, although Garrick had rejected it as "cruel, bloody and unnatural." Johnson loyally defended *Cleone* but added that he thought perhaps there was "more blood than brains" in it. As a publisher, Dodsley also founded several important literary periodicals, *The Museum, The World* and *The Annual Register,* the last under the editorial aegis of Edmund Burke. Out of all this manifold activity he is best known for two valuable collections which he edited and published, the *Select Collection of Old Plays,* published in twelve volumes, and *A Collection of Poems by Several Hands,* in three volumes, both indicative of his genuine literary perception. These two works alone guarantee Robert Dodsley a permanent place in English literary history.

PRINCIPAL WORKS: *Poems:* Servitude, 1729; The Muse in Livery: or, The Footman's Miscellany, 1732; An Epistle to Mr. Pope, Occasion'd by His Essay on Man, 1734; Colin's Kisses, 1742; Pain and Patience, 1742; Public Virtue, 1753; Melpomene, 1757; Trifles (2 vols.) 1745-77. *Plays:* The Toy Shop, 1735; The King and the Miller of Mansfield, 1737; Sir John Cockle at Court, 1738; The Blind Beggar of Bethnal Green, 1741; The Triumph of Peace, 1749; Cleone, 1758. *Miscellaneous:* A Select Collection of Old Plays (ed.) 1744 (W. C. Hazlitt, ed. 1874-76); A Collection of Poems by Several Hands (ed.) 1748; Select Fables: In Three Books, 1761; The Works of William Shenstone (ed.) 1764.

ABOUT: Chalmers, A. Biographical notice, *in* Chalmer's Works of English Poets; Courtney, W. P. Dodsley's Collection of Poetry, Its Contents and Contributors; Straus, R. Robert Dodsley, Poet, Publisher, and Playwright.

DONNE, JOHN (1573?-March 31, 1631), poet and religious prose writer, was born in London, the eldest son of John Donne, a prosperous ironmonger of Welsh descent, and of Elizabeth Heywood, daughter of John Heywood, the epigrammatist and writer of interludes. Mrs. Donne was a collateral descendant of Sir Thomas More. The family name was pronounced—and sometimes spelled—Dunne.

The older Donne died when the boy was four, and he was reared by his mother. Undoubtedly he was reared a Roman Catholic, though secretly, because of the disabilities attaching to adherents to the old faith under Elizabeth. He and his brother were sent to Hart Hall, Oxford, when John was only eleven—students under sixteen did not have to take the oath of allegiance to the Anglican Church; but because of the allegiance requirement he could not obtain a degree. At Oxford he became the lifelong friend of Henry Wotton *qv*; later Izaak Walton was his closest friend. In 1586 Donne is believed to have transferred to Cambridge. He is reputed also have traveled in Spain and Italy; it may be that his family had some thought of his becoming a priest, or entering the service of some Roman Catholic monarch. In any event, by 1591 he was entered in Thavies Inn, London, a sort of preparatory school for law students, and a year later in Lincoln's Inn. It was at this time that his brother was imprisoned and died in Newgate, for protecting a Catholic priest from arrest. Certainly Donne's intense concern with religious questions dates from this period.

He was in some way in the service of the Earl of Essex in the next few years—sympathy with the outlawed Catholics was one of the grounds of the ex-favorite's conviction for treason. Donne accompanied him as a volunteer in his expeditions to Cadiz in 1596 and to the Azores in 1597. There is no record of his having been admitted to the bar. Instead, in 1601 he became secretary to Sir Thomas Egerton, Lord Keeper of the Great Seal.

There was living with Egerton his dead wife's niece, a sixteen-year-old girl named Anne More (not, so far as known, a descendant of Sir Thomas). Donne, ten or twelve years her senior, fell violently in love with her. They were secretly married, and when the secret was exposed, Donne was ruined. Anne's father had him and the friends who had helped him arrested, Sir Thomas discharged him, and the young couple, without an income, lived from hand to mouth, on the bounty of friends and ac-

I. Oliver (?)

JOHN DONNE

quaintances, in quarters so cramped that Donne called them a "hospital" and a "prison." Gradually Donne gained the patronage and help of a few sympathetic persons of influence—the Earl of Somerset, the Countess of Bedford, Sir Robert Drury (on the death of whose young daughter he wrote *The Anatomy of the World* and the ensuing "Anniversaries"). This time of humiliation and poverty lasted for some twelve or thirteen years. James I was interested in the young poet, but refused to give him any preference except through the church. Donne was finally ordained in 1614. It is probable, though the exact date is not known, that he had become an Anglican convert before 1600, but it cannot be said that he was a wholehearted or enthusiastic one. Donne's nature was so complex, and there were so many causes for the doubts and torments that beset his soul, that one cannot put a finger on any one factor; but without question his complicated theological history left a lasting effect on a man whose twin preoccupations were religion and sensuality.

In any event, he was now a made man so far as practical affairs went. An ardent Londoner, he refused some fourteen livings that would have compelled him to leave the capital, but in the course of the next few years he did become rector of several churches which he served *in absentia* by a curate, Sevenoaks being the principal one.

157

DONNE

(There was then no reproach attached to pluralism.) In 1616 he was named divinity reader of Lincoln's Inn, and in 1619 and 1620 he served in Germany as chaplain to the Earl of Doncaster. Finally in 1621 he became Dean of St. Paul's, the position he held with spreading fame to the day of his death. Had he lived longer, he was certainly destined for a bishopric.

Anne Donne had died in 1617. In the sixteen years of her married life, she had borne twelve children (of whom only seven survived her), and she was only thirty-two when she died in childbed. Once before, when he was in Paris with Sir Robert Drury, her husband had had a vision of her with a dead child in her arms, and at that very hour she suffered a miscarriage. Donne loved her passionately, and his love poems after he met her are all to her. The fact that he reared his large family without remarrying—almost an unknown thing in his day—attests to his lasting love and grief.

In 1623 Donne himself was very ill with typhoid fever. It was during this time that he wrote his beautiful *Devotions*—one of which Ernest Hemingway's *For Whom the Bell Tolls* suddenly brought into public attention in 1940. They are all worthy of similar resurrection. Donne's prose, including even his enormous number of sermons, is magnificently sonorous and concentrated in its fierce preoccupation with death and decay and the fires of damnation.

Except for a brief flurry when Archbishop Laud cast a glance of jaundiced suspicion on his orthodoxy, Donne's outward career from the time he became Dean of St. Paul's was uneventful. His sermons crowded the cathedral; he was without doubt the greatest preacher of his time. It did him no harm also that he was markedly handsome and had a most musical voice. His extraordinary memory enabled him to draw upon never-failing stores of learning. He felt his responsibilities to his church duties keenly, and though from 1629 to his death he was practically an invalid, living with his widowed (later remarried) daughter and forced to spare himself all possible activity, he rose actually from his deathbed to preach his last sermon. It was shortly before this that he had stood (not sat) to a sculptor, draped in a funeral shroud, for the monument which an admirer later had erected to his memory in St. Paul's. It was one of the few monuments which escaped both the Great Fire of London and the bombing of World War II.

This is the man whose influence Sir Edmund Gosse considered "malign." Probably there would have been no school of "metaphysical poets" without Donne, and certainly Dryden cleared the air of a great deal of frigid extravagance and knotted nonsense which this school perpetrated at its worst. But Donne himself is not open to such criticism. Behind his most crabbed paradoxes and startling images is implicit the passion of one of the most strongly endowed, emotionally, of all English poets. If Dryden broke the tradition Donne founded, then Donne had broken first the outworn tradition of the Elizabethan lyric. Donne's viewpoint was Roman, not Italian; straightforwardly physical, not sentimental. He thought with his body and felt with his mind. The cynicism and insolence of his earliest poems gave way to direct rapture and sometimes, direct anger. He rarely idealized, and he was never didactic.

The same ardor is in his religious poems; the very asceticism of his later years is as passionate as was the self-indulgence of his youth. He "married passion to reason," said one critic, and another called him "naturally artificial." Many other poets tried to emulate Donne's subtlety, the intricacy of his wit; but the best of them never quite succeeded. They lacked the inextricable fusion of body and mind which was his salient characteristic.

His prose, as has been said, was majestic, melancholy, complex, and beautiful. He was the silkworm who draws beauty from its living self—a metaphor he himself would have liked. His mind was medieval, but his nature was modern—modern not only for his own time, but for ours. He is abrupt and harsh, extravagant and intense, erudite and full of dissonant music. In prose and poetry alike, he is a very great writer.

PRINCIPAL WORKS: *Poetry*: An Anatomy of the World, 1611; Elegie on Prince Henry, 1613; The Progresse of the Soule, 1633; Poems, 1633 (revised 1635); Poetical Works, 1779; Complete Poems (A. B. Grosart, ed.) 1872-73; Holy Sonnets (E. Gosse, ed.) 1899; The Poems of John Donne (H. Grierson, ed.) 1912. *Prose*: Pseudo-Martyr, 1610; Ignatius His Conclave (translation from his own Latin version) 1611; Devotions upon Emergent Occasions, 1624; 45 Sermons upon Special Occasions, 1625; Juvenilia, or Certain Paradoxes and Problemes, 1633; 156 Sermons (3 vols.) 1640-61; Biathanatos, 1648; Letters to Several Persons of Honour, 1651; Collected Works (H. Alfred, ed.) 1839.

ABOUT: Bennett, J. Four Metaphysical Poets; Bradford, G. A Naturalist of Souls; Coffin, C. M. John Donne and the New Philosophy; Dark, S. Five Deans; Dowden, E. New Studies in Literature; Fausset, H. L. John Donne, A Study in Discord; Gosse, E. The Life and Letters of John Donne, Hardy, E. Donne, A Spirit in Conflict; Jessopp, A. John Donne, Sometime Dean of St. Paul's; Johnson, S. Lives of the Poets; Keynes, G. L. Bibliography of John Donne; Leishman, J. B. The Metaphysical Poets; Lightfoot, J. B. Donne the Poet-Preacher; Moloney, J. M. John Donne, His Flight from Mediaevalism; Sharp, R. L. From Donne to Dryden: The Revolt against Metaphysical Poetry; Simpson, E. M. A Study of the Prose Works of John Donne; Spencer, T. (ed.) A Garland for John Donne; Symons, A. Figures of Several Centuries; Walton, I. The Life of Dr. Donne; White, H. C. The Metaphysical Poets: A Study in Religious Experience; Williamson, G. The Donne Tradition.

DORSET, Earl of, Baron Buckhurst. See SACKVILLE, THOMAS

DORSET, Earl of, Lord Buckhurst. See SACKVILLE, CHARLES

DOUGLAS, GAVIN or GAWIN (1474?-September 1522), Scottish poet, was the third son of Archibald Douglas, fifth Earl of Angus, the Scottish baronial leader popularly known as "Bell-the-Cat." Educated at St. Andrews and abroad, young Douglas served as a clergyman for a number of years and in 1501 was appointed provost of the collegiate church of St. Giles at Edinburgh. During the twelve years following he devoted himself to writing as earnestly as to his ecclesiastical duties, but after the disastrous battle of Flodden in 1513, his personal life was caught up in the tangle of Scottish politics and his literary career came to an abrupt end.

The three allegorical poems and the translation of the *Aeneid* for which Douglas is remembered were all written between his twenty-sixth and his thirty-eighth year. His earliest work was the long "dream-poem" *The Palice of Honour,* an allegory modeled on Chaucer's *Hous of Fame.* This was followed by *King Hart,* a far more mature poem in which the full psychological power of the writer sustains a similar allegorical scheme. His third poem was a four-stanza conceit called *Conscience,* written in the fashion of the period and less remarkable than the two longer pieces.

Most important of all his work was his translation of Virgil, the first version of a great classic poet in English vernacular, which reveals Douglas as a man of extensive and accurate learning as well as a poet of extraordinary vigor. Here is a curious meeting of the classic and the medieval. Douglas has rendered the Latin verse into heroic couplets, introducing each book with an original prologue, characteristically Scottish in tone and exuberant in expression. Quite apart from its poetic brilliance, the language is of considerable philological interest—"a diction drawn from all sources, full of forgotten tags of alliterative romance, Chaucerian English, dialectical borrowings from Scandinavian, French, Latin."

On the basis of his translation of Virgil, many critics have considered Douglas a forerunner of the Humanism of the Renaissance. According to G. Gregory Smith in the *Cambridge History of English Literature,* however, "Douglas is in all important respects even more of a medievalist than his contemporaries . . . strictly a member of the allegorical school and a follower of Chaucer's art."

After the battle of Flodden, Douglas put aside his poet's pen and became identified with the fortunes of the English party in Scotland. When his nephew, the Earl of Angus, married the widow of James IV, Douglas came into close relations with the court and for the next eight years found himself in a maze of plot and counter-plot involving the fate of Angus and the Queen. In 1515 he was made bishop of Dunkeld against strong opposition, but six years later having been sent to England to ask for aid, he was deprived of the bishopric and forced to remain in exile. In 1522 he died of the plague, then raging in England, and was buried in the Church of the Savoy.

PRINCIPAL WORKS: The Palice of Honour, c. 1553 (J. G. Kinnear, ed.) 1827; King Hart (folio ms.) (J. Pinkerton, ed.) 1786; Conscience (folio ms.); The XIII Bukes of Eneados of the Famose Poete Virgill Translated into Scottish Metir, 1553 (G. Dundas, ed.) 1839; Select Works of Gavin Douglas, 1787; The Poetical Works of Gavin Douglas, Bishop of Dunkeld (J. Small, ed.) 1874.

ABOUT: Hunter, W. An Anglo-Saxon Grammar, with an Analysis of the Style of Gavin Douglas; Millar, J. H. *Literary History of Scotland*; Small, J. *The Life of Gavin Douglas, Bishop of Dunkeld*; Watt, L. M. *Douglas's Aeneid*.

DOWLAND, JOHN

DOWLAND, JOHN (1563?-1626?), song writer, lutanist, was an Irishman according to a reference in the preface to his song book, *Pilgrime's Solace*, but his birthplace is unknown. When he was about eighteen he went abroad, traveling in France, Germany and Italy, where he came to know many of the noted musicians of the day. He must already have begun to compose for he was well received wherever he went and in 1588 the degree of Mus. Bac. was conferred on him at Oxford along with Thomas Morley.

Although Dowland lived abroad for long intervals, he became one of the best known and best loved of the Elizabethan song writers, and is still today sung more than any other Elizabethan composer. In 1597 he published his *First Booke of Songes or Ayres of Fowre Partes*, which won a popularity greater than any musical work published before that time in England. Dowland's songs were for the most part not madrigals but harmonized tunes for three or more voices, perfect in their melodic beauty, and leading directly to that peculiarly English product, the glee.

Dowland occasionally wrote his own verse, but the poets more often identified with his songs were Fulke Greville, George Peele, Sir Edward Dyer and Nicholas Breton. In contrast to some of the other Elizabethan song writers, he adhered closely to the form of the poem in his music. He was also a performing musician of the highest quality. His proficiency on the lute was celebrated in a contemporary sonnet by Barnfield (sometimes attributed to Shakespeare) which runs "Dowland to thee is deare; whose heauenly tuch/Upon the Lute, doeth rauish humaine sense."

The title page of his *Seconde Booke of Songs or Ayres* names him as lutanist to the King of Denmark. While few facts about his life are known, this is further evidence that he lived many years abroad. Dowland himself complains in a preface that he had been forgotten during his residence abroad and was considered old fashioned. It is true that his last years were passed in obscurity and neither the place nor the exact date of his death is known.

PRINCIPAL WORKS: The First Booke of Songes or Ayres of Fowre Parts, 1597 (W. Chappell, ed. 1844); The Seconde Booke of Songs or Ayres, 1600; The Third and Last Booke of Songs or Aires, 1603; A Pilgrime's Solace, Wherein Is Contained Musicall Harmonie of 3, 4, and 5 parts, 1612; Collected Madrigals (E. H. Fellowes, ed.) 1920-25; Fifty Songs (E. H. Fellowes, ed.) 1925.

ABOUT: Chappell, W. Life, *in* The First Book of Songes (1844 ed.); Fellowes, E. H. English Madrigal Composers; Fellowes, E. H. Songs of Dowland; Grove, Sir G. Dictionary of Music and Musicians.

DRAYTON, MICHAEL

DRAYTON, MICHAEL (1563-1631), poet, was born at Hartshill, Warwickshire, the son of prosperous tradespeople—his father may or may not have been a butcher. As a boy of ten he became a page in the family of Sir Henry Goodere, at Polesworth. The experience had a lasting influence on him. Sir Henry taught and encouraged the precocious boy, who already had an ambition to become a poet. In charming verses he tells how he begged:

> O my deare master! cannot you (quoth I)
> Make me a Poet, doe it if you can.

Nature had done it already, but Sir Henry introduced him to Virgil, and the lad was fired to imitation.

Still more influential on Drayton's life was the Goodere's younger daughter, Anne (later Lady Rainsford), who seems undoubtedly to have been the one love of his life, and the "Idea" of his many pastorals. Apparently Drayton never married, and it was Anne Goodere to whom he wrote so many poems, including that masterpiece of his sonnets, "Since there's no help, come let us kiss and part."

About 1590—with the bare possibility that he may have sampled one of the universities in the years between—Drayton arrived in London, the Mecca of all aspiring young Elizabethan writers. Though he held no public offices, he was in favor with Elizabeth, and he seems to have had some sort of quasi-connection with the court. His first book, *The Harmonie of the Church*, was suppressed—rather mysteriously, since it was entirely orthodox—but his pastorals and historical poems found a receptive public. From 1597 to 1602, for some unknown reason—perhaps the need for money—he turned to writing for the stage, according to the method of multiple collaboration then in vogue. No play entirely of his authorship is known to have been acted, but he probably had a hand in the writing of the first part at least of *Sir John Oldcastle*, a play which has also been attributed in part to Shakespeare.

When Elizabeth died, Drayton made a tactical error; he rushed into print with a congratulatory poem to James I before he had even arrived in England. The king considered the action in extremely poor taste, which it was, and pointedly ignored the poet. Stung, Drayton retorted with a clumsy satire, *The Owle*. His hurt feelings were a little assuaged when, in the same year (1603), Sir Walter Aston became his patron and made Drayton one of his esquires. This honor, to the lowborn Drayton, was a triumph; thenceforth all his published works included the word "esquire" after his name in large letters on a separate line.

By merely living from the reign of Elizabeth to that of Charles I, and remaining constantly at work during this half century or so, Drayton became in a sense the literary mirror of his time, from Shakespeare to Milton. His admirers called him "golden mouthed," but the usual adjective applied to him was "virtuous." This virtue, however, was not puritanical, if the former vicar of Stratford was correct in saying that Shakespeare died after a drinking bout with Ben Jonson and Drayton. He may even have been the "rival poet" of Shakespeare's sonnets, though this is most unlikely. However,

1599

MICHAEL DRAYTON

there seems to be little doubt that he and Shakespeare were personal friends. They came from the same part of England, from the same social class, they were nearly of an age, and they arrived in London, intent on literary careers, about the same time; they had much in common.

The early literary influences on Drayton were primarily Spenser and Sidney. The poet to whom he is usually compared is Daniel *qv*; however, he had far more vigor and variety than Daniel ever displayed. He wrote in many styles—pastoral, heroic (he was one of the pioneers of the ode), historical; and, in his old age, he developed a style of whimsical fantasy which anticipated the Cavalier poets. His best poems are the charming *Nimphidia*, the sonnet alluded to above, and the stirring *Ballad of Agincourt* (not to be confused with his heavy *Battaile of Agincourt*); but the poem for which he was best known in his own time was the ponderous *Poly-Olbion*.

This massive poetical survey fell completely flat on the appearance of its first part, and it was difficult to find a publisher for the remainder, but eventually it won its way if only by overwhelming its readers. Its nature is shown by its subtitle: "A Chorographicall Description of . . . this renowned Isle of Great Britaine, with intermixture of the most Remarquable Stories, Antiquities, Wonders, Rarityes, Pleasures, and Commodities of the Same." He finished the English and Welsh portions, but never got to Scotland. There is no evidence that he did any traveling to obtain first-hand knowledge of the places of which he treated, or that he was familiar with many of them, but he relied on written sources for his material. He did, however, try to vary the treatment and avoid monotony, and to some extent he succeeded. There was merely too much of it. He had been planning the work since 1598, though it did not begin to appear until 1617. By this time he was an embittered, left-over Elizabethan, longing for the days of his youth, for the ebullient self-confidence and swelling patriotism of those great ascendant years—a kind of patriotism which now was no longer in fashion. So many of the fiery young writers who had been the companions of his youth had burnt themselves out tragically early, that Drayton, who never

161

lived to be seventy, yet felt himself a venerable old man.

He rallied, however, to produce his fairy fantasies, and to publish his three religious poems, on Moses, Noah, and David. The rest of his work, the pastorals, the sonnets, the interpolated songs, the historical poems, the heroic epistles and odes with their echo of the Welsh harper to whom he had listened as a child at Polesworth, all this was behind him. The little swarthy man who perhaps had drunk deep with Shakespeare found himself acclaimed "a model of virtue," praised for his dogged, persevering epics, his clumsy construction and weakness in grammar forgiven for the sake of his earnestness and patriotic zeal. He died at sixty-eight and was buried in Westminster Abbey—but not in the Poets' Corner, though there is a bust erected to him there.

PRINCIPAL WORKS: The Harmonie of the Church, 1591 (as A Heavenly Harmonie of Spiritual Songs, 1610); Idea, the Shepheards Garland, 1593; Piers Gaveston Earle of Cornwall, 1594?; Matilda, 1594; Ideas Mirrour, 1594; Endimion and Phoebe, 1595; The Tragicall Legend of Robert Duke of Normandy, 1596; Mortimeriados, 1596 (as The Barrons Wars, 1603); Englands Heroicall Epistles, 1597; To the Majestie of King James, 1603; The Owle, 1604; A Paean Triumphall, 1604; Moyses in a Map of his Miracles, 1604 (as Moses, His Birth and Miracles, 1638); Poems Lyrick and Pastorall (including Odes) 1605; The Legend of Great Cromwel, 1607; Poly-Olbion, 1613; Elegies upon Sundry Occasions (including The Battaile of Agincourt, Nimphidia, the Quest of Cinthia, The Shepheards Sirena, The Moone-Calfe) 1627; The Muses Elizium (with Moses, Noahs Floud, David and Goliah) 1630; Complete Works (W. Oldys, ed.) 1748; Complete Works (R. Hooper, ed.; unfinished) 1876.

ABOUT: Aubrey, J. Lives of Eminent Men; Bullen, A. H. Elizabethans; Elton, O. Michael Drayton, A Critical Study; Newdigate, B. H. Michael Drayton and His Circle.

DRUMMOND OF HAWTHORNDEN, WILLIAM (December 13, 1585-December 4, 1649), Scottish poet, historian, pamphleteer, was born at Hawthornden, near Edinburgh, the oldest son of Sir John Drummond, the first laird. He was educated at the Edinburgh High School and at the newly founded University of Edinburgh (M.A., 1606). He then, after visiting his father in London (where Sir John was serving as gentleman usher to James VI of Scotland), studied law, in a rather desultory way, in Bourges and Paris. In 1610 his father died in England, and Drummond immediately ceased the study of

law and retired to Hawthornden, where he spent the remainder of his life. He was a recluse and a melancholy man by nature, and this tendency was strongly reinforced by the death in 1615 of his sweetheart, Mary Cunningham, just before their marriage. (They were not, as some authorities say, already married.) Though he showed no bitterness of feeling, death became his inspiration—"death since grown sweet, begins to be desired." In 1632, he did marry, his wife being Elizabeth Logan; they had five sons and four daughters, but only two sons and a daughter survived him. He practically ceased to write poetry, but busied himself with his duties as laird of Hawthornden, with rebuilding his house, with mechanical inventions (including weapons, an instrument to observe the strength of wind, a means of abstracting the salt from sea water, and a device to measure distances at sea), and with the writing of his history of Scotland. When the civil wars began in 1640, Drummond did his best to keep the peace and stay out of trouble; he signed the Covenant for his own protection, and performed some slight military duties with the greatest reluctance, and when he was called before the Covenanting Committees because of some satires he had written against the Presbyterians, he claimed freedom of speech and escaped prosecution. At heart he was a Tory and a convinced royalist, and later he aided Montrose against the Covenanters.

Much of Drummond's real life was lived in his mind and at a distance from personal contacts. He began corresponding with Michael Drayton [qv] in 1618, and continued until Drayton's death in 1631; they became close friends though they never met. Ben Jonson visited him in 1618, but in spite of mutual admiration their natures were quite incompatible. Unfortunately after their deaths the private and not very complimentary opinions each man held of the other appeared in print, to the detriment of both of them. Drummond's was a sensitive, introspective, independent mind; he sought in his study and writing to find a solution to his personal problems, and when he had solved them to his own satisfaction he ceased to write about them. He had no desire to reform or edify others. He read widely—he had a large library, which he gave to the

G. Jamesone (?)
WILLIAM DRUMMOND OF HAWTHORNDEN

University of Edinburgh—and he was contemplative by nature; in time this contemplative habit gave place to settled gloom.

Drummond has been called "the Scottish Petrarch," and the ascription is not unfitting, for the Italian influence was strong on his poetry, especially on his sonnets. His poetry reminds one often of Sidney's and Spenser's —sometimes, indeed, of Shelley's; he had the same ethereal idealism and aspiration as the later poet, but not his passion for moral reform. As Ward says, Drummond was notable for "his stately diction, love of beauty, and fanciful vein of moralizing." The prose *Cypresse Grove* has almost the magnificent and musical eloquence of Sir Thomas Browne. He would have bestowed a benefit on posterity had he continued a poet, instead of devoting the energies of his later years to royalist and anti-democratic pamphlets; but he had emptied his heart as much_as so seclusive and self-oriented a man could do so in public, and he had no concern to continue singing merely in the hope of fame or glory.

PRINCIPAL WORKS: Teares on the Death of Moeliades, 1613; Poems: Amorous, Funerall, Divine, Pastorall, 1616; Forth Feasting: A Panegyricke to the King's Most Excellent Majestie, 1617; Flowers of Sion, with A Cypresse Grove, 1623; An Entertainment of the High and Mighty Monarch Charles, 1633; To the Exequies of the Honourable Sir Antonye Alexander, 1638; Irene: or a Remonstrance for Concord, Amity, and Love Amongst His Majesties Subjects, 1638; The History of Scotland from 1423 to 1542, 1655; Poems (E. Phillips, ed.) 1656; The Works of William Drummond of Hawthornden (J. Sage and T. Ruddiman, eds.) 1711; Poems (W. C. Ward, ed.) 1894; A Cypress Grove (A. H. Bullen, ed.) 1907.

ABOUT: Fogle, F. R. A Critical Study of William Drummond of Hawthornden; Jonson, B. Conversations with William Drummond of Hawthornden; Ward, W. C. Memoir, *in* Poems, 1894; Whibley, C. Literary Portraits.

DRYDEN, JOHN (August 9, 1631-May 1, 1700), poet, dramatist, critic, was born at Aldwinkle, near Oundle, Northamptonshire, in the home of his maternal grandfather, who was rector there. The family on both sides was Parliamentarian in its sympathies. His father, Erasmus Dryden, was the poor younger son of a good "county" family, and lived for the most part in his wife's home instead of on his badly mortgaged estate at Blakesley in the same county. His mother had been Mary Pickering.

Dryden was a king's scholar at Westminster, and in 1650 entered Trinity College, Cambridge, where he received his B.A. in 1654. His M.A. was conferred on him at the request of James I in 1668. His father died in 1654, leaving him the small estate at Blakesley, but he stayed on in Cambridge for three years more, when he went to London. Snobbish rivals later sneered that he had been secretary or clerk to a relative of his there, and "journeyman to a bookseller" (he does seem to have lived for several years with his first publisher), but though his fortune was so small that it was necessary for him to earn his living as a writer, neither of these allegations seems to be true. Some of the time-serving of which he was later accused—and in some instances justly—may be traced to his constant need to make his way by his pen. Certainly he became an associate on equal terms of the best known intellectuals of his time (later, preceding Dr. Johnson, he was for all practical purposes their dictator), and his standing is sufficiently verified by the fact that he was made a Fellow of the Royal Society in 1662.

In 1663 Dryden married Lady Elizabeth Howard, daughter of Lord Berkshire. His wife was certainly his superior in social status, but her name had been the subject of scandal and there was something peculiar about the fact that her parents gave formal assent to the marriage though she was over twenty-one. After Dryden's death she became insane or senile, but there is no evidence that she was not mentally competent in her youth. Supposedly the marriage was unhappy, and Dryden is said to have had the actress, Ann Reeve, as his mistress for many years. But he and his wife seemed to be on friendly terms, though in later years they did not see a great deal of each other. In any event they became the parents of three sons, all of whom later were in the service of the Pope in Rome. Lady Elizabeth was not an heiress, and Dryden continued to write for a living. For a long time the stage was his principal medium, first in comedies, then in heroic tragedies.

In 1667 he was retained as writer to the King's Theatre, and the next year he became poet laureate. His heroic dramas were extremely successful, and at this period there is no doubt that he was a bit touched by the arrogance of success after long striving. The famous *Rehearsal*, a burlesque written by a number of local wits, was particularly aimed at him. More seriously, he was assailed and badly beaten by hoodlums in the employ of the king's favorite, Rochester, though the satire on Rochester which was the presumed reason for the attack was not Dryden's work at all, but that of Lord Mulgrave.

Actually, Dryden's pen during the latter years of the reign of Charles II was at the service of the king, and his satires were aimed at Monmouth and Shaftesbury, not at Rochester. Even had this not been his personal attitude, he was the official poet laureate, and he had always had a great reverence for constituted authority. He had ceased to write for the stage, and during this period was making his living for the most part by translations of the Roman poets, the principal one at this time being Ovid (1680). In 1683 he was appointed collector of the customs, and his financial difficulties were eased.

In 1685 Charles died and James II, who was a Roman Catholic, succeeded him. Dryden, who had begun his poetic career by a respectful elegy on Cromwell, and who only three years before had professed, in *Religio Laici*, an almost rationalistic Protestant creed, announced himself as a convert to Rome. It is easy to regard this as pure time-serving, and it was widely so regarded; but in all probability the conversion was

Sir G. Kneller, c. 1698
JOHN DRYDEN

sincere. Dryden's wife had already become a convert. When the bloodless revolution of 1688 took place, and William and Mary came to the throne, he did not revert to the Church of England. Instead, he saw himself deprived of the laureateship and saw it given to his enemy Thomas Shadwell (the "hero" of *MacFlecknoe*); and though all his pensions were also lost, he refused to swear allegiance to the new monarchs and later refused to dedicate a book to the king in spite of strong hints that it would be to his advantage to do so.

The Earl of Dorset came to his aid, but it was not enough. In 1690 he returned to writing for the stage, at nearly sixty. Once again he turned also to translations. Greatest of these was his translation of Virgil, in 1697—the book he refused to dedicate to William III. At this period also he wrote his "revival" of Chaucer; he himself said he had "scrubbed up" the great poet, and it may be said that he very effectively de-Chaucerized him! (He also made an "opera" of *Paradise Lost*, and "adapted" *The Tempest*.)

In his last years Dryden became almost a fixture in his favorite seat at Will's Coffee House, where the younger writers—Congreve, Wycherley, Addison—came to do him honor. It was there that young Alexander Pope, his greatest disciple, gazed awestruck at him. Nearly all his time was spent in London; occasionally he would go to Blakesley, where he enjoyed fishing and even sometimes played bowls with the villagers. A quiet, reserved, retiring man, who had all his life avoided quarrels and never felt it necessary to explain himself or his personal life or beliefs, he never posed as the Great Panjandrum of literature as Ben Jonson had done before him and as Samuel Johnson was to do after him, but with quiet self-confidence he knew he had won his commanding position in the literary world by dint of solid achievement. In appearance, he was short, stout, and florid, with a noticeable mole on his right cheek. There are few personal anecdotes about him—except the statement that he believed devoutly in astrology, even after he became a Roman Catholic; he was of too reticent and slow moving a temperament to display any of the eccentricities which make some great authors come alive long after their death.

Dryden died of what was called gout, followed by gangrene—probably a diabetic ailment. His final illness was short. He was buried in Westminster Abbey, in Chaucer's grave. It was twenty years before a plain monument, paid for by the Duke of Buckinghamshire, was erected in his memory.

Dryden, who so manfully defended the use of rhyme in the drama, and who was thought of in his lifetime primarily as a poet, is today at least as famous as "the father of modern English prose." His direct and lucid style, with its economy and order, was indeed the forerunner of the prose of the Augustinians. His verse, too, became the model of that of the next generation—MacFlecknoe, for example, directly gave Pope the idea of The Dunciad. As a satirist he was never delicate, but blunt and hard hitting; his weapon was not a rapier but a bludgeon. Absalom and Achitophel is perhaps the greatest political satire in English. Under the transparent guise of the Biblical story, it was aimed at the rebellion of Monmouth and the conspiracy of Shaftesbury, and it went straight home to the Whigs. Shadwell had the temerity to "answer" it, and its follower, The Medall, and was rewarded by MacFlecknoe.

In non-satiric poetry, Dryden is best known for the poems written after he became a Roman Catholic—The Hind and the Panther (written, like most of his poetry, in heroic couplets), A Song for St. Cecilia's Day, and Alexander's Feast. There is also the touching poem to the memory of Anne Killigrew, expressing his contrition for the indecency of his early comedies. The hymns ascribed to him may or may not be his. In the drama, his great achievement was in the field of heroic tragedy, beginning with The Indian-Queen. Don Sebastian, one of his last plays, was also one of his very best in this vein. It is interesting to note that the anti-clerical Spanish Fryar, written toward the end of his pedestrian Protestantism, was later revived by Queen Mary herself, much to his embarrassment.

More important than the plays are the prefaces to them, which contain some of the best of Dryden's prose writing. These essays, for that is what they were in essence, give him his standing as a critic, and a very high standing it is. Dryden was not a man to write spontaneously; he had to have occasion, some sort of religious or political enthusiasm, to spur him to expression. Arthur Ward has called him "the least original of all great English poets." His was not a creative mind; but fired to his subject, he could handle it with felicity and wit, and make of it a new and original thing by sheer force of treatment. In a sense he was the sublimation of the hack writer or of the journalist; given his assignment, he could manage it superbly, without it he was speechless. It is this, and not the venality of which he was accused, which enabled him to write so powerfully from so many viewpoints—to eulogize Cromwell, then to turn in Astraea Redux to praise of Charles II, next to hail in Britannia Rediviva the birth of the child who was to become the Old Pretender. It brought him from Religio Laici to The Hind and the Panther. But his heart went with his pen; they were not at the service of William and Mary. (Besides which, he hated the Dutch with a lifelong hatred.) He was not for sale, even in his most unfortunate comedies, one of which was removed from the notorious Restoration stage because of its obscenity. He was a faulty human being, and sometimes he was a faulty writer. But he was also on the whole a fine human being, and very often he was a truly great writer.

PRINCIPAL WORKS: *Poems*—Heroick Stanzas Upon the Death of Oliver, Lord Protector, 1659; Astraea Redux, 1660; Panegyrick to His Sacred Majesty, 1661; Absalom and Achitophel, 1681 (Part II, with N. Tate, 1682); The Medall, a Satyre on Sedition, 1682; MacFlecknoe, 1682; To the Pious Memory of . . . Mrs. Anne Killigrew, 1686; The Hind and the Panther, 1687; A Song for St. Cecilia's Day, 1687; Annus Mirabilis, 1688; Britannia Rediviva, 1688; Alexander's Feast, 1697; Fables Ancient and Modern, with Original Poems, 1700; Original Poems and Translations, 1701; Occasional Poems and Translations (T. Broughton, ed.) 1743. *Plays* (dates of publication)—The Rival-Ladies, 1664; The Indian-Queen (with R. Howard) 1665; The Wild Gallant, 1669; The Conquest of Granada, 1672; Marriage-à-la-Mode, 1673; Amboyna, 1673; Aureng-Zebe, 1676; All for Love, or the World Well Lost [adaptation of Antony and Cleopatra] 1678; The Spanish Fryar, 1681; Don Sebastian, 1690; Amphytrion, 1691; Comedies, Tragedies, and Operas, 1701; Dramatick Works (W. Congreve, ed.) 1717. *Prose*—Essay of Dramatick Poesie, 1668; Essay of Heroick Plays, 1672; Religio Laici, 1682; Life of Lucian, 1711; Critical and Miscellaneous Prose Works (E. Malone, ed.) 1800; Essays (W. P. Ker, ed.) 1900. *Collections*—Works, 1695; Miscellaneous Works (S. Derrick, ed.) 1760; Works (W. Scott, ed.) 1808.

ABOUT: Beljame, A. Le Public et les Hommes de Lettres en Angleterre, 1660-1744; Bredvold, L. I. The Intellectual Milieu of John Dryden; Collins, J. C. Essays and Studies; Garnett, R. The Age of Dryden; Hazlitt, W. English Poets; Hollis, C. Dryden; Johnson, S. Lives of the Poets; Lowell, J. R. Among My Books; Lubbock, A. The Character of John Dryden; MacDonald, H. John Dryden: A Bibliography; Masson, D. The Three Devils and Other Essays; Nicoll, A. Dryden and His Poetry; Pepys, S. Diary; Raleigh, W. Some Authors; Russell, T. W. Voltaire, Dryden, and Heroic Tragedy; Saintsbury, G. Dryden; Scott, W. Life of John Dryden; Sharp, R. L. From Donne to Dryden: The Revolt Against Metaphysical Poetry; Smith, D. N. John Dryden; VanDoren, M. John Dryden: A Study of His Poetry; Ward, A. W. History of English Dramatic Literature.

DUGDALE, Sir WILLIAM

(September 12, 1605-February 10, 1686), antiquary, historian, was born at Shustoke near Coleshill, Warwickshire, the son of John Dugdale, formerly bursar and steward at St. John's College. William went to school in Coventry, breaking off his education to marry at the age of seventeen. He lived with his wife's family until the death of his father in 1624, when he retired to the Warwickshire estate which he had inherited. Two acquaintances of these early years had a great influence on his later career: one, Sir Symon Archer, an antiquary who was collecting materials for a history of Warwick-

shire; the other, Sir Christopher Hatton, comptroller to Charles I, who encouraged him to carry out an independent study of Warwickshire antiquities.

Dugdale accompanied Archer to London where he became known at court and was rewarded with a high heraldic office which enabled him to examine the records in the Tower and Cotton collection of manuscripts. In 1641 Sir Christopher Hatton, anticipating a civil war, commissioned him to list and describe all the monuments and epitaphs in Westminster Abbey and the principal English churches. When war broke out, Dugdale attended the king at Oxford, the royalist headquarters, remaining there until the surrender in 1646. At the time of the Restoration, he resumed his heraldic functions, holding the office of Norroy king-at-arms and garter principal king-at-arms, and in 1677 he was knighted.

All of Dugdale's important antiquarian works were written between 1649 and 1675. With Roger Dodsworth he collaborated on the *Monasticon Anglicanum*, a history of English monasteries which is still of great interest as a source book. At the same time he was working on his archaeological and topographical masterpiece, the *Antiquities of Warwickshire*, of which Anthony à Wood wrote, "This summer [1656] came to Oxon *The Antiquities of Warwickshire* &c written by William Dugdale, and adorn'd with many cuts. This being accounted the best book of its kind that hitherto was made extant, my pen cannot enough describe how à Wood's tender affections and insatiable desire of knowledge were revish'd and melted downe by the reading of that book." A modern judgment might be somewhat less rhapsodic, but it is undoubtedly true that Dugdale's work—painstaking, methodical, industrious—set a new standard and became a model for later antiquarian histories.

PRINCIPAL WORKS: Monasticon Anglicanum (3 vols.) 1655-73; Antiquities of Warwickshire, 1656 (W. Thomas, ed. 1730); The History of St. Pauls Cathedral in London, 1658; The History of Imbanking and Drayning of Divers Fenns and Marshes, 1662; Origines Juridiciales, 1666; The Baronage of England, 1675-76; The Life of Sir William Dugdale (autobiography) 1713; The Life, Diary and Correspondence of Sir William Dugdale (W. Hamper, ed.) 1827.

ABOUT: Dugdale, W. The Life of Sir William Dugdale; Hamper, W. ed. The Life, Diary and Correspondence of Sir William Dugdale; Wood, A. à, Athenae Oxonienses.

DU JON, FRANÇOIS. See JUNIUS, FRANCIS

DUNBAR, WILLIAM (1465?-1530?), Scottish poet, was probably born in East Lothian. This is in the English-speaking Lowlands, as opposed to the then Gaelic-speaking Highlands; Dunbar is about as difficult for a modern to read as Chaucer is, but no more, in spite of the many Scottish words. He may have been born as early as 1460, and the date of his death is quite uncertain, except that it was certainly by 1530, since in that year Sir David Lyndsay, in *Testament and Complaynt of the Papyngo,* wrote of him as dead. He received a B.A. degree from St. Andrew's in 1475, M.A. in 1479. He then became a member of the Observantine Franciscan Order, and spent several years in France and Picardy as a begging friar. Very soon Dunbar regretted his vows, for the life of a wandering friar was most antipathetic to his nature. He came of a noble family, probably related to the Earl of March, and the humility required of a begging friar seems to have irked him badly. Somehow he managed to resign from the Order, and when he returned to Scotland about 1500 he was a fully ordained secular priest. Meanwhile he had had some slight connection with the Scottish embassy to France to find a wife for James IV, and probably went with the same commission when it finally secured the promise of the hand of Margaret, the daughter of Henry VII of England. On that occasion he was spoken of by English chroniclers as "the rhymer of Scotland," but this does not mean that he was in any sense the Scottish laureate —no such office existed.

He did, however, become a permanent attaché of the court, in the service particularly of the new queen. He received a pension, which was several times augmented, but what he really wanted was a regular benefice, and he kept wheedling the king to grant one to "the king's grey horse, auld Dunbar." James was quite content to have Dunbar at court, and made no move to grant his request. He was essentially a court poet, writing purely for the small, relatively cultured circle gathered around the king.

The last years of Dunbar's life are obscure. He may even have fallen at Flodden Field, or it is possible that after that catastrophe the queen succeeded in finding a safe harbor for him somewhere. If the *Orisone* is his, then he was alive in 1517, four years after Flodden Field; but it is probable that he died before 1522.

The two great influences on Dunbar's verse were English (Chaucer) and French (Villon). Yet he is unmistakably a Scottish "makar" or poet. His poems may be divided between the allegorical and religious, and the occasional, and most of his best work belongs to the latter category, including the prothalamium for James and Margaret, *The Thrissill* [thistle] *and the Rois* [rose]. But the one thing that distinguishes Dunbar from other courtly rhymers of his time is his robust humor, too satirical to be called Chaucerian, but fierce, wild, and boisterous. The alliterative *The Twa Marritt Wemen and the Wedo* is like *The Wife of Bath's Tale* told by a misogynist. The celebrated "flyting" (or flaying, a common Scottish form of verbal duel between rival poets) written against Walter Kennedy (who yet was and remained his friend) is a masterpiece of scurrility, personal as well as literary. Yet Dunbar had his mellower moments, as witness *In Honour of the Citie of London, The Golden Targe,* and *Lament for the Makaris. The Ballad of Kynd Kittok* and *The Dance of the Sevin Deidly Synnis* show Dunbar again in his more vigorous vein.

Though Dunbar hardly deserves Sir Walter Scott's encomium of being "unrivaled by any which Scotland ever produced," yet he has immense vitality, displays shrewd observation and originality of imagination, and achieves an unforgettable melodiousness despite the harshness of the dialect in which he wrote.

PRINCIPAL WORKS: Poems, 1508; Select Poems of Will. Dunbar, 1788; The Poetical Works of William Dunbar (D. Laing, ed.) 1834 (supplement 1865); Poems (J. Small, ed.) 1884-93.

ABOUT: Laing, D. Memoir *in* Poetical Works; Millar, J. H. Literary History of Scotland; Russell, G. and Mackay, J. G. Memoir, *in* 1884 ed.; Schiffer, J. William Dunbar, sein Leben und seine Gedichte; Smeaton, O. William Dunbar; Smith, A. Dreamthorp.

DUNS, JOANNES SCOTUS (1265?-1308?), philosopher, known as "Doctor Subtilis," took his name from his birthplace—but

DUNS

JOANNES SCOTUS DUNS

that birthplace may have been Dun (Down), Ulster, Ireland; Dunse, Berwickshire, Scotland; or Dunstane, Northumberland. His tombstone in Cologne says (translated): "Scotland bore me, England reared me, France taught me, Cologne receives me." But whether Ireland was ever known as Scotia in the thirteenth century is a matter of controversy. It is certain that he was a Franciscan monk, and that about 1300 he was lecturing at Oxford, where he may have been a fellow of Merton College. In 1304 he was in Paris, and received some degree there— but whether B.A., M.A., or D.D. is not known. He seems to have taught in the University of Paris till 1307, but probably never was its "regent." He is said to have died of apoplexy in Cologne on November 8, 1308, but even this is in doubt. His birth date, moreover, may have been as late as 1274.

Duns Scotus, the greatest British philosopher of the Middle Ages, was as a Franciscan the great enemy of the Dominican Thomas Aquinas and his Thomistic philosophy. However, his own theories deviated considerably from orthodox Scholasticism. Alfred Weber says that he was the first to attempt to prove the credibility of the Bible instead of taking it on faith. He exalted free will at the expense of divine grace, and put reason in second place to will. He thus "hastened the breach between science and dogma." Though he left his disciples (principally Occam) who became known as Scotists, actually he was

stronger in criticism than in original constructive power. He had remarkably broad learning for his time, and wrote voluminously on logic, metaphysics, theology, and grammar, being the first to consider grammar as a whole without reference to a particular language. Very much in the 1639 *Complete Works* is not his; the *De Rerum Principio* especially has been proved spurious. To a certain extent he incorporated Platonic and neo-Platonic ideas into the orthodox Aristotelianism. There is no question of his subtle, acute, and original mind.

In the sixteenth century Thomism triumphed, and Duns Scotus fell into such disrepute that at Oxford they boasted in print that his writings were used for toilet paper! It is from this period that the word "dunce" derives, a dunce being a "Duns man," hence a fool. Gradually his position in philosophy improved, until he became acknowledged again as the equal and rival in thought of Thomas Aquinas.

All of Duns' twelve volumes were written in Latin, which was his own habitual tongue as it was that of all scholars of his era. He therefore belongs more to the history of philosophy than to that of English literature. However, his influence on later thinkers and writers (*e.g.* Gerard Manley Hopkins, the Jesuit poet) gives him claim to attention in the latter field as well. He has not had the revival and modernization which his rival philosopher has achieved; he has nothing to say to modern philosophers except historically. His "realism" (in the unrealistic medieval sense), his conceptualist logic, his deprecation of reason as against faith and his insistence on the independence of the body from the soul, are all as medieval as his firm belief that the Ptolemaic system of astronomy alone could account for observed phenomena. Nevertheless, his theories are an intrinsic part of the historical corpus of philosophy, and his grammatical theory of universals had its repercussions on later researches into philology.

His twelve folio volumes were of course all in manuscript, printing being yet unknown.

PRINCIPAL WORKS: Complete Works (L. Wadding, ed.) 1639.

ABOUT: Longpré, E. Le Philosophie du B. Duns Scot; Samaniego, X. Vida del Padre J. Dunsio Escoto; Wadding, L. Life, *in* Complete Works; Weber, A. History of Philosophy; Werner, C. Die Scholastik des späteren Mittelalters.

DUNTON, JOHN (May 4, 1659-1733), publisher, pamphleteer, miscellaneous writer, was the son of the rector of Graffham, Huntingdonshire, formerly a fellow of Trinity College. His mother, Lydia Carter, died soon after his birth and the boy was left to the care of friends in England while his father went to Ireland. He went to school at Dungrove near Chesham and on his father's return was educated to be a clergyman.

As Dunton wrote later, he was always "distracted by love and politics," in both of which fields he seems to have been somewhat precocious. He fell in love when he was thirteen to the detriment of his studies and a year later was apprenticed to a London bookseller, Thomas Parkhurst. Strongly Whig in sympathy, he organized an association of a hundred fellow apprentices for whom he gave a banquet to celebrate the "funeral" of his own apprenticeship when he went into business for himself.

At twenty-three he married Elizabeth Annesley (Defoe is supposed to have married her sister and the father of John Wesley, another sister). The pair called each other Philaret and Iris and lived happily enough at the Black Raven on the proceeds of several successful publishing ventures until the depression of 1685 when financial difficulties persuaded Dunton to sail for America. In Boston he collected £500 owing to him, sold his surplus stock of books and spent several months in travel studying the customs of the American Indian. He returned to England the next year and in 1688 opened a shop at the Black Raven. According to his own account, he published six hundred books during the next ten years, only seven of which he repented. He was also the publisher of a weekly paper, the *Athenian Gazette,* an early *Notes & Queries.*

When his first wife died in 1697 he married Sarah Nicholas, the daughter of a woman of property, but they soon quarreled because his new mother-in-law refused to settle his debts. In his autobiography, *The Life and Errors of John Dunton,* he writes that his income would not support him "could he not stoop so low as to turn author," and turn author he did with a vengeance. In addition to the autobiography, which is of a good deal of interest in its record of the period, he wrote satires, articles of a decidedly eccentric turn, and a series of odd political pamphlets, strongly Whiggish. During the last thirty years of his life he grew increasingly queer to the point of actual derangement, living alone and as he put it "incognito," until he died in obscurity at the age of seventy-four.

PRINCIPAL WORKS: The Dublin Scuffle, 1699 (J. Nichols, ed. 1818); The Life and Errors of John Dunton, Late Citizen of London, Written by Himself, 1705 (J. Nichols, ed. 1818); Dunton's Whipping-Post, or a Satire Upon Everybody, 1706; Athenianism, or the New Projects of John Dunton, 1710; Mordecai's Memorial, or There Is Nothing Done for Him, 1716; An Appeal to His Majesty (with a list of political pamphlets) 1723.

ABOUT: Dunton, J. The Life and Errors of John Dunton; Nichols, J. B. Memoir, *in* The Life and Errors of John Dunton (1818 ed.); Nichols, J. B. Literary Anecdotes.

D'URFEY, THOMAS (1653-February 26, 1723), dramatist, song writer, known as Tom D'Urfey, was born at Exeter of Huguenot parentage. He was educated as a lawyer but "the fairy-field of poetry" attracted him and he began to write verse and plays, composing a rhymed tragedy, *The Siege of Memphis, or The Ambitious Queen,* which was produced when he was twenty-three. A year later the comedy, *Madam Fickle, or The Witty False One,* brought him popular success and for thirty years he continued to write boisterous farces and bombastic melodramas at top speed.

At best D'Urfey's plays were brisk and good-humored horse-play, distinguished only by the songs which he liked to introduce into the action. As a balladist, he had a sure touch in devising lyrics on current topics and although his serious work was not highly regarded, his songs were widely popular. Given to stuttering, he once said "The Town may da-da-damn me as a poet but they sing my songs for all that." Jeremy Collier attacked both D'Urfey and Congreve for immorality on the stage and proceedings were brought against them. Certainly D'Urfey's plays were no broader than those written by the better remembered Restoration dramatists, but for wit they substituted mere boisterousness.

Tom D'Urfey's gaiety and good nature won him many friends, some of them in high places. Through four reigns he enjoyed favor at court. Addison has described Tom D'Urfey and Charles II together, Tom humming one of his current songs while the king leaned on his shoulder. James II was a friend. William and Mary liked to hear him sing and he was enormously popular with the Princess Anne for whom he composed a song lampooning Princess Sophia, her rival to the throne, which began "The crown's far too weighty For shoulders of eighty." Addison and Steele were both his friends as were Henry Purcell and Thomas Farmer, both of whom set some of his songs to music.

During his lifetime D'Urfey published a great deal, both plays and collections of songs and poems. Some years before his death, however, he fell into obscurity and lived in poverty. In 1713 Addison and Steele revived one of his early comedies, *A Fond Husband*, for a benefit performance at the Drury Lane. Ten years later he died at the age of seventy.

PRINCIPAL WORKS: *Plays* (dates of publication): The Siege of Memphis, or, The Ambitious Queen, 1676; Madam Fickle, or, The Witty False One, 1677; A Fond Husband, or, The Plotting Sisters, 1677; The Fool Turn'd Critick, 1678; Trick for Trick, or, The Debauch'd Hypocrite, 1678; Squire Oldsapp, or, The Night-Adventurers, 1679; The Virtuous Wife, or, Good Luck at Last, 1680; Sir Barnaby Whigg, or, No Wit Like a Woman's, 1681; The Royalist, 1682; The Injured Princess, or, The Fatal Wager, 1682; A Commonwealth of Women, 1686; The Banditti, or, A Ladies Distress, 1686; A Fool's Preferment, or, The Three Dukes of Dunstable, 1688; Love For Money, or, The Boarding School, 1691; Bussy D'Ambois, or, The Husband's Revenge, 1691; The Marriage-Hater Match'd, 1692; The Richmond Heiress, or, A Woman Once in the Right, 1693; The Comical History of Don Quixote, Three Parts, 1694-96; The Intrigues at Versailles, or, A Jilt in All Humors, 1697; The Campaigners, or, The Pleasant Adventures at Brussels, 1698; The Famous History of the Rise and Fall of Massaniello, 1700; The Bath, or, The Western Lass, 1701; The Old Mode and the New, or, Country Miss with Her Furbeloe, 1703; Wonders in the Sun, or, The Kingdom of the Birds, 1706; The Modern Prophets, or, New Wit for a Husband, 1709. *Other Works*: A New Collection of Songs and Poems, 1683; Choice New Songs Never Before Printed, 1684; Several New Songs, 1684; A Third Collection of New Songs, 1685; A Compleat Collection of Mr. D'Urfey's Songs and Odes, 1690; A Choice Collection of New Songs and Ballads, 1699; Tales Tragical and Comical, 1704; Stories, Moral and Comical, 1707; Songs Compleat, Pleasant and Divertive (5 vols.) 1717; Wit and Mirth: or, Pills to Purge Melancholy (6 vols.) 1719-20; New Operas, with Comical Stories, and Poems, on Several Occasions, 1721; The Songs of Thomas D'Urfey (C. L. Day, ed.) 1933.

ABOUT: Baring-Gould, S. Devonshire Characters and Strange Events; Chappell, W. The Ballad Literature and Popular Music of the Olden Time; Forsythe, R. A Study of the Plays of Thomas D'Urfey.

DYER, Sir EDWARD (1543?-May 1607), poet, was the son of Sir Thomas Dyer, Kt., by his second wife. He was born at Sharpham Park, Somersetshire, and educated at either Balliol or Broadgates Hall, Oxford. He left without taking a degree, and after some travel on the Continent appeared at the court of Elizabeth in 1566. His patron at this time was the Earl of Leicester. Elizabeth at times showed favor to the young man, at other times he was under her displeasure; once she was induced to forgive him by the representation by his friends that he was "sick of a consumption" from grief at her disfavor. He held various offices, going on diplomatic missions to the Netherlands in 1584 and to Denmark in 1589, and he was appointed to search out concealed and forfeited lands. The queen gave some of these forfeited estates to Dyer, though she was not pleased by the way he did the work. In 1596, however, she appointed him chancellor of the Order of the Garter, and knighted him.

Dyer was an intimate friend of Sir Philip Sidney, who bequeathed half of his books to him. Some attempt has been made to find an allusion to him in Shakespeare's Sonnet CXI, but it seems far fetched. His poems were much admired at court, but they were never collected, and existed entirely in manuscript except for inclusion in some of the anthologies of the day—*The Phoenix Nest, England's Helicon,* and *The Paradyse of Daynty Devises.* With Sidney and Spenser he belonged to the group known as the Areopagus, the aim of which was to "Latinize" English poetry by basing it on quantity; nevertheless his own work was in rhyme and meter.

According to Aubrey, Dyer was a Rosicrucian, and dabbled in alchemy. He seems to have lived a rather wastrel life, and to have run through his fortune. There is no mention of his ever having been married, and as he made his sister his heiress, he probably died a bachelor.

The best known of Dyer's works are the "moral" poem, *My Mynd to Me a Kingdome Is,* the sonnet, *The Shepheards Conceite of Prometheus,* and the whimsical prose tract, *The Prayse of Nothing.* George (or Richard) Puttenham, in *The Arte of English Poesie,* said that Dyer was "for Elegie most sweete, solempne, and of high conceit"; and

Spenser in 1579 rather amazingly called him "in a manner our only Inglishe poett." Posterity has not confirmed this praise; Dyer is one of the most minor court poets of the Elizabethan era. His close connection with the domestic intrigues of Elizabeth's court circle, and his own assumption that he was even more closely in the confidence of the queen and her intimates than he actually was, doubtless induced his contemporaries to flatter him rather beyond his modest deserts. Spenser, however, does not belong in this category; and the friendship he and the noble-minded Sidney felt for Dyer makes one believe that he must have been a better man and even a better writer than any existing evidence would indicate. It is only fair to Dyer to add that much of his writing is lost; perhaps if we had it all we should admire him more greatly.

PRINCIPAL WORKS: Works (A. B. Grosart, ed.) 1872.

ABOUT: Aubrey, J. Lives of Eminent Men; Brooks, A. Will Shakespeare and the Dyer's Hand; Grosart, A. B. Introduction to Collected Works; Sargent, R. M. At the Court of Queen Elizabeth: The Life and Lyrics of Sir Edward Dyer; Wood, A. à, Athenae Oxonienses.

DYER, GEORGE (March 15, 1755-March 2, 1841), poet, critic, was the son of a watchman, born in London. By the charity of a group of dissenting ladies, he was sent to school at Christ's Hospital where he proved himself an excellent scholar and became a protégé of Anthony Askew, physician-in-residence. When he was nineteen he entered Emmanuel College and took his B.A. degree four years later. After several posts in provincial grammar schools, he went back to Cambridge to tutor in the family of Robert Robinson, minister of a dissenting congregation, through whom he became deeply interested in unitarianism.

Dyer was in his mid-thirties when he gave up teaching and moved to London where he lived at Clifford's Inn and contributed poems and articles to the *New Monthly* and *Gentleman's Magazine*. His poetry was of little merit although he believed himself that "a poem was a poem, his own as good as anybody's and anybody's as good as his own." His scholarship was of a higher order. As a collaborator on Valpy's 141-volume edition of the classics, he worked hard and long for twenty years, contributing much that was original. He also spent many years collecting materials for a bibliographical work which was never published, meanwhile supplementing his income with routine chores of indexing and proofreading, until his eyesight failed.

Dyer is remembered chiefly as the friend of Charles Lamb who speaks of him in his letters as a gentle and kindly eccentric. One of Lamb's *Essays of Elia*, the "Amicus Redivivus," tells a characteristic story about Dyer. Dyer had been visiting Lamb and on his departure walked straight into the river—as much apparently from absent-mindedness as from myopia—and had to be rescued from drowning. Lamb loved to tease him for his absent-mindedness and his general disorderliness, all of which Dyer accepted with sweetness and a total lack of humor. Both in dress and in his surroundings he was notoriously untidy until a fading widow, Mrs. Mather, took pity on him and married him in his latter years. He died at Clifford's Inn shortly before his eighty-sixth birthday, his wife surviving him by nearly twenty years.

PRINCIPAL WORKS: Poems, Consisting of Odes and Elegies, 1792; The Complaints of the Poor People of England, 1793; Account of New South Wales and State of the Convicts, 1794; A Dissertation on the Theory and Practice of Benevolence, 1795; Memoirs of the Life and Writings of Robert Robinson, 1796; The Poet's Fate, a Poetical Dialogue, 1797; An Address to the People of Great Britain on the Doctrines of Libel, 1799; Poems, 1802; Poems and Critical Essays, 1802; Poetics, or a Series of Poems and Disquisitions on Poetry, 1812; Four Letters on the English Constitution, 1812; History of the University and Colleges of Cambridge, 1814; The Privileges of the University and Colleges of Cambridge, 1824; Academic Unity, 1827.

ABOUT: Lucas, E. V. The Life of Charles Lamb; Robinson, H. C. Diary, Reminiscences and Correspondence.

DYER, JOHN (1699?-December 15, 1758), poet, was born in Aberglasney, Carmarthanshire, South Wales, the son of a solicitor named Robert Dyer. His birth date may be a year or two before or after the date given. He was educated at Westminster, and then put in his father's office. The law was not to his liking, and immediately after his father's death he left the office to study painting. For some years he was an itinerant painter—not a very good or successful one—in southern Wales and northern England. He then went to Italy for further study of art, and returned with malaria, which permanently injured his

JOHN DYER

health. Finally, in 1741, in his forties, he gave up painting and was ordained as a clergyman. Through the patronage of Lord Hardwicke he was named vicar of Calthorp, Leicestershire; then in 1751 resigned and received the living of Belchford, Lincolnshire. This he exchanged in 1752 and 1755 for two livings in the same county, Coningsby and Kirkby-on-Bane. In 1752, by royal mandate, he was named LL.B. of Cambridge. In 1741 he married a Miss Ensor, who he liked to believe was a collateral descendant of Shakespeare; they had a son and three daughters. Dyer died at Coningsby of what may have been tuberculosis or a flare-up of his old malaria.

Dyer was the author of three long poems and a number of shorter ones, but one only has survived to find any readers today—*Grongar Hill*, a poem of 150 lines. It is a description of the view from a hill in the Vale of Towy, where he was born—the first poem in its time to deal *exclusively* with nature. It is written in octosyllabic couplets which are a return to an earlier mode, so that in form it is a revival of the old, in matter an anticipation of the romantic new. Wordsworth, in his sonnet to Dyer, says truly that "a grateful few shall love thy modest Lay." It is the sweetness and simplicity of Dyer's style in this poem which endears him to the reader and even disarmed Dr. Johnson, who

so hated descriptive verse. A couplet chosen at random gives the flavor of Dyer's style:

A various journey to the deep,
Like human life, to endless sleep.

Of his other two long poems, *The Ruins of Rome* and *The Fleece*, the less said the better. *The Ruins of Rome* was the fruit of his sojourn in Italy, and is a conscientious attempt to describe ancient Roman architecture in pedestrian verse. *The Fleece* is a truly overpowering metrical description of the wool industry, from raising the sheep to selling the cloth. It was greatly admired by his contemporaries—chiefly, one supposes, by those in the wool business—but is quite unreadable today.

Nevertheless, in *Grongar Hill* Dyer did prove himself a poet, and one possessed of freshness of feeling and a quaint charm. The shortness of the poem saves it from the tediousness and monotony which marked Dyer's longer works, and his painter's eye enabled him to see in the landscape its minutest beauties and to communicate them to his readers.

PRINCIPAL WORKS: Grongar Hill (an Irregular Ode, *in* Miscellaneous Poems and Translations, R. Savage, ed.) 1726; Grongar Hill (revised) 1727; The Ruins of Rome, 1740; The Fleece, 1757; Shorter Poems, 1761; The Poetical Works of Armstrong, Dyer, and Green (G. Gilfillan, ed.) 1858; Poems (*in* Welsh Library, E. Thomas, ed.) 1903; Grongar Hill (R. C. Boys, ed.) 1941.

ABOUT: Boys, R. C. Introduction, 1941 ed. Grongar Hill; Gilfillan, G. Memoir *in* Poetical Works; Johnson, S. Lives of the Poets; Seccombe, T. The Age of Johnson.

EADMER (1060?-1124?), historian and biographer, was probably of English parentage. Except that from childhood he kept a journal of ecclesiastical matters, nothing is known of his life until, in his thirties, a monk at the Monastery of Christ Church, Canterbury, he became the close associate of Anselm. When Anselm became Archbishop of Canterbury in 1093, Eadmer served as his assistant, remained his intimate friend throughout his lifetime, and after his death wrote a *Life of St. Anselm*.

A man of great integrity and strong national sympathies, Eadmer became personally involved in the bitter struggle for supremacy between the English and Scottish churches when, in 1120, he was nominated Archbishop of St. Andrews by King Alexander of Scotland. He accepted upon condition that he be consecrated by Archbishop Ralph of Canterbury. Alexander refused to allow consecration to a Scottish see by an English primate, and neither would retreat from his position. Eadmer returned to Canterbury, and later formally resigned all claims to the archbishopric. He apparently remained at Canterbury until his death in 1124.

His *Historiae Novorum in Anglia*, a history of England for a period almost identical with his own lifetime (from 1066 to 1122), is at least as important for its influence upon other writers as for its content. Making use of his compendious notes, Eadmer wrote chiefly an ecclesiastical history, but incorporated valuable political and social material.

His style is classical, his approach to his material fresh and vivid. One contemporary speaks of the "chastened elegance" of his style, another of its "sober festivity." His use of firsthand authority, his avoidance of irrelevant detail, and his omission of alleged miracles greatly influenced the work of historians who followed him.

In addition to the Anselm biography, he wrote lives of saints and many other ecclesiastical pieces.

PRINCIPAL WORK: Historia Novorum in Anglia (M. Rule, ed.) 1884.

ABOUT: Bale, J. Index Britanniae Scriptorum; Collier, J. P. Ecclesiastical History, vol. 2; Wright, T. Biographia Britannica Literaria.

EALWHINE. See ALCUIN

EARLE, JOHN (1601?-1665) miscellaneous writer, was born at York. He matriculated at Christ Church, Oxford, but transferred to Merton, where he received his B.A. in 1619 and his M.A. in 1624.

A commemorative poem written in 1630 on the death of William, third Earl of Pembroke, brought the young divine to the attention of William's brother, Philip, chancellor of Oxford, who appointed him his personal chaplain. In 1641 he became chaplain and tutor to Prince Charles, and the rest of his life was devoted to the service of the royal family.

Charming, witty, a delightful conversationalist, incorruptible, just and generous, he was equally popular with the court he supported and with the non-conformists who were its enemies. He himself never had a personal enemy, and his last breath was spent protesting the harsh measures proposed against the non-conformists.

Following Cromwell's victory, Earle went into exile with the court of Charles II, acting as close companion to the king, and giving both financial and personal aid to the cause of the restoration. Upon the victorious return to England, he became dean of Westminster, bishop of Worcester, and, in 1663, dean of Salisbury, where his special function was conciliating the non-conformists. He died while attending the king and queen at Oxford during the great plague, November 17, 1665.

Earle's principal literary work, published in 1628, was a collection of sketches of people and institutions entitled *Microcosmography*. Such sketches were a popular form of the day, but Earle carried them beyond the witty satire which was their usual purpose, exploring deeper moral values, and emphasizing the significance and influence of familiar and commonplace elements of everyday life. Like their author, these sketches enjoyed wide popularity, ten editions being published during his lifetime.

PRINCIPAL WORK: Microcosmography, or a Piece of the World Discovered; in Essays and Characters, 1628.

ABOUT: Burnet, G. History of my Own Time; Clarendon, E. H. History of the Rebellion and Civil Wars in England; Clarendon, E. H. Autobiography.

EDEN, RICHARD (1521?-1576), translator, was born in Herefordshire and received his education at Queens' College, Cambridge, where he excelled at languages.

It was the age of great voyages of discovery. Spain and Portugal had taken the lead in extending the boundaries of the known world, and Eden was fired with a patriotic desire to have England take part in exploring uncharted seas. He was convinced that lack of knowledge held England's seamen back, and he therefore spent a large part of his lifetime translating into English first-hand accounts of exploration. He accompanied the publication of some of these with eloquent appeals to the merchant fleet to carry the flag of England into the new world.

He worked in the English treasury for several years following his graduation, taking a position in the English treasury of the

Prince of Spain in 1554. For the eleven years following 1562 he accompanied Jean de Ferrières, vidame of Chartres, on extensive European travels, barely escaping the St. Bartholomew massacre in Paris in 1570, and returning to London in 1573. He remained in London until his death in 1576.

An excellent scholar and scientist, Eden translated and revised Geminus' *Anatomy*, and translated Martin Cortes' *Art of Navigation*. His contributions to the literature of maritime discovery began in 1553, with the publication of *A Treatise of the New India*, which he translated and adapted from Sebastian Munster's *Cosmography*. Following publication in 1555 of *The Decades of the New World*, a collection of stories by several explorers, he was cited for heresy by the Bishop of Lincoln, and was deprived of his office in the treasury. His two final translations, John Taisner's *De Natura Magnetis* and Ludovico Barthema's *Travels in the East in 1503*, were published a year after his death under the title *History of Travel in the East and West Indies*.

PRINCIPAL WORKS: A Treatyse of the Newe India (translated from the Latin of Sebastian Munster) 1553; The Decades of the Newe Worlde or West India (translated from the Latin of Peter Martyr) 1555; Arte of Navigation (translated from the Spanish of Martin Cortes) 1561; The History of Travayle in the East and West Indies, 1577.

ABOUT: Arber, E. The First Three English Books on America; Cooper, C. H. Athenae Cantabrigienses; Oldys, W. The British Librarian.

EDWARDS, RICHARD (1523?-1566), musician and playwright, was born in Somersetshire. In 1540 he entered Corpus Christi College, Oxford, receiving his B.A. and a fellowship in 1544. In 1547 he received an M.A. at Christ Church. Although he entered Lincoln's Inn Field in 1564, he apparently never practiced law.

Edwards had studied music with George Etheridge, one of England's most distinguished musicians. In 1561 he was appointed master of the children of the Chapel Royal, where in 1565 he produced his music drama, one of the earliest in that form, *Damon and Pithias*, acted by the choir boys of the chapel. The following year a second play, *Palamon and Arcite*, was performed at Christ Church, Oxford, before Queen Elizabeth. The queen was heartily amused by the play and promised to reward its author,

but a month later, before he could enjoy her patronage, Edwards died.

A collection of short poems, *A Paradise of Dainty Devices*, compiled by Edwards and published ten years after his death, contains many of his own poems. Musically, he is best known for a charming madrigal. *In Going to My Naked Bed*, of which he wrote both words and music, and for a song, *In Commendation of Music*, part of which is quoted in *Romeo and Juliet*.

Damon and Pithias, the only extant play, is of interest chiefly because of its place in the development of romantic drama in England. For the first time, classical material was used in a modern fashion. The characters and theme were borrowed from the Roman theatre, but the form and language of the play are those of Elizabethan England. The quality of the poetry is inferior, and scenes of vulgar farce are crudely juxtaposed to those of tragedy. This use of comic relief in a tragedy was, however, one of Edwards' real contributions to later dramatic form. In spite of the shortcomings of his style, there is sufficient emotional intensity in the writing to explain the play's success with contemporary audiences.

PRINCIPAL WORKS: Damon and Pithias, 1571; (compiler and contributor) A Paradise of Dainty Devices, 1576.

ABOUT: Bradner, L. Life and Poems of Richard Edwards; Collier, J. P. History of English Dramatic Poetry.

ELLIS, GEORGE (1753-1815), publisher and miscellaneous writer, was the only son and namesake of a member of the Assembly of St. George in the West Indies. He was educated at Westminster School and at Trinity College, Cambridge.

In 1777 and 1778 he published, anonymously, lively and amusing poetic satires on manners and customs, the fashionable form of literary expression of the day.

When a group of young rebels began publishing *The Rolliad*, a series of satires attacking the Pitt administration, Ellis joined them, his contributions being higher than average both in wit and style. Sometime during the next twenty years he reversed his political stand, emerging in the late '90's as a fervent Tory. Repentant of his *Rolliad* career, he now published, with George Canning and William Gifford, a political sheet called *The Anti-Jacobin,* to which he contributed as trenchant satires defending the administration as those with which he had formerly attacked it. During the intervening years his interest was chiefly in antiquarian matters, and he became a Fellow of the Royal Society and of the Society of Antiquaries.

His most valuable literary contribution was his scholarly research in the field of early English poetry and drama. His compilation and publication of *Specimens of the Early English Poets* and *Specimens of Early English Metrical Romances* rescued much important material from neglect or oblivion. In 1796 he edited an English translation of a collection of *Fabliaux* of the twelfth and thirteenth centuries.

A diplomatic mission with Lord Malmesbury to The Hague in 1784 gave him knowledge and insight into Dutch politics. When revolution broke out there the following year he was able to interpret the events, and in 1789 his *History of the Dutch Revolution* was published anonymously.

Ellis married in 1800. He had no children. He was one of the closest friends of Sir Walter Scott, who called him "the first converser I ever saw."

PRINCIPAL WORKS: Poetical Tales by Sir Gregory Gander, 1778; History of the Late Revolution in the Dutch Republic, 1789; (ed.) Specimens of the Early English Poets, 1790; (ed.) Specimens of Early English Metrical Romances, 1805.

ABOUT: Elliott, Sir G. Life and Letters; Malmesbury, 1st Earl of, Diaries and Correspondence.

ELLWOOD, THOMAS (October 1639-March 1, 1713), Quaker, religious writer, autobiographer, was born in Crowell, Oxfordshire, the youngest child of Walter Ellwood, a country gentleman, and Elizabeth Putnam. Four years of his childhood were spent in London; then he was sent to the free school in Thame, but taken out because his father could no longer afford the charges. He was an athletic boy, fond of field sports, but in no sense "wicked," as he later felt himself to have been. His mother and older brother both died when he was very young. With his father, in 1659, he paid a long visit to the latter's old friend Isaac Pennington (later William Penn's father-in-law), where they found the family had become Quakers.

Young Ellwood was then twenty, and impressionable. To his father's anger and disgust he listened avidly to accounts of the new sect, heard Edward Burroughs preach, and announced his conversion. His father kept him a prisoner at home, and beat him soundly for keeping his hat on in his presence, but nothing availed. By 1660 he was actively a Quaker and several times was imprisoned for short periods. In 1662, recovering from smallpox, he went to London, and there through Pennington was engaged as a reader to the blind Milton. His story that he suggested *Paradise Regained* to Milton as a sequel to *Paradise Lost* has been doubted. Later he was Milton's reader again for a brief period. From 1663 to 1669 he lived with the Penningtons, acting as Latin tutor to their children and manager of their country estates. During this period he was arrested many times. In 1669 he married Mary Ellis, sixteen years his senior, who died in 1708.

During his last years Ellwood lived more or less in retirement in Amersham; however, he engaged constantly in controversies with dissident factions of the Society of Friends, and busied himself also with the editing of the *Journal* of George Fox,*qv* whose literary executor he was. It was at this time that he wrote his own life. He fancied himself as a poet, published one long religious poem, and frequently interspersed his autobiography with hymns and verses, unfortunately nothing but doggerel. If he resembled Bunyan in this respect, he also resembled that great writer in his capacity for racy, vivid prose; his "characters" of the people he knew are little gems, full of shrewd insight into human nature and displaying a gift for concise description. Aside from his autobiography and the two volumes in which he compiled the historical portions of the Bible, Ellwood's writings were all controversial religious tracts, of interest to the modern reader only as documents in the history of Christianity in England. He was an intimate friend of William Penn, who wrote the preface to his edition of Fox's *Journal.*

PRINCIPAL WORKS: An Alarm to the Priests, 1660; Forgery No Christianity, 1674; The Foundation of Tithes Shaken, 1678; A Discourse Concerning Riots, 1683; Rogero-Mastix: A Rod for William Rogers (verse), 1685; Truth Defended, 1695; Sacred History, or the Historical Parts of the Old Testament, 1705 (New Testament, 1709, combined

1720) ; A History of the Life of Thomas Ellwood, Written by His Own Hand (supplement by J. Wyeth) 1714; A Collection of Poems on Various Subjects (n.d.).

ABOUT: Brown, A. K. Thomas Ellwood, the Friend of Milton; Budge, F. A. Thomas Ellwood and Other Worthies; Ellwood, T. History of the Life of Thomas Ellwood; Webb, M. The Penns and the Penningtons.

ELYOT, Sir THOMAS (1490?-March 20, 1546), political writer, translator, was born in Wiltshire, the son of Sir Richard Elyot, judge of the court of common pleas, and of Alice Fynderne. Though he has been claimed both by St. Mary's Hall, Oxford, and Jesus College, Cambridge, he himself said that he was educated at home, and from the age of twelve taught himself. He may also have read medicine with Thomas Linacre; he certainly had some medical knowledge. In 1511 he accompanied his father on the western circuit as clerk of assize, a position he held until he resigned in 1528. His father died in 1522, and he inherited a large estate, making his home at Combe (now Long Combe), Oxfordshire. In this same year he married Margaret Barrow (or Abarrow), a pupil of Sir Thomas More, who became Elyot's close friend. The marriage was childless. After his death his widow married Sir John Dwyer.

In 1523 Cardinal Wolsey appointed Elyot clerk of the privy council, but did nothing about paying him a salary; when he was de-

posed in 1530 he was still asking for arrears of pay. In 1527 he was high sheriff of Oxfordshire and Berkshire. His *Boke Called the Governour*, a treatise on the education of statesmen, which was immensely popular, was dedicated to Henry VIII, and led to his being sent (against his will) as ambassador to the court of Charles V, with the double mission of securing the emperor's support for Henry's divorce from Catherine of Aragon, and of trying to capture William Tyndale, who was in hiding there. He returned, unsuccessful in both quests, in 1532, and tried to retire and devote himself to writing; but in 1535 he was sent to Charles V again for a year. He accepted the Anglican reform, and was in no danger of the martyrdom which overtook his friend More. In 1542 he sat for Cambridge in Parliament, and in 1544 was sheriff for Cambridgeshire and Huntingdonshire. He died at Carleton, Cambridgeshire.

Though he had no originality, Elyot was a learned writer, strongly influenced by the "New Learning," and a real scholar. He translated much from the Greek, including works by Plutarch and Isocrates. Some of his books (*e.g., The Bankette of Sapience*) were made up largely of aphorisms from the Greek writers. His *Castel of Helth*, though ridiculed by the medical men, was much read. It is significant that all his books were written in the vernacular—though his friend Roger Ascham *qv* said that he had projected a history of England in Latin. His translations were distinguished by their "elegance"; they were really nearer derivative versions than strict translations. His real interest was in political philosophy and history. Probably, however, his best claim to remembrance is as author of the first Latin-English dictionary, a monumental work which he finished in two years of intensive effort.

Elyot was knighted in 1530, when he was deprived of his post in the privy council—practically his only reward, he remarked bitterly, for seven years' hard and responsible labor.

SIR THOMAS ELYOT

After H. Holbein

PRINCIPAL WORKS: The Boke Called the Governour, 1531 (H. H. S. Croft, ed. 1883; F. Watson, ed. 1937) ; Pasquyl the Playne, 1533; Of the Knowledge Which Maketh a Wise Man, 1533; The Castel of Helth, 1534; The Bankette of Sapience, 1534; The Dictionary of Sir T. Elyot, Knyght, 1538; The Image of Governaunce, 1540; The Defence of Good Women, 1545; A Preservative Agaynst Deth, 1545.

ABOUT: Crofts, H. H. S. Introduction, 1883 ed. The Governor; Fuller, T. Worthies of England; Watson, F. Introduction, 1937 ed. The Governor.

ERCELDOUNE, THOMAS (fl. 1220?-1297?)

seer and poet, has acquired a half-legendary, half-historical role in Scottish folk lore. That he lived and wrote at least some of the tales attributed to him is indisputable. Sometimes calling himself Learmont, sometimes The Rhymer, he owned property on a tributary of the Tweed River which to this day is known as Rhymer's Land. The Russian poet Lermontov believed himself a descendant of The Rhymer.

The earliest poem which bears his name is a version of the legend of the elf-queen who loves a mortal and carries him off to her own country. The hero's name is Thomas, and a variation of the usual form of the legend has Thomas endowed with the power of prophecy upon his return home.

Soon after Thomas' death, prophecies made in his name became so popular that it is impossible to know which were his own. The most famous is that of the death of King Alexander III in 1285. Asked what the following day would bring, Thomas replied in vague oracular terms which some authorities, including Sir Walter Scott, believe to be merely a weather prediction. The king's death the next morning seemed to give the prediction of "dire and calamitous news before the hour of noon" explicit meaning, and Thomas' reputation was established.

For at least three centuries, his name was often used to gain credence for fabricated prophecies. A set of seventeen prophecies, supposed to have been his, on the outcome of the Scottish-English war, which was first published in England on the eve of the Battle of Bannockburn in 1314 and which predicted the defeat of the Scots in that battle, is probably a forgery and an early example of psychological warfare.

It is generally accepted that Thomas was the author of one of the earliest versions of the Tristram story, although the first known manuscript dates from 1450.

PRINCIPAL WORKS: Sir Tristram (Sir W. Scott, ed.) 1804.

ABOUT: Brandl, A. Thomas of Erceldoune; Geddie, J. Thomas the Rymour and his Rhymes; Murray, J. A. H. The Romances and Prophecies; Scott, Sir W. Minstrelsy of the Scottish Border.

ERIGENA, JOHN. See DUNS, JOANNES SCOTUS

ESTCOURT, RICHARD (1688-1712)

actor and dramatist, was born at Tewkesbury and educated at the local grammar school. At fifteen he ran away from home to join a company of strolling actors. When his father came to fetch him, the boy fled in the costume of the feminine role he was playing. Eventually captured and returned home, he was apprenticed to an apothecary by his practical father, but once more he slipped away. After two years of wandering around England, he went to Dublin and was accepted in the company of the Smock Alley Theatre, where he played for several years.

During this period he wrote his one full-length play, *The Fair Example*, a comedy of manners adapted from the French play *Les Bourgeoises à la Mode* by Dancourt and Sainctyon. Produced at Drury Lane for one performance on April 10, 1703, the play met with no success.

In 1704 Estcourt himself appeared at Drury Lane. For eight years he was a favorite in that company, especially in comedy roles, where his exceptional talent for mimicry made him successful. He was equally popular in the social and literary circles of London. His scintillating wit was legendary even in the company of such men as Swift and Congreve, who were among his close friends.

In 1708 Drury Lane produced Estcourt's only other composition, an interlude entitled *Prunella*, played between two acts of another drama. A burlesque on fashionable opera companies of the period which produced florid Italian operas sung in a variety of languages, Estcourt's piece presented an English woman being wooed by an Italian suitor, neither of them understanding the other's language. This was also a failure.

In June 12, 1712, he played his last role at the Drury Lane and died in August of that year, at the age of forty-four.

PRINCIPAL WORKS: The Fair Example, or The Modish Citizen, 1703; Prunella, 1705.

ABOUT: Chetwood, W. R. General History of the Stage; Genest, J. Some Account of the English Stage.

ETHEREGE, or ETHEREDGE, Sir GEORGE (1634?-1691?)

author of comedies, seems to have come of an Oxfordshire

family, though Chancery papers evidence that his grandfather (who apparently spelt the name without the "d") lived in Maidenhead, Berkshire. The grandson may possibly have attended Cambridge University briefly, and have spent a still briefer time at the Inns of Court. He almost surely lived for some time in France. All that is known certainly about his early life is that he appeared in London before 1664 and in that year became famous over night as the author of *The Comical Revenge, or* [the title by which it is usually known] *Love in a Tub.* In a sense this is the first comedy in the strict Restoration tradition.

Etherege was already by this time a member of the dissolute, witty, fashionable circle surrounding the Earl of Rochester.*ᵛ* He was involved with Rochester in a disgraceful melee with the watch at Epsom, which ended with one of the group of aristocratic hoodlums dead and the rest in temporary retirement. This apparently happened about the time of the production of Etherege's second comedy, *She Would If She Could,* a satire on the Jubilee pilgrimage to Rome. Somewhere around this time Etherege married a wealthy widow, and was knighted—according to one story, he bought the title in order to get her to marry him, according to another, he was knighted in recognition of his marriage to a fortune. Neither explanation is very creditable either to Etherege or to Charles II. The fortune he married was lost in the civil war.

There is some possibility that Etherege was secretary to the English ambassador at Constantinople in 1668. He may also have had a diplomatic post in Sweden. In any event, Charles sent him to The Hague in a diplomatic capacity some time before 1671, when he was again in London; and from 1685 to 1689 he was English representative at Ratisbon (Regensberg), Bavaria. There he succeeded in offending the middle-class Germans by his debauchery, and he finally departed abruptly for Paris, leaving his post unfilled and his secretary unpaid. He died in Paris around 1690, though the story that he was killed by a fall downstairs while drunk is probably untrue.

"Gentle George," "Easy Etherege," is thus seen to be no admirable character. Yet he was very typically a member of his class

and age—"an almost legendary type of beau and wit of the day," said Gosse. He described himself in one of his letters: "Nature . . . intended me for an idle fellow, and gave me passions and qualities fit for that blessed calling; but fortune has made a changeling of me and necessity forces me to set up for a fop of business." He was incurably lazy and procrastinating; it took a remark by Rochester, in *The Session of the Poets,* in which he was described as having "fancy, sense, judgment, wit" but being "idle," to force out of him his last comedy, *The Man of Mode.* Aside from these three plays, he wrote nothing but letters and occasional poems.

Yet this *flaneur* had talent almost amounting to genius, a gift for vivid characterization, a turn for brilliant prose dialogue. He paraded his idleness—to make a fuss about anything was not good form. Superficial though his writing was, it was instinct with wit, gaiety, and candor. He was one of the first to use heroic couplets on the stage; more importantly, he was instrumental in turning comedy from the fustian to the natural. He was familiar with the French drama, and the French influence on his own plays is strong.

A contemporary describes him as a "fair, slender, genteel man, but [he] spoiled his countenance with drinking." He had no children by his wife, who survived him; but he had a daughter (who died young) by Mrs. Barry, the actress, who had been Rochester's mistress and whom he took over on Rochester's death.

PRINCIPAL WORKS: The Comical Revenge, or Love in a Tub, 1664; She Would If She Could, 1668; The Man of Mode, 1676; The Works of Sir George Etheredge, Containing His Plays and Poems, 1704; Works (A. W. Verity, ed.) 1888; Works (H. F. B. Brett-Smith, ed.) 1927.

ABOUT: Dobrée, B. Restoration Comedy; Gosse, E. Seventeenth Century Studies; Verity, A. W. Introduction, *in* Works, 1888.

EUSDEN, LAURENCE (1688-September 27, 1730), poet laureate, was the son of a Yorkshire clergyman. In 1708 he received his B.A. from Trinity College, Cambridge, and in 1712 his M.A. and a fellowship.

He was a member of the group of writers identified with the *Spectator,* although he probably wrote very little for it. At one time he served as assistant to Steele in its publication, and a letter published in a 1711 edition under the title "Idols," which received wide attention, was attributed to him.

Although he was an inferior poet and an undistinguished translator, he contrived to further his career by the most obvious flattery of those in a position to grant favors. He obtained the patronage of Lord Halifax by translating into Latin Halifax's poem on the Battle of the Boyne, and then calling attention to his translation in an obsequious poem dedicated to Halifax, published in 1714 in Steele's *Poetical Miscellany.*

His appointment in 1718 to the post of poet laureate, which was publicly ridiculed by contemporary writers, was the result of a poem written on the occasion of the marriage of the Duke of Newcastle, who as Lord Chamberlain controlled the appointment. His poems commemorating state occasions were mediocre in quality. Thomas Cooke said in 1725 that Eusden had been "by fortune rais'd, by very few been read, by fewer prais'd."

Between 1722 and 1725, he took orders in the Church of England, becoming private chaplain to Richard, Lord Willoughby de Broke, and later retiring to the rectory of Coningsby in Lincolnshire, where, after a few dissolute years, he died in 1730. He spent these last years working on a life of Tasso and a translation of some of the poet's works, which he left unfinished.

Thomas Gray said of him, "Eusden was a person of great hopes in his youth, though at last he turned out a drunken parson."

PRINCIPAL WORKS: Original Poems and Translations, 1714; Translations from Claudian and Statius, 1714; Ode for the New Year, 1720.

ABOUT: Austin, W. S. and J. Ralph. Lives of the Poets Laureate; Cibber, C. Poets; Nichols, J. Illustrations of Literary History.

EVELYN, JOHN (October 31, 1620-February 27, 1706), dilettante, diarist, miscellaneous writer, was born at Wotton House, near Dorking, Surrey, the second son of Richard Evelyn and Eleanor Standsfield. His father, a wealthy landowner, was high sheriff of Sussex and Surrey. At the age of five he was sent to live with his maternal grandmother at Southover, and rather than leave her he refused to be sent to Eton but remained in the free school of Southover until he entered Balliol College, Oxford, in

R. Nanteuil

JOHN EVELYN

1637; the following year he was entered in the Middle Temple. He neither took a degree nor was admitted to the bar; his mother had died in 1635 and his father followed her in 1640, leaving both his sons a considerable fortune. John Evelyn immediately left for the Continent for a year of travel, his college days over.

When the civil war broke out, he adhered to the Royalist cause, but in his usual cautious manner took no active part. He was actually an officer in the king's army for three days, but retired to Wotton and "no one knew about it." He did, however, act as a messenger for the royal family, transmitting correspondence in cipher. In France in 1643, he became acquainted with Sir Richard Browne, Charles I's resident in Paris. In 1647 he married Sir Richard's daughter Mary, who was then a child of twelve. Leaving her in her mother's care, he returned to England, and in 1648 succeeded in securing tenancy of Sayes Court, a house in lease to the Brownes. During most of the Revolution Evelyn lived here quietly, absorbed in improvements to the house and gardens, though he did do a great deal of "underground" work for the Royalist cause. (This is the house which, to the painful damage of the gardens, was sublet to Peter the Great when he was inspecting the shipyards at Deptford; it is now an almshouse and the grounds are a public garden.) Evelyn's first publication, a translation of *Liberty and Servitude*, by de la Mothe le Vayer, caused him to be regarded with suspicion by the Parliamentarians, but he escaped serious trouble.

In 1651 he brought his wife to England, and two years later was able to buy Sayes Court. With the Restoration his public career, such as it was, began; he was highly regarded by Charles II, and served faithfully in several minor civil appointments, but his dignity and austerity of morals did not accord with the rowdy court. His chief office was as commissioner in charge of the sick, wounded, and prisoners of the Dutch War—when he remained in London in active service through the plague and the great fire—and later (from 1695 to 1703) as treasurer of Greenwich Hospital, for old sailors. He also acted briefly as a commissioner to execute the office of the Lord Privy Seal. Evelyn was a notably public-spirited and public-minded man; almost all his writings were evoked by economic or social needs and problems, and he was called upon naturally whenever such needs or problems arose. His *Silva* practically saved the English navy, in the days of wooden ships, by its advocacy of reforestation.

For some years he had been living with his family at his birthplace, Wotton, when in 1694 his brother died and left the estate to him. It was there that he died at eighty-six. He and his wife had had six sons and three daughters, but only one son and two daughters lived to grow up, and only one daughter survived him. (Another daughter, who died early, is supposed to have written most of *Mundus Muliebris*.) "Father, lover, friend, and husband," his child bride had called him; and in a dissolute age John Evelyn was remarkable for his nobility of spirit, his humaneness, his loyalty, his benevolence, and his virtue. He was one of the founders of the Royal Society, and its secretary; he was a notable art collector, over-generous with his treasures; he had a commanding knowledge of gardening, of antiquities, and of what is now called city planning. His diary, covering almost his entire life, is no "confession" like that of Pepys; it is impersonal, but historically invaluable. (It remained in manuscript till 1818.) The most

moving of his books is his tribute to Margaret Blagge, Mrs. Godolphin, whose beauty of character shone like a gem in Charles II's court—as did that of her biographer.

PRINCIPAL WORKS: The French Gardener, 1658; A Character of England, 1659; An Apology for the Royal Party, 1659; Tyrannus, or the Mode, 1661; Fumifugium: or the Inconvenience of the Aer and Smoak of London Dissipated, 1661; Sculptura: or the Historie and Art of Calcography, 1662; Silva, or a Discourse of Forest-Trees, 1664; Kalendarium Hortense: or the Gard'ners Almanack, 1664; A Philosophical Discourse of Earth, 1676; Mundus Muliebris: or the Ladies Dressing-Room Unlock'd, 1690; Numismata, or a Discourse of Medals, 1697; Acetaria: a Discourse of Sallets, 1699; Memoirs . . . Comprising His Diary from 1641 to 1706, and a Selection of His Familiar Letters (W. Bray, ed.) 1818 (A. Dobson, ed.) 1906; Miscellaneous Writings (W. Upcott, ed.) 1825; The Life of Mrs. Godolphin (S. Wilberforce, ed.) 1847.

ABOUT: Dobson, A. Introduction, 1906 ed Diary; Keynes, G. John Evelyn; Pepys, S. Diary; Ponsonby, A. P. John Evelyn; Wood, A. a, Athenae Oxonienses.

FABYAN, ROBERT (d. February 28, 1513) historian and chronicler, was a member of a middle-class Essex family of cloth merchants. The family business took him to London, where he married Elizabeth Pake, daughter of a wealthy clothier who presented the couple with a large estate in Essex and a considerable fortune.

Fabyan entered actively into the mercantile and public life of London. As a member of the Drapers' Company, he was one of a group who petitioned the king, in 1496, on the subject of Flemish taxes on English cloth. He served first as sheriff and later, from 1497, as alderman of the City of London, withdrawing from the latter post in 1502 on the grounds that he could not afford the upkeep that went with the office. He was nevertheless a rich man when he retired to his Essex estate that same year. Upon his death eleven years later, he left a minutely detailed will containing instructions for his funeral and distribution of his wealth to his wife and the six of his sixteen children who survived him.

Three years after his death, his *New Chronicle of England and of France* was published. For the period from the days of Brutus to his own day, Fabyan had compiled miscellaneous accounts by several earlier writers, with little regard for their veracity or style, and with no attempt to coordinate or edit them.

His account of the history of his own time, amounting to an expanded personal diary, although it showed little ability to relate events to the currents of history, is a valuable source of information on life in the London of his day. He was especially fond of pomp and ceremony, and included excellent and extensive reports of public festivities.

The first edition of the *New Chronicle*, which ended with the reign of Richard III, was followed by others which carried the account on to 1511. Whether this additional material was Fabyan's or not is unknown. An anonymous historian eventually, in the fourth edition, carried the history forward to the accession of Queen Elizabeth.

PRINCIPAL WORK: The New Chronicle of England and of France (Sir H. Ellis, ed.) 1811.

ABOUT: Busch, W. England Under the Tudors; Ellis, Sir H. Introduction to The New Chronicle; Kingsford, C. L. Chronicles of London.

FAIRFAX, EDWARD (1580?-January 27, 1635), translator, was the second son of Sir Thomas Fairfax of Denton, Yorkshire.

When he was twenty years old, young Fairfax published the first complete translation of Tasso's *Gerusalemme Liberata*, under the English title of *Godfrey of Bulloigne*. This is considered the finest English version of the work, and is an example of free and creative translation which set a high standard for other writers of the time. The quality of the poetry has been compared with that of Spenser. King James declared it his favorite English poem, and Charles I is said to have read it often during his imprisonment. A contemporary critic terms the work "an idea of the chivalrous past of Europe, as seen through the medium of Catholic orthodoxy and classical humanism."

Fairfax led the quiet, retired life of a scholar, helping his older brother with the affairs of the family estate, and coming into the public eye only in one spectacular instance.

He was convinced that certain hysterical manifestations in his two young daughters were the result of witchcraft. In a document remarkable as an example of admirable prose written by a man of temperate character and otherwise enlightened intelligence, on the subject of demonology, he seriously records and interprets the symptoms of his children's "seizures."

Twelve original eclogues which he wrote lay for years among other papers in his study. Once he copied them as a gift for the Duke of Richmond, but the copy was accidently burned. After Fairfax' death in 1635 his son came across the forgotten poems, and two of them were eventually published. The remaining ten, together with a history of Edward, the Black Prince, have been lost.

PRINCIPAL WORKS: Godfrey of Bulloigne, or the Recovery of Jerusalem, 1600; A Discourse of Witchcraft, 1621.

ABOUT: Cooper, E. Muses' Library; Grainge, W. Biographical Introduction to Daemonologia (pub. Philobiblon Society, 1882); Hunter, J. Chorus Vatum Anglicanorum.

FALCONER, WILLIAM (February 11, 1732-1769), poet, was born in Edinburgh, the son of a poor barber and wigmaker. His brother and sister were both deaf mutes. He had very little schooling, but went to sea as a boy as servant to the purser on a man-of-war, who noticed and encouraged his taste for reading. He progressed in seamanship until he became second mate of the "Britannia," which was wrecked off Cape Colonna, Greece, with only three survivors, of whom he was one. This was the incident which inspired his poem, *The Shipwreck*, exceedingly popular in its own day. Falconer had previously published only an elegy on the death of the Prince of Wales (in 1751) and a few poems in the *Gentleman's Magazine*.

The Shipwreck was dedicated to the Duke of York, who advised Falconer to enter the Royal Navy, which he did as a midshipman. In 1763, when he was purser on a frigate, he married a Miss Hicks, daughter of a surgeon. The next year he republished *The Shipwreck*, together with *The Demagogue*, which attacked Wilkes, Chatham, and Charles Churchill. Falconer was always a staunch Tory and an ardent patriot; in his *Marine Dictionary*, for example, he defined the word "retreat" as "A French manœuvre, not properly a term of the British marine."

On September 20, 1769, he sailed as purser on the "Aurora" to India. The ship rounded the Cape of Good Hope but was never heard from again; undoubtedly it was wrecked with the loss of all hands.

Short, slight, heavily pockmarked, with blunt, awkward manners but a kindly and pleasant disposition, Falconer was much more the sailor than the poet, though in his own time he was praised for "the exquisite harmony of his numbers." It is hard to find any charm in his labored, monotonous style today; the best that can be said of *The Shipwreck* is that it is technically accurate—far too much so for interest of the lay reader. He was essentially a didactic versifier, and scarcely a hint of his personality or his private feelings escapes into his work. With no schooling beyond elementary reading, writing and arithmetic, he nevertheless took advantage of every opportunity offered his intelligent mind, and taught himself, gaining a speaking knowledge of French, Italian, Spanish, and (says a contemporary commentator) "even German." He is quite forgotten today, though so much admired during his lifetime, and no edition of his complete works has been published since 1836. His *Marine Dictionary*, however, is still useful, if only as an historical source-book on the British Marine.

PRINCIPAL WORKS: The Shipwreck: A Poem in Three Cantos, by a Sailor, 1762 (J. S. Clarke, ed. 1864; W. H. D. Adams, ed. 1887); The Demagogue, 1764; A Universal Dictionary of the Marine, 1769; Poetical Works (J. Mitford, ed.) 1836.

ABOUT: Adams, W. H. D. Life, in 1887 ed. The Shipwreck; Clarke, J. S. Life, in 1864 ed. The Shipwreck; Irving, D. Lives of Scotish [*sic*] Authors; Mitford, J. Life, in Poetical Works.

FANSHAWE, Lady ANNE (March 25, 1625-January 30, 1680), memoirist, the spirited daughter of Sir John Harrison, an ardent Royalist, led the carefree life of a young lady of fashion until her fifteenth year. Her mother's death in that year, which sobered Anne's high spirits, was closely followed by the death of a brother and the imprisonment of her father. The family fortune had all been spent in the Royalist cause, as had that of Sir Richard Fanshawe, whom Anne married when she was nineteen.

In the following years she bore fourteen children (of whom five survived), lived in almost constant danger and abject poverty, accompanied her husband on daring missions in the service of the king, and performed heroic deeds in her own right. When her husband was captured and imprisoned at the Battle of Worcester, she went to his prison

window at four o'clock each morning to talk with him, and eventually, appearing herself before the council to plead his case, obtained his release on bail.

Following the Restoration she and the children accompanied Sir Richard to an ambassador's post at Madrid, where he died in 1666. Rejecting an offer from the Spanish queen mother of wealth and honor if she became a Catholic and remained in Madrid, Anne sold enough possessions to obtain the necessary funds and with her children, the youngest a year-old baby, and the body of her husband, made her way with great difficulty back to England.

Never able to collect all of the money due to her husband, and never quite recovering from his death and that of her father a few years later, she devoted the remainder of her life to her children and to the completion of her *Memoirs*. This chronicle of a life of courage, devotion and high adventure, while sometimes inaccurate as to date and detail, is lively and entertaining, and written in a clear and simple style of great charm.

PRINCIPAL WORK: Memoirs (H. C. Fanshawe, ed.) 1905.

ABOUT: Clarendon, E. H. Autobiography; Evelyn, J. Diary.

FANSHAWE, Sir RICHARD (1608-June 26, 1666), diplomat, poet and translator, was the son of Sir Henry Fanshawe, remembrancer of the exchequer, of Ware Park, Hertfordshire.

Discarding the legal career his mother had chosen for him, he entered in 1635 upon an arduous and hazardous career in the service of the Royalist cause. Joining King Charles at the outbreak of the civil war, he was for a time secretary of war to the Prince of Wales, later became treasurer of the Navy and engaged in several diplomatic missions abroad. Serving as Charles' personal secretary, he was taken prisoner in the Battle of Worcester, and confined to Lord Stafford's estate in Yorkshire until 1658, when, due largely to the efforts of his extraordinarily resourceful wife, he was released to rejoin the king in Paris.

Following the Restoration, he and his family, who had lived in poverty and distress throughout the war, seemed to be destined for more prosperous times. Lady Anne Fanshawe,*qv* in her *Memoirs*, attributed her husband's continued ill fortune to the enmity of the king's close adviser, the Earl of Clarendon.

With Lady Anne and the surviving five of their fourteen children, Fanshawe went to Madrid as ambassador to Portugal and Spain. In spite of his popularity with the people and court of Spain, he received a recall to England two days before he died of ague.

During this eventful life Fanshawe found time to write a few poems of real merit, and to do several noteworthy translations, including some of Horace's odes, the Spanish poets de Mendoza and Guarini, and Camoens' Portuguese epic, the *Lusiad*.

Sir John Denham, in a preface to Fanshawe's English version of Guarini's *Il Pastor Fido*, extolled him as the forerunner of a new school of creative adaptation as opposed to literal translation:

> That servile path thou nobly dost decline
> Of tracing word by word and line by
>   line . . .
> They but preserve the Ashes, thou the
>   Flame,
> True to his sense but truer to his fame.

PRINCIPAL WORKS: The Pastor Fido, 1647; Selected Parts of Horace, 1652; The Lusiad, 1655; To Love Only for Love's Sake, 1670.

ABOUT: Clarendon, E. H. State Papers; Fanshawe, Lady Anne. Memoirs; Mackail, J. W. Sir Richard Fanshawe.

FARQUHAR, GEORGE (1678-April 29, 1707), dramatist, who may be said to have ended the Restoration drama as Etherege [qv] began it, was born in Londonderry, Ireland, the son of a clergyman. In 1694 he entered Trinity College, Dublin, as a sizar, and was intended for the church. Already, at fourteen, he had published a Pindaric ode, and he must have realized early that his affinity was with the world of art, not with that of religion. He is said to have left college in 1695, on the death of his patron, and to have worked as a proofreader for the press; in any event, he was not graduated, and he soon found himself at Smock Alley Theatre, Dublin, as an actor—with Othello as his first part! He was not much of an actor, he suffered badly from stage-fright, and when he almost killed a fellow player accidentally during a stage duel, he abandoned acting altogether. The manager, Robert Wilks who remained through his life his closest friend

GEORGE FARQUHAR

and who played the leading roles in all his dramas, advised him to turn to writing comedy instead. This was a happy choice; Farquhar was a born comic poet.

He went to London in 1698, and his first play was an instant success. His second and third were better constructed, and again successful, but his next two were failures. The Earl of Orrery had secured a commission for him in 1700 as lieutenant in the militia and he had served briefly in Holland. In 1705 he served for a year in Shrewsbury. With *The Recruiting Officer*, based on his military experiences, Farquhar came into his own. It was the beginning of a new drama— no more "town fops" and gallants, but real people, presented as their cheerful, amusing, lively selves. Combining this with his turn for sentimental romance, Farquhar in his later comedies influenced the English novel as much as he did the English stage.

Unfortunately this light-hearted, easy-going, kind-hearted man, with his fits of melancholy, his quick temper, his diffidence and his stoical courage, was born unlucky. The Duke of Ormonde persuaded him to sell his commission, promising him a captaincy; the duke never kept his promise. A young lady fell in love with him, and in order to secure his hand pretended to be an heiress; he married her frankly for her money—he was always poor and in debt—then found she had none. He had never pretended to love her; his love was the actress Mrs. Oldfield, whom he had "discovered" as a girl of sixteen and who was for many years his mistress.

The Beaux' Stratagem, Farquhar's masterpiece, was written when he knew he was dying. He had been paid in advance for it, and he worked against time. His friends had given him several benefits (at one, in 1704, he played his own "Sir Harry Wildair," the last time he appeared on the stage), and the last of these was given on the very day of his death. He was only twenty-nine when he died, leaving a pathetic note to his friend Wilks. In spite of Wilks' help, his widow and two daughters were left in abject poverty.

Farquhar was in no sense a literary man; he was a writer for the stage. (And this in spite of his early writings in verse and prose.) He took his plots where he found them (*The Inconstant* is Fletcher's *Wild Goose Chase*), and used any threadbare theatrical trick. But his people are real and alive, his dialogue is crude but sincere, his frankness open heartedness, and humaneness are implicit in all his work. *The Beaux' Stratagem*, the "first sketch" for which was the one-act *Stage Coach*, is evidence of how far his flair for comedy might have carried him had he lived to fulfill his promise.

PRINCIPAL WORKS: *Plays*—Love and a Bottle, 1699; The Constant Couple, 1699; Sir Harry Wildair, 1701; The Inconstant, 1702; The Twin Rivals, 1703; The Stage Coach, 1705; The Recruiting Officer, 1706; The Beaux' Stratagem, 1707; Comedies, 1710; Dramatic Works (A. C. Ewald, ed.) 1892. *Miscellaneous*—The Adventures of Covent Garden, 1699; Love and Business: . . . Occasional Verses and Epistolary Prose, with a Discourse upon Comedy in Reference to the English Stage, 1702; Barcellona (verse) 1707; Works, Containing All His Poems, Letters, and Comedies, 1728; Works (W. Archer, ed.) 1908.

ABOUT: Archer, W. Introduction, *in* Works, 1908; Cibber, C. Lives of the Poets; Connely, W. Young George Farquhar: The Restoration Drama at Twilight; Gosse, E. Gossip in a Library; Guiney, L. I. A Little English Gallery; Hunt, L. Life, *in* Dramatic Works of Wycherley, Congreve, Farquhar, and Vanbrugh, 1849; Perry, H. T. The Comic Spirit in Restoration Drama; Thackeray, W. M. English Humorists of the Eighteenth Century; Wilkes, T. Life, *in* 1775 ed. of Works.

FELL, Dr. JOHN (June 23, 1625-July 10, 1696), publisher, editor, was born in Longworth, Berkshire, the son of Samuel Fell, dean of Christ Church, Oxford, and Margaret Wyld. He entered Christ Church at

After Sir P. Lely

DR. JOHN FELL

the age of eleven, receiving his M.A. at eighteen. During the civil war he was an ensign in the Royalist army. He was ordained in 1647, and the next year the Parliamentarians ejected him from his college. During the revolution he lived with a friend in Oxford, secretly observing the rites of the Established Church. With the Restoration his rise was rapid: in 1660 he was made prebend of Chichester, canon and (four months later) dean of Christ Church, master of St. Oswald's Hospital, Worcester, chaplain to Charles II, and D.D. of Oxford by royal letter. The university had fallen into practical chaos during the revolution, and he restored discipline zealously. From 1666 to 1669 he was vice chancellor of Oxford; he was a great builder (the Sheldonian Theatre was one of his enterprises), and particularly interested in the University Press. Every year he had one of the Church Fathers, or a Greek classic, annotated by himself, published and presented on New Year's Day to each student of his own college. He was a renowned philologist, and translated much from the Greek, his edition of Cyprian in 1682 becoming the standard.

In 1676 Fell became Bishop of Oxford. One of his most unpleasant duties was having to expel John Locke from his fellowship in 1685, by direct order of James II. A strict conformist and anti-papist, he was nevertheless also strictly obedient to the royal command. Besides a few original works, he was the author of a Latin book on grammar and logic, and he translated Anthony a Wood's history of Oxford—making so many changes that the author called him a "meddler." He may have been part author also of the noted religious work, *The Whole Duty of Man*, which he certainly edited and published. He died unmarried, and his heir, a nephew, gave his fine collection of books to the Bodleian Library.

Perhaps today Fell is known principally through the famous squib beginning, "I do not love thee, Dr. Fell." This was written by Tom Browne *qv* when, as a student at Christ Church, he was about to be expelled. Told he would be pardoned if he made an extempore translation of an epigram of Martial's, he produced this quatrain—and it is to the victim's credit that he kept his word and reinstated Browne. Perhaps more interesting is the statement by John Evelyn *qv* in his diary that Fell habitually preached his sermons in blank verse! He did not, however, publish any volumes of poetry. In 1675 he brought out a critical edition of the New Testament.

PRINCIPAL WORKS: The Interest of England Stated, 1659; The Life of Dr. Henry Hammond, 1661; The Vanity of Suffering, 1674.

ABOUT: Evelyn, J. Diary; Thompson, H. L. Chirst Church; Wood, A. a, Athenae Oxonienses.

FELLTHAM, OWEN (1602?-1668), es-
sayist, was the son of Thomas Felltham of Mutford, Suffolk. Very little is known of his life. He was attached in some capacity to the household of the Earl of Thomond, probably serving either as chaplain or secretary. He died at the Thomond estate at Great Billing, Northamptonshire, in 1668.

His literary reputation is based on two quite dissimilar works. He was chiefly known as a writer of extremely moral and rather dull essays. His style in these was formal and full of far-fetched conceits. He was an ardent Royalist, referring to the dead Charles II as "Christ the Second." While he seems to have written most of these essays as much to clarify and strengthen his ideas for himself as for publication, one hundred of them were published under the title of *Resolves, Divine, Moral and Political*, and met with immediate success. Many editions were published, some additional essays being included in subsequent editions.

The eighth edition, published in 1661, included forty of his poems under the title *Lusoria*.

The other work of importance is *A Brief Character of the Low Countries*, written in 1652 after he had visited Flanders, and subtitled "Being Three Weeks' Observations of the Vices and Virtues of the Inhabitants." This is in an informal and witty style, much more acceptable to modern taste than the heavy moralizing of his essays which so captivated the readers of the seventeenth century.

Felltham wrote an essay attacking Ben Jonson and the ideas he had expressed in "Come, leave the loathed stage." However, after Jonson's death, he wrote an elegy praising the playwright.

Felltham said of his own work, "My books have been my delight and recreation, but not my trade, though perhaps I could wish they had."

PRINCIPAL WORKS: Resolves, Divine, Moral and Political, 1638; A Brief Character of the Low Countries, 1652; Lusoria, 1661.

ABOUT: Gifford, W. Jonson; Hallam, H. Introduction to the Literature of England; Langbaine, G. English Dramatic Poets.

FENTON, ELIJAH (1683-1730), poet
and dramatist, was the son of John Fenton, an attorney. Educated at Cambridge, he intended to enter the clergy but found that moral scruples prevented him from taking the requisite oaths. Instead he became a school master and tutor.

A lifelong friendship with Alexander Pope led to the most important activity of his career, when Pope, who had been commissioned to translate the *Odyssey*, hired Fenton and his friend William Broome to do half of the translation for him. Pope not only paid them a ridiculously small share of the £4500 he had received for the work, but tried to conceal their collaboration. A bitter quarrel ensued between Pope and Broome, but the mild and easy-going Fenton remained on the best of terms with them both.

Although he had a reputation in London's "Spectator" group of young writers as a wit, and although his portion of the *Odyssey* translation is indistinguishable from that of Pope, Fenton's two volumes of original poems were without distinction. In 1723, possibly with the aid of Southern, he wrote a play, *Mariamne,* which showed evidence of greater talent than his poems had, and which achieved considerable success. His most popular work was an edition of the works of Milton, for which he wrote a biographical introduction.

After various tutoring positions, Fenton took over the education of the son of a wealthy widow, Lady Trumbull, who, after her son's departure for school, maintained Fenton in luxury to the end of his life. Upon his death in 1730, Pope, in spite of his expressed opinion that his friend had died of "lack of exercise," furnished an epitaph for his tomb.

PRINCIPAL WORKS: Oxford and Cambridge Miscellany Poems, 1707; Miscellaneous Poems, 1717; Mariamne, 1723.

ABOUT: Hulme, W. H. Two Early Lives of Milton; Johnson, S. Lives of the Poets; Lloyd, W. W. Elijah Fenton, His Poetry and His Friends.

FENTON, Sir GEOFFREY (1539?-1608), translator, was born in Nottinghamshire. He evidently received an excellent education, and may have spent some early years abroad, although little is known of his life until, living in Paris in 1566, at about the age of twenty-six, he published the first and most important of several translations. This was an English version of a group of Italian novels by Matteo Bandello, which had theretofore been current only in a French edition by François de Belleforest. The work was a notable influence in the literary circles of the day.

During the next fourteen years he translated several French works, mainly philosophical and religious, including a tract which was widely used in the Puritan attacks on the English drama in 1574. Curiously, the arguments for the drama which Fenton's article, *Form of Christian Policy,* attacked were the same ones used in defense of the novel in the earlier Bandello work. In 1579 he published his last and most ambitious translation, a *History of the Wars of Italy* from the French of Guicciardini, which was extremely popular.

The following year Fenton turned his back on literature and embarked on a successful political career. Through the influence of a relative, Lord Burghley, he was sent to Ireland as secretary to the lord deputy of that country. Although he was never popular with his colleagues, he rose

rapidly in the favor of Queen Elizabeth, to whom he made confidential reports on other members of the Irish government. Elizabeth gave him a life tenure in his post, and although he quarreled with nearly every lord deputy under whom he served, he proved invulnerable, in one instance returning to England to take part in the impeachment of one of his enemies. He successfully defended himself against charges that he had profited personally at Ireland's expense. He married the daughter of a former high chancellor of Ireland in 1585, was knighted in 1589, and died in Dublin in 1608.

PRINCIPAL WORKS: Tragical Discourses, 1566; Monophylo, 1572; Golden Epistles, 1575; History of the Wars of Italy, 1579.

ABOUT: Boyle, R. Autobiography; Chalmers, A. Biographical Dictionary; Lloyd, D. State Worthies; Visitation of Nottinghamshire (Harleian Society Publications).

FERGUSSON, ROBERT (September 15, 1750-October 16, 1774), Scottish poet, was born in Edinburgh, the son of William Fergusson (by some authorities called Sir William), who was at the time a haberdasher's clerk and later became managing clerk of a large drapery shop. Both his parents came from Aberdeenshire. He was educated in the Dundee Grammar School and in 1765 entered St. Andrews University as a bursar. He was intended for the ministry but soon abandoned that idea; medicine was the next objective, but though he was interested in science he could not endure the thought of surgery. He ended as a copying clerk in the commissary clerk's office, and there he remained for the rest of his active life, except for a short time in the sheriff's clerk's office, which he left because he could not bear having any connection with executions. In many ways Fergusson's life resembles that of Charles Lamb, even to its turn for conviviality and its inebriety. From 1771 on he was a constant contributor to Thomas Ruddiman's *Weekly Magazine or Edinburgh Amusement,* and he became exceedingly popular among both the literary groups and the less ponderous social circles. His father had died in 1767, and he had to support his mother. He became increasingly addicted to drink, excusing himself by saying: "Anything to forget my poor mother and these aching fingers." His health began to fail, and concurrently he suddenly became devout, burnt most of his unpublished manuscripts, and refused to read anything but the Bible. He continued to drink, however, and finally a fall downstairs injured his head so severely that he became hopelessly deranged. He died in Darien House, the public hospital for the insane. In 1787 Robert Burns had a stone erected over his grave.

Fergusson's chief claim to remembrance, indeed, is his influence on Burns—though he was hailed by his contemporaries as "the successor to Allan Ramsay" *qv*. *The Farmer's Ingle* gave birth to *The Cotter's Saturday Night*, and *Leith Races* to *The Holy Fair*. Most of Fergusson's poems were in Scottish dialect; the others which added most to his celebrity were *Caller Oysters*, *Braid Cloth*, and *Auld Reekie*, inspired by the Cape Club, of which he was a prominent member. He had keen powers of observation, an eye for drama, real wit and humor both, and a capacity for pathos and tenderness; all that he lacked was genius to blend these into living and lasting poetry. He was noted in Edinburgh for his witty conversation, and until his fatal accident appears to have been as harmless and lovable as he was irresponsible. It is characteristic that from his best days his friends spoke of him as "poor, unfortunate Fergusson." The promise of his youth, when he published his first poem at fifteen (an elegy on a deceased school master), was unhappily not fulfilled; but by lending inspiration to Burns he did his part to redeem his weaknesses and add to the glory of Scottish literature.

PRINCIPAL WORKS: Poems, 1773; Poems on Various Subjects, 1779; Works, 1800; Works, 1807; Poems (R. Aitken, ed.) 1917; Poetical Works (R. Ford, ed.) 1917.

ABOUT: Aitken, R. Introduction, Poems, 1917; Campbell, A. Introduction to the History of Poetry in Scotland; Ford, R. Introduction, Poetical Works; Grosart, A. B. Robert Fergusson; Irving, D. Life, *in* Works, 1800; Peterkin, A. Life *in* Works, 1807; Ruddiman, T. Life, *in* Poems on Various Subjects.

FERRAR, NICHOLAS (1592-December 4, 1637), theologian, was the son of a prominent London merchant and an intensely religious mother who instilled her own zeal and devotion in her children at an early age.

Graduating from Cambridge, where he studied medicine, in 1610, Ferrar was advised to travel for his health. As a member of the party accompanying the daughter of James I, Princess Elizabeth, he spent six years in travel, visiting Germany, Prague, Venice, Rome, and Marseille. After a walking tour through Spain, he returned to England in excellent health, in 1618, and entered his father's business world as an executive of the Virginia Company.

After five years in business and a short term as a Member of Parliament, he found public life so inimical to his taste that, purchasing and renovating a ruined estate at Little Gidding, he retired there with a married brother and sister and their combined families of seventeen children.

Ordained a deacon in 1626 by Archbishop Laud, Ferrar maintained his family as a religious colony, with an austere but gracious tradition of prayer, devotion, intellectual activity, and homely occupations. The purity and piety of the life at Little Gidding became widely celebrated, but also incurred the disfavor of the rising Puritan movement, which labeled it a "Protestant nunnery." Ten years after Ferrar's death in 1637, the colony was dispersed and the manorhouse wrecked by troops under the direction of Parliament.

Ferrar translated a few religious works, made several "harmonies" of the gospels, and wrote the *Story Books of Little Gidding*, in five manuscript volumes. These last record dialogues and discourses on a variety of subjects which were part of the communal life, and reflect a high degree of intellectual integrity as well as the severe, simple piety of the colony.

PRINCIPAL WORKS: Divine Considerations (translated from Juan de Valdez), On Temperance (translated from Lessio), Story Books of Little Gidding, 1631-32.

ABOUT: Blackstone, B. The Ferrar Papers; Carter, J. F. M. Nicholas Ferrar; Marshall, E. Haunts of Ancient Peace; Peckard, G. P. Memoirs of the Life of Nicholas Ferrar.

FIELD, NATHAN (1587-1620?), actor and playwright, has been so confused by biographers with his older brother Nathaniel that it is often difficult to disentangle the events of their separate lives.

Nathan was born a year before the death of his father, John Field, a famous preacher and crusader against those "sincks of synne," the theatres. When he was twelve he was taken from St. Paul's Grammar School for the children's theatre of the Chapel Royal, where, for two years, he attained extraordinary fame. Both Chapman and Jonson, in whose plays he starred, were deeply impressed by his acting. Jonson taught him Latin and probably coached him dramatically as well, and their close relationship continued when Field left the Chapel players, first for the group known as the King's Men, and later to succeed Burbage as England's foremost actor, at the Hope and Globe theatres.

Field wrote two plays, *A Woman Is a Weathercock* and, in apology to the sex, *Amends for Ladies*, which have considerable merit. He had a free, imaginative use of language which has been compared (at a distance) with Shakespeare's. His comedy, although indebted to Jonson, is original, sprightly, and occasionally outrageous. In the style of the day, the plays are overwhelmed with too many plot details. The maturing development of style in the second play would indicate that, had he taken this part of his career seriously, Field might have been a major playwright. He collaborated with Massinger and Fletcher on several plays, notably Massinger's *Nero* and *Fatal Dowry*.

He took an active part on one occasion in the controversy which had preoccupied his father. When a preacher named Sutton published a sermon denouncing the stage, Field wrote him an eloquent reply defending the theatre and protesting against the popular conception of the corrupt lives of actors.

Although many biographers have assigned him Nathaniel's profession of bookseller, Nathaniel's several children, and Nathaniel's death date of 1633, there is actually no record of Nathan beyond the year 1620.

PRINCIPAL WORKS: A Woman Is a Weathercock, acted 1609?, printed 1611; Amends for Ladies, acted 1611, printed 1618.

ABOUT: Brinckley, R. F. Nathan and Nathaniel Field; Collier, J. P. History of English Dramatic Poetry; Langbaine, G. English Dramatic Poets.

FIELDING, HENRY

FIELDING, HENRY (April 22, 1707-October 8, 1754), novelist, essayist, dramatist, was born at Sharpham Park, near Glastonbury, Somerset, the son of Lieutenant (later Major General) Edmund Fielding, and of Sarah Gould, a judge's daughter. (The family, which had aristocratic connections, in its other branches spelled the name Feilding; Henry Fielding said his branch was the first which knew how to spell!) His sister was Sarah Fielding, author of *David Simple*, his half-brother (by his father's second marriage) Sir John Fielding, blind from birth, Henry Fielding's assistant and successor as a magistrate. Lady Mary Wortley Montagu *qv* was his second cousin.

When he was four the family moved to East Stour, Dorsetshire. At thirteen he went to Eton, whence he derived his classical knowledge—according to his own estimate of his learning, "Tuscan and French are in my head, Latin I write, and Greek—I read." He had certainly left there by 1725, when the guardian of a girl with whom he was violently in love hurried her to Devonshire and married her off there lest Fielding abduct her. He expressed his "revenge of an injured lover" by translating a satire of Juvenal.

In 1728 he was in Leyden, studying law at the university. The next year he arrived in London, living the gay life of a young man about town (to the future ruin of his health) and making his way by writing farces, comedies, and burlesques, with Congreve and Wycherley as his models. In 1734 he married Charlotte Cradock, the beloved wife who became Amelia and Sophia Western in her husband's novels (even to the accident which had permanently deformed her nose). For a year or two the bride and groom, thanks to a legacy from her mother, lived in retirement at East Stour; then they returned to London and Fielding leased the "little theatre" in the Haymarket and became its manager and chief playwright. The licensing Act of 1737 ended his theatrical career, already discouraging after his comedy, *The Wedding Day*, was hissed even with Garrick as its hero. He dismissed his company and abandoned the drama for the law, entering the Middle Temple and being called to the bar in 1740.

But he did not abandon literature; from playwriting he turned to journalism, editing, with James Ralph, a paper in imitation of *The Spectator* and *The Tatler*, called *The Champion*. This lasted from 1739 to 1740, and was followed by the *True Patriot* (1745-46), the *Jacobite's Journal* (1747-48 the title was satirical—Fielding was always a staunch Whig), and the *Covent Garden Journal* (1752), source of his best occasional writing.

HENRY FIELDING

But hard on the heels of *The Champion* came Fielding's first novel, *Joseph Andrews*. This was started as a parody on Richardson's *Pamela*, and Joseph was supposed to be Pamela's brother with the roles of pursuer and pursued reversed. (Richardson was not pleased.) But the author's genius ran away with him, and soon the remarkable clergyman, Parson Adams, one of the great characters of fiction, stole the show. Fielding himself called the book "a comic epos in prose," and said it was written in imitation of *Don Quixote.* It stems rather from Bunyan, Defoe, Addison, and Steele. It is a brilliant *tour de force*, but not yet integrated; it was not until *Tom Jones* that Fielding became truly "the father of the English novel." Meanwhile he produced a three-volume "miscellany," the third part of which was the Swiftian *Jonathan Wild the Great*, which V. S. Pritchett has called "the most dazzling piece of sustained satirical writing in our language."

About 1744 Fielding's adored wife died in his arms, leaving him heartbroken. Of their several children, at least one had died, but more than one survived (this period of Fielding's life is obscure), for when in 1747 he married his wife's maid, Mary Daniel (or McDaniel), it was avowedly to secure a mother for his orphaned children. She bore him two sons and three daughters more.

In 1748 he was appointed principal justice of the peace for Westminster and Middlesex; he owed the appointment to the good offices of his lifelong friend Lord Lyttleton, and to the favorable reception by the government of the *True Patriot* and the *Jacobite's Journal.* Fielding took his duties very seriously. His pay came entirely from fees ("the dirtiest money in England") and by refusing to take money from the poor he brought his income below subsistence level, and was obliged to support his family by the help of Lyttleton and other friends. In 1749 he was chairman of the quarter session at Westminster, and he wrote a series of pamphlets on the causes and cure of crime, in defense of some of his rulings, and in advocacy of workhouses for paupers — a cruel suggestion now, but condemned then for its liberality. His remarkable blind half-brother became his assistant.

But Fielding the author could not be suppressed. In 1749 appeared his greatest work, and one of the glories of English literature—*Tom Jones.* In spite of a few structural defects, *Tom Jones* stands unchallenged as the first true novel in English, the first to display artistic unity. Pritchett has pointed out that Fielding's dramatic experience taught him how to break with dialogue "the monotony of flat, continuous narrative." Tom himself, Squire Western, Sophia, Blifil, Square, Thwackum, are immortal. Fielding presented life as it is, and ordinary people—"*l'homme moyen sensuel*"—as they are. He himself said he endeavored "to laugh mankind out of their favorite follies and vices." He hated hypocrisy, cruelty, pretentiousness, meanness; he had no subtlety, he was utterly candid and sincere; and if he condoned the weaknesses of generosity and the excesses of youth (to which he himself had been prone), he had the robust morality of a man who knew common human nature as have few other authors since Chaucer and Shakespeare. Above all, he could tell a, story and he was master of a great ironic style. Gibbon said truly: "That exquisite picture of human manners will survive the palace of the Escurial and the imperial eagle of the House of Austria." It has already survived the latter!

Amelia, Fielding's last novel, shows the ebbing strength of a tired man, long struggling vainly against increasing illness. But it has a mellowness, pathos, and insight that arose from the same source. Fielding was paid in advance for it and he needed the money. He was already a dying man. He had long suffered from gout; now asthma, dropsy, and jaundice were added. He tried every nostrum, including Bishop Berkeley's tar water, in vain. In 1753 he resigned his office, and the next year he left his house in Fordhook and, with his wife and his daughter by his first marriage, set sail for Portugal in search of a better climate. He reached Lisbon in August, sending back his last book, the journal of his voyage; two months later he was dead. He is buried in the English cemetery there; a monument was erected to his memory in 1830.

Tall (he was six feet one inch), strong, handsome Harry Fielding had shrunk and bloated to a painfully creeping invalid long before he died. But what Coleridge called his "sunshiny, breezy spirit" had stayed with him to death—and his gallant courage, his geniality, his humaneness, the sweetness of his temper. He had led a wild youth, and he paid for it—he was an old man when he died at forty-seven. But taken as a whole, his life achieved nobility. His pot-boiler plays are negligible—synthetic and deliberately bawdy. (But they are funny—*Tom Thumb* most of all.) His novels, despite their realistic frankness which shocked the nineteenth century but delighted his century and delights ours, are truly moral in purpose, as he intended them to be. What is more, they are highly readable; *Tom Jones* at least is part of the heritage of every literate reader of English. And above all, Fielding was one of the major ironists of literature. He stands at least shoulder to shoulder with the great Victorian novelists whose spiritual father he was.

PRINCIPAL WORKS: *Plays*—Love in Several Masques, 1728; The Temple Beau, 1730; The Author's Farce, and The Pleasures of the Town, 1730; Rape upon Rape (The Coffee House Politician), 1730; Tom Thumb, 1730; The Letter-Writers, 1731; The Welsh Opera, or The Grey Mare the Better Horse, 1731; The Lottery, 1732; The Modern Husband, 1732; The Covent Garden Tragedy, 1732; The Old Debauchees, 1732; The Mock Doctor, 1732; The Miser (from Molière's L'Avare), 1733; Don Quixote in England, 1734; The Intriguing Chambermaid, 1734; An Old Man Taught Wisdom, 1735; The Universal Gallant, 1735; Pasquin, 1736; Tumble-Down Dick, 1736; The Historical Register for the Year 1736, 1737; Miss Lucy in Town, 1742; Eurydice, and the Wedding Day (in Miscellanies), 1743; The Fathers, or The Good-Natured Man, 1778. *Novels and Miscellaneous*—The History of the Adventures of Joseph Andrews and His Friend Mr. Abraham Adams, 1742; Miscellanies: 1. Poems and Essays, 2. A Journey from This World to the Next, Eurydice, The Wedding Day, 3. The Life of Jonathan Wild the Great, 1743; The History of Tom Jones, a Foundling, 1749; Amelia, 1752; The Journal of a Voyage to Lisbon, 1755; Works, 1762; Novels, 1831; Works (L. Stephen, ed.) 1882.

ABOUT: Banerji, H. K. Henry Fielding, His Life and Works; Blanchard, F. T. Fielding the Novelist; Cordasco, F. Henry Fielding: A List of Critical Studies; Dobson, A. Henry Fielding: A Memoir; Godden, G. M. Henry Fielding; Hazlitt, W. Lectures on the English Comic Writers; Jenkins, E. Henry Fielding; Jones, B. M. Henry Fielding, Novelist and Magistrate; Lawrence, F. The Life of Henry Fielding; Pritchett, V. S. The Living Novel; Raleigh, W. The English Novel; Scott, W. Life, *in* Novels; Stephen, L. Introduction, Works, 1882; Thackeray, W. M. The English Humourists of the Eighteenth Century; Willcocks, M. P. A True-Born Englishman.

FIELDING, SARAH (November 8, 1710-1768), novelist, is better known as the sister of Henry Fielding than in her own right. She was born in East Stour, where she spent a few happy years of childhood before her mother died in 1718. Her father remarried and had several children by his second wife, so that he was never able to assist the older children. Sarah was apparently given an excellent education, but seems to have been poor all her life.

She lived in London with her celebrated brother following the death of his first wife, while he was composing *Tom Jones*. How much of his help she had in the writing of her first novel, *David Simple*, can only be conjectured, but it is her only work of real merit. The book was published anonymously in 1744, and was widely attributed to Henry. Angry because all kinds of anonymous writings were being laid at his door, Fielding wrote a preface to the second edition of his sister's novel, denying its authorship and overpraising the author by saying that "some of her touches might have done honor to the pencil of the immortal Shakespeare." Two sequels to the work appeared in the next few years.

On Henry's second marriage, Sarah moved to Bath where she was for years an active figure in local society, turning out occasional romances, and depending partly on the charity of friends for her living. In 1762 she published a translation of Xenophon's *Memoirs of Socrates* which evidenced admirable scholarship, but her original works were not distinguished.

She died at Bath in 1768, and the monument erected by her friend Dr. John Hoadley (upon which her birth date and her father's name are incorrect) bears the epitaph:

Her unaffected manners, candid mind,
　Her heart benevolent, and soul resigned,
Were more her praise than all she knew or thought
　Though Athens' wisdom to her sex she taught.

PRINCIPAL WORKS: The Adventures of David Simple, 1744; The Governess, 1749; The Cry, a Dramatic Fable (with Jean Collier) 1754; Lives of Cleopatra and Octavia, 1757; The History of Ophelia, 1760; Xenophon's Memoirs of Socrates, translated from the Greek, 1762.

ABOUT: Dobson, A. Fielding; Nichols, J. Literary Anecdotes of the 18th Century; Richardson, S. Correspondence

FINCH, ANNE. See WINCHILSEA, ANNE FINCH, Countess of

FISHER, JOHN (1459?-June 22, 1535), author of theological works, was born in Beverley, Yorkshire, the son of Robert Fisher, a wealthy mercer, who died when his son was thirteen. He entered Michael House, Cambridge, in 1484, received a B.A. 1487, M.A. 1491, and took orders. He was senior proctor of the university to 1494, master of Michael House in 1497, and vice chancellor of Cambridge in 1501. He became Bishop of Rochester in 1504, but continued to reside at Cambridge. As confessor of Margaret, Countess of Richmond, Henry VII's mother, he pushed through her bequest of the foundation to be known as St. John's College. Fisher infused new life into Cambridge, held the first Margaret Chair of divinity, and founded fellowships and the Lady Margaret preachership for evangelical instruction of the laity. Preaching in the vernacular, which had fallen into disuse, was his special interest, and he himself continued to preach even in old age, when he was obliged to preach sitting down. He was president of Queens' College from 1505 to 1508. In 1504 he was elected chancellor of the university, and was re-elected annually for ten years and then for life, though when Henry VIII ascended the throne in 1509, he offered to give the chancellorship to Henry's favorite, Cardinal Wolsey.

This offer does not mean that Fisher admired Wolsey; as an austere and ascetic man he hated the pomp and luxury of the famous cardinal, and he disapproved of and did not hesitate to criticize his political views. Fisher was one of the fathers of the "New Learning," who brought Erasmus to Cambridge, encouraged the teaching of Greek and himself studied the language, and engaged in Biblical criticism; on the other hand, he was violently opposed to Luther and the Reformation. As Catherine of Aragon's confessor, confidant, and almost her only friend, he set his face from the beginning against the divorce. In 1534 he was brought before Parliament on charges of misprision of treason and of collusion with Elizabeth Barton, the visionary "Maid of Kent" who was executed for prophesying against the divorce, and on this occasion his sentence was compounded by a £300 fine. But a few months later, when with Sir Thomas More [qv] he refused to accept all the provisions of the oath of compliance, he was thrown into the Tower. There he was deposed from his bishopric and chancellorship and attainted with misprision of treason for refusing again to acknowledge the king as the supreme head of the church in England. His health broke under mistreatment, but he remained steadfast. Pope Paul III innocently sealed his fate by making him a cardinal. "If the pope sends Fisher a hat," raged Henry, "there shall be no head for it." He was condemned first to be hanged, drawn, and quartered at Tyburn, but finally was beheaded on Tower Hill (just two weeks

After H. Holbein

JOHN FISHER

before More) and his head hung on London Bridge and then thrown into the Thames. In 1886 he was beatified by Pope Leo XIII, and is a saint of the Roman Catholic Church.

Fisher's best known writings are his sermons, particularly the ones given in 1509 at the funerals of Henry VII and his mother. He was a conscious stylist, sometimes homely, sometimes far fetched in his conceits, but always displaying literary skill. More said of him: "In this realm no one man, in wisdom, learning, and long approved vertue together, is mete to be matched and compared with him."

PRINCIPAL WORKS: This treatyse concernynge the fruytful sayngs of Davyd the Kynge and prophete, etc., 1508; This sermon . . . compyled & sayd in the Cathedrall churche of saynt Poule, etc., 1509; Hereafter followeth a Mornynge Remembraunce, etc., 1509; The sermon . . . made agaynst ye pernicyous doctryn of Martin Louther, 1521?; A Confutation of the Lutheran Assertyon, 1523; A Defence of the Christiane Priesthoode, 1524; A Sermon had at Paulis . . . concernynge certayne heretickes which thā were abjured for holdynge the heresies of Martyn Luther, 1525?; A Defense of Assertio Septem Sacramentorum [Henry VIII's treatise in refutation of Luther], 1525; Opera J. Fisheri, 1595; English Works (J.E.B. Mayor, ed.) 1876.

ABOUT: Anon. The Life and Death of that Renowed John Fisher, Bishop of Rochester; Bridgett, T.E. Life of Blessed John Fisher; Hall, R. (R. Bayne, ed.) The Life of Fisher; Kerker, M. John Fisher, sein Leben und Wirken; McCann, P. A Valiant Bishop Against a Ruthless King: The Life of John Fisher; Smith, R. L. John Fisher and Thomas More: Two English Saints.

FITZRALPH, RICHARD (d. 1360), preacher and religious writer, was born at Dundalk in Louth. He received his education at Oxford, being a fellow of Balliol College and apparently being chancellor or vice chancellor of the University around 1333. From this time on he advanced through a succession of appointments, favored because of papal influence in his behalf. In 1347 he went to Ireland as Archbishop of Armagh.

In both England and Ireland he was highly respected for his sermons and tracts on school theology, but on one of his frequent trips to the papal seat in Avignon, in 1349, he entered into a controversy which clouded the last years of his life. He had been called there on another matter, the dispute between the Armenian Church and the pope, on which Fitzralph wrote a nineteen volume dissertation that brought him

world-wide fame among orthodox Catholics.

Becoming interested in the controversy between the clergy and the rising orders of mendicant friars, Fitzralph published a treatise attacking the idea of mendicancy as being "without warrant in scripture or primitive tradition."

On his return to Ireland the friars persuaded the king that Fitzralph had presumed unduly on the favoritism of the pope, but popular riots in his behalf in Dublin prevented any action being taken against him. Six years later, on a visit to London, he again plunged into the heat of the controversy, preaching sermons so strong in their opposition that the friars succeeded in forcing a papal judgment on his position. His self-defense was a sermon expressing his general views of the relationship of humanity to God, which has been widely printed.

Before the judgment was announced, Fitzralph died at Avignon. Whether or not he would have been condemned is not known, but the friars won the privileges for which they had been struggling.

Natives of Dundalk, reporting miracles at his tomb, have always regarded Fitzralph as a saint, although he was never canonized.

PRINCIPAL WORKS: Richardi Radulphi Summa in Quaestionibus Armenorum, 1349 (printed in Paris in 1511); De Pauperie Salvatoris, 1349.

FITZSTEPHEN, WILLIAM (d. 1190?), biographer of Thomas a Becket, was one of Becket's closest associates for several years. In 1154, when Becket became Archdeacon of Canterbury, FitzStephen was already in his service, and the next year, when Becket was appointed chancellor by Henry II, FitzStephen became sub-deacon of his chapel. He read all letters and petitions addressed to the chancellor, and was empowered to make legal decisions on most matters, although sometimes he was appointed advocate of one party to a dispute when the case was argued before Becket himself. It is clear that Becket often consulted him, and there are recorded occasions when he gave the archbishop excellent advice.

He accompanied Becket to the Council of Northampton, where the quarrel between the archbishop and the king flared into open charges resulting in Becket's exile. FitzStephen did not accompany him abroad, but presented to the king a rhymed Latin petition for pardon, which was granted.

When Becket returned to England in 1170, FitzStephen rejoined him, and was present when, less than a month after his return, Becket was murdered in Canterbury Cathedral by partisans of the king.

With his brother Ralph, FitzStephen served as sheriff of Gloucester from 1171 to 1190, and was appointed to a judgeship by Henry in 1176. He was an itinerant justice in 1189 and 1190, when he is believed to have died.

His biography of Becket is valuable for much first-hand information. While he was biased in favor of his patron, he was scrupulously honest in reporting facts. A remarkable preface to the biography gives a detailed, vivid picture of the city of London during the twelfth century which is the chief authority for information about the life of that period.

PRINCIPAL WORK: Life of Thomas Becket.

ABOUT: Foss, E. Biographia Juridica; Hardy, Sir T. D. Descriptive Catalogue of Mss. Materials for History of Great Britain; Hutton, W. H. Thomas Becket; Madox, T. History of the Exchequer.

FLATMAN, THOMAS (1637-1688), poet and miniature painter, was born in London, and studied at Winchester and at New College, Oxford. He was a fellow of his college, but left without obtaining his degree. Ten years later he was created M. A. of Cambridge by royal decree.

He settled in London and followed his main bent toward miniature painting, occasionally writing a poem which appeared in a publication or collection. Only one volume of his poems was published, and most of them survive only in anthologies.

An early antipathy to marriage was erased when, in 1672, he met a "fair virgin" with a considerable fortune. The anecdote is told that on their wedding night, Flatman was serenaded by his friends with a song which he himself had composed in his earlier, misogynist days, beginning:

Like a dog with a bottle tied close to his tail,
Like a tory in a bog, like a thief in jail. . . .

Flatman and his wife lived on a small estate at Tishton, near Diss. They had at least one son. Flatman died in London in 1688, at the age of fifty-one.

The quality of his miniatures is as highly praised today as it was during his own lifetime. He painted many portraits, including two of himself. Critical opinion of his poetry, on the contrary, has fluctuated. Much of it was admired by his own contemporaries. The Duke of Ormonde was so delighted by an ode written by Flatman on the death of Ormonde's son, the Earl of Ossory, that he sent the poet a diamond ring.

Critics of the following generations depreciated his verses, probably too harshly. One of his poems, *A Thought of Death*, was imitated by Pope. Three others, *Death, a Song, Hymn for Morning* and *Hymn for Evening* have merit, and his lighter verses have finish and style. Two anonymous works, *Montelion's Almanack for 1661-62* and a mock romance, *Don Juan Lamberto*, have been attributed to him.

PRINCIPAL WORK: Poems and Songs, 1674.

ABOUT: Granger, J. Biographical History of England; Redgrave, S. Dictionary of Artists; Walpole, H. Anecdotes of Painting; Wood, A. à, Athenae Oxonienses.

FLECKNOE, RICHARD (d. 1678?), poet and miscellaneous writer, was probably born in Ireland and may at one time have been a priest. In 1640, to escape the civil war, he went to Ghent where he remained for three or four years. In 1645, on a mission to obtain papal permission for the marriage of Béatrix de Cusance to Charles IV, he went to Rome, where he remained for two years, "chiefly occupied," he said, "with pictures and statues." He then journeyed to Constantinople, Portugal, Brazil, Flanders and back to England. Beyond these facts, which we know from his own published account, *Ten Years' Travel*, we know nothing of his life.

Of his character, as reflected in his own and contemporary literature, we have a series of rather contradictory pictures. He was a friend and adherent of royalty, yet shortly after Cromwell's death he wrote a flattering book about him. The next year following the Restoration, he wrote equally flattering "Heroic Portraits" of the Stuarts. He professed extreme distaste for the theatre, particularly for the immorality of the English stage, and yet he wrote a number of plays. The only one produced, *Love's Kingdom*, was announced as being "written for the reformed stage."

Most of his poems were printed for private distribution, and he is credited with having said he thought it genteel "rather to affect a little negligence than too great curiosity" in his writings. The poetry, often on religious themes, was clever, shallow, neither very good nor wholly bad. That he personally was vain, snobbish and heartily disliked by most of his contemporaries seems indisputable. Andrew Marvell, who wrote *Flecknoe, an English Priest at Rome,* after he had visited the poet there, was most unflattering. Dryden's more virulent dislike of him has never been explained. Flecknoe's attacks on the stage, his personal conceit, or the quality of his poetry are conjectured causes. Others believe that in the biting satire, *Mac Flecknoe,* Dryden was attacking the poet laureate Shadwell rather than Flecknoe himself.

PRINCIPAL WORKS: Love's Kingdom, 1654; Ten Years' Travels in Europe, Asia, Affrique and America, 1656; The Idea of His Highness Oliver, 1659; Heroic Portraits, 1660; Epigrams, 1669.

ABOUT: Langbaine, G. Dramatic Poets; Southey, R. Omniana; Ware, Sir J. Writers of Ireland.

FLETCHER, GILES, the elder (1549-March 1611), diplomat, historian, poet, was born in Watford, Hertfordshire, the son of Richard Fletcher, a clergyman. His brother later became Bishop of London. He was educated at Eton and at King's College, Cambridge, which he entered in 1565. He became a fellow in 1568, received his B.A. in 1569, M.A. in 1573, and (after a study of civil law), LL.D. in 1581. In 1577 he was deputy orator of Cambridge, and in 1580 became commissary chancellor of the diocese of Ely. In 1582 he was chancellor of the diocese of Chichester.

After sitting in Parliament for Winchelsea in 1585, Fletcher entered the diplomatic service. He went to Scotland with the English ambassador, then to Germany, and finally to Russia, to try to secure a trade agreement for England from Czar Theodore. He was treated with some rudeness and abuse, which elicited a protest from Queen Elizabeth, but returned to England in 1589 with the agreement. The book he wrote on Russia was considered offensive by the Russia Company, organized for trade with that country, and by its influence was suppressed for some time, though portions appeared in

both Hakluyt's *Voyages* and *Purchas His Pilgrimes.* In 1596 Fletcher was made extraordinary master of requests in ordinary and secretary or "remembrancer" to the city of London. The next year he became treasurer of St. Paul's.

In 1600 his brother the bishop died, and Fletcher, who was his executor, was in danger of imprisonment as surety for his brother's debts. He was saved through the good offices of the Earl of Essex, and the next year, when Essex was tried and executed, Fletcher expressed sufficient sympathy with him to earn himself a term of private imprisonment lasting a year or more. He had no further difficulties, but this was the end of his public service until 1610, when James I employed him in some negotiations with Denmark.

Fletcher married Joan Sheafe in 1581. They had a daughter and three sons, two of whom, the younger Giles and Phineas,[qqv] became known as poets.

In his principal poetry, the sonnet sequence called *Licia,* Fletcher said quite frankly that he wrote "to the imitation of the best Latin poets and others," and also that this work was based on no real love, but was merely following the fashion of the time. He himself said he preferred a style of "English homespun," but no evidence of this appears in his fanciful and allegorical verse. Like his sons, he was a disciple and follower of Spenser.[qv]

PRINCIPAL WORKS: Of the Russe Common Wealth, 1591 (as History of Russia, 1643); Licia, or Poemes of Love in Honour of the Admirable and Singular Vertues of His Lady, Whereunto Is Added the Rising of the Crowne of Richard III, 1593; De literis antiquae Britanniae (P. Fletcher, ed.) 1633; An Essay upon some probable grounds that the present Tartars near the Cyprian Sea, are the Posterity of the Ten Tribes of Israel (in Israel Redux, S. Lee, ed.) 1677; Complete Poems (A. B. Grosart, ed.) 1876.

ABOUT: Cory, H. E. Spenser, the School of the Fletchers, and Milton; Grosart, A. B. Memorial-Introduction, Complete Poems; Lee, S. Elizabethan Sonnets.

FLETCHER, GILES, the younger (1588?-November 1623), poet, was born in London, the son of Giles Fletcher, the elder,[qv] and Joan Sheafe. Phineas Fletcher,[qv] his older brother, long outlived him. Giles may have been born as early as 1584. He was educated in Westminster School and Trinity College, Cambridge (B.A. 1606), was appointed minor fellow in 1608, reader in Greek grammar 1615, and reader in Greek language 1618. He then took orders and was named vicar of Alderton, Suffolk, perhaps through Francis Bacon ^{qv}. Here he spent the remainder of his short life—he died before he was forty. He pined away among the country "clodhoppers," though his sermons became famous and popular. Besides his principal work, *Christes Victorie,* Fletcher contributed to an anthology on the death of Elizabeth and the accession of James, called *Sorrowes Joy,* for which he wrote *A Canto upon the Death of Eliza;* in addition to a prose tract he wrote *An Elegy on Prince Henry's Death* and *A Description of Encolpius* (the latter in rhymed couplets). Like his brother, he was a follower of Spenser, and had some influence on Milton. He edited the *Remains* of his cousin, Nathaniel Pownall, in 1612.

Christes Victorie has lyrical passages of great beauty and drama; it is lofty and vigorous; but its general impression is one of exaggeration and even grotesqueness, because of the too ingenious conceits with which it is filled, and because of the unsuitability of its subject for its poetic form. Giles Fletcher, the younger, nevertheless constitutes a link in the chain between Spenser and Milton.

PRINCIPAL WORKS: Christes Victorie, or Triumph in Heaven and Earth, Over and After Death, 1610; The Reward of the Faithful (prose) 1623; Complete Poems (A. B. Grosart, ed.) 1876; Giles and Phineas Fletcher: Poetical Works (F. S. Boas, ed.) 1908.

ABOUT: Cory, H. E. Spenser, the School of the Fletchers, and Milton; Fuller, T. English Worthies; Grosart, A. B. Introduction, Complete Poems.

FLETCHER, JOHN (December 1579-August 1625), dramatist, collaborator with Francis Beaumont ^{qv}, was born in Rye, Sussex, where his father was then rector. The father, Richard Fletcher, later became Dean of Peterborough (in which capacity in 1587 he tormented Mary Queen of Scots in her last hours), and when he died in 1596 was Bishop of London. He died heavily in debt, and his executor, his brother Giles (father of the poets Giles and Phineas Fletcher ^{qqv}) was almost imprisoned as his surety.

John Fletcher was educated at Bene't (Corpus Christi) College, Cambridge. His father's death cut his education short, and

JOHN FLETCHER

he next turned up in London, where he became a member of the brilliant group of Elizabethan dramatists. Like most of them, he was dependent for his living on his pen, but he never forgot or omitted to mention the fact that, unlike most of them, he was a gentleman by birth. So was his great collaborator Francis Beaumont, whom he met about 1607. The young men became close personal friends as well as collaborators; according to Aubrey, they lived together and shared everything in common, even to their joint mistress. This may be a canard, but there is no doubt of their careless Bohemian mode of life. Nevertheless Fletcher moved in sufficiently self-respecting circles to be favorably regarded by Ben Jonson, who hailed him as one of his "sons."

Philaster was the first successful joint play of Beaumont and Fletcher. After Beaumont ceased writing for the stage, about 1614 (he died two years later), Fletcher carried on alone or with other collaborators, principally Philip Massinger ^{qv}. Both men had also written a few early plays of their own. *The Faithfull Shepheardess,* which has been called "the sweetest of English pastoral plays," and which strongly influenced Milton's *Comus,* was certainly entirely Fletcher's own work.

Fletcher died of the plague, and was buried in the same grave as Massinger. To his acquaintances he was equally well known for his personal modesty, for his brilliant wit, and for his impecuniousness.

For three hundred years scholars have been trying to establish the canon of the Beaumont and Fletcher plays, to discover exactly who wrote each of them. The problem is complicated by the fact that when the plays were printed, they were often ascribed to both collaborators when actually they were written by one, or to one when written by both. Others were revised later by other playwrights. Fletcher probably collaborated with Shakespeare on *Henry VIII*, and may have written most of *The Two Noble Kinsmen;* there is also a lost play, *Cardenius,* which was certainly written by Fletcher and Shakespeare together. The consensus is that he was probably sole author of fifteen plays out of fifty-two, wrote eight or nine with Beaumont, and wrote twenty-two with others, sixteen of these with Massinger. The remainder are in doubt.

The princ:pal way by which a play is judged as likely to be by Fletcher is by consideration of its metric form; Fletcher's blank verse almost always stops at the end of each line, without a carry-over, and he was unusually addicted to feminine line-endings—a device he adopted for its dramatic effect. However, there are other less technical considerations. His bent was for "mixed" comedy, with no tendency toward farce; on the other hand his pure tragedies are inferior to those of Beaumont. He had no turn for the intense and even morbid tragedy so dear to Webster and Marlowe. He also had a marked lyrical gift, and his interpolated songs are graceful and deft. He was careless in characterization, brilliant in dialogue, with an aptitude for splendid rhetoric and a feeling for "good theatre." He was a skilled craftsman and a rapid worker, but inclined to leave loose ends and gaping holes in the plot. The plays written with Beaumont have original stories, which Beaumont must have created, since Fletcher's later plots are taken from various sources. Swinburne summed up the work of Fletcher by noting his "bright exuberant speech," the "fresh air and sunshine" of his prevalent mood, and the "buoyant and facile grace" of his style. Undoubtedly the plays of Beaumont and Fletcher constitute the most considerable body of Elizabethan drama except Shakespeare's.

PRINCIPAL WORKS: (dates of publication) (*By Fletcher alone*)—The Faithfull Shepheardess, 1609; Cupids Revenge (?) 1615; With or Without Money, 1629; Monsieur Thomas, 1639; The Night-Walker, 1640; Rule a Wife and Have a Wife, 1640; The Elder Brother, 1651; The Wild-Goose Chase, 1652; The Chances, 1682; The Loyal Subject, 1700; The Tragedie of Valentinian, 1717; A Wife for a Month, 1717; The Tragedie of Bonduca, 1718. (*With Beaumont*)—The Knight of the Burning Pestle, 1613; The Captain, 1613; The Scornful Ladie, 1616; A King and No King, 1619; The Maides Tragedie, 1619; Philaster, or Love Lyes a Bleeding, 1620; Four Playes or Morall Representations in One, 1647. (*With Massinger*)—Thierry and Theodoret, 1621; The Custome of the Countrie, 1647; The Little Frenche Lawyer, 1647; The Lovers Progress (The Wandering Lover), 1647; The Beggars Bush, 1661; Sir John Van Olden Barnevelt, 1883. (*With others*)—Henry VIII (with Shakespeare) 1623; The Two Noble Kinsmen (with Shakespeare and Massinger) 1634; The Bloody Brother (with Jonson) 1639; Loves Pilgrimage (with Jonson) 1647. *Collections*—Comedies and Tragedies Written by Francis Beaumont and John Fletcher, Gentlemen, 1647; Fifty Comedies and Tragedies by Francis Beaumont and John Fletcher, Gentlemen, 1679; The Works of Francis Beaumont and John Fletcher (A. H. Bullen, ed.) 1904; The Works of Beaumont and Fletcher (A. Glover and A. R. Waller, eds.) 1905.

ABOUT: Aubrey, J. Letters Written by Eminent Persons; Cibber, T. Lives of the Poets; Coleridge, S. T. Literary Remains; Gayley, C. M. Beaumont, the Dramatist, with Some Account of His . . . Association with John Fletcher; Hazlitt, W. Lectures on the Elizabethan Drama; Mason, J. M. Comments on the Plays of Beaumont and Fletcher; Maxwell, B. Studies in Beaumont, Fletcher, and Massinger; Oliphant, E. H. C. The Plays of Beaumont and Fletcher; Saintsbury, G. History of Elizabethan Literature; Sprague, A. C. Beaumont and Fletcher and the Restoration Stage; Swinburne, A. C. Studies in Prose and Poetry; Wallis, L. B. Beaumont, Fletcher, and Company, Entertainers to the Jacobean Gentry; Wilson, J. H. The Influence of Beaumont and Fletcher on Restoration Drama.

FLETCHER, PHINEAS (April 1582-1650), poet, was born in Cranbrook, Kent, where his father, Giles Fletcher, the elder[qv], was then rector. His mother was Joan Sheafe. His younger brother was Giles Fletcher, the younger.[qv]

He was educated (like his father) at Eton and at King's College, Cambridge, which he entered in 1600, receiving his B.A. in 1604, M.A. in 1608, and later B.D. He was a fellow some time before 1611, but resigned in 1616 because of resentment in some forgotten quarrel. He then became chaplain to Sir Henry Willoughby until 1621, when Willoughby secured for him the rectory of Hilgay, Norfolk, which was thenceforth his home. In 1621 he married Elizabeth Vincent; they had two sons and four daughters. He died at the end of 1650.

Phineas Fletcher, like his brother, was steeped in Spenser's poetry. Indeed, for a long time *Brittains Ida* was attributed to Spenser himself—though probably deliberately, by the publisher. This erotic poem, which Fletcher called "these raw essayes of my very unripe years," was printed without its pious author's consent, and he deplored its publication, though later acknowledging it as his. In the same light vein were his *Sicelides*, which was acted in King's College in 1631, and the *Piscatorie Eclogs*, which conceal his father, brother, and friends under allegorical names—all the Fletchers were ardent fishermen. The poem by which Fletcher desired to be remembered was *The Purple Island*, which is a labored allegory of man's body as an island, and a much more skillful allegory of his mind. *Locusta*, the poem against the Roman Catholics which he published both in Latin and in English, contains some lines of almost Miltonic majesty, but is marred by its bitter partisanship. The simplest and hence the most beautiful of Phineas Fletcher's poems is the *Elisa*, an elegy on the "unripe demise" of Sir Antonie Irby—written, according to some authorities, at Lady Irby's request when she was about to be remarried!

Though Phineas Fletcher never attains his brother's occasional sublimity of diction, he has color and melody, and the rural descriptions in his pastorals possess great charm. His style is too mannered for sustained beauty. Francis Quarles *qv* called him "the Spenser of this age," and this is true though not in the wholly complimentary sense in which Quarles intended it: Fletcher is so like Spenser that his work becomes an image or echo of the greater poet. His poems had a very strong influence on the young Milton, and there are echoes of both the brothers in Milton's earlier, lyric poems.

Fletcher wrote two prose religious tracts, and contributed also to the Cambridge anthology, *Sorrowes Joy, or a Lamentation for our late deceased Sovereigne Elizabeth, with a triumph for the prosperous succession of our gratious King, James* (1603). *A Father's Testament*, published posthumously, was a combination of prose and verse, the latter

mostly translations from the classics. As may be seen by his lighter works, Phineas Fletcher was capable of both wit and fancy (as neither his father nor his brother was), but he sternly suppressed these in favor of poetry in the lofty vein he considered more fitting both to his clerical office and to his literary tastes.

PRINCIPAL WORKS: Locusta, vel pietas Jesuitica (The Locusts or Apollyonists) 1627; Brittains Ida, 1628; Sicelides: A Piscatory (pastoral play) 1631; Joy in Tribulation, or Consolations for Afflicted Spirits (prose) 1632; The Way to Blessedness, a Treatise on the First Psalme (prose) 1633; Sylva Poetica, 1633; The Purple Island: or the Isle of Man: together with Piscatorie Eclogs and Other Poetical Miscellanies, 1633; Elisa, or an Elegie upon the Unripe Demise of Sir Antonie Irby, 1633; A Father's Testament, 1670; Poems (A. B. Grosart, ed.) 1868; Giles and Phineas Fletcher: Poetical Works (F. S. Boas, ed.) 1908.

ABOUT: Cory, H. E. Spenser, the School of the Fletchers, and Milton; Grosart, A. B. Memoir, *in* Poems; Langdale, A. B. Phineas Fletcher, Man of Letters, Science, and Divinity.

FLORENCE of WORCESTER (d. 1118),

chronicler of English history, was a monk who died on July 7, 1118. These are the only facts known about the life of one of the most important links in that chain of chroniclers who passed along England's earliest recorded history from generation to generation.

Florence's minor contributions to the record were a list of English deacons, and a compilation of the genealogies of English kings. His great work, *Chronicon ex Chronicis*, was the first "universal" history written in England, being an attempt to encompass the story of all nations and all time from creation to the year 1117.

For the bulk of the work, up to his own time, Florence relied principally upon the writings of Marianus Scotus, an Irish scholar who, borrowing largely from Bede, had brought his chronicle up to the year 1082. Florence's additions to Marianus' manuscript, up to his own lifetime, were drawn chiefly from Eadmer's *Historia Novorum*, the *Lives* of Dunstan, Oswald and Aethelwold, Bede, Asser's *Life of Alfred*, and the *Anglo-Saxon Chronicle*.

In the case of the latter two, Florence's text has been especially valuable. The authenticity of versions of Asser's work which have survived has often been in dispute, and it is by reference to Florence's use of the original text that such questions have been solved. The version of the *Anglo-Saxon Chronicle* which he used has been lost, so that his work is the only clue to its contents, which gives it extraordinary value.

For the period of his own lifetime, Florence, never a historian in the modern sense, was an unimaginative but accurate reporter. The *Chronicle* was extended by John of Worcester to 1141, by Henry of Huntingdon to 1152, and by the monks of St. Edmundsbury to the end of the thirteenth century.

PRINCIPAL WORK: Chronicon ex Chronicis (B. Thorpe, ed.) 1848.

ABOUT: Green, J. R. Conquest of England; Hardy, Sir T. D. Descriptive Catalogue of Manuscript Materials for the History of Great Britain; Ordericus Vitalis, Ecclesiastical History of England.

FLORIO, JOHN (or GIOVANNI), 1553?-August 1625, translator, lexicographer, was born in London, the son of Michael Angelo Florio, a Protestant (Waldensian) from Florence who had fled to England from religious persecution. The older Florio was a lay preacher, and later a teacher, translator, and writer in Italian. The boy was perhaps educated on the Continent, but was reared in Oxford, where as early as 1576 he tutored a son of the Bishop of Durham. He became associated with Magdalen College by 1581, when he was a teacher of French and Italian to the university. He found patrons among the wealthy nobles, being attached at various times to the Earls of Leicester, Southampton, and Pembroke. By 1600 he has settled in London, and in 1603 James I made him reader in Italian to the queen and Prince Henry, and the next year gentleman extraordinary and groom of the privy chamber. From 1620 to his death he lived in Fulham. He married Rose Daniel, sister of the poet Samuel Daniel,*qv* and they had at least one daughter.

Florio's great work was his translation of Montaigne, which made him one of the most famous translators in English literature. It was anything but a literal version; Florio was a man intoxicated by words, and the spare style of the great French essayist was not for him. He loved words for their own sake, invented neologisms, indulged in eccentric fantasies, extravagant alliteration, pomposities, and pedantries—and created a living book. His dedications (each part was dedicated to a different person) are marvels of euphuism gone wild. "Resolute John Florio," as he called himself, was a stylist in his own right, and did not hesitate to include some things which Montaigne would have written, if he had happened to think of them! Nevertheless, Ben Jonson was glad to call him his "loving father and loving friend," and if he perhaps falsified the literal meaning of Montaigne, he demonstrated his spirit brilliantly and vividly.

Two copies of the translation now in the British Museum have a special historical interest; one contains Jonson's authentic autograph, the other, one of Shakespeare now known to be a forgery, but considered genuine until the eighteenth century.

Florio's other important work is his Italian-English dictionary, which is a curiosity of literature through its author's love of fantastic and high-flown language. His other books were textbooks and dialogues for use in the teaching of Italian.

It has been suggested that Florio was caricatured by Shakespeare as Holofernes in *Love's Labour's Lost,* but this seems unlikely, since Florio was never a country school master, and though his written style is often pompous and pedantic, there is no evidence that he himself was either. The friends and patrons he attracted were not likely to be drawn to a rustic pedant. There is, however, some reason to believe that Shakespeare and

W. Hole, 1611

JOHN FLORIO

Florio were personal acquaintances, perhaps in the poet's early obscure days in London.

PRINCIPAL WORKS: Florio's First Fruites, with a Perfect Induction to the Italian and English Tongues, 1758; Florio's Second Fruites, 1591; A World of Wordes (Italian-English Dictionary) 1598; Essayes on Morall, Politike, and Millitarie Discourses of Lo. Michaell de Montaigne, 1603.

ABOUT: Acheson, A. Shakespeare's Lost Years in London; Chambrun, L. Giovanni Florio; de-Chambrun, P. Shakespeare et Florio (in French); Upham, A. H. The French Influence in English Literature from the Accession of Elizabeth to the Restoration; Whibley, C. Literary Portraits; Wood, A. à, Athenae Oxonienses; Yates, F. A. John Florio; the Life of an Italian in Shakespeare's England.

FLUDD (or FLUD), ROBERT (1574-September 8, 1633), physician, author of treatises on medical mysticism, was born in Milgate or Bearsted, Kent, the son of Sir Thomas Fludd, Kt. (Elizabeth's treasurer of war in France and the Low Countries), and Elizabeth Andros, both of Welsh descent. He entered St. John's College, Oxford, in 1591, and received his B.A. in 1596, M.A., 1598. He then spent six years on the Continent studying medicine (and alchemy), making his living by tutoring in noble families, then returned to Oxford, to Christ Church securing his M.B. and M.D. in 1605. With some reservations, he was qualified by the College of Physicians in 1606; twice in the same year he was called before them and admonished for "contempt of Galen," but he became a Fellow of the College of Physicians in 1609, and later served four terms as one its censors. He practiced in London, where he was noted as having his own apothecary and his own amanuensis living with him in his house. He was also celebrated for the curious automata he constructed. However, his fame was much greater abroad than in England, thanks to his controversies with other scientists. He died in London, unmarried.

Fludd wrote sometimes under the names of Joachim Frizius, Rudolf Otreb (an anagram on his own name), and Robertus de Fluctibus. If this was intended to be a Latin translation of his name, he knew no Welsh; for the word in that language means not "flood" but "grey." Practically all of his writing was in Latin.

He was a medical mystic, an anti-scholastic, who sought evidence of a "universal science," derived from the Bible and regarding man as a microcosm, and the world as a macrocosm, with the universe itself proceeding from and returning to God. He was a disciple of Paracelsus, and attacked Copernicus, Kepler, and Galileo. He was a Rosicrucian, and wrote much in defense of that order; DeQuincey thought he was also a founder of the Free Masons. He believed firmly in the "weapon-salve" of Sir Kenelm Digby.[qv]

In spite of the materialistic pantheism of some of Fludd's views, he himself held that "all true science is rooted in revelation"—specifically, Genesis. He set his face firmly against the developing scientific discovery of his own era, and the greater part of his writing which is not in defense of the Rosicrucians is devoted to controversy with Kepler and Galileo, and with others who rejected the Ptolemaic for the Copernican astronomy. He was given to fantastic speculations and felt no need for proof of his sometimes contradictory assertions. In other words, even in his own time he looked toward the past rather than toward the future. Since little of his work appeared in English or was translated later, he belongs rather to the history of science or philosophy than to that of English literature.

PRINCIPAL WORKS: Apologia Compendaria, Fraternitatem de Rosea Cruce Suspicionis, 1616; Utriusque, Cosmi Majoris Scilicet et Minoris, 1617-24; Veritatis Proscenium, 1621; Monochordon Mundi Symphoniacum, 1622; Philosophia Sacra et Vere Christiania, 1626; Medicina Catholica, 1629; Doctor Fludds Answer vnto M. Foster, or the Squesing of Pastor Fosters Sponge, 1631; Clavis Philosophia et Alchymiae, 1633; Philosophia Moysaica, 1638 (as The Mosaic Philosophy, 1659); Works, 1638.

ABOUT: Craven, J. B. Robert Fludd, the English Rosicrucian; DeQuincey, T. Historico-Critical Inquiry into the Origin of the Rosicrucians and the Freemasons; Fuller, T. Worthies of England; Hunt, J. Religious Thought in England; Waite, A. E. History of the Rosicrucians.

FOOTE, SAMUEL (January 1720-October 21, 1777), dramatist, was born in Truro, Cornwall, the son of Samuel Foote, a commissioner in the prize office and a former Member of Parliament and mayor of the town. His mother was Eleanor Goodere, who had inherited a fortune after one of her brothers murdered the other and was hanged for it. Both his parents died while he was young. Foote was educated in the Collegiate School of Worcester and entered Worcester College, Oxford, in 1737, but left without

After Sir J. Reynolds

SAMUEL FOOTE

a degree. He was also entered in the Temple, but was never called to the bar. Instead, he lived the life of a wealthy young man about town. He soon wasted his fortune and turned to the stage, appearing first with Charles Macklin in *Othello* in 1744. Though he acted in both Covent Garden and Drury Lane and in Dublin, he was a complete failure as a tragedian. About 1750 an uncle died and left him another fortune; he went to Paris and soon ran through it there. Returning to England in 1752, he began writing his long series of plays—really farces though called comedies—which for the most part were played as after-pieces. He himself acted in them in both Drury Lane and Covent Garden, as well as in Ireland and Scotland, and as a comedian was very popular. He was constantly in hot water, however, because of his bold satire of living persons. In 1760 he opened an unlicensed theatre in the Haymarket, keeping away from the law by advertising his performances as "a concert of music," "an auction of pictures," etc., or inviting the public to take "a dish of chocolate" with him.

In 1766 a party of which the Duke of York was one played a joke on him by mounting him on a dangerous horse; he was thrown and so badly injured that his leg had to be amputated. In reparation, the duke gave him a life-patent on a new theatre in Westminster. He kept on acting, adapting

his plays (*The Devil on Two Sticks, The Lame Lover*) to his condition. Worse was to befall him: he satirized the Duchess of Kingston, who had been accused of bigamy. She had the play suppressed, so he turned on her chief associate, a Dr. Jackson. Jackson in revenge suborned a servant of Foote's to charge him with criminal assault. The dramatist was acquitted, but the ordeal broke his health. He started for the south of France to recuperate, but died suddenly in Dover. He was buried in Westminster Abbey.

Though Foote once stated that he had married "his washerwoman" in Worcester, no evidence of his marriage exists. He left his estate to two illegitimate sons.

He was a famous wit, to whom every current good story was attributed. He was also utterly unscrupulous, stole ideas wherever he could find them, was wildly extravagant, and was utterly selfish and vain. But this short, fat, flabby man was an inspired mimic, who lampooned celebrities like Garrick unmercifully (he also sponged on him equally unmercifully) and could make even the disapproving Dr. Johnson laugh. His plays are too topical for modern readers to enjoy, but in their day they were enormously popular. He was, as a dramatist, a disciple of Fielding, [qv] who in turn was a disciple of Congreve [qv]; but he introduced an element of satire which neither of his predecessors employed. *The Minor*, for example, is an attack on Methodism, and the puppet play, *Purity in Pattens, or the Handsome Housemaid* (1773), burlesques sentimental romance on the stage. He had great animation and a marked sense of "good theatre," but was deficient in characterization or creative originality.

PRINCIPAL WORKS: *Plays*—(dates of publication) Taste, 1752; The Englishman in Paris, 1753; The Knights, 1754; The Englishman Return'd from Paris, 1756; The Author, 1757; The Minor, 1760; The Orators, 1762; The Lyar, 1764; The Mayor of Garret, 1764; The Patron, 1764; The Commissary, 1765; The Lame Lover, 1770; The Bankrupt, 1776; The Devil upon Two Sticks, 1778; The Maid of Bath, 1778; The Nabob, 1778; The Cozeners, 1778; A Trip to Calais, 1778; Dramatic Works, 1787?. *Miscellaneous*—A Treatise on the Passions So Far As They Regard the Stage, 1747; The Roman and English Comedy Consider'd and Compar'd, 1747; Works, 1799; Works (J. Badcock, ed.) 1830.

ABOUT: Badcock, J. Essay on the Life, Genius, and Writings of the Author, *in* Works, 1830; Cooke, W. The Memoirs of Samuel Foote, with a Collection of his Genuine Bon Mots, Anecdotes, Opinions, etc.; Fitzgerald, P. Samuel Foote, A Biography; Russell, A. P. Characteristics: Sketches and Essays; Wilkinson, T. Memoirs.

FORD, JOHN (April 1586-1640?), dramatist, was born in Islington, Devonshire, the son of Thomas Ford, who was in the commission of the peace; his mother was the sister of Lord Chief Justice Popham. Almost nothing is known of his life. He may have spent a year in Exeter College, Oxford. He was entered in the Middle Temple in 1602, but was never called to the bar. By 1613, when his first play, *An Ill Beginning Has a Good Ending* (now lost) was acted, he was a regular writer for the London stage. Apparently, however, he had some private income, and was never dependent, as were so many dramatists of the time, on his writing for his daily existence. Therefore he was never a regular member of any of the "stables" of collaborators kept by the licensed theatres, though he did collaborate with Dekker, Webster, and Rowley.*qqv* We have fewer than half of his plays by which to judge him; some which were published have disappeared, and the manuscripts of several were burnt by Bishop Warburton's cook.

After 1639 Ford simply vanished from the London scene. He may have died, or he may have retired to his old home in Devonshire, as a local tradition says. Of his private life we know nothing. We can, however, learn a good deal about his personality from his writings. He was certainly a champion of lost causes and of the underdog, as witness his first publication, a eulogy (written without hope or desire of monetary return) of the notorious Duke of Devonshire, whom he had not known. A lost work, prose or verse, on Sir Thomas Overbury is another indication of his defiance of popular fashions in heroes. We know, too, that he was an intense and passionate man, sensual, romantic, yet capable of tenderness and delicacy. He was influenced strongly by Sidney, and still more strongly by Burton's *Anatomy of Melancholy*. The theme of all his plays—he was a complete fatalist—is the helplessness of human beings against the power of passion. Already this was foreshadowed in his early prose work, *Honor Triumphant*.

All Ford's plays written wholly by himself are (with the exception of the comedy, *The Fancies, Chast and Noble*) what were later called "problem plays." Even *The Fancies* has a very artificial problematical social situation as its basis. He utterly ignored conventionalities and taboos: his masterpiece, *Tis Pitty Shees a Whore,* concerns incest, and another lost play dealt with homosexuality. His catastrophes have the violence of nightmares; his tragedies are all carried on the single note of intensity, sometimes so exaggerated that it barely escapes bathos. He is capable of coarse buffoonery, of joyless grossness; but he can also ascend to the most exquisite sweetness, sympathy, and grace. It is no wonder that a later, more prudish age took him as representative of the decadence of the Elizabethan drama.

Yet he is much more than that. His technical skill grew gradually but surely; more than most dramatists of his time he created his own plots instead of, as many writers did, borrowing them. His "chronicle history," *Perkin Warbeck,* which harks back to an earlier style, has formal dignity and substance, quite unlike the carelessness of his other plays. *The Witch of Edmonton* (written in 1621 though published much later) is a true romantic-realistic drama of its own time, and though it is not known how much of it is Ford's, a good part of it certainly is. The obscurity and affectedness of his early verse grew into the grave, burning beauty of the poetry of his maturity. He never overcame his tendency to exaggeration and rhetoric, but his daring, his fatalistic melancholy, his tenderness, his human sympathy, make of his work something much finer than the "bad dream" to which some of his critics have compared it. In sheer tragic gift, though in that alone, Ford stands with Marlowe and Webster next to Shakespeare.

PRINCIPAL WORKS: *Plays*—(dates of publication) The Lovers Melancholy, 1629; The Broken Heart, 1633; Loves Sacrifice, 1633; Tis Pitty Shees a Whore, 1633; The Chronicle Historie of Perkin Warbeck, 1634; The Fancies, Chast and Noble, 1638; The Ladies Triall, 1639; The Sun's-Darling (masque, with T. Dekker) 1656; The Witch of Edmonton (with T. Dekker and W. Rowley) 1658; Dramatic Works of Massinger and Ford (H. Coleridge, ed.) 1840; Plays (H. Ellis, ed.) 1888. *Miscellaneous*—Fame's Memorial, or the Earle of Devonshire Deceased, 1606; Honor Triumphant (prose) with The Monarches Meeting (verse) 1606; A Line of Life, Pointing Out the Immortalitie of a Vertuous Name (verse) 1620; Works (W. Gifford, ed.) 1827 (revised, A. Dyce, ed. 1869).

ABOUT: Gifford, W. Life, in Works; Lamb, C. Specimens of the Dramatic Poets; Swinburne, A. C. Essays and Studies; Wolff, M. John Ford, ein Nachahmer Shakespeares.

FORTESCUE, Sir JOHN (1394?-1476?), the first English constitutional lawyer, and author of legal treatises, was a member of an ancient Devonshire family. Graduating from Exeter College, Oxford, he became, in 1430, a king's sergeant-at-law and, in 1442, chief justice of the king's court. He served in this capacity, acquiring a reputation for unquestionable impartiality, until the fall of Henry IV.

Loyal to the house of Lancaster, he accompanied Henry, Queen Margaret, and young Prince Edward into exile, and was among those charged with treason by the first parliament of Edward IV. While abroad, he was in charge of the education of the young prince, and wrote two of his most famous works for Edward's edification. The first of these was a philosophical and rather abstract discussion of "natural" forms of government, *De Natura Legis Naturae*. The second, written after he had observed the governments of Scotland and France, was a remarkable and practical defense of the laws of England, *De Laudibus Legum Angliae*. In both he upheld the Lancastrian claims to the throne. Taken prisoner at the battle of Tewkesbury, in which Prince Edward was killed and Henry finally defeated, he acknowledged the inevitable and recognized Edward IV as king. In return for a formal retraction of his arguments supporting Lancaster, he was pardoned and his property was returned to him.

His third great treatise, published under the title *The Governance of England*, was also called *The Difference Between an Absolute and a Limited Monarchy*, and reiterated the theme of *De Laudibus*: "[a king] is appointed to protect his subjects in their lives, liberties and laws; for this very end and purpose *he has the delegation of power from the people*, and he has no just claims to any power but this."

Fortescue spent the last years of his life at Ebrington. His final work was *Understanding and Faith*, a meditation on the duty of resignation.

PRINCIPAL WORKS: De Natura Legis Naturae, c. 1463; De Laudibus Legum Angliae, c. 1470; On the Governance of England, c. 1471.

ABOUT: Foss, E. Biographia Juridica; Plummer, C. Biographical Introduction to Governance of England (ed. 1885); Thomas, Lord Clermont. Life and Works of Sir John Fortescue.

FOWLER, WILLIAM (fl. 1603), Scottish poet, attended St. Leonard's College, St. Andrew, between 1574 and 1578. He studied civil law in Paris until 1581, when, he claimed in a pamphlet entitled "An Answer to the Calumnious Letter and erroneous Propositions of an apostate named M. John Hamilton," that he was driven from France by the Jesuits. The pamphlet, addressed to Francis, Earl Bothwell, is an attack on "the errors of Catholicism."

The friend of many prominent Scottish statesmen, Fowler served as a burgess of Edinburgh, and eventually was appointed secretary and Master of Requests to Queen Anne, wife of James VI. In 1603 he went to England in Anne's train, and was reappointed there to his two posts. In 1609 he was rewarded for his services with a grant of two thousand acres in Ulster. He probably died about 1614.

Fowler wrote poetry as a leisure pastime, and none of it was published. Much of it is preserved in manuscript form, however, having been bequeathed to Fowler's nephew, the poet William Drummond. Two volumes of manuscript poems are with Drummond's papers at the Society of Antiquaries of Scotland. The manuscripts of Fowler's two most interesting works are in the library of the University of Edinburgh. These are a collection of seventy-two sonnets, entitled *The Tarantula of Love*, and a translation from the Italian of *Triumphs of Petrarch*. His poetry is graceful, but is overloaded with the affectations of the period. Flattering sonnets by contemporaries, including one by James VI, are prefixed to his work. In turn, Fowler wrote a prefatory sonnet for the King's work, *Furies*.

PRINCIPAL WORKS: The Tarantula of Love, 1587; Triumphs of Petrarch.

ABOUT: Irving, D. History of Scottish Poetry; Masson, D. Drummond of Hawthornden; Nichols, J. Progresses of James I.

FOX, GEORGE (July 1624-January 13, 1691), founder of the Society of Friends, author of a journal, and religious writer, was born at Drayton-in-the-Clay, Leicestershire, the son of Christopher Fox, a prosperous weaver, and Mary Lago. He had little or no schooling, though at first his Puritan parents had intended him for the ministry. Instead, he was apprenticed to a shoemaker, who also acted as a grazier and wool dealer, in which capacity Fox became his trusted agent. In 1643, outraged by the frivolities of a fair, he heard a "divine call," and for nine months he disappeared, roaming around the country while he wrestled with his soul, in darkness and despair. He wrote later that he had tried to find help from both "priests" and Puritans, but found them both to be "empty, hollow casks."

The Society of Friends may be dated from 1647, when Fox first began preaching his doctrine of the "inner light." At first he was an occultist as well as a mystic, falling into long trances and doing "spiritual healing." This phase soon passed, and Fox, who was no fanatic, fought consistently against the "lunatic fringe" that attached itself to his new group. He was first imprisoned in Nottingham in 1649; thereafter he served eight prison sentences, one of three years (1663-66), one of fourteen months. The society, at first called "Truth's Friends," was dubbed "Quakers" by Justice Gervase Bennett in 1650; later the Friends accepted the epithet, which arose from Fox's statement that men should "tremble at the word of the Lord." Until his health broke in his last years, Fox traveled everywhere in England, Wales, Scotland, and Ireland, and visited North America, the West Indies, and Holland, preaching his doctrine and imposing discipline against the "ranters" who at first infested the society.

One of his early helpers was Margaret Fell, who was ten years his senior and the wife of Cromwell's chancellor for the Duchy of Lancaster. Judge Fell was friendly, though not a Quaker, and his home, Swarthmore Hall, became the headquarters of the Friends. After Fell's death Fox married the widow. During his last years he lived for the most part in London, where his wife visited him, though occasionally he rested at Swarthmore Hall. A "bulky" man with long straight hair, noted for his abstemiousness, Fox was respected even by his enemies; while he was in prison he was offered a captaincy in the Parliamentary Army, which,

GEORGE FOX

because of the Quaker opposition to war, he declined.

His *Journal* was dictated, not written; Fox was almost illiterate, could not spell, and was innocent of the rules of grammar. He had read little outside of the Bible. Nevertheless, he had a turn for narrative (he was a famous preacher), and his mind was original and spontaneous. He was a prolific pamphleteer, his followers editing his tracts before they were published. His style was uncouth, but his intense conviction brought life to his writing. Accused of everything from immorality to sorcery, George Fox actually was a great organizer, a true mystic but never a visionary, a genuine ascetic yet full of the common sense of the lower middle class to which he belonged and to which his doctrine at first chiefly appealed. His *Journal* is justly the most celebrated of all the numerous Quaker autobiographies.

PRINCIPAL WORKS: The Great Mistery of the Great Whore Unfolded, 1659; A Battle-Door for Teachers and Professors to learn Singular and Plural: *You* to many and *Thou* to one, 1660; A Journal or Historical Account of the Life, travels, sufferings, Christian experiences, and labour of love, in the work of the ministry of the ancient, eminent, and faithful servant of Jesus Christ, George Fox (T. Ellwood, ed.; preface by W. Penn) 1694 (T. B. Harvey, ed., 1911); A Collection of Epistles (2d part of Journal) 1698; Gospel Truth Demonstrated, in a Collection of Doctrinal Books (3d part of Journal) 1796; Works, 1831.

ABOUT: Ash, E. George Fox, His Character, Doctrine, and Work; Beck, W. Six Lectures on

George Fox and His Times; Bickley, A. C. George Fox and the Early Quakers; Brayshaw, A. N. The Personality of George Fox; Croese, G. Historia Quakeriana; Fox, G. Journal; Hodkin, T. George Fox; Janney, S. M. Life of George Fox; Jones, R. M. George Fox, an Autobiography; Newman, H. S. The Autobiography of George Fox from His Journal; Rowntree, J. S. The Life and Character of George Fox; Spurgeon, C. M. George Fox; Tuke, H. Life of George Fox.

FOXE, JOHN (1516-April 1587), martyrologist, religious writer, was born in Boston, Lancashire. When he was a child his father died and his mother married Richard Melton. He probably entered Brasenose College, Oxford, in 1533, but soon transferred to Magdalen. He received his B.A. in 1537, became a fellow in 1539, M.A. in 1543. Always Puritanical in his views, he refused to attend chapel or to take orders, and objected to the regulation that fellows must remain celibate; he was accused of heresy, but was not expelled as has been stated; he and five other fellows resigned in 1545. Reduced to extreme poverty, he went to London. In 1547 he married Agnes Randall; they had three sons and two daughters. From 1548 to 1553 he was tutor to the two sons of the Earl of Surrey, who had been executed shortly before; the boys' grandfather, the Duke of Norfolk, a Roman Catholic, was in prison during Edward VI's reign, and their aunt, the Duchess of Richmond, favored Foxe's Puritanical beliefs and became his patroness. His pupils grew much attached to him (though they themselves were inclined toward Roman Catholicism) and their estate at Reigate became his home. In 1550 he was ordained deacon, and at once became a volunteer preacher at Reigate. But in 1553, when Mary ascended the throne, the old duke was released, and his first act was to get rid of Foxe.

Foxe escaped first to Frankfurt, then to Basel, where he became press reader for the printer Johann Herbst (Oporinus). Thenceforth he was closely connected with the printing trade, and later in England worked with John Day. In 1559 he returned to England, and again found refuge with his former pupil, now Duke of Norfolk following his grandfather's death. (This is the Duke of Norfolk who was executed in 1572.) In 1560 Foxe was ordained priest, and three years later was made a prebend of Salisbury Cathedral and given a lease on the Shipton

1587

JOHN FOXE

vicarage; for a year (1572-73) he was a prebend of Durham. But in both posts, he refused to wear the surplice or to perform his clerical duties. His last years were spent in London, where he died.

Foxe had good classical learning; he wrote a work on grammar; was an early student of Anglo-Saxon and published the Gospels with Day. He wrote a mystery play and a number of religious tracts in both Latin and English. But the main work of his life was the *Actes and Monuments*, commonly called the Book of Martyrs. So overwhelmingly popular was this work that the 1570 edition was ordered chained in all cathedral churches for the use of the congregation. For a century at least it was practically required reading in every English-speaking Puritan household, often the only book owned except the Bible. Probably no single book has caused so many neuroses as has this one. Foxe was a fanatical Protestant, wrote with feverish energy, was completely credulous, and reveled in horror. No detail is too small or too dreadful to be described minutely, and no invective too violent to be applied to the Roman Catholics—for to his mind there were no martyrs except Protestants. His only theme is suffering, and he mangles his readers' nerves with one long monotony of agony and terror. Fuller said that "in good earnest. . . . Mr. Foxe hath done everything, leaving posterity nothing to work on," but Anthony à Wood remarked more acutely that Foxe "believed and reported all that was told him." Reproached for the inaccuracies of his book, he replied: "I should have taken more leisure and done it better. I graunt and confesse my fault: such is my vice."

On the credit side of this lover of horror, it may be said that he was extremely charitable, served devotedly during the plague of 1564, loved dogs in an age notably cruel to animals, and was outwardly at least a cheerful and kindly man. His great work is a mixture of "gossip, document, and exhortation," full of vilification of "the persecutors of God's truth, commonly called papists," but it is also dramatic, only too vivid, and written in a straightforward homely style. It has been called "the longest pamphlet on record."

The *Life* published in 1641, attributed to his son, is not by him and is most inaccurate.

PRINCIPAL WORKS: An Instruccyon of Christen Fayth, 1550?; Tables of Grammar, 1552; Christus Triumphans (play) 1556 (R. Day, 1578); Commentarii Rerum in Ecclesia Gestarum (first draft of Actes and Monuments) 1559: Syllogisticon, 1563; Actes and Monuments of these latter and perilous dayes, touching matters of the Church wherein are comprehended and described the great persecutions & horrible troubles, that have bene wrought & practised by the Romishe prelates, speciallye in this Realme of England, and Scotlande, from the year of our Lorde a thousand, unto the tyme now present, 1563 (J. Pratt, ed. 1877); A Sermon of Christ Crucified (on the excommunication of Queen Elizabeth) 1570.

ABOUT: Fuller, T. Church History of Britain; Gairdner, G. The English Church in the Sixteenth Century; Hagstotz, G. D. and H. B. Heroes of the Reformation; Maitland, S. R. Six Letters on Foxe's Acts and Monuments; Pratt, J. Preface to 1877 ed. Acts and Monuments; Winters, W. Biographical Notes on John Foxe; Wood, A. à, Athenae Oxonienses.

FRANCIS, FRANZ. See JUNIUS, FRANCISCUS

FRANCIS, Sir PHILIP (October 22, 1740-December 23, 1818), reputed author of *Letters of Junius* and political pamphleteer, was born in Dublin, and studied at St. Paul's School, London. Starting with a junior clerkship in the office of the Secretary of State in 1756, when he left school, he rose through a series of political positions to a principal clerkship in the War Office in 1762.

Lively controversies on constitutional questions were being carried on in the public press during the next few years, many of them arising out of the Wilkes case. Unable to resist taking part, in spite of his official position, Francis wrote an indeterminable number of letters and pamphlets signed with pseudonyms. From January 1769 to January 1772 the famous series of letters from "Junius" appeared, evidently written by someone with an intimate knowledge of events and personages in high places. Interest in the letters and their anonymous author was intense. Francis never acknowledged their authorship, but both internal evidence and his own behavior indicate that he was probably the writer.

In 1772 he resigned from his War Office position and took a continental tour. The next year he was appointed to the newly formed supreme council of Bengal. For the next ten years he waged a bitter and celebrated struggle with the governor-general, Warren Hastings, which culminated in a duel. Francis was wounded, but recovered and returned to England.

He was elected to Parliament in 1748, and worked unceasingly for Hastings' impeachment. When Hastings was acquitted, Francis gave up his dream of the governor-generalship, and, after being twice defeated for Parliament, retired to comparative obscurity.

In spite of his personal arrogance, vindictiveness, and occasional unscrupulousness, Francis was an able and liberal politician. He opposed slavery, advocated a constitutional government, sympathized with the aims of the French Revolution, and was one of the founders of the Society of the Friends of the People.

PRINCIPAL WORKS: Letters of Junius (?); Plan of a Reform in the Election of the House of Commons; Proceedings in Commons on the Slave Trade, 1796; Reflections on the Abundance of Paper in Circulation and the Scarcity of Specie, 1810; Historical Questions Exhibited, 1818.

ABOUT: Cordasco, F. Junius Bibliography; Forrest, G. W. Selections from the State Papers of India; Francis, B. and Keary, E. The Francis Letters; Parkes, J. and Merivale, H. Memoirs of Sir Philip Francis.

FRAUNCE, ABRAHAM (fl. 1587-1633), poet, was born in Shropshire and educated at Shrewsbury and at St. John's College, Cambridge. He was called to the bar in

1588, and practised law in the Welsh courts. During the five years from 1587 to 1592, he published a large body of writing which won respectful admiration from most of his fellow writers. He apparently spent the last several years of his life in the service of John Egerton, first Earl of Bridgewater, and confined his composition to epithalamia for the earl's daughters.

Fraunce was a leader of a movement to impose Latin forms on English poetry. All of his work is written in hexameters, which, while it seems an awkward and artificial form to the modern reader, was generally commended by Spenser, Gabriel Harvey, and other contemporaries including his patron, Sir Philip Sidney. Among those on the other side of the "battle of the hexameters" was Ben Jonson, who said bluntly, "Abram Francis in his English hexameters was a fool."

While still at Cambridge, Fraunce wrote a Latin metrical play, *Victoria*, based on the Italian prose play *Il Fedele* of Luigi Pasqualigo, to which he added an episode from the *Decameron*.

In 1587 he published an English version of the Latin poem *Amyntos* written by his close literary associate, Thomas Watson. The next year he wrote *The Lawyer's Logic* and the popular *Arcadian Rhetoric*, which, unlike most of the then fashionable rhetorics, used examples from modern as well as classical writings. The *Rhetoric* is noteworthy for containing quotations from the *Faerie Queene* by Fraunce's close friend Spenser, a year before that poem was published.

Under the sponsorship of Sidney's sister Mary, Countess of Pembroke, following Sidney's death, he wrote a series of short tales with the title *The Countess of Pembroke's Ivychurch*, with which he published translations of Tasso's *Aminta*, some of Virgil's *Ecologues*, a short portion of Heliodorus. In 1591 he published *The Countess of Pembroke's Emanuell*, a poem on the nativity and passion of Christ, with versions of several Psalms in hexameter.

PRINCIPAL WORKS: Victoria; Lamentations of Amintas (translation from the Latin of Thomas Watson) 1587; The Lawyer's Logic, 1588; Arcadian Rhetoric, 1588; The Countess of Pembroke's Ivychurch, 1591; The Countess of Pembroke's Emanuell, 1591; The Third Part of the Countess of Pembroke's Ivychurch, 1592.

ABOUT: Collier, W. F. History of English Literature; Cooper, C. H. Athenae Cantabrigienses; Grosart, A. B. Miscellanies of the Fuller Worthies Library; Smith, G. C. Moore, College Plays Performed in the University of Cambridge.

FULLER, THOMAS (June 1608-August 16, 1661), historian, religious writer, was born in Aldwinkle, Northamptonshire (Dryden's birthplace), the son of Thomas Fuller, rector of St. Peter's, and Judith Davenant, sister of the Bishop of Salisbury. He entered Queens' College, Cambridge (where his uncle had previously been president) in 1621, but failing to secure a fellowship transferred to Sidney Sussex College—where he was also unsuccessful, in spite of his uncle's influence. He received a B.A. 1625, M.A. 1628, B.D. 1635. He had been ordained in 1631, and his uncle immediately made him a prebend of Netherbury, Salisbury, and perpetual curate of St. Bene't's, Cambridge, then in 1634 rector of Broadwindsor, Dorset. (His father had meanwhile died, in 1632.) However, he remained for most of the time in Cambridge. With the civil wars, though he was not ousted from his positions, he abandoned them temporarily, and went to London, where he became a very popular preacher at the Savoy. Denounced by his fellow Royalists as being too "moderate" and unenthusiastic in the cause, he became chaplain to Sir Ralph Hopton's army. For most of the time before the Restoration he wandered from one Royalist estate to another, sometimes living in Oxford, and at one time in Exeter as chaplain to the new-born Princess Henrietta.

With the Restoration, he recovered his offices (though he left the intruder at Broadwindsor as curate), was made D.D. by royal edict, and became chaplain extraordinary to Charles II. His wit, amiability, and cheerfulness made him a popular figure, but he does not seem to have been able to make a living by his clerical offices. He was one of the first authors in England to earn his living by his pen. A contemporary describes him as "running around London with his big book under one arm and his little wife the other, recommending himself as a dinner guest by his facetious talk." The "big book," for which he was soliciting patrons for each section, was *The Worthies of England* (arranged by the shires in which they were

After D. Loggan

THOMAS FULLER

born), a monumental work which is today a mine of biographical information.

The "little wife" was not his first, whom he married around 1638 and who died in 1641 at the birth of his only child, a son. She was Mary Roper, sister of Viscount Baltinglas, whom he married in 1651; they had no children. Tall, heavy set and blond, usually rumpled and slovenly, absent minded but with a prodigious memory for names and facts, "Tom" Fuller is more of an eighteenth century "character" than a typical seventeenth century figure. He was no time server or truckler, but he was a mild man who disliked controversy, and who was almost Puritanical in his religious beliefs though he was whole-souledly for the king. Coleridge said that wit was "the sum and substance of Fuller's intellect," but it was a wit peculiar to its own time—an addiction to emblematic conceits that seem strange and far fetched today. He had remarkable narrative ability (*The Holy State and the Prophane State* is almost a volume of short stories), and if there had been such a thing in his day, he would surely have been an historical novelist or a writer of "fictionalized" biography. He was preaching when he was stricken with fever (probably typhus), and he was bled so heavily by the physicians that he died within a few hours. His heart was in his writing, and on his death-bed he asked for pen and ink. His verse is very bad, and he even promised in one of his books to write no more of it; but his prose has, as Coleridge said, beauty and variety, and beneath the extravagant conceits there is a born writer of stories.

PRINCIPAL WORKS: Davids Hainous Sinne (verse) 1631; The Historie of the Holy Warre [the Crusades] 1639; Josephs Party-Coloured Coat, 1640; The Holy State and the Prophane State, 1642; Truth Maintained, 1643; Good Thoughts in Bad Times, 1645; Andronicus, 1646; The Cause and Cure of a Wounded Conscience, 1647; Great Thoughts in Worse Times, 1649; A Pisgah-Sight of Palestine, 1650; The Church-Historie of Britain, 1655; The Appeal of Injured Innocence, 1659; Mixt Contemplations in Better Times, 1660; The Historie of the Worthies of England, 1662; Poems and Translations in Verse . . . [with] Unpublished Epigrams (A. B. Grosart, ed.) 1868; Collected Sermons (J. E. Bailey and W. E. Axon, eds.) 1891.

ABOUT: Bailey, J. E. The Life of Thomas Fuller; Broadus, E. K. Selections . . . with Introduction; Coleridge, S. T. Literary Remains; Fuller, M. Life and Writings of Thomas Fuller; Lamb, C. Specimens from the Writings of Fuller; Lyman, D. B. The Great Tom Fuller; Pepys, S. Diary; Rogers, H. An Essay on the Life and Genius of Thomas Fuller; Russell, A. Memorials of the Life and Works of Thomas Fuller; Tovey, D. C. Reviews and Essays in English Literature.

GAGER, WILLIAM (fl. 1580-1619), Latin dramatist, wrote for and defended the university theatre which flourished in the late sixteenth and early seventeenth centuries.

While still an undergraduate at Christ Church, Oxford, from 1574 to 1581, Gager proved to be a facile writer of Latin verse. In the ten years following he wrote four Latin plays which were successfully produced at the university.

Meleager was produced in 1581 for a distinguished audience including Sir Philip Sidney, whose *Exequies* Gager edited in 1587. In 1583 two of his plays, *Rivals*, a comedy, and *Dido*, a tragedy, were performed for the entertainment of the visiting prince palatine of Poland, Albert Alasco. The most successful of the four, *Ulysses Redux*, was performed in 1591.

Gager was a prolific writer, although only a small body of his work survives. The plays *Ulysses* and *Meleager* were printed at Oxford in 1591. A volume in the British Museum contains a miscellaneous collection of his writings, including Latin translations, verses and epigrams, excerpts from the otherwise lost *Dido*, parts of an unfinished play, *Oedipus*, and a Latin prose essay *In Praise of Eloquence*.

Dr. John Rainolds, of Queen's College and Corpus Christi, who had publicly denounced the theatre, was taken by a friend to the performance of *Ulysses Redux,* in which Gager satirized the Puritan arguments which Rainolds had used. A public correspondence between Gager and Rainolds resulted, in which Gager eloquently and convincingly defended the production of plays at universities. He was, however, contemptuous of the commercial theatre.

In 1608 Gager debated at Oxford on the positive side of the thesis, "That it is lawful for husbands to beat their wives."

From 1601 until his death in 1619, he held minor church positions, at first in the diocese of Ely where his friend, Martin Heton, was Bishop, and later as vicar-general to Bishop Andrews.

PRINCIPAL WORKS: Meleager, 1581; Rivals, 1583; Dido, 1583; Ulysses Redux, 1591.

ABOUT: Boas, F. A Defense of Oxford Plays and Players (Fortnightly Review, August 1907); Halliwell-Phillips, J. O. Dictionary of Old English Plays; Wood, A. à, Athenae Oxonienses.

GAIMAR, GEOFFREY (fl. 1140?), author of *Lestorie des Engles,* was probably a Norman living in Lincolnshire. His name may have been derived from that of a town near Caen, now named Gémare, which was called Gaimara in the twelfth century. It seems from evidence in his writings that he knew King Henry I and his queen, Adelaide of Louvain, and the king's illegitimate son, Robert, Earl of Gloucester. He wrote his only extant work at the request of Custance, wife of Ralf Fitzgilbert, who was probably an illegitimate member of the family of Gilbert of Ghent, the Earl of Lincoln.

An early work of Gaimar's has been lost, although there are numerous references to it in his later history. This was a translation into Anglo-Norman verse of a *History of the Kings of Britain,* written by Geoffrey of Monmouth, which purported to be based on secret records which had been made available to him alone by Walter, Archdeacon of Oxford. Actually, the work was largely an imaginary history, an attempt to create a romantic past for England.

Gaimar's *Lestorie des Engles* was a history in French verse of England from the period following King Arthur to the death of William II. It was based chiefly on the *Anglo-Saxon Chronicle,* although there are

errors due to mistranslation, and deliberate interpolations. Two of the latter have to do with the history of the East Anglian section where Gaimar lived. One is an account of a hero named Hereward, for which there is some historic evidence, although this version differs from others. The second is the recounting of a mythical story of a kingdom founded in East Anglia by Havelock the Dane.

While the section of *Lestorie des Engles* which deals with the reign of William II is told from personal knowledge, there are chronological errors in it which cast some doubt on the validity of other details. Its chief value lies in its description of social manners and customs.

PRINCIPAL WORK: Lestorie des Engles.

ABOUT: Freeman, E. A. History of the Norman Conquest; Petrie, H. Materials for the History of Britain; Wright, T. History of Domestic Manners and Sentiments in England, and Biographies of Literary Characters of Britain.

GARRICK, DAVID (February 19, 1717-January 20, 1779), actor, dramatist, was born in Hereford, the third son of Peter Garric, an army captain on recruiting service in the town, and of Arabella Clough, of Irish descent and daughter of a choral vicar in Lichfield Cathedral. The family name, originally de la Garrique, suggested its Huguenot origin three generations back. Garrick was reared in Lichfield and educated at Lichfield Grammar School. His first appearance as an amateur actor was at eleven. He was sent to an uncle in Lisbon to learn the wine business, but soon returned. Then his father, back from service in Gibraltar, sent him and his brother, in 1736, as the first pupils of the "academy" started in Lichfield by Samuel Johnson.[qv] The school died in six months, and teacher and pupil together set out for London. Garrick was entered in Lincoln's Inn, lived for a while in Rochester with John Colson, the mathematician, then through legacies from his father, mother, and uncle (all of whom died within the year) was able to open a wine business with his brother Peter in London.

Unfortunately for the business, his heart was entirely with the theatre. He began trying his hand at writing plays, did amateur acting, appeared professionally for the first time at Ipswich in 1741, and suddenly burst into glory as Richard III in the authorized theatre in Goodman's Fields. The wine business failed and his brother was outraged, but "Garrick fever" swept the town. It swept Garrick into Drury Lane, then to Dublin with the famous Peg Woffington, long his mistress, and finally, in 1748, to joint management of Drury Lane. In 1749 (he had quarreled with Mrs. Woffington meanwhile) he married Eva Maria Violetti (real name Veigel), an Austrian dancer. Thenceforward they were never separated; the marriage, though childless, was supremely happy. From 1763 to 1765 the Garricks were in France and Italy for their health, feted by all the great from Diderot to Beaumarchais; otherwise his life was a long succession of successes as an actor, minor successes as a playwright, money-making (he left £100,-000), and quarrels with fellow actors. He was one of the founders of the celebrated Literary Club, and a close friend of many of its noted members—Johnson, Goldsmith, Reynolds, above all Burke. In 1776 he appeared on the stage for the last time, and sold his lease of Drury Lane to Richard Brinsley Sheridan,*qv* retaining some interest. He died in his house in Adelphi Terrace, of a combination of gout, stone, and shingles, and was buried at the foot of Shakespeare's statue in Westminster Abbey—the last actor to be buried there. His widow joined him there in 1822, at the age of ninety-eight.

(His brother George, his invaluable assistant in the theatre, died a few days after him.)

Below average height, with a mobile face and flashing eyes, "little Garrick" was the first of the natural, realistic actors in England. Pope said he never had had his equal and would never have a rival. He had his faults—he was hot-tempered, vain, a poor loser; but he was not (as he was accused of being) mean or stingy; he was prudent, but quietly very generous. As a writer, the best that can be said of him is that he was sprightly and had an instinctive knowledge of "good theatre." It is thanks to Garrick that Shakespeare returned to popularity after a century of near-oblivion — though his "adaptations" of Shakespeare's plays were most unfortunate. In 1769 he organized a huge Shakespeare Festival at Stratford-on-Avon. Mercurial, witty, ebullient, his real literary gifts came out rather in his brilliant private letters than in his plays. Primarily he was an actor—the greatest of his time.

PRINCIPAL WORKS: *Plays*—The Lying Valet, 1742; Lethe, 1745; Miss in Her Teens, 1747; Lilliput, 1757; The Male-Coquette, 1757; The Guardian, 1759; The Enchanter, 1760; The Farmer's Return from London, 1762; The Clandestine Marriage (with Colman, G. [the elder]) 1766; Neck or Nothing, 1766; Cymon, 1767; A Peep Behind the Curtain, 1767; The Irish Widow, 1772; A Christmas Tale, 1774; Bon Ton, 1775; May-Day, and The Theatrical Candidates, 1775; Dramatic Works, 1768. *Miscellaneous* — An Ode upon Dedicating a Building . . . to Shakespeare, 1769; Poetical Works, 1785; Private Correspondence, 1831-32; Some Unpublished Correspondence (G. P. Baker, ed.) 1907.

ABOUT: Baker, G. P. Introduction, Some Unpublished Correspondence; Barton, M. Garrick; Davies, T. Memoirs of the Life of David Garrick, Esq.; Fitzgerald, P. H. The Life of David Garrick; Goldsmith, O. Retaliation; Knight, J. David Garrick; Martin, T. Monographs (includes Fitzgerald's Life); Murphy, A. The Life of David Garrick, Esq.; Parsons, F. M. Garrick and His Circle; Stein, E. P. David Garrick, Dramatist.

GARTH, Sir SAMUEL (1661-January 18, 1719), poet, physician, was the eldest son of a Yorkshire landowner. He received his early schooling at Ingleton in Yorkshire and entered Peterhouse College, Cambridge, in 1676. He obtained his B.A. there in 1679 and his M.A. in 1684. In 1687 he went to Leyden to study medicine; later he returned to Cambridge and received his M.D., 1691. Elected a Fellow of the Royal College of Physicians, London, in 1693, he became a Censor of the College, 1702.

R. E. Pine

DAVID GARRICK

His chief work, a burlesque poem entitled *The Dispensary*, humorously recounts the College's efforts to set up a dispensary for the poor of London against the determined opposition of the apothecaries, who refused to supply medicines cheaply, though the physicians gave their services free. All the leading men on both sides of the controversy appear in the poem under fictitious names and fight an epic but indecisive battle. *The Dispensary* went through ten editions in a little over forty years.

Garth's politics were Whig and he was the friend and physician of the leading men in his party, becoming a member of the famous Kit-cat Club. At the accession of George I (1714), the Whigs regained power and Garth was appointed Physician-in-Ordinary to the King and Physician-General to the Army. He was knighted the same year. Until his death in 1719 he continued to write verse and to increase his lucrative medical practice. He left one child, a daughter, and was buried beside his wife at Harrow.

Garth, though not a very distinguished poet, loved literature. He admired Dryden and encouraged Pope—Tories and Catholics both—besides being a close friend of his fellow Whigs Addison and Steele. Jovial, fond of good living, a freethinker, by his charity and concern for the poor he won the admiration of many devout Christians.

PRINCIPAL WORKS: The Dispensary, 1699; A Poem to the Earl of Godolphin, 1710; A Prologue for the 4th of November, 1711; A Poem upon His Majesty's Accession, 1714; Claremont, 1715; Ovid's Metamorphoses (ed.) 1717. Collected Poems in Johnson's, Anderson's and Chalmers' editions.

ABOUT: Bond, R. P. English Burlesque Poetry 1700-1750; Johnson, S. Lives of the Poets.

GASCOIGNE, GEORGE (1525?-October 7, 1577), pioneer in various branches of literature, plays, poems, critical essays, was the eldest son of Sir John Gascoigne and Margaret Scargill, and was related to Sir Martin Frobisher. He was born between 1525 and 1535 at Cardington, Bedfordshire. He left Trinity College, Cambridge, without a degree, and at some time before 1548 was entered in the Middle Temple. He was never called to the bar, but led a notoriously wild life, recklessly extravagant, dissipated, and frequently in prison for debt. His father finally disinherited him of all his patrimony which he had not already sold by post obits.

In spite of this, he served in Parliament from 1557 to 1559, sitting for Bedfordshire. With the excuse of being unsettled by "an early disappointment in love," the young man wandered around England and France during most of the 1560's; it was on one of his aimless journeys that he met Lord Grey de Wilton, who later was his chief patron. His first writing was the poem, the *Complaynt of Philomene*, which he wrote in 1562 during one of these journeys, but which was not published until *The Stele Glas* came out in 1576. His first appearance in print was with a sonnet published in 1566.

Somewhere around 1568, to recoup his fortune, Gascoigne married a wealthy widow, Elizabeth (Bacon) Breton, thus becoming the stepfather of the poet Nicholas Breton [qv] and her three other children; he himself had none. He soon spent her fortune, salvaging only the house in Walthamstowe, which was his home thenceforth. When in 1572 he was elected to Parliament for Midhurst, his creditors kept him from sitting by accusing him not only of debt, but also of manslaughter, atheism, and of being "a common rymer and a deviser of slanderous pasquils." Instead of going to Parliament he went to Holland, to fight against the Spaniards with the army of the Prince of Orange; known there as "the Green Knight," he got into trouble by his command of languages and easy manners, was accused of treachery but exonerated; joining an English reinforcement, he was captured by the enemy but released in four months. He returned to England in 1574.

In his absence, a volume of his poems and prose pieces had been published without his authority; he therefore brought out a revised volume under his own name (or initials) in 1575. He was constantly in hot water for allegedly attacking well-known persons in his writings, but was sufficiently in favor to have been one of those chosen by Leicester to write masques and "entertainments" for Queen Elizabeth when she visited Kenilworth in 1575. One of his poems, which he had written in four languages, was stolen by Abraham Fleming and published as his own in 1579. Gascoigne by this time was an invalid, thanks to the hardships of his service in Holland but still more to the excesses of his early life, and he cer-

After R. Hudson

GEORGE GASCOIGNE

ainly was not, as claimed, at the Siege of Antwerp in 1576. He died while on a visit to George Whetstone, in Stamford, Lincolnshire.

This not very edifying person was one of the great pioneers in English literature. His *Supposes* is the first extant prose comedy in English, his *Jocasta* is the second earliest blank verse tragedy, his *Stele Glas* is the first verse satire, and his *Certayne notes of instruction concerning the making of verse or ryme in English* (included in *The Posies*) is both the earliest English critical essay and the earliest writing on English prosody. He himself took Chaucer for his master, and his verse has a smoothness and sweetness that reflect those of the great poet. For a while he was extremely popular, and his poems appeared regularly in such anthologies as *The Paradise of Daintie Devices* and *Englands Parnassus*, while he was commended for his "gifts of wit and natural promptness" (W. Webbe) ; but he soon fell into desuetude and was practically forgotten. His only original play was *A Glasse of Government*; *Jocasta* is from Ludovico Dolce and *The Supposes* from Ariosto. *The Droomme of Doomes-day* is taken from Pope Innocent III, while *A Delicate Diet for daintie-mouthde Droonkardes* is from St. Austine. Nevertheless, whether by chance or design,

Gascoigne was the founder of half a dozen varieties of writing in English.

PRINCIPAL WORKS: The Supposes (play) 1566; Jocasta (with F. Kinwelmersh) 1568; A hundreth Sundrie Flowres bound up in one small Poesie, 1572; The Posies of G. G., Esq. (including Certayne notes of instruction, A Discourse of the Adventures of Master F. J., Don Bartholomew of Bath) 1575; A Glasse of Government (play) 1575; The Princelie Pleasures at the Courte of Kenelwoorth (with others) 1576; The Stele Glas, with The Complaynt of Philomene, 1576; The Droomme of Doomes-day, 1576; A Delicate Diet for daintiemouthde Droonkardes, 1576; Whole Works of G. G. (A. Jebbes, ed.) (including The Fruites of Warres and Gascoignes voyage into Holland) 1587; Complete Poems (W. Hazlitt, ed.) 1868-69; Complete Works (including The Tale of Hemetes the heremyte) (J. W. Cunliffe, ed.) 1907-10.

ABOUT: Hazlitt, W. Memoir, *in* Complete Poems; Herford, C. H. Studies in the Literary Relations of England and Germany in the Sixteenth Century; Prouty, C. T. George Gascoigne, Elizabethan Courtier, Soldier, and Poet; Schelling, F. E. The Life and Writings of George Gascoigne.

GAUDEN, JOHN (1605-September 20, 1662), bishop, presumably author of the *Eikon Basilike* which purported to be the meditations of King Charles I, was born at Mayland, Essex, where his father was a vicar. He was educated at Bury St. Edmunds and St. John's College, Cambridge. When he was about twenty-five he went to Oxford as tutor to the two sons of Sir William Russell and ten years later was appointed vicar of Chippenham.

Even against the sharply contrasting patterns of religious and political events during the reigns of the first and second Charles, Gauden's life and character appear as oddly ambiguous. A chaplain to Robert Rich, the second Earl of Warwick, he seems to have shared the earl's sympathies with the parliamentary party although he was a friend of Charles I; and as a holder of a number of preferments, including the deanery of Bocking in Essex, he conformed to the Presbyterian movement even while he published books on behalf of the Church of England. Shortly before the civil war he preached to the House of Commons; yet in his later writings he attacked Cromwell and pled the cause of the king.

Most curious of all the controversial aspects of his life and work is his supposed authorship of the *Eikon Basilike, The Portraicture of His Sacred Majestie in His Solitudes and Sufferings*, which was published at the time of the execution of

211

Charles I as the work of the unfortunate king. Quite understandably the book went through forty-seven editions and caused a tremendous stir. After the Restoration, when Gauden was made chaplain to Charles II and bishop of Exeter, he complained to the Earl of Clarendon about the poverty of the see allotted to him and asked for the bishopric of Winchester as a reward for some secret service to the crown, presumably the invention of the *Eikon.*

Gauden's claim to authorship was apparently admitted at the time by Clarendon and others, but controversy raged around the book for many years. Some witnesses claimed to have seen the manuscript in the king's handwriting; others claimed to have been consulted by Gauden while he was engaged in its composition. The accounts of Mrs. Gauden Anthony Walker (his curate) and Gauden himself, while contradictory in many aspects, agree that Gauden sent the manuscript to Charles I for approval during his imprisonment; and both internal and external evidence gives strong support to Gauden's authorship.

Whatever the truth of its origin, the *Eikon* became famous both on its own merits and on account of the answers it provoked, including Milton's attack in *Iconoclasts.* The work is a masterpiece in its expression of Charles' principles, personal feeling, and prejudices, and by making a martyr of this Stuart king, exercised a considerable influence on English history.

PRINCIPAL WORKS: The Love of Truth and Peace, 1641; Three Sermons Preached upon Severall Publicke Occasions, 1642; Eikon Basilike, The Portraiture of His Sacred Majestie in His Solitudes and Sufferings, 1649; The Case of Ministers Maintenance by Tithes, Plainly Discussed in Conscience and Prudence, 1653; Ecclesiae Anglicanae Suspiria, or the Tears, Sighs, Complaints of the Church of England, 1659; Cromwell's Bloody Slaughter-House: or his Damnable Designs in Contriving the Murther of His Sacred Majestie, King Charles I Discovered, 1660; Anti-Baal-Berith, or The Binding of the Covenant and All Covenanters to Their Good Behavior, 1661.

ABOUT: Wood, A. à, Athenae Oxonienses; Wordsworth, C. Who Wrote Eikon Basilike?

GAY, JOHN (September 1685-December 4, 1732), dramatist, poet, balladist, was born in Barnstaple, Devonshire, of an impoverished family. His father, William Gay, died when the boy was ten; his mother had died the year before. He was reared by his paternal uncle, Thomas Gay, who, after sending him to the Free Grammar School of Barnstaple, could think of nothing better to do with him than apprentice him to a silk mercer in London. That did not last long for a boy whose head was full of dreams and whose hands were congenitally idle; he left his apprenticeship and went back to Barnstaple, where he lived for a while with a paternal uncle, Reverend John Hanmer, a dissenting minister, before returning to London on his own—presumably as soon as he attained his majority. Just how he lived is not known—perhaps it was then that he acquired the knowledge of the ways of the underworld put to use in *The Beggar's Opera,* but more probably he was living on the Bohemian fringes of the literary world and beginning his long siege to secure attention at court.

The writers Eustace Budgell and Aaron Hill took an interest in him, and he may for a while have served as quasi-secretary to the latter. His first publication, a blank verse production in praise of wine-drinking, did nothing to help him financially; neither did his contribution of a translation from Ovid to Lintot's *Miscellany* of 1712, though it gained him the acquaintance of his great model, Pope, who had been represented in it by his famous *Rape of the Lock.* By the offices of friends he was appointed domestic steward to the Duchess of Monmouth, widow of the duke executed in 1685. Gay paid very little attention to the duties of his office, and was summarily dismissed in 1714. By this time both Pope and Swift had become his close friends, and Swift had him appointed secretary to Lord Clarendon, who was going to Hanover as English envoy extraordinary. The death of Queen Anne caused Clarendon's recall and ended Gay's position. For a while he lived with Pope at Binfield and with Lord Burlington in his native Devonshire; in 1717 he was with William Poultney (later the Earl of Bath) at Aix, and in 1718 with Lord Harcourt at Nuneham. For the remainder of his life he lived as a sort of half-guest, half-retainer with various patrons.

Meanwhile he was enabled to bring out a book of poems by subscription in 1720; his mock pastoral, *The Shepherd's Week,* and his *Trivia* had spread his fame; and he ctually was possessed at one time of £20,-00—all of which he promptly lost by speculation in the notorious South Sea Bubble. The disappointment threw him into actual Illness, and it is from this time that he seems to have held the fixed idea that the court owed him recognition and a living. Just why, it is hard to understand, except that George I and II were both generous patrons of authors. He did have a sinecure post as lottery commissioner from 1722 to 1731, and was given lodgings in Whitehall from 1722 to 1729, but this was far from enough. When in 1727 he was named gentleman usher to a three-year-old princess he was deeply offended, declined immediately, and thereafter made no efforts to secure court benefactions.

Meanwhile his last and most devoted patrons, the Duke and Duchess of Queensberry, had taken him in hand. For the rest of his life Gay lived with them, the duke saved his money for him (so that he was able to leave £6,000 to his two sisters), and the duchess managed his personal life. He died suddenly of "an inflammatory fever," at forty-seven, and was buried in Westminster Abbey, where the loyal Queensberrys erected a monument, bearing an epitaph by Pope followed by Gay's own lines:

Life is a jest, and all things show it.
I thought so once, and now I know it.

This admittedly lazy and idle man, constantly complaining of his lot, a "gentle parasite," amiable and compliant, was almost the only friend with whom neither of those difficult characters, Pope and Swift, ever quarreled. Swift called him "a most refractory, honest, good-natured man." Congreve and Arbuthnot qqv were his constant friends, Arbuthnot his physician as well. Everybody seems to have liked him—except Walpole, who managed to have the sequel to The Beggar's Opera barred from the stage, and was probably behind the dismissal from court of the Duchess of Queensberry for soliciting subscriptions for its publication. This, however, was part of a political controversy; Gay, so far as he had any politics at all, was a Tory, like his friends. He summed his own nature up in his Fables, when he spoke of

The hare who in a civil way
Complies with everything, like Gay—

and it is significant that the quotation most familiar from all his work is the phrase, "while there's life, there's hope." He was hardly an admirable man, but fundamentally an amiable, harmless sycophant.

The first of Gay's writings to have any real merit was The Shepherd's Week, which started as a parody on Ambrose Phillips,qv but ended by being entertaining in its own right—though Swift remarked dryly (of Rural Sports, but it was equally true of The Shepherd's Week) that this "pastoral" poet did not know rye from barley! The What d'ye Call It was, like The Rehearsal, a burlesque of current plays; it earned Gay the loss of the friendship of Steele,qv to whose Guardian he had been a contributor, but who was among the butts of his wit. Trivia is perhaps Gay's most notable poem, not only for its dry humor but for its antiquarian interest. His worst work is undoubtedly the scabrous Three Hours after Marriage, which had the collaboration of Pope and Arbuthnot. But of course to moderns Gay is primarily the author of The Beggar's Opera, the first popular hit on the English stage after the Restoration dramatists. It is still revived occasionally, and its wit, its social satire, its rousing ballads, and its charm are still fresh. It became the rage

After C. F. Zincke

JOHN GAY

in London, went to the provinces and even to the colonies, and everywhere there were plaudits for the delightful Polly Peachum, the heroine; the unknown actress who first played the part was catapulted into fame and finally into marriage to a peer. Unfortunately the sequel, *Polly*, was, as related, kept from the stage. The other of Gay's works which deserves special mention is the *Fables in Verse*, written for one of the child princes. Far inferior to La Fontaine, loosely and colloquially constructed, they are nevertheless the best of their kind in English verse, and have been much translated. Some of Gay's songs, notably "Black-eyed Susan," have also had a lasting life. This "spoiled child," "pliant parasite," and "king of idlers" nevertheless left a substantial legacy to posterity.

PRINCIPAL WORKS: *Poems*—Wine, 1708; The Fan, 1713; Rural Sports, 1713; The Shepherd's Week, 1714; Epistle to a Lady, 1714; A Journey to Exeter, 1715; Trivia, or The Art of Walking the Streets of London, 1716; Poems on Several Occasions, 1720; An Epistle to the Duchess of Marlborough, 1722; Fifty-one Fables in Verse, 1727-28; Gay's Chair (H. Lee, ed.) 1820; Poetical Works (J. C. Faber, ed.) 1926. *Plays* (dates of publication)—The Mohocks, 1712; The Wife of Bath, 1713; The What D'ye Call It, 1715; Three Hours After Marriage (with A. Pope and J. Arbuthnot) 1717; The Captives (tragedy) 1724; The Beggar's Opera, 1728; Polly (sequel) 1729; Acis and Galatea (opera, music by Handel) 1732; Achilles (opera) 1733; The Distressed Wife, 1743; The Rehearsal at Goatham, 1754. *General*—Works, 1770; Poetical, Dramatic, and Miscellaneous Works, 1793.

ABOUT: Baller, J. Biographical Sketch, *in* Gay's Chair; Benjamin, L. S. Life and Letters of John Gay; Cade, W. Life of Gay; Gaye, P. F. John Gay, His Place in the 18th Century; Hazlitt, W. Lectures on the English Poets; Irving, W. H. John Gay, Favorite of the Wits; Melville, L. Life and Letters of John Gay; Sherwin, O. Mr. Gay; Thackeray, W. M. English Humourists of the 18th Century.

GEOFFREY of MONMOUTH (1100?-1154),

historical chronicler, received his appellation either from his birth in Monmouth or from his being educated at the Benedictine priory there. It is possible that he was of Breton descent (the priory was founded by Bretons), but much more likely that he was Welsh. His father's name (significantly enough) was Arthur, and he himself signed his name Geoffrey Arthur or Gaufridus Arturus. Probably he himself was a monk. He was reared by his uncle, who was first archdeacon and then bishop of Llandaff, Glamorgan, Wales; but his great patron was Robert, Earl of Gloucester. Geoffrey father, Arthur, is said to have been "famil priest" of Robert's father.

About 1140 Geoffrey himself becam archdeacon of Llandaff, succeeding his uncl who had been made bishop. In 1147 or 114 both his uncle and his patron died, and h came under the patronage of the Bishop o Lincoln. He claimed also to have engage the interest of King Stephen. Through th influence he was named bishop of St. Asaph Wales, in 1152—though he was ordaine priest, at Westminster, only a short tim before that. Geoffrey never saw his see though his exact birth date is not known, h was by this time an old man by twelfth cen tury standards, and he remained in Llandaff Here he died suddenly, according to som accounts while he was celebrating mass.

Geoffrey might more properly be terme not an historical chronicler but a writer o romance. His principal work, the *Histor of the Kings of Britain*, he claimed to b founded on a mysterious secret book i Cymric which he said was given him b Walter (Calenius), archdeacon of Oxford There was such a man, and Geoffrey wit nessed a charter with him at Oxford in 1129 Whether there ever was such a book is an other question; no one ever saw it, and the great probability is that Geoffrey, shrewd man, realized the great public appe tite for knightly romances, realized also what it would mean for the English to have their own hero as the French had Charle magne; and from Bede, Nennius, and othe chroniclers, plus floating popular legends an perhaps some shreds of Cymric writings constructed what is now known as the Ar thurian Cycle.

Actually, only three of Geoffrey's twelv books deal with Arthur. Nevertheless, i them is contained all that later writers wer to know about the exploits of this probably mythical British King and his Round Table In the book Geoffrey also incorporated th *Prophecies of Merlin*, translated into Latii from the Cymric. It is also the source fo the stories of Lear and Cymbeline and fo many others used by Wace in the *Roma de Brut*; by Layamon; in the earliest Eng lish tragedy *Gorbuduc* (1565); by Shakes peare, Spenser, Milton, and even Words worth. As early as 1148 Geoffrey had been translated into Anglo-Norman verse. He did not lack contemporary opponents, principally William of Newburgh, who said he "cloaked fables about Arthur under the honest name of history." Nevertheless, the so-called *History* has been rightly called "the most significant literary product of the twelfth century." The *Life of Merlin* (in Latin) formerly attributed to him is thought by modern scholars not to be his—on the ground that it is too well written. Geoffrey had culture, and charm of manner, but he was a faulty scholar, and his "prose epic" is stiffly and clumsily written.

PRINCIPAL WORKS: Historia Regum Britanniae (Historia Britonum), c. 1139 (first printing 1508; J. A. Giles, ed., 1844; S. Evans, tr., 1903; L. Paton, tr., 1912).

ABOUT: Chambers, E. K. Arthur of Britain; Fletcher, R. H. The Arthurian Material in the Chronicles; Keeler, L. Geoffrey of Monmouth and the Late Latin Chroniclers; Warton, T. History of English Poetry.

1587

JOHN GERARD

GERARD, JOHN (1545-February 1612), herbalist, was born in Nantwich, Cheshire, and educated at Williston (Wisterson), where he studied medicine. He traveled in Scandinavia and Russia, and perhaps in the Mediterranean countries as well. In 1562 he was apprenticed to Alexander Mason, a London surgeon, and in 1569 he became a freeman of the Barber Surgeons' Company. Although once he was called before the company to answer a complaint, he rose high in its ranks; he was a member of the court of assistants, junior warden, twice an examiner of candidates, and in 1607 became master. His reputation as a herbalist grew after he became superintendent of the gardens of Lord Burghley, both in London (where rich men then could have large gardens) and in Hertfordshire, and later he became "herbarist" to James I. One of his projects, which failed of success, was a herbal garden to be constructed by the Barber Surgeons' Company itself under his supervision; but his own garden in Holburn was a sort of unofficial substitute.

In 1596 he issued a Latin catalogue of this garden, and the following year he brought out his *Herball*. This was scarcely an original work, since it was directly based on the *Stirpium historiae pemptades* of the Dutch botanist, Rembert Dodoens (1583),

and its woodcut illustrations were borrowed from the *Icones plantarum* of Jacob Theodor Bergzabern (Tabernaemontanus), published in 1590. However, Gerard did not merely translate Dodoens; he paraphrased him and added his own remarks, adapting the book to English climate and conditions.

The book has no particular literary merit, but it is a mine of useful information on the condition of botany and of gardening in the sixteenth century. Gerard's aim was strictly scientific, but he swallowed quite a bit of folklore and botanical superstition, which makes his book all the more valuable to later students. (It is interesting also to observe that in his day what we would now call a landscape gardener was master of the guild or company which included both surgeons and barbers.) He was undoubtedly a good practical gardener, who knew everything that was to be known in his own time about the then rudimentary science of botany. The great Linnaeus thought sufficiently highly of him to name in his honor the (chiefly American) flowering plant Gerardia.

PRINCIPAL WORKS: Catalogum arborum, fruticum, ac plantarum . . . in horto Ionnis Gerardi, 1596 (B. D. Jackson, tr., 1876); The Herball, or generall historie of plantes, 1597 (T. Johnson, revised and enlarged, 1633).

ABOUT: Jackson, B. D. Life in Catalogue, 1876; Johnson, T., Preface, Herball, 1633; Woodward, M. Gerard's Herball, the Essence Thereof Distilled.

GIBBON, EDWARD (April 27, 1734-January 16, 1794), historian, was born in Putney-on-Thames, in a Kentish family related to the ancestors of another historian, Lord Acton. His father was Edward Gibbon, a Member of Parliament and London alderman, his mother Judith Porten. All five of his brothers were named Edward after their father, to insure a namesake and heir, but every one of them, and his sister, died in infancy. Edward himself was a sickly child, precocious (especially in arithmetic) but often unable to attend school. What schooling he had was first at Kingston and then at Westminster, where during his sporadic attendance he was beaten and bullied.

His invalid mother had died in 1747, and his father moved to Buriton, near Petersfield, Hampshire; the boy's later school years were spent in the charge of his maternal grandmother and his aunt, Catherine Porten, who even opened a boardinghouse at Westminster so that he could attend school there, after her father had become bankrupt. He was deprived of normal family life and thrown upon his own inner resources. In a sense he was self-educated, for he read omnivorously, especially in history, and when he was entered at Magdalen College, Oxford, in 1752, he combined a remarkable fund of knowledge with great gaps of ignorance. The nineteen months he spent in Oxford were sheer waste of time. Always interested in religion (though without much emotional attachment) he was easily converted to Roman Catholicism at Oxford, and joined the church in 1753, when he was only nineteen. His outraged father immediately removed him from the university and after an abortive attempt to change his mind at home, sent him to Lausanne, Switzerland, to live with a Calvinist minister, Pavillard.

The object was accomplished, and within a year Gibbon was a Protestant again. He adopted French as his second language, with subsequent effects on his English style. He engaged himself to Suzanne Curchod, daughter of a Swiss Protestant pastor, and in 1758 returned to England to secure his father's consent to their marriage—for though he had attained his majority he was entirely dependent on his father for his living. Edward Gibbon, Sr., promptly opposed the marriage, and his son, an indifferent lover, as promptly

H. Walton
EDWARD GIBBON

abandoned the whole idea. Suzanne waited five years for him; when he returned to Lausanne in 1763 he treated her with such studied coldness that they parted in anger. Subsequently she became Mme. Necker, wife of the famous French minister of finance, and still later the mother of the future Mme. de Staël. Eventually she and Gibbon became cool friends again, and he even visited the Neckers in Paris. He never showed an interest again in any woman.

Meanwhile, back in England, both he and his father had become officers in the Hampshire militia, and during the war with France he was in active service, though he was never sent abroad. By the time the militia was abandoned he was a colonel. Already he had determined to devote his life to the writing of history, but during these years he had little time for serious study or writing. For a long while he hesitated among various subjects, beginning and abandoning a history of Swiss liberty and other projects. Finally he settled on what was at first to be a history of Rome, the city, itself. In 1763 he returned to the Continent, spent a year in archaeological research, and finally reached Italy. On June 15, 1764, "musing amidst the ruins of the Capitol," he came upon the developed idea. From then until the equally momentous date of June 27, 1787, when he took "everlasting leave of an old and agreeable companion," the life of Edward Gibbon was the life of *The Decline and Fall of the Roman Empire.*

However, he also had to live. He had in 1758 found his father newly remarried, to Dorothea Patton, who became almost a second mother to him; in 1770 the father died, leaving his fortune impaired and his affairs in confusion, so that Gibbon had to spend much time in untangling them. In 1772 he left Buriton and established himself in London, two years later securing a seat in Parliament for Liskeard, Cornwall. He was a completely silent member, who voted consistently for Lord North's administration—in other words, for the Tories who lost England her American colonies. He lost his seat in 1781, but was then elected for Lymington. In 1779 he had his reward, in the sinecure office of commissioner of trade and plantations, but in 1782 North fell, and Burke immediately abolished the office. (Gibbon and Burke were fellow members of the famous Club, but there was no love lost between them.) He tried vainly to be appointed secretary to the British embassy in Paris, and finally in 1783 went back to Lausanne, this time to live with his devoted friend Georges Deyverdun. He did not see England again until the final completion of his great work, when he spent 1788 in his native land. The following year Deyverdun died, but Gibbon continued to live in Switzerland until 1791, when his other close friend, J. B. Holroyd (later Lord Sheffield) persuaded him, in view of his failing health, to return home. For the remainder of his life, he lived with Holroyd either in London or in Essex, died in his home, and was buried in his family graveyard.

To return to *The Decline and Fall*, the first volume, issued in 1776, was a sensational success. Gibbon found himself at once generously admitted to the ranks of important historians by their recognized leaders, David Hume and William Robertson.[qqv] He anticipated controversy, but when it came it was based chiefly on the celebrated fifteenth and sixteenth chapters, dealing with the origin of Christianity. These partisan religious attacks Gibbon ignored, but when H. E. Davies, in 1778, accused him of inaccuracy and plagiarism—that is, censured him as an historian—he replied with his

Vindication, and as further justification of his work decided to go on and include the history of the Eastern as well as the Western Empire.

When the six great volumes of the completed work were finally published, Gibbon knew that he had neither the time nor the energy for any further major book, and thenceforth devoted himself only to minor "historical excursions" and to the writing of his unfinished autobiographical memoirs. These, with his early French book on literature; a government-inspired protest (in French) against French help to the Americans in the American Revolution; and his acute and charming private letters, make up the sum of Gibbon's writing. He is really in essence a man of one book, but of a book which might well take up any man's lifetime.

Little Gibbon, with his big head, his ugly face, his grossly obese body, and his affectations of speech and manner, nevertheless led a full social life and was the darling of salons both in London and in Paris. Boswell hated him, and called him "ugly" and "disgusting," but that was partly the typical Boswellian jealousy. Though Gibbon could never be described as lovable, and was the least emotional of men, he was a devoted son and nephew and a loyal and constant friend. It is true that he looked on government office primarily as a source of income, but according to his lights he was a good patriot. But in more than one way he was like an iceberg—90 per cent of his being was submerged in the ocean of history. As the Duke of Gloucester so grotesquely commented, it was "always scribble, scribble, scribble" to produce "another damned thick book."

The Decline and Fall, in Horace's phrase, is assuredly "more lasting than bronze." Time has marked it, and later researches have invalidated many of its conclusions, but it remains an everlasting monument. The great orotund periods of eighteenth century prose (in Gibbon's case rendered still more "classic" by his intimate feeling for French) are admirably suited to the grandeur and dignity of his subject. It is history in the grand style, but it can be exciting as well as noble. Indeed, few books have been more admirably fitted to the period of their composition; not only was Gibbon's lifetime, as Hume said, "an historical age," but there is a close affinity between the *Zeitgeist* of Rome under the Empire and of England in the eighteenth century: not for nothing has this been dubbed the Augustan Age. When the Royal Historical Society commemorated the centennial of Gibbon's death in 1894, it was paying tribute to one of the greatest of historians.

Gibbon left numerous unpublished manuscripts, many of which are still unprinted, in the British Museum. His various attempts at autobiography were carefully and efficiently pieced together by Lord Sheffield, and the man and his work may be seen as a consistent whole. As surely as Robert Browning determined in boyhood to give his life to poetry, so did Edward Gibbon determine to devote his to history. His conscientious research, his multitudinous preliminary synopses, his serious classical studies, were all shaped to the single end of one great, enduring work. For nearly twenty years, a third of his lifetime, he trod one long, purposeful road to an exact goal. By mental bent and by temperament he was born to record history. It is therefore a benefaction but no marvel that the end-product was the most magnificent single historical work in the English tongue.

PRINCIPAL WORKS: Critical Observations on the Sixth Book of the Aeneid, 1770; The Decline and Fall of the Roman Empire (6 vols.) 1776-88; Mémoire justicatif, 1779; A Vindication of some Passages in the 15th and 16th Chapters, 1779; Memoirs of my Life and Writings (J. B. Holroyd [Lord Sheffield] ed.) 1796; Miscellaneous Works (J. B. Holroyd, ed.) 1796-1814; Antiquities of the House of Brunswick, 1814; Private Letters of Edward Gibbon (R. E. Prothero, ed.) 1896.

ABOUT: Bagehot, W. Estimates of Some Englishmen and Scotchmen; Black, J. B. The Art of History; Cecil, A. Six Oxford Thinkers; Dawson, C. H. Edward Gibbon; Gibbon, E. Memoirs of my Life and Writings; Hawkes, C. P. Authors-at-Arms; Low, D. M. Edward Gibbon; Morison, J. A. C. Gibbon; Mowat, R. B. Gibbon; Norton, J. E. A Bibliography of the Works of Edward Gibbon; Paul, H. W. Men and Letters; Quennell, P. Four Portraits; Robertson, J. M. Gibbon; Ste. Beuve, C. A. Causeries de Lundi; Stephen, L. Studies of a Biographer; Strachey, G. L. Biographical Essays; Young, G. M. Gibbon.

GILBERT, WILLIAM (of Colchester)

(1540-November 30, 1603), scientist, author of *De Magnete*, first great work of physical science published in England, was born at Colchester. His father, Hierome Gilbert (also spelled Gilberd or Gylberde), de-

scended from an ancient Suffolk family, was the official recorder for Colchester. William was educated at St. John's College, Cambridge, where he took his B.A. and M.A. degrees and was elected a senior fellow in 1569.

After traveling in Europe, he settled in London as a physician and was admitted to the College of Physicians about 1576, serving on a committee engaged in the preparation of the *Pharmacopoeia Londinenses.* He was elected president of the College of Physicians in 1600, and the following year was appointed personal physician to Queen Elizabeth. On the death of the queen, he was reappointed to serve as physician to her successor, James I, but died shortly thereafter and was buried at Colchester. His books, instruments, globes, and a collection of minerals were willed to the College of Physicians, but all were destroyed in the great London fire of 1666.

Lasswitz, the German scientist, has called Gilbert "the first real physicist and the first trustworthy methodical experimenter." This judgment was made on the basis of his great work, *De Magnete, Magneticisque Corporibus et De Magno Magnete Tellure,* written in Latin and published first in 1600. A treatise on magnetism summarizing many years of research on magnets, magnetic bodies and electrical attraction, this work was the foundation of the modern theory of magnetism and electricity. Both in his faithful adherence to an inductive method and in his original conception of the earth as itself a great spherical magnet, Gilbert opened a revolutionary path through contemporary notions of physical science. It is not strange then that he was one of the first advocates of the Copernican theory in England, and it is interesting that with the term *vis electrica* he was actually the first man to give electricity its name.

Gilbert's second published work, *De Mundo Nostro Sublunari Philosophia Nova,* was edited by his brother from two manuscripts and published posthumously. During his lifetime and increasingly in the first half of the seventeenth century, the value of Gilbert's contribution was recognized both in England and on the continent. Donne was well acquainted with *De Magnete* and acknowledged its influence on his ideas in *Essayes in Divinity.* Galileo was a great admirer. Francis Bacon, while he refers to Gilbert in *Novum Organum,* never appreciated his importance. Dryden wrote what is perhaps the most fitting epitaph for this distinguished Elizabethan scientist—"Gilbert shall live till lodestones cease to draw."

PRINCIPAL WORKS: Guilielmi Gilberti Colcenstrensis, medici londinensis, De Magnete, Magneticisque Corporibus, et De Magno Magnete Tellure; Physiologia Nova, Plurimus et Argumentis, et Experimentis Demonstrata, 1600 (P. F. Mottelay, tr. 1893) (S. P. Thompson, ed. 1900); De Mundo Nostro Sublunari Philosophia Nova (W. Gilbert, ed.) 1651.

ABOUT: Thompson, S. P. William Gilbert and Terrestrial Magnetism; Thompson, S. P. Gilbert of Colchester, An Elizabethan Magnetizer.

GILDAS (surnamed **SAPIENS** or **BADONICUS**) (516?-570?) the earliest of Welsh historians and presumably a contemporary of King Arthur, was born the year of the battle of Mount Bedon, which according to the *Monumenta Historica Britannica* was about the year 516. Actually our sources for the biographical facts of Gildas' life come from three separate manuscripts: his own historical work, *De Excidio et Conquestu Britanniae,* an eleventh century biography written by a monk of Rhuys, and a twelfth century biography presumably by Caradoc of Lancarvan. There is a good deal of contradiction, however, between these various accounts and it seems probable that two or more persons by the name of Gildas were confused through the centuries.

"Gildas the Wise" was in all probability a monk and a scholar who lived abroad a good part of his life, apparently in Brittany, where he became known as a saint and is reputed to have founded the monastery of St. Gildas at Rhuys later made famous by Abelard. According to his own account, after ten years of preparation and delay he finally composed his only surviving work, the history of Britain from the Roman invasion to the coming of the Saxons. As it has come down to us, the work is divided into three parts: a preface, largely personal; the history proper; and longest and least important, a collation of scriptural passages which he used to castigate the wickedness and corruption of the British state and church in his time.

Gildas' account follows no strict chronological sequence and is often obscure in detail; neither is it of any great literary merit;

yet it remains the only historical account of Britain from the fifth century to the time of its writing. Gildas tells us much of his material was drawn from "foreign sources," which may account for the lack of sharp detail. Moreover, it is not even certain that the full text has come down to us. The treatise existed in manuscript until it was first published, with numerous alterations and omissions, in 1525 by Polydore Vergil in London. The first English version, with a more complete text, was published in 1638.

Gildas is referred to by Beda and by Alcuin, both of whom apparently consulted his manuscript, and it seems probable that he was the author of other works which have been lost. *De Excidio,* according to Montague Rhodes James of King's College, is little more than an "uncouth fragment." Yet it is one of the earliest indigenous British literary works, and, for lack of other contemporary authorities, of great historical value.

PRINCIPAL WORKS: Gildae Sapientis de Excidio et Conquestu Britanniae, 1525 (J. Stephenson, ed. and tr. 1838; T. Mommsen, 1898; J. A. Giles, 1901).

ABOUT: Caradoc, Vita Gildae (T. Mommsen, ed.); Gross, C. Sources of English History; Petrie, H. and Sharpe, J. (eds.) Monumenta Historica Britannica; Stephenson, J. Preface and Notes, *in* De Excidio (1838 ed.).

GILPIN, WILLIAM (June 4, 1724-1804), author of picturesque travel series, miscellaneous writer, was born near Carlisle, Cambridgeshire, the son of Captain John Gilpin and Matilda Langstaffe. Artistic ability ran in the family; his brother and nephew were painters, and Benjamin West was a cousin. He entered Queen's College, Oxford, in 1740, received his B.A. in 1744, was ordained in 1746, and became curate at Irthington, where his uncle was vicar. Soon after he returned to Oxford, where he secured his M.A. in 1748. To pay off college debts, he wrote his *Life of Bernard Gilpin,* the first of a series of biographies of religious reformers. For a while he was a curate in London; then about 1749 he took over a school at Cheam, Surrey, where he abolished corporal punishment, and instituted such reforms as the study of the pupils' own language and their exercise in practical gardening. He had already denounced his own training at Oxford as "solemn trifling." About this time he married his first cousin,

Margaret Gilpin (a common practice in his family). They had two daughters who died in infancy, and two sons, one of whom emigrated permanently to Massachusetts. During the summer vacations he went on sketching tours, from which grew his series of travel books, illustrated by himself.

In 1777 he gave up the school and became vicar at Boldre in the New Forest, his home thereafter. He refused the offer of another living, not believing in pluralities, and lived on his small income, giving the profits from his books to build a new poorhouse and a parish school. His original drawings for his books he auctioned for the benefit of the school. He did accept a prebend at Salisbury Cathedral. He became a victim of gout, and finally had to give up preaching and engage a curate. He died of dropsy at eighty.

An estimable man, with advanced ideas on education and poor-law reform, Gilpin also introduced a new style of travel books. Though he was satirized by William Combe as "Dr. Syntax," actually his books showed no "nature-faking" or false enthusiasm. His avowed interest was solely in the picturesque, and his style (partly in prose and partly in verse) was rather high flown, but he did a great deal to interest Britons in their own country and its beauties. His drawings, however, seemed more like studies for sketches than finished pictures. His other writing, outside of books written for the guidance of his curate when he could no longer undertake his clerical duties, was chiefly an uninspired but conscientious series of biographies of religious pioneers from the time of Wycliffe. He was also much interested in genealogy (he was probably a collateral descendant of Bernard Gilpin, the sixteenth century "Apostle of the North"), and his book on his family included an autobiographical section, which is the chief source of information concerning his life.

PRINCIPAL WORKS: *Travel books*—Observations on the Wye, and several parts of South Wales, 1782; Observations relative chiefly to Picturesque Beauty . . . on . . . the Mountains and Lakes of Cumberland and Westmoreland, 1786; Observations, etc., on the High-lands of Scotland, 1789; Remarks on Forest Scenery, and other Woodland Views, . . . Scenes of the New Forest, 1791; Observations on the Western Part of England . . . [and] the Isle of Wight, 1798; Observations on the Coasts of Hampshire, Sussex, and Kent, 1804; Observations on Several Parts of England, 1808; Observations on Several Parts of the Counties of Cambridge, Norfolk, Sussex, and Essex, 1809. *Miscellaneous*—Life of Bernard Gilpin, 1753; Life of Latimer, 1755; Life of Wycliffe, 1765; Life of Huss, 1765; Life of Jerome of Prague, 1765; Essay on Prints, 1768; Lectures on the Church Catechism, 1779; Life of Cranmer, 1784; Moral Contrasts, 1798; Sermons to a Country Congregation, 1799-1800; Dialogues on Various Subjects, 1807; Memoirs of Dr. Richard Gilpin . . . and his Posterity, with a Life of the Author, 1879.

ABOUT: Gilpin, W. Memoirs of Dr. Richard Gilpin, etc.

GIRALDUS CAMBRENSIS (Giraldus de Barri) (1146?-1220?), Welsh churchman, medieval historian, was born at Manorbier Castle, Pembrokeshire, which he later called "the sweetest spot in Wales." Through his mother, Nesta, he was descended from a prince of southern Wales; his father was William de Barri; and his uncle, David Fitzgerald, was bishop of St. David's.

As a youth he was sent abroad to be educated in Paris. There he studied and wrote Latin poems until he was in his mid-twenties, when he returned to Wales as collector of the tithes. In 1175 he was appointed archdeacon of Brecon and the following year, after the death of his uncle, an attempt was made to elect him to the bishopric of St. David's. Henry II, however, opposed the support of native Welsh elements and saw to it that a Norman bishop succeeded Fitzgerald. Disappointed, Giraldus went abroad, studying theology and lecturing in Paris for three years.

Returning again to Britain, he was appointed commissary to the bishop of St. David's in 1180, and four years later became one of the king's chaplains. During a visit to Ireland as companion to Prince John, he wrote the first of his important chronicles, *Topographia Hibernica*, to which we owe most of our knowledge of medieval Ireland, and *Expurgatio Hibernica*, an interesting, if often strongly prejudiced, history of events from 1169 to 1185.

In 1188 Giraldus accompanied the Archbishop of Canterbury on a trip through Wales, preaching the Third Crusade. Although he spoke in French or in Latin, which most of the common people could not understand, his eloquence was said to be so great that his audiences were moved to tears. On the same mission Giraldus went abroad to march with the Crusaders and write a history of the Crusade, but on the death of Henry II, he was sent back to Wales to keep

From the tomb
GIRALDUS DE BARRI

order. Refusing the ecclesiastical honors offered him, he retired to Lincoln for six years where he wrote *Gemma Ecclesiastica,* a learned and lively canonical work which gives a vivid picture of the state of morality and learning in Wales. At last in 1198 he was elected bishop of St. David's over the opposition of the Archbishop of Canterbury, but the four years following proved a long struggle in which Giraldus fought for the independence of St. David's from Canterbury, making three visits to Rome, only to have the Pope bring the controversy to an end with an order for a new election. The prior of Llanthony was elected in his place, and Giraldus lived the rest of his life in retirement, devoting all his time to writing.

Among the important works of this latter period were the *Descriptio Cambriae,* an itinerary and description of Wales of great ecclesiastical and philological, as well as topographical, interest; *De Rebus a Se Gestis,* an autobiography; and *De Instructione Principis,* which includes a number of sketches of personages in the royal family.

Giraldus lived certainly until the year 1216, probably until the year 1220, and was buried in the cathedral of St. David's. He was an excellent Latinist and a vivid writer, although as a historian his violent party spirit and burning patriotism frequently biased his judgement. His work reflects the

eloquence and humor, as well as the naive vanity, of the writer. Friend of many of the great men of his day, keen observer of the social and intellectual trends of his time, Giraldus was able to set down a unique impressionistic panorama of the scenes, the traditions, and the customs of medieval Britain. Writing in the *Cambridge History of English Literature,* Professor W. Lewis Jones says that "of all the chroniclers none has contrived to blend information and entertainment more successfully than Giraldus Cambrensis. A scholar trained in Paris, an insatiably curious student of men and books and every form of odd lore, a fighter and an intriguer to his finger-tips, an inveterate gossip, yet a man capable of high ideals and far-reaching schemes of public policy, the intimate friend of kings and statesmen, popes and prelates, yet withal a passionate lover of his own native little Wales—Gerald is one of the most romantic figures in all mediaeval literature."

PRINCIPAL WORKS: Itinerarium Cambriae: Seu Laboriosae Baldvini Cantuar, 1585; Cambriae Descriptio, 1585; Topographia Hiberniae, sive de Mirabilibus Hiberniae, 1602; Opera (J. S. Brewer, J. F. Dimock, and G. F. Warner, eds. 8 vols. Rolls Series) 1861-91.

ABOUT: The Autobiography of Giraldus Cambrensis (H. E. Butler, ed. and tr.); Brewer, J. S. Preface to Opera (Rolls ed.).

GLANVILL, JOSEPH (1636-November 4, 1680), philosopher, occultist, was born in Plymouth, Devonshire, the son of Nicholas Glanvill. He entered Exeter College, Oxford, in 1652, received his B.A. in 1655, then transferred to Lincoln College from which he received his M.A. in 1658. He then became chaplain to Francis Rous, provost of Eton, who was an official of Oliver Cromwell's. Rous died in 1659, and Glanvill returned to Oxford. In spite of his connection with the Puritans, he conformed at the Restoration, and that same year, 1660, through his brother, a London merchant, was given the rectory of Wimbush, Essex. Two years later he succeeded the vicar of Frome Selwood, Somersetshire, who had been expelled for nonconformity. This vicarage he exchanged in 1672 for Streat and Walton, Somersetshire; in 1666 he had also been made vicar of the Abbey Church in Bath. He was named chaplain-in-ordinary to Charles II in 1672, and in 1678, through the

Marquis of Worcester, a relative by marriage, became a prebendary of Worcester. He was married twice, first to Mary Stocker and after her death to Margaret Selwyn. By his first marriage he had two children, by his second three.

Glanvill's interest in natural science was early and remained keen. He was an early associate of the Royal Society and became a Fellow in 1664. In general his philosophical leanings were anti-Aristotelean, but though he was a close friend and admirer of Henry More, leader of the Cambridge Platonist, he was not a Platonist either. He distrusted, in fact, all dogma, and said that what he sought was to find truth "in the great book of nature." The chief philosophical influence on him was that of Descartes. He opposed equally the materialism of Hobbes and the emotional faith of the dissenters (though he was friendly to Richard Baxter, who in turn called him "a man of more than ordinary ingeny"). He engaged also in a long controversy with Thomas White, the English Roman Catholic priest who collaborated with Sir Kenelm Digby *qv*.

His best-known work is *The Vanity of Dogmatizing*, which contains a curious prophecy of the electric telegraph, and is also of interest because of its story of the "Scholar Gypsy," which gave Matthew Arnold the subject of his well-known poem. Glanvill's essay, *Antifanatick Theologie, and Free Philosophie*, was designed by the author to be a continuation of Bacon's *New Atlantis*. Yet this enemy of dogma and avowed skeptic believed implicitly in witchcraft, which he claimed to prove empirically, and called those who disbelieved "modern Sadducees." He also believed in the preexistence of souls, and very firmly in apparitions of the dead. He and More together investigated a number of what would be called today psychic phenomena, and in each case testified to their authenticity. In other words, his philosophical skepticism very often was used merely to bolster and vindicate his faith; he remained throughout an orthodox clergyman of the Anglican Church.

Glanvill's style is rich and colorful. Sometimes, in its more rhetorical passages, it recalls the great organ music of Sir Thomas Browne's prose.

PRINCIPAL WORKS: The Vanity of Dogmatizing: or Confidence in Opinion, 1661 (as Scepsis Scientifica: or, Confest Ignorance the Way to Science, 1665; J. Owen, ed. 1885); Plus Ultra: or the Progress and Advancement of Science since the days of Aristotle, 1668; Philosophia Pia: or, a discourse of the religious temper, etc. 1671; Essays on Several Important Subjects in Philosophy and Religion, 1676; Sadducimus Triumphatus, or, Full and Plain Evidence concerning Witches and Apparitions, 1681.

ABOUT: Greenslet, F. J. Glanvill; Hallam, H. Literature of Europe; Lecky, W. Rationalism in Europe; Owen, J. Preface, 1885 ed. Vanity of Dogmatizing; Wood, A. à, Athenae Oxonienses.

GLAPTHORNE, HENRY (fl. 1639), dramatist, was the author of a number of plays and poems, but of his life nothing is known. He is one among the later dramatists of the Jacobean age who are of importance only because they introduced the type of play which was to develop into the "heroic drama" of the Restoration period.

Glapthorne's best play, *Argalus and Parthenia*, was a pastoral tragedy founded on an episode from Sir Philip Sidney's *Arcadia*. It was acted at court before Charles and Henrietta, neither of whom seems to have been a discriminating critic, and later at the Drury Lane. A second tragedy, historical in subject-matter, was *The Tragedy of Albertus Wallenstein*, based on the life of the German military leader. Two tragedies entered in the Stationer's Register for September 1653, *The Duchess of Fernandina* and *The Vestal*, were performed but never printed. He was also the author of three comedies, *The Hollander, Wit in a Constable*, and *The Ladies Priviledge*. The latter, while it ends as a comedy, belongs, according to Ronald Bayne writing in the *Cambridge History of English Literature*, "to the type of tragi-comedy in which extravagant sentiment insists upon submitting itself to absurd tasks in the effort to prove its heroism."

Two other plays are listed in the Stationer's Register as the work of Glapthorne, *The Paraside, or Revenge for Honor*, which has also been attributed to George Chapman; and *The Noble Trial*, which is probably the same as *The Lady Mother*, printed in A.H. Bullen's *Collection of Old English Plays*. Glapthorne also published a volume of *Poems*, dedicated to the Earl of Portland, in 1639, addressing a number of verses to an unidentified lady by the name of Lucinda. Three years later he published *Whitehall, a Poem, with Elegies*, and edited a volume of poems written by his friend, Thomas Beedome.

Glapthorne's range was ambitious but his talent was minor, although certain passages in the plays are written with considerable felicity. According to Emile Legouis, "he does not lack a certain grace, but his debased blank verse is like halting prose and awakens a longing for prose"; and again according to Ronald Bayne, his work illustrated "the enervating and disintegrating effect of heroic sentiment" on English drama.

PRINCIPAL WORKS: Argalus and Parthenia, 1639; The Tragedy of Albertus Wallenstein, Late Duke of Fridland, and Generall to the Emperor Ferdinand the Second, 1639 (C. Baldwin, ed., *in* Old English Drama, 1825); The Hollander, 1640; Wit in a Constable, 1640; The Ladies Priviledge, 1640 (C. Baldwin, ed., *in* Old English Drama, 1825); The Lady Mother (A. H. Bullen, ed., *in* Old English Plays,) 1883; The Plays and Poems of Henry Glapthorne (R. H. Shepherd, ed.) 1874.

ABOUT: Shepherd, R. H. Memoir, *in* The Plays and Poems of Henry Glapthorne; Retrospective Review, vol. 10.

GLOVER, RICHARD (1712-November 25, 1785), poet, was the son of a Hamburg merchant residing in London. He was born in St. Martin's Lane, Cannon Street, and went to school at Cheam in Surrey. When he was only sixteen he wrote a poem on Sir Isaac Newton which was much admired by a Dr. Henry Pemberton who used it as a preface to his book, *A View of Newton's Philosophy.*

Richard went into his father's business, but continued to write poetry, and in 1737 published *Leonidas,* an epic poem in blank verse. Considered a poetical manifesto against Walpole, then prime minister, Glover's epic went through four editions, was translated into French and German, and in 1770 was enlarged and republished. Glover's opposition to Walpole took more political form in a petition to the Lord Mayor protesting the inadequate protection of British commerce, evidence for which he presented to the House of Commons. On the strength of his fame both as a writer and as a good British patriot, the Duchess of Marlborough willed him £500, to write a life of the Duke of Marlborough with David Mallet—a task which he refused. In 1751 he was defeated as a candidate for the office of chamberlain to the city of London, but his career as a poet and as a man

of commerce continued to flourish. Ten years later he was elected to Parliament from Weymouth.

Glover married Hannah Nunn, a lady of considerable property, from whom he was divorced in 1756. He remarried later and was survived by his wife and several children when he died at the age of seventy-three.

In addition to *Leonidas,* he wrote two long poems in blank verse: *London, or the Progress of Commerce,* published in 1739; and the *Athenaid,* which was published by his daughter posthumously. He also wrote several plays in blank verse, *Boadicea,* produced at the Drury Lane, *Medea,* and *Jason.* A ballad, *Hosier's Ghost,* inspired by Admiral Hosier's unfortunate expedition in 1726, was republished in Percy's *Reliques,* and is still readable. Although Glover was praised by such contemporaries as Lord Lyttelton and Fielding, his work has been long since, and quite deservedly, forgotten. As George Saintsbury has said, "Glover belongs to the 'tumid and gorgeous' blank-verse division. It is difficult to imagine, and would hardly be possible to find, even in the long list of mistaken 'long-poem' writers of the past two centuries, more tedious stuff than his."

PRINCIPAL WORKS: *Poems:* Leonidas, a Poem, 1737; London: or, the Progress of Commerce, A Poem, 1739; Admiral Hoser's Ghost, 1740; The Athenaid, a Poem, 1787. *Other Works:* Boadicea, a Tragedy, 1753; Medea, a Tragedy, 1761; Jason, a Tragedy, 1799; Memoirs by a Celebrated Literary and Political Character, Written by Himself (R. Duppa, ed.) 1813.

ABOUT: Chalmers, A. Life, *in* Works of the English Poets; Glover, R. Memoirs (R. Duppa, ed.); Schaaf, J. G. Richard Glover.

GODWIN, MARY WOLLSTONE-CRAFT (April 27, 1759-September 10, 1797), author of *A Vindication of the Rights of Woman,* was born, probably at Hoxton, London, the daughter of Edward John Wollstonecraft and Elizabeth Dixon, both of Irish descent. The father was a drunken bully, who after losing his patrimony had tried unsuccessfully to be a small farmer, and moved six times in her childhood, here and there from Yorkshire to Wales. What schooling the three girls among the six children got was by their own efforts. In 1778, at nineteen, Mary started working as a companion. In 1780 their mother died,

J. Opie
MRS. MARY WOLLSTONECRAFT GODWIN

scripts, writing for the magazines, and translating from French and German. In 1791 she first met William Godwin—but he disliked her at sight, because she talked so much she silenced Thomas Paine, who was also present!

The French Revolution had begun, and Mary Wollstonecraft, like so many others of the young English intellectuals of the time, was aflame for it. She wanted to go to Paris to see it at first hand. Another inducement to leave England may have been her alleged unrequited passion for Henry Fuseli, the painter, who was married; but this whole story has been disputed. In any event, she went alone, and there almost at once she met Captain Gilbert Imlay, an American from New Jersey, a Revolutionary officer, and a thorough scoundrel. They fell in love, and probably legal marriage would have been impossible in France at the time, even if Mary's principles had not forbidden it. He soon tired of her (though he continued to exploit her), and left for Havre; she joined him there in 1794 and there her daughter Fanny was born—the girl who was later one of Godwin's incredible household, and who poisoned herself at twenty-two.

Mrs. Wollstonecraft, as she now called herself, returned to England with her child in 1795, still following Imlay. He used her to travel on his (rather questionable) business affairs in Scandinavia, they were separated and reunited, and finally she discovered he was carrying on an intrigue with another woman in their own home, and tried unsuccessfully to drown herself. They were finally parted in 1796; she refused any money from him for herself, but accepted a bond for Fanny's support—and even on this he defaulted. Mary went back to hack writing for a living.

It was at this time that she met Godwin again, and so far as that cold creature could love anyone, he fell in love with her. She could give him nothing to compare with her passion for Imlay, but they became lovers, and finally—and most reluctantly—were legally married in March 1797, when she was three months pregnant. In September her daughter Mary was born, and eleven days later Mary Wollstonecraft Godwin died. She was buried in St. Pancras churchyard; it was by her grave that her daughter and Shelley pledged their love and planned

and to escape the father, Everina went to keep house for a brother. Eliza made a hasty and unfortunate marriage, and Mary joined the household of her close friend Fanny Blood, helping Fanny's mother work as a seamstress—for here again the father was dissolute, brutal, and improvident. After shocking experiences, Eliza, now Mrs. Bishop, finally secured a legal separation, and she and Mary set up a small school, first in Islington and then in Newington Green, which failed in 1785 after two years of effort.

Fanny Blood meanwhile had married (unhappily) and gone with her husband to Lisbon. At her plea, Mary hastened there to be with her at the birth of her child, but before she arrived Fanny was dead. Thus far all Mary Wollstonecraft's observation of men and marriage had been disillusioning and embittering; it is no wonder she became a rebel and a feminist.

She next became a governess in the family of Lord Kingsborough, later the Earl of Kingston, in 1787. In a year she was discharged because the children had grown too fond of her and the rattlepated Lady Kingsborough was jealous. (Margaret, one of the pupils, later Lady Mountcashel, had an interesting career of her own and was a friend of the Shelleys in Italy.) Mary went to London and soon found work as a literary hack for Johnson, the publisher, reading manu-

their elopement. In 1851 her grandson, Sir Percy Shelley, had her body removed to Bournemouth.

This passionate, beautiful woman, with her dark red hair and her ardent eyes, is one of the most appealing persons in all literary history. She was a child of her revolutionary era, compact of enthusiasm, generosity, adoration of freedom, and reckless courage. Yet she was no mere emotionalist, for her mind was alert and she wielded an eloquent (though often a stilted) pen. She was a pioneer in education as well as in feminism; she advocated national free schools and a Froebel-like system of combined work and play for children. Much of her writing was merely competent hack journalism done to order to earn a living, but her principal work, the *Vindication of the Rights of Woman*, is worth reading quite apart from its thesis.

It created a major scandal in its day, yet actually its doctrine is mild; the real reason for the heated attacks it aroused was first the unconventional life of the author, and second the plain speaking she employed in a mealy-mouthed age. A disciple of Rousseau in all else, and not a little tarred by his sentimentality, in her discussion of the relations of men and women she opposed violently his masculine contempt and advocated equality and companionship. Above all, she wanted women educated, given a chance as individuals, allowed to be something more than playthings or despised drudges. The most she asked, economically, was that unmarried women without male relatives to support them be trained to support themselves by useful work! Any of the feminists of a later era would have considered her most radical demands hopelessly reactionary. But instinct in her appeal is her anger at injustice, and there is warmth in the most rhetorical of her sentences—the same warmth that is in her heartbreaking letters to Gilbert Imlay.

PRINCIPAL WORKS: Thoughts on the Education of Daughters, 1787; Mary, a Fiction, 1788; The Female Reader (compiled) 1789; An Historical and Moral View of the Origin and Progress of the French Revolution, 1790; Elements of Morality for the Use of Children (tr. from C. G. Salzmann) 1790; Original Stories from Real Life, 1791; A Vindication of the Rights of Woman, 1792; A Vindication of the Rights of Man, in a Letter to Edmund Burke, 1793; Letters Written During a Short Residence in Sweden, Norway, and Denmark, 1796; Posthumous Works (W. Godwin, ed.) 1798; Letters to Imlay (C. Kegan Paul, ed.) 1879; Love Letters to Gilbert Imlay (R. Ingpen, ed.) 1908; Select Works (C. Jebb, ed.) 1912.

ABOUT: Bowen, M. (George R. Preedy) This Shining Woman; Clough, E. R. A Study of Mary Wollstonecraft and the Rights of Woman; Godwin, W. Memoirs of the Author of a Vindication of the Rights of Woman; James, H. R. Mary Wollstonecraft; Kegan Paul, C. William Godwin, His Friends and Contemporaries; Linford, M. Mary Wollstonecraft; Peabody, J. Portrait of Mrs. W. (play); Pennell, E. R. Mary Wollstonecraft Godwin; Taylor, G. R. S. Mary Wollstonecraft: A Study in Economics and Romance.

GOLDING, ARTHUR (1536?-1605?), translator, was the younger son of John Golding, an auditor of the exchequer, and his second wife, Ursula Merston. He was probably born in London and there is some evidence that he attended Queens' College, Cambridge, although he never took a degree. When Arthur was eleven or twelve his father died and the boy was placed in the service of Protector Somerset. His half-sister, Margaret, had married John de Vere, the Earl of Oxford, and through this connection he became receiver for John de Vere's son Edward. Golding and the young poet-earl seem to have shared quarters for a time in the home of Sir William Cecil, a well-known patron of literature. Moving in aristocratic circles, Golden was able to find a number of wealthy friends who made it possible for him to carry out the work of translating the classics which became his major interest.

His first important work, a translation of Caesar's *Commentaries,* appeared in 1565 and was dedicated to Sir William Cecil. Two years later he finished the translation of Ovid's *Metamorphoses,* considered by contemporary critics to be among the best translations of the age. His only original work, with the exception of a few prefatory verses, was a prose piece, *A Discourse upon the Earthquake That Happened Throughe This Realme of England and Other Places of Christendom the First of April 1580,* in which he considered this natural upheaval as a judgment of God to punish wickedness.

One of his closest friends was Sir Philip Sidney. When Sidney left England for the Low Countries, he entrusted an unfinished translation of De Mornay's treatise on the truth of Christianity to his friend, asking him to complete and publish it. In 1589 after Sidney's death, Golding published *A Woorke concerning the Trewnesse of the Christian Religion Begunne to Be Translated by Sir Philip Sidney.*

Praised by Thomas Nashe and William Webbe, Golding achieved an enviable reputation and in his latter years became increasingly prosperous. Shortly before his death in 1605, an order was issued to the Archbishop of Canterbury and the Attorney General giving Golding the sole right to print such works as they held to be beneficial to the church and the commonwealth.

His translation of Ovid, certainly his best work, is a conscientious rendition in ballad meter—rapid, fluent and inescapably monotonous. Charles Whibly, writing in the *Cambridge History of English Literature,* says that Golding was "never a poet and never a shirk"—a phrase which points to the faultless mediocrity of his verse.

PRINCIPAL WORKS: The Historie of Leonard Aretino, Concerning the Warres Betwene the Imperialles and Gothes for the Possession of Italy (tr.) 1563; Thabridgemente of the Histories of Trogus Pompeius, Collected and Wrytten by Justine (tr.) 1564; The Eyght Bookes of Caius Julius Caesar, Conteyning His Martiall Exploytes in Gallia and the Countries Bordering (tr.) 1565; The XV Bookes of P. Ovidius Naso, Entytled Metamorphoses (tr.) 1565-67 (W. H. D. Rouse, ed. *in* King's Library Series, 1904); Psalms of David (tr.) 1571; The Lyfe of the Most Godly Capteine Jasper Colignie Shatilion, by Jean de Serres (tr.) 1576; A Tragedie of Abraham's Sacrifice, by Theodore Beza (tr.) 1577 (M. W. Wallace, ed. 1906); A Discourse Upon the Earthquake, 1580; The Worke of Pomponius Mela, the Cosmographer, Concerninge the Situation of the World (tr.) 1585; Politicke, Moral and Martial Discourses, by Jacques Hurault (tr.) 1595.

ABOUT: Warton, T. The History of English Poetry; Wood, A. à, Athenae Oxonienses.

GOLDSMITH, OLIVER (November 10, 1730-April 4, 1774), dramatist, poet, novelist, was Irish by birth, though of English descent. On both sides his immediate ancestors were clergymen of the established church. His father, Charles Goldsmith, was a poor curate who eked out his income by desultory farming; his mother, Ann Jones, was the daughter of a vicar. It was probably at his maternal grandfather's home, Elphin, Roscommon, that he was born, though his birthplace may possibly have been his father's little farm near Ballymahon, Longford. In any event, in his infancy the family moved to Kilkenny West, near Lissoy (one of the progenitors of "sweet Auburn, loveliest village of the vale"), West Meath.

He was the fifth child and second son, and received little care or encouragement from his harassed family. Whatever resources they had went to his older brother Henry. Early in childhood Oliver suffered from smallpox, which left him badly pitted; he was besides ungainly, awkwardly built, and in no way a prepossessing figure. His speech was slow and hesitating, with a lifelong brogue, he was a born blunderer with a kind of innocence that was made to be bilked and ridiculed, and in spite of his precociousness in verse and a certain aptitude in athletics, he was the butt of his schoolmates as he was later of his adult acquaintances. The effect of this on an almost morbidly sensitive nature was to make him abnormally shy, with bursts of chattering aggressiveness which today's psychology would call over-compensation of an inferiority complex. Nothing could change the sweetness, kindness, and generosity of his heart.

His first schooling was with a half-literate ex-army sergeant who stuffed him full of Irish legends and fairy tales. Then relatives sent him to a succession of schools at Elphin, Athlone, and Edgeworthtown, and finally he was ready for Trinity College in Dublin. But his father had exhausted his resources in entering his brother there, and Oliver had to go as a sizar, a half-menial who lodged in a garret and paid for his schooling by his services. Moreover, his tutor, the wonderfully named Theaker Wilder, was interested only in mathematics and was a brute besides. It is not remarkable that Goldsmith's college career was notable chiefly for scrapes and punishments; however, he did achieve a B.A. in 1749, and returned to Lissoy to play his flute, idle around, and wait for his relatives (particularly his kind uncle, Thomas Contarine) to decide what to do next with him.

Divinity went glimmering when he presented himself to the bishop for examination clad in scarlet breeches. Law proved beyond him: nothing was left but medicine. In between he tutored occasionally and wrote a little. Once he set off for America and succeeded only in being cheated of his horse and money. (It was on this or a similar occasion that he himself made the ludicrous mistake which is the basis of *She Stoops to Conquer*.) En route to Dublin to study law, he got only as far as a gaming table. At last, in 1752, he set out for Edinburgh to study medicine, at the expense of Uncle Contarine. He acquired very little learning, but in 1754 he managed to go to the Continent, ostensibly to the University of Leyden. When he came back two years later, he called himself "M.B.," and set up in London as a physician; he never saw Ireland again. Where, if anywhere, Goldsmith acquired his medical degree is unknown; he certainly knew very little medicine. But he did travel all over France and Italy, playing the flute and being fed at monastery doors, and he brought back the experiences later embodied in *The Traveller*—some of them most certainly apocryphal.

In London, without any money, he tried almost everything. He was perhaps an actor, though it seems incredible; he was certainly an apothecary's assistant, an usher in a poor school, and finally, after all else had failed, a literary hack, proof reader, general critic, contributor to privately owned magazines, and compiler of pamphlets and books for various publishers, mostly for John Newbery, first considerable writer of books for children. (Goldsmith may be the author of Newbery's famous story of *Goody Two Shoes*.) He had been an ignominious failure when first he tried to practice medicine; he was promised a job as surgeon in one of the East India Company's factories and lost it; and he was even refused a post as "hospital mate" (i.e., orderly) as being "not qualified." The only way he could possibly earn a living (and even then he was in debt most of the time) was by grinding labor with his pen. All his writings before *The Traveller* were anonymous or under a pseudonym; *The Citizen of the World* was his first real success.

Meanwhile, however, in 1761 he had met Samuel Johnson, and thereafter the great literary dictator was his loyal if censorious friend. He was one of the original members of the famous Club, in 1764, and Reynolds and Burke became his devoted friends as well. Unfortunately, since he aspired to write plays, he had managed to antagonize Garrick by some of his remarks in *An Enquiry into the Present State of Polite Learn-*

After Sir J. Reynolds (?) 1770
OLIVER GOLDSMITH

ing in Europe, and so his first comedy, *The Good-Natur'd Man,* was refused by Drury Lane and delayed at Covent Garden to make way for a silly sentimental play which the audiences much preferred. He had to keep on doing hack work, compiling anthologies, writing scissors-and-paste histories for the young, translating from the French. (He had a really good knowledge of French—and of Latin as well—and his translation of the *Memoirs* of the persecuted Protestant, Jean Marteilhe, is first-rate work.) Even *The Vicar of Wakefield* was delayed in publication for four years after its purchase, so little drawing power did Goldsmith's name have. (The story of Johnson's selling the manuscript to rescue Goldsmith from an importunate landlady was probably much exaggerated by the jealous Boswell.) *She Stoops to Conquer* actually was extremely successful and brought him a fair sum of money—which as usual he squandered in fancy clothes, expensive lodgings, and indiscriminate charity.

In 1770 Goldsmith spent a short time in Paris with his friends the Hornecks, whose daughter Mary, the "Jessamy bride," was the nearest approach to a love-interest in his life. In 1772 he was very ill, and he never entirely recovered. His finances were in chaos, he could not make order or sense out of his irresponsible life, and probably he had not much will to live. "Is your mind at ease?" the doctor asked the dying man. "No, it is not," were Goldsmith's last words. He was forty-three years old.

He was buried in the Temple Church, and two years later his friends erected a memorial to him in Westminster, with a ponderous Latin epitaph by Dr. Johnson. That was the mortal end of a kind, merry, melancholy, soft-hearted, vain, imprudent, foolish, wise, and lovable man. As Austin Dobson said, he gave to English literature "some of the most finished didactic poetry in the language; some unsurpassed familiar verse; a series of essays ranking only below Lamb's; a unique and original novel; a comedy which besides being readable is still acted to delighted audiences." There is something fragmentary and unfinished about the best of Goldsmith's work: *The Vicar of Wakefield* is disjointed and full of irrelevant material; *The Deserted Village* is, as Macaulay pointed out, English in its prosperity, Irish in its ruin; he made grotesque errors of geography, history, and natural science, and never bothered to correct them. But even the unfriendly Macaulay has to acknowledge that "no writer was ever more uniformly agreeable." "His life and works interpret each other," Forster remarked, and it is true. The good vicar of Auburn is his brother Henry, the great house mistaken for an inn is from his own boyhood error, Dr. Primrose is probably his own father. Goldsmith put himself into his books and wrote from his heart. Moreover, the reasoned conclusions are obviously the work of a mind much keener than his slow tongue could express (though he had a pretty wit in conversation, when sufficiently goaded; and the posthumous *Retaliation* shows that the outward docility with which he took his friends' gibes covered a very sharp understanding and resentment). All Goldsmith's work is like a tapestry, raveled in places, sometimes astonishingly inept, but threaded through with glowing images and tender beauty. "Let not his frailties be remembered," said Dr. Johnson. "He was a very great man."

PRINCIPAL WORKS: An Enquiry into the Present State of Polite Learning in Europe, 1759; The Bee (essays) 1759; The Citizen of the World, or, Letters from a Chinese Philosopher, 1762; History of Mecklenburgh, 1762; The Mystery Revealed, 1762; The Life of Richard Nash, of Bath, Esquire, 1762; A History of England in a Series of Letters from a Nobleman to His Son, 1764; The Traveller, or a Prospect of Society (verse) 1765; The Vicar of Wakefield, a Tale, 1766; The Good-Natur'd Man, a Comedy, 1768; The Roman History, 1769 (abridged, 1772); The Deserted Village (verse) 1770; The Life of Thomas Parnell, 1770; The Life of Henry St. John, Lord Viscount Bolingbroke, 1770; Threnodia Augustalia (verse) 1772; She Stoops to Conquer, or The Mistakes of a Night, a Comedy, 1773; Retaliation, a Poem, 1774; A History of the Earth and Animated Nature, 1774; Miscellaneous Works (W. Osborne and T. Griffin, eds.) 1775; The Haunch of Venison, a Poetical Epistle to Lord Clare, 1776; A Survey of Experimental Philosophy, 1776; The Miscellaneous Works of Oliver Goldsmith (S. Rose, ed.) 1801; The Captivity, an Oratorio, 1866.

ABOUT: Black, W. Goldsmith; Boswell, J. Life of Samuel Johnson; Dobson, A. Life of Goldsmith; Elwin, W. Some 18th Century Men of Letters; Forster, J. The Life and Adventures of Oliver Goldsmith; Gwynne, S. K. Oliver Goldsmith; Hunt, L. Classic Tales; Irving, W. Life of Oliver Goldsmith; King, R. A. Oliver Goldsmith; Macaulay, T. B. Biographies; Moore, F. F. Oliver Goldsmith; Percy, T. Memoir, *in* Miscellaneous Works, 1801 ed.; Prior, J. The Life of Oliver Goldsmith; Thackeray, W. M. English Humourists of the 18th Century; Thomas, A. Oliver Goldsmith (play); Thrale, H. Autobiography.

GOOGE, BARNABE (June 11, 1540-February 1594), translator, poet, was born at Alvingham, Lincolnshire, on St. Barnabas Day, 1540. His mother was Margaret Mantell and his father Robert Googe, recorder of Lincoln. Although he took no degree, Barnabe attended both Christ's College, Cambridge, and New College, Oxford, after which he entered the service of Sir William Cecil, a relative.

Googe translated and published a number of works during his lifetime, but his only original work was a book of poems, *Eglogs, Epytaphes and Sonnetes*, which were apparently written before he was twenty-one. In 1561 he went abroad, leaving the manuscript of the *Eglogs* with a friend named Blunderstone. When he came back to England he found the poems had been sent to press without his knowledge and "all togyther unpolished." He was able, however, to retrieve the manuscript and correct the poems before they were published in 1563.

Appointed one of the queen's gentleman-pensioners, Googe looked about for a wife and was about to marry Mary Darrell, when her parents announced that she was already engaged to someone else. Sir William Cecil came to his aid, bringing the influence of Archbishop Parker to bear on the Darrell family and the marriage took place about 1564. In 1574 Cecil sent Googe to Ireland as his representative, and eight years later he was appointed provost-marshall of the presidency court of Connaught. He resigned his post in 1585 and returned to England where he died at the age of fifty-four, leaving a widow and eight children.

In addition to the poems, which are among the earliest examples of the pastoral in English, Googe published four translations. He was highly thought of by contemporary critics both for his scholarship and for his poetry. William Webbe commended him in his *Discourse of English Poetrie*, calling him "a painfull furtherer of learning." His eclogues are interesting for their curious mixture of the classic pastoral with Googe's own strongly Protestant disapproval of the pagan view of love and heroism, but as poetry they are feeble.

PRINCIPAL WORKS: The Zodiake of Life written by the Godly and Zealous Poet Marcellus Pallingenius [Pierre Angelo Manzoli] stellatus (tr.) 1560; Eglogs, Egytaphes and Sonnettes, 1563 (E. Arber, ed. 1871); The Popish Kingdome, or Reigne of Antichrist, written by Thomas Naogeorgos [Kirchmayer] (tr.) 1570 (R. C. Hofe, ed. 1880); Foure Bookes of Husbandrie, collected by Conradus Heresbachius (tr.) 1577 (rev. G. Markham, as The Whole Art of Husbandry, 1631); The Proverbs of the noble Sir James Lopez de Mendoza (tr.) 1579.

ABOUT: Arber, E. Introduction to Googe's Eglogs (1871 ed.); Hofe, R. C. Introduction to The Popish Kingdome (1880 ed.); Warton, T. History of English Poetry (W. C. Hazlitt, ed.).

GOSSON, STEPHEN (April 1554-February 13, 1624), writer against the stage, was born in Canterbury, the son of Cornelius Gosson, of a Kentish family. He entered Corpus Christi College, Oxford, in 1572, and received his B.A. in 1576. He then went to London, and tried unsuccessfully to establish himself as an actor and playwright. His three plays, *Catalines Conspiracy*, *Praise at Parting*, and *The Comedie of Captain Mario*, all seem to have been failures. The result was *The Schoole of Abuse*, in which he got his own back at the theatre which had repudiated him. The style of his anti-stage books is flippant and worldly, not at all Puritan, and there is a strong probability that they were equally compounded of revenge and a desire for publicity—though he claimed to have "founded the schoole and made the first lecture of all" of the Puritan diatribes against the stage. Both this book and his next were dedicated to Sir Philip Sidney *qv*, who was so far from pleased (Gosson in-

veighed also against music and poetry) that he was inspired to write his *Apologie for Poetrie*. Thomas Lodge *qv* also wrote his *Defence of Poetry, Music, and Stage-Playes* in answer to Gosson. It is significant that Gosson grants that the stage and the actors themselves may be quite respectable, though their plays are not, and that there are "good playes and sweet playes" (i.e., those by Stephen Gosson) available. The actors took their vengeance by reviving Gosson's plays, which were again flat failures; no copy of them now exists.

Somewhere before 1584 Gosson took orders, became a lecturer in the parish church in Stepney, London, and in 1591 was named queen's rector at Wigborough, Essex. This he exchanged for the rectory of Botolph Bishopsgate, London, where he lived the remainder of his life, died, and was buried.

Francis Meres praised Gosson's pastorals highly, but as none remains and his surviving poetry is negligible, no modern judgment can be made. His *Triumph of Warre* was a sermon preached at St. Paul's, justifying the war with Spain. The *Pleasaunt Quippes for Upstart New-fangled Gentlewomen*, which in all probability is his, is a coarse satire on women's styles. It is possible also, though not certain, that he wrote *A Short and Profitable Treatise of Lawfull and Unlawfull Recreations*, published in 1592.

In style, Gosson was a Euphuist, and all his books are written in the high-flown and artificial style made popular by John Lyly *qv*. Thomas Gosson, publisher of *Playes Confuted in Five Actions*, may have been Stephen Gosson's brother.

PRINCIPAL WORKS: The Schoole of Abuse, 1579; The Ephemerides of Phialo, and a Short Apologie of the School of Abuse, 1579; Playes Confuted in Five Actions, 1582; Pleasaunt Quippes for Upstart New-fangled Gentlewomen, 1595; The Triumph of Warre, 1598.

ABOUT: Lodge, T. A Defense of Poetry, Music, and Stage-Playes; Ringler, W. A. Stephen Gosson, A Biographical and Critical Study; Wood, A. à, Athenae Oxonienses.

G O W E R, J O H N (1330?-September ?, 1408), scholar, poet, came of a good Kentish family, and may have had the rank of esquire. His name was pronounced to rhyme with "power." Though not a wealthy man, he was comfortably well off, owning manors in Norfolk and Suffolk, from which he re-

JOHN GOWER

The purpose of all his work was didactic, though his best-known poem, the *Confessio Amantis*, seduced him into story telling (112 stories) by way of illustration. The *Vox Clamantis* (in Latin) was political in origin. The first version was dedicated to Richard II, and at this period (around 1380) Gower was undoubtedly a protege both of the young king and of the family of John of Gaunt. In spite of his social position, Gower's sympathies were with the peasants in the uprising of 1381, and as Richard's reign deteriorated he grew increasingly bitter against the king whom at first he had excused on the ground of his youth. The final version was dedicated to Richard's cousin and rival, Henry of Lancaster, later Henry IV. In consequence Gower earned for himself the reputation of a timeserver, though actually he seems to have been impelled by motives of pure conviction.

For centuries Gower and Chaucer were named together as if they were equals. They are not. Chaucer was a genius, Gower a cultured man with a gift for story telling. It is true that Gower helped to establish standard literary English; it is also true that he had technical mastery, that he could combine rhetorical artifice with simplicity and naturalness; and that his French poems have grace and beauty. His stories were of course borrowed from the classics—from the Bible to Ovid—but he could tell a story well. Nevertheless, his mind was essentially medieval, his long digressions and "edifying" glosses injured the readability of his work, and, as Lowell has remarked, he "raised tediousness to the precision of a science." G. C. Macaulay has perhaps judged Gower most justly by saying: "If his genius moves within somewhat narrow limits, yet, within those limits, it moves securely," ("genius" here being used merely in the sense of "inspiration"). He had a pure English style, and his moral aims were always of the highest (though he included some very dubious examples in the *Confessio Amantis*, as Chaucer did not hesitate to remind him); but his interest today is historical, not literary.

Gower seems to have employed a copying staff to distribute his writings, but of his three principal works, but one copy remains of the *Speculum Homini* or *Speculum Meditantis* (in French), under the title *Mirour de*

ceived rents, while living most of the time in London. Nothing is known about his education; the legends that he attended Oxford and was entered in the Inner Temple have no confirmation. He was almost certainly a layman. In all probability he had traveled in France, and he wrote with equal facility in Latin, French, and English. He was certainly a friend of Chaucer ("moral Gower," Chaucer called him), and there is no real foundation for the tradition that their friendship ended in a quarrel. He was Chaucer's senior, but he outlived the greater poet by eight years.

In his old age, in 1397, Gower married Agnes Groundolf, who seems to have been his second wife. There is no record of his having had children by either marriage. He lived at this time at the Priory of St. Mary Overies (now St. Saviour's), in Southwark, of which he had long been a benefactor. In his last years he was an invalid, and finally he became blind and ceased to write. He was buried at the Priory in a magnificent tomb.

Gower apparently did not start writing until middle age, except for his *Cinkante Balades* in French, and perhaps some earlier lost "amorous poems" of which he later avowed himself ashamed. His first writing was in French, his next in Latin, and it was only reluctantly that he finally ventured into English, not yet a respectable literary tongue.

l'Omme. He also wrote *Cronica tripartita* (in Latin) and an English poem, *In Praise of Peace*, both addressed to Henry IV.

PRINCIPAL WORKS (dates of printing): Confessio Amantis, 1483; In Praise of Peace, 1532; French Ballades (two series) 1818 (H. O. Coxe, ed. 1850); Works (G. C. Macaulay, ed.) 1899-1902.

ABOUT: Courthope, W. J. History of English Poetry; Ker, W. P. Essays in Mediaeval Literature; Lowell, J. R. My Study Windows; Morley, H. English Writers; tenBrink, B. History of Early English Poetry; Todd, H. J. Illustrations of the Lives and Writings of Gower and Chaucer.

GRAINGER, JAMES (1721?-December 16, 1766), physician, poet, was the son of John Grainger of Houghton Hall, Cumberland, and his second wife. So far as is known he was born at Dunse in Berwickshire, where his father held a civil service position after unsuccessful mining speculations had forced him to sell his estate. When John Grainger died, James' half-brother sent him to school. Studying medicine at Edinburgh University, he apprenticed himself to a surgeon, George Lauder, and before taking his degree entered the army medical service. He served honorably in Holland, reading the Latin poets in his leisure moments, and after the peace of Aix-la-Chapelle in 1748, left the army to travel in Europe. In 1753 he took his M.D. degree at Edinburgh and settled in London.

Although he seems to have been an excellent doctor, he failed to find patients and took to writing for a living. His friends were nearly all from the literary world—Johnson, Shenstone, Dodsley, Smollett (with whom he was later to have a bitter quarrel), Glover, Percy, and Oliver Goldsmith, whom he first introduced to Percy. He published a poem, *Ode on Solitude* in 1755, and as a regular contributor to the *Monthly Review* wrote on poetry, drama, and medicine. The feud with Smollett began when Grainger published his *Poetical Translation of the Elegies of Tibullus and of the Poems of Sulpicia*, which received an unfavorable notice in Smollett's *Critical Review*. Grainger revenged himself in a blistering public letter. Smollett retaliated by calling him a miserable hack, and there followed a resounding exchange of insults characteristic of a fulldress literary battle.

In 1759 Grainger set out on a tour to the West Indies with John Bourryau, a former pupil. The first stop was the island of St. Christopher, where Grainger married a Miss Daniel Mathew Burt, whose mother he had attended for smallpox on the voyage out. He remained in St. Christopher to practice medicine and take care of the estates belonging to his wife's family. While driving about the island on his doctor's calls, he composed a poem in four books on the cultivation of the sugar cane. Four years later when the death of his brother took him back to England, *The Sugar-Cane* was published. Apparently even his friends did not receive the poem with any great seriousness. Flat in diction and formal in argument, it is according to Louis Cazamian, the French critic, "the least readable among the technical poems of an age fertile in errors of similar nature."

Returning to the West Indies. Grainger died of a fever when he was in his mid-forties, bequeathing his manuscripts to Thomas Percy, who later arranged for the publication of a complete edition of his poetical works.

PRINCIPAL WORKS: A Poetical Translation of the Elegies of Tibullus and of the Poems of Sulpicia (tr.) 1759; The Sugar-Cane: A Poem, 1764; The Poetical Works of James Grainger (R. Anderson, ed.) 1836.

ABOUT: Anderson, R. Life *in* The Poetical Works; Chalmers, A. Biographical Dictionary; Knox, R. A. A Neglected Poet (London Mercury, vol. 8, 1923).

GRAMMATICUS, AELFRIC. See AELFRIC called GRAMMATICUS

GRAVES, RICHARD, the younger (May 4, 1715-November 23, 1804), novelist, poet, the second son of Richard Graves the elder, an antiquary, was born at Mickleton, Gloucestershire. An excellent Greek scholar, he won a scholarship at Pembroke College, Oxford, when he was seventeen. There he made friends with William Shenstone, the poet, and William Blackstone, the jurist, and on his graduation in 1736, was elected to a fellowship at All Souls' College. He began the study of medicine but gave it up after a long nervous illness. Receiving his M.A. degree from Oxford in 1740, he was ordained and became chaplain at Tissington Hall in Derbyshire, a district he was to describe later in his novels.

Through a relative, Graves was appointed curate of Aldworth near Reading about 1744. He lived at the home of a gentleman-farmer named Bartholomew and fell in love with the youngest daughter of the household, Lucy, a lovely and untutored girl of sixteen. Over the protest of his relatives he married her and sent her to London to be educated, although the marriage cost him his fellowship. The young couple lived in very straitened circumstances until Graves was given the rectory of Claverton near Bath through the influence of friends. He remained at Claverton for the rest of his life, receiving several additional preferments. Supplementing this income by his writing, and taking pupils to be educated along with his own children, he managed to make a very comfortable living. Among his pupils were Ralph Allen Warburton, son of the bishop, Prince Hoare, the artist, and Malthus, the political economist, who said later he "was taught little but Latin and good behavior."

A kindly eccentric, a conscientious cleric, and a Whig, Graves became a member of the literary coterie of Warwickshire (the most prominent member of which was his friend, Shenstone) and wrote great quantities of essays, prose tales, and verse. Marked by a lively, unaffected style, his prose works were very popular in their day, but they have been almost entirely forgotten except for one novel, *The Spiritual Quixote*. This tale of a young country squire and his mild adventures on a tour of the midlands is of considerable interest for its gentle satire on Methodism as well as for its clear account of rural life and manners.

Graves was nearly ninety years old when he died, attended by Malthus, his former pupil, who sat at the bedside of his master and administered the holy sacrament.

PRINCIPAL WORKS: The Festoon: A Collection of Epigrams, Ancient and Modern, 1766; The Spiritual Quixote: or, The Summer's Ramble of Mr. Geoffrey Wildgoose, 1773; The Love of Order: a Poetical Essay, 1773; The Progress of Gallantry: a Poetical Essay, 1774; Euphrosyne: or, Amusements on the Road of Life, 1776-80; Columella: or, The Distressed Anchoret, a Colloquial Tale, 1779; Eugenius: or, Anecdotes of the Golden Vale, 1785; Recollections of Some Particulars in the Life of the Late William Shenstone, Esq., 1788; The Rout: or, A Sketch of Modern Life, 1789; Plexippus: or, The Aspiring Plebeian, 1790; The Reveries of Solitude: Consisting of Essays in Prose, 1793; The Coalition: or, The Opera Rehears'd, a Comedy, 1794; The Farmer's Son: a Moral Tale, 1795;

Senilities: or, Solitary Amusements: In Prose and Verse, 1801; The Triflers: Consisting of Trifling Essays, Trifling Anecdotes, and a Few Poetical Trifles, 1805.

ABOUT: Hill, C. J. The Literary Career of Richard Graves; Hutton, W. H. Burford Papers.

GRAY, THOMAS (December 26, 1716-July 30 1771), poet, was born in Cornhill, London. His father, Philip Gray, was a "money scrivener" (i.e., an exchange broker), something of a rascal, and a good deal of a brute, as is evidenced by the documents left from an abortive attempt his wife made to secure a separation from him. Thomas Gray's mother was Dorothy Antrobus, who with her sister conducted a millinery establishment; it was she who saw to the education of her son. She had already saved his life by courageously bleeding him herself during an attack of croup. He was all she had in her abused and unhappy life—the only one of her twelve children who lived.

Gray's first teacher was his uncle, William Antrobus, a fellow of Peterhouse College, Cambridge. He was a good deal of a prodigy, bookish, and delicate, and he found friends like himself when in 1727 he went to Eton, where his tutor was his mother's other brother, Robert. These friends were Horace Walpole, Thomas Ashton, and Richard West (the closest to him), who died young. They formed a little group which kept superciliously aloof from the hearty athletic boys of the student body; Gray was besides an oppidan, living with his uncle, and so more or less removed from student activities. In 1734 he entered Cambridge, enrolling first at Pembroke College but soon transferring to Peterhouse. He took no degree at this time, but spent most of his hours making himself into a sound Greek and Latin scholar when he was supposed to be studying law; he became eventually one of the university's finest Hellenists. In Cambridge he formed another lasting friendship, with Thomas Wharton. In 1739 he set out for a tour of Europe as Walpole's guest; eventually when the atmosphere of patronage grew too galling, he deserted Walpole and went on by himself. They were not reconciled until 1745.

In 1741 Gray returned to London, wrote his first English verse (he had already written some Latin alcaics), and began an unfinished tragedy, *Agrippina*. That year his father took his insane temper out of this world, and surprisingly left him a small legacy. His mother and aunt moved to Stoke Poges, and he followed them. This is the site of the churchyard of the famous *Elegy*. West died in 1742, his friend's first great grief. Soon after, Gray returned to Cambridge, and this time achieved his LL.B., in 1744. He never, however, was called to the bar or practised law. Cambridge remained his headquarters thenceforth, though he frankly detested the place and everything in it, and tolerated it only for its libraries where he could work, and for the cheapness with which he could live on his tiny income. He was not a fellow of any college, but since he never married (Miss Speed, later Countess Viry, the only woman in whom he ever showed the faintest interest, was a very minor concern indeed), the quiet, studious life of a middle-aged fellow-commoner suited him very well. When he was not studying Greek he was writing and rewriting, never satisfied, constantly pruning and altering his work, frequently leaving it unfinished. Walpole insisted on having some of it to print on the new press he was playing with at Strawberry Hill, and other slim volumes were published, but actually Gray had no ambition, no desire for public acclaim, and thought of himself as a gentleman who wrote poetry rather than as a poet.

His life could scarcely have been more uneventful. He was often with his mother and two aunts at Stoke Poges. He traveled a good deal in England and Scotland, after his mother died in 1753, and discovered the beauties of the Lake Country before Wordsworth did. He had a terror of fire, and when some students played a joke on him by pretending a conflagration at his lodgings, he moved indignantly from Peterhouse to Pembroke (in 1756). When the British Museum was opened in 1759, he spent the better part of two years in London so that he could work in the great library. In 1762 he had applied for the chair of history and modern languages at Cambridge, but was unsuccessful; when the successful candidate was killed, two years later, Gray was given the post. It was a sinecure; he did no teaching, but he had to pay out of his salary for teachers of French and Italian. (The Italian teacher he chose was the grandfather of

J. G. Eccardt

THOMAS GRAY

Emma Isola, whom Charles and Mary Lamb adopted.) The only other result of his appointment was his writing of the *Installation Ode* when the Duke of Grafton became chancellor of the university.

The last personal interest of Gray's life was the young Swiss, Victor de Bonstetten, who attended Cambridge in 1770 and became his protege. He promised to visit de Bonstetten when he returned to Switzerland, but by 1771 he was too ill to travel. He had had an operation in 1764 from which he never really recovered, and he finally died at fifty-five of what was described as "gout in the stomach." He was buried beside his mother at Stoke Poges.

Most of Gray's contemporary reputation rested on his unpublished manuscripts, copied by himself many times over in his beautiful handwriting. He called himself indolent, but actually he was merely reluctant to put his energies into anything that did not interest him, and public praise decidedly did not. Though he had a fund of quiet playful humor, he was given to melancholy; seclusion, retirement, peace for study and meditation, were all he wanted of life. He was offered the laureateship in 1757, but declined it hastily. Gray's world was the world of the mind.

His poetic themes constantly echoed his current interests—Welsh poetry was reflected in *The Bard,* Norse in *The Fatal Sisters* and *The Descent of Odin.* The "Ossian" hoax took him in for only a short time, but he retained an enthusiasm for the pseudo-Celtic epic even when he realized its imposture. With the egregious William Mason (who served him as a posthumous editor almost as scurvily as Griswold served Poe, not hesitating to change his work whenever he pleased) he contemplated a history of English poetry which never came to completion, but which would probably have been an extremely interesting book. (Incidentally, if poor young Thomas Chatterton had sent his poems to Gray instead of to Walpole he might have had a happier fate.)

Gray's Pindaric odes were real Pindarics, with none of the formlessness into which this kind of poetry so often falls. Though he loved simple poetry and the homely poets of nature, his own work in the more elaborate odes was stately, classical, full of what Tovey called "heraldic splendor." The most faultless of the odes was probably the *Hymn to Adversity,* but since he was never satisfied with any of his work, what faults remain in any of it (outside of the printing errors of which he was a victim) are evidence only that he never considered it to be really finished. His Latin verse was spontaneous and fluid. And he was one of the world's great letter writers.

Today, Gray tends to become the poet of one poem, the great *Elegy.* It seems odd to think that this limpid, exquisite poem, almost Greek in its purity and classical simplicity, was denounced by Johnson and even by Goldsmith as turgid, confused, and even revolutionary! Undoubtedly its sentiments did not please the Tory Johnson. It remains nevertheless one of the most familiar but never hackneyed gems of literature, probably the source of more quotations than any poem in English except for Shakespeare's plays and some of the poems of Pope. Gray's passion for perfection may be seen in the four rejected stanzas, printed in 1924; they are quite inferior to the remainder.

Gray died without having achieved recognition except among a limited group of connoisseurs. His *Ode on a Distant Prospect of Eton College* was published anonymously; the *Elegy* was finally printed under his name only because a pirated edition contained so

many errors; he subordinated the poems themselves in the title of one volume to the drawings made to illustrate them; and in all his life the only money he ever received from writing was forty guineas for two odes. This proud, shy, sensitive man, completely out of harmony with the robust century in which he lived, was fortunate in his lifelong retreat from the world. His poetry lives on not through his efforts but despite them. No one could ever call Gray a major poet; he is too limited in range, too sparse in output: but one of the language's finest minor poets he indisputably is.

PRINCIPAL WORKS: Ode on a Distant Prospect of Eton College, 1757; Elegy Wrote [*sic*] in a Country Churchyard, 1751; Designs by Mr. R. Bentley for Six Poems by Mr. T. Gray, 1753; Odes by Mr. Gray, 1757; Pindaric Odes (Progress of Poesy, The Bard) 1758; Specimens of Welsh Poetry, 1764; Poems by Mr. Gray, 1768; Ode Performed in the Senate-House at Cambridge (Grafton Installation Ode) 1769; The Poems of Mr. Gray (W. Mason, ed.) 1775; English and Latin Poems (J. Mitford, ed.) 1844; The Correspondence of T. Gray with W. Mason (J. Mitford, ed.) 1853; Works (E. Gosse, ed.) 1884; Gray's Letters (D. C. Tovey, ed.) 1900-12.

ABOUT: Cecil, Lord D. Two Quiet Lives: Dorothy Osborne and Thomas Gray; Elwin, W. Some 18th Century Men of Letters; Gosse, E. Gray; Jack, A. A. Poetry and Prose; Johnson, S. Lives of the Poets; Jones, W. P. Thomas Gray, Scholar; Ketton-Cremer, R. W. Thomas Gray; Mason, W. Memoirs of Life and Writings, *in* Poems, 1775 ed.; Mathias, T. J. Observations on the Works and on the Character of Mr. Gray; Tovey, D. C. Gray and His Friends; Walpole, H. Horace Walpole's Correspondence with Thomas Gray, Richard West and Thomas Ashton; Woodberry, G. S. The Inspiration of Poetry.

GREEN, MATTHEW (1696-1737), poet, was apparently brought up with puritanical strictness by a dissenting family. In his youth he seems to have rebelled against this background, taking up "some free notions on religious subjects," but he remained close to one or another of the non-conformist sects throughout his life. The story is told that Green was swimming in a river when a fellow bather insultingly called him "Quaker!" Asked by a friend how his religious affiliation could be determined without his clothes, Green answered "By my swimming against the stream." Later, however, in a poem called *Barclay's Apology* he indicated that while he admired the Quakers he never actually belonged to their sect.

For many years Green worked in the customhouse where he became a trusted employee and found leisure to write occasional verse. Very few details are known of his life, but at least one anecdote recorded from the period reveals him as a whimsical and witty personality. When the government was about to cut off the allowance which provided milk for the customhouse cats, Green composed a petition in their name and won a reprieve.

The only poem he wrote of any lasting interest was *The Spleen*, published posthumously in 1737 with a preface by his friend, Richard Glover. Written in Swift's favorite octosyllabic meter, *The Spleen* praises the simple contemplative life as a cure for boredom. Light, witty and fluent, it is a pleasant example of the minor verse of the period. Another poem, *The Grotto,* on Queen Caroline's grotto at Richmond, was privately printed in 1732.

These two with several other poems by Green were included in the first volume of Dodsley's collection published in 1749. They were subsequently reprinted in Johnson's, Chalmers' and other collections of English poetry. Although his work was praised by Pope and admired by Gray, Green was very much a "one-poem" poet even in his own century, so much so, indeed, that he came to be known as "Spleen-Green."

PRINCIPAL WORKS: The Grotto, a Poem, 1732; The Spleen, An Epistle Inscribed to His Particular Friend Mr. C. J. (R. Glover, ed.) 1737.

ABOUT: Aiken, J. Essay, *in* The Spleen and Other Poems; Dodsley, R. Biographical notice, *in* A Collection of Poems; Sanford, E. Life, *in* The Poetical Works of Matthew Green (*in* The Works of the British Poets).

GREENE, ROBERT (July 1558-September 3, 1592), dramatist, pamphleteer, romancer, was born in Norwich, Norfolk. He entered St. John's College, Cambridge, in 1575, received his B.A. in 1579, transferred to Clare Hall, and was given his M.A. there in 1583. Just where he was and what he was doing for the next five years is unknown; he was incorporated as an M.A. of Oxford in 1588, and spoke of himself as "of either university." He undoubtedly did some traveling during this period; he himself says he was familiar with Spain, Italy, France, Poland, Germany, and Denmark. It is certain also that he was neither a clergyman nor an actor, both of which statements have been made of him. Probably, after some time on the Continent, he merely came to London and drifted into the Bohemian circles of the professional playwrights. He had written some plays as early as his Cambridge days, and had probably already written some of the romances which made his enemy Gabriel Harvey *qv* call him "the Ape of Euphues."

One must discount both Harvey's vicious attacks on Greene's way of life and moral character, and Greene's own sensational exaggerations. Nevertheless, there seems no doubt that he led a very debauched and unedifying existence. Red-haired Robert Greene had been reared in a rigidly virtuous and unsympathetic family (whose ethical standards continued to prick his conscience). He was a highly impressionable and emotional young man (he died at thirty-four), and he was not proof against the temptations which assailed him at the university and overwhelmed him in London. About 1585 he was married—perhaps in a runaway match—begat a son, and then deserted his wife and child. The letter he wrote her on his deathbed, however, shows that they were never unacquainted with each other's whereabouts.

We know one thing: he was an exceedingly hard and industrious worker. Most of his plays seem to be lost, or not recognized as wholly or partly his; but the huge number of pamphlets and brief romances he turned out could not have been produced by a man who was spending all his time in dissipation.

ROBERT GREENE

235

Nevertheless, it seems evident that he did die in abject poverty, deserted by all his friends, even by Thomas Nashe, who hastily disclaimed any intimacy with him. We may make every allowance for the malice displayed in Harvey's account of Greene's death in *Fovre Letters,* but the main facts seem to be there—the poor shoemaker and his wife who took him in, the two drabs who were his only visitors (one of them, sister of a hanged cutpurse, his mistress and mother of his illegitimate child), and the heartbreaking letter he sent his abandoned wife: "Doll, I charge thee by the love of our youth, and by my soules rest that thou wilt see this man [the kindly shoemaker] paide, for if hee and his wife had not succoured me I had died in the streetes." It is a story of wasted talents and blasted hopes of which the annals of literature are only too sadly full.

All of Greene's work was published in the last five years of his life or after his death. His plays were not acted or printed in the order in which they were written. Their correct order of writing seems to be: *Alphonsus,* the *Looking Glasse* (with Lodge), *Orlando Furioso, Friar Bacon and Friar Bungay*—by far the best, full of humorous life and vivid characterization, though a wild burlesque of the real Roger Bacon—and *James IV.* He also probably wrote some of the early plays which coalesced into Shakespeare's *Henry VI.* Other plays were attributed to him, including *Selemis* (1594) and *George-a-Green the Pinner of Wakefield* (1599); the latter may actually be his. He had a mastery of complicated plot, and a gift for social portraiture. Incidentally, his romance *Pandosto* contains practically the entire story of *A Winter's Tale.*

His romances ("love-pamphlets") range from the highflown Euphuism of his early work to the Defoe-like realism of *Never Too Late.* His "social" pamphlets are expanded broadsides, sharp pictures of the London underworld and its "cony-catchers"—criminal argot for confidence men. His semiautobiographical pamphlets—*A Groatsworth of Wit* is the best known of them—stem equally from a real (if perhaps temporary) repentence for his evil ways and a keen sense of the popular interest in sensation.

Two of these pamphlets possess also an adventitious interest. *A Qvip for an Upstart Courtier* earned Greene the vindictive enmity of Gabriel Harvey, whose brothers and father were attacked in it. *A Groatsworth of Wit* contains the supposed attack on Shakespeare, coupled with appeals to Marlowe, Peele, and Nashe to reform their wicked lives. It would be natural that a man of higher social class, with a university background, should resent the success of a nobody. But an examination of the famous passage—the "upstart crow beautified with our feathers" who is "in his owne conceyte the only shake-scene in a countrey" makes it probable that the person alluded to is some unnamed actor, and not any of Greene's fellow-dramatists.

Interspersed in many of Greene's "love-pamphlets" and in the plays are lyrical verses which display his finest gift. He was essentially a lyrist, and his songs are exactly what the word implies. One wonders if in the tenderest of these, *Sephestia's Lullaby* ("Weep not, my wanton, smile upon my knee"), there was an echo of the far-off day when he too had "left his pretty boy."

PRINCIPAL WORKS: *Plays* (dates of publication)—The Historie of Orlando Furioso One of the Twelve Pieres of France, 1594; A Looking Glasse for London and England (with T. Lodge) 1594; The Honorable Historie of Friar Bacon, and Friar Bongay, 1594; The Scottish Historie of James the Fourth, Slaine at Flodden, Entermixed with a pleasant Comedie, presented by Oboram King of Fayeries, 1598; The Comicall Historie of Alphonsus King of Aragon, 1599. *Romances*—Mamillia, 1583; Morando, 1584; The Myrrour of Modestie, 1584; Arbasto, 1584; Planetomachia, 1586; Penelope's Web, 1587; Perimedes the Blacke-Smith, 1588; Pandosto: The Triumph of Time, 1588; Alcida, 1589; Menaphon (Greenes Arcadia) 1589; Greenes Never Too Late, 1590; Philomela, 1592; The Anatomie of Love's Flatteries, 1594. *Pamphlets*—Greenes Mourning Garment, 1590; Greenes Farewell to Folly, 1591; A Notable Discovery of Coosnage, 1591; The Blacke Bookes Messenger, 1592; The Defence of Conny-Catching, 1592; A Disputation between a Hee Conny-Catcher and a Shee Conny-Catcher, 1592; A Qvip for an Upstart Courtier, 1592; Greenes Groatsworth of Wit, together with a Million of Repentance, 1592. *Miscellaneous*—Plays and Poems (J. C. Collins, ed.) 1905; Complete Works (A. B. Grosart, ed.) 1881-86.

ABOUT: B[arnfield], R.I. ? Greenes Funeralls; Bernhardi, W. Robert Greene's Leben und Schriften; Brown, J. M. An Early Rival of Shakspere; Castle, E. J. Shakespeare, Bacon, Jonson, and Greene: A Study; Chapman, W. H. William Shakespeare and Robert Greene: the Evidence; Collins, J. C. Life, Plays and Poems; Gayley, C. M. Representative Comedies; Grosart, A. B. Introduction, Complete Works; Harvey, G. Fovre Letters and certaine sonnets, especially touching Robert Greene and other parties by him abused; Jordan, J. C. Robert Greene; Jusserand, J. J. The English Novel in the Time of Shakespeare; Nashe, T. Strange News; R[ich], B.? Greenes Newes both from heaven and hell; Schelling, F. E. The Queen's Progress; Storojenko, N. (B. Hodgetts, tr.) Robert Greene: His Life and Works.

GREVILLE, Sir FULKE (Lord Brooke), 1554-September 30, 1628, dramatist, poet, biographer, was born at Beauchamp Court, Warwickshire, the only son of Sir Fulke Greville and Anne Neville. In 1564 he entered the newly founded Shrewsbury School on the same day as Sir Philip Sidney, who became his lifelong friend. Together they entered Jesus College, Cambridge, in 1568, and together they went to Elizabeth's court in 1577. Greville at once became a great favorite of Elizabeth, and she forbade him to travel abroad, though once or twice he incurred her displeasure by disobeying. (He was with Sidney in Heidelberg in 1577, and in 1591 he served briefly under Henry of Navarre in Normandy. He wanted to accompany Sidney to the Netherlands in 1583, but Elizabeth refused; Sidney was killed there.)

In 1583 he was made secretary to the principality of Wales, in 1597 "treasurer of the wars," in 1598 treasurer of the navy. He served four terms in the House of Commons for Warwickshire between 1592 and 1620. James I on his accession made him a Knight of the Bath, he was chancellor of the exchequer from 1614 to 1621, in 1618 commissioner of the treasury, and in 1621 James raised him to the peerage as Baron Brooke, a title held by his ancestors the Willoughbys. It will be seen that Fulke Greville was primarily a statesman; his writing (nearly all done in his youth) was strictly the avocation of a courtier, and none of his work was published before his death except his tragedy, *Mustapha*, an elegy on Sidney in *The Phoenix Nest* (1593), and two poems in *Englands Helicon* (1600). Nevertheless his interest in literature was real and deep. At Oxford he, with Sidney and Sir Edward Dyer,[qv] had belonged to Gabriel Harvey's "Areopagus," which sought to introduce Latin meters into English verse. He was the patron of many men of letters, including Samuel Daniel and Sir William D'Avenant.[qv] He also endowed a chair of history at Cambridge.

SIR FULKE GREVILLE

Greville does not seem to have married. His title was remaindered to a favorite cousin, Robert Greville. In February 1628 he wrote a will leaving his entire estate to this cousin. One of the witnesses was an old servant, Ralph Haywood, who had always expected a legacy of his own. Brooding over this slight, on September 1st he stabbed his master as he lay in bed, then immediately killed himself. Greville lingered for a month before dying of the wound. He wrote his own epitaph, which is on his tomb: "Fulke Grevil—Servant to Queene Elizabeth—Councellor to King James—and Frend to Sir Philip Sydney."

As Lamb remarked, Greville "makes passion, character, and interest of the highest order subservient to the expression of state dogmas." He was a devoted "servant" of Elizabeth, whose death cast him into misery and apprehension of England's future; but he supported James I (with one exception) in his most high-handed procedures. He contemplated, it is said, expanding his biography of Sidney into a history of Elizabeth's reign, but opposition by Lord Cecil, who had possession of the state papers, and his own careful loyalty restrained him. He himself knew his limitations as an author: "For my own part I found my creeping genius more fixed upon images of life than images of wit." His so-called "sonnets" (*Caelica*, of which Elizabeth is the protagonist if any exist) are not sonnets in the modern sense; his plays were never meant to be acted. His mind and his true interests were philosophical, not literary. His poetry is only metric prose. But he was a seminal influence, and in his personal character not far from the heights reached by his noble-hearted "frend."

PRINCIPAL WORKS: The Tragedy of Mustapha, 1609; Certaine learned and elegant workes of the Right Honourable Fulke, Lord Brooke, written in his Youth and familiar exercise with Sir Philip Sidney, 1633; The Life of the renowned Sr Philip Sidney, 1652 (N. Smith, ed., 1907); The Remains of Sir Fulk Grevill, Lord Brooke, 1670; The Works in Verse and Prose Complete of the Lord Brooke (A. B. Grosart, ed.) 1868.

ABOUT: Grosart, A. B. Memorial Introduction, Works; Hazlitt, H. Table Talk; Lamb, C. Specimens of the Dramatic Poets; Stopes, C. C. Shakespeare's Warwickshire Contemporaries; Walpole, H. Royal and Noble Authors.

GRIFFIN, BARTHOLOMEW (fl. 1596)
poet, whose single sonnet-sequence, *Fidessa, More Chaste Than Kinde*, was published in 1596, has bequeathed us his name only as B. Griffin, but he is usually identified with Bartholomew Griffin of Coventry who was buried December 15, 1602, at Holy Trinity. According to his will, Bartholomew left a widow, Katherine, and a son called Rice. It seems probable that he was related to the Griffin family of Dingley, Northamptonshire.

Fidessa, a series of sixty-two love sonnets in the traditional Elizabethan pattern, was dedicated to William Essex of Lambrone, Berkshire, and is prefaced by an epistle which gives us the only slender clues we have to the personality of its author. Griffin styles himself a "gentleman" and addresses himself to gentlemen of the Inns of Court, which suggests that he may have been a lawyer. There is mention of an unfinished pastoral which he had intended "for varietie sake" to publish with *Fidessa*, but its publication was evidently postponed and no trace of this second work has been found. Of *Fidessa* only three original copies are extant, those in the Bodleian, the Huth and the Lamport libraries.

The third sonnet of the *Fidessa* sequence, which begins "Venus and young Adonis sitting by her," was included with a good deal of variation in the text in the miscellany, *The Passionate Pilgrime*, published by W. Jaggard in 1599 as the work of Shakespeare.

Concerning this curious bit of literary history Sidney Lee writes in the *Cambridge History of English Literature*, "A definite, if slender, interest attaches to Bartholomew Griffin's *Fidessa*, a conventional sequence of sixty-two sonnets. Griffin was exceptionally bold in imitating home products and borrowed much from Daniel and Drayton's recent volumes. But it is worthier of remembrance that one of his sonnets, on the theme of *Venus and Adonis*, was transferred with alterations to Jaggard's piratical miscellany of 1599, *The Passionate Pilgrime*, all the contents of which were assigned to Shakespeare on the title-page."

PRINCIPAL WORKS: Fidessa, More Chaste Than Kind, 1596 (P. Bliss, ed 1815; A. B. Grosart, 1876; Sir S. Lee, in Elizabethan Sonnets, 1904).

ABOUT: Dowden. E. Introduction to The Passionate Pilgrime, in Shakespeare Quarto Facsimiles; Grosart, A. B. Introduction, in Fidessa (1876 ed.).

GRIMALD, Grimalde, or Grimoald, NICHOLAS (1519-1562), poet, dramatist, translator, was born in Huntingdonshire, probably the son of Giovanni Baptista Grimaldi, a clerk, and the grandson of a Genoese merchant who came to England about 1485. His mother, Annes, has been lovingly memorialized in what is probably Grimald's best poem, *Funerall Song Upon the Deceas of Annes His Mother.*

Grimald was educated at Christ's Church, Cambridge, and at Oxford, taking an M.A. degree in 1543-44. He became chaplain to Bishop Nicholas Ridley when he was about twenty-eight, was licensed as a preacher and recommended for preferment. When Ridley was imprisoned for his reformist views during the reign of Queen Mary, he corresponded regularly with his young friend, sending him copies of all he wrote and instructing him to carry out certain Latin translations. This association led to the arrest of Grimald in 1555. He appears, however, to have recanted his Protestant beliefs for the sake of a pardon and there were rumors that he acted as a spy during the religious persecutions of the latter part of Mary's reign. Of his defection Ridley wrote to a friend, "I fear me he escaped not without some becking and bowing of his knee unto Baal." Grimald did not live many years after the accession of Elizabeth, the date of his death being marked with an epitaph written by his friend, Barnabe Googe,[qv] which was published in 1562.

Grimald wrote both in English and in Latin. Forty of his English poems were published in *Tottel's Miscellany*, which first appeared in 1557, and there is some evidence for believing he was associated with Tottel as an editor. In the second edition of the *Miscellany* only ten of the original Grimald poems appear and these are signed with initials only. Although his poems were certainly inferior to those of Wyatt and Surrey, both of whom were first published in the *Miscellany*, they were above the average of the other contributors and no satisfactory explanation has ever been offered for this omission. Grimald is perhaps more interesting as a translator of Cicero and Virgil, and as the author of two Latin dramas, *Christus Redivivus* and *Archipropheta*. In his genuine appreciation of the economy of Latin verse, Grimald stands as a forerunner of the later classical influence on English diction and construction.

PRINCIPAL WORKS: Christus Redivivus, Comœdia Tragica, 1543: Archipropheta, Tragœdia, 1548; Marcus Tullius Ciceroes thre bokes of duties, to Marcus his sonne, turned oute of latine into English (tr.) 1556; Poems, *in* Tottel's Miscellany, 1557 (H. E. Rollins, ed. 1928); Nicolai Grimoaldi viri Doctis. In P. V. Maronis quatuor libros Georgicorum in oratione soluta Paraphrasis elegantissimus, 1591.

ABOUT: Merrill, L. R. The Life and Poems of Nicholas Grimald; Wood, A. à, Athenae Oxon:enses.

GROSE, FRANCIS (1731?-May 12, 1791),

antiquary, draughtsman, miscellaneous writer, was born at Greenford, Middlesex, the eldest son of a well-to-do jeweler, Francis Grose (or Grosse) and Ann Bennett. His father was a native of Berne, Switzerland, who had come to England early in the eighteenth century and had won himself the honor of making the coronation crown for George III. Young Francis was given a classical education and studied art at Shipley's drawing school, exhibiting at the Royal Academy and with the Incorporated Society of Artists.

Grose has been described as "an antiquarian Falstaff"—hearty, good-humored and enormously corpulent. Although he was fond of high living, his interests were scholarly, finding expression in a series of works on the antiquities of England, Wales,

Scotland and Ireland, as well as in the admirable tinted drawings of architectural remains, several of which are in the British Museum. In 1755 he became Richmond herald and later adjutant and paymaster for the Hampshire militia. His account books, according to his own story, were his right and left hand pockets, into one of which went money received, from the other of which money was paid out. That his talent for accountancy was slight is perhaps borne out by the speed with which he dissipated the not inconsiderable fortune left him by his father.

The Antiquities of England and Wales, his first important work, was published in six volumes from 1773 to 1787, winning him a solid reputation as an antiquary. In 1789 he began a tour of Scotland which resulted in *The Antiquities of Scotland*. During this visit he met Robert Burns, who addressed several poems to him, among them one containing the famous lines, "A child's amang you taking notes/ And, faith, he'll prent it." Two years later he left England again for a tour of Ireland which was cut short by his death in Dublin. *The Antiquities of Ireland* was completed and published by his friend, Dr. Edward Ledwick.

In addition to his antiquarian works, Grose wrote a number of humorous essays, several satirical pieces, and a slang dictionary, the *Classical Dictionary of the Vulgar Tongue*. Not only was he an excellent scholar and a first-rate draughtsman, but a man of versatile talent and great wit.

PRINCIPAL WORKS: *Antiquarian*—The Antiquities of England and Wales, 1773-87; Military Antiquities Respecting a History of the English Army, From the Conquest to the Present Time, 1786-8; A Treatise on Ancient Armour and Weapons, 1786-9; The Antiquities of Scotland, 1789-91; The Antiquities of Ireland (E. Ledwick, ed.) 1791. *Miscellaneous*—Advice to the Officers of the British Army, 1782; A Guide to Health, Beauty, Riches and Honour, 1783; A Classical Dictionary of the Vulgar Tongue, 1785; A Provincial Glossary, 1787; Rules for Drawing Caricatures, 1788; The Grumbler, 1791; The Olio, 1793.

ABOUT: Nichols, J. Literary Anecdotes; Noble, M. History of the College of Arms.

GUNNING, Mrs. SUSANNAH (1740?-

August 28, 1800), novelist, was born Susannah Minifie of Fairwater, Somersetshire. Before her marriage to John Gunning she had written three novels but the details of her life remained obscure until the escapades of the Gunning family brought her into the limelight of scandal.

John Gunning was the son of an aristocratic family who followed a military career and rose to be a lieutenant-general after distinguishing himself at the battle of Bunker Hill. His two sisters, Elizabeth and Maria, were famous beauties who became respectively the Countess of Coventry and the Duchess of Hamilton and Argyll. The Gunnings were married on August 8, 1768, and a year later their daughter, Elizabeth, was born. Elizabeth grew to be a beautiful young woman who first drew attention to herself by carrying on simultaneous flirtations with two marquises, Lord Lorne and Lord Blandford. The wanderings of her heart resulted in a complicated drama of letters exchanged and intercepted, several of which, presumably written by Elizabeth, appear to have been forgeries. A Mrs. Bowen sent certain letters to General Gunning in which Elizabeth declared her passion for Lord Lorne at the same time the General was trying to arrange a marriage with Lord Blandford. The General thereupon disowned his daughter who fled to the Duchess of Bedford in London. Mrs. Gunning followed and took up her pen to defend her daughter, publishing A Letter Addressed to His Grace the Duke of Argyll, in which she declared the letters a forgery fabricated by Mrs. Bowen and her husband, Captain Essex Bowen.

The affairs of the Gunning family made excellent fodder for the scandal-hungry and the public prints were full of squibs on what Walpole called the "Gunningiad." A second scandal broke when General Gunning was accused of an intrigue with a Mrs. Duberly and the lady's husband was awarded £5000 damages. Gunning and his mistress left England and lived in Naples where he died in 1797, bequeathing an estate in Ireland and £8000 to his wife and daughter.

Mrs. Gunning wrote a number of novels after her separation, one of which, Memoirs of Mary, was supposed to contain allusions to the family scandals. Elizabeth also wrote novels scarcely distinguishable from her mother's, and published several translations from the French. Of the novels, popular in their day and long since forgotten, it has been said they "are exceedingly harmless, an absence of plot forming their most original characteristic."

PRINCIPAL WORKS: The Histories of Lady Frances S— and Lady Caroline S—, 1763; Family Pictures, 1764; Barford Abbey, 1768; The Count de Poland, 1780; Anecdotes of the Delborough Family, 1792; Memoirs of Mary, 1793; Delves: a Welch Tale, 1796; Fashionable Involvements, 1800; The Heir Apparent (E. Gunning, ed.) 1802.

ABOUT: Baker, D. E. Biographia Dramatica; Rivers, D. Literary Memoirs of Living Authors of Great Britain.

GURNEY, THOMAS (March 7, 1705-June 22, 1770), inventor of the Gurney system of shorthand, was born at Woburn, Bedfordshire. His father was John Gurney, a miller. Although the elder Gurney tried to make Thomas a farmer, the boy was fond of books and displayed considerable mechanical aptitude. Twice he ran away from neighboring farms where he had been sent to work and managed to give himself an education and learn clockmaking. His later profession of shorthand-writer began with a happy accident. Curious about astrology, he bought a box of books at an auction for the sake of a volume on astrology and found among them a copy of William Mason's Shorthand. So assiduously did he study Mason's system that by the time he was sixteen he could take down whole sermons in shorthand and had begun to make certain improvements in method which he later incorporated in his own system.

In 1737 he went to London, after teaching school for several years, and was appointed shorthand-writer at Old Bailey, the first official court stenographer in English history. Gurney reported criminal trials, proceedings in both houses of Parliament, and taught shorthand to a select number of pupils. To supplement his income, which apparently was not large, he also conducted a clockmaking business and designed calico patterns for a manufacturer. By 1750 he had brought his original revision of the Mason system to a point of perfection which moved him to publish Brachygraphy, or Swift Writing Made Easy to the Meanest Capacity, a book which went through many editions well into the nineteenth century. For his system he claimed, "The whole is founded on so just a plan, that it is wrote with greater expedition than any yet invented, and likewise may be read with the greatest ease." An early practictioner of Gurney's system, Erasmus Darwin, was sufficiently impressed to contribute several commendatory verses to the second edition.

Gurney married Martha Marsom and had a son, Joseph, who became his assistant and successor as shorthand-writer in Parliament and English courts of law. Together they published stenographic reports of state trials and *causes célèbres* in pamphlet form and brought out successively improved editions of the *Brachygraphy*. Throughout the lifetime of his son and his grandson, Thomas Gurney's method remained the official English system of shorthand.

PRINCIPAL WORKS: Brachygraphy, or Swift Writing Made Easy to the Meanest Capacity, 1750.

ABOUT: Gurney, D. The Record of the House of Gournay; Levy, M. History of Shorthand; Rockwell, J. E. Literature of Shorthand.

HABINGTON, WILLIAM (November 4 or 5, 1605-November 30, 1654), poet, dramatist, was born at Hindlip Hall, Worcestershire, where his father, Thomas Habington, an antiquary and a Catholic, was famous for hiding priests banished under the edict of James I. His birth date coincides with the discovery of the Gunpowder Plot against James and his Parliament, made known to Lord Monteagle in an anonymous letter which, according to contemporary gossip, was written by William's mother.

William was educated by Jesuit priests at St. Omer's and in Paris and for a time considered becoming a priest himself. Instead, he returned to England and when he was about twenty-five married Lucy Herbert, youngest daughter of the first baron of Powis. In her praise he wrote a series of elegant and unimpassioned love poems first issued anonymously in 1634 under the title *Castara*. A second edition carried the author's name and added a number of new poems, among them eight elegies on his friend, George Talbot—also three prose "characters" introducing the three sections. The final edition, published in 1640, added twenty-two sacred poems and another character, "A Holy Man." Essentially a religious poet even when he wrote of earthly love, Habington talks at great length about both Castara's chastity and the chastity of his own verse. In the preface he writes, "In all those flames in which I burned I never felt

a wanton heate, nor was my invention ever sinister from the straite way of chastity."

Habington was also the author of a play, *Queen of Arragon,* first published in 1640 and revived at the time of the Restoration with a prologue and an epilogue by Samuel Butler. Butler states that Habington gave the play to Philip, Earl of Pembroke, who arranged for it "to be acted at court, and afterwards published against the author's consent." His two prose works were *The History of Edward the Fourth King of England,* compiled from notes collected by his father, and *Observations Upon Historie.*

As a person not much is known of this Catholic poet and his role in the complex drama of religious and political conflict that held the stage through most of his lifetime. Anthony à Wood says he took the republican side during the civil war and became known to Cromwell, which is understandable in view of the temporary alliance between Catholic and Puritan under James I. As a poet, we can perhaps assess him best by his own judgment in the preface to *Castara*: "If not too indulgent to what is my owne, I think even these verses will have that proportion in the world's opinion that heaven hath allotted me in fortune; not so high as to be wondered at, nor so low as to be contemned." In Habington's lyrics one can hear the accents of the sonneteers, with an echo of Spenser's art and Sydney's wit, but they are often mere empty rehearsal of metaphysical fancies lacking the ardor of a true poetic imagination. As he said himself, what his poetry needed was "more sweate and oyle."

PRINCIPAL WORKS: Castara, 1634, 1635, 1639-40 (E. Arber, ed. 1870); The Queene of Arragon. A Tragi-Comedie, 1640 (W. C. Hazlitt, ed., *in* Dodsley's Old Plays, 1875); The Historie of Edward the Fourth, 1640; Observations Upon Historie, 1641.

ABOUT: Hazlitt, W. C. Memoir, in Dodsley's Old Plays; Wood, A. à, Athenae Oxonienses.

HAKLUYT, RICHARD (1553?-November 23, 1616), collector and publisher of accounts of English maritime explorations, was born in London; his family, from Herefordshire, was of Welsh descent—not of Dutch, as has been claimed. While he was still a pupil (queen's scholar) at Westminster School, he read some accounts of explorations in the Middle Temple chambers of his cousin and namesake, Richard Hakluyt, and "resolved to prosecute that knowledge and kind of literature." He entered Christ College, Oxford, in 1570, proceeded B.A. in 1574, M.A. in 1577, and took orders. While at Oxford he lectured publicly on navigation and geography, and began the writing of *Divers Voyages*. Sir Edward Stafford, ambassador to France, became interested in Hakluyt and took him to Paris as his chaplain in 1583; there he wrote *A Particuler Discourse Concerning Westerne Discoveries* (not printed for nearly three hundred years), which came to the attention of Queen Elizabeth and earned him a prebend at Bristol.

Hakluyt's next enterprise was the publication of Peter Martyr of Anghiera's *De Orbe Novo*, which gave the elements of astronomy for the use of navigators; he tried also (in vain) to have a scientific lectureship for seamen founded. Not succeeding in this, he took on the "heavy burden, great charges, and infinite care" of his major work, the *Principall Navigations*. This he said he undertook "to stop the mouths of our reproachers" who accused English explorers of "sluggish security." The fact is that most early English explorations were made by private commercial interests, which had no desire to share their findings with the world. Hakluyt, however, was indefatigable in overcoming this attitude and making public what England had done and was doing.

The first edition of the *Principall Navigations* paid tribute to the victorious battle of Cadiz; in the second edition, this allusion was removed, because of the fall of Essex. Both editions included the destruction of the Spanish Armada and some other naval battles. Hakluyt himself, in his introduction, said truly that the book "brought to light many rare and worthy monuments which long have lien miserably scattered in mustie corners, . . . and were very like for the greatest part to have been buried in perpetuall oblivion."

In 1599 Hakluyt became rector of Wetheringsett, Suffolk (later he was rector of Gedney, Lincolnshire, as well), in 1602 a prebendary, and in 1603 archdeacon of Westminster. But though he attended faithfully to his clerical duties, exploration remained his first love. In 1601 he was an adviser to the East India Company, and in 1606 was one of the prime movers behind

the petition to James I for patents for the colonization of Virginia. He was one of the chief "adventurers" of the South Virginia Company, and was promised the living of Jamestown when a church should be founded there. (However, he never saw Virginia.)

Hakluyt was married twice, the first time in 1594 and again in 1604, his first wife having died about 1597. By his first marriage he had one son (who unfortunately became a disreputable profligate). He died in London in his middle sixties, and was buried in Westminster Abbey. He left enough manuscripts for another book; some of this material was used by Purchas,[qv] the rest is now in the Bodleian Library at Oxford. The Hakluyt Society, founded in 1846, perpetuates his name by publication of rare books of travels.

As Froude has said, the *Principall Navigations* is "the prose epic of the modern English nation." It has been remarked that England was more indebted to Hakluyt than to any man of his time for its American possessions. Hakluyt himself not only was a skilled translator, but his own prose style is vigorous, lucid, and dignified, evidencing fine imaginative power and real literary talent.

PRINCIPAL WORKS: Divers Voyages touching the Discoverie of America and the Islands adjacent unto the same, 1582; A notable historie containing foure voyages made by certayne French captains unto Florida (tr.) 1587; The Principall Navigations, Voiages, and Discoveries of the English Nation made by Sea or Over Land to the most remote and farthest distant quarters of the earth at any time within the compasse of these 1500 years, 1589 (second edition, . . . these 1600 years, 1598-1600); The Discoverie of the world from their [*sic*] originall unto the yeere of our Lord 1555 (tr. from A. Galvano) 1601; Virginia Richly valued by the description of the maine land of Florida, her next neighbour (tr.) 1609; A Particular Discourse concerning Westerne Discoveries, 1877.

ABOUT: Froude, J. A. Short Studies on Great Subjects; Fuller, T. Worthies of England; Raleigh, W. The English Voyages of the 16th Century; Tyler, P. F. Historical View of the Progress of Discovery on the More Northern Coast of America; Watson, F. Richard Hakluyt; Williamson, J. A. Richard Hakluyt and His Successors (in Centenary Volume Hakluyt Society, E. Lyman, ed.); Wood, A. à, Athenae Oxonienses.

HALE, Sir MATTHEW (November 1, 1609-December 25, 1676), judge, legal and religious writer, was born at Alderly, Gloucestershire, the only son of Robert Hale and Joan Poyntz. His father, a lawyer, died be-

fore Matthew was five and the boy was brought up by a guardian, Anthony Kingscote, who as a Puritan saw to it that his ward received an education strictly according to his own principles. In 1626 he entered the Magdalen Hall, Oxford, with the intention of taking holy orders, but his fondness for sports and the theatre changed his mind. Although he had always had the greatest contempt for lawyers, a friend, Serjeant Glanville, now succeeded in interesting him in the law. Accordingly he entered Lincoln's Inn in 1628 and by studying sixteen hours a day became the star pupil of William Noy, jurist and author.

Hale's career as lawyer and jurist was one of the most distinguished of his century from the outset, when he acted as counsel in several important state trials, until he was appointed chief justice of the king's bench in 1671. He was sergeant-at-law and justice of the common pleas under Cromwell. He served twice in Parliament, in 1654 and again in 1658. At heart he was a royalist— yet he took the engagement to be faithful to the Commonwealth required of all lawyers and served on an important committee for law reform. He also played a major role in the restoration of Charles II, again serving on several legal committees. After the Restoration he was made lord chief baron of the exchequer and later was knighted.

Through all political weathers, Hale maintained a strict and objective impartiality on the bench, which was recognized even by his enemies. During his lifetime he published a number of solid legal summaries and religious treatises, and two scientific works of dubious value. The bulk of his writing was left in manuscript when he died, the most notable being *A History of the Common Law of England* and *Historia Placitorum Coronae*.

Hale was twice married and fathered ten children, all but two of whom died during his lifetime. He died on Christmas in 1676 some ten months after he had resigned as chief justice of the bench under Charles II.

PRINCIPAL WORKS: London's Liberties, 1650; Difficiles Nugae: or Observation Touching the Torricellian Experiment, 1674; Observations Touching the Principles of Natural Motions, 1677; Pleas of the Crown, 1678; Sacra Coronae: or The King's Rights and Prerogatives Defended, 1680; Historia

Placitorum: or History of the Pleas of the Crown, 1685; History of the Common Law of England, 1713; Jurisdiction of the House of Lords, 1796; Works Moral and Religious (T. Thirlwall, ed.) 1805.

ABOUT: Burnet, G. Life and Death of Sir Matthew Hale; Williams, J. B. Memoirs of the Life, Character and Writings of Sir Matthew Hale; Wood, A. à, Athenae Oxonienses.

HALES, JOHN (April 19, 1584-May 19, 1656), author of sermons and religious tracts, was born in Bath, where his father, also John Hales, was steward of a wealthy family. After attending the Bath Grammar School he entered Corpus Christi College, Oxford, proceeding B.A. in 1603. In 1605 he became a fellow of Merton College, where he secured his M.A. in 1609 and took orders. In 1612 he was public lecturer in Greek at the university. In 1613 he was made a fellow of Eton College, but from 1616 to 1619 he was in Holland as chaplain to the English ambassador, then returning to Eton. In 1639 he was named one of the chaplains of Archbishop Laud, and canon of Windsor. As a Royalist, he was ruined by the civil war; Parliament ejected him from his canonry in 1642, and his fellowship at Eton was rescinded in 1649. Hales hid first in Buckinghamshire and then in Eton itself, where he secreted the college keys and documents and endeavored to keep a "sort of college" going. There he died, in dire poverty, four years before the Restoration. He does not seem to have been married.

This "pretty little man," gentle, cheerful, and courteous, was called by his friend Andrew Marvell *qv* "one of the clearest heads and best-prepared breasts in Christendom." He was known as "a walking library," and was usually spoken of as "the ever memorable Hales." He preached the funeral sermon of Thomas Bodley, founder of the Bodleian Library, and for a long time kept the records of books in the library after Bodley's death. Hales refused to write for publication, and anything of his published before his death was unauthorized.

PRINCIPAL WORKS: A Tract concerning Schism and Schismatiques, 1642; Golden Remains of the Ever Memorable Mr. John Hales, 1659; Works, Now First Collected (H. Dalrymple [Lord Hailes], ed.) 1765; Several Tracts, 1677.

ABOUT: Aubrey, J. Lives of Eminent Men; Elson, J. H. John Hales of Eton; Wood, A. à, Athenae Oxonienses.

HALIFAX, Marquis of. See SAVILE, Sir GEORGE

HALL, EDWARD (d. 1547), chronicler, born probably about 1498, was the son of John Hall of Northall, Shropshire, and his wife, Catharine Gedding. He was educated at Eton College and at King's College, Cambridge, where he took a B.A. degree in 1518.

Hall read law at Gray's Inn and embarked directly on a legal and political career. He held a number of official positions in London, served as sergeant of the city in 1532, and later as a judge in the sheriff's court. An ardent supporter of Henry VIII, he drew the pattern both of his political activity and of his writings to the designs of his monarch. As a member of Parliament, he seems to have been always a mouthpiece for the king. As a historian, he maintained the most extreme theory of royal supremacy. There is some evidence that he was associated with the reforming party, presumably under the influence of his mother who was a close friend of several martyrs of the period, but his lawyer's caution kept him always within the bounds of the king's own religious views.

As a chronicler, Hall has frequently been underestimated. His single long work, *The Union of the Noble and Illustre Families of Lancastre and York,* covers a period of English history from the accession of Henry IV to the death of Henry VIII, and while it is in many sections an uncritical glorification of the house of Tudor, and more particularly of Henry VIII, it is also an authority of great value on the social life and opinion of Henry's reign. Actually, the work falls into two distinct parts: an overly elaborated chronicle of earlier events compiled from traditional authorities, and an eyewitness account of the court of Henry VIII, fresh, original, and wonderfully vivid. The passion for pageantry and pomp which lived in this hardheaded politician transformed his prose into an instrument of flexibility and power when he came to describe the magnificence of the royal show.

Hall's chronicle was banned in 1555 under Queen Mary and as a consequence became exceedingly rare. Nevertheless, it survived to become a source for Shakespeare in the historical dramas and a model for the later chronicles of Grafton, Holinshed, and Stow.

PRINCIPAL WORKS: The Union of the Two Noble and Illustre Families of Lancastre and York, 1548, 1550 (Sir H. Ellis, ed. 1809).

ABOUT: Brewer, J. S. The Reign of Henry VIII (J. Gairdner, ed.); Gairdner, J. Chroniclers of England, *in* Early Chronicles of Europe Series; Pollard, A. F. Edward Hall's Will and Chronicle, Bulletin Institute of Historical Research IX, 1931-32; Tanner, T. Bibliotheca Britannico-Hibernica.

HALL, JOHN. See STEVENSON, JOHN HALL-

HALL, JOSEPH (July 1, 1574-September 8, 1656), satirist, religious and miscellaneous writer, was born near Ashby-de-la-Zouch, Leicestershire, the son of Winifred Bambridge, who was a strict Puritan, and John Hall, an employe of the Earl of Huntingdon. Indeed, on leaving the grammar school the boy was about to be trained for the Puritan ministry when a relative intervened and arranged for him to enter Emmanuel College, Cambridge, in 1589. There he proceeded B.A. in 1592, M.A., 1606, B.D. in 1603, D.D. in 1612, and was a fellow in 1595, taking orders soon after. For a while he gave public lectures on rhetoric.

In 1603 he married Elizabeth Winiffe, who died in 1652, leaving two daughters and six sons; four of the sons were clergymen, and one became Bishop of Chester. Hall was given the living at Halsted, Essex, by Sir Robert Drury, but was treated so meanly he was glad to receive from the Earl of Norwich the living of Waltham, Essex, in 1608. In 1616 he became one of the chaplains of the Prince of Wales, and also chaplain of Lord Doncaster, ambassador to France. The next year he accompanied James I to Scotland, and helped him establish the liturgy of the Established Church there. He was made dean of Worcester, then, after refusing the bishopric of Gloucester, Bishop of Exeter in 1627. In 1624 he had been one of the English deputies at the Synod of Dort. In 1641 he was transferred to the see of Norwich.

However, by then Hall's troubles had already begun. He was no stranger to controversy—his claim in his early poems to be "the first English satirist" (ignoring Wyatt, Gascoigne, and Lodge [qqv]) having been hotly disputed by Marston.[qv] The rise of

JOSEPH HALL

Puritanism and the coming of the civil war involved him in far more serious difficulties. A peaceful compromiser by nature, with Calvinist leanings, he was essentially a Low Churchman, against whom the enmity of the extremists of both sides was directed. Milton especially attacked him virulently. Worse was to come. In December 1641 he was one of the thirteen bishops sent to the Tower on charges of high treason. The charge was lessened to one of praemunire, but all his property was confiscated, and after a while he did not even receive the small stipend allocated to the condemned "malignant" bishops. The Cathedral was looted by Parliamentary forces, he was ejected from the bishop's palace, and even his wife's clothing and his children's belongings were taken from them. He and his family were left entirely penniless. He found refuge in Higham, where at first he was forbidden to preach and then became physically unable to do so. He died there at eighty-two, patient, sweet tempered, and charitable to the last, even in his poverty.

That this fundamentally amiable man should also be a pungent and sometimes a scurrilous satirist seems strange, though most of his satires were written in youth— as was most of his verse. He took as his model not the urbane Horace but the savage Juvenal. The first, or "toothless" part of his *Virgidemiarum* attacks institutions, such as

medicine, astrology, fashion, and the romantic literature of such poets as Spenser and Marlowe. The second or "byting" part deals roughly, though with great moral earnestness, with actual contemporary individuals, thinly disguised. His *Mundus alter,* primarily a satire on the Roman Catholics, gave Swift some hints for *Gulliver's Travels.* His later "characters" recall those of Theophrastus, though they are sketches of moral virtues and faults where Theophrastus dealt with social evils. The *Virgidemiarum* even earned the accolade of an order by Archbishop Whitgift of Canterbury that it should be burned, but it was "reprieved" before the sentence could be carried out.

Hall's style in his satires, particularly in the verse portions (in heroic couplets) is marked by refined irony and sophisticated ridicule. His *Characters,* despite some eloquent passages, tends to monotony, especially when it deals with virtues instead of vices. His controversial writings were no better and no worse than others of their era; if anything, he was less violent and scurrilous than were his opponents, including Milton. As for his religious writings, Fuller called him "our English Seneca, for the purenesse, plainnesse, and fulnesse of his style."

PRINCIPAL WORKS: Virgidemiarum (prose and verse) 1597-98; An Italian's dead Bodie stucke with English Flowers (verse) 1600; The King's Prophecie: or Weeping Joy (verse) 1603; Mundus alter et idem, 1605 (as Discovery of a New World, J. Healey, tr. 1608); Meditations and Vowes, 1606; Heaven upon Earth, 1606; Holy Observations, 1607; Six Decads of Epistles, 1607-10; Characters of Vertues and Vices, 1608; Solomons Divine Arts, 1609; Quo Vadis? A Iust Censure of Travell, 1617; Paraphrase of Hard Texts from Genesis to Revelation, 1633; An Humble Remonstrance to the High Court of Parliament, 1640; Episcopacie by Divine Right Asserted, 1640; The Devout Soul, 1644; Christ Mysticall, 1647; Hard Measure, 1647; The Shaking of the Olive Tree, 1660; Complete Works (J. Pratt, ed.) 1808; Complete Poems (A. B. Grosart, ed.) 1879.

ABOUT: Fuller, T. Worthies of England; Grosart, A. B. Occasional Issues; Hall, J. Hard Measure, Observations of Some Specialties of Divine Providence (in Shaking of the Olive Tree); Jones, J. Memoirs of Bishop Hall; Lewis, G. Life of Joseph Hall, D. D.; Warton, T. History of English Poetry.

HALL-STEVENSON, JOHN. See STEVENSON, JOHN HALL-

HAMILTON, ANTHONY (1646?-April 21, 1720), author of memoirs and tales, was the grandson of the Earl of Abercorn, the son of Sir George and Mary Hamilton, born probably in Roscrea, Tipperary. Of his six brothers and three sisters, all seem to have been exceptional, the gentlemen distinguishing themselves in court and on the battlefield, the ladies by their beauty and their aristocratic marriages.

Anthony seems to have accompanied his older brother, George, to France about 1667. At any rate he was in Limerick a few years later with a French captain's commission, recruiting for his brother's corps. Returning again from France, he was appointed governor of Limerick in 1685, served on the privy council in 1686, and attained the rank of major general in command of a regiment of dragoons. He fought in the battle of Newtown Butler and in the decisive battle of the Boyne, after which he seems to have retired to France, spending most of his time at the court of St. Germaine-en-Laye. He never married but was apparently much attached to Henrietta Bulkeley, a sister of the Duchess of Berwick, "la belle Henriette," to whom he wrote a number of charming letters.

Anthony Hamilton's reputation is unique in English letters as the author of what is generally acknowledged to be a masterpiece of French literature, his *Mémoires de la vie du Comte de Grammont*. Both his early years in France and his intimate connections with the Frenchified court of Charles II had given him the eye and ear of a French gentleman; and when his sister, Elizabeth, married the Comte de Grammont, Hamilton chose to make him the central figure in this wonderfully witty picture of amorous intrigue and court scandal, the author of which Voltaire declared to be the first writer to discover the essential genius of the French language. How much of a part the Comte himself played in this account of his adventures cannot be readily determined, and the *Memoirs* are too much a work of art for any reader to be overly concerned about their historical accuracy. Grammont died in 1707 and Hamilton's book appeared anonymously in 1713, to become what Chamfort called it—*"le bréviaire de la jeune noblesse."* It was first translated into English by Abel Boyer and later touched up by Sir Walter Scott.

Hamilton was also author of four French "contes" written for the entertainment of his friends, *Le Bélier, Histoire de Fleur d'Épine*, satirizing popular imitations of Arabian Nights "plus Arabe qu'en Arabie," *Les Quatres Facardines*, and *Zénéyde*, which influenced Voltaire in France and later Thomas Love Peacock in England.

PRINCIPAL WORKS: Mémoires de la Vie Du Comte de Grammont, 1713 (A. Boyer, tr. 1714; P. Quennell, ed. 1930); Select Tales, 1760; Œuvres Complètes du Comte Antoine Hamilton, 1804.

ABOUT: Auger, L. S. Biography, *in* Œuvres Complètes; Hartmann, C. H. Introduction, *in* Memoirs (Quennell, tr.); Scott, Sir W. Biographical sketch, *in* Memoirs (Scott, tr.).

HAMILTON, WILLIAM, of Gilbertfield (1665?-May 24, 1751), Scottish poet, was born in Ladyland, Ayrshire, the second son of Captain William Hamilton and Janet Brisbane Hamilton. Following the career of his father, young William went into the army and served a number of years on the continent before he retired with the rank of lieutenant to devote himself to the life of a country gentleman.

Hamilton's first poems appeared in Watson's *Choice Collection of Comic and Serious Scots Poems*, published in 1706, where they were noticed by Allan Ramsay, most brilliant figure of the popular lyric revival in Scotland during the first half of the eighteenth century. Ramsay gave credit to Hamilton's lyrics for the inspiration of his own early work and the two poets became good friends, exchanging verse epistles which Ramsay published as *Seven Familiar Epistles Which Passed Between Lieutenant Hamilton and the Author*. Hamilton's contributions to this correspondence are direct and lively with considerable metrical ingenuity.

Other poems by Hamilton appeared in Ramsay's *Tea-Table Miscellany*, signed usually with the initials W.W. standing for the soubriquet "Wanton Willy" first adopted in the *Familiar Epistles*. One of these, Willy Was a Wanton Wag (probably suggested by the English song Oh, Willy Was So Blythe a Lad) is a witty and original sketch of a Scottish gallant, which holds a unique place in Scottish song for its vivacious drollery. Another, Hamilton's elegy on his dog Bonny Heck became very well known and served as model for Ramsay's Lucky Spence's Last Advice.

Hamilton also modernized and abridged Blind Harry's famous poem on Sir William Wallace. Although not entirely successful from a literary point of view, his version of "Wallace" was long popular in Scotland and had its influence on Robert Burns who said it "poured a Scottish prejudice" into his veins. Little is known of Hamilton's later years except that he lived at Gilbertfield and moved to nearby Latrick, where he died when he was in his eighties.

PRINCIPAL WORKS: Poems, in Watson's Choice Collections of Comic and Serious Scots Poems, 1706-11; Poems, in Allan Ramsay's Familiar Epistles Between Lieutenant Hamilton and the Author (G. Chalmers, ed. in Ramsay's Works, 1800); Sir William Wallace (adaptation) 1722; Poems, in Ramsay's Tea-Table Miscellany, 1724-37.

ABOUT: Anderson, W. The Scottish Nation; Chalmers, G. Introduction to Ramsay's Works, 1800 ed.; Wilson, J. Poets and Poetry of Scotland.

HAMILTON, WILLIAM, of Bangour

(1704-March 25, 1754), Scottish poet, was the second son of a lawyer, James Hamilton, born in Bangour, Linlithgowshire. When his elder brother died, William inherited his father's estate which made him a man of considerable means. On account of delicate health he appeared little in fashionable circles, however, and devoted a great deal of time to writing poetry. From 1724 to 1727 he contributed verse to Allan Ramsay's Tea-Table Miscellany, usually conventional love lyrics addressed to one charming lady or another. Such was the ardor of his poetic sentiment, so the story goes, that one lady consulted his friend, Lord Kames, as to how she should best meet his passion. Kames advised her to profess a return of affection, which she accomplished so well that Hamilton was frightened into speechless reserve.

Hamilton followed the Stuart cause and was forced by his Jacobite activities into hiding, during which period he composed the troubled Soliliquy Wrote in June 1746. With other Jacobites he escaped to France a short while later. Through the influence of friends he was eventually allowed to return to Scotland, but his health had been seriously affected by these adventures and he died of tuberculosis in Lyons when he was fifty. His body was brought back to Scotland and buried in the Abbey Church at Holyrood. Hamilton left a son, James, by the first of his two wives.

An unauthorized collection of Hamilton's poems was printed in 1748 while he was abroad, and reprinted in 1749 under the title Poems on Several Occasions. According to T. F. Henderson writing in the Cambridge History of English Literature, "he mainly confined his poetic efforts to the celebration, in bombastic conventional form, of the charms of fashionable ladies." Nevertheless, he wrote one or two notable poems, the best of which is the well-known Braes of Yarrow, with the opening line, "Busk ye, busk ye, my bonny bonny bride." Gladsmuir, written to celebrate the Jacobite victory at Prestonpans, was set to music and became widely popular. He also made a number of translations from Greek and Latin poets, one of which The Parting of Hector and Andromache from the Iliad, is the earliest translation of Homer into English blank verse.

PRINCIPAL WORKS: The Faithful Few, 1734; Contemplation, 1747; Poems on Several Occasions, 1748; Poems and Songs (J. Patterson, ed.) 1850.

ABOUT: Chambers, R. Eminent Scotsmen; Irving, D. Lives of Scottish Poets; Biography, in Poems on Several Occasions.

HAMMOND, HENRY (August 18, 1605-

April 25, 1660), theological writer, was born in Chertsey, the youngest son of a physician, Dr. John Hammond. Dr. Hammond must have had close connections with the court, for Henry, Prince of Wales, was presumably the boy's godfather. He was educated at Eton and went to Magdalen College, Oxford, when he was thirteen. With a B.A. and an M.A. degree, he was elected a fellow of the college in 1625 and remained at Oxford to take his D.D. degree in 1639. The Earl of Leicester was impressed by a sermon that Hammond preached at court and rewarded him with the living of Penshurst, Kent.

Hammond's life might well have been that of a quiet country clergyman and scholar had he not been caught up in the troubled political events of his time. Loyal to the king during the civil war, Hammond, now archdeacon of Chichester, helped raise a troop of horse to fight for the king, and, after the defeat of the royal forces by the parliamentary party at Tonbridge, a reward of £100 was offered for his capture. Forced to leave Penshurst in disguise, he fled to Oxford, the king's headquarters. After the surrender of Oxford in 1646, Charles I asked Parliament for Hammond and another chaplain to attend him. When Charles was taken to Childersley by the army, Hammond was permitted to join him. Through the offices of Hammond's nephew, then governor of the Isle of Wight, the king made his escape to the Isle along with Hammond and several others. In 1647 he went again to Oxford where Samuel Fell, dean of Christ Church, had been imprisoned and carried on the management of the college until he too was taken into custody. He was kept under "light restraint" at the home of Sir Philip Warwick in Clapham, where he devoted himself to literary work and the relief of the ejected clergy. Ironically, Hammond died on the very day that Parliament voted for the reinstatement of the king.

Hammond published two important theological works during his lifetime, *A Practical Catechism* and *A Paraphrase and Annotations Upon the New Testament*, which gave him claim to the title "the father of English Biblical criticism." His sermons were models of the best Caroline prose in their simplicity and clarity, but he is perhaps best remembered today through John Fell's memoir, one of the most charming biographical pieces in the English language, and John Keble's beautiful eulogy written in 1819 after a visit to Hammond's tomb.

PRINCIPAL WORKS: A Practical Catechism, 1645; The Christians Obligations to Peace and Charity, 1649; A Paraphrase and Annotations Upon the New Testament, 1653; A Paraphrase and Annotations Upon the Books of the Psalms, 1659; Sermons, 1664; The Works (W. Fulman, ed.) 1684; The Miscellaneous Theological Works (N. Pocock, ed.) 1847-50.

ABOUT: Fell, J. The Life of Dr. Henry Hammond; Perry, G. G. Life of Henry Hammond; Wood, A. à, Athenae Oxonienses.

HANNAY, PATRICK (d. 1629?), poet, was presumably the son of Alexander Hannay of Kirkdale and the grandson of Donald Hannay "well known to th' English by his sword." Early in the reign of James I, Patrick and a cousin, Robert, visited the English court where they attracted the favorable attention of Queen Anne, and in 1620 both young men received grants of land in county Langford, Ireland.

After a visit to Sweden, Patrick went to Ireland where he was given a clerkship in the office of the Irish privy council at Dublin. Political rivals made several attempts to oust him. These had apparently succeeded when Charles I (son of James I and Queen Anne) officially reinstated him in view of his "having done our late dear father good and acceptable service beyond the seas with great charge and danger of his life, and having been recommended to us by our dear mother." In 1627 he was appointed master of chancery in Ireland, and according to contemporary reports was lost at sea two years later. Apparently he never married and beyond his work nothing more is known of his life.

Hannay's first published poem, written in imitation of Thomas Overbury's *A Wife*, was *A Happy Husband*, or *Directions for a Maide to Choose Her Mate*, which appeared in 1618. A year later there followed *Two Elegies on the Late Death of Our Sovereign Queen Anne*. In 1622 Hannay published a collected edition of his works, reprinting the earlier poems and adding *The Nightingale, Sheretine and Mariana*, and *Songs and Sonnets*. Of these the most interesting is probably *Sheretine and Mariana*, a tragic story of inconstant love narrated by the ghost of the heroine. He also wrote a long version of the legend of Philomela, nearly 1700 lines in curious lyrical form intended apparently to be sung.

Hannay's verse was graceful and smoothly written in a literary English strongly colored with Scoticisms, but the volume of his collected works is now chiefly prized for its frontispiece engraved by Crispin de Pass with a portrait of the author.

PRINCIPAL WORKS: (Collection) The Nightingale, Sheretine and Mariana, A Happy Husband, Elegies on the Death of Queen Anne, Songs and Sonnets, 1622 (E. V. Utterson, ed. 1841; D. Laing, ed. 1875).

ABOUT: Corser, T. Collectanea Anglo-Poetica; Laing, D. Memoir, *in* Hannay's Poems (Hunterian Club reprint).

HARINGTON, JAMES. See HARRINGTON, JAMES

HARINGTON, Sir JOHN (1561-November 20, 1612), satirist, miscellaneous writer, was born in Bath, the son of John Harington, a confidential under-treasurer to Henry

VIII, and his second wife, Isabella Markham. The family estate had been inherited from the first wife, an illegitimate daughter of the king. Queen Elizabeth was the boy's godmother, for both his parents had suffered in her cause and been imprisoned in the Tower with her. She never failed to take an interest in him, though often her notoriously short temper was sorely tried.

Harington was educated at Eton and entered Christ's College, Cambridge, in 1578. He left without a degree, and about 1583 was entered in Lincoln's Inn, but his future lay in the court, not at the bar. In 1584 he married Mary Rogers, who survived him with seven of their nine children. In 1592 he was high sheriff of Somerset. But he spent as little time as possible away from the court, where he became a kind of licensed buffoon, though subject to sharp reproof when his exuberant personality got away with him. It is said that his paraphrase of Ariosto's *Orlando Furioso* was written at Elizabeth's command because he had translated one of its most indecent sections, and she thereupon ordered him to redeem himself by translating the whole. *Ajax* further angered the queen, not because of its indelicacy, but because of a slur on the Earl of Leicester, and she banished Harington from court. He was thus "exiled" till 1598, and his next blunder was to accompany the Earl of Essex on his expedition to Ireland. There

Essex had the audacity to knight Harington, himself, on the field, and the queen was furious. Harington scuttled back to Bath, and by way of further exculpation furnished Elizabeth with his highly critical journal of Essex's campaign (published in *Nugae Antiquae*).

When Elizabeth was dying, Harington hastened to curry favor with James, but without success. In 1605 he actually had the presumption to offer himself to fill a vacancy for chancellor of Ireland—and even, though a layman, as archbishop! His letter was filed without comment. However, he did finally become a sort of informal tutor to young Prince Henry. And in excuse of his unjustified aspirations for high office, it may be said that his views on the government of Ireland were remarkably tolerant for their day. His private life at the same period was marked by an unseemly scramble for his mother-in-law's fortune; Harington's eye was always on the main chance, and he was by no means scrupulous about means.

Utterly without restraint or reticence, Harington nevertheless was a real wit, albeit an extremely dirty one. *The Metamorphosis of Ajax*, his best known work, was not merely a disquisition on the history of water-closets ("Ajax"—"a jakes"), but also advocated a new and improved variety which apparently he invented. His epigrams were much admired, but are a bit too coarse for modern taste. His *Tract on the Succession to the Crown* was his bid to ingratiate himself with the future James I. The *Nugae Antiquae*, edited by a descendant, is a compilation of his miscellaneous writings.

PRINCIPAL WORKS: Orlando Furioso, 1591; A New Discourse of a stale subject called the Metamorphosis of Ajax, 1596 (with Ulysses upon Ajax, An Anatomie of the Metamorphosed Ajax, An Apologie for the Metamorphosis of Ajax, 1929); The Englishman's Doctor, or the Schoole of Salerne, 1609; The most elegant and witty Epigrams of Sir John Harrington [*sic*], 1615; A briefe View of the Church of England, 1653; Nugae Antiquae (H. Harington, ed.) 1769; A Short View of the State of Ireland in 1605, 1879; Tract on the Succession to the Crown (M. Markham, ed.) 1880.

ABOUT: Fuller, T. Worthies of Somerset; Harington, H. Introduction, Nugae Antiquae; Markham, M. Memoir, *in* Tract on the Succession of the Crown; Reynolds, R. Cleanliness and Godliness; Strachey, G. L. Biographical Essays.

HARRINGTON, or **HARINGTON, JAMES** (January 7, 1611-September 11,

SIR JOHN HARINGTON

1677), political theorist, author of a political romance *The Commonwealth of Oceana,* was born at Upton, Northamptonshire, the eldest son of Sir Sapcotes Harrington and his first wife, Jane Samwell. He entered Trinity College, Oxford, as a gentleman-commoner in 1629, but left without a degree. After the death of his father, his grandmother, Lady Samwell, took James as her ward.

As a young man he traveled abroad in Holland and France, to Rome, where it is said he refused to kiss the Pope's toe, to Venice and back to England where he devoted himself to the education of his younger brother and two sisters. With Sir Thomas Herbert he attended Charles I as a groom of the bedchamber, and although he played no active part in the civil war, he was with Charles on the Isle of Wight and accompanied him to Hurst Castle. Republican in principle, he seems nevertheless to have been devoted to the king and was deeply shocked by his death.

In 1656 Harrington published *The Commonwealth of Oceana,* expounding his own political theories in an imaginary history of Oceana (England) in which Olphaus Megalitor (Oliver Cromwell) set up the constitution of a new republic. His reference to contemporary affairs was so thinly disguised that the book stirred up an immediate controversy and was both attacked and defended in a series of pamphlets for several years. After Cromwell's death, Harrington founded a club, the "Rota," which met at Mile's coffee-house to discuss political reform. With the Restoration he was arrested and committed to the Tower on the charge of having attempted to change the form of government. His two sisters had petitioned for a trial when he was abruptly sent off to St. Nicholas Island in Plymouth harbor. Later he was allowed to live in Plymouth and seems to have received lenient treatment, but unfortunately on the advice of a Dr. Dunstan, he took heavy doses of guaiacum, which so injured his nervous system that he never fully recovered. He died at Westminster in his sixty-sixth year, leaving a widow whom he had married late in life.

Oceana reads more like a state paper than a romance, but although it has none of the imaginative quality of *Utopia* or *New Atlantis,* it is of genuine interest in its political analysis. Long famous, it was noted by Hume as the "only valuable model of a commonwealth" then extant.

PRINCIPAL WORKS: The Commonwealth of Oceana, 1656 (H. Morley, ed. 1887) ; The Prerogative of Popular Government, 1658 ; The Art of Lawgiving: in III Books, 1659 ; Aphorisms Political, 1659 ; Political Discourses: tending to the introduction of a free Commonwealth in England, 1660 ; The Oceana and other Works collected by John Toland, 1700.

ABOUT: Herbert, Sir T. Memoirs ; Toland, J. Life, *in* The Oceana and Other Works ; Wood, A. à, Athenae Oxonienses.

HARRISON, WILLIAM (April 18, 1534-1593), chronicler, was born in Cordwainer Street, London. He studied first at Cambridge, then at Oxford, where he took a B.A. degree in 1556 and an M.A. four years later. As chaplain to Sir William Brooke, he was given the rectory of Radwinter in Essex about 1558, and for a period of eleven years he also served as vicar of Wimbush.

Harrison's topographical and antiquarian interests had won him something of a reputation when Reginald Wolfe, printer to Queen Elizabeth, consulted him in connection with his project for a "universal Cosmographie of the whole world with particular histories of every knowne nation." Harrison began work on a *Description of England,* and after Wolfe's death in 1576 was instrumental, with Holinshed and others, in revising the scheme of the projected work, limiting its field to England, Scotland, and Ireland. Harrison's *Description of England* was actually completed sometime before the publication of the Holinshed *Chronicles,* but both the *England* and his translation of Bellenden's Scottish version of Boece's *Description of Scotland* were first printed in Holinshed. Two unprinted works by Harrison also belong to this scheme, his "Chronologie which he had gathered and compiled with most exquisite diligence" from the Creation to the year 1592, and a much corrected manuscript on Hebrew, Greek, and English weights and measures.

No work of the time contains so vivid and picturesque a sketch of life in the Elizabethan period as Harrison's *Description of England.* His subject matter in what he liked to call "this foule and frizeled Treatise of mine" ranged from food, dress, and housing, to agriculture and economics. On contemporary fashions in dress he wrote, "except it were a dog in a doublet, you shall not see anie so disguised as are my countriemen of England"—and again, deploring the cookery of the aristocratic class, that the cooks of the nobility were "for the most part musicall-headed Frenchmen and strangers." An ardent patriot, Harrison was nevertheless a shrewd and humorous critic of the English scene. Both amiable and scholarly, his work remains the most quoted and the most trustworthy authority on life in the England of Elizabeth and of Shakespeare.

PRINCIPAL WORKS: An Historicall Description of the Island of Britayne (in Raphael Holinshed's Chronicles of England, vol. 1) 1577-78; The Description of Scotlande, from Hector Boethius (in Holinshed's Chronicles of England, vol. 1) 1577-78; Harrison's Description of England in Shakespeare's Youth (F. J. Furnivall, ed.) 1877-78; Elizabethan England (L. Withington, ed.) 1902.

ABOUT: Cooper, C. H. Athenae Cantabrigienses; Furnivall, F. J. Introduction to Harrison's Description of England.

HARTLEY, DAVID (June, 1705-August 28, 1757), philosopher, was born in Halifax (but not on August 30, 1705, as his son wrote). His father was David Hartley, a clergyman; his mother, who died soon after his birth, was Evereld Wadsworth. His father remarried when the child was two. He seems to have been reared in a foster home, at Bradford (both towns are in Yorkshire), where he attended Bradford grammar School. In 1722 he entered Jesus College, Cambridge, proceeding B.A. 1726 and M.A. 1729; in 1727 he became a fellow, but lost his fellowship the following year because of his marriage. He gave up the study of divinity because of scruples about signing the Articles, and set up as a physician, though he never had a medical degree. He practised first at Newark, then at Bury St. Edmunds, then in London, and finally, from 1742 to his death, in Bath. He was twice married, his second wife being an heiress whom he married in 1735. He had children by both marriages—his son by his first wife, also David Hartley, becoming Benjamin Franklin's friend who signed with him the treaty ending the American Revolution.

Hartley had many interests—mathematics, music, history, poetry, and he was a shorthand enthusiast. Himself a sufferer from the disease, he took up the cudgels for "Mrs. Stephens's medicine for the stone,"

After Shackelwell
DAVID HARTLEY

in defense of which he wrote several pamphlets. But it was as a philosopher that he was chiefly celebrated; Priestley and James Mill were among his disciples, and Coleridge thought so highly of him that he named his son Hartley in his honor. "He of mortal kind," the poet called him

Wisest, he first who marked the ideal tribes
Up the fine fibres thro' the sentient brain
Pass in fine surges.

This was a fair description of Hartley's "associationist" theory, drawn from Newton and Locke, and forming the psychological portion of his Observations on Man. (The theological portion was badly outmoded.) According to this theory, there is no thought without a brain; the soul is the thinking subject. The contact of the supposititious ether on the medulla sets up vibrations which result in sensations, and leaves traces which give rise to memory, emotions, reason, and action. The mind is blank prior to sensation, and soul-life depends on association of ideas. His system failed, however, to account for such mental phenomena as judgment and belief. Hartley is not only the founder of the Associationist School of philosophers, he is also the father of eighteenth century deism, and he made the first systematic attempt to establish a theory of physiological psychology. Though rationalist in his thought, he was not a materialist, and he remained a practicing Christian. His system would have been more logical had he had any knowledge whatsoever of his contemporaries in philosophy, including Berkeley and Hume.[qqv] As it is, it remains like its author, neat, methodical, rather fussy, highly ethical, and completely dated.

PRINCIPAL WORKS: Conjecturae quaedam de sensu motu et idearum generatione [Certain conjectures concerning motor activity and the origin of ideas] 1746; Observations on Man, his frame, his duty, and his expectations, 1749; Theory of the Human Mind, on the Principle of the Association of Ideas, 1775.

ABOUT: Albee, E. History of English Utilitarianism; Bower, G. S. Hartley and James Mill; Hartley, D. (son) Sketch of Life, in 1791 ed. of Observations on Man; Ribot, T. English Psychology; Schönlank, B. Hartley und Priestley (in German); Stephen, L. History of English Thought in the 18th Century; Weber, A. History of Philosophy.

HARVEY, GABRIEL (1545?-1630), poet, critic, rhetorician, was born in Saffron-Walden, Essex, the son of a prosperous master ropemaker. Two of his brothers were also minor literary figures of the time. He entered Christ's College, Cambridge, in 1566, and proceeded B.A. in 1570. The same year he became a fellow of Pembroke College, where he met Edmund Spenser.[qv] Harvey was an ardent advocate of the substitution of Latin prosody for English "barbarous and balductum [trashy] rymes with artificial verses," and he tried his best, by a sort of intellectual bullying, to force Spenser's genius into accordance with his theories. He very nearly killed off *The Faerie Queene* before its birth, but Spenser evaded the commands of Harvey's "Areopagus" (formed to spread his views). Nevertheless, they not only remained friends, but Spenser celebrated Harvey as Hobbinall in *The Shepheards Calendar*.

When Harvey was eligible for an M.A. in 1573, his arrogant and conceited nature had so antagonized the other fellows of Pembroke that they delayed for three months giving him the necessary "grace." The same result of his unfortunate disposition continued to impede his career. He became a college tutor, and a reader in rhetoric in 1576, but the actual office was denied him. In 1578 he became a fellow of Trinity College, which implied the study of law, but instead he angered the authorities by publishing satirical poems. He blamed

Spenser for this, though apparently he himself had had them published. In 1583 he was junior proctor of Cambridge, and in 1585 was made master of Trinity, only to have his appointment quashed at court. In 1585 he was made a D.C.L. of Oxford.

His London years, after this, were chiefly marked by his bitter controversy with Robert Greene.[qv] Greene had offended him mortally by scornful allusions to Harvey's lowborn family, and he pursued the playwright even after Greene's wretched death. Thomas Nashe [qv] then took up the battle, until finally Archbishop Whitgift ordered all the books in the controversy suppressed. About the beginning of the century Harvey returned to Saffron-Walden, where according to Nashe he practised both medicine and astrology.

Harvey wished to be "epitaphed as the Inventour of the English Hexameter"—which died with him. He was an extremely unpleasant person, censorious of others, puffed up about his own abilities, spiteful, and morbidly sensitive. He was nevertheless a really good scholar, even if he displayed his learning overmuch. Quarrelsome, surly, and selfish, he seems to have had no real friends, except for the patient Spenser, who died in 1599; and he never married. There is evidence that a good writer and even a good poet went to waste, drowned in a sea of malice and bad temper; but his controversial works are written in what has been dubbed "a crab-tree cudgel style."

PRINCIPAL WORKS: The Story of Mercy Harvey, 1575: Rhetor (Latin) 1577: Ciceronianus (Latin) 1577: Gratulationes Valdinenses (verse, Latin) 1578; Smithus (verse, Latin) 1578; Letters to and from E. Spenser, 1579; Foure Letters, and Certaine Sonnets, 1592; A New Letter of Notable Contents, 1593; Advertisement to Papp-Hatchet 1593: Peirces Supererogation, 1593; The Trimming of Thomas Nashe, Gentleman, 1597; The Letter Book of Gabriel Harvey, 1573-80 (E. J. L. Scott ed.) 1884; Complete Works (A. B. Grosart, ed.) 1884-85; Marginalia (G. C. Stone-Smith, ed.) 1913

ABOUT: Disraeli, I. Calamities of Authors Grosart, A. B., Memorial Introduction, Complete Works; Haslewood, J. Essays upon English Poet and Poesie; Morley, H. Clement Marot, and Othe Studies; Warton, T. History of English Poetry.

HARVEY, WILLIAM (April 1, 1578 June 3, 1657), physician, medical theorist was born at Folkestone, Kent, in a hous which he later bequeathed to his college a Cambridge. (His house at Burwash, Sussex he gave to the Royal College of Physicians.

WILLIAM HARVEY

His father was Thomas Harvey, a prosperous yeoman, his mother Joane Halke, the second wife. He was educated at the King's School, Canterbury, then entered Gonville and Caius College, Cambridge, in 1593, proceeding B.A. in 1597. He then went to Padua, where he studied medicine under the famous Fabrizio (Fabricius), and received his M.D. there in 1602. Returning to England, he was given a Cambridge M.D. the same year, and settled in London as a physician, Francis Bacon being among his patients. In 1604 he married Elizabeth, the daughter of Dr. Lancelot Browne, Queen Elizabeth's physician. He became a Fellow of the College of Physicians in 1607, and in 1609 physician at St. Bartholomew's Hospital. In 1615 he was named Lumleian lecturer at the College of Physicians, and the following year he gave the first of his lectures demonstrating the circulation of the blood. The manuscript of his notes is now in the British Museum; the work was not published until 1628.

Though Harvey was almost pure scientist, and had no interest in politics, the civil war disrupted his life and work badly. As physician first to James I and then to Charles I, his affiliations were with the Royalists, and he accompanied the king to Oxford in 1645. There Charles named him warden of Merton College. It is said that during the battle of Edgehill he had charge of the young princes,

and that throughout the battle he sat on the sidelines, reading! His house was looted and his fine anatomical collections were destroyed. He returned to London, but his services at St. Bartholomew's had ended. He devoted himself to building a library for the College of Physicians; this was done anonymously, but a statue was erected to him by the College in 1652. Unfortunately this library was burnt in the Great Fire of London. He served on the council of the College in 1655 and 1656, and indeed had been elected president in 1654 but declined because of age and failing health. Long a sufferer from gout, he had practically ceased to practice and lived with his brother, a London merchant. He finally died of a stroke, at seventy-nine. He was buried at Hempstead, Essex, with his three principal books deposited in his sarcophagus and displayed on the monument. In his honor the College of Physicians established the annual Harveian Orations, which are still given, and deal with some aspect of Harvey's work.

This "little choleric man," as Aubrey called him, was one of the great pioneers of biology. As Dryden put it: "The circling streams once thought but pools of blood . . . from dark oblivion Harvey's name shall save." He established all the main facts concerning the circulatory system of animals, with the exception that the capillaries were not discovered until the invention of the microscope, when Malpighi made them known. To quote Cowley, in his Ode to Harvey, he "wisely thought 'twas fit not to read comments only, . . . but on th' original itself to look." His other great interest, mammalian reproduction, produced less important and valid results, again because of lack of the microscope. Though Harvey was well read, especially in the classics (he seems to have been familiar with none of his great English contemporaries in literature), he had no pretensions to literary style, and belongs in a history of literature only because of the profound effect and influence of his work. He was, however, one of the greatest men in the history of science.

PRINCIPAL WORKS: Exercitatio anatomica de motu cordis et sanguinis in animalibus [Anatomical treatise on the motion of the heart and the blood in animals] 1628; Exercitationes duae anatomicae de circulatione sanguinis [Two anatomical treatises on the circulation of the blood] 1649 (R. Lowndes, tr., 1653); Exercitationes de generatione animalium

253

[Treatises on the generation of animals] 1651; Works (T. Willis, tr.) 1847; Unpublished Letters (G. E. Paget, ed.) 1848.

ABOUT: Aubrey, J. Lives of Eminent Men; Coxe, J. R. An Inquiry into the Claims of Dr. William Harvey; Keynes, G. Personality of William Harvey; Malloch, A. E. William Harvey; Moore, N. History of the Study of Medicine in the British Isles; Nordenskiöld, E. The History of Biology; Willis, R. Life of Harvey: Wyatt, R. B. H. William Harvey.

HAUGHTON, WILLIAM (fl. 1598), dramatist, was one of the men associated with John Day, Thomas Dekker, Henry Chettle and others in Philip Henslowe's "stable" of successful playwrights. Beyond the notations in Henslowe's *Diary* and two plays which survive, almost nothing is known of him. In Cooper's *Athenae Cantabrigienses* he is identified with a William Haughton who took degrees from both Oxford and Cambridge, but there is no other evidence to support this assumption.

He is first mentioned by Henslowe in 1597 as "yonge Horton," which would seem to indicate that he was considerably younger than the dramatists with whom he worked. He is listed as sole author of five or six plays and as a frequent collaborator. Only one play has come down to us as indisputably his, *English-Men for My Money: Or, A Woman Will Have Her Will;* but another, *The Devil and His Dame,* has been identified with *Grim the Collier of Croyden* and is usually assigned to Haughton. In 1599 he was at work on a lost play, *The Poor Man's Paradise,* and later in the year collaborated with John Day on the *Tragedy of Merry* and *Cox of Collumpton,* both lost. With Dekker and Chettle he wrote *Patient Grissil,* published in 1603. He may also have collaborated in Marlowe's *Lust's Dominion* and Yarrington's *Two Lamentable Tragedies.*

Henslowe notes that Haughton was imprisoned in the Clink (probably for debt) and was released when Henslowe magnificently advanced him ten shillings. A few months later he received five shillings from Henslowe "in earnest of a Boocke which he wold calle the *Devell and his Dame.*" If this work may be identified with *Grim the Collier of Croyden,* we have two plays by Haughton which seem to represent two different stages in his development as a writer of comedies. *Grim the Collier* is character-

istic of the sixteenth century when a clear comedy form had not yet emerged. *A Woman Will Have Her Will* is more typical of the seventeenth century of manners, without the earlier trappings of a chronicle or interlude. Haughton, so far as we can judge, was a mediocre dramatist, but he is interesting as a link between this earlier form of comedy and that which flowered in the comedies of Jonson.

PRINCIPAL WORKS: English-Men For My Money: Or, A Pleasant Comedy Called, A Woman Will Have Her Will, 1616 (in Robert Dodsley's Collection of Old Plays, W. C. Hazlitt, ed. 1874-76); Grim the Collier of Croyden: or, The Devil and His Dame: With the Devil and St. Dunstan, 1662.

ABOUT: Alleyn, E. The Alleyn Papers; Henslowe, P. Diary.

HAWES, STEPHEN (1474?-1523?), poet, was probably born in Suffolk, attended Oxford and perhaps some foreign university as well, and in 1502 became a groom of the chamber of Henry VII. Henry's was a very French court—his poet laureate was no Englishman, but the blind Bernard André de Toulouse—and Hawes had undoubtedly traveled in France. He was noted for his prodigious memory—he could, for example, recite all the works of his master John Lydgate *qv* by heart, and was known in court circles as a wit. Moreover, he had undoubted classical learning. He was certainly dead before 1530, for in that year Thomas Feylde wrote of "young Stephen Hawes, whose soul God pardon, Treated of love so clerkely and well." But if he died "young" (in an era when fifty was a venerable age), then the date of 1474 for his birth, implied by himself, may be considerably too early, or the accepted date of his death considerably too late. Bale called "his whole life . . . an example of virtue." He was married, and his wife survived him.

There are no extant manuscripts of Hawes' poems, but *The Example of Vertu* was probably written in 1503 or 1504; his principal work, *The Passetyme of Pleasure,* about 1505 or 1506; *The Cövercyon of Swerers* before 1509; and *A Ioyfull Meditacion* in that year, when Henry VIII ascended the throne.

Hawes' mind was essentially medieval; he was born too late for the theory of poetry to which he adhered—that all poetry must be allegorical or didactic, or both, that the poet is primarily a teacher. With this standard in mind, he could say truly that he was "the only faithful votary of poetry"—though on the whole it was a singularly unpoetic age. He called Lydgate "the chefe originator of my learning," though he owed something to Gower and rather less to Chaucer. (*The Passetyme*, for example, is a long allegorical account, bringing in all the orthodox machinery of romance, of the "education" of the knight Graund Amoure in search of his love, La Bel Pucell—which merely means the search of love for a beautiful maiden.) The sameness of Hawes' style in all his poems is relieved by occasional flashes of sharp observation of contemporary life and by passages of real humor; on the whole, however, it is vitiated by careless construction, confused meter, and bizarre and artificial wording. Nevertheless, Hawes had an appreciable influence on Spenser (how much is a matter of controversy), and echoes of *The Passetyme* may be heard in *The Faerie Queene*.

PRINCIPAL WORKS (dates of publication): The Passetyme of Pleasure, 1509; The cövercyon of swerers (on a riband), 1509; A Ioyfull medytacion to all Englonde of the coronacyon of our moost naturall sovereyne lorde kynge Henry the eight, 1509(?); The boke called the example of vertu, 1512; The comfort of Lovers(?).

ABOUT: Bale, J. Illustrium Maioris Britanniae Scriptorum Catalogus; Browning, E. B. The Greek Christian Poets and the English Poets; Courthope, W. A. History of English Poetry; Minto, W. Characteristics of English Poets; Morley, H. English Writers; Saintsbury, G. The Flourishing of Romance and the Rise of Allegory; Southey, R. The English Poets; Wood, A. à, Athenae Oxonienses.

HAWKESWORTH, JOHN (1715?-November 16, 1773), miscellaneous writer, was born in humble circumstances and, according to his own account, became "a hired clerk to one Harwood, an attorney in Grocer's Alley in the Poultry."

His first published work appeared in *Gentleman's Magazine* to which he contributed verse from 1746 to 1749. There is some evidence that he also compiled parliamentary debates for the same magazine, succeeding Samuel Johnson. After the success of Johnson's *The Rambler*, Hawkesworth together with Johnson, at that time a close friend, and two others, founded a similar publication, *The Adventurer*, which Hawkesworth edited for two years and to which he contributed some seventy essays in the style of Johnson. Encouraged by the success of this venture, he edited and published the *Works of Jonathan Swift* in 1755.

Hawkesworth first became known as a dramatist when David Garrick asked him to revise Dryden's *Amphitryon*, which was acted with considerable success at the Drury Lane. Even more successful was his adaptation of Thomas Southerne's *Oroonoko* originally based on the novel by Aphra Behn. His original works for the theatre included two oratorios for which John Stanley wrote the music, and *Edgar and Emmeline*, which became very popular.

In 1756 he was given an honorary LL.D. degree for his literary efforts and considered taking up practice in the ecclesiastical courts. Instead he decided to devote his time to managing the prosperous school for young ladies conducted by his wife at Bromley. In 1771 Garrick recommended him to Lord Sandwich, first lord of the Admiralty, for the task of revising and publishing the official accounts of recent voyages to the South Seas. Hawkesworth seems to have made a good thing of this assignment, selling the completed work to Cadell and Strahan, publishers, for £6000. When, however, the *Account of Voyages in the Southern Hemisphere* was published, Hawkesworth became the target for merciless criticism. He was attacked for inaccuracy, for indecency and for the general irreligious tenor of his introduction. Much disturbed, Hawkesworth retired to the home of a friend, Dr. Grant, where he died only a short time after the publication of the *Voyages*. Gossip had it that he had ended his own life by an overdose of opium.

PRINCIPAL WORKS: *Plays*—Amphitryon: or, The Two Sosias altered from Dryden, 1756; Oroonoko, by Thomas Southerne, with alterations, 1759; Edgar and Emmeline, A Fairy Tale in a Dramatic Entertainment, 1761; The Fall of Egypt, An Oratorio, 1774; Zimri, An Oratorio, 1780(?). *Other Writings*—The Adventurer (ed. and contrib.) 1752-54; The Works of Jonathan Swift (ed.) 1754-55; Almoran and Hamet, An Oriental Tale, 1761; Letters Written by Jonathan Swift (ed.) 1766; An Account of the Voyages Undertaken in the Southern Hemisphere, Drawn Up From the Journals Which Were Kept by the Several Commanders and From the Papers of Joseph Banks, Esq., 1773.

ABOUT: Chalmers, A. Biographical Dictionary; Chalmers, A. British Essayists; Hawkins, Sir J. Life of Samuel Johnson.

HAYWARD, Sir JOHN (1564?-June 27, 1627), historian, was born near Felixstowe, Suffolk. He was educated at Pembroke College, Cambridge, taking a B.A. in 1580, an M.A. in 1584, and some time later an LL.D.

By a curious chain of circumstances, his first published work, a history of the first year of Henry IV's reign, involved him in a mesh of suspicion and accusation. Because the work was dedicated to the Earl of Essex in the most laudatory terms, Queen Elizabeth was led to believe by enemies of Essex that the book was a veiled attack on her own policies. The fact that Hayward included a detailed description of the deposition of Richard II was interpreted as a treasonable allusion to the fate which might await the queen herself. Actually there appears to have been no justification for such suspicion. When the queen suggested to Bacon that there might be "places in it that might be drawn within case of treason," Bacon answered wittily enough that Hayward had borrowed so much from Tacitus that there might be grounds for felony, but not treason. Nevertheless, Hayward was brought before the Star Chamber and imprisoned, and later when Essex was tried for treason, Bacon as counsel for the crown argued that the Earl had aggravated his offenses by accepting Hayward's dedication.

Under the rule of James I, Hayward came into favor. He published one treatise justifying the succession and another arguing for the union of England and Scotland, both of which were flattering to the king. With Prince Henry as his official patron, he also wrote lives of the Norman kings. In 1610 he was appointed, along with William Camden, as historiographer of Chelsea College, newly founded by James I. In 1616 he was admitted to the College of Advocates and three years later he was knighted.

Hayward was married to Jane Pascall and had one daughter. The character of the marriage is indicated in his will bequeathing certain property to his wife which, he says, "in regard to her unquiet life and small respect towards me is a great deal too much."

As historian, Hayward was considerably more than a chronicler. He had the scholar's critical eye for the task of recording history, and showed more interest in the evolution of policies than in persons and events as such. Following the classical models, he wrote analytically and with genuine style, opening the way to modern historical method.

PRINCIPAL WORKS: The First Part of the Life and Raigne of King Henrie the IIII, 1599; An Answer to the First Part of a Certaine Conference Concerning Succession, 1603; A Treatise of the Union of England and Scotland, 1604; The Lives of the III Normans, Kings of England, 1613 (T. Parks, ed. *in* Harleian Miscellany, 1809-12); The Life and Raigne of King Edward the sixt, 1630; Annals of the First Four Years of the Reign of Queen Elisabeth (J. Bruce, ed.) 1840.

ABOUT: Bruce, J. Introduction to Hayward's Annals of Queen Elizabeth; Wood, A. à, Fasti Oxonienses.

HAYWOOD, Mrs. ELIZA (1693?-February 25, 1756), playwright, novelist, miscellaneous writer, was a Miss Fowler, the daughter of a London tradesman. She apparently married very young and had two children who, according to her enemies, were illegitimate, but according to her friends were legally fathered and cruelly abandoned by Mr. Haywood. Whatever the facts of her early life, Haywood had disappeared by the time Eliza first came to notice in literary circles.

She made an appearance as an actress in Dublin about 1715 and came to London shortly after. According to the editors of *The Tatler*, Mrs. Haywood was the "Sappho" described by Steele in 1709 as "a fine lady who writes, sings, dances, and can say and do whatever she pleases without the imputation of anything that can injure her character." Mrs. Haywood dedicated a collection of novels to Steele a good many years later, but it is doubtful whether she was actually his Sappho.

In 1721 she was employed by Rich, a theatrical manager, to rewrite a tragedy in blank verse, *The Fair Captive*, which was acted without much success. Two years later she wrote a comedy, *A Wife to Be Lett*, produced at the Drury Lane, in which according to contemporary accounts Mrs. Haywood stepped into the role of heroine at the last moment. She also wrote another tragic drama and collaborated with William Hatchett on *The Opera of Operas, or Tom Thumb the Great*, adapted from Fielding.

Eliza Haywood was best known, however, as a writer of fiction, turning out quantities of novels and "secret histories" most of which dealt with the trials and temptations of virtuous ladies, and all of which sold exceedingly well. Two of her books, *Memoirs of a Certain Island Adjacent to Utopia* and *The Secret History of the Present Intrigues of the Court of Caramania,* aroused the indignation of Pope. Both related scandalous episodes in the life of well-known personages who could be easily identified in spite of fictitious names by means of a key in back. Pope called her a "shameless scribbler" and worse—some of the coarsest lines in the *Dunciad* were devoted to making her ridiculous. Swift joined him in calling her a "stupid, infamous, scribbling woman." It must be remembered, however, that this was a period when professional women writers were not well thought of and, even though her novels have been long since forgotten, Mrs. Haywood belongs in the company of Mrs. Manley and Mrs. Behn —women with the energy and the courage to support themselves by their pens at the cost of an unsavory reputation.

PRINCIPAL WORKS: *Novels*—Love in Excess: or, The Fatal Enquiry, 1719; The Battle of the Authors, 1720; The Perfidious Brethren, 1720; The British Recluse: or, The Secret History of Cleomira, 1722; Idalia: or, The Unfortunate Mistress, 1723; Lasselia: or, The Self-Abandon'd, 1723; A Spy Upon the Conjurer: or, A Collection of Surprising Stories Relating to Mr. Duncan Campbell, 1724; Memoirs of a Certain Island Adjacent to the Kingdom of Utopia, 1725; The Mercenary Lover: or, The Unfortunate Heiresses, 1726; The Fruitless Enquiry, 1727; The Secret History of the Present Intrigues of the Court of Caramania, 1727; The History of Miss Betsey Thoughtless, 1751; The History of Jemmy and Jenny Jessamy, 1753. *Plays* —The Fair Captive (revision) 1721; A Wife to Be Lett, 1724; Frederick, Duke of Brunswick-Lunenburgh, 1729; The Opera of Operas: or, Tom Thumb the Great (with William Hatchett) 1733. *Miscellaneous*—Poems on Several Occasions, 1724; The Works of Mrs. Eliza Haywood, 1724; Secret Histories, Novels and Poems, 1725; The Female Spectator, 1744-46 (J. B. Priestley, ed. 1929).

ABOUT: Chalmers, A. Biographical Dictionary; Whicher, G. F. The Life and Romances of Mrs. Eliza Haywood.

HEARNE, THOMAS (July 1678-June 10, 1735),

historical antiquary, was born at Littlefield Green in the parish of White Waltham, Berkshire, where his father was parish clerk. The family was in such straitened circumstances that Thomas had to be put to day labor while his father taught him as best he could, until Francis Cherry of Shottesbrooke, impressed by the boy's ability, undertook to provide for his education. In 1695 he was sent to Oxford, where he took a B.A. in 1699 and an M.A. in 1703.

Turning down an opportunity to go to Maryland as a missionary, Hearne spent most of his time studying manuscripts at the Bodleian library, where his diligence attracted the attention of the librarian, John Hudson. Hudson helped to get him the position of assistant keeper in the library. Hearne immediately went to work revising the book catalogue and completed the coin catalogue, all the while enriching his store of antiquarian knowledge. He was offered chaplaincies at Corpus Christi and at All Souls' College, but he preferred the work in the library and in 1712 was advanced to second keeper. A year later he was offered the librarianship of the Royal Society, but again he refused to leave Oxford and the Bodleian. In 1715 Oxford elected him archi-typographer and esquire bedell in civil law, but when the chief librarian claimed he could not hold these offices and continue in his library work, he resigned the new offices. This record of singleminded devotion was broken when in 1716 he was deprived of the library office because of his refusal to support the new Hanoverian dynasty.

Living in retirement at Edmund Hall, Hearne continued the historical work which he had begun during his years at the Bodleian, editing and publishing an invaluable series of antiquarian volumes, most of them from original manuscripts never before available. In his earlier years he had been devoted to classical literature, but his later interests were English history and antiquities. Again positions of honor were offered him—the Camden professorship of history, the post of chief archivist, and finally the head librarianship of his beloved Bodleian— all of which he let go by because of his steadfast refusal to take an oath of allegiance to the Hanoverian regime.

Hearne had actually no great grasp of history, but his persistent and fanatical passion for the documents of the English past led him to edit and publish his long series of English chronicles, opening a treasure house of material to students of history. He also carried on extensive correspondence with the antiquaries and literary men of his time and kept a voluminous diary running to 145 volumes, which has been preserved and which is of interest for its sharp comment on his contemporaries.

PRINCIPAL WORKS: Reliquiae Bodleianae, or Some Genuine Remains of Sir Thomas Bodley, (ed.) 1703; Ductor Historicus, or A Short System of Universal History and an Introduction to the Study of It, 1704-05; The Itinerary of John Leland the Antiquary (ed.) 1710-12; Joannis Lelandi Antiquarii de Rebus Britannicis Collectanea (ed.) 1715; A Collection of Curious Discourses Written by Eminent Antiquaries Upon Several Heads in our English Antiquities (ed.) 1720; The History and Antiquities of Glastonbury, 1722; Historia Vitae et Regni Ricardi II (ed.) 1729; The Works of Thomas Hearne, 1810; Remarks and Collections of Thomas Hearne (C. E. Doble, and D. W. Rannie, eds. Oxford Historical Society) 1885-1921.

ABOUT: Bliss, P. (ed.) Reliquiae Hearneanae, the Remains of Thomas Hearne; Curll, E. (ed.) Impartiale Memorials of the Life and Writings of Thomas Hearne; Huddesford, W. (ed.) The Lives of Leland, Hearne and Wood.

HENDERSON, ROBERT. See HENRYSON, ROBERT

HENLEY, JOHN (August 3, 1692-October 14, 1756), orator, theologian, grammarian, was born at Melton Mowbray, Leicestershire, the son of Reverend Simon Henley, vicar of the parish. He entered St. John's College, Cambridge, in 1709 and took his B.A. in 1712, his M.A. four years later. Ordained, he became a curate in his native town.

Henley's career as an eccentric London preacher and reformer began when he went to London in 1721 as reader at the church of St. George the Martyr. Even at Cambridge he had been concerned with new methods of communicating both secular and religious knowledge, considering the teaching methods of the college unduly restrictive. In London his unconventional ideas of preaching led him into difficulties and he was forced to retire in 1724 to the living of Chelmondiston in Suffolk.

Feeling that his talents were not sufficiently appreciated by the church, he decided to break off all orthodox religious connections and preach as he saw fit. In 1726 he rented rooms in the Newport Market in London and established what he called the "Oratory Chapel." Running a series of provocative advertisements on Saturdays, he preached on Sundays and lectured on Wednesdays to large crowds of the curious. On one occasion he drew an audience of shoemakers by advertising that he could show them a new and speedy method for making shoes. His method, revealed from a gold and velvet pulpit, was to cut the tops off high boots.

There is little doubt that his showmanship was excellent even though his peculiarities made him a favorite subject for ridicule. Hogarth satirized him in two humorous plates, *The Oratory* and *The Christening of the Child.* Pope attacked him in *The Dunciad,* "Oh great restorer of the good old Stage / Preacher at once, and Zany of thy age!"

In the midst of oratorical didoes, he also wrote voluminously, editing, translating, publishing pamphlets, sermons, handbooks, and grammars. In 1730 he approached Sir Robert Walpole and was employed at £100 to conduct a periodical ridiculing the arguments of the opposition journal, *The Craftsman.* This periodical, the *Hyp Doctor,* appeared at intervals for nine years. In 1746 he was arrested on the charge of "endeavoring to alienate the minds of his Majesty's subjects from their allegiance by his Sunday harangues," but he was soon released on bail and apparently never brought to trial.

PRINCIPAL WORKS: Esther, Queen of Persia, an Historical Poem, 1714; The Complete Linguist with a Preface to Every Grammar, 1719-21; The Works of John Sheffield (ed.) 1722; An Introduction to an English Grammar, 1726; The Primitive Liturgy for the Use of Oratory, 1727; Letters and Advertisements, 1727; The Appeal of the Oratory and the First Stages of Christianity, 1727; The Art of Speaking in Public, 1727; Oratory Transactions, 1728-29; The Orators' Miscellany, 1731; A Course of Academical Lectures on Various Subjects, 1731; Select Discourses on Several Subjects, 1737; Why How Now, Gossip Pope? Or, the Sweet Singing Bird of Parnassus Taken Out of its Pretty Cage to be Roasted, 1743.

ABOUT: Dibdin, T. F. Bibliomania; Disraeli, I. Disappointed Genius, in Calamities of Authors.

HENRY OF HUNTINGDON (1084?-1155), historian, was born between 1080 and 1085, the son of Nicholas, who seems to have been archdeacon of Huntingdon. According to his own account he was brought up by a patron, Robert Bloat, then bishop of Lincoln. Nothing is known of his education except that he mentions Albinus of Angers as his master.

About 1109 he was made archdeacon of Huntingdon, a position which he probably held for the rest of his life. At the request of Alexander of Blois, who had succeeded his earlier patron as bishop of Lincoln,

Henry undertook to write an English history following Bede and other early chroniclers. In 1139 he accompanied Archbishop Theobald to Rome and on the return journey met Robert de Monte, the Norman historian, who was then a monk at the monastary of Bec. De Monte introduced him to the *Historia Britonum* of Geoffrey of Monmouth.

Henry's *Historia Anglorum* was apparently composed between 1125 and 1130. In its first version it covered British history up to the year 1129, and with later additions up to 1154. The early part was drawn from the *Anglo-Saxon Chronicles*, Bede, and other familiar sources, enlarged partly from oral tradition and partly by the author's own invention. The second part covering events after 1127 was written contemporaneously with the events described and is probably entirely original. Later editions of the work contain two added books, *De Miraculis*, an account of the miracles of nineteen saints, and *De Summitatibus*, an epilogue with three epistles. According to Leland, he also wrote eight books of epigrams, only two of which are now known. The *Historia* was first published in 1596 in Savile's *Scriptores Post Bedam*, and a section was later included in the *Monumenta Historica Britannica*.

Henry of Huntingdon was a facile writer who liked to enliven his narrative with outbursts of poetry, but as a historian he was inclined to be careless and vague as to detail. Of the early twelfth century chroniclers, he was for generations one of the most widely read, second only to William of Malmesbury in reputation, but modern criticism has found him wanting both in accuracy and in style.

Henry apparently died shortly after the completion of the final version of his *History*, since the records show that there was a new archdeacon of Huntingdon in the year 1155.

PRINCIPAL WORKS: Historia Anglorum, 1596 (T. Arnold, ed. Rolls Series, 1879); Epigrammata (T. Wright, ed. *in* Anglo-Latin Satirical Poets, Rolls Series, 1879).

ABOUT: Arnold, T. Introduction to Historia Anglorum; Leland, J. De Scriptoribus Britannicis.

HENRY THE MINSTREL, or BLIND HARRY or HARY (fl. 1470-1492), Scottish poet, was probably a native of Lothian, Scotland, since his *Wallace* is written in the Lothian dialect, which was the best Scots of the time. Supposedly he was a wandering minstrel, who earned his bread by reciting his poem in the courts of nobles. He was said to have been blind from birth, and he may have dictated his epic to an amanuensis. The treasury accounts of James IV show payments made to him from 1490 to 1492, and since James usually kept on paying his pensioners throughout their lifetime, presumably he died at the latter date. Dunbar *(qv* in *Lament for the Makaris* proves that he was dead by that year (1506).

In a sense, Blind Harry's *Wallace* and John Barbour's *Bruce* may be said between them to have created Scottish nationality as a self-conscious thing. No book in Scotland has gone through as many editions as the *Wallace*; up to the nineteenth century it was in every Scottish home, together with the Bible. Burns speaks of it as one of the first two books he ever "read in private," saying it "gave me more pleasure than any read since." *Wallace* helped to heal the wounds to Scottish pride given by Flodden; its ardent patriotism, its hot defiance of England, its glorification of the thirteenth century hero and his exploits (always victorious in this version) were balm to a beaten nation.

This national epic has survived in just one manuscript, of eleven books and 11,853 lines, which is now in the Advocates' Library in Edinburgh. This manuscript, bound with Barbour's *Bruce*, was written by John Ramsay in 1488. If Blind Harry was actually a "burel man"—a simple, unlearned peasant—as he calls himself, then Ramsay certainly edited the poem, for it bears evidence of some classical learning, and at least the ability to read Latin which would be gained by a few years in a monastery school. How a man blind from birth would have acquired this ability is a question. On the other hand, Ramsay represented himself merely as a copyist, and there is no sign of similarity between the styles of the two poems in his manuscript, so that one cannot deduce from internal evidence that the same hand had been at work on them both. It is a question which can never be settled, unless by some chance a second contemporary manuscript should somehow come to light.

The rhymed heroic meter of the poem displays very little of the alliteration which later, by its excess, really disfigured Scottish (and English) poetry. It is perhaps a bit too sanguinary and violent for our modern tastes, and it is, of course, quite unrealistic, based on folk tales and legends, with no attempt to picture the historic Wallace. But its simple, running style, its eloquence, and its ardor for liberty, make it something more than an antiquarian document. It is interesting to note that the author constantly defends Wallace as a member of the lesser gentry—the first entry into Scottish literature of Burns' proud statement that "a man's a man for a' that."

PRINCIPAL WORKS: The Actis and deidis of the illustre and vailyeand campioun Schir William Wallace Knichte of Ellerslie, 1508 (first printed edition extant, 1570; J. Jamieson, ed. 1820; J. Moir, ed. 1889).

ABOUT: Eyre-Todd, G. Early Scottish Poetry; Henderson, T. F. Scottish Vernacular Literature; Irving, D. History of Scottish Poetry; Jamieson, J. Preliminary Remarks, in 1820 ed.; Millar, J. H. A Literary History of Scotland; Moir, J. The Wallace: A Critical Study of Blind Harry; Schofield, W. H. Mythical Bards.

HENRYSON or HENDERSON, ROBERT

(1430?-1506?), Scottish poet, may possibly have been born as early as 1420; Dunbar,[qv] in Lament for the Makaris, calls him "very old"—though of course a septuagenarian would be "very old" in the fifteenth or sixteenth century. Incidentally, the death date given for him is merely based on the fact that he was dead when Dunbar's poem appeared in 1506. He is supposed to have entered the University of Glasgow in 1462, but already, by that time, to have been a Bachelor or Master of Arts from some European university, probably Paris or Louvain; he is always referred to as "Master" or "Magister." He is also said to have been a schoolmaster at Dunfermeling (Dunfermline), Fifeshire, and there was a Benedictine abbey there in which he may have taught. If he is the same Robert Henryson who was a notary public, then he was at least in lower orders, since only the clergy then acted as notaries. His poems were all, apparently, written after 1450. This is all that is known about Henryson's life.

Henryson has been called "the most Chaucerian of the makaris or bards." His longest and by far his best work is the Fables, the matter of which is of course not original, being taken from Æsop, but the treatment is markedly fresh, full of vivacious

spirits and felicitous turns of phrase. His "local atmosphere," introduced into the old fables, is wholly realistic, characterized by humor, good taste, contemporaneity, and keen observation of the world about him. If he imitated Chaucer, he imitated him well.

It was in the Testament of Cresseid that he came (openly and avowedly) nearest to the great English poet of the preceding century, and this poem is not unworthy of being published together with Chaucer's Troilus. In fact, it was once supposed actually to be Chaucer's. Henryson's repentant Cresseid, stricken with leprosy and seeing her Troilus once more before she dies, when he rides by and throws her a coin, only to be smitten with horror when he realizes who she is, is conceived in a fine dramatic tradition.

Henryson is noted for the variety of his themes and treatments. The lament of Orpheus in his poem of that name is a beautiful lyric—in fact, he was the first pure lyrist among the Scottish poets. His mastery of cadence is superb. His thirteen shorter poems range from allegory, religion, and personal meditation to the "pastoral dialogue," Robene and Makyne, almost a true ballad, and the scathing Sum Practysis of Medecyne, in which he pays off his grudge against the doctors in the true invective style of the Scottish "flytings." (See Dunbar, W.) Being a man of his century, and probably a clergyman as well, Henryson is of course highly didactic, with long morals appended to all his poems, not merely to the Fables. Nevertheless, he is no mere preacher in verse, but a skilled and talented poet, with an original mind and a gift for true music.

PRINCIPAL WORKS (dates of publication): The Testament of Cresseid (with Chaucer's Troilus and Cressida) 1532; The Morall Fabillis of Esope the Phrygian, 1570; Orpheus and Eurydice, 1827; The Poems and Fables of Robert Henryson (D. Laing, ed.) 1865; The Poems of Robert Henryson (G. G. Smith, ed.) 1906; The Poems of Robert Henryson (W. H. Metcalfe, ed.) 1917.

ABOUT: Diebler, A. R. Henryson's Fabeldichtungen; Eyre-Todd, G. Medieval Scottish Poetry; Gordon, R. K. The Story of Troilus; Irving, D. Lives of the Scotish [sic] Poets; Metcalfe, W. H. Introduction, Poems, 1917; Morley, H. English Writers; Saintsbury, G. History of English Prosody; Stearns, M. W. Robert Henryson.

HERBERT, Lord EDWARD, of Cherbury

(March 3, 1583-August 20, 1648), philosopher, historian, poet, was born at

Eyton-on-Severn, Shropshire, the oldest son of Richard Herbert, sheriff of Montgomeryshire, Wales, and his second wife, Magdalen Newport. There were seven sons and three daughters in all; George Herbert ^{qv} was his younger brother. Richard Herbert died in 1596, and the widow married Sir John Danvers, a man twenty years her junior. Because of inherited epilepsy, Edward was taught at home, but he entered University College, Oxford, the year of his father's death and remained there (without a degree) to 1600. In 1599, at sixteen, his family married him to a cousin, Mary Herbert, aged twenty; they had two sons and two daughters, and the marriage seems to have been happy enough, considering the circumstances.

Herbert went to London and entered court circles; in 1603 James I, on his accession, made him a Knight of the Bath, and in 1605 he, like his father, was sheriff of Montgomeryshire. From 1608 to 1610 he made two extended trips to France and Italy, and from 1614 to 1617 he was a soldier in the army of the Prince of Orange—actually a soldier of fortune for any prince who would hire him. In 1619 he became ambassador to France; he quarreled with his superiors and with the French officials, was once recalled and reinstated, and finally dismissed in 1624, though he had done much to negotiate the marriage of the future Charles I and Henrietta Maria. He was awarded the Irish peerage of Castle Island, but it was not until 1629 that he became an English peer as the first Baron Herbert of Cherbury. When the civil war started, he fluctuated wildly, refused several times to join the king, finally surrendered to the Parliamentarians to save his property. The remainder of his life was divided between writing (history to regain the royal favor, philosophy and poetry for their own sakes), and frantic efforts to hold on to his vanishing estates and fortune.

Herbert was a strange mixture of braggart and thinker, adventurer and scholar. Extremely handsome, he was also extremely vain, quarrelsome and quick on the draw (he was a famous duelist), and a lady-killer who boasted that even a queen was not unmoved by his charms. His autobiography, which goes only to 1624, does him disservice at his own hands. Gassendi and Descartes would not have been influenced by the man he

W. Larkin, 1608
LORD EDWARD HERBERT

describes there, nor would his mother's friend, John Donne, ^{qv} have esteemed him, nor would Ben Jonson ^{qv} have praised his "learning, wit, valour, and judgment."

Though Herbert is to be admired for going to the original documents for his history, the result is negligible, since his primary object was to please the king. His poetry imitates the obscurity and harshness of his master Donne, though he is capable of an occasional lyric not unworthy of Herrick. It is as a philosopher that he is most important. He is in a sense the father of the Scottish school of intellectualist philosophers, and the foreshadower of eighteenth century deism. His *De Veritate* is a search for the causation of knowledge and the conditions of truth, with universality of belief as the test. In his *De Religione Gentilium* he was a pioneer in the study of comparative religion, finding all present theological systems "corruptions of the pure and primitive rational worship." Even in the midst of his career as a soldier of fortune, he took time out to visit the philosophers and scientists near whom he found himself; and he had a turn for invention, particularly of military equipment. Fundamentally he was a man with a ranging and searching mind which warred with his extroverted personality. He was never an original thinker, but his writing, especially in philosophy, is distinctly not

261

that of a mere amateur, but the serious work of a man of talent and ability.

PRINCIPAL WORKS: *Philosophy*—De Veritate [Concerning truth] 1624; De Causis Errorum [Concerning the causes of errors] 1645; De Religione Gentilium [Concerning the religion of peoples] 1663; A Dialogue between a Tutor and his Pupil, 1768. *History*—The Life and Raigne of King Henry the eighth . . . [with] A General History of the Times, 1649; Expeditio Buckinghami ducis in Ream insulam [expedition of the Duke of Buckingham to the Isle of Rhé] 1656 (in English, 1860). *Miscellaneous*—English and Latin Poems (H. Herbert, ed.) 1665 (J. C. Collins, ed. 1881); (C. C. M. Smith, ed. 1923); Life of Herbert of Cherbury, Written by Himself (H. Walpole, ed.) 1764 (S. Lee, ed. 1906).

ABOUT: Aubrey, J. Lives of Eminent Men; Güttler, C. Lord Herbert von Cherbury; Herbert, E. Life of Herbert of Cherbury, Written by Himself; Rémusat, C. Lord Herbert de Cherbury; Wood, A. à, Athenae Oxonienses.

HERBERT, GEORGE (April 3, 1593-March 1633), poet, miscellaneous writer, was

born in Montgomery Castle, Montgomeryshire, Wales, the fifth of the seven sons of Richard Herbert and his second wife, Magdalen Newport, later Lady Danvers. He was the younger brother of Lord Edward Herbert of Cherbury,^{qv} and born in the same year as Izaak Walton, his biographer, and Nicholas Ferrar, his editor. He attended Westminster School, and entered Trinity College, Cambridge, in 1609, was given his B.A. in 1613, M.A. in 1616 (in which year he also became a fellow), was appointed reader in rhetoric in 1618, and orator of the university in 1619. He had hoped that the oratorship, with its opportunities of meeting royalty, would mean political preferment, as it often did; the death of James I in 1625 put an end to these hopes, and he finally resigned the post in 1627. He had retired to a friend's house in Kent to make up his mind whether or not to continue his studies in divinity; while there he was appointed a prebend of Layton. Ecclesia (Leighton Bromswold), Huntingdonshire. As a layman, he could not perform all the duties of the office, and he devoted himself therefore to rebuilding the church itself.

Ferrar was a clergyman near by and this influence (though in actuality they met only once, years later), together with that of Herbert's mother's friend, John Donne,^{qv} decided the issue. Exactly when Herbert was ordained is not clear, but in 1630 he became rector of Fugglestone-with-Bemer-

GEORGE HERBERT

ton, Huntingdonshire, his home thenceforth. In 1629 he had married Jane Danvers, a distant relative of his stepfather; they had no children. Herbert's life as a clergyman was that of a saint. What little time was taken from his clerical duties and his writing he gave to a daily walk to Salisbury Cathedral, where he joined in singing in the choir; he was a true musician, not only a singer but also a performer on the viol and the lute. Tall, gaunt, ascetic in appearance, he did not have long to live; for years he had been a victim of tuberculosis, which killed him at forty. His widow married Sir Robert Cook.

Herbert's early poetry—the Latin elegies on Prince Henry and Queen Anne in the Cambridge collections, the satirical answer to the attacks of Andrew Melville, even the poems written on his mother's death—are of slight value. They were written by the courtier who flattered James I and hoped to cut a figure in the world, not by the dedicated "priest of the temple." His translation from Cornaro has only an antiquarian interest. His *Outlandish Proverbs* displays another side of his nature—his wry humor and homely common sense. His chief prose work is *A Priest in His Temple*, which is in a sense a companion piece to or commentary on the poems collected by Ferrar and published under the title of *The Temple*—and it is by these poems that he is remembered.

The intimacy of feeling in Herbert's religious poetry in *The Temple* has frequently been commented on. "Of God found and known here and now in the little passages of daily life and the small circumstances of our common environment, Herbert has the most to say of any seventeenth century poet I know," writes Helen C. White. ". . . This intimacy of consciousness is revealed in the peculiar homeliness of the terms in which Herbert tries to communicate his sense of the divine. There is splendor in Herbert, and some of that startling magnificence that is to be found in practically all writers of this period. . . . There is that happy, effortless felicity that, gathering up much meaning in a phrase, yet has leisure for charm, the essence of the classic spirit. But the distinctive contribution of Herbert to the poetic style of the period is to be found in none of these, but rather in a peculiar combination of homeliness and grace." He owed much to Donne—some of whose faults, such as an excess of ingenuity he inherited—but his genius and his humility are his own. In art, as in life, he had a passion for perfection which made him rewrite and alter incessantly. Richard Baxter said that Herbert "speaks to God like a man who really believeth in God," and William Cowper, in his deepest melancholia, found comfort only in reading and re-reading Herbert's poems.

It should be noted that nothing whatever of Herbert's was published in his lifetime, except the Cambridge elegies and the Latin and English poems (*Parentalia*) on the death of his mother which were printed in 1627 with Donne's *Sermon of Commemoration of the Lady Danvers*. Ferrar and Walton between them made him known to the public, as the retiring and highly sensitive poet himself would never have done. The two famous older men who had been his admirers, Francis Bacon and Lancelot Andrewes,*qqv* had predeceased him by seven years.

All Herbert's books and manuscripts were burnt during the civil war, so that there may be major work of his that has been lost forever. He occupies a lasting place in the history of English literature, and a still higher one in the small list of poets whose subject is the soul and its relation to God.

PRINCIPAL WORKS: The Temple, Sacred Poems and Private Ejaculations (N. Ferrar, ed.) 1633; Hygiasticon (tr.) 1634; Outlandish Proverbs, selected by Mr. G. H. (Jaculata Prudentum) (*in* Witts Recreations) 1640; A Priest in his Temple, or, the Countrey Parson, his Character and Rule of Holy Life (with Jaculata Prudentum *as* Herbert's Remains) 1652; Complete Works (A. B. Grosart, ed.) 1874; English Works (G. H. Palmer, ed.) 1905; Works (F. E. Hutchinson, ed.) 1941.

ABOUT: Bennett, J. Four Metaphysical Poets; Beresford, J. Gossip of the 17th and 18th Centuries; Coleridge, S. T. Biographia Literaria; Daniell, J. Life of George Herbert; Hutchinson, F. E. Introduction, Works, 1941; Hyde, A. G. George Herbert and His Times; Leishman, J. B. The Metaphysical Poets; More, P. E. Shelburne Essays; Oley, B. Biographical Notice, Herbert's Remains; Palmer, G. H. The Life and Works of George Herbert; Tannenbaum, S. A. and D. George Herbert: A Concise Bibliography; Walton, I. The Life of Mr. George Herbert; White, H. C. The Metaphysical Poets: A Study in Religious Experience.

HERRICK, ROBERT

HERRICK, ROBERT (August 1591-October 1674), poet, was born in London, the sixth of the seven children of Nicholas Herrick, a goldsmith from an old Leicestershire family of Norse descent, and of Julian (Stone) Herrick. When he was a year old his father died, apparently by suicide (he fell or jumped out of a window), in consequence of which part of his estate was confiscated. The children were placed under the guardianship of their uncle, Sir William Herrick, the richest goldsmith in England, and jeweler to the king. Their mother moved with them to Hampton, Middlesex, where the poet was reared. (To this period belongs his earliest known poem, "A Country Life.") He was educated at his uncle's expense at Westminster School, and then, in 1607, apprenticed to him for ten years.

But obviously it soon became apparent that Robert would never be a good goldsmith, and it probably was easy for him to secure his uncle's permission to enter St. John's College, Cambridge, in 1613. In 1616 he transferred to Trinity Hall, where he secured a B.A. in 1617, and M.A. in 1620. Ostensibly he was studying law, but he made no headway at it, and his letters deal with no subject except his constant impecuniousness.

There followed seven years in which Herrick is lost to sight. He may have been in London, consorting with the court musicians for whom he wrote songs afterwards, or he may have been with his mother in

263

HERRICK

ROBERT HERRICK

Middlesex. Some time during this period he took holy orders. In 1627 he became military chaplain to the Duke of Buckingham, and accompanied him on his expedition to the Isle of Rhé. In 1629 his pleasant life in his beloved London came to an abrupt end, when Charles I gave him the living of Dean Prior, near Totnes, in Devonshire.

At first Herrick was very homesick, felt himself an exile, and lamented bitterly his banishment to the West Country. Soon, however, he became interested in the rural traditions and customs of "dull Devonshire," and reconciled to his fate. He even found that he had written his "Farewell unto Poetry" most prematurely. Some stories are told of his irascibility, provoked by his rough and apathetic parishioners—such as the writing of scurrilous epigrams about them, and even once throwing his sermon in their faces —but on the whole he was well liked. Some of his poems which no longer existed even in manuscript were remembered by and later collected from the country people. And he consoled himself by occasional visits to London, a long one in 1640.

As a convinced Royalist, Herrick refused to subscribe to the Solemn League and Covenant, and consequently he was ejected from his living by the Long Parliament. He returned gladly to London, settled in Westminster, resumed the lay habit, and until the

Restoration lived on the ready charity of his rich relatives and friends. In 1662 he ousted his successor and returned to Dean Prior for the rest of his life, resuming his peaceful life with his spaniel and his other pets, all cared for by his old servant Prudence Baldwin. He never married, and the probability is that Julia, Anthea, and the rest of the ladies in his love poems were purely creatures of the imagination.

Herrick's only volume during his lifetime was brought out in 1648, when he first returned to London. His poems, besides being set to music for the court, had appeared in various anthologies—anonymously in *A Description of the King and Queen of Fayries* in 1635, in *Lachrymae Musarum* in 1649, and sixty-two of them in *Witts Recreation* in 1650. So careless was he of them that two of them were ascribed to Carew in one of that poet's volumes, and some were thought to be Shakespeare's. After the 1200 poems of *Hesperides*, divided into "unbaptised rhymes" and "noble numbers" (i.e., secular and divine), Herrick wrote very little, and the body of his work is still contained in various editions of the *Hesperides*. After his death he was totally forgotten until the end of the eighteenth century, when John Nichols rediscovered him.

Herrick, though he is usually classed with the Cavalier Poets, was far from typical of them. They are romantic, he is classical, harking back to Horace, Catullus, and even Theocritus, though his immediate master was Ben Jonson, one of whose "sons" he was. He was no admirer of Petrarch or the other Italians, and he preferred Marlowe to Spenser. Almost alone of his generation he was completely unaffected by Donne. He was fastidious, a deliberate, careful reviser; as he wrote, "Better 'twere, my book were dead, / Than to live not perfected." His range is limited, but within that range he is supreme; as Gosse said, "As a pastoral lyrist he stands first among English poets." F. W. Moorman called him "one of the most pagan of English poets, . . . more of a Roman flamen than a Christian priest." He was indeed steeped in Roman poetry, and he has the singing throat of Catullus, though nothing of the Roman's naked passion. Herrick is the poet of spring and of youth, of gentle melancholy at inevitable death, of rural rites and immemorial observances, of flowers new-sprung, of love that is graceful and delicate rather than (except in one poem, "To Anthea, Who May Command Him Anything") burning or passionate. Spontaneous, fresh, sensuous, sometimes naive and homely, these are the adjectives to describe his poetry. To quote Moorman again, "Among the singers of a day when England was a nest of singing birds, Herrick stands as king."

PRINCIPAL WORKS: Hesperides: or, the Works, both Humane and Divine, of Robert Herrick, Esq., 1648 (W. C. Hazlitt, ed. 1869; A. W. Pollard, ed. 1891; G. Saintsbury, ed. 1893; F. W. Moorman, ed. 1921); Complete Poems (A. B. Grosart, ed.) 1876; Chrysomela: Selections from the lyrical poems of Robert Herrick (F. T. Palgrave, ed.) 1877.

ABOUT: DeLattre, F. Contribution à l'Étude de la poesie anglaise au XVIIe siècle; Easton, E. Youth Immortal; Gosse, E. 17th Century Studies; Grosart, A. B. Memorial-Introduction, in Complete Poems; MacLeod, M. L. A Concordance to the Poems of Robert Herrick; Moorman, F. W. Robert Herrick, a biographical and critical study; Saintsbury, G. Introduction, Hesperides, 1893 ed.; Swinburne, A. C. Preface, Hesperides, 1891 ed.; Tannenbaum, S. A. and D. Robert Herrick: A Concise Bibliography.

HERVEY, JAMES (February 26, 1714-December 25, 1758), cleric, devotional writer, was born in Hardingstone near Northampton. His father was the rector of Collingtree, a neighboring village. Young James was educated at Lincoln College, Oxford, under the tuition of Dr. Hutchins, then rector of the college. In his second or third year he came under the influence of the Oxford Methodists, particularly John Wesley, who was a fellow and tutor at Lincoln College. In 1736 he received his B.A. degree and took holy orders.

After assisting his father for a time, he went to London and served as curate at Dummer in Hampshire. In 1738 he became chaplain to Paul Orchard of Stoke Abbey, Devonshire, and was godfather to Orchard's eldest son. Apparently he began the composition of his *Meditations Among the Tombs* about this time, and when the complete *Meditations and Contemplations* appeared several years later, the second volume was dedicated to his godson.

He became curate of Bideford, North Devon, in 1740 and was so well thought of by his parishioners that when a new rector dismissed him three years later they offered to maintain him at their own expense. Hervey went, however, to Weston Favell to assist his father, and when his father died, he succeeded to the livings of Weston Favell and of Collingtree which combined amounted to £180 a year. In order to qualify for this new position he took his M.A. at Cambridge in 1752. Hervey had already suffered one breakdown from overwork, and the zeal with which he now attacked both his parochial and his literary duties led to a long illness. He died before he was forty-five.

Hervey's writings were extremely popular in their day, although to modern readers they are impossibly platitudinous. He wrote in the over-inflated style which the most sincere religious writers of the time seemed to assume with their pulpit manner. In addition to *Meditations and Contemplations,* he published *Dialogues Between Theron and Aspasio,* which took him squarely into the Calvinist controversy then at its height, and brought him a sour criticism from John Wesley. A pious, gentle, unworldly soul, Hervey was as modest and simple in his life as his literary style was elaborate and artificial.

PRINCIPAL WORKS: Meditations and Contemplations, 1746-47; Theron and Aspasio, or A Series of Dialogues and Letters Upon the Most Important and Interesting Subjects, 1755; Collected Works, 1769.

ABOUT: T. W. Life, in Meditations and Contemplations; Tyerman, L. Oxford Methodists.

HERVEY, Lord JOHN (October 15, 1696-August 5, 1743), Baron Hervey of Ickworth, memoirist, was the son of John, the first Earl of Bristol, by his second wife. He was educated at Westminster School and Clare Hall, Cambridge, where he took an M.A. in 1715.

Leaving Cambridge, he went abroad first to Paris and then to the court of George I at Hanover where he ingratiated himself with Prince Frederick. On his return to England, instead of going into the army as his father wished, he spent most of his time at Ickworth in "the perpetual pursuit of poetry." Visiting the court of the prince and princess at Richmond, he met and fell in love with Mary Lepell, whom he married in 1720.

Hervey was elected to the House of Commons in 1725, where he sided with Pulteney against Walpole until Walpole became minister, when he found it expedient to switch his loyalties and was rewarded with the office of vice chamberlain to the royal household. With Pulteney he carried on a lively battle of pamphlets which came to a climax in a duel, Hervey nearly meeting a violent end at the point of Pulteney's rapier. In 1733 he entered the House of Lords, where he was an invaluable instrument to Walpole through his influence with Queen Caroline. In 1740 he was appointed lord privy seal, a post which he held until after Walpole's resignation. He died when he was only forty-six and was buried at Ickworth.

Hervey, "a virtuoso in defamatory epithets," was a clever, cynical, unprincipled man who seemed to delight in making enemies. Even Walpole disliked him, having recorded privately that though Hervey was "too ill to go to operas, yet, with a coffin-face, is as full of his dirty little politics as ever." He could exert great wit and charm when he so desired and was extraordinarily popular with the ladies, even though the Duchess of Marlborough describes him as having "a painted face and not a tooth in his head." He quarreled with the Prince of Wales over the favors of one of the queen's ladies in waiting. He quarreled with Pope over the good graces of Lady Mary Wortley Montagu, whereupon Pope named him "Lord Fanny" in his famous imitation of a Horace satire and referred to Lady Mary as "furious Sappho."

Hervey had eight children and when he died he left the manuscript of his *Memoirs* to his eldest son, who determined that they could not be published until after the death of George III. Actually the *Memoirs* did not appear in print until 1848. They offer a minute portrait of the court of George II, highly polished, cynical, satiric, and venomous. In presenting the wicked comedy of court intrigue, Hervey often comes close to the type of classical Roman satire.

PRINCIPAL WORKS: Observations on the Writings of the Craftsman, 1730; Remarks on the Craftsman's Vindication of His Two Honble. Patrons, 1731; An Epistle From a Nobleman to a Doctor of Divinity, 1733; Letters Between Lord Hervey and Dr. Middleton Concerning the Roman Senate, 1778; Memoirs of the Reign of George the Second (J. W. Croker, ed.) 1848 (R. Sedgwick, ed. 1931).

ABOUT: Croker, J. W. Biographical notice, *in* Memoirs; Walpole, H. Catalogue of Royal and Noble Authors.

HEYLYN, PETER (1600-May 8, 1662), writer on ecclesiastical history, was born at Burford in Oxfordshire, the second son of a country gentleman, Henry Heylyn. A precocious scholar, he entered Hart Hall, Oxford, at the age of fourteen, and later attended Magdalen College, where he took a B.A. in 1617 and an M.A. three years later. Elected a fellow of Magdalen, Heylyn gave lectures on cosmography and historical geography and in 1624 took holy orders.

All his life Heylyn was a lively and frequently acrimonious controversialist. While he was still at Oxford he carried on a series of audacious disputations with John Prideaux, the regius professor of divinity, on the visibility and infallibility of the church. Later he assailed the arguments of Bishop John Williams in two pamphlets, *A Coal From the Altar* and *Antidotum Lincolnese;* and assisted William Noy in preparing a case against William Prynne for the publication of *Histriomastix,* a fierce attack on plays and actors and on the court which supported them.

In 1628 Heylyn risked his ecclesiastical future by marrying Letitia Highgate. Nevertheless he continued to enjoy the king's favor and was appointed a court chaplain. In 1631 he was given the prebendary of Westminster Cathedral under Bishop Williams and two years later the rectory of Alresford, Hampshire. During the civil war Heylyn made himself useful to the royalist party in various ways, joining the king at Oxford where he edited a vivacious but virulent news sheet, *Mercurius Aulicus.* As a result of his royalist activities, the rectory at Alresford was plundered and his library dispersed. Under the Commonwealth Heylyn spent several years wandering about the countryside in disguise, suffering from poverty and failing eyesight, until 1653 when he settled at Lacy's Court, Abingdon, where he was left undisturbed by the government.

In spite of near blindness, he wrote his most important works during these latter years, a series intended to furnish a complete survey of the ecclesiastical questions of his time. Most notable were his *History of the Reformation of the Church of England,* and *The History of the Life and Death of William Laud,* a defense of Laud which has become a valuable biographical authority. At the Restoration Heylyn returned to residence at Westminster, where he was consulted with great respect on ecclesiastical matters. He died when he was sixty-two, leaving a widow and eleven children.

PRINCIPAL WORKS: Microcosmus, or A Little Description of the Great World, 1621; A Survey of France, 1625; The History of the Sabbath, 1636; Ecclesia Vindicata, or The Church of England Justified, 1657; A Short View of the Life and Reign of King Charles, 1658; Examen Historicum, 1659; Ecclesia Restaurata, or The History of the Reformation of the Church of England, 1661 (J. C. Robertson, ed. 1849); Cyprianus Anglicus, or The History of William Laud, Archbishop of Canterbury, 1668; Aerius Redivivus, or The History of the Presbyterians, 1670; Historical and Miscellaneous Tracts, 1681.

ABOUT: Barnard, J. Life, in Ecclesia Restaurata (J. C. Robertson, ed.); Vernon, G. Life of Dr. Peter Heylyn; Wood, A. à, Athenae Oxonienses.

HEYWOOD, JOHN (1497?-1580?), epigrammatist, dramatist, was probably born in London, and his father may have been William Heywood, coroner of Coventry. He may also have lived during his childhood in Hertfordshire. None of these things is certain, but what is certain is that at an early age he became a chorister in the service of Henry VIII, singing and playing the virginals, and acting in interludes, largely for the entertainment of the future Queen Mary. It is possible that after his voice changed he was sent to Pembroke College (then Broadgates Hall), Oxford. He was a Roman Catholic, and he married Joan (or Eliza) Rastell, whose mother was the sister of Sir Thomas More. They had a daughter and two sons, Ellis (Elizaeus) and Jasper, both of whom became Jesuit priests, and the latter of whom wrote tragedies and poems.

When Mary reached the throne, Heywood was one of her greatest favorites. She gave him an estate in Yorkshire, the rents from which later became his main support. Heywood had been undisturbed during the reign of Edward VI, and Elizabeth as a princess had been his friend, but he became apprehensive of his safety after her accession, and in 1564 he felt it wiser to leave for France, where he settled at Malines. From 1575 to 1578, a very old man by this time, he lived at the Jesuit College in Antwerp, where his son Ellis was a preacher. In the last named year, a mob besieged the college, and all the residents, including Heywood and his son, were expelled. The remainder of his life

was spent in Louvain. The exact date of his death is not known, but in 1587 Thomas Newton spoke of him as "dead and gone."

Heywood's plays grew naturally from the popular interlude form. They were in a sense not plays at all in our modern meaning, but dramatic dialogues or debates on a set subject. *The Foure P.P.*, a contest in lying, among a palmer, a pardoner, a "potycary," and a peddler, approaches most nearly to the dramatic form. But in the exuberant gaiety and spontaneity of his plays, Heywood is a forerunner of true comedy. His characterization was realistic and he dealt with contemporary types, much as Chaucer did. When he did not, as in *A Play of the Wether*, which is concerned with the Greek gods on Olympus, he remains realistic still. It is going rather too far, however, to call him, as Symonds did, "a prose Chaucer." In a way —though he had a genuine love of learning and was something of a reformer, with some spirited shafts of satire aimed at theological abuses—Heywood's position at court was little better than that of a high class jester, and his plays had to be adapted to their audience.

In his productive years, Heywood was celebrated not only for his plays and his epigrams, but also for his ballads, most of which have been lost. One was referred to by Shakespeare in *Hamlet*. His proverbs and epigrams display him much better as a poet

1562

JOHN HEYWOOD

than do his so-called plays; they have pathos as well as humor, poignancy as well as wit. He himself was modest about his achievements, and said of himself merely

> Longe have I bene a singinge man
> And sondrie partes oft I have songe.

He may have been referring only to his career as an actual chorister, but the description applies equally well to his writing.

The first two plays ascribed to Heywood do not bear his name, but must be his, for the reason that no one else at that time was writing this particular kind of dialogue. Most of the plays were published by William Rastell, who was Mrs. Heywood's uncle—another way of establishing the canon.

The influence of the early French farces (French companies played often at the English court) is apparent on all Heywood's plays. They are written in lively verse; in all but one virtue triumphs over vice, thus making them legitimate successors to the ancient morality plays; and they are what he claimed for them, "new and very mery enterludes."

PRINCIPAL WORKS: *Plays*—A Mery Play betwene Johan Johan, Tyb his Wyfe, and Syr Jhān the Preest, 1533; A Mery Play betwene the Pardner and the Frere, the Curate and Neybour Pratte, 1533; The Play of the Wether, 1533; A Play of Love, 1534; The Playe Called the Foure P.P., 1543?; Wytty and Wytless (as A Dialogue on Wit and Folly, F. W. Fairholt, ed.) 1846; Dramatic Writings (J. S. Farmer, ed.) 1905. *Miscellaneous*—A Dialogue Conteining the Number of the Effectuall Proverbs in the English Tongue, 1549 (J. Sharman, ed. 1874); An Hundred Epigrammes, 1550; Two Hundred Epigrammes, upon the Hundred Proverbs, with a Thyrde Hundred Newly Added, 1550; The Spider and the Flie (verse) 1556; A Fourth Hundred of Epygrams, Newly Invented, 1560; John Heywoodes Woorkes [Epigrams and proverbs] 1562.

ABOUT: Bolwell, R. W. The Life and Works of John Heywood; Collier, J. P. History of English Dramatic Poetry; Fairholt, F. W. Some Account of John Heywood and his Interludes; Reed, A. W. Early Tudor Drama; Sharman, J. Introduction, Proverbs, 1874 ed.; Symonds, J. A. Shakespeare's Predecessors in the English Drama.

HEYWOOD, THOMAS (1572?-August 1641), dramatist, miscellaneous writer, was born in Lincolnshire, of a well-connected family. Very little is known about his life. According to his own say-so, he was educated at Cambridge, though the statement that he was a fellow of Peterhouse seems definitely mistaken. It is not known just when he came to London, but by 1598 he was a member of Philip Henslowe's Lord Admiral's Company. He was an actor for thirty years, and during that same period says that he wrote all or parts of some two hundred and twenty plays. Only a small portion of these has survived. He was a careless worker, who wrote on the back of tavern bills, let his manuscripts vanish when the play had been performed, and was reluctant to publish, because he had no time for revision.

Heywood did not stay with Henslowe's company, but during his professional career was identified with several others. In all cases he seems to have taken a share in the profits, since he was paid no salary. He spent the remainder of his life in London, though whether he was married is unknown. He loved the city ardently, and was the appropriate person to be chosen to write five of the pageants for the installation of the new Lord Mayor, between 1631 and 1639. He was also a fervent patriot and a strong adherent of Protestantism, though in general he avoided controversial political or religious matters. He was a fair scholar, who translated Sallust, Ovid, and Lucian, but he was never an associate of the "university wits" who held themselves aloof from the common workaday people of the theatre. When he died at about eighty he left uncompleted a proposed "lives of all the poets, in all lands and all times." He was buried in Clerkenwell.

Heywood's forte is the domestic drama, the *comédie larmoyante* which combines smiles and tears. His masterpiece is in that genre—it is *A Woman Kilde with Kindnesse*. *The English Traveller* is not far behind it. He liked also the romantic drama with patriotic overtones, such as *The Fair Maid of the West*. Unfortunately he was also addicted to broad farce, which was less successful, and he was given to complicated by-plots which only weakened his main theme. It is said that Beaumont and Fletcher had his *Foure Prentises of London* in mind when they wrote their burlesque *Knight of the Burning Pestle*.

About 1635 Heywood ceased to write for the stage; and in fact throughout his life he had done a good deal of non-dramatic writing, both in prose and in verse. It is as a dramatist, however, that he lives. Lamb even called him "a prose Shakespeare," with special reference to his gift for dramatization of character. Certainly he was no lyrist, and his interpolated songs are poor. The German critic J. L. Tieck appraised him most justly by calling him "the model of a light and rapid talent," and "a man of facile and felicitous endowment." His virtuosity and flexibility, which enabled him always to follow the latest fashion in plays, injured his literary reputation—but then he never thought of his plays as literature, or of himself as a serious author. He was a remarkably modest man, who spoke of himself as a tyro when he had long been established. It is his very unaffectedness and sincerity which most commend him. His regular motto for all his printed plays shows the nature of the man and his modest aspirations—"Aut prodesse solunt aut delectare"—"they are wont either to profit or to please."

PRINCIPAL WORKS: *Plays* (dates of publication)—King Edward the Fourth (chronicle play) 1600; If You Know Not Me, You Know No Bodie, 1605 (2d part, 1606); A Woman Kilde with Kindnesse, 1607; The Rape of Lucrece, 1608; The Golden Age, 1610; The Silver Age, 1613; The Brazen Age, 1613; A Marriage Triumph (masque) 1613; The Foure Prentises of London, with The Conquest of Jerusalem, 1615; The Iron Age, 1632; The English Traveller, 1633; A Mayden-Head Well Lost, 1634; The Late Lancashire Witches (with R. Brome) 1634; A Challenge for Beautie, 1636; Love's Maistresse, 1636; The Royall King, and the Loyall Subject, 1637; The Wise-Woman of Hogsden, 1638; Fortune by Land and Sea (with W. Rowley) 1655; The Captives, 1883; Best Plays (A. W. Verity, ed.) 1888. *Non-Dramatic Works*—Troicus Britannicus, or Great Britain's Troy (verse) 1609; An Apology for Actors, 1612; The Life and Death of Hector (verse) 1614; England's Elizabeth, 1632; The Hierarchie of the Blessed Angells (verse) 1635; The Life of Merlin, surnamed Ambrosius, 1641; Exemplary Lives and Memorable Acts of Nine of the Most Worthy Women of the World, 1656; Gynaikeon, or Nine Books of Various History, concerning Women, 1657.

ABOUT: Chambers, E. The Elizabethan Stage; Clark, A. M. Thomas Heywood, Playwright and Miscellanist; Collier, J. P. Introduction, Apology for Actors, 1841 ed.; Cromwell, O. Thomas Heywood: A Study in the Elizabethan Drama of Everyday Life; Lamb, C. Specimens of Early Dramatic Poetry; Symonds, J. A. Shakespeare's Predecessors; Tannenbaum, S. A. and D. John Heywood: A Concise Bibliography; Ward, W. History of English Dramatic Literature.

HIGDEN, RANULF (d. 1364), chronicler,

was born in the western part of England and took his vows as a Benedictine monk at St. Weburg's, Chester, in 1299. His name appears in several variant spellings: Hydon, Hygden, Hikeden; the first name: Ranulphus, Ralph, and Randle. He is sometimes identified with Randle Higgenet, the alleged author of the Chester plays, but there is no satisfactory supporting evidence for such an assumption.

Higden seems to have traveled a good deal in England before he undertook the composition of his long chronicle, *Polychronicon*, a universal history from the Creation to his own time. Beyond this monumental work, and a number of other manuscripts in Latin, nothing is known of him. *Polychronicon* was apparently written about 1350. Of the one hundred or more manuscript copies extant, some end with the year 1327, while some carry the chronicle as far as 1342. Any continuations beyond that date seem to have been added by other hands.

The work is divided into seven books, of which a good portion of the final book was written contemporaneously with the events described. It is, however, of scant interest as an original authority, but valuable rather as a compendium of the historical, geographic, and scientific knowledge of the age. Higden, like most medieval scholars, drew from many traditional sources, building up a vast structure of fact and legend. As the most exhaustive history of its time, the *Polychronicon* was read and studied for two centuries, becoming itself a source for later chronicles.

The first English version was made in 1387 by John Trevisa at the request of Thomas, Lord Berkeley. Trevisa's translation was printed by Caxton in 1482 with a continuation, which appears to have been written by Caxton himself, carrying the history up to 1460. Another English translation was made in the following century, which is the basis for the Rolls Series edition published in 1865.

WORKS: Polychronicon, 1350? (C. Babington, and J. R. Lumby, eds. 9 vols. Rolls Series, 1865-86).

ABOUT: Babington, C. and Lumby, J. R. Prefaces, *in* Polychronicon (Rolls Series); Gairdner, J. Early Chroniclers of England.

HILL, AARON (February 10, 1685-February 8, 1750), poet, dramatist,

was born at Beaufort Buildings, Strand, the son of George Hill of Malmesbury Abbey, Wiltshire. His father died when he was an infant and the boy was brought up by his mother and Mrs. Gregory, his grandmother. With financial assistance from Mrs. Gregory, he left school when he was about sixteen and sailed to Constantinople to visit a relative, Lord Paget, who was then British ambassador. Paget found a tutor for the boy and sent him to travel throughout the East. As a result he published *A Full Account of the Ottoman Empire* on his return to England in 1709, a work of youthful enthusiasm which he later deprecated. In the same year he published a poem, *Camillus,* dedicated to Lord Peterborough, who was so pleased he offered to take him abroad. Recently married, Hill declined the invitation and settled down to a double career of financial speculation and literature.

Although Hill apparently had the greatest confidence in his own capacities in both these fields, he was successful in neither. Involved in a series of grandiose speculative schemes, all of which called for large amounts of capital, and all of which collapsed, he went heavily into debt. Interested in the theatre, he wrote a bombastic tragedy, *Elfrid, or the Fair Inconstant,* which was produced at the Drury Lane and later published as *Athelwold,* winning him nothing but ridicule. He also translated and produced an opera and several plays, and continued to write poetry. A poem, *The Northern Star,* dedicated to Peter the Great, so complimented the Czar that he ordered a gold medal to be presented to Hill, but the medal was never received.

About 1738 he left London (probably because of pecuniary difficulties) and planted vineyards at his wife's estate in Essex. Twelve years later, Frederick, Prince of Wales, commanded a benefit performance of Hill's translation of Voltaire's *Merope,* but the unfortunate author died the night before the play was performed.

Hill seems to have been a first-rate bore, although he was liked for his kindness and liberality. Pope lists him as one of the "bad authors" in the *Miscellanies,* characterizing him as a "flying fish" who could make only brief flights out of the deep; and again in the *Dunciad* he is referred to in a highly dubious compliment as "not quite a swan, not wholly a goose."

PRINCIPAL WORKS: A Full Account of the Present State of the Ottoman Empire, 1709; The

Works of the Late Aaron Hill, Esq., 1753; The Dramatic Works of Aaron Hill, Esq., 1760.

ABOUT: Brewster, D. Aaron Hill, Poet, Dramatist, Projector; Dobson, A. Rosalba's Journal and Other Papers; Ludwig, H. The Life and Works of Aaron Hill.

HOBBES, THOMAS (April 5, 1588-December 4, 1679), philosopher, was born in Westport, now part of Malmesbury, Wiltshire. His father, a half-educated clergyman, caused such a scandal by a fight at the door of his church that he deserted his wife and three children and was never heard from again. Hobbes himself had been born prematurely because of his mother's fright over the approach of the Armada; as he said, "she brought forth twins, myself and fear," and he was constitutionally timid and apprehensive. His paternal uncle, a glover and alderman, undertook the boy's education, and after schools in Westport and Malmesbury (where he showed a precocious aptitude for the classic languages), sent him in 1603 to Magdalen Hall, Oxford. Hobbes had little use for the scholasticism then pervading Oxford, and he idled away his time there, but did secure his B.A. in 1608.

He then began his lifelong association with the Cavendish family, starting with his appointment as tutor, secretary, and companion to William Cavendish, later the second Earl of Devonshire, who was very little his junior, and became his devoted friend. In 1610 he made the grand tour with his pupil, and learned to speak French and Italian. Most of his time he spent with the young earl (as he became in 1626), either at Hardwick, the Cavendish family seat, or in London, where Hobbes became the associate of such men as Bacon, Jonson, Cowley, Digby, d'Avenant, Waller, and Herbert of Cherbury. For a while he seems to have acted as Bacon's amanuensis.

In 1628 the young earl died, and his son being still too young for tutelage, Hobbes went to the Continent with another pupil, the son of Sir Gervase Clifton. It was at this period that he first began to think along the lines of philosophy and statecraft (a short *Tract on First Principles* was circulated in manuscript among his acquaintances), and that, to his wonder and delight, he discovered geometry. Mathematics thenceforth shared his interest with philosophy, though he never became so expert as he assumed himself to be. His only previous writing had been a translation of Thucydides.

About 1630 Hobbes returned to England and became tutor and mentor of the future third earl, then a child. In 1634 he went with his charge to the Continent again, and it was in this three-year stay that he made the acquaintance of Mersenne, Descartes, Gassendi, and, above all, Galileo, from whom his philosophical theories were directly descended. Anonymous criticisms of Descartes led to the latter's contemptuously refusing to communicate with Hobbes further; it was the first of Hobbes' experiences in controversy.

Hobbes left England again for Paris in 1640; as a protégé of the Cavendishes he was of course a royalist, and his first tentative expressions of opposition to theocratic interference with government, even though they were formally unpublished, made him apprehensive of Puritan wrath. He joined the exiled court, and for a while tutored the future Charles II in mathematics. But once again his timidity drove him away; he had made enemies among both the English court and the French clergy. Caught between two fires, he returned secretly to England in 1651, submitted to the Commonwealth, and received permission to live quietly in London. Soon the earl also submitted, to recover his estates, and Hobbes joined him. With the Restoration, Charles himself was friendly, but Hobbes was unwelcome at court and knew it. In 1667 he received a real fright when a bill was passed by the Commons (though killed by the Lords) against "blasphemous" books, one of which was his own masterpiece, *Leviathan*. It is said that he burned many of his papers, and began to attend church regularly (though he always turned his back on the sermon!); in any event, it is certain that he was refused permission to print thereafter anything bearing on religion or politics.

Leviathan and its predecessors had of course drawn an immense number of articles and books attacking it and its author. So far as possible Hobbes avoided replying, although ten years after the book's publication he was stung into a wrangle with Dr. Bramhall, the Bishop of Londonderry. Where he

J. M. Wright

THOMAS HOBBES

did rush into controversy was unfortunately in the field where he was weakest—mathematics. He had paid his compliments to Oxford in previous books, and Oxford was quick to resent it. Hobbes's belief that he could square the circle, and other mathematical aberrations he professed, gave the opportunity to such men as Robert Boyle and John Wallis. In this long-drawn-out dispute Hobbes was thoroughly worsted.

The remainder of Hobbes' long life was spent with the Cavendish family; it was in Hardwick that he died. His mind remained vigorous to the last; when he was forbidden to write on his philosophical theories, he wrote an autobiography in Latin verse and translated the *Iliad* and *Odyssey*. He was still active at ninety-one, when he suffered a paralytic stroke and died. Sickly in his childhood, he proved unusually tenacious of life. He was tall (over six feet), with brilliant eyes, black hair, and a ginger mustache; he shaved his beard because he said he did not want to "look like an austere philosopher." His life had always been temperate (though he recollected "having been drunk a hundred times in ninety years"), and after the age of seventy he eschewed meat and wine. He still smoked a pipe, however, and he played tennis when he was seventy-five. He was never married, but he acknowledged and supported an illegitimate daughter.

In his own day Hobbes' philosophy, except for the clerical attacks on it, was of far higher reputation abroad than at home. It was revived by James Mill and the Utilitarians. Hobbes is the father, as Weber has said, of "materialism, criticism, and modern positivism; he occupies a position between pure empiricism and Cartesian rationalism." He derives from neither Bacon nor Descartes, but from Galileo. At the bottom of his system is *motion*, and motion activates not only material bodies but also men's minds and the societies men construct. The "motions of the mind" which we call thought have physical causes. His greatest book, the *Leviathan* (society itself is that artificial monster), to which all his previous work led, deals first with man, then with the Commonwealth, then with the Christian Commonwealth, and finally with "the Kingdom of Darkness." Man to Hobbes is no "noble savage," as he was to Rousseau; he is inherently anarchic and truculent, with war and murder his natural expression of being. (Is there an echo here of the timid child born prematurely from his mother's fright?) Government exists, by a social contract, to curb this aggressive creature. Good is what the government says it is; religion is law; man's duty is not to follow his own light, but to obey. This is a complete revolt against the individualistic urge of both the Renaissance and the Reformation, and its closeness to contemporary fascism is apparent; Hobbes was no democrat. Above all, the church has no right to share in the secular state—which, with his materialism, is where Hobbes ran afoul of the religious of all sects. Philosophically, his influence on Spinoza and Leibnitz was enormous, and though much of his system was superseded by that of Locke,[qv] he was undoubtedly the greatest enzyme in the body of English thought until the nineteenth century and Darwin.

England has been fortunate in that so many of her greatest philosophers were also great stylists. Hobbes is one of the greatest. He was not a wide reader, but he read deeply; "if I read as much as the learned do," he said, "I should be as ignorant as they are." He had imaginative power and logical ability in even balance. His style is simple, direct, vigorous, and arresting, unsurpassed in its feeling for structure. His fame rests on the *Elements of Law*, the *Philosophical Rudiments*, and above all on the *Leviathan*. He is one of the giants of philosophy and of the science of government, however antipathetic his conclusions may be to contemporary liberal thought; and irrespective of his views, he is one of the finest prose-writers in the English language.

PRINCIPAL WORKS: Elementorum Philosophiae . . . de Cive, 1647 (as Philosophical Rudiments concerning Government and Society, 1651); Humane Nature (1st part Elements of Law) 1650; Epistolica dissertatio de principiis justi et decori (A dissertation in the form of a letter concerning the principles of the right and proper) 1651; Leviathan Or the Matter, Forme, and Power of A Commonwealth Ecclesiasticall and Civil, 1651; Of Liberty and Necessity (unauthorized) 1654; Elementorum Philosophiae . . . de Corpore Politica (2d part Elements of Law) 1655 (as Philosophical Rudiments concerning the Political Body, 1656); The Questions concerning Liberty, Necessity, and Chance, 1656; Elementorum Philosophia . . . de Homine (Philosophical rudiments concerning man) 1658; Dialogus Physicus, 1661; Seven Philosophical Problems and Propositions of Geometry . . . with an Apology for Himself and His Writings, 1662; Problematica Physica, 1662; Mr. Hobbes considered in his loyalty, religion, reputation, and manners, 1662; De Principiis et Ratiocinatione Geometrarum (The principles and rationale of geometry) 1666; Opera Philosophica (Latin works) 1668; Three Papers presented to the Royal Society against Dr. Wallis, 1671; Decameron Physiologicum; or Ten Dialogues of Natural Philosophy, 1672; Behemoth: The History of the Civil Wars of England, 1679 (complete, 1682); Thomae Hobbes Malmesburiensis Vita (The life of T. H. of Malmesbury) (Latin verse) 1679; An Historical Narration concerning Heresie and the Punishment thereof, 1680; A Dialogue between a Philosopher and a Student of the Common Laws of England, 1681; The Whole Art of Rhetoric, 1681; Historia ecclesiastica (Latin verse) 1688, (Ecclesiastical History, 1722); Moral and Political Works, 1750; Complete Works (W. Molesworth, ed.) 1839-46; The Elements of Law Natural and Politique (F. Tönnies, ed.) 1889.

ABOUT: Aubrey, J. Lives of Eminent Men; Collingwood, R. G. The New Leviathan; Croom Robertson, G. Hobbes; Graham, W. English Political Philosophy from Hobbes to Maine; Hobbes, T. Mr. Hobbes considered, T. H. Malmesburiensis Vita; James, D. G. Life of Reason: Hobbes, Locke, Bolingbroke; Laird, J. Hobbes; Lyon, J. La Philosophie de Hobbes; Mondolfo, R. La Morale de T. Hobbes; Oliver, P. Saints of Chaos; Rickaby, J. Free Will and Four English Philosophers; Stephen, L. Hobbes; Strauss, L. The Political Philosophy of Hobbes; Taylor, A. E. Hobbes; Thorpe, C. D. The Aesthetic Theory of Hobbes; Tönnis, F. Hobbes, Leben und Lehre; Weber, A. History of Philosophy.

HOBY, Sir THOMAS (1530-July 13, 1566), diplomatist, translator, was the son of William Hoby of Leonminster, Herefordshire, and Katherine Forden, his second wife. He was educated at St. John's College, Cambridge, and possibly also at Oxford. For several years he traveled on the Continent, perfecting his accomplishments as a linguist. On his return to England he married Elizabeth, the daughter of Sir Anthony Cooke, and devoted himself to reading and translating the classics.

Hoby's translation of Castiglione's *Il Cortegiano*, published as *The Courtyer* in 1561, was widely popular and brought him an immediate reputation as a translator. He seems to have been a man of universal interests as well as a voracious reader. Roger Ascham admired his scholarship, writing that he was in "many ways well furnished with learning and very expert in knowledge of divers tongues." Lady Hoby was also a linguist, publishing several translations of her own.

Hoby was knighted in 1565 and shortly thereafter went to France as ambassador. On the day he landed at Calais, a French soldier at the town gate shot down the English flag. Hoby demanded redress for the insult and after some delay obtained satisfaction, but this inauspicious beginning seems to have colored the period of his service. He died in Paris when he was only thirty-six years old, survived by Lady Hoby, two sons and two daughters.

His translation of *The Courtyer* had a cosmopolitan vogue on the Continent as well as in England. As a picture of the "perfect man" of the Renaissance, it became the final word on a gentleman's behavior and undoubtedly exercised an indirect effect on higher education in England. It was said that Sir Philip Sidney never ventured abroad without a copy of *The Courtyer* in his pocket. Whatever the truth of this story, it became certainly the source from which Elizabethan gallants drew their principles of courtliness.

PRINCIPAL WORKS: The Courtyer of Count Baldessan Castilio (tr.) 1561 (W. H. D. Rouse, ed. Everyman's Library, 1928); A Booke of the Travaile and Lief of Me, 1564 (E. Powell, ed. Camden Miscellany, 1902).

ABOUT: Cooper, C. H. Athenae Cantabrigienses; Lowndes, W. T. Bibliographical Manual.

HOCCLEVE, THOMAS. See OC-CLEVE, THOMAS

HOLCROFT, THOMAS (December 10, 1745-March 29, 1809), playwright, novelist, miscellaneous writer, was born in London, the son of Thomas Holcroft, a shoemaker who also rented out horses, but who failed at both trades and had to take to the roads as a peddler. His family accompanied him, and Thomas had a wandering childhood. At thirteen he was a stable boy at Newmarket. In the evenings he studied languages and music, and this was all his education. In 1761 the father returned to London and set up again as a cobbler, and his son joined him as helper. He tried all sorts of occupations without success—as teacher in a small school in Liverpool, back in London as a shoemaker, finally as resident tutor in a home from which he was dismissed for "constantly attending a reading room or sporting club," whose great vice was that it gave "dramatic recitations." Meanwhile Holcroft had begun writing, in the form of articles in the *Whitehall Evening Post*.

In 1770 he seized a chance opportunity to become prompter in a Dublin theatre, and for the next eight years he was a strolling actor in the provinces. His first novel, *Alwyn*, was based on this experience. His first play, *The Crisis*, was produced at Drury Lane in 1778. In 1783 he was in Paris as correspondent of the London *Morning Herald*; he attended a performance of Beaumarchais' *Marriage of Figaro*, memorized

J. Opie

THOMAS HOLCROFT

the play completely, and when he returned to England wrote a translation of it, in which he appeared at Covent Garden in 1784. This was his last appearance on the stage.

When the French Revolution began, Holcroft was among its most ardent admirers and supporters. He joined the revolutionary Society for Constitutional Information, and accordingly was one of thirteen indicted for treason in 1794. He was kept in Newgate for two months, when the first defendant, Thomas Hardy, having been acquitted, Holcroft and the others were discharged without trial. In 1799, being very hard up (mostly through losses as a picture dealer), he sold his books and pictures and went to live in Hamburg, where he started a magazine, *The European Repository*, which ran for only two numbers. He then spent two years in Paris, returning to England in 1803. There he started a printing plant with his brother-in-law, which also failed as did all his business ventures. He died in London after a long illness.

Holcroft was married four times and had several children. His daughter Fanny became a novelist. His last wife, Louisa Mercier, later married James Kenney, a playwright.

Holcroft was a very prolific writer, contributing to many magazines besides pouring out a stream of books. He had a great influence on William Godwin and is said to have inspired the writing of *Political Justice*. Paine, Coleridge, Hazlitt, and Lamb were among his friends; stern and irascible though he was, Lamb called him "candid, upright, and single-meaning." His plays are artificial melodramas, full of outright plagiarism; like his novels, they were intended to extend his radical views. The best known of them are *The Road to Ruin* and *The Deserted Daughter*. His novels are hard reading, though they have traces of both humor and sentiment; they are not quite so dull, however, as they seemed to Saintsbury, who called them "dreary declamation and propagandist puppet-mongering" (in the *Cambridge History of English Literature*). His autobiography, much of which was written by Hazlitt from Holcroft's notes, is his most readable book today.

PRINCIPAL WORKS: *Plays*—The Crisis, 1778; Duplicity, 1781; The Noble Peasant (comic opera) 1784; The School for Arrogance, 1791; The Road

to Ruin, 1792; The Deserted Daughter, 1795; The Man of Ten Thousand, 1796; A Tale of Mystery, 1802; The Lady of the Rocks, 1805. *Novels*—Alwyn, or the Gentleman Comedian, 1780; The Family Picture, 1783; Tales of the Castle (tr. from the French of Mme. de Genlis) 1785; Anna St. Ives, 1792; The Adventures of Hugh Trevor, 1794-97; Memoirs of Bryan Perdue, 1805. *Miscellaneous*—Human Happiness (verse) 1783; The Life of Baron Frederic Trenck (tr. from the German) 1792; Travels from Hamburg, through Westphalia, Holland, and the Netherlands to Paris, 1804; Tales in Verse, 1806; Memoirs (continued by W. Hazlitt) 1816 (E. Colby, ed. 1925).

ABOUT: Colby, E. Bibliography of Thomas Holcroft; Hazlitt, W. Memoirs of the late Thomas Holcroft, written by himself, continued . . . by William Hazlitt; Lamb, C. Letters; Mitford, M. R. Recollections of a Literary Life; Paul, C. K. William Godwin, His Friends and Contemporaries.

HOLINSHED or **HOLLINGSHEAD, RAPHAEL** (d. 1580?), chronicler, probably came of a Cheshire family, where the name of Raphael or Ralph was common. He may possibly have entered Christ's College, Cambridge, in 1544, and according to some authorities he was an ordained clergyman. He probably came to London about 1560, but the first thing definitely known about him was that he entered the employ of Reginald or Reyner Wolfe, a publisher, who died in 1573. Holinshed remarked that he was "singularly beholden" to Wolfe. Since 1548 Wolfe had been planning and preparing a chronicle history of Great Britain and Ireland, and this was the task to which he set Holinshed, who became editor-in-chief. His principal assistant was William Harrison,*qv* to whom we owe the vivid description of England in the *Chronicles*. Harrison also translated the *Scotorum Historiae* of Hector Boece for the Scottish section, while the section on Wales was done by Richard Hooker and that on Ireland by Edmund Campion. Since Campion was a Jesuit, and was described by Holinshed as "my first friend and inward companion," it is unlikely that the latter was actually an Anglican clergyman—though the *Chronicles* show a Protestant bias.

On Wolfe's death, the project was taken over by three other publishers jointly, and finally brought out in one volume in 1578 (in two volumes in 1587; revised in 1808). Holinshed did no further literary work, but became steward to Thomas Burdet of Bramcote, Warwickshire, to whom, by his will, he left all his manuscripts and notes.

Holinshed himself wrote (or compiled) the section of the *Chronicles* giving the history of England—from Noah and the Flood to almost his own time. He said: "The histories I have gathered according to my skill, . . . having had more regard to the manner than the apt penning." He showed some evidences of scholarship, often citing his authorities, though he was entirely uncritical when it came to the period before the Norman Conquest. Some of the contemporary allusions caused temporary expurgations, for political reasons, the full work not being republished until the 1808 edition. The style is on the whole clear but pedestrian; Holinshed apologized for its "plainness," but was unable to restrain himself from an occasional Elizabethan flourish of style. The work was highly popular, being ardently patriotic in an era of nascent nationalism.

It is not for itself, however, that the *Chronicles* has claim to fame, but for the writers who plundered it for plots. Spenser said justly that "Master Holinshed hath much furthered and advantaged me," while Shakespeare took from the *Chronicles* the plots of most of his historical plays, besides those of *Macbeth, Lear,* and *Cymbeline.* (It should be noted, however, that the stories of the last two named were also given by Geoffrey of Monmouth *qv* three centuries earlier.)

PRINCIPAL WORK: The Chronicles of England, Scotlande, and Irelande, 1578.

ABOUT: Boswell-Stone, W. G. Shakespeare's Holinshed: the Chronicle and the Historical Plays Compared.

HOLLAND, PHILEMON (1552-February 9, 1637), classical scholar, translator, was born at Chelmsford, Essex. John Holland, his father, was a Protestant clergyman who had fled with Miles Coverdale to the continent during the reign of Queen Mary and who, after the accession of Elizabeth, became rector of Dunmow Magan in Essex. Philemon was educated at Trinity College, Cambridge, where he took a B.A. in 1570 and an M.A. in 1574. He subsequently studied medicine, receiving his M.D. about 1595, probably from a foreign university.

Holland settled in Coventry where he built up a modest medical practice and devoted the greater part of his time to translating the classics. His knowledge of Greek and Latin was accurate and thorough; his English, although sometimes marred by the ornate style characteristic of the Elizabethan period, had individuality and color. His earliest translation, the *Romane Historie* of Livy, was published in 1600, to be followed a year later by Pliny's *Historie of the World*, a gigantic labor which won him the respect of his contemporaries. He also translated Plutarch, Suetonius, and Xenophon, working straight from the original texts without pedantry and without distortion. Perhaps his most interesting work was a translation of William Camden's *Britannia* first printed in 1610, twenty-four years after its original publication in Latin. Since Camden was a friend and fellow scholar, Holland was able to work closely with the author on his text.

In 1608 Holland was appointed an usher in the Coventry free school, where George, Lord Berkeley, was a pupil, and some twenty years later he became the headmaster. Although his works were surprisingly popular, Holland was never a wealthy man and during his latter years he suffered poverty. The council of the corporation of Coventry bought several of his translations and in 1632 the city voted him a small pension. Two years before his death the president of Magdalene College, Cambridge, authorized a charitable allowance to Holland and his family. He died at the age of eighty-five after a long period of illness.

PRINCIPAL WORKS: The Romane Historie Written by Titus Livius of Padua (tr.) 1600; The Historie of the World, Commonly Called the Natural Historie of C. Plinius Secundus (tr.) 1601; The Philosophie, Commonly Called the Morals of Plutarch (tr.) 1603 (E. H. Blakeney, ed. Everyman's Library, 1911); The Historie of Twelve Caesars, by Suetonius (tr.) 1606 (J. H. Freese, ed. 1923); Britannia, by William Camden (tr.) 1610; Cyrupaedia, The Institution and Life of Cyrus, by Xenophon (tr.) 1632.

ABOUT: Colville, F. L. Warwickshire Worthies; Fuller, T. The Worthies of England; Wood, A. à, Fasti Oxonienses.

HOLLAND, Sir RICHARD (fl. 1450), Scottish poet, lived during the reign of James II and became a partisan of the Douglas clan in their struggle against that monarch. Nothing is known of his life and only one of his poems has survived, *The Buke of the Howlat.*

Holland tells us at the beginning of the poem that it was written for "Ane Dow [Dove] of Dunbar, dowit with ane Douglas." This must have been Elizabeth Dunbar, daughter of the Earl of Moray, who married Archibald, the seventh Earl of Douglas. Since she was married about 1442 and the Douglas family met its final disaster in 1452, the poem must have been composed between these dates. Apparently when James, Earl of Douglas, and his followers fled to England in 1455, Holland accompanied them. An act of the Scottish parliament offering pardon to those who would return to their allegiance specifically mentions "Schir Richard Holland," excepting him from pardon. He is believed by some authorities to have acted as chaplain to the Earl of Moray, killed in battle with James II.

The Buke of Howlat has been preserved in two manuscripts, the Asloan dating from about 1515, and the Bannatyne, 1568. The poem itself is judged to be fifty to seventy years older than the earliest manuscript. Written in a long alliterative line, it tells a familiar allegory of the owl in borrowed plumes, on the surface a satire of pride, underlaid by personal and possibly political allusions. Like most of the early Scottish alliterative poems, it is extremely tedious to the modern ear, but it contains a good deal of interesting antiquarian material in its references to heraldic blazons, musical instruments of the time, as well as several of the highland bards. Holland was highly esteemed by later Scottish poets. Blind Harry, William Dunbar, and Sir David Lyndsay all refer to him.

Holland's poem was edited from the Bannatyne manuscript by David Laing in 1823, and both Laing and Irving in his *History of Scottish Poetry* have offered lengthy explanations as to the meaning of its allegory.

PRINCIPAL WORKS: The Buke of the Howlat (Asloan MS.) 1515, (Bannatyne MS.) 1568 (D. Laing, ed. 1823; F. J. Amours, ed. *in* Scottish Alliterative Poems, 1891-92).

ABOUT: Irving, D. History of Scottish Poetry; Laing, D. Preface to The Buke of the Howlat.

HOLLINGSHEAD, RAPHAEL. See HOLINSHED, RAPHAEL

HOME, HENRY, Lord KAMES (1696-December 27, 1782), Scottish judge, critic, and miscellaneous writer, was born at Kames, Berwickshire. His mother was a granddaughter of Robert Baillie, principal of the University of Glasgow, and his father, George Home, was a prosperous country gentleman. Henry was educated at home by a private tutor who apparently taught him very little. When, later, he determined to become an advocate after a meeting with Sir Hew Dalrymple, president of the Court of Session in Edinburgh, he had to study hard to fill the gaps in his early training. Called to the bar in 1724, he practiced law without much success until the publication of *Remarkable Decisions of the Court of Session* in 1728 brought him favorable notice.

Home rose from lawyer to judge, in 1752 receiving an appointment as ordinary lord of session with the title Lord Kames. For the next thirty years he sat on the bench, for nearly twenty of them holding the position of lord of the judiciary court. Although his language on the bench was frequently considered unseemly, he won the respect of both colleagues and criminals for his honesty, his impartiality, and his good humor. When the session closed for Christmas vacation in 1782, Kames said a cheerful good-by to his fellows, "Fare ye a' weel, ye bitches!" and went home where he died two days later at the age of eighty-six.

Kames was a prolific writer, digging into the fields of law, psychology, metaphysics, agriculture, and literary criticism with equal assurance. Although his style was crabbed and monotonous, and his scholarship frequently inaccurate, he enjoyed a considerable literary reputation in Scotland. Boswell, who admired Kames and at one time planned to write his biography, records a conversation with Johnson in which, boasting of Scottish literary accomplishment, he said, "But, sir, we have Lord Kames," to which Johnson retorted, "You *have* Lord Kames. Keep him!"

The publication of his *Essays on the Principles of Morality and Natural Religions* led to suspicions of Kames' orthodoxy, although it had been intended as a refutation of Hume's most unorthodox doctrines. A charge of heresy was brought against him before the presbytery of Edinburgh, but was later dismissed. Kames was married to Agatha Drummond, by whom he had one son.

PRINCIPAL WORKS: Remarkable Decisions of the Court of Sessions From 1716 to 1728, 1728; Essays Upon Several Subjects Concerning British

Antiquities, 1747; Essays on the Principles of Morality and Natural Religion, 1751; Introduction to the Art of Thinking, 1761; Elements of Criticism, 1762; Sketches of the History of Man, 1774; The Gentleman Farmer, 1776; Loose Hints Upon Education, 1781.

ABOUT: Chambers, R. Biographical Dictionary of Eminent Scotsmen; Tytler, A. F. (Lord Woodhouslee) Life of Lord Kames.

HOME, JOHN (September 21, 1722-September 5, 1808), Scottish minister, dramatist, was born in Leith, the port of Edinburgh, where his father was town clerk. Preparing for the ministry, he attended the University of Edinburgh where he made friends with William Robertson and Adam Ferguson, both of whom were to become well known as ministers and historians.

Home was licensed a probationer of the kirk by the presbytery of Edinburgh in 1745, the year of the second Jacobite rebellion. He immediately enlisted in a college company of volunteers for the defense of Edinburgh and later, as a lieutenant in a company of Glasgow volunteers, was taken prisoner and incarcerated in Donne Castle.

Leaving military exploits behind, Home was inducted into the ministry at Athelstaneford, East Lothian, when he was twenty-five, and allied himself with the broad church party. Interested in literature, he began to write verse tragedies which led him shortly into difficulties with the presbytery. His first play, *Agis*, founded on Plutarch, was rejected by Garrick in London. The same thing happened with his second play, *Douglas*, based on old Scottish ballads, but with the help of friends *Douglas* was produced in Edinburgh in 1756, where it had a long and successful run. The ruling party in the kirk was so incensed by the spectacle of a Presbyterian minister in the role of successful dramatist that proceedings were initiated against Home and a bitter war of pamphlets ensued. A year later *Douglas* was performed at Covent Garden with spectacular success and Home resigned from the ministry.

Home became private secretary to the Earl of Bute, then Prime Minister, and tutor to the Prince of Wales. In this powerful position he was able to demand London production for all his plays—the formerly rejected *Agis*, *The Siege of Aquileia* and *The Fatal Discovery*, none of which was as well received as *Douglas*. *Alonzo*, produced by Garrick in 1773, was more successful.

One of Home's most intimate friends was David Hume, the Scottish philosopher. A few months before Hume's death in 1776, Home accompanied him to Bath where he kept a diary recording all of the philosopher's conversation. Hume was an admirer, as well as a keen critic, of his friend's plays, considering him at least potentially as a Scottish Shakespeare. Even the best of the tragedies, however, the picturesque and profoundly Scottish *Douglas*, was harshly criticized by Samuel Johnson, who said there were not "ten good lines in the whole play."

PRINCIPAL WORKS: Douglas, 1756 (H. J. Tunney, ed. in Acting Drama 1924); Agis, 1758; The Siege of Aquileia, 1760; The Fatal Discovery, 1769; Alonzo, 1773; Alfred, 1778; The History of the Rebellion in 1745, 1802; Collected Works (H. Mackenzie, ed.) 1822.

ABOUT: Chambers, R. Biographical Dictionary of Eminent Scotsmen; Gipson, A. E. John Home: A Study of His Life and Works; Mackenzie, H. Life, in Collected Works.

HOOKER, RICHARD (1554?-November 2, 1600), theologian, was born near Exeter, Devonshire, the son of Roger Vowell or Hooker (the family had used the two names interchangeably for some time), a man of good family fallen on evil days. Through family connections the boy was enabled to attend the Exeter grammar school and then to enter Corpus Christi College, Oxford. His patron was the Bishop of Salisbury, and after his death the Bishop of London, whose son Hooker tutored. He received his B.A. in 1573 and M.A. in 1577, when he also became a fellow. Two years later he was appointed reader in Hebrew, and soon after, he took orders. In 1581, when he was preaching at St. Paul's Cross, London, he married his landlady's daughter, Joan Chambers, and had to resign his fellowship. According to contemporary accounts, Mrs. Hooker was an ill-favored shrew and the marriage was disastrous; however, her husband made her his sole executrix and was on the best of terms with his father-in-law, so much of this may be discounted as malicious gossip. In any case Hooker was the mildest and meekest of men, the typical "absent-minded professor," and so lost in his studies that doubtless he never noticed any domestic friction. They had four daughters.

In 1584 Hooker became vicar of Drayton-Beauchamp, Buckinghamshire, and the

RICHARD HOOKER

next year master of the Temple, in London. There he was drawn into a long controversy with Walter Travers, one of the readers, who was inclined to Presbyterianism; but on both sides it was marked by dignity and personal courtesy. However, it exhausted Hooker, who also had begun contemplation of his great book, and at his own request in 1591 he was allowed by Archbishop Whitgift to resign and to take a country rectorship—that of Boscombe, near Salisbury. In 1595 he exchanged this for Bishopsbourne, near Canterbury, where he lived for the remainder of his life. His health began to fail, and a cold caught on a journey proved fatal. Sir William Cowper, grandfather of the poet, erected a monument to him and wrote an epitaph in which he called him "the judicious Hooker."

Hooker is the greatest apologist of the Anglican church. Lancelot Andrewes [qv] said truly on his death that "behind him he hath not left anie neere him." He laid down, in his *Ecclesiastical Polity*, the line thenceforth taken by the church, steering it between the twin extremes of Puritanism and Roman Catholicism. In an age of scurrility he has been called "a Knight of Romance among caitiff brawlers." His tolerance, his broadmindedness, his moderation, and his calmness in controversy would have made him notable even if he had not also had great literary gifts. But Hooker was both a scholar

and an artist; though he was far from a popular preacher, in written form he was eloquent and often majestic in style, and capable of quiet satire. The impress of a fine and profound mind is on all his work.

Of the eight books of the *Ecclesiastical Polity*, five were published in Hooker's lifetime. The seventh and eighth are obviously made up of his own notes, though unskillfully arranged. The sixth is suspect; it does not even deal with the same subject outlined for that book in Hooker's long introduction, and was probably foisted on him by another (anonymous) writer.

The man himself, small, weak-sighted, was marked by what Fuller called "dovelike simplicity." He had no guile and suspected no one else of it. He was purely a man of study, painfully shy outside of it, modest and patient, but instinct with the quiet dignity of the dedicated scholar.

PRINCIPAL WORKS: Of the Laws of Ecclesiastical Polity (8 books) 1594-1662; A Learned Discourse of Justification, etc., 1612; A Learned Sermon of the Nature of Pride, 1612; The Answere to a Supplication preferred by Mr. Travers, etc., 1612; A Remedy against Sorrow and Fear, 1612; A Learned and Comfortable Sermon of the Certaintie and Perpetuitie of Faith in the Elect, 1612.

ABOUT: Fuller, T. Church History; Hallam, H. Introduction to the Literature of Europe; Hook, W. F. Ecclesistical Biography; Hunt, J. Religious Thought in England from the Reformation; Hurst, J. F. Literature of Theology; Landor, W. S. Imaginary Conversations; Maurice, J. F. D. Modern Philosophy; Passerine d'Entreves, A. The Mediaeval Contribution to Political Thought; Sisson, C. J. The Judicious Marriage of Mr. Hooker and the Birth of the Laws of Ecclesiastical Polity; Stanley, V. Richard Hooker; Stephen, J. F. Horae Sabbaticae; Thornton, L. S. Richard Hooker, A Study of His Theology; Walton, I. Life of Mr. Richard Hooker; Wood, A. à, Athenae Oxonienses; Wordsworth, C. Ecclesiastical Biography.

HOPKINS, MATTHEW (d. 1647), author of *The Discovery of Witches*, was the son of James Hopkins, a minister at Wenham, Suffolk. Little is known of him before 1644 when he began his spectacular career as a "witchfinder," but he apparently lived at Manningtree, Essex, where he may have practiced law.

The hunting down and hanging of witches was a cruel and curious manifestation of the religious hysteria bred in England's civil war; and Hopkins, the "Witch Finder Generall," emerges from the records as a monster of impudent sadism. According to his own account, Hopkins' experience with witches began in March 1644, when he discovered that seven or eight witches living near him at Mannington were holding meetings to offer sacrifices to the devil. Shortly thereafter he set himself up as England's official witch-seeker and traveled by horseback from town to town with two assistants, a man and a woman. He charged twenty shillings in expense money to each town visited, rounding up those suspected of witchcraft and, with the full cooperation of the local authorities, harrying them into confessions which condemned them to the scaffold.

Hopkins' technique was unbelievably brutal. If the accused refused to confess, he or she was "searched" for the supposed mark of a witch, a third teat on some part of the body. He was then placed bound and cross-legged on a table in a closed room, with a hole in the door by which the "imps" could enter, for twenty-four to forty-eight hours without food or sleep. Or he was thrown into a pool with thumbs and toes tied together. Presumably the possession of a "witch's teat" would prevent sinking, so if the unfortunate victim managed to swim and stay afloat, he was sentenced to hang. Not surprisingly these methods led frequently to confession and execution. In 1645 a special commission was appointed to try witches at Bury St. Edmunds and according to Hopkins' testimony, at least sixty witches from Essex alone were hanged in one year.

Hopkins' witch-hunting activities were exposed by a courageous vicar, John Gaule, a Puritan and a Cromwellian, who believed in witchcraft but not in Hopkins. Gaule published a book of sermons on the subject in 1646 which led to queries presented to the judges at Norfolk suggesting that Hopkins himself might be a witch. In his own defense, Hopkins wrote and published *The Discovery of Witches*, explaining the symptoms of witchery and detailing his accomplishments. By the most dramatic of ironies, the witch-hunter was taken into custody shortly thereafter and tried by his own methods. Thrown into a pool, he "swam" and was hanged as a witch in August 1647.

PRINCIPAL WORKS: The Discovery of Witches: in Answer to Severall Queries Lately Delivered to the Judges of Assize for the County of Norfolk, and Now Published by Matthew Hopkins, Witchfinder, 1647 (M. Summers, ed. 1928).

ABOUT: Gaule, J. Select Cases of Conscience Touching Witches and Witchcrafts; Granger, J. Biographical History of England; Hutchinson, F. Historical Essay Concerning Witchcraft.

HORMAN, WILLIAM (d. April 12, 1535), vice provost of Eton, author of a volume of Latin aphorisms, was born at Salisbury and went to school at Winchester. According to some authorities, he attended King's College, Cambridge, but Anthony à Wood says he was a fellow of New College, Oxford, from 1477 to 1485, when he became a master at Eton.

In 1494 Horman was appointed to the rectory of East Wrotham, Norfolk, where he remained for nine years. He was elected a fellow of Eton in 1502 and later served as vice provost. An excellent scholar and critic, Horman wrote voluminously in the time he could borrow from academic and clerical duties. Only two of his writings are known to have been printed, *Vulgaria* and *Antibossicon*, but he apparently wrote some thirty other works, many of them compendia for school use. The *Vulgaria*, a valuable collection of aphorisms in Latin and English, was first printed by Pynson in 1519, and again by De Worde in 1540. *Antibossicon*, which may have been written partly by Robert Aldrich, was an attack in the form of a dialogue on the grammatical works of Robert Whitynton, who had abused Horman's friend, William Lily, in a series of verses under the pseudonym, "Bossus." Unfortunately the major part of the work written by this scholarly divine has not survived.

Horman died at Eton on April 12, 1535 and was buried in the college chapel. A memorial bearing his effigy and an epitaph suggests that he lived to be nearly one hundred years old.

PRINCIPAL WORKS: Vulgaria, 1519 (M. R. James, ed. 1926).

ABOUT: Gillow, J. Dictionary of English Catholics; Wood, A. à, The History and Antiquities of Oxford.

HOWARD, FREDERICK. See CARLISLE, FREDERICK HOWARD, Fifth Earl of

HOWARD, HENRY. See SURREY, Earl of

HOWARD, Sir ROBERT (1626-September 3, 1698), dramatist, was the son of Thomas Howard, first Earl of Berkshire, and Elizabeth, daughter of William Cecil, Lord Burghley. According to Wood, he was educated at Magdalen College, Oxford, but there is some confusion on this point and he may instead have been a student of Magdalene College, Cambridge.

During the civil war he fought with the Royalists and was knighted in 1644 for bravery in the field. After the establishment of the Commonwealth he was imprisoned at Windsor Castle for a time, but the Restoration brought him again into favor. Under Charles II he was elected to Parliament and held a number of important government posts, among them the extremely lucrative one of auditor of the exchequer. In the good graces of the Stuart court he lived with considerable style at his Surrey estate, dabbling in art and literature, and enjoying a variety of feminine companionship. Sir Robert was four times married—his fourth wife, Annabella Dives, a maid of honor to the queen.

Dryden became Howard's brother-in-law, marrying Lady Elizabeth Howard, and the two established a polite if not cordial relationship. Howard had published a collection of *Poems* in 1660, which Scott later called "productions of a most freezing mediocrity," and in 1665 he brought out a volume of four plays, *The Surprisal, The Committee, The Indian Queen,* and *The Vestal Virgin. The Indian Queen,* a tragedy in heroic verse, had been considerably revised by Dryden but Howard offered no acknowledgment. His preface to the *Foure New Plays* provoked an ironic response from Dryden in an *Essay of Dramatic Poesy* and initiated a well-mannered literary controversy between the two on the merits of blank verse as against rhymed verse in tragic drama.

The best of Howard's plays was a comedy, *The Committee,* which satirized the doings of the Puritan party. An indifferent piece of dramaturgy, it borrowed interest from the character of an Irish butler well liked by actors and long played on the London stage. While Howard enjoyed a certain amount of success, he was not respected by his contemporaries. Shadwell ridiculed him as Sir Positive At-All in a play, *The Sullen Lovers,* and John Evelyn echoed the opinion of Dryden and others in regard to Howard as "pretending to all manner of arts and sciences—not ill-natured, but insufferably boasting."

PRINCIPAL WORKS: *Plays*—Foure New Plays: The Surprisal, The Committee, The Indian Queen, The Vestal Virgin, 1665; The Great Favourite, Or, The Duke of Lerma, 1668. *Other Writings*—Poems, 1660; The Duell of the Stags, A Poem, 1668; An Account of the State of His Majesties Revenue, 1681; The Life and Reign of King Richard the Second, 1681; Historical Observations Upon the Reigns of Edward I, II, III, and Richard II, 1689.

ABOUT: Arundell, D. D. Dryden and Howard; Genest, J. Account of the English Stage; Spingarn, J. E. (ed.) Critical Essays of the Seventeenth Century.

HOWELL, JAMES (1594?-November 1666), author of historical and political pamphlets, letters, and essays, was a Welshman, born probably at Abernant, Carmarthenshire, where his father, Thomas Howell, was rector. He received a B.A. degree from Jesus College, Oxford, in 1613 and ten years later was elected a fellow.

Howell's first position was that of manager for a glassware factory in London. Traveling on the continent in search of materials and workmen, he perfected his linguistic accomplishments and turned to secretarial and diplomatic employment. In 1626 he became secretary to Lord Scrope, residing in York, from which district he was elected to Parliament a year later. On a political mission for Strafford, lord-deputy of Ireland, he remained in London where he made the acquaintance of some of the chief literary men of the time, among them Ben Jonson. A year later he published his "maiden fancy," a political allegory in prose entitled *Dodona's Grove.*

During the civil war he was arrested by order of the Long Parliament and imprisoned in the Fleet (whether for political activity or for debt is not clear). Remaining in prison for eight years and deprived of all other means of livelihood, he devoted himself to writing historical and political tracts, poems, and letters. Howell was one of the first Englishmen to make his living by his pen, and although he had little imagination, his command of language and his lively observation gave interest to everything he wrote.

Released from the Fleet in 1651, Howell sought the favor of Cromwell with a pamphlet on the Long Parliament. Nine years later at the time of the Restoration, his writings took on an appropriately Royalist tone and Charles II created for him the post of Historiographer Royal of England at £100 a year.

The work by which Howell is remembered, *Epistolae Ho-Elianae*, written while he was in prison, is a series of easy and entertaining essays in letter form containing philosophic reflections, political, social, and domestic anecdotes. Thackeray, who rated the *Epistolae* among his favorite bedside books, compared Howell to Montaigne, and wrote that he never tired of "the artless prattle of the priggish little clerk of King Charles' council."

PRINCIPAL WORKS: Dodona's Grove, or, The Vocall Forrest, 1640; Instructions for Forreine Travell, 1642 (E. Arber, ed. 1869); England's Teares for the Present Wars, 1644; Epistolae Ho-Elianae, Familiar Letters Domestic and Forren, 1645-55 (A. Repplier, ed. 1907); Londinopolos: An Historicall Discourse or Perlustration Of the City of London and Westminster, 1657; A Perfect Description of the Country of Scotland, 1659; A Brief Character of the Low Countries, 1660; Poems on Several Choice and Various Subjects (P. Fisher, ed.) 1663.

ABOUT: Repplier, A. Introduction to Epistolae Ho-Elianae; Vann, W. H. Notes on the Writings of James Howell; Wood, A. à, Athenae Oxonienses.

HOYLE, EDMOND (1672-August 29, 1769), author of a *Short Treatise on the Game of Whist*, has been described as a native Yorkshireman, but it seems probable that in this case his identity was confused with that of another Edmond Hoyle. He was presumably a lawyer, although nothing is actually known of his life until 1741, when he was living in Queen Square, London, giving lessons in whist.

Hoyle began to circulate among his pupils a handbook on the principles of whist which proved so helpful that he was encouraged to publish it. The first edition of the famous *Short Treatise on the Game of Whist* appeared in 1742, to be followed by fourteen successive editions during Hoyle's lifetime, with innumerable revisions and reprintings after his death. Hoyle was the first to write scientifically on a card game and his work was so popular in its time that his name has come to be used as the authority for any rulebook on games.

In the early editions of the *Treatise* Hoyle offered to disclose the secret of his "artificial memory which does not take off your Attention from your Game" for one guinea. How many buyers he had for this secret has not been recorded, but the sale of the book was enormous. A contemporary skit titled *The Humours of Whist* satirized Hoyle and his pupils, portraying the dismay of card sharpers whose secrets were thus exposed.

Hoyle followed his first success with similar manuals on backgammon, piquet, quadrille, brag, and chess; and continued to revise the original work on whist until he died at the age of ninety-seven. Hoyle was inclined to be careless as an editor, but he wrote in vigorous, original style, and his calculations on the laws of chance are still basic for a number of card games. There are many literary references to Hoyle, both contemporary and in later centuries—in Fielding's *Tom Jones*, in Alexander Thomson's poem on whist, in Byron's *Don Juan*—and in the still current expression "according to Hoyle."

PRINCIPAL WORKS: Short Treatise on the Game of Whist, 1742.

ABOUT: Jones, H. Article on Whist, Encyclopaedia Britannica.

HUCHOUN (fl. 14th century), Scottish author of romances in verse known as Huchoun of the Awle Ryale, is an almost legendary figure of early British literature to whom are attributed a number of manuscript works. Scholars have indulged in considerable controversy as to the life and works of Huchoun but completely satisfactory conclusions have not yet been reached.

Huchoun is first mentioned in Wyntoun's *Orygynale Cronykil* written about 1420. In describing the conquests of King Arthur, Wyntoun writes that "Huchoun of the Awle Realle In til his Gest Historyalle" has treated the same subject. From further evidence in Wyntoun, this *Gest Historyalle* must have been an alliterative poem and all the authorities are now agreed that it is the poem called *Morte Arthure* in the Thornton MS. of Lincoln Cathedral—a kind of historical novel in alliterative verse written about 1365.

Two other works are mentioned by Wyntoun: the *Epistill of Suete Susane* and the *Adventures of Gawain*. It seems fairly certain that the first of these may be identified with *The Pistill of Susane*, a fourteenth century version of the story of Susannah in the Apocrypha, which has been preserved in five

MSS. under variant spellings. The *Adventures of Gawain* is believed to be either *The Awntyres off Arthure at the Terne Wathelyne* or *Golagros and Gawane*.

One of the curious things about the works attributed to Huchoun is a dialect coloring which makes it uncertain whether the poet was actually Scottish or English. George Neilson, the chief authority on Huchoun, attaches to his name a whole cycle of additional poems usually regarded as of early English origin. John Pinkerton in the eighteenth century suggested that Huchoun be identified with the "gude Sir Hew of Englintoun" who is listed with other poets in Dunbar's *Lament for the Makaris*, and who was a statesman or knight in the reigns of David II and Robert II. Since the name Huchoun was a familiar Scotch diminutive meaning "little Hugh" this identification seems plausible.

Whatever the truth of these scholarly speculations, we have Wyntoun's first-hand judgment on his work. Apologizing for differing from Huchoun in certain details of the life of King Arthur, he goes on to say:

> And men of gud discretioun
> Suld excuss and loif Huchoun
> That cunnand was in litterature
> . . . He was curyouss in his stile
> Faire and facund and subtile. . .

PRINCIPAL WORKS: Golagros and Gawane (J. Pinkerton, ed. *in* Scotish Poems) 1792; The Pistill of Susan (5 MSS.) (D. Laing, ed.) 1822; The Awntyrs off Arthure at the Terne Wathelyne (3 MSS.) (D. Laing, ed.) 1822; Morte Arthure (Thornton MS.) (J. O. Halliwell, ed.) 1847; (M. M. Banks, ed.) 1900.

ABOUT: Neilson, G. Huchoun of the Awle Ryale; Weston, J. L. Romance, Vision and Satire.

HUDSON, THOMAS (fl. 1610), poet, was presumably born in Scotland or in the northern part of England. Very little is known of his life and his name is remembered for only one work, a poem translated from the French of the Huguenot poet, Du Bartas, whose writings were greatly admired in the Elizabethan period.

Thomas Hudson's name first appears with three other "Hudsones" (probably his brothers) on a list of those in the service of James VI of Scotland for the year 1567. All four names appear again in *The Estait of the King's Hous* with details as to their liveries and the salaries paid them. It is also on record that Hudson was installed as master of the Chapel Royal on June 5, 1586, and his appointment ratified by two separate acts of Parliament.

Hudson's translation from Du Bartas was probably suggested by the king to whom it is dedicated, and James VI himself contributed a commendatory sonnet. Titled *The Historie of Judith in Forme of a Poeme: Penned in French by the Noble Poet, G. Salust, Lord of Bartas: Englished by Tho. Hudson*, the work was first published in 1584. It was reissued in 1608 with Joshua Sylvester's more extensive translation of Du Bartas.

Hudson was also a contributor to *England's Parnassus* which appeared in 1600 and was probably the T. H. who contributed a sonnet to James VI's *Essays of a Prentise*. That he was not immune from contemporary criticism seems to be indicated in a line from a satirical piece played at Cambridge in 1606, *The Return from Parnassus*. Hudson and another writer, Henry Lock, are advised to let their "books lie in some old nooks amongst old boots and shoes." Sir John Harington, however, in his notes on *Orlando Furioso*, describes the *Historie of Judith* as written in "verie good and sweet English verse."

PRINCIPAL WORKS: The Historie of Judith (tr.) 1584.

ABOUT: Irving, D. Lives of Scotish Poets and History of Scotish Poetry; Ritson, J. Bibliographia Poetica.

HUME, DAVID (April 26, 1711-August 25, 1776), philosopher, political economist, historian, was born in Edinburgh, the younger son of Joseph Hume, a country gentleman of small estate, who died in David's infancy, and of Catherine Falconer. He was educated at home until he entered the University of Edinburgh at twelve, to study law. According to his own statement, university training in Scotland at that time usually ended at the age of fourteen or fifteen, and Hume does not seem to have stayed even so long. He continued intensive study, however, to such a degree that he suffered a nervous breakdown about 1729, which he proposed to cure by the odd method of going into business. A few months in 1732 in a merchant's office in Bristol showed him how inefficacious that would be, and in 1734 he took what little money he had inherited and went to France, where he settled at La Flèche, in Anjou, and for three years devoted himself entirely to reading and writing.

It was there, indeed, that he wrote his first and most important book, *A Treatise of Human Nature,* from which all his philosophy was developed, and he returned to England to have it published. It fell absolutely flat—indeed, it was not until his *Essays Moral and Political* appeared that Hume won any wide recognition—and there was nothing for him to do but to join his elder brother on the family property, Ninewells, in Berwickshire. He made constant efforts to find some extra-literary means of livelihood; he tried in vain to secure the professorship of "ethics and pneumatic philosophy" at Edinburgh and of logic at Glasgow, and in 1745 he actually went as tutor to the Marquis of Annandale, a literary-minded eccentric who was afterward declared insane. After a year Hume escaped from this impossible position—made even more difficult by the insolence of the Marchioness' cousin, who acted as manager of the estate—and he had to sue in court to get his back pay. Next he accompanied General St. Clair as his secretary on his expedition to France in 1746, and his mission to Vienna and Turin in 1748. From 1751 to 1763, his brother having married, he lived with his sister in Edinburgh, while history and political economy gradually superseded philosophy in his writing. During this period his income was a little augmented by appointment as keeper of the Library of Advocates, in spite of loud opposition because of his unorthodoxy in religion.

In 1763 he became secretary of the British embassy in Paris, under the Earl of Hertford, and remained there for more than two years. This was the time when Hume blossomed out, and became "le bon David," the darling of the French salons, the friend of D'Alembert and Turgot—much to the astonishment of the British, who had noticed him only to try (vainly) to draw him into controversy. He returned at the beginning of 1766 with Rousseau and his Thérèse, whom he had befriended. Back in England he exerted himself to find a refuge and help for the French philosopher, but he was no match for Rousseau's paranoid suspicions. Rousseau soon turned against him, and pub-

After A. Ramsay

DAVID HUME

licly accused him of every variety of enmity and persecution, stinging even the pacific and bewildered Hume into reply.

In the midst of this long-drawn-out quarrel Hume became under-secretary of the Foreign Office in London, and remained in that post until 1769. By that date, he had been making a fairly good living from his writing for at least ten years, in spite of the many attacks upon him, and he decided to settle permanently in Edinburgh. Again with his sister, he built a house (on what has since been named for him St. David's Street —a strange compliment to a heretic!), and looked forward to many useful years. But he was soon attacked by what seems to have been cancer of the liver, and after a long illness he died, about six weeks after the American colonies, whose cause he had befriended, declared their independence.

Hume is generally conceded to be the greatest English philosopher—though in later years he grew so ardently Scottish and anti-English that he would not have relished the appellation. Locke anticipated his theory in part, but Hume covered a much wider field. Though he himself later disclaimed his great *Treatise on Human Nature* (not cowardice but an itch for fame was the cause of the disclaimer) and suppressed some of his more outspoken essays, he could not repudiate his own words in his autobiography, that from youth he possessed "a certain boldness of temper which was not inclined to submit to any authority [in philosophy], but led me to seek out some new medium by which truth might be established."

W. R. Sorley has called Hume "Hobbes inverted." Just as Hobbes derived all thought and the structure of society itself from physical nature, so Hume derived them from the human senses, from what he called ideas and impressions. He did not, however, follow Berkeley in contending that physical objects would not exist without a mind to realize them. His skepticism was not absolute, in other words, but he was the father of criticism and positivism. He did not deny the existence of metaphysics, but to him psychology was philosophy. His philosophy influenced Comte just as his economics influenced Turgot. Alfred Weber called him "the spiritual father of Kant" as well. His whole system was in the *Treatise of Human Nature*, and after this book he merely expanded or particularized; he did not develop it further.

In economics, Hume in some respects anticipated Ricardo and his own friend Adam Smith. His economic views were closely woven into his historical work, his two main preoccupations after 1751. His *History of Great Britain,* long a standard textbook, is marred in its later volumes by his obsession against the Whigs and what became almost a persecution mania about the English attitude toward Scotland. Nevertheless, it is the first history to present social and literary events as at least as important as political and military.

Hume was no proselytizer or missionary; he made no attempt to "carry the Gospel to the heathen" and gathered no disciples. His philosophy—which implied at the most a vague deism in religion, and in fact was much nearer what (thanks to T. H. Huxley) we call today agnosticism—satisfied him as an explanation of phenomena and provided him with strength by which to live and die. Even his clerical enemies could not fail to note his entire calm in the face of inevitable death. As Adam Smith said of him, "he approached . . . the character of a perfectly wise and virtuous man."

But he himself remarked that literature, not philosophy, had from the beginning been "the ruling passion of my life, and the great source of my enjoyment." His chief fault, outside of a rather excessive dislike of controversy or disturbance, was a frank longing for celebrity, and chiefly not as a philosopher but as a writer. His style was indeed admirable, in the rather heavy, dignified way of the Augustan era, with its rolling Latin periods in the mode of Gibbon—though Smollett went rather too far in calling him "one of the best men, and undoubtedly the best writer, of the age."

However, Smollett may be excused, for he was one of several young writers whom Hume befriended generously. Indeed, he was the most amiable and friendly of men. His geese were all swans, his friends could do no wrong, and even in the writings of his enemies he could find something to praise. Despite his own rather childlike longing for fame, he had not a tinge of envy in his huge body. Physically, he was far from attractive —fat, clumsy and never overcame his broad Scottish accent, but (as he had proved in Paris) he knew how to handle social acclaim, and was as much at his ease in a drawing room as in his beloved club of cronies in Edinburgh. The best minds of his day honored him, and he was the very antithesis of the recluse philosopher, even though he never married or founded a family, but died a bachelor living with his spinster sister.

PRINCIPAL WORKS: A Treatise of Human Nature, Being an Attempt to Introduce the Experiment Method of Reasoning into Moral Subjects, 1739-40 (J. M. Keynes and P. Straffa, eds. 1938); Essays Moral and Political, 1741-42; Philosophical Essays Concerning Human Understanding, 1748; An Enquiry Concerning the Principles of Morals, 1751; Political Discourses, 1752; Essays and Treatises on Several Subjects, 1753-54; The History of Great Britain, 1754-78; Four Dissertations: 1. The Natural History of Religion, 2. Of the Passions, 3. Of Tragedy, 4. Of the Standard of Taste, 1757; The Life of David Hume, Esq., Written by Himself (A. Smith, ed.) 1777; Two Essays (Suicide & Immortality) (D. Hume [nephew], ed.) 1777; Dialogues concerning Natural Religion, 1779.

ABOUT: Black, J. B. The Art of History; Burton, J. H. Life and Correspondence of David Hume; Calderwood, H. David Hume; Church, R. W. Hume's Theory of the Understanding; Francke, C. J. W. David Hume (in Dutch); Greig, J. Y. T. (John Carruthers) David Hume; Hendel, C. W. Studies in the Philosophy of Hume; Hume, D. Life; Huxley, T. H. Hume; Jode, F. Leben und Philosophie Humes; Knight, W. Hume; Laing, B. M. David Hume; Maund, C. Hume's Theory of Knowledge; Morris, C. R. Locke, Berkeley, Hume; Mossner, E. C. The Forgotten Hume, le bon David; Rickaby, J. Free Will and Four English Philosophers; Smith, A. H. A Treatise on Knowledge; Sorley, W. R. History of English Philosophy; Stephen, L. English Thought in the 18th Century; Thomsen, A. David Hume, Sein Leben und seine Philosophie; Weber, A. History of Philosophy.

HURD, RICHARD (January 13, 1720-May 28; 1808), critic, editor, bishop of Worcester, was born in Congreve, Straffordshire, the second son of John Hurd, a well-to-do farmer. He was educated at Emmanuel College, Cambridge, taking his B.A. in 1738 and his M.A. in 1742. Two years later he was ordained as a priest.

A moderate Tory and an orthodox churchman, Hurd divided his time between ecclesiastical duties and literary pursuits, achieving a solid, if not spectacular, reputation in both fields. He published critical and theological works, among them a commentary on the *Ars Poetica* of Horace which won him the patronage of William Warburton. Through Warburton's influence he was appointed Whitehall preacher in 1750 and proceeded to the curacy of St. Andrew the Little at Cambridge three years later. Hurd edited Warburton's *Remarks on Hume's Natural History of Religion*, earning the resentment of the Scottish philosopher by the flippant tone of his commentary.

Hurd's two most important works were the *Moral and Political Dialogues*, introducing historical personages as interlocutors, and *Letters on Chivalry and Romance*, which dealt with the origins of knight-errantry and attempted to vindicate Gothic art and literature from the charge of barbarism. Both books were much praised although Johnson deplored the "woefully whiggish cast" of the *Dialogues*.

From the rectory of Thurcaston in Leicestershire, Hurd was appointed to the sinecure rectory of Folkton, Yorkshire, in 1762. Five years later he was made archdeacon of Gloucester, delivering the first Warburton lectures at the Lincoln's Inn chapel. A favorite of George III, he was nominated to the see of Lichfield and Coventry in 1774 and seven years later, having acted as preceptor to the Prince of Wales, was transferred to Worcester. In 1783 he was offered the primacy, an honor which he declined.

Hurd acted as editor for the works of William Warburton, his lifelong friend, as well as the works of Cowley and Jeremy Taylor. Gibbon, with whom he had carried on a spirited theological controversy, criticized his style but added that he knew "few writers more deserving of the great, though prostituted, name of the critic."

PRINCIPAL WORKS: Moral and Political Dialogues, 1759; Letters on Chivalry and Romance, 1762 (E. J. Morley, ed. 1911); An Introduction to the Study of the Prophecies Concerning the Christian Church, and in Particular Concerning the Church of Papal Rome, 1772; Works of William Warburton (ed.) 1788; Collected Works, 1811; The Correspondence of Richard Hurd and William Mason, and Letters of Richard Hurd to Thomas Gray (E. H. Pearce and L. Whibley, eds.) 1932.

ABOUT: Evans, A. W. Warburton and the Warburtonians; Kilvert, F. Memoirs of the Life and Writings of Bishop Hurd.

HUTCHESON, FRANCIS (August 8, 1694-1746), Scottish philosopher, was born near Saintfield, County Down, Ireland, but of a Scottish family stemming from Ayrshire. His father, John Hutcheson, was a Presbyterian minister (at Armagh), and so was his grandfather. He lived at Ballyrea, near Armagh, until he was eight, then with his brother was sent to his grandfather in Saintfield, to be educated at the academy of Killeleagh. From 1710 to 1716 he was a student at the University of Glasgow, and was licensed to preach in the last named year. He established a private academy in Dublin, and refused all preferment in the Presbyterian church because of increasing religious doubts. In 1729 he was appointed professor of moral philosophy at Glasgow, the first British philosopher to occupy a full professorial chair. There he remained for the rest of his life, in 1745 refusing a more lucrative offer from Edinburgh. In 1738 he had been called before the presbytery for questioning on theological issues, but no attempt was made to displace him. His lectures—he was a much better speaker than writer—did much to influence the Scottish taste for philosophical study and discussion.

Hutcheson married a Miss Wilson, and had one son, who was a physician and also (under the name of Francis Ireland) a popular musical composer. He died of a fever at fifty-one.

His purely philosophical views are not very striking or profound, but he was one of the first modern writers on aesthetics, and his ethical writings (which really constitute a psychological study of the moral faculties) are important. In general, he was a forerunner of Bentham and the Utilitarians, even anticipating, in another form, Bentham's famous definition of virtue as "the greatest

285

F. Bartolozzi

FRANCIS HUTCHESON

good of the greatest number." Hutcheson equated virtue with universal benevolence and his standard of moral goodness was the general happiness of others. He was an optimist firmly opposed to the self-centered philosophy of Hobbes. Hume was strongly influenced by him, while he himself was a disciple of the third Earl of Shaftesbury; in his theory of logic he closely followed Locke.

In character, Hutcheson adhered to his own views; he was an extremely warm-hearted, kindly, generous man, who allowed poor students to attend his lectures without pay and found ways of assisting them to live. Though noted for his quick temper, he was in essence sweet natured and lovable. The orthodox Presbyterians objected strongly to his belief that man can have a knowledge of good and evil without a previous knowledge of God (he was a professed deist), but they could do nothing to lessen his popularity in the university or the high esteem in which he was held by his colleagues and his students.

His *Logicae Compendium*, which was published posthumously, was not intended by him for publication and was not completed.

PRINCIPAL WORKS: An Inquiry into the Original of Our Ideas of Beauty and Virtue, 1725; An Essay on the Nature and Conduct of the Passions and Affections, with Illustrations on the Moral Sense, 1728; Philosophiae moralis institutio compendaria, 1742 (English, 1747); Metaphysical Synopsis, 1742; A System of Moral Philosophy (F.

Hutcheson [son], ed.) 1755; Logicae Compendium, 1756.

ABOUT: Fowler, T. Shaftesbury and Hutcheson; Leechman, W. Life, *in* A System of Moral Philosophy; McCosh, J. Scottish Philosophy; Scott, W. R. Francis Hutcheson; Smith, A. Theory of Moral Sentiments; Stephen, L. History of English Thought in the 18th Century.

HUTCHINSON, Mrs. LUCY (January 29, 1620-?), author of a volume of memoirs, was born in the Tower of London of which her father, Sir Allen Apsley, was chief lieutenant. Lucy seems to have been a precocious child, learning French, Latin, Greek, and Hebrew, reading theology and the classics. Of her own childhood she writes "My father and mother, fancying me beautiful and more than ordinarily apprehensive, spared no cost to improve me in my education. When I was about seven years of age, I remember, I had at one time eight tutors in several qualities—language, music, dancing, writing, and needlework."

When Lucy was eighteen she married John Hutchinson, a Puritan who was later to play an important role on the side of Parliament during the civil war. In whatever leisure she could spare from domestic duties the young wife continued her study of the classics and translated six books of Lucretius. "I turned it into English," she wrote, "in a room where my children practiced the several qualities they were taught with their tutors, and I numbered the syllables of my translation by the threads of the canvas I wrought in." Under Puritan influence, however, Mrs. Hutchinson came to believe that the study of "pagan poets and philosophers" was a "great means of debauching the learned world" and took no pride in her earlier accomplishment.

Hutchinson was made governor of Nottingham Castle during the civil war and, although he did not approve of Cromwell's policies, was one of those to sign the death warrant of Charles I. At the Restoration only the heroic efforts of Mrs. Hutchinson saved his life. Again when he was arrested in 1663 on suspicion of being involved in the Yorkshire plot, she complained to the Privy Council of his unjust imprisonment and paid daily visits to Sandown Castle where he was imprisoned. Hutchinson died the following year, leaving this message for his wife: "Let her, as she is above other women, show herself in this occasion a good Christian, and above the pitch of ordinary women."

During the next seven years Mrs. Hutchinson wrote the biography of her husband which two centuries later was recognized as a masterpiece of its kind. She was inclined to overrate his political importance, but the dignity and candor of her portraiture against the acutely sketched background of her times give genuine literary distinction to these memoirs. The date of Mrs. Hutchinson's death is unknown and her *Memoirs of the Life of Colonel Hutchinson* remained unpublished until 1806.

PRINCIPAL WORKS: Memoirs of the Life of Colonel Hutchinson, Governor of Nottingham, to Which Is Prefixed the Life of Mrs. Hutchinson Written by Herself, A Fragment, 1806 (C. H. Firth, ed. 1885, 1906).

ABOUT: Guizot, F. P. G. Monk's Contemporaries: Biographical Studies on the English Revolution; Hutchinson, L. Life of Mrs. Hutchinson, prefixed to Memoirs.

INCHBALD, Mrs. ELIZABETH (October 15, 1753-August 1, 1821), novelist, dramatist, actress, was born Elizabeth Simpson, at Bury St. Edmunds, Suffolk, the daughter of John Simpson, a farmer, who died when she was eight. What education she had came merely from her own reading. Her brother became an actor, and she longed to emulate him. In 1772, at eighteen, she ran away to London. Frightened by the kind of advances made to her—she was very pretty, tall, fair, and slender—a few months later she married Joseph Inchbald, an actor much her senior, to secure protection. He did more; he gave her her chance on the stage. She appeared as Cordelia to his Lear in Bristol. She continued to act until 1789, for the most part in Ireland, Scotland, and in the provinces (her first London appearance was in 1780), and took such major roles as Juliet, Imogen, and Desdemona, but she was never a successful actress, largely because she suffered from an impediment in her speech.

Inchbald died suddenly in 1779 in Leeds, and his widow never remarried. She had plenty of opportunities—William Godwin, for one, wanted to marry her after his first wife, Mary Wollstonecraft, died—and she was an unconscionable flirt, but she seems to have been one of those women whose only interest in the other sex lies in coquetry. In an age when actresses were not "accepted" in good society, her reputation was unblemished —perhaps because she was all her life a devout Roman Catholic.

Mrs. Inchbald had kept on improving her education, studying French and painting, twice visiting Paris, becoming the close friend of such intellectually minded people of the stage as Mrs. Siddons with all her Kemble relatives. She turned to writing soon after her husband's death. Her first play, *The Mogul Tale,* produced in 1784, was her best; her plays on the whole were rather thin—topical, with clever dialogue and pleasant humor, but injured by complicated plots and absurd improbabilities. It was as a novelist that she made her real contribution to literature. Her two novels, dealing seriously with real problems, are tender, touching, sincere, and curiously "modern" in tone. *A Simple Story* at least is still quite readable. It is said to have given Charlotte Brontë her first idea for *Jane Eyre.*

From 1806 to 1809 Mrs. Inchbald edited the twenty-five volumes of *The British Theatre,* and she selected plays for further compilations. She also contributed to the *Edinburgh Review.* She was remarkably well paid for her era, and since she was also prudent and thrifty—though she was lavishly generous—she left a fortune of some six thousand pounds. In her last years she had started writing her memoirs, but destroyed the manuscript—it is said at the advice of a

G. Dance, 1794

MRS. ELIZABETH INCHBALD

Roman Catholic bishop, who perhaps was alarmed by the liberality of her political and economic views, however orthodox her religious tenets. It is unfortunate, since she had known all the "intelligentsia" of her day, and her memoirs should have been instructive and delightful.

PRINCIPAL WORKS: *Plays* (dates of publication)—I'll Tell You What, 1786; Such Things Are, 1788; Everyone Has His Fault, 1793; Wives as They Were, 1797; To Marry or Not to Marry, 1805; The Mogul Tale, 1824. *Novels*—A Simple Story, 1791; Nature and Art, 1796.

ABOUT: Boaden, J. Memoirs of Mrs. Inchbald, Including Her Familiar Correspondence; Kemble, F. Records of a Girlhood; Littlewood, S. R. lizabeth Inchbald and Her Circle: the Life Story of a Charming Woman; Scott, E. W. Preface, A Simple Story, 1880 ed.; Smith-Dampier, J. L. East Anglian Worthies.

JAGO, RICHARD (October 1, 1715-May 8, 1781), poet, was born at Beaudesert, Warwickshire, the son of the Reverend Richard Jago and Margaret Parker. He was educated at Solihull, where he met William Shenstone,*qv* who became his lifelong friend. As his father was in straitened circumstances, he entered University College, Oxford, in 1732 as a servitor. He proceeded B.A. in 1736, M.A. 1739. He was ordained in 1737 and was a curate at Snitterfield, Warwickshire, until 1746, when he received the two small livings of Harbury and Chesterton in the same county. In 1744 he had married Dorothea Fancourt, who died in 1751, leaving three sons and four daughters. In 1758 he married Margaret Underwood, who survived him; there were no children from this marriage.

Having this large family to support, Jago was delighted in 1754 to become vicar of Snitterfield, where he had been curate. He resigned his two small livings in 1771, when through Lord Willoughby de Brooke he received the rectory of Kimcote, Leicestershire. He continued, however, to live at Snitterfield, and spent the remainder of his life there. Outside of his clerical duties and his poetry, his chief pursuit was the improvement of the grounds and buildings of his rectory. He lived the life of a literary recluse, his only associates a small group of Warwickshire poets centering around the Duchess of Somerset, and including Richard Graves and William Somerville.*qqv* His prevailing mood was that of melancholy—

and in later years he became acutely irritable, a typical dyspeptic—but his sprightly letters show that he was capable of cheerfulness and even of wit.

Jago was a very minor poet, of the nature-graveyard-moralism school, but his work was pleasant and unaffected, and frequently he displayed powers of keen observation of natural objects. His poems have long remained unread, and they have little vigor or originality, being primarily the avocation of a rural clergyman. The best of them is *Edge-Hill*, which in spite of its didacticism contains some simple and pleasing passages.

He was frequently the victim of theft of his poems, and of their ascription to others. Some of them were long accredited to Shenstone. One appropriator of a poem of his excused himself by saying that "Iago" was not the name of a real person!—from which it appears that the name may have been pronounced in the Italian manner, and may have been of remote Italian origin.

Volumes of his sermons on special occasions were published in 1755 and 1763.

PRINCIPAL WORKS: Edge-Hill: or, the Rural Project Delineated and Moralized, 1767; Labour and Genius, 1768; Poems, Moral and Descriptive, 1784.

ABOUT: Anon. Some Account of the Life and Writings of Mr. Jago, *in* Poems Moral and Descriptive; Graves, R. Recollections.

JAMES I (July 1394-February 20, 1437), king of Scotland, poet, was the younger son of Robert III and of his queen, Annabella Drummond. He was born in Dunfermline. His mother died in 1402, and he was sent to St. Andrews in the charge of Bishop Henry Wardlaw. Soon after, his older brother was killed, probably at the instigation of the boys' uncle, the Duke of Albany. Robert was an invalid and far from a strong character; he did not feel he could protect James, and he arranged for him to be reared in France. He set sail, probably early in 1406. Unfortunately the ship was intercepted by the English, and the child became a prisoner of Henry IV. At first he was kept in the Tower of London, then at Nottingham Castle, at Evesham, and finally for the most part at Windsor Castle. Though he was kept under strict custody—he was being held for 60,000 marks ransom, a quite usual procedure—he was well treated and well educated, and his

JAMES I OF SCOTLAND

tastes for poetry and music were indulged. He had fellow prisoners, including the son of Owen Glendower, ruler of Wales, and later Charles of Orleans (also a poet), though it is unlikely that James and Charles were allowed to associate.

His father had died soon after James was captured, and Albany had been appointed regent. Naturally, he was none too eager to have the new king return to Scotland, and nothing much was done about raising his ransom. Henry IV died, and James remained the prisoner of Henry V. He accompanied the English king to France in 1420, was unable, as he had been expected to do, to get the Scottish allies of the French to raise the siege of Melun, and had the humiliation of seeing them executed as rebels. Again he accompanied Henry V to France in 1422, this time to Rouen, and stayed there until after the king's death, returning to England as prisoner of Henry VI. But his long imprisonment was almost at an end; Albany died the same year, and in 1423 James was released, on the promise of payment of the ransom.

One of the conditions of his release was that he was to marry an English noblewoman. This was Joan or Jane Beaufort, daughter of the Earl of Somerset, whom James had first beheld walking in a garden under his window, and whom he had loved from that moment. It is practically certain that it is she who was the inspiration of *The Kingis Quair*. They remained devoted lovers to the end; almost alone among Scottish kings James had no mistresses. Six daughters (one of whom became the queen of Louis XI of France) and twin sons (one of whom died in infancy, the other of whom succeeded his father as James II) were born of the marriage.

James was crowned in 1424, and proceeded immediately to reform his kingdom. Twenty-six of the kinfolk and followers of Albany were put to death. In effect the king declared war on the feudal lords of the Highlands, and drew his adherents from the church and the burghers. He introduced statute law into Scotland. In the thirteen years of his reign he had frequent trouble both with the pope and with England (the ransom was never paid). In 1435 an English invading force was beaten and driven back. But his chief danger was from the rebel Highland chiefs. At Christmas time, 1436, he went to Perth and stayed in the Charterhouse there, disregarding warnings of a conspiracy against him, led by Sir Robert Graeme (or Graham). On February 20, one of the conspirators left the door unbarred, Graeme and his followers burst in, and the king was stabbed to death. (A poetic account of the assassination may be found in Rossetti's *The King's Tragedy*.)

James was an authentic poet, one of the leaders of the so-called "Scottish Chaucerians." *The Kingis Quair* ("quair" means "book") has passages which are not unworthy of its author's master—James may indeed have written Fragment B of Chaucer's *Romaunt of the Rose*. Two other poems sometimes ascribed to him, *Christis Kirk of the Grene* and *Peblis to the Play*, probably belong to a later period. He did, however, write *Sen trew Vertew encreeses dignytie*, also called *The Ballad of Good Counsel*. But *The Kingis Quair* is his true legacy to posterity, and needs no extraneous interest to recommend it.

PRINCIPAL WORKS: The Kingis Quair (manuscript) 1488 (W. W. Skeat, ed., 1884); Poetical Remains of James the First, King of Scotland (W. Tytler, ed.) 1783.

ABOUT: Andrew of Wyntoun. The Orygynale Cronykil of Scotland; Balfour-Melville, E. W. M. James I, King of Scots; Brown, J. T. T. The Authorship of the Kingis Quair; D'Israeli, I. The Literary Character; Jusserand, J. J. The Romance of a King's Life; Lang, A. History of Scotland; Millar, J. H. A Literary History of Scotland; Ross, J. M. Scottish History and Literature.

JAMES I (James VI of Scotland) (June 19, 1566-March 27, 1625), king of England, 1603-25, author of political and theological works, was the only child of Mary Queen of Scots and her second husband, Henry Stuart, Lord Darnley, and was born in Edinburgh Castle. By Mary's forced abdication in 1567, the infant became king of Scotland, with his uncle, the Earl of Moray, and his paternal grandfather, the Earl of Lennox, as successive regents. He was reared at Stirling Castle by the Earl of Mar, and educated by tutors, chiefly George Buchanan.[qv] They made the precocious child a fair scholar and an egregious pedant. His childhood was a chaos of civil war, he himself being kidnapped at fourteen. His policy fluctuated between currying favor with Catholic Spain and Protestant England; England won when he attained his majority in 1587 and for fear of alienating Elizabeth let his mother be executed almost without protest. Nevertheless, he was a good king of Scotland—though later a bad enough king of England. In 1589 he married Anne of Denmark (they had two sons—Henry, who died in 1612, and Charles, later Charles I, and two daughters) and the queen's secret conversion to Roman Catholicism increased his difficulties. She died in 1619.

In 1603 he ascended the English throne, after unnecessary intriguing for it. His boasted "kingcraft" was merely a playing of one rival government or party against the other; he was a coward, a boor, coarse in language though careful in conduct, heedless of the gross corruption of his court, slovenly, garrulous, opinionated, and narrow minded. He believed implicitly in witchcraft, was superstitious and stubborn, and created scandal by his subservience to handsome masculine favorites like George Villiers, Duke of Buckingham. On the other side of the ledger must be placed the facts that he was a generous patron of Scottish poetry, that he authorized the great King James version of the Bible, and that he was genuinely interested in literature and learning.

James was the most prolific author in the annals of the English monarchy except Alfred the Great. Most of his books were anonymous, and most of them were written in the Scottish dialect—he never learned to speak southern English without an accent. He wrote in advocacy of the theory of the divine right of kings, in opposition to tobacco, which he loathed, and in defense of witchcraft and demonology. Unfortunately he was a mediocre writer, and nothing he wrote could remotely be designated as literature. The *Basilikon Doron*, his best-known book, was written for the instruction of his oldest son, Prince Henry. In his youth he was devoted to poetry, and published some of his own, in no way notable. His "meditations" on portions of the Bible were commonplace. In an age when the English language attained its great glory, the king of England stood almost alone as a stiff, awkward, and involved writer.

PRINCIPAL WORKS: Treatise of Poetry, 1584; The Essays of a Prentise in the Divine Art of Poesie, 1584; A Fruitful Meditation [on] Revelation, 1588; Poetical Exercises at Vacant Hours, 1591; Daemonologie, 1599; Basilikon Doron, 1599; The True Law of Free Monarchies, 1603; A Counterblaste to Tobacco, 1604; A Discourse of the Manner of the Discovery of the Powder Treason, 1605; An Apology for the Oath of Allegiance, 1607; The King's Majesties Declaration to his Subjects concerning Lawful Sports to be used, 1618; Prose Works (J. Montague, ed.) 1619; Meditations on the Lord's Prayer, 1619; Meditations on. . . St Matthew, 1620; Meditations on. . . Chronicles, 1620; New Poems by James I of England (A. F. Westcott, ed.) 1911.

D. Mytens

JAMES I OF ENGLAND

ABOUT: Aikin, L. Memoirs of the Court of King James the First; Harris, W. An Historical and Critical Account of the Life and Writings of James I; Henderson, T. F. James I and VI; Lang, A. History of Scotland; Linklater, E. Ben Jonson and King James; McLaurin, C. Mere Mortals; Rait, R. S. Lusus Regius; Smith, G. G. Elizabethan Critical Essays; Steeholm, C. and H. James I of England, the Wisest Fool in Christendom; Williams, C. James I; Williamson, H. R. King James I.

JENYNS, SOAME (January 1, 1704-December 18, 1787), miscellaneous writer, was born in London. His mother was a daughter of Sir Peter Soame and his father was Sir Roger Jenyns of Bottisham Hall. Jenyns entered St. John's College, Cambridge, when he was eighteen but left three years later without a degree.

His first publication was a poem, *The Art of Dancing*, which appeared anonymously in 1727. In the next few years he continued to write verse, much of which was first printed in *Dodsley's Miscellany*, and in 1752 he published a collection of *Poems*. Jenyns also played a modest role in political affairs. In 1742 he was elected to Parliament and thirteen years later served as a commissioner on the Board of Trade and Plantations.

Two prose works by Jenyns attracted wide attention, the first *A Free Inquiry into the Nature and Origin of Evil*, and second *A View of the Internal Evidence of the Christian Religion*, which ran through ten editions. Both these treatises, the latter in particular, provoked lively controversy, writers and clerics stepping forward to attack and defend the author with equal spirit. Samuel Johnson wrote a brilliant and blistering review of *A Free Inquiry* for the *Literary Magazine*, and although Jenyns was ordinarily a man without malice, he resented Johnson's attack and cherished a long dislike that continued even after Johnson's death with the publication of a disparaging epitaph. Hannah More, on the other hand, admired Jenyns' work although with reservations. She claimed to know a "philosophical infidel" who had been converted by reading *A View*; nevertheless she was inclined to feel that the author "brings too much ingenuity into his religion."

Jenyns' prose was usually considered a model of ease and elegance by contemporary critics. He was commended by such writers as Burke and Boswell. In a long perspective, however, Johnson's judgment has proved more accurate. Jenyns' speculative inquiries were of the shallowest and his prose had more grace than grasp.

PRINCIPAL WORKS: Poems, 1752; A Free Inquiry into the Nature and Origin of Evil, 1757; Miscellaneous Pieces in Prose and Verse, 1761; The Objections to the Taxation of Our American Colonies Considered, 1765; Miscellanies, 1770; A Scheme for the Coalition of Parties, 1772; A View of the Internal Evidence of the Christian Religion, 1776; Disquisitions on Several Subjects, 1782; Thoughts on Parliamentary Reform, 1784; The Works of Soame Jenyns (C. N. Cole, ed.) 1790.

ABOUT: Cole, C. N. Memoir, in The Works of Soame Jenyns.

JEROME, STEPHEN (fl. 1604-1650), miscellaneous writer and author of *Origen's Repentance*, was a graduate of St. John's College, Cambridge, receiving his B.A. degree in 1604 and an M.A. three years later. Beyond this fact there is little record of his life, but he apparently took holy orders. The preface to *Origen's Repentance*, published in 1619, is dated by Jerome "from my house at Newcastle, May 12th," where he was a preacher at St. Nicholas' Church. Some five years later, writing from Ireland, he describes himself as "domesticke chaplain to the Right Honorable Earl of Corke."

Copies of Jerome's two most important works are extremely rare and have become more interesting to bibliophiles as literary curios than valuable to students of literature. The full title of the first of these gives something of its flavor, *Origen's Repentance: After He had Sacrificed to the Idols of the Heathen: Gathered from Svidas, Nicephorus, Osiander, and the Greeke and Latine Coppies in Origen's Works: Illustrated and Applied to the Case of Every Poore Penitent Who in Remorse of Soule Shall Have Recourse to the Throne of Grace*. It is a long tract written in doggerel verse, divided into three sections each consisting of a "century of stanzas."

The second of his better known works is *Ireland's Jubilee: or Ioye's Io-paean, For Prince Charles His Welcome Home*, published in 1624. Presumably written to commemorate the return of the Prince of Wales from Spain, it is a curious pastiche of scriptural quotations and allusions referring more often to Biblical events and personages than to his contemporary world. According to

Thomas Frognall Dibdin, an early nineteenth century bibliophile, Jerome's *Ireland's Jubilee* is second in rarity only to Cranford's *Teares of Ireland*.

PRINCIPAL WORKS: Moses His Sight of Canaan, 1614; Origen's Repentance, 1619; Seaven Helps to Heaven, 1620; Ireland's Jubilee, 1624; A Minister's Mite, 1650.

ABOUT: Cooper, C. H. Memorials of Cambridge; Hazlitt, W. C. Handbook to Early English Literature, 1st series.

JOHN of SALISBURY (d. October 25, 1180),

ecclesiastic, politician, classical writer, took his name from his birthplace, Salisbury (Old Sarum). He was probably born some time between 1115 and 1120. All that is known of his childhood is his statement that the priest who taught him the Psalms tried to use him as an assistant in experiments in black magic, but he resisted. He seems to have been small in stature, and was dubbed "Parvus." From 1136 to 1138 he was in Paris, as a pupil of Abelard, "the first important representative of England in the schools of Paris." He spent the next two years in Chartres, studying "grammar" (the analysis of Latin literature) and rhetoric to supplement the logic learned from Abelard. Early in 1141 he returned to Paris and remained there as a student until 1145. In 1148, at the Council of Rheims, he met, through Bernard de Clairvaux, Theobald the incumbent Archbishop of Canterbury, and two years later he became Theobald's secretary. His duties were also diplomatic, and he made many visits to Rome, where the only English pope, Adrian IV, was his close friend. It was through John that Henry II of England secured from the pope jurisdiction over Ireland, the beginning of a long and troubled history.

John soon fell out of favor with the king, however, since he was an ardent advocate of the supremacy of the church over the state. It was at this period that he wrote both his most important books, the *Policraticus* and the *Metalogicus*. The latter he dedicated to Thomas à Becket, then chancellor. When Becket became Archbishop of Canterbury in 1162, John entered his service. Within a year Becket and the king were bitter enemies, and when Henry returned from France in 1163, John (who was already in the king's bad graces, had followed all Becket's procedures loyally, and was consti-

tutionally timid) decided he would be safer out of England. He fled to his old friend, Peter de la Celle, abbot of Rheims. Becket followed him into exile the following year.

In 1170 John returned to England, a short time before Becket, and was in the cathedral when Thomas was murdered there. It is said that he ran and hid, but returned before the end and was splashed with Becket's blood. He wrote immediately a life of Becket in which he urged his canonization (afterwards accomplished); he had already written two biographies of St. Anselm. John remained in the service of Becket's successor, and in 1174 acted as treasurer of Exeter Cathedral.

In 1176 John was named Bishop of Chartres, and he spent the remainder of his life there. (It must be remembered that in this era a large part of France belonged to England.) His last activity was at the Council of the Lateran in 1179. The next year he died at Chartres.

Besides the books already mentioned, John wrote an unfinished *Historia Pontificalis* in verse, a satirical ecclesiastical history from 1148 to 1152 (at least, these years are all that remain extant). He also wrote a didactic poem, *Eutheticus de dogmate philosophorum*. All his work, of course, was in Latin, and it appeared before the age of printing. The *Metalogicus* dealt with grammar and logic, and was a sort of compound of Augustinian and Aristotelian philosophy. The *Policraticus* was a "statesman's handbook," in which the state is compared to the human body, with the clergy as the soul, the prince as the head, and so on down to the peasants as feet. John, says J. E. Sandys, was "the first of modern writers on the philosophy of politics," and the *Policraticus* was "the earliest of all the mediaeval theories on the nature and functions of the state." Calm common sense and moderation were his salient characteristics; he was a true humanist in spirit before the days of Renaissance humanism. His model in style was Cicero, and his Latin is unsurpassed for purity.

PRINCIPAL WORKS: (dates of modern printing): Eutheticus de dogmate philosophorum (C. Paterson, ed.) 1843; Joannes Saresberiensis Opera (J. A. Giles, ed.) 1848; Policraticus (C. C. J. Webb, ed.) 1909; Historia Pontificalis (R. L. Poole, ed.) 1927.

ABOUT: Demimuid, M. Jean de Salisbury; Jusserand, J. J. Literary History of the English People; Lloyd, R. B. The Golden Middle Age; Norgate, K. England Under the Angevin Kings; Poole, R. L. Illustrations of the History of Mediaeval Thought; Sandys, J. E. History of Classical Scholarship; Schraaschmidt, C. Johannes Saresberiensis nach Leben und Studien, Schriften und Philosophie; Ueberweg, F. History of Philosophy; Wright, T. Biographia Britannica Literaria.

JOHNSON, RICHARD (1573-1659?), writer of prose romances, was baptized in London on May 24, 1573. Little is known of his life but from the title of his dirge *A Servant's Sorrow for the Loss of His Late Royal Mistres*, written in 1619, it may be conjectured that he was connected with the household of James I.

Johnson's most widely read work was *The Most Famous Historie of the Seaven Champions of Christendome, St. George of England, St. Denis of France, St. James of Spain, St. Anthony of Italy, St. Andrew of Scotland, St. Patricke of Ireland, and St. David of Wales*, the oldest known copy of which is dated 1597. Since the *Historie* was registered at Stationer's Hall a year earlier, it is probable that this was a second edition. According to contemporary accounts Johnson's book achieved great popularity, and encouraged by its "great acceptance" he added a second part in 1608 recounting the noble achievements of "St. George's three sons, the lively sparks of nobility." Still a third part was published in 1616, and a poetical version by Sir George Bluc appeared six years later.

Two other works by Johnson may be mentioned. *The Most Pleasant History of Tom a Lincoln, That Renowned Soldier, the Red-Rose Knight* is a good example of the early prose romance of the "Euphues" type, and as such holds a certain interest for literary scholars. *The Pleasant Conceites of Old Hobson, the Merry Londoner*, clustering a number of contemporary anecdotes around the name of William Hobson, a well-known London haberdasher of the period, has both literary and antiquarian interest. In this the author professes to relate diverting episodes in the life of Hobson while he makes his own comment on events during the reigns of Edward VI, Mary, and Elizabeth.

Johnson also wrote a number of vividly titled pamphlets and social satires. An edition of his *A Crowne-Garland of Goulden Roses*, first published in 1612, appeared in the year 1659, but it seems probable that this was a posthumous publication. On the whole Johnson was a competent hack writer of his time, but hardly more.

PRINCIPAL WORKS: The Nine Worthies of London, 1592; The Most Famous Historie of the Seaven Champions of Christendome, 1596-97; Anglorum Lachrimae, 1603; The Pleasant Conceites of Old Hobson, 1607 (J. O. Halliwell, ed. 1843); A Crowne-Garland of Goulden Roses, 1612 (W. Chappell, ed., 1842); Looke on Me, London, I Am an Honest Englishman Ripping Up the Bowels of Mischief Lurking in Thy Suburbs and Precincts, 1613 (J. P. Collier, ed., *in* Illustrations of Early English Popular Literature, 1864); The Golden Garland of Princely Pleasures and Delicate Delights, 1620; The History of Tom Thumbe, the Little, 1621; The Most Pleasant History of Tom a Lincolne, That Renowned Soldier, the Red-Rose Knight, 1631 (W. J. Thomas, ed., *in* Early English Prose Romances, 1828).

ABOUT: Chappell, W. Preface to A Crowne Garland; Corser, T. Collectanae Anglo-Poetica; Ritson, J. Bibliographia Poetica.

JOHNSON, SAMUEL (September 18, 1709-December 13, 1784), man of letters, editor, poet, biographer, lexicographer, was born in Lichfield, in a house now the Johnson Museum, the son of Michael Johnson, a bookseller and once sheriff, and Sarah (Ford) Johnson. He was a precocious child, but very early he contracted scrofula (his parents took him to Queen Anne for the "king's touch"), which left him scarred and almost blind. This, added to partial deafness, a huge, ungainly body, and the nervous effects of the disease—grimacing, gesturing, muttering to himself—determined much of Johnson's future, and deepened his natural melancholy into almost melancholia. When the extreme poverty of his early London years left its marks of slovenliness, voracity, and surly manners, the unprepossessing exterior was complete. It hid a warm, generous, loyal heart and a brilliant, inquiring mind.

Johnson was sent to school at Lichfield and Stourbridge, and then was taught his father's trade. He hated being a tradesman; fifty years later, he stood in the rain in his father's stall at Uttoxeter Market, to make up for the day he was too proud to accompany his father there. By the promise of help—not kept—from a rich neighbor, he was enabled to enter Pembroke College, Oxford, in 1728. He was grindingly poor, and devilishly proud, a rebel against all regulations. He left in a year (with possible occasional residences for two years more), without a degree. Later Oxford gave him both an M.A. and an LL.D. His first publication was while he was at Pembroke—a Latin verse translation of Pope's *Messiah*, in a college anthology.

His father died, practically bankrupt, in 1731. Johnson took a miserable job as usher at Market Bosworth, Leicestershire, tried in vain for one at his old school at Stourbridge, and then went for three years to live in Birmingham, where he subsisted by writing for a newspaper. There in 1735 he married Elizabeth Porter, twelve years his senior, a widow with grown children. But it was a marriage for love; until she died in 1752, his "Tetty," who to others was a ridiculous, affected provincial, was to Johnson everything beautiful and charming.

His wife had a little money, so that Johnson was able to open a school of his own near Lichfield. Only eight pupils ever came to it; it was a complete failure. In 1737 Johnson gave up, and with one of his pupils, David Garrick, set out for London. Having no profession, he became a hack writer. In a few months he was able to bring his wife from Lichfield (leaving her daughter to live with his mother), but years of desperate poverty and actual destitution were before him. His first writing was all anonymous, and much of it was hack journalism. Beginning in 1738 he was more or less regularly employed by the *Gentleman's Magazine*. This magazine had been publishing Parliamentary debates, a practice that was later forbidden; Johnson then devised "debates in the Senate of Magna Lilliputia," written from a reporter's notes; to his amazement these were taken as actual transcripts—often much more eloquent than the actual speeches! He did some work in the classifying of the Harleian Library, and his poem *London* (the first of two based on Juvenal's satires) and his biography of the poet-imposter Richard Savage, who had shared his days of direst need, attracted some attention. When he came to London it was with a tragedy, *Irene*, in his pocket. It was twelve years before Garrick produced it. It ran only nine nights, but gave him some money; Johnson had no flair for drama, and the play has been described as "a moral poem in dialogue." For two years, 1750-52, he issued

After Sir J. Reynolds, 1769
SAMUEL JOHNSON

the semi-weekly *Rambler*, in which he wrote all the material; it had only five hundred circulation, but it made him a reputation. A few days before the last number appeared, his wife died.

The idea of a new dictionary of the English language had been with Johnson since 1745 or so. In 1747 he issued his prospectus, and eight years later the work was done. For the eight years' work he received 1500 guineas—about $887 a year—and out of this he had to pay his six amanuenses. His famous letter to Lord Chesterfield, which is said to have been a death-blow to the patronage system, explained why the dictionary carried no dedication. Outmoded as it is now, Johnson's was by far the best dictionary thus far issued.

From 1756 to 1757 Johnson edited the *Literary Magazine* and wrote his *Idler* essays. His next important book was *Rasselas* ("a sort of prose *Vanity of Human Wishes*") which he wrote in twenty-four hours to defray his mother's funeral expenses. In 1762, with the election of a Tory government, he, the arch-Tory, at last received a pension. (Gratitude probably inspired his series of rather inept political pamphlets, a decade or more later, hotly opposing the nascent rebellion of the American colonists.) The next three years were important ones in Johnson's personal life: in 1763 he met Boswell, his perfect biographer; in 1764 he and Sir Joshua Reynolds founded the famous Club, from which time dates Johnson's growing ascension as "the Great Cham of Literature," in Smollett's phrase; and in 1765 he met Henry and Hester Thrale, whose houses in London and Streatham became his home for at least half the time. His close friendship with them was broken only by Thrale's death and by Mrs. Thrale's remarriage to the Italian musician Piozzi, which Johnson never forgave—though by that time he was near his own death.

In the next decade he made his only excursions outside of England—to Scotland and the Hebrides with Boswell, to North Wales and to France with the Thrales. In France he spoke not French, but Latin; he had been from boyhood a fine and fluent Latinist. (One of his uncompleted projects was an edition of the Latin poems of Politian.) In Scotland he tried to overcome his emotional prejudice against the Scots, and took time out to see through and expose the fakery of the celebrated poems of "Ossian."

After the exhausting labor of his edition of Shakespeare's plays, which despite its editor's bias is the basis of all the variorum editions, Johnson had decided to undertake no more major projects on his own initiative. However, in 1777 one came to him—the proposal that he edit the works of fifty-two English poets of the seventeenth and eighteenth centuries. The work was finished by 1781, and the prefaces (as *Lives of the Poets*) were then issued separately. The best of these brief critical biographies—e.g., Dryden, Pope, Cowley—are unsurpassed; Johnson's invincible prejudices badly injured some of the others, notably the life of Gray.

This was the last of his books to be published during his lifetime, and his last major work. He was a dropsical semi-invalid from 1781 on—though always able to rally for an evening with his friends at a tavern. His house in Johnson's Court (not named for him), Fleet Street—now the address of the Rationalist Press Association, which would have cut the extremely religious Johnson to the quick—was filled with his quarreling aged pensioners, whom he supported and endured. In 1783 he had a stroke. He rallied enough to make last visits to his old haunts—Lichfield, Birmingham, Oxford—

and to contemplate a trip to Italy to avoid the English winter. But this plan came too late. In the autumn of 1784, feeling the approach of death, he destroyed all his personal papers. In December he, who had always feared death so terribly, met it with calm resignation. He was buried in Westminster Abbey.

Samuel Johnson was a strange compound of disparate traits—indolent and industrious, kindly and irascible, superstitious and sensible. He was, as Ben Ray Redman called him in a book review, "a boor and a bully—a Tory of Tories." Macaulay remarked the dichotomy of his "kind and generous heart with his gloomy and irritable temper." As Louis Kronenberger has put it, he was "a scarred and sick and deeply melancholy man," half insane and in terror of madness all his life, yet a skeptic as well as a bigot, "ill humored but not ill natured," lonely, longing to be loved, a hater of cant, courageous, fiercely independent. "No man of such narrow views ever had broader sympathies," says Kronenberger. "He had a larger nature, a truer benignity, a profounder humaneness than any other English writer of his age."

As for the famous Latinate style, it is not always pompous, and Johnson was quite capable of simple, homely statement. To quote Thomas Seccombe, "He sacrificed expression rather too much to style, and was perhaps over conscious of the balanced epithet. But he contributed both dignity and dialectical force to the prose movement of his period." As a poet, he is nearer his model Juvenal than to any English poet; in the grand style of eighteenth century poetry Johnson is not the least considerable.

PRINCIPAL WORKS: A Voyage to Abyssinia (tr. from French) 1735; London: A Poem, 1738; Marmor Norfolciense, 1739; An Account of the Life of Mr. Richard Savage, 1744; An Account of the Life of John Philip Barretier, 1744; The Plan of a Dictionary of the English Language, 1747; The Vanity of Human Wishes (Poem) 1749; Irene: A Tragedy, 1749; The Rambler, 1752; A Dictionary of the English Language, 1755 (abridged, 1756); The Prince of Abissinia (Rasselas) 1759; The Idler, 1761; The Plays of Shakespeare (ed.) 1765; The False Alarm, 1770; The Patriot, 1774; Taxation No Tyranny, 1775; A Journey to the Western Islands of Scotland, 1775; The Works of the English Poets (ed.) 1779-81 (The Lives of the Most Eminent English Poets, 1781); Prayers and Meditations, 1785; Works (J. Hawkins, ed.) 1787-89; Letters to and from the Late Samuel Johnson, LL.D. (H. L. Piozzi, ed.) 1788; Sermons on Different Subjects (J. Taylor, ed.) 1788-89; An Account of the Life of Dr.

Samuel Johnson, from his birth to his eleventh year, written by himself (R. Wright, ed.) 1805; A Diary of a Journey to Wales (R. Duppa, ed.) 1816; Collected Works (9 vol.) 1825; Letters (G. B. Hill, ed.) 1897; The Portable Johnson and Boswell (L. Kronenberger, ed.) 1947.

ABOUT: Anderson, R. The Life of Samuel Johnson, LL.D.; Bailey, J. C. Dr. Johnson and His Circle; Boswell, J. Life of Samuel Johnson, LL.D.; Broadley, A. M. Dr. Johnson and Mrs. Thrale; Bronson, E. H. Johnson Agonistes and Other Essays (Johnson and Boswell); Brown, J. E. Critical Opinions of Dr. Johnson; Carlyle, T. Heroes and Hero-Worship; Croker, J. W. (ed.) Johnsoniana; Elwin, W. Some 18th Century Men of Letters; Hawkins, J. The Life of Samuel Johnson; Hill, G. B. Dr. Johnson, His Friends and His Critics; Hilles, F. W. ed. Age of Johnson; Hollis, C. Dr. Johnson; Houston, P. H. Dr. Johnson, A Study in 18th Century Humanism; Johnson, S. Account of [his] Life from his birth to his eleventh year; Kronenberger, L. Introduction, Portable Johnson and Boswell; Krutch, J. W. Samuel Johnson; Lunn, H. K. (Hugh Kingsmill) Johnson without Boswell, Samuel Johnson; Lynd, R. Dr. Johnson and Company; Macaulay, T. B. Biographies; McNair, Sir A. D. Dr. Johnson and the Law; Pearson, H. and Lunn, H. K. Skye High; Piozzi, H. L. Anecdotes of the late Samuel Johnson; Raby, J. T. (ed.) Bi-Centenary of the Birth of Dr. Samuel Johnson; Raleigh, W. Six Essays on Johnson; Reade, A. L. Johnsonian Gleanings; Roberts, S. C. Dr. Johnson; Roscoe, E. S. Aspects, of Dr. Johnson; Salpeter, H. Dr. Johnson and Mr. Boswell; Scott, W. Life of Johnson; Seccombe, T. The Age of Johnson; Smith, C. and N. Bibliography of the Works of Samuel Johnson; Stephen, L. Samuel Johnson; Struble, M. C. A Johnson Handbook; Vuliamy, C. E. Ursa Major: A Study of Dr. Johnson and His Friends; Watkins, W. B. C. Perilous Balance.

JONES, Sir WILLIAM (September 28, 1746-April 27, 1794), oriental scholar and philologist, was born in Westminster. The boy was only three when his father, William Jones the mathematician, died and his training was left to his very able mother. He entered Harrow School in 1753 where he became known as a brilliant scholar, mastering Latin, Greek, French, Italian, and the elements of Arabic and Hebrew before he was eighteen. Although he was recommended for law he rejected the idea of a law career on the ground that old English law books were frequently written in bad Latin, and entered University College, Oxford, in 1764. There he was elected a fellow of the College and graduated B.A. in 1768, taking his M.A. five years later.

While he was still a student Jones added to his slender income by acting as a tutor to Lord Althorp, son of the first Earl Spencer. During the six years of his connection with the Spencer family he made several trips on the Continent, studying Arabic, Persian and Chinese, as well as German, Spanish, and Portuguese. The first fruit of his lifelong interest in oriental languages came to maturity in two works, a translation from the Persian of a life of Nadir Shah, and a *Grammar of the Persian Language*, first published in 1771. Both books added to his growing prestige as an oriental scholar and won him membership in the Royal Society and the Literary Club of which Dr. Johnson was the moving spirit.

In spite of the brilliance of his reputation, however, Jones found his means insufficient and before he was thirty turned again to law. Called to the bar at the Middle Temple in 1774, he became a capable jurist and published a number of legal works. He interested himself also in politics but his liberal opinions, particularly his opposition to the American war, made him an unsuccessful candidate for Parliament.

Combining his two lines of interest Jones sought and finally obtained an appointment as judge of the high court in Calcutta. Knighted in 1783, he married Anna Maria Shipley and sailed for India where he found the opportunity to extend his oriental studies. Jones' contribution during his ten years in India were of inestimable importance both to the development of Anglo-Indian understanding and to philology. He founded the Bengal Asiatic Society and contributed to the society's publication *Asiatic Researches*, a monument in the study of Indian language, literature, and philosophy. He translated a number of Asiatic classics, bringing them for the first time to the attention of the English-speaking world. He was the first English scholar to master Sanskrit, laying a foundation stone in the science of comparative philology. Aiming to be "the Justinian of India" he projected and partially carried out a digest of Hindu and Mohammedan law. Jones died when he was only forty-eight leaving behind him a reputation both for extraordinary scholarship and for amiability of character.

PRINCIPAL WORKS: Grammar of the Persian Language, 1771; Poems Consisting Chiefly of Translations From the Asiatic Languages, 1772; The History of the Life of Nadir Shah, King of Persia (tr.) 1773; Poeseos Asiaticae Commentariorum Libri Six, 1774; The Speeches of Isaeus in Causes Concerning the Law of Property (tr.) 1779; The Muse Recalled, 1781; Essay on the Law of Bailments, 1781; The Moallakat, or the Seven

Arabian Poems Which Were Suspended on the Temple at Mecca, 1783; Discourses to the Bengal Asiatic Society, 1784-94; The Asiatic Miscellany Consisting of Original Productions, Fugitive Pieces, Imitations and Extracts, 1785-86; Sacontala, or The Fatal Ring: An Indian Drama by Calidas (tr.) 1789; Institutes of Hindu Law, 1796; Poetical Works, 1810.

ABOUT: Cary, H. F. Lives of English Poets; Shore, J. Memoirs of Sir William Jones.

JONSON, BEN (1572-August 6, 1637), dramatist, poet, was born in Westminster, London, where he now lies buried in the Poets' Corner of the Abbey. According to his own account, he was descended from the Johnstones of Annandale, Scotland, and he used their coat of arms. His paternal grandfather, he said, was a Scottish gentleman who entered the service of Henry VIII; his father, "having lost his fortune, became a minister." Jonson was born a month after his father's death. His mother's name is not known, but she was an energetic and redoubtable woman, for whom her son always had great respect; she died very old but still active. When the boy was two she married again, her second husband being a master bricklayer.

Jonson was christened Benjamin, but was always known as Ben. His stepfather sent him to a school in St. Martin's Lane, and after this he was enabled to enter Westminster School by the kindness of its master, William Camden. He was then apprenticed to his stepfather's trade; in all likelihood he never saw either Cambridge or Oxford until both conferred honorary degrees on him. Bricklaying was not much to his taste; he soon escaped by enlisting as a soldier, and served for a year or two in Flanders. About 1592 he was married, not happily. His wife, he said (her name is unknown), was "curst but honest"—that is, virtuous but a shrew. They had several children, none of whom survived him, and he seems to have had real affection for them, but for five years at least he and his wife were separated.

Somewhere around 1595 he first appeared as an actor in Philip Henslowe's company. He had no talent for acting, and Henslowe soon employed him primarily in his "stable" of playwrights. He collaborated with Dekker, Marston, Chapman, Chettle, and others, and he seems to have written some early tragedies of his own that have been lost. Later on he became a free lance, writing for

After G. Honthorst
BEN JONSON

various dramatic companies. He was still with Henslowe, however, when in 1598 he killed a fellow actor, Gabriel Spenser, in a duel. He escaped the gallows on a felony charge by pleading the right of clergy (i.e., that he could read and write), but he suffered confiscation of what goods he had, and branding on his right thumb. He endured no obloquy because of this mishap (any more than for his later imprisonments on political suspicions arising from his plays), and indeed it was at this very time that his first important and successful play, *Every Man in His Humour*, was first performed. It was at the Globe, and Shakespeare was one of the actors in it, as he was later in others of Jonson's plays.

While in prison, Jonson had been converted to the Roman Catholic Church. He remained in it for twelve years, when he reverted to Anglicanism. He was still a Catholic at the time of the Gunpowder Plot, in 1605, and documents discovered later prove that he was a government agent in its investigation.

Jonson was notoriously a quarrelsome man, sensitive and quick to take offense, though soon over his anger. While he was on the outs with anyone, his revenge always took the form of lampooning his enemy in a play. The first important victim of this sort of attack was Dekker, who retorted in *Satiro-Mastix*, but Jonson did not keep up

297

the feud. In the same way he quarreled later with both Marston and Chapman, yet both in the end became his friends and admirers. In fact, they wrote *Eastward Ho* together, and when his two collaborators were arrested because of alleged treasonable statements in the play, Jonson insisted on going to prison with them.

His great period, both artistically and in the matter of prosperity, was now beginning. Some of his greatest plays—*Volpone, The Silent Woman, The Alchemist, Bartholomew Fayre, Catiline*—belong to this decade. He was in high favor with James I, who engaged him as principal writer of all his masques—and Jonson boasted not without reason that nobody could write a masque as he could. This was the time when he was one of the immortal crew at the Mermaid Tavern—just as later he lorded it over the Apollo Room in the Devil Tavern, with the young men, his "sons, sealed to the tribe of Benjamin," sitting awestruck at his feet. He quarreled with his fellow writers as easily as ever, and he did not hesitate to criticize them all, but that does not mean that they were his enemies. Jonson was vain, but he was never jealous. Later commentators have built up an enmity between him and Shakespeare, which was all nonsense. Jonson did gibe at Shakespeare, but he also praised him warmly, and if they were never intimate friends, they were for the most part on good terms; though the story may or may not be true that Shakespeare died from the after-effects of a drinking bout with Jonson and Drayton.

James thought so highly of Jonson that he wanted to knight him, but Jonson refused. The king did give the poet a pension, though a small one. In 1613 Jonson had to supplement it by going to France as tutor to Sir Walter Raleigh's eldest son. Then in 1619 he made a triumphal tour of Scotland (this was when he met Drummond of Hawthornden), and he followed it by a trip to Oxford to receive his honorary M.A.

In the last fifteen years of Jonson's life his good fortune failed him. In 1623 all his books and unpublished manuscripts were destroyed by fire, an irreparable disaster. Then when James died in 1625 and was succeeded by Charles I, learning was more valued at court than was pageantry or wit, and Jonson, though not completely out of favor, was treated capriciously. He did have

his pension raised, after much difficulty, and he acted unofficially as Poet Laureate from 1629 on. (He seems never to have had the official title, though he received the Poet Laureate's pay, including the butt of canary.) In 1628 he was given the post of city chronologer; he regarded it as a sinecure, and lost it because he made no attempt to carry out its duties, but Charles ordered it restored. He had also secured the reversion of the Mastership of the Revels, in 1621, but he had no advantage of that, for he predeceased the incumbent Master.

Charles ordered no masques from him until 1628, and then Jonson quarreled so violently with Inigo Jones, who designed the scenery for them, that he was asked to write no more. His last plays were failures—Dryden called them "mere dotages." *The New Inne* was actually hissed off the stage before its ending. In 1626 and again in 1628 he suffered paralytic strokes, he became palsied and dropsical. He could drag his huge body to the Devil Tavern, with the help of his servant and "son," the poet Richard Brome, but his great days of hearty drinking and brilliant talk were over. His last work he left unfinished; it was the tender and beautiful *Sad Shepherd*, his only pastoral. When he was interred in Westminster Abbey, the troubles leading to the civil war had begun, and there was no one to build him a monument; the remark of Sir William Young, "O rare Ben Jonson!," was inscribed instead on the slab over his grave.

It is often said that Ben Jonson occupied the position in the seventeenth century held by Samuel Johnson in the eighteenth—that of literary dictator, final arbiter, critic, and patron. That is true, but temperamentally he reminds one still more of a (lesser) literary figure of the twentieth century, G. K. Chesterton. He was more vain and more quarrelsome, but he had Chesterton's physical bulk, bibulousness, scholarliness, brilliance, and ebullience. (Also, for a while, he shared Chesterton's religious faith.) He was in every sense of the word a great man. And yet he did not belong entirely to his time—he was at once a throwback and an anticipation.

Jonson lived in the midst of the Romantic Era, the Age of Elizabeth, yet he himself was a realist and a satirist, with no touch of the romantic about him. He was a conscious classicist, and his tragedies, *Catiline* and *Sejanus*, were written almost as propaganda for the Aristotelian rules of dramatic unity and for adherence to strict historical fact. He thought of himself primarily as a reformer of the stage, appointed to bring it back from the extravagance and eccentricity of the Romantic poets to realism and classicism. His great comedies were all written with the depiction of life as their aim—the important thing was not the plot or the poetry, but the characterization. It is not true that Jonson's characters in the comedies are merely types, each an embodiment of a "humor" or trait of personality, but he did emphasize these ruling passions, thus leading directly to the comedy of manners of the Restoration.

His masques are ingenious, elaborate, and (without their music, scenery, dances, and costumes) rather dull. In poetry again he was a strict classicist; he translated Horace's *Ars Poetica,* and he abode by its rules. As if by indirection, two or three limpid and tender lyrics, in the true Elizabethan mode, escape from his rather stiff verse; but the best (and best known) of these, *To Celia* ("Drink to me only with thine eyes") has been shown to be a free translation of Philostratus. It is only in the unfinished pastoral he left behind him that he is completely fresh and charming. In his comedies Jonson reads almost like an eighteenth century writer. And he is very English; no matter where his plays are laid, their heart is in London.

Not only are many of his early plays lost, but also some of his poetry—many of the *Epigrams,* and a *Discourse on Love.* One folio of his miscellaneous works was published during his lifetime, in 1616, another in 1640. Relatively few of his plays, and little of his poetry, were published separately. Of all his work, *Volpone* remains most durable, having enjoyed current revival on both stage and screen.

PRINCIPAL WORKS: *Plays* (dates of publication): Every Man Out of his Humour, 1600; Every Man in his Humour, 1601; The Fountaine of Selfe-Love, or Cynthias Revels, 1601; The Poetaster, 1602; Sejanus his fall, 1605; Volpone Or the Foxe, 1609; The Case is Alterd, 1609; Catiline his Conspiracy, 1611; The Alchemist, 1612; Epicœne, Or, the Silent Woman, 1620; The New Inne, 1629; Bartholomew Fayre, 1631; The Magnetick Lady, 1640. *Masques:* Masque of Blacknesse, 1605; Hymenaei, 1606; The Characters of Two Royall Masques, 1608; The Masque of Queenes, 1609; Lovers Made Men, 1617; The Masque of Augures, 1621; Neptunes Triumph, 1623; The Fortunate Isle, 1624; Loves Triumph through Callipolis, 1630; Chloridia, 1630. *Miscellaneous:* The Workes of Ben Jonson (the 1616 and 1640 folios) including (besides plays and masques): Underwoods (verse), The Forrest (verse), Horace, His Art of Poetrie, The English Grammar, Timber, Or, Discoveries made upon Men and Matters, The Execration against Vulcan (verse), Epigrams (verse); Works (W. Gifford, ed.) 1816 (F. Cunningham, ed. 1875).

ABOUT: Aubrey, J. Letters Written by Eminent People; Baudissire, W. H. T. Ben Jonson und seine Schule; Bentley, G. E. Shakespeare and Jonson; Castelain, M. Ben Jonson: l'Homme et l'œuvre; Chetwood, W. R. Memoirs of the Life and Writings of Ben Jonson; Drummond of Hawthornden, W. Conversations with Ben Jonson; Dryden, J. Essay on Dramatic Poetry; Fuller, T. Worthies of England; Gifford, W. Biographical Memoir, Works, 1816 ed.; Gosse, E. 17th Century Studies; Greenwood, G. G. Ben Jonson and Shakespeare; Hazlitt, W. Lectures on the Dramatic Literature of the Age of Elizabeth; Johnston, G. B. Ben Jonson: Poet; Linklater, E. Ben Jonson and King James; Palmer, J. L. Ben Jonson; Schelling, F. E. Elizabethan Drama; Smith, G. G. Ben Jonson; Steegmüller, F. (Byron Steele) O Rare Ben Jonson; Stoll, E. E. Poets and Playwrights; Swinburne, A. C. A Study of Ben Jonson; Symonds, J. A. Ben Jonson; Wendell, B. The Temper of the 17th Century in English Literature.

"JUNIUS." See FRANCIS, Sir PHILIP

JUNIUS, FRANCISCUS, FRANCIS, FRANZ, or DU JON, FRANÇOIS (1589-November 19, 1677), philologist, antiquary, was born in Heidelberg, the son of a French Huguenot theologian, Francis Junius (or Du Jon). When the boy was three or four years old the family moved to Leyden where he was under the tutelage of a circle of distinguished men, among them his father and his brother-in-law, Gerhard Johann Vossius. The latter had a strong influence on his mind and guided his interests into the field of philology at an early age.

Junius first visited England in 1621, after serving as pastor at Hillegondsberg for several years. There he met Thomas Howard, the Earl of Arundel, who employed him as librarian and tutor. In this position he had easy access to the Bodleian Library and was able to learn Anglo-Saxon, which had long interested him in connection with a comparative study of Teutonic and northern languages. Junius was an indefatigable scholar whose custom it was to rise at four and work steadily until one in the afternoon and again, after an hour or two of recreation, from three until eight in the evening. This scholarly routine was broken by several years of European travel as tutor to the family of the Earl of Oxford. After a visit to his sister in the Netherlands, he determined to leave England in 1651 and live with her in Amsterdam and The Hague. During this residence he found the opportunity to visit Friesland, studying the Friesian language.

Junius' first publication was an impressive three-volume work, *De Pictura Veterum Libri Tres,* printed in 1638. This was followed by a number of philological works, an edition of Caedmon, and an extremely valuable Gothic glossary, all of which were published between the years 1655 and 1665. His *Etymologicum Anglicanum,* first edited and published in 1743, was used by Dr. Johnson for the etymologies in his *Dictionary.*

Junius returned to England in 1674 and three years later went to live with his nephew, Dr. Isaac Vossius, canon of Windsor. He died at Windsor at eighty-eight, leaving his valuable philological collections to the Bodleian. He also left a unique collection of Gothic and Saxon type to Oxford to be used by the Oxford Press.

PRINCIPAL WORKS: De Pictura Veterum Libri Tres, 1638; Caedmonis Monachi Paraphrasis Poetica Genesios (ed.) 1655; Gothicum Glossarium, Quo Argentii Codicis Vocabula Explicantur, 1664; Moeso-Gothic Text of Ulphilas (ed.) 1665; Quatuor D.N.I.C. Evangeliorum Versiones Perantiquae Duae, Gothica Scilicet et Anglo-Saxonica (tr. and ed. with Thomas Marshall) 1665; Etymologicum Anglicanum (E. Lye, ed.) 1743.

ABOUT: Graevius, J. G. Life, *in* De Pictura Veterum; Lye, E. Life, *in* Etymologicum Anglicanum; Wood, A. à, Athenae Oxonienses.

KAMES, Lord. See HOME, HENRY

KELLY, HUGH (1739-February 3, 1777), dramatist, miscellaneous writer, was the son of a Dublin tavern keeper, born in Killarney. Although he had little education, he acquired an early appreciation of literature and drama from the actors who frequented his father's tavern. Among them were several English actors who recognized the young man's talents and urged him to go to London for a literary career.

Kelly arrived in London in 1760 and set up shop as a staymaker. His theatrical friends brought him a steady stream of business but his unskilled workmanship lost him

old customers as fast as new ones appeared. Forsaking corsets, he began to contribute to newspapers and in 1761 became an editor of two publications, the *Court Magazine* and the *Ladies' Museum.* With chambers in Middle Temple Lane, Kelly settled down to the career of a hard working literary hack, writing essays, verse, a novel, theatrical criticism, and finally drama.

David Garrick encouraged him to write his first comedy, *False Delicacy,* which was finished in 1768. Garrick at this time was in difficulties with Oliver Goldsmith, whose *Good-Natured Man* was nearly ready for production, and as a threat to Goldsmith he made himself loving sponsor to Kelly's play. *False Delicacy* was produced at the Drury Lane six days before *The Good-Natured Man* went on at the Covent Garden. Bolstered by the much publicized rivalry between the two dramatists, Kelly's play achieved a great success, although as Johnson was not slow to point out this moralistic little comedy-drama was "totally devoid of character."

Small and fat, fond of food and drink, the new playwright enjoyed his success to the full, appearing publicly in "a flaming broad silver-laced waistcoat, bag-wig, and sword."

Kelly wrote a second comedy, *A Word to the Wise,* no less insipid and equally successful, which provoked riots between his friends and his political opponents and was finally run off the stage. Three other plays, a verse tragedy *Clementina, A School for Wives,* and *The Man of Reason* were produced during the next five years. After the production of the latter play, which was roundly damned, Kelly gave up playwriting to study law. He was called to the bar in 1774 and practiced at Old Bailey and Middlesex Sessions. Although he had made a considerable fortune on his plays, his law career proved a failure and he went heavily into debt. He died when he was only thirty-eight, leaving a widow and five children.

PRINCIPAL WORKS: *Plays:* False Delicacy, 1768; A Word to the Wise, 1770; Clementina, 1771; The School for Wives, 1774. *Miscellaneous:* Thespis: or, A Critical Examination into the Merits of All the Principal Performers Belonging to Drury Lane Theater, 1766; Thespis: or, A Critical Examination into the Merits of All the Principal Performers Belonging to Covent Garden Theater, 1767; Memoirs of a Magdalen, 1767; The Babler, 1767; The Works of Hugh Kelly, 1778.

ABOUT: Life, *in* The Works of Hugh Kelly; Baker, D. E. Biographia Dramatica; Schorer, M. Hugh Kelly: His Place in the Sentimental School, Philological Quarterly 1933.

KEN or KENN, THOMAS (July 1637-March 19, 1711), one of the fathers of English hymnology, bishop of Bath and Wells, was born at Berkhampstead, Hertfordshire. His father was Thomas Ken, an attorney at Furnival's Inn, London, and his mother was the daughter of the poet, John Chalkhill. Both his parents died before he was fourteen and it seems probable that he went to live in the home of Izaak Walton who had married his half-sister, Anne, in 1646. Ken was educated at Winchester and New College, Oxford, graduating B.A. in 1661 and taking an M.A. three years later.

He began his ecclesiastical career in 1663 as rector of Little Easton, Essex, moving upward in the next six years to the prebendary of Winchester. There he took delight in playing the organ and began to compose the hymns which have made his name known throughout the Protestant world. In 1674 he published his *Manual for Winchester Scholars,* which contained the well-loved morning, evening, and midnight hymns. The closing verse of one of these hymns beginning "Praise God from whom all blessings flow" is still sung in Protestant churches as the Doxology.

After receiving the degree of D.D. in 1679 he was appointed chaplain to Princess Mary, sister of the king and wife of William II, Prince of Orange. He lived at The Hague for a time but difficulties in his relations with the Prince led him to return to England. The story is told that when King Charles came to visit Winchester in 1683 Ken refused his residence to Nell Gwynne, the king's mistress, saying "A woman of ill repute ought not to be endured in the house of a clergyman." A year later Charles sought him out as "the good little man who refused his lodging to poor Nell," and appointed him bishop of Bath and Wells.

Ken was one of the seven non-juring bishops who refused to publish the "Declaration of Indulgence" reissued by James II in 1688. For this he was committeed to the Tower on a charge of high misdemeanor. After his acquittal came the revolution and William of Orange ascended the throne. When Ken refused to take the oath of allegiance to the new king he was relieved of his bishopric. The last years of his life were spent with Thomas Lord Weymouth, a college friend, at Longleat, Wiltshire. The good man died when he was seventy-three, leaving behind a few notable sermons and letters, some rather undistinguished poetry, and the three great hymns.

PRINCIPAL WORKS: Manual of Prayers for the Use of Winchester Scholars, 1674; Hymns for Morning, Evening, Midnight, 1695; The Works, Published from Original Manuscripts (W. Hawkins, ed.) 1721; The Prose Works (J. T. Round, ed.) 1838.

ABOUT: Bowles, W. L. The Life of Thomas Ken; Gilman, F. G. The Evolution of the English Hymn; Hawkins, W. Life, *in* The Works; Plumpter, S. H. The Life of Thomas Ken.

KENNEDY, WALTER (1460?-1508?), Scottish poet, was born into one of the most prominent noble families of western Scotland. Through his grandmother, Mary, a daughter of Robert III, he was directly related to the royal house. His father was Gilbert, the first Lord Kennedy. His uncle, James Kennedy, was bishop of St. Andrews and a regent during the minority of James III. A niece, Janet, became the mistress of James IV who created her Lady Bothwell and granted her the castle and forest of Darnaway.

Walter entered Glasgow College in 1475, taking a B.A. and an M.A., and in 1481 was elected an examiner. From evidence in his poems it seems likely that he took holy orders and he was probably the Walter Kennedy who became provost of Maybole in Ayrshire, a collegiate church founded by one of his ancestors.

Not much of Kennedy's poetry survives. His most important work, as well as the few biographical facts we have, are to be found in *The Flyting of Dunbar and Kennedie,* written about 1504. Chiefly antiquarian in interest, this curious work is a versified battle between the two poets, Kennedy and William Dunbar. Written in a spirit of rough fun, the poem consists of a lively exchange of taunts which expresses not only the different opinions of two men but the rivalry between the English east of Scotland and the Gaelic west. Dunbar considered his rival a half-barbarous Celt who wore highland dress and spoke the Gaelic dialect. He describes Kennedy as looking like a leper with a lean neck, a shriveled throat and a dry, yellow skin. Kennedy, on the other hand, as a devout man and a staunch adherent of old doctrines, accuses Dunbar of favoring the English influence of the reforming Lollards.

References in the work of other Scottish poets indicate that Kennedy was highly esteemed by his contemporaries. Unfortunately for modern readers, the five poems which survive in manuscript are for the most part conventional and dull, and his reputation must rest on the portions of *The Flyting* attributed to his authorship.

The approximate date of the poet's death is marked by two lines in Dunbar's *Lament for the Makaris,* written before 1508: "Good Maister Walter Kennedy in poynt of dede lies verraly."

PRINCIPAL WORKS: The Praise of Age (Bannatyne and Maitland MSS.); Ane Agit Manis Invective Against Mouth Thankless (Bannatyne and Maitland MSS.); Ane Ballat in Praise of Our Lady (Asloane MS.); Pious Counsale (Bannatyne and Maitland MSS.); The Passioun of Christ (Howard MS.); The Flyting of Dunbar and Kennedie, in Scottish Poems (Chepman and Myllar, eds.) 1508 (G. Stevenson, ed. 1918); Collected Poems, *in* The Poems of William Dunbar and the Minor Makars (D. Lang, ed.) 1834.

ABOUT: Laing, D. Notes and Memoirs, *in* Poems of William Dunbar.

KID, THOMAS. See KYD, THOMAS

KILLIGREW, HENRY (February 11, 1613-March 14, 1700), author of a play *The Conspiracy,* was born at the manor of Hanworth near Hampton Court. His mother, Mary, was the daughter of Sir Henry Woodhouse and his father was Sir Robert Killigrew. Under the tutorship of Thomas Farnaby he entered Christ Church, Oxford, in 1628 where he took his B.A. and M.A. degrees and some years later a D.D.

Killigrew wrote *The Conspiracy* to be performed before the court in celebration of the marriage of the eldest son of the Earl of Pembroke and the daughter of the Duke of Buckingham. The play was registered at Stationer's Hall in March 1638, and the same year was published in an imperfect version while Killigrew was traveling in Italy. Fifteen years later the author published a corrected version under the new title, *Pallantus and Eudora.*

During the civil war Killigrew acted as chaplain to the king's army and subsequently to James, Duke of York. The Restoration brought him several posts of honor, among them the rectorship of Wheathamstead, Hertfordshire. In 1663 he was appointed master of the Savoy Hospital, a famous charitable institution in London. Apparently there was a good deal of graft involved under his administration and some authorities attribute the final ruin of the Savoy to Killigrew's improvidence. Other evidence, however, has shown him to be a conscientious and charitable administrator, and it is possible that the greed of Charles II was responsible for the ousting of its chaplains and the dissolution of the Savoy in 1702, two years after Killigrew's death.

Killigrew had two brothers, Thomas, and Sir William, who were also dramatists. By his wife, Judith, he had a number of children, three of whom, Anne, Henry, and James, carried on distinguished careers of their own. *The Conspiracy,* his one play, shows considerable skill and, since he was in his early twenties when he wrote it, gave signs of a promise which was never developed. According to the preface, Ben Jonson praised the play, and Sir Charles Sedley, the Courtier poet, later made an adaptation titled *The Tyrant King of Crete.*

PRINCIPAL WORKS: The Conspiracy, 1638; Pallantius and Eudora (a version of The Conspiracy) 1658; Sermons, 1685.

ABOUT: Genest, J. History of the English Stage; Loftie, W. J. Memorials of the Savoy; Wood, A. à Athenae Oxonienses.

KILLIGREW, THOMAS (the elder) (February 7, 1612-March 19, 1683), dramatist, was born in London, the son of Sir Robert Killigrew and Mary Woodhouse. In 1633 he became a page in the court of Charles I, and remained a favorite of the king and later of his son Charles II. As a Royalist, he was imprisoned from 1642 to 1644, then joined the king, first at Oxford and then in Paris. In 1651 Charles made him English resident in Venice, but was forced to recall him because Killigrew's debauchery and financial irregularities caused a scandal. With the Restoration he became a fixture at the court, as a groom of the bedchamber. Pepys says that he was actually and formally the king's jester, with cap and bells; this seems unlikely for a man of Killigrew's social class, but it is certainly true that he used absolute freedom of speech

After Sir A. Van Dyck
THOMAS KILLIGREW THE ELDER

with Charles, who disliked criticism but was disarmed by Killigrew's ready wit.

Most of Killigrew's plays were written and some were acted before the civil war and before the Puritans closed the theatres. His passion for the theatre had begun in boyhood, when he used to volunteer as an "extra." Charles gave Killigrew and D'Avenant licenses to erect new theatres, to the anger of Sir Henry Herbert, who had had a monopoly as master of the king's revels. D'Avenant continued the feud, but Killigrew compromised with Herbert, and in 1673, on Herbert's death, succeeded him. Meanwhile he had established his own theatre, the Red Bull, later Drury Lane. He died in London and was buried in Westminster.

Killigrew was twice married, in 1636 to Cecilia Crofts, who died in 1638, leaving one son, and in 1654 to Charlotte de Hesse, a Hollander, who after being naturalized became, in 1662, first lady of the queen's privy chamber. By his second marriage he had four sons and two daughters, one of whom was Thomas Killigrew the younger.*qv* His two brothers, Sir William and Henry, also wrote plays.

Thomas Killigrew's most popular play was *The Parson's Wedding*, an exceedingly obscene but also a very amusing comedy. It was always acted exclusively by women, even in the men's parts, to permit it to be produced at all. In general, Killigrew was not much of a dramatist; some of his so-called plays were not meant to be acted, but only to be read, and he borrowed far and wide for his plots. Though Pepys enjoyed the plays, and called Killigrew a "merry droll," actually he was far more noted for his spoken repartee than for anything he wrote. Sir John Denham expressed the general opinion in a couplet:

> Had Cowley ne'er spoke, Killigrew
> ne'er writ,
> Combined on one, they'd made a
> matchless wit.

PRINCIPAL WORKS (dates of publication): The Prisoners, and Claracilla, two tragaecomedies, 1641; Comedies and Tragedies (including Bellamira her Dream, The Pilgrim, The Princess, Thomaso, or, the Wanderer) 1664.

ABOUT: Harbage, A. Thomas Killigrew, Cavalier Dramatist; Pepys, S. Diary; Summers, M. The Playhouse of Pepys.

KILLIGREW, THOMAS (the younger) (February 1657-July 1719), author of a comedy, *Chit Chat,* was born in London, the son of Thomas Killigrew the elder and his second wife, Charlotte de Hesse. Practically nothing is known of his life—not even if he was married—beyond the fact that he was a gentleman of the bedchamber to the Prince of Wales, later George II, and that in 1692 he fought a duel which attracted some attention.

Killigrew played a bit at writing, and the year after his death a story by him appeared in an anthology. Aside from this, his only known production was *Chit Chat,* which, though amusing in a pleasant, gossipy way, had no plot and could hardly be called anything but a prolonged dialogue—exactly what its name implied.

This piece of writing was published early in 1719 and dedicated to the Duke of Argyll, who was so gratified that he procured its production at the Drury Lane (Killigrew's father's theatre), and "press agented" it so well that it brought its author upwards of a thousand pounds. Colley Cibber and the famous Mrs. Oldfield were among the actors. This was in February, and five months later Killigrew died.

PRINCIPAL WORKS: Chit Chat, a Comedy, 1719; The Fable of Aumilius and the Statue of Venus (*in* Miscellanea Aurea, or the Golden Miscellany) 1720.

ABOUT: Baker, D. E. Biographia Dramatica; Genest, J. Some Account of the English Stage from 1660 to 1830.

KILLIGREW, Sir WILLIAM (1606-October 1695), dramatist, was the eldest of three playwriting brothers belonging to a noble Cornish family. Son and heir of Sir Robert Killigrew, he was baptized at Hanworth, Middlesex, on May 28, 1606, and entered St. John's College, Oxford, in 1623. Three years later he was knighted and after leaving the university, made the customary "grand tour" of Europe.

Like his brothers, Thomas and Henry Killigrew, Sir William was an intimate of the court of Charles I. He served as gentleman-usher to the king and commanded one of the troops of horse guarding the monarch during the civil war. Among his numerous posts of honor was the governorship of Pendennis Castle and Falmouth Haven. He was twice elected to Parliament, the first time in 1628 and again after the Restoration in 1642. Charles II restored him to his former post as gentleman-usher of the privy chamber and later appointed him vice chamberlain to Queen Catherine, a position which he held for twenty-two years.

Sir William was the author of *Three Playes: Selindra, Pandora,* and *Ormasdes,* first published in 1665. *Selindra,* a tragicomedy, was performed at the Theatre Royal. *Pandora,* presumably written as a tragedy, was played as a comedy at Lincoln's Fields Theatre where it enjoyed considerable success. So far as the records show, the third play, *Ormasdes* was never produced. In 1666 he published a second collection of plays, reprinting *Selindra* and *Pandora,* and adding a new version of *Ormasdes* rewritten under the influence of heroic drama and titled *Love and Friendship.* The only completely new drama in this collection was *The Siege of Urbin,* which has been fairly described as "a capable and sympathetic play."

He was also author of miscellaneous works of prose and verse, two collections of which were published. After the year 1682 Sir William took no further part in the life of the court and little more is known of his life. He died in 1695, leaving a widow and four children, and was buried in the Savoy Chapel.

PRINCIPAL WORKS: Three Playes: Selindra, Pandora, Ormasdes, 1664; Four New Playes: The Siege of Urbin, Selindra, Love and Friendship, Pandora, 1666; Midnight Thought, By a Person of Quality, 1681; Midnight and Daily Thoughts in Prose and Verse, 1694.

ABOUT: Boase, G. C. and Courtney, W. P. Bibliotheca Cornubiensis; Genest, J. History of the English Stage; Lawrence, W. J. Sir William Killigrew's The Siege of Urbin, Times Literary Supplement, October 1928.

KINASTON, Sir FRANCIS. See KYNASTON, Sir FRANCIS

KING, HENRY (1592-September 30, 1669), poet, bishop of Chichester, was the eldest son of John King, bishop of London, and the great-grandnephew of Robert King, first bishop of Oxford. The exact date of his birth is unknown but according to the records he was baptized at Worminghall, Buckinghamshire, on January 16, 1592. Educated at Westminster and Christ Church, Oxford, where he took his B.S. in 1611 and his M.A. three years later, Henry was appointed to the Prebendary of St. Pancras, St. Paul's Cathedral.

King's rise in the order of the clergy was steady and before his eventual advance to the episcopal bench he held many preferments, among them the rectory of Chigwell, Essex, the archdeaconry of Colchester, the rectory of Fulham, and a royal chaplainship. When he was thirty-one he was made a canon of Christ Church; fifteen years later he became dean of Rochester; and in 1641 he was given the see of Chichester along with the rectory of Petworth in Sussex.

A collection of poems written by him was first published in 1657. Along with the writings of Richard Corbett, bishop of Oxford and Norwich, King's work is a good example of the upper-class poetic taste of the day. An intimate friend of both Ben Jonson and John Donne, he owed his poetic inspiration more to the former, but he was undoubtedly very close to Donne, and served as executor for his estate. He was also a good friend of George Sandys, Sir Henry Blount, and Izaak Walton. King was married to Anne Berkeley and had several children by her. She died when she was only twenty-four and one of his loveliest poems is an elegy written for her.

When Chichester was surrendered to Parliament in 1643, Bishop King's library was seized and his estates sequestrated. For the next seventeen years he lived in virtual retirement with friends and relatives. In

1660 he returned to Chichester, where he died at the age of seventy-seven.

PRINCIPAL WORKS: Psalmes of David Turned Into Meter, 1651; Poems, Elegies, Paradoxes, and Sonnets, 1657; Sacred Poems (J. Hannah, ed.) 1843; Selected Profane Poems (J. R. Tutin, ed.) 1904; The Poems of Bishop Henry King (J. Sparrow, ed.) 1925.

ABOUT: Hannah, J. Biographical Preface, in Sacred Poems; Mason, L. The Life and Works of Henry King.

KING, WILLIAM (May 1, 1650-May 8, 1729), archbishop of Dublin, religious writer, was born in Antrim, Ireland, the son of James King, an Aberdeen man. He was a student of Trinity College, Dublin, taking his B.A. in 1670 and his M.A. in 1673. The following year he was ordained a priest and held several ecclesiastical posts, receiving an appointment as dean of St. Patrick's in 1689.

An Irish patriot and a Whig, he was at the same time a high churchman, fighting to prevent the spread of Roman Catholicism on the one hand, and battling against Presbyterianism on the other. Under the Jacobite government he was arrested and imprisoned for a time. After the revolution, as bishop of Derry, he worked to erase the scars of war and restore the church to efficiency and respectability. In 1691 he published *The State of the Protestants in Ireland under King James's Government*, an able analysis of the principles of the revolution.

In 1702 he was made archbishop of Dublin. As an ardent believer in the rights of the Church of Ireland, he came to know Swift well, and carried on a voluminous correspondence with both Swift and Parnell. In King's opinion, Swift was a clergyman of highly unclerical habits, of considerable ability, but of overweening egotism.

Bishop King's chief work was *De Origine Mali*, published both in Dublin and in London in 1702, and dedicated to Sir Robert Southwell. An attempt to reconcile the existence of evil with the idea of an omnipotent and beneficent deity, *De Origine Mali* attracted considerable attention on the continent, but was largely neglected in England until it was translated by Edmund Law in 1729. It seems probable that King's book was carefully read by Pope and influenced the *Essay on Man*.

After having once been reported dead at the age of forty-six when the rumor was spread that a severe attack of gout had proved fatal, King lived to be seventy-nine. He died, unmarried, leaving nearly £17,000 to public charities.

PRINCIPAL WORKS: The State of the Protestants in Ireland Under King James's Government, 1691; De Origine Mali, 1702 (E. Law, tr. 1729); A Key to Divinity, or a Philosophical Essay on Free Will, 1715.

ABOUT: King, Sir C. S. A Great Archbishop of Dublin, William King; Ware, Sir J. The History of the Bishops of Ireland (W. Harris, ed.).

KING, WILLIAM (1663-December 25, 1712), miscellaneous writer, humorist, was the son of Ezekiel King, the owner of a small estate in Middlesex, who resided in London. He was educated at the Westminster School and at Christ Church, Oxford, taking a B.A. degree in 1685 and an M.A. in 1688. Four years later he took the degree of a Doctor of Civil Law and became an advocate at Doctor's Commons.

Dr. King's talents as a humorous writer were first displayed in the amusing *Dialogue Shewing the Way to Modern Preferment* published in 1690. He next published *Animadversions on a Pretended Account of Denmark*, a reply to an attack on the Danish system of government written by Robert Molesworth, a Whig, in return for which Prince George of Denmark obtained for him an appointment as secretary to Princess Anne. During the next few years he carried on a controversy, along with Swift and others, against Richard Bentley over the genuineness of the *Epistles of Phalaris*. His *Dialogues of the Dead*, published in 1699, was a clever attack on Bentley. In the same year there appeared his *A Journey to London in the Year 1698*, a travesty on a then current book on Paris, which King considered his best work.

In 1701 King was appointed a judge of the admiralty court in Ireland, but apparently he devoted more time to writing burlesque poems (among them *Molly of Mountown* and *Orpheus and Eurydice*) than to his duties on the bench. He was appointed keeper of the records for Birmingham Tower at Dublin Castle, but again he refused to take his duties seriously and resigned to return to England. Having spent all his small private fortune, King was now forced to eke out a precarious living by writing poems and pamphlets. In 1708 he was paid £32 5s for *The Art of Cookery, in Imitation of Horace's Art* of Poetry, and a year later he received the same amount of *The Art of Love, in Imitation of Ovid*. Debts piled up and he was apparently confined in Fleet prison for a time, until Swift recommended him to succeed Steele as a gazetteer at £200 a year. He resigned in 1712 and lived with friends and relatives until his death.

Both in his life and in his work Dr. King was a strict Tory and a high churchman, although found of drink and convivial companionship. (Pope wrote of him "I remember Dr. King would write verses in a tavern three hours after he could not speak.") His *Useful Miscellanies*, a collection of verse and prose published in 1712, reveals the contradictory sides of his personality and remains a curious and amusing compilation of his scattered works.

PRINCIPAL WORKS: A Dialogue Shewing the Way to Modern Preferment, 1690; Animadversions on a Pretended Account of Denmark, 1694; A Journey to London in the Year 1698, 1698; Dialogues of the Dead, 1699; The Transactioner, with some of His Philosophical Fancies, 1700; Miscellanies in Prose and Verse, 1705; The Art of Cookery, in Imitation of Horace's Art of Poetry, 1708; The Art of Love, in Imitation of Ovid, 1709; Useful Transactions in Philosophy and Other Sorts of Learning, 1709; Useful Miscellanies, 1712; Remains of Dr. William King (J. Brown, ed.) 1732; The Original Works of William King (J. Nichols, ed.) 1776; The Poetical Works of Dr. King, 1781.

ABOUT: Johnson, Samuel. The Lives of the Poets; Nichols, J. Memoir, *in* Original Works; Williams, G. G. Dr. William King, Humorist, Sewanee Review, 1927.

KIRKE, EDWARD (1553-November 10, 1613), critic, friend of Edmund Spenser, is remembered for his commentary on Spenser's *Shepheards Calendar*, the first "critical introduction" in English literature. Little is known of his life. He entered Pembroke Hall, Cambridge, as a sizar in 1571, and there made friends with Spenser and Gabriel Harvey. Transferring to Caius College, he graduated B.A. in 1574 and took his M.A. degree three years later.

Ordained as a minister, Kirke was presented by his patron, Sir Thomas Kynaston, to the rectory of Risby, Suffolk, in 1580. Seven years later he was also made rector of Lackford. The few facts relevant to his life and work are drawn largely from the three-way correspondence between Spenser, Gabriel Harvey, and Kirke. From these letters it has been satisfactorily established that the

E. K. who provided a preface and commentary to Spenser's *The Shepheards Calendar* was indeed Edward Kirke, and not Spenser himself as some critics have maintained.

The Shepheards Calendar, first published anonymously and inscribed to Sir Philip Sidney, appeared in 1579. It opened with E. K.'s preface addressed to "his verie special and singular good friend," Gabriel Harvey, in which the writer praised the poet whose worthiness "shall soon be sounded by the trump of Fame." The preface falls into two parts: the first, a defense of the poet's archaic diction; the second, a description of the whole pattern of the poem, supplying argument, notes and commentary. According to the evidence in a letter from Spenser to Harvey, Kirke may also have edited another of Spenser's works in the same manner. This was perhaps *Muiotaphia* or *Visions of Du Bellay*, although more probably it is one of the lost works.

Kirke died at Risby in his sixtieth year. His widow, Helen, was named as executrix of his will and there is also mention of a son-in-law, Richard Buckle, and a godson, John Kirke, possibly the dramatist.

PRINCIPAL WORKS: Introduction and Notes to Shepheards Calendar by Edmund Spenser, 1579 (H. O. Sommer, ed. 1890).

ABOUT: Letters and Notes *in* Spenser's Works (A. B. Grosart, ed.).

KNOLLES, RICHARD (1550?-1610), author of *Generall Historie of the Turkes*, was probably the son of Francis Knolles, or Knowles, of Cold Ashby, Northamptonshire. The records show that he attended Lincoln College, Oxford, graduating B.A. in 1564-5, and taking an M.A. degree five years later. Elected a fellow of his college, he remained in residence until Sir Peter Manwood heard of his abilities and called him from the university to take the mastership of a grammar school at Sandwich, Kent. Manwood also encouraged him to write his *Generall Historie of the Turkes*, which after twelve years of scholarly labor was published in 1603.

Knolles' monumental work, 1200 pages in folio, is of little historical value but is an interesting example of the prose style of the period, ornate and colored with fabulous detail. Although the author lists a number of Byzantine authorities, his chief source seems to have been Boissard's *Vitae et Icones*

Sultanoram Turcicorum. The book went through numerous editions and was highly praised by no less a critic than Dr. Johnson, who wrote "None of our writers can in my opinion justly contest the superiority of Knolles, who in his *History of the Turks* has displayed all the excellencies that narration can admit. His style, though somewhat obscured by time, and sometimes vitiated by false wit, is pure, nervous, elevated, and clear." Knolles' limited reputation Johnson attributed to his choice of a subject "of which none desire to be informed."

A later admirer of Knolles' book was Lord Byron, who noted shortly before his death, "Old Knolles was one of the first books that gave me pleasure when a child; and I believe it had much influence on my future wishes to visit the Levant, and gave perhaps the oriental coloring which is observed in my poetry."

Apart from one or two translations, Knolles wrote only the *History*, devoting the greater part of his time to teaching. He died at Sandwich and was buried in St. Mary's Church on July 2, 1610, "leaving behind him the character of an industrious, learned, and religious person."

PRINCIPAL WORKS: The Generall Historie of the Turkes From the First Beginning of that Nation, 1603.

ABOUT: Wood, A. à, Athenae Oxonienses.

KNOX, JOHN (1505?-November 24, 1572), minister, religious writer, was born in Haddington, East Lothian, Scotland, the son of William Knox, a peasant farmer. His mother's maiden name was Sinclair. In 1522 he went to Glasgow University, but left without a degree. He studied law as well as divinity, and for some time acted as a notary, which means he must have been in minor orders of the church, as were all notaries at that time. He then became a tutor to the sons of the members of a group which was beginning to be affected by the ideas of the Reformation. Knox himself was converted by George Wishart, who was burnt at the stake in 1546. His execution led to the assassination of Cardinal Beaton, and Knox's employers (including Sir David Lindsay), who were sympathizers with the assassination, entrenched themselves in Beaton's Castle St. Andrews, with Knox as their minister. The French captured the castle, and all in it, including Knox, were taken prisoner and sent to the galleys at Rouen in 1548. The next year, on their release, he went to England, where under Edward VI he was permitted to preach—indeed he is said to have been offered and to have declined the bishopric of Rochester.

With Mary's accession in 1553, however, England became untenable for him, and he fled first to Dieppe, then to Geneva, where he met Calvin, thereafter his guide and leader. For the next year or two he was minister of the English exiles in Frankfort, then after two surreptitious visits to Scotland he returned to Geneva. In 1559 he came back to Scotland, where after a year of fighting and constant danger the Protestants were able to effect a compromise whereby they were tolerated and permitted to preach. During these years Mary of Lorraine had been regent of Scotland for her daughter, Mary, Queen of Scots—both of them, of course, being Roman Catholics. Mary now came to Scotland, and her long quarrel with Knox began, ended only by her abdication in 1567. Knox by this time was the undisputed head of the Calvinists or Presbyterians in Scotland, and in some sense almost a rival of the queen herself. In 1570 he suffered a stroke of apolexy, and he finally died in Edinburgh two years later.

Two of Knox's many books—all brought out by immediate practical occasions—were

JOHN KNOX

outstandingly important. One was his *First Blast of the Trumpet against the Monstruous Regiment of Women,* which earned him the enmity of Elizabeth, though it was the Roman Catholic queens, Mary Tudor, Mary of Lorraine, and Catherine de Medici, against whom he inveighed. The other was his *History of the Reformation in Scotland,* vivid, vigorous, and by far his most noted work from a literary standpoint. It was Knox also who gave Scotland its bent toward education—"a school in every parish, a college in every town, three universities, all state-owned and free"—and all making education completely subservient to piety.

This narrow, bigoted, harsh man, who was yet completely direct and single-minded, epitomized in himself the dour strictness which later became the hallmark of Puritanism. He was capable of tenderness, and he had a keen sense of humor, but these characteristics were overwhelmed by a fanaticism which knew no bounds. He did much harm to Scotland, yet much good, and he left it, in his history, its first original prose work in the vernacular. (His Scottish vernacular, however, was heavily tinctured by his years in England and Switzerland.)

Knox was twice married, in 1553 to Marjory Bowes, who died in 1560 leaving two sons, and in 1564 to Margaret Stuart, a sixteen-year-old belonging to an obscure branch of the royal family, and by her Knox had three daughters. She survived him to marry Richard Ker.

PRINCIPAL WORKS: An Epistle to the Congregation of the Castle of St. Andrews, 1548; A Confessioun and Declaration of Praiers upon the Death of Edward VI, 1554; A Faithfull Admonition ... unto the Professors of God's Faith in England, 1554; Two Comfortable Epistles to [the] Afflicted Brethren in England, 1554; The Copie of a Letter Sent to the Ladye Mary Dowagiere, Regent of Scotland, 1556?; The First Blast of the Trumpet against the Monstruous Regiment of Women, 1558; An Answer to ... Blasphemous Cavillations Written by an Anabaptist, 1560; An Answer to a Scottish Jesuit, 1572; The Historie of the Reformation of Religioun within the Realme of Scotland, 1586; Works (D. Laing, ed.) 1846-64.

ABOUT: Brown, P. H. John Knox, a Biography; Carlyle, T. Heroes and Hero Worship; Glasse, J. John Knox, a Criticism and an Appreciation; Lang, A. John Knox and the Reformation; McCrie, T. The Life of John Knox; Melville, J. Memoirs; Stevenson, R. L. Men and Books.

KYD, or KID, THOMAS (November 1558-1594), dramatist, poet, was born in London, the son of Francis Kyd, a scrivener

or notary. In 1565 he entered the newly founded Merchant Taylors' School, one of his classmates being Edmund Spenser. Very little is known about his subsequent life; in fact, his name was almost forgotten until the end of the eighteenth century. Apparently he was apprenticed to his father's profession, but did not remain long in it. The John Kyd who published two pamphlets, one certainly by Thomas and one probably so, and who died in 1592, seems to have been his brother. Thomas Kyd became a part of the Bohemian literary set of the day, most of them dramatists since that was the most popular literary form. Thomas Nashe jeered at him and his "Senecan tragedy" drawn from English translations of Seneca; but Kyd seems to have known French and Italian well, and Spanish fairly so, though his Latin was admittedly bad. He was certainly a close associate of Christopher Marlowe in Marlowe's last enigmatic years, and they had the same patron—though whether that patron was the Earl of Sussex, Lord Pembroke, or Lord Strange is unknown.

When Marlowe was arrested in 1593, some of Kyd's private papers were found "shuffled" in among his. Kyd was therefore arrested and put to the torture, on charges of immorality and atheism. He secured his release by writing a letter "to purge himself from these aspersions," but his patron promptly dropped him, and he spent the last year of his life in the deepest poverty. Nashe, implacable, called him "a shifting companion that ran through every art and throve by none."

Kyd is nevertheless one of the most important of the pre-Shakespearian Elizabethan playwrights. His *Spanish Tragedy* (written between 1585 and 1588) held the stage for at least a century after his death, though it was considerably "refurbished," probably by Ben Jonson. It had seven editions between 1599 and 1638. Kyd was long the best known Elizabethan dramatist abroad.

His "swelling bombast of bragging blank verse" (Nashe again) was confessed by Kyd himself when he declared his preference for "a stately written tragedie." Like Marlowe's, his prevailing mood was somber, though, unlike Marlowe, he was capable also of subtle humor. His plays are melodramatic "tragedies of blood," but though they are sensational they do not plumb the lowest depths of horror and revulsion. Kyd is a master of dramatic surprise and of stage-craft, with an instinct for realism and a power of character development. But on the whole the interest of his work is less literary than historical.

Shakespeare undoubtedly knew Kyd's plays, if not the man himself, and drew from them. *Titus Andronicus*, if it is not partly Kyd's, is certainly in his style. The principal question concerning Shakespeare and Kyd, however, relates to *Hamlet*. It is: Did Shakespeare base his *Hamlet* on a lost play (the "Ur-Hámlet") by Kyd? There is a good deal of evidence that he did. On the other hand, Shakespeare may have drawn some of *Hamlet* from *The Spanish Tragedie* itself.

In general, it is difficult to establish the canon of Kyd's plays. It is almost sure that *The First Part of Ieronimo*, published in 1605, is not by Kyd, though it gives the earlier history of the characters of *The Spanish Tragedie*. It reads instead like a burlesque of the latter play, and it is inconceivable that Kyd could have written some of the passages in it. There is some question also whether he was the author of *Solimon and Perseda*, but in this case the probability is in Kyd's favor.

Though his contemporaries despised him and rejected him as merely the author of "two-penny pamphlets," Kyd was a dramatist of considerable importance in the history of the English theatre.

PRINCIPAL WORKS: *Plays*—The Spanish Tragedy of Don Horatio and Bellimperea, with the pittiful Death of Old Hieronimo, 1592; Pompey the Great, his Faire Corneliaes Tragedie (tr. from French of R. Garnier) 1594; The Tragedie of Solimon and Perseda, 1599. *Miscellaneous*—The Householders Philosophie (tr. from Italian of T. Tasso) 1588; The Truethe of ... the Murthering of John Brewer, Goldsmith, 1592; The True Report of the Poisoninge of Thomas Elliott, Tailor, 1592; Works of Thomas Kyd (F. S. Boas, ed.) 1901.

ABOUT: Boas, F. S. Life, *in* Works; Coleridge, S. T. Table Talk; Crawford, C. Concordance to the Work of Thomas Kyd; Henslowe, P. Diary; Lamb, C. Specimens of the English Dramatic Poets; Nashe, T. Preface to Menaphon (by R. Greene); Sarrazin, G. Thomas Kyd und sein Kreis; Schelling, F. E. Elizabethan Drama.

KYNASTON, or KINASTON, Sir FRANCIS (1587-1642), poet, scholar, was born at Oteley, Shropshire, the eldest son of Sir Edward Kinaston. He was a student of both Oxford and Cambridge Universities,

taking his B.A. from St. Mary Hall, Oxford, in 1604, and his M.A. from Trinity College, Cambridge, five years later. He was a good linguist and an outstanding scholar, but, according to Wood, more addicted "to the superficial parts of learning, poetry and oratory (wherein he excelled), than to logic and philosophy."

Kynaston was called to the bar at Lincoln's Inn in 1611. He became an intimate of court circles, holding several posts of honor, served as M.P. for Shropshire for a year, and was knighted by James I. Under Charles I he gathered around him a brilliant circle of literary dilettantes to found an academy of learning called the Musaeum Minervae. The king himself contributed £100 to the Musaeum, which was "to give language and instruction, with other ornaments of travel, unto our gentlemen before their undertaking long journeys into foreign parts." Only nobility and gentry were admitted and instruction was carried out in Sir Francis's own house, which was furnished with "books, manuscripts, musical and mathematical instruments, paintings, statues, etc." Sir Francis was regent of the school and his friends were the teachers, the regent himself undertaking to teach heraldry, law, antiquities, coins, and husbandry. This fantastic enterprise apparently survived seven years, perishing with its founder's death in 1642.

Kynaston's principal literary work was a curious metrical romance, *Leoline and Sydonis*, first published in 1642, which, along with the works of other minor Caroline poets, has remained almost unknown until collected by Saintsbury. He also published a translation of Chaucer's *Troilus and Cressida* in Latin rime royal with commentary, and a series of sonnets addressed to his mistress, Cynthia, which display considerable lyric excellence.

PRINCIPAL WORKS: Amorum Troili et Cresidae (tr.) 1635; The Constitutions of the Musaeum Minervae, 1636; Leoline and Sydonis with Cynthiades, 1642.

ABOUT: Wood, A, à, Athenae Oxonienses.

LANGLAND, WILLIAM (1330?-1400), poet, may never have existed at all. One of the theories about *Piers Plowman* is that the three versions are the work of five unknown writers, one of whom may have been named John But, a scribe or minstrel, three of whom were priests, and one a monk. On the other hand, the author may have been Langland (or Langley) who may have been a serf, or he may have been the son of Stacy de Rokayle, or Rokesle, a franklin or farmer, of Shipton-under-Wychwood, Oxfordshire. He may have been born at Clebury Mortimer (Clibery), near Shrewsbury, Shropshire, and educated at the Benedictine monastery at Malvern, near Worcester. This Langland, who was nicknamed "Long Will" because of his height, took minor orders, but never progressed in the church, probably because he was married. His wife's name was Kitte and he had a daughter. From 1362 he lived in London, and earned most of his living by copying legal documents. Toward the end of his life he lived in Bristol. Or the author may have been Robert Langland, or Langley, a priest, who was educated at Oxford or Cambridge.

The "Langland myth" theory is that of J. M. Manly, the earlier William Langland theory that of W. W. Skeat. All that is certain is that the author or authors of this famous poem wrote in a dialect which suggests origin in Oxfordshire or Shropshire. If one man wrote the three versions of the poem, he may or may not also have been the author of *Mum, Sothsegger* ("Quiet, Soothsayer!") written about 1399, also known as *Richard the Redeless* ("without good sense"), which treats of the last days of Richard II and is unfinished.

Granting the existence of William Langland, the first version seems to date from about 1362. The next text dates from 1377, the third from 1393 or 1398. In any event, it seems quite certain that the third *section* of the poem is wholly or partly by an imitator of the first two sections, since it is quite different both in style and in philosophy. (The three sections alluded to are in all three manuscript texts.)

The full title of the poem is *The Vision of William concerning Piers the Plowman, together with Vita de Do-wel, Do-bet, et Do-best, secundum Wit et Resoun*—a strange mixture of English and Latin. The first manuscript contains 2567 lines, the second 7242, the third 7357.

Piers, the protagonist of the poem, is conceived of as the coming reformer who will remedy the vices and corruption of the church. In the various versions he becomes more exalted in nature until at the end he is identified with Christ—"Petrus est Christus." In the beginning he is a simple plowman who leads a group of penitents in search of truth. Piers appears only in the second section; the first is a vision of a field, representing the world, the church, and "Lady Meed," the third a search for Do-well, Do-better, and Do-best. In the first manuscript the dreamer dies of fever with the search uncompleted, in the second and third he survives.

Piers Plowman is a revival of the old Teutonic alliterative verse, without rhyme. There is no doubt that if more than one man wrote the different versions, the first was the only real poet. He has verve and picturesqueness, the people in his allegory are real and vivid, and he has dramatic power. The second version is wholly different; it is satirical and is more a debate than an allegory. For the simplicity of the first version it substitutes elaborate figures of speech and long discussions of fine points of theological dogma. It is also far angrier than the first—perhaps influenced by Wycliffe. The third version is primarily a revision of the second.

The question of authorship may never be settled. But *Piers Plowman* remains one of the monuments of English literature.

PRINCIPAL WORK (date of publication): The Vision of Piers Plowman, 1550 (as The Vision of William concerning Piers the Plowman, together with Richard the Redeless, W. W. Skeat, ed., 1867-85).

ABOUT: Bale, J. Scriptores Illustres Majoris Britanniae; Bright, A. H. New Light on Piers Plowman; Chadwick, D. Social Life in the Days of Piers Plowman; Dawson, C. H. Mediaeval Religion; Hort G. Piers Plowman and Contemporary Religious Thought; Jusserand, J. J. Piers Plowman: A Contribution to the History of English Mysticism; Manly, J. M. Piers the Plowman and Its Sequence; Milman, H. H. History of Latin Christianity; Morley, H. English Writers; Poole, R. L. Illustrations of the History of Mediaeval Thought; Ten Brink, B. Early English Literature.

LATHAM, SIMON (fl. 1618), seventeenth century authority on falconry, was probably the nephew of Lewis Latham of Elstow, Bedfordshire, who was under-falconer and later serjeant-falconer to the king. Almost nothing is known of his life except from the testimony of his two volumes on the art of falconry.

Latham tells us he derived his "art and understanding" from Henry Sadleir of Everley, Wiltshire, who was the son of Sir Ralph Sadleir, grand falconer to Queen Elizabeth. As a young man Latham served as one of the officers under the master of the hawks and the elaborate ritual of falconry, which was the favorite recreation of the aristocracy in the middle ages, became his practice and his passion. Urged by his friends, he wrote the treatise *Latham's Falconry: or the Faulcons Lure and Cure*, first published in 1615, which became the authoritative work on the subject for the seventeenth century. The work was in two books, "the first, concerning the ordering of all Hawks in generall, especially the Haggard Faulcon Gentle. The second, teaching approved medicines for the cure of all Diseases in them."

Encouraged by the success of his book, which went through a number of editions, Latham published a *New and Second Booke of Faulconry* in 1618, and some years later *The Gentleman's Exercise, or Supplement to the Bookes of Faulconry* (1662) was published under his name. To the modern reader Latham's works are little more than curiosities, although they remain a rich source of information for anyone interested in the history of falconry.

PRINCIPAL WORKS: Latham's Falconry: or the Faulcons Lure and Cure, 1615; New and Second Booke of Faulconry, 1618.

ABOUT: Harting, J. E. Biblioteca Accipitraria; Latham's Falconry.

LATIMER, HUGH (1485?-October 16, 1555), preacher, religious writer, was born in Thurcaston, Leicestershire, the son of Hugh Latimer, a yeoman farmer. In 1497 he fought against the Cornish rebels, which makes it probable that he was born as early as 1480; on the other hand, he did not enter Clare Hall, Cambridge, until 1506. He secured his B.A. in 1510, M.A. in 1514, and B.D. in 1524. He was ordained a priest and licensed to preach, and in 1522 he was crossbearer for the university. He was opposed to the Reformation, until 1524, when he became a convert to Thomas Bilney, later executed for his faith. For some time Cardinal Wolsey was tolerant of the little group of Cambridge Protestants, and even after an attack on him by Robert Barnes in 1525 caused their suppression, he allowed Latimer

1555

HUGH LATIMER

to return to Cambridge and to preach there. His first Protestant sermons were those "on the cards," in 1529. However, he was on a commission to investigate heretical books in 1530, and since he favored Henry VIII's divorce he remained safe. He received the living of West Kingston, Wiltshire, in 1531, and though he was called before the convocation in 1532, he recanted and was unpunished. He became royal chaplain in 1534, in 1535 Bishop of Worcester, with a seat at Hartlebury, and in 1536 an examiner of heretics.

But in 1539 he refused to sign the Act of Six Articles, and resigned his bishopric. For a year he was under arrest, in custody of the Bishop of Chichester. He was saved from execution by intervention of Cardinal Cromwell. In 1540 he was released, but with the fall of Cromwell he was ordered to leave London, not to preach, and not to visit either the university or his old diocese. He was rearrested and kept in the Tower in 1546 and 1547. With the accession of Edward VI, Latimer was back in favor and became court preacher; he refused to reapply for his bishopric although the House of Commons requested him to do so. Latimer's real danger began when Mary came to the throne. He was given every opportunity to flee, being by then an old and sick man, but he refused, and was imprisoned again in the Tower in 1553. His trial did not come until 1554, part of his imprisonment being spent in Oxford. Finally, together with Nicholas Ridley he was condemned to be burned. It was at the stake that he said those famous words: "Be of good cheer, Master Ridley, and play the man; we shall this day light such a candle, with God's grace, in England as I trust shall never be put out." He seemed to "embrace the fire," and died quickly.

Latimer's writings were all sermons, and he was a noted preacher. His sermons were unconventional, homely, and vivid; they were "good talking," easy, natural, and full of practical illustrations. Unfortunately, they were also full of repetition, which makes them wearying to read. He was a true friend of the poor, and eager to right social as well as religious wrongs. His is one of the great names in the history of freedom of religion.

By nature Latimer was somewhat timid, reluctant to take part in controversy, and a lover of peace. His steadfast courage under martyrdom, therefore, was all the more to his credit than if he had been naturally a pugnacious man.

PRINCIPAL WORKS: A Notable Sermō (the "Plough Sermon") 1548; 27 Sermons Preached by Hugh Latimer, 1562; Fruteful Sermons by Hugh Latimer, 1571; The Sermons of Master Hugh Latimer, 1758; Sermons of Hugh Latimer Arranged (J. Watkins, ed.) 1824; Complete Works (G. E. Corrie, ed.) 1844-45; Sermons (H. C. Beeching, ed.) 1906.

ABOUT: Beeching, H. C., Introduction, Sermons, 1906; Carlyle, R. M. and A. J. Hugh Latimer; Demaus, R. Hugh Latimer: A Biography; Foxe, J. Book of Martyrs; Stowe, J. Chronicle; Tulloch, J. Leaders of the Reformation; Watkins, J. Life in Sermons, 1824.

LAUD, WILLIAM (October 7, 1573-January 10, 1645), religious writer, was born in Reading, the son of William Laud, a clothier, and Lucy (Webbe) Robinson, another clothier's widow. He attended Reading Free School, and in 1589 entered St. John's College, Oxford, securing a scholarship in 1590 and a fellowship in 1593, which he resigned in 1610. He secured his B.A. in 1594, M.A. in 1598, B.D. in 1604, and D.D. in 1608. He was ordained priest in 1601, was one of the university proctors in 1603, and in 1605 became chaplain of the Earl of Devonshire. In 1607 he was vicar of Stanford, Northamptonshire, and in 1610 received the living of Cuxton, Kent. From 1611 to 1621 he was president of St. John's. In 1616 he was made Dean of Gloucester, and the next year accompanied James I to Scotland. In 1621 he was appointed a prebendary of Westminster, and the same year became Bishop of St. David's. His great patrons were the future Charles I and his friend the Duke of Buckingham, so that from Charles' accession in 1625 Laud began to reach his real predominance in the church and nation. With utter devotion to the king he fought for him against Parliament, and at the same time endeavored to use Charles to compel reforms in the church.

In 1626 he was Dean of the Chapel Royal and Bishop of Bath and Wells, in 1629 chancellor of Oxford (winning the right to oversee both universities), and finally in 1633 Archbishop of Canterbury. He took part in the proceedings of the notorious Star Chamber, and was a harsh and tyrannical judge. It is natural, therefore, that when the long struggle between king and Parliament began, Laud should be detested by Puritans and liberal churchmen alike. By 1640 he was being attacked by mobs, and the next year the Long Parliament impeached him on a charge of treason. He was imprisoned in the Tower for three years before he finally came to trial, and the House of Commons refused to recognize a pardon from the king. The best he could gain was permission to be beheaded instead of suffering the full penalty for treason. His execution took place the following January.

It is difficult to see Laud himself through the mass of invective aimed at him. It is undoubtedly true that he was blamed for much of which Charles himself was guilty, yet it was Laud who proclaimed that resistance to the doctrine of the divine right of kings would bring damnation as its punishment. He was equally ruthless and tactless, a hard, masterful man; but he was not vindictive and he was personally upright. His one aim was to compel conformity, obedience, and order, in church and state alike. Precedent was to him "part of the divine order of the world."

As a preacher (all his writing except his interesting diary consisted of sermons) Laud was a disciple of Lancelot Andrewes, but he lacked Andrewes' gift for eloquence. His sermons were reasoned and logical; in his view the Church of England had deserted "not the body but the errors" of the Roman

After Sir A. Van Dyck
WILLIAM LAUD

Catholic Church. What he hated most was the "disorderly" faith of the Dissenters—yet his persecution caused as many churchmen as Puritans to emigrate to America.

He was not a noted literary figure—his sermons were marked by their historical allusions and their dependence on the daily lessons or Psalms, but they had little value as literature. Yet he was a link between the literature of Elizabeth and that of Charles. He belonged in mentality to the days of the Tudors, though he preached Donne's funeral sermon in 1631.

PRINCIPAL WORKS: Conference with Fisher, 1624 (C. H. Simpkinson, ed. 1901) ; Seven Sermons, 1651; Diary (H. Wharton, ed.) 1695; Collected Works (H. and E. Wharton, eds.) 1695-1700; Collected Works (W. Scott, and W. Bliss, eds.) 1842-60.

ABOUT: Benson, A. C. William Laud, Sometime Archbishop of Canterbury; Collins, W. F. (ed.) Archbishop Laud Commemoration; Duncan-Jones, A. S. Archbishop Laud; Hutton, W. H. William Laud; Laud, W. Diary; Longueville, T. Life of Laud, by a Romish Recusant; Rogers, J. E. T. Historical Gleanings; Simpkinson, C. H. Life and Times of William Laud, Archbishop of Canterbury; Wharton, H. The History of the Troubles and Tryal of William, Archbishop of Canterbury; Wood, A. à, Athenae Oxonienses.

LAW, WILLIAM (1686-1761), religious writer, mystic, author of treatises on practical morality, was born in King's Cliffe, near Stamford, Northamptonshire, one of the eleven children of Thomas Law, a small landowner, and Margaret Farmery. He entered Emmanuel College, Cambridge, in 1705, as a sizar, and took his B.A. in 1708, and M.A. in 1712. He was ordained and appointed a fellow of the college in 1711, but three years later, on the accession of George I, he lost both his fellowship and his possibility of service in the church by refusing to take the oath of allegiance to the king and abjuration of the Stuarts. This action, resulting from objection to selection of a king by Parliament instead of by "divine right," made him one of the first of the second generation of non-jurors.

He had at one time been a curate, now he was rescued by Edward Gibbon, grandfather of the historian, who made him tutor to his son. Law accompanied the younger Gibbon to his own Cambridge college in 1727, and when the young man went abroad in 1730 became a member of the Gibbon household at Putney. The family was broken up by the elder Gibbon's death in 1737, and Law retired to his family estate at King's Cliffe. Here he was joined in 1740 by Gibbon's maiden sister and by a Mrs. Hutcheson, a wealthy widow. They took a house together and formed a sort of lay religious foundation. Though they had a considerable fortune among them, they lived most austerely and gave all their money to schools, poorhouses, and for alms, clothes, and food for the poor. The neighbors complained of the influx of beggars, but they held fast and continued their life of "retirement and good deeds" under Law's regulation. Law died here suddenly at seventy-five in the very act of singing a hymn.

Law's writings may be divided into three categories. As a controversialist he was one of the ablest of an era of controversy, lucid, pointed, and terribly sincere. He disputed with latitudinarians, skeptics, and deists, the most famous of his controversies being with Benjamin Hoadley, Bishop of Bangor. He also took on Bernard Mandeville, the pessimistic skeptic, and Matthew Tindal, the optimistic deist.

As a practical moralist his fame rests with the *Serious Call,* a famous book in its day, which by its influence on the Wesleys helped to found Methodism, though its author was an ardent high churchman. This book first established Law's fame throughout Europe. It was probably the most influential religious work of the century.

In the third category, as a mystic, Law is the principal English exponent of the German, Jacob Boehme. To him body and soul were expressions of the same state of being —in other words, he was a spiritual monist. The root of life is the will to die, be reborn in the new and become one with God. Nature and law are one, and true knowledge can come only from within—though Law was no enemy of any except barren scholastic learning.

In every category he was a great prose writer—though his mystical writings were most unpopular. His style is like himself, stiff and formal on the outside, richly emotional and even witty beneath, grave, clear, and rhythmical. His mind was essentially logical, and he treated feeling with logic, never losing himself or the thread of his argument in even his most mystical writings. He was a saintly, devoted man, loving animals, children, and music, and living all his years a more austere life than any monk of the early days of Christianity.

PRINCIPAL WORKS: Three Letters to the Bishop of Bangor, 1717-19; Remarks upon. . .The Fable of the Bees, 1724; The Absolute Unlawfulness of the Stage-Entertainment Fully Demonstrated, 1726; A Practical Treatise upon Christian Perfection, 1726; A Serious Call to a Devout and Holy Life, 1729; The Case of Reason, or Natural Religion, Fairly and Fully Stated, 1731; The Grounds and Reasons of Christian Regeneration, 1739; An Appeal to All that Doubt, 1740; The Spirit of Prayer, 1749-50; The Way to Divine Knowledge, 1752; The Spirit of Love, 1752-54; Of Justification by Faith and Works, 1760; A Collection of Letters, 1760; An Humble, Earnest, and Affectionate Address to the Clergy, 1761; Letters to a Lady Inclined to Enter into. . .the Church of Rome, 1779; A Serious and Affectionate Address to All Orders of Men, 1781; Works (G. B. Morgan, ed.) 1892; Liberal and Mystical Writings of William Law (W. Scott-Palmer and W. P. DuBose, eds.) 1908.

ABOUT: Abbey, E. J. The English Church in the 18th Century; Baker, E. W. Herald of the Evangelical Revival; Gibbon, E. Miscellaneous Works; Hobhouse, S. H. William Law and 18th Century Quakerism; Overton, J. H. William Law, Non-juror and Mystic; Stephen, L. English Thought in the 18th Century; Talon, H. William Law: A Study in Literary Craftsmanship; Tighe, R. A Short Account of the Life and Writings of William Law; Walton, C. Notes and Materials for an Adequate Biography of William Law; Whyte, A. Character and Characteristics of William Law, Non-juror and Mystic.

LAYAMON or **LAWEMON** (fl. 1200), historian, chronicler in Middle English, has told us a good deal about himself in his own work. He was of pure Anglo-Saxon descent, his father being Leovenath, a version of an old Saxon name, and he was born in the Welsh Marches, probably in Worcestershire. Layamon was a priest at Ernley (Areley Regis) in that county. His learning was limited, especially as to geography and history, and his Latin was poor. But he was a great lover of learning, who "traveled far and wide over the country and procured the noble books which he took for his model."

He paid lip service to the Venerable Bede and others as his "models," but actually his *Brut* is a paraphrase (by no means a mere translation) of the French *Roman de Brut*, by Wace. It is fairly certain that Layamon was not acquainted with Wace's own original, the *Historia Regum Britanniae* of Geoffrey of Monmouth.

Layamon's intention was to tell the history of Britain "from the time of the Flood," but actually he began with the Fall of Troy and the arrival in Britain of the legendary Brut (Brutus), and ended with the death of Cadwalader in 869. He included the Arthurian legend and the stories of Lear, Cymbeline, and Locrine. Layamon's Arthur is much more of a Christian knight than is Geoffrey's.

Layamon is the first important writer in Middle English. He represents also the first perfect fusion of the Teutonic and Celtic elements in English. (His *language*, of course, being Middle English of a southwestern dialect, has large Norman French components, but the Normans themselves were originally Teutons.) He was also the first to make an extensive use of French legendary material—e.g., Arthur's voyage to Avalon after his death—while still retaining the Old English mode of writing, in unrhymed alliterative verse (as in *Beowulf*).

The *Brut* exists in two manuscripts, both apparently dating from the early thirteenth century (though the poem itself was probably written in the late twelfth century), and both in the same dialect. The later one, however, has some modernization of spelling, substitutes other forms for words which had become obsolete, and includes occasional rhyme and assonance.

In spite of the Celtic background of the legend, and the free use of Breton (i.e., French Celtic) elements, Layamon and his poem are unmistakably English, pointing straight to the next century and the coming of Chaucer. He has the English fondness or proverbs and adages, the English love for a good plain story, and the English fancy for high-sounding, resonant verse.

The imaginative tale that Layamon was a hermit who lived in a cave on the Severn River may be dismissed. He had far too much experience of the world around him and far too much liking for his fellowmen. The priest of Ernley comes down to us through the centuries as the earliest of the English breed of nonprofessional writers to whom writing, though an avocation, is a passion which ultimately consumes most of their lives.

PRINCIPAL WORK (date of publication): Brut (F. Madden, ed.) 1847.

ABOUT: Gillespy, F. L. Layamon's Brut, a Comparative Study in Narrative Art; Morley, H. English Writers; Ten Brink, B. Early English Literature.

LEARMONT, THOMAS. See ERCEL-DOUNE, THOMAS

LEE, HARRIET (1757-August 1, 1851), novelist, dramatist, was born in London, the daughter of John Lee, an actor. When her father died in 1781 she joined her older sister Sophia, who was already an established playwright, in running a private school for young ladies at Belvidere House, Bath. The Lee sisters combined their pedagogic duties with the tireless pursuit of literature, publishing novels and plays in quantity.

Harriet's first novel, *The Errors of Innocence*, ran to five volumes and was published in 1786. The following year she had a comedy produced at the Drury Lane entitled *The New Peerage, or Our Eyes May Deceive Us*, of which Genest gently remarked that it was "on the whole a poor play." She published another play, *The Mysterious Marriage, or The Heirship of Rosalva*, which was never acted, and a novel, *Clara Lennox*. Collaborating with Sophia she wrote *The Canterbury Tales*, a collection of twelve stories told by travelers brought together by accident. All but two of these tales were Harriet's work and it may at least be said that her style is superior in quality to that of Sophia. Lord Byron later dramatized one of the tales as *Werner, or The Inheritance*, acknowledging his debt to Harriet, and her own dramatization of the same story was produced at Covent Garden in 1825 under the title, *The Three Strangers*.

Harriet's lively personality was considerably more interesting than her literary work. William Godwin met her at Bath after the death of Mary Wollstonecraft and was so impressed by the wit and force of her conversation that he determined to marry her. The courtship ran through a curious correspondence from April to August 1798, in which Harriet frequently rebuked her famous suitor for his egotism. When he again visited Bath to make a formal proposal, Harriet refused him on the ground that his radical religious views would make a happy marriage impossible. She lived in single blessedness to the age of ninety-four, enjoying the friendship of many of the prominent literary persons of her time who admired her for her sprightliness, her excellent memory and her good judgment.

PRINCIPAL WORKS: *Plays*—The New Peerage, or Our Eyes May Deceive Us, 1787; The Mysterious Marriage, or The Heirship of Rosalva, 1798; The Three Strangers, 1826. *Novels*—The Errors of Innocence, 1786; Clara Lennox, 1797; The Canterbury Tales, 1797-1805.

ABOUT: Baker, D. E. Biographia Dramatica; Littell's Living Age, 1851; Paul, K. William Godwin.

LEE, NATHANIEL (1653?-May 1692), playwright, was born in London, one of the eleven children of Richard Lee, a Presbyterian minister who later became an Anglican clergyman. He was educated at Westminster School, and in 1665 entered Trinity College, Cambridge, receiving a B.A. in 1668. While at the university he contributed an English ode to a collection of Cambridge verse.

Lee returned to London and endeavored to become an actor, but stage fright made him a complete failure, though he had a good voice and some acting ability. He was in the habit of reading his own plays aloud to the actors who were to play in them, and it is said they always sounded better then than they did on the stage.

Unfortunately this handsome young man "of ingenious conversation" was also an alcoholic. He was taken up by the wild fashionable set around Buckingham and Rochester, and thoroughly debauched. He alienated his patrons by drunken scenes, and finally in 1684 he had gone so far downhill that he was committed to Bedlam. Even there it is said that he carried on witty conversations with his visitors. After five years he was released, and the Theatre Royal gave

NATHANIEL LEE

him a small pension, but he was beyond cure, and he died of alcoholism before he was forty.

Lee's plays were drawn mostly from historical sources, freely treated or (in the case of the comedy, *The Princess of Cleve*) from the French novels of Mme. de Lafayette, which he coarsened unpardonably. Writing was purely a source of livelihood to him, and he had no literary ambitions. When *Lucius Junius Brutus* offended the court by its pro-Whig sentiments, he promptly turned out *The Duke of Guise,* which was as strongly pro-Tory. He himself said, "I abound in ungoverned fancy," and Rochester, in *The Session of the Poets,* said of him that he had "a musical note, but sometimes strained so hard that it rattled in the throat." *The Rival Queens* and *Theodosius* were his most successful plays, but in them as in the rest, occasional grandeur of phrase is marred by constant hysterical ranting and absurd confusion. Theophilus Cibber, who granted Lee "a few great beauties, . . . with extravagant blemishes," dismissed him on the whole as a turgid writer of "furious fustian." Actually his plays were meant to be acted, not read, and undoubtedly they lose from being deprived of voices and stage accessories.

There must, however, have been some literary good in a man whom Dryden constantly collaborated with, for whom he wrote prologues and epilogues, and whom he spoke of affectionately as "poor Nat Lee." Lee had no sense of measure, no true humor (his comedy was plain indecency), no ability in characterization, no delicacy, and his heroic tragedies in blank or rhymed verse have no standing as poetry; but his "white hot passion" sometimes attained real nobility. He wrote whatever was the fashion and likely to be immediately popular, and when he strained after Elizabethan heights (he was a close student of the Elizabethan dramatists) he only exposed how far below them he was. Today he is practically unreadable. But so fastidious a critic as Addison found much in him to admire. "Lee's thoughts," he said, "are frequently lost in . . . a cloud of words . . . He has infinite fire, but it is so involved in smoke that it does not appear in half of its luster."

PRINCIPAL WORKS: The Tragedy of Nero, 1675 (as Piso's Conspiracy, 1676); Sophonisba, or Hannibal's Overthrow, 1676; Gloriana, or the Court of Augustus Caesar, 1676; The Rival Queens, or the Death of Alexander the Great, 1677; Mithridates, King of Pontus (epilogue by Dryden) 1678; Œdipus (with J. Dryden) 1679; Caesar Borgia, 1680; Theodosius, or The Force of Love, 1680; Lucius Junius Brutus, 1681; The Duke of Guise (with J. Dryden) 1683; Constantine the Great (epilogue by Dryden) 1684; The Princess of Cleve (prologue and epilogue by Dryden) 1689; The Massacre of Paris, 1690; Works, 1722, 1734-36.

ABOUT: Addison, J. Spectator Essays; Cibber, C. Apology; Cibber, T. Lives of the Poets; Ham, R. G. Otway and Lee: Biography from a Baroque Age; Langbaine, G. Account of the English Dramatic Poets; Mosen, R. Über N. Lee's Leben und Werke.

LEE, SOPHIA (1750-March 13, 1824), novelist, dramatist, was born in London, the daughter of John Lee, an actor. Her mother died when she was still a child and Sophia took entire charge of the domestic duties of the household, acting as foster mother to her younger sisters. She also found time to write a three-act opera based on Diderot's *Père de Famille.* Her opera, *The Chapter of Accidents,* was sent first to Harris, the manager of the Covent Garden, who gave it long and serious consideration, finally suggesting that she cut the serious passages and turn it into an afterpiece. Sophia next sent the work to Colman of the Haymarket who advised her to write it as a five-act comedy. She followed Colman's advice and the play was produced in 1780 with great success.

When her father died in 1781 Sophia used the profits from her play to establish young ladies' seminary at Bath, where she could continue to write and give a home to her sisters. She proved herself an excellent teacher and the school was a success from the start. In 1785 she published a three-volume novel, *The Recess, or A Tale of Other Times*, dedicated to Sir John Elliot, a physician who had encouraged her in literary pursuits. The novel was well received and Sophia was inspired to write a long, dull ballad, *A Hermit's Tale*, which she published two years later.

With her sister, Harriet Lee, who also became a writer, she collaborated on a collection of stories, *The Canterbury Tales*, contributing an introduction and two of the tales. A second drama, this one a tragedy in blank verse entitled *Almeyda, Queen of Granada*, was produced at the Drury Lane with Mrs. Siddons in the title role, but not even the skill of that great actress could save it and *Almeyda* closed after four performances.

Sophia gave up her school in 1803 and a year later published *The Life of a Lover*, a series of epistles which was supposed to contain a good deal of personal history. Sophia was widely known and liked, a woman of considerable wit and good sense, who became with her sister "almost famous" for plays and novels of no literary worth.

PRINCIPAL WORKS: The Chapter of Accidents (play) 1780; The Recess, or A Tale of other Times, 1783-85; A Hermit's Tale (poem) 1787; Almeyda, Queen of Granada (play) 1796; The Canterbury Tales (with Harriet Lee) 1797-1805; The Life of a Lover, in a Series of Letters, 1804; Ormond, or the Debauchee, 1810.

ABOUT: Boaden, J. Memoirs of Mrs. Siddons; Tompkins, J. M. S. The Popular Novel.

LELAND or **LEYLAND, JOHN** (1506?-April 18, 1552), antiquary, was a descendant of John Leland, the elder, a Latin writer and grammarian who died in 1428. He was born in London and educated at St. Paul's School under William Lily. Finding a patron in Thomas Myles, he went to Christ's College, Cambridge, graduating B.A. in 1522, and studying further at All Soul's College, Oxford. A first-rate classical scholar who also knew French, Italian, and Spanish, he finished his studies in Paris under Sylvius (Francois Dubois) and took holy orders.

Leland first attracted favorable notice in court circles by his elegant Latin verses and was appointed royal chaplain and librarian to King Henry VIII in 1530. In the same year he was presented with the rectory of Pepeling in the marches of Calais, asking the privilege of absentee rectorship a few years later in order to carry out his antiquarian researches. Commissioned the "king's antiquary," he spent six years on an antiquarian tour of England collecting material for a monumental work to be titled *History and Antiquities of This Nation*.

Although Leland was never able to complete this projected work, an elaborate prospectus presented to the king as a New Year's gift in 1545 indicates the scope of his labors. The scheme was to include a topography of England, an account of adjacent islands, an account of the British nobility, as well as a history of British antiquities. Very little of Leland's work was published during his lifetime and the bulk of his writings remained in manuscript, of which various copies were made and used by antiquarians of the sixteenth and seventeenth centuries. His *Commentarii de Scriptoribus Britannicis*, edited by Anthony Hall, was first published at Oxford in 1709. *The Itinerary of John Leland* and the *Collectanea* were edited and published by Thomas Hearne several years later. In spite of their fragmentary form, these works made up an impressive repository of facts to be consulted by such later writers as Bale, Dugdale, and Camden, and confirmed his title as the first antiquary of England.

In 1542 Leland was appointed to the rectory of Haseley, Oxfordshire, and to the canonry at King's College, Oxford. A few years later he became incurably insane, according to Wood, "upon a foresight that he was not able to perform his promise," the completion of his projected work.

PRINCIPAL WORKS: Assertio Inclytissimi Arturii Regis Britanniae, 1544 (W. E. Mead, tr. and ed. 1925); The Laboryouse Journey and Serche of Johan Leylande, Geven of Hym as a Newe Yeares Gyfte to Kynge Henry the VIII, 1549 (W. A. Copinger, ed. 1895); Commentarii de Scriptoribus Britannicis (A. Hall, ed.) 1709; The Itinerary of John Leland the Antiquary (T. Hearne, ed.) 1710-12 (L. Toulmin-Smith, ed. 1906-10); Leland's Collectanea (T. Hearne, ed.) 1715.

ABOUT: Burton, E. Life of Leland, with Notes and Bibliography; Huddesford, W. Lives of Leland, Hearne and Wood; Toulmin-Smith, L. Introduction to The Itinerary.

L'ESTRANGE, Sir ROGER (December 17, 1616-December 11, 1704), journalist, political pamphleteer, was born in Hunstanton, Norfolkshire, the son of Sir Hamon L'Estrange and Alice Stubbe. He may have attended Cambridge, but took no degree. He was a talented musician, and played the violin well. He seems to have followed no profession until the beginning of the civil war, when as a convinced Royalist he was imprisoned in Newgate for more than three years on a charge of espionage. Once condemned to death, he was reprieved and then allowed to escape. While in prison he began writing the long series of political pamphlets. communications, defenses, apologies, and broadsides—eighty-four in all—which he kept up for most of the rest of his life.

From prison he fled to Germany and Holland. On his return in 1653 he made some sort of compromise with Cromwell which was afterwards one of the indictments against him. He continued as a pamphleteer against the Puritans after the Restoration, but received no recognition from Charles II until 1663, when he was appointed one of the licensers of the press and surveyor of the imprimeries. In effect, this made him censor of the press, and he was a severe and harsh one, condemning at least one man to death He was also given a monopoly of the news, and to 1666 he published the *Intelligencer*

After Sir G. Kneller

SIR ROGER L'ESTRANGE

and the *News*, one number of each weekly. Then Henry Muddiman's *Gazette* drove him from the field.

In 1679 L'Estrange took the field as an opponent of the Earl of Shaftesbury and an advocate of the Roman Catholics—he was, indeed, suspected of secretly belonging to that faith, but this was not true. This naturally brought him into favor with James II, but in 1681 he was falsely accused of procuring the perjury of a witness in the Titus Oates case, and, though he was acquitted, the popular outcry against him was so great that he fled again to Holland for several months. He also lost his seat in Parliament, to which he had been elected in 1680 for Middlesex. In 1684 he was again elected for Winchester. From 1681 to 1687 he published the *Observator;* James was obliged to suppress this, but secretly gave him a sizable grant in compensation. He was knighted in 1685, and sent on a mission to Scotland in 1686, but with the Revolution of 1688 his good fortune came to an end. He was several times arrested and imprisoned, dismissed from his post as licenser; his health broke after a stroke in 1692; his wife (Mary Doleman) died, completely ruined by gambling; his daughter turned Roman Catholic; his son was an invalid, who died soon after his father; and with all his money gone he ended as a booksellers' hack.

His translations, however, which were the principal work of his later years, were by no means hack work; they were sound and thorough. He translated from the French and Spanish, and also from the Latin of Cicero, Seneca, Terence, Tacitus, and Erasmus. His great work as a translator was his edition of Aesop, which without his moral "reflections" is still a standard one. As a translator L'Estrange was fresh and lively, using contemporary colloquialisms and even slang, indulging in light irony to the point of flippancy. This made him eminently readable, but of course also "dated" his work badly. Though Hallam considered him "a pattern of bad writing," his contemporary Evelyn called him "a person of excellent wit, abating some affectations." His political and ecclesiastical pamphlets were bitter, dogmatic, prejudiced and often scurrilous—as when he jeered at Milton's blindness. (Yet later he subscribed to an edition of *Paradise Lost.*) It is as a journalist that he is most important—the foremost English journalist before Defoe.

PRINCIPAL WORKS: L'Estrange His Apology, 1660; Considerations and Proposals in order to the Regulation of the Press, 1663; Discourses of the Fishery, 1674; The Fables of Aesop and other Eminent Mythologists: with Moral Reflexions, 1692; Fables and Storyes Moralized, 1699.

ABOUT: Clarendon, E. (Earl) The History of the Rebellion; Evelyn, J. Diary; Hallam, H. Literature of Europe; Kitchin, G. Sir Roger L'Estrange: a Contribution to the History of the Press in the 17th Century; Pepys, S. Diary.

LEYLAND, JOHN. See LELAND, JOHN.

LILLO, GEORGE (February 4, 1693-September 3, 1739), dramatist, was born in London, the son of a Dutch father and an English mother. His father was a prosperous jeweler, and the son was apprenticed to the trade and was for many years the father's partner. The family were Dissenters. Little is known of his private life, not even if he was married. He is described as a modest, affable man, rather good looking, though he was blind in one eye. Most of his life was spent in London; at one time he seems to have lived at Rotherhithe. His closest friend was the bookseller John Gray, to whom he assigned many of his manuscripts.

Lillo's importance is as a pioneer; he was the first to write prose domestic comedy in English. His influence on Diderot in France, Lessing in Germany, and Fielding (and even Thackeray, who burlesqued him) in England was considerable.

The great landmark in his work was *The London Merchant*, produced at Drury Lane in 1731. This didactic dramatization of the tradesman's world, "in artless strains, a tale of private woe," was based on an old ballad, and told of the downfall of a guileless apprentice lured to crime by a prostitute. Kemble and Mrs. Siddons were glad to play in it, and for many years it was performed in the holiday season as an example and warning to apprentices.

Lillo experimented in other forms also. He revived the masque, dead for a century, to celebrate the marriage of the Princess Royal to William IV of Orange. (The result has been called "patriotic but inane.") In *Marina* he produced a new version of *Pericles, Prince of Tyre. Fatal Curiosity,* though domestic in scene, was written in

blank verse, and so was *Elmerick,* which he left to John Gray at his death and which was played and published posthumously. Lillo's blank verse was his weakest work, a sort of "frigid declamatory."

Moreover, though it is true that he "broke the old shackles of verse tragedy," his own stilted prose often reads as if a real break were beyond his powers. His prose is sometimes ornate to the point of grotesqueness as representing the actual speech of ordinary people. His characterization is crude, and his plots are often inconsistent. Nevertheless, Lillo marks a milestone in the history of the English drama. His aim was frankly moral, "thoughtless youth to warn." In *The London Merchant* at least he wrote out of his own experience, about the world he himself knew best.

Arden of Feversham, also drawn from a ballad, was left unfinished at Lillo's death, and was completed by another hand. The *Life of Scanderberg* (George Castriot, the Albanian chieftain) appended to *The Christian Hero,* was not written by Lillo himself, but by some unknown person. His first play, *Silvia,* he called a "ballad opera," and throughout his work one sees the strong influence of the folk ballads which were the earliest domestic poetry of England.

PRINCIPAL WORKS: Silvia 1731; The London Merchant, or, The History of George Barnwell, 1731; The Christian Hero, 1735; Fatal Curiosity, 1737 (as The Shipwreck, 1784); Marina, 1738; Elmerick, 1740; Britannia and Batavia (masque) 1740; Arden of Feversham (with J. Hoadly) 1762; Works of the Late Mr. George Lillo (T. Davies, ed.) 1775.

ABOUT: Cibber, T. Lives of the Poets of Great Britain and Ireland; Davies, T. Some Account of His Life, *in* Works; Hoffman, L. George Lillo (in German); Hudson, W. H. A Quiet Corner in a Library; Lamb, C. Specimens of the English Dramatic Poets.

LILLY, WILLIAM (May 1, 1602-June 9, 1681), astrologer, author of pamphlets and almanacs, was born in Diseworth, Leicestershire, the son of William Lilly, a yeoman farmer, and Alice Barham, who died when he was sixteen. In 1613 he was sent to the Grammar School at Ashby-de-la-Zouche, where he received a fair classical education. His father now having lost his entire property, the boy went to London in 1618 as servant to a wealthy but illiterate merchant, Gilbert Wright, soon becoming his accountant and factotum, as well as nurse and ama-

teur surgeon to Mrs. Wright, who died in 1624. Wright remarried, one Grace Whitehead, but died in 1627, and a few months later Lilly married the widow, thus taking over the "corner house in the Strand." In 1632 he became a pupil of Rhys Evans, the Welsh astrologer, and seems really to have believed in this pseudo-science (though he never failed to get information for his "predictions" anywhere he could). His youth was filled wth "dreams of salvation and damnation," and he was a good deal of a neurotic.

Mrs. Lilly died in 1633, leaving him a tidy fortune, and the next year he married Jane Rowley, who turned out to be a shrew and whose unlamented death occurred in 1654, when he promptly married Ruth Needham; he had no children by any of these marriages.

In 1634 Lilly participated in an inglorious attempt to locate "hidden treasure" under Westminster Abbey. He taught astrology in London until 1637, when, afflicted by melancholia (probably hypochondriacal) he retired to a house he bought at Hersham, Surrey. In 1641 he returned to London, and in 1644 published his first almanac; these were continued annually till his death. During the civil war he played a dubious role; though in 1648 he helped Charles II to escape from Carisbrook Castle, he was undoubtedly a spy for the Parliamentarians and wrote in their behalf; and after the Restoration he was twice arrested and examined. He was pardoned after a fine, but his reputation was always suspect thereafter and he was frequently in trouble. After the fire of 1666 he lived in Hersham, where he studied medicine, and practiced it (with astrological trimmings) the rest of his life; he was licensed to practice in 1670. He died at seventy-nine after a paralytic stroke.

Lilly was the only astrologer of his time to predict specific events, and he often caused much disturbance by his prophecies of disaster; but they were couched in such vague terms that they might mean anything. From 1648 he conducted a long feud with the naval almanac-maker, George Wharton, and hired John Hall to write pamphlets against Wharton. As a writer, in any sense of style, he did not exist, though his autobiography has historical interest. He is re-

membered chiefly because Samuel Butler lampooned him as "Sidrophel" in *Hudibras*.

PRINCIPAL WORKS: Collections of Prophecies, 1646; Christian Astrology Modestly Treated, 1647 (as An Introduction to Astrology, "Zadiel" [R. J. Morrison] ed. 1852, 1927) ; The English Merlin Revived, 1649; Monarchy or No Monarchy, 1651; Secret Observations on the Life and Death of Charles, King of England, 1651; Annus Tenebrosus. or The Dark Year, 1652; Anima Astrologiae, or a Guide for Astrologers, 1676; Strange News from the East, 1677; The History of Lilly's Life and Times, Written by Himself, 1715.

ABOUT: Butler, S. Hudibras; Lilly, W. The History of Lilly's Life and Times; Pepys, S. Diary.

LINACRE, THOMAS (1460?-1524), author of grammatical and medical works, received the beginnings of his classical education at Canterbury, under William de Selling, and at Oxford, where he probably studied under Vitelli, the first teacher of Greek in England. The rest of his education was obtained in Italy, where he studied for a year under the tutors of the sons of Lorenzo de Medici, was influenced by the great scholar Hermolaus Barbarus to read Aristotle and the classical medical writers, and was graduated from the University of Padua as an M.D. with a brilliant record. After further medical and classical study under Nicolaus Leoncenses, he returned to England with an exceedingly high reputation as a physician and as one of the foremost scholars of the country.

At Oxford he taught and worked with such celebrated men as Erasmus, Thomas More, John Colet, and William Grocyn. These men were his life-long friends, drawn to him by his estimable character and his enthusiastic devotion to the causes he espoused.

The greatest achievement of his life was the founding of the College of Physicians, which for the first time established standards for the study and practice of medicine in England. He helped organize the college along the lines of similar institutions he had observed in Italy, was its first president, contributed the buildings in which it was housed, and willed it his extensive medical library. He also established three lectureships in medicine, two at Oxford and one at Cambridge.

Linacre's services won him favor at court. He received appointment as tutor to Prince Arthur and as physician to the king, was granted a succession of financially rewarding ecclesiastical preferments, and, toward the end of his life, became physician and tutor to five-year-old Princess Mary. In 1520 he gave up his active medical practice and took priest's orders, in order to devote more time to study and writing.

Much of his literary work was the translation of the medical works of Galen and other Greek writers. Many of these, including an unfinished translation of Aristotle, were never published. He also wrote a Latin grammar in English, which, translated into Latin by Thomas Buchanan, was long a standard text in France.

Linacre died at about the age of sixty-five, and was buried in the old cathedral of St. Paul's School.

PRINCIPAL WORKS: Linacri Progymnasmata Grammatices Vulgaria, 1525?; Rudimenta Grammatices (no date).

ABOUT: Munk, W. The Roll of the Royal College of Physicians; Osler, Sir W. Thomas Linacre; Wood, A. à, Athenae Oxonienses.

LINDSAY, Lady Anne. See BARNARD, Lady ANNE (LINDSAY)

LINDSAY, or LYNDSAY, Sir DAVID (1490?-1555?), Scottish poet, was the son of Sir David Lindsay of the Mont, who had estates in both Fife and Lothian. It is not known in which of these he was born. Little also is known of his education, though he probably attended a school in Haddington, Lothian, and seems to have been a graduate of St. Andrews University by 1508. In the same year he entered the service of James IV, and four years later became usher and general playfellow of the infant who was to be James V. He remained the future king's close companion until the latter's death in 1542.

In 1522 Lindsay married Janet Douglas, a seamstress at court. They had no children, and rumor says the marriage was unhappy. From 1526 to 1528 James was practically a prisoner of the powerful Douglases (Lindsay's wife did not belong to this great branch of the family), but when he regained power he appointed Lindsay Lyon King of Arms, or chief herald. Lindsay also undertook several diplomatic missions for James, to Brussels and Paris, and after the king's death to England and Denmark for his successor, the young James VI (James I of

England). The exact date of Lindsay's death is not known, but it was probably some time in 1555.

Lindsay has been called "the last of the Makars" and "the last Scottish Chaucerian." Neither appelation is accurate. Though all his writing is in verse, he was really no poet; he was a satirist and a reformer who in another age would certainly have written in prose. He was a firm advocate of the use of the vernacular even in religious and legal writings. Primarily what he did was to put into verse his advice to the king (though he was never James' tutor) and his opinions on contemporary politics with special reference to corruption and vice. The only one of his poems which at all suggests Chaucer is *The Historie of the Squyer William Meldrum*, and that suggestion is purely in form, not in spirit.

Lindsay's principal work was the only complete Scottish morality play, *The Pleasant Satyre of the Thrie Estaitis*, first played in 1540. It is a curious mixture of allegory and depiction of real life, with very coarse farcical interludes. Like all Lindsay's work, it is brilliant, witty, and sententious; Lindsay himself acknowledged that he had no real poetic gift. In many ways this play is a forerunner of actual comedy.

Though he never left the Roman Catholic Church, Lindsay's sympathies were with the reformers, and he was an unsparing critic of religious corruption. When Cardinal Beaton was assassinated, his sympathy was not with his classmate at St. Andrews, but with the murderer. The king had at first seemed inclined toward reform, but under the influence of Beaton and of his second queen, Mary of Guise, he reverted to strict orthodoxy. Nevertheless no attempt was ever made to silence Lindsay, who enjoyed unexampled freedom of speech—he even engaged with the king himself in a "flyting" (a Scottish mode of verse invective). He was very definitely oriented away from the Middle Ages and toward the Renaissance. He was no humanist, however; his interest was solely in reform, not in art or learning.

At first very popular, Lindsay soon lost ground, because of his difficult dialect, his frequent coarseness, and his failure to become an outright Protestant. He remains nevertheless the first literary voice of the Reformation in Scotland. As for his personality, George Buchanan called him "a man of unsuspected [i.e., undoubted] probity and veracity."

In 1542 Lindsay completed a *Register of Arms of the Scottish Nobility*, still the most authoritative document on heraldry in Scotland, though it never appeared in print until 1821.

PRINCIPAL WORKS (dates of printing): The complaynte and testament of our Soverane Lordis Papyngo [parrot] 1530; The Tragicall Death of [Cardinal] David Beaton, 1547; Ane Dialog betuix Experience and Ane Courteour (The Monarche) 1553?; The Dreme, 1558; Warkis of the famous and Worthie Knicht Schir David Lyndsay of the Mont, 1568; The Pleasant Satyre of the Thrie Estaitis, 1602; Poetical Works (G. Chalmers, ed.) 1806; Poetical Works (D. Laing, ed.) 1879.

ABOUT: Chalmers, G. Life, *in* Poetical Works, 1806; Laing, D. Memoir, *in* Poetical Works, 1879; Millar, J. H. Literary History of Scotland; Tytler, P. F. Life of Lyndsay.

LITTLETON, Sir THOMAS (1422-1481), judge and legal author, was the son of Thomas Westcote and of Elizabeth, daughter of Thomas de Littleton. As heir to his maternal grandfather's considerable estate, he was baptised in his mother's maiden name.

He entered upon an active legal career in his early twenties, holding a succession of public offices and becoming entangled in the involved political struggles of the next twenty years. He became an extremely wealthy man, his own fortune augmented by income from his many offices and by his marriage to a rich widow, daughter of Sir William Burly, speaker of the House of Commons. They had two daughters who never married, and three sons whose descendants included several distinguished men.

It was for the edification of his second son, Richard, who also determined upon a legal career, that Littleton wrote the treatise, *Tenures*, which brought him lasting fame. It is of antiquarian interest that this is the first work in English law to be printed, and is one of the ten earliest books published in London. The first scientific classification of land laws, which at that time were the only laws in England, the work defines land rights by giving illustrative cases, some actual and some hypothetical. It is complete and concise, and remained for a long time the chief authority on the subject.

One hundred and fifty years after it was written, Sir Edward Coke, devoting the first volume of his *Institutes of the Laws of England* to a comment on *Tenures*, called it "the most perfect and absolute work that ever was written in any human science."

High in the favor of Edward IV, Littleton continued his legal career, was made Knight of the Bath in 1475, and died at his estate in Frankley, Worcestershire, in 1481.

PRINCIPAL WORKS: Tenures (c1480).

ABOUT: Bridgeman, R. W. A Short View of Legal Bibliography; Foss, E. Biographia Juridica; Wambaugh, E. Littleton's Tenures in English.

LLOYD, ROBERT (1733-1764), poet, was the son of the second master of Westminster School, Pierson Lloyd. Among young Robert's classmates when he attended Westminster were many who were later to become distinguished in various fields of English life. Chief among these in importance to Robert Lloyd was Charles Churchill, who, for a few years, was to become one of the most telling satirists of his day. Churchill and Lloyd went together to Cambridge, where their irregular behavior as "brother rakes" and their poetic careers had simultaneous beginnings. After receiving his M.A. in 1758, Lloyd became an usher at Westminster School, an uncongenial task which he soon resigned in favor of a writing career.

His first publication, a poem titled *The Actor*, gained him wide reputation and the poetry editorship of a magazine called *The Library*. A second publication, a collection of poems, resulted in his being named editor of the new *St. James Magazine*. Neither the magazine nor its editor was a success, and a year and a half later Lloyd resigned his position and was immediately clapped into debtors' prison. Churchill, who had once been extricated from a similar predicament by his old schoolmaster Pierson Lloyd, now rescued his benefactor's son, and having fared better financially than his friend, settled a weekly allowance on Robert.

Lloyd was a witty, friendly young man of unquestioned scholarship and some talent, most of whose creative energies were spent on hack-work in a futile effort to stay out of debt. Dissolute lives and the strain of poetry had affected the strength of both friends. Churchill, Lloyd, and Churchill's sister, Patty, whom Lloyd was to have married, all died within a few months in 1764, when Lloyd was only thirty-one.

PRINCIPAL WORKS: The Actor, 1760; Poems, 1762; The Capricious Lovers, a comic opera, 1764.

ABOUT: Chalmers, A. British Essayists; Forster, J. Historical and Biographical Essays; Nichols, A. Literary Anecdotes.

LOCKE, JOHN (September 29, 1632-October 28, 1704), philosopher, was born in Wrington, Somersetshire, the son of John Locke, a solicitor, and Agnes Keene. He was educated at Westminster School and at Christ Church, Oxford, which he entered in 1652. The Aristotelian atmosphere of Oxford did not much suit Locke, and he devoted himself largely to the study of medicine and science in general, which latter was not then among the formal subjects offered. (His interest in science continued; he became a Fellow of the Royal Society in 1668.) However, in 1659 he was appointed to a studentship, in 1660 was lecturer in Greek and in 1662 in rhetoric, and was censor of moral philosophy in 1663. In 1666 he secured a dispensation exempting him from having to take orders. His connection with Oxford continued, with frequent absences, until 1684, when he was deprived of his studentship, *in absentia*, for "contumacy." In about 1666 he began to specialize in the study of medicine, but he never had an M.D. degree, and was not even an M.B. until 1674. What little practicing he did in later years was chiefly in the household of his friend and patron, Lord Ashley, later the first Earl of Shaftesbury.

The first interruption of Locke's university residence came in 1665, when he was secretary to Sir Walter Vane, the English ambassador to Brandenburg. After his return he became a member of Shaftesbury's household when he was not at Oxford, and served as family doctor, confidential friend, and general factotum, even to helping arrange marriages of members of the family. When Shaftesbury became Lord Chancellor in 1672, he made Locke secretary of presentations, and in 1673 he was secretary to the Board of Trade. As secretary to the Lords Proprietor of Carolina from 1669 to 1672, he drew up the colony's first constitution (never enacted), envisaging a highly aristocratic state, with slave labor, and religious toleration for believers only. (As will be

J. Closterman after Sir G. Kneller
JOHN LOCKE

seen, this last was Locke's permanent view on the subject.)

Shaftesbury became involved in conspiracies looking to the ousting of James II, and his ministry fell in 1675. This, combined with Locke's always delicate health, induced him to go to France to live. He stayed in Montpelier until 1679, when Shaftesbury for a brief time was again Lord Chancellor. With the Rye House Plot and other overt evidences of the coming revolution (which placed William and Mary on the throne), Locke had nothing to do; nevertheless when his patron fled England in 1682 Locke soon found his own position untenable. He went to Holland, and for some time lived in hiding under an assumed name, in actual danger of his life. James offered him a pardon, but he refused it on the ground that he had committed no crime for which to be pardoned. Up to this time Locke had published nothing, but he was already at work on what later became the *Essay on Human Understanding*. His first actual publication was a series of contributions to the *Bibliothèque Universelle*, in 1687, when he was already fifty-five years of age.

He returned to England in 1689, after the bloodless revolution of the year before, and was offered by the new sovereigns an ambassadorship at either Berlin or Vienna. He declined, both because he disliked Germany and its climate, and because he had very different work in view. Instead, he accepted the commissionership of appeals, almost a sinecure, which with the small property left him by his father (who had died in 1660, soon followed by his only brother), enabled him to live while he wrote. He held this post to his death, when he was succeeded by Joseph Addison.

Shaftesbury had died soon after his flight in 1682, and Locke made his permanent home after 1691 with Sir Francis and Lady Masham, on the same terms of familiarity and intimacy as with his former patron. After a long illness, he died suddenly at their estate, Oates, Essex, while Lady Masham was reading to him from the Psalms, and was buried in their family graveyard at High Laver, with a Latin epitaph, written by himself, on his tombstone. He never married, but in later years he acted *in loco parentis* to a number of aspiring young men, chief of them his godson, Peter King.

Besides pure philosophy, Locke wrote works of considerable importance on economics and education. His economic writing was elicited by contemporary problems and deals mostly with specific topics. In his view, the state is an outgrowth of a voluntary contract by free citizens, instead of a natural or divine thing in itself. In education, his emphasis was on utility, and beyond that on the building of moral character. Its object, he thought, was to fit men for life in the real world. Locke is often spoken of as the apostle of toleration, and in some sense this is true; as he said, "truth certainly would do well enough if she were once left to shift for herself." This he applied to both the political and the religious fields; however, he denied toleration both to Roman Catholics and to atheists. In general, his political ideal was the early Roman Republic, as he conceived it to have been constituted.

It is, of course, in the field of pure philosophy that Locke is greatest—one of the most important if not the most important, of English philosophers. He was a forerunner of Kant and his "critical method." What he undertook was a systematic investigation of the nature of human understanding, in order to determine the nature of knowledge. He presented no theory as to the origin of mind, but, mind being granted, he believed that the self, the world, and God were properly the objects of human knowl-edge. The means of understanding he called ideas, by this term comprehending what today are called presentation, representation, precept, and concept. He is thus the founder of epistemology, or the theory of knowledge.

To Locke, the mind of the infant was a blank page, a *tabula rasa*; in other words, no innate ideas exist (the Platonic belief). Reflection and self-consciousness are the original source of knowledge. He assumed the existence of God and the self, as of the mind, and again made no attempt to account for their origin; indeed, one of his primary aims was to fix the limits of knowledge and its possible attainments. David Hume carried on from this point, tracing both self and God as concepts to human sensation itself.

Essentially, Locke's mind was scientific; he did not endeavor (as did Hobbes, for example) to be all-inclusive, but confined his theory to what he considered provable argument. Naturally this approach and the conclusions drawn from it aroused heated and long-drawn controversy, into which Locke entered when it seemed to him worthy of his fire. His scientific interest extended beyond medicine to anthropology, botany, and archaeology. Fundamentally, as Albert Weber has said, Locke was an exponent of "anti-mystical and positivist tendencies." He never, however, made the final step into outright negation of the existence of a divine power, as Hume came very near to doing.

As a writer, Locke was not a great stylist, but he did make philosophy speak the language of ordinary educated people, with no strained and intricate terminology. His own nature, reflected in his style, was characterized by forthrightness, candor, and common sense.

PRINCIPAL WORKS: Epistola de Tolerantia, 1689 (W. Popple, tr. 1689.); A Second Letter concerning Toleration, 1690 (A Third Letter, 1692); An Essay Concerning Humane Understanding, 1690; Some Considerations of the Lowering of Interest and Raising the Value of Money, 1691 (Further Considerations, 1695); Some Thoughts Concerning Education, 1693; The Reasonableness of Christianity as Delivered in the Scriptures, 1695; A Vindication of the Reasonableness of Christianity ... from Mr. Edwards' Reflections, 1695 (a Second Vindication, 1697); A Letter to the ... Bishop of Worcester [Edward Stillingfleet] Concerning Some Passages Relating to the Essay on Humane Understanding, 1697 (Mr. Locke's Reply to ... the Bishop of Worcester, 1697, Mr. Locke's Answer to the Second Letter, 1699); A Paraphrase and Notes on the Epistle of St. Paul to the Galatians, 1705; Posthumous Works, 1706; Some Familiar Letters, 1708; A Collection of Several Pieces of Mr. John Locke

(A. Collins, ed.) 1720; Original Letters (T. I. M. Forster, ed.) 1830; The Philosophical Works of John Locke (J. A. St. John, ed.) 1843.

ABOUT: Aaron, R. I. John Locke; Alexander S. Locke; Bastide, C. John Locke (in French); Bourne, H. R. F. The Life of John Locke; Cousin, V. Elements of Psychology; Forster, T. I. M. Analytical Sketch, in Original Letters; Fraser, A. C. Locke; Gibson, A. G. Locke; James, D. G. Life of Reason: Hobbes, Locke, Bolingbroke; Lamprecht, S. P. The Moral and Political Philosophy of John Locke; Leibnitz, G. W. New Essays Concerning Human Understanding; MacLean, K. John Locke and English Literature of the 18th Century; Morris, C. R. Locke, Berkeley, Hume; Pollock, F. Locke's Theory of the State; Rickaby, J. Free Will and Four English Philosophers; Santayana, G. Some Turns of Thought in Modern Philosophy; Stephen, J. F. Horae Sabbaticae; Webb, T. E. The Intellectualism of Locke; Weber, A. History of Philosophy; Wood, A. à, Athenae Oxonienses.

LODGE, THOMAS (1558?-1625), poet, playwright, author of romances in verse, was the son of Sir Thomas Lodge, Lord Mayor of London. He was probably born in his father's house in West Ham. In 1571 he attended the Merchant Taylors School, and in 1573 entered Trinity College, Oxford. He graduated B.A. in 1577, M.A. in 1581. In 1578 he was entered at Lincoln's Inn, but he soon deserted the law for literature, becoming an associate of such well-known writers as Lyly, Greene, Daniel, and Drayton. He accompanied an expedition to Terceira and the Canaries in 1584, and Thomas Cavendish's voyage to South America in 1591. Apparently by this time he was at odds with his family; his mother died in 1579 leaving him a legacy for the express purpose of studying law, which he forfeited, and when his father died Thomas was not mentioned in his will.

After 1596 Lodge wrote no further imaginative literature. As he said, he had determined to "cease to ravel out his wits in rhyme." He had become a convert to Roman Catholicism, and he settled in London as a physician, though seemingly without much success, since he was imprisoned for debt in 1619. Wood says he had obtained an M.D. degree at Avignon in 1600, and he certainly had one from Oxford in 1602. He was married twice, and his second wife, Jane Aldred, a widow, was a Roman Catholic and is supposed to have converted him. At one period, about 1616, he was obliged to leave England and live in Holland to avoid punishment as a recusant. His later years were largely devoted to translations of Josephus, Seneca,

and Du Bartas. He died in London toward the end of 1625, leaving one daughter by his first wife.

Lodge started writing as a playwright—a poor and monotonous one. Though he wrote a defense of the stage against Stephen Gosson's attack, actually he himself despised the theatre. In prose he was an ardent disciple of Lyly and wrote in a languid, highflown Euphuistic style. His romances are chiefly notable because *Rosalynde* gave Shakespeare his plot for *As You Like It*—just as *Glaucus and Scilla* inspired him to *Venus and Adonis*. The second part of *Henry VI* (together with other plays of the period) has been attributed to him, but probably in error. His satire is fairly flat, and as a lyrist he cloys with his "sugared sweetness." He is best in his pastorals and eclogues. In short, Lodge tried every current mode of writing, and having little creative talent of his own, became a sedulous imitator of others. Lyly, Greene, Spenser, Sidney, Kyd, Marlowe, and Ronsard are all directly echoed in his verse and prose.

What might have been his most interesting work has been lost—a *Sailor's Kalendar* which might have given us a first-hand view of his voyages. He also wrote a book on domestic medicine which was never published. His lyrics appeared in most of the fashionable anthologies of the time—such volumes as *Englands Helicon, Englands Parnassus, The Phoenix Nest*, etc. His translations are heavily weighted with his religious bias. In 1581 he was called before the Privy Council for questioning in connection with his pamphlet in defense of the stage (which had not been licensed and was printed privately), but he seems to have got off with nothing more than censure.

The best of his romances is the realistic prose work, *The Life and Death of William Longbeard*. The best known of his lyrics is *Rosalynde*.

PRINCIPAL WORKS: *Plays*: The Wounds of Civill War, 1594; A Looking Glass for London and England (with R. Greene) 1594. *Romances*: Forbonius and Prisceria, 1584; Rosalynde, Euphues Golden Legacie, 1590; The History of Robert ... the Divell, 1591; Euphues Shadow, 1592; The Life and Death of William Longbeard, 1593; A Margarite of America, 1596. *Miscellaneous*: A Defence of Poetry, Music, and Stage Plays, 1580?; An Alarum against Usurers, 1584; Scillaes Metamorphosis (Glaucus and Scilla) 1589; Catharos, Diogenes in his Singularity, 1591; Phillis (sonnets) with the Tragical Complaynt of Elstred, 1593; A Spiders

Webbe (verse) 1594; A Fig for Momus (verse) 1595; Wits Miserie and Worlds Madnesse, 1596; The Divel Conjured, 1596; Paradoxes, 1602; A Treatise of the Plague, 1603; Works, except Translations (E. Gosse, ed.) 1878-82.

ABOUT: Chambers, E. K. The Elizabethan Stage; Fraser, M. E. N. Thomas Lodge as a Dramatist; Gosse, E. Thomas Lodge; Gregg, W. W. Lodge's Rosalynde; Jusserand, J. J. English Novels in the Time of Shakespeare; Paradise, N. B. Thomas Lodge: the History of an Elizabethan; Richard, E. C. Über Thomas Lodge's Leben und Werke; Sisson, C. J. Thomas Lodge and Other Elizabethans; Wood, A. à, Athenae Oxonienses.

LOGAN, JOHN (1748-1788), Scotch divine and poet, was the son of a Midlothian farmer whose mental instability (he drowned himself "while of unsound mind") may have accounted for some of his son's misfortunes.

Young Logan, a promising pupil at Edinburgh University, was aided in his studies by Lord Elibank, studied for the ministry, and tutored Sir John Sinclair. Following his ordination in 1773, he received a parish in South Leith, where his distinguished intellect, brilliant rhetoric and comprehensive views made him an extremely popular preacher. He contributed much of the material for the revision of the Biblical paraphrases and hymns of the Scottish church. In 1779 and 1781, he lectured at Edinburgh University.

In spite of his attainments, he was evidencing a growing mental instability and was drinking more heavily than his parishioners could countenance. When a tragedy he had written, *Runnamede*, was produced at Edinburgh in 1783, this worldly activity was used as an excuse to retire him on an annuity. He moved to London and in spite of his melancholia carried on an active literary life, contributing articles to *The English Review*. He died in 1788, at the age of forty.

In 1770, Logan published a book of poems written by a school friend, Michael Bruce, "and others." In 1781 he published a volume of his own work, which included some of the paraphrases and hymns, and some of the poems from the earlier book, including the celebrated "Ode to the Cuckoo." Following his death, two volumes of his sermons, paraphrases, and poems were published, whereupon unsubstantiated charges of plagiarism from the work of Bruce were made. Much of his poetry is distinguished, and his paraphrases of scripture are especially successful. An analysis of his Edinburgh lectures, which he published under the title of *Elements of the Philosophy of History*, gives evidence of wide knowledge and a philosophic mind.

PRINCIPAL WORKS: Elements of the Philosophy of History, 1781; Poems, 1781; An Essay on the Manners and Governments of Asia, 1782; Runnamede, 1783.

ABOUT: Chambers, R. Eminent Scotsmen; Scott, Sir W. Fasti; Whedon, D. D. Biographical introduction, Logan's Sermons, pub. 1855.

LOVELACE, RICHARD (1618-58), poet, was born in Woolwich, of an old Kentish family, the son of Sir William Lovelace, who was killed in Holland in 1628, leaving a large family of whom Richard was the eldest. He was educated at Charterhouse, and in 1624 entered Gloucester Hall, Oxford. Only two years later he was given an M.A. degree at the solicitation of a lady of the court who was struck with his "most amiable and beautiful person, innate modesty, virtue, and courtly deportment." He must have had some learning also, for he was incorporated in Cambridge in 1637.

In 1639 and 1640 he served in the Scottish campaigns as ensign and then captain; then having attained his majority, entered into the large family estates in Kent. He was from the first one of the court circle and an ardent Royalist. In 1642, as a member of the commission of peace, he dared to present to Parliament the Kentish petition for the restoration of the bishops, and consequently spent seven weeks as a prisoner in the Gatehouse. (There he wrote his famous "To Althea, from Prison.")

During most of the civil war Lovelace was a prisoner on parole, unable to leave London, though he outfitted his two soldier brothers with horses and arms. He finally joined Charles at Oxford, and after the siege was lost raised a regiment and served as colonel under the French king against Spain in 1646, and was badly wounded at Dunkirk (nearly three hundred years before that coastal town again became a famous military place). In 1648 he returned to England and he and his brother were imprisoned in Petre House, Aldgate, until December 1649, after the execution of Charles I.

Lovelace had completely ruined himself and "consumed his whole patrimony in useless efforts to serve his sovereign" (Anthony

RICHARD LOVELACE

à Wood), and the remainder of his life was spent in the direst poverty, on the charity of his friends, and in deepest melancholy. He died in a London slum, near where Chatterton also died more than a century later, and was buried at St. Bride's, which was burned in the great fire of 1666.

Lovelace's famous Lucasta (the name comes from Lux Casta, pure light) has been identified by guess as one Lucy Sacheverell. Legend says that she thought him killed at Dunkirk and married another. Another story is that he thereupon married Althea, whoever she was, which is sheer nonsense; he never married anyone.

Lovelace is one of the most peculiar figures in literature. The great mass of his work is frigid, tasteless, fantastically extravagant, tortured in style—and this deliberately, since he worked and reworked his writing. He was assiduous and fastidious in his revisions, and over-elaborated until his poems read almost like a burlesque of Donne. Yet somehow out of this earth grew a few miraculous flowers. "To Althea, from Prison" ("Stone walls do not a prison make"), "To Lucasta, Going Beyond the Seas," and above all "To Lucasta, Going to the Wars" seem like miracles in their perfection of noble simplicity. Many of his poems were set to music in their day, but for a long time he was almost forgotten, the superb with the bad, until he was revived in Percy's *Reliques*.

Then he became a marked influence on such later poets as Campbeil and Byron.

Aubrey called him "a handsome man, but prowd," and said that when he had money he "lived in great style." He was the close associate of Andrew Marvell, of Henry Lawes, the noted musician, and probably of Sir John Suckling. Two comedies he wrote, *The Scholar* (performed at Oxford in 1636) and *The Soldier*, have both been lost. In the total content of his work, Lovelace is far behind others of the Cavalier Poets, but none of them except perhaps Herrick ever surpassed the beauty of his two or three greatest lyrics.

PRINCIPAL WORKS: Lucasta: Epodes, Odes, Sonnets, Songs, etc. to which is added Amaranthe, a Pastorall, 1649; Lucasta: Postume Poems of Richard Lovelace, Esquire (D. P. Lovelace [brother] ed.) 1659; Lucasta: the Poems of Richard Lovelace (W. L. Phelps, ed.) 1921; The Poems of Richard Lovelace (C. H. Wilkinson, ed.) 1930.

ABOUT: Aubrey, J. Lives of Eminent Men; Courthope, W. J. A History of English Poetry; Hartmann, C. H. The Cavalier Spirit and its Influence on the Life and Writings of Richard Lovelace; Phelps, W. L. Introductory Note, Lucasta, 1921 ed.; Schelling, F. E. A Book of 17th Century Lyrics; Wendell, B. The 17th Century in English Literature; Winstanley, W. Life of Richard Lovelace, Esquire; Wood, A. à, Athenae Oxonienses.

LUDLOW, EDMUND (1617?-1692), memoirist, was born in Wiltshire, son of Sir Henry Ludlow, a passionate advocate of republicanism and one of the most radical members of the popular party in the Long Parliament. Espousing his father's views following his graduation from Oxford at nineteen, young Ludlow joined the bodyguard of the Earl of Essex and plunged into active military leadership in the rebellion. He was one of the judges of the king, signed his death warrant, and helped plan and organize the first councils of state.

In 1646 he was elected to Parliament by Wiltshire and, like his father, championed the cause of republicanism, opposing Cromwell whenever the principle of self-government was threatened by the Protector's policies. He was appointed second in command to Ireton with the army in Ireland and, upon Ireton's death, practically completed the conquest of Ireland before the new commander arrived.

He was arrested on his return to England for his anti-Cromwellian activities, and, appearing before Cromwell, demanded ". . . that which we fought for, that the nation might be governed by its own consent." Although Wiltshire desired to return to Parliament, the government and the clergy succeeded in preventing his election until after Cromwell's death, when Ludlow was instrumental in the overthrow of Richard Cromwell and the recalling of the Long Parliament. He was in Ireland, reorganizing the army and government on republican principles, when the Long Parliament was once more expelled, and Ludlow was charged with treason.

Upon the Restoration, he escaped arrest as a regicide by going into an exile that lasted for the remaining thirty years of his life. Although there were many rumors of his revolutionary activities and frequent attempts were made upon his life, he refused to take an active part in insurrection, and died an exile, at Vevey, when he was seventy-three.

During his exile, he wrote his *Memoirs*, a chronicle of the revolution in which his sincere devotion to the cause of self-government counterbalances occasional inaccuracies and prejudices. As a statement of the purposes of the republican party, and a record of the incorruptible and stubborn courage of one of its leaders, this is one of the important documents of English history.

PRINCIPAL WORKS: Memoirs, 1698-99.

ABOUT: Guizot, F. P. G. Monk's Contemporaries; Thurloe, J. State Papers.

LYDGATE, JOHN (1370?-1451?), poet, took his name from his birthplace, Lydgate, near Newmarket, Suffolk. He may possibly have studied at Oxford, and almost certainly traveled in France, though probably not as a student. He entered the church at fifteen, and became a monk at St. Edmund's Bury. He was ordained subdeacon in 1389, deacon in 1393, and priest in 1397. However, he spent relatively little time at the monastery, but lived for the most part in London, where he devised pageants for the various guilds. In 1423 he was made prior of Hatfield Broadoaks (Hatfield Regis), but paid little attention to the post, and in 1434 was relieved from it and permitted to return to Bury. In 1426 he was certainly in Paris. His great patron was Duke Humphrey of Gloucester, uncle of Henry VI, from the date of whose accession Lydgate was considered the official court poet, but he was in favor with Henry V also, and received a

JOHN LYDGATE

pension in 1431. Half of this pension went to the treasurer of Bury, and the last time it was paid in this form was in 1449, so Lydgate is assumed to have died around 1450. His last work, the *Secreta Secretorum*, was left unfinished.

"My master, Chaucer," Lydgate always said, and claimed to have known Chaucer in his last years and to have been a friend of the poet's son Thomas. However that may have been, it was a strange aberration of taste which for many years grouped Lydgate with Chaucer and Gower as a sort of poetic trinity. Gower may indeed have had some claim to this eminence, but few less poetic poets than Lydgate have ever written. He was extremely prolific as well as sadly prolix—his work runs to some 140,000 lines —and for the most part his writing is slovenly, tedious, platitudinous, tasteless, and prosy. "A barbarous jangle," James Russell Lowell called it. Most of his work is still in manuscript and likely to remain there. As John Methane put it, his books were "indicted [indited] with terms of rhetoric, and half-changed Latin, with conceits of poetry." Even his pedantry is without foundation, for he knew no Greek and had small acquaintance with the Latin classics; his learning was mostly second-hand.

Yet *The Story of Thebes* was actually printed with *The Canterbury Tales*; *The Temple of Glass* was long attributed to

Stephen Hawes, a much better poet; and Coleridge, Chatterton, and above all Gray admired him extravagantly. There are beautiful passages in Lydgate, but they are choked in a mass of polysyllabic verbiage. He has neither vividness of style, power of pathos, nor mastery of prosody, in all of which Chaucer is supreme. He does have humor, and he is usually fairly lucid and easy to understand if not to read, but his chief characteristic is dullness. All his longer poems were either translations or paraphrases; the *Falls of Princes* was from Boccaccio, *The Troy Book* from della Colonna, *The Pilgrimage of the Life of Man* (a remote collateral ancestor of *Pilgrim's Progress*) from de Guileville.

Lydgate is at his best in his beast fables, his ballads, and in such brief humorous poems as *London Lickpenny* (not "Lackpenny," as sometimes given). Perhaps if he had written less and learned a little more from his "master, Chaucer" he would have given himself a chance to write better poetry. It may be added that he looks back to the Middle Ages, not forward to the Renaissance; his special adoration of the Virgin and his exaggerated horror of death are both essentially medieval.

PRINCIPAL WORKS (dates of publication): The Temple of Glass, 1477; Stans Puer ad Mensam (Rules of Breeding: literally, The Boy Standing at the Table) 1479?; The Court of Sapience, 1481; Life of Our Lady, 1484?; Falls of Princes, 1494; Assembly of Gods, 1498; Horse, Goose and Sheep, 1499; The Troy Book, 1513; The Damage and Destruction of Realms (prose) 1520; Albon and Amphabel, 1534; The Story of Thebes (in The Canterbury Tales) 1561; Minor Poems, 1840; Secreta Secretorum, or Secrets of Old Philosophers (B. Burgh, completed; R. Steele, ed.) 1894; Pilgrimage of the Life of Man (F. J. Furnivall and K. Lockok, eds.) 1899-1904; Nightingale Poems (O. Glauning, ed.) 1900; Reason and Sensuality (E. Sieper, ed.) 1901-03.

ABOUT: Browning, E. B. The Greek Christian Poets and the English Poets; Gray, T. Works; Lowell, J. R. My Study Windows; MacCracken, H. N. The Lydgate Canon; Saintsbury, G. History of English Prosody; Warton, T. History of English Poetry.

LYLY, JOHN (1554?-November 1606), dramatist, author of prose romance "Euphues," whose name is also spelled "Lilly" and "Lylie," was born in the Weald of Kent about 1553 or 1554. He entered Magdalen College, Oxford, in 1569, and received a B.A. 1573, M.A. 1575. In 1574 he tried in vain to obtain a fellowship. In general, he was somewhat neglectful of his studies, but was already "a noted wit." After the university he came to London and began his long and notably unsuccessful effort to obtain court patronage. In spite of frequent and pathetic letters to Elizabeth, nothing at all happened. He did find patrons, first Lord Delaware, then the Earl of Oxford, and he seems to have been in the service of Oxford's father-in-law, Lord Burghley, in 1580. But even there he met with some unknown difficulty, which led him to ask for an interview to prove his "honesty." He seems to have secured a theatrical lease at Blackfriars, but this venture was probably a failure, since in 1583 he was in prison for debt, and Oxford got him out.

Finally he was appointed vice master of the children (choristers) who performed plays at the Chapel Royal and St. Paul's, on the strength of the plays he had written for them. This he accepted gladly, since he hoped it would lead to the post he wanted, that of Master of the Revels. He may even have had the reversion of this, but it did him no good, as the current holder lived for over thirty years more.

In 1589 he injected himself into the notorious "Marprelate" controversy, with an anti-Puritan pamphlet, thereby involving himself with the redoubtable Gabriel Harvey. This, perhaps as much as the craze for Euphuism, made Nashe and Greene his devoted disciples, since Harvey was their enemy as well. Simultaneously his popularity as playwright and novelist waned, and he wrote nothing more of importance. Lyly served in Parliament, sitting for Hindon in 1587, Aylesbury in 1593 and 1601, and Appleby in 1597. By his marriage to Beatrice Browne he had a daughter and two sons, one of whom died in infancy. A small man, usually seen puffing a pipe, Lyly seems to have been rather overwhelmed by the furore his novels and plays aroused, and to have been badly disappointed by their failure to bring him wealth and more than temporary fame.

As a writer of comedies, he was much esteemed, though the charming lyrics with which his plays are interspersed may or may not be his own. These plays are a sort of polite allegory, not very interesting now, but very popular with the court, since real members of the court circle were supposed to be hidden behind the classical names. His chief service to drama was to establish prose as a medium for comedy. (Not, however, prose plus the domestic scene; that was left for George Lillo.)

But it is, of course, as the creator of *Euphues* (before he became a dramatist at all) that Lyly's name has come down to us. If we were not experienced in fads and crazes ourselves, it would be difficult to understand how mad all England went over the high-flown, artificial language of Lyly's two semi-novels. As Edmund Blount put it, "Our nation are in his debt, for a new English which hee taught them. Euphues and his England began first that language; All our Ladies were then his Schollers; and that Beautie in Court which could not Parley Euphueisme, was as little regarded as shee which now there speakes not French." (It must be remembered that Blount was Lyly's editor, and that this is a "blurb.")

Actually, Lyly was less of a creator than an adapter. As Harvey meanly remarked, "young Euphues hatched the egges, that his elder freends laide." The real source of Euphuism was North's *Diall of Princes,* itself a translation from the Spanish of Antonio de Guevada. The two books were hardly novels at all; on a thread of the thinnest of plots they strung dissertations and letters, with two long essays on education and religion. Lyly's aim was frankly didactic, to refine the English prose of his day, and "to heare finer speech than the language would allow." Hence this balanced, ornate writing, with its constant allusions to classical authors, its pomposity, artificiality, and self-consciousness. What Lyly added on his own were elaborate puns and plundering of Pliny's "unnatural natural history."

He was nevertheless an artist of intellect and feeling, who raised the drama to the level of literature, and who, in both his novels and his plays, by adding delicacy and subtlety to English prose purged it of the super-masculinity of the Elizabethans and gave it a feminine charm. He had a feeling for style, and his compilation from Cicero, Marcus Aurelius, Erasmus, and North (for that is what the two books of *Euphues* really amount to) actually foretold the true novel of manners and of love. He was interested in contemporary life and people in a manner quite unlike the writers of medieval romances. As a fad, Euphuism became ridicu-

lous, and Shakespeare caricatured it well in *Love's Labour's Lost;* nevertheless, there is an echo of Lyly in both *Much Ado About Nothing* and *As You Like It.* Sidney gave the final quietus to it. But Lyly left English literature different from the way he found it.

PRINCIPAL WORKS: *Plays*: Alexander, Campaspe, and Diogenes, 1584; Sappho and Phao, 1584; Endimion, the Man in the Moone, 1591; Gallathea, 1592; Midas, 1592; Mother Bombie, 1594; The Woman in the Moone, 1597; Loves Metamorphosis, 1601; Lyly's Comedies (E. Blount, ed.) 1632; Dramatic Works (F. W. Fairholt, ed.) 1858. *Novels*: Euphues and his Anatomie of Wit, 1579; Euphues and his England, 1580. *Miscellaneous*: Pappe with an Hatchet, 1589; Complete Works (R. W. Bond, ed.) 1902.

ABOUT: Ainger, A. Lectures and Essays; Asher, E. Euphues; Boas, F. S. Shakespeare and his Predecessors; Feuillerat, A. John Lyly (in French); Harvey, G. Advertisement to Papp-Hatchet; Jusserand, J. J. The English Novel in the Time of Shakespeare; Landmann, F. Der Euphuismus; Morley, H. English Writers; Sisson, C. J. (ed.) Thomas Lodge and Other Elizabethans; Symonds, J. A. Shakespeare's Predecessors in the English Drama; Ward, A. W. English Dramatic Literature; Wilson, J. O. John Lyly; Wood, A. à, Athenae Oxonienses.

LYNDSAY, Sir DAVID. See LINDSAY, Sir DAVID.

LYTTLETON, Lord GEORGE (1709-1773), literary patron and miscellaneous writer, was the son of Sir Thomas Lyttleton, a descendant of the jurist Thomas Littleton. He attended Eton and Christ Church, Oxford, took the traditional Grand Tour of the Continent, and returned to England to play a fairly important role in politics and letters.

For a time he was personal secretary to Frederick, Prince of Wales, and was able to assist many of his literary friends to sinecures through his royal patron. He was elected to the House of Commons, took his seat in the House of Lords upon the death of his father, served as Chancellor of the Exchequer in 1755 and was created First Baron Lyttleton in 1756. His political career was stormy. Although he was lanky and awkward looking and his speech and manner were usually disagreeable, he wielded considerable influence in the House of Lords. He lost the preferment of the Prince of Wales, but through family connections was a member of a powerful clique which included Pitt and Grenville. Some of his opportunistic actions, however, antagonized this "cousinhood," as it was called.

His literary career began with poems written at school, letters from abroad, and four eclogues, *The Progress of Love*, strongly reminiscent of Pope. His earlier prose works were influenced by Montesquieu and Fénelon; his later work, following his conversion from deism to Christianity, was sober and heavy handed. His one poem which was popular during his lifetime and which still retains some interest because of its intensity of feeling, is *Monody*, a lament for the death of his young wife Lucy who died at twenty-nine after five years of happy marriage, during which she bore him three children. A later unhappy marriage resulted in separation. The *History of Henry II*, a life-time work, was conscientiously accurate but painfully dull.

Lyttleton, an amiable, unworldly, absent-minded, benevolent, prejudiced man, was both hated and loved by many of the leading writers of his day. Lord Chesterfield speaks of his "distinguished inattention and awkwardness." He was reviled and ridiculed by Walpole, Johnson and Smollett. On the other hand he was a close friend and patron of many writers, including Pope. Fielding's *Tom Jones* is dedicated to him, and James Thomson made him his literary executor.

He died at his estate at Hagley at sixty-four, and is buried in the parish churchyard.

PRINCIPAL WORKS: Letters from a Persian in England, 1735; Monody, 1747; Conversion and Apostleship of St. Paul, 1747; Dialogues of the Dead, 1760; History of the Life of Henry II, 1767-71.

ABOUT: Johnson, S. Life of Author, *in* Selected Poems of George, Lord Lyttleton; Martins, A. Biographical Notes, *in* Poetical Works of Lyttleton; Walpole, H. Letters; Walpole, H. Memoirs.

MACKENZIE, HENRY (August 1745-January 14, 1831), Scottish author of sketches, novels, and plays, was born in Edinburgh, the son of Joshua Mackenzie, a prominent physician, and Margaret (Rose) Mackenzie. He was educated at the Edinburgh High School and University, and then articled to a solicitor. After a period in London in 1765 studying exchequer law, he returned to his native city, eventually became partner of his former employer, and on the latter's death succeeded him as attorney for the Crown. In 1804 he became comptroller of taxes for Scotland. He was active in the Highland Society, and headed its committee which in 1805 gave a qualified acquiescence in the authenticity of the "Ossian" poems. For many years he was the literary dictator of Edinburgh, and since he lived to eighty-five, with his mental abilities unimpaired, he actually spanned the period from Burns to Scott. An excellent critic, he did much for them both, raising money to keep Burns from having to emigrate, and becoming the friend and advocate of Scott, who dedicated *Waverly* to him. As president of the famous literary club of Edinburgh, Mackenzie edited its occasional magazines, the *Mirror* from 1779 to 1780, the *Lounger* from 1785 to 1787. These were collections of essays, in *Spectator* style, of which Mackenzie wrote forty-two of the hundred and ten in the former, and fifty-seven of the hundred and one in the latter. Scott called him "the northern Addison," and he was that in a different sense from the one intended.

The Man of Feeling, Mackenzie's most famous novel, which gave him an entirely undescriptive sobriquet, was really less a novel than a disjointed series of episodes and scenes, a la "Sir Roger de Coverley." This was the period of "sensibility," and no more mawkishly sentimental hero ever appeared in print. Compared with even the sentimentality of Sterne, Mackenzie's "man of feeling" was lackadaisical, crude, and clumsy—a true

Sir H. Raeburn
HENRY MACKENZiE

child of the worst of Rousseau. For years Mackenzie hawked the book about, but publishers would not take it even as a free gift. Published anonymously, it became immensely popular. Thereupon a clergyman in Bath named Eccles claimed it as his, and presented a written manuscript (copied from the book) full of changes and erasures to prove his authorship! Mackenzie was then obliged to acknowledge it, but Eccles still kept some partisans, and had his claim engraved on his tombstone.

Mackenzie's second novel, *The Man of the World*, was not much better, equally humorless but with the addition of a melodramatic villain. His third novel, *Julia de Roubigne*, was by far his best. Mackenzie's true love, however, was the theatre, though only *The Prince of Tunis* was even a partial success. *The Force of Fashion* and *The White Hypocrite* both failed at Covent Garden in 1789, and were never published separately. *The Shipwreck* is merely a version of *Fatal Curiosity*, by George Lillo.

In 1807 a volume of Mackenzie's collected works was published without his knowledge and with no publisher's name. He therefore brought out his own edition the following year.

In 1776 Mackenzie married Penuel Grant; they had eleven children. A spry, withered little man who somewhat resembled Voltaire in appearance, a great hunter, briskly active to the last, Mackenzie, though kindly and affectionate, was actually a hardheaded, practical lawyer, and in no way resembled his silly "man of feeling."

PRINCIPAL WORKS: *Novels*: The Man of Feeling, 1771; The Man of the World, 1773; Julia de Roubigné, 1777; Collected Novels, 1823. *Plays*: The Prince of Tunis, 1773; The Shipwreck, 1784; Works, 1807, 1808.

ABOUT: Scott, W. Prefatory Memoir, *in* Collected Novels; Thompson, H. W. A Scottish Man of Feeling: some account of Henry Mackenzie, Esq., of Edinburgh, and of the golden age of Burns and Scott; Wilson, J. Noctes Ambrosianae.

MACKLIN, CHARLES (1697?-July 11, 1797), actor, dramatist, was born in Northern Ireland to William and Alice McLaughlin. The date and place of his birth, like most of the facts about his early life, cannot be accurately established. We know that his father died in 1704, and that his mother moved to Dublin, where she married Luke O'Meally, landlord of the Eagle Tavern,

Werburgh Street. Macklin's stepfather was kind, but subject to fits of rage. Charles received his only regular schooling from a Scotsman named Nicholson at Islandbridge, just outside Dublin. He stole money from his mother and ran away to London, where he worked in a public house, entertained the customers by his gift of mimicry, and is said to have married the iandlady. Located and brought back to Dublin, he ran errands as a "badgeman" at Trinity College in 1713. Later he ran away again to become a strolling player in England.

We know he performed often in Bristol, made his first London appearance in 1725, and played in the capital again in 1730. His first big opportunity came in 1733, when the leading actors deserted Drury Lane Theatre. Macklin and his first acknowledged wife took over the leading parts there; they were regular members of the company almost continuously until 1748. He first played Shylock, his greatest part, at Drury Lane in 1741. He went to the Smock Alley Theatre, Dublin, in 1748, returned to London to play at Covent Garden Theatre, and made a "farewell" appearance at Drury Lane in 1753.

Some disastrous years as a tavern keeper and public lecturer followed. He returned to the Drury Lane stage, 1759, in Shylock and his own two-act farce, *Love-a-la-Mode*. The remaining years of his acting career were divided between Dublin and London. On May 7, 1789, at Drury Lane, he made his last stage appearance—as Shylock—forgetting his lines after the first few speeches.

Macklin was the greatest comic actor of his day, but failed in the tragic parts that he insisted on playing in later years. Next to Shylock, his best part was Sir Pertinax McSycophant, the scheming Scot in his own masterpiece, *The Man of the World*, which he first played in its final form when over eighty. With his deeply lined face, robust body, powerful voice and natural style of playing, he revolutionized English acting. He was the greatest stage manager and teacher of acting of his day, his daughter Maria being his best pupil.

Dogmatic, hot tempered, uncooperative, he quarrelled with Garrick and Quin, his chief acting rivals. In 1735 he killed Thomas Hallam in a backstage argument about a wig. In 1775 he won a famous law case against some rioters who had driven him off the

Covent Garden stage, and then treated them with great magnanimity.

Arthur Murphy edited and published Macklin's best two plays in 1793, assuring him a decent income for his few remaining years. He hung around the London theatres to the last, feeble in mind but strong in body, and passed away quietly of extreme old age. He was buried in St. Paul's Church, Covent Garden. His second wife, whom he married in 1759, survived him, but his talented daughter and spendthrift son were already dead.

PRINCIPAL WORKS: Henry the Seventh, 1746; Love-à-la-Mode, 1784, 1793; The True Born Irishman, 1793; The Man of the World, 1785, 1793.

ABOUT Congreve, F. A. Authentic Memoirs of the late Mr. Charles Macklin; Cooke, W. Memoirs of C. M.; Kirkman, J. T. Memoirs of the Life of C. M.; Parry, E. A. Charles Macklin.

MACPHERSON, JAMES (October 27, 1736-February 17, 1796), collector, "translator" of Gaelic Ossian poems, historian, was born in Ruthven, Inverness, Scotland, the son of Andrew Macpherson, a small farmer. In 1753 he entered King's College, Aberdeen University, transferring later to Marischal College, and then to the University of Edinburgh. At none of these did he secure a degree, and though he studied divinity he was never a clergyman. During his college years he wrote some four thousand lines of verse, little of which was ever published. His first poem to appear, The Highlander, was a failure, and he tried to have it suppressed. After doing some hack literary work in Edinburgh, and serving as schoolmaster in his native Ruthven, Macpherson became tutor to the son of Graham of Balgowan, later Lord Lynedoch.

It was on a visit to Moffatt in 1759 with his pupil that he met John Home and through him first learned of the existence of the traditional Ossianic poems in Gaelic. From this small beginning grew an enormous controversy. Macpherson was not much of a Gaelic scholar, but he was an ardently patriotic Scot. He thought little of the original poems, but he did believe that anything Scottish must outdo anything in other Celtic lands, particularly Ireland. Soon he had produced a "translation," The Death of Oscar, which Home showed to Hugh Blair. Blair showed it to a number of "people of rank as well as taste," notably the Earl of

After Sir J. Reynolds, 1772
JAMES MACPHERSON

Bute, and they became all afire to have the whole of this unknown body of Scottish poetry translated into English. Macpherson, the unsuccessful poet, was delighted. Financed by Bute and others, he journeyed through the Highlands and the outlying Scottish islands, and came out with the epic of Fingal (the Irish Finn). In Macpherson's version Fingal, the great Scottish hero, conqueror of the Romans, always came to the rescue of the Irish and was in every way their superior.

It is impossible to exaggerate the effect of Fingal, its successor Temora, and the final complete "translated" works of Ossian, Fingal's bard. They strongly influenced the whole romantic movement in European literature. Goethe, Klopstock, and Schiller were immensely influenced by them, and (in Italian) they were Napoleon's favorite reading. Only in Ireland and England were voices raised in skepticism. The first was that of Samuel Johnson, who in his Journey to the Western Islands of Scotland flatly denounced Macpherson as an impostor. The controversy raged, with hot assailants on both sides (Hume was one of the defenders, Gray one of the attackers) until in 1805 the Highland Society of Edinburgh appointed a committee of investigation. It reported that though there were undoubtedly genuine Ossianic poems in Gaelic, Macpherson had not translated them; he had not even written

333

paraphrases. The poems were his own, on Celtic themes, and even some of the sources he had cited did not exist. Moreover, he had had to create Gaelic originals of his own to prove his good faith! In other words, what had started perhaps as a practical joke had turned into downright forgery—though of course Macpherson never in his life acknowledged this.

Yet he was something more than a mere forger, for the poems themselves, in spite of their turgid bombast, do have passages of exalted sublimity, and they do capture the misty romanticism of the Celtic past. As has been remarked, Macpherson "won his great success fairly, by unfair means." Perhaps the greatest harm he did was quite unwitting; his example inspired poor Thomas Chatterton to his fatal imposture.

Macpherson meanwhile went on to worldly success. Though he was so passionate a "Caledonian," he was also a strong advocate of union with England and a die-hard Tory. In 1764 he was made secretary to the governor of East Florida, and when after a year in Pensacola he quarreled with the governor and returned to England, he was allowed to keep the same salary for life, as a pension. He moved to London and became a political correspondent for the Tory government, and supervisor of the government's newspapers. When the American colonies revolted he was the official spokesman and pamphleteer against them and for Lord North. From 1780 to his death he was a Member of Parliament for Camelford, Cornwall. In 1781 he became agent to Mohammed Ali, Nabob of Arcot, a post which made him extremely wealthy. Finally, his health failing, he returned to Scotland, built a large house, and spent his last years in secluded domesticity and fervent religiosity. By his own request, his body was brought from Scotland and buried in Westminster Abbey.

He was a big, handsome man whose private life was most irregular; he left four illegitimate children at his death. He had the touchy Highland pride (though his father was a poor farmer, he was closely related to the head of his clan), reserved, hot tempered, and easily offended. Even Hume, who believed fully in his pretensions, called him "a strange and heteroclite mortal, and most perverse and unamiable." When Dr. Johnson remarked that it was "easy to abandon

one's mind to write such stuff," Macpherson threatened him physically, and Johnson sent word that he had a stout club ready for him. With his monomania about Scottish superiority, and his absurd ethnological theories to exalt the Scots, it is probable that the root of his entire imposture was the fact that "his Highland pride was alarmed at appearing to the world only as a translator."

As an historian, he was above all a Tory apologist, and though he had access to original papers, his work must always be read with that bias in view. His prose style, in complete contradiction to the high-flown decorativeness of his poetry, was choppy and abrupt, with very short sentences. His prose translation of the *Iliad* was widely ridiculed.

Yet when all is said and done, the Ossian poems (which must now be considered Macpherson's own) have, in their outworn *genre*, great beauty. Though the influence of Biblical style is readily apparent—and some outright plagiarisms, especially from Milton, have been discovered—yet the Ossianic poems do in their own right display depth of imagination and sentiment, and magnificence of language. In fact, these very facts should have aroused suspicion from the beginning, since the genuine early Gaelic poems are rough and barbarous.

PRINCIPAL WORKS: *Poetry:* The Highlander, 1758; Fragments of Ancient Poetry collected in the Highlands of Scotland, and translated from the Galic [*sic*] or Erse language, 1760; Fingal, 1762; Temora, 1763; The Works of Ossian, translated by James Macpherson, 1765-77; The Poems of Ossian, containing the poetical works of James Macpherson (M. Laing, ed.) 1805. *History:* An Introduction to the History of Great Britain and Ireland, 1771; The History of Great Britain from the Restoration to the Accession of the House of Hanover, 1775; Original Papers (Secret History of Great Britain) 1775; A Short History of the Opposition during the last session of Parliament, 1779; The History and Management of the East India Company, 1779. *Miscellaneous:* The Iliad of Homer translated into prose, 1773; The Rights of Great Britain Asserted against the Claims of America, 1776.

ABOUT: Nutt, A. Ossian and the Ossianic Literature; Saunders, T. B. Life and Letters of James Macpherson; Shaw, W. Inquiry into the Authenticity of Ossian; Sinclair, J. A Dissertation on the Authenticity of the Poems of Ossian; Smart, J. S. James Macpherson: An Episode in Literature.

MAIR, JOHN. See MAJOR, JOHN.

MAJOR or MAIR, JOHN (1469?-1550?), classical scholar, historian, was born in Glenhornie or Gleghornie, East Lothian, Scotland, some time between 1469 and 1479, probably nearer the earlier date. In 1493 he entered God's House (now Christ's College), Cambridge, but after about a year went to the University of Paris, where with other English and Scottish students he was enrolled in the "German nation," becoming its procurator and quaestor. He remained in Paris until 1518. He became Master of Arts in 1496, Doctor of Theology in 1505; he was made a regent and lectured at the colleges of Navarre, Montaigu, and the Sorbonne. He then returned to Scotland and until 1525 was lecturer on logic and theology first at the University of Glasgow and then at St. Andrews. Buchanan and Knox were among his pupils. He was also vicar of Dunlop, Ayrshire, and canon of the Chapel Royal at Stirling.

After refusing an offer from Cardinal Wolsey to head the new Christ Church College, Oxford, Major spent the next six years in Paris again, returning to Scotland in 1531. From 1533 to his death he was provost of St. Salvator College, St. Andrews.

Major has been called "the last of the Schoolmen." He described himself as "by name indeed a Scot, but by profession a theologian." He became "the champion of Mediaevalism against the new learning," and was hated and derided by Humanists and Protestants alike; however, though always faithful to the old church, he was by no means illiberal. He was a keen critic of corruption within the church, and in political matters held that civil authority was derived from the will of the people.

All of his books were scholastic treatises except for his *History of Greater Britain*, in which (in the midst of war) he advocated the union of Scotland with England. He felt strongly that the historian's first duty was to tell the truth as he saw it, and though he did not do much historical research he kept that principle in view throughout his history. In theology he sought to reconcile the two theories of nominalism and realism; Knox, who became Major's bitter enemy, said that his word was "holden as an oracle in matters of religion." He was indeed, as has been said, "a storehouse of all the learning of the Middle Ages."

All Major's writing was in Latin—the crabbed, cramped Latin of the Middle Ages, the so-called Sorbonne style. He apologized for his undecorated style, and actually he has standing only as a theologian and an historian, not at all as a literary figure. However, his shrewd practical sense and his independence of judgment made his history of value far beyond his time.

PRINCIPAL WORKS: Exponabilia, 1503; Inclitarum artium libri, 1506; Commentary on the Four Books of the Sentences of Peter Lombard (in Latin) 1509-17; Insolubilia, 1516; Historia Majoris Britanniae, tam Angliae quam Scotiae, 1521 (A History of Greater Britain, A. J. G. Mackay, ed., A. Constable, tr., 1892); Ethics of Aristotle (in Latin) 1529; Commentary on the Four Gospels (in Latin) 1529.

ABOUT: Brown, P. H. Life of George Buchanan; Mackay, A. J. G. Life, *in* A History of Greater Britain.

MALLETT or MALLOCH, DAVID

(1705?-1765), poet and miscellaneous writer, was the son of a Scottish farmer, a tenant on the estates of Lord Drummond at Perthshire. He was educated at the local parish school, worked as janitor at the Edinburgh High School, and supported himself while studying at the University of Edinburgh by tutoring. One of the major influences in his life was his friendship with a classmate, James Thomson, author of *The Seasons*.

In 1723 he left the University without a degree, and for the next eight years tutored the sons of the Duke of Montrose. During this period he wrote several poems, including the ballad *William and Margaret*, his best work. Charges that it was plagiarized from Marvell were never substantiated.

In 1731 his first play, *Eurydice*, was produced at Drury Lane. In that same year he became tutor to the stepson of John Knight, with whom he had studied at Oxford. In 1734 he received an M.A. from Edinburgh, and both a B.A. and an M.A. from Oxford.

His literary output was varied. In addition to the early poems, patterned after Pope and Thomson, he wrote several fairly successful plays, an inferior *Life of Bacon*, and a patriotic masque, *Alfred*, in collaboration with Thomson. The latter contains the song *Rule Britannia*, which, after Thomson's death, Mallet claimed as his own.

Much of his success was based on shameless opportunism. A friend of Pope, he attacked Pope after his death and was rewarded with the editorship of Bolingbroke's works. The Duchess of Marlborough bequeathed him £1000 for a biography of her husband, which, although he "prepared" for it for years, was never written. As a result of pamphleteering for the Tory party, he received the sinecure of a lifetime government position.

Upon the death of his first wife, Susanna, he remarried within a year. His second wife, Lucy, retaining control of her considerable dowry, spent much of it dandifying the appearance of her short, corpulent, exceedingly vain husband. Early in his career he had anglicized his name and his accent. His conversation matched his clothes in elegance, but he was heartily disliked by most of his contemporaries.

He died at about the age of sixty and was buried in St. George's cemetery, London.

PRINCIPAL WORKS: Pastoral, 1720; William and Margaret, a ballad, 1720; The Excursion, 1726; Eurydice, 1730; Mustapha (play) 1739; Life of Bacon, 1740; Alfred, a masque (with J. Thomson) 1740; Poems on Several Occasions, 1743; Britannia, a masque, 1755; Poems on Several Occasions, 1762; Elvira (play) 1763.

ABOUT: Boswell, J. Life of Johnson; Genest, J. Accounts of the Stage; Johnson, S. Lives of the Poets.

MALLOCH, DAVID. See MALLETT DAVID

MALONE, EDMOND (October 4, 1741-April 25, 1812), literary critic, Shakespearian scholar, was born in Dublin, the son of Edmond Malone, barrister and member of the Irish House of Commons, and of Catherine Collier. His uncle was Chancellor of the Exchequer. He was educated at a private school, where he took an active part in the school theatricals, and in 1756 entered Trinity College, Dublin, securing a B.A. degree. In 1759 he made his first trip to England, with his mother, who remained there; in 1763 he was entered at the Inner Temple. It was at this time that he first met Samuel Johnson, and he soon became a member of the Johnson circle, though it was 1782 before he was admitted to the famous Club. Malone spent 1766 in France, then returned to Dublin and was called to the Irish bar in 1767. He joined the Munster Circuit, but met with small success, so eked out his living by writing for the newspapers. In 1774 his father died (his mother had died in 1765), and he inherited sufficient property not to need any longer to practice his profession. He moved

Sir J. Reynolds. 1778
EDMOND MALONE

permanently to London in 1777 and thenceforth devoted his entire time to literary criticism and editing.

He was a close friend of Burke and Walpole; he edited Goldsmith's works (1780); he erected the monument to Johnson in Westminster; helped to revise the famous Life of Johnson; and Boswell dedicated to him the Tour of the Hebrides. It was he who exposed the forgeries of Chatterton and of Samuel Ireland. In 1793 Oxford gave him a D.C.L. degree; in 1801 Dublin bestowed an LL.D. on him. He died unmarried, in London, a mild-tempered, good-humored man with "elegant manners," a noted book collector, and an intimate of nearly all the important literary figures of his time. In spite of his Irish birth he was a Unionist, and was opposed to Catholic Emancipation.

Malone's interest in Shakespeare began about 1777. His estimate of the order of the plays has never been superseded, though his main field of research was in Shakespeare's biography and in the history of the Elizabethan stage. As a matter of fact, he was much more of an antiquary than of a true critic. In 1780 he issued a two-volume supplement to Johnson's edition of Shakespeare, with an appendix in 1783. This was to the version by George Steevens, a clever but unscrupulous man, then Malone's friend, later his bitter enemy. Malone himself exhibited scrupulous fidelity; Henry Hallam

raised his "candor and love of truth." He
was hotly attacked by Steevens' friends for
alleged ignorance and bad taste, but neither
accusation was justified. It must be said,
however, that Malone was unfailingly dull.
His own monumental edition of Shakespeare
was left uncompleted at his death, and was
finished by Boswell's son James. (This is
known as the Third Variorum Edition.) In
1800 he published an edition of Dryden's
critical and miscellaneous prose, with an
"account of the life and writings of the
author."

PRINCIPAL WORKS: An Attempt to Ascertain
the Order in which the Plays of Shakespeare Were
Written, 1778; The Plays of Shakespeare (ed.)
11 vol.) 1785-92 (J. Boswell, Jr., ed. 21 vol.
1821); A Dissertation on . . . King Henry VI,
787.

ABOUT: Boswell, J., Jr. Memoir, in 1821 ed.;
Hardinge, G. The Essence of Malone; Prior, J.
Life of Edmond Malone, Editor of Shakespeare.

MALORY, Sir THOMAS (?-March 14,
1471), author of *Le Morte d'Arthur,* was
first identified by Professor George Lyman
Kittredge of Harvard as Sir Thomas Malory
of Newbold Revel, Warwickshire. If this
identification, now generally accepted by
scholars, is correct, we possess a reasonable
amount of biographical information about
the first master of English prose.

The Sir Thomas Malory in question was
the son of Sir John Malory and Phillipa
Revell; his father was a person of importance in Warwickshire, being High
Sheriff or Member of Parliament for the
county on several occasions.

Thomas served at Calais in his youth
under Richard de Beauchamp, Earl of Warwick, supplying one lance and two archers;
various dates have been suggested, but all we
know for certain is that this occurred during
the reign of Henry V (d. 1422). Malory
must have been very young at the time.
About 1442 he became a Member of Parliament for Warwickshire, a distinction which
carried with it the title of Knight. Besides
his seat at Newbold Revel (or Fenny Newbold), he inherited the Manor of Winwick
from his father.

In 1451 Sir Thomas was arrested by Sir
William Mountford, Sheriff of Warwickshire and Leicestershire, for acts of hostility
against the Priory of Monks Kirby. He and
his servant John Appelby broke out of
Mountford's custody at Coleshill, swam the

moat, and escaped. They were later rearrested and a number of charges were
brought against them at an inquisition held
at Nuneaton, August 23, 1451, by Humphrey,
Duke of Buckingham. They were alleged to
have broken into Coombe Abbey and carried
off valuables, and to have lain in wait for
Duke Humphrey; Malory was further accused of the rape of Joan, wife of Hugh
Smyth. Later, Malory pleaded not guilty to
all these charges before King Henry VI and
was released. Further imprisonments in
1456 and 1460 followed.

Malory was again in prison in 1468, this
time on a charge of sedition, having taken
the Lancastrian side in the Wars of the
Roses. He was exempted by name from a
general pardon granted by Edward IV in
that year. Internal evidence shows that part
or all of *Le Morte d'Arthur* was written in
prison; the concluding lines of the work state
that it was finished in the ninth year of Edward IV's reign—that is, between March 4,
1469 and March 3, 1470.

Whether released from Newgate before
his death or not, Malory died in London and
was buried in the church of St. Francis at
Greyfriars. He left no estate, having probably deeded his property to a friend in trust
for his heir, lest it be confiscated. We know
that Malory's wife's name was Elizabeth;
his son Robert died young, so that the heir
was his grandson Nicholas, who died without
male issue in 1513.

Le Morte d'Arthur, Malory's translation
and adaptation of various French and English romances to make a connected story,
was the longest and best prose work which
had appeared in English up to that time. It
was first printed by Caxton, who divided it
into twenty-one books, in 1485.

PRINCIPAL WORKS: Le Morte d'Arthur (W.
Caxton, ed.) 1485 (Wynkyn de Worde, ed. 1529;
E. Strachey, ed. 1884; H. O. Sommer, ed. 1889-91;
A. W. Pollard, ed. 1890; F. J. Simmons, ed. 1893-
94).

ABOUT: Altick, R. The Scholar Adventurers;
Hicks, E. Sir Thomas Malory, his Turbulent
Career; Vinaver, E. Malory.

MANDEVILLE, BERNARD DE (1670?-
January 1733), physician, satirist, was born
in Dort (Dordrecht), Holland, the son of
Michael de Mandeville, a prominent physician. After the Erasmus School, Rotterdam, he entered the University of Rotterdam

in 1685, and received his M.D. degree at the University of Leyden in 1691. He then went to England, ostensibly to "learn the language"—which he did so well many persons refused to believe he was a foreigner. He settled in London as a physician, but actually had very little practice, and there is reason to believe he must have had some semi-official connection with the Dutch government, since he was supported by a pension from Dutch merchants. He also did what would now be called "public relations" work for the distilling industry. Through associations in London literary society he met such people as Addison and Benjamin Franklin, who called him "a most entertaining facetious companion."

Mandeville's chief work was *The Fable of the Bees,* originally issued as *The Grumbling Hive.* From a literary viewpoint this was mere doggerel, but it was important as expressing the views of Descartes and Hobbes against the facile optimism of Shaftesbury. To Mandeville, as to Hobbes, mankind was actuated only by his material interests, which were the stimulants to progress, whereas so-called virtues were merely fictions devised by rulers and clergymen to put men under their domination. "The moral virtues are the political offspring which flattery begets upon pride."

The book in its various editions aroused a long and heated controversy. The grand jury of Middlesex County presented it as a nuisance; Francis Hutcheson, William Law, and Bishop Berkeley were among those who wrote opposing its thesis. On the other hand, it was extremely popular, and Dr. Johnson, for one, said that it had "opened his views into real life." It was certainly coarse, but it also had vigor and fluency, and its ingenious paradoxes were pointed and acute. It revealed the author's acquaintance with the work of Locke, and it pointed the way to Bentham and the doctrine of utilitarianism.

Mandeville's other books, outside of a rather sensible medical treatise on what was then called "the vapors" and a free translation of Æsop, were more or less "follow-ups" on *The Fable of the Bees.* He was nothing of a poet, and his serious verse was pretty bad. In a coarse age he was extremely outspoken and even vulgar, though part of his reputation in that line was due to his open discussion of subjects—such as capital punishment and prostitution—which then were not thought fit for public print. In consequence he had ascribed to him several books and pamphlets, pornographical in nature, which were certainly not his.

Mandeville was himself not a pleasant person, overbearing and arrogant. He died in London and was buried there, never again seeing his native land and even losing most of his familiarity with his native tongue after some forty years' residence in England. His work has no standing as literature, but it is a constituent part of the philosophical ferment of the eighteenth century, and he did a good deal to clear the road for a more scientific view of both philosophy and economics.

PRINCIPAL WORKS: Typhon in Verse, 1704; The Planter's Charity (verse) 1704; Esop Dressed, or a Collection of Fables Writ in Familiar Verse, 1704; The Grumbling Hive, or Knaves Turn'd Honest, 1705 (as The Fable of the Bees; or, Private Vices, Public Benefits, with an Inquiry into the Original of Moral Virtue, 1714; with An Essay on Charity and Charity Schools, and A Search into the Nature of Society, 1723 (F. B. Kaye, ed. 1924); The Virgin Unmask'd, 1709; Treatise of the Hypochondriack and Hysterick Passions, 1711; Free Thoughts on Religion, the Church, and Natural Happiness, 1720; An Inquiry into the Causes of the Frequent Executions at Tyburn, 1725; A Conference on Whoring, 1725; The Origin of Honour, and the Usefulness of Christianity in War, 1732.

ABOUT: Bain, A. Moral Science; Hawkins, J. Life of Johnson; Kaye, F. B. Commentary, *in* Fable of the Bees, 1924 ed.; Newman, J. W. Lounger's Commonplace Book; Robertson, J. M. Pioneer Humanists; Sakmann, P. Mandeville und die Bienenfabel-Controverse; Stephen, L. English Thought in the 18th Century.

MANLEY, Mrs. MARY DE LA RIVIERE (April 7, 1663-July 11, 1724), novelist, playwright, pamphleteer, periodical writer, was the daughter of Sir Roger Manley, who fought on the Royalist side in the civil war and spent fourteen years in Holland as an exile; after the Restoration he held several military commands, including the Lieutenant-Governorship of Jersey, 1667-74. His younger daughter, Mary de la Riviere, is believed to have been born either in Jersey or at sea off the Jersey coast. She inherited her literary talent from her father, who was the author of two valuable historical works; at his death in 1688 she also inherited the sum of £200 and a share in the residue of his estate.

Her troubles seem to have begun just after her father's death. She was then inveigled into a bigamous marriage by her cousin John Manley, whose first wife was still living; about six years later he deserted her. The Duchess of Cleveland, a former mistress of Charles II, took pity on her and sheltered her for six months. Then the Duchess accused Mrs. Manley of having an affair with her son and turned her out. For the next two years Mrs. Manley seems to have strayed, morally and physically, up and down the West of England. In 1696 she blossomed forth as an authoress publishing a volume of letters and having two plays produced in London. *The Lost Lover*, a comedy, was a failure, but her tragedy, *The Royal Mischief*, succeeded.

She now became a celebrated London figure and the mistress of more than one person in the public eye. Her affair with Sir Thomas Skipworth, lessee of Drury Lane Theatre, may be regarded as an offshoot of her dramatic career; she found another protector in John Tilly, Warden of the Fleet prison. By 1705 her charms must have been fading, for she took to literature again, producing the first of her collections of contemporary scandal thinly disguised as fiction. This was *The Secret History of Queen Zarah*. Her most notorious work in this genre, *Secret Memoirs and Manners of Several Persons of Quality of Both Sexes. From the New Atalantis, an Island in the Mediterranean*, appeared in 1709 and was an instant success.

The *New Atalantis* contained scandal about every important member of the Whig party, which was then in power. Pride of place was given to the Duke of Marlborough's youthful intrigue with Mrs. Manley's former friend, the Duchess of Cleveland. Mrs. Manley was arrested and generously obtained the release of the publishers and printers of the *New Atalantis* by acknowledging its authorship. She refused, however, to reveal the sources of her scandalous information and was discharged early in 1710.

She now collaborated with Swift in various Tory pamphlets, and succeeded him in the editorship of *The Examiner*, 1711. After the return of the Tories to power in 1711, Swift, who described her as "very homely and very fat," recommended that she be rewarded for her services. Her autobiographical *Adventures of Rivella* appeared in 1714, and is the chief authority for the facts of her early life.

The Tories went out of office in 1714, so that Mrs. Manley's last years were ones of further struggle; in her later writings she took care not to fall foul of the law. She died at the London printing house of Alderman Barber whose mistress she was.

Mary Manley is a sympathetic figure, generous and good natured; Swift and Steele both had a genuine affection for her. Her unfortunate "marriage" made her a social outcast; having no reputation to lose, she exploited the popular taste for scandal, as did better and more reputable writers of her day. Her Tory principles were genuine enough; in that respect she was her father's daughter, though she tended to mix pornography with politics. In *Rivella* and *The Power of Love* she helped to create the realistic traditions of the English novel; we may regard her as a feminine counterpart to Defoe.

PRINCIPAL WORKS: *Plays*: The Lost Lover, or The Jealous Husband, 1696; The Royal Mischief, 1696; Almyna, 1707; Lucius, the First Christian King of Britain, 1717. *Novels and Memoirs*: Letters Written by Mrs. Manley, 1696; The Secret History of Queen Zarah, 1705; The New Atalantis, 1709; Memoirs of Europe, 1710; Adventures of Rivella, 1714; The Power of Love, *in* Seven Novels, 1720.

ABOUT: Hudson, W. H. Idle Hours in a Library; Jerrold, W. C. Five Queer Women.

MANNYNG, ROBERT (fl. 1288-1338), poet, is more commonly known as Robert of Brunne—Brunne or Brunnewake being the modern Bourne, Lincolnshire. At an early age he joined the monastery of the Gilbertine Order (founded in 1139) at its parent house in Sempringham, some six miles from Bourne. In all probability he was not a monk, but a lay brother. At one time he lived in Cambridge, where he knew Robert Bruce, the great Scottish leader, and his brothers; he may possibly have been a student at the university but it is more likely that he was merely staying at the Gilbertine priory there. Later he lived in the priory at Sixille (Six Hills), also in Lincolnshire. All these things we learn from his own poems, and that when he began to write in "englysch rime" he had already been fifteen years at

Sempringham. This is practically all we know of Mannyng's life.

With the exception of the doubtful ascription to him of a free translation from Bonaventura of "medytacyuns" on the Eucharist and the Crucifixion, the only surviving poems by Mannying are his version of the *Manuel des Pechiez* by William of Wadington (originally written for the use of Norman settlers in Yorkshire), which Mannying called *Handlyng Synne,* and his *Chronicle of Inglande,* the first part taken from the *Historia Regum Britanniae* of Geoffrey of Monmouth, in its translation by Wace, the second part from the *Chronicle* of Peter Langtoft, an Anglo-Norman canon of the Augustinian priory at Bidlington. In both cases Mannyng's poems are not so much translations or even paraphrases as free fantasias on a theme.

He is a born story teller, who added and subtracted as he pleased to or from his original, omitting dull discussions of theory and adding narratives of his own observation or invention. How he wrote *Handlyng Synne* at Sempringham it is difficult to imagine, since the residents were allowed no books and could write only by permission of their superiors. Mannyng's object was to draw the minds of common men and women from unedifying frivolities to spiritual things, and he knew the way to do this was to write "in simple speech for love of simple men." He was democratic in his approach, harsh in his satire and invective against the vices of the upper classes, the clergy, and women. In his *Chronicle* he emblemizes the evolving Englishman, no longer Saxon or Norman but unitedly and patriotically English. He is in a sense a combined homilist and troubadour, obviously influenced by the French *fabilaux,* simple, direct, with pithy proverbs and homely speech.

Though Mannyng apologizes for his "foul Englysche and feeble rime," actually he is, as Furnivall has said, "a language reformer who helped make English flexible." In the rough alexandrines of the second part of the *Chronicle,* he "foreshadowed the heroic couplet," and he has real poetic feeling. Chaucer, Gower, and Langland may all have been familiar with his work, though only three manuscripts have survived. The *Chronicle* runs from the legendary Brut to

the end of the reign of Edward I, and in its latter portion is of great historical interest. In the stories in *Handlyng Synne,* Mannyng sometimes reaches almost Chaucerian verve and penetration. As Kington-Oliphant said, he "foreshadowed the path that English literature was to tread from that time forward."

PRINCIPAL WORKS: Handlyng Synne (F. J. Furnivall, ed.) 1862; Medytaciuns of ye Soper of our Lorde Jhesu, etc. (J. M. Cooper, ed.) 1875; The Chronicle of Inglande (F. J. Furnivall, ed.) 1887 (Peter Langtoft's Chronicle, as Illustrated and Improved by Robert of Brunne, T. Hearne, ed. 1725).

ABOUT: Boerner, O. Über die Sprache Robert Mannyngs von Brunne und ihr Verhaltnis zur Neuenglischen Mundart; Furnivall, F. J. Prefaces, Handlyng Synne and The Chronicle of Inglande; Hellmers, G. Über die Sprache Robert Mannyngs; Kington-Oliphant, T. L. Old and Middle English; Ten Brink, B. Early English Writers.

MAP or **MAPES, WALTER** (fl. 1200), author of a satirical miscellany, was probably Welsh by birth. His parents were friends of Henry II, and, on his return to England after having studied in Paris under Girard la Pucelle, he became a clerk of the royal household. He remained closely connected with the court until the death of Henry, his position increasing in importance from itinerant justice, through a series of offices, until, following Henry's death, he became archdeacon of Oxford in 1197.

His reputation, both as a wit and as a serious writer, far exceeds any direct evidence which remains. If, as legend has it, he was either solely or in large part responsible for the long prose romances, *Lancelot, Death of Arthur,* and *Quest of the Holy Grail,* on which all later forms of the Arthurian legend were based, he is a major figure in English literature. Proof is absent, but the persistence of the ascription by contemporary and later writers makes his authorship seem probable. He is also reputedly the author of many of the "Goliardic" poems, witty Latin satires on church corruption.

The one undisputed work of Map's which survives is *De Nugis Curialium* (of courtiers' triflings), a sort of sketchbook in which, during ten busy years of court life, he jotted down a miscellany of material at the request of Henry II. There are gossipy anecdotes, bits of Welsh folk-lore, clever satires on church and state, and some passages of serious historical value, including an evaluation of the lives and accomplishments of the Anglo-Saxon kings. The work gives evidence of a lively, worldly, perceptive mind, versed in the classics, law, and theology as well as in the sophisticated life of the court.

From evidence given by his loyal friend Giraldus Cambrensis, who fostered the memory of Walter's verbal brilliance, it appears that he died about 1209.

PRINCIPAL WORK: De Nugis Curialium.

ABOUT: Foss, E. Biographia Juridica; Nutt, A. Studies in the Legend of the Holy Grail; Wright, T. Biographia Britannica Literaria.

MARKHAM, GERVASE or JERVIS

(1568?-1637), miscellaneous writer, was the youngest son of Robert Markham of Cottam, Nottinghamshire. Following a few years of soldiering in the Low Countries and in the service of the Earl of Essex in Ireland, he became what has been called "England's first hackney writer," although this is probably too harsh a judgment.

He was something of a scholar, learning Latin, French, Italian, Spanish, and Dutch, and building up a respectable personal library. He occasionally essayed serious literature, including several poems based on Biblical themes, and a narrative poem on the fight of the "Revenge" which Tennyson used as a basis for his poem on that subject.

But it is for his "commercial" writing that he is best remembered. Extremely prolific, unabashedly opportunistic, he turned out book after book, sometimes reissuing practically the identical book under a new title for additional sales. His subject matter included military tactics, husbandry, housewifery, angling, the breeding of fighting cocks, and all phases of breeding, raising, and training of horses. To his considerable knowledge of these subjects he added an engaging assumption of infallibility, and he wrote in an easy, familiar style which invested his instructions with charm and authority, and which gives the modern reader a remarkably immediate sense of the spoken language and everyday life of the time.

Markham was especially at home in the field of horsemanship, establishing an excellent stable of his own, and importing the first Arabian horse into England. He was an adept at dedications, publishing one work, *Cavelarice*, in seven volumes, each dedicated to a different, presumably financially grateful, patron. The booksellers, realizing that he was flooding his own market, once obtained his signature to an agreement not to publish any further books on farriery, an agreement which he broke a few years later.

Markham was married but had no children. He was about sixty-nine when he died, and is buried at St. Giles' Church, Cripplegate, in London.

PRINCIPAL WORKS: Poem of Poems, the Song of Solomon, 1592; Discourse on Horsemanship, 1593; The Most Honorable Tragedy of Sir Richard Grinville, 1595; Virtue's Tears, a Lament for Henry III of France and Walter Devereux, 1597; Tears of the Beloved, or Lamentations of St. John, 1600; Marie Magdalene's Lamentations, 1601; The English Arcadia, 1607; Cavelarice, or the English Horseman, 1607; Country Contentments, 1611; The English Housewife, 1611; The Pleasures of Princes, 1615; Hunger's Prevention, 1621; The Art of Archery, 1634.

ABOUT: Baker, D. E. Biographia Dramatica; Brydges, Sir S. E. Censura Literaria; Fleay, F. G. A Biographical Chronicle of the English Drama; Langbaine, G. Dramatic Poets; Ritson, G. Bibliographica Poetica.

MARLOWE, CHRISTOPHER

(February 6, 1564-May 30, 1593), dramatist, was born in Canterbury. His father, John Marlowe (the name was also spelled Marley, Morley, Marlin, and in half a dozen other ways) was a shoemaker and tanner; his mother, Catherine Arthur, was the daughter of a clergyman. He attended the King's School in Canterbury and in 1580 entered Bene't (now Corpus Christi) College, Cambridge. He received a B.A. in 1584, and M.A. in 1587.

A few obscure years followed. Modern research has established that Marlowe's M.A. degree was given him without delay at the request of the queen, through the Privy Council. It has been rumored that Marlowe, like Jonson, was a soldier in the Low Countries; the probability is that he was not a soldier, but a spy, from before the Armada to the end of his life. He was certainly a close friend of Sir Walter Raleigh's; and the three men with him when he died, one of whom was supposed to be his murderer, were all known government spies.

In any event, by 1589 he was in London, and was an occasional actor and a regular dramatist for the Lord Admiral's Company. His previous writing had been confined to a translation of Ovid's *Amores*. His first play (dates of publication are not the same as dates of production) was *Tamburlaine*. In spite of the unevenness of this great tragedy, it is extraordinary for a first play by an unknown dramatist. It aroused much scandal among the classicists, since it marked the first appearance of true blank verse—not mere unrhymed decasyllables—on the stage. It began the attacks on and ridicule of Marlowe for "bombast"—attacks entirely undeserved and resented and answered by his friends, Nashe, Greene, Peele, Kyd, and the others.

Dr. Faustus came next, then *The Jew of Malta.* Then Marlowe turned from romantic tragedy to history, with *Edward II* and *The Massacre at Paris. Edward II* was the first true historical play in English, as distinguished from chronicle plays. It was also Marlowe's first to show sustained power instead of patches of brilliance interspersed with more plodding and less inspired passages.

It must be remembered that all Marlowe's output was condensed into the work of four years. At his death, besides these plays, he left the unfinished *Dido,* completed by Nash, the poem *Hero and Leander,* unnecessarily finished by George Chapman, and his translations of Lucan and Ovid. That is all, except for one short pastoral poem and a brief verse published in *Englands Parnassus* (1600), beginning, "I walked along a stream for pureness rare."

That is all, but it includes three at least of the greatest tragedies in English, a fine historical play, and a lovely lyric. Shakespeare was two months younger than Marlowe; in 1593 he had written only *Henry VI, Richard III, The Comedy of Errors,* and *Venus and Adonis,* besides some of the sonnets. That is not to say that Marlowe was greater than Shakespeare, or even as great; but it gives some idea of what the world lost by Marlowe's early death.

In addition to his own plays, Marlowe undoubtedly collaborated with many of his colleagues, probably including Shakespeare. With the wholesale borrowing and intricate multi-auctorial playwriting of the time, it is impossible to say definitely to just which plays of which authors Marlowe lent a hand. Among those of Shakespeare which have been suspected to owe something either to Marlowe's collaboration or to lost plays of

his are *King John, Henry VI, Titus Andronicus,* and *The Taming of the Shrew.*

Marlowe was less than thirty when he was killed. Thanks to the remarkable researches of Leslie Hotson, and those of an English scholar, Roderick Eagle, we know a little more of what happened than did all but a few of his contemporaries, but there is much which is still shrouded in mystery. One fact is that Marlowe's religious views were distinctly unorthodox, though whether he was technically an atheist has not been established. In any event, a warrant for his arrest on charges of "atheism and immorality" was certainly sworn out in May, 1593. (Kyd, some of whose papers were found mixed with Marlowe's, was put to the torture and recanted.) Marlowe escaped to Deptford, now a London slum but then a country town four miles from London.

There, on May 30th, he spent the day in an inn with Robert Poley, Nicholas Skeres, and Ingram Frizer or Frezer. At the end of that day Marlowe was dead of stab wounds. Whether there was a quarrel over the bill, or whether the killing was really a political assassination is unknown. As said above, all these three were proved spies and Marlowe might possibly have wanted to leave a service from which there is no withdrawing. The story by Francis Meres that Marlowe and Frizer quarreled over the favors of a "lewd love" is definitely disproved. It is certain that Frizer was pardoned a few days later. Eagle's theory is still more startling. It is that Marlowe was not killed at all, but that the so-called murder was a pretense, enabling Marlowe to go to Rheims secretly on an errand of espionage, while word was spread that he was dead and an unknown corpse, attired in his clothes, was taken to the coroner. There are some grounds for this rather bizarre idea—for example, Gabriel Harvey wrote that Marlowe died of the plague, which may have been one of the stories circulated; and no one knows where he is buried. However, even Eagle says he never came back from Rheims, but was caught and killed there, so for all practical purposes he died in 1593. The whole venturous, romantic, exuberant spirit of the Age of Elizabeth is epitomized in this son of a Canterbury shoemaker.

Whatever happened to Marlowe the man, Marlowe the poet left enough work behind him to give him immortality. His friend Michael Drayton wrote well that he was "all air and fire," creator of "brave translunary things." He made a full break with tradition, he gave new capacity to blank verse, instinct with a towering imagination. He loved words for their own sake, delighted in them consciously; in fact, one of the salient points of Marlowe's plays is that they are less dramatic than literary, and it was in literary and not in dramatic development that he was a pioneer.

He had many faults, and they were not merely the faults of youth. His plays revolve always around a single character, and the minor characters are left as mere sketches. He could not draw a living woman. He had little sense of humor, and the comedy in his plays is grotesque and clownish and may indeed have been interpolated by others because he was incapable of doing it himself. Though it is not true that he is bombastic, he does indulge in much hyperbole and extravagance of speech.

But when all that is granted, there is left a great genius. His verse, as Edward Thomas has said, is "almost uncontrollably sweet and swift." Swinburne called him "the most daring and inspired pioneer in all our poetic literature." He was indeed, as Peele, named him, "the Muses' darling," the chosen author of Jonson's "mighty line. . . fitter for admiration than for parallel." His rich and vigorous imagination aspired always beyond the bonds of language; in Symonds' fine phrase, the wellspring of his poetry was "love of the impossible." To read *Tamburlaine, Dr. Faustus, The Jew of Malta*, is a crucial experience in the reader's life. Webster perhaps came nearest to his spirit; of Shakespeare's plays, perhaps *Lear* and *Macbeth* most nearly approximate the Marlovian fire. In his only completed nondramatic poem, *The Passionate Shepheard to his Love* (published as Shakespeare's in *The Passionate Pilgrim*, 1599, as Marlowe's own in *Englands Helicon* in 1600, with a witty rejoinder by Raleigh), he has left an almost perfect thing of its kind. If Hotson's or Eagle's conjectures are correct, it seems that Queen Elizabeth unwittingly did England a disservice indeed when she picked young Christopher Marlowe for the dangerous job of spying on the Spaniards.

PRINCIPAL WORKS (*Dates of publication*): Tamburlaine the Great, 1590; The Troublesome Raigne and Lamentable Death of Edward the Second, King of England, 1594; The Tragedie of Dido Queene of Carthage (with T. Nash) 1594; Certaine of Ovid's Elegies, 1597? (C. Edmonds, ed. 1870); The Massacre at Paris, with the Death of the Duke of Guise, 1598; Hero and Leander (finished by G. Chapman) 1598; Lucans First Booke, Translated Line for Line, 1600; The Tragicall History of Dr. Faustus, 1604; The Famous Tragedie of the Rich Jew of Malta, 1633; Collected Works (A. H. Bullen, ed.) 1884-85 (H. Ellis, ed. 1887; F. T. Brooke, ed. 1910); Plays (E. Thomas, ed.) 1909.

ABOUT: Bakeless, J. E. Christopher Marlowe, the Man in his Time, The Tragicall History of Christopher Marlowe; Beard, T. Theatre of God's Judgement; Boas, F. S. Christopher Marlowe, a Biographical and Critical Study, Marlowe and His Circle; Brooke, C. F. T. The Marlowe Canon; Bullen, A. H. Introduction, Collected Works, 1883-85 ed.; Clark, E. G. Raleigh and Marlowe; Dowden, E. Transcripts and Studies; Eccles, M. Christopher Marlowe in London; Ellis-Fermor, U. M. Christopher Marlowe; Hazlitt, W. Dramatic Literature of the Age of Elizabeth; Henderson, P. And Morning in his Eyes; Hotson, J. L. The Death of Marlowe; Ingram, J. H. Marlowe and his Associates; Kocher, J. H. Christopher Marlowe: A Study of his Thought, Learning, and Character; Lamb, C. Specimens of the English Dramatic Poets; Lewis, F. G. Christopher Marlowe, an Outline of his Life and Works; Meres, F. Palladis Tamia; Norman, C. The Muses' Darling; Robertson, J. M. Marlowe, a Conspectus; Schelling, F. E. Elizabethan Drama; Swinburne, A. C. A Study of Shakespeare; Symonds, J. A. Shakespeare's Predecessors; Thomas, E. Introduction, Plays, 1909; Vaughan, W. The Golden Grove; Verity, A. W. Marlowe's Influence on Shakespeare.

MARMION, SHACKERLEY (1603-1639),

dramatist and poet, the son of a minor law official, was born near Brackly, Northamptonshire. His father impoverished the family when young Marmion was in his teens, but he entered Wadham College, Oxford, as a commoner, and obtained his B.A. in 1622 and his M.A. in 1624.

After a year in the army, he lived in London, associating himself with both the literary world and the underworld. He was involved in a street brawl in 1629 in which he was accused of stabbing a man, although he was never arrested for the offence. His literary career was greatly influenced by his friends Ben Jonson and John Suckling. He wrote three comedies, all weak imitations of Jonson in style, although one, *The Antiquary*, had some originality of conception. The contemporary audience, especially the courtiers, applauded these fairly outrageous satires on the vices of their own society. The setting of one of the plays, *Hollands Leaguer,* was a notorious Blackfriar's brothel of that name.

Marmion's best work was a poem in heroic couplets based on Apuleius' story of Cupid and Psyche. Adhering closely to the original story, Marmion avoided the plot extravagances of which most of the minor Carolinian poets were guilty.

In 1638 Suckling raised a company for an expedition to Scotland. Marmion joined this expedition, became ill, and was returned to London, where he died at the age of thirty-six. He was buried at the Church of St. Bartholomew.

PRINCIPAL WORKS: Hollands Leaguer, 1632; A Fine Companion, 1633; The Antiquary, 1636; The Legend of Cupid and Psyche, 1637.

ABOUT: Dodsley, R. Old English Plays; Fleay, F. Biographical Chronical of the English Drama; Wood, A. à, Athenae Oxonienses.

MARSHALL, STEPHEN (1594?-1655),

Presbyterian divine, one of the authors of *Smectymnuus,* was the son of a poor glover of Godmanchester, Huntingdonshire. He entered Emanuel College, Cambridge, as a pensioner, graduating with a B.A. in 1618; although he was not a remarkable scholar, he supported himself by tutoring and lecturing until he obtained an M.A. and a B.D. He was an unprepossessing man personally.

He became vicar of Finchingfield, Essex, and in 1642 took the additional task of morning lecturer at St. Margaret's, Westminster. He moved steadily toward support of liberalizing reform in the church, beginning in 1636 when, although he carefully observed all rules and forms, he was accused of having "an incomformable heart." Later he was one of the strongest advocates of the parliamentary cause during the civil war, and for church reform under Cromwell.

He was a chaplain in the army of the Earl of Essex, and an important member of the Westminster Assembly of Divines, which worked with the Scottish church for the establishment of presbyterianism in England. In 1641 he was one of five divines who wrote a famous appeal for church reforms addressed to the House of Commons. The tract, titled *Smectymnuus* (combining the initials of the authors), did not result in immediate action, but was one of the first factors toward abolition of the episcopacy.

His everyday sermons were persuasive because of their homely, colloquial, earnest style, he occasionally delivered exceptionally eloquent and well written sermons, of which twenty-five were published. For the last few years of his life Marshall was town preacher at Ipswich, where he died of tuberculosis in 1655. He was buried in Westminster Abbey, but following the Restoration his bones were exhumed and thrown with those of other anti-Royalists into a dishonored pit in St. Margaret's churchyard.

PRINCIPAL WORKS: Smectymnuus (co-author with four divines) 1641; A Peace Offering to God, 1641; Reformation and Desolation, 1641; A Sacred Panegyrick, 1643.

ABOUT: Brook, B. Lives of the Puritans; Fuller, T. Church History of Britain; Fuller, T. History of the Worthies of England; Walker, C. History of Independency.

MARSTON, JOHN (1575?-June 25, 1634),

dramatist, satirist, clergyman, was probably born at Coventry, Warwickshire. His father, also named John, was a country gentleman who had had considerable legal training—so much that he was appointed Reader of the Middle Temple, 1592. The dramatist's mother was Maria Guarsi, member of an Italian family which had settled in London, where her father and grandfather were successful surgeons.

Young John entered Brasenose College, Oxford, early in 1592 and graduated B.A. almost exactly two years later. He then studied law, in accordance with his father's wishes, but did not find it to his taste and turned to literature. Attracted by Joseph Hall's success in the same medium, he published two collections of verse satires in 1598. These contained some slighting references to Hall, but Marston was not destined to outshine his predecessor. In 1599 the Archbishop of Canterbury ordered both books of satires to be burned, mainly because of the licentiousness of a poem entitled *The Metamorphosis of Pygmalion's Image.*

Marston next took up play writing, and again made an inauspicious start by attacking one of his seniors. The anonymous *Histriomastix* (1599), which is certainly Marston's, contained a character named Chrysoganus; not only was Chrysoganus modeled on Macilente in Ben Jonson's *Every Man Out of His Humour,* but he could be taken as a gentle caricature of Jonson himself. Jonson replied to the supposed attack in his next play, and Marston in the two following years wrote *Jack Drum's Entertainment* and *What You Will*, both containing hits at Jonson. Their rivalry was fostered by the fact that they were writing for the two rival companies of child actors alluded to in *Hamlet;* Marston was writing for the Children of Paul's, Jonson for the Children of Blackfriars.

In 1601 Jonson determined to annihilate Marston and brought out his *Poetaster.* Crispinus in this play is a devastating caricature of Marston. He is represented as having red hair and small legs, wearing a long feather in his cap, and using an outlandish vocabulary in his writings—this last a very just criticism. As a punishment for his sins against poetry, Crispinus is in the final scene forced to vomit his vocabulary. Jonson also claimed to have taken a more direct revenge on Marston; he told Drummond of Hawthornden that he beat the rival poet and took his pistol away from him. Marston did not answer *Poetaster* himself, but Dekker was hired to write *Satiromastix*, which proved so effective a reply that Jonson gave up play writing for a couple of years.

The quarrel must have been made up later, for in 1604 Marston dedicated his best-known play, *The Malcontent*, to Jonson. Moreover, in 1605 Chapman and Marston collaborated on a play entitled *Eastward Ho;* certain passages satirizing the Scots and—by implication—the Scottish James I, were thought to be by Jonson. Chapman and Marston were imprisoned and Jonson "voluntarily" imprisoned himself with them, according to his own account. Whether Jonson was guilty or innocent, this was certainly a friendly act. Marston was in jail again in 1608, on what charge we do not know. About this time he gave up play writing permanently.

Marston's malcontent career ended with his marriage and the taking of holy orders. We do not know the dates of these events, but there must have been some connection between them, for his wife Mary was the daughter of a clergyman, the Reverend William Wilkes, chaplain to James I. On October 10, 1616, Marston was appointed to the living of Christchurch, Hampshire, which

he resigned on September 13, 1631, perhaps because of ill health. It is likely that he spent his retirement in London, for he died in Aldermanbury parish there and was buried in Temple Church beside his father.

Marston's quarrelsome early career suggests an insecure personality, ambitious but unable to find a proper outlet for very real talents. One cannot resist identifying him with the leading character in his own *Malcontent*—Malevole, an exiled Duke, who returns to his own Court of Genoa in disguise. Like Jaques in *As You Like It*, he is treated there as a privileged jester, entitled to abuse all and sundry. Finally he appears in his true colours and regains his dukedom.

Marston's plays, particularly *The Dutch Courtesan* and *The Insatiate Countess* (a fragment later completed by William Barksted), are full of bitter satire on womankind. It is pleasant to imagine that his wife reconciled him to her sex; certainly he was a good husband to her, for her will contains affectionate references to him and she was buried by his side on July 4, 1657.

Though not a great playwright, Marston will always be remembered as a personality. Impatient, bitter, satirical, all his plays—good and bad—bear the unmistakable stamp of his character. Malevole in *The Malcontent* is the ultimate expression of a personality type very common in Elizabethan life and literature. T. S. Eliot alone among the critics refuses to regard *The Malcontent* as Marston's best play, preferring *The Wonder of Women.* This may well have been Marston's own favorite, for he calls it a "tragedy which shall boldly abide the most curious perusal," whereas in most of his other work he gives the impression of writing down to his audience.

No portrait of Marston is extant. It is an odd sidelight on Marston—if indeed he answers to Jonson's description—that his plays contain many slighting references to people with red hair. It suggests that Marston's dissatisfaction with the world at large sprang from inner dissatisfaction with himself.

PRINCIPAL WORKS: *Plays*: The History of Antonio and Mellida, 1602; Antonio's Revenge, 1602; The Malcontent, 1604; The Dutch Courtesan, 1605; Parasitaster, or The Fawn, 1606; The Wonder of Women, or The Tragedy of Sophonisba, 1606; What You Will, 1607; The Insatiate Countess (with Barksted) 1613. *Satires*: The Metamorphosis of Pygmalion's Image and Certain Satires, 1598; The Scourge of Villainy, 1598; The Plays of John Marston (H. H. Wood, ed.) 1934.

ABOUT: Allen, M. S. The Satire of John Marston; Eliot, T. S. Elizabethan Essays.

MARVELL, ANDREW (March 31, 1621-August 18, 1678), poet, satirist, was born in Winestead, Yorkshire, his father, also Andrew, being the vicar there. His mother was Anne Pease When the child was three, the father became master of Hull Grammar School, where the son received his first education. In 1633 Marvell entered Trinity College, Cambridge, as a sizar. He received his B.A. in 1638, but remained at the university until 1641. In 1640 his father was drowned. Apparently on his small inheritance, Marvell traveled in Holland, France, Italy, and Spain from about 1642 to 1646; he learned the languages of all these countries, and all his life had some sort of business affairs in Holland.

Marvell's earliest poems appeared (one in Greek, one in Latin, both addressed to Charles I) in a Cambridge anthology in 1637. Throughout his lifetime he was far better known as a satirist and pamphleteer than as a poet; except for a few fugitive appearances in print (a poem in the 1674 edition of *Paradise Lost,* for example), his poems were circulated only in manuscript. (His poem on Richard Flecknoe, an Irish

ANDREW MARVELL

priest, written in Rome in 1645, inspired Dryden's satire on Shadwell, in 1682.)

The civil war and the Commonwealth posed a problem for a young man who, though broad in his religious and political views, was not really a Puritan and never left the Church of England. Marvell's ruling passion was a longing for law and order; he admired strong people, and Cromwell was among his greatest admirations. From 1650 to 1652 he was tutor in the family of Lord Fairfax, who was a Parliamentary general; most of his beautiful garden poems were written at the Fairfax estate, Nun Appleton, Yorkshire. In 1653 Milton, his great friend (but it must be noted that his other close friend was Lovelace, who was a Royalist) tried in vain to secure Marvell's appointment to assist him as Latin or foreign language secretary to Cromwell; instead, another got the post and Marvell became tutor to Cromwell's ward, William Dutton. In 1657 he finally secured the secretaryship, and held it until the Restoration.

In 1659 Marvell was elected to Parliament for Hull, and continued to hold the seat till his death, though in 1663-65 he was abroad as secretary to the Earl of Carlisle in his embassy to Russia and Scandinavia. For his constituents, Marvell issued regular *News Letters,* which constituted nearly all the writing published under his own name in his lifetime. As a member of the House of Commons, he was instrumental in saving Milton from any punishment after the Restoration. At first Marvell had high hopes of Charles II, but events soon led him to the firm belief that the Stuarts could not learn by experience. His broadsides and controversial pamphlets and his satirical poems, though all anonymous, were nevertheless widely credited to him (besides a number which he did not write). Actually he was a republican, and the Commonwealth had seemed to him the ideal state. His *Account of the Growth of Popery*, which was a direct attack on the king and court, created a sensation; £100 was offered for apprehension of the anonymous author, without success. Marvell's life was threatened, and was probably in real danger. It is easy to understand why, when he died suddenly at only fifty-seven, there were rumors that he had been poisoned.

Actually, however, he died of tertian fever, or malaria, helped out of life by "an old conceited doctor" who bled him and gave him opiates instead of prescribing quinine, which was well known by then as Peruvian bark. He died in London and was buried in St. Giles-in-the-Field.

Marvell was not known to be married, but his poems were issued the next year by a woman calling herself Mary Marvell, his widow. As she was also given executorship of his estate, she must have had some proof of their marriage. In any event, he left no children.

He was a man of medium size and warm coloring, with brown hair and hazel eyes. He was fond of wine, but refused "to play the good fellow in any man's company in whose hands I would not trust my life"—another evidence that he was far too cautious to have permitted himself to be poisoned. Though Marvell's satire sometimes descends to scurrilous lampooning, there is no doubt of his complete integrity. He scornfully turned down offers of court positions and royal bribes. In a time of religious fanaticism he was markedly tolerant, advising "prudence toward dissenters," but being so open to argument at the other end of the hierarchy that once in his college days a Jesuit at Cambridge influenced him to desert the university. (His father found him in a bookshop in London and brought him back to Cambridge.)

Swift called Marvell "a great genius," but it was Marvell the pamphleteer whom he hailed; he did not know Marvell the poet at all. Wordsworth did, and celebrated him in a sonnet; so did Charles Lamb, who said that "all his serious poetry is full of a witty delicacy." Marvell was one of the earliest English poets to love nature for its own sake, and to celebrate its beauty without a moral tagged on. His English guide was Donne, but his real master was Horace; Horace is instinct in every poem Marvell wrote, and the famous *Horatian Ode* to Cromwell reads as if the great Roman himself had written it. (Actually, Marvell sometimes wrote his poems—not this one—in Latin and then translated them into English.) Francis Turner Palgrave said that Marvell had written "more in Milton's style than any other poet," but in fact Milton,

even in his youthful lyrics, could never have written *A Garden* or *The Definition of Love* or, above all, *To His Coy Mistress*—that curiously modern poem (though it has echoes of Donne) which is one of the immortal amatory lyrics. If Marvell must be classified, he belongs much more with Herrick and Lovelace than with Waller or the later poets of the Restoration.

PRINCIPAL WORKS: *Prose*: The Rehearsal Transprosed [*sic*] 1672-73; Mr. Smirke, or the Divine in Mode, 1676; An Account of the Growth of Popery, and Arbitrary Government in England, 1678; A Defence of John Howe on God's Prescience, 1678; Remarks upon a Late Disingenuous Discourse, 1678. *Poetry*: The First Anniversary of the Government under His Highness the Lord Protector, 1655; The Character of Holland, 1655; Clarendon's House Warming, 1667; Dialogue between Two Horses, 1675; Advice to a Painter, 1678; Miscellaneous Poems, 1681; A Collection of Poems on Affairs of State, 1689; Poems and Satires (G. A. Aitken, ed.) 1892. *Miscellaneous*: Works, 1726; Works (E. Thompson, ed.) 1776; Complete Works (A. B. Grosart, ed.) 1872-75.

ABOUT: Aubrey, J. Brief Lives of Eminent Men; Bagguley, W. H. Andrew Marvell, Tercentenary Tributes; Birrell, A. Andrew Marvell; Bradbrook, M. C. and Lloyd Thomas, M. G. Andrew Marvell; Coleridge, H. The Worthies of Yorkshire and Lancashire; Cooke, T. Account of Life, *in* Works, 1726; Dove, J. The Life of Andrew Marvell; Grosart, A. B. Memorial Introduction, Complete Works; Hood, E. P. Andrew Marvell, His Life and Writings; Landor, W. S. Imaginary Conversations; Poscher, R. Andrew Marvells Poetische Werke; Rogers, H. Essays; Sackville-West, A. M. Andrew Marvell; Thompson, E. Life *in* Works, 1776; Wood, A. à, Athenae Oxonienses.

MASON, WILLIAM

MASON, WILLIAM (1724-1797), poet, was born at Kingston-on-Hull, son of a vicar and descendant of a long line of public officials. He received his B.A. and M.A. from St. John's College, Cambridge, and was appointed a Pembroke fellow in 1747. In 1754 he resigned his fellowship to act as chaplain to the Earl of Holderness, and became vicar of Aston in Yorkshire. Three years later he was appointed chaplain-in-ordinary to the king, and was made a prebend of York Cathedral. He lived three months of the year at York, made an annual visit to London, and remained at Aston the rest of the time. Tiring of this routine, he resigned the royal chaplaincy, quarreled with Holderness, and spent most of his time on an estate he had inherited in East Riding. He married in 1764, but his wife died of tuberculosis three years later. Mason died as the result of an injury to his foot in 1797.

He was a good example of the cultivated clergyman of his day, with a sound classical education and some talent in music, art, and writing. His considerable literary output was ambitious of aim, but pretentious and barren in execution. His close friendship with Thomas Gray, who made him his literary executor, undoubtedly gave Mason an inflated sense of his own ability, many of his poems being imitations of Gray's. He wrote two plays "in the classical manner," frank and feeble imitations of Sophocles, which were performed at Covent Garden.

Gray was patronizingly fond of his friend, of whom he said, "He has much fancy, little judgement . . . a good, well-meaning creature." A mild liberal politically, a loyal, virtuous, philanthropic man, Mason nevertheless had the current reputation of being a pompous, priggish fool. As one of his contemporaries phrased it, he was "a very small poet and a somewhat absurd person."

PRINCIPAL WORKS: Musaeus, a Monody on the Death of Pope, 1744; Isis, a poem, 1748; Elfrida, 1752; Caractacus, 1759; Sappho, an opera, 1778.

ABOUT: Baker, D. Biographica Dramatica; Chalmers, A. English Poets; Coleridge, H. Lives of the Northern Worthies; Genest, J. History of the Stage.

MASSINGER, PHILIP (1583-1640), dramatist, was a son of Arthur Massinger, faithful servant of Henry and William Herbert, second and third Earls of Pembroke respectively. His father was house steward at Wilton, the Herberts' big mansion near Salisbury; he was no mere servant, but the trusted friend of his employers, and a scholar and a gentleman to boot, having been a fellow of Merton College, Oxford; late in life he became a Member of Parliament.

Philip was baptized at Salisbury, November 24, 1583. It has been conjectured that he was a page at Wilton, but nothing definite is known of his early life until we find him entered at St. Alban Hall, Oxford, in 1602. He left Oxford in 1606 without taking a degree. While at college, he is said to have paid more attention to contemporary literature than to the scholastic curriculum.

Massinger went from Oxford to London, and there became friendly with several dramatists of the time. He may have collaborated anonymously with all of them, but he was most closely associated with Fletcher, whose intimate friend he became. We may date the beginning of his collaboration with Fletcher from 1613, when Beaumont married, or from Beaumont's death in 1616. In any case, he is believed to have had a share in a number of plays attributed to Fletcher. These were written for the King's Men, the acting company for which Massinger wrote during almost his entire career.

In 1623 Massinger broke away and wrote for the Queen's company, for the first time under his own name. *The Parliament of Love*, *The Bondman* and *The Renegado* belong to this period. When Fletcher died in 1625, Massinger rejoined the King's company, and was one of their regular playwrights until his death.

He did not derive a large income from his plays; there is a letter extant in which he, Nathaniel Field, and Robert Daborne appeal to Philip Henslowe, the famous theatre manager, for a loan of five pounds to bail them out. Perhaps they had been arrested for debt. Massinger had, however, several patrons among the nobility. The Herberts, mindful of his father's services, stood by him; Philip, the fourth Earl of Pembroke, allowed him an annual pension of thirty or forty pounds. This was afterwards paid to Massinger's widow, but we do not know her name, the date of the marriage, or how many children there were. There must have been some issue, for a woman claiming descent from Massinger died during the late eighteenth century.

Massinger died in his sleep at his home near the Globe Theatre, Southwark. He had gone to bed apparently in perfect health. His burial took place in St. Saviour's churchyard, March 18, 1640; the actors for whom he had written so many plays attended his funeral. He may have been buried in the same grave as Fletcher.

Massinger's personality is something of a mystery; very little about it can be deduced from his plays. His portrait is not particularly attractive. His brow is lofty and somewhat bald; his eyes are large; his nose, too, is large and has a wart on it; what

After T. Cross

PHILIP MASSINGER

really spoil the face, though, are the small, rather indecisive mouth and chin, with their thin growth of moustache and beard.

His plays are well constructed, but wanting in poetry; no one of the period wrote blank verse which was closer to prose in its rhythm and vocabulary. Massinger's forensic tone has often been commented upon; every speech sounds like a lawyer arguing a case. This is particularly true of his own favorite among his plays, *The Roman Actor*.

He was more successful in romantic comedy than in tragedy. Swinburne gave high praise to one play of the former type, *A Very Woman*, and another, *The Great Duke of Florence*, is admired by Cruickshank. But it is generally conceded that Massinger was at his best in true comedies like *The City Madam* and *A New Way to Pay Old Debts*.

The latter play must be regarded as Massinger's masterpiece; it held the stage for nearly two hundred years, and is still worth a revival. Massinger had very little power to create believable characters, but Sir Giles Overreach, the villain, is so consistent and monstrous a monomaniac that one is finally forced to take him seriously. He amasses wealth by the most unscrupulous means with the one aim of marrying his daughter Margaret to a lord. When his plans are frustrated and she marries a commoner, he goes

mad. Wellborn, his nephew, who finds the "new way to pay old debts," is hardly a character at all. He hoodwinks Sir Giles into believing that he is about to marry a wealthy widow; Sir Giles advances him money, planning to plunder him once more when he is safely married; thus Wellborn is able to pay his debts. The two plots, of Margaret's marriage and Wellborn's rehabilitation, are very skilfully interwoven, but every one of the characters is completely transparent; one finds it very hard to believe that anyone except a Massinger character could be taken in by any of the various deceptions practiced.

When T. S. Eliot speaks of Massinger's "defective sensitiveness," he puts his finger on the fault that prevented him from ever becoming a great playwright. Massinger is a great rhetorician, but he is completely insensitive to the finer shades of human nature. His tragedies and tragicomedies anticipate the "heroic plays" of Dryden, where ideas rather than characters conflict with one another. In comedy he is more successful, because it is possible to make a workable comic character out of a single idea; Justice Greedy in *A New Way to Pay Old Debts* is incarnate gluttony, for example; to see what Massinger lacks, one has only to compare Greedy with Falstaff.

PRINCIPAL WORKS: *Plays*: The Virgin Martyr, 1622; The Duke of Milan. 1623; The Bondman, 1624; The Roman Actor, 1629; The Picture, 1630; The Renegado, 1630; The Emperor of the East. 1632; The Fatal Dowry, 1632; The Maid of Honour. 1632; A New Way To Pay Old Debts, 1633; The Great Duke of Florence, 1636; The Unnatural Combat. 1639; The Bashful Lover. 1655; The Guardian, 1655; A Very Woman, 1655; The City Madam, 1658; Believe As You List (T. C. Crocker. ed.) 1849; The Parliament of Love (K. M. Lea, ed.) 1928.

ABOUT: Cruickshank, A. H. Philip Massinger; Eliot, T. S. The Sacred Wood; Eliot. T. S. Elizabethan Essays; Lowell, J. R. Latest Literary Essays and Addresses; Stephen, Sir L. Hours in a Library.

MATHIAS, THOMAS JAMES (1754?-August 1835), satirist, Italian scholar, was the son of the court treasurer, Vincent Mathias. After attending school at Kingston-on-Thames and Eton, he entered Trinity College, Cambridge, where he won high honors for his Latin discourses, and where under Agostino Asola he pursued those studies in Italian which later earned him the reputation of being the best English scholar of Italian since Milton.

349

He became court treasurer and librarian after leaving Cambridge, a sinecure which left him ample time to devote to literary pursuits. He published many satires, most of them personal, and rather coarse than clever. From 1794 to 1797, the four parts of *Pursuits of Literature* were published anonymously, and the work immediately became the most widely read and the most bitterly resented book of the day. The 16th edition was published in 1812; by that time it was generally known that Mathias was the author.

Pursuits of Literature is a short poetic work of criticism, extended to enormous size by ten times its own length in prose prefaces and notes. It is written with ostentatious pedantry, obvious spite, ill-will, and partiality, but it served in its own day to indicate the unhealthy and parasite-ridden state of English literature.

In 1814 Mathias published an edition of the works of Thomas Gray, whom he greatly admired. Published at too high a price to sell, the venture reduced him to poverty, and, falling ill, he sought health and fortune in Italy, where he remained for the rest of his life. He translated and edited much Italian literature, and wrote two noteworthy books of criticism in Italian, *Poesie Liriche* and *Canzoni Toscane.* He died at Naples in 1835.

PRINCIPAL WORKS: Pursuits of Literature, 1794-97; An Imperial Epistle from the Emperor of China to George III, 1794; The Political Dramatist, 1795; An Equestrian Epistle in Verse to the Earl of Jersey, 1796; Observations on the Writings and Character of Mr. Gray, 1815; Poesie Liriche (no date); Canzoni Toscane (no date).

ABOUT: Brydges, Sir E. Restituta; Halkett, S. and Laing, J. Dictionary of Anonymous and Pseudonymous English Literature; Wordsworth, S. Scholae Academicae.

MAY, THOMAS (1595-November 13, 1650), poet, translator, dramatist, eldest son of Sir Thomas May of Sussex, graduated from Cambridge in 1612 and began the study of law at Gray's Inn in 1615. A speech impediment and the loss of the family fortune turned him from the profession of law to that of letters.

The first part of his literary career was conventional and won the approval of Charles I, who promised May a pension, and recommended him for poet laureate. Besides writing four plays, (one a comedy, the others based on classic tragic themes), he translated Virgil, Martial, and Lucan's historical poem, *Pharsalia,* and wrote a continuation of the latter.

Either because of conviction or pique at his royal sponsor's failure to deliver either pension or laureateship, May espoused the Parliamentary cause during the civil war, and became its chief literary exponent. He lived in Parliament's quarters, was one of its two paid secretaries, and drew up many important state documents. His greatest contribution was his *History of the Long Parliament,* and a later *Breviary of the History of the Parliament of England.* Using current newspaper accounts and the official publications of the republican and Royalist parties as his material, he wrote a remarkably honest and objective history, although he never concealed his own bias in favor of radical republicanism. Charges of self-interest and parasitism were made against May by his enemies, but even they brought no stronger charge against the history than that it was "adroitly partial." Unfortunately, in spite of its factual basis, and a certain elegance of style, the history is a flat, colorless document.

May was also charged by his enemies with free living, debauchery, and atheism, and when he died in 1650 it was said by some that he died of drunkenness, by others that he strangled himself by tying his nightcap strings too tightly "under his fat chin and cheeks." He was buried in Westminster Abbey, but following the Restoration his body was exhumed and buried, with other anti-Royalists, in an obscure pit in St. Margaret's churchyard.

PRINCIPAL WORKS: The Heir, a comedy, 1620; Georgics of Virgil, a translation, 1628; Lucan's Pharsalia, a translation, 1627-35; Selected Epigrams of Martial, a translation, 1629; Antigone, 1631; Agrippina, 1639; Cleopatra, 1639; History of the Long Parliament, 1647; A Breviary of the History of the Parliament of England, 1650; The Old Couple, 1658.

ABOUT: Biographia Britannica; Winstanley, J. England's Worthies; Wood, A. à, Athenae Oxonienses.

MEDWALL, HENRY (fl. 1486), writer of interludes, was chaplain to John Morton, the Archbishop of Canterbury.

In the British Museum is a very small fragment of a printed interlude, the oldest secular play in English of whose existence we have direct proof. It was written by Medwall about 1490, and printed by John Rastell, a printer so devoted to the drama that he produced plays in his own home. This ancient interlude may have been the source of Shakespeare's *Rape of Lucrece*, its title being *A Godely Interlude of Fulgens, Cenatoure of Rome, Lucres his Daughter, Gayus Flaminius and Publius Cornelius*. A copy of the complete edition, printed by Rastell between 1513 and 1519, was discovered in 1919 and is now in the Huntington Library.

An interlude of which only the title survives was *Of the Finding of Truth, Carried Away by Ignorance and Hypocrisy*. The legend is that Henry VIII, watching this play at Richmond, was pleased by the novel introduction of a jester, but walked out before the end of the presentation.

Another of Medwall's interludes, *Nature*, is extant, one of the earliest morality plays of which we have the entire text. It is essentially an attack on the clergy and church, and like other early moralities combines a strong comic element and striking realism of action and dialogue, with broad allegorical meaning. In *Nature*, Man is separated from Reason by Sensuality, reunited with Reason by Age, and, at the end of his life, again separated by Avarice.

PRINCIPAL WORKS: Fulgens and Lucres (F. S. Boas and A. W. Reed, eds. 1926); Nature, an interlude (no date).

ABOUT: Ames, J. Typographical Antiquities; Collier, J. P. The History of English Dramatic Poetry; Warton, T. History of English Poetry.

MERES, FRANCIS

MERES, FRANCIS (1565-January 29, 1647), literary historian, critic, was born in Kirton, Lincolnshire, the son of Thomas Meres or Meers. He received his B.A. degree at Pembroke College, Cambridge, in 1587, M.A. 1591, and was incorporated as an M.A. of Oxford in 1593. John Meres, the high sheriff of Lincolnshire, was his cousin, and the young man endeavored to secure his patronage and influence, but apparently without much success. He was in London by 1597, casting about for a means of livelihood, and somewhere along the road he must have taken orders, for in 1602 he was named rector of Wing, Rutlandshire. Here he remained for the rest of his life, and was succeeded by his only son. In addition to his clerical duties he ran a private school. His wife, Maria, died in 1631.

Meres' first appearance in print was with some verses in *The Paradise of Daintie Devices* (1595), but for the most part he wrote in prose. He published one of his sermons, and two works of devotion translated from the Spanish of Luis de Granada, but probably by way of a French translation from the Spanish, since there is no evidence that he had any knowledge of the latter tongue.

His chief work was *Palladis Tamia*, which constituted the second volume of a series of four, by various hands, with the over-all title of *Politeuphuia: Wits Commonwealth*. These books consisted of apothegms, short reflections, and literary comments. The important part of Meres' contribution was his "comparative discourse" on English poets, a sort of imitation of Plutarch, each English author being compared to a Greek, Latin, or Italian one. In all, he reviewed briefly a hundred and twenty-five English authors from Chaucer to his own day, thus rendering a great service to the history of English literature. One of his inclusions was a contemporary list of Shakespeare's plays. He was not always accurate by any means; his account of the death of Marlowe was grotesquely wrong even on the information he himself could have obtained.

The *Palladis Tamia* was famous in its time, with three editions under differing titles in forty years. The 1634 edition was announced and used as a text for schools.

Meres was a Euphuist, and all his writing was done in that high-flown and artificial style, with balanced periods and constant citation of classical authorities. His interest to modern readers is solely as a source of contemporary information on the writers of his own period.

PRINCIPAL WORKS: Gods Arithmetick, 1597; Palladis Tamia: Wits Treasurie, being the second part of Wits Commonwealth, 1598 (as Wits Commonwealth, second part: A Treasure of Divine, Moral, and Philosophical Similes, 1634; as Witts Academie, 1636); Granados Devotion, 1598; Sinners Guide (from Granados) 1614.

ABOUT: Smith, G. G. Elizabethan Critical Essays; Wood, A. à, Fasti Oxonienses.

MERRY, ROBERT

MERRY, ROBERT (April 1755-December 14, 1798), miscellaneous writer and dilettante, was born in London. Son of the wealthy governor of the Hudson's Bay Company, he attended Harrow and Christ's College, Cambridge, but his ne'er-do-well tendencies asserted themselves while he was still an undergraduate, and he left college without graduating. Freed from all responsibility by his father's death, he bought and sold a commission in the horse guards, quickly ran through his fortune, and joined the English colony in Florence after a few years of aimless travel.

Merry was an immediate success in both the frivolous society and the superficial literary life of the colony. His verses were included in the *Florence Miscellany*, and he was elected a member of the Della Cruscan Academy. But the open scandal of his affair with a Countess Cowper, in which his rival was the Grand Duke Leopold, was too much for his fellow emigrés, and he returned to London to embark on the most spectacular period of his career.

A preposterously stylized letter entitled *Adieu and Recall to Love*, and signed "Della Crusca," appeared in *The World*. An equally extravagant reply was forthcoming, signed "Anna Matilda," and this public correspondence not only flourished but bore and nourished a flock of tasteless imitators, who carried to the wildest extremes the worst features of Della Crusca's style, lacking his "irregular touch of genius." Merry finally met "Anna Matilda" and the original correspondence terminated, but whether because the public taste was finally offended, or because of Merry's disappointment in the charms of Mrs. Hannah Cowley,[qv] twelve years his senior, is not recorded.

A romantic interest in the French Revolution led Merry to write *Laurel of Liberty* and an anniversary ode on *The Fall of the Bastille*. In 1791 a play of his was produced at Covent Garden, and he married an actress, Elizabeth Brunton. She left the stage at the behest of Merry's family, but after the failure of his next play and three reckless, debt-ridden years in Paris and London, she accepted an acting engagement in the United States. Grown fat and lazy, Merry basked for two years in the American limelight of his wife's success and his own inflated reputation, talking of the revolutionary epic he planned to write. He died of apo-

plexy in Philadelphia in 1798, at the age of forty-three.

PRINCIPAL WORKS: Paulina, 1787; Diversity, 1788; Ambitious Vengeance, 1789; Laurel of Liberty, 1790; Lorenzo, 1791; The Magician no Conjuror, 1792.

ABOUT: Baker, D. Biographia Dramatica; Dunlap, W. History of the American Stage; Genest, J. Account of the English Stage.

MICKLE, WILLIAM JULIUS (September 28, 1735-October 28, 1788), poet, was born at Longholm, Dumfriesshire, in Scotland, the son of the parish minister. He left Edinburgh high school at fifteen to work in a brewery owned by his father, which he eventually inherited and nearly ruined by poor business judgment.

Turning to letters as a means of livelihood, Mickle went to London. His first major work was a didactic play, *The Concubine, or Sir Martyn*. For five years he devoted himself to a translation of Camoen's *Lusiad*, a translation so free and creative that it ranks as an excellent poem in itself.

In spite of the success of the *Lusiad*, he was not making a secure living by his writing, and in 1779 he sailed for Portugal as secretary to the commander of a squadron of British warships. Besides receiving more literary acclaim in Portugal than he had in England, Mickle's share in the financial returns of the expedition gave him a comfortable income for life, to which he added the large dowry of May Tonkins, whom he married in 1781.

He retired to an estate near Oxford. Of his later writings only two items are noteworthy. In 1777 an undistinguished ballad, *Cumnor Hall*, was published, which for some reason caught the fancy of young Sir Walter Scott. He found a "peculiar enchantment" in the rhythms of the first stanza, and years later used the ballad as the cornerstone of *Kenilworth*.

Although there is some doubt about it, Mickle probably wrote a tender ballad called *The Mariner's Wife*, more popularly known by its first line, "There's nae luck about the hoose." If he wrote it, it is his masterpiece. It was in the simpler forms of balladry that he excelled. Scott said of him that he would have been a better writer "had he known his own strength, and trusted to the impulses of his heart, instead of his ambition."

He died at the age of fifty-three, while on a visit to Forest Hill.

PRINCIPAL WORKS: The Concubine, 1767; Voltaire in the Shades, 1770; Lusiad, a translation, 1771-75; Prophecy of Queen Emma, 1782.

ABOUT: Chambers, R. Biographical Dictionary of Eminent Scotsmen; Johnson, J. The Scotish Musical Museum.

MIDDLETON, CONYERS (December 27, 1683-July 28, 1750), biographer and religious writer, was the son of a well-to-do rector of Yorkshire. He received a B.A., an M.A., and a D.D. from Trinity College, Cambridge, and was a fellow of Trinity until his first marriage in 1710.

He engaged in two celebrated public feuds, the first a long-drawn-out affair with Richard Bentley, Master of Trinity College. Fined for libel because of a pamphlet charging Bentley with graft and mismanagement of the college, Middleton was rescued from penury when his friends managed to have him appointed chief librarian of Cambridge, with the impressive and especially invented title of Protobibliothecarus. He immediately renewed his attack on Bentley, was again fined, and in disgust left England to spend two years in Italy.

Here he developed the interest in Catholic dogma and pagan myths that was to lead to his second feud and most controversial writings. He returned to England, was appointed Woodwardian Professor of Mineralogy at Cambridge, and began a pamphlet controversy with Daniel Waterland on the subject of the deist attacks on the church. While maintaining his orthodoxy, he admitted skepticism of the authenticity of some of the legends and miracles of the Bible, inviting a storm of criticism and nearly losing his Cambridge degrees.

An extremely partisan but excellently written biography of Cicero, published in 1741, was popular enough to give him financial security for the last few years of his life. He lived at Cambridge, spending his evenings in the coffee-houses or with friends at his home, which Thomas Gray declared to be the only place at Cambridge where he could enjoy good conversation. He had married three times, and the granddaughter of one of his wives was the future Mrs. Montagu, "Queen of the Bluestockings," whose precocious childhood he influenced greatly.

He died at sixty-seven, while he was preparing a defense of his iconoclastic treatise on miracles. Saintsbury called him the "most distinguished representative of the absolutely plain style."

PRINCIPAL WORKS: Letter from Rome, 1729; Life of Cicero, 1741; Introductory Discourse, 1747; A Free Enquiry into the Miraculous Powers, 1749-50.

ABOUT: Monk, J. H. Life of Richard Bentley; Nichols, J. Literary Anecdotes.

MIDDLETON, THOMAS (1570?-1627), dramatist, is one of the most inscrutable figures of the Elizabethan period. Neither his plays nor the one extant portrait of him give any satisfactory clue to his character. The portrait shows a broad, serious face with wide-set penetrating eyes, large unshapely nose, small feminine mouth; the hair is long and curling; a trim moustache and tiny beard provide an almost foppish contrast to the square, solid lines of jaw and chin. The combination of masculine and feminine characteristics in the face is remarkable and prepares one for Middleton's extraordinary insight into his women characters, but there is nothing in the portrait's expression that gives any hint as to his temperament.

The same obscurity surrounds most of the details of his presumably uneventful life. We do not know the date of his birth, but he was the son of William Middleton and Anne Snow, and it is presumed that he was born in London. Of his father we know nothing, except that he had a coat of arms and was a gentleman. Thomas had one sister, Amy; he married Mary Morbeck, daughter of one of the six chancery clerks; he had one child, Edward, who was nineteen in 1623; he may have married twice, for his widow's name is given as Magdalen; these are absolutely all the facts known about his family life.

Middleton entered Gray's Inn, probably in 1593, but soon took to literature, like so many of his contemporaries who were educated for the law. His first known work is a poor poem entitled "The Wisdom of Solomon Paraphrased." His first play, *The Old Law*, probably dates from 1599 and marked the beginning of a long and prolific career as a dramatist; it is hard to establish which plays ascribed to him are entirely his, for he collaborated a great deal, notably with Rowley and Dekker. Aside

THOMAS MIDDLETON

behalf of the Mayor and Corporation for services rendered or "for his better encouragement."

The date of Middleton's death is not known, but he was buried at Newington Butts on July 4, 1627. His widow was given financial help by the City of London that same year; she survived him only a year, being buried on July 18, 1628.

Middleton first became known for his realistic prose comedies of contemporary London life; among the better ones are *Blurt Master-Constable, Michaelmas Term, A Chaste Maid in Cheapside,* and *The Roaring Girl.* This last contains his greatest and most original comic character, Moll Cutpurse, based on a real underworld figure of the time who always wore men's clothes, smoked a pipe, and committed highway robberies. Middleton idealizes her as a sort of early feminist, coarse in speech, but chaste, sincere, independent, and firmly opposed to the slavery of marriage.

His best comedies of a more conventional type are *A Mad World, My Master* and *A Trick to Catch the Old One.* In the latter, a young spendthrift passes off a prostitute as a rich widow, and gets his miserly uncle to propose marriage to her. The plot and the whole tone of this play foreshadow Restoration comedy.

Middleton's deservedly high reputation as a tragic dramatist rests on two plays in blank verse, *The Changeling* and *Women Beware Women,* which are indisputably his and decidedly similar in style to each other; they do not, however, bear the slightest resemblance to any of his comedies.

Beatrice-Joanna, the heroine of *The Changeling,* employs De Flores to murder her betrothed so that she can marry Alsemero. The repulsive De Flores, who is madly in love with her, forces her to become his mistress in return. He commits further crimes to shield her, so that she grows more and more dependent on him and ends by being more his than Alsemero's. Beatrice and De Flores are finally unmasked and perish together.

In *Women Beware Women,* Livia by her guile entices Bianca away from Leantio and makes her the Duke's mistress; she also persuades Hippolito and Isabella, uncle and niece, that their love for each other is not

from his plays and the poem mentioned above, he published two satirical prose pamphlets, *The Black Book* and *Father Hubbard's Tales,* in 1604, and *Microcynicon* (satires in verse) in 1599.

Only two aspects of Middleton's career are well documented—his work as "Chronologer and Inventor of Honourable Entertainments" for the City of London, and the suppression of his daring and original political play, *A Game at Chess,* in 1624. The latter satirized the diplomatic relations between Spain and England and was literally a nine days' wonder; after a run of nine performances at the Globe it was taken off as a result of the protests of the Spanish Ambassador. The theatre was closed and the author and players were summoned before the Privy Council; Middleton did not appear, and a warrant was issued for his arrest. His son Edward later gave himself up and was released on bail. The king's players pleaded that the play had been duly licensed by the Master of the Revels. Perhaps because this was true, they were allowed to reopen their theatre soon afterwards, but were forbidden ever to perform *A Game at Chess* again.

Middleton wrote, directed and produced many pageants for the City of London, the first one in 1613. He became Chronologer of the City in 1620, and there are records of many sums of money paid to him on

incestuous; finally she herself falls in love with Leantio, Bianca's discarded husband; the Duke and Bianca arrange for Hippolito to kill Leantio; Livia plots to avenge Leantio's death during the festivities at the Duke's marriage to Bianca; other people have similar plans, and practically the entire cast of characters — including Livia — is wiped out in the last act. The rapid corruption of Bianca by wealth and luxury receives the same sort of painstaking analysis as Beatrice's downfall does in *The Changeling*; *Women Beware Women* would not be tolerable otherwise.

Middleton's verse is plain, solid and powerful; it contains a minimum of imagery, but is always magnificently appropriate to the matter in hand. However improbable his tragic plots may seem, their construction is sound and workmanlike. T. S. Eliot writes with admiration of his "steady impersonal passionless observation of human nature," which gives him the right to be called a realist in tragedy as well as in comedy. Middleton was a fine craftsman, of that there can be no doubt; because he has put so little of himself into his work, some might question his right to be called a great artist.

PRINCIPAL WORKS: *Plays*: Blurt Master-Constable, 1602; The Phoenix, 1607; Michaelmas Term 1607; A Trick to Catch the Old One, 1608; The Family of Love, 1608; A Mad World, My Masters, 1608; Your Five Gallants, 1608; The Roaring Girl (with Dekker) 1611; A Fair Quarrel (with Rowley) 1617; A Game at Chess, 1625; A Chaste Maid in Cheapside, 1630; The Widow (with Jonson and Fletcher) 1652; The Changeling (with Rowley) 1653; The Spanish Gipsy (with Rowley) 1653; The Old Law (with Massinger and Rowley) 1656; More Dissemblers Besides Women, 1657; Women Beware Women, 1657; No Wit (Help) Like a Woman's, 1657; The Mayor of Quinborough, 1661; Anything for a Quiet Life, 1662; The Witch, 1778.

ABOUT: Dyce, A. Introduction to his edition of Middleton's Works; Eliot, T. S. For Lancelot Andrewes; Eliot, T. S. Elizabethan Essays.

MILTON, JOHN (December 9, 1608-November 8, 1674), poet, author of pamphlets and prose papers, was born in Cheapside, London. His father, also John Milton, came of an Oxfordshire family which had disinherited him because he turned from its Roman Catholicism to the Church of England; though his chief interest was music, he earned his living as a scrivener or notary. His mother was Sarah Jeffrey.

Few sons in the seventeenth century had such kindly and admiring fathers. The boy was given a private tutor who stayed with him even after he entered St. Paul's School in 1620, and he was carefully taught music as well. He was a studious lad who turned his hand early to the writing of verse, both in Latin and in English.

In 1625 he entered Christ's College, Cambridge. There his delicate good looks and his natural hauteur earned for him the sobriquet of "the Lady of Christ's," and he himself says he was an "indocile" student. Certainly he had some trouble with his tutor, and for a while (less than a term) absented himself from the university. But there he met his great friend, Charles Diodati, and he was still a student there when he wrote his great sonnet on Shakespeare, affixed to the Second Folio in 1632. He received his B.A. in 1629, his M.A. in 1632. (In 1635 he was admitted as M.A. of Oxford also.)

His father meanwhile had been able to retire from business and had moved to Horton, Buckinghamshire. There for five years Milton lived at leisure, able to devote his entire time to study and writing. It is to this period that we owe nearly all the great miscalled "minor" poems—"L'Allegro," "Il Penseroso," "Arcades," which was in a sense a sketch for *Comus*, and *Comus* itself. His mother died in 1637, but his brother married and came to live with their father, so this admirable parent agreed to let his older son take the Grand Tour abroad which was expected to round off the education of cultured young men. He was on the Continent for nearly two years, meeting Grotius in France, Galileo in Italy, and writing sonnets in Italian to an unknown (or imagined) lady of Bologna. Here also he wrote two of his greatest poems, both elegies: one, the well known *Lycidas*, in memory of a college mate, Edward King, who was drowned in 1637, the other, not well known because it is in Latin, *Epitaphium Damoni*, on the death of Diodati in 1638.

Affairs in England were fast reaching the point of civil war. Milton, who always took himself and his abilities with the utmost seriousness, decided that he had no right to live a life of leisure abroad when men who could be of service were needed at home.

355

He returned by slow stages, and the household at Horton having been broken up, settled finally in Aldergate, London.

There his sister, who had been widowed and remarried, sent him her two sons by her first marriage to educate, and gradually a few others of his friends did the same, so that he had a number of resident pupils, though he was never really a teacher by profession. For twenty years thereafter, Milton the poet was in abeyance; only a few familiar verses in Latin and some sonnets belong to this period of his life. Instead, heart and soul for the Republic—though he was never, religiously, an exact adherent of the Puritans—he wrote nothing but controversial pamphlets and—later on—state papers and letters in Latin.

Since it is impossible to understand Milton without going into his marital misfortunes, the painful story must be told. In 1643, when he was thirty-four, he married a girl of seventeen, Mary Powell. Just how the marriage came about, no one knows—except that her father owed Milton money. The Powells were Royalists, and Mary was reared in a different world from the one into which she was now thrust. After a month she begged to be allowed to visit her home. She stayed for two years, and it would have been far better for her if she had never been forced to ask on her knees for forgiveness and reinstatement. Milton was formal, arrogant, and cold; he despised all women and most of all his wife; to him the ideal wife was a combination of guardian angel and slave. Mary did not qualify. Moreover, her Royalist family by this time was in poverty and distress, with the triumph of Cromwell, and all of them moved in as well—together with the nephews and other pupils and Milton's own father. Mary bore three daughters and a son (who died in infancy), and then with the fourth daughter she died, at twenty-six.

It is to the years when she had left her husband that Milton's pamphlets in favor of divorce belong. They brought him objurgation and unpleasant notoriety, and there is no doubt that they stemmed from no theoretical belief in divorce but from his own private troubles. (He even proposed marriage to another woman in this period, but she had the good sense to say no.) But their general arguments are still cogent, and

W. Faithorne, 1670

JOHN MILTON

the difficulties they encountered gave rise to the noble *Areopagitica*, one of the world's greatest pleas for freedom of the press.

In 1656, four years after his first wife's death, Milton married Catherine Woodcocke. She died the next year in childbirth, and so did her daughter. Milton had three growing girls to raise. These unhappy creatures were treated without affection or understanding. (They were taught just enough to enable them, for example, to read to their father in languages they did not understand.) Being human, they rebelled and hated him. At a loss what to do, Milton married again in 1663. His third wife was Elizabeth Minshull, who survived him. She was a good wife and suited him well, but she did not help the domestic impasse; the daughters united in hating their stepmother as well. Finally they were sent out to learn fine embroidery and other arts by which they might make their living; eventually two of them married.

We are now, however, far ahead of the chronological history of Milton's life. In 1649 he became Cromwell's Latin secretary for foreign affairs, a post he held until the Restoration; after 1657 Andrew Marvell was his necessary assistant. For in 1652 the poet had become completely blind (which was the reason for his daughters' long hours of reading to him in Latin and Greek and

Syriac). The appearance of his eyes was unchanged, and though the cause of his blindness is not known, it is thought to have been glaucoma. His sight had never been good, and his secretarial duties strained his eyes finally beyond endurance.

Why Milton was not hanged when Charles II came to the throne is a mystery. The probability is that he was saved through the offices of Marvell and of D'Avenant. His pamphlets and prose books were burned by the public hangman, he himself went into hiding, and he was even arrested, but not held. Naturally he lost his salary and much of his property, but he was thrifty and was never really poverty stricken. He had moved many times in London, but finally lived in Bunhill Fields. Here the blind old man prepared once more to be a poet.

For many years he had been dreaming of an English epic, perhaps with the subject taken from history or from the Arthurian legends. The final decision was on a Biblical theme, and the result was *Paradise Lost*. It was followed by *Paradise Regained*, and then by *Samson Agonistes*, and then Milton's work was done. In his last years he lived quietly with his third wife, a neat, carefully dressed figure, fond of smoking and moderately given to wine, his fingers swollen with what was then called gout and what we now call arthritis. He attended no religious services and inclined more to Quakerism than to any other sect. He died finally of "gout stuck in," and was buried with his father in St. Giles-in-the-Fields.

"Of all other writers of the highest class, he most resembled Dante," George Saintsbury has said. It is true that *Paradise Lost* is "alone in its kind of greatness"; and *Paradise Regained* is not far behind it, though curiously it has never had quite so high a position in public esteem. *Samson Agonistes* David Masson has called "the most powerful drama in the English language after the severe Greek model." Certainly nothing can exceed the majesty and sublimity of Milton's great religious epic.

But for pure poetry, one must turn to his "minor" poems. Spenser was an early influence, but Milton's lyrics and sonnets are peculiarly his own. They are too familiar; they have grown hackneyed: but the stateliness and fire of the great sonnets, the exquisite sweetness of passage after passage in *Lycidas, Comus,* "L'Allegro," "Il Penseroso," cannot be surpassed in the work of any other English poet. Milton the man is in many ways most unattractive; Milton the poet has few rivals, in his combination of magnificence and ease.

As much cannot be said for Milton the prose writer. Too often (always excepting the *Areopagitica* and perhaps the *Eikonoklastes* which answered that celebrated paean of praise to Charles I, the *Eikon Basilike*), in his controversial works Milton is confused, excited, chaotic, illogical, anarchistic. He is stubborn, disdainful, utterly without tact or diplomacy—in other words, he was a completely self-centered man and his prose writing shows it. He has been justly accused of offensive "rude railing and insolent swagger." And his Latin style, except in the state papers, is very much akin to his English one. It is a far cry from the "loftiness of mind, and majesty" (Dryden) of his poetry.

It is hard to see how anyone loved John Milton, except perhaps in his boyhood; it is hard to sympathize with or admire a great part of his prose writing. But as a poet, he has earned the verdict of posterity, which has placed him next to the pinnacle of all English literature, William Shakespeare.

PRINCIPAL WORKS: *Poetry*: A Maske Presented at Ludlow Castle [Comus] 1637; Lycidas, 1638; Poems of Mr. John Milton, both English and Latin, 1645 (as Poems, etc., upon several occasions, 1673); Paradise Lost, 1667; Paradise Regained, with Samson Agonistes, 1671; Poetical Works (T. Tickell, ed.) 1695; Latin and Italian Poems (W. Cowper, tr.) 1808. *Prose*: Prelatical Episcopacy, 1641; Of Reformation touching Church-discipline in England, 1641; Animadversions upon the Remonstrants' Defence, 1641; The Reason of Church Government urged against Prelaty, 1642; An Apology against a Pamphlet called a Modest Confutation of the Animadversions, 1642; The Doctrine and Discipline of Divorce, 1643; Of Education, 1644; Areopagitica, . . . a Speech for the Liberty of Unlicensed Printing, 1644; Tetrachordon, 1645; Eikonoklastes, 1649; The Tenure of Kings and Magistrates, 1649; Observations on the Articles of Peace, 1649; Pro Populo Anglicano Defensio (defense of the English people) 1651; Defensio Secunda (second defense) 1654; Treatise of Civil Power in Ecclesiastical Causes, 1659; The Readie and Easie Way to Establish a Free Commonwealth, 1660; Accedence Commencement Grammar, 1669; History of England to the Norman Conquest, 1670; Religion, Haeresie, Schism, Toleration, 1673; A Brief History of Moscovia, etc., 1682; Republican Letters, 1682; Letters of State, 1694; De Doctrina Christiana (R. Sumner, tr.) 1825; Works (J. Mitford, ed.) 1851.

ABOUT: Aubrey, J. Lives of Eminent Men; Bagehot, W. Literary Studies; Belloc, H. Milton; Birrell, A. Obiter Dicta; Bowra, C. M. From Virgil to Milton; Bridges, R. Milton's Prosody; Coleridge, S. T. Seven Lectures on Shakespeare and Milton; De Quincey, T. Essays; Dowden, E. Transcripts and Studies; Emerson, R. W. Natural History of Intellect and Other Papers; Firth, C. H. Milton as an Historian; French, J. M. ed. Life Records of John Milton; Fuller, E. John Milton (bibliography, J. P. Anderson); Garnett, R. Life of John Milton; Hanford, J. H. John Milton, Englishman; Hanford, J. H. A Milton Handbook; Hulme, W. H. Two Early Lives of Milton; Hutchinson, F. E. Milton and the English Mind; Johnson, S. Lives of the English Poets; Larson, M. A. The Modernity of Milton; Lowell, J. R. My Study Windows; Macaulay, R. Milton; Mackail, J. W. The Springs of Helicon; Masson, D. The Life of Milton; Murry, J. M. Heroes of Thought; Pattison, M. Milton; Phillips, E. The Life of Milton; Racine, L. (K. John, tr.) Life of Milton; Raleigh, W. A. Milton; Raymond, D. N. Oliver's Secretary; Rossetti, W. M. Lives of Famous Poets; Saintsbury, G. A History of English Prosody; Saurat, D. Milton, Man and Thinker; Tulloch, J. English Puritanism and its Leaders; Ward, A. W. (ed.) Tercentenary of the Birth of John Milton; Whiting, G. W. Milton's Literary Milieu; Williams, C. The English Poetic Mind; Wood, A. à Fasti Oxonienses; Woodberry, G. E. The Torch.

MINOT, LAURENCE (1300?-1352?), poet, is known only from the fact that he twice mentions his own name in the eleven war ballads discovered in a fifteenth century manuscript in the British Museum by Thomas Tyrwhitt late in the eighteenth century. His poems all deal with the wars of Edward III, and as the first event celebrated occurred in 1333 and Minot spoke of himself as then being "not very young," it is presumed he was born somewhere around 1300. The last event mentioned (the siege of Guisnes) occurred in 1352, so that after that Minot either died or ceased to write, or his later poems have been lost. From the fact that he wrote in the dialect of Yorkshire and Norfolk, and that there is a Minot family of that period in that part of England (though the name itself is Norman French), he is supposed to have been a native of that district. He may have been a professional gleeman, possibly even a king's minstrel; statements that he was a monk or priest are not to be credited. Apparently he followed the army and entertained the soldiers, but he certainly was not always present at the sieges and battles he describes, for frequently he makes obvious mistakes. He names the king and others as being present where they were not, and sometimes he rejoices

prematurely in a victory that turned out to be a defeat.

Throughout Minot is fiercely patriotic, intensely loyal to the king, and scornful of Scots and Frenchmen alike. He has two distinct styles, which may have followed each other chronologically but more probably were used according to the audience to be appealed to—the old long alliterative line, which the soldiers would favor, or rhymed meters with refrains which would appeal more to the court. One remarkable point is that nowhere does he indulge in a single metaphor, simile, or other figure of speech. There is something of the folk song about his poems, with their conventional alliterative tags.

It is likely that some if not all of the poems were composed extemporaneously, perhaps on the very scene. In his brief output Minot seems to embody the militant England of the fourteenth century, and he dwells lovingly on every detail of horror and brutality, as well as on the glory of war. The only time he shows any compassion is in telling the story of the famous burghers of Calais. Though he has only the single theme, he is saved from monotony by the vigor and energy of his style and by the variety of his meters.

PRINCIPAL WORKS: Poems on Interesting Events in the Reign of King Edward III (J. Ritson, ed.) 1795; The Poems of Laurence Minot (J. Hall, ed.) 1887.

ABOUT: Hall, J. Introduction, Poems of Laurence Minot; Scholle, W. Quellen und Forschungen.

MITFORD, WILLIAM (February 10, 1744-April 27, 1827), historian, was born in London, the elder son of a wealthy lawyer. A handsome, strong youth, he showed no interest in his studies, left Queen's College, Oxford, without graduating, and, although he studied at the Middle Temple, never practiced law.

He inherited estates from both his father and mother, married in 1766, and virtually retired to the family home at Exbury, Hampshire. Here he pursued the two great interests of his life, the study of Greek, and his membership in the South Hampshire Militia. It was his fellow member of the militia, the historian Gibbon, who suggested that he write the history of Greece to which he devoted twenty-six years, and which for some time remained the standard English work on that subject.

Mitford was a member of Parliament for thirty-three years, where his only occasional function seems to have been to speak in favor of the militia. He was a professor of ancient history at the Royal Academy, and a member of the Society of Antiquaries. He died at the age of eighty-three on his estate at Exbury, leaving five sons and one daughter.

His *History of Greece* is a curious example of a work written from an obviously partisan viewpoint, which nevertheless, because of the author's conscientious research, contains enough accurate material to counteract his biased conclusions. An avowed enemy of democracy, Mitford denigrated and distorted the accounts of Athenian democracy whenever possible. There are some historical inaccuracies, but generally the work is ahead of its time in terms of scholarship. The style varies from simple clarity to unintelligible obscurity. Byron listed the author's virtues as, "learning, labor, research, wrath and partiality," and adds, "His great pleasure consists in praising tyrants, abusing Plutarch, spelling oddly and writing quaintly."

PRINCIPAL WORKS: Treatise on the Military Force (no date); Essay on the Harmony of Language, 1774; History of Greece, 1784-1810; Considerations on the Corn Laws, 1791; Observations on the History of Christianity, 1823; Principles of Design in Architecture, 1824.

ABOUT: Allibone, S. Dictionary of English Literature; Burke, Sir J. B. Landed Gentry; Redesdale, Lord, Biographical memoir, *in* Mitford's History of Greece, 1829 ed.

MONBODDO, JAMES BURNETT

(1714-May 26, 1790), Scottish judge, pioneer in anthropology, was born James Burnett, in Monboddo, Kincardineshire, Scotland. He was educated at the Universities of Aberdeen and Edinburgh, at the latter of which he studied law. In 1767 he was made Lord of Session (judge), with the courtesy title of Lord Monboddo.

Without real scientific training, Monboddo curiously anticipated much of modern evolutionary theory. He believed that man and the apes were akin; in fact, he considered man a species of orangoutang. He held that human beings had gradually evolved from a purely animal state to one

in which the mind could exist independently of the body. The social state he considered a natural process, brought about by "the necessities of humanity." Language, however, was not "natural," but was a consequence of the demands of social life.

It may be imagined what his contemporaries thought of him. When Dr. Johnson made his famous tour of Scotland with Boswell, they visited Monboddo, and Boswell's *Life of Johnson* contains much interesting material about him. Monboddo apparently was an eccentric, outside of his theories, and some of his compatriots even believed he was a wizard, with a monkey as his familiar. In more cultured circles he was considered merely an object of ridicule. More than most persons of whom it can be said, he was born before his time; solely by what cannot be called other than lucky guesses, and by the application of reason to problems, he hit upon many ideas which Darwin and his followers were later to prove. In others of his theories he anticipated Kant. He was a remarkable figure, but has no particular standing as a writer, though his style is clear and persuasive.

PRINCIPAL WORKS: The Origin and Process of Language, 1773; Antient Metaphysics, 1779-99.

ABOUT: Boswell, J. Life of Dr. Johnson; Knight, W. A. Lord Monboddo and Some of His Contemporaries.

MONTAGU, ELIZABETH

(October 2, 1720-August 25, 1800), essayist, literary critic, was born Elizabeth Robinson, the daughter of Matthew Robinson and Elizabeth Drake, a cousin of Laurence Sterne. Though she was born in York, most of her childhood was spent at Coveney, Cambridgeshire, with her maternal grandmother, whose second husband, Conyers Middleton, was librarian of Cambridge University. The pretty, precocious child was made much of, and given a better education than was usual among girls in her day. Through the young Duchess of Portland, she was included in literary circles at a very early age; in fact, she made her debut, in Bath and Tunbridge, when she was only thirteen, and was bored with "society" before she was twenty. In 1742 she married Edward Montagu (cousin of Edward Wortley Montagu); she was twenty-two and he was fifty-one, but she was cold and practical by nature, and had

After Sir J. Reynolds
MRS. ELIZABETH MONTAGU

already remarked that "gold is the chief ingredient in worldly happiness." Their only son died in infancy in 1744, and from that time she devoted herself exclusively to a social and literary life.

Mrs. Montagu was the first and long the "queen" of the bluestockings—though nobody knows the real origin of this term for literary ladies of the eighteenth century. Her receptions were entirely given over to conversation; no card-playing was allowed. Her salons were held first in the magnificent house Montagu built on Hill Street, Mayfair, then after he died in 1775 and she inherited his large fortune, in a still grander house on Portman Street. She had a genuine interest in literature, and was extremely generous to impecunious authors; Hannah More called her "the female Maecenas of Hill Street." In 1776 she paid a long and triumphant visit to Paris. Thereafter she lived in London or in her other mansion near Newbury and continued her salons until extreme old age, though she was almost blind in her last years. She was universally acknowledged as "the Mme. du Deffand of the English capital," and in spite of her affectations and pretensions she did do much to refine the barbarous and frivolous society of the time.

Outside of a large correspondence, Mrs. Montagu's writing was all anonymous,

though everyone knew who did it. She wrote three of Lord Lyttleton's *Dialogues of the Dead* (1760), and one at least of these is witty and vivaciously satirical. Her own major production was her *Essay on the Writings and Genius of Shakespeare*, written to confute Voltaire, and actually damaging to his critical reputation. Though Fanny Burney acclaimed this as achieving "the Parnassian heights of female British literature," George Saintsbury described it more justly as "well intentioned but feeble." Nevertheless, with all her vanities and absurdities, Mrs. Montagu had a good mind. Dr. Johnson, who first gave her her title of "queen," said of her: "That lady exerts more mind in conversation than any person I ever met with."

Mrs. Montagu reared and adopted a nephew to whom she left her entire fortune. He edited her letters, and his great-granddaughter wrote her biography.

PRINCIPAL WORKS: Essay on the Writings and Genius of Shakespeare, compared with the Greek and French dramatic poets, with some remarks upon the misrepresentations of M. de Voltaire (anon.) 1769; Letters (M. Montagu, ed) 1809-13; Bluestocking Letters (R. B. Johnson, ed.) 1926.

ABOUT: Blunt, R. Mrs. Montagu, "Queen of the Blues"; Climenson, E. J. (great-grandniece) Elizabeth Montagu, the Queen of the Bluestockings; Doran, J. A Lady of the Last [18th] Century; Huchon, R. Mrs. Montagu and her Friends; Saintsbury, G. History of Criticism.

MONTAGU, Lady MARY WORTLEY (May 1689-August 21, 1762), author of poems and letters, was born the Honorable Mary Pierrepont, the daughter of Evelyn Pierrepont, who in 1690 became the Earl of Kingston and in 1713 the Duke of Kingston, and the Honorable Mary Feilding, daughter of the Earl of Denbigh, and a collateral relative of Henry Fielding. Her mother died when the child was five, and the clever, pretty little girl was "brought up carelessly in a library." Her father was proud of her and liked to show her off, but any encouragement in educating herself came from her uncle and from Bishop Burnet. Another influence on her girlhood was her friendship with Mary Astell, the pioneer feminist.

Another of her close friends was Anne Montagu, granddaughter of the Earl of Sandwich. Anne had a brother, Edward Wortley Montagu, who took part in his sister's correspondence with her friend, and after Anne's death in 1709 conducted it alone. The two young people fell in love, though in a manner that suggests pride and stubbornness more than passion, but they were refused assent to their marriage because Montagu would not entail his estate. Accordingly, they eloped in 1712. For a few years they lived in relatively straitened circumstances; then the Whigs came into power and Montagu was elected to Parliament and in 1716 was made ambassador to the Porte, charged with reconciling Turkey and Austria, which were at war. His wife, who had been shining in court society, accompanied him, learned the Turkish language, and wrote her impressions of that then quite unknown country in witty and acute letters. When they returned in 1718, she also brought back the practice of inoculation (not vaccination), of which she was an enthusiastic advocate—her own beauty having been marred by smallpox.

The Montagus had a son, who became a traveler and writer like his mother, and a daughter who married the Earl of Bute in 1739. Immediately after, Lady Montagu left for the Continent, and lived alone until 1761 in various parts of Italy. She never saw her husband again, though they continued to correspond on affectionate terms. He developed into a complete miser, who at his death left nearly a million and a half pounds—an immense fortune for the time.

Lady Montagu's early poems (imitations of Pope, but some of them excellent imitations) had been published without her authorization. She had written a translation of the *Enchiridion* of Epictetus, but she did not think of that, any more than of her letters, as publishable. Her very valuable diary was burned by her daughter about 1794. Her literary fame therefore was posthumous, but her current reputation decidedly was not. Pope, who had been her ardent admirer, became her bitter and vindictive enemy; the guess is that he declared his love for her and was laughed at. Horace Walpole hated her as well; and it is thanks to these two that Lady Montagu was depicted as dirty, avaricious, heartless, and eccentric to the point of insanity. Eccentric she certainly was, but fundamentally she was a lonely, unhappy, warmhearted woman

After F. Zincke

LADY MARY WORTLEY MONTAGU

whose aristocratic pride prevented her from protesting against traducement. She came back to England after her husband had died and left her most of his great fortune, but it was only to die of cancer.

This "she meteor," "the cleverest woman of her day," "second only to Mme. de Sévigné as a letter writer," was actually one of the first Western women to live in the Near East; for the remainder of her life she was known popularly as "the female traveler." Her letters are not so much brilliant as spirited; she had an easy style and a keen eye for her surroundings. Her main characteristics are her faculty for description and her "glorified common sense." She was not a bad critic; she admired Fielding and Smollett, and had far less admiration for Richardson in spite of his appeal to her emotions. Her letters were copied and edited, and it is not certain how many of them are now in their original form.

PRINCIPAL WORKS: Court Poems by a Lady of Quality, 1716 (as Town Eclogues, 1747); Nonsense of Common-Sense, 1737-1738 (R. Halsband, ed. 1947); Constantinople Letters, 1763; Letters of Rt. Hon. Lady M...y W...y M...e (*sic*), 1763; Poetical Works (I. Reed, ed.) 1768; Works, including Correspondence, Poems, and Essays, 1803; Letters and Works (Lord Wharncliffe [great-grandson], ed.) 1837; Letters from the Levant (J. A. St. John, ed.) 1838; Letters and Works (W. Moy Thomas, ed.) 1861.

ABOUT: Bagehot, W. Lady Mary Wortley Montagu (*in* Hutton, R. H. Literary Studies); Barry, I. Portrait of Lady Mary Wortley Montagu;

Benjamin, L. S. ("Lewis Melville") Lady Mary Wortley Montagu, her Life and Letters; Cove, J. W. Admirable Lady Mary: The Life and Times of Lady Mary Wortley Montagu; Dilke, C. W. Papers of a Critic; Moy Thomas, W. Life in Letters and Works, 1861; Nichols, J. Literary Anecdotes of the 18th Century; Symonds, E. M. ("George Paston") Lady Mary Wortley Montagu and her Times; Walpole, H. Letters.

MONTGOMERIE, ALEXANDER

(1556?-1610?), Scottish poet, was born "Eister day at morne," probably in 1556, at Hessilhead Castle, Ayrshire, the son of Hugh Montgomerie and of the daughter of "Houston of Houston." His brother Robert later became the titular Archbishop of Glasgow. He was privately educated, probably in Argyleshire, perhaps in Galloway as well, and became attached to the court of the regent Morton. When Morton was superseded by James VI after his release from England, Montgomerie remained in the king's service. He had the appelation of "captain," and was spoken of as *eques montanus*, which means "mounted knight," but actually he was never knighted. He was the unofficial poet laureate of the court, and is said to have been the king's chief teacher in the art of versification, though this is probably an exaggeration, since James was rather his superior as a poet before he left England.

In any event, he received a regular pension, and in 1586 was given permission to travel for five years in France, Flanders, and Spain. In one of these countries he got into some kind of trouble and was imprisoned, causing his disgrace at the Scottish court and suspension of his pension, which was recovered only after a lawsuit and numerous supplications. He was married, and had a son and a daughter, the latter of whom was tried for witchcraft in 1622. Nothing is known of his last years, but he is supposed to have died about 1610.

Montgomerie was a great experimenter in metrics, writing what James called "cuttit and broken verse." In this he was a disciple of Alexander Scott, but went beyond him. With several others, he has been called "the last of the Makaris," but the English influence was strong on his verse. He was especially fond of fourteen-line stanzas, and wrote some seventy more or less regular sonnets. He had a good ear for rhythm, and his poems are full of homely turns of phrase, but in general, though he is simple and unaffected, he is also dull. His verse has no feeling, and reflects the gloomy, pessimistic, languid nature of its writer, contrasting oddly with its jingly rhythm.

In 1579 Montgomerie wrote two royal pageants, *The Navigatioun* and *A Cartell of Three Ventrous Knichts*, which were acted at court. His best known poem is "The Cherrie and the Slae," in which the cherry represents virtue and the sloe represents vice. In the common Scottish style, he wrote a *Flyting*, or acrimonious and abusive verse debate, with Sir Patrick Hume of Polwarth. The most poetic of his verses is "The Nicht Is Near Gone." Though his familiar poems to his friends show good taste, his verses relating to his lawsuit are viciously bitter, and he displayed a sickening servility in his poems to James, who liked neither gross flattery nor cringing. The manuscripts of his surviving poems are now in the University of Edinburgh.

PRINCIPAL WORKS (dates of publication): The Cherrie and the Slae, 1597; The Mindes Melodie, 1605; The Flying betwixt Montgomerie and Polwart, 1621; Works (D. Irving, ed.) 1821; Poems (J. Cranstoun, ed.) 1887; Poems (G. Stevenson, ed.) 1910.

ABOUT: Brotanek, R. Alexander Montgomerie (in German); Cranstoun, J. Biographical Sketch, in Poems, 1887 ed.; Hoffmann, O. Studien zu Alexander Montgomerie; Melville, J. Diary.

MOORE, EDWARD (March 22, 1712-February 28, 1757), poet, dramatist, periodical writer, was born at Abingdon, Berkshire, the son of a nonconformist clergyman who died when the boy was about ten years old. Edward received his education from his uncle at the nonconformist academy and seminary, Bridgewater, Somerset. After a brief period at another such school in East Orchard, Dorset, he was apprenticed to a wholesale linen draper in London. When his apprenticeship was completed, he spent some years in Ireland as a factor with another linen merchant. Returning to London, he set up in business with an Irish partner, but was unsuccessful.

Moore took to writing as a last resort; his "marriage with the muses," he says, "like most other marriages into that noble family, was more from necessity than inclination." Throughout his career he was a successful writer of songs, and his first major work was *Solomon, a Serenata*, to the music of Dr. Boyce. *Fables for the Female Sex*, a rather conventional collection of verse tales in the manner of Gay, gave him his first literary success and ran into twenty editions before the end of the century.

The theatre seemed to offer better prospects of financial reward; in five years he wrote two comedies, *The Foundling* and *Gil Blas,* and a prose tragedy, *The Gamester.* His friend Garrick produced and acted in all three; *The Gamester* alone is important, for it marks a step toward the modern drama. Complex in plot, it has for hero one Beverley, a man of the middle classes, who is undone by gambling and evil companions. Translated into French, German, Dutch, Spanish, Italian, it was adapted or imitated by Diderot, D'Alembert, Iffland, and many other Continental dramatists. It has been called "the most modern English tragedy written in the eighteenth century."

Moore also wrote poems defending Garrick and his own political patrons—Lord Lyttleton and Pelham—as well as numerous pieces best termed *vers de société.* His love for a well-born and beautiful girl named Jenny Hamilton created quite a flutter in London society during 1749-50. The couple finally scraped together enough money to marry in May 1750.

From January 1753 to December 1756 Moore edited a weekly paper, *The World,* published by Dodsley, to which he contributed sixty-one numbers. Most of the essays

EDWARD MOORE

dealt with high society; such aristocratic stylists as Horace Walpole and Lord Chesterfield contributed to it. Moore announced the death of his pseudonymous personality, Adam Fitz Adam, in the last number. Two months later he himself was dead of rheumatic fever. No monument marked his grave in Lambeth Parish burying ground. Lord Chesterfield paid for the education of Moore's only son and presented him with £500 when he reached the age of sixteen.

Moore's face is described as round and pleasant, with large eyes and a sharp nose. He kept the strict moral code of a nonconformist, but had a good sense of humor and was popular in good society. He lacked the character and conviction to be a satirist rather than a humorist. All that was strongest in his upbringing, his character, and his literary talent went into that one play, *The Gamester.*

PRINCIPAL WORKS: *Poems:* Fables for the Female Sex, 1744; The Trial of Selim the Persian, 1748; An Ode to David Garrick, 1749; An Ode on the Death of Mr. Pelham, 1754. *Plays:* The Foundling, 1748; Solomon, A Serenata, 1750; Gil Blas, 1751; The Gamester, 1753. *Miscellaneous:* Poems, Fables and Plays, 1756; Collected Poems in Anderson's and Chalmers' editions.

ABOUT: Caskey, J. H. The Life and Works of Edward Moore.

MOORE, FRANCIS (January 29, 1657-1715?), physician, astrologer, schoolmaster, author of almanacs, was born in Bridgnorth, Shropshire. Nothing is known of his education, or of his life until he came to London toward the end of the seventeenth century. He was a student of and then an assistant to John Partridge, a well known astrologer of the time. In 1698 he was licensed to practice physic, though it is doubtful that he had a medical degree from any college. He settled in Lambeth, where he combined the conducting of a private school, the practice of medicine, and the casting of horoscopes.

In connection with his medical practice, Moore made up his own pills for his patients; and to advertise these pills, he published in 1698 a sort of almanac called the *Kalendarium Ecclesiasticum.* In this he made no predictions except of the weather for the year. Two years later, however, he published a real almanac, under the title of *Vox Stellarum* (the voice of the stars).

363

This was on the same pattern as many others published at the time, all issued by the Stationers' Company, and included such items as "the influence of the moon on peace and war and on sickeness, the revolutions of kings and princes, eclipses and comets," and the general horoscopes of those born under the different signs of the zodiac.

The first of Moore's regular almanacs came out in July 1700 for 1701, and they were published thereafter every July for the coming year. Moore died some time between July 1714 and July 1715, for the prognostications for 1716 came out under a different authorship. The almanacs, however, were continued; and indeed are continued to this day, having for many years been published under the title of *Old Moore's Almanac.* The first to continue them after Moore's death was Tyche Wing, the second Henry Andrew.

Nothing more is known about Moore himself, except that in 1702 he had moved to Southwark. A portrait printed in one issue shows him as an obese old man with chubby face. It is not known whether he was married or left descendants.

The almanacs, of course, had no pretensions to literary quality, and all that can be said about Moore as a writer is that he was at least able to read and write, and apparently had some elementary knowledge of Latin, which he used freely in his annual volumes.

PRINCIPAL WORKS: Kalendarium Ecclesiasticum, . . . a new Two-fold Kalendar, 1698; Vox Stellarum . . . or Almanack, 1700-1715.

MOORE, Dr. JOHN (1729-March 15, 1802), novelist, miscellaneous writer, was born at Stirling and baptized on December 7, 1729. His mother was Marion Anderson of Glasgow and his father, Charles Moore, a Presbyterian minister. After the father's death, the family moved to Glasgow where John was educated at the University. He studied literature, history, philosophy, and at the same time was apprenticed to Dr. John Gordon, a surgeon, who also taught Tobias Smollett.

When he was little more than eighteen, Moore found practical medical experience in the army, serving first as a surgeon's mate in the regiment of the Duke of Argyll, and then as assistant surgeon with the Earl of Albemarle, Colonel of the Coldstream Guards. He came back from active service in 1749, attended the lectures of Dr. William Hunter, the Scottish physician and anatomist, and later traveled to Paris with William Fordyce for further study. On his return to England he was appointed surgeon to the household of the Earl of Albemarle, then British ambassador. On the invitation of his former teacher, Dr. Gordon, Moore went back to the practice of medicine in Glasgow, taking his M.D. at the University in 1770. During his residence there he married Miss Simson, the daughter of a professor of divinity.

Dr. Moore traveled extensively, first with his friend Smollett (Smollett's *The Adventures of Peregrine Pickle* was written as a result of a French tour he made with Dr. Moore in 1750), and then with the Duke of Hamilton, whom he had attended as a physician. His first literary productions, written after he had settled in London, were travel books describing his journeys in letter form. These won him considerable reputation and brought him into contact with prominent literary figures of his time, including Robert Burns and Dr. Johnson. In 1786 he published a successful novel, *Zeluco,* "tracing the windings of vice and delineating the disgusting features of villany." A second novel, *Edward,* was the reverse of *Zeluco,* portraying the admirable side of human nature, which the good doctor managed to make extraordinarily dull. Moore also edited the works of Smollett and wrote a biographical preface.

A wise physician and a mediocre writer, Moore seems to have been an attractive personality well liked by his many friends. During the latter years of his life he suffered from poor health and retired with his family to Richmond, Surrey, where he died at the age of seventy-three.

PRINCIPAL WORKS: A View of Society in France, Switzerland, and Germany, 1779; A View of Society and Manners in Italy, 1781; Zeluco: Various Views of Human Nature Taken From Life and Manners, Foreign and Domestic, 1786; A Journal During a Residence in France, 1793-94; Edward: Various Views of Human Nature Taken from Life and Manners Chiefly in England, 1796; A View of the Commencement and Progress of Romance (prefixed to Smollett's Works, J. Moore, ed.) 1797; Mordaunt: Being Sketches of Life, Character, and Manners in Various Countries, 1800.

ABOUT: Anderson, R. Life of John Moore, M.D.; Chalmers, A. Biographical Dictionary.

MORE, HENRY (1614-September 1, 1687), Platonist, poet, philosophical writer, was born in Grantham, Lincolnshire, the son of Alexander More, a gentleman of moderate fortune. Both his parents were strict Calvinists, but their son said later that he "never could follow that hard doctrine." About 1628 he entered Eton, and in 1631 Christ's College, Cambridge. (That was Milton's last year there, but there is no evidence that they were acquainted.) More received a B.A. in 1635, M.A. in 1639, and in the same year took holy orders and became a fellow and tutor of the college. He lived there for the remainder of his life, except for long periods spent visiting his ex-pupil, Viscount Conway. Lady Conway, who also became his pupil, was an enthusiast who ended as a Quaker, and it is to her influence that More's mystical and theosophical tendencies in later years have been traced. At the Conway estate, in Ragley, Warwickshire, he loved to wander in the woods, and there many of his books were composed.

More refused all preferment in the church, including offers of appointment as master of his college, dean of Christ Church, Oxford, provost of Trinity College, Dublin, dean of St. Patrick's, Dublin, and two bishoprics. He finally accepted a prebendary at Gloucester, only to resign immediately in favor of a friend. He ascribed these refusals to "pure love of contemplation and solitude," and to the feeling that he could "do the church of God better service in private than public station." But though he was as saintly a man as ever lived, he was no recluse or ascetic; he loved music, played the theorbo, and liked to play at bowls. He was so charitable that his lodgings were likened to an asylum for the poor. He had courage also; throughout the civil war and the Commonwealth he remained steadfastly loyal to the royal family, and took the risk of danger to himself, though actually he never was molested.

At the time he entered Cambridge, the university was deep in enthusiasm for Descartes, but after a short period of mild skepticism More discovered Plato, "immersed himself head and ears in the study of philosophy," and remained thereafter the chief English voice of Platonism and Neoplatonism. Gradually the rationality of his earlier writings gave way to a misty vagueness,

After D. Loggan
HENRY MORE

until Tulloch, who found him interesting historically and as a person, described him as completely unreadable.

In 1679, persuaded by innocent vanity that his English reputation was destined to grow into international fame, More took on the onerous task of translating all his English writings into Latin. He was financed in this by a legacy left him by a barrister friend. He was mistaken in his estimate, but to his preface to this Latin edition we owe most of the knowledge we have about his private life and nature.

Humble, kindly, dreamy, with his chief defect a certain precipitancy of judgment, More is an attractive figure, though few except experts in the history of Christian Platonism read his works today. Coleridge, who had a certain intellectual affinity with him, greatly admired More's "original, enlarged, and elevating views," but to modern readers the chief alleviation of his vagueness and dullness as a writer is a sort of radiance of thought that shines through it, the reflection of his saintly character. His early poetry is better philosophy than it is poetry.

PRINCIPAL WORKS: Psychozoia Platonica: Or a Platonical Song of the Soul (verse), 1642; Philosophical Poems, 1647; An Anti-dote against Atheism, 1653; Conjectura Cabbalistica: A Conjectural Essay Interpreting . . . the Mind of Moses, 1653; Enthusiasmus Triumphans: The Natural Causes, Kinds, and Cures of Enthusiasme, 1656; The Immortality of the Soule, 1659; An Explanation of the Grand Mystery of Godliness, 1660; A Collection of several Philosophical Writings, 1662; Apology, 1664; Enchiridion Ethicum (in Latin) 1667; Divine Dialogues, 1668; Enchiridion Mysticum (in Latin) 1671; Opera Omnia (in Latin) 1679; Apocalypsus Apocalypseos, or the Revelation . . . unveiled, 1680; A Plain and Continued Exposition of the . . . Prophecies . . . of Daniel, 1681; A brief Discourse of the Real Presence, 1681; A Collection of Aphorisms, 1704; Philosophical Works (F. I. McKinnon, ed.) 1925.

ABOUT: Benson, A. C. Essays; Hallam, M. Moral and Metaphysical Philosophy; McKinnon, F. I. Introduction, Philosophical Works; More, H. Praefatio Generalissima, in Opera Omnia; Tulloch, J. Rational Theology; Ward, R. Life of the Learned and Pious Dr. Henry More; Zimmermann, R. Henry More und die vierte Dimension des Raums.

MORE, Sir THOMAS (February 7, 1478-July 6, 1535), judge, classical scholar, miscellaneous writer, author of *Utopia,* was born in London, the only surviving son of Sir John More, barrister and later justice of the King's Bench, and his first wife, Alice Graunger. He was educated at St. Anthony's School, and then in 1491 placed in the household of Archbishop Thomas Morton, Lord Chancellor of England. Struck with the boy's precocity, Morton had him entered the next year at Canterbury Hall (afterwards absorbed into Christ College), Oxford. It was there that he first came under the influence of the Humanists, particularly John Colet. In fact, his lawyer father, fearing the effect on his son's career of too much interest in the classics, took him from the university after two years and entered him at Lincoln's Inn. He was called to the bar in an unusually short time, and became reader-in-law at Furnival's Inn. In 1504 he was a member of Parliament, and in spite of his youth frustrated one of the projects of Henry VII, who in revenge threw More's father in the Tower and fined him £100.

Although More was an under sheriff of London in 1510, his real public career did not begin until 1516. From 1499 to 1503 he underwent a period of absorption in religion, contemplated joining the Carthusians or Franciscans, and lived a life of extreme asceticism. Then he suddenly rejoined the world, became active in his profession, and built up a large private practice. All his life, however, he wore a hair shirt next to his skin, and the twin impulses of practical living and religious seclusion were always at war within him. In 1505 he married Jane Culte—it is said that he preferred her younger sister, but would not offend her by passing her over. In any event, his family life was notably happy. He had three daughters—the oldest his beloved Margaret, who married William Roper—and a son who seems to have been a bit subnormal mentally. Mrs. More died in 1511, and within a month, by special dispensation, More married a widow with one daughter, Alice Middleton, seven years his senior and without any intellectual pretensions. Probably the motive was to secure someone to care for his small children, but she made him a loyal and devoted wife.

It was not long before More was singled out for attention by Henry VIII. After diplomatic and commercial missions to Flanders and France, he was made Master of Requests (1518), subtreasurer (1521), speaker of the House of Commons (1523), high steward of Cambridge and chancellor of the Duchy of Lancaster (1525), and finally Lord Chancellor in 1529. More knew well, especially after the downfall of Wolsey, how dangerous was the fickle king's special favor, but he tried every ruse in vain to circumvent it. As the first layman to become Lord Chancellor, he was unavoidably in the limelight. He made on the whole a just, efficient, honest, and fair minded judge—though no harsher persecutor of heretics ever lived.

As a member of the Privy Council, More had voted to impeach Wolsey, but events were rapidly forcing him to take a stand against the king. He acquiesced silently in the divorce from Catherine of Aragon, but in 1534 he refused to swear to the Act of Succession, which would have involved him in support of the supremacy of the king over all rulers, including the Pope. Already he had found himself in trouble the year before, when he was almost indicted for treason because of his advocacy of the so-called Holy Maid of Kent, Elizabeth Barton. Now he was thrown in the Tower, all his property confiscated and given to Elizabeth (who kept it all her life), and though at first he was treated leniently, after it was discovered that he was communicating with his fellow prisoner, John Fisher, he was kept in isolation. His trial on a charge of high treason finally took place on July 1, 1535, and five days later, calm and gently humorous to the

After H. Holbein, 1525
SIR THOMAS MORE

last, he was executed. The best he could secure for himself was beheading instead of hanging. His body was buried in the Tower (not in Chelsea, where his home was, as he had wanted) and his head was exhibited on London Bridge. It is almost certain that his daughter Margaret managed to rescue it and that it was buried with her.

More's writing, outside of his famous *Utopia* (originally in Latin) was (except for minor and mediocre verse) either controversial or devotional in nature. Erasmus, his great friend (*The Praise of Folly* was written by Erasmus in More's house), said that in his youth More had written comedies, but none of these has survived. Though he was unmistakably a Humanist, More was undeviatingly orthodox in religion. His controversial work, in both English and Latin, is marred by frequent scurrility. His Latin style is impeccable, classical rather than medieval, his English style brilliant and witty. More's was a contradictory nature— he had a fund of gentle humor, he had charm and gaiety, he was whimsical and lovable; and at the same time he was deeply devout, with a streak of religious melancholy which marks even many of his epigrams. He was by nature kind, yet he could be extremely cruel; he had courage and steadfastness, yet he never rushed rashly into danger; he was just and honest, yet he yielded a little to the prevalent corruption of the courts.

He loved music and played well, he was an art patron and a friend of the painter Holbein, was austere to the point of asceticism. The handsome courtier and the shrewd lawyer battled within him always with the pious devoté, who could not live without assurance of spiritual support.

The only one of More's books that is alive today—except perhaps for his translations of Lucian and the epigrams of the Greek Anthology—is of course the *Utopia*. This famous romance of "Nowhere" (which is the literal translation of the Greek word) was derived from many sources—from Plato's *Republic*, from Augustine's *City of God*, from the account of the voyages of Amerigo Vespucci, and from More's own memories of the wide, clean streets of the Netherlands cities. More's "perfect commonwealth" includes both monarchy and slavery, the women of Utopia are subservient to the men, and though there is religious toleration it does not extend to unbelievers. On the other hand, More's attitude toward war, penology, and economics is so far ahead of his time that the world has not yet caught up with much of it.

More was made a saint of the Roman Catholic Church in 1886. His execution aroused the hot indignation of many of his contemporaries, and produced a literature of its own. The most interesting example is *The Tragedy of Sir Thomas More* (1590), which by some critics has been attributed to Shakespeare.

PRINCIPAL WORKS: Life of John Picus, Earle of Mirandula, 1510; Utopia (in Latin) 1516 (translations: R. Robinson, 1551, G. Burnet, 1684, A. Cayley, 1808); A Dyaloge, 1528; Supplicacyon of Soulys, 1529; Confutacyon of Tyndale's Answere, 1532; The Apology of Sir Thomas More, 1533; Deballacyon of Salem and Bizance, 1533; A Letter Impugnynge the erronyouse wrytyng of John Fryth, 1533; History of Richard III (incomplete) 1543; A Dyaloge of Comfort against Tribulation, 1553; The Workes of Sir Thomas More, Knyght, written by him in the Englysh tonge (W. Rastell [nephew] ed.) 1557; Thomae Mori . . . Lucubrationes, 1563; Opera Omnia, 1689; The Correspondence of Sir Thomas More (E. D. Rogers, ed.) 1948.

ABOUT: Ames, R. A. Citizen Thomas More and His Utopia; Bridgett, T. E. Life and Writings of Blessed Thomas More; Campbell, W. E. Erasmus, Tyndale, and More; Campbell, W. E. More's Utopia and his Social Teaching; Cecil, A. A Portrait of Thomas More, Scholar, Statesman, Saint; Chambers, R. W. The Saga and Myth of Sir Thomas More; Chambers, R. W. Thomas More; Clayton, J. Sir Thomas More; Hollis, C. Sir Thomas More; Lee, S. L. Great Englishmen of the 16th Century; Maynard, T. Humanist as

Hero: the Life of Sir Thomas More; More, Sir T. Correspondence of Sir Thomas More; Routh, E. M. Sir Thomas More; Sargent, D. Thomas More and his Friends; Seebohm, F. The Oxford Reformers; Smith, R. L. John Fisher and Thomas More: Two English Saints; Sullivan, F. and M. P. Moreana, 1478-1945.

MORGANN, MAURICE

MORGANN, MAURICE (1726-March 28, 1812), essayist, was born in London, the descendant of an old Welsh family. Little is known of his life and he is remembered only for a single work, *An Essay on the Dramatic Character of Sir John Falstaff,* published in 1777 and widely praised.

During the administration of 1782, Morgann served as undersecretary of state to William Fitzmaurice Petty, Earl of Shelburne and later Marquis of Lansdowne. He seems to have been highly esteemed by Lord Lansdowne who on several occasions allowed Morgann to entertain literary friends at his estate while he was away. One of these friends was Dr. Johnson. Morgann also served as secretary to the embassy for ratifying peace with America in 1783.

Apparently Morgann wrote a number of pamphlets on burning questions of the day which were issued anonymously, but since all his papers were destroyed after his death by the instructions in his will, none of his work survives, except the essay on Falstaff. According to a friend, Dr. Symmons, "thus were lost various compositions in politics, metaphysics, and criticism, which would have planted a permanent laurel on his grave."

The *Essay on the Dramatic Character of Sir John Falstaff* pleads in witty fashion for a vindication of Falstaff's courage. Dr. Johnson made ironic comment on this thesis, "Why, sir, we shall have the man come forth again; and as he proved Falstaff to be no coward, he may prove Iago to be a very good character," but actually there is evidence that Johnson respected Morgann's argument, which on a deeper level subjected the whole character of Falstaff to subtle analysis in relation to the dramatic art of his creator. The book was twice republished after Morgann's death at Knightsbridge in 1802, and can still be read with considerable interest.

PRINCIPAL WORKS: An Essay on the Dramatic Character of Sir John Falstaff, 1777 (W. A. Gill, ed. 1912).

MOTTEUX, PETER ANTHONY (February 18, 1660-February 18, 1718), editor, translator, dramatist, was born in Rouen, Normandy, probably the son of Antoine le Motteux, a merchant. He came to England in 1685 among many hundreds of French refugees at the time of the revocation of the Edict of Nantes. Living with his godfather, Paul Dominique, in London, Motteux quickly mastered the English language and began a double career as East India merchant and literary jack-of-all-trades.

In 1692 he founded and edited *The Gentleman's Journal,* a periodical of miscellaneous contents more like a modern magazine than any periodical for years to come, publishing news, stories, poems, and criticism. When the *Journal* languished in little more than a year, Motteux turned his willing pen to writing plays, operas, poems, translations, and so-called musical interludes.

The only work of any importance which he accomplished was a translation of the fourth and fifth books of Rabelais, concluding the translation made by Urquhart and others. He also wrote a life of Rabelais to serve as introduction and edited the entire series. Although Motteux' version of Rabelais is racy and readable, it frequently distorts the intention of the original in its use of London slang. With Ozell, John Phillips, and others, Motteux also made a translation of *Don Quixote.* His plays, of which he wrote and produced a great many, were cut to the fashionable pattern, and had not the smallest distinction.

Although he won the liking of Dryden, he earned the contempt of Pope who wrote of him among those "obscure authors, that wrap themselves up in their own mud, but are mighty nimble and pert." Indeed it would seem that this Frenchman turned Englishman came to understand too well the ways of Grub Street.

Motteux died scandalously on his fifty-eighth birthday in a house of ill fame under circumstances which have never been fully explained. The proprietress of the house and several inmates were accused of murder and tried at the Old Bailey, but all were acquitted.

PRINCIPAL WORKS: *Plays:* Love's A Jest, 1696; Beauty in Distress, 1698; The Island Princess, 1699; The Four Seasons, or Love in Every Age, 1699; The Masque of Acis and Galtea, 1701;

Arsinoe, Queen of Cyprus, 1705; The Temple of Love, 1706; Thomyris, Queen of Scythia, 1707. *Other Works*: The Works of F. Rabelais (tr. and ed.) 1694, 1708; The History of the Renown'd Don Quixote (tr. and ed.) 1700-12.

ABOUT: Cunningham, R. N. Peter Anthony Motteux: a Biographical and Critical Study.

MOTTLEY, JOHN (1692-1750), dramatist, biographer, compiler, was born in London. His birth, according to his own account, was the only fruit of a secret mission undertaken by his father, Colonel Thomas Mottley, on behalf of the exiled James II. The colonel, it seems, found an opportunity to visit his wife, who, when her husband followed his king into exile in 1688, had chosen to remain in England. She was a Guise, and her family had long opposed the Stuart dynasty. Colonel Mottley died leading his French regiment at the Battle of Turin, 1706.

John was educated at St. Martin's Library School, founded by Archbishop Tennison, and entered the Excise Office as a clerk when not quite sixteen. In 1720 he gave up his job on Sir Robert Walpole's promise of a better one in the Exchequer; the new post never materialized, and Mottley had to earn his living by writing. His career began with two poorly received tragedies; in opera, farce and comedy he was more successful. The comedy, *The Widow Bewitched*, was his best independent work; with Charles Coffey he wrote a comic opera, *The Devil to Pay*, which was revived many times.

He compiled or edited various works under pseudonyms; as Elijah Jenkins he was responsible for *Joe Miller's Jests, or the Wit's Vade Mecum*, often reprinted or imitated in the two hundred years since its appearance. He also wrote biographies of Peter the Great and Catherine the Great of Russia.

Mottley is assumed to have compiled the *Complete List of All the English Dramatic Poets and of All the Plays Ever Printed in the English Language to the Present Year 1747*, which forms an appendix to Thomas Whincop's tragedy, *Scanderbeg;* his own biography is certainly the longest and fullest in the list, not excepting Shakespeare's. We learn there that he was suffering from gout in the right hand and had "not been above twice out of his lodgings these two years

past." Gout may have caused his death in London three years later. The wretched engraving at the head of his biography gives him a large shapeless nose, thick lips, and a conceited expression. The tone of his remarks about himself certainly does not belie this last trait.

PRINCIPAL WORKS: *Plays*: The Imperial Captives (tragedy) 1720; Antiochus (tragedy) 1721; The Craftsman (farce) 1729; The Widow Bewitched, 1730; The Devil to Pay, 1731. *Other Writings*: Joe Miller's Jests, 1739; The History of the Life of Peter I, Emperor of Russia, 1739; The History of the Life and Reign of the Empress Catherine of Russia, 1744.

ABOUT: Whincop, T. Scanderbeg (edition of 1747. but see above).

MUDDIMAN, HENRY (February 5, 1629-March 1692), journalist, was born in London, the son of Edward Muddiman by his first wife, Alice. He attended the choir school of St. Clement Danes, and in 1641 entered St. John's College, Cambridge, but left without a degree. For a while he was a schoolmaster. When the trouble started between the king and Parliament, Muddiman—though he was no controversialist and avoided argument—was considered to be a "safe man" and the Rump Parliament gave him a monopoly of news letters, with free postage for both himself and his correspondents.

These news letters were not newspapers, but folios, written by hand by Muddiman's clerks, and sent to subscribers at a minimum of five pounds a year, to inform them of governmental activities and developments. Muddiman held this monopoly throughout the civil war and after the Restoration; in later years he became a Jacobite, and in 1687 William III took away his privileges.

To accompany these news letters, Muddiman began in 1659 printing a supplementary sheet, called the *Parliamentary Intelligencer*. From 1660 to 1700 actual reports of Parliamentary procedure were forbidden, and Muddiman's paraphrases were therefore extremely valuable. Muddiman had succeeded Marchamont (or Marchmont) Nedham. His first paper was under the protection of the Parliamentary general, George Monck. Its name was soon changed to the *Kingdom's Intelligencer*. In 1663 Charles II gave the monopoly of the printed news to Sir Roger L'Estrange, but by this time Muddiman's written letters were so much more profitable that he did not care; in any event L'Estrange soon lost the monopoly.

In 1665 Muddiman began to publish the *Oxford Gazette* twice a week, licensed by Lord Arlington. The next year this became the *London Gazette*, which is still issued every Tuesday and Friday, as the official organ of the government. It was the same size and shape as Muddiman's written news letters, and accompanied them to subscribers. After 1687, when the news letters were discontinued, Muddiman, who was growing old, lost interest, and after 1689 he ceased to write at all.

He spent his last years at his country house, "Coldherne," at Earls Court. It is interesting to realize that this, now a part of metropolitan London, was then a remote suburb, and throughout his years of activity Muddiman "commuted" to his office in the Strand, on horseback, armed with sword and pistols to repel very possible bandits!

Muddiman was the most famous journalist of the seventeenth century. Pepys, who distrusted his political views, nevertheless called him "a good scholar." He was hardly that, though he knew enough Latin to translate Erasmus; but he was a competent journalist, and he paved the way for Defoe and through him for modern newspapers.

PRINCIPAL WORKS: Sir Politique Uneased, 1660; The Colloquies and Familiar Discourses of Desiderius Erasmus of Rotterdam (tr.) 1671.

ABOUT: Muddiman, J. G. The King's Journalist: Studies in the Reign of Charles II; Pepys, S. Diary.

MULCASTER, RICHARD (1530?-April 15, 1611), schoolmaster, author of books on education, was born at Carlisle or near by on the river Line, the son of William Mulcaster. He went to school at Eton under Nicholas Udall and studied at both Cambridge and Oxford, taking his M.A. at Christ Church, Oxford, in 1556.

As a schoolmaster in London his reputation was such that the newly founded school of the Merchant Taylors appointed him first headmaster in 1561. There he remained for the next twenty-five years, developing the theories of education, many of them well in advance of their time, which were contained in his two books, *Positions* and *The Elementarie*.

Writing in the *Cambridge History of English Literature*, W. H. Woodward calls Mulcaster "the uncouth prophet of a new order." In the midst of the Elizabethan age and in spite of his harshness as a teacher, he was genuinely dedicated to the education of the rising burgher class, aware of a new world and the new approach to education which it demanded. For one thing, he stressed the importance of teaching students to write English in a period when Latin was still the language of the gentleman and the scholar. His own works are written in a straightforward English prose which did much to search out the linguistic resources of the language. "I love Rome, but London better," he wrote, "I favour Italy, but England more, I honour Latin, but worship English." He also advocated the special training of teachers at universities and asserted the right of girls to a higher education.

Resigning from the Merchant Taylors school, Mulcaster held several preferments before he accepted the head mastership of St. Paul's School in 1594. There he remained until five years before his death. Both by his teaching and his writings Mulcaster was probably the most famous schoolmaster of his time. Queen Elizabeth, interesting herself in his career, gave him the rectory of Stanford Rivers, Essex, and invited him on a number of occasions to present masques at court which were performed by his pupils. One of his early students was the poet, Edmund Spenser. Shakespeare probably knew him and he is sometimes identified with the caricature of a schoolmaster in *Love's Labour's Lost*.

PRINCIPAL WORKS: Positions, 1581 (R. H. Quick, ed. 1888); The Elementarie, 1582 (E. T. Campagnac, ed. 1925); The Educational Writings of Richard Mulcaster (J. Oliphant, ed.) 1903.

ABOUT: Oliphant, J. Critical Preface to The Educational Writings; Quick, R. H. Biography in Positions; Wilson, H. B. History of Merchant Taylors School.

MUNDAY, ANTHONY (1553-1633), dramatist, poet, balladist, pamphleteer, compiler, was born in London, the son of Christopher Munday, draper. He did not go to either Oxford or Cambridge, but received a good education at some London school. He may have been on the stage in his teens; in 1576 he was apprenticed to John Allde, a stationer. Twenty-three was late in life to become a mere apprentice; one wonders

whether Anthony's correct age was given on his tombstone, which makes him eighty years old at his death and is the only authority for the year of his birth.

While apprenticed to Allde, he began to write verses. According to his own account he obtained an introduction to Edward de Vere, Earl of Oxford, who suggested that he travel on the Continent and learn languages. Anthony seems to have decided that the cheapest way of doing this was to offer himself as a potential Catholic convert and thus make his way to Rome. Accordingly, some time in 1578 he obtained a release from Allde and sailed for Boulogne with Thomas Nowell, who later became a Catholic priest. Helped by funds from various English priests on the Continent, Munday reached the English College at Rome where, he says, he led a mutiny among the students.

On his return to England Munday entered the service of the Earl of Oxford, and may have acted with his lordship's company of players. He now began his writing career in earnest—and a remarkable career it is. First he imitated the *Mirror for Magistrates* in two gloomy poems, *The Mirror of Mutability* and *The Pain of Pleasure*. Then he imitated Lyly's *Euphues* in his prose romance *Zelauto*. Next, he turned informer against his Catholic friends and was instrumental in having several of them executed. In 1581-82 he wrote several anti-Catholic pamphlets and *The English-Roman Life*, an account of his Continental trip. As a "Messenger of the Queen's Bedchamber" he hunted Catholics periodically down to 1596.

Meanwhile, his literary career took a new turn. He wrote ballads and lyric poetry, including "Beauty Bathing," which first appeared in *England's Helicon* and is now in the *Oxford Book of English Verse*. Having learnt French and Italian moderately well, he set about translating some of the great Continental romances of chivalry. *Palmerin of England* was registered in 1581, though the first extant copy dates from 1596. *Palmerin d'Oliva*, *Amadis of Gaul* and others followed.

About 1585 there seemed to be money in the drama, so Munday started writing plays. He was one of Philip Henslowe's

"stable" of dramatists, 1592-1602, and was described as "our best plotter" by Francis Meres, 1598. Nevertheless, audiences were becoming more sophisticated and some of the brilliant men now taking to playwriting satirized Munday's old-fashioned work— Marston in *Histriomastix*, Ben Jonson in *The Case Is Altered*.

Munday gave up the stage about 1602, and may have set up shop as a draper. He had been a member of the Drapers' Company since 1585. During the last thirty years of his life his literary work found an audience mainly among his fellow bourgeois of the City of London. He wrote many pageants for the City, the last in 1623. He also continued Stow's *Survey of London*, bringing out the edition of 1618, and contributing a good deal to that of 1633, which appeared soon after his death.

Munday married twice, his first child being baptized in 1584. His second wife's name was Gillian, and he left everything to her in his will, since his children were by now better off then he was himself.

Apart from the one lyric mentioned above, Munday was an uninspired literary hack. It is hard to believe now that he was considered the obvious person to write *Sir John Oldcastle* as a counterblast to Shakespeare's Falstaff. Yet for at least a quarter of a century he had his finger on the literary pulse of England, and nothing that he wrote could fail to sell.

PRINCIPAL WORKS: *Plays*: Fidele and Fortunio, 1585; The First Part of the True and Honourable History of the Life of Sir John Oldcastle, 1600; The Downfall of Robert, Earl of Huntington, 1601; The Death of Robert, Earl of Huntington, 1601; Sir Thomas More (A. Dyce, ed.) 1844; John a Kent and John a Cumber (J. P. Collier, ed.) 1851. *Poetry*: The Mirror of Mutability, 1579; The Pain of Pleasure, 1580; A Banquet of Dainty Conceits, 1588: *Translations*: Palmerin D'Oliva, 1588; The First Book of Amadis of Gaul, 1590; The First Part of Palmerin of England, 1596 (Second Part, 1596; Third Part, 1602.) *Pamphlets*: A Brief Discourse of the Taking of Edmund Campion, 1581; A Discovery of Edmund Campion, 1582; The English-Roman Life, 1582; A Watchword to England to Beware of Traitors, 1584. *Romance*: Zelauto, 1580.

MURPHY, ARTHUR (December 27, 1727—June 18, 1805), playwright, actor, translator, periodical writer, was born at Clooniquin, County Roscommon, Ireland. His father, a Dublin merchant, went down with one of his own ships which foundered

with all hands aboard in 1729. Mrs. Murphy sold all her property in Ireland and moved her family from Dublin to London in 1735. The next year Arthur was sent to his aunt, Mrs. Plunkett, in Boulogne, France. From 1738 to 1744 he attended the English Jesuit College at St. Omer and received an excellent classical education, standing first in his class for five years.

On Arthur's return to England his maternal uncle, Jeffrey French, was horrified at his ignorance of arithmetic and his habit of attending Mass. Arthur remedied both these shortcomings to the best of his ability. He studied accountancy and became a clerk in a Cork counting-house, 1747. In 1749 he turned down Jeffrey French's offer of a position on a Jamaica plantation, and took a post in a London bank.

At the end of 1751, Murphy gave up business for literature. The next year he started writing a weekly paper, *The Gray's Inn Journal,* where his theatre notices, particularly those praising Garrick, attracted much attention. Jeffrey French died in 1754, leaving nothing to Murphy, who was by then £300 in debt. The young critic decided to become an actor, and made his first appearance—as Othello—on October 18, 1754. He was well received by his audiences, and was hired for Garrick's company the following season. At the end of this season he retired from the stage, having paid his debts and cleared £400 besides, thanks to a comedy he had written, *The Apprentice.*

Murphy now turned to the law, while continuing his career as a playwright and doing some political journalism as well. In 1762 he was called to the bar, and practiced his profession, not very successfully, until 1787, when he retired. He was a Commissioner of Bankrupts on two different occasions. In 1803 he was given an annual pension by George III, so that the last years of his life were free from money worries. His death was tranquil and he was buried beside his mother in Hammersmith Church.

Murphy was an amazingly prolific playwright, producing farces, comedies and tragedies. *The Way to Keep Him* is a brilliant comedy, worthy to rank beside all but the best of Goldsmith and Sheridan. *Know Your Own Mind,* his last comedy, is regarded by some as even better than *The*

Way to Keep Him. Murphy also wrote the life of his hero, Garrick, and an essay on the life and genius of his friend, Dr. Johnson. His complete translation of Tacitus is still reprinted.

A tall, portly man, with a plump, handsome face, dark complexion and a fine Roman nose, Murphy was attractive to women, but never married. His greatest love was Ann Elliot, a young actress of humble birth whom he protected and wrote several leading parts for. She died at twenty-five. Murphy was at one time engaged to a girl of his own class who also died young. There is much that is endearing about Murphy—for example his loyalty to Mrs. Thrale after her marriage to Piozzi—and both his character and his dramatic ability have just recently begun to receive their due.

PRINCIPAL WORKS: *Plays:* The Apprentice, 1756; The Upholsterer, 1758; The Orphan of China (tragedy) 1759; The Way to Keep Him, 1760; All in the Wrong, 1761; The Citizen, 1763; What We Must All Come To, 1764; The Grecian Daughter (tragedy) 1772; Know Your Own Mind, 1778. *Other Writings:* The Gray's Inn Journal (collected edition in 2 vols.) 1756; An Essay on the Life and Genius of Samuel Johnson, 1792; The Works of Tacitus, 1793; The Life of David Garrick, 1801; The Works of Sallust Translated, 1807.

ABOUT: Dunbar, H. H. The Dramatic Career of Arthur Murphy; Emery, J. P. Arthur Murphy; Foot, J. The Life of Arthur Murphy, Esq.

MURRAY, LINDLEY (April 22, 1745-January 16, 1826), grammarian, was American-born, the eldest son of a Pennsylvania Quaker family. His father, Robert Murray, conducted an extremely successful mercantile business in New York which he hoped to pass on to his son. When Lindley was fourteen, having proved himself an indifferent student, he entered his father's counting-house, but finding commerce unattractive, he ran away to pursue his real interests, which were literature and languages. He enrolled himself in a boarding school in Burlington, New Jersey, but was discovered shortly by his family and brought back to New York, where he took up the study of law. Called to the bar he practiced in New York and was married at twenty-two to Hannah Dobson.

After a brief trip to England in 1770, he settled in New York and by the end of the Revolutionary War had built up a large and lucrative practice. Suffering from ill health, he went again to England in 1784 and bought an estate at Holgate near York, where he lived the rest of his life. As a gentleman of leisure he devoted himself to study and literature. A petition from the teachers of a Friends' school for girls near York led him to compose the English grammar which, published in 1795, achieved enormous success and gave him claim to the title, "the father of English grammar." The book ran through nearly fifty editions and became a standard textbook in both England and America. Murray followed his *Grammar* with a number of other textbooks, the *English Exercises*, the *English Reader, Lecteur Français*, and an *English Spelling Book*, all of which sold widely.

Murray was the first to introduce system into the teaching of grammar, although unfortunately his own style exhibited many of the faults against which he warned his readers. While his methods were universally accepted in their day, they have long been superseded. J. W. Adamson writing in the *Cambridge History* calls him "the originator of that formal, logic-chopping treatment of its subject which long made English grammar the least profitable of school studies."

PRINCIPAL WORKS: English Grammar, Adapted to the Different Classes of Learning, 1795; English Exercises, 1797; English Reader, 1799; Lecteur Français, 1802; An English Spelling Book, 1804; Memoirs of the Life and Writings of Lindley Murray, Written by Himself (E. Frank, ed.) 1826.

ABOUT: Egle, W. H. Life of Murray; Frank, E. (ed.) Memoirs; Moon, G. W. The Bad English of Lindley Murray and Other Writers.

NAPIER or **NEPER, JOHN** (1550-April 4, 1617), Scottish mathematician, the inventor of logarithms, author of several books, was born at Merchiston near Edinburgh, the eldest son of Sir Archibald Napier and Janet Bothwell. He was educated at St. Salvator's College, St. Andrews, and spent several years in study and travel on the Continent. When he was twenty-two he married Elizabeth Stirling and took charge of his estate as the eighth laird of Merchiston. Widowed five years later Napier married Agnes Chisholm.

As a landowner Napier was concerned with the political and agricultural questions of his day, and as a strict Calvinist he supported the Protestant cause, crossing swords with Roman Catholic apologists. His first publication was a theological work, the *Plaine Discovery of the Whole Revelation of Saint John*, important as one of the first interpretations of scripture to be published in Scotland. His deepest interest, however, was in mathematics and invention. For several years he seems to have been engaged in inventing secret instruments of war for defense against the anticipated invasion by Philip of Spain, and his arithmetical calculating rods, called "Napier's bones," represent the earliest attempt at the invention of a calculating machine. *Rabdologia*, a treatise outlining the method of using the calculating rods, was published in 1617.

Napier's most important work, *Mirifici Logarithmorum Canonis Descriptio*, published in 1614, first presented the mathematical theory of logarithms to the world. His original table of logarithms was subsequently studied and improved by Henry Briggs, professor of geometry at Gresham College, in whom Napier found an enthusiastic disciple and collaborator. A work explaining the calculation of the table, *Canonis Constructio*, was published posthumously by Napier's son.

Worn out from overwork and suffering from severe gout, Napier died when he was sixty-seven, having made a contribution of commanding importance to the development of mathematics.

PRINCIPAL WORKS: Plaine Discovery of the Whole Revelation of Saint John, 1593; Mirifici Logarithmorum Canonis Descriptio, 1614 (E. Wright, tr. 1616); Rabdologiae Seu Numerationis Per Virgulas Libri Duo, 1617; Mirifici Logarithmorum Canonis Constructio, 1619; De Arte Logistica (M. Napier, ed.) 1839.

ABOUT: Hobson, E. W. John Napier and the Invention of Logarithms; Napier, M. Memoirs of John Napier.

NASH or **NASHE, THOMAS** (November, 1567-1601), author of an adventure novel, plays, poems, satires, miscellaneous works, was born in Lowestoft, Suffolk, the son of William Nash, a poor curate of a Hertfordshire family, and his second wife, Margaret. He entered St. John's College, Cambridge, in 1582 as a sizar, and was given a B.A. in 1586. In 1588 he left the university under a cloud, apparently expelled. This may have been a late consequence of a play, *Terminus et Non Terminus*, of which he was coauthor and in which he acted, which was offensive to the authorities.

THOMAS NASH

In any event, like so many other young men of his time, he went to London and endeavored to make his way by writing. He tried everything, from plays for Henslowe's company to anti-Puritan pamphlets, but though he became one of the recognized "university wits," and the associate of such men as Greene, Lodge, and Daniel, he was always miserably poor. As an illnatured critic remarked after his death, "he never in his life paid shoemaker or tailor," and he himself commented bitterly, "the seven liberal sciences and a good leg will scarce get a scholar bread and cheese."

It is as a pioneer realistic novelist, the precursor of Defoe, that Nash is most important. His plays are negligible. They include a satirical masque, *Summers Last Will and Testament*, written at Croydon in 1592 when he had left London because of the plague, and a lost comedy written with others, *The Isle of Dogs*, which caused the closing of the theatre and the jailing of several persons, including Ben Jonson, for "seditious and slanderous" utterances. Whether Nash himself was among those cast into the Fleet is doubtful; it is certain that he was banished from London for a time. Later he spent some time in the Isle of Wight.

Nash's other play was the mere finishing (no one knows how much he did) of Marlowe's *Dido, Queen of Carthage*, left un-

completed at Marlowe's death. Nash was not much of a dramatist, and his view of the drama was that it was a mere vehicle for moral teaching.

His entrance into the famous "Marprelate controversy" embroiled him in enmity with that redoubtable fighter, Gabriel Harvey, especially after Greene's death, when Nash rather halfheartedly took up his friend's cause. No one knows just which of the "Marprelate" pamphlets were his, but he is supposed to have been the controversialist writing as "Pasquil." He was violently anti-Puritan, perhaps in reaction to his early training, since both his parents were inclined to Puritanism.

Nash's other satirical pamphlets were aimed not so much at vice and crime as at "respectable roguery," affectation, and superstition. He wrote a first class parody of the annual prognostications of the astrologers under the pseudonym of "Adam Fouleweather." His first publication, the preface to Greene's *Menaphon* (1589), was a sharp criticism of many of his contemporaries, chiefly Kyd, but he lost his satirical vein in honest praise of those he admired, Daniel and Drayton, most of all. An unauthorized edition of Sidney's poems which he was hired to edit in 1591 was immediately suppressed because he had included his friends' poems among Sidney's. But eager satirist as he was, he was not a good hater; he even made overtures to Harvey in *Christes Teares over Jerusalem*. They were scornfully refused, and the fight went on until all the "Marprelate" pamphlets were suppressed in 1599.

But Nash's great accomplishment was the picaresque novel, *The Unfortunate Traveller*. Nash had apparently at some time traveled in France and Italy, and he took his rogue-hero, Jack Wilton, there and then back to England. Wilton is more of a rogue than a criminal, and is of better class than are the protagonists of French and Italian picaresque romances. This is the very first historical novel in English; Erasmus, Luther, and Sir Thomas More are among its characters.

Nash himself may be seen most clearly in his *Pierce Pennilesse*—for "Pierce Pennilesse" read "Thomas Nash." He spent himself in efforts to secure patrons, but never kept one long; his complaints and his bitterness alienated them. To keep alive, he wrote what he called "toys for gentlemen"—i.e., indecent poems and songs; one of these, *The Choosing of Valentines*, which has survived, is so obscene that it has never been printed. He was not given to overmodesty, and boasted of his originality and his "swelling boystrous" style. But he actually did have a hard life, and his boasting did have a foundation. What he really was, was a journalist born too early who tried his hand at everything and wrote "as fast as my hand could trot."

After an early attraction to Euphuism, Nash became the chief scorner of that high-flown mode of writing; his own prose was natural and forceful, and his few lyrics evidence the influence of Sidney and Spenser, both of whom he admired. Isaak Walton called him "a man of sharp wit, and the master of a scoffing, satirical, and merry pen." His tragedy was apt to degenerate into melodrama, but his comedy was always sure and to the point. As Drayton put it, Nash "a branch of laurel well deserved to bear."

Nash's last years are obscure, and the date of his death is fixed only by an elegy written in 1601. So far as known, he was never married.

PRINCIPAL WORKS: *Plays*: Dido, Queen of Carthage (with C. Marlowe) 1594; A Pleasant Comedie Called Summers Last Will and Testament, 1600. *Novel*: The Unfortunate Traveller, or The Life of Jacke Wilton, 1594 (E. Gosse, ed. 1892). *Pamphlets*: The Anatomie of Absurditie, 1589; A Countercuffe Given by Martin Junior, 1589; The Return of . . . Pasquill, 1589; The First Parte of Pasquill's Apologie, 1590; A Wonderfull Strange and Miraculous Astrologicall Prognostication, 1591; Four Letters Confuted, 1592; Pierce Pennilesse his Supplication, 1592; The Apologie of Pierce Pennilesse, 1593; Christes Teares Over Jerusalem, 1593; Terrors of the Night, 1594; Have with You to Saffron Walden, 1596; Lenten Stuffe, 1599. *Collections*: Complete Works (A. B. Grosart, ed.) 1883-85; Works (R. B. McKerrow, ed.) 1904-10.

ABOUT: Dekker, T. Newes from Hell; D'Israeli, I. Quarrels of Authors; Grosart, A. B. Memorial Introduction, Complete Works; Harman, F. G. Gabriel Harvey and Thomas Nash; Jusserand, J. J. The English Novel in the Time of Elizabeth; Meres, F. Palladis Tamia.

NENNIUS (fl. 796), Welsh historian, the traditional author of *Historia Britonum*, is a shadowy figure of whose life almost nothing is known. A dedicatory epistle to the *Historia* indicates that the work was completed at the end of the eighth century, probably about 796, and refers to the counties of Brecknock and Radnor as the home of the author.

The *Historia Britonum* exists in thirty different manuscript versions, a North Welsh group represented by the eight Cambridge manuscripts, a South Welsh group covered in seventeen manuscripts in the Harleian collection, and an English group in the five Vatican manuscripts. So confused is the character of the work owing to later interpolations and variations in text that critics have not been able to agree on either its authenticity or its authorship. Until Heinrich Zimmer published his *Nennius Vindicatus*, some scholars considered Nennius merely a transcriber and attributed the work of compilation to other authors, among them Monk, an Irish bishop of the ninth century, and Gildas. The weight of Zimmer's evidence, however, seems to prove that Nennius was either the original compiler or editor and that the work was completed in 796. It was then apparently sent to Elbodug, Bishop of Bangor, North Wales (who may have been the teacher of Nennius), after which numerous revised versions were made by other writers.

In its fullest form the *Historia* falls into the following parts: two *Prologues* (of which the first may be spurious), the *Calculi* or *De Sex Aetatibus Mundi*, the *Historia* proper, *Genealogiae Saxonicae*, and *Mirabilia*. Some of these parts are undoubtedly later additions. While of little value as an original authority, the *Historia* is an interesting summary of early tradition drawn apparently from both Roman and early Saxon and Irish sources, and contains some of the oldest legends relating to the victories of King Arthur.

PRINCIPAL WORKS: Historia Britonum, 796? (T. Mommsen, ed. 1898; J. A. Giles, tr. and ed. 1901).

ABOUT: Liebermann, F. Nennius the Author of the Historia Britonum; Zimmer, H. Nennius Vindicatus.

NEPER, JOHN. See NAPIER, JOHN

NEWBERY, JOHN (1713-December 22, 1767), publisher, author and originator of juvenile literature, was a farmer's son, born at Waltham St. Lawrence, Berkshire. Except for brief attendance at the village school, he had no formal education, but his great love of reading successfully made up for this lack.

When he was seventeen Newbery found a position as assistant to William Carnan, the proprietor and editor of a provincial newspaper, the *Reading Mercury*. Carnan died after several years and left the paper to his brother and Newbery. As a newly established publisher, Newbery married the widow of his former employer and set out to extend his business. After a brief tour of England he opened a warehouse in London in 1744, and a year later moved to the Bible and Sun in St. Paul's Churchyard where he became well known as a publisher, bookseller, and vendor of patent medicines.

During the next fifteen years Newbery established several newspapers and magazines, *The Universal Chronicle or Weekly Gazette*, which first published Dr. Johnson's *Idler* essays; the *Public Ledger*, in which Oliver Goldsmith's *Citizen of the World* first appeared; and *The Christian Magazine*, the first periodical entirely devoted to religious matters. He was known as a good friend to authors, always willing to make small advances, but with such men as Goldsmith and Johnson on his publishing list it would appear that he was more shrewd than philanthropic. Goldsmith has left an unforgettable portrait of this bustling bookseller in his *Vicar of Wakefield*, a "red-faced, good-natured little man who was always in a hurry."

Newbery is chiefly remembered, however, as the first publisher to make books for children an important branch of the publishing business. His *Juvenile Library* initiated a long series of miniature volumes attractively bound in flowered and gilt paper, appealing to the young reader with such titles as *The History of Little Goody Two Shoes, Tommy Trip and His Dog Jowler,* and *The Renowned History of Giles Gingerbread*. The authorship of Newbery's juveniles is still a matter of dispute. They were published anonymously, but undoubtedly Newbery planned and wrote a number of them himself, although Goldsmith, Giles Jones, and even Dr. Johnson, probably wrote some. At any rate Newbery deserves the full credit for opening a new field of

literature, and endeavoring to please children as well as to instruct them.

PRINCIPAL WORKS: *Essays:* The Art of Poetry Made Easy, 1746; Essay on Perfecting the Fine Arts in Great Britain and Ireland, 1767. *Juveniles:* A Little Pretty Pocket Book, 1744; The Circle of the Sciences, 1745-46; The History of Little Goody Two Shoes, 1766; The Twelfth-Day Gift, or The Grand Exhibition, 1767; The Renowned History of Giles Gingerbread, 1769.

ABOUT: Knight, C. Shadows of the Old Booksellers; Welsh, C. A Bookseller of the Last Century, Being Some Account of the Life of John Newbery.

NEWCASTLE, MARGARET (LUCAS) See CAVENDISH, MARGARET

NEWCASTLE, WILLIAM CAVENDISH, First Duke of. See CAVENDISH, WILLIAM

NEWTON, Sir ISAAC (December 25, 1642-March 20, 1727), philosopher, physicist, was born at Woolsthorpe, near Grantham, Lincolnshire, the son of Isaac Newton, who died three months before his son's birth, and of Hannah Ayscough, who in 1646 remarried, her second husband being Barnabas Smith, a clergyman. The child was left in the care of his maternal grandmother, and attended Grantham Grammar School, where he displayed very early his genius for mathematics. In 1656, when he was fourteen, his stepfather died; his mother returned to Woolsthorpe and immediately took her son out of school to help her on the farm. Instead, he spent most of his time on mathematics, and in 1660, through the good offices of his uncle, his mother was persuaded to let him follow his natural bent.

In 1661 he entered Trinity College, Cambridge, as a subsizar. He became a scholar in 1664, and received his B.A. in 1665. The plague then closed the university for over a year, and he studied at home. The next two years, 1665 and 1666, were Newton's greatest; during them he made his epochal discovery of the law of gravity and began his work in optics. Even his work in differential calculus (fluxions) was started at this period. In 1667 he became a fellow of Trinity, and in 1669 Lucasian professor of mathematics. The first reflecting telescope was invented in 1668. In 1672 he became a Fellow of the Royal Society, whose presi-

J. Vanderbank
SIR ISAAC NEWTON

dent he was to be for the last twenty-five years of his life.

The three books of the *Principia*, "the greatest single triumph of the human mind," appeared in 1687, after Newton several times almost gave up in despair the idea of completing it. He was involved in long and acrimonious disputes, based on rival claims, with Boyle and Hooke—as later with Leibnitz on fluxions—and his aberrant devotion to theology always threatened to divert him from his real path. It was largely thanks to Locke, who offered to subsidize it if necessary, that the great work finally was published. In 1689 Newton was elected to Parliament as a Whig, for Cambridge; in 1696 he became warden of the Mint, and in 1699 its master, resigning his professorship and living thenceforth in London. He was knighted by Queen Anne in 1705. He was still in his office as master of the Mint when he died of stone. He was buried in Westminster Abbey.

Though Newton had endured much illness—including what was at least a "nervous breakdown"—he had never worn glasses and still had all his own teeth when he died at eighty-five. He never married, his half-nephews and nieces being his heirs. Notoriously absent-minded and untidy, modest, charitable, he was of the abstracted thinker type. He had no pretensions to literary fame;

the *Principia* and much of his other work first appeared in Latin. From a literary viewpoint, it is his influence—e.g., that of his (mistaken) optical theories on the eighteenth century poets—that counts.

But Voltaire well said that "if all the geniuses of the universe assembled, he should lead the band." Macaulay believed that "in no other mind have the demonstrative faculty and the inductive faculty coexisted in such supreme excellence and perfect harmony." And Sir Arthur E. Shipley has remarked that "his supreme genius has insured him a place in the very small list of the world's thinkers of the first order."

PRINCIPAL WORKS: Principia, 1687; Opticks, 1704; Arithmetica universalis, 1707; The Chronology of Ancient Kingdoms Amended, 1728; Observations upon the Prophecies of Daniel and the Apocalypse, 1733; Method of Fluxions, 1736.

ABOUT: Andrade, E. N. da C. Isaac Newton; Brewster, D. Memoirs of the Life, Writings, and Discoveries of Sir Isaac Newton; Broad, C. D. Sir Isaac Newton; Brodetsky, S. Sir Isaac Newton; Craig, Sir J. H. M. Newton at the Mint; Dampier-Whetham, W. C. D. A History of Science; De Villamil, R. Newton: the Man; Gray, G. J. Bibliography; Greenstreet, W. J. Isaac Newton; More, L. T. Isaac Newton, a Biography; Nicholson, M. H. Newton Demands the Muse; Sullivan, J. W. N. Isaac Newton.

NICHOLS, JOHN (February 2, 1745-November 26, 1826), printer, biographer, bibliographer, antiquary, was born in Islington, now part of London, the son of Edward Nichols, a baker, and Anne Wilmot. He attended the local school, and was intended for the navy, but an uncle who could have helped him having died, he was apprenticed instead in 1757 to William Bowyer, "the learned printer." From Bowyer he learned far more than how to set type; he secured a good classical training and was encouraged to write verse and to publish some of it in 1763. In 1766 he became his master's partner. They were close friends, and later Nichols was to write his biography and name his surviving son for him. Bowyer died in 1777, leaving the residue of his estate to Nichols.

In 1766 Nichols married Anne Craddock, who died ten years later. In 1778 he married Martha Green, who died also after ten years of marriage. By his second marriage he had two sons (one died in infancy) and six daughters. His second wife was from Leicestershire, and inspired the *History and*

Antiquities of that county, which he called "my most durable monument."

In 1778 Nichols became, with David Henry, editor of the *Gentleman's Magazine,* contributing to it frequently, and editing it alone from 1792 to his death. His acquaintance with Dr. Johnson began only in the latter's last year, but during that time he was a devoted and useful friend. He published Johnson's *Lives of the Poets.* Nichols' interests were multifarious: he edited Swift, revised a biographical dictionary, published an edition of Shakespeare, wrote a series of biographical literary anecdotes, and compiled several purely antiquarian volumes. Though he hated political disputes, he was a member of the London Common Council for various periods between 1784 and 1811. He retired from business in 1803, and the next year received what he considered his greatest honor by becoming master of the Stationers' Company. His last years were spent with his six daughters in Islington, and were full of misfortune; he broke his leg, his sight failed, and a disastrous fire destroyed his stock of books. He died suddenly at eighty-one, and was buried in his native borough.

Though Nichols was lampooned for "ignorance" and undue pretensions, largely by those who could not grant ability to one without a formal education, he actually was a sound antiquarian and historian. His collections of "literary anecdotes" are a mine of biographical material. His last collection was left unfinished, and was completed by his son and grandson.

PRINCIPAL WORKS: Islington: A poem, 1763; Bibliotheca Topographica Britannica (with R. Gough) 1780-1800; A Collection of Royal and Nobel Wills, 1780; Biographical Anecdotes of Mr. Hogarth, 1781; Biographical Anecdotes of William Bowyer and his Literary Friends, 1782; The Progresses and Public Processions of Queen Elizabeth, 1788-1821; History and Antiquities of the Town and County of Leicestershire, 1795-1815; Brief Memoirs of John Nichols, 1804; Literary Anecdotes of the 18th Century, 1812-16; Illustrations of the Literary History of the 18th Century, 1817-28 (completed by J. B. and J. G. Nichols, 1828-58); The Progresses, Processions, and Festivities of King James I and His Court, 1828.

ABOUT: Chalmers, A. Memoir, *in* Illustrations of the Literary History of the 18th Century, 1858 ed.; Dobson, A. Rosalba's Journal and Other Papers; Nichols, J. Brief Memoirs.

NIGEL called **WIREKER.** See WIREKER, NIGEL

NORRIS, JOHN (1657-1711), author of philosophical essays and poems, was born at Collingbourne-Kingston, Wiltshire, where his father, John Norris, was the rector. He was educated at Winchester and at Exeter College, Oxford, graduating B.A. in 1680 and taking an M.A. four years later. An excellent scholar, he was appointed a Fellow of All Soul's College, where he began the voluminous writings on metaphysical subjects which were continued throughout his career as clergyman, philosopher, and poet.

Norris was ordained soon after his graduation and in 1689 he accepted the living of Newton St. Loe, Somerset. Two years earlier he had published his most popular book, the *Miscellanies,* which included both poems and essays largely religious in character. He was a decided churchman, opposed to both non-conformists and Whigs, but his real devotion was to the more mystical realm of Platonic philosophy. Quite naturally his religious theories brought him into controversy with a number of his contemporaries, among them several prominent Quakers and the philosopher John Locke.

Married and with a growing family, Norris moved to the rectory of Bemerton near Salisbury, where he received something between £200 and £300 a year. According to his own account, however, his clear in-

After H. Eldridge
JOHN NICHOLS

come was little more than £70 and the world ran "strait and hard with him." He died at Bemerton in his mid-fifties, leaving a widow and three children.

Norris's chief philosophical work, *An Essay Towards the Theory of an Ideal and Intelligible World*, was published in two parts, the first in 1701 and the second three years later. The *Essay* is of interest as a last outcropping of the Cambridge school of Platonism, as well as an attempt to embody the religious and philosophical theories of the French Cartesian, Nicolas de Malebranche, whose work the English rector greatly admired. Although Locke refers to him slightingly as "an obscure, enthusiastic man," John Norris was a writer not without impact in his day.

PRINCIPAL WORKS: Poems and Discourses, 1684; A Collection of Miscellanies, 1687; The Theory and Regulation of Love, 1688; Christian Blessedness to which is added Reflections Upon a Late Essay Concerning the Human Understanding, 1690; Letters Concerning the Love of God, 1695; An Account of Reason and Faith in Relation to the Mysteries of Christianity, 1697; An Essay Towards the Theory of the Ideal or Intelligible World, 1701-04; A Philosophical Discourse Concerning the Natural Immortality of the Soul, 1708; Collected Poems (A. B. Grosart, ed.) 1871.

ABOUT: Mackinnon, F. I. The Philosophy of John Norris of Bemerton; Powicke, F. J. A Dissertation of John Norris; Wood, A. à, Athenae Oxonienses.

NORTH, ROGER (September 3, 1653-March 1, 1734), lawyer, historian, biographer, was born at Tostock, Suffolk, the youngest son of Dudley, the fourth Baron North. He was brought up at his grandfather's house in Kirtling under the tutorship of the clergyman of the parish. When he was fourteen Roger entered Jesus College, Cambridge, where an elder brother, John, was a Fellow. After two years he left the university and entered the Middle Temple to study law.

The North family seems to have been an extraordinary one. As Roger himself later wrote, "The Norths were a numerous flock, and no one scabby sheep in it." An older brother, Sir Francis, served first as Chief Justice of the Court of Common Pleas and then as Lord Keeper of the Great Seal under James II. Under the patronage of Sir Francis, young Roger embarked on an outstandingly successful law career in 1675, was appointed when he was only twenty-five as personal steward and legal adviser to

William Sancroft, the Archbishop of Canterbury. As king's counsel four years later he was called to the bench at Middle Temple, rising to the position of solicitor-general to the Duke of York and attorney-general to the Queen. According to his own account he received an income of over £4000 a year from his practice.

With the revolution and the death of his brother, Sir Francis, Roger North gave up hope of any further advancement in his career and retired to an estate at Rougham, Norfolk, where he devoted himself exclusively to his family and his literary interests. In 1696 he married the daughter of Sir Robert Gazer, who brought him a considerable fortune. The household also included his brother, Montague, and the children of his three deceased brothers.

Leading the life of a country gentleman, North spent his leisure in research on law, history, music, philosophy, and wrote the biographies of his three elder brothers which have become classic in English historical literature. He lived to be eighty-one, a wise and respected man, who was called Solomon by his country neighbors. On his death he left a mass of manuscript notes, as well as *The Life of Francis North, Baron of Guilford, The Life of Sir Dudley North and Dr. John North*, and his own *Autobiography*, all of which were published posthumously. These *Lives* both for charm and candor of style, and for their importance as history, hold an enduring place in English literature.

PRINCIPAL WORKS: A Discourse of Fish and Fish Ponds, 1713; Examen: or, An Enquiry into the Credit and Veracity of a Pretended Complete History, 1740; The Life of Francis North, Baron of Guilford, 1742; The Life of Sir Dudley North and of Dr. John North, 1744; A Discourse on the Study of the Laws, 1824; Memoirs of Musick (E. F. Rimbault, ed.) 1846; Autobiography (A. Jessopp, ed.) 1887; Lives of the Norths (including the three lives and the autobiography) (A. Jessopp, ed.) 1890.

ABOUT: North, R. Lives of the Norths.

NORTH, Sir THOMAS (1535?-1601?), translator, was the second son of Edward, the first Lord North, and his first wife, Alice Squyer. He may have been a student at Peterhouse, Cambridge; in 1557 he was entered at Lincoln's Inn. He was never called to the bar, however, and soon left the law for literature. Although his father left him a sizable legacy, and his brother, when he became Lord North, constantly helped him,

North for some reason was always hard up. About 1568 he seems to have had some sort of position in Cambridgeshire, and in 1574 he accompanied his brother on the latter's embassy to Henri III of France. When the Armada threatened England, North was a captain in the army against invasion, and in consequence was knighted by Elizabeth about 1591. From 1592 to 1597 he was on the commission of peace of Cambridgeshire. In 1601 the queen (to whom his Plutarch was dedicated) finally bestowed a pension on him. He died soon after. He was married twice to widows, first to Elizabeth (Colville) Rich, then to Judith (Vesey) Bridgwater, who survived him and later married John Courthope. According to some authorities he had a son by one of his marriages, but if so the child died in infancy.

Leicester, writing to Burghley in North's behalf, said of him: "He is a very honest gentleman, and hath many good things in him which are drowned only by poverty." The best of these good things was his Plutarch, "the most famous Elizabethan translation." North wrote nothing of his own, but devoted himself entirely to translation. His mastery of Greek and Latin was shaky, and all his translations were done from French, Italian, or Spanish. His *Diall of Princes,* from the Spanish of Guevara, was ornate and mannered, and set the fashion which culminated in Lyly's *Euphues.* But by the time he brought out his version of Plutarch's *Parallel Lives of the Greeks and Romans,* through the French translation by Jacques Amyot, he had become, as Charles Whibley has said, "a master of noble English," who "played upon English prose as upon an organ whose every stop he controlled with an easy confidence."

North has been called "the first master of English prose." But he was more: he had a natural aptitude for characterization, which made his (or Plutarch's) Greeks and Romans into Englishmen, but into vivid, living human beings as well. Shakespeare seized on North with joy. Sometimes almost word for word, he transmuted North's prose into some of the world's greatest poetry. *Julius Caesar, Coriolanus,* and above all *Antony and Cleopatra* came straight out of North, and parts of *Pericles, Timon of Athens,* and *A Midsummer Night's Dream* as well. Thus indirectly as well as directly,

North contributed immeasurably to the glory of English literature.

PRINCIPAL WORKS: The Diall of Princes (from the Spanish of Guevara) 1570; The Morall Philosophie of Doni (from the Italian) 1570; Lives of the Noble Grecians and Romanes (from the French of Amyot) 1579 (enlarged eds. 1595, 1603); Shakespeare's Plutarch, being a Selection from the Lives in North's Plutarch which Illustrate Shakespeare's Plays (W. W. Skeat, ed.) 1875.

ABOUT: Bushby, F. Three Men of the Tudor Time; Hazlitt, W. Shakespeare's Library; Whibley, C. Literary Portraits.

NORTON, THOMAS (1532-March 10, 1584), lawyer, poet, dramatist, translator, was born in London. He was the eldest son of Thomas Norton, a wealthy merchant, and received a good education. We do not know the dates of his residence at Cambridge University, but he received an M.A. from there in 1570; probably he had taken his B.A. degree many years earlier. Certainly in 1550, at the age of eighteen, he was enough of a scholar to be entrusted with the translation of a Latin letter written by Peter Martyr to the Duke of Somerset. The Duke, who was Lord Protector of England during the minority of Edward VI, employed young Norton as an amanuensis. Whether his love for the Reformation was the cause or the effect of his employment by Somerset, Norton's whole life thenceforward was molded by his zeal for the Protestant religion.

He entered the Inner Temple to study law in 1555. The same year, he married Margery, a daughter of Archbishop Cranmer, leader of the Reform party in the Church of England. The Catholic Mary Tudor was then Queen of England and in 1556 Cranmer was burnt at the stake for his religious views. Norton escaped persecution; soon afterwards the Protestant Elizabeth came to the throne. In 1558 he was a Member of Parliament for Gatton; in 1562, as Member for Berwick, he served on a committee that recommended Queen Elizabeth's marrying to ensure the Protestant succession. His doctrinal position was made very clear when, in 1561, his translation of Calvin's *The Institution of Christian Religion* appeared.

Norton had a successful legal career, particularly as what we should now call a corporation lawyer; he handled the legal business of two powerful London guilds—the Stationers Company and the Merchant

Taylors Company. In 1571 he was appointed Remembrancer of the City of London and represented the City in Parliament. But no amount of other business could keep him from advocating, on the one hand, his own extreme form of Calvinism, on the other, the persecution of English Catholics. In 1570 he translated Nowell's *Catechism;* in 1579 he went to Rome at his own expense to investigate Catholic plots against England. The Bishop of London made him Licenser of the Press in 1581 and he was active in the interrogation (which included hideous torture) of numerous Catholic prisoners from that year until his death. Unhappily for him, his own religious views were too radical for the taste of Queen Elizabeth and her advisers, who thought the Reformation had gone far enough. In 1582 and again in 1584 he himself was imprisoned for short periods. The second incarceration ruined his health and he died shortly after his release. The fate of his second wife, Alice Cranmer, a cousin of the first, whom he married in 1568, was no less tragic. She had always showed a tendency to religious mania, and went completely mad in 1582.

Norton owes his place in the history of English literature to some verses in *Tottel's Miscellany* (1557) and to his joint authorship with Thomas Sackville [qv] of *The Tragedy of Gorboduc*—the first blank verse play in English. Performed at the Inner Temple on Twelfth Night 1562, and again before Queen Elizabeth on January 18, 1562, this sententious play is a stern warning against the evils of an uncertain succession to the English throne. It may legitimately be read as propaganda for the queen's marriage, which Norton advocated in Parliament that year. Norton has also, independently of Sackville, the distinction of being the third person to employ blank verse in English— in his translation from Calvin. Both the above considerations suggest that Norton had at least as big a share as Sackville in the conception and execution of this seminal play, which was destined to have so many remarkable progeny.

PRINCIPAL WORKS: Calvin's The Institution of Christian Religion (tr.) 1561; The Tragedy of Gorboduc, 1565 (pirated 1571); Nowell's Catechism (tr.) 1570.

ABOUT: Baker, H. Induction to Tragedy; Cooper, W. D. Introduction to his edition of Gorboduc (Shakespeare Society 1847).

OCCAM, WILLIAM of. See OCKHAM, WILLIAM of

OCCLEVE or HOCCLEVE, THOMAS (1370?-1450?), poet, probably took his name from Hockliffe, Bedfordshire, which may well have been his birthplace. What little we know of him comes from his own numerous autobiographical passages and allusions in his poems. He had studied divinity, but never took holy orders. For some thirty-five years he was a clerk in the office of the Privy Seal in London. His salary was very small, and the pension he received in addition after 1390 was usually in arrears, giving rise to various plaints and pleas. Finally in 1424 he received a "corrody," or a charge on the funds of a monastery (Southwick, Hampshire), which enabled him to resign. It also relieved him of the danger of having "to trotte unto Newgate" for debt.

According to Occleve's own account, his "misruly" youth was a period of rather mild dissipation, marked by physical cowardice, gluttony, and over-drinking, though the worst he alleges against himself is his fondness for treating to sweet wine and wafers "Venus femel lusty children deer." About 1411, when he was more than middle-aged by the standards of his time, he married, and presumably thereafter his wife kept him in order. At one period he was, he says, actually insane, and in later years he became almost blind, but was "too proud" to wear spectacles. He probably was just the sort of man he portrays—amiable, feckless, garrulous, egotistical, likable, but a nuisance to his friends and patrons; with a real love of literature and some talent, but not enough to have brought him any renown except in the very unpoetical era in which he lived. He admired Chaucer greatly, and may have known him in the great poet's last years; his name is always coupled with Lydgate's, but it is probable the two never met.

Occleve is not quite so dull as Lydgate, but neither is he so learned or so industrious, and he utterly lacks Lydgate's occasional humor. He could, however, tell a story quaintly well, if pompously, and he has good single lines. His most poetic and dignified poem is his *Ars Sciendi Mori* (the art of knowing death); his longest—5,500 lines —the *De Regimine Principium* (rule of princes), a hodgepodge addressed to Henry

THOMAS OCCLEVE

V in his roistering days as Prince Hal, and doubtless never glanced at by its recipient. Its main object in any case was to advance the author's chances for a better pension. *La Male Règle*, written about 1406, was Occleve's ingenuous confession of the sins of his youth. He wrote some hundred and sixty minor poems, mostly ballades, many of them familiar verses addressed to various patrons or patrons aspired to. *The Mother of God* was long attributed to Chaucer, but though it is one of Occleve's best it is far from Chaucerian. Occleve also translated into English verse Christine de Pisan's *Letter of Cupid to Lovers,* and two stories from the *Gesta Romanorum, The Tale of Jonathas* and *The Emperor Jereslaus's Wife.* He was long neglected, until in the seventeenth century he found an admirer in William Browne, who included one of his poems in *The Shepheards Pipe* (1614). There have since been several editions of his poems.

Occleve may have been born as early as 1368, and may have died as early as 1446; however, if a doubtful poem of 1448 is his, he may have survived to as late as 1450. He died, as he had lived most of his life, in London, probably in his house in the Strand.

PRINCIPAL WORKS: Poems (G. Mason, ed.) 1796; De Regimine Principium (Regement of Princes) (T. Wright, ed.) 1860; Works (F. J. Furnivall, ed) 1892-1907.

ABOUT: Browne, W. Works (W. C. Hazlitt, ed.); Furnivall, F. J. Introductions, Works; Ten Brink, B. Early English Writers.

OCKHAM or **OCCAM, WILLIAM** of (1280?-1349?), philosopher, took his name from Ockham, Surrey, of which he was probably a native. There is no justification for the common spelling of "Occam." He studied at Oxford, perhaps at Merton College or perhaps at the Franciscan house there, since he was a Franciscan monk. He was in any case a pupil of Duns Scotus. It was at Oxford he received his B.D. degree and he may have taught there for a few years, but his D.D. degree was secured at Paris. He never saw England again. He became involved in the great controversy between the Emperor Ludwig of Bavaria and Pope John XXII, and in 1327 the pope had him and other Franciscans, including Michael de Cesena, general of the order, imprisoned at Avignon. They escaped, after about a year and a half, to Italy, and put themselves under Ludwig's protection. He took them with him to Bavaria, and in the Franciscan monastery at Munich Ockham spent the remainder of his life. (He probably did not know that at one time Ludwig offered to give him up for punishment to John's successor, Benedict XII; the offer was not accepted.) John had excommunicated Ockham; when the emperor also was excommunicated, Ockham came to his defense. Michael de Cesena died in 1342 and for a while Ockham claimed to be his successor as general, but later he gave up the claim. When Ludwig also died, Ockham made overtures toward reconciliation to the then Pope, Clement VI, and abjured some of his "heresies."

Ockham, known as "the Invincible Doctor," was one of the last of the greater Schoolmen, the apostle of nominalism as against the realism of Thomas Aquinas. In other words, he held there was no real existence of universals: only individuals are real, and "entities must not be multiplied unnecessarily." He taught also that Christian doctrines rest on faith, and are not provable by reason: "moral laws are good only because God wills them, and not in their own right." But the heart of his long struggle was the Franciscan doctrine of evangelical poverty —that Christ and the disciples rejected the ownership of property—a doctrine that attacked the existing power and organization of the church. Ockham not only "shattered realism" but he also had an immense influence on both the church and the schools.

He wrote on logic, philosophy, and political theory. His *Commentary on the Sentences* (of Peter Lombard), which was at least begun while he was at Oxford, Poole called "an epoch in logical theory." Wycliffe admired him so greatly he refused to call him a heretic, while Alfred Weber said Ockham was "a precursor of Locke." His *Dialogue,* written about 1333, was a masterly summing up of the balance of power between emperor and pope. It is no wonder that the other appellation bestowed on him by his contemporaries, besides Doctor Invincibilis, was Venerabilis Inceptor (venerable teacher). The final victory of the secular over the theological power was in great part due to the teaching and influence of Ockham.

All Ockham's writing was in Latin, the universal language of scholars in his time. The dates given are of first printings of the original manuscripts.

PRINCIPAL WORKS: Opus nonaginta dierum (the work of ninety days) 1481; Adversus errores Johnnis XXII (against the errors of John XXII) 1481; Quodlibeta septem (seven miscellanies, literally, "anythings") 1487; Summa logices (summary of logic) 1488; De Sacramento altaris, and De Corpore Christi (on the sacrament of the altar, and on the body of Christ) 1491; Quaestiones ... Sententiarum, and Centilogium theologicum (questions on the Sentences [of Peter Lombard], and A hundred records of theology) 1495; Dialogus ... de Imperatorum et Pontificum Potestate (dialogue concerning the power of the emperors and the popes) 1495; Expositio Aurea super totam Artem Veterem (the golden exposition of the whole art of the ancients) 1496; Summulae ... physicorum (little summaries of physics [of Aristotle]) 1506; Defensorium contra Johnnes XXII (defense against John XXII) 1513; De Jurisdictione Imperatoris (concerning the jurisdiction of the emperor) 1598; Quaestiones ... physicorum (questions of physics) 1637.

ABOUT: Carré, M. H. Realists and Nominalists; Little, A. J. Grey Friars in Oxford; Moody, E. A. The Logic of William of Ockham; Poole, R. L. Illustrations of the History of Mediaeval Thought; Riezler, S. Die literarischen Widersacher der Päpste zur Zeit Ludwig des Baiers; Überweg, F. History of Philosophy; Weber, A. History of Philosophy; Wood, A. à, Athenae Oxonienses.

OGILBY, JOHN (November 1600-September 4, 1676) printer, translator, was born in Edinburgh of a prosperous family which had lost its wealth. His father was imprisoned, presumably for debt, and there was no money for the boy's education. John went to work and with his savings invested in a lottery for the development of the Virginia colony. He won enough money to obtain his father's release and set himself up as an apprentice to a dancing master in London.

Ogilby became favorably known both as a teacher and as a performer. He danced in the Duke of Buckingham's masque at court, but retired from active performance when an injury left him slightly lame. In 1633 he accompanied Thomas Wentworth, Earl of Strafford and Lord-deputy of Ireland, to Dublin as tutor to his children. There he was appointed deputy master of the revels and built a theatre which proved very successful. His theatre was destroyed during the civil war and after many hardships he found himself again penniless in London.

In his forties he studied Latin and in 1649 published a translation of Virgil which sold well and gave him a small income. This was followed by a verse paraphrase of Aesop's *Fables.* Indefatigable, he then studied Greek with an usher in the school of James Shirley, the dramatist, and published translations of the *Iliad* and the *Odyssey.*

With the Restoration Ogilby came into favor at the court of Charles II. He was in charge of the "poetical part" of the coronation ceremonies in 1661, and a year later again won appointment as master of the revels in Ireland. During the latter part of his life he engaged in the publishing business, translating, editing, and printing many fine books. The great fire of 1666 destroyed both his house and his business, but with William Morgan (his wife's grandson by an earlier marriage), he rebuilt the printshop and continued to publish handsome editions, particularly books of geography with maps and engravings by Hollar and others.

Although ridiculed by Dryden and Pope as a bad poet, Ogilby was a competent translator; his Virgil and Homer were both widely read until superseded by later and better translations.

PRINCIPAL WORKS: The Works of Publius Virgilius Maro (tr.) 1649; The Fables of Aesop Paraphras'd in Verse (tr.) 1651; Homer His Iliads (tr.) 1660; Homer His Odysses (tr.) 1665.

ABOUT: Wood, A. à, Athenae Oxonienses.

OLDHAM, JOHN (August 9, 1653-December 9, 1683), poet, author of *Satires Upon the Jesuits,* was born at Shipton, Gloucestershire, the son of a nonconformist clergyman. He was educated first at home and then at Tetbury school, where a Bristol alderman paid for his education. He entered St. Edmund Hall, Oxford, in 1670 and graduated B.A. in 1674. He would have liked to stay on at the University, but his father could not afford it.

Oldham spent the next year or so at home in the country; with plenty of time on his hands, he took to poetry and fell in love. His first known poem, "To the Memory of My Dear Friend, Mr. Charles Morwent," was written in 1675, though not published until after his death. In 1676 and 1677 he wrote some love poems to a lady whom he called Cosmelia; she has never been identified. Four of these poems were written in September 1676; since they mention parting and absence, it is probable that this was the date at which Oldham took a post as usher in Archbishop Whitgift's School, Croydon, Surrey.

Here he was near London, but very badly paid for uncongenial work; none the less he preferred teaching to taking holy orders, perhaps because of his nonconformist upbringing. "A Satire to a Friend about to Leave the University" gives Oldham's views on earning a living and is one of his pleasantest poems besides. In 1677 his poem *Upon the Marriage of the Prince of Orange* was published anonymously, while others of his works found their way about London in manuscript. As a result, a group of aristocratic wits came to Croydon to visit the talented schoolmaster—Rochester, Sedley, Dorset and others—and he in turn probably found his way to Will's Coffee-house.

In 1678 he left the Croydon school and became tutor to the family of Judge Thurland at Reigate. *Garnet's Ghost*, the first of Oldham's *Satires Upon the Jesuits*, was written, and pirated, in 1679. This was based on the "Popish Plot" forged by Oates and Tonge and "revealed" by Titus Oates, which resulted in the death of the magistrate before whom Oates had first sworn to its truth. All four *Satires* were published with a Prologue in an authorized edition two years later. This book firmly established Oldham's reputation.

In 1681 he became tutor to the son of Sir William Hickes. The Earl of Kingston offered to make Oldham his chaplain soon afterwards; the poet refused, whereupon the

After W. Dobson

JOHN OLDHAM

earl invited him to come and live with him as a guest and an equal. He did so and died of smallpox at the earl's country seat near Nottingham.

Oldham's death created a greater demand for his poetry than ever. A collected edition of his *Works* and *Remains* appeared in 1684; the latter were preceded by a number of commemorative poems, of which Dryden's, beginning, "Farewell, too little and too lately known," was the finest. The elder poet commented upon the "harsh cadence" of Oldham's verse, but added that it is:

A noble error, and but seldom made,
When poets are by too much force betrayed.

Oldham's satire is certainly forceful; see especially "Loyola's Will" and "St. Ignatius's Image," the third and fourth of the *Satires Upon the Jesuits.*

Oldham was tall and thin, with a long and rather ugly face. There is a certain amount of obscene language in his poetry; his life during the Croydon period was not entirely above reproach, either, but there is a letter extant in which he announces his reformation. The last years of his short life seem to have been exemplary. His integrity was such that he never dedicated a single poem to a patron, refusing to owe his livelihood to any form of servility. Such an attitude provides a striking contrast to Dryden's, but one is forced to admit that Oldham was by no means the equal of Dryden as a poet.

PRINCIPAL WORKS: Upon the Marriage of the Prince of Orange, 1677; Garnet's Ghost Addressing to the Jesuits, 1679; A Satire Against Virtue, 1679; Satires Upon the Jesuits Written in the Year 1679, 1681; Some New Pieces, 1681; Poems and Translations, 1683; Remains of Mr. John Oldham, 1684; The Works of Mr. John Oldham, 1684.

ABOUT: Bell, R. Memoir in The Poems of John Oldham, 1854; Thompson, E. Memoirs in The Compositions in Prose and Verse of Mr. John Oldham, 1770.

OLDMIXON, JOHN (1673-July 9, 1742), Whig historian and pamphleteer, was the son of John Oldmixon, a gentleman of the manor of Oldmixon near Bridgwater. His mother, Elinor, was a sister of Sir John Bawden.

Oldmixon began his literary career as a poet and dramatist, publishing considerable unimportant verse and several plays or "pastorals" which were produced with fair success. His last and best play, The Governor of Cyprus, was performed in 1703. Five years later he came into prominence as a historian with the publication of The British Empire in America, a work heavily weighted by the Whiggish principles of its author.

Pope describes him as having been "all his life a virulent Party-writer for hire." Certainly his career was marked by ill-tempered controversy and his historical perspective was limited by the bounds of his political beliefs. In 1712 he published The Secret History of Europe, a fierce attack on the Tory government for its subservience to France, and was rewarded with the post of port collector of Bridgwater on the accession of George I. His most important work, The Critical History of England, embodied an attack on Clarendon's History which led to a long and bitter controversy. The book was prefixed by an Essay on Criticism in which he also attacked Dryden, Addison, Pope, and the historian, Echard.

Oldmixon's Bridgwater post was inadequately and irregularly paid, and for a number of years he tried to get the post of poet laureate, without success. Complaining of slights and insults from the Jacobites, Oldmixon finally gave up his position and resigned himself to years of gout and poverty. In addition to a number of political pamphlets published anonymously, he wrote a continuous History of England, covering the

period from the reign of William and Mary through that of Queen Elizabeth. His Memoirs of the Press, published posthumously, is of some biographical interest, but all his work is marred by the contentious and opinionated nature of his personality and point of view.

PRINCIPAL WORKS: Poems on Several Occasions, 1696; Thyrsis, A Pastoral, 1697; The Grove or Love's Paradise, 1700; The Governor of Cyprus, 1703; The British Empire in America, 1708; The Secret History of Europe, 1712-15; The Critical History of England, Ecclesiastical and Civil, 1724-6; The History of England During the Reigns of the Royal House of Stuart, 1730; The History of England During the Reigns of King William and Queen Mary, Queen Anne, King George I, 1735; The History of England During the Reigns of Henry VIII, Edward VI, Queen Mary, Queen Elizabeth, 1739; Memoirs of the Press, Historical and Political, 1742.

ABOUT: Oldmixon, J. Memoirs of the Press.

OLDYS, WILLIAM (July 14, 1696-April 15, 1761), antiquary, bibliographer, biographer, born in London, was the son of Dr. William Oldys, chancellor of London, by his mistress, Ann. Both the boy's parents died before he was sixteen and he came under the guardianship of Benjamin Jackman, a friend of his mother.

From earliest youth Oldys collected rare books and manuscripts. In 1724 he moved to Yorkshire, leaving a large part of his library in the care of his London landlord, Burridge. When he came back to London six years later, he found that Burridge had sold a number of valuable books and manuscripts, among them an annotated copy of Langbaine's Dramatick Poets, which contained notes made by Oldys and later used by Cibber for his Lives of the Poets. In 1731 Oldys sold his collection to Edward Harley, Earl of Oxford, to whom he subsequently acted as literary secretary for three years.

During this period, working in Oxford's library, Oldys edited Raleigh's History of the World, writing a Life of Raleigh which solidly established his reputation in the field of letters. He was consulted as an authority by many writers and, when on the death of Harley the earl's celebrated library was sold, Oldys and Dr. Johnson were appointed editors to draw up a catalog of the library. From this grew the Harleian Miscellany, a reprint of the most interesting tracts and pamphlets in Harley's library. Oldys also contributed twenty-two articles to the *Biographia Britannica,* and wrote a *Life of Charles Cotton,* which was prefixed to Sir John Hawkins' edition of *The Compleat Angler.*

After Harley's death Oldys worked for various booksellers, but found himself unable to make a living and spent three years in the Fleet Prison as a debtor. His release was finally arranged by friends, and through the good graces of the Duke of Norfolk, he received an appointment as Norroy king-at-arms. Oldys died when he was sixty-four, leaving behind a mass of notes for a projected *Life of Shakespeare* and a number of annotated texts which have been used extensively by later scholars.

PRINCIPAL WORKS: A Dissertation upon Pamphlets, 1731; Life of Sir Walter Raleigh (prefixed to Raleigh's History of the World) 1736; The British Librarian, 1737; Catalogus Bibliotheca Harleianae (with Samuel Johnson) 1743; The Harleian Miscellany (ed. with Samuel Johnson) 1744-46 (T. Park, ed. 1808-13); Biographia Britannica (contrib.) 1747-60; Some Account of the Life and Writings of Charles Cotton, 1760.

ABOUT: Corney, B. Facts Relative to William Oldys, Esq., Norroy King at Arms; Davies, T. A Catalogue of the Library of the Late William Oldys; Yeowell, J. A Literary Antiquary, Memoir of William Oldys (with Oldys' Diary).

ORFORD, EARL OF. See WALPOLE, HORACE, Fourth Earl of Orford

ORM or **ORMIN** (fl. 1200?), Augustinian monk, author of "Ormulum," is known only by one manuscript, apparently in his own hand, consisting of 20,000 lines and covering thirty-one homilies out of two hundred and forty-two he said he had written. His name comes from his own statement that his work was called the *Ormulum* "because Orm made it." Internal evidence suggests that he was of Danish descent, that he came from the northern Midlands, perhaps from Lincolnshire, and that he was an Augustinian monk perhaps from the monastery of Elsham, on the Humber. He had a brother Walter, who was also a monk in the same monastery and who encouraged him in his writing.

The *Ormulum* is a series of metrical paraphrases of the Gospel of the day from Annunciation to Acts (the portion preserved), with expositions following. It is written in rhymeless iambic meter, with alternating lines of seven and eight syllables.

The orthography is Orm's own, phonetic spelling invented by himself, and is of great value as showing how words were pronounced in Middle English; for example, he doubles all consonants following short vowels.

The writing itself is simple and direct, free from mysticism but running to strained conceits and plays upon words and even upon individual letters. Apparently the monastery in which Orm lived was a religious backwater; his every orthodoxy is outdated and he combats heresies long since dead. He seems unacquainted with contemporary theology and harks back to the Venerable Bede. The *Ormulum,* despite its Middle English language, is a pure continuation of Old English thought.

Orm's poetic style was wooden, with everything else sacrificed to regularity of rhythm. He was a modest man, a paragon of industry, humbly proud of his accomplishment, and pathetically eager that future copyists of his manuscript exercise extreme care and accuracy. Unfortunately, the book seems to have had little influence and attracted little attention outside his own monastery, and so far as is known nobody ever copied it at all. The fragmentary manuscript in the Bodleian Library is probably the only one that ever existed.

Orm's sources were Bede, Gregory, and perhaps Josephus; he could therefore read Latin. He was a pedant rather than a scholar, but touchingly scrupulous and exact. His work has no literary merit except that of simplicity, but to philologists it is of extreme importance. It represents the first Anglian (northern English) literature after the Norman Conquest, and historically is second in value only to Layamon's *Brut.*

PRINCIPAL WORK: Ormulum (R. M. White, ed.) 1852 (R. Holt, ed. 1878).

ABOUT: Kölbing, E. Englische Studien; Napier, A. S. A History of the Holy Rood Tree; Saintsbury, G. History of English Prosody; Schofield, W. H. English Literature from the Norman Conquest to Chaucer; Ten Brink, B. Early English Literature.

OTWAY, THOMAS (March 3, 1652-April 10, 1685), playwright, poet, was born at Trotton, Sussex, where his father Humphrey was either rector or curate at the time. Some years later the father was appointed rector of the neighboring parish of Woolbeding, where he died in harness, 1670. Elizabeth, the poet's mother, survived her husband many years.

In 1668 Otway was a boarder at Winchester School; the following year he entered Christ Church College, Oxford; he left without taking a degree in 1672. His interest in the stage must have begun early, for there is a story that he was given a small part in Aphra Behn's first play, *The Forced Marriage*, 1670; he had such a bad attack of stage fright on the first night that he could not say his lines; a professional actor took over the part and Otway never appeared on the stage again.

After leaving the university, Otway went to London. Both at Winchester and at Oxford he had known the young Anthony Cary, Viscount Falkland, who probably introduced him to such aristocratic patrons of literature as the Earl of Plymouth and the Earl of Rochester. We do not know how Otway, whose father was very poor and left him nothing, managed to pay his fees at Winchester and Oxford; in London he probably lived off his patrons and learnt their habits of drunkenness and debauchery.

His first play, a tragedy entitled *Alcibiades*, was performed in 1675. Like all his later plays, it was put on at Dorset Garden by Betterton, the leading actor of the day. Though *Alcibiades* was not particularly successful, Betterton stood by him; *Don Carlos*, produced the next year, was an outstanding success. Otway next made English versions of Racine's *Bérénice* and Molière's *Les Fourberies de Scapin*; the success of the latter encouraged him to write an original comedy, *Friendship in Fashion*. Later he utilized his military experience in two further comedies, *The Soldier's Fortune* and *The Atheist*.

Otway's gift for tragedy steadily matured; he abandoned rhyme for blank verse in *The History and Fall of Caius Marius*, which borrowed heavily from *Romeo and Juliet*; two original tragedies in blank verse, *The Orphan* and *Venice Preserved*, followed. These two plays are easily his best and both held the stage for over a century. In them the influence of Racine predominates over that of Shakespeare; like Racine, Otway created better women's roles than men's.

After J. Riley

THOMAS OTWAY

Though his career as a dramatist was, broadly speaking, a succession of triumphs, Otway's personal life was a long-drawn-out tragedy. The extreme sensitiveness that made him a failure as an actor and contributed so much to his power as a dramatist ultimately destroyed him. He fell hopelessly in love with Mrs. Barry, Betterton's leading lady; she, who would give herself to any man for money, was quite incapable of returning his love. Some of his pitiful letters to her are extant; in one he says that he has vainly pursued her for seven years. His plays suggest that he had strong masochistic tendencies; probably the agonies she made him suffer were the most irresistible part of her attraction for him.

In 1678 he seems to have tried to break her spell in the traditional romantic manner, for he took an ensign's commission in the Duke of Monmouth's regiment and fought in Holland. The war ended that year, however, and he was soon back in London, penniless. With her cruelty as an excuse, he became what we would now call a chronic alcoholic. He was always in debt and finally hid from his creditors—and his friends—in an ale-house on Tower Hill, where he either starved or drank himself to death. A tragedy which he was supposed to be working on at the time disappeared and has never been recovered.

Otway was about five feet seven in height and rather fat; his manner is said to have been gentle and charming; some writers have described him as good looking, but the most familiar portrait of him shows a rather pudgy, flat face with a snub nose.

Such further details as we know about his life reveal a sensitive, chivalrous, impulsive nature. He challenged the poet Settle to a duel, believing him to be the author of *The Session of the Poets*; the cruel satire on Otway in that poem was, however, written by Lord Rochester; the fact that Mrs. Barry was Rochester's mistress for a time may have caused a quarrel between Otway and his patron. Otway once rebuked Churchill, later Duke of Marlborough, for ill treating an orange girl at the theatre; this led to a duel between them. About a year before his death, Otway pursued the murderer of a friend of his on foot as far as Dover; the fever which resulted is said to have seriously injured his health.

Monimia in *The Orphan* and Belvidera in *Venice Preserved* are the two characters by which Otway's name is still remembered; it is ironical to think that these tender, sympathetic roles were first played by the cruel Mrs. Barry, his evil genius.

PRINCIPAL WORKS: *Plays*: Alcibiades, 1675; Don Carlos, 1676; Titus and Berenice and The Cheats of Scapin, 1677; Friendship in Fashion, 1678; The History and Fall of Caius Marius, 1680; The Orphan, 1680; The Soldier's Fortune, 1681; Venice Preserved, 1682; The Atheist, 1684. *Poems*: The Poet's Complaint of his Muse, 1680; Windsor Castle, 1685.

ABOUT: Dobrée, B. Restoration Tragedy; Gosse, E. Seventeenth Century Studies; Ham, R. G. Otway and Lee; Summers, M. Introduction to The Complete Works of Thomas Otway.

OVERBURY, Sir THOMAS (June 1581-September 15, 1613), author of miscellaneous works in verse and prose, and center of one of the most sensational murder stories in English history, was born in Ilmington, Warwickshire, the home of his maternal grandfather. His father was Nicholas Overbury, knighted in 1621, a bencher of the Middle Temple, later a judge in Wales and a Member of Parliament; his mother was Mary Palmer. In 1596 Overbury entered Queen's College, Oxford, and graduated B.A. in 1598, after which he was entered in the Middle Temple. However, his objective was not the law, but the royal court.

In 1601, on a pleasure trip to Edinburgh, Overbury met Robert Carr, who became his nemesis. Carr, later Viscount Rochester and then Earl of Somerset, was a favorite of James VI of Scotland, who became James I of England. He and Overbury became inseparable friends, and when Carr went to London with the accession of James, Overbury received the benefits of the association. He was appointed sewer to the king in 1607, knighted in 1608. Feeling that his advancement was not rapid enough, he spent two years, 1609 and 1610, in the Low Countries and France. For a while he was, through Carr, the avenue to the king's ear; even Bacon, it is said, "stooped and crouched" before him.

All this changed when Overbury, who had first approved and then opposed Carr's liaison with the notorious Frances Howard, Countess of Essex, seemed to the jealous and angry countess an obstacle in the way of her marriage to her lover, after her divorce. At first Rochester (as he was by now) hesitated to act—probably because Overbury had damaging information about him; he induced James to give Overbury a diplomatic post abroad, but Overbury refused it. Then Rochester turned the king against Overbury, by alleging the latter's opposition to his accession and his "disrespectful" remarks; and the queen, too, was offended by Overbury's "disrespect." He was accordingly sent to the Tower, as a temporary expedient to get him out of the way until the marriage. But the countess had other ideas. Through accomplices planted as his jailers she began systematically poisoning the food of the wretched man. They finally dispatched him with corrosive sublimate, and a compliant physician attested that he had died of "consumption due to melancholy." He was buried immediately, but there was a vast hue and cry, and all concerned were put on trial for murder three months later. The accomplices were hanged; the countess' wicked great-uncle, the Earl of Northampton, who had helped her, had died meanwhile; the two principals, now man and wife, were convicted, then pardoned—it was said because James himself was involved. Overbury died unmarried; Ben Jonson said that he was in love with Sidney's daughter, the Countess of Rutland.

After I. Oliver
SIR THOMAS OVERBURY

This unfortunate man was a sincere lover of literature and art and culture. His murder at thirty-two prevented any real fruition of his undoubted talent. He was among the earliest known writers of "characters," brief descriptions in prose and verse of typical figures—the farmer, the squire, the clergyman, and so on. (In a sense, Chaucer's brief descriptions of the Canterbury pilgrims are "characters," with stories appended; Overbury's have no story.) Best known was *The Wife*, to which, in subsequent editions, other sketches by himself and his friends were added, until it is impossible to say which are his. They are artificial and involved, full of elaborate conceits, but they started a fashion, and they display witty observation and a wide if supercilious knowledge of human beings.

PRINCIPAL WORKS: A Wife Now the Widdow, 1614; The first and second part of the Remedy of Love, 1620; Sir Thomas Overbury his Observations in his Travailes, 1620; The Miscellaneous Works in Verse and Prose of Sir Thomas Overbury, Knight, 1756

ABOUT: Amos, A. The Great Oyer of Poisoning; Gardiner, J. Studies in English History; Jonson, B. Conversations with William Drummond of Hawthornden; Niccols, R. Sir Thomas Overburies Vision; Parry, E. A. The Overbury Mystery; Whibley, C. Essays in Biography; Wood, A. à, Athenae Oxonienses.

OWEN, JOHN (1560?-1622), author of several volumes of Latin epigrams, was a Welshman, born in Plas Dû, Carnarvonshire, where his father, Thomas Owen, was the sheriff. Jane Owen, his mother, was a sister of Sir William Morris. John attended the Winchester School under Thomas Bilson and proceeded to New College, Oxford, graduating as a Bachelor of Civil Law in 1590.

After leaving the university Owen taught school for several years at Trelech, Monmouthshire, and in 1594 was appointed headmaster of King Henry VIII's school at Warwick. In the sixteenth century the making of Latin verses was an essential part of the curriculum in an English grammar school and Owen soon gained a reputation for his Latin epigrams pointed with contemporary reference and full of lively wit. His first collection of epigrams, published in 1606, won great popularity both in England and on the Continent, and was reprinted within a month. During the next six years he published several additional collections, creating the best known body of Latin epigrams since Martial, to whom he was often compared.

"Little Owen the epigrammaker" aimed his barbs at institutions, books, and prominent people of the day, as well as at such conventional figures as the poor author, the miser, the degenerate noble, the atheist, and the uxorious husband. At least one of his volumes of epigrams was placed on the Roman Index for points scored against the Church, and it is said that an uncle who was a Roman Catholic "dashed his name" from his will for this imprudence.

Five English translations of Owen's epigrams appeared before 1678 and they were also widely translated abroad, particularly in Germany, where they exerted a remarkable influence on German epigrammatists of the seventeenth century. The epigrams still may be read for their point and brevity, their playful punning, and what Wood called "an ingenious liberty of joking."

In spite of earlier successes, Owen was apparently supported by his kinsman, Lordkeeper Williams, during the last years of his life. He died, unmarried, in London when he was about sixty.

PRINCIPAL WORKS: Epigrammatum Libri Tres, 1606; Epigrammatum Liber Singularis, 1607; Epigrammatum Libri Tres, 1612; Epigrams of That Most Wittie and Worthie Epigrammatist Mr. John Owen, Gentleman (J. Vicars, tr.) 1619.

ABOUT: Colvile, F. L. Worthies of Warwickshire; Wood, A. à, Athenae Oxonienses.

OXFORD, EARL of. See VERE, EDWARD DE

PAINTER or PAYNTER, WILLIAM

(1540?-February 1594), translator, compiler of *The Palace of Pleasure*, was born either in London or Kent, and was possibly the son of William Paynter, a wool comber. He entered St. John's College, Cambridge, as a sizar in 1554, soon secured a scholarship, but left without a degree. He appeared next as headmaster of a school at Sevenoaks, in spite of a requirement that the master must be a bachelor of arts from one of the universities. In 1560 he was ordained deacon, and the next year became clerk of the ordnance in the Tower of London. This post he held to his death, in spite of confessed malfeasance—he confessed in 1586 that he had borrowed £1000 from the public funds to build up his private fortune, and in 1591 his son acknowledged (though he denied) further misconduct. Painter married Dorothy Bonham, by whom he had one son and four daughters. He died and was buried in London.

Painter's *Palace of Pleasure* served as a means of introducing English readers to the Italian *novelle* (short stories, by him translated as "novels"). The first volume of his anthology contained sixty stories, the second thirty-four, the 1575 edition seven more, a hundred and one in all. Though some were taken from Livy, Herodotus, and Aulus Gellius, his main source was Italian, chiefly the stories of Boccaccio and Bandello. The dramatists of the time, including Shakespeare, ransacked his book thoroughly—though it is significant that from Painter Shakespeare took only bare plots, never characterizations or actual words, as from North or Holinshed. The book was the source of *Romeo and Juliet, All's Well That Ends Well, Coriolanus, Timon of Athens,* and *The Rape of Lucrece,* as well as of Webster's *Duchess of Malfi* and plays by Jonson, Peele, Shirley, Beaumont and Fletcher, Marston, Massinger, and others. It inspired Ascham's acid comment in *The*

Scholemaster about "ungratious bookes, made in Italie, and translated in English." Ascham's objection was to the prevalence of blood and sex; but Painter succeeded in Italianizing a whole generation of English literature.

Painter's book was extremely popular, and deservedly so; he was a born story teller, often improved on his plots, and was a clear, direct, and vivid writer. To paraphrase Bacon, he took all fiction of and before his time to be his province. The only other book known to have been of his authorship was *The Cytie of Cyvelite* (1562), but this is thought to have been an earlier version of *The Palace of Pleasure* under another title; if not, it is completely lost.

PRINCIPAL WORKS: Antiprognosticon (tr. from Latin of W. Fulke) 1560; The Palace of Pleasure, Pleasaunt Histories and Excellent Novells, Selected Out of Divers Good and Commendable Authors, 1566-67, 1575 (J. Haslewood, ed. 1813, J. Jacobs, ed. 1890).

ABOUT: Haselwood, J. Preface, Palace of Pleasure, 1813 ed.; Jacobs, J. Biography, Palace of Pleasure, 1890 ed.

PALEY, WILLIAM (1743-May 25, 1805),

philosopher, theologian, was born at Peterborough, the eldest son of a Church of England clergyman who from 1745 until his death was headmaster of the Giggleswick grammar school. Young Paley inherited his common sense and his propensity to thrift from both father and mother. His mental powers were early recognized by his father, whose school he attended, but his physical coordination left much to be desired. Being no good at games, he early became studious, absent minded and fond of fishing.

He studied mathematics for a year before going up to Christ's College, Cambridge, in 1759. There he won numerous scholarships and was Senior Wrangler (first in mathematics in the whole university) in 1763. Three years of school teaching at Greenwich followed, during which period he took holy orders and became curate of Greenwich. In 1766 he was made a Fellow of his college, where he lectured in philosophy, leaving mathematics to his good friend John Law.

Law's father became Bishop of Carlisle in 1768; in 1775 he made Paley rector of Musgrave, Cumberland. Meanwhile Paley and his lectures had become very popular at

Cambridge. Leaving the University, Paley married a Carlisle girl and won rapid advancement in the Carlisle diocese, of which he became Archdeacon, 1782, and Chancellor, 1785.

In 1785 he published his first major work, *Principles of Moral and Political Philosophy*, which at once became a Cambridge textbook, based as it was on his Cambridge lectures. *Horae Paulinae*, a work of Biblical criticism, appeared in 1790. In 1794, he brought out his *Evidences of Christianity*, the work with which his name will always be associated. It, too, became a textbook. In it, Paley undertook to prove the truth of Christianity with the help of common sense alone. If a savage found a watch, Paley argued, he would assume that this intricate mechanism had a maker, though he saw no one nearby; so, too, the Universe must have a Maker. Paley's works on morals and theology are really a summing-up of English eighteenth century thought on these subjects.

The *Evidences* earned Paley a number of lucrative benefices, bringing his annual income to well over £2,000, but he never rose to be a bishop. His first wife, by whom he had eight children, died in 1791; in 1795, he married another Carlisle woman, who survived him. From this year until his death, he lived mainly at Monkwearmouth, having become rector of Bishop-Wearmouth in Durham diocese. He died at Lincoln, where

After G. Romney

WILLIAM PALEY

he was Sub-Dean of the Cathedral, but was buried in the Cathedral of Carlisle.

Paley was tall and heavy, with a large head and pronounced features. He was extremely literal-minded, but had a good sense of humor which enabled him to laugh at his own foibles, particularly the besetting one of absent-mindedness. He did much of his thinking during his erratic daily walks—usually with the end of his walking stick in his mouth. Fishing, too, gave him plenty of time for thought.

PRINCIPAL WORKS: Principles of Moral and Political Philosophy, 1785; Horae Paulinae, 1790; Reasons for Contentment, Addressed to the Labouring Part of the British Public, 1790; A View of the Evidences of Christianity, 1794; Natural Theology, 1802; Sermons and Tracts, 1808.

ABOUT: Meadley, G. W. Life of William Paley.

PALTOCK, ROBERT (1697-March 20, 1767), author of the adventure-romance, *The Life and Adventures of Peter Wilkins*, was the only son of Thomas Paltock of St. James's, Westminster, and his third wife, Anne. After the death of his father in 1701, Robert moved to Enfield, Middlesex, with his mother, who died ten years later.

Forced to make his own way, Paltock eventually became an attorney, practicing at Clement's Inn, London, and writing in his leisure. His only interesting work was the Utopian romance, *The Life and Adventures of Peter Wilkins*, first published in 1751. In the account of its hero's travels, "relating particularly his shipwreck near the South Pole; his passage thro' a subterraneous cavern into a kind of New World; his there meeting with a Gawry or Flying Woman, whose life he preserv'd, and afterwards married her; his extraordinary conveyance to the Country of the Glums and Gawrys," the book was undoubtedly influenced by both *Gulliver's Travels* and *Robinson Crusoe* but achieves a fanciful imaginative quality quite its own. Coleridge, Charles Lamb, and Leigh Hunt all admired it, and Southey wrote that the winged people of the book "are the most beautiful creatures of imagination that were ever devised."

Paltock's book (dedicated to Elizabeth, Countess of Northumberland, presumed to be the prototype of his heroine) ran through four editions before 1800 and at least sixteen later. A musical pantomime based on the book was produced in 1800 and a play in 1827. The only other work attributed to the creator of Wilkins is *Memoirs of the Life of Parnese, A Spanish Lady,* an extremely dull book published under the initials, R.P. Paltock was married to Anna Skinner, the daughter of an Italian merchant, by whom he had four children. He died in London when he was nearly seventy.

PRINCIPAL WORKS: The Life and Adventures of Peter Wilkins, a Cornish Man, 1751 (A. H. Bullen, 1884).

ABOUT: Bullen, A. H. Introduction to The Life and Adventures of Peter Wilkins (1884 ed.).

PARIS, MATTHEW (d. 1259), historian, monk, was connected from 1217 to his death with the Benedictine monastery of St. Albans, on Watling Street, the old Roman road from London to Wroxeter, near Shrewbury. Though he never became abbot, he was much more than an ordinary monk; he was the monastery's official historiographer (St. Albans was the center of monastic learning and culture in the thirteenth century), was a familiar at court in the reign of Henry III, on terms of intimacy with the king's brother, Earl Richard, and was, in fact, a diplomat, a courtier, and a man of the world. In 1248, so high was his reputation for probity and ability, Pope Innocent IV sent him to the Benedictine monastery at Holm, Norway, to reform unsatisfactory conditions there, and this at the request of the Norwegian monks themselves. He stayed for eighteen months and accomplished his mission successfully.

Besides being a writer, Paris was a painter, and a skilled worker in gold and silver. Tradition says that he had a "foreign teacher" in these arts. The quaint illustrations of his chronicles were all made either by him or under his supervision.

He was also a born historian. His first act on becoming historiographer of the monastery in 1238 was thoroughly to revise the work of his predecessor, Roger of Wendover. He then transformed the chronicle into a sort of state journal, which in effect constituted a history of England and the Continent to 1259. The chronicle then stopped abruptly, and it is presumed that the reason was the author's death. He had correspondents and informants in high places, and used their information constantly and intelligently. He abridged his own major

chronicle in the *Historia Minor,* and in so doing softened a few of the aspersions of the longer version.

For Paris was above all an outspoken, fearless critic of the king, the nobles, the clergy, and the pope. He was an English patriot, and he never hesitated to fight against tyranny or greed whether directed from London or from Rome. Easily fired with moral indignation, he named names and applied scathing adjectives to them. Yet in spite of his freedom of speech, both the pope, and, particularly, the king frequently showed him favor and apparently regarded him as a sharp but upright mentor. Essentially he was a genial, warmhearted man with a rough tongue and an utter lack of fear. His only prejudice—natural to an Augustinian—was against the begging friars.

Paris is often prolix and given to long-drawn-out rhetorical figures, but because he had an instinct for orderly arrangement and readable style, he is never boring, and he keeps strictly to his subject. He wrote, of course, exclusively in Latin, in a scholarly, clear, and vigorous style. He verified his sources, never sacrificed accuracy to picturesqueness (though the picturesqueness is there, notably in the illustrations), and, in a word, had a concept of the art of history almost unique in the Middle Ages. The *Chronica Majora* constitutes a masterly survey of English and, to a certain extent, European history in the mid-thirteenth century.

PRINCIPAL WORKS: Historia Anglorum (Historia Minor) (F. Madden, ed.) 1866-69 (J. A. Giles, tr. 1852-54); Chronica Majora (H. R. Laurd, ed.) 1872-73

ABOUT: Jessopp, A. Studies by a Recluse; Luard, H. R. Introduction, Chronica Majora; Madden, F. Preface, Historia Anglorum; Ten Brink, B. Early English Literature.

PARK, MUNGO (September 10, 1771-1806?), travel writer, was born at Fowlshiels or Foulshiels, a farm on the estate of the Duke of Buccleigh, in Selkirkshire, Scotland. He was seventh of the thirteen children of Mungo Park. After Selkirk Grammar School, he was apprenticed at fifteen to a surgeon named Anderson, and in 1789 entered Edinburgh University, where he studied medicine and botany and received his surgical diploma. At the end of 1791 he went to London, where his brother-in-law,

After H. Eldridge, 1798
MUNGO PARK

James Dickson, a market gardener turned botanist, introduced him to Sir Joseph Banks, president of the Royal Society. Through Banks he secured a post as assistant medical officer on an East Indiaman.

Park spent 1792 and 1793 mostly in Sumatra, studying the botany of the island and sending specimens home to Banks. When he returned to England, Banks interested the African Association in naming Park as successor to Major Daniel Houghton, who had disappeared while exploring the Niger River. Park was in Africa from 1795 to the end of 1797; he had a dangerous and adventurous experience, including a bout of fever, robbery of all his possessions, and imprisonment by an Arab chief. The report he turned in was made by him into a book which immediately became popular; it was a simply written narrative, but full of incident and excitement.

Failing another appointment, however, there was nothing for Park to do but return to Fowlshiels. There he married the daughter of Anderson, his old master; they had a son and three daughters. Negotiations were under way for him to return to Africa, but they hung fire, and he moved to Peebles and started the practice of medicine. It was at this time that he met Sir Walter Scott, who became much interested in him.

Finally, in January 1805, Park set out for Africa again. This time he was commissioned a captain, and his wife's brother went with him as a lieutenant. In Africa they were joined by a regular lieutenant and a detachment of soldiers, a party of thirty-five in all. By August only eleven of the thirty-five were still living; fever and dysentery had accounted for the rest, including his brother-in-law and a friend who had been his first companions. The last heard from Park was a letter in November, telling of his making a boat by combining two canoes.

It was not until 1812 that searchers from England found what had happened. By the beginning of 1806 there were only five Europeans left in the party, including Park himself—and one of those was insane. At some time early in the year the party was met by hostile natives; to escape them Park and the others jumped into the river and were drowned. His journal was lost. The only survivor was a native slave who gave what few details he recalled. In 1827 Park's son went to Africa to try to complete his father's exploration, and died there of fever.

Park was a tall, handsome man, of a cold and reserved temperament. He was not primarily a writer, but his unaffected and straightforward style made him and his only book famous in their day.

PRINCIPAL WORKS: Travels in the Interior of Africa, 1799.

ABOUT: Carlyle, T. Montaigne and Other Essays; Gwynn, S. L. Mungo Park and the Quest of the Niger; Hewitt, W. H. Mungo Park; Machlachlan, T. B. Mungo Park; Mitchell, J. L. Niger: the Life of Mungo Park; Scott, J. G. Mungo Park; Thomson, J. Mungo Park and the Niger.

PARKER, MATTHEW (August 6, 1504-May 17, 1575), theologian, was born in Norwich, the son of William Parker, a "calenderer of stuffs," and Alice Monins. His father died when Matthew was twelve, and his mother married John Baker, who reared the boy. Parker entered Corpus Christi College, Cambridge, in 1522; he also did part of his university work in St. Mary's Hostel. In 1503 he was made Bible-clerk, and he received his B.A. in 1525. In 1527 he was ordained deacon and priest and became a fellow of Corpus Christi, proceeding M.A. in 1528. He became associated with the little group (including Latimer and others) known as the "Cambridge Reformers," but, inde-

MATTHEW PARKER

pendent, moderate, and tolerant by nature, he did not follow them all the way. Cranmer licensed him to preach in 1533, and two years later he became, reluctantly, Anne Boleyn's chaplain.

The post included, as its principal duty, deanship of the college for secular canons, St. John the Baptist, at Stoke-by-Clare, Suffolk, and this occupied most of Parker's attention for the next twelve years. He became B.D. in 1535, D.D. in 1538, and in 1537 was made chaplain to Henry VIII. In 1539 he was accused of heresy, but acquitted, and he lost none of the royal favor; indeed in 1542 he was given a prebendary at Ely and a living at Ashdon, Essex, which two years later he exchanged for one at Burlingham, Norfolk. At the end of 1544 he was named, for his "approved learning, wisdom, and honesty," master of Corpus Christi. The next year he became vice chancellor of Cambridge, and accepted another living at Landbeach, Cambridgeshire.

In 1547 Parker married Margaret Harleston, who died in 1570, leaving four sons and a daughter. Throughout the reign of Edward VI he continued to advance (though marriage was a detriment to his career in the church), becoming dean of Lincoln in 1552. But with the accession of Mary I, he naturally found himself in trouble; not only was she a Roman Catholic, but he had espoused the cause of Lady Jane Grey. All

his preferments were taken from him, and he lived in hiding, often in danger; a fall from a horse while "on the run" permanently injured his health. With Elizabeth his sun shone again. But Parker was a shy and unambitious man, and became Archbishop of Canterbury in 1559 very much against his will; he would have preferred to live out his life in Cambridge. Nevertheless, he was recognized as leader of the Anglican party, midway between Roman Catholicism and Puritanism; he revised the Articles of the church to the present thirty-nine, and had much to do with the so-called "Bishops' Bible." Elizabeth especially frowned on his marriage, and was even royally rude to his wife, while accepting their magnificent hospitality. Parker died at seventy-one of arthritis and the stone, and was buried in his palace at Lambeth.

Primarily Parker was a scholar, "the head of the race of modern book collectors." He was interested in the revival of Old English, collected Saxon chronicles, and bequeathed a fine collection of manuscripts to the library of Corpus Christi. He was also a patron of printing, and kept a bookbinder as part of his private household. He was an energetic, industrious man, reserved but benevolent, a hard and conscientious worker. What little writing of his own he did was on ecclesiastical matters, and most of this is still in manuscript at his old college. Many prayers written by him also appear in various collections and anthologies, while his version of the Psalms shows a real feeling for rhythm.

PRINCIPAL WORKS: De Antiquitatis Britannicae Ecclesiae (concerning the antiquity of the British church) 1572; The Whole Psalter translated into English Metre (no date); Correspondence (J. Bruce, and T. T. Perowne, eds.) 1853.

ABOUT: Gee, H. Elizabethan Clergy; Kennedy, W. M. Archbishop Parker; Perry, E. W. Under Four Tudors; Strype, J. The Life and Acts of Matthew Parker.

PARKINSON, JOHN (1567-August 1650), herbalist, was probably born in Nottinghamshire, although very few details of his life are known. From his work it appears that he was practicing as an apothecary before the year 1616, and had a garden in Long Acre "well stored with rarities."

Parkinson is remembered as the author of one of the greatest of early herbals, *Theatrum Botanicum, The Theatre of*

Plantes, published in 1640. The most complete work on the subject until John Ray, Parkinson's herbal described some thirty-eight hundred different plants, illustrated by specially cut woodblocks. An earlier work on garden flowers, the *Paradisi in Sole, Paradisus Terrestris*, described nearly a thousand different plants, of which seven hundred eighty were illustrated.

Highly regarded at court, Parkinson served as apothecary to James I, and on the publication of *Paradisus Terrestris* received the title of "Botanicus Regius Primarius" from Charles I. He is known to have introduced at least seven new species of plants into England and added thirteen species to the recorded flora of Middlesex. Parkinson died when he was over eighty and was buried on August 6, 1650, at St. Martin's-in-the-Fields.

The name of Parkinson has been variously remembered. Pulteney speaks highly of his work in *Sketches of the Progress of Botany*; Charles Plumier, the French botanist, honored his memory by naming a genus of Central American tree after him; and as late as 1884 a Parkinson Society was founded in England to search out and cultivate old varieties of garden flowers.

PRINCIPAL WORKS: Paradisi in Sole, Paradisus Terrestris, or A Garden of All Sorts of Pleasant Flowers, 1629; Theatrum Botanicum, The Theatre of Plantes, or An Universall and Complete Herball, 1640.

ABOUT: Pulteney, R. Sketches of the Progress of Botany; Smith, Sir J. E. Life, *in* Rees' Cyclopaedia.

PARNELL, THOMAS (1679-1718), poet, divine, was born in Dublin, where his father had moved from Congleton, Cheshire, on the Restoration of Charles II in 1660. The Parnell family had been among the wealthier citizens of Congleton for more than a generation and ardently supported the Parliament against Charles I in the civil war; this partisanship was undoubtedly the reason for the father's removal to Ireland. The poet's mother was an Irishwoman and the family remained in Ireland after the father's death in 1685.

Parnell was educated at Dr. Jones' school in Dublin and entered Trinity College at the early age of thirteen. He graduated B.A., 1697; M.A., 1700. His scholarship in Greek and Latin was outstanding; this probably accounts for his being admitted to deacon's orders in 1700, though he was under the canonical age, twenty-three. Rapid promotion in the Church of Ireland followed; he took priest's orders in 1703, became a minor canon of St. Patrick's Cathedral in 1704, and was made Archdeacon of Clogher diocese in 1706. In the same year he married Anne Minchin, by whom he had two sons and a daughter; her death in 1711 was a blow from which his extremely sensitive nature never recovered; his sons both died in childhood.

Parnell had inherited a good deal of money and was unhappy in Ireland, so that he was in the habit of making frequent visits to London; there he associated with literary men. Under Swift's influence he gave up his family's traditional Whig politics and became a Tory in 1711, about the time that the Tories came into power. Beloved by Swift, Pope, Gay and Arbuthnot, he was a member of their Scriblerus Club. He addressed a poetical *Essay on the Different Styles of Poetry* to the Tory Minister Bolingbroke, 1713, and published the same year a *Poem on Queen Anne's Peace* which was definitely Tory propaganda. In 1712 and 1713 he contributed nonpolitical essays to the Whig *Spectator* and *Guardian*. In truth, politics can have interested him very little; Swift's efforts to get him ecclesiastical preferment from the Tory Government were bound to fail.

THOMAS PARNELL

395

In 1712 Parnell was made a Doctor of Divinity; he later received the prebend's stall at St. Patrick's Cathedral which Swift vacated to become Dean. In 1716 he was made vicar of Finglas, near Dublin. On his way home from a visit to London in 1718, he died at Chester and was buried there on October 24.

Pope published a carefully selected edition of Parnell's *Poems* in 1721. This volume shows him to have possessed a very minor talent, rising to greatness only in the concluding lines of "A Night-Piece on Death." He clearly owed his position in the inner circle of Pope and Swift not to his literary ability or political convictions, but to that elusive quality, "Irish charm." Pope also found his scholarship very useful in preparing the translation of the *Iliad,* for which Parnell wrote an essay on Homer.

By temperament lazy and unstable, Parnell was always either overflowing with gaiety or plunged in gloom. His sorrow at the death of his wife is said to have made him a drunkard; he was very subject to headaches, and may have died of a nervous disorder. His portrait shows a very handsome, sensitive, youthful face, full of that sweetness which made him so delightful a companion and was the outstanding characteristic of his otherwise undistinguished poetry.

PRINCIPAL WORKS: *Poems*: Essay on the Different Styles of Poetry, 1713; Poem on Queen Anne's Peace, 1713; Homer's Battle of the Frogs and Mice (tr.) 1717; Poems (A. Pope, ed.) 1721; Posthumous Works of Thomas Parnell, 1758. *Prose*: Essay on the Life, Writings and Learning of Homer (prefixed to vol. I of Pope's Iliad) 1715; Life of Zoilus (*in* Homer's Battle, etc.) 1717.

ABOUT: Goldsmith, O. The Life of Dr. Parnell; Johnson, S. Lives of the Poets.

PARR, SAMUEL (January 26, 1747-March 6, 1825), Latin scholar, pamphleteer, was born at Harrow-on-the-Hill, the son of an apothecary, Samuel Parr, who was descended from Catherine Parr. He was educated at Harrow where he proved himself a precocious student, and at Emmanuel College, Cambridge. On the death of his father he was forced to leave the university, but later returned to take an M.A. and an LL.D.

Ordained a deacon in 1769 and a priest several years later, Parr divided his time between his duties as a clergyman and as a pedagogue. In 1766 he held the post of first assistant at the Harrow School, where Richard Brinsley Sheridan was one of his pupils, and five years later borrowed money to found a school of his own. He subsequently held the headmastership of the Colchester and the Norwich grammar schools, and during the last forty years of his life served as perpetual curate and private tutor at Hatton in Warwickshire. Although he held a number of preferments, his advance in the ecclesiastical field was hampered by the strong Whig principles taught him by his father. Known as "the Whig Johnson," he gained a reputation for great erudition and an effective literary style although he had neither the force nor the humor of Johnson.

Parr first won fame both as a Latinist and as a political writer with his preface written in elegant and difficult Latin to his own edition of a treatise on Cicero written by Bellenden. The high quality of scholarship therein displayed brought him to the attention of Charles James Fox, then a powerful figure in the cabinet, of whom he later wrote in *Characters of the Late Charles James Fox.* Parr's first wife, Jane Morsingale, died in 1810 after a series of domestic tragedies, and six years later he married Mary Eyre, the sister of an old friend.

In spite of his occasional rashness and his many eccentricities of manner, Parr had a large circle of friends whom he liked to serve—among them the scholar Richard Porson, who spent a winter at Hatton studying in Parr's library, and the philosopher, Jeremy Bentham. Yet with all his erudition, Parr accomplished little of permanent value, and his English writings are now largely unreadable because of their mannered verbosity.

PRINCIPAL WORKS: A Discourse on Education and On the Plans Pursued in Charity Schools, 1786; Praefatio to G. Bellendini de Statu Libri Tres (ed.) 1787-88; Characters of the Late Charles James Fox, 1809; The Works of Samuel Parr, with Memoirs of His Life and Writings (J. Johnstone, ed.) 1828.

ABOUT: Barker, E. H. Parriana, or Notices of the Reverend S. Parr; Blunt, J. J. Essays Contributed to the Quarterly Review; Field, W. Memoirs of the Life, Writings and Opinions of Samuel Parr; Nicoll, H. J. Great Scholars.

PAYNTER, WILLIAM. See PAINTER, WILLIAM

PEACHAM, HENRY (1576?-1643?), miscellaneous writer, author of *The Compleat*

Gentleman, was born in North Mimms, Hertfordshire. His father, Henry Peacham the elder, was a clergyman and classical scholar, author of a book on rhetoric. Educated at Trinity College, Cambridge, where he took his B.A. in 1594 and his M.A. four years later, young Peacham became a school master, teaching for several years at Wymondham, Norfolk.

A man of varied accomplishments, Peacham wrote Latin and English verse, painted, composed, and was a student of botany, heraldry, and mathematics. His first published work was a treatise on art. Although he professed to dislike teaching, he was always intensely interested in his own pupils and had definite notions as to what they should be taught. His best known work, *The Compleat Gentleman,* written for William Howard, the youngest son of Lord Arundel, is a quaint medley of Peacham's own interests projected as a plan for the proper education of a young gentleman. The book is of interest chiefly for the survey of contemporary English art, literature, and science which it includes.

Peacham spent several years in foreign travel as tutor to the three elder sons of the Earl of Arundel, and on his return to London devoted all his time to literature. In 1620 he published *Thalia's Banquet,* a book of epigrams, and two years later *The Compleat Gentleman,* which went through a number of editions. A Cavalier and a polemic in the Royalist cause, he wrote a series of political and social pamphlets in his later years, all of which are now forgotten. His old age was spent in poverty and the story is told that he wrote books for children at a penny each in order to keep himself alive. Unmarried and given to melancholy, he died a year or two after the publication of a last tract, *The Worth of a Peny,* in 1641.

PRINCIPAL WORKS: Minerva Britannia: or a Garden of Heroycal Devices, 1612; The Art of Drawing With the Pen and Limning in Watercolors, 1616; Thalia's Banquet, 1620; The Compleat Gentleman, 1622 (G. S. Gordon, ed. 1906); The Worth of a Peny, or A Caution to Keep Money, 1641; The Art of Living in London, 1642.

ABOUT: Darling, J. Cyclopaedia Bibliographica.

PEARSON, JOHN (February 18, 1613-July 16, 1686), scholar, theologian, bishop of Chester, was born at Great Snoring, Norfolk. His father, Robert Pearson, was rector of Great Snoring and later archdeacon of Suffolk. Joanna, his mother, was the daughter of Richard Vaughan. John went to Eton and to Queens' College, Cambridge, for a year, moving on to King's College, where he was elected a fellow. He graduated B.A. in 1635, M.A. in 1639, and proceeded to take holy orders.

As a young clergyman he was appointed to the rectory of Thorington in Suffolk, but interrupted the steady progress of his career to join the remnants of Charles I's party, acting as chaplain to the Royalist forces at Exeter. After the civil war he lived quietly in London, preaching at St. Clement's, Eastcheap, and giving most of his time to study. During this period he wrote his most important theological work, *Exposition of the Creed,* which became a standard book in English divinity.

His reputation for scholarship solidly established, Pearson's ecclesiastical career again moved forward after the Restoration. Under the patronage of Bishop Wren, he was made successively rector of St. Christopher-le-Stocks in London, prebend of Ely, archdeacon of Surrey, a royal chaplain, and master of Jesus College, Cambridge. In 1662 he was appointed master of Trinity College, a position which he held until he was consecrated bishop of Chester eleven years later. He died at Chester when he was seventy-three.

In addition to *An Exposition of the Creed,* which was undoubtedly the masterpiece of doctrinal exposition in its period, Pearson wrote another work of interest, *Vindiciae Epistolarum S. Ignatii,* in which he defended the authenticity of the Epistles of St. Ignatius. Not only was Pearson a notable preacher and an able theologian, he was a man of such unfailing equanimity and virtue that even his opponents respected him. Not many years after his death Richard Bentley wrote of "the most excellent Bishop Pearson, the very dust of whose writings are gold."

PRINCIPAL WORKS: An Exposition of the Creed, 1659 (T. Chevallier and R. Sinker, eds. 1882); Vindiciae Epistolarum S. Ignatii, 1672 (E. Churton, ed. 1844); The Minor Theological Works (E. Churton, ed.) 1844.

ABOUT: Churton, E. Life, *in* Minor Theological Works; Smith-Dampier, J. L. East Anglian Worthies.

PECOCK, REGINALD (1395?-1460?), theologian, bishop of St. Asaph and of Chichester, was a Welshman, born probably in the diocese of St. David's. At Oriel College, Oxford, where he took his B.D. in 1425, Pecock established such a brilliant record that he attracted the attention of Humphrey, Duke of Gloucester, who brought him to London and introduced him to the court. In 1431 he was elected master of Whittington College and rector of St. Michael's in Riola, and little more than a decade later he was promoted to the bishopric of St. Asaph.

Pecock's career and ultimate fate were shaped by an irony of his time. As a defender of the orthodoxy of the church against the reforming Lollards, he chose arguments and methods which brought him into conflict with the very clergy which he proposed to defend. In his earliest extant work, *The Reule of Crysten Religioun*, he set out to win over the heretical Lollards by persuasion, exalting the authority of reason and asserting natural law higher than that of the scriptures. Although he managed thus to offend both strict churchmen and reformists, his political position as an adherent of the house of Lancaster was sufficiently secure to save him from any immediate retaliation. In 1450 he was elevated to the bishopric of Chichester, and four years later he was made a member of the privy council.

Writing in English when English was still considered a vulgar tongue, Bishop Pecock continued to antagonize the clergy with theological works of a profoundly skeptical and rationalist temper, the *Donet*, the *Book of Faith*, and most important, the *Repressor of Overmuch Blaming of the Clergy*. With the rise of the Yorkist party to power, Pecock's enemies seized the politically expedient moment to organize against him and demand his public censure. In 1457 Archbishop Bourchier called on Pecock's accusers to appear before him. Pecock's works were examined and he was charged with having set natural law above the scriptures, with disregarding the authority of the pope and the saints, and (most interesting of all) with writing on great matters in English. Pecock was given the choice of public recantation or burning at the stake. He chose the former and before the archbishop and thousands of spectators abjured his own works and delivered fourteen of his books to be burnt.

Deprived of his bishopric and expelled from the privy council, Pecock was sent to Thorney Abbey in Cambridgeshire, where he was confined without books or writing materials for the last years of his life. Many of his writings have disappeared, and some exist only in manuscript, but of the printed works, the *Repressor* remains an expression of a forceful and independent intellect as well as a monument of fifteenth century English prose.

PRINCIPAL WORKS: The Repressor of Overmuch Blaming of the Clergy, c. 1450 (C. Babington, ed. 1860); The Book of Faith, 1456 (H. Wharton, ed. 1688; J. L. Morison, ed. 1909).

ABOUT: Babington, C. Introduction to The Repressor; Gairdner, J. and Spedding, J. Studies in English History; Green, V. H. H. Bishop Reginald Pecock, A Study in Ecclesiastical History and Thought; Hannick, E. A. Reginald Pecock; Lewis, J. The Life of Dr. Pecock.

PEELE, GEORGE (1558?-1597?), playwright, poet, was the son of James Peele, Clerk of Christ's Hospital, and may have been born inside the walls of that institution. In 1565 and again in 1570 George is mentioned in the records as a pupil at Christ's Hospital Grammar School; his father is allowed free books for him. Some idea of the father's status and abilities may be gathered from the fact that he was the author of two works on bookkeeping, the first ones to appear in English.

George Peele went to Oxford University in 1571, being a student first at Broadgates Hall and then in 1574, at Christ Church. He graduated from there B.A., 1577; M.A., 1579. He seems to have stayed on at Oxford until 1581; a deposition made by him in March 1583 says that he had been in London almost two years, had spent nine (not ten) years at Oxford, was twenty-five years of age, married, and owned some land "in the right of his wife."

Peele's literary career began at Oxford, where he translated a play of Euripides into English verse and perhaps wrote original poetry too. He seems to have been a gay dog at the University, though he cannot have had much money of his own; the governors of Christ's Hospital contributed £5 toward his B.A. degree expenses.

In 1583 Peele revisited Oxford and had some hand in the production of two Latin plays. "For provision for the plays at Christ Church" he was paid eighteen shillings. There is reason to believe that he was by then both an actor and a playwright; *The Arraignment of Paris*, a pastoral play, was published the next year. This work is worthy of a talented poet, learned in Latin and Greek, but some of his later plays are peculiar hodgepodges. The most successful is *The Old Wives' Tale*, a romantic fantasy largely based on folk material. Milton's *Comus* shows some indebtedness to this play.

At the end of 1585 or the beginning of 1586 Peele's father died; during his last illness he had to ask his employers for help; they gave him £5. Peele therefore inherited nothing from his father; in general, his life seems to have been one of poverty and dissipation, though he tried all sorts of expedients to earn money by his pen. He wrote some pageants for the London Lord Mayor's Show and numerous congratulatory poems such as *A Farewell* to Sir John Norris and Sir Francis Drake; *An Eclogue Gratulatory* to the Earl of Essex on his return from Portugal; *The Honour of the Garter*, addressed to the Earl of Northumberland on his receiving the order of the Garter. For this last poem he received £3 from the earl. Lord Burghley seems to have been a good patron of Peele's; the poet wrote speeches as part of an entertainment given to Queen Elizabeth at Theobalds, Burghley's country seat, in 1591.

In 1592 Robert Greene on his deathbed wrote *Greene's Groatsworth of Wit*, in which he warned his friends Marlowe and Peele, among others, that they, like him, would come to a bad end if they relied on the fickle actors for their livelihood. His prophecy was fulfilled. The struggle against disease and poverty soon became too much for Peele. In 1595 he sent Lord Burghley a copy of *A Tale of Troy*, accompanied by a letter which mentioned that long sickness has enfeebled him and that his messenger is "my eldest daughter and necessity's servant." No doubt he hoped Burghley would relieve his necessity.

By 1598 Peele was dead; in *Palladis Tamia*, published that year, Francis Meres speaks of him as having died of the pox, i.e.

syphilis. Peele was a byword for wit, trickery and debauchery; *The Merry Conceited Jests of George Peele*, while possibly none of them authentic, present a just picture of his current reputation in London before and after his death. Nothing is known of his personal appearance, unless certain hints in the *Jests* are to be taken seriously.

Peele is remembered in literary history mainly as an immediate predecessor of Shakespeare in the drama; Shakespeare no doubt learnt much from his work, as he did from all those who preceded him, but specific indebtedness is harder to trace.

PRINCIPAL WORKS: *Plays and Masques*: The Arraignment of Paris, 1584; The Famous Chronicle of King Edward the First, 1593; The Battle of Alcazar, 1594; The Old Wives' Tale, 1595; The Love of King David and Fair Bethsabe, 1599; The Hunting of Cupid (W. W. Greg, ed.) 1911; Two Elizabethan Stage Abridgments: The Battle of Alcazar and Orlando Furioso (W. W. Greg, ed.) 1922. *Poems, Pageants, etc.*: The Device of the Pageant, 1585; A Farewell and A Tale of Troy, 1589; An Eclogue Gratulatory, 1589; Polyhymnia, 1590; Descensus Astraeae, the Device of a Pageant, 1591; The Honour of the Garter, 1593; Merry Conceited Jests of George Peele, 1607.

ABOUT: Bullen, A. H. Introduction to his edition of Peele's Works; Cheffaud, P. H. George Peele (in French).

PENN, WILLIAM (October 14, 1644-July 30, 1718), Quaker founder of Pennsylvania, author of religious and miscellaneous writings, was born in London, the son of Admiral William Penn (knighted in 1660) and of Margaret Jasper, a native of Holland. He was reared at Wanstead, Essex, a center of Puritanism, educated at the near-by school in Chigwell, and entered Christ Church, Oxford, in 1660. There he was noted for athletic prowess, and contributed a Latin poem to a college anthology. In 1662, however, he was expelled for nonconformity. His father whipped him and turned him out of the house, then relented and sent him abroad to try to cure his religious aberrancy. For a while he was a figure at the court of Louis XIV (he even fought a duel), then attended the Protestant College at Saumur, and went on to Turin. He returned apparently a conventional young gentleman, fought briefly in the Dutch War, and was entered at Lincoln's Inn in 1665. Then his father sent him to Ireland, to manage his estate there and to serve on his naval staff; his original interest in Quakerism revived, and

WILLIAM PENN

he was arrested in 1667 in connection with a Quaker meeting at Cork.

His father recalled him to London, and soon he was a minister of the Quaker faith, wearing their garb and refusing to doff his hat except to God. He began to preach in 1668, and his *Sandy Foundation Shaken* landed him in the Tower; he was released through the influence of the Duke of York (later James II) only to land in Newgate for six months. His father died in 1670. Penn made the first of three missionary tours to the Continent, then retired as a country gentleman, first to Hertfordshire, then to Sussex. He kept on preaching, however, wrote innumerable tracts against Roman Catholics, Baptists, and other non-Quakers, and participated in his last public controversy in 1675, with Richard Baxter.

In 1676 Penn had been made trustee of half of New Jersey; by 1682 he had a grant of the other half, and also of the country west of the Delaware River. Against his protests, this territory was called Pennsylvania, in honor of his father. The rent was two beaver skins a year and a fifth of all gold and silver found there! In 1682 he sailed for America, founded Philadelphia, made a treaty with the Lenni Lenape Indians, and wrote a remarkably liberal constitution for the province. He returned to England in 1684 because of a boundary dispute with Lord Baltimore, and did not return until

1699. In the interim, quarrels arose with the Assembly, the constitution was largely abrogated, and his son, left behind, became ringleader of all the malcontents and semicriminals in the territory. From 1692 to 1694 he was actually deprived of the governship, and he was constantly in trouble under William and Mary because of his friendship with the deposed James II. But he kept on writing and preaching—on one occasion to Peter the Great of Russia.

Penn lived in Pennsylvania again from 1699 to 1701, then returned to England permanently. In 1707, thanks to misjudgment of a man who swindled him, he was imprisoned in the Fleet for debt. He mortgaged his province, but his sons inherited the proprietorship. After a series of apoplectic strokes, he died at Field Ruscombe, Berkshire, and was buried near Chalfont St. Giles, Buckinghamshire. He was twice married: in 1672 to Gulielma Springett, who died in 1694, leaving three sons and four daughters, and in 1695 to Hannah Callowhill (a street in Philadelphia is named for her), who survived him. By his second marriage he had four sons and two daughters.

Penn was sanguine and optimistic by nature, rather practical than mystical, a bit gullible where others' good intentions were concerned. Though puritanical in his beliefs, he was a great friend of education; and though he kept slaves he improved their lot. He was an able controversialist, but most of his tracts are boring and tedious, with no literary merit. The exception is *Some Fruits of Solitude*, which is epigrammatic and pithy.

PRINCIPAL WORKS: Truth Exalted, 1668; The Sandy Foundation Shaken, 1668; Innocency with her Open Face, 1669; No Cross No Crown, 1669; (J. D. Hilton, ed. 1902); The Great Case of Liberty of Conscience, 1671; Quakerism a New Nickname for Old Christianity, 1672; Reason against Railing and Truth against Fiction, 1673; Some Account of the Province of Pennsilvania in America, 1686; Letters on the Penal Laws, 1687; The Reasonableness of Toleration, 1689; A Key opening a way to every common Understanding, 1692; Some Fruits of Solitude, 1693 (E. Gosse, ed. 1901); A Brief Account of the Rise and Progress of the People Called Quakers, 1694; Primitive Christianity Revived, 1696; The Christian Quaker and his Divine Testimony Stated and Vindicated, 1699; A Collection of the Works of William Penn (J. Besse, ed.) 1726.

ABOUT: Beatty, E. C. O. William Penn as Social Philosopher; Brailsford, M. R. The Making of William Penn; Buell, A. C. William Penn as the Founder of Two Commonwealths; Channing, E. William Penn; Clarkson, T. Memoirs of the Public and Private Life of William Penn; Comfort,

W. W. William Penn, A Tercentenary Estimate;
Dixon, W. H. A History of William Penn; Dobrée,
B. William Penn, Quaker and Pioneer; Fisher,
J. F. A Discourse . . . on the Private Life and
Domestic Habits of William Penn; Fisher, S. G.
The True William Penn; Graham, J. W. William
Penn; Grant, C. Quaker and Courtier; Hull, W.
D. William Penn, A Topical Biography; Janney,
S. M. The Life of William Penn; Oliphant, M. O.
W. Historical Sketches of the Reign of Queen
Anne; Pepys, S. Diary; Stoughton, J. William
Penn; Street, L. His Excellency, William Penn;
Trueblood, B. F. William Penn's Holy Experiment
in Civil Government; Vulliamy, C. E. William
Penn.

PENNANT, THOMAS (June 14, 1726–
December 16, 1798), naturalist, antiquarian,
travel writer, was born in Downing, Flintshire, Wales, the son of David Pennant and
Arabella Mytton. From the age of twelve
he showed an interest in natural science.
After school at Wrexham and Hadley, he
entered Queen's College, Oxford, in 1744,
but left without a degree. From 1746 his
scientific interests focused on geology and
what would now be called palaeontology,
though his first publication, in 1750, was on
a local earthquake. In 1754 he was made a
fellow of the Society of Antiquaries, but he
resigned in 1760. He was a correspondent
of Linnaeus, and Gilbert White's famous
Selborne arose in the form of letters between
White and Pennant and Daines Barrington.

In 1757 Pennant was elected to the Royal
Society of Upsala, by Linnaeus' influence,
and in 1767 he was made a fellow of the
Royal Society. In 1771 he received an honorary D.C.L. from Oxford. The profits from
his *British Zoology*, which was long a standard textbook, he gave to establish a Welsh
school in London. Meanwhile he lived at
Downing, was high sheriff of Flintshire, and
in 1763 succeeded to his father's estate. In
1765 he traveled on the Continent and met
Voltaire and Buffon. In all his journeys,
throughout England in Ireland, Scotland,
and in Wales, he kept elaborate journals,
which later he expanded into books.

In 1759 Pennant married Elizabeth Falconer, who died in 1764, leaving a daughter;
in 1777 he married Anne Mostyn, by whom
he had another daughter and a son. Until
he was nearly seventy he had never had an
ill day; then his health failed but his mind
remained keen and active to the last. He
died and was buried in Downing. Pennant
described himself as "a moderate Tory,"

After T. Gainsborough, 1776
THOMAS PENNANT

while Horace Walpole, though calling him
"a smatterer, who picks up his knowledge as
he rides," nevertheless added that he was "a
very honest and good natured man," though
"too lively and impetuous."

As a naturalist Pennant was quite inferior
to Buffon, but he had a gift for making dry
subjects interesting. His own favorite of his
books was the *History of Quadrupeds*. Dr.
Johnson greatly admired Pennant's *Tour in
Scotland*, and called him "the best traveler
I ever read: he observes more things than
anyone else does." Thomas Bell, one of
Gilbert White's editors, thought Pennant
"vain and self-seeking," but actually he gave
full credit when the information he used had
been obtained from others. It is certain that
he never wrote a travel book about a place
he had not seen, or a tour he had not taken
(on horseback). It may be added that on
many of his journeys he took a botanist and
an illustrator with him, and the hundreds of
illustrations, many of them valuable, in his
books were all made under his immediate
supervision.

PRINCIPAL WORKS: The British Zoology, 1766-
70; A Tour in Scotland, 1771; Synopsis of Quadrupeds, 1771 (enlarged as History of Quadrupeds,
1781); A Tour in Wales, 1778-81; The Journey
from Chester to London, 1782; Arctic Zoology,
1784-87; Of London, 1790; Indian Zoology, 1790;
Literary Life of the late [*sic*] Thomas Pennant,
Esq., by Himself, 1793; The History of the
Parishes of Whiteford and Holywell, 1796; Outlines
of the Globe (4 of 14 projected volumes) 1798-

401

1800; A Tour from Downing to Alston Moor, 1801; A Tour from Alston Moor to Harrowgate and Brimham Crags, 1809.

ABOUT: Pennant, T. Literary Life; Walpole, H. Letters; Wood, A. à, Athenae Oxonienses.

PEPYS, SAMUEL (February 23, 1633-May 26, 1703) (the name is pronounced Peeps), diarist, was probably born in London, though perhaps in Huntingdonshire. His father, John Pepys, though a tailor, was the younger son of a good family, and the father's first cousin was Sir Edward Montagu, the first Earl of Sandwich, who was Samuel's lifelong friend and patron. His mother, Margaret Knight, was of a lower social class.

The boy seems to have been boarded out as a small child; then he attended Huntingdon Grammar School and St. Paul's, and in 1650 entered Trinity College, Cambridge, soon transferring to Magdalene College, as a sizar. There he soon won scholarships, and graduated B.A. in 1653, and M.A. in 1660.

In 1655, at twenty-two, he married Elizabeth St. Michael, daughter of a Huguenot French father, and only fifteen. The young couple lived for a while in Montagu's house, Pepys serving as a sort of upper steward or factotum. In 1658 he was "cut for the stone," a date he observed annually, major operations being the soul-searing events they were in those days. The same year Montagu secured a position for him as clerk to George Downing (after whom Downing Street is named); Downing ("to save the salary," Pepys thought) had him made clerk of the council.

The Restoration was the turning point in Pepys's official career. Though he had indulged in Roundhead sentiments in his youth, he was by this time a thorough Royalist, and Montagu's friendship stood him in good stead. He was appointed secretary to the two generals of the fleet, Montagu himself and Monk, and for the first time met the Duke of York, afterwards James II, who became a helpful friend. Through Montagu again, he became clerk of the privy seal and clerk of the acts (also a justice of the peace), and held these posts from 1660 to 1662, when he resigned. Through these offices Pepys became rich—not from his salary, but from fees. By his own lights and those of his colleagues, he was unswervingly

honest; like all of them, he took bribes, but he did not let them influence him.

In 1665 he became surveyor general of the victualing office of the Navy, with a house in the Navy Office. It is said that when Pepys entered the Navy Offices he did not so much as know the multiplication table; nevertheless, he was one of the most efficient and effective employees it ever had. In 1668 he defended the Navy in a speech before the bar of the House of Commons. Unfortunately, his sight was failing, and had been since 1664; he never became blind, but it was necessary to ask for a leave of absence. He spent nearly a year in France and Holland with his wife, and soon after their return, in November 1669, Mrs. Pepys died of a "fever," at only twenty-nine. Her husband's grief was real, and he sought consolation in unremitting work.

In 1672 he was appointed Secretary of the Admiralty, the Duke of York then being Lord of the Admiralty. In 1676 he was Governor of Christ's Hospital and Master of the Trinity House (again in 1685), and in 1677 he was Master of the Clothworkers' Company—a compliment to his tailor father. In 1679 he sat in Parliament for Harwich. But both the Duke (whose known ally he was) and Pepys had bitter enemies; that same year they involved him in a baseless accusation of secret Roman Catholicism and "Popish conspiracy," and for a few months he was actually in the Tower. The charge was dismissed without even a trial, when one of the conspirators confessed on his deathbed. However, Pepys had lost his office, though not the royal favor. In 1682 he went with the Duke of York to Scotland, and the next year to Tangier with Lord Dartmouth. In 1684 he became Secretary of the Admiralty again—the period in which he instituted his greatest reforms and became known as "the right hand of the Navy." Charles II himself had succeeded his brother as Lord of the Admiralty. In 1685 he was once more a Member of Parliament for Harwich, and in 1684 and 1685 he was president of the Royal Society, of which he had been a Fellow since 1664. At this period he lived in York Buildings, in great prosperity and some magnificence, though alone except for servants, as he never remarried and had no children.

J. Hayls, 1667

SAMUEL PEPYS

But the Revolution of 1688, which ousted James and brought in William and Mary, ended Pepys' official career. He was accused of sending Navy information to the French, and imprisoned in the Gatehouse, Westminster, as "an enemy to the state" (he who was called by now "the Nestor of the Navy"); his friends secured his release, but he was under technical arrest until 1690, and of course he had been relieved of his office. Charles and James between them owed him £28,000 which he never got.

In 1700, a semi-invalid, he retired to Clapham, living with his friend and ex-clerk, William Hewer, and there he died of the stone, for which he had been "cut" nearly half a century before. He was buried beside his wife in St. Olav's, and left his entire estate to his sister's son. His library, after his nephew's death, he bequeathed to Magdalene College; it included a priceless collection of broadsides, tracts, newspapers, and prints. Most of his own manuscripts are now in the Bodleian Library in Oxford.

During his lifetime the only things Pepys had published were a report on Christ's Hospital and a memoir on the Navy, part of a projected history of the Navy which never got farther. But of course what has created the immortal fame of Samuel Pepys was not his public, but his private, self—the diary, written in a mixture of shorthand,

Latin, Greek, Spanish, French, and German, and just plain cypher, which he kept from 1659 to 1669 for his own secret use. The failing sight which made him reluctantly close the diary in 1669 was one of the great misfortunes of English literature.

For here, perhaps for the only time in history, is a whole man, not as he would like to be or as he would like the world to think him, but as he is. Vanity, scandal, weakness—the vows to give up over-drinking and theatre-going, his philandering eye, his quarrels and temper, his frank opinion of his acquaintances both great and small, his love of music and his religious fervor, his heroic deeds during the plague and the great fire and his flirtations and infidelities, his intimate life at home with his wife and servants, his journeys around London, his insatiable curiosity—they are all here. And the style, piquant, brilliant, candid, is exactly suited to the matter. Here, as Wheatley has said, is "not only a picture of the life and manners of the time, but also the dissection of the heart of a man."

Pepys's diary has been so much quoted and misquoted, parodied and burlesqued (Franklin P. Adams has done one of the best of these parodies, and in 1926 J. B. Fagan wrote an entire play on Pepys); isolated phrases have become such common tags—"and so to bed," "my wife, poor wretch"—that if it were possible to stale the diary it would long ago have been done. Pepys was no literary man like Evelyn, but a man of action, a careful and methodical executive, who by divine grace was also colloquial, garrulous, sociable, and completely candid at least to himself in secret. The diary is unique, indescribable to those who do not know it, and beyond all price to those who do.

Its translation in part from cypher and shorthand ("tachygraphy") was a four-year job for the Reverend John Smith in the early nineteenth century, and he translated only such portions as would not shock the contemporary reader. Some of it is still unpublished and indeed undeciphered. What it would have meant if Pepys could have had his sight corrected as would have been done today, and had been able to continue the diary for the last quarter-century of his life!

PRINCIPAL WORKS: Letters upon the present state of Christ's Hospital, 1688; Memoires relating to the State of the Royal Navy of England for ten years, 1690; Memoirs of Samuel Pepys, Esq., comprising his diary from 1659 to 1669 (deciphered by J. Smith) (R. Braybrook, ed.) 1825, (H. B. Wheatley, ed. 1893-99); An Account of His Majesty's Escape from Worcester, 1830; The Life, Journals, and Correspondence of Samuel Pepys, Esq., F.R.S. (J. Smith, ed.) 1841; Private Correspondence of Samuel Pepys (J. R. Tanner, ed.) 1926; Further Correspondence (J. R. Tanner, ed.) 1929.

ABOUT: Bradford, G. The Soul of Samuel Pepys; Bridge, F. Samuel Pepys, Lover of Musique; Bryant, A. Samuel Pepys; Drinkwater, J. Pepys, His Life and Character; Evelyn, J. Diary; Hudson, W. H. Idle Hours in a Library; Jeffrey, F. On Pepys's Diary; Lubbock, P. Samuel Pepys; Lucas-Dubreton, J. (H. J. Stenning, tr.) Samuel Pepys: A Portrait in Miniature; Pepys, S. Diary; Ponsonby, A. A. W. H. Samuel Pepys; Stevenson, R. L. Familiar Studies of Men and Books; Tanner, J. R. Mr. Pepys: An Introduction to the Diary, together with a Sketch of his Later Life; Wheatley, H. B. Samuel Pepys and the World He Lived In, Pepysiana; Whibley, C. The Real Pepys (The Pageantry of Life); Whitear, W. H. More Pepysiana.

PERCY, THOMAS (April 13, 1729-September 30, 1811), poet, antiquarian, editor of the *Reliques of Ancient English Poetry*, bishop of Dromore, was born at Bridgnorth Shropshire, where his grandfather had been a grocer and probably his father also. He later claimed descent from the great Percy family, Earls of Northumberland; no satisfactory proof or refutation of this claim has ever been put forward.

He was educated at Bridgnorth Grammar School and won an exhibition from there to Christ Church, Oxford, in 1746. He graduated B.A., 1750, M.A., 1753. In the latter year he took holy orders and was appointed by his college to the parish of Easton Maudit, Northamptonshire. He stayed on at the University until 1756 when, having been given the adjoining parish of Wilby as well, he went to live at Easton Maudit. In 1759 he married Anne Gutteridge, daughter of a Northamptonshire squire, a charming, sensible and tactful woman to whom he had written some poems during their courtship including "O Nancy, Will You Go with Me?"

Percy's literary career began soon after his marriage. In 1761 there appeared a translation from the Chinese edited by him. He undertook editions of the works of the Duke of Buckingham and the Earl of Surrey, which were printed, but never published. In 1763 he issued some translations of Icelandic runic poetry and, in 1765, his *Reliques of Ancient English Poetry*. The latter was Percy's *magnum opus*, of tremendous importance to antiquaries and poets alike. Forty-five of the poems were drawn from an old manuscript which he had rescued from destruction at a friend's house in Shropshire, probably while still in his teens. The other poems were drawn from many sources, both manuscript and printed, discovered by Percy and his friends.

After the publication of the *Reliques* Percy became famous and sought after. He had dedicated the work to the Duchess of Northumberland—a Percy—and in 1766 was made tutor to her younger son and chaplain to the Duke. He had to attend on the family at Alnwick and London, leaving his wife and children at Easton Maudit. In 1768 he edited *The Household Book of the Earl of Northumberland in 1512*, which prompted the publication by others of many similar documents valuable to the social historian.

Percy became chaplain to King George III in 1769; his wife was already nurse to the young Duke of Kent. He now spent about eight months of every year in London and was an important member of the "Club" founded by Reynolds, to which he was elected in 1768. Dr. Johnson and Percy were good friends, but once had a famous quarrel which Boswell patched up; Percy's best friend among the Club members was Oliver Goldsmith.

THOMAS PERCY

In 1770 Percy became a D.D. of Cambridge. He was appointed dean of Carlisle in 1778 and bishop of Dromore, Ireland, in 1782. He moved his family to Carlisle in 1780, but retained his Northamptonshire livings until 1782. The next move took the Percys to the small town of Dromore, County Down, where the episcopal palace was Percy's home for the rest of his life.

Percy's religious tolerance made him popular in Ireland and he came through the Rebellion of 1798 unscathed. He voted for the Union of Ireland with England in 1800. In 1783 his only son Henry died of consumption. Percy's hopes now centered on his nephew, Thomas, who edited the fourth edition of the *Reliques* in 1794, and died in 1808.

Percy's eyesight had been bad all his life and began to fail completely in 1803. In 1806 his wife died and was buried in Dromore Cathedral. He himself lived five years longer and was buried beside her. Of his nine children, two daughters survived him.

Portraits of Percy show a long, lean, rather aristocratic face with a quizzical mouth. He was decidedly tactless and hot-tempered in his youth; in later years he bore the loss of his sight, and of all those he held most dear, with truly Christian resignation.

Percy was a scholar rather than a man of letters; he loved research for its own sake and seemed reluctant to publish. Genealogy was almost a mania with him. His own poetic talent was of a very minor order, but his rediscovery of older English poetry was destined to inspire the poets of the Romantic revival in Germany as well as England.

PRINCIPAL WORKS: *Original*: O Nancy will you go with me? (Dodsley's Collection of Poems, Vol. VI) 1758; A Key to the New Testament, 1766; The Hermit of Warkworth, a Northumberland Ballad, 1771; An Essay on the Origin of the English Stage, 1793; Memoir of Goldsmith, 1801. *Edited or Translated*: Hau Kiou Choaan, or The Pleasing History, 1761; Miscellaneous Pieces Relating to the Chinese, 1762; Five Pieces of Runic Poetry, 1763; The Song of Solomon Newly Translated, 1764; Reliques of Ancient English Poetry, 1765; The Household Book of the Earl of Northumberland in 1512, 1768; Northern Antiquities, with a Translation of the Edda and Other Pieces from the Ancient Icelandic Tongue, 1770; Bishop Percy's Folio MS (J. W. Hales and F. J. Furnivall, eds.) 1867-68.

ABOUT: Gaussen, A. C. C. Percy: Prelate and Poet; Percy, T. Percy Letters: The Correspondence of Thomas Percy and Richard Farmer.

PERCY, WILLIAM (1575-May 1648), poet, dramatist, was the son of Henry Percy, eighth Earl of Northumberland, born probably at Topcliffe near Thirsk, Yorkshire. As a student at Gloucester Hall, Oxford, he became friendly with Barnabe Barnes, the son of the bishop of Durham. When Barnes published a sonnet sequence in 1593, Percy hastened to follow his example and a year later published a collection of twenty poems, *Sonnets to the Fairest Coelia*. Although he promised in his preface "ere long to impart unto the world another poem more fruitful and ponderous," the promise was apparently never fulfilled; the only other verse attributed to Percy is a madrigal printed in Barnes' *Foure Books of Offices*.

Percy was also the author of six plays which exist in manuscript, two of which were printed for the Roxburghe Club in 1824: *The Cuck-Queanes and Cuckolds Errant, or The Bearing Down the Inn*, a prose comedy, and *The Fairy Pastoral, or Forest of Elves*, in blank verse. The four unpublished plays were entitled *Arabia Sitiens, or A Dream of a Dry Year*; *The Aphrodisial or Sea Feast*; *A Country's Tragedy in Vacuniam, or Cupid's Sacrifice*; and *Necromantes, or The Two Supposed Heads*. Percy's plays, apparently intended for amateur production by the children of St. Paul's, show none of the skill one would expect from even a second-rate professional dramatist.

Little is known of Percy's life, although it apparently followed a troubled course. The records show that he was once committed to the Tower on a charge of homicide, and after 1638 he seems to have lived in obscurity at Oxford "drinking nothing but ale." He died "an aged bachelor" in Pennyfarthing Street, after he had lived a melancholy and retired life many years. His plays have been completely forgotten; his verse is remembered only as an example of some of the worst features of the Elizabethan school of sonneteering.

PRINCIPAL WORKS: Sonnets to the Fairest Coelia, 1594 (Sir S. Lee, ed. *in* Elizabethan Sonnets, 1904); The Cuck-Queanes and Cuckolds Errant, or The Bearing Down the Inn (J. Haslewood, ed.) 1824; The Fairy Pastoral, or Forest of Elves (J. Haslewood, ed.) 1824.

ABOUT: Fleay, F. G. Biographical Chronicle of the English Drama; Ritson, J. Bibliographia Anglo-Poetica; Scott, J. G. Les Sonnets Élisabéthains.

PETTIE, GEORGE (1548-July 1589),

writer of romances, was the son of John Le Petitie, or Pettie, of Oxfordshire, and Mary Charnell. He entered Christ Church, Oxford, in 1564 and took his B.A. five years later. At the university he was a close friend of William Gager, the Latin dramatist, who encouraged his literary ambitions.

After several years of foreign travel and a period of military service abroad, Pettie published *A Petite Pallace of Pettie His Pleasure*, which was modeled on William Painter's extremely successful *The Palace of Pleasure*. Apparently his publisher, Richard Watkins, and not Pettie himself, was responsible for the close similarity in titles. The book was a collection of twelve "pretie Hystories," adaptations of familiar classical stories to the contemporary taste, which became widely popular and went through a number of editions. Pettie also published a translation from the French of Guazzo's *Civile Conversation*.

Pettie's brother, Robert, became the father of Mary Pettie whose son was Anthony à Wood.[qv] Writing of his granduncle's work, Wood says Pettie "was as much commended for his neat style as any of his time," but in Wood's own opinion *A Petite Pallace* was "so far from being excellent or fine that it is more fit to be read by a schoolboy or a rustical amorata than by a gentleman of mode and learning." Actually Wood's judgment seems to the modern critic unduly harsh. Pettie was interested in the enrichment of the English language, and while his work is of no great importance in itself, the romances of the *Petite Pallace* introduced certain structural and ornamental characteristics which undoubtedly influenced Lyly and the whole school of Euphuism.

Pettie died, according to Wood, "in the prime of his years, at Plymouth, being then a captain and a man of note."

PRINCIPAL WORKS: A Petite Pallace of Pettie His Pleasure: Contayning Many Pretie Hystories By Him Set Foorth in Comely Colours and Most Delightfully Discoursed, 1576 (Sir I. Gollancz, ed. 1908; H. Miles, ed. 1930); The Civile Conversation of M. Steeven Guazzo (tr.) 1581 (Sir E. Sullivan, ed. *in* Tudor Translations, 1925).

ABOUT: Pettie, G. Preface to A Petite Pallace; Wood, A. à, Athenae Oxonienses; Wood, A. à, Life and Times (A. Clark, ed.).

PETTY, Sir WILLIAM (May 26, 1623-

December 16, 1687), political economist, was born at Romsey, Hampshire, where his father was a clothier. At the Romsey grammar school he displayed an early taste for mathematics and applied mechanics, but left school at an early age to go to sea. Apparently his fellow seamen disliked him for his learning and he found himself deserted on the French coast with a broken leg. After his recovery he remained in France, studying at the Jesuit College in Caen. Later he studied medicine at Leyden, and with several years of travel behind him, returned to England.

In London he won a somewhat spectacular reputation for reviving the corpse of a woman hanged for murder and pronounced dead. This led to his appointment as a fellow of Brasenose College in 1649, and two years later as deputy professor of anatomy at Oxford. In 1654 he was sent to Ireland as an army physician and there undertook for the Commonwealth a survey of lands forfeited in 1641. The resulting "Down Survey" completed in thirteen months, was the first attempt at a large-scale, scientific survey, and in every way a remarkable accomplishment.

Petty bought an estate in county Kerry where he set up several business enterprises, and acted as commissioner of distribution for the lands he had surveyed. He also acted as secretary to Henry Cromwell, clerk of council, judge of Admiralty for Ireland, and in 1658 was elected to Richard Cromwell's parliament. After the Restoration, so solid was his position that Charles II received him favorably and eventually knighted him. During this period he profited by several inventions (a manifold letter-writer, a double-bottomed ship), all of which seem to have proved themselves practical. He was also a founder of the Royal Society, to which he contributed a number of papers on economic matters.

With all this bewildering versatile array of accomplishment, Sir William's real importance was as a pioneer in the science of comparative statistics, or what he liked to call "political arithmetic." He was the first to apply the quantitative method to social data, such as vital statistics on Ireland amassed during his survey. He was among the first political economists to study the origin of wealth, in his *Treatise of Taxes and Contributions* stating the doctrine that value and price depend on the labor necessary for production. He had, moreover, extraordinarily advanced ideas on money, on rent, on free trade, and a truly statesmanlike understanding of the real strength of a nation. Along with Thomas Hobbes, who became his intimate friend, Petty set one of the foundation stones for the modern school of political economy.

PRINCIPAL WORKS: Reflections Upon Some Persons and Things in Ireland, 1660; A Treatise of Taxes and Contributions, 1662; Sir William Petty's Quantulumcumque Concerning Money, 1682; Observations Upon the Dublin Bills of Mortality, 1683; An Essay Concerning the Multiplication of Mankind, 1686; Five Essays in Political Arithmetick, 1687; Political Arithmetick, 1690; The Political Anatomy of Ireland, 1691; The Economic Writings of Sir William Petty (C. H. Hall, ed.) 1899.

ABOUT: Aubrey, J. Brief Lives; Fitzmaurice, Lord. Life of Sir W. Petty; Wood, A. à, Athenae Oxonienses.

PHAER or PHAYER, THOMAS (1510?-August 1560), translator, writer on law and medicine, was probably the son of Thomas Phaer of Norwich. He received his education at Oxford and at Lincoln's Inn, entering the law and practicing with considerable success. Later in life he also studied medicine, taking an M.D. at Oxford in 1558 or 1559.

Phaer was the author of two handbooks popularizing contemporary legal methods, *Natura Brevium*, published in 1535, and *Newe Boke of Presidentes . . . in Maner of a Register*, published in 1543. His efforts in this field were rewarded by an appointment as solicitor in the court of the Welsh marches. In 1544 he published a popular medical treatise, *The Regiment of Life*, which was derived from the French *Regimen Sanitatis Salerni* translated by Thomas Paynell some years before. Phaer added considerable material of his own: a dissertation on the pestilence, on the veins and related diseases, and *A Book of Children*. With this work he claimed to have first made medical science intelligible to Englishmen in their own language.

Living in Kilgerran (Cilgerran) Forest with his wife, Ann, and three daughters, Phaer continued to practice both law and medicine, spending his leisure time in writing. His most important contribution to English literature was a translation of Virgil's *Aeneid*. While he was not much of a poet, he was the first Englishman to attempt a complete translation of Virgil and for twenty years, until Stanyhurst published a new translation, Phaer's version enjoyed considerable prestige. He died after translating the first nine books and part of the tenth, a labor which occupied him for five years. The translation was completed by Thomas Twyne in 1584.

PRINCIPAL WORKS: Natura Brevium, 1535; A Boke of Presidentes Exactelye Written in Maner of a Register, 1543; The Regiment of Lyfe, 1544; The Seven First Bookes of the Eneidos of Virgill, 1558; The Nyne Fyrst Bookes of the Eneidos With So Much of the Tenthe Booke As Could Be Founde (W. Wightman, ed.) 1562.

ABOUT: Fuller, T. The Worthies of England; Phillips, J. R. History of Cilgerran; Wood, A. à, Athenae Oxonienses.

PHILIPS, AMBROSE (1675?-June 18, 1749), poet, was born in Shropshire of a Leicestershire family. There was a Sir Ambrose Philips, serjeant-at-law, who may or may not have been his father. He was educated at Shrewbury, and in 1693 entered St. John's College, Cambridge, as a sizar. He graduated B.A. in 1696, M.A. 1700, and was a fellow of the college from 1699 until he resigned his fellowship in 1708. Up to that time he had lived in Cambridge; now he moved to London and began a career to advance himself. He became a sort of pet or protégé of Addison and Steele and their Whig circle, which embroiled him in what Dr. Johnson called "a perpetual reciprocation of malevolence" with Gay and Pope and their Tory friends. Pope ridiculed him in the *Dunciad* and Philips retorted, to his own discredit, by publicly threatening to beat the dwarfed and crippled little "wasp of Twickenham."

Philips' desire to please won him some solid favors from the Whigs. In 1714 he was made justice of the peace for Westminster, in 1717 commissioner of the lottery, and in 1724 he accompanied the new bishop of Armagh to Ireland, where he became a member of the Irish Parliament, secretary to the Lord Chancellor in 1726, and judge

After M. Ashton, 1735
AMBROSE PHILIPS

of the prerogative court (though he was not a lawyer) in 1733. He returned to London in 1748, and the next year died of a stroke.

Swift, who was once Philips' friend, spoke of him as "poor pastoral Philips," who was "party mad." He was a dandified, pompous man, who took criticism very ill. His nickname of "Namby Pamby" came from his sentimental poems to the infant children of the noblemen he wooed for patronage. But though he was tedious, cloyingly sweet and arch, frigid and frequently mawkish, Philips had a real feeling for verbal music and real sensibility. He was harmed rather than helped by Steel's injudicious overpraise in the *Guardian.* He had some scholarship; he translated Sappho, Pindar, and Anacreon; and in 1723 he published one of the earliest collections of old English ballads. He began writing English verse in Cambridge, had his *Epistle to Lord Dorset* in the *Tatler* in 1709, and the next year his pastorals appeared with Pope's in Tonson's *Miscellany.*

In 1718 and 1719 Philips edited a weekly paper in imitation of the *Spectator,* called the *Freethinker*—though he was careful to explain in the first issue that the name had no religious or irreligious connotations. He was secretary of the Hanover Club, an organization which advocated the succession of George I, and seems to have been quite sincere, though with an eye to his own welfare, in his extreme partisanship. He wrote three verse tragedies, only one of which had any success—*The Distrest Mother,* a version of Racine's *Andromaque.* (This is the play to which old Sir Roger was taken by his friend in *The Sir Roger de Coverley Papers.*)

PRINCIPAL WORKS: Life of John Williams (abridged from Bishop Hacket) 1700; The 1001 Days: Persian Tales (tr. from the French of F. Pétit de la Croix) 1709; Pastorals and Other Poems (*in* Tonson's Miscellany) 1710; The Distrest Mother (tragedy) 1712; On the Accession of George I (verse) 1714; Epistle to James Craggs (verse) 1717; The Briton (tragedy) 1722; Humfrey, Duke of Gloucester (tragedy) 1723; Pastorals, Epistles, Odes, and Poems, 1748.

ABOUT: Cibber, T. The Lives of the Poets of Great Britain and Ireland; Johnson, S. Lives of the English Poets; Saintsbury, G. A History of English Prosody.

PHILIPS, JOHN (December 30, 1676-February 15, 1709), poet, was born at Bampton, Oxfordshire, the son of Mary Cook and Stephen Philips, archdeacon of Shropshire and vicar of Bampton. John went to school at Winchester and entered Christ Church, Oxford, in 1697. There he became known as a wit as well as a scholar, and along with his best friend, Edmund Smith (called "Captain Rag, the handsome sloven"), he flouted college regulations the while he wrote promising verse, winning for himself great personal popularity.

Abandoning his earlier intention to go into medicine, Philips devoted all his time to poetry, although he was slow to publish. His first poem, *The Splendid Shilling,* is probably also his most famous. Written in facetious imitation of Milton's lofty blank verse, the poem opens "Happy the Man, who void of Cares and Strife,/ In Silken, or in Leathern Purse retains/ A Splendid Shilling . . ." and proceeds to ring a series of witty and unexpected changes on its small and shining subject. Addison (with perhaps somewhat rash enthusiasm) called it "the finest burlesque poem in the British language." Other admirers were Robert Harley and Henry St. John of the Tory government. So great, indeed, was the fame won by this first poem that its author was employed by the Tories to write acclamatory verses on the battle of Blenheim, with far less happy results. The poem *Blenheim,* published in 1705, attempted to make serious use of Milton's style and resulted in a kind of unconscious burlesque which added nothing to Philips' reputation.

Probably his best work is the long poem *Cyder*, written in light-hearted imitation of the *Georgics* and celebrating the joys of country life. In its love of nature and the concrete details of rural pleasures *Cyder* foreshadows the work of James Thomson. The body of Philips' work is slight, but he holds a position of some importance in the history of English literature as the first poet after Milton to reintroduce blank verse, rebelling against the heroic couplet of the period. Philips did not live long enough to carry out his more ambitious plans and his best work remains that in the vein of parody. He died of consumption and asthma at thirty-three at his mother's house in Hereford.

PRINCIPAL WORKS: The Splendid Shilling, 1705; Blenheim, 1705; Cyder, A Poem in Two Books, 1708; Poems By Mr. John Philips (J. Sewell, ed.) 1712; Poems of John Philips (M. G. Lloyd Thomas, ed.) 1927.

ABOUT: de Maar, H. A History of Modern English Romanticism; Johnson, S. The Lives of the Poets; Lloyd Thomas, M. G. Introduction to Poems; Sewell, J. Life, *in* Poems.

PHILIPS, KATHERINE (January 1, 1631-June 22, 1664), called the "matchless Orinda," founder of a literary salon, author of verse, was born in Bucklesbury, London, the daughter of John Fowler, a merchant, and Katherine Oxenbridge. She received her first education from a cousin, and was sent to boarding school at eight. At sixteen she married her stepbrother, James Philips; her father had died and her mother had married Hector Philips, of The Priory, Cardiganshire, Wales. Her life thereafter was spent between Wales and London. Her first publication was a verse prefixed to the poems of Henry Vaughan in 1651, and it is from this date that she began to be well known. In both Cardigan and London she conducted literary salons, and her friends included such people as Jeremy Taylor, Cowley, and Vaughan. In 1666 she visited Ireland in connection with her husband's claim to some lands there, and again made for herself a circle of admiring friends. It was the custom in all these groups to use fanciful names by which they addressed one another, and Mrs. Philips' was Orinda; it was Dryden who added the "matchless."

MRS. KATHERINE PHILIPS

In 1663 her translation of Corneille's *Pompée* was produced in Dublin; she also translated part of the same dramatist's *Horace*. An unauthorized edition of her poems was brought out in 1664, much to her annoyance, and she secured their withdrawal. Soon after, she died of smallpox, in London, leaving her husband and a son and daughter. An authorized edition of the poems came out posthumously.

Mrs. Philips was one of the earliest women in England to receive recognition as a poet. Much of the admiration accorded her was on the principle of Dr. Johnson's dancing dog—not that she did it so well, but that she did it at all; nevertheless she did have talent if not much power. Nearly all her poems were addressed to women friends, usually under their "salon names." Saintsbury speaks of their "curious 'magic music' of sound and echo and atmosphere." Her letters to Sir Charles Cotterel, a member of her group, display ability and wit, and give an excellent picture of mid-seventeenth century literary society. She was imitative and derivative, but she was a pioneer. As a person she seems to have been independent and forthright, no submerged appendage to a husband as were most women of her time, though not an open feminist like the slightly later Mary Astell. Though she lived through the civil war and the Commonwealth, she appears to have been completely unaffected

409

by political affairs, and her salons continued, untouched by war and revolution.

PRINCIPAL WORKS: Pompey (tr. from the French of P. Corneille) 1663; Poems by the Incomparable Mrs K. P., 1664; Poems, 1667; Letters of Orinda to Poliarchus (Sir Charles Cotterel) 1705-1709; Selected Poems (L. I. Guiney, ed.) 1904.

ABOUT: Gosse, E. 17th Century Studies; Saintsbury, G. Minor Poets of the Caroline Period; Souers, P. W. The Matchless Orinda.

PHILLIPS, EDWARD (1630-1696?),
critic, miscellaneous writer, nephew of John Milton, was born in London. His mother, Ann, was Milton's only sister, and his father, Edward Phillips, was an official of the crown office in court of chancery. After the death of the senior Phillips, his widow married Thomas Agar, her husband's successor in the crown office, and both Edward and his younger brother, John, were brought up and educated by Milton. Edward went to Oxford in 1650 but left without a degree to make a living as a hack writer in London.

The most interesting thing about Phillips was probably his relation to Milton, with whom he maintained an intimate connection, although his religious, political, and moral views diverged widely from those of his early training. He was privileged to read *Paradise Lost* in manuscript as it was written, and was first to praise it in print. From Milton's papers and notes he drew nearly all his own critical judgments and in later years he became the chief original source of information about his uncle.

Edward Phillips' most important work was the *Theatrum Poetarum*, published after Milton's death, a list of the chief poets of all ages and countries, particularly English poets, with short critical notes. The excellent prefatory *Discourse of the Poets and Poetry* is usually ascribed to Milton. He also published *A New World of Words, or A General Dictionary*, a wandering excursion into the field of lexicography; a translation of Milton's *Letters of State* with a valuable memoir; and an entertaining but frequently licentious piece, *The Mysteries of Love and Eloquence*.

John Evelyn, the diarist, whose son Phillips tutored for several years, described him as "a sober, silent, and most harmless person." Wood, on the other hand, gives a lengthy but by no means flattering account of both Edward and John Phillips. According to Wood, Edward eventually "married a woman with several children, taught school in the Strand, lived in poor condition, though a good master; wrote and translated several things merely to get a bare livelihood." He died in obscurity sometime after the publication of the fifth edition of his *World of Words* in 1696.

PRINCIPAL WORKS: A New World of Words, or A General Dictionary, 1658; Theatrum Poetarum, Together With a Prefatory Discourse of the Poets and Poetry In Generall, 1675 (Sir S. E. Brydges, ed. 1800); The Mysteries of Love and Eloquence, 1685.

ABOUT: Evelyn, J. Diary; Godwin, W. Lives of Edward and John Phillips; Wood, A. à, Athenae Oxonienses.

PHILLIPS, JOHN (1631-1706), miscellaneous writer, translator, editor, was the posthumous son of Edward Phillips, and a nephew and godson of John Milton. With his elder brother, Edward, he was educated by Milton, who took over the training of both boys after the death of their father.

John acted as assistant to his uncle while Milton served as Latin secretary to Cromwell, and precociously put his classical training to work with the publication in 1649 of a treatise on learning Latin. Three years later his *Pro Rege et Populo Anglicano*, a defense of Milton in reply to an anonymous attack, first revealed the controversial spirit and slashing wit which were to become his stock-in-trade as a tireless pamphleteer.

Revolting against the strict discipline of his uncle's household, Phillips wrote a scathing satire on Puritanism, *Satyr Against Hypocrites*, which made his reputation and enabled him to earn a livelihood. A collection of bawdy verse edited by Phillips, *Sportive Wit, The Muses' Merriment*, involved him along with his publisher in charges of having produced a licentious book, and served to estrange him entirely from his uncle. He also wrote *Montelion, or The Prophetical Almanack*, a burlesque of the astrological almanacs of William Lilly in which he ridiculed anti-monarchical views; and *Maronides, or Virgil Travestie*, an extremely witty Hudibrastic burlesque of the fifth and sixth books of the *Aeneid*.

An untiring and able linquist, Phillips translated, in whole or part, works of Grelot, Plutarch, Lucian, Tavernier and others; the best known is the spirited but irreverent and inaccurate translation of *Don Quixote*.

As editor, and for the most part author, of *Modern History or A Monthly Account of All Considerable Occurrences,* and a similar periodical translated from the French, *The Present State of Europe,* he added to the more respectable side of his literary reputation.

Phillips again brought disgrace on himself when he was hired by the infamous Titus Oates to vindicate Oates' part in the so-called "popish plot." Apparently both his political and his moral views shifted with expedience, but his mind and his pen remained sharp under all masters. Shortly before his death Phillips was described by John Dunton as a gentleman of great learning who would "write you a design off in a very little time if the gout and claret don't stop him."

PRINCIPAL WORKS: Joannis Philippi Angli Responsio ad Apologiam Anonymi Cujusdam Tenebrionis Pro Rege Et Populo Anglicano Infantissimam, 1652; A Satyr Against Hypocrites, 1655; Sportive Wit, The Muses' Merriment (ed.) 1656; Montelion or The Prophetical Almanack, 1660; Maronides or Virgil Travestie, 1672-73; Dr. Oates's Narrative of the Popish Plot Vindicated, 1680; Modern History or A Monthly Account of All Considerable Occurrences, 1687-89; The Present State of Europe, or the Historical and Political Monthly Mercury, 1690-1706.

ABOUT: Darbishire, H. The Early Lives of Milton; Godwin, J. The Lives of Edward and John Phillips; Wood, A. à, Athenae Oxonienses.

"PINDAR, PETER." See WOLCOT, JOHN

PIOZZI, Mrs. HESTER LYNCH THRALE,

(January 16, 1741-May 2, 1821), author of *Anecdotes of the Late Samuel Johnson,* was born at Bodvel, Carnarvonshire, the only child of John Salusbury and his wife Hester Cotton. Her parents quarreled constantly, but were both devoted to her in their different ways. Her father, hot tempered to the point of insanity, had few methods for supporting his family other than waiting for his relatives to die and leave him their money. Two attempts to seek his fortune—in Nova Scotia and in Ireland—were failures; meanwhile his wife looked for a suitable husband for Hester. The man she chose was Henry Thrale, a brewer of low birth and considerable wealth who had been educated at Eton and Oxford. He was fifteen years older than Hester and by no means in love with her. Hester and Henry finally married in 1763, but not before John Salusbury had dropped dead in one of his fits of rage and anxiety about the marriage.

Thrale was cold, kind, and unfaithful to Hester; he occupied himself chiefly with his brewery, which had its ups and downs. Hester bore him twelve children, of whom five daughters lived, and set up a little salon for literary men and musicians in his house at Streatham. She met Dr. Johnson in 1764 and soon became his closest friend. When Thrale died in 1781, leaving her wealthy and free, many people expected her to marry Johnson. The man who won her heart, however, was an Italian music teacher of her own age named Gabriel Piozzi, a Roman Catholic. By September or October 1782 she was passionately in love with him. None of her friends or children approved of the match, and early in 1783 she said good-by to Piozzi and sent him back to Italy. After a year of separation, she was in such bad health that her eldest daughter relented, Piozzi was recalled, and they were married in July 1784. Hester's health at once recovered and they lived very happily together, first in Italy and then in England, until his death in 1809. They adopted a nephew of his under the name of John Piozzi Salusbury, who became the sole heir of both. Mrs. Piozzi lived on for another twelve years, retaining to the end her enormous

G. Dance, 1793
MRS. HESTER LYNCH THRALE PIOZZI

vitality and her capacity for giving rise to gossip.

Hester was four feet eleven in height, with chestnut hair, a good complexion, a prominent nose, large gray eyes, and an extremely intelligent and vivacious expression. She might not have been beautiful, but she was unmistakably alive. It is not at all surprising that a woman of her temperament, who had made a loveless first marriage, should fall passionately in love at forty-one and inspire love in return.

She was well educated in a scattered sort of way and worthy to be the friend of intellectual men and women, but her writings are of little value as literature. They are read for the light they throw on two fascinating personalities—Dr. Johnson and herself.

PRINCIPAL WORKS: Anecdotes of the Late Samuel Johnson, 1786; Letters to and from the Late Samuel Johnson, 1788; Observations and Reflections Made in the Course of a Journey through France, Italy and Germany, 1789; British Synonymy, 1794; Retrospection, 1801; Thraliana, the Diary of Mrs. Hester Lynch Thrale (K. C. Balderson, ed.) 1942.

ABOUT: Clifford, J. L. Hester Lynch Piozzi; Vulliamy, C. E. Mrs. Thrale of Streatham.

POMFRET, JOHN (1667-November 1702), poet, was born at Luton, Bedfordshire. His mother was Catherine Dobson and his father was Thomas Pomfret, vicar of Luton, presumed to be the author of *Life of Lady Christian, Dowager Countess of Devonshire.* John became a student at the Bedford grammar school and at Queens' College, Cambridge, where he graduated B.A. in 1686, and M.A. four years later.

Taking holy orders, Pomfret was given the rectory of Maulden in Bedfordshire, and later of Millbrook. He first began to write poetry with an elegy on the death of Queen Mary, which was published in 1699 along with a number of other pieces as *Poems on Several Occasions.* A year later he won sudden fame with the publication of *The Choice: A Poem Written By a Person of Quality. The Choice* is an exposition in neat verse of the epicurean tastes of a cultivated man of the day. It is not easy to understand why it became so popular, widely anthologized throughout the eighteenth and even the nineteenth century. Like Lady Winchilsea,[qv] to whose verse his may be compared, he was greatly overpraised in his own time. When Dr. Johnson was approached by

the booksellers on the scheme for *Lives of the Poets,* Pomfret was one of three poets added by Johnson as "a favorite of readers."

Pomfret was recommended to the bishop of London for preferment, but a line from *The Choice,* in which the poet frankly declared his wish to "have no wife," so displeased the bishop that his preferment was refused. Pomfret's wife was Elizabeth Wingate, whom he married in 1692, and by whom he had a son who became rougecroix - pursuivant - of - arms. Pomfret died while still in his thirties and was buried at Maulden on December 1, 1702.

Although his poems were frequently reprinted and widely read, they are largely forgotten today. He is interesting only as an example of "the cultivated, poetizing, archaeologizing, chess-playing divines of the eighteenth century."

PRINCIPAL WORKS: Poems on Several Occasions, 1699; The Choice, A Poem Written By A Person of Quality, 1700; A Prospect of Death, 1700; Reason, 1700; Miscellany Poems on Several Occasions, 1702.

ABOUT: Johnson, S. Lives of the Poets; Kellett, E. E. Pomfret's Choice, in Reconsiderations.

POPE, ALEXANDER (May 21, 1688-May 30, 1744), poet, translator of Homer, editor of Shakespeare, was born in Lombard Street, London, the only child of Alexander Pope, a prosperous linen merchant, and his second wife Edith Turner. Both parents were Roman Catholics; the poet's paternal grandfather was a Church of England clergyman; we do not know the date or occasion of the father's conversion to Catholicism.

The year 1688 was a bad one for English Catholics; the Catholic James II was driven from his throne, to be succeeded by the Protestant William III. Pope's father is believed to have retired from business that year and moved to Hammersmith; in 1698 he bought a small house and estate at Binfield in Windsor Forest, to which the family moved about 1700; the old gentleman had an adequate income from investments and devoted the rest of his life to gardening.

The future poet had little regular education; an aunt taught him to read; he began Greek and Latin with a priest named Banister or Taverner; at the age of eight he went to a Catholic school at Twyford near Winchester; unhappy there, he was brought nearer home to Thomas Deane's school in London. When the family went to Binfield, Pope left school for good. Except for some lessons from a priest at Binfield, he was self-educated thereafter, until when nearly fifteen he went to London for lessons in French and Italian; he quickly learned to read these languages, but could not speak them.

Pope was a healthy child, but between twelve and sixteen his health deteriorated rapidly; a tubercular condition known as Pott's disease was the cause; too much study and too little fresh air and exercise aggravated it; he was very near death when some sensible medical advice enabled him to check the progress of the disease. His growth, however, had been stunted and curvature of the spine had set in; he was never more than four feet six in height, and grew steadily more hump-backed. His face was handsome —particularly the big, expressive eyes—but the lines of strain about the mouth became more pronounced with the years.

Pope took to poetry very early—certainly before the age of twelve—and was encouraged by his father and by a Binfield neighbor, Sir William Trumbull, a former Secretary of State. In 1705 the Chevalier Wogan, a fellow Catholic, introduced him to London literary society at Will's coffee-house. There he met the survivors of Dryden's circle, including the dramatists Wycherley and Congreve and the poet Walsh. Wycherley particularly admired his talents; Walsh (d. 1708) helped him to revise his poems and advised him to aim at "correctness" in poetry.

Pope's genius was recognized quickly, not only by writers, but by the bookseller Tonson, who made an offer for his *Pastorals* as early as 1706. These poems, which Pope claimed to have written in 1704, were finally published in Tonson's sixth *Miscellany*, 1709. The *Essay on Criticism*, his first separate publication, appeared two years later; it was praised by Addison in the *Spectator*, and established Pope's reputation once and for all. The first version of *The Rape of the Lock* quickly followed and, in 1713, *Windsor Forest*. The favorable references to the forthcoming Peace of Utrecht in the latter poem were the first public announcement of Pope's Tory politics. He already was a leading member, with Swift and Gay, of the

W. Hoare (?)
ALEXANDER POPE

Scriblerus Club, a Tory group of writers formed in opposition to Addison's Whig circle at Button's. The friendship between Pope and Addison, never very warm, rapidly cooled under the influence of party politics.

The second phase of Pope's literary career began in October 1713, when he issued proposals for his translation of the *Iliad*, to be published by subscription. Nearly six hundred subscribers were forthcoming, Whigs as well as Tories; Pope made over £5000 by the work, but the translation and notes took him longer than he expected; the first volume appeared in 1715, the sixth and last in 1720.

In 1718, thanks to the success of his translation, Pope was able to lease his famous villa and garden at Twickenham, where he and his mother lived the rest of their lives. His father had died in 1717, aged seventy-one; his mother died in 1733, aged ninety-one. Pope was a model son of them both.

Having completed the *Iliad*, he undertook an edition of Shakespeare with introduction and notes. This appeared in 1725. He completed his version of Homer by bringing out the *Odyssey*, of which he had translated only half; this kept him hard at work until 1725.

Pope by now had an assured income of £800 a year; the subscriptions to the *Odyssey* had brought in almost as much as those to the *Iliad*. For the rest of his life he wrote only to please himself; though the Tories went out of power in 1714 and never regained it in Pope's lifetime, his ability placed him above politics; he was free to honor his old friends the Tory Ministers Oxford and Bolingbroke; he could ask favors from the Whig Prime Minister Walpole or criticize him, as he pleased.

Pope's career as a satirist now really begins; the first version of *The Dunciad*, in which he pilloried all the minor writers who had attacked him, appeared in 1728. A fourth "book" was added in 1742, and the final version came out in 1743. The "hero" of the first version was Theobald, a better, if duller, Shakespeare scholar than Pope; his place was taken in the last version by Colley Cibber, a talented actor and dramatist but a very feeble poet, who had incurred Pope's wrath by being made Poet Laureate. The fourth book of *The Dunciad*, in which Dulness triumphs over Learning, Literature, Law, Church and State, is by far the most readable part of the poem today.

Pope expounded his theological and moral beliefs in the *Essay on Man*; the later *Moral Essays* (or *Ethic Epistles*) and *Satires* can be regarded as practical applications of the theories set forth there; they are, of course, much more entertaining than the *Essay on Man*. Nevertheless, that *Essay* was Pope's most ambitious original poem; no student of his work can afford to pass it by.

Pope's later career is one of diminishing activity and growing ill health. Except for the fourth book of the *Dunciad*, he wrote no original poetry after 1738, but revised and corrected his earlier work with the help of Warburton. From the beginning of May 1744, it was clear that his death was approaching. Spence, his Boswell, watched over him, and Bolingbroke visited him regularly. He received the last rites of the Catholic Church and died peacefully. He was buried at Twickenham near his father and mother.

In analyzing Pope's complex and much discussed character, one has to distinguish very carefully between his private friendships and his literary ones. The former were lifelong and unshakable, the latter temporary and subject to sudden change.

Among his literary friendships, those with Wycherley and Addison were ill fated; the older men admired Pope's talents, and he theirs; elaborate compliments were exchanged on paper, but temperamental affinity was lacking. Politics was the real cause of the breach with Addison; but when he supported Tickell's translation of the *Iliad* against Pope's, Pope felt that any revenge was justified; the lines on Atticus were the result. Pope's "affair" with Lady Mary Wortley Montagu was mainly a matter of literature; he admired her intelligence and wrote her complimentary letters; when he tried to make love to her she laughed at him; because his affection for her was not very real, he afterwards was able to caricature her as Sappho in *Of the Characters of Women*.

His literary enmities had no sounder basis than his literary friendships; any fool, he felt, was a natural enemy. Thus, he made unkind remarks about the critic Dennis in his *Essay on Criticism* without having any personal spite against him; when Dennis replied bitterly, Pope was stung, and from then on his animosity was personal. Theobald became an enemy by criticizing Pope's edition of Shakespeare; many lesser men met a similar fate for similar reasons. In other words, Pope would enter a friendship or a quarrel on intellectual grounds; then his very sensitive feelings would be hurt and one more would be added to the number whom he regarded as personal enemies.

Typical of his many personal friendships, on the other hand, is his life-long one with Martha Blount; he met her when they were both about nineteen; she was a Catholic and very fond of Pope, yet she refused to marry him because of his appearance; he never quarreled with her as he did with Lady Mary; when he died he left her most of his estate, though in his last years she had not treated him very well.

Some of Pope's literary friends became his personal friends, too. He was always loyal to Swift and Gay, and helped the latter financially. After Thomas Parnell's death he edited and published his *Poems*, 1721.

Pope's snobbish love for lords and ladies, his readiness to attack anyone who criticized him, his vanity, and the constant attendance he demanded from friends and servants, must all be seen against the background of his physical deformity and ill health. To a modern observer the wonder is, not that he had so many failings, but that he had so few.

Pope's reputation as a poet, which stood next after Shakespeare, Milton and Dryden in the eighteenth century, suffered severely in the nineteenth. He has now been restored to a place not so very far below his former one. The best modern assessment of his genius is F. R. Leavis'. His poetry other than satirical may be summed up in his own line:

> What oft was thought, but ne'er
> so well expressed.

His satirical poems and *The Rape of the Lock* are the best things of their kind in the English language. As Mr. Leavis points out, it is not the bitterness of the satires which is admirable, but their consummate grace and skill. The *Epistle to Dr. Arbuthnot* is regarded by most modern critics as the best example of Pope's satirical powers.

PRINCIPAL WORKS: *Poems*: An Essay on Criticism, 1711; Windsor Forest, 1713; The Rape of the Lock, 1714; The Temple of Fame, 1715; Verses to the Memory of an Unfortunate Lady, Eloisa to Abelard (Works) 1717; The Dunciad, 1728; An Essay on Man, 1733; An Epistle to Dr. Arbuthnot, 1735; Of the Characters of Women, 1735; The Works of Mr. Alexander Pope, Containing his Epistles and Satires, 1737; Poems and Imitations of Horace, 1738; One Thousand Seven Hundred and Thirty Eight, 1738; The New Dunciad, 1742; The Dunciad, in Four Books, 1743. *Translations*: The Iliad of Homer, 1715-20; The Odyssey of Homer, 1725-26. *Letters*: Letters of Mr. Pope, 1735; New Letters of Mr. Pope, 1737; *Works*: (W. Warburton, ed.) 1751; (W. Elwin and W. J. Courthope, eds.) 1871-89.

ABOUT: Ault, N. New Light on Pope; Carruthers, R. The Life of Alexander Pope; Courthope, W. J. The Life; Dobrée, B. Alexander Pope; Johnson, S. Lives of the Poets; Leavis, F. R. Revaluation; Sherburn, G. The Early Career of Alexander Pope; Sitwell, E. Alexander Pope; Spence, J. Anecdotes (S. W. Singer, ed.); Stephen, L. Alexander Pope; Strachey, L. Characters and Commentaries; Thornton, F. B. Alexander Pope: Catholic Poet.

PORSON, RICHARD (December 25, 1759-September 25, 1808), classical scholar, critic, man of letters, was born in East Ruston, Norfolk, the son of Huggin Porson, worsted weaver and parish clerk, and Anne Palmer. From earliest childhood he exhibited a phenomenal memory and was a mathematical prodigy. His father intended him to follow his own trade, but also supervised his studies carefully. By the influence of

wealthy neighbors, he was sent to Eton in 1774, then in 1778 to Trinity College, Cambridge, where he soon won a scholarship and in 1782 became a fellow and first chancellor's medalist. He graduated B.A. in 1782, M.A. in 1785. In 1792 he was obliged to resign his fellowship; by its terms he had to take orders, and the only lay fellowship was given by the master of Trinity to his own nephew. Porson's wealthy friends then raised an annuity of £100 a year for him; at his death the principal was used to establish the Porson Prize and Porson Scholarship at Cambridge. He was also made regius professor of Greek.

Porson did not lecture in his professorship, but spent most of his time in London pursuing his classical studies. In 1796 he married a Mrs. Luman, a widow whose brother was editor of the *Morning Chronicle*, but she died in five months, of tuberculosis. In 1806 he was appointed principal librarian of the London Institution, with rooms in the library. His marvelous memory began to fail early in 1808, and in September he suffered an apoplectic stroke on the street and was taken to the workhouse; his assistant recognized him from a newspaper story and took him back to the library. There he died six days later. He was buried in Trinity College.

Porson was the greatest classical scholar of his day. He was also an eccentric, the

After T. Kirby

RICHARD PORSON

center of stories not all of which were accurate. He was a proud, sensitive, touchy man, naturally warm hearted and benevolent, slovenly and careless in his appearance, indolent in everything except his studies, and working on them (he actively disliked writing) in bursts of industry. He was a born wit, full of dry humor not unlike that of Swift, whom he admired immensely, but quite able to be a silent bore in "society," which he hated. He was also unfortunately, a genuine alcoholic, and this defect undoubtedly shortened his life.

Porson's finest criticism is in his edition of Euripides, which was left unfinished. His masterly edition of Aeschylus was published without mention of his name, and an edition of Aristophanes which he was to have made was rendered impossible by the stupid ignorance of its projectors. He himself said: "I am quite satisfied if, three hundred years hence, it shall be said that one Porson lived towards the close of the eighteenth century, who did a good deal for the text of Euripides." His Greek handwriting was so beautiful that it became the basis of the "Porson type" of the Cambridge University Press.

Porson also did a good deal of general writing, mostly in the form of essays in the *Gentleman's Magazine* and letters to the papers, in which his native irony and satire were well displayed; he was especially good in parody. His unpublished papers are preserved in the library of Trinity. His great achievement as a classicist was in textual criticism; his work throughout was predicated on his worship of accuracy and truth.

PRINCIPAL WORKS: Xenophon's Anabasis (ed.) 1786; Appendix to Toup, 1790; Letters to Travis, 1790; Aeschylus (ed.) 1795-1806; Euripides (ed.) 1797-1802; The Odyssey (collated, *in* The Grenville Homer) 1801; Adversaria (J. H. Monk, and C. J. Blomfield, eds.) 1812; Tracts and Miscellaneous Criticisms (T. Kidd, ed.) 1815; Aristophanica (P. P. Dobrée, ed.) 1820; Notes on Pausanias, 1820; The Lexicon of Photius (P. P. Dobrée, ed.) 1822; Notes on Suidas, 1834; Correspondence (H. R. Luard, ed.) 1867.

ABOUT: Barker, E. H. Porsoniana; Clarke, M. L. Richard Porson, a Biographical Essay; Kidd, T. Imperfect Outline of the Life of R. P., *in* Tracts and Miscellaneous Criticisms; Nicoll, H. J. Great Scholars; Sandys, J. E. History of Classical Scholarship; Watson, J. S. The Life of Richard Porson.

PORTER, HENRY (fl. 1596-1599), dramatist, is probably the Henry Porter from London, son of a gentleman, who matriculated at Brasenose College, Oxford, on June 19, 1589, aged sixteen. He seems not to have graduated, and may be the same Henry Porter who in 1591 was pardoned at Westminster for killing one John Cotterell in self-defense.

Porter is mentioned no fewer than twenty-four times in the diary of Philip Henslowe, the theatre manager, between 1596 and 1599. Payments and loans in respect of five plays written wholly or partly by him are there recorded. He is listed as the sole author of *Love Prevented*, of the Second Part of *Two Angry Women of Abington*, and of *Two Merry Women of Abington;* this last play may never have been completed, as there is no record of a final payment for it. He also wrote *Hot Anger Soon Cold* with Chettle and Jonson and *The Spencers* with Chettle. The only extant play by Porter is *Two Angry Women of Abington*, published in 1599 and described on the title page as having been "lately played" by the Admiral's company, for which all the plays listed above were written. This comedy must be the First Part of *Two Angry Women*, which is not mentioned in Henslowe's diary (unless it be identical with *Love Prevented*).

The last mention of Porter in the diary occurs on May 26, 1599, when he borrowed ten shillings from Henslowe. His constant need to borrow small sums suggests that he was extremely poor and leading a very dissipated life. It is probable that he died in 1599.

Two Angry Women of Abington, though praised by Lamb and several times reprinted, reads like a mere piece of hack work. One of the angry women suspects that her husband has had relations with the other; a quarrel arises which prevents the marriage of the latter's son with the former's daughter. When the play has gone on long enough, the two women are unconvincingly persuaded to make up their quarrel.

PRINCIPAL WORKS: A Pleasant Comedy of the Two Angry Women of Abington, 1599 (W. W. Greg, ed. 1912).

ABOUT: Greg, W. W. (ed.) Henslowe's Diary; Shear, R. E. New Facts about Henry Porter (Publications of the Modern Language Association, Vol. XLII, 1927).

PRESTON, THOMAS (1537-June 1, 1598), dramatist, was born at Simpson,

Buckinghamshire, presumably of good family, for he received his early education at Eton. His career at King's College, Cambridge, was unusually brilliant, since he entered as a Scholar in 1553 and became a Fellow of the College in 1556, a year before taking his B.A. degree. He graduated M.A. in 1561.

Preston had more to recommend him than his scholarship; when Queen Elizabeth visited Cambridge in 1564 he put on a dazzling performance. He delivered a Latin oration, took part in a public disputation, and even acted a part in the tragedy of *Dido* with outstanding success. No wonder the queen allowed so accomplished a young man to kiss her hand and gave him a pension of £20 per annum, though she was usually freer with gracious gestures than with hard cash.

In 1572 King's College needed someone to lecture in law; Preston was ordered to study the subject and duly obtained his L.L.D. in 1576. Five years later he resigned his fellowship in order to practice law; in 1584 he was back at the University again, though not at his old college. Trinity Hall had appointed him Master—the highest office in that college. This post he held for the rest of his life. In 1589-1590 he acted temporarily as Vice Chancellor of the University. He is buried in the chapel of Trinity Hall, where his wife Alice set up a monument to him.

Preston owes his niche in literary history to his only known play, *A Lamentable Tragedy Mixed Full of Pleasant Mirth Containing the Life of Cambises, King of Persia*, entered for publication by John Allde in 1569. Anyone who happens to read *Cambises* may well wonder how such an absurd piece of doggerel could save its author from oblivion. The answer is that this happens to be one of the very few surviving plays of the period. If anyone less important had written it, it would probably never have been printed.

The "play" has no plot; King Cambises performs one act of justice, several of injustice, and dies as the result of an accident. Ambidexter, corresponding to the "Vice" of the morality plays, strolls on and off the stage urging various characters to acts of double-dealing; he is involved in some of the usual slapstick comedy and gets several sound beatings. Ambidexter and the other comic characters speak rhyming doggerel; the "serious" characters employ rhymed fourteeners, of which the following is not an unfair example (Cambises is speaking):

> Dispatch with sword this judge's life,
>   extinguish fear and cares:
> So done, draw thou his cursèd skin,
>   straight over both his ears.

Such lines as these cannot be described as bombastic; they are merely flat.

In *Henry IV, Part I*, Falstaff says, "I must speak in passion, and I will do it in King Cambises' vein," which suggests that Preston's play was a by-word for rant in Shakespeare's time. Falstaff, however, goes on to speak in blank verse, not fourteeners, and it is possible that some later play on the same subject is meant. Oddly enough, there is a scene of low comedy between soldiers and a prostitute in *Cambises* that reminds one just for a moment of *Henry IV*.

PRINCIPAL WORK: A Lamentable Tragedy . . . the Life of Cambises, King of Persia, 1570.

PRICE, RICHARD (February 23, 1723-April 19, 1791), Unitarian minister and writer on moral, political, and financial subjects, was born in Tynton, Glamorganshire, Wales, the son of Rice Price, a bigoted, morose, Calvinist minister. Richard's later liberality in religion stemmed from early rebellion against his childhood environment. After attending a number of small schools, he was sent to an academy of semi-religious nature in London in 1741. For a while he was chaplain and companion to one Streatfield, in Stoke Newington, a London borough, and at the same time preached in various dissenting chapels. In 1756 both his employer and an uncle died and left him a little money, enabling him to give more attention to the public questions which most interested him. In 1757 he married Sarah Blundell; they had no children. The next year he moved to Newington Green, one of several places where he had congregations.

By 1769 Price was sufficiently well known for the University of Glasgow to bestow an honorary D.D. degree upon him. His writings in favor of the American Revolution elicited an invitation from Congress in 1778 to come to America; he declined, but wrote that he looked to the new republic

417

After B. West

RICHARD PRICE

"as the hope, and likely soon to be the refuge of mankind." In 1783 he was accorded an LL.D. at Yale at the same time as George Washington.

Price declined an offer to be private secretary to the Earl of Shelburne (later the Marquis of Lansdowne), who had been his friend and patron since 1769, and instead remained a minister to his death. His wife died in 1786, and the remainder of his life was one of illness and melancholy, cheered only by foundation of the Unitarian Society in 1791 (he was one of the original members) and by the beginnings of the French Revolution.

Price's writing may be divided into political, financial, and philosophic or ethical. In politics he was a leading spokesman of the radicals; it was his advocacy of the French Revolution which inspired Burke's bitter *Reflections on the Revolution in France*. In finance, he developed the theory of life insurance, and gave impetus to reestablishment of the sinking fund as a means of wiping out the national debt; he was a competent mathematician with a power of dealing with abstractions. He was best known in his lifetime for his *Review of the Principal Questions and Difficulties in Morals*. Philosophically he attacked both Locke and Hume, holding that "the understanding has its own ideas, and does not depend on sense impressions." The source of ideas,

including those of right and wrong, is in reason; they are "perceived by immediate intuition" and "morality is a branch of necessary truth." He was thus a precursor of intuitional ethics, and the exact antithesis of Paley. Though in some ways he was also in profound disagreement with Priestley, they were intimate friends, and Priestley preached his funeral sermon.

PRINCIPAL WORKS: A Review of the Principal Questions and Difficulties in Morals, 1767; Observations on Reversionary Payments, 1771; An Appeal to the Public on the Subject of the National Debt, 1772; Observations on the Nature of Civil Liberty, the Principles of Government, and the Justice and Policy of the War on America, 1776; Additional Observations, 1777; The General Introduction and Supplement to the Two Tracts on Civil Liberty, 1778; An Essay on the Population of England, 1780; Observations on the Importance of the American Revolution, and the Means of Rendering it a Benefit to Mankind, 1784; A Discourse on the Love of Our Country, 1789.

ABOUT: Franklin, B. Memoirs; Morgan, W. [nephew] Memoir of the Life of Dr. Richard Price; Stephen, L. A History of English Thought in the 18th Century.

PRIESTLEY, JOSEPH (March 13, 1733-February 6, 1804), scientist, philosopher, was born at Fieldhead, near Birstall, Yorkshire, the oldest of six children of Jonas Priestley, cloth-dresser, and his first wife, Mary Swift. Both his parents were Congregationalists. At nine he was adopted and reared by his paternal aunt, Sarah Keighley, a strict Calvinist. After Batley Grammar School and several years as pupil of a Congregational minister, John Kirby, he was sent to Daventry Academy in 1751. By 1755 he was assistant and soon successor to a superannuated Presbyterian minister at Needham Market, Suffolk, and in 1758 secured a better congregation at Nantwich, Cheshire, though he was not ordained until 1762. In 1761 he became classical tutor at Warrington Academy, and remained there until 1767; he taught languages, oratory, natural philosophy, logic, and civil law. Priestley was a natural linguist, familiar with French, German, Italian, Latin, Greek, Hebrew, Syriac, Chaldee, and Arabic.

In 1762 he had married Mary Wilkinson; they had three sons and a daughter. In 1767 he became a minister at Leeds, taking pupils also and founding the Leeds circulating library. Lord Shelburne (later the Marquis of Lansdowne) made him his librarian, "literary companion," and tutor to his sons in

418

1773; the next year he traveled with his employer on the Continent and met Lavoisier. This was just after Priestley had first isolated oxygen, the nature of which he did not understand; it was left for the French chemist to develop his discovery. Priestley had no scientific training, and thought of oxygen merely as "a different kind of dephlogisticated air." He and Shelburne parted company amicably in 1780, but he continued to receive an annuity from his patron for life.

Priestley moved to Birmingham, where his friends contributed to his livelihood so that he could go on with his scientific experiments—though he also was minister of a church there. He was a Unitarian from about 1783, and was one of the founders of the Unitarian Society in 1791. Erasmus Darwin and James Watt, the inventor of the steam engine, were among his Birmingham friends. He was by this time a famous man who had been elected to the Academies of Science of France, Russia, Italy, and Holland. His advocacy first of the American and then of the French Revolution had, of course, made him many enemies. In 1791 mobs rioted in Birmingham against the radicals, burnt Priestley's church and sacked his house, destroying most of his papers and scientific equipment. He settled in London and for a time served a church in Hackney,

but in 1794 he and his wife followed their sons (the daughter was married) to America. After short stays in New York and Philadelphia, they settled in Northumberland, Pennsylvania, his home for the remainder of his life. He lectured occasionally in Philadelphia, but declined the offer of the presidency of the new college, now the University of Pennsylvania. Though never naturalized, he was active in the party of the Jeffersonian Democrats. His wife died in 1786, his youngest son before that, his second son quarreled with him and left for Louisiana, and he made his home, in failing health, with his oldest son's family. There he died and was buried in the Quaker cemetery.

Priestley was a warm hearted, generous, companionable man, strongly independent in spirit. From his boyhood, as he said of himself, he "saw reason to embrace what is generally called the heterodox side of almost every question." Hampered by a bad stammer, he nevertheless spent his life as a public speaker; with "no ear," he yet played the flute assiduously. As a writer, he was direct and vigorous, with a gift for epigram. Philosophically, he was an empirical materialist, a disciple of Hartley except that he held that thought and the soul are products of the brain itself. Yet he held fast to the belief that his views could be reconciled with Christianity. In economics, he was a precursor of Bentham and the Utilitarians; societies exist "for mutual advantage" and happiness is "the great standard by which everything relating to the state must finally be determined."

PRINCIPAL WORKS: A Treatise on the History and Present State of Electricity, 1767; An Essay on the First Principles of Government, 1768; A Free Address to Protestant Dissenters as Such, 1769; Institutes of Natural and Revealed Theology, 1772-74; Experiments and Observations on Different Kinds of Air, 1774-82; Disquisitions Relating to Matter and Spirit, 1777; The Doctrine of Philosophical Necessity Illustrated, 1777; A Free Discussion on the Doctrines of Materialism [correspondence with R. Price] 1778; History of the Corruption of Christianity, 1782; Observations on the Importance of the American Revolution, 1784; General History of the Christian Church, 1790; Letters to Edmund Burke, 1791; Experiments on the Generation of Air and Water, 1793; Memoirs of the Year 1795 (with a Continuance to the Time of his Decease by his Son Joseph Priestley, 1809); Theological and Miscellaneous Works (J. T. Rutt, ed.) 1817-32.

ABOUT: Aykroyd, W. R. Three Philosophers; Holt, A. A Life of Joseph Priestley; Huxley, T.

Mrs. Sharples

JOSEPH PRIESTLEY

H. Science and Education; Lodge, O. (J. H. Muir-head, ed.) Nine Famous Birmingham Men; Peacock, D. H. Joseph Priestley; Priestley, J. Memoirs of the Year 1795, etc.; Rutt, J. T. Life and Correspondence of Joseph Priestley; Thorpe, T. E. Joseph Priestley; Weber, A. History of Philosophy; Weiser, H. B. Priestley and the Discovery of Oxygen.

PRIOR, MATTHEW (July 21, 1664-September 18, 1721), poet, diplomatist, was born in Winborne Minster, East Dorset, the son of George Prior, a carpenter and joiner. While he was still a small child the family moved to London. He was sent to Westminster School, but taken out on his father's death and apprenticed to his uncle, a tavern keeper. There in 1680 the Earl of Dorset found the boy reading Horace as he stood at the bar, and interested himself in sending him back to Westminster. Against his patron's wishes (he wanted Prior to go to Oxford), he entered St. John's College, Cambridge, in 1683, the next year became King's Scholar, secured his B.A. in 1686, and in 1688 was made a fellow. He and his friend Charles Montagu had attracted attention by a satire on Dryden's pro-Roman Catholic *The Hind and the Panther,* and in 1691 he was rewarded by being sent as secretary to the English ambassador, Lord Dursley (later the Earl of Berkeley), to The Hague. He remained until 1697, and William III (who was also Prince of Orange) made him a gentleman of the king's bedchamber. In 1698 he was sent to Paris, where he pleased Louis XIV as much as he had William. The next year he returned to England as under secretary of state, and he succeeded Locke as one of the commissioners of trade and plantations. Cambridge bestowed an honorary M.A. on him.

For one brief term, in 1701, Prior was a Member of Parliament for Grinstead, and there he, who had been a protégé of the Whig lords, voted for their impeachment in connection with the Partition Treaty. From this time on he was permanently on the Tory side, and though he had been reared a Presbyterian became High Church as well. On Anne's accession the Whigs regained the government, and he lost both his posts. He spent his "exile" as secretary to the Bishop of Winchester, and he and Swift founded the Tory *Examiner.* His collected poems were first published at this time, in an un-

After J. Richardson, c. 1718
MATTHEW PRIOR

authorized edition, which he followed by an authorized one.

The Tories came into power again in 1711, and Prior re-entered the diplomatic service. He was actually chosen as ambassador to France, but refused confirmation because of his humble birth. He went to Paris as a sort of upper secretary to Lord Bolingbroke, then as acting ambassador, and finally as actual plenipotentiary. In 1714 Anne died and Prior immediately lost his embassy post and also the commissionership of customs, to which he had been appointed. In 1715 he was impeached by Sir Robert Walpole and kept under custody of the sergeant-at-arms of the House of Commons for two years. To ease his miseries his friends published a sumptuous folio edition of his poems, including his two most ambitious efforts, *Alma* and *Solomon.* The proceeds enabled him to buy Down Hall, Essex, his home thenceforth.

By this time, however, he was aging, deaf, and ill, and he died at fifty-seven, while visiting the Earl of Oxford at Wimpole, Cambridgeshire. He was buried in Westminster Abbey, "at the feet of Spenser," and left money for a monument to be erected to him in the Poets' Corner.

Prior, like many self-made men, was a bit of a sycophant and opportunist and very adaptable to the wishes of the great. He was an extremely versatile writer whose genius was for light verse, parody, and persiflage. He had a serious interest in metrics, however, and thought of himself as essentially a poet. He said: "Poetry, which by the bent of my Mind might have become the Business of my life, was by the happyness [accident] of my Education only the Amusement of it." Thackeray compared him to his master Horace, and thought him "among the easiest, richest, and most charmingly humorous of English lyrical poets."

PRINCIPAL WORKS: The Country-Mouse and the City-Mouse (with C. Montagu) 1687; Hymn to the Sun, 1694; Carmen Seculare, 1699; Pallas and Venus, 1706; Poems on Several Occasions, 1707; Collected Poems, 1716; The Dove, 1717; The Conversation (prose tale) 1720; A New Miscellany of Original Poems by Mr. Prior, Mr. Pope, etc., 1720; A Supplement to Mr. Prior's Poems, 1722; Down Hall, 1723; The Turtle and the Sparrow, 1723; A New Collection of Poems on Several Occasions, 1725; Miscellaneous Works (A. Drift, ed.) 1740; Poetical Works (T. Evans, ed.) 1779; Works (J. Mitford, ed.) 1835 (G. Gilfillan, ed. 1858); Selected Poems (A. Dobson, ed.) 1889; The Writings of Matthew Prior (A. R. Waller, ed.) 1905-07; Shorter Poems (F. L. Bickley, ed.) 1923.

ABOUT: Bickley, F. L. The Life of Matthew Prior; Eves, C. K. Matthew Prior, Poet and Diplomatist; Johnson, S. Lives of the English Poets; Legg, L. G. W. Matthew Prior: A Study of his Public; Saintsbury, G. History of English Prosody; Thackeray, W. M. The English Humourists of the 18th Century.

PROCTOR, THOMAS (fl. 1578-1584), poet, was probably the son of John Proctor (d. 1584), an Oxford graduate and a clergyman, who was headmaster of the grammar school at Tunbridge, Kent, from 1553 to 1559, and who became rector of St. Andrew's, Holborn, London, in 1578.

Thomas was apprenticed to the London printer John Allde; he received the freedom of the Stationers' Company in 1584. Anthony Munday was also an apprentice of Allde's; when Proctor's poetic miscellany, *A Gorgeous Gallery of Gallant Inventions,* appeared in 1578, Munday prefixed some commendatory verses to it. Proctor in his turn prefixed similar verses to Munday's *Mirror of Mutability* in the following year. Both performed the same office for one "T. F., Student," whose *News from the North* appeared in 1579.

Proctor seems to have taken over the compilation of *A Gorgeous Gallery* from one Owen Roydon. No poems by Proctor occur until page 79, where there is a poem called *Proctor's Precepts;* ten of the remaining

twenty-one poems are initialed "T.P." All his contributions are grave, sententious, and moralistic. The pessimistic tone and alliterative style of most of the verse in *A Gorgeous Gallery* were already going out of fashion.

Proctor also wrote *Of the Knowledge and Conduct of Wars* and *The Triumph of Truth,* the latter published by himself; it is probable that he set up shop on his own after becoming a fully fledged Stationer. The date of his death is unknown, but he is generally believed not to have been the Thomas Proctor who wrote *A Profitable Work to This Whole Kingdom in 1610, The Right of Kings,* 1621, and *The Righteous Man's Way,* 1621. The author of fairly competent but old fashioned poetry which failed to secure a hearing in' *A Gorgeous Gallery* (the book was not reprinted until the nineteenth century), Proctor probably decided that a literary career was not for him and turned to surer ways of earning a living.

PRINCIPAL WORKS: A Gorgeous Gallery of Gallant Inventions, 1578; Of the Knowledge and Conduct of Wars, 1578; The Triumph of Truth, 1585 (?).

ABOUT: Rollins, H. E. Introduction to his edition of A Gorgeous Gallery, 1926.

PRYNNE, WILLIAM (1600-October 24, 1669), Puritan pamphleteer, was born in Swainswick, Somersetshire, the son of Thomas Prynne and his second wife, Marie Sherston. He was educated at Bath Grammar School and entered Oriel College, Oxford, in 1618, graduating B.A. in 1621. He was then entered in Lincoln's Inn and called to the bar in 1628.

Prynne was the archetype of the seventeenth century Puritan—narrow, bigoted, fierce, self-righteous, and fanatical. His *Histrio-mastix,* a bitter condemnation of the stage (though written in dramatic form, with acts, scenes, and choruses), appeared in 1632. It aroused a storm. In his exaggerated way, he had called all actresses "notorious whores." Unfortunately, Queen Henrietta Maria was fond of amateur dramatics, and took the phrase as a personal insult. In 1634 Prynne was pilloried, his ears cropped, his Oxford degree and his membership in Lincoln's Inn rescinded; he was fined £5000, and ordered imprisoned for life. In 1637, on his further attacking the stage and sports,

WILLIAM PRYNNE

1640

he was again brought before the Star Chamber, again pilloried, his cropped ears further trimmed, and he was branded on his cheeks as a seditious libeler. In 1640 his fine and imprisonment were cancelled and in 1641 Parliament made what amends it could to him. His chief persecutor, he felt, had been Archbishop Laud, and thenceforth he pursued Laud with vindictive fury. It must be added that except in this respect Prynne endured his ills with patience and courage.

Though he was a Puritan, he was not a Republican. He was the spokesman of Parliament against the army, opposed the execution of Charles I, and (he had sat in Parliament in 1648 for Newport, Cornwall) was one of those expelled in Pride's Purge, in 1649. He tried to regain his seat in 1659 without success, but finally reentered Parliament for Bath in 1660. Charles II made him keeper of records of the Tower. He died in Lincoln's Inn, unmarried, and was buried there.

Prynne was an extremely prolific writer, author of some two hundred works. *Histrio-mastix* alone contains 1100 pages, with numerous marginal notes. Historically his work is of value because it contains so much material otherwise unobtainable; but this material is carelessly arranged, and Prynne's writing has no literary merit; it is merely pedantic, exaggerated, and heavy. He attacked Milton on divorce, he attacked the

Roman Catholics and the Presbyterians (though he himself later became a Presbyterian), and above all he attacked Laud. *Histrio-mastix*, his best known book, has been called "a gigantic monument to misplaced energy and zeal," and much the same might be said of all his work.

PRINCIPAL WORKS: Health's Sicknesse: the Unloveliness of Lovelocks, 1628; Histrio-mastix, the Players Scourge, or Actors Tragœdie, 1632; Mount Orgueil (verse) 1641; The Antipathy of English Lordly Prelacy, 1641; The Sovereign Powers of Parliaments and Kingdoms, 1643; A Breviate of the Life of William Laud, Arch-bishop of Canterbury, 1644; Hidden Workes of Darknes Brought to Publicke Light, 1645; Canterburie's Doome, 1646; The First Part of an Historical Collection of the Ancient Councils and Parliaments of England, 1649; A Legal Vindication of the Liberties of England, 1649; The Republican and Other Spurious Good Old Cause Briefly and Truely Anatomised, 1659; Animadversions on the Fourth Part of Coke's Institutes, 1669; An Exact Abridgment of the Records in the Tower of London, 1689.

ABOUT: Aubrey, J. Letters from the Bodleian Library; Gardiner, S. R. (ed.) Documents Relating to the Proceedings against William Prynne in 1634 and 1637 (Biographical Fragment, J. Bruce); Hazlitt, W. The English Drama and Stage; Kirby, E. W. William Prynne; Pepys, S. Diary; Wood, A. à, Athenae Oxonienses.

PURCHAS, SAMUEL (1577-1626), writer on religion and travel, was born at Thaxted, Essex, the son of George Purchas, a yeoman farmer. He was educated at St. John's College, Cambridge, whence he graduated M.A. in 1600. He took holy orders and became curate of Purleigh, Essex, in 1601; in that year he married Jane Lease, a yeoman's daughter, one of the servants at the parsonage.

Purchas was appointed vicar of Eastwood, Essex, in 1604; in 1614 he became chaplain to the Archbishop of Canterbury and was made rector of St. Martin's, Ludgate, London, by John King, Bishop of London. Probably these latter appointments were made in recognition of his first book, *Purchas his Pilgrimage, or Relations of the World and the Religions Observed in All Ages and Places.*

He found his London benefice not only more satisfactory for his health and pocket, but also much more convenient for his researches. In 1615 he became a B.D. of Oxford. In 1618 his brother-in-law William Pridmore and his favorite brother Daniel died, both leaving encumbered estates. Purchas was by no means a rich man, but he managed to straighten out their affairs; his will, made in 1625, mentions about thirty acres of land at Thaxted, a house, a mill, a valuable collection of books, and other items.

Purchas his Pilgrim, Microcosmus, or the History of Man, a religious work, appeared in 1619. Purchas' best known work, however, is *Hakluytus Posthumus, or Purchas his Pilgrims, Containing a History of the World in Sea Voyages and Land Travels by Englishmen and Others,* which appeared in 1625. Purchas had apparently worked with Hakluyt in collecting materials for a continuation of the latter's *Voyages;* Hakluyt bequeathed him his papers at his death in 1616. The engraved title page of *Hakluytus Posthumus* contains a portrait of Purchas, aged forty-eight, which gives him a round, plump face, a naïve expression, and a lofty, balding forehead. He died the year after the publication of his *magnum opus,* being survived by his wife, his son Samuel and his daughter Martha.

PRINCIPAL WORKS: Purchas his Pilgrimage, 1613; Purchas his Pilgrim, Microcosmus or the History of Man, 1619; The King's Tower (a sermon) 1623; Hakluytus Posthumus, or Purchas his Pilgrims, 1625.

ABOUT: Publishers' Note to 1905 (Glasgow) edition of Hakluytus Posthumus, or Purchas his Pilgrims.

PUTTENHAM, GEORGE (1529?-1590),

putative author of *The Arte of English Poesie,* was the son of Robert Puttenham and Margery, sister of Sir Thomas Elyot. The authorship of the anonymous *Arte* has also been attributed to his elder brother, Richard Puttenham, and to Lord Lumley. Any identification of the author must base itself on a number of autobiographical references in the work, none of which is incompatible with what is now known of George's career.

George Puttenham entered Cambridge University in 1546; the passage in the *Arte* which seems to say that its author was a scholar at Oxford is decidedly ambiguous. No record of George's graduation exists. In 1556 he entered the Middle Temple to study law. Between leaving Cambridge and taking up law he may well have traveled on the Continent.

About 1560 he married Lady Elizabeth Windsor, widow of William, second Lord Windsor. In 1563 he was in Flanders. In 1570 he was accused of conspiring against Cecil, Queen Elizabeth's chief minister. By this time he was also notorious for an evil life and for unorthodox religious views. It is hardly surprising that he and his wife separated. In 1578 the quarrel between him and his wife's family came to a head; he had not paid her allowance for the past five years; he was arrested and brought before the Privy Council. A settlement was reached in 1579, and in 1585 the Council awarded him £1000 in redress of some of his grievances. Sir John Throckmorton, husband of his sister Margery, was his long-suffering advocate and friend.

In 1588 Queen Elizabeth rewarded him, probably for his manuscript *Justification* defending her conduct in the case of Mary, Queen of Scots. If he was the author of the *Arte,* he wrote many other MS. works mentioned therein, including *Partheniades*—poems addressed to the Queen. The *Arte,* published in 1589, is easily the most learned and substantial of Elizabethan critical treatises, though stylistically not the equal of Sidney's *Apology for Poetry.* George died in London, bequeathing all he had to Mary Symes, a servant.

PRINCIPAL WORKS: The Arte of English Poesie, 1589; A Justification of Queene Elizabeth in Relation to the Affair of Mary Queen of Scots (*in* Acounts and Papers Relating to Mary Queen of Scots) 1867.

ABOUT: Willcock, G. D. and A. Walker. Introduction to their edition of The Arte of English Poesie, 1936.

PUTTENHAM, RICHARD (1520?-1601?),

literary critic, reputed author of *The Arte of English Poesie,* was the son of Robert Puttenham and Margery Elyot, sister of Sir Thomas Elyot. As the book accredited to him (and to his brother George among others) was anonymous, any statements based on it may or may not apply to either of the Puttenhams. Thus, there is no record that either of them was a student at Oxford, as the anonymous writer claims. He says also that he has traveled in France, Italy, and Spain—which Richard Puttenham did twice, once with his uncle as a boy, later when he was a fugitive from justice; whereas George Puttenham may possibly never have left England. This was one of the reasons why H. H. S. Crofts in 1883 claimed Richard as the author, instead of George, the usual ascription previously. It is certain that Richard Puttenham had some connection with the court of Elizabeth, and he may at one time have been a Yeoman of the Guard. It is also certain that he was convicted of rape in 1561, pardoned in 1563, fled to the Continent until 1566, returned to England, and by 1588 was in prison again, apparently until his death. The second charge was probably also what the law-books call a "sexual offense," for in his will in 1597 he left his estate (what remained of it; he had long ago spent his legacy from his uncle) to a "reputed" daughter. He was married when very young to Mary Warham, and they also had at least one daughter.

The author of *The Arte of English Poesie* claims to have written plays, poems, and essays, none of which has survived if they existed. George Puttenham did write a defense of Elizabeth in her treatment of Mary, Queen of Scots. George, incidentally, was the third husband of Elizabeth Coudray, Lady Windsor, and for years was involved in violent litigation with her family; he was imprisoned and finally won £1000 recompense for unjust imprisonment. Whichever brother wrote the book, it was rushed into print to provide money for legal expenses.

The book is a combined history of English poetry, the first philosophic criticism of English poets, and a treatise on metrics. The writer knew and admired Wyatt and Surrey, Spenser, and Sidney, and was familiar with Sidney's still unpublished *Apologie for Poesie*. Historically it is of great interest, and its criticism (except for the earliest periods) is good and to the point; Harington, Jonson, and Meres all relied on it. The metrics is another matter: the author had little genuine poetic feeling, but seemed to consider poetry a sort of puzzle; he made elaborate diagrams of figures of speech, and admired extravagantly the "forms" (verses printed to represent objects) which were dear to the metaphysical poets of the following century. This is the "ornament" to which the third section is devoted.

Whoever wrote *The Arte of English Poesie* was something of a scholar, acquainted with the classics, an elderly man at the time of publication (George Puttenham died in 1590, Richard supposedly in 1601), and a "gentleman pensioner" of the queen, with a fondness for literature and intellectual pursuits. Somehow this does not sound like either of the turbulent Puttenhams, and a different and quite unknown person may be the real author, possibly Lord Lumley.

PRINCIPAL WORK: The Arte of English Poesie, Contrived into Three Bookes: The First of Poets and Poesie, the Second of Proportion, the Third of Ornament, 1589 (J. Haslewood, ed. 1811; E. Arber, ed. 1869; G. D. Willcock and A. Walker, eds. 1936).

ABOUT: Bolton, E. Hypercritica; Crofts, H. H. S. Introduction, 1883 ed. The Governour (T. Elyot); Haslewood, J. Ancient Critical Essays; Saintsbury, G. History of Criticism; Schelling, F. E. Poetic and Verse Criticism of the Reign of Elizabeth.

PYE, HENRY JAMES (February 20, 1745-August 11, 1813), poet laureate, miscellaneous writer, was born in London the son and heir of Henry Pye, a country gentleman who was Member of Parliament for his county (Berkshire) from 1746 to his death in 1766. Young Pye was educated at Magdalen College, Oxford, graduating M.A. in 1766. At his father's death he inherited an estate heavily encumbered with debt. For many years he struggled to retain his estate and carry out the duties of a landowner. He was a justice of the peace, a militia officer, and, from 1784 to 1790, a Member of Parliament for Berkshire.

He was finally forced to sell his property; he lost his seat in Parliament in 1790, but was appointed Poet Laureate the same year, mainly as a reward for political services. He had written poetry industriously since his Oxford days, much of it about country pursuits, and was ready to produce New Year and birthday odes annually, as the conditions of the Laureate's tenure then required.

Byron's "Better to err with Pope than shine with Pye" is one of the kinder estimates of his work; *Alfred*, his "masterpiece," is smoothly versified, but never for a moment surprises; Rogers and Campbell, whom Byron admired, wrote several poems equally "correct" and now equally unreadable. Pye's official odes, however, are surpassed in insipidity by Colley Cibber's alone.

Pye served as a police magistrate for Westminster from 1792 to his death; his life, public and private, was without blemish; he wrote or edited some useful works of reference and translated much from the classical and modern languages; but he lacked the spark that turns verse into poetry.

Pye married twice and was survived by his second wife, three daughters, and a son.

PRINCIPAL WORKS: *Poems*: Beauty, 1766; Elegies on Different Occasions, 1768; The Triumph of Fashion, 1771; Faringdon Hill, 1774; Six Olympic Odes of Pindar . . . Translated, 1775; The Progress of Refinement, 1783; Shooting, 1784; Aeriphorion, 1784; Amusement, 1790; The War Elegies of Tyrtaeus Initiated, 1795; Lenore (tr.) 1796; Naucratia, 1798; Alfred, an Epic Poem in Six Books, 1801; Verses on Various Subjects Written in the Vicinity of Stoke Park, 1802; Collected Poems, 1810. *Prose and Drama*: The Poetics of Aristotle (tr.) 1788; The Spectre, 1789; The Siege of Meaux, A Tragedy, 1794; The Democrat, 1795; The Aristocrat, 1799; Adelaide, A Tragedy, 1800; A Prior Claim, A Comedy, 1806; The Sportsman's Dictionary, 1807; Comments on the Commentators of Shakespeare, 1807; Summary of the Duties of a Justice of the Peace out of Sessions, 1808.

ABOUT: Austin, W. S. and J. Ralph. Lives of the Laureates; Broadus, E. K. The Laureateship.

QUARLES, FRANCIS (1592-September 8, 1644),

poet, essayist, aphorist, was born at Romford, Essex, the third son of James and Joan Quarles. His father was a gentleman by birth, Clerk of the Green Cloth and Purveyor of the Navy to Queen Elizabeth. Francis received his early education at a country school and proceeded to Christ's College, Cambridge, from which he graduated B.A. in 1608. He next spent some years studying law at Lincoln's Inn, London. In 1613 he was appointed cupbearer to Elizabeth of Bohemia, daughter of James I, and spent some time at her court in Germany.

Back in England again, he published his first poem in 1620. This was *A Feast of Worms Set Forth in a Poem of the History of Jonah*, the first of many Biblical paraphrases by Quarles—nearly all with equally colorful titles.

The poet's next post was that of secretary to Archbishop Ussher, Primate of All Ireland, a scholar and a statesman. Quarles lived with him in Dublin for some years, returning to Essex about 1632. His famous *Emblems*, a book of moral and devotional poetry, first appeared in 1635 with illustrations by William Marshall.

In 1640 he was appointed chronologer to the City of London, where he appears to have spent the rest of his life. The manuscript *Chronicle of the City of London* which he kept has since disappeared.

The outbreak of civil war between Charles I and the Parliament placed Quarles in a very unhappy position. He was a loyal son of the Church of England, but had numerous Puritan friends, including the family of his godfather, Sir Francis Barrington. His extreme piety, too, resembled that of the Puritans and made his works popular among them both in his lifetime and after. There was much in Charles' conduct that he did not approve of, but he finally chose the Royalist side, as his pamphlet, *The Loyal Convert*, relates. The chief motive for his decision was his belief in the divine right of kings.

Living in London, the Parliamentary stronghold, Quarles was forced to keep his views to himself. *The Loyal Convert* appeared anonymously, but someone must have got wind of the poet's opinions. In 1644 "a petition, full of unjust aspersions, was preferred against him by eight men (whereof he knew not any two, nor they him, save only by sight)." So writes his wife, who further tells us that "the first news of it struck him so to the heart, that he never recovered from it." One of the charges was that he might be a Roman Catholic. Whatever the other charges were, Quarles seems to have been cleared of them all, but he died soon afterwards.

W. Dobson

FRANCIS QUARLES

425

During his last illness he refused the services of a certain doctor because he happened to be a Roman Catholic. The approach of death led Quarles to search his conscience very thoroughly, but he died with his mind at rest, in the bosom of the Church of England.

Quarles died a pauper, leaving behind his wife Ursula and nine living children out of eighteen that had been born to him. He was a very loving father and husband; his adoring wife wrote *A Short Relation of the Life and Death of Mr. Francis Quarles*, which was prefixed to his *Solomon's Recantation*. She did her best to support her family by publishing his remaining manuscripts, but in some cases she seems to have been cheated by the booksellers.

In preference to a career at Court, Quarles spent the greater part of his life in prayer, meditation, study and the composition of his numerous edifying works in verse and prose. As his writings show, he had a profound knowledge of the Bible, which he consulted at every crisis of his life. Originality was not his chief concern and many of the aphorisms in his *Enchiridion* are borrowed from such worldly authors as Bacon and Machiavelli. The last three books of his *Emblems* are based on the Latin poems of a Jesuit, Hermann Hugo.

Quarles is famous for his far-fetched "conceits," many of which were inspired by the abstruse symbolism of the "emblems" or illustrations which they describe. His syntax is often extremely involved, also. At moments, however, he can be astonishingly simple and direct; he is sometimes passionate and always sincere. In the eighteenth century Pope and others made his name a byword for dullness, but the whole Metaphysical school of poetry was then out of fashion. Besides, Quarles was still reverenced by unsophisticated readers, which did his reputation no good among the cultured.

With the return of the Metaphysicals to favor, Quarles has had a little more justice done him, but he is certainly one of the lesser poets of the group. He often exaggerates characteristic Metaphysical traits to the point of absurdity and beyond.

The best known portrait of Quarles might be the likeness of almost any solid Puritan of the period and has nothing individual about it. Of his lighter side we know only that he was a keen fisherman, like his contemporary Izaak Walton.

PRINCIPAL WORKS: *Poems*: A Feast of Worms, 1620; Hadassa, History of Esther, 1621; Job Militant, 1624; Sion's Elegies, Wept by Jeremy the Prophet, 1625; Sion's Sonnets, Sung by Solomon the King, 1625; Alphabet of Elegies, 1625; Argalus and Parthenia, 1629; History of Samson, 1631; Divine Fancies, 1632; Divine Poems, 1633; Emblems, 1635; Hieroglyphics of the Life of Man, 1638; Solomon's Recantation, 1645; The Shepherd's Oracles, 1646. *Prose*: Enchiridion, 1640; Observations Concerning Princes, 1642; Barnabas and Boanerges, 1644; The Loyal Convert, 1644; Judgment and Mercy for Afflicted Souls, 1646.

ABOUT: Haight, G. S. Francis Quarles in the Civil War (Review of English Studies, vol. 12); Quarles, U. A Short Relation (*in* Solomon's Recantation, 1645).

RADCLIFFE, Mrs. ANN (WARD) (July 9, 1764-February 7, 1823), novelist, was born in London, the only daughter of William Ward, a merchant, and Ann Oates. Her mother was a cousin of the classical scholar, Dr. Samuel Jebb, and in an age when tradespeople were not "received" she was enabled to move in upper class circles through relatives among the gentry. Like most girls in the eighteenth century, she had little or no formal education, but in her cousins' homes she met such well-known figures as Hester Thrale Piozzi, Lady Mary Wortley Montagu, and Josiah Wedgwood, and they helped to form her taste and to interest her in literature.

In 1787, when she was twenty-three, she married William Radcliffe, then a law student but later owner and editor of the *English Chronicle*. Her first novel appeared two years later. Mrs. Radcliffe's entire career as an author was confined to about ten years. Then, for no apparent reason except that she was "written out" and had no financial compulsion, she simply ceased to write for publication. Rumors spread that she was dead, and even that she was insane and being kept in seclusion. Actually, she was never in better health and spirits; she and her husband traveled a great deal, and in any case she had always disliked publicity. So completely did the world lose sight of her that in 1815 an anonymous editor brought out a volume of poems from her novels, and even added some of his own, thinking her dead!

In actual fact she lived for several years after that, and died at fifty-eight of asthma, from which she had suffered for many years. She was a cheerful, equable person, fond of music and musically gifted, and in contrast to the vicissitudes of her heroines, she lived a peaceful, uneventful life. She received then unprecedented sums for her later novels —£500 for one, £800 for another. Even so, they made her publishers rich.

Nowadays it is difficult to understand why Scott admired her extravagantly, or why that exquisite poet, Christina Rossetti, wanted to write her biography. (She had to give the idea up, for lack of usable material.) Scott himself said that her prose was poetry and her poetry was prose. She was, indeed, a prose poet, in both the best and the worst senses of the phrase. The romantic landscape, the background, is the best thing in all her books; the characters are two dimensional, the plots far fetched and improbable, with "elaboration of means and futility of result."

The truth seems to be that Mrs. Radcliffe came at exactly the right time; in her hands the Gothic novels of her contemporaries, "Monk" Lewis and Horace Walpole, became wildly romantic, ancestors of a whole school, finding its culmination, perhaps, in America, in the supernatural and macabre stories of Poe and of Charles Brockden Brown. Schedoni, in *The Italian*, was the legitimate ancestor of the Byronic hero; her influence on both Byron and Scott was incalculable.

The best three of Mrs. Radcliffe's novels, by far, are *The Romance of the Forest, The Mysteries of Udolpho*, and *The Italian;* yet even in these there is the same dreary succession of trials of a persecuted heroine, conventionally represented, of dangers and terrors that peter out to nothing, and of final victory over the lady's enemies. Her one historical novel, published posthumously, is very bad. Nevertheless, Mrs. Radcliffe was a mistress of suspense, an ingenious weaver of intricate incident, and a real artist in the description of the wild scenery she loved. (Incidentally, she never saw Italy, scene of several of her books.) She introduced the "poetical landscape" into the modern novel. She is practically unreadable today, but she was a seminal influence in English fiction.

PRINCIPAL WORKS: The Castles of Athlin and Dunbayne, a Highland Story, 1789; A Sicilian Romance, 1790; The Romance of the Forest, 1791; The Mysteries of Udolpho, 1794; A Journey Made . . . through Holland and Germany, 1795; The Italian, or the Confessional of the Black Penitents, 1797; Poems, 1815; The Novels of Mrs. Ann Radcliffe, 1824; Gaston de Blondeville, or, the Court of Henry III, 1826.

ABOUT: Birkhead, E. The Tale of Terror; Hunt, L. Men, Women, and Books; Jeaffreson, J. C. Novels and Novelists from Elizabeth to Victoria; Lang, A. Adventures among Books; Le Fèvre-Deumier, J. Célébrités anglaises; MacIntyre, C. F. Ann Radcliffe in Relation to her Time; Scarborough, D. The Supernatural in Modern English Fiction; Scott, W. Memoir of the Life of the Author, *in* The Novels of Mrs. Ann Radcliffe.

RALEIGH, Sir WALTER (1552?-October 29, 1618), voyager, explorer, author of poems, history, and accounts of expeditions, was born in Hayes Barton, Budleigh, Devonshire, the son of Walter Raleigh, a country gentleman, and his third wife, Katharine (Champernown) Gilbert. The name was spelled in some seventy ways, and the one way Sir Walter never spelled it was "Raleigh," the common modern form! It was pronounced "Rawly." Raleigh was a true Devonshire man—he retained a broad Devon accent all his life—tall, handsome, dark, impetuous, full of energy, proud, quarrelsome, courageous, and an unconscionable liar. Not much is known of his early life; he spent three years from about 1566 at Oriel College, Oxford, but left without a degree; he was with the Huguenot army in France in 1569, and by 1576 he was in London, where he entered the Middle Temple but did not study law. He it was who first suggested the famous gatherings at the Mermaid Tavern (indeed, he is one of the many to whom Shakespeare's plays have been attributed); Ben Jonson called him his 'father' in literature; he was a close friend of Spenser and introduced him at court; he was even a member of the Society of Antiquaries. But his true forte was action. In 1578 he made a voyage with his half-brother, Sir Humphrey Gilbert, against the Spaniards, whom he always hated. In 1580 he was twice arrested for dueling. Later in 1580 he was a captain in Ireland, and was ruthless in suppressing the "rebels." Sent to court with dispatches in 1581, he caught Elizabeth's eye—perhaps, as alleged, by spreading his cloak over a puddle for her to walk on. He became one of her pets, and she kept him at

SIR WALTER RALEIGH
c. 1586

home as much as possible. In 1584 she knighted him, and in 1585 made him Lord Lieutenant of Cornwall; she heaped him with estates, patents, and monopolies—including the monopolies of sweet wine and tin. There is no denying that Raleigh was greedy and ambitious; with all his charm he was unscrupulous. But he had a genuine interest in exploration and a genuinely patriotic desire to enlarge England's dominions. He was rich by now, and he financed and backed the exploration and colonization of Virginia—though the queen would not let him accompany the colonists and he never saw Virginia. (He might have been lost with the Roanoke settlers if he had.) He introduced tobacco and potatoes into England.

Raleigh's downfall—or his first downfall—came in 1592, when it was rumored that he had married, or was about to marry, Elizabeth Throgmorton, a maid of honor. Elizabeth hated to have either her favorites or her maids of honor marry, and most of all each other. She threw them both in the Tower, then banished them from court. They did marry, very happily, and had two sons. (Raleigh may have had an illegitimate daughter as well.) It was 1597 before he was restored to favor; meanwhile he had joined expeditions to Cadiz and to Portugal, and made his first voyage to Guiana (Venezuela), in search of gold. He had served in Parliament for the second time. After Eliza-

beth forgave him, he and Essex made an expedition to the Azores, then in 1600 he was made governor of Jersey.

The end of all his hopes and ambitions came with Elizabeth's death and the accession of James. That fanatical believer in the divine right of kings stored in his heart every rebellious or slighting word. Raleigh was accused of participation in a conspiracy to murder the king (he probably did know about it, but was not of it), was tried—very unfairly—by Coke, sentenced to death, then reprieved. He was a prisoner in the Tower until 1616. However, it was easy imprisonment—his family could be with him, he had books and even a chemical laboratory where he concocted a quack "elixir." It was here that he wrote his famous history—though he reached only 130 B.C.

In 1616 he did a very foolish thing. In desperation, he offered to go again to South America, to find gold in territory not claimed by Spain. The expedition was a complete failure, and his son was killed on it. Immediately on his return he was rearrested, tried again on the old conspiracy charge, again condemned to death (this time by Bacon), and finally beheaded. He was buried in Westminster.

Raleigh's was far from a faultless character, but it was a fascinating one. He is a sort of epitome of the Elizabethans. He was widely rumored to be a freethinker, and to conduct a "School of Atheism," and he was involved in Marlowe's arrest, but his writings are full of devout religion. His history is the first attempt in English at a unitary history of the world, treating all the past as a whole, with its interrelations and correlations. And he was a true poet, "most lofty, insolent, and passionate," as *The Arte of English Poesie* puts it. He has magnificence of phrase, and that grand bronze clangor by which the Elizabethans celebrated life, and death as the crown of life. He was an indefatigable reader, and few men so constantly occupied physically have found time to write so much. If there could be but one completely typical Englishman of the Age of Elizabeth, it would be Sir Walter Raleigh.

PRINCIPAL WORKS: The Discoverie of the Large and Bewtiful Empire of Guiana, 1596 (W. M. Panzer, ed 1928); Report of the Truth of the Fight about the Isles of the Azores, 1596; The History of the World, 1614; The Prerogatives of Parliaments in England, 1628; To-day a Man, To-morrow None, 1644; Judicious and Select Essayes and Observations, 1650; Remains of Sir Walter Raleigh (Maxims of State, The Arts of Empire, The Cabinet Council) 1651; Observations, Touching Trade and Commerce, 1653; Works (T. Birch, ed.) 1751; The Poems of Sir Walter Raleigh (E. Brydges, ed.) 1813.

ABOUT: Anthony, I. Raleigh and his World; Bradbrook, M. C. The School of Night; Brushfield, T. N. Bibliography of Sir Walter Raleigh; Brydges, E. Biographical and Critical Introduction, Poems; Cayley, A. The Life of Sir Walter Raleigh, Kt.; Chidsey, D. B. Sir Walter Raleigh, that Damned Upstart; Clarke, E. G. Raleigh and Marlowe; Creighton, L. Life of Sir Walter Raleigh; de Sélincourt, H. Great Raleigh; Edwards, E. The Life of Sir Walter Raleigh; Fuller, T. Worthies of England; Gosse, E. Raleigh; Harlowe, V. T. Raleigh's Last Voyage; Hume, M. A. S. Sir Walter Raleigh, the British Dominion of the West; Kingsley, C. Plays and Puritans; Lee, S. Great Englishmen of the 16th Century; Napier, M. Lord Bacon [sic] and Sir Walter Raleigh; Naunton, R. Fragmenta Regalia; Ober, F. A. Sir Walter Raleigh; Pemberton, H. Shakspere and Sir Walter Raleigh; Quinn, D. B. Raleigh and the British Empire; Rodd, J. R. Sir Walter Raleigh; Sabatini, R. Heroic Lives; Southey, R. English Seamen; Stebbing, W. Sir Walter Raleigh; Strathmann, E. A. Sir Walter Raleigh: a Study in Elizabethan Skepticism; Thompson, E. J. Sir Walter Raleigh, the Last of the Elizabethans; Waldman, M. Sir Walter Raleigh; Wood, A. à, Athenae Oxonienses.

RAMSAY, ALLAN (October 15, 1685?-January 7, 1758), Scottish poet, was born at Leadhills, Lanarkshire; his father, John Ramsay, overseer of the Earl of Hopetown's lead mines, died in May of 1685, as his testament dative proves; it follows that 1686, traditionally given as the year of Ramsay's birth, is too late, for the poet's birthday was undoubtedly October 15. Ramsay's early biographers were very careless about checking their statements; readers are referred to Burns Martin's book, listed below.

Ramsay's father died in debt; poverty forced his mother to marry again soon afterwards. Allan received his education at some local school; about 1700, probably as a result of his mother's death, he went to Edinburgh, where he was apprenticed to a periwig maker in 1704. His brother Robert had been apprenticed to the same wig maker nine years earlier. Allan became a burgess of Edinburgh in 1710. He set up for himself as a wig maker, married Christian Ross in 1712, and became the father of a son—also named Allan and afterwards a celebrated painter—in 1713. Several other children followed in due course.

After W. Aikman, 1723
ALLAN RAMSAY

From 1712 to 1715 Ramsay and his friends met regularly as "The Easy Club." Clubs of this kind were useful centers for mutual education—and admiration—in provincial cities and towns during the eighteenth century. The members read the *Spectator* to one another; their other activities included the publication of Ramsay's first effort, *Poem to the Memory of the Famous Archibald Pitcairn, M.D.*, 1713. Ramsay was elected poet laureate of the Club in 1715; the group had a Scottish nationalist tone and the Jacobite Rebellion may have had something to do with the Club's demise in 1715.

Ramsay's dialect poems appeared more and more frequently, usually in broadside form, from 1716 onwards. No attempt has been made to list the individual titles in the bibliography below, which confines itself to important collected editions issued in the poet's lifetime. Special mention must be made, however, of *Christ's Kirk on the Green*, a poem attributed to James I of Scotland; Ramsay issued this, adding a second canto of his own, in 1716; Burns used this poem as a model for the structure and meter of his *Hallowe'en* and *The Holy Fair*. Ramsay's burlesque *Elegies on Maggy Johnston, John Cowper and Lucky Wood*, 1718, and the *Epistles* exchanged by him and William Hamilton of Gilbertfield were also fruitful models for Burns.

Ramsay became his own publisher; the subscribers' edition of his *Poems* in 1721 sold four hundred copies at a guinea each. In 1719 he successfully appealed to the Town Council of Edinburgh against the pirating of his works. He was becoming a person of importance in the city, having been chosen a constable in 1716 and a lieutenant in the trainbands (i.e. militia) in 1718.

About 1722 he abandoned wig making for bookselling and started the earliest circulating library in the British Isles about 1725. He was very much interested in the theatre. *The Gentle Shepherd* was not at first intended for performance, but he turned it into a ballad opera in 1728 by the addition of songs. It had its first London performance in 1730. In 1736 he opened the New Theatre in Carruber's Close, but the Licensing Act of 1737 forced him to close down at considerable personal loss. He published no new poetry after 1730, fearing that his gift was deserting him, but he still wrote a good deal. In 1737 he published his last collections of Scots folklore, probably to recoup his loss on the theatre.

In spite of reverses, he was able in 1740 to retire from business to his new octagonal house on Castle Hill. Because of its shape, the house was known locally as "The Goose-Pie." He transferred his property to Allan junior in 1741; his wife died in 1743. When Prince Charlie and his men came to Edinburgh in 1745, the poet was very opportunely out of town, but the rebels used his house as a "strong point" during the fight with the English garrison.

Ramsay enjoyed a happy and honored old age, except that he suffered badly from scurvy of the gums, which may have caused his death. Like many another self-made man, he was vain and garrulous, but extremely likable. About five feet four in height, with a rugged Scots countenance, he grew rather fat in later years.

Both as an original poet and as a rather unscholarly editor Ramsay helped to preserve the continuity of Scots poetry from Dunbar and Henryson to Robert Fergusson and Burns. His *Ever Green* was a collection of Scots verse written prior to 1600; the various volumes of *The Tea Table Miscellany* preserved a great number of Scots songs. Fergusson and Burns surpassed him in realism, but could not have done all that

they did without his stimulating example before them. Both acknowledged their debt on many occasions.

PRINCIPAL WORKS: *Original Poetry*: Scots Songs, 1718; Poems, 1720 (Octavo), 1721 (Quarto); Fables and Tales, 1722; The Gentle Shepherd, A Scots Pastoral Comedy, 1725; Poems, Vol. II, 1728; A Collection of Thirty Fables, 1730. *Anthologies*: The Ever Green, 1724; The Tea Table Miscellany, Vol. I, 1724 (Vol. II, 1726; Vol. III, 1727; Vol. IV, 1737); A Collection of Scots Proverbs, 1737.

ABOUT: Gibson, A. New Light on Allan Ramsay; Martin, B. Allan Ramsay.

RANDOLPH, THOMAS (June 15, 1605-1635), dramatist, poet, was born at Newnham-cum-Badby, Northamptonshire, the second son of William Randolph, steward to Lord Zouch, and his first wife Elizabeth Smith. Thomas had a brilliant academic career, first at Westminster School, where he became a King's Scholar, and then at Trinity College, Cambridge, which he entered in 1624. He graduated B.A. in 1628, was elected a Fellow of the College in 1629, and was given an M.A. in 1631. At Cambridge he was famous not only for his charm of manner and his skill in Latin and English poetry, but also for his English comedies in imitation of the classical dramatists, full of scholarly wit. Such were *Aristippus, The Conceited Peddler, The Nurses' Looking-glass, Hey for Honesty*—an adaptation of the *Plutus* of Aristophanes—and *The Jealous Lovers*.

While at the University, Randolph made frequent trips to London. By 1628 he was a protégé of Ben Jonson; among his other friends were the dramatist Shirley and various courtiers with literary tastes. About 1632 Randolph gave up his fellowship and went to London, probably as manager and playwright for one of the theatre companies. His new career was not a financial success, however, though his *Amyntas* was performed at Court. About 1634 he left London for the country, apparently hoping to give up his dissipated and extravagant ways. He finally settled at Blatherwick, Northamptonshire, as tutor to the children of William Stafford, nephew of his friend Anthony Stafford. There he died; he was buried in the parish church on March 17, 1635.

Precociously talented, Randolph accomplished a great deal before his early death; his comedies, though formless, show considerable originality; none of his poems is worthless, and a few, written with more care than usual, are immortal. *His Ode to Master Anthony Stafford, to Hasten Him into the Country* and his *Eclogue to Master Jonson* are generally considered his masterpieces.

PRINCIPAL WORKS: Aristippus, 1630; The Jealous Lovers, 1632; Poems, with The Nurses' Looking-glass, and Amyntas, 1638; Hey for Honesty, 1651; The Drinking Academy (H. E. Rollins and S. Tannenbaum, eds.) 1930; Poetical and Dramatic Works (W. C. Hazlitt, ed.) 1875; Poems (G. C. Moore Smith, ed.) 1929.

ABOUT: Moore Smith, G. C. Thomas Randolph (British Academy Publications); Tannenbaum, S. A. Thomas Randolph: A Concise Bibliography.

REDFORD, JOHN (fl. 1535), musician, poet, dramatist, was educated in the choir school of St. Paul's Cathedral, London; he later became vicar-choral, organist, almoner, and choirmaster of the Cathedral. His name is more important in the annals of music than in those of literature, for some authorities consider him the finest English composer of instrumental music of his day. Most of his music is written for the organ, but some vocal music also exists.

Redford made his first appearance in literary history in 1848, when J. O. Halliwell edited for the Shakespeare Society a British Museum manuscript containing the incomplete text of *The Play of Wit and Science,* a morality play by Redford, as well as a number of lyrics written by him and others.

Wit and Science is of no particular dramatic merit, but so few plays survive from this period that each one has at least a scarcity value. One of Redford's duties as choirmaster of the St. Paul's boys was probably to write such plays and direct their performance.

The lyrics at the end of the manuscript are much better poetry than the play. It is not clear just how many are meant to be credited to Redford, but apparently at least ten are his, including three songs from *Wit and Science.* Most of the ten deal with moral or religious topics; the noblest is *Nolo Mortem Peccatoris.* Two songs are relevant to Redford's career as a musician. One, which goes on to praise the "mean" or middle register—and hence the Golden Mean—begins with the line, "Long have I been a singing man." The other is a comic *Lamen-*

tation of Boys Learning Prick-Song, in which the boys complain of their captious choirmaster and how often he beats them.

Nothing is known of Redford's life besides his name and official positions at St. Paul's. He is believed to have died between 1540 and 1547, aged somewhere between fifty and sixty.

PRINCIPAL WORKS: The Moral Play of Wit and Science and Early Poetical Miscellanies, 1848.

ABOUT: Pfatteicher, C. F. John Redford.

REEVE, CLARA (1729-December 3, 1807), novelist, was born and died at Ipswich, where her father was a Church of England clergyman. From him she received her entire education, which seems to have been an unusually good one. He died in 1755, and Clara, with her mother and two younger sisters, moved to Colchester, where some of her earlier works were published.

Her first work to appear, at the ripe age of forty, was a volume of poems; next came *The Phoenix,* a translation of a Latin romance; her first original novel was *The Champion of Virtue, a Gothic Story,* in imitation of *The Castle of Otranto,* but designed to "keep within certain limits of credibility" that she felt Horace Walpole's novel had transgressed.

Under its second edition title of *The Old English Baron* Miss Reeve's first novel had a very gratifying success, being reprinted as late as 1883, and probably helping to inspire the novels of Mrs. Radcliffe and others. She wrote several other novels on contemporary and historical themes, but none had a success equal to the first. Her critical study *The Progress of Romance* was reproduced in facsimile at New York in 1930 because of its value as a contemporary appreciation of the new trend in fiction.

One of Miss Reeve's best friends was Mrs. Bridgen, daughter of Samuel Richardson; the revised edition of *The Old English Baron* is dedicated to her.

The etched portrait of Miss Reeve in the 1883 edition of *The Old English Baron* shows a plump, placid English face; the nose is definitely snub, and the complexion appears to be pink-and-white.

No authoritative biography and no adequate bibliography of Miss Reeve appear to exist. The *Memoir* by Scott is scanty and inaccurate; later writers have repeated one or more of its errors and added some of their own.

PRINCIPAL WORKS: Poems, 1769; The Phoenix, 1772; The Champion of Virtue (The Old English Baron) 1777; The Two Mentors, a Modern Story 1783; The Progress of Romance, 1785; The Exiles, 1788; The School for Widows, 1791; The Memoirs of Sir Roger de Clarendon, 1793; Destination, 1799.

ABOUT: Scott, Sir W. Memoir prefixed to 1823 edition of The Old English Baron (Ballantyne's Novelists' Library).

REID, THOMAS (April 26, 1710-October 7, 1796), philosopher, was born in Strachan, Kincardineshire, Scotland, the son of Lewis Reid, a Presbyterian minister, and Margaret Gregory. He entered Marischal College, University of Aberdeen, in 1722 and was graduated in 1726; he then studied divinity and was licensed to preach in 1731. From 1733 to 1736 he was librarian of Marischal; then he spent a year in England with his close friend, John Stewart, professor of mathematics. In 1737 King's College, Aberdeen, presented Reid with a living at New Machar, near by; the congregation was at first very hostile, and even ducked him once in a pond, but his benevolence and charity finally won it over. In 1740 he married his first cousin, Elizabeth Reid; they had a large family, but only one daughter survived him.

Reid's first writing, *An Essay on Quantity*, appeared in the *Philosophical Transactions* in 1748. In 1751 he was appointed

After J. Tassie

THOMAS REID

professor of philosophy at King's College, though his duties included teaching mathematics, physics, logic, and ethics as well as philosophy. In 1762 Marischal made him a Doctor of Divinity, and two years later he left Aberdeen to succeed Adam Smith as professor of moral philosophy in Glasgow. In 1758 he had been one of the founders (and first secretary) of the Aberdeen Philosophical Society, nicknamed "the Wise Club."

Reid retained his university post to his death, but in 1780 he turned his teaching duties over to an assistant, to devote all his time to the writing of philosophy. His last years were unhappy; his wife died in 1792, he lost his hearing, and his memory failed, though to the end he retained his keen interest in mathematics. His married daughter cared for him until he died of an apoplectic stroke at eighty-six. He was a small but strong and athletic man, prudent but outstandingly generous, warm hearted and much loved.

Thomas Reid was the founder of the so-called Scottish School or "common sense school" of philosophy. He was no precursor of pragmatism, however; to him common sense, which was the foundation of his system, meant "the beliefs common to rational beings," or "one branch or degree of reason." He was the only adequate critic of Hume; he pointed out cogently that neither Hume, Locke, nor Berkeley had given any *proof* of his contentions, but all had started out from premises taken for granted. To Reid, ideas had no existence as entities; he argued for "immediate perception" and "natural and original judgment." His mind was naturally scientific, he wrote clearly and simply as well as earnestly. His great defect, however, was clumsy terminology; he used words frequently in senses different from those commonly ascribed to them, and thus rendered it difficult to elicit his exact meaning. He was an eminently fair controversialist, submitting every question to the test of logical proof. He wrote relatively little, but his philosophy, expressed in his books and in his university lectures, secured disciples and actually founded a school of thought.

PRINCIPAL WORKS: An Essay on Quantity, 1748; An Inquiry into the Human Mind on the Principles of Common Sense, 1764; A Brief Account of Aristotle's Logic (*in* H. Home [Lord Kames] History of Man) 1784; Essays on the Intellectual Powers of Man, 1785; Essays on the

Active Powers of Man, 1786; Works (W. Hamilton, ed) 1846 (H. L. Mansel, ed. 1863).

ABOUT: Ferrier, J. F. Lectures; Fraser, A. C. Reid; Jones, O. M. Empiricism and Intuitionism in Reid's Common Sense Philosophy; McCosh, J. Scottish Philosophy; Pringle, P. A. S. Scottish Philosophy; Stewart, D. Life, *in* 1846 ed. Works.

RERESBY, Sir JOHN (April 14, 1634-May 12, 1689), author of memoirs and travel sketches, was the son and heir of Sir John Reresby, baronet, a Cavalier who died in 1646 as a prisoner of the Parliament. Young John was born at Thribergh Hall, Yorkshire, where he lived until 1649; in this year his mother brought the family to London, where he attended school for the first time. Later he went to another school at Enfield Chase; in 1651 he became a student of Gray's Inn.

Making poor progress in his legal studies, Reresby decided he would like to travel; in 1654 he left England for France; he stayed on the Continent over four years, visiting Switzerland, Italy, Austria, Germany, Holland, Belgium, and returning again to France before going home to England. In 1659 he was back in France again, and found favor at the court of Queen Henrietta Maria, widow of Charles I. Soon after the restoration of Charles II to the throne of England in 1660, Reresby returned home and was presented to the king.

Thereafter Reresby often attended at court, but held no office. He became a Member of Parliament in 1675, and sat in most of the parliaments from that year until his death. In Parliament he was a moderate supporter of Charles II, who appointed him Governor of Bridlington in 1678 and Governor of York in 1682. After the accession of James II, Reresby, a sound Protestant, was less strongly Royalist, but remained loyal. A conspiracy led by the Earl of Danby seized York and made Reresby a prisoner soon after the landing of William of Orange in 1688. The following year Reresby made his peace with William, but died suddenly at Thribergh not long afterwards.

Reresby was small, and lame as the result of a fall in childhood; these handicaps made him extremely aggressive, and he was involved in numberless duels. A good linguist and a talented musician, he had little literary ability; his *Travels* and *Memoirs*, written only for his family's eyes, are how-ever, fairly important historical documents. He married for love; his wife, Frances Browne, bore him nine children; he seems to have been a faithful husband and a kind father.

PRINCIPAL WORKS: Memoirs, 1734; Travels and Memoirs, 1813.

(NOTE: The MS. of the *Travels* has been lost; the only reliable and complete edition of the *Memoirs* is that edited by Professor Andrew Browning, Glasgow, 1936.)

ABOUT: Browning, A. Introduction to Memoirs of Sir John Reresby.

RHYMER, THOMAS the. See ERCEL-DOUNE, THOMAS

RICH, BARNABE (1540?-November 10, 1617), romancer, pamphleteer, was a distant relative of Lord Rich and was probably born in Essex. He received little education, enlisting in the army about 1555. He served in the Low Countries, rose to the rank of captain, and was sent to Ireland in 1573; the greater part of his remaining years was spent there and he died in Dublin.

In 1574, during a visit to London, he renewed acquaintance with literary men, like Churchyard and Gascoigne, who had served with him on the Continent. They introduced him to Lodge and others. Rich decided to take to writing himself and his first book, *A Right Excellent and Pleasant Dialogue Between Mercury and an English Soldier*, appeared the same year.

Rich spent much of his service in Ireland at garrison duty, usually in Dublin. In 1584-85 he was in command of a hundred men at Coleraine in the North of Ireland. Most of these men were killed in a fight with the Scotch-Irish in November 1585, while Barnabe was safe in Dublin.

In 1589 Queen Elizabeth granted him a pension of half-a-crown a day for life; probably this marked the end of his active military career; the grant seems to have been renewed by James I in 1606, and the payment continued regularly until his death. In 1616 he received a royal gift of £100 as the oldest army captain in Ireland.

Rich was a very loyal Englishman and a fanatical Protestant. Many of his pamphlets are concerned with the state of Ireland; they complain about the corruption of the English government there and its undue toleration of Roman Catholics or—as

433

Rich would call them—"Papists." He became a determined enemy of Adam Loftus, Archbishop of Dublin, Lord Chancellor of Ireland, and first Provost of Trinity College in Dublin, who was notorious for his misappropriation of government funds. As a result, Rich was assaulted by Loftus' men on several occasions and finally fled to England, believing that his life was in danger. He remained in London from about 1594 to 1600 or later, though in 1599 he begged Sir Robert Cecil to send him back to Ireland "in any able sort."

When he did return to Ireland, Rich once more became the self-appointed adviser of the English government on Irish affairs. He had written letters on the subject to Lord Burghley and Sir Robert Cecil, afterwards Earl of Salisbury; in 1612 we find him sending to Sir Julius Caesar, Chancellor of the Exchequer, a manuscript entitled *Remembrances of the State of Ireland*; a further one called *The Anothomy (Anatomy?) of Ireland* was sent in 1615.

Rich's work is important in three ways: his pamphlets on the soldier's lot are valuable to the military historian; his writings on Ireland, both published and manuscript, are of value to historians of that country, in spite of their fierce anti-Irish and anti-Catholic bias; finally, one of the romances in *Rich His Farewell to Military Profession* gave Shakespeare the plot for *Twelfth Night*, Rich himself having found the story in a novel by Bandello.

The previous paragraph would seem to imply that Rich's work is not worth reading for its own sake, nor is it; the same is true of most Elizabethan prose, of which Rich's is not a bad example. His verse, however, is very poor.

PRINCIPAL WORKS: *Romances*: Rich His Farewell to Military Profession, 1581; The Strange and Wonderful Adventures of Don Simonides, 1581; The Second Tome of the Travels and Adventures of Don Simonides, 1584; The Adventures of Brusanus, Prince of Hungaria, 1592. *Pamphlets*: A Right Excellent and Pleasant Dialogue, 1574; Alarm to England, 1578; The True Report of a Late Practice Enterprised by a Papist, 1582; A Pathway to Military Practice, 1587; A Martial Conference, 1598; A Soldier's Wish to Britain's Welfare, 1604; Faults, Faults and Nothing Else but Faults, 1606; A Short Survey of Ireland, 1609; Room for a Gentleman, 1609; A New Description of Ireland, 1610; A True and a Kind Excuse, 1612; A Catholic Conference, 1612; The Excellency of Good Women, 1613; Opinion Defied, 1613;

The Honesty of This Age, 1614; The Irish Hubbub, 1617.

ABOUT: Ghall, S. Barnabe Rich in Ireland (Dublin Magazine, 1926).

RICH, MARY. See WARWICK, MARY RICH, Countess of

RICHARDSON, SAMUEL (1689-July 4, 1761), novelist, seems to have been born in Derbyshire, one of nine children of a prosperous joiner or cabinetmaker, originally from Surrey. The family moved to London when he was a small child. The obscurity about his early life is due to his own reticence; Richardson was a bit of a snob and rather ashamed of his beginnings. Apparently he had been intended for the Church, but his father lost his money and could not afford the necessary education. Richardson's schooling, wherever it took place (he was never a student at Christ's Hospital, as has been claimed) was certainly very meager. He was a precocious child, who from early boyhood wrote love letters for all the illiterate servant girls of his acquaintance. At seventeen he was apprenticed to a printer named Wilde, and in true "industrious apprentice" style, by 1719 he was in business for himself. In 1721 he married Martha Wilde (who was not his old master's daughter, as has been stated); they had five sons and a daughter, all of whom died early; she died in 1731. He then married Elizabeth Leake, and they had one son and five daughters, but the son and one daughter died as children—not at all an unusual record for the eighteenth century.

Richardson prospered as a printer, becoming printer to the House of Commons and half-owner of the patent as law printer to the king. Toward the end of his life he was master of the Stationers' Company, and he was able to build a new printing plant, with home attached, and a country house at Hammersmith. This money came primarily from his trade; his fame, of course, came from his writing. Though all his books were anonymous, their authorship was an open secret.

Pamela, which may be called the mother or grandmother of the novel of sentiment, originated in a request from two colleagues that Richardson (with his experience as a vicarious letter writer) do a volume of letters for them to be used as copies on various occasions. (Actually this book was written and published; it was the only work of Richardson's he never acknowledged.) Becoming interested in the ostensible authors of these "model letters," he conceived the idea of using them in a novel. *Pamela*, in two volumes (two more were added later to describe the heroine's married life), was the result.

It is impossible to exaggerate the furore caused by the plump, florid little printer's first novel. *Pamela* was read from the pulpit; church bells were rung to celebrate the heroine's final victory, when her would-be seducer at last married her legally. It was the first authentic voice of the emerging middle class, of its ethics, its religion, and its sentimentality. It was essentially puritanical in its viewpoint; "virtue" was "rewarded" by strictly bourgeois concepts, and even its rather surprising sexual frankness was drowned in a syrup of sentimentality. But it would never have been the remarkable success it was, if the artist hidden in Richardson had not outweighed the moralist. What made its readers laugh and weep and sympathize was the vivid realism of the writing, and the uncanny knowledge of feminine psychology displayed by the author.

The book gave birth to a flood of "continuations," skits, plays, and parodies. Most famous of these was Fielding's *Joseph Andrews* (supposedly Pamela's brother), which started out as a burlesque, and ended as a novel in its own right. Richardson was bitterly offended, and he never forgave Fielding. Later he wrote *Sir Charles Grandison* as a direct answer to *Tom Jones*; he would show a hero who was a gentleman and a Puritan. What he really showed was an overwhelming prig. However, between these two came *Clarissa* (often miscalled "Clarissa Harlowe"). Both *Clarissa* and *Grandison* are, incidentally, much better novels than *Pamela*.

Pamela is a wish-fulfilment dream; *Clarissa* a warning of the "distresses" attendant on "misconduct in relation to marriage." It is a tragedy, and the persecuted heroine finally dies at the end of seven volumes. But here is the same instinctive psychological insight, the same vividness, and for the first

J. Highmore, 1750
SAMUEL RICHARDSON

time a really good study of subsidiary characters. Its agony is overdone, its obstacles are frequently factitious, and much of it is in the poorest possible taste, but it was a *succès fou*. So was *Grandison*, much the most didactic of the three, but also the only one with much real humor and some wit.

Richardson, like all the writers of his age, suffered much from unscrupulous piracy of his work; he wrote an indignant pamphlet about it, which did no good in the absence of an adequate copyright law. But aside from this, he reveled in the esteem and glory that came to him. He became the center of a circle of admirers, mostly middle-aged ladies, to whom he gave little breakfasts while he read aloud his latest writing. He was a ridiculously vain little man, who adored being praised and flattered. But this must not blind us to the fact that he was also a major novelist. Ill planned, careless, and chaotic his novels might be, but they were works of genius—a genius strictly limited, but genuine. Like Dickens, he was a born story teller, and he had the same easy, varied style—with very much the same flaws of taste and pretentiousness. He looked silly when he tried to describe an aristocratic society he had never experienced, but within his own world he displayed an insight that few novelists have equaled.

435

The influence of Richardson's novels is almost incalculable. In England, Sterne, Fanny Burney, and even Jane Austen owed much to him; in France and Germany he practically created a literary genre. Rousseau was his disciple in fiction, and even Goethe echoed Richardson in *Werther.* "Pamela's daughters" indeed invaded every civilized western country, and her descendants were a long time in dying. One may call Richardson himself a prig, a milksop, a snob—and justly; but even his private character was not all foolish—he was kindly, practically generous to many needy young authors, amiably absent-minded, but a shrewd business man and a just employer. He would bore most modern people abominably, and his books do bore them and are seldom read now except by students of literary history, but what he did for the English novel (and for the European novel as a whole) gives him a permanent right to the admiration of posterity. Even he would be satisfied with his fame.

PRINCIPAL WORKS: Pamela, or Virtue Rewarded. In a Series of familiar Letters from a Beautiful Young Damsel to Her Parents, 1740-44; Letters written to and for particular Friends, 1741; Tour through the Whole Island of Great Britain, 1742; Clarissa: or the History of a Young Lady, 1747-48; Meditations Collected from the Sacred Books . . . Mentioned by Clarissa for Her Own Use, 1750; The History of Sir Charles Grandison, 1753-54; A Collection of the Moral and Instructive Sentiments, Maxims, Cautions, and Re- (A. L. Barbauld, ed.) 1804; Works (E. Mangin, ed.) 1811; Novels (W. Scott, ed) 1824; (L. Stephen, ed. 1883).

ABOUT: Barbauld, A. L. Biographical Account *in* Correspondence; Diderot, D. Éloge de Richardson; Dobson, A. Richardson; Downs, B. W. Richardson; Hazlitt, W. Lectures on the English Novelists; Hudson, W. H. A Quiet Corner in a Library; Jusserand, J. The English Novel; Krutch, J. W. Five Masters; McKillop, A. D. Samuel Richardson, Printer and Novelist; Mangin, E. Sketch of Life and Writings, *in* Works; Sale, W. M. Samuel Richardson: a bibliographical record of his literary career, with historical notes; Schmidt, E. R. Richardson, Rousseau, und Goethe (in German); Scott, W. Life, *in* Novels, 1824 ed.; Stephen, L. Prefatory Chapter, *in* Novels, 1883 ed.; Thomson, C. L. Samuel Richardson, a Biographical and Critical Study; Utter, R. P. Pamela's Daughters.

RIDLEY, NICHOLAS

RIDLEY, NICHOLAS (1500?-October 16, 1555), author of theological treatises and prayers, was born at Unthank Hall, near Willemoteswick, Northumberland, the son of Christopher Ridley and Anne Blenkinsop. After school at Newcastle-on-Tyne, he entered Pembroke Hall, Cambridge, about

1518, his uncle, a clergyman, paying all his expenses. He made himself into an outstanding Greek scholar, graduated B.A. in 1522, became a fellow of his college, and received an M.A. in 1526. After this he studied at the Sorbonne and at Louvain, and in 1530 returned to Cambridge as junior treasurer of his college. In 1534 he was made proctor and chaplain of the university, having meanwhile been ordained. Already he was beginning to lean toward the Reformation, though he never declared himself openly until his uncle's death in 1536. He secured his B.D. degree in 1537, and became chaplain of the Archbishop of Canterbury, Thomas Cranmer. In 1538 he was given the living of Herne, Kent. Two years later he received his D.D. and was appointed master of Pembroke. In 1541 he was made canon of Canterbury and one of Henry VIII's chaplains; in 1545 he was canon of Westminster, in 1547 Bishop of Rochester, and in 1548 made a visitation to Cambridge (he still retained his mastership of Pembroke) to establish the Anglican reform there.

As early as 1534, Ridley had been accused of heresy, but had been acquitted. Now under Edward VI he was in high favor. He helped compile the Book of Common Prayer, and he became the young king's adviser, inspiring him to relieve the poor by establishment of Christ's, St. Thomas', and Bethlehem Hospitals. (Bad as these were by

NICHOLAS RIDLEY

modern standards, they were far better than nothing at all.) In 1550 he was one of the commissioners who deposed the Bishop of London, whom he succeeded.

But with the accession of Mary, Ridley's doom was sealed. Very indiscreetly (his enemies said, on the promise of the bishopric of Durham), he attached himself openly to the cause of Lady Jane Grey, and in 1553 went so far as to preach a sermon in which he declared both Mary and her half-sister Elizabeth to be illegitimate. What made him think Mary would ever forgive this cannot be imagined, but on her accession he immediately threw himself on the queen's non-existent mercy. She responded by having him thrown in the Tower, and seeing that he was excepted from the later amnesty. In 1554 he was sent, with Cranmer and Latimer, to Oxford to defend his religious views. He was declared a heretic and excommunicated (from the Roman Catholic Church), and when he refused to recant, was tried in September 1555, sentenced to the greater excommunication and to degradation, and handed over to the secular law. With Latimer and Cranmer he was burnt at the stake on October 16, but unlike them he did not die easily, but only after horrible tortures, which he endured bravely.

Ridley was a really great scholar. He was also a pulpit orator whose sermons were greatly admired, but nearly all of them have disappeared. Very little of his writing remains, and most of that was first collected by Foxe. He had no literary pretensions, but wrote his tracts only in advocacy of the reform movement.

PRINCIPAL WORKS: Injunctions Given in the Visitation, 1550; A Brief Declaration of the Lorde's Supper, 1555; Certen Godly, Learned and Comfortable Conferences between N.R., late Bysshope of London, and Hughe Latimer, . . . [with] a Treatise ag^t the Error of Transubstantiation, 1556; A Friendly Farewell (J. Foxe, ed.) 1559; A Pitious Lamentation of the Miserable Estate of the Church of Christ in England, 1566; Works (H. Christmas, ed.) 1813.

ABOUT: Foxe, J. Actes and Monuments; Ridley, G. Life of Bishop Ridley.

RITSON, JOSEPH (October 2, 1752-September 23, 1803), literary antiquary, historian, bibliographer, was born at Stockton-on-Tees, Durham, the son of Joseph Ritson and Jane Gibson. His father and mother were both for a time in domestic service; later his father became a struggling farmer.

Young Ritson received his entire education at Stockton, and was apprenticed to a solicitor there at an early age. Soon afterward he was apprenticed to a conveyancer. About 1775 he left Stockton for London; after working in a conveyancing office there for five years at a salary of £150 a year, he set up in business for himself. At first he did not prosper, but his business grew with time; in 1784 he became Bailiff of the Liberty and Franchises of the Savoy, London; in 1786 this post was secured to him for life, giving him an annual income of something less than £100. He would have been well-to-do, were it not for his heavy expenditure on books, his generous support of his relatives, and his unfortunate speculation on the stock market.

Ritson's interest in literature and archaeology began in his Stockton days; he went on an antiquarian walking tour in Scotland, 1773; the library facilities in London and his greater leisure after 1784 fathered an immense body of work, chiefly in the fields of English folk poetry and other folklore. Ritson was the first "scientific" editor of such material, and he was savagely critical of editors who (like Percy) "improved" their originals or (like Pinkerton) actually wrote spurious folk poetry. He was also impatient with the various contemporary editors of Shakespeare.

Ritson was a little, thin, stooped man with a long, sharp nose; he never married, but brought up his nephew Joseph Frank like a son. A vegetarian and an atheist, Ritson was a Jacobite in 1778, but became a thorough revolutionary after a visit to Paris in 1791. He was always very critical of priests and lawyers, though himself called to the Bar in 1789. He had his own eccentric system of spelling, too. A chronic nervous condition, probably hereditary, grew worse after 1790; in 1802 he had a stroke; in September 1803 he became definitely insane, but mercifully died after a few days' confinement.

PRINCIPAL WORKS: Observations on the Three First Volumes of the History of English Poetry, 1783; Remarks . . . on the Text and Notes of the Last Edition of Shakespeare, 1783; a Select Collection of English Songs, 1783; Gammer Gurton's Garland, or the Nursery Parnassus, 1784; The Quip Modest, 1788; Ancient Songs, 1790; Pieces of Ancient Popular Poetry, 1791; Cursory Criticisms on the Edition of Shakespeare published by Edmond Malone, 1792; The English

Anthology, 1793-94; Scotish (*sic*) Songs, 1794; Law Tracts, 1794; Poems . . . by Laurence Minot, 1795; Robin Hood, 1795; Bibliographia Poetica, 1802; An Essay on Abstinence from Animal Food as a Moral Duty, 1802; Ancient Engleish (*sic*) Metrical Romancees (*sic*) 1802; Northern Garlands, 1810; The Office of Bailiff of a Liberty, 1811; The Caledonian Nurse, 1821; The Life of King Arthur, 1825; Memoirs of the Celts or Gauls, 1827; Annals of the Caledonians, Picts, and Scots, 1828; Fairy Tales, 1831.

ABOUT: Bronson, B. H. Joseph Ritson, Scholar-at-arms; Burd, H. A. Joseph Ritson, a Critical Biography; Nicolas, H. Memoir prefixed to The Letters of Joseph Ritson, 1833.

ROBERTSON, WILLIAM (September 19, 1721-June 11, 1793), Presbyterian minister, historian, was born in Bothwick, Midlothian, the son of William Robertson, a Presbyterian minister, and Eleanor Pitcairne. He was educated at Dalkeith Grammar School and in 1733 went to the University of Edinburgh (which gave him an honorary D.D. in 1758). In 1741 he was licensed to preach, and two years later he succeeded his uncle as minister at Gladsmuir, East Lothian. In 1745 his parents both died, and he had to care for and educate a number of younger brothers and sisters; in consequence, he had to wait eight years to marry his cousin, Mary Nisbet, also a minister's daughter. They had three sons and two daughters.

In 1745 Robertson fought as a volunteer against the Pretender, and in recognition of his services he was elected next year to the General Assembly. He became the leader of its "moderate" faction, and was its moderator from 1763 to 1769. In 1750 he became minister at Lady Yester's Chapel, Edinburgh, and in 1759 became chaplain of Stirling Castle. This was the year he published his *History of Scotland*, which brought him immediate acclaim. In 1761 he was minister of Old Greyfriars, Edinburgh, and the next year was made king's chaplain in Scotland. In 1762 also he was appointed principal of Edinburgh University (a post he held until 1792) and the next year he was made historiographer royal.

For his *History of the Reign of Charles V*—the first attempt in English to present a large-scale general view of European history —Robertson received £4500, the largest sum paid to that time for an historical work. It gave him a European reputation, and he was elected a member of the official Academies of Madrid, Padua, and St. Petersburg. He died of jaundice at seventy-two.

After Sir J. Reynolds
WILLIAM ROBERTSON

Robertson, though a staunch Presbyterian, was distinctly liberal in his views, as may be seen from the fact that he was the close friend of Hume, and was intimate also with Adam Smith, Garrick, and Gibbon. He even defended the theatres, though he himself never attended one. In 1779 his house was attacked by a Calvinist mob because he had approved the lifting of penalties on Scottish Roman Catholics. He was a charter member of the Select Society, which gathered the best minds in Edinburgh for discussion. The deaf old gentleman in his old-fashioned dress, with his strong Scottish brogue, was a familiar figure in Edinburgh. He was the correspondent of Voltaire and Catherine II of Russia, yet he remained always a true Scottish provincial.

As an historian, Robertson gave an enormous impetus to the writing of history in Scotland. He had the historical sense of unity and interrelation, but he used his authorities inaccurately and was too uncritical and superficial. Nevertheless, he broke ground that no one else had covered. His style, which he modeled on Tacitus, Juvenal, and Swift, was heavily "Johnsonian" and full of Latinisms. But he had a gift for rhetorical narrative and was capable of lucidity as well as of sonority. His philosophical comments were mere commonplaces; his talent was for pure exposition.

Robertson's *History of America* deals entirely with the Spanish explorations and colonizations; the American Revolution prevented his going on to the colonial history of North America.

PRINCIPAL WORKS: The Situation of the World at the Time of Christ's Appearance, 1755; History of Scotland during the Reigns of Queen Mary and of King James VI till his Accession to the Throne of England, 1759; History of the Reign of the Emperor Charles V, 1770; History of America, 1777 (2 vols.) 1778 (3 vols.); An Historical Disquisition concerning the Knowledge the Ancients Had of India, 1791; Works (8 vols.) (D. Stewart, ed.) 1817.

ABOUT: Black, J. B. The Art of History; Brougham, H. Lives of Eminent Men of Letters; Gleig, G. Account of the Life and Writings of William Robertson; Stewart, D. Account of Life *in* Works.

ROCHESTER, Earl of. See WILMOT, JOHN, Second Earl of Rochester

ROLLE of HAMPOLE, RICHARD

(c. 1300-September 30, 1349), author of religious works, was born at Thornton-le-Dale in Yorkshire, the son of William Rolle. He went to school early and his ability there attracted the attention of Thomas de Neville, Archdeacon of Durham, who sent him to Oxford University, paying all his expenses. Thirteen was the usual age for entering the university then; Rolle remained at Oxford until he was in his nineteenth year, making excellent progress in his studies and concentrating on theology rather than secular learning.

Suddenly he decided to quit the University and become a hermit—he was at home for the summer vacation at the time. From two of his sister's dresses and his father's rain hood he made himself a hermit's garb. His sister cried out that he was mad, so he ran away, never to return home again.

That evening he was recognized as an Oxford contemporary by the sons of John de Dalton, a local squire, whose wife had seen him praying in her place in the church. The next day, the Feast of the Assumption, Richard preached a sermon which so impressed John de Dalton that he undertook to support the would-be hermit, whose father he knew.

Once established in his cell, Richard took up a life of contemplation in earnest. He was soon rewarded by the beginnings of mystical experience; this experience reached

its climax some four years later; its whole course is described in *The Fire of Love*, originally written by Rolle in Latin.

Later he left the Daltons' neighborhood and traveled about the North of England, finally settling near a small nunnery at Hampole, close to Doncaster. His writings refer to various persecutions that he suffered from the regular clergy, but at Hampole he seems to have been untroubled; it was there that he died, probably of the plague.

In later life, Rolle cured a certain Margaret de Kirkeby, a recluse, of what seems to have been a hysterical seizure. Other miracles were attributed to him after his death, and a cult grew up at Hampole.

Rolle wrote devotional and moral works in English as well as in Latin, hoping thereby to reach a wider circle of readers, especially among women, who could not usually read Latin even if they were nuns. He translated portions of the Bible into English —notably the Psalms. He also wrote English poetry; *The Prick of Conscience*, a long poem, has always been attributed to him, but Miss H. E. Allen, the great modern authority on Rolle, says he did not write it.

Rolle's authentic works were all written before the invention of printing, so only modern editions are listed below. Many works have been attributed to him that are not his, and many that are his have never been printed.

Besides his importance to the development of a vernacular English literature, Rolle is a very significant figure in other ways. He was without a doubt the greatest English mystic, and, as such, he has been much written about and translated in the present century. He is also, like Wycliffe, symptomatic of the coming of the Reformation. He translated part of the Bible, he was critical of the regular priesthood, he never belonged to any religious order; these things do not make him a Protestant, but they do make him part of a very important movement within the Catholic Church itself which antedated both Reformation and counter-Reformation.

PRINCIPAL WORKS: *Modern Editions of the English Works*: The Prick of Conscience (R. Morris, ed.) 1865; Hampole's English Prose Treatises (G. G. Perry, ed.) 1866; The Psalter by Richard Rolle of Hampole (H. R. Bramley, ed.) 1884; Yorkshire Writers, Richard Rolle of Hampole (C. Horstmann, ed.) 1895-96. *Translations and Modernizations*: A Book of the Love of Jesus (R. H. Benson, ed.) 1904; Meditations on the Passion (E. Burton, ed.) 1906; The Form of Perfect Living (G. E. Hodgson, ed.) 1910; The Mending of Life (D. Harford, ed.) 1914; The Fire of Love and The Mending of Life (F. M. M. Comper, ed.) 1914; Some Minor Works of Richard Rolle (G. E. Hodgson, ed.) 1923.

ABOUT: Allen, H. E. Writings Ascribed to Richard Rolle, Hermit of Hampole, and Materials for his Biography; Comper, F. M. M. The Life and Lyrics of Richard Rolle; Hodgson, G. E. The Sanity of Mysticism.

ROPER, WILLIAM (1496-January 4, 1578), biographer of Sir Thomas More, was the eldest son of John Roper, who owned estates at Eltham and Canterbury in Kent and was clerk of the pleas to the court of king's bench at Canterbury. William inherited the greater part of his father's estate at the latter's death in 1524, and also succeeded to his court clerkship.

In 1525 William married Margaret, favorite daughter of Sir Thomas More, a gentle, charming woman, extremely intelligent and very well educated. Like all More's family circle, Roper was devoted to the future martyr and saint. After More's execution in 1535, Roper wrote a biography of him, intended for circulation chiefly among his immediate family and friends; the work was not printed until long after Roper's death.

Roper was a Member of Parliament for various Kentish constituencies at different times during the reigns of Henry VIII and Edward VI. Like his father-in-law, he remained a staunch Catholic until death, so it is not surprising to find that he sat in every parliament during the brief reign of the Catholic Mary Tudor. After Elizabeth's accession in 1558 Roper sat no more in Parliament. Indeed, his known Catholicism made him an object of suspicion to the Privy Council; in 1568 and 1569 he had to appear before that body on charges of being accessory to treasonous behavior, but suffered no serious inconvenience. In 1577 he resigned his legal post in favor of his eldest son. The following year he died and was buried in St. Dunstan's Church, Canterbury, along with the decapitated head of Sir Thomas More. Margaret had died in 1544; she bore him two sons and three daughters.

Roper's *Life of Sir Thomas More* is an extremely readable little book, full of humorous and pathetic anecdote. It is too art-less a work to claim consideration as literature, but is better worth reading than many more pretentious biographies.

PRINCIPAL WORKS: The Life, Arraignment and Death of that Mirror of All True Honor and Virtue, Sir Thomas More, 1626.

ROSCOMMON, WENTWORTH DILLON, Fourth Earl of (1633?-January 1685), critic, translator, was born in Ireland, the son of Sir James Dillon and Elizabeth Wentworth. His maternal uncle was the Earl of Strafford, then lord deputy of Ireland. Educated as a Protestant, the boy was sent abroad to a Protestant university in Caen, Normandy, at the time of Strafford's impeachment. He continued to live on the Continent until after the Restoration, when he returned to England. At this period in his life he has been described as a "scholar, an honest man and something of a prig."

In 1662 he married Lady Frances Boyle and became a member (usually *in absentia*) of the Irish parliament. Although he played a gentleman's role in public life both in Ireland and in London, his greatest ambition was to found a literary academy. This project he was able to carry out at least partially, bringing together a distinguished group of writers and translators who read and criticized each other's work. His own contribution was an *Essay on Translated Verse*, of which the kindest thing to be said is that it reads like an exercise presented to an academy of letters, which is no doubt what Roscommon intended. For his efforts the earl received an honorary degree of LL.D. from Cambridge in 1680 and a D.C.L. from Oxford three years later.

Roscommon also translated Horace and Ovid and wrote a number of poems, hymns, and critical essays. His greatest claim to fame is as the first English critic to praise Milton's *Paradise Lost*. Perhaps because he was a friend of Dryden, perhaps because Dr. Johnson (rather grudgingly) admired him, Roscommon's talents were overrated in his own time and in the eighteenth century.

According to Johnson's account, the earl decided on religious grounds to retire to Rome after the accession of James II, saying "it would be best to sit next to the chimney when the chamber smoked." This would seem to be apocryphal, however, since he died a few months before the death of

Charles II. It is also told that he rose from his sickbed to hear a sermon preached by a friend, calling it his own funeral oration, and on his deathbed wrote the first half of a divine poem which he left as a legacy to his second wife, Isabella. Probably Dr. Johnson's estimate of Roscommon's work is as just as any—"he improved taste, if he did not enlarge knowledge, and may be numbered among the benefactors to English literature."

PRINCIPAL WORKS: Horace's Art of Poetry, Made English by the Earl of Roscommon (tr.) 1680; An Essay on Translated Verse, 1684 (J. E. Spingarn, ed. 1909); Ovid's Art of Love (tr.) 1692; A Prospect of Death: a Pindarique Essay, 1704; The Miscellaneous Works of the Late Earls of Rochester and Roscommon, 1707; A Collection of Divine Hymns and Poems, 1709; Poems by the Earl of Roscommon, 1717; The Christian Poet, or Remains by Wentworth Dillon, the Earl of Roscommon, 1735.

ABOUT: Johnson, S. The Lives of the Poets (G. B. Hill, ed.); Kippis, A. Biographia Britannica; Sanford, E. Life, in Select Poems of the Earl of Roscommon.

ROSS, ALEXANDER (April 13, 1699-May 20, 1784), Scots poet, was born in Kincardine-O'Neil parish, Aberdeenshire, the son of a tenant farmer. He attended the local school and won a bursary to Marischal College, Aberdeen, in 1714; he graduated M.A. in 1718. For a time he was a private tutor and then became a parish schoolmaster; though very devout, he chose not to enter the Church. He taught first at Aboyne, then at Laurencekirk; finally, in 1732 or 1733, he settled at Lochlee in Glenesk, where he spent the remainder of his long life. He was reader and precentor of the parish, session clerk and notary public, as well as schoolmaster. Nevertheless he found plenty of time for reading and study, and wrote a great deal of poetry—mainly devotional, but including some popular songs and two "pastoral tales" in Scots dialect.

In 1766 Ross revisited Aberdeen to seek a publisher for his poems. James Beattie, poet and philosopher, selected *Helenore* and a few songs as best suited for publication, and they were published by subscription two years later. Ross made £20 from the edition. In 1778 a second edition appeared, dedicated to the Duchess of Gordon, who invited Ross to visit her and gave him a present of £15 on his departure.

Ross married Jean Catanach, a Catholic, in 1726. She bore him seven children, of whom four lived to adulthood; they were all brought up as members of the Church of Scotland. Jean died in 1779, aged seventy-seven. Her husband died five years later, after an unusually long and uneventful life.

Ross's *Helenore* is modeled on Allan Ramsay's *The Gentle Shepherd*, but has a certain originality and truth to life of its own. It will always hold a place in the history of Scots literature, but the ordinary reader is hardly likely to have the patience to grapple with the Highland Scots dialect through a poem of four thousand lines. Ross's songs are unimpressive.

In person Ross was small, but neatly formed. By temperament he was lively and good humored.

PRINCIPAL WORKS: The Fortunate Shepherdess, a Pastoral Tale, 1768; Helenore, or the Fortunate Shepherdess (2d ed. of the preceding) 1778; The Scottish Works of Alexander Ross . . . consisting of Helenore, or The Fortunate Shepherdess, Songs, The Fortunate Shepherd, or The Orphan (M. Wattie, ed.) 1938.

ABOUT: Wattie, M. Life in The Scottish Works of Alexander Ross.

ROWE, NICHOLAS (1674-December 6, 1718), dramatist, poet, was born at Little Barford, Bedfordshire, the eldest child of John and Elizabeth Rowe. His father was a successful London barrister; his mother died when he was only five years old. Educated at a private school and then at Westminster School, Rowe was intended for the law; his father took him from Westminster at fifteen and entered him as a law student at the Middle Temple. Rowe completed his studies and was called to the Bar, but never practiced. Meanwhile his father had died in 1692 and left him £300 a year, which was more than enough to live on. Rowe decided to follow his own inclinations and become a dramatist.

In 1700 his first play, *The Ambitious Stepmother*, was performed with some success. Rowe became a friend of Addison and Pope; the latter was particularly attached to him. During his play writing career, which lasted until 1715, he was probably the outstanding tragedian in England, though *The Biter*, his one attempt at farce, was an utter failure. *Jane Shore*, which he described as

After Sir G. Kneller

NICHOLAS ROWE

"Written in Imitation of Shakespeare's Style," was his best work, though *The Fair Penitent*, which gave the world the character of "gay Lothario," was almost equally popular during the century following his death.

In 1707 Rowe revealed his political sympathies by publishing *A Poem upon the Late Glorious Successes of Her Majesty's Arms*, dedicated to Lord Godolphin; his support of the war policy and his choice of a patron showed that he was a Whig. From 1709 to 1711 he held a government post under the Whigs as Under-Secretary of State for Scotland. Later, when the Whigs regained power at the accession of George I, he was made poet laureate. Several other lucrative official positions came his way in the three following years, but he did not live long to enjoy his political favor. The laureateship may be said to have put an end to his literary career, though he ground out various New Year and birthday odes. His work as a translator from Latin and Greek deserves some mention, if only because he produced an English version of Lucan's epic, the *Pharsalia*.

Rowe was the first textual editor and the first true biographer of Shakespeare. His six-volume edition of the plays, which appeared in 1709, contained many notes and emendations that have been accepted by later scholars.

He was a very merry man for a writer of tragedy; he laughed a great deal and could make others laugh too—in conversation, not in the theatre. His portrait shows him to have been decidedly handsome. He married twice. His first wife, Antonia Parsons, died in 1706, after bearing him a son; his second, Anne Devenish, whom he married in 1717, bore him a daughter, outlived him and married again.

As editor, as translator, as dramatic poet, Rowe has a triple claim on the gratitude of posterity. The author of *Jane Shore* and first editor of Shakespeare was not unworthy of his last resting place—the Poets' Corner of Westminster Abbey.

PRINCIPAL WORKS: *Plays*: The Ambitious Stepmother (tragedy) 1701; Tamerlane (tragedy) 1702; The Fair Penitent (tragedy) 1703; The Biter (farce) 1705; Ulysses (tragedy) 1706; The Royal Convert (tragedy) 1708; The Tragedy of Jane Shore, 1714; The Tragedy of the Lady Jane Grey, 1715. *Poems and Translations*: A Poem upon the late Glorious Successes, 1707; Callipaedia (tr.) 1712; Poems on Several Occasions, 1714; Ode for the New Year, 1716; Lucan's Pharsalia (tr.) 1718.

ABOUT: Broadus, E. K. The Laureateship; Johnson, S. Lives of the Poets.

ROWLANDS, SAMUEL (1570?-1630?),

writer of satirical and devotional tracts in prose and verse, is an author dearer to book collectors than to lovers of literature; all the original editions of his works are of a tantalizing rarity. This rarity is probably due to the fact that he wrote for semi-literate readers of the London lower middle classes, who would re-read what few books they owned until these fell to pieces.

Nothing is known of Rowlands aside from his works. The first of these, a collection of devotional poems entitled *The Betraying of Christ*, appeared in 1598; the last, *Heaven's Glory*, in 1628. With his second pamphlet, *The Letting of Humour's Blood in the Head-Vein*, he began his satirical onslaught upon the society of his time; *A Merry Meeting*, in similar vein, followed. Both these pamphlets were burned by the authorities in 1600. *Greene's Ghost Haunting Coney Catchers*, a prose pamphlet first printed in 1602, imitates similar works by Greene, Nash and others in revealing the tricks used by Elizabethan "confidence men" to fleece the unsuspecting "gull" or "coney." *'Tis Merry When Gossips Meet*, which was published the same year, is an amusing account, realistic rather than satirical, of the conversation that passes between a widow, a wife, and a maid of the shopkeeping class over their wine.

The titles listed above exemplify the main types of writing practiced by Rowlands. He also wrote "occasional" poems on current events such as the death of Queen Elizabeth, and produced a version of *The Famous History of Guy, Earl of Warwick.*

In spite of the seeming variety of his poetical undertakings, Rowlands practically always employed the same six-line stanza, whatever his subject matter. He used it most effectively in certain twelve-line epigrams in *The Letting of Humour's Blood.*

Since no new work by Rowlands appeared after 1628, he presumably died shortly thereafter, having by then some twenty-five titles to his credit or discredit.

PRINCIPAL WORKS: The Complete Works of Samuel Rowlands, 1598-1628, Now First Collected (Hunterian Club) 1880; Ave Caesar, God Save the King (Hunterian Club) 1886; The Bride (A. C. Potter, ed.) 1905.

ABOUT: Gosse, E. Seventeenth-Century Studies.

ROWLEY, SAMUEL (d. 1633?), dramatist, first appears in the *Diary* of Philip Henslowe, the Elizabethan theatre owner, as witness to a loan made by Henslowe on August 3, 1597. On November 16, 1598, he and one Charles Massey became "covenanted servants" of Henslowe, signing a bond not to perform at any other playhouse but his until a year from the following Shrovetide. Before and after this period of indenture Rowley and Massey appear in the *Diary* as members of the Lord Admiral's company of players.

In 1601 Henslowe paid Rowley and William Birde £6 for a play named *Judas.* The following year Rowley received £7 for *Joshua,* of which he was apparently sole author. He and Birde received £4 between them for "additions" to Marlowe's *Dr. Faustus* later in 1602. These additions were undoubtedly some of the naïve comic scenes in the play as we now have it. Neither *Judas* nor *Joshua* is now extant.

Rowley is not mentioned in the *Diary* after 1602, but there is no doubt that he continued with the Admiral's Men, who became

successively the Prince's Men in 1603 and the Palsgrave's Men in 1613. Rowley's name appears in all the known lists of this company, the last of which is dated January 4, 1613.

Rowley's one extant play is *When You See Me, You Know Me, or the Famous Chronicle History of King Henry VIII,* printed in 1605. It had already been acted by the Prince's Men. He wrote other plays for the company of which he was so long a member: *Hymen's Holiday,* acted at court in 1612 and 1633; *A French Tragedy of Richard III* and *Hard Shift for Husbands,* both licensed in 1623. *The Noble Soldier,* a tragedy "by S.R.," was published in 1634, the author being then dead, according to the preface. Dekker is believed to have had a larger share than Rowley in the writing of this play.

The most distinctive portion of *When You See Me* is the low comedy of King Henry's fool, William Summers. We may conclude that Rowley's main talent was for comedy; H. Dugdale Sykes (see below) credits him with the authorship of two plays prior to 1590 which gave comic hints to Shakespeare.

PRINCIPAL WORKS: When You See Me, You Know Me, 1605; The Noble Soldier, or A Contract Broken, Justly Revenged, 1634.

ABOUT: Dugdale Sykes, H. The Authorship of "The Taming of a Shrew," "The Famous Victories of Henry V" and the Additions to Marlowe's "Faustus"; Greg, W. W. Henslowe's Diary.

ROWLEY, WILLIAM (1585?-1642?), dramatist, was probably born in London of humble parentage. The first mention of his name occurs on the title page of *The Travels of the Three English Brothers.* The next mention is in the patent issued to the Duke of York's new company of players, March 20, 1610, where Rowley's name stands second in the list. He had probably been an actor for some years previously. The payments made to the company for Court performances in 1612 and 1613 were received by Rowley, which suggests that he was an important member of the group. The company changed its name to the Prince's Men in 1613.

This company and the Lady Elizabeth's Men amalgamated in 1614 and played together for two years at the Hope Theatre,

Paris Garden. Middleton was a leading dramatist of the Lady Elizabeth's company and his collaboration with Rowley probably began at this time. After the two companies separated again, the Prince's Men played *A Fair Quarrel* and *The World Tost at Tennis* at the Curtain Theatre, while the Lady Elizabeth's Men played *The Changeling, The Spanish Gipsy,* and *All's Lost by Lust* at the Cockpit Theatre. All these plays, except the last, which is by Rowley alone, are results of the Rowley-Middleton collaboration.

Rowley was present at the funeral of King James I as one of the Prince's Men; the Prince now became King Charles I, and Rowley was mentioned in the patent issued to the King's Men, 1625. He does not appear in the patent list of 1629 and may have left the stage at Middleton's death in 1627. In the period 1632-38, four plays were published with Rowley's name alone prefixed; all the other plays credited to him are joint efforts. He must have been in great demand as a collaborator, and probably had a hand in many plays which were never printed.

In 1637, Rowley married Isabel Tooley at Cripplegate. He is supposed to have died before the civil war between Charles I and the Parliament began.

We know nothing of Rowley's personal appearance or character, though Langbaine says he was "beloved of . . . Shakespeare, Fletcher and Jonson." Neither do we know for certain what share he had in the plays on which he collaborated. The general opinion of scholars seems to be that he drafted the plots and supplied the comic scenes. Like Dekker, he had the knack of writing realistic London dialogue.

All's Lost by Lust, the only tragedy that Rowley wrote alone, is not particularly distinctive. It is solidly plotted, like most of the Middleton-Rowley plays, but one misses the ruthless dissection of character, particularly feminine character, that is to be found in *The Changeling*—or in *Women Beware Women,* which Middleton wrote alone. One must admit, however, that *The Changeling* is better than any play written by Middleton without Rowley's help. Perhaps it was Rowley's critical rather than his creative power that made him so good a collaborator. His experience as an actor, too, would be of the greatest value. This is all conjecture; William Rowley, in spite of the facts that are known about him, remains only a name.

PRINCIPAL WORKS: *Plays:* The Travels of the Three English Brothers (with Day and Wilkins) 1607; A Fair Quarrel (with Middleton) 1617; A New Wonder, A Woman Never Vext, 1632; A Match at Midnight, 1633; A Tragedy Called All's Lost by Lust, 1633; A Shoemaker a Gentlemen, 1638; The Changeling (with Middleton) 1653; The Spanish Gipsy (with Middleton) 1653; Fortune by Land and Sea (with Heywood) 1655; The Old Law (with Massinger and Middleton) 1656; The Witch of Edmonton (with Dekker and Ford) 1658; The Birth of Merlin (supposedly with Shakespeare) 1662. *Masque:* The World Tost at Tennis (with Middleton) 1620. *Pamphlet:* a Search for Money, 1609.

ABOUT: Stork, C. W. Introduction to William Rowley, his All's Lost by Lust, etc.; Symons, A. Studies in the Elizabethan Drama.

RYMER, THOMAS (1641-December 14, 1713), collector of historical documents, dramatist, critic, was born at Yafforth Hall, Brafferton, Yorkshire, the son of Ralph Rymer, who was hanged for high treason after the "Presbyterian uprising" in 1663. After school at Danby-Wiske, he entered Sidney-Sussex College, Cambridge, in 1658, but left without a degree. He was entered in Gray's Inn in 1666, and called to the bar in 1673. However, he devoted much more time to literature than to the law. He translated Ovid, Plutarch, and wrote some poetry —a series of elegies to Edmund Waller in 1688, and a number of "sportively amorous" poems in various anthologies. He first gained public notice, however, as a critic of the drama and poetry.

Rymer may well have been (by modern standards at least) what Macaulay called him, "the worst critic that ever lived." He believed fanatically in the classical drama with its observance of unities by the Aristotelian formula, and that "the Ancients are and ought to be, our masters." From this standpoint he attacked the great Elizabethan dramatists, including Shakespeare, Jonson and Beaumont and Fletcher. He spoke of *Paradise Lost* as something "which some are pleased to call a poem." He was a pompous learned bigot, who loved to show off his narrow erudition. To him, the greatest dramatic poetry in English was "as rude as our architecture"—said architecture being the Gothic which naturally he also disapproved. Dr. Johnson said that Rymer's criticism had "the ferocity of a tyrant," and even Pope, who in most points agreed with him, thought him "rather too severe" in "demolishing Shakespeare."

To exemplify his views, Rymer himself wrote a play, *Edgar, or the English Monarch*, one of the last strictly classic, rhymed tragedies in English. Unfortunately for him, it was not a success.

Rymer's work of real value began in 1692, when he was made historiographer royal, and given the commission to collect all the treaties and international conventions made by England from the twelfth century. This work (in which Leibnitz helped him by correspondence) was never entirely completed, but the fifteen volumes he himself produced and the five done after his death by others are of immense historical importance. His expenses outran the subsidy paid him, and he spent his last years in extreme poverty, but never pausing in his disinterested labors. He died in London, and was buried in St. Clement Danes. He was unmarried, but seems to have had a long attachment to one "Mrs. Anna Parnell, spinster," to whom he left all his property. This consisted entirely of manuscripts, which she sold to various libraries.

As a critic or a dramatist, Rymer has no standing whatever, but his historical work entitles him to a place in the memory of posterity. This would doubtless have given him satisfaction, as his one aim was to be known as a scholar.

PRINCIPAL WORKS: Cicero's Prince (tr.) 1668; Reflections on Aristotle's Treatise of Poesie (from the French of Rapin) 1674; The Tragedies of the Last Age Consider'd and Examin'd by the Practice of the Ancients, and by the Common Sense of All Ages, 1678; Edgar, or the British Monarch, A Tragedy, 1678; Of the Antiquity, Power, and Decay of Parliaments, 1684; A Short View of Tragedy: Its Original, Excellency, and Corruption, with Some Reflections on Shakespeare and Other Practitioners for the Stage, 1693; Foedera, Conventiones, Literae, Et. . . Acta Publica, etc. (treaties, conventions, letters, and public acts) (15 vols.) 1704-13 (5 more vols., R. Sanderson, et al., 1714-35).

ABOUT: Hardy, T. D. Memoir, *in* Syllabus of Foedera, 1869; Johnson, S. Lives of the English Poets; Macaulay, T. B. Critical and Historical Essays.

SACKVILLE, CHARLES (January 24, 1643-January 29, 1706), sixth Earl of Dorset, fourth Earl of Middlesex, poet, balladist, was the son of Richard Sackville, fifth Earl of Dorset, and Frances Cranfield, daughter of the first Earl of Middlesex. When his father inherited the earldom in 1652, Charles received the courtesy title of Lord Buckhurst. He attended Westminster School for a time, but in 1658 he went to France with a tutor and during the next two years "completed" his education by making the Grand Tour of Europe.

After the restoration of Charles II, Buckhurst became a Member of Parliament, but he was better known as a drunkard, a debauchee, a wit, and a member of the King's intimate circle. With Sir Charles Sedley and Sir Thomas Ogle he took part in the obscene and blasphemous frolic at the Cock Tavern, June 16, 1663. He appeared before a magistrate afterwards, but suffered no punishment.

Buckhurst took part in the great naval victory of the English over the Dutch on June 3, 1665. The night before the battle, he is reputed to have composed his one immortal work, the gay ballad "To All You Ladies Now at Land." On the other hand, he is also supposed to be the Eugenius of Dryden's *Essay of Dramatic Poesy;* the fictitious conversation there set down is described as taking place near London on the day of the battle.

In 1667 Nell Gwynn left the stage for a time to become Buckhurst's mistress. Other amours brought him three or four illegitimate children. In 1674 he became Earl of Middlesex and married the Countess of Falmouth, said to be a former mistress of Charles II. In 1677, at the death of his father, Middlesex became Earl of Dorset. In 1679 his first wife died. In 1685 he married Lady Mary Compton, a beauty of seventeen, and finally gave up his dissipated habits.

Having been in favor throughout the reign of Charles II, Dorset fell from grace at the accession of James II in 1685, and was one of those who helped bring over William III to depose James in 1688. He was Lord Chamberlain to William until 1697 and received the Order of the Garter in 1691, the year his second wife died. The last years of his life were passed in retirement. In 1704 he married Anne Roche, a woman of humble family. At his death his only son Lionel, born 1687, succeeded to his titles.

Sackville's poetical output was small and by no means important; he better deserves to be remembered in the annals of literature as the patron of Dryden, Otway, Congreve,

and Prior—besides many lesser figures—
and as one of the first to recognize the genius in Butler's *Hudibras* and Milton's *Paradise Lost.*

PRINCIPAL WORKS: Pompey the Great, a
Tragedy, Translated out of French by Certain
Persons of Honour (with Waller, Sedley, Godol-
phin, Filmer) 1664; The Works of the Earls of
Rochester, Roscommon, Dorset, etc. 1714; The
Works of the Most Celebrated Minor Poets, vol.
I, 1749.

ABOUT: Harris, B. Charles Sackville; Johnson,
S. Lives of the Poets.

SACKVILLE, THOMAS (1536-April 19,
1608), first Earl of Dorset, poet, dramatist,
was born at Buckhurst, Sussex, the eldest
son of Sir Richard Sackville. His father,
a first cousin of Henry VIII's Anne Boleyn,
held various government positions under
Henry VIII, Edward VI, Mary and Elizabeth, and greatly enriched himself thereby.
Thomas received an excellent education, first
at some local grammar school, then at Hart
Hall, Oxford, and finally at St. John's College, Cambridge, from which he graduated
M.A. He also studied law at the Inner
Temple.

On Queen Elizabeth's coming to the
throne he became a Member of Parliament,
serving in her first two parliaments 1557-59,
and again in 1563. In the early years of
Elizabeth's reign he was very high in her
favor, partly because of his great ability and
partly because he was her second cousin. He
was constantly in private attendance on her
person. These were the years when his literary work was done. *The Tragedy of Gorboduc,* which he wrote conjointly with
Thomas Norton,[*qv*] was performed before the
queen January 6, 1561. In about 1560,
Sackville seems to have planned to take over
The Mirror for Magistrates, a lugubrious
series of poems about the downfalls of great
men that various hack writers were turning
out at the time. He wrote an *Induction* or
introduction for the series and *The Complaint of Henry, Duke of Buckingham,*
which were printed in the edition of 1563,
but not at the beginning of the series, where
they belonged. Until recently the original
plan of the series was thought to be Sackville's, but Baldwin and Ferrers seem to
have been at work on the idea since 1553,
when Sackville was only seventeen, and he
had no share in the first volume that appeared.

THOMAS SACKVILLE, 1st EARL
OF DORSET

After the death of his father in 1566,
Sackville had no time for poetry; he was in
Rome at the time, having gone on a tour of
Europe to complete his education. He hurried home, took over the management of the
great estates he had inherited, and on June
8, 1567, was knighted and created Baron
Buckhurst. He vacated the position of Grand
Master of the Freemasons, which he had
held since 1561, and plunged into affairs of
state.

In 1568 he was Elizabeth's ambassador
to negotiate her marriage with the Duke of
Anjou, which never took place; in 1571 he
again represented her on a special embassy
in France. He also became a member of her
Privy Council at about the same time. In
1586, he was chosen to convey the news of
sentence of death to Mary, Queen of Scots;
he seems to have carried out this unpleasant
mission as humanely as was possible.

In 1587, his career underwent a setback;
sent to the Low Countries by the queen to
investigate the military and political conduct
of the Earl of Leicester, he returned with
an unfavorable report on the reigning favorite. The queen made him a prisoner in his
own house for some nine months, but took
him back into favor after Leicester's death,
in 1588. The following year he was made
a Knight of the Garter and conducted an
embassy to the Low Countries. In 1591 he
negotiated a peace with France; the same

year he was elected Chancellor of Oxford University.

The apex of his career came in 1599, when he became Lord Treasurer of England, a post that he held for the rest of his life. Being wealthy enough not to wish to enrich himself at the public's expense, he carried out the duties of this and all his other offices with the strictest integrity. As Lord High Steward, he presided at the trial of the Earl of Essex and passed sentence on him in 1601. The coming of James I to the throne in 1603 did not affect his position at all. In 1604, he negotiated a peace with Spain and was created first Earl of Dorset. In 1608 his career came to a fitting close; he died at the Privy Council table during a session of that body.

Sackville married, in 1555, the daughter of a Privy Councillor, Cicely Baker, who bore him four sons and three daughters and outlived him. The marriage seems to have been a happy one. A portrait of him done in his later years shows a long, serious face with deep-set eyes and long, drooping moustaches.

Sackville, besides being joint author of the first blank verse play in English, has the distinction of having written one of the best longer poems to appear in English between Chaucer and Spenser—the *Induction*. Spenser recorded his admiration of Sackville's poetry in a sonnet accompanying a presentation copy of *The Faerie Queen*.

PRINCIPAL WORKS: Induction and The Complaint of Henry, Duke of Buckingham, in the Mirror for Magistrates, 1563; The Tragedy of Gorboduc (pirated 1565) 1570.
ABOUT: Sackville-West, R. W. Introduction to The Works of Thomas Sackville, 1859.

ST. JOHN, HENRY. See BOLINGBROKE, HENRY ST. JOHN, First Viscount

SALE, GEORGE (1697?-November 13, 1736), orientalist, translator of the *Koran*, was the son of Samuel Sale, a London merchant. In 1720 he entered the Inner Temple as a law student, and eventually set up in business as a solicitor. It so happened that the Society for the Promotion of Christian Knowledge, located nearby in the Middle Temple, began in 1720 to prepare an Arabic translation of the New Testament. Through the Society, Sale got in touch with the men who taught him Arabic, but whence his interest in the East originated we do not know.

By 1726 he knew enough Arabic to correct the Testament for the S.P.C.K., of which society he became a member and officer. He now plunged deeper into Oriental studies, while at the same time struggling to keep up his legal business, which undoubtedly suffered from his love for scholarship. About this time he married Marianne d'Argent, who was to bear him seven children before his early death.

In 1734 appeared Sale's translation of the *Koran*, notable not only for its accuracy, but for the wide familiarity with Moslem literature, history, and theology displayed in the introduction and notes.

After the appearance of his *magnum opus*, Sale set to work on a contribution to the *Universal History*, and also helped to found the Society for the Encouragement of Learning. No doubt he would have added many more scholastic achievements to his already breath-taking record if a fever had not carried him off in eight days when he was barely middle aged.

Sale has been accused of being a secret believer in the faith of Islam, but there does not appear to be any justification for this view. His calm, unbiased exposition of that faith, however, won him the admiration of Voltaire.

PRINCIPAL WORKS: The Koran, Translated into English Immediately from the Original Arabic, to which Is Prefixed a Preliminary Discourse, 1734.
ABOUT: Davenport, R. A. A Sketch of the Life of George Sale, prefixed to some editions of the Koran.

SANDERSON, ROBERT (July 27, 1660-December 25, 1741), historian, was the son of a landowner in County Durham. He was educated at St. John's College, Cambridge, and at the Inns of Court. He obtained a position as a clerk in the Rolls Chapel, where many important legal records were preserved. It is not surprising that Thomas Rymer, the historiographer royal of the time, employed him as a research assistant in his monumental compilation, *Foedera*, a collection of all the treaties made by the English Crown with foreign governments since the Norman Conquest.

Sanderson was a subordinate of Rymer's in the years 1696-1707, but in the latter year he became Rymer's assistant; after Rymer's death in 1713 he continued the work alone, editing volumes sixteen and seventeen, which brought the collection down to the year 1625.

Later he added three further volumes of documents, to 1654; these supplementary volumes contained papers relative to domestic as well as foreign affairs, contrary to Rymer's original plan. Sanderson, by printing the journals of Charles I's first parliament, got himself into trouble with the House of Commons; he was forced to suppress the volume in which this breach of parliamentary privilege occurred.

Sanderson, who had four wives but no children, passed his last years in comparative wealth. A younger son, he inherited a good deal of property in the north of England from an older brother in 1727; the previous year he had been appointed Usher of the High Court of Chancery and Master of the Rolls.

After the twentieth and last volume of the *Foedera* appeared in 1735, Sanderson does not seem to have undertaken any further historical research. His career must be regarded chiefly as a pendant to Rymer's.

Born at Eggleston Hall, Durham, he died and was buried in London.

PRINCIPAL WORKS: Original Letters from King William III (tr. and ed.) 1704; Foedera, vols. XVI-XX, 1715-35.

SANDYS, GEORGE (March 2, 1578-March 1644), poet, translator, was the seventh and youngest son of Edwin Sandys, Archbishop of York, and Cicely Wilford. He entered St. Mary Hall, Oxford, in 1589, but left without a degree. Nothing is known of his life until in 1610 he traveled to Turkey, Egypt, and Palestine, producing on his return a book that was a real contribution to the geography and ethnology of a region then little known in England. This, like all his books, was dedicated to Charles I, either as Prince of Wales or as king.

Sandys' elder brother, Sir Edwin, was treasurer of the Virginia Company, and Sir Francis Wyat, who had married Sandys' niece, was governor of the colony. Thus George Sandys became involved in colonial enterprises. At one time he held shares in the Bermuda Company, but sold them when his application for appointment as governor was turned down. In 1621, however, he went to Virginia as colonial treasurer of the Virginia Company. Before he left, he had begun his translation of Ovid's *Metamorphoses*, which he finished in America. From 1624 to 1628 he was a member of the council in Virginia (besides owning and running a plantation), but he seems to have been of rather a quarrelsome disposition, and after many differences with his fellow members and with his neighbors he returned to England for good in 1631.

Charles made him a gentleman of the privy chamber, but most of his subsequent life was spent in long visits to the country houses of friends and relatives, while he continued his translations—the first book of the *Aeneid*, and then a long series of metrical paraphrases of the Bible. Drayton had long been his friend, and now he became acquainted with Carew and Waller. Many of his Biblical paraphrases were set to music by the famous composer Henry Lawes. In 1638 he was appointed agent of the legislative assembly of Virginia in London, but he exceeded his instructions, and soon ceased to have any active part in the duties of his office. He died unmarried at Boxley Abbey, Kent (the home of his niece, now widow of Sir Francis Wyat), soon after his sixty-sixth birthday. It is interesting to note that Thomas Fuller, meeting Sandys in 1641, spoke of him as "a very aged man with a youthful soul in a decayed body." He was then sixty-three!

GEORGE SANDYS

Sandys' translation of Ovid was very popular for a century after his time; Pope, for one, "liked it extremely." It is occasionally too much ornamented, but on the whole is faithful, melodious, and as literal a translation as could be attained in rhymed couplets. He had a gift for writing colloquially without baldness. His *Christ's Passion* is an imitation, almost a translation, of a Latin tragedy by Grotius. His Biblical paraphrases, of the Psalms, Lamentations, Ecclesiastes, the Song of Songs, etc., are, as Dryden called them, "ingenious and learned," if scarcely more.

The name is pronounced "Sands."

PRINCIPAL WORKS: A Relation of a Journey begun An. Dom. 1610, etc., 1615; The First Five Books of Ovid's "Metamorphoses," etc., 1621 (complete, 1626); A Paraphrase upon the Psalmes and Hymnes dispersed throughout the Old and New Testaments, 1636; A Paraphrase upon the Divine Poems [including the Psalms] 1638; Christ's Passion, a tragedy, 1640; A Paraphrase upon the Song of Solomon, 1641; Selections from the Metrical Paraphrases (H. J. Todd, ed.) 1839; Poetical Works (R. Hooper, ed.) 1872.

ABOUT: Brown, A. Genesis of the United States; Hooper, R. Memoir *in* Poetical Works; Todd, H. J. Memoir *in* Selections; Wood, A. à, Athenae Oxonienses.

SAPIENS. See GILDAS

SAVAGE, RICHARD (d. August 1, 1743), poet, dramatist, is one of the strangest figures in English literature. His writing amounts to very little, and would long have been forgotten had it not been for his personal history. He was born, probably of humble parentage and probably in London, somewhere around 1697. Nothing is known of him until 1716, when he claimed (probably without foundation) to be the author of a comedy produced that year, *Woman's a Riddle*, adapted from the Spanish. The next year he published a doggerel poem, called *The Convocation*, of which even he was ashamed later, and the existing copies of which he tried to destroy.

But his real career began in 1718, when he announced that he was the illegitimate son of Richard Savage, Earl Rivers, by the Countess of Macclesfield. Now, the Earl of Macclesfield had indeed divorced his wife for adultery, and she did have a son and daughter by Rivers. Nothing is known of either beyond infancy, but the weight of evidence goes to show that they both died

young. The countess had remarried a Colonel Brett, and Savage now began to blackmail her. She always considered him an impostor, and so he has been proved to be by numerous errors in his alleged history. Nevertheless, he persuaded Pope, Steele, and Johnson, among others, of the justice of his claim; Johnson, with whom he had shared the terrible poverty of the lexicographer's early days in London, wrote his *Life of Savage*, repeating the story in good faith; Steele planned to marry Savage to his own illegitimate daughter (the deal fell through when Steele could not raise the promised dowry); and Pope believed in him almost to the end and contributed to his support. (Pope was, indeed, indebted to him for much of the scurrilous gossip about other writers in *The Dunciad*.)

Savage kept on writing, and in 1723 appeared on the stage in the title role of his *Sir Thomas Overbury*, but he was a complete failure as an actor. In 1727 he killed one James Sinclair in a drunken brawl, and was condemned to death, but was pardoned the next year through the influence of the Countess of Hertford. In 1730 he was actually promised the poet laureateship by George II, but the king was overruled and Colley Cibber got the appointment. Nothing daunted, he secured a pension from Queen Caroline from 1732 to her death in 1737, and thereafter styled himself the "volunteer laureate."

His poem, *The Bastard*, in which he attacked Mrs. Brett unmercifully, appeared in 1728, and he was probably also the anonymous author of *Nature in Perfection, or The Mother Unveiled*. To keep him quiet, Viscount Tyrconnel, Mrs. Brett's nephew, took him into his household and gave him a pension, but he soon quarreled with his patron, left, and kept on talking. In 1735 his prose libel on the Bishop of London, *The Progress of a Divine*, earned him a trial for obscenity, but he was acquitted. Finally, in 1740, Pope and others promised him a pension if he would go to live in Bristol. He quarreled with even these last benefactors, and they withdrew the money. In 1743 he was arrested for debt and died of a fever in prison. He is buried in St. Paul's, Bristol.

Savage was a blackmailer, an ingrate, an impostor, a drunkard, and a thoroughly bad egg. As a writer he was negligible. Even

449

Johnson could say no more than that *The Wanderer* (which was strongly influenced by Thomson) was "a heap of shining materials thrown together by accident." Saintsbury has called him "as mediocre a mediocrist" as ever wrote. His poetry was rhetoric, when it was not abuse or whining. He seems to have had some wit, and Johnson was attracted by his prevailing melancholy. That is the best that can be said for him.

PRINCIPAL WORKS: The Convocation, or the Battle of Pamphlets, 1717; Love in a Veil (comedy, from the Spanish) 1719; Sir Thomas Overbury, a Tragedy, 1724; Miscellaneous Poems and Translations, 1726; The Bastard, 1728; The Author to Be Let (prose) 1728; The Wanderer, 1729; The Progress of a Divine (prose) 1735; London and Bristol Delineated (prose) 1744; Various Poems, 1761; Works, 1775.

ABOUT: deFord, M. A. Love Children: A Book of Illustrious Illegitimates; Johnson, S. Lives of the English Poets; Makower, S. V. Richard Savage, a Mystery in Biography; Saintsbury, G. History of English Prosody; Whitehead, C. Richard Savage (novel).

SAVILE, Sir GEORGE (Marquis of Halifax) (November 11, 1633-April 5, 1695), political pamphleteer, was born at Thornhill, Yorkshire, the son of Sir William Savile, Bart., and Anne Coventry, daughter of the Lord Keeper of the Seal. His childhood was spent in the Civil War, his mother being his first teacher. His father was royalist governor of York and Sheffield, and when he was killed in 1644, his mother held out in the siege of Sheffield Castle until a mutiny of the garrison forced her to surrender. The boy never attended an English university, but may have studied in Paris or Louvain.

In 1656 he married Dorothy Spencer, daughter of the Earl of Sunderland, who died in 1670, leaving three sons and a daughter. Two of the sons were later killed in war. In 1672 Savile married Gertrude Pierrepoint, by whom he had a daughter who became the mother of Lord Chesterfield. It was for her that he wrote his *Advice to a Daughter*.

In 1667 Savile was a captain in Prince Rupert's regiment of horse, and the next year his long political career began when he was put on a commission to inquire into financial scandals in Charles II's government. From then until 1692, Savile (Charles made him successively baron, earl, viscount, and marquis of Halifax) was the leader of the Whigs, first in the House of Commons, then in the House of Lords. He was actively opposed to the succession of James II, because of the Roman Catholic issue, and after failing to make peace between Charles and his illegitimate son Monmouth, Savile became an advocate of the accession of William and Mary; he did not actually take part in the revolution of 1688, but as speaker of the House of Lords he officially welcomed the new king and queen. At various times in his turbulent career he was a privy councilor, president of the council, and Lord Privy Seal. His relations with Charles, Rochester, and Shaftesbury fluctuated, and he was even accused of Jacobite connections. On the whole, however, he was a consistent Whig liberal, and it is certain that he was utterly incorruptible. After he was stricken off the council rolls he retired to his estate in Acton, but he died at Halifax House, which he had built in London, and was buried in Westminster.

Savile was a brilliant pamphleteer and essayist, subtle, pithy, candid, direct, possessed of "a bold and happy use of metaphor." His *Character of a Trimmer* has been called "worthy of Montaigne," and indeed Montaigne was consciously his master. His cynicism is largely on the surface; beneath it he was patriotic, loyal, and broadly tolerant if seldom warm. His pamphlets were written, not to entertain, but to convince; they are literature, as it were, accidentally. He had a great reputation as an orator, and the same eloquence often appears in his written words. His integrity in an age of corruption would alone make him outstanding.

He is supposed to have been the "natural" father of Henry Carey, the poet, and thus the great-grandfather of the actor Edmund Kean.

PRINCIPAL WORKS: A Letter to a Dissenter Upon Occasion of His Majesties late Gracious Declaration of Indulgence, 1687; The Character of a Trimmer, 1688; A Lady's Gift, or Advice to a Daughter, 1688; The Anatomy of an Equivalent, 1689; Essay upon Taxes, 1693; Miscellanies, 1700; Character of Charles the Second [with] Political, Moral, and Miscellaneous Thoughts and Reflections, 1750; Observations upon a Late Libel . . . concerning the King's Declaration (H. Macdonald, ed.) 1940.

ABOUT: Foxcroft, H. C. Character of the Trimmer: Being a Short Life of the First Marquis of Halifax; Foxcroft, H. C. Life and Letters of Sir George Savile, First Marquis of Halifax; Paul, H. W. Men and Letters; Walpole, S. Essays Political and Biographical.

SAVILE, Sir HENRY (November 30, 1549-February 19, 1622), classical scholar, translator, was the second son of Henry Savile and Elizabeth Ramsden. He was born at Bradley, Yorkshire, and entered Brasenose College, Oxford, about 1561. He graduated B.A., 1566; M.A., 1570. In 1565, while still an undergraduate, he became a Fellow of Merton College; twenty years later he became Warden (president) of the same college. Prior to this important appointment he had lectured in mathematics at Oxford, traveled on the Continent, and become Greek tutor to Queen Elizabeth.

About 1592 he married Margaret Dacres, by whom he had a son and a daughter. The son died in 1604, aged eight, but the daughter lived to become the mother of Sir Charles Sedley.

In 1595-96 Savile earnestly sought the provostship of Eton College, though he was not in holy orders. The queen finally gave him the post, which he held concurrently with the wardenship of Merton for the rest of his life. He was a stern but effective head of both institutions, and well deserved the knighthood bestowed on him by James I in 1604.

After the death of his son, Savile devoted himself wholeheartedly to scholarship. He had already, in 1591, translated some books of Tacitus into English. He now took a share in the preparation of the King James Bible and produced his monumental edition of the *Works* of St. Chrysostom in Greek. The latter, like other editions of Greek and Latin authors that he later published, was brought out at his own expense. In 1619 he endowed the Savilian Professorships of Geometry and Astronomy in the University of Oxford.

Savile was a tall man and in his youth extremely handsome. He died at Eton and was buried there. Monuments at Eton and Merton College commemorate the greatest English classicist of his day, who devoted much of his personal fortune to the furtherance of learning.

PRINCIPAL WORKS: *Translation*: The End of Nero and Beginning of Galba. Four Books of the Histories of C. Tacitus, 1591. *Editions*: Rerum Anglicarum Scriptores post Bedam Praecipui, 1596; S. Johannis Chrysostomi Opera, Graece, 1610-13; Xenophontis de Cyri Institutione, 1613; Thomae Bradwardini . . . de Causa Dei contra Pelagium, 1618. *Mathematical Lectures*: Praelectiones Tresdecim in Principium Elementorum Euclidis, 1621.

ABOUT: Maxwell-Lyte, H. C. A History of Eton College; Wood, A. à, Athenae Oxonienses.

SCOTT or **SCOT, MICHAEL** (1175?-1234?), Scottish scholar, translator, author of works on astronomy and alchemy, probably came from the Scottish border, though he may have been born in Fifeshire. He studied at Oxford and Paris (where he received the title or degree of "mathematicus"), then in Bologna and Palermo. He was probably ordained in Paris. In Sicily he became attached to the court of Frederick II, first in the service of the king's clerk register. He proceeded to Toledo, where he is said to have studied Arabic, which later enabled him to translate Averroes (only recently dead) and Avicenna—though Roger Bacon, perhaps with scholarly jealousy, claimed that Scott's Arabic came by way of "Andrew, a Jew." In any event, Scott returned to Palermo with his translation from Arabic to Latin of Aristotle's *Natural History*. Frederick inspired or ordered most of his subsequent writings, on mathematics, medicine, alchemy and astronomy (really astrology).

Scott apparently held some benefices in Italy, and two succeeding popes tried in vain to secure some preferment for him in England. Honorius II did name him Archbishop of Cashel, in Ireland, against the wishes of the Irish canons, but Scott declined on the ground that he was not familiar with the Irish language. In 1230 he was in Oxford again, as part of a mission from Frederick to introduce Aristotle to all the European universities.

Nothing more is known definitely of his life; he was dead by 1235, as evidenced by a poem by Vincent of Beauvais. He may have died in Italy, or returned before his death to his native Scotland; one legend is that he is buried in Melrose Abbey. His study of alchemy led to all sorts of legends of his learning and magical powers, and he was mentioned by Dante, Boccaccio, and (as "Auld Michael") by Sir Walter Scott. Allan Cunningham wrote a novel about him, and Coleridge contemplated a play on the same subject. There are tales of his prophecies, of his magical subjugation of the king of France, of his "iron helmet," worn because he had predicted his death by a falling pebble, and of his lifting the helmet in church at the elevation of the Host, where-upon a pebble fell from the roof and killed him. All of them, needless to say, are apocryphal.

Scott was, nevertheless, one of the best known scholars of his time. He was also renowned as a physician, and many of his remedies were preserved and used during the Middle Ages. His writing was all, of course, in Latin, and was done before the age of printing; only one of his works (and that one doubtfully his) has been translated into English. Most of his writing (including some translations of Aristotle and Averroes) is still in manuscript, in the Bodleian Library of Oxford, the Vatican, the Sorbonne, and elsewhere. He was styled Frederick's "court astrologer," though this does not seem to have been an official appointment.

PRINCIPAL WORKS (dates of printing): Liber Physiognomiae et Hominis Procreationis (Liber de Secretis Naturae) (book of physiognomy and of human generation, or book of the secrets of nature) 1477; De Animalibus (translation of Aristotle's Concerning Animals) 1493; Super Auctorem Spherae (above the author of the globe) 1495; Mensa Philosophica, 1602 (as The Philosopher's Banquet, 1614); Quaestio Curiosa de Natura Solis et Lunae (curious question about the nature of the sun and moon—a book on alchemy) 1622.

ABOUT: Bacon, R. Opus Maius, Opera Minora; Brown, J. W. Life and Legend of Michael Scot; Bruce, J. Life of Michael Scott; Duhem, P. Le Système du Monde; Haskins, C. Studies in the History of Mediaeval Science; Thorndike, L. History of Magic and Experimental Science.

SCOTT or **SCOT, REGINALD** (1538?-October 9, 1599), author of *The Discovery of Witchcraft*, was the son of Richard Scot and Mary Whetenall. Both his parents were members of old and influential families in the county of Kent. He entered Hart Hall, Oxford, in 1555, but took no degree. In 1568 he married Jane Cobbe and settled down to the life of a Kentish country squire. His intellectual equipment, however, was entirely unusual for a man in his position.

In 1574 he published *A Perfect Platform of a Hop-garden*, the first book to deal systematically with the great Kentish industry of hop growing. Its value was at once appreciated, and new editions appeared in 1576 and 1578.

In 1584 Scott's *The Discovery of Witchcraft. . . Whereunto Is Added a Treatise upon the Nature and Substance of Spirits and Devils* first appeared in print. This re-markable work was the product of wide reading and no less wide practical experience—perhaps in part obtained as a Justice of the Peace in his native country. Scott strove to prove that the belief in witchcraft was both heretical and unsupported by facts —alleged witches and their persecutors being the victims of self-deception. More than a century was to pass before the majority of his fellow countrymen accepted his viewpoint, and his work was attacked by King James I and other writers on witchcraft.

In 1588 he became a Member of Parliament, this being the peak point of his public career. In his latter years he seems to have been in financial difficulties, from which he extricated himself by marrying a widow named Alice Collyar. His first wife had died some years before; by her he had one daughter, Elizabeth, who survived him, as did his second wife and his stepdaughter. He died at Smeeth, Kent, which was probably also his birthplace.

PRINCIPAL WORKS: A Perfect Platform of a Hop-Garden, 1574; The Discovery of Witchcraft, 1584.

ABOUT: Nicholson, B. Introduction to his edition of The Discovery of Witchcraft, 1886.

SCOTUS, JOHANNES. See DUNS, JOANNES SCOTUS

SCOTUS or **ERIGENA, JOHN** (fl. 850), philosopher, was certainly Irish and not Scottish. To make this plain, he used "Erigena" or "Eriugena" as his pseudonym. It is therefore incorrect to call him "John the Scot."

Very little is known of his life. He was probably born about 810, and went to France some time between 840 and 847. There Charles the Bald (Emperor Charles II, king of the West Franks) made him head of the Schola Palatina, or Palatine Academy, in Paris. He may never have actually been a priest, though probably he was. He was on terms of close intimacy with the king, who never seems to have resented some pretty free speech; William of Malmesbury, commenting on this, called him "little in person and of a merry wit." Certainly the emperor, who had inspired most of his writings, protected him well from a succession of charges of heresy. The synods of 855 and 859 both condemned his greatest work, *De Divisione*

Naturae, the first contemptuously calling it "Scots porridge." Popes in 1050, 1255, and as late as 1585 condemned it and ordered it burnt. Fortunately some copies escaped this fate.

Nothing is known of his end; William of Malmesbury said that King Alfred brought him to England as abbot of Malmesbury, and that the monks killed him with their "styles" (pens), but he seems to be confusing Scotus with another John.

John Scotus Erigena was a remarkable man. Alfred Weber said he "resembles Origen in the breadth of his mind, and is much superior to his times. . . . His learning rises far beyond the scientific level of the Carlovingian epoch. . . . He possessed wonderful powers of speculation and boldness of judgment." Bertrand Russell called him "one of the most astonishing persons of the ninth century."

He was not so much a Scholastic as the predecessor, by his dialectical method, of the Scholastics; and not so much a mystic or pantheist as a neo-Platonist. The Bible and the Church fathers were his final authority, but, he said, "reason and revelation cannot conflict, both being true, but if they seem to conflict, reason is to be preferred." He dealt freely with both the letter and the spirit of Christian doctrine. God to him is the final cause, the alpha and omega; reality is divided into four classes, the first and last of which are God. Matter exists only through thought (thus anticipating Descartes), and it will cease to be when distinction of sex disappears and man returns to the primal unity. All this, of course, is heretical, and John was lucky to have the protection of a powerful monarch.

John's translation of the pseudo-Dionysius (done by order of the emperor) from Greek into Latin is a storehouse of modern mystical theories. His book on (and against) predestination was written as part of an ecclesiastical controversy; to him predestination was "incompatible with the unity of God." He was also the author of a number of curious poems, written in a combination of Greek and Latin, in the so-called macaronic (burlesque) style.

It should be added that not only was John or Johannes Scotus confused with another John, but also during the later Middle Ages it was frequently supposed that John Scotus and John Erigena were two different persons!

PRINCIPAL WORKS (dates of printing): De Divisione Naturae (concerning the division of nature) 1681; De Divina Praedestinatione (concerning divine predestination) (G. Maugin, ed.) 1850; (Complete works *in*) Patrologia Latina (H. J. Floss, ed.) 1853; Expositiones (expositions [on Dionysius]) 1871; (Poems *in*) Poetae Latini Aevi Carolinae (Latin poets of the Carlovingian age) (T. Taube, ed.) 1896.

ABOUT: Bett, H. Johannes Scotus Erigena: a Study in Mediaeval Philosophy; Christlieb, T. Leben und Lehre des Johannes Scotus Erigena; Dräseke, J. Johannes Scotus Erigena und Seine Gewährsmänner; Gardner, A. Studies in John the Scot; Poole, R. L. Mediaeval Thought; Russell, B. History of Western Philosophy; Tallandier, St. R. Scot Erigène et la Philosophie Scholastique; Weber, A. History of Philosophy; William of Malmesbury, Gesta Pontificum.

SEDLEY, Sir CHARLES

SEDLEY, Sir CHARLES (1639?-August 20, 1701), playwright, poet, was born in London and baptized in St. Clement Danes, March 5, 1639. His father, Sir John Sedley, baronet, of Southfleet, Kent, had died in August 1638, leaving his extensive landed property in trust for his eldest son, Henry. Both Henry and another son, William, died without issue, so that Charles quite unexpectedly became heir to the estates and the title in 1656.

Charles had grown up, without a father to control him, in the disturbed and anxious period of the civil war; at one time his mother was actually in prison, at another the whole family moved to France; it is not surprising, therefore, that he did not make the best possible use of his sudden wealth. He was, in fact, for some years a notorious rake, but an extremely literate one; his mother, Lady Elizabeth Sedley, was an intelligent woman, who saw that he got a thorough grounding in Latin from a private tutor and sent him to Wadham College, Oxford, in 1656. Charles only spent about a year there, as the attractions of London life proved too strong.

On February 9, 1657, he married Katherine Savage, a younger sister of his brother William's widow. In December 1657 she gave birth to a daughter, Katherine, who afterwards became the mistress of the Duke of York (later King James II) and was created by him Countess of Dorchester.

Soon after the restoration of Charles II in 1660, Sedley became one of the king's intimate circle, all of whom were noted for

SIR CHARLES SEDLEY

their debauchery and atheism. Sedley's most notorious prank occurred in 1663, when he, Lord Buckhurst, and Sir Thomas Ogle stripped themselves naked on the balcony of the Cock Tavern; after some obscene clowning, Sedley delivered a drunken and blasphemous oration to the large crowd which had collected; a shower of stones finally forced the unprotected "wits" to retire. Sedley was fined 2,000 marks and given a week in jail.

Soon afterward Sedley met two other aristocratic men of letters, Lord Rochester and Sir George Etherege, with whom his name will always be associated. His first literary effort was his share in translating a play of Corneille's with Waller, Buckhurst, Filmer, and Godolphin; this was played without success as *Pompey the Great.*

Sedley appears as Lisideius, one of the four disputants in Dryden's *Essay of Dramatic Poesy,* 1668, and he was probably a better critic than dramatist. He wrote *Antony and Cleopatra,* a stilted rhyming tragedy in the manner of Corneille, and two prose comedies, *The Mulberry Garden* and *Bellamira, or the Mistress,* which are certainly not comparable with Wycherley's work, let alone Congreve's. His lyric poetry is neat and pointed, but hardly moving.

Lady Katherine became insane; she was a Roman Catholic and in or about 1672 retired to a convent at Ghent; that year Sedley went through a form of marriage with

Ann Ayscough, a woman of his own class, who lived with him as his wife thereafter. She bore him two sons, the first of whom, named Charles, lived until 1701; the second died in infancy. Under Ann's influence, Sedley gradually gave up his old habits of dissipation, took care of his estate, and began to shoulder his responsibilities as a Member of Parliament—a position he had held since 1668.

In 1680 the roof of a tennis court fell on a group of players which included Sedley and Etherege. Sedley's skull was fractured and he nearly died of his injuries, but recovered to continue his parliamentary career. He was a moderate supporter of King William III after the Revolution of 1688, and much opposed to political corruption. His beloved son made a runaway marriage in 1695 which turned out happily, but died a few months before his father in 1701, probably hastening the latter's end. Sedley, having passed his later life as a model "husband" and father, "died like a philosopher without fear or superstition." Both his lawful wife and the remarkable Ann Ayscough survived him.

PRINCIPAL WORKS: The Mulberry Garden, 1668; Antony and Cleopatra, 1677; Bellamira, or the Mistress, 1687; The Happy Pair, or a Poem on Matrimony, 1702.

ABOUT: Pinto, V. de S. Sir Charles Sedley.

SELDEN, JOHN (December 16, 1584-November 30, 1654), lawyer, orientalist, miscellaneous writer, was born in Salvington, Sussex, the son of John Selden, a yeoman farmer, also known as a musician or "minstrell." His mother, Margaret Baker, was of a higher social class and had some fortune. He was educated at Chichester Grammar School, and entered Hart Hall, Oxford, in 1600, but left without a degree to be enrolled in Clifford Inn in 1602, migrating two years later to the Inner Temple. He was called to the bar in 1612, and for the most part engaged only in conveyancing cases, though occasionally he appeared in other cases requiring special knowledge. He became a bencher in 1633. Scholarship was always his first love, and he became eventually "the great dictator of English learning."

From the time when Selden became steward to the Earl of Kent in 1629, his relations with the Earl and Countess were very close. He spent much of his time in either their town house or their country home, managed the estate after the earl's death in 1629, and reputedly was married to the widowed countess, though no official evidence of this exists.

His *Historie of Tythes*, with its denial of divine law in tithing, caused a furore; he was forced to recant, the book was suppressed, and he was forbidden to answer its attackers. This in a sense began his public career, which continued when, though not a member of Parliament, he wrote the famous protestation to the House of Commons in 1621. This earned him a short imprisonment in the Tower. In 1623 and 1626 (and again, for Oxford, in the Long Parliament) he was a member of the House; he helped impeach Buckingham and he defended Hampden. In 1629 he found himself in the Tower again, and he was imprisoned there and elsewhere until 1631. Yet in most matters he was on the king's side, and won sufficient favor from Charles to be appointed keeper of the rolls and records of the Tower in 1645. After the king's trial he withdrew from politics, his only action being to protect the universities during the civil war.

Selden's scholarship was impressive. He was an antiquary as well as an historian, and an authority on constitutional law as well. He had a thorough knowledge of Hebrew and a good working mastery of Arabic. He was in no real sense a philosopher or metaphysician, but he held that law must be derived from authority, hence cannot have its source in reason, though all human beings possess a natural moral sense. He was really a follower of Erastus, and like him was a skeptic who never entirely deserted religion —both Archbishop Ussher and the materialist Hobbes were his friends, and both of them claimed domination of his deathbed. He died in London just before his seventieth birthday, and was buried in the Temple Church.

Selden was a better speaker than a writer; an eloquent orator, his written style is harsh and obscure. He is best known today by his *Table Talk*, collected after his death, which reveals the man as he was—tolerant, moderate, broad-minded, erudite, and a bit ponderous. His learning was unsurpassed in his day, and much of his work is still of value in spite of later researches. His *De Dis*

JOHN SELDEN

Syriis (he wrote impartially in Latin or English) was perhaps the earliest inquiry into the heathen religions of the Old Testament period. His *Mare Clausum*, which argued that the sea around England belonged to England and not to the world, was an answer to Grotius' *Mare Liberum;* James I forbade its publication, but twenty years later Charles I had it issued as almost a state paper. Besides his published works, he wrote some Latin verses, and did a treatise on the Jews in England for Purchas. When it appeared he felt it had been mutilated, and he quarreled permanently with Purchas. In 1623 he edited Eadmer's *History,* and in 1647 published the first modern edition of *Fleta,* an Old English lawbook. His valuable collection of Oriental manuscripts is now in the Bodleian Library, Oxford.

PRINCIPAL WORKS: Jani Anglorum facies altera (the other Face of the English Janus) 1610; England's Epinomis (partial translation) 1610; The Duello or Single Combat, 1610; Titles of Honour, 1614; Analecton Anglo-Britannicon, 1615; De Dis Syriis (concerning the Syrian gods) 1617; Marmora Arundeliana (the Arundel marbles) (with P. Young [Junius] and R. James) 1628; Mare Clausum, seu de dominio maris (closed sea, or concerning the dominion of the ocean) 1635; De successionibus in bona defunctorum ad leges Ebraicorum (concerning succession in property of the dead by Hebrew law) 1638; De jure naturali et gentium juxta disciplinam Hebraeorum (concerning natural and international law according to Hebrew law) 1640; Brief Discourse of the Powers of the Peers and Commons, 1640; Privileges of the Baronage of England, 1642; De anno civili et calendario veteris ecclesiae seu reipublicae Judaicae (concerning the civil year and calendar of the ancient Jewish church or state) 1644; Uxor Ebraica (the Hebrew wife) 1646; De Synedris veterum Ebraeorum (concerning the legislators of the ancient Hebrews) 1650-55; Vindiciae (vindications) 1653; Decem historiae Anglicanae Scriptores (ten writings of English history) (with R. Twysden) 1653; Table Talk (R. Milward, ed.) 1689 (S. H. Reynolds, ed. 1892); Opera Omnia (D. Wilkins, ed.) 1723.

ABOUT: Clarendon, E. Life; Johnson, S. Memoirs of John Selden; Paul, H. W. Men and Letters; Wilkins, D. Vita (life) in Opera Omnia; Wood, A. à, Athenae Oxonienses.

SETTLE, ELKANAH (February 1, 1648-February 12, 1724), dramatist, poet, was

born in Dunstable, Bedfordshire, the son of Josias Settle. In 1666 he entered Trinity College, Oxford, but a few years later left for London without a degree. He is said at that time to have had a tidy fortune, which he wasted. He was well known as "Recanting Settle," being first a Tory, then a Whig, then a Tory again, all in the hope of money and patronage which were not forthcoming. For a while he was a trooper in the army of James II (though previously Otway had fought a duel with him over his attacks on James), and at one time he published a weekly newspaper in the Tory cause. With the Revolution of 1688, he returned to the Whigs once more. All these changes of coat having failed to do anything for him, Settle abandoned politics and secured the appointment in 1691 as city poet, which involved the writing of pageants for Lord Mayor's Day.

Settle's celebrity as a dramatist was thanks to Rochester, who patronized him and pushed him ahead in order to annoy Dryden. *Cambyses* and *The Empress of Morocco* were therefore great successes; Settle's head was turned, and he began to think of himself as Dryden's rival and equal. Dryden annihilated him in *Absalom and Achitophel*, where as Doeg he was characterized as "free from all meaning, whether good or bad," and (with Shadwell) as one of "two fools that crutch their feeble sense on verse." Settle's attempts at retaliation were feeble, and Pope completed his annihilation in *The Dunciad*. Once his factitious vogue was over, his bombastic, doggerel rhymed plays ceased to make him a living; for *The City-Ramble* he actually received just three pounds and ten shillings! His post as city poet paid very little, and he fell

so low that he wrote love-letters for servants, ballads to be hawked around the streets, and drolls for Bartholomew Fair. Pope says he even acted in these, playing the part of a dragon! He kept on hand a stock of elegies, complimentary poems, and so on, which he adapted for individual requirements.

At last, completely destitute, he was taken as a "poor brother" in the Charterhouse, where he died soon after his seventy-sixth birthday. He was married (in 1674) to Mary Warner, but it is not known what became of her or whether they had any children.

Settle's poems and plays were utterly negligible; he was only a tool in the hands of the vindictive Rochester. He was a pitiful hack, whose orotund dramas, inaccurate historically and full of high-flown nonsense, have not survived even as laughing-stocks or bad examples. Yet he had the audacity to "revise and rewrite" Beaumont and Fletcher's *Philaster,* and he thought of himself to the end as one of the leading poets of his era. In the end he was rehashing his own earlier plays.

PRINCIPAL WORKS: *Plays:* Cambyses, Knight of Persia, 1671; The Empress of Morocco, 1673; Love and Revenge, 1675; The Conquest of China by the Tartars, 1676; Ibrahim, the Illustrious Bassa, 1677; Fatal Love, or the Forc'd Inconstancy, 1680; The Female Prelate: being the History of the Life and Death of Pope Joan, 1680; The Heir of Morocco, with The Duke of Gayland, 1682; Distress'd Innocence, or the Princess of Persia, 1691; The Ambitious Slave, or a Generous Revenge, 1694; The World in the Moon (opera) 1697; The Virgin Prophetess, or the Fate of Troy (opera) 1704; The Siege of Troy, 1707; The City-Ramble (comedy) 1711?; The Lady's Triumph (opera) 1718. *Miscellaneous:* Some Notes and Observations on the Empress of Morocco revised, 1674; The Life and Death of Major Clancie, the Grandest Cheat of this Age, 1680; Character of a Popish Successor, 1681; Absalom Senior or Achitophel Transprosed, 1682; Heroick Poem on the Coronation of the High and Mighty Monarch James II, 1683; Reflections on Several of Mr. Dryden's Plays, 1687; A Narrative of the Popish Plot, 1693; The Compleat Memoirs of . . . that Notorious Impostor, Will. Morrell, etc., 1694; Minerva Triumphans (verse) 1701; Carmen Irenicum, . . . an Heroic Poem, 1702.

ABOUT: Brown, F. C. Elkanah Settle, his Life and Works; Johnson, S. Lives of the English Poets; Wood, A. à, Athenae Oxonienses.

SEWARD, ANNA (December 12, 1742-March 25, 1809), poet, was born in Eyam,

Derbyshire, near the peak celebrated in Scott's *Peveril of the Peak.* (The *Dictionary of National Biography* erroneously gives her birth year as 1747.) She was the eldest daughter of the Reverend Thomas Seward (pronounced See-Ward), rector of Eyam and later Prebendary of Salisbury and Canon of Lichfield in Staffordshire, where all her life was spent, after the age of seven. Her mother was Elizabeth (Hunter) Seward, whose father was Head Master of the Free School in Lichfield, and who was remotely related to Samuel Johnson, a pupil of his. At three Anna (called Nancy) was reading Milton and Shakespeare; at nine she could recite verbatim the first three books of *Paradise Lost*; and she began to compose verse of a semi-religious character when she was twelve. Reading constantly all her life, she was largely self-educated, though completely non-conversant with Greek and Latin. (This did not prevent her from essaying metrical versions of Horatian odes later in life.) She continued writing verse, encouraged by Dr. Erasmus Darwin (grandfather of Charles), till her father, who had some literary pretensions of his own, made her desist. Thereafter she led an active social life, with tea parties, callers, and concerts planned by John Saville, vicar choral of the Cathedral, and the object of Anna Seward's life-long devotion, though she never married.

During a summer visit in 1769 to Buxton, Miss Seward met John André, the ill-starred young Genevese who became involved in the Benedict Arnold conspiracy, and who was hanged as a spy at Tappan, New York, in 1780. This elicited her best-remembered poem, the *Monody on the Death of Major André*, written in vigorous couplets. George Washington, whom she assailed, later went to some trouble to prove to her that she was wrong. Dr. Darwin said of Miss Seward that she invented the epic elegy, in which a form of narrative was combined with lamentation; she turned out many poems that answer to this description. Her other works included an *Elegy on Captain Cook*, praised by Dr. Johnson, whom she cordially disliked and constantly belittled; and a poetical novel, *Louisa*. John Gibson Lockhart called her posthumous *Poetical Works* (edited by Sir Walter Scott) "a formidable monument of mediocrity" and Margaret Ashmun, her chief biographer, concedes that her style was high flown and overwrought. Frederick Pottle

describes Anna Seward as "a tall, stout, handsome woman with the imperious bearing of Queen Elizabeth, but with a heart that was utterly enthusiastic and sentimental; a woman with a genius for inaccuracy but apparently no consciousness of malice." She died at sixty-six and was buried in the choir of the Cathedral.

PRINCIPAL WORKS: Elegy on Captain Cook, 1780; A Monody on the Death of Major André, 1780; Louisa, 1784; Poetical Works, 1810; Letters of Anna Seward, Written Between the Years 1784 and 1807, 1811.

ABOUT: Ashmun, M. The Singing Swan; Lucas, E. V. A Swan and her Friends; Meynell, A. C. T. The Second Person Singular; Nichols, J. Illustrations of the Literary History of the Eighteenth Century; Pearson, H. The Swan of Lichfield; Ritchie, Lady, From the Porch; Church Quarterly, 1937.

SHADWELL, THOMAS (1642?-November 19, 1692), dramatist, poet, was born at either Broomhill or Santon Hall, Norfolk; both these places were country seats of his father, John Shadwell, a gentleman who lost much of his property during the civil war through his loyalty to the king. Thomas received his early education at home and at the King Edward VI Grammar School, Bury St. Edmunds. He entered Caius College, Cambridge, December 17, 1656, when his age was given as fourteen. In 1658 he left Caius to become a member of the Middle Temple and study law, as his father had done before him. Later he seems to have traveled on the Continent; in his twenty-fourth year he spent some months in Ireland, where his father was Recorder of Galway and Attorney General for Connaught, 1665-70.

Some time between 1663 and 1667, Shadwell married an actress named Ann Gibbs; in May 1668 his first play, *The Sullen Lovers*, an adaptation from Molière, was performed at the Duke of York's Theatre, with Mrs. Shadwell in a leading role. The comedy was a success, though Shadwell claimed he had written it very hastily; this encouraged him to make play writing his career. He did not, however, have any marked success again until *Epsom Wells* was performed in 1672. This and *The Squire of Alsatia*, produced in 1688, were his most successful pieces.

Right at the beginning of his literary career, in the preface to *The Sullen Lovers*, Shadwell crossed swords with Dryden,

After W. Faithorne

THOMAS SHADWELL

claiming that the latter underestimated the comic powers of Ben Jonson. Dryden and Shadwell kept up a friendly controversy for some years; in 1674 they banded together to attack Settle, a rival playwright, in *Notes and Observations on the Empress of Morocco.* We do not know what later inspired Dryden to write his merciless satire on Shadwell, *Mac Flecknoe,* which seems to have circulated in manuscript for some time prior to its publication in 1682 and may have been written as early as 1678.

Personal reasons must have caused the writing of *Mac Flecknoe,* but the motive for its publication was political. English party politics, with the names "Whig" and "Tory," were born toward the end of Charles II's reign. The Whigs favored a Protestant heir to the throne in place of the Duke of York, who was a Catholic. Shadwell, unlike his father, opposed the king and took the Whig side. His *The Lancashire Witches* contained bitter satire on the Catholics. In 1682 he wrote *The Medal of John Bayes* in answer to *The Medal,* Dryden's second anti-Whig poem. It was in large part a personal attack on Dryden, probably in revenge for *Mac Flecknoe;* Dryden's crushing answer was to have the latter poem printed. He also caricatured Shadwell as Og in the second part of *Absalom and Achitophel.*

The upshot of these literary battles was that Dryden and his friends used their in-

fluence to keep Shadwell's plays off the stage during the rest of Charles II's reign and almost the entire reign of James II. When William III became King of England in 1689, he appointed Shadwell poet laureate in place of Dryden; the substitution was a matter of politics and of course implied no comparison of their poetic merits.

During the later years of his life Shadwell suffered greatly with gout, and took opium to deaden the pain. He died suddenly, as the result, it was said, of an overdose of opium.

Shadwell was an amiable, fat, lazy, deep-drinking man. He depended on the theatre for a considerable part of his income, and when his work was not performed or failed to please, he was often very poor. Yet his plays were almost all written in a hurry, in response to urgent demand from the actors. Among his patrons were William Cavendish, first Duke of Newcastle, the Earl of Dorset and Sir Charles Sedley. All of them helped him financially and he in return helped the Duke to write comedies. The Duke had been the patron of Ben Jonson, and probably fostered Shadwell's inordinate admiration for the older dramatist. All that is best in Shadwell's work, indeed, comes from Jonson. He lacked the wit, polish and skill in construction of Wycherley, Etherege and Congreve, but his comedies contain a rich variety of eccentric characters, each carefully drawn from the life.

PRINCIPAL WORKS: *Plays:* The Sullen Lovers, 1668; The Royal Shepherdess (tragi-comedy) 1669; The Humorists, 1671; The Miser, 1672; Epsom Wells, 1673; The Tempest (opera) 1674; Psyche (opera) 1675; The Libertine (tragedy) 1675; The Virtuoso, 1676; The History of Timon of Athens (tragedy) 1678; A True Widow, 1679; The Woman-Captain, 1680; The Lancashire Witches, 1682; The Squire of Alsatia, 1688; Bury Fair, 1689; The Amorous Bigot, 1690; The Scourers, 1691; The Volunteers, 1692. *Other Writings:* Notes and Observations on the Empress of Morocco, 1674; The Medal of John Bayes, 1682; Satire to his Muse, by the Author of Absalom and Achitophel, 1682; The Tenth Satire of Juvenal, 1687.

ABOUT: Borgman, A. S. Thomas Shadwell: His Life and Comedies; Broadus, E. K. The Laureateship; Dryden, J. Mac Flecknoe.

SHAFTESBURY, ANTHONY ASHLEY COOPER, Third Earl of (February 26, 1671-February 4, 1713), author of treatises on moral philosophy, was the grandson of the famous first Earl Shaftsbury, Charles I's Lord Chancellor and Dryden's "Achito-

phel." His father, the second earl, seems to have been slightly subnormal mentally; at any rate, he was kept under the constant supervision of his father's friend, John Locke, who married him off at seventeen to Lady Dorothy Manners, daughter of the Earl of Rutland, attended the lady when her son was born, and remained as superintendent of the boy's education. When the child was two his grandfather was made his legal guardian. The grandfather's ruin came in 1681, and when he died two years later the boy's parents immediately took him away from Locke and sent him to Winchester College. He was miserable there, and three years later he was allowed to leave and go with two friends and a tutor to the Continent, eventually settling in Italy. His health was already frail, and he had no further formal schooling.

In 1695 he was elected to Parliament, as a Whig, from Poole, but though he was an ardent partisan his health kept him from being active, and he resigned in 1698. The next year his father died and he succeeded to the title. As a member of the House of Lords he attended sessions but was unable to do more; William III offered him a secretaryship of state, but he was obliged to decline. The only office he held was that of vice admiral of Dorsetshire, and when Anne ascended the throne, with Tory sympathies, she took that away from him. He retired to the family estate in Dorsetshire, coming occasionally as near London as Chelsea (then a separate town), but because of his asthma was unable to endure the smoke of the city. All his time from then on was given to study and writing.

Shaftesbury had always been an ardent student of philosophy, particularly of Plato, Epictetus, and Marcus Aurelius. His viewpoint was very near that of the last named; though he was counted with the Deists, actually he never left the Church of England, and had a respect for established religion, though none for its priests. His first publication (1698) had been a preface to the sermons of Benjamin Whichcote, the Cambridge Platonist, and he was much influenced by that school. He hated fanaticism and the persecution to which fanaticism gives rise, but he was so little aggressive that he advocated combating "prejudice" by

ridicule alone. Yet with all his dislike of "enthusiasm," he was himself an enthusiast, whose emotions often overcame his reason.

Except for the successive publication of his moral treatises (all issued anonymously —and the first surreptitiously, by a bookseller whom he had befriended), Shaftesbury's life contained little of the eventful. His friends persuaded him that he ought to be married and carry on the family line, and after a vain courtship of a girl to whom he was really attracted, he married, in 1709, one whom he had scarcely met, Jane Ewer. He said openly that the marriage had taken place merely to "satisfy" his friends, but it turned out well enough. The couple had one son, who became the fourth earl.

Continued ill health finally drove Shaftesbury from England again in 1711. He died in Naples two years later, at nearly forty-two, and was buried at St. Giles, Dorsetshire. Though his writing was anonymous, its author was well known, and he had the satisfaction of contemporary celebrity, in France and Germany as well as at home.

Because of his semi-invalidism, Shaftesbury's life was lived almost entirely in the intellect. He had a turn for art, and was something of a virtuoso, especially of medals and bronzes. He was most economical, and worried needlessly about his financial status,

After J. Closterman
ANTHONY ASHLEY COOPER, 3RD EARL OF SHAFTESBURY

but he was a generous man, who constantly supported needy students at the universities he had never been strong enough to attend. Essentially he was a Whig aristocrat of the eighteenth century type, with all the virtues and limitations of that breed.

A true lover of liberty and of his fellow-man, Shaftesbury's principal thesis (as given in his *Inquiry concerning Virtue or Merit*) was that there exists in man a "natural affection of rational creatures" which extends to everything in the universe. "The whole is harmony, the members entire, the music perfect." Mankind has a natural moral sense as it has an aesthetic sense. "The human mind is in harmony with cosmic nature."

What he most detested were cynical, egoistic views of human nature, and for this reason he attacked not only Hobbes but even his old tutor Locke. Yet Locke's antagonist Berkeley was among his severest critics. His admirers included Diderot and Leibnitz, and his theories were carried on further by Francis Hutcheson and his school. Pope also admired him, and the *Essay on Man* is an extended poetic version of Shaftesbury's *Moralists*.

Unfortunately, his very lucid views were expressed in a bombastic, turgid, artificial style, labored and overdecorated. He was at bottom purely an amateur (in the modern sense of the word) in the arts, including the art of literature. He makes hard reading today, and is important only as a fructifier of the ideas of others.

PRINCIPAL WORKS: An Inquiry concerning Virtue or Merit, 1699; Paradoxes of State, 1702; A Letter concerning Enthusiasm, 1708; The Moralists, a Philosophical Rhapsody, 1709; Sensus Communis: an Essay on the Freedom of Wit and Humor, 1709; Soliloquy: or Advice to an Author, 1710; Characteristics of Men, Manners, Opinions, Times [containing all the foregoing] 1711 (revised, 1713; J. M. Robertson, ed. 1900); A Notion of the Historical Draught or Tablature of the Judgment of Hercules, 1713; Miscellaneous Reflections, 1714; Letters to a Young Man at the University, 1716; Letters . . . to Robert, now Viscount. Molesworth, 1721; Original Letters of Locke, Algernon Sidney, and Lord Shaftesbury (T. Forster, ed.) 1830.

ABOUT: Brown, J. Essays on the Characteristics; Fowler, T. Shaftesbury and Hutcheson; Martineau, J. Types of Ethical Theory; Rand, B. Life, Letters, and Philosophical Regimen of Shaftesbury; Schönfeld, V. Die Ethik Shaftesburys; Stephen, L. Essays on Freethinking; Walpole, H. Royal and Noble Authors; Weiser, C. F. Shaftesbury und das Deutsches Geistesleben.

SHAKESPEARE, WILLIAM (April 23, 1564-April 23, 1616), dramatist, poet, was born at Stratford-on-Avon, Warwickshire, the eldest son of John Shakespeare and Mary Arden. Whether the traditional date of his birth be correct or not, he was certainly baptized on April 26, 1564. His mother was of gentle birth; John Shakespeare had been one of her father's tenants. John gave up farming, moved to Stratford, and became a successful wool dealer and glover there. He held in turn all the principal town offices, including that of chief alderman. After 1577 he held no office; it is possible that he got into financial difficulties at this time, which would explain why his talented son was not sent to either Oxford or Cambridge. William was presumably educated at the Stratford grammar school, where he would have learnt some Latin.

There is a strong Stratford tradition that Shakespeare had to leave home in early youth because of his poaching exploits among Sir Thomas Lucy's deer. Some scholars identify him with an actor named William Shakeshafte who was in Lancashire in 1581. In November 1582, Shakespeare married Anne Hathaway of Shottery, near Stratford. She was eight years older than he and already pregnant, for their eldest child, Susanna, was baptized at Stratford, May 26, 1583. The only other children of the marriage, the twins Hamnet and Judith, were baptized on February 22, 1585. Hamnet, the boy, was buried August 11, 1596, but the two daughters survived their father, as did Anne.

Anne was the daughter of a yeoman farmer and not of markedly lower social status than her husband, but the hasty marriage cannot have been very happy. She continued to live in Stratford and bring up her children, but Shakespeare seems to have spent little time at home between 1585 and 1610. He and his father took part in a business venture together in 1587, but we hear nothing more of him until 1592, when an uncomplimentary reference in Robert Greene's *Groatsworth of Wit* reveals that he was an actor in London and already had had a hand in writing *Henry VI*, thereby arousing the envy of professional playwrights like Greene.

Venus and Adonis, Shakespeare's first published work, appeared in 1593, and at once established his reputation as a poet; *The Rape of Lucrece* was published in 1594. Both these poems were dedicated to Henry Wriothesley, Earl of Southampton; the second dedication suggests that by 1594 Shakespeare was in high favor with the earl.

In 1594 Shakespeare, Richard Burbage, William Kemp, and other actors formed a company known as the Lord Chamberlain's Players. The Lord Chamberlain, their patron, was an official of the Royal Household, and the company often played before Queen Elizabeth, the first occasion being December 26, 1594, when *The Comedy of Errors* was performed. James I, when he came to the throne in 1603, granted the company a license and became its official patron; henceforward the group was called the King's Men.

All Shakespeare's plays from 1594 onward were written exclusively for this company; Richard Burbage was one of the best tragic actors of the day and Will Kemp the best low comedian. The company first owned the Theatre, Shoreditch; when the ground lease expired, they dismantled this theatre and built a new one, the Globe, on the Bankside, Southwark, in 1599; after 1608 they used the Blackfriars Theatre in winter; the Globe burned down in 1613; some of Shakespeare's manuscripts may have been lost in the fire.

As shareholder, actor, and playwright, Shakespeare drew the greater part of his income from the theatrical venture; he seems, however, to have augmented his fortune considerably by wise investments in real estate. In 1596 John Shakespeare applied for and received a coat of arms, which gave him and his sons the right to be called gentlemen. The following year William bought a large house in Stratford called New Place. In 1609 Thomas Greene, the Town Clerk, was renting this house from Shakespeare, but soon afterward the dramatist retired to it and spent his last years there.

Palladis Tamia by Francis Meres, published in 1598, lists twelve plays by Shakespeare and hails him as "among the English . . . the most excellent in both kinds (i.e. comedy and tragedy) for the stage." Meres also describes him as the reincarnation of Ovid in lyric poetry, mentioning *Venus and*

WILLIAM SHAKESPEARE

Adonis, Lucrece and "his sugared Sonnets among his private friends."

John Shakespeare died in 1601; no will of his is extant, but William owned his father's two houses in Stratford when he made his own will. In 1602 he bought 107 acres of land in Old Stratford for £320. Later the same year he acquired a cottage in Stratford town. He became part owner of a house in Blackfriars, London, in 1613, though he never lived in it. As a matter of fact, we do not know where Shakespeare resided during his London years, except that in 1604 he was a lodger in the house of Christopher Mountjoy, a Huguenot. This information comes from the records of a lawsuit between Christopher and his son-in-law in 1612; Shakespeare was a material witness.

One other important investment of Shakespeare's remains to be recorded; in 1604 he paid £440 to Ralph Hubard for the right to half the tithes of Old Stratford, Welcombe, Bushopton, and Stratford-on-Avon.

The progress of Shakespeare's career as a dramatist may be deduced from the bibliography given below, where the plays are listed in the order of their composition, as established by centuries of scholarship. It will be seen that most of the comedies and histories were written before 1600. The great tragedies—*Hamlet, Othello, Lear, Macbeth, Antony and Cleopatra*— belong to the period between 1601 and 1608. After 1608 Shakespeare tried his hand at tragi-comedy, perhaps following the example of Beaumont and Fletcher, whose work had by then become more popular than his. His last plays were written in 1611 and it is likely that he had given up acting about four years earlier. He never played leading roles; tradition has it that he acted kings' parts with great dignity, played Adam in *As You Like It* and the Ghost in *Hamlet.*

To return to events in his family life: his mother died in 1608; Susanna married John Hall in 1607 and Judith married Thomas Quiney in 1616. On March 25 of the latter year Shakespeare made his last will and testament, where he is described as "in perfect health and memory, God be praised." Now that both his daughters were married—Judith's marriage had taken place only six weeks before—it was only right that he should make a will. Though he died a month later, we need not disbelieve the remark about his health; he may have expected to live many more years; tradition says that his death was sudden. He was buried in the parish church of Stratford-on-Avon, April 25, 1616.

Shakespeare's will is the most revealing document that survives concerning him. His elder daughter, Susanna, was naturally the principal legatee, inheriting virtually all his goods and real estate. Under certain conditions Judith was to receive £300. There were substantial bequests to his sister Joan Hart and her sons, and to his niece Elizabeth Hall. He left £10 to the poor of Stratford, his sword to Thomas Combe, gifts of money to his executors Thomas Russell and Francis Collins, twenty shillings in gold to his godson William Walker. Among the recipients of money to buy mourning rings were one Hamlet Sadler and three members of the acting company—John Heminge, Richard Burbage and Henry Condell.

The only mention of his wife was the bequest to her of "my second best bed with the furniture." Too much has often been read into this apparently slighting reference, however. The best bed was probably an heirloom and so went to Susanna; Anne had

doubtless received her jointure of one-third of her husband's estate during his lifetime.

It it difficult to form a picture of Shakespeare's personality as it appeared to his contemporaries. Great personal charm he must have had, for even the envious and surly Ben Jonson "loved the man" and wrote of "my gentle Shakespeare." He also said that Shakespeare was "honest and of an open and free nature." Other contemporary references concur in this estimate.

The *Sonnets* would tell us a great deal about Shakespeare, if we could read them aright. Sonnets 1-126 were written to a man, the mysterious "Mr. W.H.," who may be Henry Wriothesley, Earl of Southampton, or William Herbert, Earl of Pembroke; Heminge and Condell dedicated the First Folio to the latter and his brother, the Earl of Montgomery. Whoever he was, the man was handsome, of higher rank and much younger than Shakespeare. The poet speaks constantly of his "love" for this beautiful youth and often of the danger of scandal.

The rest of the sonnets, except the two last, are to the "Dark Lady" who, though far from beautiful, makes the poet suffer agonies of lust. In Sonnet 144 he sums up his relationship with the two recipients of the sonnets as follows:

> Two loves I have of comfort and despair,
> Which like two spirits do suggest me still,
> The better angel is a man right fair:
> The worser spirit a woman colour'd ill.

The *Sonnets*, like the plays, run the entire gamut of human emotions; one is safe in saying that their author, in Dryden's words, "of all Modern and perhaps Ancient Poets, had the largest and most comprehensive soul."

Most of Shakespeare's plays were not published in his lifetime, since there was no such thing as dramatic copyright and the other acting companies would have been only too glad to make use of them for nothing. In 1623 Heminge and Condell brought out a folio edition of all the plays (except *Pericles*) now in the Shakespeare canon. The date of first publication is given after each play in the list below. The plays are divided into groups and the date in parentheses before each group roughly indicates when the plays in it were composed.

The Shakespeare portrait reproduced above is one of only two extant portraits which, Sidney Lee writes in the *Dictionary of National Biography*, "can be regarded as fully authenticated: the bust in Stratford church and the frontispiece to the folio of 1623 [the Droeshout engraving]."

PRINCIPAL WORKS: *Plays*: (Before 1594) Henry VI, Parts I, II, III, 1623; Richard III, 1597; Titus Andronicus, 1594; Love's Labour's Lost, 1598; The Two Gentlemen of Verona, 1623; The Comedy of Errors, 1623; The Taming of the Shrew, 1623; (1594-1597) Romeo and Juliet (pirated 1597) 1599; Richard II, 1597; A Midsummer Night's Dream, 1600; The Merchant of Venice, 1600; King John, 1623; (1597-1600) Henry IV, Part I, 1598; Henry IV, Part II, 1600; Henry V (pirated 1600) 1623; Much Ado About Nothing, 1600; Merry Wives of Windsor (pirated 1602) 1623; As You Like It, 1623; Julius Caesar, 1623; Troilus and Cressida, 1609; (1601-1608) Hamlet (pirated 1603) 1604; Twelfth Night, 1623; Measure For Measure, 1623; All's Well That Ends Well, 1623; Othello, 1622; Lear, 1608; Macbeth, 1623; Timon of Athens, 1623; Antony and Cleopatra, 1623; Coriolanus, 1623; (After 1608) Pericles, 1609; Cymbeline, 1623; The Winter's Tale, 1623; The Tempest, 1623; Henry VIII (with John Fletcher) 1623. *Poems*: Venus and Adonis, 1593; The Rape of Lucrece, 1594; The Phoenix and the Turtle, 1601; Sonnets and A Lover's Complaint, 1609.

ABOUT: *Biography*: Chambers, E. K. A Short Life of Shakespeare, with the Sources; Chambers, E. K. Sources for the Biography of Shakespeare; Chute, M. Shakespeare of London; Pearson, H. Life of Shakespeare; Raleigh, W. Shakespeare; Wilson, J. D. The Essential Shakespeare. *Criticism*: Bradley, A. C. Shakespearian Tragedy; Coleridge, S. T. Notes and Lectures upon Shakespeare; Dowden, E. Shakespeare, His Mind and Art; Granville-Barker, H. Prefaces to Shakespeare; Harrison, G. B. Introducing Shakespeare; Knight, G. W. The Crown of Life; Knight, G. W. The Imperial Theme; Knight, G. W. The Shakespearian Tempest; Knight, G. W. The Wheel of Fire; Mackail, J. W. The Approach to Shakespeare; Smith, D. N. (ed.) Shakespeare Criticism.

SHEFFIELD, JOHN, Duke of Buckingham and Normanby (April 7, 1648-February 24, 1721), essayist, poet, dramatist, was the only son of Edmund Sheffield, second Earl of Mulgrave, and Elizabeth Cranfield, daughter of the first Earl of Middlesex. He became third Earl of Mulgrave in 1655; at nine the boy had a governor who warned him never to kneel in public; the tutor's authority was rather damaged later in France, when he involuntarily knelt at a procession of the host and the boy stumbled over him. At seventeen Sheffield was a volunteer in the first Dutch war at sea, under Prince Rupert, and in 1667 was made captain of an independent troop of horse at Dover. In the second Dutch war he served as a volunteer under the Duke of York, and

was made a Knight of the Order of the Garter in April 1674. A Gentleman of the Bedchamber to Charles II, he obtained leave from the king to campaign in France with the Marshal de Turenne, and in 1680 commanded an expedition for the relief of Tangiers (in a leaky ship); he had incurred Charles' displeasure after several affairs of gallantry, and was banished from court in 1682 for two years.

He won favor with James II, becoming a privy councillor and Lord Chamberlain of the Household. His relations with William and Mary were less cordial, though in 1694 he was granted a pension of £3,000 a year and created Marquis of Normanby. Anne made him Duke of Buckingham in 1703, but Whigs soon compelled him to surrender his government posts, and he persuaded the Tory party to make some fruitless overtures to the Electress Sophia to assume the throne. The overthrow of the Whig ministry reinstated him in several posts from which he was promptly removed on the accession of George. Buckingham died at seventy-three at Buckingham House, St. James' Park. After lying in state he was buried in King Henry's chapel in Westminster Abbey; his monument bears an epitaph written by himself. He left an heir and his third wife, Catharine Sedley, the illegitimate daughter of James II.

Buckingham was a patron of Dryden, for whom he obtained the laureateship, and an enemy of Rochester, whom he challenged to a farcical duel. Tall, long-waisted, with an oval face, he figures in Dryden's *Absalom and Achitophel* as "Sharp-judging Adriel, the Muses' friend; himself a Muse." A profuse but not particularly memorable or original writer, he is remembered, if at all, for his *Essay on Satire* (which embroiled Dryden with Rochester) and *An Essay Upon Poetry*. His chief feat as a dramatist was bisecting Shakespeare's *Julius Caesar*, rewriting it, and interpolating several love scenes.

PRINCIPAL WORKS: An Essay Upon Poetry, 1682; The Temple of Death, a Poem, 1695; The Character of Charles II, 1696; The Works of the Most Noble John Sheffield, late Duke of Buckingham, 1721; Buckingham Restor'd, 1727.

ABOUT: Johnson, S. Lives of the Poets; Macaulay, W. B. History of England; Saintsbury, G. Dryden; Studies in Philology, 1937.

SHENSTONE, WILLIAM (November 13, 1714-February 11, 1763), author of miscellaneous verse and prose, was born at his famous estate of Leasowes, at Halesowen, then in Shropshire, now in Worcestershire. He was the son of Thomas Shenstone, a churchwarden, and of Anne Penn. After schools at Halesowen and Solihull, he went in 1732 to Pembroke College, Oxford, where he was a contemporary of Samuel Johnson. In the same year his mother died, and his uncle, Thomas Dolman, rector at Broome, near Kidderminster, became his guardian. His first book of poems, written at Oxford "for the entertainment of the author, and printed for the amusement of a few friends prejudiced in his favour," he later tried to have suppressed. At the university his chief friends were Richard Jago and Richard Graves, and through them he later became a member of the literary circle centering around Lady Luxborough, the Duchess of Somerset (earlier the Countess of Hertford), William Somerville, and Jago and Graves. He took no degree, but remained on the college books until 1742.

After that date Shenstone published no more poetry except occasional verse in the anthologies brought out by Richard Dodsley (later his editor), in 1748, 1755, and 1758. However, at his death it was found that he had a volume of poems ready for publica-

E. Alcock

WILLIAM SHENSTONE

tion, which were included in his collected works. He lived in Leasowes for the most part, and when his guardian died in 1745 he bought the place. The remainder of his life was one long effort to beautify it, in the formal, artificial style of the eighteenth century. Gray remarked that Shenstone's "whole philosophy consisted of living against his will in retirement, and in a place which his taste had adorned, but which he enjoyed only when people of note came to see and recommend it." Actually, however, he was one of the pioneers of landscape gardening.

A huge, obese, slovenly man, he caught cold while on a journey in winter to urge Lord Stamford's influence to secure a governmental pension for him (he had impoverished himself by his expenditures on Leasowes), and the cold developed into what was then called "putrid fever," of which he died. He was buried at Halesowen.

Shenstone never married. He was a man of warm and generous nature, but sensitive and touchy; he was a loyal friend but bore a permanent grudge against anyone who offended him. There were many such (including Horace Walpole, who called him "that water-gruel bard"), and the harsh criticism given his writing not only caused him to cease publishing it, even anonymously, but also increased his natural tendency to melancholy.

Shenstone's best known poem was *The Schoolmistress*, a burlesque imitation of Spenser, the subject being taken from his own first teacher, Sarah Lloyd. Among his other better known verses were "The Judgment of Hercules," "The Progress of Taste," and pastoral ballads and elegies. Johnson patronized him and infuriated him, but Goldsmith and Burns were among his admirers. He himself preferred his insipid letters to any of his poems. Saintsbury summed him up well in saying that he was "not a great poet, [but] very few of his contemporaries . . . had more of the root of the matter, though time and circumstance and a dawdling sentimental temperament intercepted and stunted fruit and flower. . . . The spell is never consummated, but the possibility is always there."

Shenstone did have genuine literary interests, and it was he who first suggested to Thomas Percy the collection of his *Reliques.*

PRINCIPAL WORKS: Poems on Various Occasions, 1737; The Schoolmistress, 1742; Works in Verse and Prose (R. Dodsley, ed.) 2 vols. 1764, 3 vols. (with Letters, and Essays on Men, Manners, and Things) 1769; Poetical Works (G. Gilfillan, ed.) 1854.

ABOUT: D'Israeli, I. Curiosities of Literature; Dodsley, R. Character of Shenstone, in Works in Verse and Prose; Gilfillan, G. Life, in Poetical Works; Graves, R. Recollections of Some Particulars in the Life of the late William Shenstone, Esq.; Grazebrook, H. S. The Family of Shenstone the Poet; Hecht, H. Thomas Percy and William Shenstone; Humphreys, A. R. William Shenstone: an 18th Century Portrait; Johnson, S. Lives of the English Poets; Saintsbury, G. History of English Prosody.

SHERIDAN, Mrs. FRANCES (1724-September 26, 1766), novelist and dramatist, was born in Dublin, Ireland, the daughter of the Reverend Dr. Philip Chamberlaine, prebendary of Rathmichael and archdeacon of Glendalclough, and Anastasia (Whyte) Sheridan, who died soon after Frances was born. Frances was the youngest of five children, three of them brothers who surreptitiously taught her when her father refused to allow her to learn to read or write, Walter instructing her in Latin and Richard in botany. At fifteen she wrote a two-volume romance, *Eugenie and Adelaide*, on housekeeping paper, and even attempted a sermon or two. After her father lapsed into imbecility she attended the theatre, also forbidden, where she was enraptured by Thomas Sheridan, manager of the Dublin Theatre, and defended him in *Faulkner's Journal*, with a poem called *The Owls; a Fable*, written in 1746. The occasion was "Kelly's Riot." (Kelly chased George Anne Bellamy, an actress, backstage, and was restrained by Sheridan.) In 1747 Walter married her to Sheridan. In 1758 another and more serious riot occurred, and the Sheridans moved to London, where they lived on Henrietta Street, Covent Garden. Here Dr. Johnson and Samuel Richardson (whom the elder Sheridan called "dull as a droning fly") became their friends.

Mrs. Sheridan's first successful book was *Memoirs of Miss Sidney Bidulph*, a novel in journal form, published in 1761. Dr. Johnson told her, "I know not, Madam! that you have a right, upon moral principles, to make your readers suffer so much," but others considered the book to be humorous as well as moral and pathetic. During a summer at

Windsor Mrs. Sheridan planned and wrote her best known play, *The Discovery*, which David Garrick produced at the Theatre Royal, Drury Lane, February 5, 1763, with himself as Sir Anthony Branville and Sheridan as Lord Medway. (In 1775, nine years after her death, it was revived as a rival bill to her son's *The Duenna*.) Aldous Huxley, who made a modern adaptation, called the play "a specimen at one and the same time of the eighteenth-century refinement, polish, and acuteness, and of eighteenth-century emotional crudity. It is at once high comedy and low sentiment." She was also the author of *Nourjahad*, an Oriental tale which was dramatized. Mrs. Sheridan was an unassuming woman with dark eyes, black hair, and a pronounced limp from a childhood accident. She died in France, at forty-two, of a complication of four maladies and was buried at Blois.

PRINCIPAL WORKS: Memoirs of Miss Sidney Bidulph, 1761; The Discovery, 1763; The Dupe, 1764; The History of Nourjahad, 1767.

ABOUT: Fitzgerald, P. Lives of the Sheridans; Huxley, A., ed. The Discovery; Lefanu, A. Memoirs of the Life and Writings of Mrs. Frances Sheridan; Wilson, M. These Were Muses.

SHERIDAN, RICHARD BRINSLEY BUTLER (October 30, 1751-June 29, 1816), dramatist, came of a family several members of which distinguished themselves in the arts and professions. His grandfather, the schoolmaster Thomas Sheridan, was Swift's friend; his father, also Thomas Sheridan, was an actor and theatre manager; his mother, Frances Chamberlaine Sheridan (who died when Richard was not yet fifteen), was a novelist and dramatist.

He was born in Dublin, but when he was a small child his parents moved to London and at nine he joined them there and never again saw his native country. (His ancestors were Anglo-Irish.) His father was his first teacher, but from 1762 to 1768 he was sent to Harrow, following which he was given private tutors. He never attended a university. In 1770 his father moved to Bath, where he became a teacher of elocution. Young Richard formed a close friendship with Nathaniel Holhed, then an Oxford student, and the two boys made a metrical translation of the epistles of Aristaenetus, a Greek writer of the fifth or sixth century, then wrote a farce, *Jupiter*, which they endeavored

SHERIDAN

J. Russell, 1788
RICHARD BRINSLEY SHERIDAN

in vain to have accepted by either Garrick or Foote.

In 1772, before his twenty-first birthday, Sheridan eloped to France with Elizabeth Anne Linley, a beautiful girl of sixteen and an extremely gifted singer, daughter of a well-known composer. The elopement was innocent—the object was to enable Elizabeth to enter a nunnery to escape the unpleasant attentions of one Major Matthews, reputed a married man; the two youngsters were secretly married in Calais. Both fathers were furious and hauled their children home again. Sheridan then fought two duels with Matthews, in the first of which he disarmed his opponent, but in the second of which he was badly wounded. To end the whole affair, as he thought, the elder Sheridan then sent his son to Waltham Abbey, Essex, where as a cure for love he was set to study mathematics. The next year he was entered in the Middle Temple (though he was never called to the bar); and a week later, with her father's consent but against the wishes of his own, he and Elizabeth were married again.

The young couple, without an income, set themselves up in London in the style of people of wealth; and, by a miracle, within a year Sheridan's first important play, *The Rivals*, had been produced at Drury Lane, was an enormous success, and they were made financially. Mrs. Sheridan was a re-

markable woman; though she ceased to sing in public, and refused to publish her writings, she was her husband's active assistant both in the management of Drury Lane and in his political career, and her beauty made her a noted figure; she was the original of Reynolds' "St. Cecilia." Unhappily, it was a fated beauty; she had tuberculosis and died of it in 1792, leaving one son and a heartbroken husband. This son later was the husband of Caroline Sheridan, the novelist, and their daughters included the famous beauties, Lady Dufferin, the song-writer, and Caroline Norton.

Meanwhile, in 1776, Sheridan succeeded Garrick as manager of Drury Lane, and soon after, with his father-in-law and others, became part owner of the theatre. It made him a fortune, but later it proved his financial ruin, for he paid all losses during its rebuilding in 1794, and in 1809 the new theatre burned down. Until his later years, however, he averaged £10,000 a year, and was able to live in the grandeur he loved. *The School for Scandal*, following *The Rivals*, made him a celebrity as well. He became a familiar figure in literary and artistic cricles, and in 1777 was invited into the famous Club.

After 1780 this career was duplicated by his political life. He entered Parliament for Stafford in that year, and with a few defeats served most of the time for this and other constituencies until 1813. It is said that he had to pay each burgess five guineas to vote for him (a quite normal procedure in those days), and by the latter date he could not afford it any longer. He was a strong Whig, a follower of Charles James Fox. He became one of the great orators of the House of Commons, his most celebrated effort being his speeches on the impeachment of Warren Hastings. (His first speech against Hastings was the first ever applauded by hand-clapping in the House.) He was a strong friend of the American rebels, and Congress voted him £20,000 in gratitude, but he refused the gift —perhaps he had heard that the soldiers who won the Revolution had gone unpaid. He was also an opponent of his fellow Club member Burke in supporting the French Revolution in its early days, though later, like most Englishmen, he recanted, and his last speech in Parliament was a defiance of Napoleon. Three times he held office briefly

—in 1782 as under-secretary for foreign affairs, in 1783 as secretary to the treasury, and in 1806 as treasurer of the navy and a privy councilor. He became a close friend of the Prince of Wales (later George IV), though he always resented being thought of as the prince's confidant or spokesman. At least once he refused a proffered peerage in exchange for a change of party; his integrity and truly progressive spirit were never questioned. He fought valiantly, for example, for freedom of the press, though the newspapers had often treated him scurvily. And he opposed union with Ireland, a most unpopular stand.

In 1795 Sheridan married again, his second wife being Jane Ogle, daughter of the Dean of Winchester. By this marriage also he had one son.

As long as Sheridan was in Parliament, he could not be arrested for debt. But when he lost his last election, the duns were upon him. He spent a short time in a debtor's prison in 1813, and a writ was served on him while he lay in his last illness. (He was not, however, reduced to extreme poverty, as rumor had it.) He had practically ceased to write, his last play being the melodrama, *Pizarro*, produced in 1799. Outwardly he was the soul of gaiety, which masked a deep and growing melancholy. For a while he was frequently inebriated (he was one of those unfortunates whom liquor affects unduly), but he pulled himself together and in his last years drank nothing but water. But his health had broken, and was never regained; besides a general breakdown he suffered badly from varicose veins. He died finally at sixty-four, and his funeral in Westminster Abbey was one of the largest and most magnificent ever held there.

All his life this virtuous, amiable man, whose greatest defect was a pardonable fondness for living in the grand style, was for some reason the object of calumny and malicious gossip. Even his early biographers—who are not cited here—helped to spread false stories against him. He never fought back, but he was thin skinned and badly hurt. Much of this animosity was, of course, political in origin; as a dramatist Sheridan was a shining success from the start.

When one analyzes Sheridan's three most important plays—*The Rivals, The School for Scandal,* and *The Critic* (that merciless parody of the fashionable sentimental drama), it is easy to see that neither the plots nor the principal characters are new; they are conventional stock. All those immortal creatures—Mrs. Malaprop, Sir Anthony Absolute, Sir Lucius O'Trigger, Lady Teazle, Joseph Surface, and the rest—have appeared many times before under other names. What he did was to "pour new wine into old bottles"—to rewrite Restoration drama in terms of the Georgian era. He was far from the first to deal with "drawingroom diplomacy," but he was the first to make it the *essence* of his plays; and he was the first to voice the standards, ideals, and conventions of the new society, made up of soldiers and politicians rather than of the old landowning families. He had *both* wit and humor, which seldom appear in the same man, and there was genuine feeling in his most brilliant sallies. Compare his two greatest comedies with those of, say, Wycherley or Congreve, and the difference in warmth and vitality will be apparent at once. Add a genius for stagecraft and for phrase-making alike, and Sheridan's supremacy as a writer of high comedy is accounted for. He was an extremely useful public servant, but it is a loss to posterity that all his ability did not go instead into the making of more plays like *The School for Scandal* and *The Rivals.*

PRINCIPAL WORKS: *Plays* (dates of publication): The Rivals, 1775; The School for Scandal, 1778?; The Critic, or, A Tragedy Rehearsed, 1781; A Trip to Scarborough (from Vanbrugh's Relapse) 1781; The Duenna: or the Double Elopement (from Wycherley's Country Wife) 1785; Pizarro, a Tragedy, 1795; The Forty Thieves (with G. Colman, the Younger) 1825; St. Patrick's Day, or the Scheming Lieutenant, 1829. *Poems*: Clio's Protest, or the Picture Varnished, 1771; The Ridotto of Bath, 1771; Ode to Scandal, 1819. *Collections*: Collected Works (T. Moore, ed.) 1833; (L. Hunt, ed. 1840; W. F. Rae, ed. 1902).

ABOUT: Armstrong, C. F. Shakespeare to Shaw; Cove, J. W. (Lewis Gibbs) Sheridan; Darlington, W. A. Sheridan; Fitzgerald, P. Lives of the Sheridans; Foss, K. Here Lies Richard Brinsley Sheridan; Gibbs, L. Richard Brinsley Sheridan, His Life and His Theatre; Glasgow, A. Sheridan, of Drury Lane; Moore, T. Memoirs of the Life of the Right Honorable Richard Brinsley Sheridan; Oliphant, M. O. W. Sheridan; Oliver, R. T. Four Who Spoke Out; Rae, W. F. Sheridan, a Biography, with an Introduction by Sheridan's Greatgrandson, the Marquis of Dufferin and Ava; Rhodes, R. C. Harlequin Sheridan, the Man and the Legend; Sanders, L. C. Life of R. B. Sheridan (with Bibliography by J. P. Anderson); Sichel,

SHERLOCK

W. S. The Life of R. B. Sheridan; Watkins, J. Memoirs of the Public and Private Life of the Right Honorable R. B. Sheridan.

SHERLOCK, THOMAS (1678-July 18, 1761), preacher, religious writer, was the eldest son of Dr. William Sherlock, dean of St. Paul's. After attending Eton, where his friends included Lord Townshend and Robert Walpole, he entered St. Catharine's College, Cambridge University, in 1693, receiving his B.A. in 1697, M.A. in 1701, and D.D. in 1714. Benjamin Hoadly, his lifelong antagonist, was in college at the time. It is assumed from Pope's reference to Sherlock in the *Dunciad* as "the plunging prelate" that he was a swimmer of note as a student. Elected a fellow of his college in 1678, he was ordained by Bishop Patrick in 1701. Three years later he was appointed master of the Temple, when his father resigned his office, and remained there nearly fifty years (till 1753), an extremely popular preacher. In 1711 Sherlock was made chaplain to Queen Anne; was elected master of St. Catherine Hall in 1714, and became vice chancellor of the university; obtained the deanery of Chichester in 1715; and was installed as Canon of Norwich in 1719.

The year before, his publication of *Vindication of Corporation and Test Acts*, directed against Hoadly, lost him the king's favor, and he was struck off the list of royal chaplains. The death of George I brought him back to court with Queen Caroline as his patroness, with the natural result that Sherlock became an ardent Tory and supporter of church and state politics, defending Walpole in 1741 against the Prince of Wales' party. In 1747 he seems to have refused the archbishopric of Canterbury, giving ill health as a reason, but the next year was confirmed as bishop of London. He was stricken by paralysis in 1753, but published four volumes of sermons in 1758. His wife, who was Judith Fontaine of Yorkshire, bore him no children. Sherlock died at eighty-three, and was buried in the parish churchyard of Fulham.

M. H. Hutton calls Sherlock "the most powerful opponent, and the most rational, whom the deists encountered." His anti-deist sermon. *The Use and Interest of Prophecy*, went through several editions, while *A Letter to the Clergy and People of London and*

Westminster on Occasion of the Late Earthquake (1750), with its vigorous denunciation of vice, sold 100,000 copies in less than a month.

PRINCIPAL WORKS: Remarks on the Bishop of Bangor's Treatment of the Clergy and Convocation, 1717; The Use and Intent of Prophecy, 1725; The Trial of the Witnesses of the Resurrection of Jesus, 1729; Discourses at the Temple Church, 1754-1758, 1797; Works (J. S. Hughes, ed.) 1830.
ABOUT: Carpenter, E. Thomas Sherlock, 1678-1761, Bishop of Bangor; Hughes, J. S. Divines of the Church of England Series, vol. 1; Stephen, L. History of English Thought in the Eighteenth Century.

SHERLOCK, WILLIAM (1641?-June 19, 1707), was born in Southwark, and educated at Eton and Peterhouse, Cambridge University, where he received his B.A. in 1660, his M.A. three years later. Some years elapsed before he began his career as a preacher, notable for his bewildering facility for arguing on both sides of a question. His first rectory was St. George's on Thames Street, London, in 1669. By 1680 he was a D.D., next year a prebendary in St. Paul's Cathedral, and Master of the Temple in 1685. His first publication, *The Knowledge of Jesus Christ and Union With Him* led to the baseless charge that he was a Socinian, or disbeliever in the divinity of Christ. In *The Case of Resistance to the Supreme Powers* he argued for the divine right of kings and the duty of passive obedience, but held out as long as possible against taking the oath of allegiance to William and Mary, and was considered for that reason to be a nonjuror. More prudent counsels (including possibly those of his wife) prevailed, and he took the oath in August 1690. His *Practical Discourse Concerning Death*, his most popular work, was published while he was flirting with the nonjurors. On June 15, 1691, he succeeded Tillotson as Dean of St. Paul's.

In 1690 a heady attack of Sherlock's on Socinianism laid him open to a fresh charge, that he was a tritheist, or believer that the three persons of the Trinity are three distinct gods, an opportunity which his formidable opponent, Robert South, was quick to seize. By 1696 he had extricated himself from the quandary and had begun to write against dissenters. In 1698 he became rector of Therfield, Hertfordshire. Sherlock died at Hampstead, at the age of sixty-six, and was buried in St. Paul's. His son Thomas also became a preacher of note.

PRINCIPAL WORKS: A Discourse Concerning the Knowledge of Jesus Christ, 1674; The Case of Resistance to the Supreme Powers, 1684; A Practical Discourse Concerning Death, 1689; A Vindication of the Doctrine of the Trinity, 1690; A Practical Discourse Concerning the Future Judgment, 1692; Sermons Preached upon Several Occasions. 1719.

ABOUT: Kettlewell, J. Memoirs; Lathbury, T. History of Nonjurors; Macaulay, T. B. History of England; Huntington Library Quarterly, November 1946.

SHIRLEY, JAMES (1596-1666), dramatist, poet, was probably the "James the Sonne of James Sharlie" baptized at St. Mary Woolchurch, London, September 7, 1596. James Shirley the elder—baptized at the same church, January 18, 1568—was the son of William Shirley and was buried on June 2, 1617. We do not know what his occupation or social status was.

Young Shirley entered Merchant Taylors' School, London, on October 4, 1608, and left in 1612. He is believed to have entered St. John's College, Oxford, that year, but he transferred to St. Catharine's College, Cambridge, in the Easter Term of 1615 and graduated B.A. in 1617. His father's death may have prevented him from proceeding to M.A. Anthony a Wood says that he took holy orders and was a clergyman in or near St. Albans, Hertfordshire. On June 1, 1618, he married Elizabeth Gilmet of St. Albans, who was just sixteen; her family had influence, and in November 1618 he was promised the headmastership of the St. Albans Grammar School when it next fell vacant.

Mary, daughter of James and Elizabeth Shirley, was baptized at St. Albans in December 1619. In January 1621 Shirley was appointed master of the Grammar School, a position that he held until 1624 or the beginning of 1625. According to Wood, he then became a Roman Catholic, gave up his parish, gave up school teaching too, and moved to London, where he lived in Gray's Inn and became a dramatist.

Shirley's first play, Love Tricks or The School of Compliment, was licensed for performance February 10, 1625. His eldest son, Mathias, was baptized at St. Giles, Cripplegate, on February 26, 1625, so that the move to London must have taken place by this

JAMES SHIRLEY

date. His conversion to Catholicism belongs to late 1624 or early 1625, for in February 1624 he was a Proctor in Convocation for the Archdeaconry of St. Albans and therefore still a member of the Church of England.

Shirley's prolific career as a dramatist, which continued until the closing of theatres by the Parliament in 1642, was almost uniformly successful. Queen Henrietta Maria was a Catholic, and by 1633 he was in the highest possible favor with the Court; his The Young Admiral was performed on the king's birthday that year; Charles I himself suggested the plot of The Gamester, performed at court in 1634. Shirley's masque, The Triumph of Peace, was performed before the king by the Gentlemen of the Inns of Court in the same year.

In May 1636 an outbreak of the plague caused the closing of the London theatres; Shirley took himself and his wares to Dublin, where John Ogilby had opened a theatre, the first in that city, in 1635. He wrote a number of plays and prologues for this theatre, St. Patrick for Ireland being one, of course. The London theatres reopened in October 1637; Shirley may have made one or two visits to his native city, but he did not finally leave Ireland until 1640.

On his return to London, Shirley, who had previously written almost exclusively for the queen's company of players, wrote for the King's Men, whose leading dramatist, Massinger, had just died.

After the outbreak of the civil war and the closing of the theatres, Shirley, a loyal supporter of the king, had to leave London with his wife and children. He served in some military capacity under his patron William Cavendish—later first Duke of Newcastle—until the latter left England after the battle of Marston Moor, 1644. Soon afterward Shirley "retired obscurely" to London, according to Wood, and was supported there by one Thomas Stanley. In 1646 he published some poetry and in 1647 edited a volume of plays by Beaumont and Fletcher.

Shirley now took to his old profession of school master, teaching private pupils, compiling textbooks on Latin grammar, and doing a good deal of hack work for Ogilby's translations of Homer and Virgil. Some private and semi-private theatrical performances were permitted under the Protectorate; Shirley's masque, *Cupid and Death*, was given before the Portuguese ambassador in 1653; *The Contention of Ajax and Ulysses*, which contains the famous lyric, "The glories of our blood and state . . ." was performed privately.

After the restoration of Charles II in 1660 many of Shirley's plays were revived with varying success, but he wrote no new ones. His house near Fleet Street was burned down in the Great Fire of London, 1666, and he and his second wife, Frances, were forced to move to the Parish of St. Giles in the Fields, Middlesex, where they died about two months later on the same day, as a result of their sufferings during and after the fire. They were buried together on October 29. Three sons and two daughters survived their father.

Shirley's portraits show a handsome, rather melancholy and intense face, with dark hair and a light moustache. His dress is somber but elegant. Of his personality we really know nothing, though he seems to have had many good friends, not only among the nobility and gentry but among rival poets; Massinger and Ford, with many others, wrote complimentary verses to him.

As a lyric poet, Shirley has at least one immortal poem to his credit; as a dramatist he is not unworthy to terminate the great period of English drama that began with

Marlowe. His earlier work mainly consists of realistic comedy modeled on Jonson and Fletcher; *The Lady of Pleasure* and *The Gamester* are good examples. Later he turned more to tragedy and romantic comedy in the manner of Beaumont and Fletcher and Shakespeare; *The Cardinal* was his own favorite among his tragedies and *The Traitor* has also been admired by many critics. No single play of his, however, stands out as an unmistakable work of genius.

PRINCIPAL WORKS: *Plays*: The Wedding, 1629; The Grateful Servant, 1630; The School of Compliment, 1631; Changes, or Love in a Maze, 1632; The Witty Fair One, 1633; The Bird in a Cage, 1633; The Traitor, 1635; Hyde Park, 1637; The Gamester, 1637; The Young Admiral, 1637; The Example, 1637; The Lady of Pleasure, 1637; The Duke's Mistress, 1638; The Royal Master, 1638; The Maid's Revenge, 1639; Love's Cruelty, 1640; The Opportunity, 1640; The Coronation, 1640; The Constant Maid, 1640; St. Patrick for Ireland, 1640; The Humorous Courtier, 1640; A Pastoral Called the Arcadia, 1640; Six New Plays (The Brothers, The Doubtful Heir, The Imposture, The Cardinal, The Sisters, The Court Secret) 1653; The Politician, 1655; The Gentleman of Venice, 1655; Honoria and Mammon, 1659. *Masques*: A Contention for Honour and Riches, 1633; The Triumph of Peace, 1633; The Triumph of Beauty, 1646; Cupid and Death, 1653; The Contention of Ajax and Ulysses, 1659. *Other Works*: Poems, 1646; Via ad Latinam Linguam Complanata (The Way Made Plain to the Latin Tongue) 1649; The Rudiments of Grammar, 1656.

ABOUT: Armstrong, R. L. Introduction to The Poems of James Shirley; Baugh, A. C. *in* Modern Language Review, XVII, 1922, and Review of English Studies, VII, 1931; Nason, A. H. James Shirley, Dramatist; Radtke, S. J. James Shirley: His Catholic Philosophy of Life; Tannenbaum, S. A. and D. James Shirley, a Concise Bibliography; Wood, A. à, Athenae Oxonienses.

SIDNEY, Sir PHILIP (November 30, 1554-October 17, 1586), poet and prose writer, was born in Penshurst, Kent, the son of Sir Henry Sidney, later Lord Deputy of Ireland, and Mary Dudley, daughter of the Duke of Northumberland. Sidney was born to the purple; the Earl of Leicester was his uncle, Philip II of Spain was one of his godfathers, Henry of Navarre and William of Orange were among his friends. When he was only nine his father, then Lord President of Wales, made him lay rector of a living at Wickford, Flintshire. In 1564 he entered Shrewbury School with Fulke Greville, his lifelong friend thereafter. At Christ Church, Oxford, which he entered in 1568, he became a close associate of such future celebrities as Richard Carew, Richard Hakluyt, and William Camden.

Probably no more beloved man ever lived, and he deserved his friends' devotion. Sidney has stood for centuries as the prime example of the chivalrous and noble gentleman. If he had a fault it was his undue solemnity and dislike of the light or trivial; yet he was no pompous prig. Spenser, whom he met through Gabriel Harvey, became his ardent worshiper. He was offered the vacant throne of Poland. Veronese painted his portrait. As a boy he became the honored friend of the middle-aged Protestant philosopher, Hubert Languet. And the story of his knightly death has become a legend.

From his childhood he loved learning, yet he left Oxford after three years because of the plague, and never returned for a degree. Instead, he received the queen's permission to travel abroad to learn languages, meanwhile conducting some quasi-diplomatic errands for her, though he was not yet twenty-one when he was recalled to England in 1575. For a while he was attached to the court, but Elizabeth's court was no place for the idealistic, sensitive Sidney—who was an excellent swordsman, quick to draw sword. In 1576 he had been in Ireland with the first Earl of Essex, in 1577 abroad again for Elizabeth. A private quarrel with the Earl of Oxford, and the queen's uncertain temper and high-handed way with her favorites combined to drive him away, by 1579.

He went to Wilton, where he stayed with his beloved sister, Mary, by now the countess of Pembroke. It was for her that he wrote his prose romance, the *Arcadia*. She did not obey his injunction to burn the pages as he wrote and sent them to her, and his deathbed request to have the book destroyed was also disobeyed. Why Sidney so disliked his pastoral romance is a puzzle; perhaps he felt it too trivial to represent him, perhaps he was ashamed of its youthful euphuistic extravagance. With his sister also he versified the Psalms.

But in spite of his high connections and his important services, Sidney had only a modest income and needed some sort of steady employment. Through his uncle he served in 1580 as steward to the bishop of Winchester. In 1581 (as again in 1584) he was a Member of Parliament for Kent. In 1583 he was knighted, more or less by accident—the queen was still somewhat at outs

with him for two years more. In the same year he married Frances, daughter of the famous Sir Francis Walsingham. She survived him with one daughter (another child was still-born after his death), and twice remarried.

In 1585 another uncle, the Earl of Warwick, secured for Sidney the post of master of ordnance. He had already been designated "general of horse." In 1584 he had been in France again for the queen, and had rather exceeded his instructions by ardently advocating a Protestant league against Spain. Sidney was always a devoted Protestant, and in general a devout Christian; though he met Giordano Bruno, and Bruno, captivated by him as everybody else was, dedicated his books to him, Sidney never approved of the great Italian's profound skepticism.

Most of his energies in this period were devoted to trying to make the vacillating queen agree to send an army against Spain. But another matter took up much of his interest, and that was the colonization of North America. Elizabeth never let him go on any of the voyages to the New World, but he owned large grants in the nebulous territory then known as Virginia—which stretched from Florida to Newfoundland.

Sidney's efforts to get direct action against Spain failed, but finally the queen did agree to help the Protestant Dutch with men and arms. Leicester was made commander in

SIR PHILIP SIDNEY

chief and Sidney was appointed governor of Flushing. The queen particularly refused to let him do any actual fighting. He evaded her, of course. In September 1586 came the battle of Zutphen. The story is almost too well known: how he threw away his leg armor because a friend had forgotten his, how he was wounded badly in the thigh, how he gave his last drinking water to a private soldier whose "need was greater," how (in the primitive surgical conditions of those days) he lingered for almost a month, finally dying six weeks before his thirty-second birthday.

Never has there been such an outpouring of public grief. It came from his fellow poets, his colleagues at court, the ordinary people who had learned to think of him as a sort of ideal figure, the great of every country of Europe who had been carried away by his charm and sincerity. It was not until the following February that the public funeral could be held; both his parents had died recently and the family estate was in a muddle, with no money available; but when it did occur it was an outpouring such as England has scarcely seen since. He was buried in St. Paul's. By his will he had remembered innumerable friends and retainers; his books he left to Fulke Greville and to Sir Edward Dyer.

It may be wondered whether the universal affection felt for Sidney by all who met him has not induced a rather exaggerated idea of his standing as a poet. When Nash, for example, cried at Sidney's death: "Put out your rushlights, you poets and rhymers!" Shakespeare had just begun to write. Yet discounting all the hyperbole of affection, Sidney was a fine and authentic poet. He was one of the first Englishmen to probe the lyrical possibilities of the sonnet. In this form Petrarch was undoubtedly his master— even though he said, "I am no pickpurse of another's wit."

Sidney's standing as a poet rests largely on his *Astrophel and Stella*, the lady known as Stella being Penelope Devereux, daughter of the first Earl of Essex, sister of the second, and Lady Richmond when the book was published. How much of "Astrophel's" adoration of "Stella" is genuine, how much a poetical pose, is a nice question. It is true that at one time Penelope was promised to

Sidney by her father, and some of the sonnets and songs are highly personal; yet the book was dedicated to Sidney's own wife, she edited the second edition, and neither Lady Richmond's husband nor her very touchy brother ever objected. Hazlitt found *Astrophel* "frigid, jejune, and stiff," but most readers agree rather with Lamb that it is the voice of "transcendent passion"—whether real or imaginary does not matter.

In prose, the *Arcadia*, in spite of its conceits, is charming—a sort of wish-fulfilment dream of the ideal chivalry of a pastoral golden age—which decidedly was not located anywhere near the temperamental Elizabeth. But Sidney's best prose is in the *Apologie for Poetrie*—poetry to him meaning any imaginative literature, including the drama. It is written in a simple, direct, and musical prose. It is also one of the finest known examples of false prophecy, for in it Sidney lamented that his own age was lacking in true poets! (It must be remembered that he was one of the group calling itself the Areopagus, whose object was to tie English poetry to classical meters.) The *Apologie* was a reply to Stephen Gosson's attack on the stage, though Sidney refused to enter into acrimonious controversy. He also wrote a fine defense of his father's procedure in Ireland, which still exists only in manuscript.

Shelley perhaps has the last word on Sidney; for though we can hardly grant that one as martial and militant as he was "sublimely mild," there can be no question that, in a lusty, roaring, scarcely scrupulous age, Sir Philip Sidney was indeed, by common consent, "a spirit without spot."

PRINCIPAL WORKS: A Worke concerning the trewnesse of the Christian Religion (tr. from the French of Du Plessis Mornay, finished by A. Golding) 1587; The Countesse of Pembroke's Arcadia, 1590; Syr P. S. His Astrophel and Stella, 1591 (authorized ed. 1598); Apologie for Poetrie (Defense of Poesie) 1594; Letters and Memorials of State (A. Collins, ed.) 1746; The Psalmes of David translated into divers and sundry kindes of Verse (with the Countess of Pembroke) (S. W. Singer, ed.) 1823; Correspondence of Sir Philip Sidney and Hubert Languet (S. A. Pears, tr. from the Latin and ed.) 1845; Poems (A. B. Grosart, ed.) 1873; Miscellaneous Works (W. Gray, ed.) 1893; Complete Works (A. Feuillerat, ed.) 1914-23.

ABOUT: Addleshaw, P. Sir Philip Sidney; Bill, A. H. Astrophel: or, the Life and Death of the Renowned Sir Philip Sidney; Bourne, H. R. F. Sir Philip Sidney; Denkinger, E. M. Immortal Sidney; Gray, W. Life *in* Miscellaneous Works; Greville, F. Life of the Renowned Sir Philip Sidney; Hill, H. W. Sidney's Arcadia and the Elizabethan Drama; Jusserand, J. J. The English Novel in the Time of Shakespeare; Lee, S. Great Englishmen of the 16th Century; Moffett, T. Nobilis: or, a View of the Life and Death of a Sidney; Myrick, K. O. Sir Philip Sidney as a Literary Craftsman; Pears, S. A. Memoir, *in* Correspondence with Languet; Symonds, J. A. Life of Sidney; Thaler, A. Shakespeare and Sir Philip Sidney; Wallace, M. W. The Life of Sir Philip Sidney; Warren, C. H. Sir Philip Sidney, a Study in Conflict; Wilson, M. Sir Philip Sidney.

SKELTON, JOHN (1460?-June 21, 1529), poet, dramatist, came of a family that originated in Cumberland and Yorkshire; nothing is known of his immediate ancestry or of the date and place of his birth. The first mention of him occurs in the dedication of Caxton's translation of the *Aeneid*, 1489; his Latin scholarship is there highly praised and he is described as "late created poet laureate in the University of Oxford." In other words, Skelton had received a special degree in Latin grammar, rhetoric and versification. Louvain University gave him a similar degree, as did Cambridge in 1493; the entry in the Cambridge records mentions the two previous laureations. Skelton himself says he was educated at Cambridge, and he may have graduated B.A. from there in 1480, before going to Oxford.

By 1489 Skelton was already an English poet as well as a Latinist; an elegy on the death of the Earl of Northumberland written that year is his earliest surviving poem. He may have sought favor at Court through his poetry; in 1495 he was in London; in 1498 he was ordained subdeacon, deacon and priest in rapid succession; later the same year Henry VII heard him say Mass. It is therefore not surprising to find Skelton the tutor of the future Henry VIII in 1499, a position which he may well have held since 1494 and in which he continued until about 1502. For the young prince's edification he compiled a treatise called *Speculum Principis* in 1501. A John Skelton who may have been the poet was imprisoned in the king's prison by the royal Court of Requests in 1502; this was a routine commitment for debt, however, and does not necessarily imply a fall from favor.

Henry VII about this time appointed Skelton rector of Diss in Norfolk, where he is found living in 1504; this parish provided a satisfactory income and may be considered a reward for his services as tutor, though it was admittedly rather far from Court. When

Henry VIII succeeded to the throne in 1509, Skelton sought his former pupil's favor; he appears to have lived permanently in London after 1512.

A number of ribald folk tales had Skelton as their protagonist, both in his lifetime and afterwards; there is a strong tradition that he kept a concubine while at Diss, to the scandal both of his bishop and of his parishioners. This may be true; in matters of faith, however, Skelton was strongly orthodox, as the records of Norwich diocese Consistory Court show.

After his return to London, Skelton lived mostly in the City of Westminster; John Islip, the abbot of Westminster, was a patron of his. In 1518 he was lodging in the house of Alice Newebery at Westminster.

From about 1512 onward Skelton called himself "orator regius" or royal orator. This may mean that he conducted some of the king's Latin correspondence with foreign governments, but his chief duties were those of court poet, whether or not Henry VIII ever actually appointed him poet laureate. His poetry at this period shows great variety; *A Ballad of the Scottish King* celebrates the English victory at Flodden; *Magnificence* is a morality play, probably acted at court; *Against Garnesche* is a series of abusive poems composed "by the king's most noble commandment" against Sir Christopher Garnesche, another court official, who replied in kind, the intention being to amuse the court by this mock war of words; numerous songs and comic pieces, many of which do not survive, also belong to this period.

In his earlier period of residence at court Skelton had written an allegorical satire, *The Bowge of Court*, in the Chaucerian meter of "rime royal." Toward the end of his second period of court favor, he returned to satire, now employing the type of verse known as Skeltonic, which he had apparently invented during his residence at Diss—perhaps for *The Book of Philip Sparrow*. In *Speak, Parrot*, in *Colin Clout*, and in *Why Come Ye Not to Court?* he attacked the growing power of Cardinal Wolsey with ever-increasing explicitness, though he included in his condemnation every ecclesiastic who was unworthy of his position. The plain-spoken *Colin Clout* is perhaps Skelton's masterpiece.

In 1523 Skelton published *The Garland of Laurel*, a sort of apologia for his poetic career, which lists his works to date, including *Speak, Parrot* and *Colin Clout*, and shows that he had left the court for the service of the Countess of Surrey. It seems clear that Wolsey had exercised his power and Skelton had had to flee the court. Thereafter he did his best to placate the cardinal. His last work, *A Replication Against Certain Young Scholars*, written in 1528, which vindicates orthodoxy and especially the cult of the Virgin Mary, was written at Wolsey's express command. The story that Skelton took refuge from Wolsey in Westminster Abbey and died there is mistaken; he may well have taken sanctuary there with John Islip in 1522 or 1523, but he died a free man, and was buried in his parish church, St. Margaret's, Westminster.

Both Skelton's poetry and his personal life have come in for a good deal of contempt and misunderstanding. Much of his poetry consists of invective, and a fair number of obscene words are used, but it is never pornographic. A parallel might be drawn between him and Swift as regards their obscenity, religious orthodoxy, satirical propensity, strong moral sense and occasional falling-off from their own high standards. Still, Skelton was undoubtedly gayer and more Rabelaisian than Swift, with fewer sexual inhibitions.

The Skeltonic style—one can hardly call it meter—is partly patterned on the rhymed Latin *prose* of the period. It has often been sneered at as doggerel, but several modern English poets—chief among them Robert Graves and W. H. Auden—have used it with gusto and appropriateness. Skelton had no sense of proportion, so that all his major poems lack form and most of them are too long, but he introduced a new note into English poetry. He is just as much a medieval figure as Chaucer, but his medievalism is that of the *Prologue*, not that of *The Knight's Tale;* he shows greater affinity still with the author of *Piers Plowman.*

PRINCIPAL WORKS: The Bowge of Court, 1500; A Ballad of the Scottish King, 1513; A Right Delectable Treatise upon a Goodly Garland or Chaplet of Laurel, 1523; A Replication Against Certain Young Scholars, 1528; Magnificence, 1529-32; Colin Clout, 1532-37; The Book of Philip Sparrow, 1542-46; Why Come Ye Not to Court? 1542-46; Speak, Parrot (and The Death of the Noble Prince King Edward the Fourth, A Treatise of the Scots, Ware the Hawk, The Tunning of Elinor Rumming) 1542-48; Pithy, Pleasant and Profitable Works of Master Skelton, Poet Laureate, 1568; The Poetical Works of John Skelton (A. Dyce, ed.) 1843; The Complete Poems of John Skelton (P. Henderson, ed.) 1931.

ABOUT: Edwards, H. L. R. Skelton: the Life and Times of an Early Tudor Poet; Lloyd, L. J. John Skelton: A Sketch of his Life and Writings; Nelson, W. John Skelton, Laureate.

SKINNER, JOHN (October 3, 1721-June 16, 1807), Scottish songwriter, was born at Balfour, parish of Birse, Aberdeenshire, the son of John Skinner, a parish school master; his mother died when he was a child. Taught by his father, the boy was sufficiently schooled in Latin at thirteen to win a bursary or scholarship at Marischal College, Aberdeen. After leaving school he taught for a few months in the parish school of Kemnay, then moved to the not inappropriately named town of Monymusk, where he began to write verses, including a "football idyll": "The Monymusk Christmas Ba'ing." The wife of the local grandee, Sir Archibald Grant, bart., liked the verses, and gave Skinner access to Sir Archibald's well-stocked library. The town's Episcopal clergyman completed Skinner's conversion from Presbyterianism to Scottish Episcopalianism. He was appointed tutor to the only son of Mr. Sinclair of Scalloway, Shetland, in 1740, and a year later married Grace Hunter, a clergyman's daughter. In 1742, after training at Meldrum, he was ordained at Peterhead, appointed minister of Longside, and settled down in a cottage at Linshart. His church was destroyed, and Skinner himself once imprisoned for six months during the Jacobite disturbances, on the charge of preaching in his house to an audience of more than four.

To supplement his diminished income, Skinner made an unsuccessful attempt at farming. His troubles did not extinguish his cheerful spirits, and the fame of his lyrics spread. After Robert Burns met Skinner's second son, John, bishop of Aberdeen, in the office of Chalmers, the Aberdeen printer, in 1787, the two poets began a correspondence. Burns saw to it that several of Skinner's best songs were included in Johnson's *Musical Museum*, and called his political satire, "Tullochgorum," "the best Scotch song ever Scotland saw." Mrs. Skinner died in 1799, and he retired in 1807, dying at eighty-six. He is buried at Longside.

"Tune Your Fiddle" and "Old Age," popular songs of Skinner's, are surpassed by "Ewie wi' the Crookit Horn," an elegy in a vein of pathetic humor, which Burns frankly imitated in his "Poor Mailie's Elegy."

PRINCIPAL WORKS: Ecclesiastical History of Scotland, 1788; Theological Works (J. Skinner, bp., ed.) 1809; Amusements of Leisure Hours, or Poetical Pieces Chiefly in the Scottish Dialect, 1809; Miscellaneous Collection of Fugitive Pieces, 1809; Songs and Poems, 1859; A Garland from the Vernacular, 1921.

ABOUT: Reid, H. G. Memoir in Songs and Poems; Skinner, J., bp. Memoir, in Skinner's Theological Works; Ward, T. H. English Poets.

SMART, CHRISTOPHER (April 11, 1722-May 21, 1771), poet, was born in Shipbourne, Kent, the son of Peter Smart, a native of Durham, and Winifred Griffiths, a Welshwoman. His father was steward of the Kentish estates of Viscount Vane. Smart was educated at schools in Maidstone and Durham, where his precociousness in verse gained him the patronage of the Duchess of Cleveland, who gave him a pension until her death in 1742. He entered Pembroke Hall (now Pembroke College), Cambridge, in 1739, and graduated B.A. in 1742, M.A. in 1747. His first publication was a translation of Pope's "Ode to St. Cecilia" into Latin verse. He also wrote an extravaganza, *A Trip to Cambridge*, which was acted in the college. He was made a fellow in 1745, and praelector in philosophy. Unfortunately, he was improvident and given to drink, and he lost his praelectorship when he was imprisoned in his rooms by his creditors. He retained his fellowship, but went to London, where, through Dr. Burney (father of Fanny Burney) he met John Newbery, the publisher, with whom he was frequently associated thereafter. In 1751, after a first brief incarceration in Bedlam, he married Anna Maria Carman, Newbery's stepdaughter, then returned to Cambridge without notifying the university authorities of his marriage. It was discovered, and he almost lost his fellowship, which was his only means of support; however, he had won the Seatonian Prize for two years for a poem on the attributes of the Supreme Being, and he was allowed to retain his fellowship on condition that he continue to compete for it. He won

CHRISTOPHER SMART

it five times in all. His only previous English verse had been a contribution to *The Student, or the Oxford and Cambridge Miscellany.*

By 1755 Smart had moved to London permanently, and was making his living as a bookseller's hack for Newbery. He had a gift for light verse, and wrote every variety of verse to order, even to advertisements. Much of this was anonymous or under the pseudonym of Ebenezer Pentweazle. Another pseudonym was Mary Midnight, under which name he had edited *The Midwife, or the Old Woman's Magazine,* from 1751 to 1753. At the same time he did translations of Horace and others, in prose and verse. All this brought him very little money. In 1756 he "leased" himself for ninety-nine years, as editor of the weekly *Universal Visiter [sic],* for one sixth of the profits. The magazine lasted only two years. In 1759 Garrick gave a benefit for him, because of his "much reduced circumstances." It was not enough; his wife and two daughters had to go to live with his married sister in Ireland, and he never saw them again.

In 1763 Smart was in Bedlam again for a year or more. His insanity took the form of religious mania, with constant prayer. It was during this period that, in charcoal on the walls and in key-scratches on the panels, he wrote his only really first-class poem, *A Song to David.* (Strangely enough, the first

475

collected edition of his poems omitted this, his masterpiece, as "a melancholy proof of his madness.") Dr. Johnson visited him in the asylum, and reported that Smart was harmless—he would "as lief pray with Kit Smart as with anyone," and as for the other charge that Smart did not love clean linen, the doctor had "no passion" for that himself!

Smart was released, but he was hopelessly in debt, his writing deteriorated badly, and he was unable to keep away from liquor. His debtors finally had him imprisoned in the King's Bench, and though Dr. Burney (who raised a small subscription for him) obtained permission for him to have the freedom of the rules (in other words, to move about in a limited territory), he died still under this imprisonment, the month after his forty-ninth birthday, and was buried in St. Paul's.

Poor Smart was nobody's enemy but his own; like most melancholiacs, he was capable of great gaiety, he was generous, kind-hearted, and frank, and all who knew him loved him. His translations were accurate, but uninspired; his light verse facile but ephemeral. Only *A Song to David* has the true spirit of poetry in it. Perhaps too extravagantly admired by Browning and Rossetti, it yet is full of emotion and power, and some of its lines would be worthy of William Blake at his best.

PRINCIPAL WORKS: The Horatian Canons of Friendship, 1750; On the Eternity of the Supreme Being, 1750; On the Immensity of the Supreme Being, 1751; Poems on Several Occasions, 1752; On the Omniscience of the Supreme Being, 1752; The Hilliad, 1753; On the Power of the Supreme Being, 1754; On the Goodness of the Supreme Being, 1756; Hymn to the Supreme Being on Recovery from a Dangerous Fit of Illness, 1756; The Works of Horace translated literally into English prose, 1756; A Song to David, 1763; Ode to the Earl of Northumberland, 1764; Hannah, an Oratorio, 1764; A Translation of the Psalms of David, 1765; A Poetical Translation of the Fables of Phaedrus, 1765; The Works of Horace translated into verse, 1767; The Parables of Our Lord and Savior Jesus Christ done into familiar verse, 1768; Abimelech, an Oratorio, 1768; Poems (C. Hunter, ed.) 1791.

ABOUT: Boswell, J. Life of Johnson; Burney, F. Diary; Gosse, E. Gossip in a Library; Gray, G. J. Bibliography of the Writings of Christopher Smart; Hunter, C. Memoir, *in* Poems.

SMITH, ADAM (June 5, 1723-July 17, 1790), economist, philosopher, was the son of Adam Smith, writer to the signet and comptroller of customs, and Margaret Douglas. He was a posthumous child, his father dying two months before his birth in Kirkcaldy, Fifeshire, Scotland. As a baby, he was kidnapped by tinkers, but soon rescued. He attended the University of Glasgow from 1737 to 1740, when he transferred to Baliol College, Oxford. Despite his dislike of the Jacobite atmosphere of Baliol, he remained there until 1746, graduating B.A. in 1744. Then he returned home to Kirkcaldy for two years of study, during which he gave a series of lectures on English literature under the patronage of Lord Kames. (His taste was strictly classical; he hated blank verse and preferred Racine to Shakespeare.) In 1748 he moved to Edinburgh, where he soon became one of the contemporary group of Edinburgh intellectuals, and was elected to the Edinburgh Philosophical Society.

In 1751 Smith was named professor of logic at the University of Glasgow, and the next year professor of moral philosophy. In these capacities he taught everything from *belles lettres* to science. To arrange for publication of his *Theory of Moral Sentiments* he made his first visit to London, where he met (and quarreled with) Dr. Johnson. In later years they were on better terms, and Smith even became a member of the famous Club in 1775.

In 1764 he resigned his chair at the university to go to France as tutor for the young Duke of Buccleuch and his brother, Hew Campbell Scott. This position included a lifetime annuity. In Toulouse he began the writing of his masterpiece, on the *Wealth of Nations,* and soon after, he and his pupils moved to Paris, where Smith became intimate with the Encyclopedists (d'Holbach, Diderot, Helvetius, and others), and, more importantly, with the Physiocrats (Quesnay, Turgot, and Necker). Though he differed from them in many points of economic theory, they undoubtedly had an influence on him. This life abroad was suddenly terminated by the murder of the younger of his charges, and Smith and the duke returned to Scotland. Here he settled in Kirkcaldy with his mother and a woman cousin, to finish his book. Smith's life may be divided into two parts, the first as a secluded scholar, the second, after publication of the *Wealth of Nations,* as a man of the world and a European authority on political economy. In 1778 he was appointed one of the commissioners

J. Tassie, 1787

ADAM SMITH

of customs at Edinburgh, a sinecure post which allowed him to go on studying and writing. He was made a Fellow of the Royal Society of Edinburgh in 1784. He brought his mother and cousin to Edinburgh to live with him, and spent much of his time in London, where Franklin became one of his new friends.

Smith never married, and any stories of unrequited love by or for him are probably apocryphal. His attachment to his mother was too strong to allow him any other emotional life, and when she died at ninety his intense grief astonished his friends. He had become prosperous from his books and his annuity, but most of his money went to secret charities, and he died relatively poor. In 1788 his cousin, his only other close relative, died, and his health failed rapidly. On his deathbed he ordered sixteen volumes of his manuscript writings burned; one of these was on jurisprudence, the nature of the others is unknown. His last public office had been as Lord Rector of Glasgow University, in 1787. In personality he was the extreme type of the "absent-minded professor," even when he was most occupied in public and social affairs.

Though Smith's first fame came from the *Theory of Moral Sentiments*, his philosophy is now considered the least of his achievements. Religiously he was a Deist, of the eighteenth century kind; he certainly did not share Hume's skepticism, though he defended Hume against the allegations of last-minute conversion. The *Theory* is eloquent, but loosely reasoned and diffuse; Smith's idea was that moral principles arose from sympathy, that there is no special "moral sense" but that social feeling is the basis of morality. In the end, however, he had to grant that individual conscience was the final judge.

It is as an economist that he is most important, though it is an error to call him the founder of political economy. It has been his fate to have his principles twisted to fit the tenets of quite different schools of thought, and he was cited by the *laissez faire* economists of the early industrial era in a way that he himself would almost certainly have disagreed with. Though others had written of political economy before him, he was the first to isolate economic facts and treat them scientifically as a unity. Labor was to him the foundation of wealth: "the annual labour of every nation is the fund which originally supplies it with all the necessaries and conveniences of life which it annually consumes." The landowners and the workers are alike in agreement with the best interests of society, whereas the "dealers" and merchants are against those interests. The division of labor is the first step in industrial progress. The common good arises, as it were, accidentally through the operations of self-interest. Smith objected to governmental controls and advocated "national liberty," including free trade. This "liberty," however, he conceded, must be somewhat restricted in the interest of national security and the protection of individuals.

Smith's method of exposition was by deduction from concrete instances. This rendered his writing clear, but did little to give it grace or readability. In general the effect is that of a disjointed series of monographs. His appeal was to the "informed and enlightened," and he rapidly became the main economic authority of statesmen and philosophers alike. To a certain extent outmoded, he remains nevertheless one of the standard classics of political economy.

PRINCIPAL WORKS: The Theory of Moral Sentiments [with] A Dissertation on the Origin of Languages, 1759; An Inquiry into the Nature and Causes of the Wealth of Nations, 1776; Essays on Philosophical Subjects (D. Stewart, ed.) 1795; Collected Works, 1812; Lectures on Justice, Police, Revenue, and Arms (E. Cannan, ed.) 1896.

ABOUT: Bagehot, W. Biographical Studies; Bonar, J. The Tables Turned; Clark, J. M. *et al.* Adam Smith: Lectures to Commemorate the Sesquicentennial of . . . the Wealth of Nations (University of Chicago); Farrer, J. A. Adam Smith; Ginzburg, E. The House of Adam Smith; Haldane, R. B. Life of Adam Smith; Hirst, F. W. Adam Smith; Macpherson, H. C. Adam Smith; Nicholson, J. S. A Project of Empire; Oncken, A. Adam Smith in der Culturgeschichte; Rae, J. Life of Adam Smith; Rogers, J. E. T. Historical Gleanings; Scott, W. R. Adam Smith; Small, A. W. Adam Smith and Modern Sociology; Stewart, D. Account of Life and Writings *in* Essays.

SMITH, ALEXANDER (fl. 1714-1726), biographer, called himself "Captain Smith" on the title pages of his numerous accounts of famous highwaymen, thieves, rascals and courtesans which appeared during the reign of George I, but it is unlikely that he was even a brevet officer. Practically nothing is known about his life, but his contributions to the literature of roguery were extensive, and were drawn upon heavily by later writers. Harrison Ainsworth, for instance, wrote the opening chapters of *Jack Sheppard* after study of Smith's *Comical and Tragical History of the Lives and Adventures of the Most noted Bayliffs in and About London and Westminster* (London 1723), a shilling pamphlet which had an enormous sale. Smith's *Memoirs of the Life and Times of the Famous Jonathan Wild* (1725) antedated Fielding's *Jonathan Wild* by seventeen years. His best known work is *A Complete History of the Lives and Robberies of the Most Notorious Highwaymen*, which went through numerous editions, and in which Sir John Falstaff and Moll Cutpurse appear. Smith's compilations, frequently scandalous in tone, were commissioned by the booksellers of the period, to whom they became a valuable literary property. For a time the first editions of his work also brought high prices.

PRINCIPAL WORKS: History of the Lives of the Most Noted Highwaymen, Footpads, Housebreakers, Shop-lifts, and Cheats, 1714; Secret History of the Lives of the Most Celebrated Beauties, Ladies of Quality, and Jilts, from Fair Rosamond Down to This Time, 1715; Lives of the Most Noted Bayliffs, 1723; Memoirs of The Life and Times of the Famous Jonathan Wild, Together with the Lives of Modern Rogues, 1726.

ABOUT: Chandler, F. W. The Literature of Roguery; Hayward, A. L. ed. History of the Lives of the Most Noted Highwaymen, 1926.

SMITH, CHARLOTTE (May 4, 1749-October 28, 1806), poet, novelist, was born on King Street, St. James's Square, London, the eldest child of Nicholas Turner and Anna (Towers) Turner. Her mother died when the girl was three. She was brought up by her aunt, Miss Towers, and married off at sixteen to Benjamin Smith, the erratic son of a wealthy West Indian merchant. The marriage was notable chiefly for heartbreak, discouragement, and twelve children. At various times the Smith family lived at Southgate, at Lys Farm, in "a gloomy ruin of a château" in Normandy, at Bignor Park, Sussex, and, when Smith was imprisoned for debt, at the King's Bench itself. They were finally separated, under conditions that hint at infidelity on Smith's part, and Charlotte Smith took her family to Brighton. Here she resorted to novel writing to support them, though hampered by rheumatism and other ailments. Her literary career began with the publication, at her own expense, of *Elegiac Sonnets and Other Essays*; other editions came out by subscription.

The theme of many of her sentimental and didactic novels was that of a badly married wife helped by a thoughtful sensible lover. Charlotte Smith drew on other personal experience in writing her fiction: the D'Alonville of *The Banished Man* (1794) was drawn from her rather worthless son-in-law, the Chevalier de Faville, an *émigré*, and she was accused of lampooning Hannah More in the character of Mrs. Manby in *The Old Manor House*. She was the first English novelist to deal in romantic landscape description, and her *Celestina* had considerable influence on Mrs. Radcliffe when the latter came to write *The Romance of the Forest*. James Foster calls Charlotte Smith's style "in its happiest moments clear, rapid and readable, although sometimes too poetic and slightly affected." She died at fifty-seven and was buried in the parish church at Stoke.

PRINCIPAL WORKS: Elegiac Sonnets, and Other Essays, 1784. *Novels:* Emmeline, or The Orphan of the Castle, 1788; Ethelinde, or The Recluse of the Lake, 1789; Celestina, a Novel, 1791; Desmond, 1792; The Old Manor House, 1793; The Wanderings of Warwick, 1794; The Banished Man, 1794; Montalbert, 1795; Darcy, 1796; Marchmont, 1796; The Young Philosopher, 1798; Letters of a Solitary Wanderer, 1798-1801.

ABOUT: Frisch, G. A. Der Revolutionaire Roman in England; Gregory, A. The French Revolution and the English Novel; Heilman, R. B. America in English Fiction, 1780-1800; Hilbish, F. M. A. Charlotte Smith: Poet and Novelist; Johnson, R. B. The Women Novelists; Cornhill Magazine, November 1903; Publications of Modern Language Association, June 1928.

SMITH, JOHN (1616-August 7, 1652), Cambridge Platonist, author of *Select Discourses*, was born at Achurch on the Nene, an affluent of the Ouse, within sight of Aldwinkle, Dryden's birthplace. His parents, John and Catherine Smith, were elderly and hitherto childless; his mother died a few months after his birth. The child was not baptized till February 15, 1618, a year often mistakenly given as that of his birth. Smith's early education was probably obtained at the Grammar School of Oundle, three miles from Achurch. "Divers persons of worth" assisted him to enter Emmanuel College, Cambridge University, on April 5, 1636. Here his tutor and friend, Benjamin Whichcote, also gave him "reasonable support and maintenance." Smith obtained his B.A. in 1640 and M.A. four years later; nervous breakdowns may have lengthened his stay at college. On April 11, 1644, he was one of nine nominees whom the Earl of Manchester, acting for parliament, appointed to fellowships at Queens' College, and in the same year he became Hebrew Lecturer and Censor Philosophicus. Later Smith was Greek Praelector and a lecturer in mathematics. When appointed Dean and Catechist of his college in 1650, he was expected to preach from time to time in the college chapel. There he delivered six of the ten *Discourses* which made his reputation. By this time Smith had "studied himself into a consumption," and died at thirty-six after weeks of suffering. His grave in the college chapel is unmarked. The preacher on the occasion of Smith's funeral described him as "a living library," a compendium of the six hundred books which he left for the college.

One of the most celebrated of the Cambridge Platonists and a student of Plotinus, Smith nevertheless gave first place to Christ in his *Select Discourses*, marked, in the words of Frederick Powicke, by a stately yet easy eloquence, elevation, and spiritual glow. He was praised and admired by Coleridge, Alexander Knox, and Matthew Arnold.

PRINCIPAL WORKS: Select Discourses, 1660.

ABOUT: Campagnac, E. T. The Cambridge Platonists; De Pauley, W. C. Candle of the Lord; Jones, R. M. Spiritual Reformers in the 16th and 17th Centuries; Metcalfe, W. M. The Natural Truth of Christianity; Powicke, F. J. The Cambridge Platonists, a Study; Tulloch, John, Rational Theology in the Seventeenth Century; Willey, B. Seventeenth Century Background.

SMITH, Sir THOMAS (December 23, 1513-August 12, 1577), statesman and author, was born at Saffron Walden, Essex, the eldest son of John Smith, described as "a person of good rank, quality, and wealth," who claimed descent on the sinister side from the Black Prince, and Agnes (Charnock) Smith. A rather puny child, he attended a local grammar school and was tutored at twelve by Henry Gold of Cambridge. The next year Smith entered Queens' College, where he was a King's scholar; was elected a fellow January 25, 1529/30; and, receiving his M.A. in the summer of 1533, lectured on natural philosophy and Greek. In May 1540 he went abroad for study, and obtained a D.C.L. at Padua; after he returned in 1542 and was made an LL.D. at Cambridge, he undertook, with his friend John Cheke, some reforms in the pronunciation of Greek (his faction was called "etists," their opponents, "itists").

Smith became regius professor of civil law at Cambridge in January 1543/44, and was ordained a priest in 1546. An illegitimate son was born a year later. He married Elizabeth Carkek or Carkyke in 1548, and Philippa, widow of Sir John Hampden, in 1554; neither bore him children, and he made his nephew William his heir. Well known as a Protestant sympathizer, Smith entered the service of Protector Somerset in February 1546/47 after the accession of Edward VI; became a secretary of state and an advisor on coinage reform; fell from favor and was imprisoned in the Tower for debt; and retired during Mary's reign, saved by an indulgence from the Pope from persecution. Smith returned to power and influence under Elizabeth, who sent him in September 1562 to France as joint ambassador with Sir Nicholas Throgmorton, with whom he violently disagreed. He was appointed Secretary of State in July 1572, obtaining an act for the better maintenance of learning in 1575. During his first stay in France, Smith wrote his *De Republica Anglorum* which has been called the most important description of the constitution and government of England written in the Tudor age. He died at sixty-three, his death probably hastened by his physician's drastic purging, and was buried in the chancel of the parish church of Theydon Mount, Essex. Strype states that

Smith had a large forked yellow beard at thirty-three, and shaved his head in order to wear a cap.

PRINCIPAL WORKS: De Recta et Emendata Linguae Anglicae Scriptione Dialogus, 1568; De Republica Anglorum: The Maner of Governement or Policie of the Realme of England, 1583.

ABOUT: Dixon, N. W. History of the Church of England; Hume, D. The Courtships of Queen Elizabeth; Smith, T. De Republica Anglorum (L. Alston and F. W. Maitland, eds. 1906).

SMOLLETT, TOBIAS GEORGE

(March 1721-September 17, 1771), novelist, miscellaneous writer, was born at Dalquhurn, Cardross, Dumbartonshire, Scotland. This was a farm given by his grandfather, a judge and Member of Parliament, to his youngest son, Archibald, when the latter, without profession, made an imprudent marriage with the penniless Barbara Cunningham. Archibald Smollett died when his son Tobias was two. He is described as petulant, and his wife as ill-tempered, two characteristics which their son inherited in full measure.

The boy wanted to become a soldier, but his grandfather, who was supporting him, had bought a commission for his older brother and did not care to spend the same amount on him also. So after school at Dumbarton he was sent to Glasgow, at fifteen, first to matriculate in the university and then to be apprenticed to a surgeon and apothecary, John Gordon. He must have studied well, for though he secured no degree from the university, three years later, when he went to London, he was a qualified surgeon.

His object, however, was not to practice his profession, but to secure production of a tragedy on the death of James I, *The Regicide*. Nobody would read it, and the few who glanced at it laughed. This, by all means the poorest of Smollett's literary efforts, was his darling. He hated Garrick for turning it down, and though he had to swallow his anger eight years after, when Garrick paid him handsomely for another play, he never forgave Lord Lyttleton for refusing to sponsor the tragedy, and he lampooned Lyttleton unmercifully. Smollett's whole public life, indeed, was a series of quarrels, a poor preparation for a career as a physician.

In fact, so desperate and near starvation was he that he was forced to accept an appointment as ship's surgeon in 1740 under Admiral Vernon in his ill-fated expedition to the West Indies. Smollett was at the siege of Cartagena, then went with the fleet to Jamaica, where in complete disgust he left the navy forever. He stayed in Jamaica until 1744, then returned to London and set up as a surgeon on Downing Street. In Jamaica he had fallen in love with a beautiful young heiress, Anne (or Nancy) Lascelles, and about 1747 when she came to England they were married. Smollett, who was a human porcupine in his social relations, was at home a man of deep affection and tenderness. The death of their only daughter at fifteen was a blow from which he never recovered.

This was the man who suddenly leapt to fame with the publication of *Roderick Random* in 1748. There had been other picaresque novels, and indeed this one was openly founded on *Gil Blas*. But what Smollett did was to instill new vigor and vividness into the picaresque romance, and above all to introduce a new type of character—the British sailor. No one has portrayed the "jolly tar" of his time as Smollett did. For the rest, like all his novels, this was rambling, badly constructed, with no ethical or social viewpoint, but full of farce, rough joking, and violence. Smollett, inured to blood and disease by his profession, never spared his readers.

The first thing he did with the money that poured in from *Roderick Random* was, of course, to have *The Regicide* privately printed. It fell flat.

In spite of his great success, Smollett apparently had as yet no thought of living by writing alone. In 1750 he went to Aberdeen and secured his M.D. degree at Marischal College, then set out for Paris where he collected material for his next novel, *Peregrine Pickle*. This, his longest novel, has brilliance and vivacity mingled with brutal savagery. It never seemed to occur to him that his hero was a scoundrel and an insolent bully. Many of its characters (and this is true of all his novels) were taken from life, chiefly from the ranks of his "enemies." The truth is that Smollett was basely jealous of other authors, Fielding most of all, and it was not until he felt really secure that he could hide or soften his hatred of them.

He returned to England to settle in Bath, but as a doctor he was an utter failure. He finally gave it up, moved to Chelsea, and set up what must have been the first of the "literary factories" in the Dumas style. He took on orders for histories, compilations of travel accounts, translations, and anything else he could obtain, and in addition to ruining his own health by overwork on this and his creative writing, he farmed out the hack work to a dozen poor scribblers, whom he exploited and lorded it over for starvation pay and a seat at his Sunday dinners for poverty-ridden writers. Smollett was always in need of money, no matter how much he made. (His wife's fortune was mostly lost in litigation over her father's will.) He was an extravagant host; he loved to be the generous entertainer at taverns, and he had no talent for keeping money.

Ferdinand, Count Fathom, father of the "Gothic" novel, appeared in 1753. His "factory" translated Le Sage, Voltaire, and Fenelon, he edited *Don Quixote*, he was head contributor to the *Critical Review* (1756), and he was editor of the *British Magazine* (1760) and the *Briton* (1762). In the *British Magazine* he published *Sir Lancelot Greaves* (his weakest novel, a poor imitation of *Don Quixote*) as a serial, probably the first novelist to do this. He also paid a £100 fine and spent three months in prison for libeling an admiral in the *Critical Review*. The *Briton* was founded by the Tories, led by Lord Bute; when Wilkes founded the satirical *North Briton* in reprisal, ridiculing the Scottish prime minister and the Scottish editor alike, it was discontinued, and Smollett had another man to hate—not Wilkes, but Bute.

In 1763 his daughter died, and at the same time his health, broken by overwork, failed completely. At his wife's appeal he took her away from the scene of their grief, and they spent two years in France and Italy, with the aftermath of a very lively but very acidulous travel book. It was during this trip that he met Sterne and was immortalized as "Smelfungus" in the *Sentimental Journey*. The two men could never have been friends—the one romantic, full of "sensibility," the other splenetic and violently prejudiced.

Smollett returned in better health, and was well enough to journey to Scotland in

"Italian School" c. 1770

TOBIAS SMOLLETT

1766, where he revisited his old haunts and saw his mother for the last time. But arthritis, combined with a neglected ulcer, completed the ruin of his health. He went to Bath again, this time as a patient, found no cure (whereupon he wrote a book attacking the value of the waters), and finally at the end of 1769 went to Italy. He settled first in Pisa, then in Leghorn, where he died and was buried in the English Protestant Cemetery.

There probably never was a coarser writer than Smollett. His *History of an Atom*, for example, is simply a dirty, brutal, rancorous satire on the statesmen of his day. He interpolated into *Peregrine Pickle* the unbelievably smutty (and dull) *Memoirs of a Lady of Quality*, written by the notorious Viscountess Vane and introduced into the novel for a cash fee. Even *Humphrey Clinker*, his last and in many ways most pleasant novel (it was, whether he knew it or not, influenced by Sterne), was kept from being high humor by his weakness for dirty farce. As a versifier, he was a rough and unscrupulous satirist.

Yet Smollett could create real and unforgettable characters; he had a keen eye for sham, and a shrewd logical brain. Though the pamphlet printed in 1795, purporting to prophesy the American and French Revolutions thirty years earlier, may be a fraud, he

481

did make some very accurate guesses of the same kind in his *Travels Through France and Italy.* Inevitably he is compared to Fielding and Defoe; he had neither the former's sweetness of spirit and breadth of mind nor the latter's photographic realism. But he belongs in almost the first rank of novelists —scarred and splotched, but genuine gold. He was the victim of his own inherited temperament: he diagnosed himself as having "an over-irritable nervous system," and the wonder is not that he could not suppress it in his writings, but that with such a nature he could produce his masterpieces at all.

PRINCIPAL WORKS: *Novels:* The Adventures of Roderick Random, 1748; The Adventures of Peregrine Pickle, 1751; The Adventures of Ferdinand Count Fathom, 1753; The Adventures of Sir Launcelot Greaves, 1762; The History and Adventures of an Atom, 1769; The Expedition of Humphrey Clinker, 1771. *Verse:* The Tears of Scotland, 1745; Advice: a Satire, 1746; Reproof, A Satire, 1747; Burlesque Ode on the Death of a Grandmother, 1747; The Regicide: Or, James the First of Scotland, 1749; The Reprisal: or, The Tars of Old England, A Comedy, 1757; Ode to Independence, 1773; Plays and Poems, 1777; Poetical Works, 1794. *Miscellaneous:* A Complete History of England, from the Descent of Julius Caesar to the Treaty of Aix-la-Chapelle, 1748; A Faithful Narrative of the Base and Inhuman Acts... Practic'd on the Brain of Habbakuk Hilding, etc., 1752; An Essay on the External Use of Water, 1752; Continuation of the Complete History of England, 1762-65 (revised, as The History of England from the Revolution to the Death of George the Second, 1789); A Compendium of Authentic and Entertaining Voyages, Digested in a Chronological Series, 1766; Travels through France and Italy, 1766; The Present State of All Nations, 1768-69; Miscellaneous Works, 1790.

ABOUT: Benjamin, L. S. (Lewis Melville) The Life and Letters of Tobias Smollett; Boege, F. W. Smollett's Reputation as a Novelist; Buck, H. S. Smollett as Poet. A Study in Smollett; Chambers, R. Smollett: his Life; Cordasco, F. Smollett Criticism: 1770-1945; Graham, H. Scottish Men of Letters in the 18th Century; Hannay, D. Life of Tobias George Smollett; Kahrl, G. M. Tobias Smollett, Traveler-Novelist; Knapp, L. M. Tobias Smollett: Doctor of Men and Manners; Lang, A. Adventures among Books; Martz, L. L. The Later Career of Tobias Smollett; Masson, D. British Novelists and Their Style; Raleigh, W. The English Novel; Smeaton, O. Tobias Smollett; Wershoven, F. J. Smollett et LeSage

SOMERVILLE or SOMERVILE, WILLIAM (September 2, 1675-July 19, 1742), author of poems on hunting, sports, and games, was born in Wolseley, Staffordshire, the home of his maternal grandfather. His father was Robert Somerville, his mother Elizabeth Wolseley. After attending school at Stratford-on-Avon, he entered New College, Oxford, in 1694. He was entered in the Middle Temple in 1696, but never studied law. He became a fellow of his college, and lived there until 1705, when his father died and he succeeded to the family estate of Edstone, near Henley-in-Ardon, Warwickshire. There he spent the remainder of his life, as a country gentleman, a devotee of all sports (except coursing, which he objected to), and part of a small literary coterie which included Shenstone and Richard Jago as its chief ornaments. In 1708 Somerville married Mary Bethell, who died in 1731; the marriage was childless. He was a conscientious justice of the peace, but otherwise did not give much attention to his duties and responsibilities as a landowner; he was improvident and toward the end of his life had to sell the reversion of his estate to a distant cousin in order to meet his living expenses. Shenstone says that in his later years he was extremely intemperate. One burden on his estate was an annuity to his mother, who died at ninety-eight, only a few months before him. A tall, handsome, blond man, he was popular with his friends, and among his literary acquaintances he numbered such outstanding figures as Allan Ramsay, Addison, and Pope. He died at sixty-seven at Edstone, and was buried at Wooton-Wawen, Warwickshire, beside his wife.

Though Somerville had real literary taste and was a good critic of other people's work,

Sir G. Kneller (?)
WILLIAM SOMERVILLE

he was exceedingly uncritical of his own, and permitted a vast amount of sheer doggerel, dull and full of coarse humor, to be published under his name. His one real success was with *The Chace*, a lively narrative poem on his favorite subject, the hunt. This went into a number of editions during his lifetime. *Field Sports*, his next most popular poem, dealt with hawking. *Hobbinal* was a rough burlesque in blank verse. His verse was purely an avocation to Somerville and he took it lightly. But he was something of a scholar, and his opinion was respected by other writers—rather unfortunately so in the case of (the earlier) James Thomson, whom he patronized officiously.

The chief merit of Somerville's poems to modern readers is their close personal acquaintance with the country, with rural life of the eighteenth century and the country scene of the pre-industrial era. There is little description of nature in them, however, and he does not belong to the school, soon to arise and to culminate in Gray, which took pleasure in purely descriptive accounts of the natural scenery of the countryside.

PRINCIPAL WORKS: The Two Springs, A Fable, 1725; Occasional Poems, Translations, Fables, Tales, 1727; The Chace, a Poem, 1735; Hobbinal, or the Rural Games, 1740; Field Sports, 1742; Poetical Works, 1766.

ABOUT: Gilfillan, G. Memoir *in* Poetical Works of Joseph Addison, etc., 1859 ed.; Johnson, S. Lives of the English Poets; Shenstone, W. Letters.

SOUTH, ROBERT (September 4, 1634-July 8, 1716), preacher, miscellaneous writer, was born at Hackney, the son of Robert South, a London merchant. His mother's maiden name was Berry. He was admitted in 1647 as a King's Scholar to Westminster School, where he is said to have mentioned Charles I in his prayers on the day of the king's execution. At Christ Church, Oxford, he wrote a Latin panegyric on Cromwell; he received his B.A. on February 24, 1654/55, and his M.A. in June 1657. After a trip to the Continent, South received Episcopal ordination in 1658, and an M.A. in 1659 from Cambridge University, which made him public orator August 10, 1660, a post in which he remained until 1677. He was chosen as his chaplain by Clarendon, who procured South his B.D. and D.D.; then became chaplain to the Duke of York in 1667 after

Clarendon's fall. He was installed as canon of Christ Church December 29, 1670. From his first sermon at St. Mary's, Cambridge, on July 24, 1659, South had drawn attention from the unusually humorous quality of his discourses from the pulpit.

South went to Poland in June 1676 as chaplain to the ambassador, Laurence Hyde, afterwards Earl of Rochester, and discussed the journey in a letter to Edward Pococke. In 1678 he received the rectory of Islip, Oxfordshire, turning over half the income to a curate and living at his estate at Caversham, near Reading. After the flight of James II he postponed as long as possible taking the oath of allegiance to William and Mary. It was said that he was then under the influence of William Sherlock, whom he later attacked anonymously, charging Sherlock with being a tritheist. On the death of Thomas Sprat South was offered the bishopric of Rochester and the deanery of Westminster, but refused both on the ground of infirmity. He died at Westminster at eighty-two, and was buried in the Abbey near the grave of Busby.

South's sermons, well salted with humor, and barbed with vivacious shafts of ridicule and wit, make much livelier reading nowadays than the sermons of Jeremy Taylor or John Tillotson, Archbishop of Canterbury.

PRINCIPAL WORKS: Musica Incantans, 1655; Sermons Preached Upon Several Occasions, 1679; Animadversion upon Dr. Sherlock's Book Entitled a Vindication of the Holy and Ever-blessed Trinity, 1693; Tritheism Charged Upon Dr. Sherlock's New Notion of the Trinity, 1695; Posthumous Works, 1717.

ABOUT: Birch, T. Life of Tillotson; South, R. Memoirs of His Life and Writings, 1717; Retrospective Review, 1823.

SOUTHERNE or **SOUTHERN, THOMAS** (1660-May 26, 1746), dramatist, was born at Oxmantown, near Dublin, Ireland, the third son of Francis Southerne, a prominent Dublin brewer. After graduating from the school of Edward Wetenhall he entered Trinity College, Dublin, as a pensioner on March 30, 1675/76. His college tutor was Giles Pooley. Southerne is not recorded as obtaining a B.A. degree (but was awarded an honorary M.A. in the spring term of 1696). In 1680 he crossed the Irish Sea and was admitted to the Middle Temple July 15, 1680, not in 1678 as the *Dictionary of National Biography* has it. His earliest play,

The Loyal Brother, presented at Drury Lane in 1682, contained in the character of Tachmas a flattering portrait of James II, then Duke of York. *The Disappointment* was given a command performance January 17, 1684/85, a fortnight before the death of Charles II. During the Monmouth Rebellion of 1685 Southerne held a commission in Princess Anne's Regiment of Foot. After retiring from the army in 1689 he continued his successful career as a dramatist, which proved longer than that of any other Restoration playwright. Bridging the gap between the drama of Charles II and George II, Southerne completed for Dryden an unfinished tragedy, *Cleomenes*; supported Congreve in his first dramatic attempt; recommended Colley Cibber's first play to the patentees; and lived to see David Garrick play *Richard III*. He is said to have married well. Dying at eighty-five, he was buried in St. Margaret's Church, Westminster. He had a strong, rather heavy-featured face, full eyes, large nose, and double chin.

Southerne wrote "domesticated and sentimentalized" tragedies, of which the most popular were *The Fatal Marriage* (1694) and *Oronooko* (1696), both dramatizations of romances by Mrs. Aphra Behn. Regarded as a political opportunist, he also wrote ribald comedies between 1690 and 1693 as the convention of the times required. His friends, who included Pope and Swift, called him "Honest John."

PRINCIPAL WORKS: The Loyal Brother: or The Persian Prince, 1682; The Disappointment: or, The Mother in Fashion, 1684; Sir Anthony Love: or, The Rambling Lady, 1691; The Wives' Excuse, or, Cuckolds Make Themselves, 1692; The Maid's Last Prayer, or, Any, Rather than Fail, 1693; The Fatal Marriage, or, The Innocent Adultery (based on Aphra Behn's The History: or, The Fair Vow-Breaker) 1694; Oronooko (based on a novel by Aphra Behn) 1696; The Fate of Capua, 1700; The Spartan Dame, 1719; Money and Mistress, 1726.

ABOUT: Dodds, J. W. Thomas Southerne, Dramatist; Summers, M. Essays in Petto; Modern Language Review, October 1933.

SOUTHWELL, ROBERT (1561?-February 21, 1595), poet, religious writer, was born at Horsham St. Faith's, Norfolk, the son of Richard Southwell, the illegitimate descendant of an old Roman Catholic family (but an Anglican), and of Bridget Copley, a Roman Catholic. Through his mother he was a collateral ancestor of the poet Shelley.

So beautiful was he as a small child that he was stolen from his cradle by a gypsy, but was soon recovered. Though he was short in stature, throughout life he was markedly handsome, with auburn hair and gray eyes.

When he was still very young he was sent to the Catholic college at Douay, Belgium, and at fourteen was transferred to Paris, where his teacher was Thomas Darbyshire, under Queen Mary the archdeacon of Essex. Southwell was markedly religious from his childhood, and his one ambition was to join the Jesuit order. He finally became a novice in Rome in 1578, passed his novitiate mostly at Tournay, and was received into the order in Rome in 1580, when he was appointed prefect of studies at the English College. He was ordained priest in 1584, and at his own request, two years later, was sent to England with Father Henry Garnett as a missionary for the old and proscribed faith. By a law of Elizabeth, any native Englishman who had been ordained a Roman Catholic priest during her reign was guilty of treason if he remained in England more than forty days, so Southwell knew well the risk he ran. Indeed, martyrdom was his avowed aim. For six years, however, he was not apprehended, though his presence was reported upon his arrival and he was under surveillance. He became domestic chaplain to Lady Arundel, whose husband was in the Tower on a treason charge, and he traveled throughout England as a missionary, though living principally in London.

He had become intimate with a Catholic family named Bellamy, and when they were apprehended he too was involved. By a trick he was decoyed into the house of Richard Topcliffe, chief enforcement officer of the penal laws against Roman Catholics. Imprisoned first in Topcliffe's house, then in the Gatehouse of Westminster, and finally in the Tower, he was horribly tortured— thirteen times in the Tower alone—but remained steadfast and refused to implicate others. (By this time he had converted his father and brother.) The prose treatises he had written had been widely circulated in manuscript, and he had powerful friends even outside his church. It was three years before he came to trial. There he pleaded "not guilty of treason," but was condemned, and was barbarously executed at Tyburn.

ROBERT SOUTHWELL

Most of Southwell's poems were written in prison, in full expectation of his imminent death. In writing them he had three aims— natural self-expression in a time of personal crisis; comfort to his co-religionists; and the rescue of poetry from "worldly uses." He was undoubtedly familiar with Shakespeare's *Venus and Adonis*, published in 1593, and his *Saint Peters Complaint* is in the same meter. His longer poems, showing a strong Italian influence, are full of involved conceits, contrasts, antitheses, and paradoxes; but his shorter poems display great lyrical power and vivid imagination, with simple but profound symbolism. Ben Jonson said that he would gladly have destroyed many of his own poems if he could have written Southwell's *The Burning Babe*. He had force, sweetness, and exaltation, and was primarily a lyrical poet who turned his gift to the uses of religious didacticism. Gabriel Harvey called Southwell's prose "elegant and pathetical," but to modern taste it is artificial and too much affected by the euphuistic craze. He himself was a sweet natured man, brilliant and witty, and sincere to the point of willing martyrdom.

PRINCIPAL WORKS: *Poetry:* Saint Peters Complaint, with other Poemes, 1595; Maeoniae, or, certaine excellent Poems and spirituall Hymnes, 1595; Foure-fould meditation, of the foure last things, 1606; Poetical Works (W. B. Turnbull, ed.) 1856. *Prose:* Mary Magdalens [Funeral] Teares, 1591; An Epistle of Comfort to the Reverend Priestes, 1593?; A Humble Supplication to Her Maiestie,

1595; The Triumphs over Death, 1596; A Short Rule of Good Life, 1598; Complete Works (A. B. Grosart, ed.) 1872; Hundred Meditations on the Love of God, 1873.

ABOUT: Foley, H. Records of the English Province of the Society of Jesus; Hannay, D. The Later Renaissance; Janelle, P. Robert Southwell, the Writer; Possoz, A. Vie de Père R. Southwell; Quiller-Couch, A. T. Adventures in Criticism; Saintsbury, G. A History of Elizabethan Literature.

SPALDING, JOHN (fl. 1650), Scottish historian, is the author of an unfinished, conservative and royalistic work on the history of Scotland between 1624 and 1645, and an object of commemoration by various antiquarian societies bearing his name which, however, have not unearthed many concrete details about his life. He may have been born in Aberdeen, though the name was not common there before the eighteenth century. In any case, Spalding was certainly a resident of the "Old Town," Aberdeen, where he practiced law and served as clerk to the consistorial court for the diocese. He maintained an office within the precincts of St. Machar, an old cathedral, but his papers were destroyed by fire in 1721. A document in his own handwriting, dated January 30, 1663, is extant.

Spalding's *History of the Troubles and Memorable Transactions in Scotland* plunges into a feud between the Earl of Moray and the Clan Chattan, and ends with General Baillie. It is a plain, unvarnished narrative, supported by copies of documents which probably had come under his scrutiny as clerk of the court and, while deferential to Charles I, shows a liberal viewpoint and a distaste for some of the excesses of Puritanism. It was not published until more than a century after it was written, when a two-volume octavo edition appeared in Aberdeen in 1792. William Forbes Skene, the Scottish antiquarian, edited the one-volume Bannatyne Club reprint in 1829, and Dr. John Stuart edited still another reissue in 1850 for the Spalding Club, a publishing society founded at Aberdeen in 1839. The New Spalding Club, carrying on the tradition, began operations in the same city in 1886.

PRINCIPAL WORK: History of the Troubles and Memorable Transactions in Scotland from the Year 1625 to 1645, 1792.

ABOUT: Spalding, J. History (see Preface by Dr. John Stuart in the 1850 reprint).

SPEED, JOHN (1552?-July 28, 1629), historian, cartographer, was probably born at Farringdon or Farndon in Cheshire, the son of John Speed, a tailor, and Elizabeth Cheyne Speed. He was also taught the art of tailoring, and was admitted to the Merchant Taylors' Company in 1580. Two years later he married; twelve sons and six daughters were born in course of time to John and Susanna Speed, who died a year before her husband. Their house was in Moorfields, on ground leased from the Company. In 1614 he received the patronage of Sir Fulke Greville, first Lord Brooke, who made it possible for Speed to give up the irksome task of tailoring and turn his attention to the making of maps, at first of the counties of England. He had already presented some of his maps to Queen Elizabeth in 1598. Between 1608 and 1610 he published fifty-four maps of England and Wales, collected with others in his *Theatre of the Empire of Great Britain*, which was published in 1611 and went through numerous editions.

As a member of the Society of Antiquarians, Speed met William Camden and Sir Robert Cotton, the latter of whom proved especially helpful in lending him manuscripts and coins, and reading the proofs of Speed's *magnum opus*, *The History of Great Britain* (from the Roman conquest to King James I, to whom it was dedicated). It appeared in 1611 as a continuation of *The Theatre . . . of Great Britain*, and won Speed the distinction of being termed the first real historian in the modern sense. Instead of writing a chronicle or compiling annals, he achieved a flowing narrative which was strengthened by the use of unpublished documents and which gave full credit to his predecessors, even when repeating their errors. Charles Whibley called Speed a born rhetorician whose love of words outstripped his taste. His *Genealogies Recorded in Sacred Scriptures* went through thirty-three editions before 1640. Blind, and suffering from "the stone," Speed died at seventy-seven and was buried in St. Giles', Cripplegate.

PRINCIPAL WORKS: The Theatre of the Empire of Great Britain: Presenting an Exact Geography of the Kingdomes of England, Scotland, Ireland, and the Iles Adjoyning, 1611; The History of Great Britaine, 1611; Genealogies Recorded in Sacred Scriptures, 1611?; A Cloud of Witnesses. . . Confirming unto Us the Truth of the Histories in God's Most Holie Word, 1616.

ABOUT: Biographia Britannica; Camden, W. Annales.

SPENSER, EDMUND (1552?-January 16, 1599), poet, was born in London, probably in a younger branch of the old family of Spencer in northern England. His father was probably John Spenser, a native of Lancashire, a clothier by trade but of gentle birth. The family undoubtedly was far from prosperous, for the boy was entered as a "poor scholar" at the Merchant Taylors' School (perhaps at its opening in 1561), and in 1569 entered Pembroke Hall, Cambridge, as a sizar. Exactly how old he was then is not known; he may have been born as early as 1549.

At the university he encountered some of the most potent influences of his later years. The mixture of neo-Platonism and Calvinism which distinguished his thinking came from the dominant thought of Pembroke in his day, and here too he met Gabriel Harvey, who became his exacting, arrogant friend and in a sense his master; for a while Spenser followed his criticisms and commands almost slavishly. Here also he began to write poetry, his versions of Petrarch and Du Bellay appearing in van der Noodt's *Theatre for Worldlings*.

Spenser graduated B.A. in 1573 and M.A. in 1576, and then for a year he disappeared. The probability is that he was staying with some of his relatives in Lancashire. There he met the lady known only as "Rosalind," whom he loved without return—though probably without any lasting scar on his spirit. More importantly, he was drawn through Harvey into the circle of the great Earl of Leicester, and met Leicester's nephew, Sir Philip Sidney. Spenser and Sidney became close friends for the few years the latter was still to live; Spenser dedicated *The Shepheardes Calender* to him, and mourned him later as "Astrophel," and Sidney praised his friend's first work (though with reservations) in the *Apologie for Poetrie*.

Already the idea of *The Faerie Queene* was in Spenser's mind, though Harvey—founder of the Areopagus, that association dedicated to naturalizing Latin meters into English verse—discouraged and delayed its writing. In 1578 Spenser became secretary to the bishop of Rochester; then, after the first of his several periods of frequenting

Elizabeth's court hoping in vain for preferment, he was made secretary to Lord Grey of Wilton, the new Lord Deputy of Ireland. Much of Spenser's life thereafter was spent in Ireland, and there is no point in glossing over the fact that (though individual cruelty aroused his pity) his hatred of the Roman Catholic Church made him acquiesce heartily in the policy of expropriation and wholesale "extermination" of the "natives." In 1581 he was clerk of the Dublin chancery, in 1585 clerk of the council of Munster, and the next year he secured the perpetual lease of the confiscated Kilcolman Castle in that county. His sister is supposed to have come from England to keep house for him there.

At Kilcolman Castle Spenser finished the first three cantos of *The Faerie Queene* (which is really a fragment, since twelve cantos were projected, and only eight were finished). Raleigh visited him there in 1587, was much struck by the poem, and persuaded Spenser to return to England and once more try his luck at court. It was not good; he had always as a barrier to his hopes the Earl of Burghley, Leicester's rival, who took pleasure in frustrating the ambitions of any of Leicester's adherents. Spenser's various "complaints"—*Mother Hubberds Tale, Virgils Gnat*, and so forth—were well founded. The most he ever got from Elizabeth, whom he helped to immortalize as Belphoebe, Gloriana, and Britomarte in *The Faerie Queene*, was a pension of fifty pounds a year. Finally, in 1591, thoroughly disheartened, he went back to Ireland.

There in 1594 he married Elizabeth Boyle, subject of his *Epithalamion*. She survived him with three sons and a daughter, was remarried twice, and bore a number of other children to her later husbands.

In 1595 Spenser was in England again, to see to the publication of the second three cantos of *The Faerie Queene*. He returned to Ireland in 1597, and the next year became sheriff of Cork. Disaster awaited him. In the rebellion led by the Earl of Tyrone, Kilcolman Castle was taken and burned, and Spenser and his family barely escaped with their lives. Sent to London at the beginning of 1599 with dispatches, worn out with excitement and grief, his always delicate health wrecked, and his entire property lost, he was

EDMUND SPENSER

at the end of his tether. Only a short time after his arrival he died suddenly. He was buried in Westminster Abbey, near Chaucer, though it was the next century before a monument was erected to him.

Though several portraits of Spenser survive, they are not very good, and little is known of his appearance except that he was a small man who affected a full beard. Of his nature and personality much more can be guessed. Gentle and sensitive by nature, he lived largely in a dream world of his own imagining. Though knighthood itself was dead, the spirit of chivalry remained alive in him, and as an escape from the vicissitudes and labors of his own life he dwelt in a golden past which in truth never existed. At the same time he was devoutly religious, and patriotic as only an Englishman of the Elizabethan age could be. All these factors combined to mold his masterpiece. His mind was receptive rather than creative: "All the great movements of his time are mirrored in his work," W. J. Courthope remarked. Somehow he reconciled feudalism and the Renaissance, the Christian and the pagan; he was dowered with "a modest, sympathetic disposition, an intelligence philosophic and acute, learned industry, a brilliant fancy, an exquisite ear."

Spenser is one of the most scholarly of English poets, though not always exact in his scholarship. He made a deliberate effort to enrich the language by the use of archaisms; and though his syntax was simple, it was soundly based on the syntax of Greek and Latin. In *The Shepheardes Calender*, to be sure, he employed the most ordinary of rustic speech, but that too was deliberate—and soon abandoned; in *Colin Clouts Come Home Againe* all this factitious rusticity has quite vanished.

In a sense *The Faerie Queene*, a great English epic (Spenser's avowed aim was to do for England what Ariosto did for Italy), is a failure. Too many elements are combined in it. It is a romantic allegory, yet sometimes the allegory becomes plain illustration. It is supposed to picture King Arthur's court, but the figures of that court sometimes are realistically presented, sometimes are mere names for virtues or vices. He started to "fashion a gentleman or noble person in vertuous and gentle discipline," and originally there was to have been a canto for each of twelve virtues, such as honor, chastity, justice, and courtesy. In the first three cantos he kept pretty closely to this plan; the Red Cross Knight is the militant Christian, Una the embodiment of wisdom. In the second set of three (the seventh and eighth books were not published until the folio of 1609), Elizabeth and her courtiers have supplanted Arthur and her knights: "I meane glory in my general intention but in my particular . . . our soveraine the Queene." The more the actual court disappointed him, the more he dreamed of the ideal one.

This ambiguity, this profusion and multiplicity, enrich the poem but make for lack of unity. With all its defects, however, *The Faerie Queene* is one of the most glorious of English poems. It is also one of the most seminal; its influence can be traced in a straight line all the way to the nineteenth century romantics. It is no wonder that Lamb called Spenser "the poets' poet"; he has been a source of inspiration for countless followers.

It must be noted that Spenser was a deliberate experimenter in metrics. The stanza named for him (a variation of the French *chant royal* or the Italian *ottava rima*) was an eight-line iambic pentameter with an added Alexandrine, the rhyme-scheme being a,b,a,b,b,c,b,c,c. It has been used frequently since, and effectively. He also had much recourse to alliteration, an early English verse attribute which for a long time was superseded by rhyme; Spenser combines the two.

For lofty harmony, for imagery, for rich splendor of music, Spenser is unexcelled. So far as sheer poetry is concerned (not, of course, in all other categories of poetic achievement) he stands second only to Shakespeare. The present is not one of the eras when his voice speaks most clearly; he appeals most strongly to times of burgeoning and upward growth like his own age. He remains nevertheless one of the truly great poets of our tongue, and even in the periods most neglectful of him he has never lacked devoted admirers. We do not relish long romantic allegories or epics today; we turn from *The Faerie Queene* as we do from *Paradise Lost*. The turn of both will come again, while our civilization survives. Edmund Spenser, who looked with a severe eye on the emerging poetry and drama of his own day, and longed in vain for the classical poetry of Greece and Rome, has yet become, with his younger contemporary Shakespeare, the very embodiment of the poetic genius of the age of Elizabeth.

PRINCIPAL WORKS: The Shepheardes Calender, 1579; Letters to Gabriel Harvey, 1580; The Faerie Queen, Cantos 1, 2, 3, 1589; Cantos 4, 5, 6, 1596; Cantos 7, 8 (in First Folio) 1609; Complaints, 1591; Amoretti and Epithalamion, 1595; Colin Clouts Come Home Againe, 1595; Prothalamion or a Spousall Verse, 1596; Fowre Hymnes, 1596; Second Folio (collected poems) 1611-13; Veue of the State of Ireland (prose) 1633; Works (A. B. Grossart, ed.) 1882-84.

ABOUT: Atkinson, D. F. Edmund Spenser, a Bibliographical Supplement; Bradner, L. Edmund Spenser and The Faerie Queene; Carpenter, F. I. A Reference Guide to Edmund Spenser; Church, R. W. Spenser; Cory, H. E. Edmund Spenser, a Critical Study; Courthope, W. J. The Genius of Spenser; Davis, B. E. C. Edmund Spenser, a Critical Study; Dowden, E. Transcripts and Studies; Grosart, A. B. Life *in* Works; Hazlitt, W. Chaucer and Spenser; Henley, P. Spenser in Ireland; Hughes, M. Y. Virgil and Spenser; Hunt, L. Imagination and Fancy; Jones, H. S. V. A Spenser Handbook; Judson, A. C. The Life of Edmund Spenser; Lee, S. Great Englishmen of the 16th Century; Legouis, E. Spenser; Lowell, J. R. Spenser; Renwick, W. L. Edmund Spenser: an Essay on Renaissance Poetry; Saintsbury, G. History of English Prosody; Schofield, W. H. Chivalry in English Literature; Stoll, E. E. Poets and Playwrights; Wurtsbaugh, J. Two Centuries of Spenserian Scholarship.

SPRAT, THOMAS (1635-May 20, 1713), miscellaneous writer, was born at Beaminster in Dorset, son of Thomas Sprat, minister of that parish; his mother was probably a Strode. He received his B.A. from Wadham College, Oxford, in 1654; M.A. in 1657; B.D. and D.D. in 1669, and held a fellowship at Wadham from 1657 to 1670. Here he met Seth Ward, Christopher Wren, Dr. Ralph Bathurst, and other students of science; this was the beginning of the Royal Society whose historian Sprat eventually became. His poem on the death of Cromwell, published in 1659, was later included in Dryden's *Miscellany*. Another poem, *The Plague of Athens*, appeared in 1659; modeled on Cowley's Pindaric style, it earned its author the sobriquet of "Pindaric Sprat." Through Cowley's recommendation he was appointed chaplain to the Duke of Buckingham. The diarist John Evelyn assisted Sprat in his composition of *Observations on Monsieur de Sorbier's Voyage to England*, a defense of English character. Two years later appeared his well known *History of the Royal Society of London*, written in vigorous, almost modern English and frequently republished in the next century. The title was rather elastic, since only the second part related to the Society, the other two dealing with ancient philosophy and experimental knowledge. On Cowley's death, Sprat wrote a fulsome tribute which Johnson called "a funeral oration rather than a history," but he refused to permit the publication of Cowley's familiar letters.

A divine of considerable levity, Sprat is thought to have been one of his patron Buckingham's collaborators on the latter's play *The Rehearsal*, directed against Dryden and others. His advocacy of high church doctrine and the divine right of kings insured his advancement (he was made dean of Westminster in 1683 and bishop of Rochester in 1684), but his participation in the unpopular Ecclesiastical Commission of James II (1686) was condemned, as was his permitting the reading aloud of the Declaration of Indulgence in Westminster Abbey. In May 1692 Sprat was the temporary victim of a plot which accused him of conspiring to restore James to the throne. He died of apoplexy in the palace at Bromley, survived by his wife, who was Helen Wolseley, and was buried in Westminster Abbey on the south side of St. Nicholas' Chapel.

PRINCIPAL WORKS: Three Poems upon the Death of his late Highness Oliver, Lord Protector, 1659, 1682, 1709; The Plague of Athens, 1659; Observations on Monsieur de Sorbier's Voyage into England, 1665; The History of the Royal Society of London, 1667; An Account of the Life and Writings of Mr. Abraham Cowley, 1668.

ABOUT: Fulcher, P. M. ed. Foundations of English Style; Shuster, G. N. The English Ode from Milton to Keats; Sonnischen, C. L. The Life and Works of Thomas Sprat; Spingarn, J. E. Critical Essays of the Seventeenth Century.

STANHOPE, FOURTH EARL. See CHESTERFIELD, PHILIP DORMER STANHOPE

STANLEY, THOMAS (1625-April 12, 1678), author of a history of philosophy, translations, and poems, was born at Cumberlow, Hertfordshire, the only son of Sir Thomas Sherlock and Mary (Hammond) Sherlock, a sister of the poet William Hammond and cousin of Richard Lovelace. His first tutor was William Fairfax, whose father translated Tasso, and who instilled in the boy an enthusiasm for poetry in the Romance languages. Thomas entered Pembroke Hall, Cambridge University, at thirteen, graduating M.A. in 1641, and embarking on a lengthy Grand Tour of Europe. He returned in time for the civil war, which did not interfere with his pleasant life at lodgings in the Middle Temple. Here he wrote and made his translations, and drew on his personal means to assist less fortunate writers, notably the dramatist James Shirley. His cousin Lovelace wrote a poem on the occasion of Stanley's wedding to Dorothy Enyon of Flower, Northamptonshire, by whom he had a son, Thomas.

Stanley's first volume of *Poems* (1647), which was dedicated to Love, eulogized imaginary mistresses like Celia and Doris, and included translations from Guarini, Marino, Tasso, Lope de Vega, and Petrarch. This and succeeding books were collected in the *Poems* of 1651, which also contained his rendering of Anacreon's Odes. He turned from poetry to Greek philosophy at the suggestion of his uncle by marriage, Sir John Marsham, the chronologer, and between 1655 and 1662 published the four volumes of his *History of Philosophy*, which for a long time remained the standard work on its subject, though more historical than critical in tone. In 1656 Stanley permitted John Gamble, a musician, to set several of his poems to music. Other poets whom he translated were Bion, Moschus, Johannes Secundus, Gongora, and Montalvan. Smith's translation of the *Pervigilium Veneris* was marked by a "rather uncanny grace," according to George Saintsbury, who goes on to say that while the mere list of Stanley's work "may suggest an industrious pedant, curiously combined with a butterfly poet," his work "actually possesses very considerable charm."

Winstanley called Stanley "the glory and admiration of his time," and the usually waspish Pope spoke of him respectfully. He died at fifty-three at his lodgings in Suffolk Street, Strand, and was buried in the church of St. Martin's-in-the-Fields.

PRINCIPAL WORKS: Poems and Translations, 1647; Poems, 1651; The History of Philosophy: Containing the Lives, Opinions, Actions and Discourses of the Philosophies of Every Sect, 1655-1662.

ABOUT: Hazlitt, W., ed. Lovelace's Poems; Stanley, T. Poems and Translations 1814 (see Memoir by Sir S. E. Brydges); Revue Hispanique, February-April 1920.

STANYHURST, RICHARD (1547-1618),

translator of the *Aeneid*, historian, author of devotional works, was born in Dublin, Ireland, the son of James Stanyhurst, Recorder of Dublin and Speaker of the Irish House of Commons in three parliaments. Richard was educated at Waterford prior to entering University College, Oxford, in 1563. While still an undergraduate he wrote Latin commentaries on Porphyry which were published in 1570, two years after he had graduated B.A.

He studied law in London and in 1569 returned to Ireland with Edmund Campion, his Oxford tutor, who later became a Jesuit and a Catholic martyr. Stanyhurst completed Campion's *History of Ireland* and wrote his own *Description of Ireland* for Holinshed's *Chronicles*, first published 1577.

In 1579 Stanyhurst's first wife, Janet, died in childbirth at Knightsbridge, London. Shortly thereafter he left the British Isles for good, settled on the Continent and became a Roman Catholic. In 1582, at Leyden, he published his notorious translation of the first four books of Virgil's *Aeneid* in English hexameters. It will be sufficient to quote one

line from Book II—by no means the most outlandish—

> You me bid, O Princess, to scarify
> a festered old sore.

His miscellaneous verse is almost all equally infelicitous.

Henceforward Stanyhurst wrote exclusively in Latin, producing a history of Ireland, a life of St. Patrick, and various devotional and controversial works. About 1585 he married Helen Copley, an English Roman Catholic, by whom he had two sons who later became Jesuits. From 1590 to 1595 Stanyhurst was in Spain, whence he returned to Flanders. After Helen's death in 1602 he became a Catholic priest and was appointed chaplain to Archduke Albert, Spanish Governor of the Netherlands. His last Latin work was a reply to Archbishop James Ussher, his Church of Ireland nephew. He is believed to have died at Brussels in 1618.

PRINCIPAL WORKS: A Treatise containing a Plain and Perfect Description of Ireland (*in* Holinshed's Chronicles) 1577; The First Four Books of Virgil His Aeneid Translated into English Heroical Verse, 1582.

ABOUT: Arber, E. Introduction to his reprint of Stanyhurst's Translation of Virgil's Aeneid, 1880.

STEELE, Sir RICHARD (March, 1672-September 1, 1729),

journalist, dramatist, miscellaneous writer, was born in Dublin, the son of Richard Steele, an attorney, and Elinor (Sheyles) Symes. His father died when Richard was five and his mother soon after; his uncle, Henry Gascoigne, secretary to the first Duke of Ormonde, became his guardian. He entered the Charterhouse in 1684, and there, two years later, met Joseph Addison,*qv* a few weeks his junior, with whom his name will always be associated.

In 1690 he matriculated at Christ Church, Oxford, changing in 1691 to Merton College. His first writing there, a comedy, he burned. He left without a degree to enroll as a gentleman trooper in the life guards under the Duke of Ormonde's grandson (later attainted for treason)—an action which cost him his uncle's approval and a large estate. In 1694 he dedicated an elegy on Queen Mary to Lord Cutts, and in consequence was appointed Cutts' secretary and transferred to his Coldstream regiment. By 1700 he was a captain. It was at this period that he fought a duel with one Captain Kelly, wounding him badly, an episode which turned Steele into a lifelong opponent of dueling. In 1702 he was in Lord Lucas' regiment.

This was also the period when Steele began to appear in print. His *Christian Hero,* an honest attempt to show that a man could be a gentleman, a military figure, and a Christian, all in one, only exposed him to the ridicule of his acquaintances. He turned to writing plays for Drury Lane—once again to "reconcile good breeding and wit with virtue." They were too didactic to be very witty or very successful. Steele had not yet found his métier, though he was floundering toward it.

His first marriage took place in 1705, to Margaret (Ford) Stretch, a wealthy and, it is said, an elderly widow, who died the following year. Steele's fortunes began to improve. From 1706 to the prince's death in 1708 he was gentleman waiter to Prince George of Denmark, and in 1707 he was appointed gazetteer; but Harley, whom he had satirized, came into power and threw him out in 1710.

The stodgy official *Gazette* did not give Steele much scope, and so in 1709 he founded the thrice-weekly *Tatler,* the first of his many magazines. From the first Addison was his anonymous collaborator. Steele had found his forte at last. The light, informal, yet not superficial essay was the field in which he could function best. The full list of the papers he published follows: *Tatler,* 1709-11, 271 numbers, of which Steele wrote 188; *Spectator,* 1711-12, 555 numbers, of which Steele wrote 236; *Guardian,* 1713-15 (Steele wrote most of this); *Englishman,* 1713-14 and again in 1715, of which Steele wrote all 56 numbers; *Lover,* 1714 (all 40 by Steele, including advice to the lovelorn); and five more ephemeral periodicals with from three to nine issues each—*Town Talk,* 1715-16; *Tea Table,* 1716; *Chit-Chat,* 1716; *Plebeian,* 1719; and *Theatre,* 1720. Of these, the *Spectator* is by far the best known. It was Steele who created the famous "Sir Roger de Coverley," though it was Addison who later wrote most of the essays about the old knight.

Meanwhile, Steele had married his second wife, his "dear Prue," whose real name was Mary Scurlock. He met her at his first wife's funeral, and married her the next year. He spoke of her as "Charmer," "Inspirer," "Ruler," and "Absolute Governess," all of which she was. Steele loved her and their children (they had two daughters and two sons both of whom died young), but he could no more be held down than could quicksilver. With all his sincere love of virtue, he was not made for domestic life. He had at least one illegitimate daughter, whom he once proposed to marry to Richard Savage. He was restless, weak willed, and he loved wine and good fellowship.

As a Whig, Steele prospered when the Whigs were in power. From 1710 to 1713, when he resigned, he was commissioner of stamps. His political pamphlets made him bitter enemies among the Tories. In 1713 he was elected to Parliament for Stockbridge, Hampshire, but the next year he was expelled for "uttering seditious libels" in his *Crisis.* With the accession of George I, his fortunes prospered. He was made a justice of the peace, deputy lieutenant of Middlesex, surveyor of the royal stables at Hampton Court, and (most profitable) supervisor of Drury Lane. He lost the patent in 1720, but it was restored in 1721. In 1715 he entered the House of Commons again, sitting for Boroughbridge, Yorkshire. The same year the king knighted him. He was one of the

J. Richardson, 1712

SIR RICHARD STEELE

491

commissioners to take over forfeited Jacobite estates in Scotland; and by way of social life he established a sort of lecture series, or conversaziones, which he called the Censorium. He wrote another comedy, aimed at dueling (he had already written a book against the duel). In 1722 he was reelected to Parliament for Wendover, Buckinghamshire.

But Steele's best days were over. His wife had died in 1718, and the next year he quarreled with his old friend Addison. His attempt at reconciliation was frustrated by Addison's death. Rudderless and without compass, he fell heavily into debt. Finally he compounded with his creditors, and arranged with them to retire to the country and gradually pay off his indebtedness. First he went to Herford, then to his wife's estate in Carmarthen, Wales, where he died after a stroke of paralysis, at fifty-seven. He left two fragments of comedies, and little more.

Steele was one of those charming, unstable men of whom nobody approves but whom everybody likes. He had the temperament of a Cavalier of the days of Charles I, modified by the puritanical outlook of his own period. As Utter and Needham remarked, "Steele could never be a Cavalier, for he could never leave repentance. He could never be a Puritan, for he could never learn thrift." Warm hearted, lovable, impetuous, there was still something of the eternal adolescent in him. As Lady Mary Wortley Montagu remarked of both him and Fielding alike: "They both agreed in wanting money, in spite of all their friends, and would have wanted it, if their hereditary lands had been as extensive as their imaginations; yet each of them was so formed for happiness, it is a pity he was not immortal."

In an era when women were treated with contempt and false chivalry, Steele admired and respected them as human beings capable of development. He was generous, tolerant, easy going. He must have been a difficult husband, for all his warm affection, but he was a delightful companion.

He was also a first class essayist, second only to Addison, and in some ways second not even to him. He was a master of the deft, ingratiating approach, of the moving narrative. In a sense he founded the short story, and he could have been a novelist— he could have anticipated Richardson in the epistolary novel, if he had had more staying power and less impatience. His plays, besides being ill constructed, were wildly improbable and often over sentimental, but his essays never were. Neither were they heavily didactic, though so often he had a moral lesson in view. Though the essays from the *Spectator*, and to a lesser degree from the *Tatler*, have become hackneyed through generations of use as school texts, they still have freshness and charm. Just a little more iron in his nature, and a bit less of mercury, and Sir Richard Steele would have been in the first instead of in the second rank of authors.

PRINCIPAL WORKS: *Plays* (dates of publication): The Funeral: or Grief à-la-Mode, 1702; The Lying Lover: or, The Ladies Friendship, 1704; The Tender Husband: or, The Accomplished Fools, 1705; The Conscious Lovers, 1723; Complete Plays 1759. *Political Works*: The Englishman's Thanks to the Duke of Marlborough, 1712; Letter to Sir Miles Wharton concerning Occasional Peers, 1713; The Importance of Dunkirk Considered, 1713; The Crisis, 1714; Romish Ecclesiastical History of Late Years, 1714; Letter to a Member of Parliament concerning the Bill for preventing the Growth of Schism, 1714; Mr. Steele's Apology for Himself and his Writings, 1714; Political Writings, 1715; The Crisis of Property, 1720; A Nation a Family, 1720. *Miscellaneous*: The Christian Hero, 1701; Poetical Miscellanies (with others) 1714; The Ladies Library, 1714; The Court of Honour, 1720; Letters of Mr. Steele and Mr. Pope, 1735; Epistolary Correspondence (J. Nichols, ed.) 1787; Selected Essays (A. Dobson, ed.) 1885, (L. E. Steele, ed. 1907); Letters of Richard Steele (R. B. Johnson, ed.) 1928.

ABOUT: Aitken, G. A. The Life of Richard Steele; Connely, W. Sir Richard Steele; Dilkes, C. W. Papers of a Critic; Dobson, A. Richard Steele; Forster, J. Historical and Biographical Essays; Hawkes, C. P. Authors-at-Arms; Hazlitt, W. Lectures on the English Comic Writers; Macaulay, T. B. Essays; Montgomery, H. R. Memoirs of the Life and Writings of Sir Richard Steele; Thackeray, W. M. The English Humorists of the 18th Century; Utter, R. P. and Needham, G. B. Pamela's Daughters.

STEEVENS, GEORGE (May 10, 1736-January 22, 1800) literary critic, Shakespeare commentator, was born in Poplar, London, the son of George Selden, a retired sea-captain of the East India Company and one of its directors. After school at Kingston-on-Thames and Eton, he attended King's College, Cambridge, from 1753 to 1756, but took no degree. Inheriting a small fortune, he bought a house (formerly an inn) on Hampstead Heath, which was his home thereafter; as he never married, his household was cared for by a widowed cousin and her family.

Steevens was a member of the Royal Society and of the Society of Antiquaries, and Dr. Johnson (who saw but excused his faults) even got him into the Club in 1774; but for the most part he had more enemies than friends. A vicious critic, a virulent controversialist, with a bitter tongue and not too much integrity, he came, as Johnson said, "to live the life of an outlaw." His relations with other Shakespearian critics, except his assistant Isaac Reed, were bad; he was accused of plagiarizing Edward Capell, he quarreled violently with Edmond Malone; and after earning some reputation as a textual critic of Shakespeare he ruined it by rushing into print, to spite Malone (though he had already termed himself a retired "dowager-editor") with an attempt to "restore some apparent meaning to his [Shakespeare's] corrupted lines, and a decent flow to his obstructed versification."

In his calmer moments, however, Steevens did have genuine learning, and he collected a very valuable library of Elizabethan literature. He was also a good draughtsman, and an early collector of Hogarth's prints. He was part owner of *St. James' Chronicle,* and contributed many epigrams, parodies, and burlesques to it and other periodicals. He took an active part in the unmasking of Chatterton's forgeries. He also contributed some information used in Johnson's *Lives*

G. Dance, 1793

GEORGE STEEVENS

of the English Poets, and in Hawkins' edition of Johnson's works.

Steevens was capable of amiability and even of charity, but in general he was a cantankerous, hot tempered, saturnine man, who was not above anonymous libels on his own friends and mean and silly practical jokes. His private life was most methodical; every morning before seven he walked from Hampstead to London, visited book shops, publishers, and acquaintances, and walked back again. As Henry Hallam remarked, he was clever, but possessed of an utter lack of candor or love of truth. He even went so far, in his editions of Shakespeare, as to write obscene notes and attribute them to clerical commentators with whom he was on bad terms! In a word, he was a thoroughly unpleasant person. Nevertheless, his work is a constituent part of the history of Shakespearian criticism.

PRINCIPAL WORKS: 20 of the Plays of Shakespeare, being the whole number printed in quarto during his life-time, or before the Restoration, collated where there were different copies, and publish'd from the originals, 1766; The Works of Shakespeare with the Corrections and Illustrations of Various Commentators (with S. Johnson) 1773 (with Essay on Chronology and notes by E. Malone, 1778; with Poems as supplement, 1780; revised edition, 1793; I. Reed, ed. 1803 [First Variorum]); The Genuine Works of Hogarth (with J. Nichols) 1808-11.

ABOUT: Boswell, J. Life of Johnson; D'Israeli, I. Curiosities of Literature; Hallam H. Introduction to the Literature of Europe; Nichols, J. Literary Anecdotes.

STEPHENS, JOHN (fl. 1615), author of *Satirical Essays,Characters and Others,* was probably born in Gloucester, where many generations of his family had been active in political and public life. He studied law, entered Lincoln's Inn in 1611, and practiced common law in Gloucester.

He wrote one long and rather dull play, based on Ovid and Lucan, entitled *Cynthia's Revenge, or Menander's Extasy;* it was published with verses by Ben Jonson praising the work.

Of more interest is a collection of portraits in verse, in the popular fashion of the day, titled *Satirical Essays, Characters, and Others, and quick descriptions fitted to the life of their subjects.* In the main, Stephens' "characters" followed the traditional pattern, being based on wit rather than perception, and on generalization rather than particulars. In some cases, however,

493

his sketches go beneath the surface, and become individual portraits, with more evidence of direct, personal observation of human nature than most of his colleagues showed. A few of the sketches amount to rudimentary examples of the modern short story.

A second edition, with changes and the addition of *A new satire in defense of common law and lawyers*, was published in 1615, and a reprint of this edition appeared sixteen years later.

PRINCIPAL WORKS: Cynthia's Revenge, 1613; Satirical Essays, 1615.

ABOUT: Baker, D. E. Biographia Dramatica; Lowndes, W. T. Bibliographer's Manual.

STERNE, LAURENCE (November 24, 1713-March 18, 1768), novelist, author of sermons and miscellaneous writings, was born in Clonmel, Tipperary, Ireland, where his father, Roger Sterne, an ensign in the army, was stationed. Roger Sterne was, however, purely English; his grandfather had been Archbishop of York. Laurence Sterne's mother was Agnes (Nuttle) Hebert, widow of an English army officer but herself Irish, and of much lower class socially than her husband.

The child's first two years were spent with his rich paternal grandmother at Elvington, Yorkshire, but for eight years more he, with his mother and sister, trailed after the ensign from barracks to barracks, all over England and Ireland. "My uncle Toby" and "Corporal Trim" came straight from the memories of these years. Finally, in 1723, the boy was established in school at Halifax. Then in 1731 his father, by now a lieutenant on overseas duty, died, and he had to leave school. He went back to Elvington, where after two unhappy years a cousin arranged his entrance in Jesus College, Cambridge, as a sizar. Sterne took his B.A. in 1736, his M.A. in 1740, but he was not a notable student; he confessed that his knowledge of Greek was very poor. The chief result of his college education was the acquirement of a number of debts and of a lifelong friend, John Hall-Stevenson.[qv]

His uncle, Jaques Sterne, who was a clergyman but also a keen Whig politician, advised the lad to take orders, and he did so, being ordained deacon in 1736, priest in 1738. He had no vocation whatever, and his only object was to secure a livelihood.

There was nothing unusual or reprehensible in this in his day, and Sterne was only one of hundreds of indifferent clergymen. Through his uncle he received the living of Sutton-in-the-Forest, Yorkshire, in 1738, some small court perquisites (sinecures with incomes attached) in 1741, and in 1743 the additional living of Stillington, near Sutton.

Also, in 1741, he received a prebendary stall at York Cathedral, but this was through the influence of his wife, Elizabeth Lumley, whom he had married that year. Sterne's marriage was unhappy from the start, but then it is impossible to imagine him happy in any marriage. He was a born philanderer, who made no secret of it. He was not, however, the unkind husband he has been depicted as being; when in after years he and his wife lived apart, and later separated entirely, it was by her wish more than his. She preferred residence in France to England, and he always supported her and their daughter, whom he loved tenderly. (Another daughter had died in infancy.) On another count Sterne may be absolved; Byron said he "wept over a dead ass and let his mother starve." Stern certainly could be mawkish, but he was not hard hearted. His mother was mercenary and demanding; she neglected him for eleven years, then when she heard he had married a wealthy woman (he hadn't), she arrived with his sister and for years bullied and extorted money from him. She did die in a debtor's prison, but after they had long been estranged.

Except for this family skeleton, Sterne lived with fair comfort at Sutton for twenty years. He attended to his clerical duties, but he gave as much or more time to shooting, playing the bass viol, painting (very badly), and beginning his career as a writer. He had a succession of love affairs, some platonic, more not, and a succession of quarrels in consequence with his wife. His health was never good; the probability is that he had had tuberculosis from boyhood. His friend Hall-Stevenson lived near by, and kept open house to a rather questionable and roistering crew, of whom his clerical friend cheerfully made one. Sterne was not popular with his flock, if only because he was active in securing the law which enclosed the common lands of the farmers, thereby increasing his own property at the expense of theirs. But he was in general not much of a politician, and in fact became alienated from the uncle who had been his benefactor, principally because he refused to follow the latter into his intense Whig activities.

Sterne's first published work was sermons; in this period he also wrote a satirical *roman-à-clef* which was circulated in manuscript and not published for ten years thereafter. But in 1759 there appeared the first volume of his masterpiece, *Tristram Shandy*, which the critics objurgated and the reading public took to its heart. He had journeyed to London with his manuscript, and it is said that, reading some of it to a group of friends, he suddenly discovered they were all asleep; in disgust he threw the manuscript in the fireplace, whence it was rescued, scorched. (Perhaps it was not his only copy!) His expectation after its first success was to issue two volumes "for forty years"—actually it ended (though it was never really completed) with the ninth volume, in 1767.

In 1760, through Lord Fauconberg, Sterne was made perpetual curate of Coxwold, Yorkshire, which had a much better climate than Sutton. Two years later his health broke down entirely, and he was obliged to leave for France and Italy. His wife and daughter followed later, and stayed in France when he made short returns to England. In 1766 he came back to London and settled there. For the first time he had the gratifying experience of being a literary lion, and on a later visit to Paris he repeated this pleasure. The literary result of his travels was *A Sentimental Journey*, which also was left unfinished. *Tristram Shandy* had hinted that "Mr. Yorick" (Sterne's name for himself) had sermons he would be glad to have published, so that there were yearly volumes of these—probably bewildering to the readers of his novels, for they were quite conventional.

The most celebrated of Sterne's many romances took place in this period—that with Eliza Draper, an unhappily married young woman whom he knew only from December 1766 to April 1767, but with whom he corresponded, fervently, until his death. He would undoubtedly have married her, had there not been a husband and a

LAURENCE STERNE

wife (now permanently living in France) in the way.

Sterne died in London of pleurisy, at fifty-four, and was buried in St. George's. Two days later "resurrection men" exhumed and stole his body and sold it to the anatomists. His skeleton is said to have been on display at Cambridge for years.

In spite of extenuating circumstances— his lifelong ill health, his wretched childhood, his impossible mother—Sterne's character is not an ingratiating one. His lachrymose sentimentality, coupled with sly pruriency, is not endearing. At least he was no hypocrite; his heart was worn, not on his sleeve, but on a platter held out before him wherever he went. He was gay and light hearted by nature, and could laugh as easily as he could weep. He was an exact contemporary of Rousseau, and in many ways his English counterpart, so far as personality went, though he had none of Rousseau's pathological persecution mania.

But as a writer he revolutionized the novel. He was the first to change it from a mere mirror of life to a subjective romance. He stems from Cervantes, but with none of the great Spaniard's depth or universality; and *Rasselas* and *Candide* are both among the relatives of *Tristram Shandy*; but Sterne alone took the final step. As Goethe (who fashioned *Werther* in Sterne's image) put it, he was "a model

495

in nothing, in everything an awakener and suggester." His humor—though to critics as different as Johnson, Walpole, Smollett, and Goldsmith in his own day, and to Macaulay and Thackeray in a later one, he was a mere cheap jester—is true and warm and delicate. His flexible style, his ingenious fancy, his sparkling, light-handed touch, his sure craftmanship, his real humanitarianism, extenuate his indubitable faults—his long, rambling discursiveness, which can become intolerably boring to an impatient modern reader; his ridiculous and unmanly sentimentality; above all, his cold, dry, smirking indecency. He made the novel personal, subtle, free; he was a pioneer and a great innovator. His influence is still discernible today.

PRINCIPAL WORKS: Charity Sermon, 1747; The Abuses of Conscience, 1750; The Life and Opinions of Tristram Shandy, 1759-67; Sermons of Mr. Yorick, 1760-69; A Sentimental Journey through France and Italy, 1768; A Political Romance (The History of a Warm Watch Coat) 1769; Letters from Yorick to Eliza, 1775; Letters to his Friends on Various Occasions, 1775; Letters to his Most Intimate Friends (L. S. Medalle [daughter] ed.) 1775; Works, 1779; Original Letters Never before Published, 1788; Seven Letters Written by Sterne and his Friends (W. D. Cooper, ed.) 1844; Unpublished Letters, 1855-56; Works (G. Saintsbury, ed.) 1894.

ABOUT: Behmer, C. A. Laurence Sterne und C. S. Wieland; Benjamin, L. S. (Lewis Melville) The Life and Letters of Laurence Sterne; Cordasco, F. Laurence Sterne: A List of Critical Studies; Cross, W. L. The Life and Times of Laurence Sterne; Curtis, L. P. The Politicks of Laurence Sterne; Czerny, J. Sterne, Hippel, und Jean Paul; Dilworth, E. N. Unsentimental Journey of Laurence Sterne; Fitzgerald, P. H. Laurence Sterne; Goethe, J. H. von, Spruche in Prosa; Hartley, L. C. This Is Lorence; Medalle, L. S. Memoirs, in Letters to His Most Intimate Friends; More, P. E. Shelburne Essays; Pinger, W. R. R. Laurence Sterne and Goethe; Quennell, P. Four Portraits; Rabizzani, G. Sterne in Italia; Sichel, W. S. Sterne: A Study; Stephen, L. Hours in a Library; Texte, J. J. Rousseau et les Origines du Cosmopolitisme littéraire; Thackeray, W. M. Lectures on the English Humourists; Thayer, H. W. Laurence Sterne in Germany; Traill, H. D. Sterne; Watkins, W. B. C. Perilous Balance; Yoseloff, T. A Fellow of Infinite Jest.

STEVENSON, JOHN HALL- (1718-March 1785), author of tales and verse pamphlets, was born John Hall, son of a country gentleman of Durham. He attended Jesus College, Cambridge, and there began the intimate friendship with Laurence Sterne which was one of the few positive elements of his life. He left college without graduating, took the traditional Grand Tour of the Continent, and upon his return to England married Anne Stevenson, taking her surname in order to simplify the transference of property she brought him as a dowry.

From early youth, Hall-Stevenson's only interests had been Rabelaisian wit and heavy drinking, and he now settled down to exactly the kind of life he enjoyed. From an uncle he inherited Skelton Castle, an isolated, half-ruined pile in Yorkshire, which he renamed Crazy Castle. Here he entertained literary friends from London and abroad, gathered together a library of jokes and French contes, the more obscene the better, and held drunken orgies with those local clergymen and squires whom he had organized in the "club of demoniacs."

Sterne, his life-long friend (they may have been distant relatives), defended him, and found him generous and loyal. Sterne spent much time at Skelton Castle, used its library extensively, and used its master for a model for the character of Eugenius in both *Tristram Shandy* and *Sentimental Journey*. After Sterne's death, Hall-Stevenson essayed a feeble continuation of *Sentimental Journey*, and proposed a life of Sterne, which was never written.

There are some indications that he might have been a fairly good poet, if he had chosen to be. But his work is so slovenly, so full of rancor and venom, and so tiresomely indecent that it is difficult to read. His best known work was a book in imitation of the coarser French fables of La Fontaine and his followers, called *Crazy Tales*.

So victimized by his own hypochondria that he took to his bed in mortal agony whenever the wind was in the east, beset by financial difficulties, on such bad terms with his wife that she seldom came to Skelton, his last years were dismal ones. He died at Skelton at the age of sixty-seven.

PRINCIPAL WORKS: A Nosegay and a Simile for the Reviewers, 1760; Fables for Grown Gentlemen, 1761; Crazy Tales, 1762; A Pastoral Cordial, 1763; A Pastoral Puke, 1764; Makarony Fables, 1767; Lyric Consolations, 1768; Essay upon the King's Friends, 1776.

ABOUT: Burke, Sir J. B. Landed Gentry; Nichols, J. Literary Anecdotes; Sterne, L. Correspondence.

STILLINGFLEET, EDWARD (April 17, 1635-March 27, 1699), preacher, scholar and religious writer, seventh son of an

ancient York family, was born in Cranborn, Dorset. He was a scholarship student at St. Johns College, Cambridge, became a fellow of the college after obtaining his B.A., and received his M.A. in 1656. He supported himself by tutoring, was ordained, and in 1657 became rector of Sutton.

His writings on religious subjects were already attracting wide notice. In 1665 he became rector of St. Andrews, a position he held for twenty-four years, although his popularity in London and at court grew so rapidly that his parishioners complained of the amount of time he spent away from St. Andrews. Some of his popularity may have been due to his prepossessing appearance (he was nicknamed "the beauty of holiness"), but Pepys quotes authorities as saying he was "the ablest young man to preach the Gospel since the Apostles," and a contemporary called him "the learnedest man of his age in all respects." He was a reader at the Temple, preacher at Rolls Chapel, Dean of St. Paul's, and a royal chaplain, and, following the revolution, became Bishop of Worcester.

Stillingfleet was married twice and had ten children. He amassed an extensive and valuable library of rare books and manuscripts, and was an active and prolific antiquarian. In addition to producing a remarkably large and able body of writings, he was a frequent speaker in the House of Lords, and, even after failing health rendered him less active, was often consulted by both church and state on ecclesiastical matters. He died at the age of sixty-four, and is buried in Worcester Cathedral.

He was an ardent controversialist, and most of his writing was dialectical. The best known work is an early one, *The Irenicum*, which, while it condemned nonconformity, suggested the possibility of a compromise between Episcopacy and Presbyterianism. He always maintained a tolerant attitude toward nonconformists, even while attacking their position.

One of his controversial works was written to uphold Archbishop Laud in his debate with the Jesuit, John Fisher. Following a critical article by Stillingfleet on actions of Dryden's after his conversion, Dryden attacked Stillingfleet in the fable, *The Hind and the Panther*. One of Stillingfleet's last public controversies was with Locke on the latter's interpretation of the doctrine of the Trinity.

In spite of his prodigious output and personal popularity, and the skill and scholarship that went into his writings, they were without literary distinction and achieved no lasting fame.

PRINCIPAL WORKS: The Irenicum, 1659; Origines Sacrae, 1662; A Rational Account of the Grounds of the Protestant Religion, 1663; Origines Britannicae, 1685; Miscellaneous Discourses on Several Occasions, 1735.

ABOUT: Burnet, G. History of My Own Time.

STIRLING, Earl of. See ALEXANDER, Sir WILLIAM

STOW, JOHN (1525?-April 6, 1605), chronicler, antiquary, was born in London. His father and grandfather were tallowchandlers who supplied lamp oil and candles to St. Michael's Church, Cornhill. John himself was apprenticed to a tailor and in 1547 received the freedom of the Merchant Taylors' Company or guild. We know nothing of his education and it is possible that he was mainly self-educated.

Toward middle life Stow took up those antiquarian studies which helped to make him famous. He was chiefly interested in old manuscripts, books, documents and the like, which he transcribed or—if he could afford it—bought. Since he not only spent money but neglected his trade of tailoring, he found it very difficult to make ends meet. Fortunately he had patrons, including Archbishop Parker and the Earl of Leicester. His fellows of the Merchant Taylors' Company voted him a pension, first of £4, then of £6, annually. A master tailor named Robert Dowe gave him money while alive and left him more at his death in 1602. Camden the antiquary also gave him £8 per annum and in 1604 James I authorized Stow to take up public collections.

Stow's first published work was an edition of Chaucer. Four years later he brought out a *Summary of English Chronicles*. It was not until 1580 that he brought out his *Chronicles of England*, better known as *The Annals of England*, the title of the second edition. This was an uncritical compendium of English history from the legendary days of Brutus down to the year of writing; he continued to bring it up to date, putting

JOHN STOW

in everything—details about the weather, even—until his death.

Perhaps his most original work was his *Survey of London*, which supplies a history of the city and a description of it as it was in Elizabethan times. Revised editions of this work kept appearing for a full century and a half after his death.

Stow was a friend of Ben Jonson's and a merry, philosophical character who often made light of his poverty, but he was also subject to violent hatreds. One of these was for his elder brother, Thomas Stow, also a tailor, who returned his animosity; the quarrel may have arisen over the terms of their mother's will. In 1570 Thomas charged John with being a Roman Catholic—and hence a traitor—but he was cleared by the Ecclesiastical Commissioners. Stow also engaged in a literary "war" with a rival chronicler named Grafton.

Stow was tall and thin, had good sight and a good memory. He writes of having three daughters, all apparently in domestic service. He was buried in the church of St. Andrew Undershaft, where his wife Elizabeth set up a statue to his memory. The portrait reproduced above is from the statue.

PRINCIPAL WORKS: The Works of Geoffrey Chaucer (ed.) 1561; A Summary of English Chronicles, 1565; The Chronicles of England, 1580 (The Annals of England, 1592); A Survey of London, 1598.

ABOUT: Kingsford, C. L. Introduction to The Survey of London, 1908; Whibley, C. Essays in Biography.

STRODE, RALPH (fl. 1350-1400), scholastic philosopher and logician, was probably born in the west of England. He taught philosophy and logic at Merton College, Oxford, and was widely known as an excellent teacher. One of the many legends about him is that he tutored Chaucer's son Lewis at Merton.

Enough of his writing on logic remains to justify his high reputation, although the principal work is lost. We know of his theological writing indirectly, since we have the opposite side of a controversy in which he took part. But whether or not he was a poet—whether he wrote no poetry at all, or wrote four of the most distinguished poems of the fifteenth century—has never been established.

In the field of philosophy, he took a middle-of-the-road position between the realists and the nominalists. Of his *Logica*, which had wide popularity, no copy is extant. *Consequentiae*, first printed in 1477, is a painstakingly detailed study of syllogistic thinking, and *Obligationes*, not printed until 1507, is a series of exercises in logic.

Strode's theological writings were in the nature of a public debate with John Wycliffe, with whom he had attended Merton College. We can gather, from Wycliffe's side of the friendly argument, which has been preserved, that Strode's position was that certain defects in the church and clergy must be tolerated in order to maintain the stability of the institution as a whole.

There is some slight basis for the theory that he was the author of four well known poems, printed in the fifteenth century with no clue to authorship. Of these, the finest, *The Pearl*, is an exceptionally beautiful elegy for a dead baby daughter. The others are *Sir Gawayne and the Green Knight*, and two moralistic poems, *Cleanness* and *Patience*. Chaucer dedicated *Troylus and Criseyde* to the poet John Gower, and to "philosophical Strode," and this linking of names has contributed to the belief that Strode was also a poet.

PRINCIPAL WORKS: Logica (no date); Consequentiae, printed 1477; Obligationes, printed 1507.

ABOUT: Bale, J. Index Britanniae Scriptorum.

STRUTT, JOSEPH (October 27, 1749-October 16, 1802), artist, engraver, antiquary and author of works on English customs, was the son of a wealthy miller of Springfield Mill, Chelmsford. His father died when Joseph was a baby, and his mother apprenticed him to an engraver at the age of fourteen. He studied at the Royal Academy when he was twenty-one and twenty-two, winning high honors, and in turning to the British Museum for models for his engravings he developed that combination of text and illustration which made his antiquarian works uniquely valuable.

From this point on, his life was divided into curiously spaced intervals of work. During the five years from 1773 to 1778, he published three profusely illustrated works on the antiquities and history of England. His engravings were excellent, his research accurate, and, what is most important, these were the first works of this kind to appear in England. In 1778 his young wife died, and for the next seven years he lived as a recluse. During this time he wrote a tenderly elegiac poem about his wife, did some of his best engravings, and painted industriously. Then for five years he returned to research and published the authoritative *Biographical Dictionary of Engravers.*

Once more, ill and in debt, he retired from active life, and for five years lived on a farm in Hertfordshire. Here his chief occupation was the writing of several unimportant novels and one satirical romance which was never published. He returned to London in 1795, and during the last seven years of his life published two more books based on his antiquarian research, and began a romance, *Queenhoo Hall.* He died at fifty-three, before this work was finished, and was buried in St. Andrews Churchyard in London.

Sir Walter Scott completed *Queenhoo Hall,* which is based on the history of an ancient mansion near Strutt's Hertfordshire retreat. Although Scott's conclusion of the romance was weak, it is noteworthy that it was this work which suggested to him the idea of the Waverley novels.

PRINCIPAL WORKS: The Regal and Ecclesiastical Antiquities of England, 1773; Manners, Customs, Habits, etc., of the People of England, 1774-76; Chronicle of England, 1778-80; Biographical Dictionary of Engravers, 1785; Dresses and Habits of the English People, 1796-99; Sports and Pastimes of the People of England, 1801.

ABOUT: Nichols, J. Literary Anecdotes.

STRYPE, JOHN (November 1, 1643-December 11, 1737), ecclesiastical historian and biographer, was born in Houndsditch, in London. His father, John van Strijp, had come to England to learn the silk trade from his brother, who had fled religious persecution in the Netherlands. Young John grew up in Strype's Yard, Petticoat Lane, went to Jesus College and Catherine Hall, Cambridge, and obtained a master's degree from both Cambridge and Oxford. He took holy orders, and received a series of sinecure holdings which supported him for life.

His close friend, William Hicks, great-grandson of a secretary of Lord Burghley, gave Strype some of the remarkably fine family collection of manuscripts, and loaned the rest to the publisher Richard Chiswell to be edited by Strype for publication. In 1694, when Strype was fifty-one, *The Memorials of Thomas Cranmer* was published according to this arrangement. Chiswell, financially disappointed in the results, refused to pay Strype for the editing and claimed that he had bought the manuscripts outright. Meantime, Hicks had been certified insane, and Strype, having the papers in his possession, simply retained them, issuing a long series of historical and biographical works based on the material they contained.

Strype worked hard. He amassed endless amounts of curious and important information. But he lacked literary ability, imagination, judgment, and sometimes accuracy. His books are valuable as reference works, but they earned for their author the nicknames "Dryasdust" and "Appendixmonger." Chiefly they are interesting as marking the steady growth in the early years of the eighteenth century of scholarship and research.

His later years were spent at Hackney, where he lectured from 1689 to 1724, and where he ended his days at the home of Thomas Harris, a surgeon who had married one of Strype's granddaughters. He died at ninety-four and was buried in the Leyton churchyard.

PRINCIPAL WORKS: Memorials of Thomas Cranmer, 1694; Life of Sir Thomas Smith, 1698; Life and Acts of John Aylmer, 1701; Life of Sir John Cheke, with his Treatise on Superstition, 1705; Annals of the Reformation in England, 1709-31; Life and Acts of Edmund Grindal, 1710; Life and Acts of Matthew Parker, 1711; Life and Acts of John Whitgift, 1718; Ecclesiastical Memorials, 1721.

ABOUT: Biographia Britannica; Carte, T. A General History of England; Lyson, D. Environs of London.

STUBBES or STUBBS, PHILIP (fl. 1581-1593)

, Puritan pamphleteer, was the son of "genteel parents." Little is known of his life. He attended Cambridge and Oxford, graduated from neither, and began the seven years of travel and observation throughout England which gave him material for his masterpiece.

Meanwhile he published three ballads: the first, *A fearful and terrible example of God's just judgment upon a lewd fellow, who usually accustomed to swear by God's Blood*, created a sensation; the subject of the second, one Joan Bowser of Dornington, sued him for libel; the third, *A View of Vanity*, is lost.

In 1583 he published *The Anatomy of Abuses*, his most important work. A second volume, and two works of which no copy remains, followed. In 1586 he married a fifteen-year-old girl, Katherine Emmes, who died four years later after the birth of their only child, a son named John. Stubbes' biography of young Katherine, called *A Crystal Glass for Christian Women*, was even more popular with the contemporary public than *The Anatomy of Abuses*. His last book, a collection of prayers and meditations, was published in 1592.

Stubbes' importance lies not in his puritanical criticism of society, although it was both sincere and justified, but in the quality of his mind and the painstaking detail with which he described the manners, customs, dress and pastimes of his time. His puritanism, as a matter of fact, was modified; the first edition of *Anatomy* carried a preface in which he qualified his condemnation of certain amusements, allowing that plays, private dancing, and gaming might under certain specified circumstances be tolerated. This introduction was omitted from later editions. But his sense of social justice was far beyond his time, and because of his acute observation this book is one of the chief sources of information about the everyday life of Shakespeare's England.

PRINCIPAL WORKS: Three Ballads, c. 1581; The Anatomy of Abuses, 1583; The Rosary of Christian Prayers and Meditations, 1583; The Anatomy of Abuses, part II, 1583; A Crystal Glass for Christian Women, 1591; A Perfect Pathway to Felicity, 1592.

ABOUT: Collier, J. Bibliograpical Catalogue; Furnivall, F. T. Biographical foreword, Anatomy of Abuses, 1877 ed.; Wood, A. à, Athenae Oxonienses.

STUKELEY, WILLIAM (November 7, 1687-March 3, 1765)

, antiquary, was the son of a Lincolnshire lawyer. He attended the grammar school in his native town of Holbeach, but his extreme curiosity led him to more knowledge than was to be learned in school. He studied astrology, wood carving, numismatics, nature lore and microscopy, and learned dialectics by listening to his father's learned discourses with his friends. At Corpus Christi College, Cambridge, he studied botany and anatomy, graduating with an M.B. in 1708. Two years later he began the practice of medicine in Holbeach, and in 1717 opened offices in London.

Among his numerous interests, the deepest one was the study of antiquities. In 1718 he was made a member of the Royal Society, and the following year he was one of the moving factors in the founding of the Society of Antiquaries, of which he was secretary for nine years. He was a gregarious man, with many friends among the intelligentsia of London, and a penchant for joining organizations, including the Freemasons. He received an M.D. from Cambridge in 1719, and was elected to the College of Physicians.

It was an attack of gout which launched him on a writing career. In the course of long tours about England which he undertook for the sake of his health, he investigated, sketched, and eventually wrote about most of the historic ruins of the country. The study of ancient religions impressed his rather credulous mind, and when he moved his practice to Grantham in his native Lincolnshire, he included a Druidic temple in his extraordinarily beautiful garden. He attempted to reconcile pagan mythology and sacred history, and was nicknamed "the archdruid of the age."

Eventually he took holy orders and became rector of St.-George-the-Martyr in London. He married twice, and had three daughters. He died of paralysis when he was seventy-eight, and was buried in the East Ham churchyard in Essex.

His most famous work is on the reconstruction of the temple of Stonehenge, although in this, as in his other books, some of his information is untrustworthy.

PRINCIPAL WORKS: An Account of a Roman Temple, 1720; Itinerarium Curiosium, 1724; A Treatise on the Cause and Cure of the Gout, 1734; Palaeographia Sacra, 1736; Stonehenge, 1740; Palaeographia Britannica, 1743-52.

ABOUT: Lowndes, W. T. Bibliographer's Manual; Munk, W. College of Physicians; Nichols, J. Literary Anecdotes, and Literary Illustrations.

SUCKLING, Sir JOHN (1609-1642), poet, dramatist, pamphleteer, was born at Whitton, Middlesex, the eldest son of Sir John Suckling and Martha Cranfield, sister of the first Earl of Middlesex. The elder Sir John, descended from an old Norfolk family, had a distinguished career in the government service; at his death in 1627 he was a Privy Councillor and had held the positions of Comptroller of the Royal Household and Secretary of State. The poet's mother died in 1613 and his father married again.

We do not know where Suckling received his early education; he entered Trinity College, Cambridge, in 1623 and left in 1627, without taking a degree, to enter Gray's Inn. His father died soon afterward, leaving him heir to a great estate, but he was not to gain full possession of it until he was twenty-five. In 1628 he set out on a tour of Europe, spending some time in France and Italy. In 1630 he was back in England, for Charles I knighted him that year. Thanks to his father and his uncle, the Earl of Middlesex, Suckling was always in high favor with Charles and Queen Henrietta Maria; he repaid that favor with a loyalty which, coupled with his truly Cavalier way of life, made him particularly obnoxious to the Puritans.

In 1631 he went to Germany in the Marquis of Hamilton's expedition, which fought for Gustavus Adolphus in the Thirty Years' War. Suckling returned to England next year, and was in constant attendance on the court, except when ordered by the Star Chamber to spend some time in residence on his estate (1635). He was famous for the high stakes he would wager on cards, lawn bowls, ninepins or any other game, for his many love affairs, and for his general extravagance.

In 1634 Suckling's courtship of a wealthy heiress got him into an unpleasant scrape. The king favored his suit, but the lady did not, and she employed another suitor, Sir

T. Russell after Sir A. Van Dyck
SIR JOHN SUCKLING

John Digby, to dissuade the poet. Digby, a noted swordsman, waylaid Suckling and demanded that he give up his pretensions; Suckling refused, whereupon Digby cudgelled him thoroughly. Suckling never offered to draw his sword, presumably because Digby would have been certain to kill him; he thus earned a very bad reputation for cowardice.

When Suckling's play Aglaura was produced in 1638, he spent an unprecedented amount of money on the staging and costumes; the play was a poor one, however, as were his later dramatic efforts—Brennoralt, The Goblins, The Sad One (unfinished).

For Charles' ill fated Scottish expedition of 1639 Suckling recruited and outfitted a hundred men in extremely colorful uniforms, at a cost of £12,000. When his men ran away along with the rest of the English army, it was once more suggested that he was better fitted for the boudoir than the battlefield.

Suckling was a member of the Long Parliament and strove hard to prevent a break between king and parliament. A letter of his to Henry Jermyn, printed as a pamphlet in 1641 under the title A Copy of a Letter Found in the Privy Lodgings at Whitehall, gave an extremely intelligent analysis of the political situation and advised the king to redress popular grievances on a generous scale before it was too late.

In 1641 Suckling was involved in a plot to rescue the king's impeached minister, the Earl of Strafford, from the Tower of London. Goring betrayed the plan and alleged that it was part of a larger scheme to win the army to the king's side and overthrow the parliament. Realizing that the king was no longer strong enough to protect him, Suckling fled to France—as did others in the conspiracy.

He is said to have committed suicide in Paris the following year, being unable to face poverty; this seems likely enough from what we know of his character, but there are other quite different accounts of his death.

Suckling's character is an extraordinarily complex one, full of the instability of the true gambler who plunges from the highest hope to the depths of despair. He was by turns brave and cowardly, loyal and cynical, the author of ribald lyrics and of *An Account of Religion by Reason*. His close friends included the debauched and syphilitic Davenant and Carew on the one hand, and the noble and learned Boyle and Falkland on the other.

His lyric poetry, however, is all of one piece. Lightness, grace and—above all—wit are its characteristics. The diction is always simple and clear, while the verse technique shows great virtuosity. Love is treated as a delightful game, where the pleasure of playing is more important than the result. Suckling can even appreciate chastity in women and the joys of platonic love. Cynical, witty songs like "Why so pale and wan, fond lover?" will last as long as the English language, and not one of Suckling's lyrics and epigrams is entirely lacking in wit.

Short and slight, with flowing locks, sharp nose and eager eyes, Suckling looked more intelligent and vivacious than handsome. His conversation was as full of wit as his poetry. He was the quintessence of his transitional age, a Cavalier lacking true chivalry, who clung to the old order without believing in it deeply enough to stand and fight to the bitter end.

PRINCIPAL WORKS: Aglaura, 1638; The Discontented Colonel (a tragedy later revised and titled Brennoralt) 1640; The Copy of a Letter Written to the Lower House of Parliament, 1641; A Copy of a Letter Found in the Privy Lodgings at Whitehall, 1641; Fragmenta Aurea (Poems, Aglaura, The Goblins, Brennoralt) 1646; The Last

Remains of Sir John Suckling (Letters to Several Persons of Honor, The Sad One) 1659.

ABOUT: Hazlitt, W. C. Introduction to the Poems, Plays and Other Remains of Sir John Suckling; Suckling, A. I. Life, prefixed to Selections from the Works of Sir John Suckling.

SURREY, HENRY HOWARD, Earl of

(1517?-January 19, 1547), poet, was the eldest son and heir of Thomas, third Duke of Norfolk, by his second wife, Elizabeth Stafford. The duke's first marriage had made him the brother-in-law of Henry VII and uncle of Henry VIII. Furthermore, the Howards were directly descended from Edward I through Lady Margaret Mowbray. Surrey's career and personality cannot be understood without reference to his family history and genealogy. He and all his family felt themselves very little inferior to the king in birth, breeding, power, or privilege.

The date and place of Surrey's birth are unknown; he passed most of his childhood at Tendring Hall in Suffolk and Kenninghall in Norfolk; when his father became Duke of Norfolk in 1524, he was given the courtesy title of Earl of Surrey. He received an excellent education, presumably from John Clerke, his father's secretary; he studied the Latin, French, Spanish, and Italian languages and literatures. In 1530 he became the companion of the Duke of Richmond, bastard son of Henry VIII. They were educated together at Windsor until October 1532, when they went to France and spent nearly a year at the French court.

There was at one time talk of betrothing Surrey to Princess (later Queen) Mary—a proposal made by his first cousin, Anne Boleyn. Finally Surrey was married to Lady Frances de Vere, daughter of the Earl of Oxford, in 1532, though they did not live together until 1535 because of their youth. On the friends' return from France in 1533, the Duke of Richmond contracted a similar marriage with Surrey's sister, which was never consummated, as the Duke died in 1536 to the great distress of Surrey.

Surrey's marriage turned out very happily, in contrast to his father's and mother's, which ended in separation in 1534. His first child, later fourth Duke of Norfolk, was born in 1536; another son and three daughters followed in due course.

Norfolk and Surrey were forced to take part in the trial and sentencing to death of

Anne Boleyn. Henry VIII's next wife was Jane Seymour, and the Seymour family soon became bitter enemies and rivals of the Howards. In 1537 Surrey was imprisoned for striking someone, probably Sir Edward Seymour, within the precincts of the court. It is likely that he did so in denial of the accusation that he and his father sympathized with the rebellion called "The Pilgrimage of Grace," which Norfolk had been sent north to suppress. As a matter of fact, the accusation was true; Norfolk and Surrey were against the Reformation, the absolute monarchy of the Tudors, and the newly created nobility which supported both.

Surrey was out of prison by October 1537. A period of royal favor now began for him. In 1539 he was appointed to strengthen the defenses of Norfolk because of a threat of invasion. In this and the two following years he received considerable grants of land from the king and was created a Knight of the Garter in 1541. Meanwhile the king had married Catherine Howard, another first cousin of Surrey's, in 1540. Two years later she, like Anne Boleyn, was executed for adultery. Surrey attended the execution.

In 1542 he was imprisoned for issuing a challenge to one John à Leigh. The next year Surrey was again in trouble with the Privy Council, this time for a drunken riot in the City of London. He was again imprisoned in the Fleet, but soon freed.

Surrey had had a good deal of military training and had covered himself with glory at a tourney in 1540, but it was not until 1544 that he was given his first really important command, being made Marshal of the Field in the army sent to besiege Montreuil; he was thus in charge of movement and security for an entire army. Later he led an attempt to take Montreuil by storm which was very nearly successful; he was wounded and escaped capture only with difficulty.

In 1545 he was put in command of the vanguard of the English army sent to relieve Boulogne; then he was made commander of the garrison at Guines, and finally commander of Boulogne itself, with the title of lieutenant general. He was very eager to hold Boulogne, though many of the Privy Council were against it. Many successful sorties were carried out against the French,

but the biggest one resulted in an English defeat with serious losses, though it achieved its objective of destroying a French supply train. Surrey was recalled to England early in 1546.

Henry VIII was dying and Sir Edward Seymour, now Earl of Hertford, was Norfolk's only possible competitor for the post of Protector during the minority of Edward VI. In December 1546 Surrey and Norfolk were imprisoned on trumped-up charges inspired by Hertford; the chief complaint against Surrey was that he had usurped the royal coat of arms and planned to usurp the throne. His trial was a farce, but he was found guilty of treason and executed none the less. Norfolk escaped execution, because Henry VIII died eight days after Surrey.

Surrey had no literary career as such; his poetry was written in the spare moments of an active life—some of it in prison—and not printed until ten years after his death. He and Sir Thomas Wyatt the Elder—whose work he was familiar with, though he does not seem to have known him personally—invented modern English versification and adopted or adapted many Italian verse forms, including the sonnet. Surrey, in his translations from Virgil, was the first ever to write English blank verse.

The numerous portraits of Surrey show a typical English aristocrat, with a long, Roman nose, a small, fish-like mouth, and

HENRY HOWARD, EARL OF SURREY

503

an expression combining real arrogance and seeming imbecility. Whether Surrey really planned to usurp the throne we cannot now tell, but he certainly had the pride of Lucifer, a "heady will," and a hot temper.

PRINCIPAL WORKS: Songs and Sonnets, Written by the Right Honorable Lord Henry Howard, Late Earl of Surrey, and Others ("Tottel's Miscellany") 1557; Certain Books of Virgil's Aeneis Turned into English Meter, 1557.

ABOUT: Casady, E. Henry Howard, Earl of Surrey.

SWIFT, JONATHAN (November 30, 1667-October 19, 1745), satirist, pamphleteer, writer of miscellaneous verse and prose, was born in Dublin, but of an English family. His father, also Jonathan Swift, who died seven months before his son was born, was steward of the King's Inns; his mother, Abigail Erick, came from Leicestershire, and was a cousin of John Dryden. As soon as the boy was born, his mother returned home to England, leaving him with a nurse who took him to her own home in Cumberland for three years. By this time he was able to read. He was returned to Dublin and put in the care of his uncle, Godwin Swift, who sent him to Kilkenny Grammar School (where he met Congreve) in 1673, and then, in 1682, to Trinity College, Dublin.

Already Swift's aberrant nature and the tragedy of his life were inexorably fixed. His troubled childhood, the equivocal relations with his mother, the patronizing and parsimonious attitude of his uncle, had done their work. He entered the university a bitter, fiercely proud, angry, and lonely youth. He wasted most of his time there, in a sort of subconscious retaliation on his uncle, and just managed to secure his B.A. "by special grace" in 1686. He was in constant rebellion and continually under censure, but he hung about the university until 1688, when he joined his mother in Leicestershire.

Finally he got a job as secretary to Sir William Temple in Moor Park, Surrey. Temple was not the man to understand young Swift—who could?—and at first he treated him very much *en haut*, to the secretary's fury; but in later years he made a friend and confidant of him. Swift secured an M.A. degree *ad eundem* from Hart Hall, Oxford, in 1692, and he did his first writing —Pindaric odes which impelled Dryden to

say, "Cousin Swift, you will never be a poet." In 1693 Temple, seeing his discontent and frustrated ambition, procured for him the office of Master of the Rolls, in Ireland. Swift went with bad grace, for he was very reluctant to return to his native land—he always was. But two important things, besides his first writing, had come to him in this first period with Temple. He had begun already to have the fits of giddiness which plagued him all his life; and he had met Stella. She was Hester Johnson, daughter of the companion or housekeeper to Lady Giffard, Temple's widowed sister, and at this time she was a child and Swift acted as her tutor.

In 1694, in Ireland, he was ordained deacon, in 1695 ordained priest, purely in the hope of being able to earn a living. Though Swift frequently deprecated implications that he had worldly ambitions in connection with his profession, he was bitterly disappointed by the meager rewards he received—indeed, he had reason to be. He was an orthodox enough Anglican, detesting Roman Catholics and dissenters alike, but politics was always more to his liking than the priesthood. He was made prebend at Kilroot, near Belfast, and stayed there a year, a year marked by the first of his peculiar affairs with women. This one was with Varina, Jane Waring (Swift always gave his women pseudonyms).

He returned to Temple in 1696, unable to make ends meet at Kilroot. This time, on much better terms, he stayed until Temple died in 1699, leaving Swift the task and the profit of editing his letters and memoirs. Unfortunately the publication of the last three volumes (they were issued from 1700 to 1709) earned him the undying enmity of Lady Giffard. It was during this period with Temple that Swift wrote *The Battle of the Books* and *A Tale of a Tub*, though they were not published until 1704. Stella was still there, and now she was a grown woman. There was also a distant connection of the Temples, much older, named Rebecca Dingley.

Disappointed in several legitimate hopes for advancement in England, Swift had to be content, in 1700, with another Irish living, that of Laracor, near Trim, together with the smaller vicarages of Aghar and Rathbeggan and a prebendary at Dunlavin,

C. Jervas

JONATHAN SWIFT

St. Patrick's, Dublin. His first act on returning to Ireland was to get rid of Varina by a letter full of studied insult. He spent as much time as possible in Dublin (where he received a D.D. degree) and made several visits to London. On the last of these he persuaded Stella, together with Mrs. (by courtesy) Dingley, to move to Ireland. It must be noted that though Stella acted as his hostess, he never saw her except in the presence of a third person. And even in the intimate *Journal to Stella*, he always addressed her and Mrs. Dingley together.

Between 1702 and 1704 Swift was frequently in England for long stays. In 1705 he met Addison and Steele and became active in Whig politics, contributing frequently to the *Tatler* and occasionally to the *Spectator*. In 1707 he was sent by the Irish clergy to try (unsuccessfully) to obtain "Queen Anne's bounty" for the Irish church. He stayed for two years. Gradually he had become a real political power, but no longer with the Whigs. Swift has been accused of venality in his change to the Tory party; this is nonsense. No one was more loyal than he. But he was a natural conservative, and he had never really belonged with the Whigs; his chief political interest was in the church, and the Tories were the logical friends of the Establishment. After a brief return to Ireland, he went back to London,

this time staying from 1710 to 1713. He became the right-hand man of Harley (later the Earl of Oxford) and of St. John (later Viscount) Bolingbroke, and when the two quarreled he stuck by Harley, for whom he had a deep personal affection. He edited the Tory newspaper, the *Examiner*, for over a year, and he was in a position of real authority and influence. He used most of it to obtain favors for needy friends and struggling authors—for no man with a reputation for miserliness was ever so truly openhanded and charitable.

It was in this period that Swift met Hester Vanhomrigh (Vanessa), the third of the strange triangle with Stella. Why women were so fatally attracted and devoted to a man who could never lead a normal love-life is a psychological mystery. But ten years after Swift had gone back to Dublin, Vanessa, whose mother had died, persuaded her sister to move with her to Ireland—against Swift's most urgent objections.

In 1713, in return for his inestimable benefits to the Tory cause, Swift received a very inadequate reward, the deanery of St. Patrick's. He had hoped for that much or better in England. He had been neither popular nor wanted in Dublin, and England was his chosen home. He was an efficient manager of his charge, and a good executive, but it was the last post he would have selected for himself. He had no choice, however. The next year he was back in London, and was there or in Berkshire until the middle of 1717. He was now a literary as well as a political figure, the associate of Gay and Pope, a participant in the "Martin Scriblerus" writings, a member of the club known as the Brothers. Once more he sailed back to Ireland where his situation changed completely, thanks to the "Drapier Letters," begun in 1720. (Ostensibly they were written by "M. B., Drapier.") Swift had no love for Ireland, but injustice always aroused him to a white heat of indignation. The economic exploitation of Ireland by England infuriated him. Then the printer of the "Letters" was prosecuted and Swift came to his defense, acknowledging his authorship. Suddenly he became a popular idol, and he remained so. In 1729 he received the freedom of Dublin. He was in England again in 1726 and 1727, but thenceforth he belonged to Ireland.

Stella died at the beginning of 1728. Whatever their legal relations (*if* they were married, it was probably in 1716), she was the one human being necessary to him. Because of her he had broken with Vanessa in so terrible a scene that she had died of it a few weeks later. It was the beginning of the end for him, and it was made harder by his break with his old friend Thomas Sheridan (grandfather of the dramatist), which could not be cured before Sheridan died. For ten years Swift's decline was not apparent, but then it was rapid. His cousin, Mrs. Whiteway, came to keep house for him, but very soon it was obvious that Swift was no longer capable of carrying on his career. He became paralyzed and afflicted with aphasia (he was never really insane), and by 1742 he was declared incompetent and guardians were appointed for him. The disease seems to have been labyrinthine vertigo, an affection of the inner ear, from which he had suffered since his youth. In 1742 he had his last lucid interval, following the bursting of an abscess of the eye. He died six weeks before his seventy-eighth birthday, and was buried privately beside Stella in St. Patrick's. As he had long ago prophesied, he had "died first at the top."

A library has been written on Swift's character and particularly on his mysterious sexual nature. Modern psychology can explain a good deal, but not all. It is easy to say that the simple answer is that (as he hinted more than once) he was impotent all his life: but behind his impotence, as behind his misanthropy, his public parsimony and secret benevolence, his fierce rebellion and pride, his pain and rage at injustice and cruelty, his cynical coarseness in writing contrasted with his squeamishness of speech and action, his deep tenderness inextricably mingled with brutality, lies a psychological twist buried deep in his childhood. His mother, who was herself a strange creature, in all probability made him what he was emotionally.

But intellectually, nature made him a genius, the greatest satirist of our tongue. Ironic fate has turned the bitterness of *Gulliver's Travels* into an expurgated story for children—ignoring the Struldbrugs and the Houyhnhnms and Yahoos. His political writings, cogent and strong as they were (and he was a master of commonsense persuasion and simple vigor), are outdated. His verse was never poetry in any true sense, but at its best witty satirical rhyme. He was capable of simple fun—as in the "Isaac Bickerstaff" persecution of the wretched astrologer Partridge. But the essence of Swift is in his prose satire—arid, as is all unrelieved satire, but savage, precise, and pointed with deadly barbs (*e.g.*, the *Modest Proposal*). "I hate and detest the animal called man," he said. This was the same man who wrote his own epitaph, saying that he lay now where violent anger and injustice could no longer tear his heart. It was the same man who left behind him an envelope on which was written: "Only a woman's hair."

Jonathan Swift was a tragic human being; but he had also a mind of utmost clarity and logical power, and a magnificent talent for clear, strong prose. Together they combined to put him in the very first rank of English writers.

PRINCIPAL WORKS: A Discourse of the Contests and Dissensions between the Nobles and Commons in Athens and Rome, 1701; A Tale of a Tub, with The Battle of the Books, 1704; An Argument against abolishing Christianity, 1708; Letter on the Sacramental Test, 1708; Predictions for the Year 1708 (as Isaac Bickerstaff) 1708; A Vindication of Isaac Bickerstaff, Esq., 1709; A Project for the Advancement of Religion, and the Reformation of Manners, 1709; Baucis and Philemon (verse) 1709; A Meditation upon a Broomstick, 1710; The Conduct of the Allies, 1711; Miscellanies by Dr. Jonathan Swift (unauthorized) 1711; A Proposal for Correcting, Improving, and Ascertaining the English Tongue, 1712; The Public Spirit of the Whigs Considered, 1714; Letters, Poems, and Tales, 1718; A Proposal for the Universal Use of Irish Manufacture, 1720; The Swearers-Bank or Parliamentary Security for Establishing a new Bank in Ireland, 1720; A Letter of Advice to a Young Poet, 1721; A Letter to the Shop-keepers, Tradesmen, Farmers, and Common People of Ireland (as M. B., Drapier) 1724; Fraud Detected, or The Hibernian Patriot (all the Drapier Letters) 1725; Cadenus and Vanessa (verse) 1726; Travels into Several Remote Nations of the World, by Lemuel Gulliver, First a Surgeon, Then a Captain, 1726; Letter to a Very Young Lady on her Marriage, 1727; Miscellanea, 1727; A Short View of the State of Ireland, 1727; Character of Mrs. Johnson, 1728; A Modest Proposal for Preventing the Children of Poor People from being a Burden to their Parents or the Country, 1729; The Lady's Dressing Room (verse) 1732; The Life and Genuine Character of Dr. Jonathan Swift, Written by Himself, 1733; On Poetry: A Rhapsody (verse) 1733; Works, 1735; The Legion Club (verse) 1736; A complete Collection of Genteel and Ingenious Conversation, 1737; Political Tracts, 1738; Verses on the Death of Dr. S., Written by Himself, 1739;

Poetical Works, 1740; Dean Swift's Literary Correspondence, 1741; Three Sermons, 1744; Directions to Servants in General, 1745; Works, 1755, 1787 (W. E. H. Lecky, ed. 1910); Letters [Journal to Stella] (J. Hawkesworth, ed) 1768.

ABOUT: Ackworth, B. Swift; Birrell, A. Essays about Men, Women, and Books; Churchill, R. C. He Served Humanity; Collins, J. C. Jonathan Swift: A Biographical and Critical Study; Craik, H. Life of Swift; Dark, S. Five Deans; Davis, H. J. The Satire of Jonathan Swift; Dobson, A. 18th Century Vignettes; Forster, J. Life of Jonathan Swift; Goodwin, F. S. Jonathan Swift, Giant in Chains; Gwynne, S. Life and Friendships of Dean Swift; Hardy, E. Conjured Spirit: A Study of the Relationship of Swift, Stella and Vanessa; Hay, A. Swift: the Mystery of his Life and Love; Hazlitt, W. Lectures on the English Poets; Johnson, S. Lives of the Poets; King, R. A. Swift in Ireland; Lecky, W. E. H. Biographical Introduction, Works, 1910 ed.; Leslie, S. The Skull of Swift, an Extempore Exhumation; Masson, W. D. Essays, Chiefly on English Poets; Newman, B. Jonathan Swift; Prévost-Paradol, L. A. Jonathan Swift, sa vie et ses oeuvres; Rossi M. M. and Hone, J. M. Swift: or, The Egotist; Scott. W. Memoirs of Jonathan Swift; Sheridan, T. (Jr.) Life of Swift; Sichel, W. Bolingbroke and His Times; Stephen, L. Swift; Swift, D. Essay upon the Life, Writings, and Character of Dr. Jonathan Swift; Swift, J. The Life and Genuine Character of Dr. Jonathan Swift, Written by Himself; Taylor, W. D. Jonathan Swift, a Critical Essay; Thackeray, W. M. English Humourists of the 18th Century; Van Doren, C. Swift; Watkins, W. B. C. Perilous Balance; Wilde, W. R. The Closing Years of Dean Swift's Life.

SYLVESTER, JOSHUA (1563-September 28, 1618), poet, translator, was born near Medway, Kent, the son of Robert Sylvester, a clothier. Both his parents died when he was a child, and he was adopted by his maternal uncle, William Plumbe. He was educated in a school at Southampton where all conversation was in French, so that he learned to speak that language fluently. In after years he regretted bitterly that he had been taken from school at thirteen and put into trade. All through his life he was a prolific writer of verse, but it brought him no money and he was obliged to spend most of his time as a businessman. Efforts to secure govermental or even good mercantile posts were unavailing, in spite of the influence of the great Earl of Essex, who was interested in this unusual young tradesman. At one time he was steward of one of the Essex estates at Lambourne, Staffordshire. Finally, in 1591, he joined the Merchant Adventurers' Company, and in 1606 Prince Henry of Wales (who died in 1612) became his patron, made Sylvester

After G. Van Dalen
JOSHUA SYLVESTER

groom of his chamber, and gave him a pension.

This of course lapsed on the prince's death, but the next year he became secretary of the Merchant Adventurers of Stade. Unfortunately this involved his leaving England and living at Middleburg, Zeeland. Still lamenting his exile, he died there at fifty-five.

Sylvester was married, not happily, and his wife and five or six children survived him.

Sylvester's poetry never achieved much popularity, though it appeared in such anthologies as *Englands Parnassus* (1600) and *A Poetical Rapsody* [*sic*] (1602) and though he published several volumes of verse. It was as a translator that he was known and, until the Restoration, much admired. Then he fell from popular and critical favor, and Dryden called his work "abominable fustian." It was by his translation of Du Bartas' scriptural epic of creation, *Les Semaines*, that Sylvester was best known; this was published in various parts until the completed work appeared in 1606. Sylvester translated the French poem into heroic couplets, highly artificial and full of plays upon words, but showing enthusiastic sympathy for Du Bartas' religious devotion and a certain quaint simplicity which made his translation—really more of a paraphrase —pleasant reading. Drayton and Drummond of Hawthornden admired him greatly, though Ben Jonson decidedly did not. He did have a strong influence on the young Milton and, whatever his later views, on Dryden himself.

PRINCIPAL WORKS: Divine Weekes and Workes (tr. from Du Bartas) 1590-1606; Monodia, 1594; The Profit of Imprisonment (tr. from French of Teligni) 1594; The Miracle of the Peace in Fraunce, 1599; Avtomachia, or the Self-Conflict of a Christian (tr. from Latin of G. Goodwin) 1607; Lachrimae Lachrimarum (elegy on Prince Henry) 1612; The Parliament of Vertues Royal (prose and verse) 1615; The Maiden's Blush (tr. from the Latin of Frascatius) 1620; The Wood-man's Bear, 1620; Panthea, or Divine Wishes and Meditations, 1630; Works (A. B. Grosart, ed.) 1880.

ABOUT: Dunster, C. Considerations on Milton's Early Reading; Grosart, A. B. Memorial Introduction, Works; Jonson, B. Conversations with Drummond of Hawthornden.

TADWINUS. See TATWIN

TANNAHILL, ROBERT (June 3, 1774-May 17, 1810), song writer and poet, was born at Paisley, Scotland, where his father, James, was a weaver. He had only rudimentary schooling, and at thirteen was apprenticed to his father. He was never a scholar, but liked to read songs and poetry, and rigged up a rack at the side of his loom to hold a book and a note pad.

He went to England in 1799, but returned to Paisley to take over his father's business upon the latter's death in 1802. He suffered an early unhappy love affair with a Paisley girl named Janet Tennant, and never married.

He had written some unremarkable poetry when he was a boy, but it was when he began to set new lyrics to old, forgotten melodies that he found his true métier. A neighbor musician, Robert Archibald Smith, wrote original tunes for some of his songs, and when a volume of them was published in 1807 they were immediately widely popular. Tannahill has recorded that "perhaps the highest pleasure ever I derived from these things has been hearing, as I walked down the pavement at night, a girl within doors rattling away at some one of them."

Some of the songs immortalized his unfortunate lost love, notably "Jessie, the Flower o' Dunblane" and a sequel, "The Farweel." Others dealt with imaginary lovers, or with the love of nature. Among the better known are "Bonnie Wood o' Craigie-

lee," "Sleepin' Maggie," and "The Lass o' Arranteenie." One of the greatest compliments paid the young balladist was a visit from the ancient bard James Hogg, the Ettrick Shepherd.

Tannahill was only thirty-six when a growing melancholia, which led him to believe he was being cheated and persecuted, drove him to destroy all his manuscripts and to drown himself in a culvert near Paisley. He remains the town's most celebrated son, and his popularity in Scotland is not far beneath that of Burns.

PRINCIPAL WORKS: Poems and Songs, 1807.

ABOUT: Chambers, R. Biographical Dictionary of Eminent Scotsmen; McLaren, W. Life of Tannahill; Ramsey, P. A. Biographical prefix, The Works of Robert Tannahill, 1851 ed.

TATE, NAHUM (1652-August 12, 1715), dramatist, poet, poet laureate, was born in Dublin, the son of Faithful Teate (Nahum Tate himself spelled his name this way until he went to London), an English clergyman. He entered Trinity College, Dublin, in 1668 and secured his B.A. degree in 1672. He then went to London to seek his fortune, primarily as a dramatist. Though he wrote one or two original plays, most of his work for the stage was as an editor, adaptor, or translator, and he worked frequently in collaboration in both verse and drama. He was an advocate of stage reform, and even in substantial agreement with Jeremy Collier.

Tate's "specialty" was "revision" of the Elizabethan dramatists, principally of Shakespeare. His remarkable version of *King Lear* omitted the part of the fool, and had Cordelia survive to marry Edgar! Though Addison objected hotly, Dr. Johnson was pleased, the original version having too much harrowed his feelings. Tate gave the same treatment to *Coriolanus, Richard II,* the Jonson, Chapman, Marston *Eastward Ho,* and Webster's *White Divel.* His own plays were largely ranting melodrama.

Dryden commissioned Tate to write the second part of *Absalom and Achitophel,* though he himself wrote the portraits of Settle and Shadwell and gave a finishing polish to the whole poem. Tate was a clever enough imitator or what might be called a permitted plagiarizer of Dryden's style, but as a poet in his own right he earned the place he was given in Pope's *Dunciad.* His best poem is "Panacea, a Poem on Tea" (1700), and that is none too good.

In his earlier years he prospered, under the patronage of Lord Dorset. Though he was a Tory, and the Tories were out of office, he was appointed poet laureate in 1692, succeeding Shadwell, and through Dorset's influence he also became historiographer royal in 1702. In 1715 he lost the latter office, which was by far the more lucrative, on the accession of George I and the triumph of the Whigs. Though he was honest, he fell into debt, and though Lord Dorset frequently protected him from arrest, he was in hiding from his creditors, in Southwark, when he died the following August.

Tate is known also as co-author with Nicholas Brady of the *New Version of the Psalms*, which was appointed to be read in churches. Its general level is very low, and it is unbearably dull, but the less intolerable portions in it are believed to be Tate's.

Tate's was not an engaging personality; he was taciturn, grumpy, and given to heavy drinking. There has been some question whether he was the worst or only nearly the worst of the poets laureate. On the whole, it may be said that he was a poetaster rather than a poet.

PRINCIPAL WORKS: *Plays*: Brutus of Alba, 1678; The Loyal General, 1680; The History of King Lear, 1681; The Sicilian Usurper (Richard II) 1681; The Ingratitude of a Commonwealth (Coriolanus) 1682; A Duke and No Duke, 1685; Cuckold's Haven, or an Alderman No Conjurer (Eastward Ho) 1685; The Island Princess (from Beaumont and Fletcher) 1687; Injur'd Love, or the Cruel Husband (The White Divel) 1707. *Poems*: Poems, 1677; 2d Part of Absalom and Achitophel (with J. Dryden) 1682; A New Version of the Psalms in Metre (with N. Brady) 1696 (Supplement, 1700).

ABOUT: Garnett, R. The Age of Dryden; Saintsbury, G. Dryden.

TATHAM, JOHN (fl. 1632-1664), dramatist and poet, was first known by a play he wrote in his youth, a pastoral comedy entitled *Love Crowns the End*. Ten years later another play appeared, *The Distracted State*, in which he first began the virulent attack on the Scottish people which he expressed even more violently in a play in an unidentified dialect called *The Scots' Figgaries*, written in 1592. This hiatus of ten years might mean that he had seen military service in Scotland, in the course of which he had for some reason conceived a particular dislike of its

people, although he was prejudiced against any foreigners.

He was one of the inner coterie of poets and playwrights of London, and in 1657 was appointed "city poet." This involved the annual creation of the Lord Mayor's great pageant, which was sponsored each year by a different guild (i.e., the grocers, the haberdashers, the clothmakers, etc.) and which each year rose to new heights of elaborate splendor. Tatham wrote twelve of these, the last one so extravagant in production that, with the city devastated by plague and fire, the expensive pageants were discontinued for seven years.

In 1660 he wrote the play which is most often associated with his name, a sensational and journalistic satire titled *The Rump, or The Mirror of the Late Times*. It reflects the extremely critical temper of the times toward public figures, and impudently caricatures recognizable political leaders in its cast of street pedlars. A tasteless lampoon of the members of the rump parliament was printed with the second edition of the play, and although it was anonymous it was almost certainly written by Tatham. Nothing is known of his activities after 1665.

PRINCIPAL WORKS: Love Crowns the End, 1632; Fancies Theater, 1640; The Distracted State, 1641; The Scots' Figgaries, 1652; The Rump, 1660; Ostella (no date).

ABOUT: Baker, D. E. Biographia Dramatica; Fairholt, F. W. Lord Mayor's Pageants; Fleay, F. G. Biographical Chronicle of the Stage.

TATWIN, TATUINI, or **TADWINUS** (d. 734), Archbishop of Canterbury and author of poems and Latin enigmas, was a native of Mercia, the ancient Anglian kingdom in what is now central England. Æthelbald, the Mercian king, was a cousin of the founder of the monastery of Briudun or Bredon in Worcestershire, of which Tatwin was head. Possibly this royal connection was a factor in his being named Archbishop of Canterbury, although he also was a man of excellent character, high intelligence, and learning. He was consecrated by four English bishops in 731; a legend that he broke precedent by going to Rome to receive the sign of office from the Pope is probably not true.

There are contemporary and later references to poems written by Tatwin which have not survived. Aldhelm, Bishop of Sherborne, the first important English writer in Latin, who died in 709, had written witty acrostics and puzzles in metric lines which were imitated by many followers. On this model, Tatwin wrote forty ingenious enigmas in Latin hexameter, the first and last letters of the first line of each forming a double acrostic. After his death, his friend Albinus, abbot of St. Augustine's, Canterbury, added sixty more to match Aldhelm's original group of a hundred enigmas.

Tatwin died in 734, and was buried in St. Augustine's.

ABOUT: Hook, W. F. Archbishops of Canterbury.

TAYLOR, JEREMY (1613-August 13, 1667), Bishop of Down and Connor, administrator of Dromore Diocese, religious writer, was born at Cambridge, son of a barber named Nathaniel Taylor and his wife Mary. His education began early, first under his father and then under Thomas Lovering, whom he followed to the Perse School in 1619. He entered Gonville and Caius College as a sizar or "poor scholar" in 1626, when his parents alleged that he was in his fifteenth year and had been at school about ten years; he matriculated the following year. He won first a scholarship and then a fellowship on the Perse Foundation, graduated B.A. in 1631 and M.A. in 1634. Always precocious, he took holy orders before he was twenty-one.

JEREMY TAYLOR

In 1634 he delivered some sermons at St. Paul's Cathedral, London, in place of his college roommate; they attracted the attention of many people, including Archbishop Laud, who thought him still too young for Church preferment, but had him made a fellow of All Souls' College, Oxford. Taylor remained there until his appointment as rector of Uppingham, Rutlandshire, in 1638. That year also saw his first publication, *A Sermon . . . upon the Anniversary of the Gunpowder-Treason,* which gave him the opportunity to clear himself of all suspicion of Roman Catholicism. He was, however, always extremely "high church," like his benefactor Laud. The latter's execution and the outbreak of the civil war soon followed. Taylor, by now chaplain to Charles I, naturally took the king's side and in 1642 was with him at Oxford, where he was made a Doctor of Divinity by royal command in honor of his treatise on episcopacy.

Taylor was turned out of his parish by the Puritans in 1644, went to Wales, and was captured by the parliamentary forces after a skirmish at Cardigan Castle; presumably he was acting as a chaplain to the Royalist forces at the time. He was soon released and settled in Wales with his wife, Phoebe Langsdale, whom he had married in 1639. He acted as chaplain to the Earl of Carbery at Golden Grove and taught school in the neighborhood. All his finest writing belongs to this period of retirement. He was very conscious, however, of his duty to his fellow Anglicans, now being persecuted all over the country. He visited Charles I in 1647, and from 1653 on was often in London, holding services and preaching. This activity led to two periods of imprisonment in 1655. His first wife had died in 1651 and he now took refuge on the estate of his second wife, Joanna Bridges.

In 1657 he was back in London at his post; the following year with Cromwell's permission, he went to Ireland at the request of Viscount Conway. Here he lived at Portmore, near Lisburn, County Antrim, preaching and ministering to the local Episcopalians, including the Conway family. The Presbyterians objected strongly and in 1659 he had to appear before the Puritan ecclesiastical commissioners in Dublin because of his Anglican practices. However, the next year the Restoration of Charles II took place.

Taylor went to London to greet the new king and was promptly made an Irish bishop and vice chancellor of Dublin University.

Unfortunately, as Bishop of Down and Connor, Taylor had to go back to County Antrim and do battle with the Presbyterians once more. The author of *The Liberty of Prophesying* felt himself obliged to oust thirty-six Presbyterian clergymen who refused to accept the authority of a bishop, while at the same time wishing to retain their Church of Ireland parishes and parish churches. Taylor finally got his diocese in working order again, but he was unhappy there and longed for an English bishopric. However, his old friend Sheldon, now Archbishop of Canterbury, mistrusted his volatile temperament, his shakiness on the doctrine of original sin, and the fact that, while Charles I had thought him too tolerant, Charles II found him quite the reverse. Taylor had to stay in Ireland for the rest of his life—a short time, as it turned out. He caught a fever August 3, 1667, as the result of visiting the sick, and was dead in ten days. All Taylor's four sons predeceased him, to his great sorrow; he was survived by three daughters and his second wife, who married again. He is buried in Dromore Cathedral, which he restored.

It is hard to reconcile the differing accounts of Taylor's personality and appearance; his portrait in later years shows him as an erect seated figure, tallish, with an ascetic face that is far from handsome. He seems to have been greatly beloved, but unfitted for public life—too little of a courtier, too given to rash decisions. We can imagine him as happiest leading the life of a scholar and a man of letters; in his youth he was perhaps overstudious; if his writings are any guide, the years at Golden Grove were the golden period of his life.

A Discourse . . . of Friendship is Taylor's only entirely secular work; the other writings, however, are hardly typical works of theology. Taylor is never content to appeal to the intellect alone; he must touch the heart as well—hence his sermons constitute some of his very best work. Indeed, it would not be far fetched to regard most of his treatises as expanded sermons—warm exhortations rather than coldly logical demonstrations. Always there is the oratorical cadence, the completely visualized metaphor.

Gray's biographer, William Mason, called him "the Shakespeare of English prose."

Indeed, though Taylor's immense classical and patristic learning is not in doubt, his theological position has often been regarded as inconsistent or even indefinable. The views on original sin expressed in *Unum Necessarium* were disapproved of by many besides Sheldon. However, most of the inconsistencies in Taylor's reasoning seem to be inherent in Anglicanism itself; if not the most intellectual divine of the English church, he may surely be regarded as, next to Donne, the most eloquent. *Holy Living* and *Holy Dying*, particularly the latter, are now his best known works. *The Liberty of Prophesying* is a narrower plea for religious toleration than its title suggests.

PRINCIPAL WORKS: A Sermon . . . upon the Anniversary of the Gunpowder-Treason, 1638; Of the Sacred Order and Offices of Episcopacy, 1642; Theologia Eklektike, A Discourse of the Liberty of Prophesying, 1647; The Great Exemplar of Sanctity and Holy Life, 1649; A Funeral Sermon, 1650; The Rule and Exercises of Holy Living, 1650; The Rule and Exercises of Holy Dying, 1651; Eniautos, A Course of Sermons for All the Sundays of the Year, 1653; The Golden Grove, 1655; Unum Necessarium, 1655; A Discourse of the Nature, Offices and Measures of Friendship, 1657; The Worthy Communicant, 1660; Ductor Dubitantium, 1660; A Dissuasive from Popery, 1664.

ABOUT: Gosse, E. Jeremy Taylor; Heber, R. and C. P. Eden. Life, prefixed to The Whole Works (10 vols. 1847-54); Nicolson, M. H. New Material on Jeremy Taylor (Philological Quarterly, 1929).

TAYLOR, JOHN (August 24, 1580-December 1653), writer of verse and prose, was born in Gloucester of a poor family. He was sent to the Gloucester Grammar School, but "flunked out" in Latin accidence so was taken away and apprenticed to a waterman on the Thames. Soon he was pressed into the navy, and served under the Earl of Essex, making sixteen voyages before he was invalided out with a lame leg. He went back to ferrying (hence his self-chosen appellation of "the water-poet"), and for fourteen years collected the perquisite of wine for the Tower, finally being discharged for refusing to buy from certain ships. Meanwhile he was making a reputation for himself as a writer of doggerel verse and prose satire. Witty, good-natured, and quick to defend his fellow ferrymen, he was also a master of self-advertisement. His custom was to circulate leaflets ("Taylor's bills") for subscriptions,

JOHN TAYLOR

or to give his work away and then collect from the recipients. He kept himself in the public eye by various voyages and foot journeys on wagers—once, for example, he and some companions rowed up the river in a boat made of brown paper, with stockfish for oars, and nearly drowned. Eventually he was commissioned to write and arrange some of the official Thames pageants.

In 1625 he fled to Oxford from the plague, and was permitted to live and study at Oriel College. A staunch Royalist, he went to Oxford again at the beginning of the civil war, in 1642, kept a public house there and was made a yeoman of the guard by Charles I. When Oxford surrendered, in 1645, he returned to London and again opened a tavern. His open opposition to the Puritans caused his arrest in 1649, but he was released and allowed to return to his public house. He was married, but had no children; after his death in London his widow carried on the business until she too died, in 1658.

Taylor's wit was rough and coarse, and much of his repartee is unintelligible now because of his use of current slang. He published in all some hundred and fifty separate works, sixty-eight of which he himself collected in 1630 as *All the Workes of John Taylor the Water-poet*. He carried on a long feud with Thomas Coryat, and Coryat succeeded in having one of his books burned.

Ben Jonson, whom he also travestied, was more good natured; he went so far as to say that he did not "see ever any verses in English equal to the Sculler's." Dekker and Breton were also among the amused patrons of the "literary bargee." As a matter of fact, Taylor was merely a voluminous scribbler with a facile pen, but his illimitable self-confidence and his irrepressible impudence and ingenuity made people laugh and gave him contemporary fame. He had the city man's contempt for the provincial, and the better educated man's contempt for the illiterate, and out of these and of his experiences as a traveler he made his whimsical comic broadsides and booklets.

PRINCIPAL WORKS: The Sculler (verse) 1612; Laugh and Be Fat, 1613; Fair and fowle weather (verse) 1615; Taylor's Urania (verse) 1616; The Booke of Martyrs (verse) 1617; The Pennyles Pilgrimage (verse and prose) 1618; A Kicksey-Wimsey, 1619; The Praise of Hemp-seed, 1620; Taylor's Farewell to the Tower Bottles, 1622; A Memorial of all the English Monarches (verse) 1622; The World Runnes on Wheeles, 1623; The Fearfull Sommer, 1625; John Taylor's Wit and Mirth, 1629; All the Workes of John Taylor the Water-poet, 1630; A Bawd, a Vertuous Bawd, a Modest Bawd (verse and prose) 1630; The Suddain Turne of ffortunes wheele (verse) 1631; The Old, Old, Very Old Man (verse) 1635; John Taylor the Water-Poet's Travels through London to visit all the Taverns, 1636; Drinke and Welcome (verse and prose) 1637; Taylor's Feaste, 1638; I. [sic] Taylor's Last Voyage, 1641; Englands Comfort and Londons Ioy (verse) 1641; Rebells Anathematized and Anatomized (verse) 1645; The World Turned Upside Down, 1647; Ranters of Both Sexes, 1651; The Certain Travailes of an Uncertain Journey, 1653; Works (C. Hindley, ed.) 1872.

ABOUT: Hindley, C. Introduction, Works; Wood, A. à, Athenae Oxonienses.

TAYLOR, JOHN (August 16, 1703-1772), oculist, author of treatises on the eye and an autobiography, was born in Norwich, the son of John Taylor, a surgeon and apothecary. He was apprenticed to an apothecary in London in 1722, then studied surgery at St. Thomas' Hospital, specializing in diseases of the eye. He practiced in Norwich as a general surgeon and oculist until 1727, when he began an itinerant practice. By 1733 he had traveled and treated patients all over the British Isles. In that year he received his M.D. from Basle, and the next year from Liège and Cologne, after which he traveled in France and Holland, returning to England in 1735. He was appointed oculist to George II, and Gibbon was among his patients, but he continued his travels, with

London as his headquarters. He visited and practiced in nearly every court in Europe. Known as "Chevalier" Taylor, he was a skillful surgeon, but he had the characteristics of a charlatan, advertising himself extravagantly and delivering before each treatment a bombastic oration—"in the true Ciceronian, prodigiously difficult and never attempted in our language before." (Every sentence began with a genitive and ended with a verb!) Of his autobiography Dr. Johnson remarked that it was "an instance of how far impudence will carry ignorance." In 1767 he left England permanently, and died in a convent in Prague. Curiously for an oculist, he was blind for several years before his death.

Taylor married Ann King, and had one son, who allowed his name to be used as author of a scurrilous life of his own father. In Taylor's day many satires were written about him, but he himself almost justified them in his frank autobiography. His optical treatises were quite serious and conventional.

PRINCIPAL WORKS: An Account of the Mechanism of the Eye, 1727; Treatise on the Chrystalline Humour of the Human Eye, 1736; An Impartial Enquiry into the Seat of the Immediate Organ of Sight, 1743; The History of the Travels and Adventures of the Chevalier John Taylor, Ophthalmiater, 1761.

ABOUT: Boswell, J. Life of Johnson; Nichols, J. Literary Anecdotes; Smith, J. C. British Mezzotinto Portraits; Taylor, J. History of Travels and Adventures; Walpole, H. Letters.

TEMPLE, Sir WILLIAM

(April 25, 1628-January 27, 1699), diplomat, essayist, memoirist, was born at Blackfriars, London, the eldest son of Sir John Temple, Master of the Rolls in Ireland, and his wife Mary Hammond. William's mother died in 1638 and his father never remarried. The boy received his early education first at Penshurst from his uncle, Dr. Henry Hammond, then at the grammar school in Bishop's Stortford. He left school at fifteen, and did not go to Emmanuel College, Cambridge, until 1644. There he spent two years, played much court tennis and took no degree.

In 1648 he set out for France to complete his education, met Dorothy Osborne for the first time on the way, traveled to France with her and her brother, and stayed with them at St. Malo for some time. Finally his father ordered him on to Paris; William obeyed, but he had fallen deeply in love with

Sir P. Lely

SIR WILLIAM TEMPLE

Dorothy and, though seeing each other infrequently, they carried on a correspondence for the next seven years.

Temple spent two years in France, returned to England for a brief stay, then went to Holland, Germany, and the Spanish Netherlands for a further two years; he learned Spanish, Dutch and a certain amount of German. Two years in London followed; he finally succeeded in overcoming the opposition of both families and married Dorothy on Christmas Day, 1654. Just before the marriage she contracted smallpox, which destroyed her beauty but not his feeling for her. The young couple spent the year 1655 in England; after their eldest son John was born (he committed suicide in 1689 when Secretary for War) they moved to Ireland, where they lived in retirement until the Restoration of Charles II in 1660; Temple then began to think of a political career.

He was a member of the Irish Parliament 1661-63; in 1663 he moved his family to Sheen, near London, and lived there until 1680, when he bought his famous house, Moor Park, near Farnham, Surrey. His first diplomatic post was a secret mission to the Bishop of Munster in 1665, to arrange for that prelate to take England's side in the war against the Dutch. The Bishop collected some installments of a subsidy, but concluded a separate peace with the Dutch in 1666, virtually without firing a shot.

513

In spite of this unlucky start, Temple was made English ambassador in Brussels, 1665, and a baronet, 1666. In 1668 he negotiated with admirable promptness the Triple Alliance, whereby England, Sweden, and Holland united to protect the Spanish Netherlands against Louis XIV of France. This won him the appointment of ambassador to Holland, but he was recalled in 1670; by 1672 the English were again at war with the Dutch, thanks to the bribes which Charles II received from Louis XIV. Temple was called upon once more when it was time to make a treaty with Holland in 1674.

He helped to bring about the marriage of William of Orange and Princess Mary in 1677 and took part in negotiating the Treaty of Nimeguen, 1679. From 1679 to 1681 he was a privy councillor, but he had been brought in merely to bolster an unpopular government and never possessed the king's confidence. He entered upon his final period of retirement in 1681; eight years later, when his old friend William of Orange became King of England and offered him the secretaryship of state, as Charles II had done on more than one occasion, he refused it.

He spent his retirement in gardening and writing his essays and memoirs; from 1689 until his death, except for brief intervals, he employed Jonathan Swift as his amanuensis. Swift met Stella at Moor Park.

Temple's sister, Lady Giffard, who lived with him most of her life, describes him as a model husband, father and friend, very temperate in his habits, very cultured and amiable, but given to moody fits and impatient of pain during his attacks of gout. Swift was unduly sensitive to Temple's behavior in these moody fits, but genuinely regretted his death. Temple left Swift £100 and made him his literary executor.

Temple was tall and handsome, with curly dark brown hair and gray eyes. He was a man of great gifts and great integrity, who managed to live graciously on a surprisingly small income, mainly derived from the inherited post of Master of the Rolls in Ireland. His views on foreign policy were directly opposite to those of Charles II and he lacked ambition, otherwise he might have been the greatest politician of his day. His writings are not particularly interesting, but

the excellent plain style in which they were written served as a model for Swift.

PRINCIPAL WORKS: Poems, 1670; An Essay Upon the Advancement of Trade in Ireland, 1673; Observations upon the United Provinces of the Netherlands, 1673; Miscellanea, Part I, 1680 (Part II, 1690; Part III, 1701); Memoirs, 1692; Letters (J. Swift, ed.) 1700; Memoirs, Part III, 1709; The Early Essays and Romances of Sir William Temple (G. C. Moore Smith. ed.) 1931.

ABOUT: Giffard, M. The Life and The Character *in* The Early Essays and Romances (*see above*); Macaulay, T. B. Essays; Osborne, D. The Letters; Woodbridge, H. E. Sir William Temple.

THEOBALD, LEWIS (March 1688-September 18, 1744), author of poems, essays, dramatic works, Shakespearean editor, was born in Sittingbourne, Kent, the son of Peter Theobald, a solicitor. Though he never went to school and secured his entire education from the local rector, he was a good classicist. He was left an orphan in early childhood, without any money, and it was Lord Sondes who supported him and saw to his receiving such education as he had. He was trained for the law and became a solicitor like his father, but he soon deserted the law for literature. Going to London, he spent the remainder of his life as a literary hack, though of rather a high class, for he translated, to order, Aeschylus, Sophocles, Aristophanes, Plato's *Phaedo*, and the *Odyssey* into racy colloquial prose.

Theobald tried his hand at almost every variety of writing. (For the dedication of his adaptation of Shakespeare's *Richard II* Lord Orrery gave Theobald a £100 note in a snuff-box "worth £20.") His poetry is worthless, and his plays are not much better. One of them, *The Perfidious Brother*, got him into trouble, for it had been written by Henry Meystayer and then was claimed by Theobald as his own; he said he had revised it so much that it had actually become his. Another, *The Double Falsehood*, had a strange career; Theobald claimed to have discovered it and ascribed it to Shakespeare, later critics thought it was by Shirley or Massinger, and the fact seems to be that it was almost entirely Theobald's own.

But these misadventures do not give a real picture of Theobald's standing. He was well enough thought of to be chosen to edit Wycherley's plays after his death; and he is one of the very best of Shakespearean textual critics. Unfortunately, he began his career in this field by harsh though justified criticism of Pope's edition of Shakespeare. In retaliation, "the wasp of Twickenham" pilloried Theobald as "hero" of the first version of *The Dunciad* (1728); in 1741 Colley Cibber was "promoted" to this position. Then Pope brought out a new edition, disingenuously including many of Theobald's corrections, and Theobald lost his temper; in his own edition, in 1734, he was betrayed into unmeasured abuse of Pope and what Dr. Johnson called "contemptible ostentation." The result was that for years Theobald was thought of as the dull pedant described by Pope, whereas the truth is that he was one of the sanest, most perspicacious, scholarly, and painstaking of the textual critics of Shakespeare. J. Churton Collins called him "the Porson of Shakespearean criticism."

In 1730 Theobald was almost appointed poet laureate, but Cibber snatched the honor from him at the last minute. He was working on an edition of Beaumont and Fletcher when he died, leaving no fortune but a good Elizabethan library. He was married and had one son. His name was pronounced "Tibbald."

PRINCIPAL WORKS: Life of Cato, 1713; The Persian Princess (play) 1715; The Perfidious Brother (play) 1715; The Loves of Antiochus and Stratonice (prose romance, from Corneille) 1717; Pan and Syrinx (opera) 1717; The Lady's Triumph (opera) 1718; Decius and Paulina (masque) 1718; Memoir of Sir Walter Raleigh, 1719; Harlequin a Sorcerer (pantomime) 1725; Shakespeare Restored, 1726; Apollo and Diana (opera) 1726; The Double Falsehood (play) 1728; The Plays of Shakespeare (ed.) (7 vols.) 1734; Merlin (pantomime) 1734; Orpheus and Eurydice (opera) 1740; The Happy Captive (opera) 1744.

ABOUT: Cibber, T. Lives of the English Dramatic Poets; Collins, J. C. Essays and Studies; Jones, R. F. Lewis Theobald: His Contribution to English Scholarship. Nichols, J. Illustrations of Literature.

THOMAS, THE RHYMER. See ERCELDOUNE, THOMAS

THOMSON, JAMES (September, 1700-August 27, 1748), poet, dramatist was born in Ednam, Roxburghshire, Scotland, the son of Thomas Thomson, a Presbyterian minister, and Beatrix Trotter. In his infancy the family moved to Southdean, near Jedburgh. He went to school in Jedburgh, and then entered Edinburgh University in 1715 to study divinity. His first verse appeared in the *Edinburgh Miscellany* in 1720. He seems

to have obtained an M.A. degree, and in 1725 he went to London, his original intention being to practice preaching with a view to being licensed as a minister. Soon, however, he abandoned divinity for literature, earning his living as tutor in several noble families. Thomson's habit of dedicating all his plays and his poems in successive parts to various men of note and wealth earned him some patrons, and brought him particularly to the attention of the Prince of Wales (later George II). His plays were all tendentious, aimed at what would now be called propaganda for the Tories and against the Whigs, in consequence of which *Edward and Eleonora* was suppressed by the censor. Thomson in retaliation wrote a new preface to Milton's *Areopagitica* (on freedom of the press).

In 1730 Thomson had become tutor to the son of Sir Charles Talbot, solicitor general and later lord chancellor. He was abroad in France and Italy with his pupil in 1730-31, then returned to England. The boy died in 1733. Talbot, however, had become interested in the poetic tutor, and got him the sinecure post of secretary of briefs in chancery, which he held until Talbot died in 1737. It is said that the position was held open as long as possible, in the hope that Thomson would reapply for it, but that a mixture of pride and indolence kept him from doing so until too late.

In 1736 he had retired to a little house in Richmond, where he lived with a man cousin; Thomson was never married. He was near Pope at Twickenham, and managed to remain the friend of that touchy poet and to benefit by his criticism. Now, however, he was out of employment and in real need. He fell into debt—he could never learn to live without ease and luxury—and was rescued only when Lord Lyttleton (later his indiscreet and rather presumptuous posthumous editor) managed to have him appointed to another sinecure, as surveyor general of the Leeward Islands. It was too late, however; Thomson caught a chill on a journey, came down with pneumonia, and died in Richmond just before his forty-eighth birthday.

It is doubtful if Thomson himself realized his unique place in English literature, as the first poet to treat landscape objectively (without the subjective emotionalism of the Romantics), and as such to be the precursor

J. Patoun. 1746

JAMES THOMSON

the poet of the aspiring middle class of the eighteenth century—that he has survived.

PRINCIPAL WORKS: *Poetry*: The Seasons (in parts and with successive revisions) 1726-44; A Poem Sacred to the Memory of Sir Isaac Newton, 1727; Britannia, 1729; A Poem to the Memory of Mr. Congreve, 1729; Liberty: Antient and Modern Italy, Greece, Rome, 1735; Britain, The Prospect, 1736, complete, 1736; A Poem to the Memory of... Lord Talbot, 1737; The Castle of Indolence, 1748; Poetical Works, 1773 (G. Gilfillan, ed. 1853, W. M. Rossetti, ed. 1873) *Plays:* The Tragedy of Sophonisba, 1730; Agamemnon, 1738; Edward and Eleonora, 1739; Alfred, A Masque, 1740; Tancred and Sigismonda, 1745; Coriolanus, 1749; Alfred the Great, a Drama for Music, 1753. *Miscellaneous*: Preface to Milton's Areopagitica, 1738; Works, 1736; Complete Works (G. Lyttleton, ed.) 1750-52.

ABOUT: Bayne, W. James Thomson; Cibber, T. Lives of the English Dramatic Poets; Gilfillan, G. Life *in* Poetical Works, 1853 ed.; Johnson, S. Lives of the English Poets; Macaulay, G. C. James Thomson; Morel, L. James Thomson, Sa Vie et Ses Oeuvres; Murdoch, P. Life of James Thomson; Schmeding, G. Jakob Thomson, ein Vergessener Dichter des 18en Jahrhunderts.

THRALE, Mrs. HESTER LYNCH. See PIOZZI, Mrs. HESTER LYNCH THRALE

TICKELL, THOMAS (1686-April 23, 1740), poet, was born at Bridekirk in Cumberland. His father and grandfather were both clergymen, but when he was elected a fellow of Queen's College, Oxford, in 1710, after getting his B.A. and M.A. he did not take orders. He held his fellowship by special dispensation of the king until his marriage.

All that is significant in his life stems from his friendship with Joseph Addison. His earliest poem, *Oxford*, written in 1706, contains a passage in praise of Addison, and his second publication, a panegyric entitled *To Mr. Addison, on His Opera of Rosamond*, helped obtain for him a temporary professorship of poetry at Queen's.

Addison replied by praising Tickell's poem *On the Prospect of Peace*, and by conferring on Tickell those evidences of preferment which Steele might have expected to receive after their long association. Tickell accompanied Addison to Ireland when he was appointed secretary to the lord lieutenant, became an undersecretary when Addison was secretary of state, and was finally chosen by his patron to be his literary executor.

The enmity between Addison and Pope was generated by an incident involving

of Collins, Cowper, and Gray. His own aim was to produce grandiose poems on lofty abstract themes; his *Liberty* was a complete failure, and his *Seasons* an outstanding success. In these poems, one to each season, natural description is not merely incidental to man (who indeed does not appear), but is the poet's chief concern. Thomson's observation was accurate, and his imagination, if limited, was strong; he was a poetic phrasemaker, and many of his happy phrases have passed into proverbial speech.

A self-indulgent, fat man, who never rose before noon and loved to eat and drink (*The Castle of Indolence*—an imitation of Spenser—is more or less a confession), Thomson nevertheless had great industry and spurts of energy—he was, for example, a notable walker. He has been accused (by the unreliable Savage) of lechery as well as laziness, but it is known that for many years he loved faithfully Elizabeth Young, who married another. He was a good humored, likable man, of whom his friends—particularly the actor James Quin, the most faithful and devoted of them—were warmly fond.

His plays are rhetorical and conventional, but have the distinction that they are taken from the original Greek, not sifted through French versions. He was a belligerent patriot, and there seems no doubt he wrote the words of "Rule, Britannia." But it is as the poet of the domestic landscape—peculiarly

Tickell. Tickell and Pope began translations of *The Iliad* at about the same time. Tickell, learning of Pope's project, completed only the first book, which he gave to Addison to read and criticize. When Pope came to Addison with the manuscript of his translation, Addison refused to read the first book, for fear of being accused of double dealing, but read and praised the second book. Upon simultaneous publication of the two translations, Addison and his circle praised Tickell's version highly, embittering Pope and leading to a long and acrimonious feud.

Tickell was a pleasant, inoffensive man, devoted to his wife and four children, fond of temperate but hospitable entertaining. Most of his writings were mediocre, many of them imitations of Addison, although it is probable that had he pursued an original bent he would have been a better versifier than his patron. The one work of real beauty, deep feeling and notable poetic expression is the elegy he wrote upon Addison's death, of which Macaulay said: "It would do honor to the greatest name in our literature."

PRINCIPAL WORKS: Oxford, 1706; To Mr. Addison, on His Opera of Rosamond, 1710; On The Prospect of Peace, 1712; An Epistle from a Lady in England to a Gentleman in Avignon, 1717; Elegy, 1719.

ABOUT: Cibber, T. Lives of the Poets; Johnson, S. Lives of the Poets; Ward, T. H. The English Poets.

TILLOTSON, JOHN (October 10, 1630-November 18, 1694), Archbishop of Canterbury, author of sermons and religious writings, was born in Halifax. His father was a well-to-do cloth worker; his mother was in a mental institution for many years. He graduated from Clare Hall, Cambridge, and for ten years was a fellow of the college. A noncomformist, he forfeited his fellowship, and later resigned from the rectory of Keddington in Suffolk because of the protests of his Puritan parishoners.

He carefully prepared himself for a career as a preacher, studying ecclesiastical history and writings, and listening to other preachers—at Cambridge he had heard four sermons each Sunday and one on Wednesday. His style was not rousing, but it was easy and pleasant, with a modern, liberal tone that appealed to the intellectuals and the bourgeoisie of the city. William Warburton

characterized both the man and his sermons as being "simple, elegant, candid, clear and rational." He was often invited to preach in London; in 1664 he was appointed Tuesday lecturer at St. Lawrence Jewry, where his good friend John Wilkins was rector. His popularity grew rapidly. In 1666, when he received his D.D. degree, he became a royal chaplain, dean of Canterbury, and was on the commission for revision of the prayer book.

He was reluctant to accept the archbishopric when it was offered to him in 1691. He knew and valued the strength of his influence on the middle class of London, and he knew, too, that "the people naturally love a man that will take great pains and little preferment." Finally convinced, he filled the office capably but uneventfully for three years, until his death.

Although he was an exceedingly generous, pleasant, good humored and kindly man, Tillotson's latitudinarian tendencies exposed him to the most outrageous accusations of various unlikely iniquities. He was married to John Wilkens' step-daughter, a niece of Oliver Cromwell, and had two children who predeceased him. He died a poor man, but his sermons and writings were later bought by publishers at an unusually high price, as a mark of respect. His written words, for all their simple clarity and rationality, are without literary charm and distinction, although Dryden declared that he "learned to write" by reading Tillotson.

PRINCIPAL WORKS: Sermons (14 vols.) (R. Baker, ed.) 1695-1704; The Works (3 vols.) (T. Birch, ed.) 1752; Tillotson's Sermons (G. W. Weldon, ed.) 1886; The Golden Book of Tillotson (J. Moffat, ed.) 1926.

ABOUT: Birch, T. Life of John Tillotson (included in Works); Hunt, J. Religious Thought in England; Smith, J. C. Mezzotinto Portraits; Stoughton, J. History of Religion in England.

TINDAL, MATTHEW (1657-August 16, 1733), deist, author of works on religion, was born in Devonshire (baptismal date May 12, 1657) and attended a county school there. He studied for the law at Lincoln College and Exeter College, Oxford, obtaining his B.A. in 1667, B.C.L. in 1679, and D.C.L. in 1685. He became an advocate in 1685, receiving a royal pension for services rendered to the crown in international disputes.

He had been elected to a law fellowship at All Souls in 1678. When he renounced his conversion to the Catholic church ten years later, he was accused by some of doing so in an effort to obtain the wardenship of All Souls. He soon went even farther, however, and in 1706 published *Rights of the Christian Church*, an attack on certain policies of the Church of England. The book caused a national furor, and over twenty refutations were published.

Tindal continued his attacks in pamphlets, going further and further toward rationalism. However, he called himself a "Christian deist," and somehow retained his fellowship at All Souls in the face of the most outrageous charges by his enemies, who, among other things, accused him of "gluttony, debauchery, and immorality."

When he was seventy, he published one of the most important works on deism, *Christianity as Old as the Creation; or, the Gospel a Republication of the Religion of Nature*. His stated aim was to show that "natural religion and external revelation, like two tallies, exactly answer one another without any other difference between them but as to the manner of their being delivered." The style of the book is diffuse, confused, and repetitious, but it is an effective statement of the essential deist doctrine. Again the work had wide circulation and influence, and more than thirty replies were published. A manuscript copy of a second volume of this work fell, after Tindal's death, into the hands of Bishop Gibson of London, who destroyed it.

Tindal died at his lodging in Coldbath Fields, London, when he was seventy-three, and was buried at Clerkenwall Church.

PRINCIPAL WORKS: Essay of Obedience to the Supreme Powers, 1694; Liberty of the Press, 1698; Rights of the Christian Church, 1706; Christianity as Old as the Creation, 1730.

ABOUT: Burrows, M. Worthies of All-Souls; Hearne, T. Collections of Curious Discourses; Wood, A. à, Athenae Oxonienses.

TOLAND, JOHN (November 30, 1670-March 11, 1722), Irish deist and pamphleteer, was born at Inishowen, near Londonderry. He may have been the illegitimate son of a priest. He was raised as a Catholic, became a Protestant at sixteen, and was sent to Glasgow College by a group of "eminent dissenters." He received his M.A. at the University of Edinburgh in 1690, studied in Leyden, and spent two years at Oxford.

If he had ever had enough financial security to pursue farther the scholarship for which he had real capacity and inclination, he might have been a great figure in liberalizing religious thought and doctrine. His first book, *Christianity Not Mysterious*, written in 1696, while it expressed the doubts and ideas of a freethinker and a rational theologian rather than of a deist, was the first and one of the most important weapons in the deist controversy of the following century.

From this time on, Toland's life was too often a matter of keeping out of debt by doing hack writing, and keeping out of trouble by running or hiding. He knew Locke slightly, and was greatly influenced by him, knew and was respected by Leibnitz, and he was occasionally given financial assistance by those who sympathized with his point of view, including Lord Shaftesbury. His *Letters to Serena* was dedicated to his good friend, Queen Sophie Charlotte of Prussia, whom he met on a trip abroad in 1701, when he was well received at court and by German intellectuals. For the most part he lived by writing political pamphlets to order, by editing and translating (he knew ten or more languages), and by minor government jobs for which he had to humble himself and apologize for the "youthful indiscretion" of his first (and best) book, which had been burned by Parliament.

He emerged now and then from the obscurity of this sycophantic struggle for a living to support his views aggressively, either in the coffee-houses or in print. His last work, which may have been written on order, was a prayerbook, in imitation of that of the Church of England, for the celebration of a pantheistic ritual. In all, he published about fifty works.

He spent the last four years of his life at Putney, where he died at the age of fifty-two.

PRINCIPAL WORKS: Christianity Not Mysterious, 1696; Life of John Milton, 1698; Amyntor, 1699; Vindicus Liberius, 1702; Letters to Serena, 1704; Pantheisticon, 1720.

ABOUT: Biographia Britannica; Disraeli, I. Calamities of Authors; Hunt, J. Religious Thought in England.

TONSTALL, CUTHBERT. See TUNSTALL, CUTHBERT

TOOKE, JOHN HORNE (June 25, 1736-
March 18, 1812), author of philological
works, was born in Westminster, one of the
seven children of a poulterer named John
Horne. He was educated at Eton and by
private tutors, and graduated from St.
John's College, Cambridge, with a B.A., in
1758. The great tragedy of his life was that
his father insisted upon his entering the
ministry. He was a materialist, lacking imagination and passion, but possessing great
powers of perception and logic, brilliantly
equipped for his own choice of profession,
the law.

A shrewd, witty, worldly, vain and contentious man, he was obviously unfitted for
the church. He soon left the holding his
father had bought him, and traveled on the
continent, where he met Voltaire, Sterne,
and the temporarily exiled English reformer
and agitator, John Wilkes. Returning to
London, Horne worked wholeheartedly in
the cause of Wilkes' freedom, until, losing
respect for him personally, he broke with
him politically. By espousing Wilkes' cause,
he had lost all chance of religious preferment; by opposing Wilkes, he lost his political popularity; he was excluded from practicing law because he was a clergyman. As a
climax to these misfortunes, he was jailed
for a year for raising funds to give to Benjamin Franklin to aid the American Revolution.

In 1786 he published a "philosophy" of
grammar, *The Diversions of Purley*, a significant contribution to the young science of
comparative philology. His reputation established and an income assured, he retired
to a small estate in Wimbledon, where he
gardened, entertained, and expressed his
contempt for the government by the dangerous gambit of pretending to be a spy. He
was tried for high treason, defended himself
ably, and was acquitted. He made one last
political sortie, getting elected to the House
of Commons, but his attacks on the ministry
were so troublesome that he was eliminated
by the expedient of passing a law excluding
the clergy from Parliament.

He assumed the name of his friend, William Tooke, whose estate, Purley, he had
saved from confiscation by a brilliant legal
maneuver. In return, Tooke agreed to leave
the estate to Horne, which he failed to do.

Horne Tooke died at Wimbledon at the
age of seventy-six, leaving his estate to one
of his three illegitimate children.

PRINCIPAL WORK: Diversions of Purley, 1786-
1805.

ABOUT: Coleridge, S. Table Talk; Hazlitt, W.
Contemporary Portraits; Stephens, A. Memoir of
John Horne Tooke.

TOPLADY, AUGUSTUS MONTAGUE
(November 4, 1740-August 14, 1778), divine,
writer of hymns and polemics, was born in
Farnham, Surrey. His father, Richard Top-
lady, an army major, died in 1741, and he
was raised by his mother. She took him to
Ireland, where, in 1760, he graduated from
Trinity College at Dublin.

He was ordained a deacon in 1762 and a
priest in 1764. He held in succession the
curacies of Blagdon, Farleigh, Harpford,
and Broad Hembury, retaining the last one
from 1768 until his death.

First converted to the ministry by a follower of John Wesley, Toplady soon became
the most extreme of Calvinists, and the rest
of his life was devoted to a crusade against
Wesley and Wesleyan doctrines. What is
curious is that in this violent controversy
both Wesley and Toplady, men of high
principles, broad learning, and unimpeachable
character, descended to a fish-wife level of
public disputation. Toplady's exposition of
the Calvinist point of view was brilliantly
written, his style was acute, incisive, racy,
but when he wrote of Wesley he did so with
"coarse vigour . . . and abandon." The tone
of their exchanges can be inferred from a
passage by Wesley: "Mr. Augustus Toplady
I know well; but I do not fight with chimney-
sweepers. He is too dirty a writer for me to
meddle with; I should only foul my fingers."

Along with virulent attacks on Wesley,
Toplady found time to write several hymns
of great dignity and beauty, chief among
them "Rock of Ages."

In 1775 he contracted tuberculosis, and
moved to London for medical care. He
edited the *Gospel Magazine* for over a year,
using it as an additional weapon against
Wesley, and preached at a French Calvinist
Reformed church. Two months before his
death, he preached a final sermon, silencing
rumors of a change of heart by reiterating
his doctrines and reaffirming every word he
had ever written. He died at thirty-eight,

and was buried in the Tottenham Court Chapel.

PRINCIPAL WORKS: Poems on Sacred Subjects, 1759; The Church of England Vindicated from the Charge of Armineanism, 1769; The Historic Proof of the Doctrinal Calvinism of the Church of England, 1774; The Scheme of Christian and Philosophical Necessity Asserted, 1775; A Collection of Hymns, 1776; Memoirs, 1778; Works, with Memoir by W. Row, 1794.

ABOUT: Julian, J. Dictionary of Hymnology; Row, W. Memoir prefixed to Works; Winters, W. Memoir.

TOURNEUR, CYRIL (1575?-February 28, 1626), dramatist, poet, makes no appearance in Elizabethan records prior to the publication of his first work in 1600. This is an almost impenetrable allegory entitled *The Transformed Metamorphosis*, dedicated to Sir Christopher Heydon. As Heydon was an ardent supporter of Essex, it has been thought that the Mavortio of the poem represents Essex; if this hypothesis be correct, it is still far from clear just what Essex is supposed to have achieved. On internal evidence one would say that this was the poem of a very young man—aged eighteen or twenty rather than twenty-five—who had studied Greek not wisely but too well, and was determined to Grecize the English tongue.

In 1607 was published a truly remarkable play by Tourneur, *The Revenger's Tragedy*, "as it hath sundry times been acted by the King's Majesty's Servants"—the company that Shakespeare also wrote for. Tourneur's next publication gives us a valuable clue; in 1609 appeared *A Funeral Poem upon the Death of . . . Sir Francis Vere*. Sir Francis was lieutenant governor of the fortress of Brill in Holland, a post which had previously been held by a certain Richard Turnor. Those familiar with the vagaries of Elizabethan spelling will realize that Richard probably came from the same family as Cyril Tourneur (Turnour or Turner); the poet afterwards served in Holland himself; moreover, Turnor had been a warm supporter of Essex.

In 1611 Tourneur's *Atheist's Tragedy* was published. The following year a play by him called *The Nobleman* was licensed for publication, but seems never to have been printed. It was acted at court by the King's Servants, 1612. Next year appeared *Three Elegies on the Most Lamented Death of*

Prince Henry (eldest son of James I) by Tourneur, Webster and Heywood, respectively. It is probable that these three dramatists were all known to each other, as all had written for the King's Company.

Early in 1613 Robert Daborne writes of having "given Cyril Tourneur an act of *The Arraignment of London* to write." This play was never published. In December 1613 Tourneur was paid forty-one shillings by the Lord Chamberlain for "carrying letters for His Majesty's service to Brussels." This may mark the beginning of the poet's overseas service, which must have been creditable, as he received a pension of £60 a year from the Dutch.

In 1625 Tourneur went with Sir Edward Cecil from the Hague on the ill fated Cadiz expedition which the latter commanded. (It is significant that Richard Turnor had served under Sir Edward's father at Brill.) Tourneur was to have been Secretary of the Council of War, but had to be content with the post of Cecil's personal secretary. On the way home from Cadiz Tourneur, along with a number of other sick men, was disembarked at Kinsale. He died there nearly three months later. His wife Mary, left penniless, appealed to the Council of War for assistance.

The above is the sum total of our knowledge concerning Tourneur, except for any conjectures about his personality that we can draw from his two extant plays.

Scholars have long puzzled over the question, "Which of the plays did Tourneur write first?" *The Atheist's Tragedy* is an average Elizabethan play—not only inferior in quality to *The Revenger's Tragedy*, but showing little trace of the unique personality that makes itself felt in every line of the latter. Charlemont, the injured party in *The Atheist's Tragedy*, lives to see the vengeance that he has forborne accomplished by heaven; the play is thus a natural foil to *The Revenger's Tragedy*, where Vindici takes the law into his own hands and ultimately is punished for doing so.

Most recent scholars accordingly believe that the lesser play may have been the product of a maturer Tourneur, aiming to produce a totally different mood in his audience.

There is no doubt, however, as to what mood Tourneur's genius was best fitted to produce. *The Revenger's Tragedy* is saturated with loathing for human bestiality. Vindici, who carries the skull of his murdered love about with him, seems to delight in his task of extirpating her murderers. He is a connoisseur in revenge, anxious to make the punishment fit the crime; the Duke, for instance, poisons himself by kissing the skull, which he thinks is the face of a beautiful woman who has given him a midnight rendezvous.

The Revenger's Tragedy is the most blood curdling of all Elizabethan and Jacobean plays. It is so grimly in earnest, so haunted by the loathsomeness of sex, that it makes us shiver where many of Tourneur's contemporaries would only make us laugh. No play—not even *Hamlet*—has better exemplified the death-wish.

PRINCIPAL WORKS: The Transformed Metamorphosis, 1600; The Revenger's Tragedy, 1607; A Funeral Poem, 1609; The Atheist's Tragedy, 1611; A Grief on the Death of Prince Henry (*in* Three Elegies) 1613; The Character of Robert, Earl of Salisbury, MS.

ABOUT: Collins, J. C. Introduction to The Plays and Poems, 1878; Eliot, T. S. Elizabethan Essays; Tannenbaum, S. A. and D. Cyril Tourneur, A Concise Bibliography.

TRAHERNE, THOMAS (1634?-September 27, 1674), author of religious works in prose and verse, is a man who almost disappeared from memory until his rediscovery in the twentieth century, and about whom little is known. According to Anthony à Wood, he was a shoemaker's son from Hereford, on the Welsh border, who entered Brasenose College, Oxford, in 1652, graduated B.A. in 1656, was ordained, secured his M.A. in 1661, and in 1657 became rector at Credenhill, near his birthplace. His actual birth date is unknown, and may have been as late as 1637.

In 1667 he was made domestic chaplain to Sir Orlando Bridgman, lord keeper of the seal, and at the same time served Teddington, near Hampton Court, where Bridgman's home was situated, as clergyman. Bridgman was a friend as well as an employer, and Traherne spent the remainder of his life under his roof, dying there at no more than forty, and being buried in the local church. Wood says he led a simple and devout life, accumulating no fortune except in books; in fact, this is evidenced by his will, which

goes to the extent of bequeathing an old hat to a friend. He never married.

His literary career has been a curious one. Only one book was published in his lifetime, a controversial prose work on Roman Catholic forgeries, and that was anonymous. Friends brought out two volumes of devotional prose, interspersed with verse, after his death. His poems remained in manuscript, passing from his brother's into other hands. They were found in a bookstall at the beginning of this century, by W. T. Brooke, who sold the manuscript to A. B. Grosart. Grosart thought they were Vaughan's, and intended to publish them as such, but failed to do so; he gave them to Bertram Dobell, who established them as Traherne's. Since then they have had a small group of ardent admirers; the English philosopher, W. Macneile Dixon, for example, has quoted Traherne freely in *The Human Situation*.

As a poet, Traherne belongs to the so-called metaphysical school, with Vaughan and Herbert. He had an original mind, and a power of glowing rhetoric, marred by indifferent attention to metrics and an overweening love of imperfect rhymes. All his life he was possessed of a nostalgic harking back to childhood, and the simplicity of his piety has in it something of the child. Yet, though his genius was poetic and imaginative rather than philosophical, his prose (which parallels or exemplifies his verse) is by far his finest mode of expression. There is in it almost an echo of the magnificence of Sir Thomas Browne. It has the grand roll and the startling imagery of Browne, and should not have been neglected as it has been. In prose, Traherne is never diffuse, repetitive, and didactic, as he too often is in verse.

In a sense Traherne is still an undeservedly forgotten author. His name does not even appear in the massive *Dictionary of National Biography* or in Bartlett's *Familiar Quotations*. At least one volume of his devotions and meditations still remains in manuscript, unpublished. He was not a great writer, but in his own restricted field he is himself what he called the Bodleian library—"a glory to Oxford and to this [the English] nation."

PRINCIPAL WORKS: Roman Forgeries, 1673; Christian Ethicks (with verse) 1675; A Serious and Patheticall Contemplation of the Mercies of God, 1699; Poetical Works (B. Dobell, ed.) 1903;

Centuries of Meditations (B. Dobell, ed.) 1908; Poems of Felicity (H. I. Bell, ed.) 1910.

ABOUT: Dobell, B. Life *in* Poetical Works; Leishman, J. B. The Metaphysical Poets; Quiller-Couch, A. T. From a Cornish Window; Wade, G. I. Thomas Traherne (Bibliography of Criticism by R. A. Parker); White, H. C. The Metaphysical Poets: A Study in Religious Experience; Willett, G. E. Traherne, an Essay; Wood, A. à, Athenae Oxonienses.

TRAVERS, WALTER (1548?-1635),

Puritan divine, author of religious works, was born in Nottingham, the son of a goldsmith who instilled his own Puritan ideals in his four children.

Travers graduated B.A. from Christ's Church, Cambridge, in 1565, obtained his M.A. in 1569, and the same year became a fellow of Trinity College. In 1574 an anonymous work, *Ecclesiasticae Disciplinae Explicatio*, was published which attacked the universities of England, calling them "haunts of drones—monasteries whose inmates yawn and snore, rather than colleges of students." The work, immediately recognized as Travers', established his position among the foremost spokesmen of the reformist school. On a visit to the University of Geneva he met the liberal rector of the University, Beza, whose ideas strengthened Travers' own.

He received a B.D. from Cambridge in 1576, and a D.D. from Oxford the same year, but refused to take the oaths which would enable him to be ordained. Two years later he went to Antwerp, at the suggestion of the English ambassador there, received the Presbyterian ordination, and held services for the English merchants. Returning to England a year or two later, he became Lord Burghley's chaplain and tutor to his son.

Largely on Burghley's recommendation, he was appointed afternoon lecturer at Temple. In line for the mastership when it fell vacant, Travers refused to be reordained in order to obtain the appointment, and it went to Richard Hooker, a sincere and orthodox divine, whose sister was married to Travers' brother. In spite of their friendship and mutual respect, the two divines carried on a lively controversy in the pulpit of Temple, Hooker upholding the orthodox viewpoint in the morning and evening, Travers taking the opposite stand in the afternoon. Public interest and partisanship

soon reached such a pitch that Travers was prohibited from preaching.

In 1591 he taught at St. Andrews University, and in 1595 became provost of Trinity College in Dublin. Three years later he resigned and returned to London in ill health and poverty, but when he died five years later, he left a considerable estate to various colleges and institutions.

PRINCIPAL WORKS: Ecclesiasticae Disciplinae Explicatio, 1574; A Supplication Made to the Privy Counsel, 1612.

ABOUT: Hunt, J. Religious Thought in England; Wood, A. à, Fasti.

TREVISA, JOHN de (1326-1412), trans-

lator, was born at Crocadon in St. Mellion. He was educated at Oxford, and was a fellow of Exeter College there from 1362 to 1369, and of Queen's Hall for the next ten years. In 1379, three fellows, including Trevisa, and the provost of Queen's were expelled on a charge of "unworthiness," probably because of their sympathy with the doctrines of the reformer, Wycliffe. Soon after this, Trevisa became chaplain to Thomas, Lord Berkeley, who, with his two sons, remained his patron throughout his life. He died at Berkeley at the age of eighty-six.

It was for the benefit of Lord Berkeley that Trevisa translated two medieval Latin classics whose contents comprised most of the knowledge of that time. In a *Dialogue on Translation Between a Lord and a Clerk* with which he prefaced the first work, he described Berkeley's overcoming his scruples about translating great books into the "vulgar tongue," and so making them available to the people. It was the earnestness with which he pursued this intent that gave Trevisa's translations both their chief charm and value.

The first of his major works was the *Polychronicon* of Higdon, a history of the world from creation to the middle of the fourteenth century. The second was *De Proprietatibus Rerum* of Bartholomaeus Anglicus, an encyclopedia of all natural science, compiled in the thirteenth century. Trevisa extended both with notes, and continued the history to his own time.

His determination to have the works completely intelligible to even unschooled readers led him to use an easy, racy, colloquial style far from the stiff latinate English of most translations of the day. While free and non-literal, the translations are conscientious in the extreme; when alternate meanings are possible, Trevisa gave both, and he occasionally interpreted passages which made no sense to him, with the philosophical apology, "God wot what this is to mean." Even more than the often naïve information contained in these works, their peculiarly native style had wide influence, and they have been called the cornerstone of English prose.

PRINCIPAL WORKS: Polychronicon, 1387; De Proprietatibus Rerum, 1398.

ABOUT: Ames, J. Typographical Antiquities; Blades, W. The Biography of William Caxton; Tanner, T. Biblioteca Britannico-hibernica.

TRIMMER, Mrs. SARAH (January 6, 1741-December 15, 1810), author of children's books, was born at Ipswich, the daughter of John Joshua Kirby and his wife Sarah. She was a precocious girl whose literary tendencies were encouraged by her family and by such family friends as Reynolds, Gainsborough, Hogarth, and Samuel Johnson. She was in her middle teens when she delighted Johnson one day, at the height of an argument about a passage in Milton among friends assembled at Reynolds' house, by drawing a volume of Milton from her pocket and settling the dispute.

When she was eighteen she married James Trimmer, and for the next twenty-three years devoted herself to the raising and educating of her twelve children. In 1782 she was persuaded to publish, from her experience with her own children, a study-guide to the teaching of nature lore and sacred history, which was so popular that eleven editions were published during the next twenty years.

Her exceedingly active career thereafter included the organization of Sunday schools for the poor and for underprivileged adults, the establishment of an industrial school at her home town of Brentford, and an unceasing campaign against what she regarded as the imminent danger of a French Jacobin attack upon English Christianity. "Good Mrs. Trimmer" was in the forefront of most progressive educational projects of the day. Queen Charlotte consulted her on the establishment of charity schools at Windsor. The Society for Promoting Christian Knowledge used her biblical abridgements for seventy-seven years. She edited two educational magazines, one devoted to the criticism of children's books. She opposed the use of fairy tales on unexpectedly modern psychological grounds, and introduced the use of picturebooks for the education of the preschool child.

It is mainly for one book that she has been remembered by generations of children. This is the *Fabulous Histories, Designed for the Instruction of Children, Respecting Their Treatment of Animals*, but more fondly remembered by the children who read the charming story of the robin family of Pecksy, Flapsy, Robin, and Dick, as *The History of the Robins*.

Mrs. Trimmer died at her home at Brentford at the age of sixty-nine.

PRINCIPAL WORKS: Easy Introduction to the Knowledge of Nature, 1782; Sacred History, 1782; Fabulous Histories, 1786; Instructive Tales, 1810; New and Comprehensive Lessons, 1814.

ABOUT: Elwood, A. K. Memoirs of the Literary Ladies of England; Law, J. and M. Gilbert. Some Account of the Life and Writings of Mrs. Trimmer.

TUCKER, ABRAHAM (September 2, 1705-November 20, 1774), philosopher, was born in London, the son of a merchant, originally of a Somerset family. He was left an orphan in infancy, and reared by his maternal uncle, Sir Isaac Tillard. After school at Bishop Stortford, Hertfordshire, he matriculated at Merton College, Oxford, in 1721. He left without a degree and entered the Middle Temple, but was never called to the bar, using his legal knowledge only as a justice of the peace after he bought Betchworth Castle, near Dorking, Surrey, in 1727, studied agriculture, and settled down for the rest of his life as a country gentleman.

He was indeed more of a widely read and articulate country gentleman than any philosopher in the technical sense. Retired and humorously self-deprecatory, he spent all his spare time in reading and writing, mostly on ethics. In 1736 he married Dorothy Barker, who died in 1754 leaving three daughters. Tucker did not remarry, but devoted himself to the education of his daughters, one of whom edited the posthumous conclusion of his major work, *The Light of Nature Pursued*. In 1771 he became totally blind, but this also he endured with equanimity, inventing a machine to enable him to write. He had no literary associates, and he shunned politics—even setting to music some verses written in derision of his only political venture! He has been called a "metaphysical Montaigne," and indeed he was primarily an essayist—a frank, simple, naïf man, warmhearted, affectionate, and witty, good humored and garrulous.

All his work during his lifetime was published under one of two pseudonyms, "Edward Search" and "Cuthbert Comment." His writing is full of erratic speculations, divagations, and digressions, but it also has much shrewd observation, and even (in his illustrative anecdotes) humor and pathos. He was really a moralist, and in substantial agreement with that other moralist Paley, who acknowledged his indebtedness. Though Tucker in turn owed much to Hartley, he disliked and criticized him, and though Locke was avowedly his master, he found fault with him also, as well as with Berkeley. He is an introspective, analytical psychologist, who expresses a sort of rough-and-ready mysticism in a matter-of-fact manner. His principal book is far too long, because his plan grew as he wrote and he could not resist wandering off on by-paths. In a way he is a pioneer Utilitarian, holding that common good is the road to virtue as well as to happiness, but adhering to the doctrine that these can come only "by the will of God." His style is clear and simple, and though he is long outdated, he undoubtedly prepared the public mind for more profound philosophers.

PRINCIPAL WORKS: The Country Gentleman's Advice to His Son on the Subject of Party Clubs (anon.) 1755; Freewill, Foreknowledge, and Fate (as Edward Search) 1763; Man in Quest of Himself: or a Defence of the Individuality of the Human Mind (as Cuthbert Comment) 1763; Vocal Sounds (as Edward Search) 1773; The Light of Nature Pursued (4 vols., as Edward Search) 1768 (vols. 5-7, J. Tucker, ed. [daughter] 1778; abridged, W. Hazlitt, ed. 1807; as Posthumous Works of Abraham Tucker, H. S. J. Mildmay, ed. [grandson] 1834).

ABOUT: Mackintosh, J. Dissertation on the Progress of Ethical Philosophy; Mildmay, H. S. J. Life, in Posthumous Works; Stephen, L. English Thought in the 18th Century.

TUKE, Sir SAMUEL (d. January 26, 1674), playwright, was the third son of George Tuke of Frayling, Essex. Little is known of his early years, except that he entered Gray's Inn, with an older brother, in 1635.

He played an active role in the Royalist army during the civil war, being ambitious for promotion and jealous of office. During the Protectorate, he went into exile with the royal family, attempting to attach himself to the entourage first of the Duke of York, then of the Duke of Gloucester. During this period he was converted to Catholicism.

Following the Restoration, Tuke's favor grew at court. Charles II sent him on several diplomatic missions to the French court, and in 1663 suggested to him the writing of a play based on a plot by the Spanish playwright, Calderon.

It is on this play, *The Adventures of Five Hours*, that Tuke's literary reputation is based. It was produced at the Duke's Theater and was a success, running for thirteen performances. Echard, translator of Terence, said of it, "It is one of the pleasantest stories that ever appeared upon our stage," and Pepys recorded it "the best for variety, and the most excellent continuation of the plot to the end, that ever I saw, or think ever shall."

Tuke was knighted in 1664 and created a baronet in the same year. He lived in virtual retirement the last ten years of his life, except for an occasional speech in the House of Lords in defense of loyal Catholics, and a paper contributed to the Royal Society on the history of the ordering and generation of green Colchester oysters.

He died at Somerset House in 1674. He was married twice and left one son, who was killed in the war in Ireland.

PRINCIPAL WORKS: The Adventure of Five Hours, 1663 (R. Dodsley, ed. 1744; W. C. Hazlitt, ed. 1876).

ABOUT: Dodsley, R. Old Plays; Evelyn, J. Diary and Correspondence; Gaw, A. Sir Samuel Tuke's Adventures of Five Hours in Relation to the Spanish Plot and to Dryden; Wood, A. à, Athenae Oxonienses.

TUNSTALL or TONSTALL, CUTHBERT (1474-November 18, 1559), author of religious works, was the illegitimate son of Thomas Tunstall of Lancashire, whose father, Sir Richard Tunstall, had lost his title and the family seat at Thurland Castle because of Lancastrian sympathies.

He attended Balliol College, Oxford, and King's Hall, Cambridge, and graduated LL.D. from the University of Padua. His scholarship was of a high order. He knew intimately the leading Renaissance scholars, both at home and abroad, and was a close friend of Erasmus, with whom he lived while on a diplomatic mission to Brussels.

His career was a curiously uneven one because of the sincerity and intensity of his religious convictions. He never concealed the extent of his belief in Catholic dogma and ritual, nor failed to attempt to influence legislation in a pro-Catholic direction. When such legislation went against him, he was strict in his observance of the law. But so great was his influence and prestige that his career depended to a large extent upon the religious bias of the changing rulers of England, and therefore the degree of their confidence or distrust of him.

From 1506 to 1511, he held a variety of rectorships, becoming in 1511 chancellor to Archbishop Warham, who introduced him at court. He rose rapidly, was England's representative on several diplomatic missions, was made Bishop of London in 1522 and, in 1530, succeeded Wolsey as Bishop of Durham. His influence was especially great during the period of severance of the Church of England from the Church of Rome, and Henry VIII, beginning to fear his presence at court, made him president of the Council of the North, with the particular commission of protecting the northern border against the Scots.

Edward VI was more openly antagonistic, and following an attack by the Scots in 1547, Tunstall's commission was revoked and he was arrested on a contrived charge of treason. He was imprisoned for a year, tried, and deprived of his bishopric. His fortunes turned again under Queen Mary, and he was restored to the bishopric, only to be deprived again under Queen Elizabeth. He was in the custody of Archbishop of Canterbury Matthew Parker, charged with refusing to consecrate Parker, when he died at the age of eighty-five.

His best known work, written during his imprisonment at the age of seventy-seven, is an excellent exposition of the Catholic dogma of the Eucharist.

PRINCIPAL WORKS: De Arte Supputandi Libri Quattuor, 1522; De Veritate Corporis et Sanguinis Domini nostri Jesu Christi in Eucharista, 1551; Contra Blasphematores Dei Praedestinationis Opus, 1555; Certain Godly and Devout Prayers, 1558.

ABOUT: Foxe, J. Acts and Monuments; Fuller, T. Church History of Britain; Strype, J. Works.

TURBERVILLE or **TURBERVILE, GEORGE** (1540?-1610?), poet, translator, compiler, was born at Whitechurch, Dorsetshire, the son of Nicholas Turberville, a country gentleman who had the misfortune to be murdered by his brother-in-law, John Morgan, in late 1579 or early 1580. George is said to have entered Winchester School in 1554 and to have become a fellow of New College, Oxford, in 1561; he left Oxford the next year without a degree and entered one of the Inns of Court to study law.

In 1568 he accompanied Thomas Randolph on his embassy to Russia and wrote some verse epistles descriptive of that country. He had already won a reputation as an original poet and translator; the first extant edition of his *Epitaphs, Epigrams, Songs and Sonnets* is dated 1567 and described as "newly corrected with additions"; it must therefore be at least a second edition. Turberville made good use of his popularity while it lasted, having no fewer than four books printed in 1567 and 1568.

We know nothing more of him until 1571, when the Privy Council wanted to know why "George Turbervile, who hath been always from his youth, and still is, given to his book and study and never exercised in matters of war," had been given command of a hundred soldiers in Dorsetshire.

No copy of the *Tragical Tales, Translated by Turbervile in Time of his Troubles* exists with an earlier imprint than 1587, but Rollins (see below) thinks that the "troubles" date from before 1575; the introduction to *The Book of Falconry* certainly speaks of them as over. We can only conjecture what they were. Later he had plenty of troubles—the murder of his father, the persecution of many of his relatives (and perhaps himself) as Roman Catholics, an appearance before the Privy Council "to answer certain matters objected against him."

George Gascoigne and Sir John Harington wrote verses in praise of Turberville's work; they were presumably his chief friends among the literary men of the day. Toward the end of Elizabeth's reign Turberville was regarded as a worthy poetical pioneer, but rather out of date. His chief merit lay in his excellent knowledge of Greek, Latin, and Italian, which made him not only a competent translator but an important adapter of Italian models to English purposes. He used blank verse very early, in the *Heroical Epistles.*

The last we hear of Turberville is that he was Muster Master for Warwickshire under his patron the Earl of Warwick, in 1588. Rollins thinks he was dead by 1593; at any rate he was dead when Sir John Harington (d. 1612) wrote his epitaph.

PRINCIPAL WORKS: Epitaphs, Epigrams, Songs and Sonnets, with a Discourse of the Friendly Affections of Timetes to Pindara his Lady, 1567; The Heroical Epistles of the Learned Poet Publius Ovidius Naso (tr.) 1567; The Eclogues of the Poet Mantuan, Turned into English Verse, 1567; A Plain Path to Perfect Virtue, Translated into English, 1568; The Book of Falconry or Hawking, Collected out of the Best Authors, 1575; The Noble Art of Venery or Hunting, Translated out of the Best Authors, 1575; Tragical Tales, Translated by Turbervile in Time of His Troubles (1574?) 1587.

ABOUT: Rollins, H. E. New Facts About George Turbervile (Modern Philology, 1918); Wood, A. à, Athenae Oxonienses.

TUSSER, THOMAS (1524?-May 3, 1580),

agricultural writer and poet, was born in Rivenhall, Essex. His birth date is sometimes given as 1515. He was a choir boy, first at Wallingford Castle and then at St. Paul's Cathedral. He was educated at Eton, attended King's College and Trinity Hall, Cambridge, but left the university before graduating because of ill health.

His fame rests chiefly on one work, *Five Hundred Points of Good Husbandry, United to as Many of Good Housewifery.* This is a long survey of the changing seasons in the life of the English countryside, containing pithy advice on such subjects as farming, forestry, weather, virtue, thrift, and religion. It is written in clear, straightforward doggerel, lacking in imagination and originality, but containing a remarkably complete picture of the agriculture, household economy, customs and observances of rural England in Shakespeare's boyhood. The book was used as a manual of agriculture for two centuries, and was prized by its rural readers for its easy readibility, kindly humor, and homely wisdom.

Ironically, Tusser's own life was a series of misfortunes, ill-advised ventures, and failures. The "good, honest, homely, useful old rhymer" seemed incapable of profiting by his own good advice. After leaving college,

he was at court for ten years as musician to Baron Paget. Upon his marriage he moved to a farm in Suffolk, later removing because of his wife's health to Ipswich, where his wife died. He married a second time and had four children. The Dean of Norwich helped him get a position as a singer in the cathedral, until he fell ill. Another farming project in Essex failed; he moved to London, only to be forced to flee from a plague epidemic; stayed for a while in Cambridge; and finally died in a debtor's prison in London.

Although his work has no value as poetry, he was something of a pioneer in the careful use of several metrical forms and rhyme schemes which were later adopted by more serious poets.

PRINCIPAL WORK: Five Hundred Points of Good Husbandry, 1573 (D. Hartley, ed. 1931).

ABOUT: Fuller, T. Worthies of England; Ritson, J. Bibliographia Poetica; Tusser, T. Autobiography; Warton, T. History of English Poetry.

TYNDALE, WILLIAM (1494?-1536),

translator of the Bible, religious writer, came from a family of yeoman farmers settled in and near the parish of Stinchcombe, Gloucestershire, who bore the name Hutchins as well as Tyndale. Foxe says he was educated "from a child" at Oxford University, where he was a member of Magdalen Hall (later incorporated in Hertford College). He graduated B.A., 1512; M.A., 1515. He may possibly be the "William Hychyns" ordained at Whitborne, Hereford diocese, on June 10, 1514. If not, we do not know just when or where he took orders. In 1516 or later Tyndale went to Cambridge, probably because it was less conservative than Oxford and offered better opportunities for studying Greek.

About 1522 Tyndale left Cambridge to become tutor to the children of Sir John Walsh at Little Sodbury, Gloucestershire. He also preached in the neighborhood, especially at Bristol. The local clergy, who frequently visited Sir John, were less broad minded than Tyndale's Cambridge colleagues and objected to his reformist opinions. He had to appear before the chancellor of the diocese on a charge of heresy, but nothing could be proved against him; Tyndale on his side was appalled by the ignorance and sloth of the country clergy. He made up his mind to translate the New Testament. This could not be done in Gloucestershire, so he decided to seek the patronage of the supposedly liberal Cuthbert Tunstall, Bishop of London. He parted from Sir John Walsh on good terms; the bishop, however, received him coldly; he was later a bitter enemy of Tyndale's translation.

A wealthy merchant named Monmouth who had heard Tyndale preach at St. Dunstan's-in-the-West, London, took him into his house and gave him money after the bishop proved unhelpful. Through Monmouth he must have met other merchants who helped defray his printing costs later. Tyndale finally decided that there was no hope of translating and printing the New Testament anywhere in England. With money from Monmouth he sailed for Hamburg in 1524 and thence went to visit Luther at Wittenberg, where he worked on the translation. He was never to see England again.

In 1525 Tyndale and one William Roye went to Cologne, to have the New Testament printed there. Their plan was discovered by an anti-reformer named Cochlaeus, when only part of St. Matthew's Gospel had been printed. They fled with the printed sheets to Worms. Cochlaeus sent letters of warning to Henry VIII and Bishop Fisher, but the printing was safely carried out at Worms, and the first copies reached England early in 1526.

Soon the Testament was being burnt in England and its readers persecuted, but the demand for it continued; a pirated edition was brought out; later, the authorities in England seemed likely to make a fortune for the Continental printing trade by buying up copies to burn.

Tyndale now began to sign his name to his writings, finding that scurrilous poetry attacking Cardinal Wolsey, written by Roye and one Jerome, was being attributed to him. The first book so signed was *The Parable of the Wicked Mammon*. A whole series of works by Tyndale appeared with a Marburg imprint, but it has since been discovered that they were printed at Antwerp, the false imprint being a ruse to protect the printer. Tyndale ran great risks seeing them through the press, for English agents were hunting for him all over Holland and Germany.

The Obedience of a Christian Man defends the power of kings, at the same time

WILLIAM TYNDALE

that it attacks the Church's powers of confessing and absolving, and maintains the Protestant view of the Sacraments. King Henry VIII approved of this work, but not of Tyndale's next original book, *The Practise of Prelates*, in which he attacked Cardinal Wolsey and Henry's plans for a divorce.

Meanwhile, in 1529, Tyndale had set out by sea from Antwerp to Hamburg with his version of the Pentateuch and been shipwrecked; he lost all his MSS. but with the help of Coverdale completed a new translation before the end of the year. He then returned to Antwerp, where the hunt had for the moment died down.

In 1531, after the downfall of Wolsey, the situation in England became more favorable to the reform party, most of whom upheld Henry's divorce—especially if it was going to mean a breach with the Pope. Tyndale was invited to return to England by a merchant called Vaughan, acting on the king's behalf. Tyndale, however, did not feel it safe to do so; Sir Thomas More, now Lord Chancellor of England, had lately engaged in acrimonious controversy with him, and he doubted whether the king could protect him against More and the bishops. Also, he made it a condition of his going back that the king should permit an authorized English Bible to be printed and circulated among the people.

Henry now turned against Tyndale again and strove to have him extradited or kidnapped, but failed. In 1535 Coverdale's translation of the Bible was published on the Continent and its circulation permitted in England. Tyndale had an unpleasant controversy in 1534-35 with another reformer named Joye who persisted in issuing reprints of Tyndale's New Testament altered by himself in accordance with his own views on resurrection. Tyndale then produced his own very carefully revised version.

In May 1535 an Englishman named Henry Phillips—presumably hired by one or more of the English bishops—came to Antwerp, discovered where Tyndale lived, pretended to be a Lutheran, and won his friendship. One day he invited Tyndale to dinner and handed him over to officers of the Holy Roman Empire.

Tyndale was imprisoned for sixteen months at the castle of Vilvorde, near Brussels, during which time King Henry and Thomas Cromwell tried, halfheartedly, to obtain his release. Thomas Poyntz, the merchant at whose house Tyndale had lived for the preceding year, strove very hard to the same end and was imprisoned for his pains, but escaped. After a long trial, Tyndale was convicted of heresy, defrocked and handed over to the secular power. Early in October 1536, he was strangled at the stake in Vilvorde, crying, "Lord, open the King of England's eyes!" His body was then publicly burnt.

It is difficult to be impartial in one's view of so singleminded and courageous a figure as Tyndale; Foxe ascribes all the virtues to him, but he certainly lacked one—resignation. He lashed out at his enemies in vigorous prose; yet by the controversial standards of the time he was a moderate man. As a translator he is almost beyond praise; 90 per cent of his wording is retained in the King James Bible. He was undoubtedly a fine Greek scholar and a surprisingly good Hebraist. But best of all, he was a master of colloquial English—something few other scholars of his time would deign to be.

Tyndale was short and spare of figure and rugged of countenance. In his portrait a lofty, corrugated brow dominates the lined and bearded face of a man who has suffered much but remains undaunted.

PRINCIPAL WORKS: New Testament (tr.) 1525-26; The Parable of the Wicked Mammon, 1528; The Obedience of a Christian Man, 1528; The Pentateuch (tr.) 1530; The Practise of Prelates, 1530; An Answer Unto Sir T. More's Dialogue, 1531; Jonah (tr.) 1531; The Exposition of the First Epistle of St. John, 1531; An Exposition upon the V, VI, VII, Chapters of Matthew, 1532; The Supper of the Lord, 1533; A Fruitful and Godly Treatise Expressing the Right Institution of the Sacraments, 1533 (?); A Pathway to the Holy Scripture, 1534; The Testament of W. Tracy, Esquire, Expounded, 1535; The Whole Works, 1572-73.

ABOUT: Campbell, W. E. Erasmus, Tyndale, and More; Demaus, R. William Tyndall; Foxe, J. Acts and Monuments; Mozley, J. F. William Tyndale.

TYRWHITT, THOMAS (March 27, 1730-August 15, 1786), editor, literary critic, was born in London; his father was Robert Tyrwhitt, archdeacon of London and canon of Windsor, and his mother Elizabeth Gibson, daughter of the Bishop of London. The name is pronounced "Tirrit." He entered Eton in 1741, and Queen's College, Oxford, in 1747, graduating B.A. in 1750. In 1755 he became a fellow of Merton, where he secured his M.A. in 1756. He was entered at the Middle Temple, and called to the bar in 1755, but, largely because of ill health, he never practiced law. Through Lord Barrington he was made deputy secretary for war in 1756, and held the post until 1772, but lived most of this time in Oxford. From 1762 to 1768 he was clerk of the House of Commons; for this post he gave up his fellowship and moved to London. In that capacity he published the Proceedings and Debates of the House of Commons in 1620-21 (1766). He became a fellow of the Royal Society in 1771, and a trustee of the British Museum in 1784, leaving to the latter his large library of classical authors, the books annotated by himself.

Primarily Tyrwhitt was a scholar, a great linguist, who "knew almost every European tongue." He edited Aesop, and Aristotle, Aeschylus, Sophocles, Euripides, Aristophanes, and some fragments of Plutarch; many of these editions are still in manuscript. All of his critical and scholarly work was published anonymously. He was a Shakespearean scholar who, the most generous of men, was of the greatest assistance, without acknowledgment, to Steevens, Malone, and Isaac Reed. He was also the person who definitively established the

THOMAS TYRWHITT

"Rowley" poems as being by Chatterton, helped to this opinion by his exact knowledge of the English of the fourteenth and fifteenth centuries.

But Tyrwhitt's greatest benefaction to English scholarship and literature was his rehabilitation of the poetic reputation of Chaucer. Up to his time, because of ignorance of the pronunciation of Middle English, Chaucer had been thought of as a lively writer of barbarous doggerel. Tyrwhitt discovered and established the rule of Chaucer's heroic verse, by fixing the value of "e" mute in Middle English metrics. Later grammarians have found cause for some complaint and criticism, but in his own time he was the unquestioned textual critic of the day.

Tyrwhitt never married, but lived the quiet life of a scholar among his books in London. Never strong, he died at fifty-six. His name was for the most part known only to other scholars. Retiring as he was, he had a small but warm circle of friends, and was notably charitable and free-handed. He did no original writing, but his restoration of Chaucer, a great piece of scholarship, has earned him the gratitude of every lover of English poetry.

PRINCIPAL WORKS: Translations in Verse [English to Latin, Greek to English] 1752; Observations and Conjectures upon some Passages of Shakespeare, 1766; Canterbury Tales of Chaucer, with an Essay upon his Language and Versification, an Introductory Discourse, and Notes, 1775-78; Poems, supposed to have been written at Bristol by Thomas Rowley and others in the 15th century, with an Appendix, 1777-78; Vindication of the Appendix, 1782.

ABOUT: Nichols, J. Illustrations of Literature, Literary Anecdotes.

UDALL or UVEDALE, NICHOLAS

(1505-December 1556), dramatist, scholar, was born in Hampshire, probably in Southampton, and in 1517 entered Winchester as a scholar. He matriculated in Corpus Christi College, Oxford, in 1520, graduated B.A. in 1524, and served as a tutor. In the university he was noted for his Latin verse, but still more for his interest in the Protestant Reformation, in consequence of which, though he was ordained, he did not receive his M.A. degree until 1534.

From 1537 to 1554 he was vicar of Braintree, Essex, but he did not reside there for several years. (He may possibly have written or adapted a miracle play, *Placidas, alias St. Eustace*, performed there.) He seems to have been an usher at St. Anthony's School, London, for a short time, but in 1534 he was appointed headmaster of Eton. His *Floures for Latine Spekynge* was written as an Eton textbook. He was a good teacher, though a notoriously severe whipper.

Udall left Eton in 1541 under a cloud. He was accused of conspiring with two pupils and his own servant to steal silver plate from the school; he was acquitted of that, but confessed to homosexual relations with one of the boys. In consequence, he spent a short term in the Marshalsea prison. He retired to his vicarage, where he was apparently quite acceptable, and he seems to have served for a while as a schoolmaster in Northumberland or Durham. He turned also to the writing of theological works— such as his answer to the Roman Catholic commoners of Devon and Cornwall—and to translations of religious treatises from the Latin, notably of Erasmus. He was in favor of Henry VIII's divorce, and with his close friend John Leland, the antiquary, celebrated the coronation of Anne Boleyn. His Protestant sympathies kept him in favor with Edward VI, who made him a canon of Windsor in 1551, and in 1553 rector of Caborne, Isle of Wight. He served also as "schoolmaster" for the Bishop of Windsor, and tutor of the young Earl of Durham, who was a prisoner in the Tower.

However, he was adaptable enough to be in the favor of Queen Mary also—in fact, she had collaborated with him in his translation of the first volume of Erasmus' *Paraphrase of the New Testament*. After a short time as master of the Winchester Grammar School, he was appointed headmaster of Westminster School (1553), and served until a month before his death, when Mary ordered the school re-absorbed into the original monastery. The queen also gave him a warrant to prepare "dialogues and interludes."

Most of Udall's perhaps numerous plays are lost; one of them may have been *Ezechias*, performed before Queen Elizabeth in 1554. Of the one surviving, *Ralph Roister Doister* (probably written about 1540), there was one extant copy, without a cover, which was recognized as Udall's by John Payne Collier in 1825.

This, the earliest true comedy in English on classical lines, with an organic plot, and divided into acts and scenes, is a free adaptation of Plautus' *Miles Gloriosus*, dealing with the unsuccessful courtship of a braggart soldier who thinks every woman is in love with him. But in Udall's versatile hands it became a genuine English play, with well drawn, recognizable English characters.

Udall was unmarried; he died and was buried, at Westminster. He was not an admirable character, but he is an important figure in the history of English drama.

The name was variously spelled "Udal," "Udall," "Udallus," "Öwdal," and even "Woodall." It is probable that Udall was actually descended from the ancient Hampshire family of Uvedale.

PRINCIPAL WORKS: Floures for Latyne Spekynge, selected and gathered out of Terence, 1533; Verses and Dites [ditties] Made at the Coronation of Queen Anne (Latin and English, with J. Leland) 1533; Apothegms (tr. from Erasmus) 1542; Paraphrase of the New Testament (tr. from Erasmus, with others) 1548; Ralph Roister Doister, 1567 (W. D. Cooper, ed. 1847; E. Arber, ed. 1869; W. H. Williams, and P. A. Robins, eds. 1901); Dramatic Writings (J. S. Farmer, ed.) 1906.

ABOUT: Arber, E. A Brief Note of the Life, Works, and Times of Nicholas Udall, *in* Ralph Roister Doister, 1869 ed.; Collier, J. P. History of English Dramatic Poetry; Collins, J. C. Essays and Studies; Cooper, W. D. Life, *in* Ralph Roister Doister, 1847 ed.; Nichols, J. Progresses of Queen Elizabeth; Williams, W. H. and P. A. Robins. Introduction, Ralph Roister Doister, 1901 ed.; Wood, A. à, Athenae Oxonienses.

URQUHART or **URCHARD, Sir THOMAS** (1611-1660?), translator, miscellaneous writer, was born in Cromarty, Scotland, the oldest son of Sir Thomas Urquhart and Christian, daughter of Lord Elphinstone. The father wasted or lost his ancestral fortune, until before his death he was put in restraint by his family. Urquhart inherited the same tendency. Charles I gave him a letter of protection from his creditors in 1639.

He was educated at King's College, Aberdeen, which he entered in 1622, and was then sent on the Grand Tour of the Continent. He was involved in the "Trott of Turriff" Royalist uprising in 1639, but at first kept pretty well out of the civil wars. In 1641 he was knighted by Charles, following which he spent three more years, from 1642 to 1645, on the Continent, and then returned to Cromarty. In 1648 he was named an "officer of horse and foot," and after the abortive uprising at Inverness the next year he was declared a traitor, but was discharged by the Scottish General Assembly in 1650 without imprisonment. He accompanied Charles II on his expedition to England, was wounded at the battle of Worcester, and thrown into the Tower, but transferred to Windsor and leniently treated by Cromwell. He did lose four trunks of clothes and three of manuscripts.

After G. Glover

SIR THOMAS URQUHART

After his release he returned to Scotland and buried himself in his translation of Rabelais, all but the first part of which appeared after his death. It is probable that he spent some time later in London in connection with publication of his translation. Nothing positive is known about him, however, until his brother laid claim in 1660 to the hereditary office of sheriff of Cromarty, the implication being that Sir Thomas was dead. The legend is that he died in Paris of a fit of excited laughter on hearing of the Restoration.

Except for his *Epigrams,* which are sententious and prosaic, Urquhart's original books are almost indescribable. They are written in a fantastic jargon, full of half-insane pedantry and eccentric, esoteric learning. He was euphuist run wild. The *Ekskubalauron* (usually known as "the Jewel") constituted the introduction to a long work lost with his trunks at Worcester. He also invented a universal language, and wrote one book in it. Interspersed in his works were a "vindication" of Scotland before Presbyterianism, and many fragments of autobiography. The *Pantochronocanon* traced back his ancestry in detail to Adam! The whole, however, is practically unreadable and incredibly extravagant and affected.

Yet Urquhart is perhaps the greatest translator of the Elizabethan Age. The same qualities which made his own books monuments of eccentricity enabled him to become the ideal translator of Rabelais. He had a genius for coining words, and he rendered the galimatias and gibberish of *Pantagruel* in an inspired manner, bringing to his translation shrewdness, vigor, and fertility of imagination worthy of Rabelais himself.

Urquhart seems to have been unmarried. He wrote his name indifferently "Urquhart" or "Urchard," which may be a clue to its contemporary pronunciation.

PRINCIPAL WORKS: Epigrams, Divine and Moral (verse) 1641; The Trissotetras: or A Most Exquisite Table for Resolving all Manner of Triangles, 1645; Pantochronocanon: Or, a Peculiar Promptuary of Time, 1652; Ekskubalauron: Or The Discovery of a Most Exquisite Jewel, 1652; Logopandecteision, or an Introduction to the Universal Language, 1653; The Works of Mr. Francis Rabelais, Doctor in Physick, Book 1, 1653; Book 2, 1664; Book 3, 1693; The Works of Sir Thomas Urquhart (T. Maitland, ed.) 1834.

ABOUT: Irving, D. Lives of Scottish Writers; Maitland, T. Introduction, Works; Whibley, C.

Studies in Frankness; Willcock, J. Sir Thomas Urquhart of Cromartie.

USK, THOMAS (d. March 4, 1388), author of the prose work, *The Testament of Love,* was born in London. We know nothing of his early life, but from his writing it seems that he must have received a good education and may have been in holy orders. He suddenly appears on the stage of history as private secretary to John Northampton, Lord Mayor of London from 1381 to 1383. Northampton was a follower of Wycliffe and a social revolutionary. He strove to undermine the vested power of the London guilds during his term of office. Sir Nicholas Brembre won the mayoralty from him at the end of 1383, and had him arrested for sedition early in February 1384.

Usk fled from London and perhaps from England, but thought better of it and, like many another repentant revolutionary, decided to turn state's evidence. He was imprisoned in Newgate briefly in August 1384, bore witness against Northampton, John More and Richard Northbury before King Richard II at Reading, and in September received a royal pardon for his share in Northampton's "conspiracy."

But at some time in late 1384 or early 1385 Usk was again imprisoned, this time at Ludgate, and for six months. He had again to appear before the king at Reading—on the charge of having borne false witness the first time. It was during this period of imprisonment that he wrote *The Testament of Love,* in an attempt to clear himself of the accusation of treachery and win the favor of "Margarite"—probably the queen.

Whether his book had anything to do with it or not, Usk managed to obtain an acquittal. Probably the king wished him to be innocent. He now enjoyed not only the favor of the new Lord Mayor, Brembre—who many people thought had bribed him to betray Northampton—but also that of the king. In October 1387 Richard II thanked the citizens of London for electing (under pressure, of course) Thomas Usk to be subsheriff of Middlesex. Next month, however, Brembre and others of the king's advisers were arrested, Usk along with them. This sudden change was the result of the successful rebellion of the Duke of Gloucester, uncle of the king, who claimed that Usk had been appointed sub-sheriff mainly for the purpose of arresting *him*. Usk was tried on March 3, 1388; he protested his innocence, but was sentenced, hanged, and beheaded on the following day.

The Testament of Love was found among Chaucer's manuscripts and considered to be his until 1866; in 1897 Henry Bradley discovered that the initial letters of the chapters formed an acrostic revealing the authorship of Usk. The work itself is extremely derivative, being especially indebted to Chaucer's translation of Boethius.

PRINCIPAL WORKS: The Testament of Love *in* The Works of Chaucer (W. Thynne, ed.); *in* The Complete Works of Chaucer, Vol. VII (W. W. Skeat, ed.) 1897.

ABOUT: Bressie, R. The Date of Thomas Usk's Testament of Love (Modern Philology, 1928).

USSHER or USHER, JAMES (January 4, 1581-March 21, 1656), scholar, historian and theological writer, was born in Dublin, the son of Arland Ussher, clerk of the Irish court of chancery. His parents were Protestants.

Members of his family had been active in founding Trinity College in Dublin, and when it opened in 1594 the precocious boy of thirteen was the second student enrolled. He achieved early success in disputation, received his B.A. in 1597, his M.A. in 1600, was ordained deacon and priest in 1601, and in 1609 was offered the office of provost of the university, which he declined in favor of the title "Professor of Theological Controversies."

His early literary bent was toward poetry, but upon reading Cicero's phrase, "Not to know what happened before you were born, is to be always a child," he determined to devote himself to history. The scope of his learning was astonishing, and possessing the objectivity of a scholar, he was looked to for advice by all parties and respected by all. He drafted the Articles of Faith for the Irish Church. In 1621 he was appointed Bishop of Meath and Clonmacnoise. He spent some time in England, and while there in 1626 was made Bishop of Armagh, and thus primate of Ireland.

He was in England again in 1641 when all his property in Ireland was destroyed in the revolution. He remained in England, where he was awarded the bishopric of Carlisle and voted a pension by Parliament. Although his health was failing, he preached often and vigorously, frequently at Lincoln's Inn. Cromwell and Richelieu consulted him on theological matters, and upon his death of pleurisy at the age of seventy-five, Cromwell ordered a public funeral in Westminster Abbey, the only instance of the Church of England burial service being read there during the Protectorate. Ussher's wife had predeceased him by two years; he was survived by his only daughter, Elizabeth.

His writings have no great virtue of style. They were of enormous value as compilations of authorities from Ussher's remarkably wide knowledge, but when those authorities were superseded by later ones, his works lost their popularity. Samuel Johnson said of him, "Usher was the great luminary of the Irish Church; and a greater, no church could boast of."

PRINCIPAL WORKS: De Ecclesiarum Successione, 1613; Gravissimae Quaestionis de Christianorum Ecclesiarum, 1613; A Discourse of the Religion anciently professed of the Irish, 1623; Immanuel, or the Mystery of the Incarnation, 1638; The Annals of the World, 1658; Sermons, 1659; Chronologia Sacra, 1660.

ABOUT: Clarke, S. Lives of English Divines; Granger, J. Biographical History of England; Wood, A. à, Fasti Oxonienses.

UVEDALE, NICHOLAS. See UDALL, NICHOLAS

VANBRUGH, Sir JOHN (January 1664-March 26, 1726), architect and dramatist, was born in London, the son of Giles Vanbrugh, a "sugar-baker." His grandfather, Gillis van Brugg, had emigrated from Ghent to escape the Spanish rule. The name apparently was pronounced "Vanbrook" in his day.

In his infancy the family moved to Chester to avoid the plague, and he probably attended the King's School there. He was then sent to France to study architecture. He was arrested in Calais in 1690 as a suspected spy, sent to Vincennes, and then to the Bastille on a *lettre de cachet*. It was there that he wrote the first draft of *The Provok'd Wife*. He was released late in 1692 and returned to England, where he was commissioned in the army. In 1695 he was commissioned captain in Lord Berkeley's marine regiment of foot. The enormous success of *The Relapse* in 1697 (inspired by Cibber's *Love's Last Shift*) kept him busy

After Sir G. Kneller
SIR JOHN VANBRUGH

writing and adapting plays, but it also involved him in a controversy with Jeremy Collier, the enemy of the Restoration drama, and gradually he gave more and more of his attention to architecture.

As an architect Vanbrugh's ideas were grandiose to an extreme. His building of Castle Howard, for Lord Carlisle, was a triumph, and obtained for him the post of Carlisle herald in 1703, and Clarenceaux king-at-arms (against the wishes of the rest of the College of Heralds) in 1704. He had been made comptroller of the board of works in 1702, was dismissed in 1713, but reappointed in 1715, and in 1716 was made architect of Greenwich Hospital. His dismissal from office was an outgrowth of the long dispute over Blenheim Castle, the largest domestic building in England. This was authorized by Parliament, but no funds were provided, and Lord Marlborough, to whom it was supposedly a national gift, refused to pay for it. Lady Marlborough then took over and was still more difficult; Vanbrugh finally received part of his money in 1725. He had another unhappy experience with the Queen's Theatre in the Haymarket, of which he was architect, lessee, and manager. Unfortunately its acoustics could not have been worse, his attempt to introduce grand opera failed, and he was glad at last to let the house and end the venture.

Vanbrugh was knighted by George I in 1714. In 1719 he married Henrietta Yarburgh; of their several children only a son and daughter survived. He died of quinsy at sixty-two, not in his great "Bastile House" in Blackheath, but in his house in Whitehall, now the War Office.

Though of Flemish descent, Vanbrugh was the "typical" Englishman, bluff, hearty, good-humored, energetic. Everyone liked him except Lady Marlborough—even Swift apologized after his death for having satirized him. Pope, another not given to overpraise, called him "an honest-hearted, real good man."

He was not really a man of letters at all, and cared little for style. His plays are broad, lively farces full of vivid caricature and equally vivid realistic characterization. They are undeniably bawdy, but very funny. He had a great influence on English fiction, and Thackeray's "Sir Pitt Crawley" is a lineal descendant of "Sir John Brute" in *The Provok'd Wife*. A fair adaptor of French plays, he made a botch of adapting Fletcher. Voltaire summed up the chief Restoration dramatists well in calling Congreve the wittiest, Wycherley the strongest, and Vanbrugh the gayest.

PRINCIPAL WORKS: *Plays* (dates of publication)—The Relapse, or Virtue in Danger, 1697; The Provok'd Wife, 1697; The False Friend (from Zorrilla through LeSage) 1702; The Cornish Squire (from Molière) 1704 (as Squire Trelooby, 1734); The Confederacy (from Molière) 1705; The Mistake (from Molière) 1706; The Country House (from d'Ancourt) 1715; A Journey to London (completed by C. Cibber, as The Provok'd Husband) 1725; Dramatic Works (W. C. Ward, ed.) 1893, (A. E. H. Swaen, ed. 1896). *Miscellaneous* —A Short Vindication of the Relapse and the Provok'd Wife from Immorality and Prophaneness, 1698; Justification of What He Deposed in the Duchess of Marlborough's Late Tryal, 1781; Complete Works (B. Dobrée and G. Webb, eds.) 1927-28.

ABOUT: Barman, C. Sir John Vanbrugh; Dametz, M. John Vanbrughs Lebe und Werke; Dobrée, B. Essays in Biography; Lovegrove, G. H. The Life, Work, and Influence of Sir John Vanbrugh; Perry, H. T. E. The Comic Spirit in Restoration Drama; Swaen, A. E. H. Biographical Notice, Plays, 1896 ed.; Whistler, L. Sir John Vanbrugh, Architect and Dramatist.

VANCOUVER, GEORGE (1758-May 10, 1798), explorer, author of an account of his voyages, was born in King's Lynn, Norfolk, son of the deputy collector of customs of the ancient port city. Accustomed from childhood to the seafaring life of the coast, he joined the navy when he was thirteen, and sailed with Captain John Cook when he was barely fifteen. He accompanied Cook on three of his trips of exploration, including the search for the northwest passage.

By the time he was thirty-two, Vancouver was a commander. The small settlement of Nootka, on the northwest coast of the American continent, insignificant except as the center of the sea-otter trade, had been claimed by the Spaniards as token of their sovereignty over the entire northern Pacific seaboard. Vancouver, in command of the ship Discovery, was sent to reestablish the English claim to Nootka, and incidentally to continue the explorations of the Pacific coast begun by Cook.

The voyage took five years to complete. Sailing around the Cape of Good Hope, Vancouver surveyed the southwest coast of Australia, and corrected Cook's map of the coast of New Zealand, substituting for Cook's phrase about Dusky Bay, "Nobody knows what," an accurate drawing of shoreline and the legend, "Somebody knows what." He surveyed the west coast of the American continent from San Francisco northward, writing with great interest in his logbook about the Spanish colonies and the relationship of the Spanish missionaries to the Indians. In 1795 he returned to England by way of Cape Horn.

His health had been affected by the arduous life at sea, and it is possible that he had tuberculosis. At the request of the Admiralty, he settled in the village of Petersham with his brother, John, on a government pension, to write a complete account of his voyage from his journals and records. He had nearly finished editing and proofreading the fifth and final volume when he died, at the age of forty.

PRINCIPAL WORK: A Voyage of Discovery to the North Pacific Ocean and Round the World in the Years 1790-1795, 1798.

ABOUT: Godwin, G. S. Vancouver, a Life; Laut, A. Vancouver's Voyages; Meany, E. Vancouver's Discovery of Puget Sound.

VAUGHAN, HENRY (April 17, 1622-April 23, 1695), poet, was born in Newton-on-Usk, Brecknockshire, Wales, the son of Thomas Vaughan (a man of good family but apparently of rather bad character) and Denys Gwillims, a local heiress. He is one of the very few twins known to fame; his twin brother, Thomas, also wrote poetry but was more celebrated as an alchemist. The boys were tutored together by the rector of Llangattock, and together entered Jesus College, Oxford, in 1638. Henry Vaughan, however, left without a degree and went to London to study law at the desire of his relatives. Soon he had turned to the study of medicine, and though it is not known where or how he got his degree, he practiced medicine for the remainder of his life, first at Brecon, about 1645, and then in his native town.

The early years in London, when he made the acquaintance of many of the literary figures of the time, gave rise to Vaughan's first volume of poems. After his conversion to Christianity he was reluctant to publish his secular poetry, and even tried to suppress it, feeling that his glimpse into a mildly Bohemian world was a blot on his character. It was after his return to Wales that, under the influence of George Herbert, he became the mystic and the religious poet nature had intended him to be. As a Royalist, he may have taken part in the civil war—his brother certainly did—perhaps as a surgeon. But the remainder of his life is very unfruitful of incident. He was married twice, first to Catherine Wise, then, after her death, to her sister Elizabeth; by each wife he had three daughters and a son. He was highly thought of as a physician, and gave most of his time and energy to his profession until he died in Newton just after his seventy-third birthday.

Vaughan knew that his poetry was "cross to fashion." He was at home neither among the Puritans nor among the Carolines. The influence of Donne is strong upon him, but it comes filtered through a screen of Herbert, who remained as a man and a poet the object of his humble admiration. He is perhaps technically inferior to Herbert—largely because he had little sustaining power—but he far outdoes Herbert in intensity.

Vaughan cannot always keep up to the initial glory of his poems; they often start magnificently and then ebb into the awkward and commonplace. But few poets have a wider sweep, more majesty, more genius for expressing the virtually ineffable. There are passages of almost unearthly beauty in such poems as "Friends Departed" and "The Retreat." "Remote, mysterious, timeless," he seems to bring messages from another sphere of life and thought. He is detached from earth; even the human pathos of "Friends Departed" or the nostalgic melancholy of "The Retreat" is drowned in the excess of his religious passion.

For nearly two hundred years Vaughan remained practically unknown, only one of his volumes even demanding a second edition. The worldly eighteenth century had no place for him. He was rediscovered in time to become the spiritual godfather of Wordsworth—perhaps of Tennyson too, in *In Memoriam*, though Tennyson denied it. There is no doubt whatever that the *Ode on the Intimations of Immortality* and others of Wordsworth's semi-pantheistic poems derived from Vaughan.

Vaughan himself was no pantheist, however, though he has been called one. Theologically he was strictly orthodox. His translations and original prose writings on the Church Fathers show that. But he did have a mystical rapport with nature which lent exquisite beauty to his descriptions of natural objects (always subservient to his major religious theme); and he was intimately one with his native Wales. He took the name of "Silurist" deliberately, in reference to the Silures, Tacitus' name for the aboriginal Welsh. In a play upon the name (since *silex* also means "flint") he said that he had drawn "unanticipated sparks from a flinty ground." That indeed is a very happy phrase to describe Vaughan's frequent but isolated passages of pure and high poetry.

His prose was rich and melodious, though sometimes marred by artificiality and affectation which occasionally dropped into bathos. But primarily he was a poet—by flashes only —but they are flashes of lightning. It might even be said that he had only moderate talent, but great and consuming genius.

It is interesting to note that John Aubrey, the most worldly and extroverted of men, was a cousin of this unworldly Welsh doctor. It is he who has provided most of the scanty facts of Vaughan's personal history—including the description of the poet's father as a "coxcombe" and dishonest. There was actually no definitive full-length biography of Vaughan until F. E. Hutchinson's was published in 1948.

It should perhaps be explained that *Olor Iscanus* means "the swan of Usk," the river which runs by Vaughan's birthplace; *Silex Scintillans* is "sparkling flint" (it was with this volume that Vaughan first called himself "Silurist"); *Flores Solitudinus* is "flowers of solitude"; and *Thalia Rediviva* is "Thalia [the muse] revived." This was Vaughan's last volume of poetry, and contains much early and some later work; it was published probably without his authority and possibly against his will. The titles of all these works are Latin, but the works themselves are of course in English. *Olor Iscanus* contains some prose translations besides poems; *The Mount of Olives* is made up of translations from Anselm and original devotional essays; *Flores Solitudinis*, besides translations from the Church Fathers, contains a life of Paulinus; and *Thalia Rediviva* includes also some of Thomas Vaughan's poems. Henry Vaughan also translated (1655) *Hermetical Physick* from the Latin of Nollius.

PRINCIPAL WORKS: Poems, with the Tenth Satyre of Juvenal Englished, 1646; Silex Scintillans: or, Sacred Poems and Private Ejaculations, 1650; Olor Iscanus, 1651; The Mount of Olives: or, Solitary Devotions, 1652; Flores Solitudinis, 1654; Thalia Rediviva: The Pass-Times and Diversions of a Countery-Muse, 1687; Complete Works (A. B. Grosart, ed.) 1870-71; Poems (E. K. Chambers, ed.) 1896.

ABOUT: Aubrey, J. Brief Lives of Eminent Men; Beeching, H. C. Introduction, Poems, 1896 ed.; Bennett, J. W. Four Metaphysical Poets; Brown, J. Horae Subsecivae; Grosart, A. B. Introduction; Complete Works; Guiney, L. I. A Little English Gallery; Hutchinson, F. E. Henry Vaughan; Johnson, L. Critical Essays; Leishman, J. B. The Metaphysical Poets; Marilla, E. L. comp. Comprehensive Bibliography of Henry Vaughan; Palgrave, F. T. Landscape in Poetry; Sencourt, R. Outlying Philosophy; Shairp, J. C. Sketches in History and Poetry; Wells, H. W. The Tercentenary of Henry Vaughan; White, H. C. The Metaphysical Poets: A Study in Religious Experience; Wood, A. à, Athenae Oxonienses.

VAUGHAN, THOMAS (April 17, 1622-February 27, 1666), poet, author of works on alchemy, was the descendant of an ancient Welsh family of Llansaintffraed, Breconshire. He was the twin brother of the metaphysical poet, Henry Vaughan, and the brothers were devoted to each other throughout their lives.

He graduated with a B.A. from Jesus College, Oxford, became a fellow of the college, and two years later received the living of St. Bridget's in Breconshire. He fought in the Royalist army during the civil war. He was married in 1651, and at about the same time began publishing the works on magic, alchemy, and the Rosicrucian mysteries which were the real interest of his life. In 1658 he was deprived of his rectory at St. Bridget's on charges of "drunkenness, swearing, incontinency, and being no preacher."

He now plunged into the study of chemistry, forswore his earlier profligate manner of life, and insisted he was a true scientist, searching for a solution of nature's mysteries. When the scholar Henry More called him a magician, Vaughan protested so vehemently that a public controversy, marked by extraordinary virulence, followed, much of it devoted to Vaughan's attack on, and More's defense of, Aristotle.

Some of his poetry was published with that of his brother, and while he was a far inferior poet to Henry, his own verse has poetic feeling and some of his brother's intense love of nature.

Most of his works on magic were published under the pseudonym of Eugenius Philalethes, and he has sometimes been confused with a more thoroughgoing believer in magic, Eirenaeus Philalethes, who wrote at the same time and whose identity has never been discovered. In 1895 a book titled *Mémoires d'une Ex-Palladiste* appeared in France, in which its author, Diana Vaughan, declared herself a descendant of Thomas Vaughan, identified him with Eirenaeus Philalethes, and vouched for the authenticity of a pact said to have been signed between the devil and her forebear on March 25, 1645. This was later proved to be a hoax perpetrated by five Parisian journalists.

Vaughan died at the age of forty-four, presumably from the fumes of mercury with which he was carrying on experiments at the rectory of Albury, Oxfordshire.

PRINCIPAL WORKS: Anthroposophia Theomagica, with Anima Magica Adamica, or the Antiquities of Magic, 1650; Lumen de Lumine, 1651; Aula Lucis, or the House of Light, 1652; Euphrates, 1655; The Chemist's Key to Shut, and to Open: or the True Doctrine of Corruption and Generation, 1657.

ABOUT: Aubrey, J. Brief Lives; Thurloe, J. State Papers; Waite, A. E. Introduction to Lumen de Lumine; Wood, A. à, Athenae Oxonienses.

VAUX, THOMAS, Second Baron Vaux of Harrowden (1510-1556), poet, was the eldest son of Nicholas Vaux, first Baron Vaux, and his wife Anne Green. When Thomas was thirteen his father died, and he

succeeded to the barony and immediately plunged into the life of the court which was to be the only life he knew. The thirteen-year-old boy accompanied Cardinal Wolsey on a diplomatic visit to France. He later studied at Cambridge, but did not graduate.

When he was twenty-one he took his place in the House of Lords. The following year he accompanied the court on a visit to Boulogne and Calais, and in 1533 was made Knight of the Bath. He married and had two daughters and two sons.

A member of the inner intellectual clique of the court, he indulged, as a matter of course, in the writing of short lyrics, which, like those of his fellow courtiers, were metrically adept, generally light in tone, and largely dependent on Petrarchan conceits for what charm they possessed. However, his were not only among the most accomplished of such verses, but they often have a deeper religious sensibility and a more chivalrous attitude toward love than those of his contemporaries. Some of his more reflective verses, while revealing no deeply poetic feeling, do show a touchingly devout and sincere spirit. He has been called a "brave, simple and musical writer."

Thirteen of his poems appeared posthumously in the collection, first published in 1576, entitled *The Paradise of Dainty Devices*. The two lyrics for which he was best known were love poems, "The assault of Cupid upon the fort when the lover's heart lay wounded," and "The aged lover renounces love." The latter, which legend says he wrote on his deathbed, is incorrectly sung by the First Gravedigger in *Hamlet*, as he digs Ophelia's grave.

Vaux was at one time Captain of the Isle of Jersey. He died at his home at Harrowden, Northampton, when he was forty-six years old.

PRINCIPAL WORKS: Thirteen poems, in The Paradise of Dainty Devices, 1576.

ABOUT: Burke, Sir J. B. Peerage; Ritson, J. Bibliographia Poetica; Warton, T. History of English Poetry.

"VENERABLE BEDE, THE" See BEDA

VERE, EDWARD de (April 2, 1550-June 24, 1604), seventeenth Earl of Oxford, poet, was the only son of John de Vere, Earl of

Oxford, who died in 1562. Edward at once succeeded to the title, but was a royal ward for the remainder of his minority, known as Lord Bulbeck. Queen Elizabeth's chief minister, Sir William Cecil, afterward Lord Burghley, took charge of him.

Oxford was intellectually precocious, entering Queens' College, Cambridge, before he was nine years old. After he became a ward his education was continued by his maternal uncle, Arthur Golding, translator of Ovid's *Metamorphoses.*

Oxford's entire life story is one of brilliant promise and magnificent opportunities that in the end came to nothing. First, consider his failure as a private citizen. He married in 1572, at his own insistence, Burghley's daughter Anne. Three years later he went on a long-desired Continental tour. After he had been absent six months, his wife gave birth to a daughter, which he chose on his return to consider illegitimate. The couple separated for some years, and never were on particularly good terms afterward. Anne died in 1588. He married Elizabeth Trentham in 1591 and by her had a son who lived to be his heir. Oxford left him a much-reduced patrimony, having sold a great deal of land cheap to pay for his extravagant way of life.

Oxford was in frequent attendance on Queen Elizabeth from boyhood and might have been as great a favorite as Leicester, but he forfeited her good will by many acts of disobedience. In 1572 he wanted to rescue his kinsman, the Duke of Norfolk, from the Tower; in 1574 he visited the Continent without the queen's permission. At the end of 1580 he suddenly confessed to the queen that he had become a professing Catholic on his return from his travels, as had Lord Henry Howard, Francis Southwell and Charles Arundel; he now sincerely repented this action and accused the others of treason. They brought numerous countercharges and Oxford's fortunes began to decline. Nonetheless, from 1584 to his death he received a government pension of £1000 per annum; James I made him a Privy Councillor.

He distinguished himself in his youth by his skill in military exercises, but never held any important military command. For the fight against the Spanish Armada he fitted out his own ship, but did not achieve much.

1575

EDWARD DE VERE, 17TH EARL
OF OXFORD

The most satisfactory part of his career was his patronage of literature. Gabriel Harvey, the scholar, and Lyly and Munday, dramatists and writers of euphuistic prose, were some of those he helped. Beginning in 1580 he had his own company of players. Francis Meres described him as one of the best contemporary writers of comedy, but none of his plays has survived—unless he collaborated with Lyly. Just over a score of unremarkable lyrics can be definitely attributed to him. Nevertheless, several writers have believed him to be the author of Shakespeare's plays.

Portraits of the earl in his youth show a short figure with a handsome, effeminate face, a moustache but no beard, and clothes of the utmost splendour.

PRINCIPAL WORKS: The Poems (*in* Fuller Worthies' Miscellany, Vol. IV) 1872; The Poems of Edward de Vere (J. T. Looney, ed.) 1921.

ABOUT: Looney, J. T. Shakespeare Identified in Edward de Vere; Ward, B. M. The Seventeenth Earl of Oxford, 1550-1604.

VILLIERS, GEORGE, Second Duke of Buckingham (January 30, 1628-April 16, 1687), satirist, poet, dramatist, was born in London, the second son (his older brother died in infancy) of the first duke, who was assassinated in August of that year, and of Lady Katherine Manners, who remarried the Marquis of Antrim. Charles I, who had been

Sir P. Lely

GEORGE VILLIERS, 2ND DUKE
OF BUCKINGHAM

his father's friend, reared him and his younger (posthumously born) brother at court with his own children. He was sent to Trinity College, Cambridge, where Cowley became his lifelong friend. He graduated M.A. in 1642. He and his brother then joined the king at Oxford, at the beginning of the civil war; he served for a while under Prince Rupert, then was sent, in the care of the Earl of Northumberland, to Rome and Florence. His estates were sequestered but returned, in 1647, because of his youth. In 1648 he joined the Earl of Holland in Surrey, was voted a traitor, his estates were again sequestered and his brother was killed in battle. He escaped to Holland, where Charles II made him a member of his privy council in exile in 1650. He went with Charles to Scotland, being acceptable because of his religious tolerance and friendship to the Presbyterians. By 1651 he was royalist commander-in-chief in Scotland. Then he followed Charles to England, fought at Worcester, and again escaped to Holland. There his overtures to Cromwell brought about a breach with Charles, which was complete by 1654. In 1656 he went back to England and in a whirlwind courtship married Mary, the only daughter of the parliamentary general, Lord Fairfax, who had been about to marry the Earl of Chesterfield. Thanks to his new father-in-law, he

was given only house imprisonment, but breaking his parole, he was sent to the Tower until 1659.

With the Restoration he finally renewed his friendship with Charles, became a gentleman of the bedchamber, and was readmitted to the privy council in 1662. From 1661 to 1667 he was lord lieutenant of the West Riding of York. His estates were restored to him, and he was very wealthy. But his constant plotting and intrigue kept him on uneasy terms with the king; in 1667 he served a short term again in the Tower. In consequence he brought about the downfall of his enemy Clarendon. Next he killed the Earl of Shrewsbury in a duel and openly took the Countess as his mistress. Attacked by Parliament for his scandalous and intriguing life, he reformed for a while, but his long feud with the Duke of York spelled the end of his public life when the duke ascended the throne as James II. Villiers retired to Yorkshire, a semi-invalid, it was said, because of his years of debauchery, and there he died of a chill brought on while hunting. He was buried in Westminster. He left no legitimate children, and the title became extinct.

Villiers, though he had wit, charm, and generosity, and was sincerely tolerant in religion, was a notorious roué in an uncensorious era, and was a sort of monster of vanity, instability, and unreliability. He lived in a maze of plotting and scandal, and was a thoroughly bad sort. But he did have intellectual interests (he was a member of the Royal Society and something of an alchemist), and his satire had both bite and verve. His "characters" are among the best of their kind. He was one of the authors of the immensely popular *Rehearsal*. He was a literary man, however, only very much on the side; primarily he was, as Dryden put it, "chymist, fiddler, statesman and buffoon."

PRINCIPAL WORKS: The Rehearsal (with S. Butler, et alia) 1672; Poetical Reflections . . . by a Person of Quality, 1681 (?); Poetical Reflections on a late poem entitled Absolon [*sic*] and Achitophel, 1682; The Chances (comedy, adapted from Fletcher) 1682; A Short Discourse on the Reasonableness of Men's having a Religion, 1685; The Battle of Sedgmoor (dialogue) 1704; The Militant Couple (dialogue) 1704; Miscellaneous Works (T. Brown, ed.) 1705; The Restoration (comedy, adapted from Beaumont and Fletcher) 1714; Works (T. Evans, ed.) 1775.

ABOUT: Brown, T. Miscellania Aulica; Burghclerc, W. G. George Villiers, 2nd Duke of Buckingham: A Study in the History of the Restoration; Cammell, C. R. The Great Duke of Buckingham; Chapman, H. W. Great Villiers; Coffin, R. P. T. The Dukes of Buckingham: Playboys of the Stuart World; Fairfax, B. Memoirs of the Life of George, Duke of Buckingham; Pepys, S. Diary; Walpole, H. Royal and Noble Authors.

WACE of JERSEY (fl. 1170), chronicler,

was born in Jersey, probably about 1100. He was educated in France, and became a "reading clerk," or teacher, at Caen. His writings marked a period of literary transition, since they were written by a classical scholar and churchman, but are in the "vulgar" tongue of the people. Long narrative poems written in Old French, the Romance language, they were called romances, although they were based on historical authorities and were, as far as Wace's careful and honest efforts could make them, historical rather than fictional.

Surviving are five of the romances, and a metrical translation and expansion of Geoffrey of Monmouth's *History of the Britons*, into which Wace introduced for the first time the idea of chivalry at King Arthur's court, and the first record of the institution of the Round Table.

The *Roman de Brut*, which was written in 1155 and dedicated to Eleanor of Aquitaine, tells the story of Brutus, the legendary founder of Britain. It is chiefly important because the later chronicler, Layamon, based a far better known work of the same name entirely on one of the manuscript copies of Wace's poem.

In 1160, at the request of Henry II, Wace began work on his most important chronicle, the *Roman de Rou*. His written sources for this were Dudo of St. Quentin and William of Jumièges, but much of it is based on oral information.

The first section of the poem traces the kings of England in reverse order from Henry II to Rou, or Hrolf. The second carries the history of England from Rou to Richard the Fearless, and the third brings it up to 1107. Except for its metrical form, Wace did not attempt to embellish his story with art. There are fewer legends and more facts in his chronicle than in those of most of his contemporaries, and, if his authorities differed on a given point, he included the alternate versions. Edward Freeman, author of the *History of the Norman Conquest of England*, called Wace's *Rou* the "most trustworthy narrative of the central scene of my history."

The work took ten years to write, part of which time Wace lived at Henry's court at Fécampe, part at Bayeux, where Henry had awarded him a prebend. Nothing further is known of his life after the completion of his final work, although he may have been alive as late as 1174.

PRINCIPAL WORKS: Life of St. Nicholas; Conception of the Virgin; Life of St. Margaret; Brut, 1155; Roman de Rou, 1160-70.
ABOUT: Round, J. H. Feudal England; English Historical Review, 1893-94.

WAKEFIELD, GILBERT (February 22,

1756-September 9, 1801), scholar and controversial writer, was born at St. Nicholas in Nottingham, where his father was rector of the parish. He says in his autobiography, "I, at the age of three, could spell the longest words, say my catechism without hesitation, and read the gospels with fluency." He attended Jesus College, Cambridge, as a scholarship student, won many prizes in Latin, graduated with a B.A. in 1776, and was made a fellow of the College.

Two years later, without serious theological study, he was ordained and given a curacy at Liverpool. Immediately plunging into study, he discovered in himself Arian or Unitarian convictions which forced him to resign his curacy and prevented him from further scholastic or religious employment.

He supported himself, his wife, and his six children by private classical tutoring, with two periods of teaching in liberal schools where he need not subscribe to the Articles of Faith. During these years he wrote a good deal, and translated Horace, Virgil, and Lucretius.

In 1798 he wrote an eloquent and vitriolic pamphlet in which he attacked Pitt, charged corruption in the civil and ecclesiastical systems, and opposed the war with France, defending the rights of the French revolutionaries. He was tried for seditious libel and imprisoned for two years. The conditions of his imprisonment were as lenient as possible; sympathizers raised money, his family lived near him, and he carried on his studies and a lively and scholarly correspondence. A few months after his release he died of typhus fever at his home at Hackney.

Wakefield's brilliance is unquestioned, but what might have been an extraordinarily distinguished career was ruined by his twin vices of acrimony and carelessness. His personal amiability was transformed in his writing into the most violent and bitter animosity. He was dogmatically prejudiced about trifles as well as about more serious matters, and however admirable his aims, his controversial manners were execrable. On the other hand, in his chosen field of classical scholarship, while his industry, taste, and knowledge were exceptional, he made serious errors of judgment and fact because of his headlong haste and lack of care.

PRINCIPAL WORKS: An Essay on Inspiration, 1781; The Internal Evidence of the Christian Religion, 1789; Silva Critica, 1789-94; Memoirs, 1792; An Examination of Thomas Paine's "Age of Reason," 1794; Horace, a translation, 1794; Virgil, a translation, 1796; Lucretius, a translation, 1796; Noctes Carcerariae, 1801.

ABOUT: Aikin, J. Memoir; Fox, C. J. Memoirs; Wakefield, G. Memoirs.

WALLER, EDMUND (March 3, 1606-October 21, 1687), poet, was born at Coleshill, Buckinghamshire (formerly in Hertfordshire), the eldest son and heir of Robert Waller and Anne Hampden. His father was an extremely wealthy country gentleman of a very old family, while his mother was an aunt of John Hampden, the Roundhead leader, and a relative by marriage of Oliver Cromwell. Edmund was educated by country schoolmasters, including a Mr. Dobson of Wickham (High Wycombe?). After his father's death in 1616 he went to Eton and thence in 1620 to King's College, Cambridge. He left in 1622, without taking a degree, to enter Lincoln's Inn and study law, as his father had done. He seems to have been a Member of Parliament for Amersham as early as 1621.

Left very wealthy by his father's will, Waller created a sensation in 1631 by marrying an orphan heiress, Anne Banke, who was a ward of the Court of Aldermen in the City of London. The Court objected to her marriage without its consent, and Waller would have been in serious trouble if King Charles I had not intervened on his behalf. He retired with his wife to the country after the affair had been settled; she died in childbirth, 1634, having borne him a son and a daughter.

Waller now began to enter into London literary society and to attend the court. His first celebrity as a poet dates from this period. Many of his early poems were addressed to "Sacharissa," his name for Lady Dorothy Sidney, whom he met and fell in love with about 1635. Waller was not a very passionate lover, to judge by his poems; perhaps it would be more correct to say that he was not a very passionate poet. The lady married another suitor in 1639.

Charles I was very averse to summoning parliaments, but in 1640 he needed money so badly that he summoned two—the "Short Parliament" and the "Long Parliament." Waller was a highly vocal member of both. At first he seemed to take the side of his Roundhead relatives, but in 1641 he began to move toward the Royalists. As a wealthy landed proprietor and investor, Waller had everything to lose if open war broke out between king and Parliament. When the king raised the royal standard at Nottingham in 1642, Waller sent him a large sum of money, but retained his seat in parliament. In February 1643 he was one of the parliamentary commissioners to discuss peace terms with the king at Oxford. These discussions came to nothing and Waller, on his return to London, became involved in a plot to capture the defenses of the city and hand it over to the king. On May 31, he and his accomplices were arrested.

Waller soon made a full confession of his share in the plot and strove to implicate certain noblemen, probably in the hope that parliament would be afraid to proceed against them and would therefore release him. Some of the less wealthy and distinguished plotters, including a brother-in-law of Waller's named Tomkins, were tried, sentenced, and executed with great promptness, but the parliament was not too happy about doing the same thing to one of its own members. On July 4, 1643, Waller came to plead his case at the bar of the House, wearing mourning and behaving with the utmost contrition. His speech in his own defense was a wonderful histrionic performance; it saved his life; after being kept in prison until November 1644, he was fined £10,000 and banished to France. Before leaving England he married another heiress, Mary Bracey.

Waller was by no means poor while in exile; he enjoyed at least one pleasant tour in Switzerland and Italy. From 1648 he lived in Paris with the other exiled Royalists. In 1651, probably thanks to his influence with

540

J. Riley

EDMUND WALLER

Cromwell, his sentence of banishment was revoked; he returned to England the following year. In 1653 his mother died. He was appointed a Commissioner for Trade in 1655.

Having written two poems in praise of Cromwell, he wrote a third in praise of Charles II at the Restoration in 1660. When Charles asked him why the last was so much worse than the other two, he replied, "Sir, we poets never succeed so well in writing truth as in fiction."

From 1661 until his death Waller was a member of every parliament that sat. He never held any government post, but was one of the most popular speakers, becoming in later years the "father" of the House of Commons by virtue of his age. As always, he advocated tolerance and the "middle way."

Waller continued writing poems and making speeches to the last. He was forewarned of his death by a swelling in his leg; he died at his home, Hall Barn, and was buried in Beaconsfield churchyard. His second wife had died in 1677.

A good idea of Waller's character can be gained from his behavior at critical moments of his life, as recorded above. He was a man without strong passions or strong convictions. Yet he became a favorite of men of every political party because of his gifts as a public speaker and as a private companion. He was normally a water drinker, though he fractured his skull by a fall after a merry party in 1670; his abstemiousness did not prevent him from being the liveliest member of every convivial gathering. At the approach of death he became pious and wrote some religious poetry of no great merit.

The great majority of Waller's poems are "occasional"—that is, written on some anniversary or about some topical event. It is hardly any wonder that his popularity as a poet was very high in his own lifetime and has declined steadily almost ever since. In the eighteenth century he still had a high and rather undeserved reputation as one of the inventors of the classical couplet. The smoothness of his versification was always admired. Pope in his *Essay on Criticism* recommended the true critic to:

. . . praise the easy vigour of a line,
Where Denham's strength and Waller's
    sweetness join.

But in truth the modern reader will find him very insipid. "Go, lovely rose" and a few other lyrics are immortal, but he lacked both wit and learning, one or other of which redeemed the verses of most of his Cavalier contemporaries.

PRINCIPAL WORKS: *Poetry*: Poems, 1645; Divine Poems, 1685; The Second Part of Mr. Waller's Poems, 1690. *Prose*: Speech Against Prelates' Innovations, 1641; Mr. Waller's Speech in the Painted Chamber, 1641; Speech, 4 July 1643, 1643; The Works of Edmund Waller in this Parliament, 1645.

ABOUT: Johnson, S. Lives of the Poets; Thorn-Drury, G. Introduction to The Poems of Waller.

WALPOLE, HORACE (HORATIO) (Fourth Earl of Orford) (September 24, 1717-March 2, 1797), Gothic novelist, man of letters, was born in London, the youngest child of Sir Robert Walpole, Whig prime minister and later first Earl of Orford, and of his first wife, Catherine Shorter. Because he was ten years younger than any other of the children, and so different from all of them, contemporary scandal guessed that his real father was Lord Hervey. Walpole never heard this gossip, and was unusually devoted to both his parents all his life—his mother died when he was twenty.

After private tutoring, he entered Eton in 1727, remaining there for seven years. It was there that he became a close friend of

J. G. Eccardt, 1754
HORACE WALPOLE, 4TH EARL
OF ORFORD

his cousins, the Conways, and one of the inseparable "quadruple alliance" with Richard West, Thomas Ashton, and Thomas Gray. In 1735 he entered King's College, Cambridge, but left without a degree in 1739 to make the Grand Tour of the Continent with Gray. They quarreled on the journey, not to be reconciled for years. Walpole was seriously ill in Italy, and finally cut his journey short because in his absence he had been elected a Member of Parliament for Callington, Cornwall. His first speech was in defense of his father. He served for various constituencies until 1768, when he retired. Politics never really interested him much except as a spectator. Thanks to his father, however, he held several small sinecure appointments in the Exchequer throughout his life.

In 1747 he leased a house which he called Strawberry Hill, near Twickenham, on the Thames, and in 1753 he began the building and gardening which made it a show place, a sort of combined museum and park, overrun by visitors who secured tickets to see it. Though he made some bad mistakes, he was a connoisseur and a virtuoso, and the final dispersal of his collections in 1842 brought an immense sum. In 1757 he started his own press, with a man and boy to operate it, and during his lifetime all his own books were published from it. He also published Gray's

poems, a *Life of Lord Herbert of Cherbury,* the *Mémoires de Grammont,* and other important works. He sometimes called the press his "Elzivirianum," in honor of the pioneer printer, but officially it was the Strawberry Hill Press.

Walpole made a long visit to Paris in 1765, and then first met Mme. du Deffand, the *salonnière,* twenty-five years his senior and going blind. They corresponded until her death in 1780, and she fell in love with him, which must have been most embarrassing to a man who never showed any real interest in a woman. His letters to her were destroyed, however (hers to him have been published), not because of this but because he was ashamed of his unidiomatic French.

His brother, the second earl, had died, and a nephew succeeded as third earl. This nephew, unfortunately, was insane for a good part of the time, and prodigally extravagant when he was not. It therefore devolved on the uncle to take charge of the family fortune, and a good part of his time and energy in his later years was perforce devoted to this task. In 1791 the nephew died, and Horace Walpole succeeded. He refused to enter the House of Lords, and seldom signed his name as Earl of Orford. He was always independent in such matters; christened Horatio, he always preferred the "good English name" of Horace.

In 1789 the Berry family, father and two grown daughters, became his close neighbors, and Agnes and Mary Berry became his most intimate friends. (He is reported even to have been willing to marry Mary Berry, if necessary, in order to keep them near him!) After his death Mary Berry edited his works, though in conformity to the prejudices of the time she gave her father's name as editor.

For many years Walpole's house, his garden, and his art collections were the chief occupation and interest of his life. Next to them came his correspondence. He has been called "the prince of letter writers," "the best letter writer in the English language." He made letter writing a fine art. One correspondent, Sir Horace Mann, he wrote to for forty years or more—someone has remarked, meanly, that they never quarreled because after their first meeting they never saw each other.

Indeed, it became a literary convention to speak of Horace Walpole as cynical, affected, cold, petulant, arrogant, and frivolous. (Macaulay, who disliked all Whigs, despised Walpole.) He was all these things, at least at times. He was also a very shy man. Much that repelled people in him was a mask or shield worn for protection. He was fastidious to the point of neurosis, and equally sensitive and proud. Only with a few old and close friends could he relax and be himself. His own words are unconsciously self-revelatory: "Life is a comedy to those who think, a tragedy to those who feel."

It is true that his ruthless treatment of Chatterton was the last straw that broke that unhappy youth's spirit—but considering the circumstances, Walpole's harshness seems less cruel, and he was deeply affected by the boy's suicide. He resigned from the Society of Antiquaries, of which he had been a fellow, because his fellow members criticized roughly his *Richard III*, but he was not vainglorious about his writing. He was always an amateur, and never thought of himself as a literary figure. "I want no laurels," he said, "and shall be quite content with a sprig of rosemary thrown after me, when the parson of the parish commits my dust to dust."

The laurel was due him, however, since *The Castle of Otranto*, absurd as it often is, "one vast anachronism," is yet the pioneer Gothic novel, the earliest effort to introduce supernaturalism and mystery into romance. His tragedy, *The Mysterious Mother* (which Fanny Burney called "horrible"), has been termed "the least bad of tragedies when tragedy was at its worst." His journals, diaries, and letters constitute an autobiography and a history of their time, as well as being a mine of wit. His attempt to rehabilitate Richard III, though faulty in scholarship, foreshadowed modern historical research. His letters surpassed those of his model, Mme. de Sevigné, in pure wit and as pure art.

A semi-invalid all his life, of whom it was said that "he was never very young," Walpole died of gout, his old enemy, at nearly eighty. He was the finest type of intellectual aristocrat of the eighteenth century, though probably few persons ever felt any warm affection for him.

PRINCIPAL WORKS: Aedes Walpolianae, 1747; Catalogue of Royal and Noble Authors, 1758; Fugitive Pieces in Prose and Verse, 1758; Anecdotes of Painting in England, 1762-71; Catalogue of Engravers Born and Resident in England, 1763; The Castle of Otranto, 1764-65; The Mysterious Mother, 1768; Historic Doubts on the Life and Reign of Richard III, 1768; Miscellaneous Antiquities, 1772; Miscellaneous Letters, 1778; Description of the Villa, 1784; Works (R. [M.] Berry, ed.) 1798; Reminiscences, 1819; Private Correspondence, 1820; Memoirs of the Last Ten Years of the Reign of King George II, 1822; Letters (J. Wright, ed.) 1840; Memoirs of the Reign of King George III (D. Le Marchant, ed.) 1845; Memoirs of the Reign of King George II (Lord Holland, ed.) 1846; Letters (P. Cunningham, ed.) 1857-59; Journal of the Reign of George III from 1771 to 1783 (J. Doran, ed.) 1859; Letters to George Montagu, 1881; Some Unpublished Letters of Horace Walpole (S. Walpole, ed.) 1902; Letters (Mrs. P. Toynbee, ed.) 1903; Letters (W. S. Lewis, ed.) 1926.

ABOUT: Benjamin, L. S. (Lewis Melville) Horace Walpole; Berry, M. Some Extracts of Journals and Correspondence; Chase, I. W. U. Horace Walpole: Gardenist; Cox, W. Memoirs of Horatio, Lord Walpole [sic]; De Koven, A. F. Horace Walpole and Mme. du Deffand; Dobson, A. Horace Walpole, A Memoir; Greenwood, A. D. Horace Walpole's World; Gwynne, S. L. The Life of Horace Walpole; Havens, M. A. Horace Walpole and the Strawberry Hill Press; Ketton-Cramer, R. W. Horace Walpole; Lewis, W. Collector's Progress; Macaulay, T. B. Essays; Mehrotra, K. K. Horace Walpole and the English Novel; More, P. E. Shelburne Essays; Pinkerton, J. Walpoliana; Seeley, L. B. Horace Walpole and His World; Stuart, D. M. Horace Walpole; Walpole, H. Horace Walpole's Correspondence with Thomas Gray, Richard West, and Thomas Ashton; Walpole, H. Reminiscences; Warburton, E. Memoirs of Horace Walpole and His Contemporaries; Yvon, P. Horace Walpole (in French).

WALSH, WILLIAM (1663-March 18, 1708), critic and poet, was born at Abberley, Worcestershire. He attended Wadham College, Oxford, but did not graduate. He was elected four times to parliament, serving three terms for Worcestershire and once for Richmond, but except that he spoke as a Protestant and a Whig, little is known of his parliamentary career. He was a Gentleman of the Horse at the court of Queen Anne from 1702 until his death.

His literary career would have been that of any of the light versifiers of his day except for his strong friendship with Dryden and Pope, which led them to overrate his powers both as poet and critic. Pope's own account of Walsh's influence on his work says they first met when Pope was fifteen, although Pope's habitual untrustworthiness in matters concerning his own precocity makes this questionable. Walsh's advice to Pope has become well known through Pope's quotation of it: "He used to encourage me much; and used to tell me, that there was one way left of excelling; for though we had several great poets, we never had any one great poet that was correct; and he desired me to make that my study and aim." Walsh did more than this for young Pope, editing and criticizing many of his poems in manuscript, and correcting his translation of Statius' *Thebais*. In return, Pope overpraised Walsh's verse, and Dryden called Walsh the best critic in the nation.

Walsh was a cultivated dilettante, a dandy in appearance, who declared that there was "not one folly he had not committed in his devotion to women except marriage." He wrote largely for his own amusement, publishing almost nothing during his lifetime. For the modest pastime they were with him, his erotic, epigrammatic and elegiac verses were not without elegance and charm.

His only essay in play-writing was an adaptation of a Molière play, *Monsieur de Pourceaugnac*, of which he, Vanbrugh, and Congreve each wrote one act, devoting two mornings each to the work.

Walsh died at forty-five. Most of his work was published posthumously, a collected *Works* being issued in 1736.

PRINCIPAL WORKS: Dialogue Concerning Women, Being a Defense of the Sex, 1691; Funeral Elegy on the Death of the Queen, 1695; Aesculapius, or the Hospital of Fools, 1714; Poems, 1716; Letters Amorous and Gallant, 1716; Works, 1736.

ABOUT: Cibber, T. Lives of the Poets of Great Britain; Johnson, S. Lives of the English Poets; Luttrell, N. Brief Relation of State Affairs; Pope, A. Essay on Criticism, and Epistle to Dr. Arbuthnot.

WALSINGHAM, THOMAS (d. 1422?),

monk and chronicler, may have been born in Norfolk. He was attached to the Benedictine Abbey of St. Albans, and received his education there and at Oxford. He at one time was musical director of the Abbey, but his principal office, held under Abbot Thomas de la Mare, was that of scriptorarius, or supervisor of the manuscript copying of the monks.

One of his early works, *Chronicon Angliae*, completed about 1388, expressed rather violent political opinions, including an attack on John of Gaunt. When John's son ascended the throne of England in 1399 as Henry IV, this work was suppressed by the monks for fear of reprisal. In *Gesta Abbatum*, Walsingham wrote the biographies of

the abbots of St. Albans, basing the earlier part on a chronicle of Matthew Paris.

In 1394 he became Prior of the Benedictine monastery at Wymundham, and here he rewrote the *Chronicon Angliae* in a more politic form, the resulting chronicle, untitled, being known as the *St. Albans Chronicle*.

His last two works were his greatest, the *Historica Anglicana* and the *Ypodigma Neustriae*. The former, a comprehensive history of England from 1247 to his own day, is for the most part a compilation of earlier chronicles, only the contemporary portion being of his own composition. The latter work grew out of his great admiration for Henry V. By linking Henry's career closely with that of his predecessors, the Dukes of Normandy, he attempted to justify his invasion of France. Not an historian in the modern interpretive sense, Walsingham sometimes colored or manipulated the bare facts to suit his own purpose. He is the principal authority on Henry V's French campaigns, on Wycliffe, on the Wat Tyler rebellion, and on the reigns of Richard II and Henry IV.

He returned to St. Albans in 1409. The *Historia Anglicana* ends at 1422, but whether he lived to complete it is not certain.

PRINCIPAL WORKS: Chronicon Angliae, 1388; Gesta Abbatum, 1390-94; The St. Alban's Chronicle, 1394; Ypodigma Neustriae (no date); Historia Anglicana (no date).

ABOUT: Gairdner, J. Early Chroniclers of England; Gardiner, S. and J. Mullinger. Introduction to the Study of English History; Nicolson, W. English, Scotch and Irish Historical Libraries.

WALTON, IZAAK (August 9, 1593-December 15, 1683),

biographer and author of *The Compleat Angler*, was born at St. Mary, near Stafford, the son of Jervis Walton, of a yeoman family. Nothing is known of his ancestry otherwise or of his education, though he probably attended school in Stafford. At an early age he was sent to London and apprenticed to Thomas Grinsell, an ironmonger, who later became his brother-in-law. Before he was of age he had a tiny shop in Cornhill, in 1614 "half a shop" in Fleet Street, and in 1618 he became a freeman of the Ironmongers' Company.

This residence in Fleet Street was important for Walton, for the vicar of St. Dunstan's Church in this parish, of which

Walton afterwards was a vestryman, was then John Donne. Through Donne and those to whom Donne introduced him, he met Drayton, Ben Jonson, Wotton, and other literary men of the era. He seems to have been an accepted member of the current literary group by 1619, at which date one "S.P." wrote a dedicatory poem to him. He was also a pet of the clergy, and spent much of his later life in long visits to one or another of them, "of whom he was much beloved." Except for occasional verses, the first writing he is known to have published was his memoir of Wotton, which was prefixed to a posthumous edition of Wotton's poems in 1640, but was not published separately until 1651.

When the civil wars started, Walton showed himself a quiet but trusted Royalist. In fact, after the Royalist defeat at Marston Moor in 1644, he felt it wiser to absent himself from London for a while. He bought a holding in his native Staffordshire, and though he was back in London the next year, this continued to be his occasional home. In 1651 he had custody of one of Charles II's important jewels, the "lesser George," which he returned after the Restoration. Another story of this period unhappily places Walton among the vandals who liked to scratch their names in public places; he wrote his monogram and the date in 1658 on Casaubon's tomb in Westminster Abbey!

In 1626 Walton had married Rachel Floud (or Floyd), great grandniece of Cranmer. All their seven children died in infancy, and she followed them in 1640. In 1646 he married Anne Ken, half-sister of Thomas Ken, who later became Bishop of Bath and Wells. They had two sons (one died as an infant, the other grew up to become a clergyman), and a daughter who married William Hawkins, later a prebendary of Winchester Cathedral.

Undoubtedly ironmongering had made Walton prosperous, and he devoted increasingly less time to his business until, after his second wife's death, he retired altogether. For years he lived with George Morley, the Bishop of Winchester, though he spent long periods with his friend Charles Cotton at his fishing-lodge on the Dove River, which forms the boundary between Staffordshire and Derbyshire. Fishing had been Walton's pas-

J. Huysmans

IZAAK WALTON

sion from his youth, and it was natural that he should write about it. The first edition of *The Compleat Angler* appeared in 1653, but Walton kept on adding to it and revising it until 1676. At first it was a dialogue between "Piscator" (the fisherman—himself) and "Viator" (the wayfarer). Later "Venator" (the hunter) took the place of "Viator" (his remarks were written by Cotton in later editions), and "Auceps" (the falconer) was added. In a desultory way the characters discuss their favorite sports—with "Piscator," naturally, having the last word. The rambling, charming book wanders constantly into descriptions of nature, appropriate quotations, and whimsical philosophy; it has been dear to many who have never baited a hook.

As a matter of fact, Walton has been much criticized, technically, by ardent fishermen. He himself acknowledged that he knew nothing of fly-fishing, and that subject was covered from the beginning by Thomas Bowker, a retired cook and a writer of humorous essays. Walton's field was fishing with worms, frogs, and grasshoppers. Fishing to him was not an occupation, but a leisurely recreation—and so was writing. He was never a professional author; he wrote when and as the spirit moved him.

He lived to be ninety—an excellent recommendation for the benefits of angling—

and his last years were quite uneventful—calm, busy, and happy. Occasionally he edited a book which interested him, the most important of these ventures being the poem *Thealma and Clearchus,* which he published the year before his death. Though he said plainly that the author was John Chalkhill, who lived in the Elizabethan age, some critics have thought the name a pseudonym for Walton himself. This is most improbable; there *was* a John Chalkhill, his wife's step-grandfather, and the manuscript verses probably came down through the family to her. Walton's own verse, such as his *Elegie* to Donne, in 1633, was quite inferior.

Walton died quietly in his son-in-law's house in Winchester, leaving his property at Shalford, Surrey, to be used for the benefit of the poor of Stafford. He was buried in the Winchester Cathedral.

Not only in *The Compleat Angler,* but in his *Lives* as well, Izaak Walton is the divine amateur, writing for his own pleasure as well as that of others. As George Saintsbury put it, he has a "singular and golden simplicity." His art is not all artlessness, but the purity and ease of his style, its unpremeditated, discursive grace, make of his writing a sort of poetry in prose. Occasionally he essays a higher flight, but his "purple passages" are his least happy ones. The man himself is the chief attraction of his writing, as he reveals himself unconsciously—a kindly, pious man who loved nature and music and, above all, fishing, who had much gentle humor, wide if not deep learning, and a sweetness of personality that made him beloved not only of "eminent clergymen," but of eminent authors also, and, indeed, of all who knew him.

PRINCIPAL WORKS: The Life of Sir Henry Wotton, with Reliquiae Wottonianae, 1651 (H. Nicolas, ed. 1836); The Compleat Angler: or, The Contemplative Man's Recreation, 1653 (rev. eds. 1655-1676); The Life of John Donne, 1658; The Life of Mr. Rich. Hooker, 1665; The Life of Mr. George Herbert, 1670; The Life of Dr. [Robert] Sanderson, 1678; Lives (G. Saintsbury, ed.) 1927.

ABOUT: Alexander, W. A. Journey to Beresford Hall; Landor, W. S. Imaginary Conversations; Marston, E. Thomas Ken and Izaak Walton; Marston, R. B. Walton and Some Earlier Writers on Fish and Fishing; Martin, S. Izaak Walton and His Friends; Nevinson, H. W. Books and Personalities; Nicolas, H. Memoir *in* Compleat Angler, 1836 ed.; Shepherd, R. H. Waltoniana; Tweddell, G. Walton and the Earlier English Writers on Angling; Westwood, T. The Chronicle of the Compleat Angler.

WARBURTON, WILLIAM (December 24, 1698-June 7, 1779), editor, theological writer, Bishop of Gloucester, was born at Newark, Nottinghamshire, the son of George and Elizabeth Warburton. His father was an attorney, and William, after receiving his education at the grammar schools of Newark and Oakham, Rutlandshire, was himself apprenticed to an attorney in 1714. His apprenticeship lasted five years and he seems to have practiced law in Newark for some time afterward. Meanwhile he was reading voraciously, especially in theology, and took deacon's orders in 1723. In 1727 he obtained his first parish and was ordained priest. The following year he was given the wealthy parish of Brant Broughton and granted an M.A. by Cambridge University, both thanks to the efforts of Sir Robert Sutton, a Nottinghamshire politician.

By his defense of the orthodoxy of Pope's *Essay on Man,* Warburton won the aging poet's friendship and met his benefactor Ralph Allen. In 1745 he married Gertrude Tucker, Allen's niece. Allen used his considerable political influence to obtain preferment in the Church for Warburton. Little happened at first, but in 1754 Warburton became one of the chaplains to the king and was made a D.D.; in 1757 he became Dean of Bristol; in 1759 he was appointed Bishop of Gloucester.

C. Phillips

WILLIAM WARBURTON

Ever since Warburton's first important and extremely orthodox work, *The Alliance of Church and State*, had appeared, his reputation as an author had grown, though his attempt in *The Divine Legation of Moses Demonstrated* to show why there was no mention of an after-life in the Old Testament, was not entirely successful.

Much of Warburton's reputation was undeserved and was questioned by many critics even during his lifetime. Never having had a university education, he was extremely inaccurate in matters of scholarship. Though he sneered at previous editors, his own edition of Shakespeare was inferior to theirs. Pope made him his literary executor; he edited and annotated the poems, but never got around to writing the poet's life; finally he gave the materials for it to Ruffhead, who completed the task.

Warburton was probably the most quarrelsome literary man (at least on paper) that ever lived. Some writers he fought with because they had, however gently, criticized his works; others he attacked without provocation. He may justly be regarded as the first man to perfect the footnote sneer—in his editions of Shakespeare and Pope and elsewhere.

Warburton was extremely good to his widowed mother and fatherless sisters (the father died in 1706). He was also a fond husband and father. His only child, a son, died in 1775, when he himself was already beginning to lose his faculties. His wife admired him, but was reputed to be unfaithful to him. She was much younger than he and married again after his death. A tall, powerful man, sociable and far from strait laced, with an insatiable appetite for all kinds of reading—light as well as heavy—Warburton was the perfect type of an eighteenth century bishop, scornful alike of Methodists and Rationalists, Wesley and Hume. He died in his episcopal palace and was buried in Gloucester Cathedral.

PRINCIPAL WORKS: The Alliance between Church and State, 1736; The Divine Legation of Moses Demonstrated, 1737-41; A Commentary on Mr. Pope's Essay on Man, 1739; The Works of Shakespeare with Comments and Notes by Mr. Pope and Mr. Warburton, 1747; A Letter to the Editor of the Letters on the Spirit of Patriotism, 1749; A View of Lord Bolingbroke's Philosophy, 1754-5; The Doctrine of Grace, 1762; Works (R. Hurd, ed.) 1788.

ABOUT: Disraeli, I. Quarrels of Authors; Evans, A. W. Warburton and the Warburtonians; Hurd, R. Life, prefixed to Works.

WARD, EDWARD (NED) (1667-June 20, 1731), humorist, was born in Oxfordshire, but except for an early visit to the West Indies he spent most of his life in or near London. He became a tavernkeeper, first at Moorfield's and in 1699 at Fulwood's Rents, and joined that rising school of writers which has been called the "strange underworld of letters." This was the day of the literature of the man in the street, a complete about-face from the exclusive and aristocratic elegance of the writing of the middle seventeenth century. Cockney London was asserting its personality in the coffeehouses and taverns, and a group of writers which included Ward wrote of and for this new reading public.

A burly, pleasant man, Ned Ward entertained the guests of his public house with his wit for part of each day, and spent the rest turning out a prodigious amount of vulgar, gross, racy, lively doggerel.

So Ned, divided, writes and brews
To try if darling gain accrues
More from his Mash-Tub than his Muse.

His muse was a frankly commercial one. He wrote with no literary pretensions, although the wit is real, the satire often sharp, and the picture of life in the London of Queen Anne's time is vividly brought to life in his pages.

His masterpiece was the *London Spy*, a narrative written in eighteen monthly parts. This chronicled the life of London streets and shops, public houses and alleyways, as seen through the eyes of a touring visitor. It also contains a section entitled *Voyage to New England* with a description of Boston in 1690.

Samuel Butler's *Hudibras* was a frequently imitated model for many of the satires of the period, among them Ward's *Hudibras Redivivus, a Burlesque Poem of the Times*, in which he attacked the government and the low-church party so violently that he was arrested, indicted, and punished by a fine and by being made to stand twice in the pillory.

In all, Ward wrote nearly ninety pieces in his facile, familiar verse, pieces of little more literary worth than the vivid jargon of the sporting press today, but with the value of lively, honest reportage of life in another time.

PRINCIPAL WORKS: London Spy, 1703-09; Secret History of the Calves-Head Club, 1703; Hud:bras Redivivus, 1705-07; The Diverting Works of Cervantes, 1709; The Secret History of Clubs, 1709; Nuptial Dialogues and Debates, 1710; The Life and Adventures of Don Quixote de la Mancha, 1711; The History of the Grand Rebellion, 1713.

ABOUT: Baker, D. E. Biographia Dramatica; Cibber, T. Lives of the Poets; Lowndes, W. T. Bibliographer's Manual; Troyer, H. W. Ned Ward of Grub Street; Notes and Queries, Second Series.

WARNER, WILLIAM (1558?-March 9, 1609), poet, author of prose tales, translator, was born in London. Very little is known of his life. He was educated at Magdalen Hall, Oxford, but took no degree. His profession was that of attorney of the Court of Common Pleas. He died suddenly in his bed at Amwell, Hertfordshire, and was buried in the church there, but no one knows what brought him to that part of the country. The parish register says that he was "of good years and of honest reputation." Drayton writes of him as "my old friend." *Pan His Syrinx* was dedicated to Sir George Carey, the first edition of *Albion's England* to his father, Henry Carey, first Baron Hunsdon, Lord Chamberlain; they were presumably his chief patrons.

Besides these facts, all we know of Warner is his literary work. *Pan His Syrinx* is a collection of seven prose tales. Warner's translation of the *Menaechmi* of Plautus may have been seen by Shakespeare, who borrowed the plot of this play for his *Comedy of Errors*.

Warner is chiefly remembered, however, as the author of *Albion's England*, a long poem in rhymed "fourteeners." The four books of the original edition tell the "history" of England from Noah to Henry II; the second edition contains six books and brings the story down to the end of the Wars of the Roses; the third edition in eight books brings us to the accession of Queen Elizabeth. The fourth edition, in twelve books, was finished on the first day of the thirty-ninth year of Elizabeth's reign (i.e. in 1595) and brings the story up to date. The fourth edition is the one most readily available, being reprinted in Alexander Chalmers' *English Poets*. It is noteworthy that the eleventh and twelfth books are concerned

with the Elizabethan voyages and follow Hakluyt closely. Two further expansions of the poem appeared in Warner's lifetime and a third after his death.

The subject matter of the poem is not confined to history and legend, for the historical characters frequently pause to tell each other tales which do not make even a pretense of being history. Most of them are probably folk-tales, though some may be original. They are the pleasantest portions of this naïve work.

Brute or Brutus, grandson of Aeneas, was the legendary founder of the ancient Britons, but Warner must have felt abashed at the idea of retelling the whole *Aeneid*, for he merely included a prose summary of it as an appendix to Book II. Among other legends, he gives the story of Lear and that of Gorboduc.

Francis Meres in *Palladis Tamia* ranked Warner with Spenser as an epic poet, but there is really no comparison. Warner is a mere versifier, and shows no desire to be anything more. His verse, we may be sure, owed its contemporary popularity more to middle-class readers than to learned men and courtiers.

PRINCIPAL WORKS: Pan His Syrinx, 1584; Albion's England (Bks. I-IV) 1586; I-VI, 1589; Bks. I-VIII, 1592; Bks. I-XII, 1596; Bks. I-XIII, 1602; A Continuance of Albion's England (Bks. XIV-XVI) 1606; Albion's England (Bks. I-XVI) 1612; Menaechmi, 1595.

ABOUT: Cawley, R. R. Warner and the Voyagers (Modern Philology, 1922).

WARTON, JOSEPH (April 1722-February 23, 1800), literary critic, essayist, was born in the home of his maternal grandfather at Dunsfold, Surrey, the son of Thomas Warton "the elder," poet and medievalist, and Elizabeth Richardson, the daughter of a clergyman. Thomas Warton, "the younger," was his brother. He was educated at the Basingstoke (Hampshire) Grammar School, where Gilbert White was his schoolmate, and in 1735 went to Winchester, where he became a friend of William Collins. His first verse appeared in the *Gentleman's Magazine* in 1739. The next year he entered Oriel College, Oxford, graduating B.A. in 1744, B.D. and D.D. 1760. He was ordained in 1744 and served as his father's curate at Basingstoke until the latter died the following year. Through the Duke of Bolton he

J. Flaxman

JOSEPH WARTON

received the living of Winslade in 1748, and in 1751 he accompanied the duke to France on a curious errand—to marry him to his mistress the instant the duchess, who was ill, should die! After five months the duchess was still alive, and Warton returned to England, thereby losing promised preferment in the church. In 1754 he became rector of Tunworth, but despairing of further preferment, the next year he gave up the church to become second master of Winchester.

Warton was a bad teacher and no disciplinarian at all. In 1766 he became headmaster, but he had to face three open mutinies on the part of the pupils, and after the third, in 1793, he resigned and retired to Wickham, Hampshire, the living of which, together with that of Upham, had been given him a few years before. He also had a prebendary stall in Winchester and in London. In 1748 he married Mary Daman, who died in 1772, leaving three daughters, and three sons, all of whom became clergymen; in 1773 he married Charlotte Nicholas, who survived him with one daughter.

Warton spent much of his time in London, and became part of the literary group around Johnson; though they sometimes quarreled, Johnson asked him to contribute to the *Adventurer* (from 1753 to 1756), and in 1773 he was admitted into the famous Club. In emulation of his brother, he announced in 1784 a forthcoming history of Greek, Roman, French, and Italian poetry, but it never appeared. He edited Pope, with others, in 1797, and was working on an edition of Dryden when he died.

Warton was a literary, not a philological, scholar. Though he was not a medievalist, like his father and brother, he did admire Spenser, Milton, and Dante (all half-forgotten or decried in the eighteenth century), and he was a free critic of the classical school of Pope. As a translator, he was superior to Dryden in accuracy, but inferior in power of expression; his life of Virgil, for example, is far better than his translation of the Roman poet in which it appears. He was a great and enthusiastic talker, and apparently something of a bore, though Reynolds, Burke, Garrick, Percy, and Nichols were among his friends, and he even had some admirers among his rebellious pupils at Winchester. He and Collins appeared with first volumes of odes in the same year; Collins was a failure, Warton a success; but Collins is still read, and Warton as a poet is forgotten. The portrait reproduced here is from a memorial monument by Flaxman in Winchester Cathedral.

PRINCIPAL WORKS: Ode on Reading West's Pindar, 1744; Odes on Various Subjects, 1746; The Works of Virgil in English Verse (with C. Pitt) 1753; Essay on the Genius and Writings of Pope, 1756-82; The Three Wartons: A choice of their Verse (E. Partridge, ed.) 1928.

ABOUT: Boswell, J. Life of Johnson; Densin, J. The Wartons: Studies in English Literature; Gosse, E. B. Two Pioneers of Romanticism; Nichols, J. Literary Anecdotes; Pattison, M. Pope and his Editors; Wooll, J. Biographical Memoirs of the Rev. Joseph Warton.

WARTON, THOMAS (the elder) (1688?-September 10, 1745), poet, was born at Godalming, where his father, Anthony Warton, was vicar. He studied at Hart Hall and Magdalen College, Oxford, graduating from the latter with a B.A. in 1710, obtaining an M.A. in 1712 and a B.D. in 1725. He did some writing while he was still an undergraduate, and in 1718 wrote a versified satire on George I which had wide circulation, although it has since disappeared.

He was elected Professor of Poetry at Magdalen in 1718, and while the caliber of his own verse was not high (Nicholas Amherst called him "Squeaking Tom of Maudlin"), his love of antiquity, his interest in "runic" odes, and his admiration for Milton's poetry were to have specific influence on the work of greater writers.

Some of Milton's early poems had been long neglected until Warton's praise called attention to them, and Pope is said to have first learned of *Comus* and *Il Penseroso* through Warton. Gray's interest in runic poetry was stimulated by Warton's. Principally, Warton's scholarly knowledge of English literature and his attachment to medieval art and especially to Gothic architecture, which was currently out of fashion, influenced the lives and careers of his two more illustrious sons. His son Thomas became poet laureate, and wrote an authoritative *History of English Poetry*, and carried on his father's interest in antiquity, while Joseph became a famous editor and critic.

In 1723 Warton moved from Oxford, although he retained his professorship there until 1728, and became vicar and schoolmaster at Basingstoke in Hampshire. He remained there the rest of his life, holding also three neighboring vicarages. He wrote largely for his own pleasure, and his collected poems were published by his sons after his death.

PRINCIPAL WORK: Poems on Several Occasions, 1748.

ABOUT: Cary, H. F. Lives of English Poets; Hearne, T. Collections of Curious Discourses; Nichols, J. Literary Anecdotes.

WARTON, THOMAS (the younger) (January 9, 1728-May 21, 1790), poet, critic, poet laureate, was born in Basingstoke, Hampshire, the son of Thomas Warton, "the elder," and Elizabeth Richardson; and the younger brother of Joseph Warton. His father was his teacher until he entered Trinity College, Oxford, in 1744. He graduated B.A. in 1747 and was ordained, becoming a tutor in Trinity, securing his M.A. in 1750, becoming a fellow of Trinity in 1751, and receiving a B.D. degree in 1767. He was professor of poetry at Oxford from 1757 to 1767, Camden professor of history in 1785, and in the same year was named poet laureate. In 1771, the same year he became a fellow of the London Society of Antiquaries, he was named to the living of Kiddington, Oxfordshire, but continued to reside at the university. He died there of apoplexy and was buried in Trinity chapel.

All his life Thomas Warton was an Oxford don, not a professional author. He never married, and in this as in other ways he represented a revival of the medieval Oxford. He was the first to use the medieval material in the Bodleian Library, and on his vacations he studied Gothic architecture. He lectured in Latin (some of his lectures were printed); he edited Theocritus (1770) and collections of Latin (1758) and Greek (1770) inscriptions. As a further outgrowth of his interest in neglected pre-eighteenth century literature, he edited the early poems of Milton (1785) and left uncompleted an edition of Milton's major poems.

In another way he harked back to an earlier Oxford. He was no secluded scholar, but paid little attention to his pupils and much to "ale, tobacco, low company, and going to see a man hanged." As professor he would inquire every year if anyone wished him to lecture—frequently no one did. A "little, squat, red-faced man," he spent much time in London, some of it in unedifying pursuits, but some in company with his friend Samuel Johnson, for whom he wrote several numbers of the *Idler* and others of Johnson's periodicals.

Warton's major work was the unfinished *History of English Poetry*, which was intended to run from the end of the eleventh century to the beginning of the eighteenth,

After Sir J. Reynolds
THOMAS WARTON THE YOUNGER

but actually stopped with three volumes at the close of the sixteenth century. Though this has been condemned (principally by Scott) as inaccurate and incoherent— "a total and absolute want of connection"— actually it is interesting and valuable; as Gibbon said, it shows "the taste of a poet and the minute diligence of an antiquarian."

As a poet in his own right, Warton was precocious, producing his first verse at the age of nine. In adult life, however, his forte was the humorous and mock-heroic, rather than serious poetry. He enjoyed writing burlesques such as the *Companion to the Guide* (to Oxford) and editing anthologies of humorous verse like *The Oxford Sausage*. His lives of Trinity College worthies were discovered to be based in part on forged documents, but undoubtedly Warton was imposed upon, and was not the forger.

He was an enthusiastic medievalist, like his father, "of the school of Spenser and Milton, rather than that of Pope" (though he did use the heroic couplet of Pope and his school), but he was no mere imitator. John Wilson summed him up justly in saying that he was "poetical, but no poet," and even Scott, who thought his *History of English Poetry* so bad, granted him "a head abounding in multifarious lore, and a mind unquestionably imbued with true poetic fire." More important than his own verse was his service in helping to awaken public interest in the English literature of the Middle Ages and of the Age of Elizabeth.

PRINCIPAL WORKS: The Pleasures of Melancholy (anon.) 1747; The Triumph of Isis, 1749; Newmarket, A Satire, 1751; The Union, or Select Scots and English Poems (ed.) 1753; Observations on the Faerie Queen of Spenser, 1754-62; A Companion to the Guide and a Guide to the Companion (anon.) 1760; The Life and Literary Remains of Ralph Bathurst, President of Trinity College, Oxford, 1761; The Oxford Sausage (ed.) 1764; The Life of Sir Thomas Pope, Founder of Trinity College, Oxford, 1772; The History of English Poetry (3 vols.) 1774-81; Poems, 1777 (R. Mant, ed. 1791); Specimen of a History of Oxfordshire, 1781; An Inquiry into the Authenticity of the Poems attributed to Thomas Rowley, 1782; The Three Wartons: A Choice of their Verse (E. Partridge, ed.) 1928.

ABOUT: Austin, W. S. and J. Ralph. Lives of the Laureates; Boswell, J. Life of Johnson; Densin, J. The Wartons: Studies in English Literature; Drake, N. Essays; Gosse, E. B. Two Pioneers of Romanticism; Ker, W. P. Thomas Warton; Mant, R. Memoir *in* Poems, 1791 ed.; Martin, L. C. Thomas Warton and the Early Poems of Milton; Rinaker, C. Thomas Warton:

A Biographical and Critical Study; Walpole, H. Correspondence; Wilson, J. (Christopher North) Essays: Critical and Imaginative.

WARWICK, MARY RICH, Countess of (November 8, 1625-April 12, 1678), religious writer and author of memoirs and epigrams, was born at Youghal, the thirteenth child of Richard Boyle, the first Earl of Cork. Her mother died when Mary was three and she and a younger sister were raised by Sir Randall Clayton and his wife at Mallow.

Her six older sisters made brilliant matches, and when Mary was twelve years old her father decided that she was to marry James Hamilton, later to be Earl of Clanbrassil. She steadfastly refused, enraging her father, and shortly afterward announced to him her determination to marry Charles Rich, the impecunious younger son of the Earl of Warwick. Banished to the country by her irate father, she quietly continued to see Charles, and married him when she was sixteen. Her father, relenting, gave her a large dowry.

The young couple lived at Leigh's Priory, near Felsted, Essex, the home of Charles' older brother, who had succeeded to the title. Mary had two children of her own, and helped to educate her nieces, the two families being on terms of closest friendship. Many Puritan ministers were entertained at Felsted, and influenced by them and by Anthony Walker, domestic chaplain to the Warwicks, she developed a severely pietistic character. Leigh's Priory also became a haven for visiting clergy, and Mary Rich spent a part of every day in mystic contemplation in the "Wilderness" garden of her home. She kept a diary from 1666 until just before her death, some extracts of which, expressing her devoutness, were published and circulated by the Religious Tract Society. In addition to occasional writings on religious themes, she constantly jotted down short epigrams or apothegms, touched by her deep religious feeling but also indicating a witty and ingenious mind, on any subject which struck her fancy: her children at play, her household tasks, the weather, her husband's choleric temperament.

Her husband succeeded his brother in 1659. He died of gout in 1673 leaving the estate to his wife, who died five years later at Leigh's. Her writings, annotated by her chaplain, Thomas Woodroffe, were published posthumously, some of them with the funeral sermon preached by Anthony Walker, titled *The Virtuous Woman Found, Her Loss Bewailed and Character Exemplified.*

PRINCIPAL WORKS: Rules for a Holy Life, 1847; Occasional Meditations upon Sundry Subjects, 1847; Pious Reflections Upon Several Scriptures, 1848.

ABOUT: Budgell, E. Memoirs of the Boyles; Fell-Smith, C. Mary Rich, Countess of Warwick; Palgrave, Mary E. Mary Rich, Countess of Warwick.

WATSON, RICHARD (1737-July 4, 1816), Bishop of Llandaff, theological, political and scientific writer, was born at Heversham, Westmoreland, where his father was the local clergyman and schoolmaster. He attended Trinity College, Cambridge, graduating with a B.A. in 1759 and the next year receiving his M.A. and being made a fellow of his college.

He was a versatile and accomplished man of many interests. His mind was neither profound nor brilliant, but he had amazing powers of application and a practical approach to each new subject which enabled him to master it quickly before his interest shifted. He had studied mathematics and "natural philosophy," and when the university offered him a professorship in chemistry he accepted it, knowing nothing of the subject, but wanting to "try his strength in a new pursuit." He shut himself up in a laboratory for fourteen months (blowing it up once), and became so expert that during the next five years he delivered immensely popular lectures, wrote textbooks and treatises, was consulted by the government on chemical subjects, and was elected to the Royal Society. His interest in science waning, he burned his books and notes, managed to get his D.D. degree the day before examinations took place for candidates for a chair of divinity, and was unanimously elected. His theological studies, like those in chemistry, were eminently practical. He concentrated on the Bible, and rejected all authorities except the New Testament. He soon received a series of preferments in the church, some of which he retained for purposes of income when, in 1782, he became Bishop of Llandaff. Inheriting an income several years later, he retired with his wife

and six children to Calgarth Park, where he died at the age of seventy-nine.

Watson's writings were as various as his occupations. Besides his chemical works, which were acute and ingenious, and his letters and sermons, which were polished and accomplished, he wrote a number of soundly reasoned, spirited, and liberally tolerant controversial works. He supported the American Revolution, defended religious toleration, and advocated fairer distribution of church revenues. His answers to a work by Thomas Paine and to Gibbon's *Decline and Fall of the Roman Empire* were widely popular, Gibbon declaring him to be "the man whom I should be happy to call my friend, and whom I should not blush to call my antagonist."

PRINCIPAL WORKS: On the Subjects of Chemistry, 1771; Plan of Chemical Lectures, 1771; Letters from a Christian Whig, 1772; The Principles of the Revolution Vindicated, 1776; Apology for Christianity, 1776; Chemical Essays, 1781; Apology for the Bible, 1796; Address to the People of Great Britain, 1798.

ABOUT: Biographical Dictionary of Living Authors; Hunt, J. Religious Thought in England; Mathias, T. J. Pursuits of Literature; Watson, R. Anecdotes of the Life of Richard Watson.

WATSON, THOMAS (1513-September 25, 1584), Bishop of Lincoln, humanist and author of a Latin tragedy, was born in Durham. He received his education at St. John's College, Cambridge, and was associated with the college for several years following his graduation. He received the degrees of B.A. in 1534, M.A. in 1537, B.D. in 1543, and of D.D. from both Cambridge and Oxford in 1554.

A Catholic, of broad education, high scholarship, and strong personal integrity, his severe adherence to his religious principles brought him much suffering and also the position of being the "chief superior of the English Catholic Church."

He was a fellow of St. John's for about ten years following his graduation, then became chaplain to Stephen Gardiner, the Bishop of Winchester. He supported Gardiner in a dispute with the privy council, and accompanied his superior to prison in 1550. Upon Mary's accession to the throne, his fortunes turned, and he rose rapidly in popularity and power. Following Gardiner's appointment as Chancellor of Cambridge, Watson became, in succession, Master of

St. John's College, Dean of Durham, rector of Bechingwall All-Saints, and, in 1556, Bishop of Lincoln.

With other Catholic churchmen who refused to take the oath of supremacy under Elizabeth, Watson was persecuted for the rest of his life. He was imprisoned in the Tower upon Elizabeth's accession, and deprived of his bishopric. Sixteen years later, upon giving a bond not to influence anyone "to any opinion or act to be done contrary to the laws established in the realm for causes of religion," he was released in the custody of his brother. His position of leadership among Catholics was too firmly established for such a bond to be long observed, and three years later he was again incarcerated, this time at Wisbeck Castle, where he died at the age of seventy-one.

Watson's literary reputation is based on a small body of controversial writing which had great influence in religious circles of his own day, and on an unpublished classical tragedy, *Absalom*. It was written while he was engaged at Cambridge in intensive study of Aristotle and Horace, with the leaders of the revival of Greek scholarship; the great classicist Roger Ascham pronounced it one of the two modern plays worthy to be compared with the classics. It was written in strict Senecan style, and is a vivid story of revolt in the royal house of Israel. Watson refused to publish it because, in two verses, he had used anapestic instead of iambic meter.

PRINCIPAL WORKS: Absalom, a tragedy (no date); Two Notable Sermons Concerning the Real Presence of Christ's Body and Blood in the Blessed Sacrament, 1554; Wholesome and Catholic Doctrine, 1558.

ABOUT: Cooper, C. H. Athenae Cantabrigienses; Foxe, J. Acts and Monuments; Biographical preface to Watson's Wholesome and Catholic Doctrine.

WATSON, THOMAS (1557?-September 1592), poet, classical scholar, was born in London. Nothing is known of his family, and little of his life. He may or may not have attended Oxford (he certainly had a good classical education), but if so he left without a degree. He is supposed to have been entered in one of the Inns of Court and to have been called to the bar—he frequently signed his work as "student of law" —but he did not practice. His main interests were literary, yet his attitude was always that of the amateur, not of the professional; probably he had private means. In 1581 he visited Paris, where he met Sir Francis Walsingham, who may have been more or less his patron. At one time he was employed by William Cornwallis as tutor for his son. This led to the one serious difficulty of his life; he married the daughter of another of Cornwallis' household, a man named Swift, and abetted Swift in his suit of their employer's daughter, even forging letters to help win the girl. There was a scandal and a court trial, in which Watson was accused, but he was then already dead and so no action could be brought against him.

In early youth Watson gained some attention abroad as well as at home as a writer of Latin poetry. His later celebrity came as a *soi-disant* sonneteer, one of the first of the Elizabethan age. But his so-called sonnets were really sets of three verses of six lines each. (Some of the later ones are in the orthodox fourteen lines.) His friends praised him extravagantly, and compared him to Petrarch and Ronsard, from whom he drew freely and frankly. As Sidney Lee put it, Watson drew "drops of water from Petrarch's and Ronsard's fountains." Indeed, his first book, the *Hecatompathia*, acknowledged before each poem its original source. Actually he was scarcely a poet at all, but a frigid pedant. After seeing his Latin translation of Tasso's *Aminta* translated into English by Abraham Fraunce without acknowledgment, he took the precaution of furnishing his own English translations of his Latin poems. His "love poetry" is purely a literary exercise, without the slightest feeling. He is a prime example of a man noted in his own time—his poems appeared in all the famous anthologies—and quite unreadable after it.

Watson was much interested in music, and wrote the words for many songs. Meres called him "best for tragedy," but no play of his has survived. Among his other close friends, besides Meres, were Lyly and possibly Marlowe, though his relations with Marlowe are confused and mysterious, as was so much about the life of that great poet. It is possible also that Spenser referred to him as "Amyntas" in *Colin Clout's Come Home Again*.

PRINCIPAL WORKS: Sophoclis Antigone (Latin from Greek) 1581; The Hecatompathia or Passionate Centurie of Love (Watson's Passions) 1582; Amyntas (Latin from Italian) 1585 (English tr., A. Fraunce, 1587); The First Sette of Italian Madrigalls Englished, 1590; Miliboeus (Latin) 1590 (as An Eglogue upon the Death of . . . Sir Francis Walsingham, 1590); Amintae Gaudia (Latin) 1592; The Tears of Fancie, or Love Disdained, 1593; English Works (E. Arber, ed.) 1870.

ABOUT: Eccles, M. Christopher Marlowe in London; Lee, S. An English Garner; Meres, F. Palladis Tamia; Noble, J. A. The Sonnet in English.

WATTS, ISAAC (July 17, 1674-November 25, 1748), hymn writer, author of devotional poetry and prose, was born in Southampton, the oldest of nine children of Isaac Watts, a clothier. The father, a deacon in a dissenting chapel, was in prison for his faith when the boy was born. In later years he ran a boarding school. The mother, whose maiden name was Taunton, was partly of Huguenot French descent.

Watts was educated at Southampton Grammar School, where his precociousness induced a local physician to offer to send him to a university, but he preferred to stay with the dissenters, and went instead from 1690 to 1694 to a nonconformist academy at Stoke Newington. After two years at home (during which he began writing hymns), he became tutor in the family of Sir John Hartopp, at Stoke Newington, remaining with him until 1701. At the same time he began preaching, in 1699 was made assistant pastor of an independent chapel in London, and in 1702 became the pastor. His health, however, was always poor, and he became an actual invalid "from overstudy"; he could pay little attention to his pastoral duties, and tried often, in vain, to resign. Instead, he was given first an assistant and then a co-pastor. In 1728 the University of Edinburgh gave him an honorary D.D.

From 1712 to his death Watts lived with his friends and patrons, Sir Thomas and Lady Abney, at Theobalds. Sir Thomas died in 1722, but Watts remained with the widow, and moved with her in 1735 to Stoke Newington, where he died, unmarried. He was buried in Bunhill Fields, but there is a monument to him in Westminster Abbey.

Watts was almost if not quite a Unitarian, and extremely liberal in social as well as religious views. His piety was tender, joyful, and serene. Most of his prose writing was

G. White, 1727

ISAAC WATTS

against civil establishment of a national church. It is unfortunate that he is remembered only for well worn hymns and for his now hackneyed *Divine Songs for Children*, for he was a bold experimenter in metrics, deserting the conventional heroic couplet of his age for blank verse, Sapphics, and the "poulters' measure." Amid a mass of turgid bombast and bathos (chiefly in his Pindaric odes), there are lines of true poetry. As Dr. Johnson said, "his ear was well tuned and his diction elegant and copious." His fervid, emotional hymns—"O God our help in ages past," "When I survey the wondrous cross," etc.—have survived to the present day and in their time practically made over the dissenting hymnal.

For better or worse, however, Watts is known today for his pious children's verses, on which later generations were reared. Some of his phrases have passed into the realm of proverb— "let dogs delight to bark and bite," "birds in their little nests agree," "how doth the little busy bee," "Satan finds some mischief still for idle hands to do," " 'tis the voice of the sluggard" (which "Lewis Carroll" parodied), and so many others. Nearly everyone knows the tender "Cradle Hymn"—"Hush, my dear, lie still and slumber," nearly everyone recognizes "while the lamp holds out to burn," "hark, from the tombs a doleful sound," "when I can read my title clear to mansions in the skies." They were all written, and much else familiar besides, by Isaac Watts.

PRINCIPAL WORKS: *Prose*: Sermons, 1721; Doctrine of the Trinity, 1722; Logick, 1725; The Knowledge of the Heavens and the Earth Made Easy, 1726; Catechisms, 1730; A Humble Attempt towards the Revival of Practical Religion among Christians, 1730; An Essay on Civil Power in Things Sacred, 1731; Scriptural History, 1732; Philosophical Essays, 1733; The World to Come, 1738; The Improvement of the Mind, 1741; Essays on the Freedom of the Will, 1752. *Poetry*: Horae Lyricae, 1706; Hymns, 1707; Divine Songs for Children, 1715 (as Divine and Moral Songs for Children, 1729); Psalms of David, 1719; Works, 1810.

ABOUT: Davis, A. P. Isaac Watts: His Life and Works; Gosse, E. History of 18th Century Literature; Johnson, S. Lives of the English Poets; Milner, T. The Life, Times, and Correspondence of Isaac Watts; Saintsbury, G. History of English Prosody; Wright, T. Isaac Watts and Contemporary Hymn Writers.

WEBBE, WILLIAM (fl. 1568-1591),

critic, received his B.A. from St. John's College, Cambridge, in 1573, and about 1583 was a tutor successively in the households of two landowners in Essex, one of his employers being a cousin of Lady Jane Grey. That is all that is known of his personal history, except that, to while away "the summer evenings," he wrote his only book—the first attempt at an historical survey of English poetry. He was very weak on the early portions of English literature; knew of no poet before Chaucer, Lydgate, and Gower, and was quite uncertain as to their dates. He is a storehouse of information, however, for his own period, though for the most part he admired poets whose very names, let alone their works, are now quite unknown, and denigrated those who were the glory of the age. He did admire Spenser if for the wrong things. For Webbe belonged to the school of thought of which Gabriel Harvey was the chief figure, which wanted English poetry to eschew "this tinkerly verse which we call rhyme" and to turn to classical meters instead. To illustrate his contentions, he turned the poems of others, including Spenser, into lame sapphics and limping hexameters. This process was known as "versing," and Webbe was ardently devoted to it.

Nevertheless, as Saintsbury said, Webbe was "enthusiastic for poetry according to his lights," even though "his judgment was too uncertain to be much relied on." Only two copies of the original edition of his book remain, but it was reprinted nearly two centuries later.

PRINCIPAL WORK: A Discourse of English Poetrie, Together with the Authors Judgment Touching the Reformation of Our English Verse, 1586 (E. Arber, ed. 1870).

ABOUT: Morley, J. English Writers; Saintsbury, G. History of Criticism; Schelling, F. E. Poetic and Verse Criticism of the Age of Elizabeth; Spingarn, J. E. A History of Literary Criticism in the Renaissance; Wylie, L. J. Studies in the Evolution of English Criticism.

WEBSTER, JOHN (1580?-1625?), dram-

atist, was born in London, the son of John Webster, a freeman of the Merchant Taylors' Guild, and hence himself "born free" of that guild, though it is doubtful whether he—or even his father—ever held a needle. He was almost certainly not the John Webster who was Clerk of St. Andrew's, Holburn; nor was he the John Webster who married Isabell Sutton in 1590 and had a daughter. He may possibly have been the John Webster, "cloth-worker," who died in September 1625. He may perhaps have had a classical education, but it is more likely that he picked up his scraps of classical learning from the better educated playwrights with whom he associated; he was one of Philip Henslowe's "stable" of playwrights as early as 1602, and he collaborated more or less, in his early days, with Dekker, Drayton, Rowley, Ford, Chettle, Middleton, Chapman, Heywood, and others. He was alive in 1624 when, the city poet Middleton being unavailable, he wrote the masque for the installation of the new Lord Mayor, John Gore; he was probably selected because Gore was himself a Merchant Taylor.

That is literally all that is known of Webster's life. A little more of his character can be gleaned from his work. We know from Henslowe that he was a very slow worker. He was a great tragic poet, but not much of a playwright so far as plot construction is concerned. His nature was somber, brooding, and moody, and spiritually he was much akin to Donne. He was a lover of strange bits of forgotten erudition, a born antiquary, like Burton and Browne. He admired and to some extent followed Shakespeare. He was obsessed by the idea of vengeance, but his sympathy was not with the avenger, but with the victim. He had many warm personal friends in the literary circle of his day, and he returned their affection. He had dignity and self-respect, and one of the evidences of this is the modesty and reserve which kept his private life away from the public gaze, so that we know so little about him.

His work was divided into three periods —one of apprenticeship and collaboration; the period of his two supreme tragedies; and a period of failing powers and an unfortunate preoccupation with comedy, which was not his forte. Although he was primarily a poet, his only known non-dramatic poem (except for a few occasional verses) is an elegy on the Prince of Wales, Henry, whom so many Elizabethan writers mourned.

There are only three plays (besides the masque) which are certainly and entirely Webster's own—but two of these are among the greatest treasures of English literature. He probably wrote *Appius and Virginia*, but it is not altogether certain. He almost certainly did not write any of *The Thracian Wonder*, published in 1661, though another John Webster may have had a hand in it. In the dedication to *The Devils Law-case* he speaks of a play of his called *The Guise*, which has been lost. He probably wrote some part, from the major portion to a mere few lines, of many plays ascribed in part to others of Henslowe's playwrights, some of these plays still extant, some lost—*A Cure for a Cuckold*, *Sir Thomas Wyat* (Webster probably wrote all the second part of *Lady Jane*, from which this play was made), *West-Ward Ho* and *North-Ward Ho* (written in answer to *Eastward-Ho*), *The Weakest Goeth to the Wall*, *The Malcontent*, *A Late Murther of the Sonne upon the Mother*, *Caesar's Fate*, *Christmas Comes but Once a Year*. It would be impossible now to unravel Webster's contribution (if any) from any of these which survive.

The Devils Law-case, a tragicomedy, shows occasional flashes of the true Webster, but they appear in his swift lyric lines, not in the play's cumbersome form or awkward plotting. (He never, in his greatest work, learned to fashion a good plot.) But to all intents and purposes, John Webster must be judged by *The White Divel* (later often called *Vittoria Corombona*), and above all by *The Dutchesse of Malfy*.

In these two magnificent tragedies his genius, second only to that of Shakespeare, soars untrammeled. His deep tragic sense, his white heat of bitter wrath, his preoccupation with death and his power of presenting a catastrophe of horror by the slow accumulation of small events, his pictorial imagination which thought in symbols as did Donne's, his sudden flashing phrases, like lightning in a murky sky—all are here in all their power. Webster had indeed a "demonic forcefulness of phrase," and Nathan Drake, in the rational eighteenth century, did well to shudder away from his "more than earthly wildness." The two great plays are in the classical Greek sense a purge or a catharsis. Webster could *illuminate* horror, making it shine.

It is not strange that he was long ignored and neglected—though his own contemporaries, in the gorgeous, excited, unrestrained Age of Elizabeth, gave him his proper due and rank—until Lamb rediscovered him, as he did so many. Webster is strong meat for the squeamish. But for those who love sustained music, pregnant imagery, beauty tempered by severity, and the fearless facing of utmost terror with no shield except cosmic anger at life's cruelty and injustice, Webster belongs in the topmost sphere of the literary galaxy.

PRINCIPAL WORKS: The White Divel: Or, the Tragedy of Paulo Giordano Ursini, Duke of Brachiano, With the Life and Death of Vittoria Corombona the Famous Venetian Curtizan, 1612; A Monumental Columne Erected to the Living Memory of the Ever-glorious Henry, Late Prince of Wales, 1613; The Tragedy of the Dutchesse of Malfy, 1623 (produced by 1614); The Devils Law-case, or, When Women Goe to Law, the Devill is Full of Businesse, 1623; Monuments of Honor (masque), 1624; Appius and Virginia (?), 1654; Works (A. Dyce, ed.) 1830; Dramatic Works (W. Hazlitt, ed.) 1857; Plays of Webster and Tourneur (J. A. Symonds, ed.) 1888; Works (W. L. Lucas, ed.) 1927.

ABOUT: Bax, C. The Life of the White Devil; Brooke, R. John Webster and the Elizabethan Drama; Crawford, C. Collectanea; Gosse, E. 17th Century Studies; Haworth, P. English Hymns and Ballads and Other Studies in Popular Literature; Lamb, C. Specimens of the English Dramatic Poets; Stoll, E. E. John Webster, the Periods of His Work; Swinburne, A. C. The Age of Shakespeare.

WESLEY, CHARLES (December 18, 1707-March 29, 1788), Methodist divine and hymn writer, was born at Epworth Rectory, Lincolnshire. He was a younger brother of

John Wesley, the founder of Methodism, and shared with him much of the labor, though little of the fame, of this work. Except that, as he declared, he was born to be a follower, and his brother to be a leader, Charles' part in the movement was as active as, and often more stable than, that of John. His greatest distinction is that he was not only the "poet of the Revival," but the most prolific hymn writer of all time. He wrote over 6500 hymns many of them still sung today.

Leaving Christ Church, Oxford, where he received his B.A. in 1730 and his M.A. in 1733, Charles accompanied his brother to America in 1735, acting as secretary to James Edward Oglethorpe, Governor of Georgia. His ill health, his inability to get along with Oglethorpe, and his general disinclination for missionary work sent him back to England within a year.

Charged by the church with irregularity, Charles, like his brother, became an itinerant minister, and for seventeen years traveled all over England, preaching and helping to establish groups of followers. When, in 1749, he married Sarah Gwynne, she joined his travels, leading the singing of her husband's hymns in an exceptionally fine voice. An odd, absent-minded little man, Charles Wesley's warm, frank, simple personality and the great intensity of his conviction were effective factors in his preaching. Poor health forced him to give up his itinerant life in 1756, and he lived his last years at Bath and London, preaching to the end of his life. Although he had ideological differences with his brother, their strong and loyal affection was lifelong.

Thirty-one volumes of his own hymns were published, as well as eight volumes on which his brother collaborated. Considering this prodigious output, the quality of the songs is remarkably high. Probably the best known is "Jesus, Lover of My Soul." Wesley's two surviving sons were musical prodigies, one of them playing the organ at three and writing an oratorio when he was eight years old.

PRINCIPAL WORKS: Hymns on God's Everlasting Love, 1741; Elegy, 1742; On The Lord's Supper, 1745; For Our Lord's Resurrection, 1746; Poetical Works, 1768-72; Sermons, 1816.

ABOUT: Baker, T. Charles Wesley as Revealed by His Letters; Edwards, M. L. Family Circle: A Study of the Epworth Household; Jackson, T. Life of the Rev. Charles Wesley; Julian, J. Dictionary of Hymnology; Telford, J. Life of the Rev. Charles Wesley; Whitehead, J. The Life of the Rev. John Wesley.

WESLEY, JOHN (June 17, 1703-March 2, 1791), preacher, leader of Methodism, hymn writer, author of miscellaneous prose works, was the fifteenth of the eighteen children (his brother Charles was the eighteenth) of the Reverend Samuel Wesley and his wife, Susanna Annesley, and was born at Epworth Rectory, in Lincolnshire. His early schooling was under his very strict mother, but at eleven he entered the Charterhouse, and in 1720 went on a scholarship to Christ Church, Oxford. He graduated B.A. in 1724, was ordained deacon in 1725, became M.A. in 1727, and was ordained priest in 1728. As a deacon he served as his father's curate; then in 1726 he became a fellow of Lincoln College. However, he remained in Epworth until called to residence at Lincoln in 1729. There he found his brother Charles and a few of his friends had formed a group devoted to devout practices and good deeds, and he himself became the leader of this "Holy Club." Already they were dubbed "methodists," because of their methodical rules of living, but it was many years before they broke with the Church of England; John, indeed, was an almost fanatical High Churchman.

In 1735 the two brothers (their father had recently died) went to Georgia on a mission for the Society for the Propagation of the Gospel. Charles was secretary to James Oglethorpe, and stayed only a year; John remained for nearly three years. The mission was a failure, Wesley's English parishoners were irked by his insistence on the minutiae of High Church rites. He left actually involved in a suit for defamation arising from one of his rather equivocal courtships. But he had already begun his inimitable journal and diaries (which have "all the charm of a pious Pepys"), and he had begun his lifelong habit of itinerant preaching, traveling by horseback in the wilderness. Small and frail, he was yet a great horseman, walker, and swimmer. In later years he rode five thousand miles a year, and preached fifteen sermons a week.

Wesley had become a disciple of the Moravians in Georgia; his "conversion" to

N. Hone

JOHN WESLEY

the doctrine of individual grace through Christ's atonement, which is the heart of his dogma, he dated from 1738. He traveled to Germany and Holland to talk with the Moravian leaders, and he began, reluctantly, both outdoor preaching and the sending out of itinerant preachers, many of them laymen. The first Methodist chapel was in Bristol in 1738, the first London "society" was founded in 1739, and the first Methodist conference was held in 1774, but it was 1784 before Wesley gave the Methodists a legal constitution, ordained bishops, and finally separated from the Established Church.

After two strange and unsuccessful courtships, one in America and one in England, Wesley married Mary Vazeille, in 1751, a widow with four children. The marriage was most unhappy from the start, and she finally deserted him in 1776, and died in 1781. Wesley was seldom in his unfriendly home; he was constantly on evangelical journeys throughout England, in Ireland, Scotland, and Holland. From 1778 to his death he edited the *Arminian Magazine*. In 1788 Charles died, and his brother did not long outlive him. In his later years, he had lived much in London, where he died (of diabetes). Much of his time he spent pouring out tracts—not on religion alone, but on medicine, philology, physics, history, even condensations of novels—the profits of which he used to further his charitable works.

From the beginning he and his followers had devoted much time to visiting the prisons, and to succoring the sick and the poor, including debtors, and the last letter he ever wrote was an attack on slavery. Though he called himself a "Bible bigot," he was much broader in his views than were later Methodists—he danced, played cards, read novels, and had no condemnation for the stage. Equable and unsentimental, strongly antimystical after a youthful attraction, he had a calm, strong mind and a gift for direct and simple writing. He wrote like an orator, which he was. It is hard to tell his hymns from his brother's, but he had not Charles Wesley's poetic talent. He was a real linguist, and something of a scholar, and above all he had a genius for organization and administration.

PRINCIPAL WORKS: Collection of Psalms and Hymns (with C. Wesley) 1737-38; Journal, 1739 (N. Curnock, ed. 1909); Works, 1771-74; A Calm Address to our American Colonies, 1775; A Calm Address to the Inhabitants of England, 1777; Poetical Works of John and Charles Wesley, 1868-72; Letters (G. Eayrs, ed.) 1915; Standard Sermons (E. H. Sugden, ed.) 1921.

ABOUT: Baines-Griffiths, D. Wesley the Anglican; Baker, E. W. Herald of the Evangelical Revival; Bebb, E. D. Wesley: A Man with a Concern; Birrell, A. Wesley, His Life and Times (in Letters); Bowen, M. (M. C. Long) Wrestling Jacob; Cadman, S. P. The Three Religious Leaders of Oxford and their Movements; Cell, G. C. The Rediscovery of John Wesley; Dobrée, B. John Wesley; Edwards, M. L. Family Circle: A Study of the Epworth Household; Edwards, M. L. John Wesley and the 18th Century; Harrison, G. E. Son to Susanna: the Private Life of John Wesley; Herbert, T. W. John Wesley as Editor and Author; Hutton, W. H. John Wesley; Laver, J. Wesley; Lee, U. The Lord's Horseman; Lipskey, A. John Wesley, a Portrait; Lunn, A. H. M. John Wesley; McConnell, F. J. John Wesley; Simons, J. S. John Wesley, the Master Builder; Southey, R. The Life of Wesley and the Rise and Progress of Methodism; Vulliamy, C. E. John Wesley; Wade, J. D. John Wesley.

WHETSTONE, GEORGE (1544?-1587?), author of miscellaneous verse and prose tales, dramatist, was born in London, the son of Robert Whetstone, who died when the son was a young boy, and of Margaret Bernard. Nothing is known of his education, but in early manhood he appeared at court, and soon was noted for his wild life. He dissipated his inheritance in gambling and other vices, then undertook a long and ruinous lawsuit to try to recover some of his fortune; when he had lost that, he was left with just enough to retire to France to live. By 1572 he was in England again, commissioned as an army captain, and was sent to fight in the Low Countries against Spain. There he met George Gascoigne and Thomas Churchyard, whose personal histories were much like his own, and who advised him to have recourse to writing for a livelihood.

He returned to London in 1574, and applied for help in vain to his more prosperous relatives. He decided to take his friends' advice. What he did was to paraphrase various French and Italian romances (perhaps adding some of his own invention), in prose and verse. On the side, he wrote panegyrics to various courtiers who he thought (contrary to the result) would reward him materially. Gascoigne became his close friend; Whetstone's first published verses were in a preface to Gascoigne's poems; Gascoigne died while on a visit to Whetstone.

Whetstone appeared in the anthology, *A Paradise of Daintie Devices*, in 1578, and the same year published his play in rhymed verse, *Promos and Cassandra*. It was from a prose version of this play, in *An Heptameron of Civill Discourses*, that Shakespeare took the plot of *Measure for Measure*. Whetstone meanwhile, without seeing his play through the press (it was never acted), left on an unfortunate expedition to Newfoundland captained by Sir Humphrey Gilbert. In 1580 he was in Italy, then returned to England to try his hand at the book—a description of the vices of London, which he knew only too well—by which he is best known—*A Mirrour for Magistrates of Cityes*. In 1585 he was in Holland, and was present at the battle of Zutphen, in which Sir Philip Sidney was killed; later he wrote a curious biography in verse of Sidney. After that nothing is known of him, but he is supposed to have been dead by 1587. So far as is known, he was never married.

Whetstone, though he had no talent, was a pioneer in both the romantic play and the prose romance in English. He was an early advocate of reform of the drama, though he never went so far as did Gosson, for instance, in excoriating it. He had some feeling for dramatic structure and design but his writing in general was crude and clumsy. George Steevens, in his unamiable way, called him "the most quaint and contemptible writer, both in prose and verse" that he had ever read.

PRINCIPAL WORKS: Rocke of Regard (prose and verse) 1576; A Remembraunce of . . . George Gaskoigne, 1577; Promos and Cassandra, 1578; Remembraunce of . . . Sir Nich. Bacon, 1579 (A. Boswell, ed. 1816); Riche his Farewell to the Militarie Profession (prose) 1581; An Heptameron of Civill Discourses (prose and verse) 1582; Remembraunce . . . of Sir James Dier, 1583; Remembraunce . . . of Thomas, Earle of Sussex, 1583; A Mirrour for Magistrates of Cityes (with A Touchstone for the Time) 1584 (as The Enemie to Unthryftiness, 1586); The Honorable Reputation of a Soldier, 1585; Remembraunce of Francis, Earle of Bedford, 1585; The English Myrror (prose) 1586; Sir Philip Sidney (verse) 1587; The Censure of a Loyall Subject [on the Babington conspiracy] 1587; Frondes Caducae (A. Boswell, ed.) 1816.

ABOUT: Izard, T. C. George Whetstone, Mid-Elizabethan Gentleman of Letters.

WHICHCOTE or WHITCHCOTE, BENJAMIN (May 4, 1609-1683), author of religious works, was born at Stoke in Shropshire. He attended Emmanuel College, Cambridge, as a scholarship student, his tutor being Anthony Tuckney. Upon being ordained in 1636, he was appointed to the very influential post of Sunday afternoon lecturer at Trinity Church, largely attended by members of Cambridge, which he retained for twenty years.

Whichcote's was a Baconian philosophy, a firm reliance on truth, arrived at through induction, as a supporter of religious revelation. Devoutly religious, he insisted that the principles of Christianity could only be strengthened by rational examination and independent thought. He was therefore accused by the orthodox of "enthusiasm," or the assumption of an inspired right to interpret Scripture.

In 1644 he became provost of King's College, and in 1649, vice chancellor of Cambridge. A speech he made at Commencement instigated a famous correspondence with his old tutor, Tuckney, in which the current controversy between Puritan orthodoxy and rational theology was thoroughly expressed. At the Restoration, Whichcote, along with most university leaders installed during the Protectorate, was dismissed. On the day of his leave taking, he wrote, "I fail for truth's sake, whereto alone I acknowledge myself addicted." Upon complying with the Act of Uniformity he was, however, restored to favor, and appointed vicar of St. Lawrence

Jewry. He lived, during the latter part of his life, at Milton in Cambridgeshire, whose rectorship he had held for some years. He was married to the widow of the Governor of Massachusetts, Mathias Craddock, but had no children. During his later years he was constantly identified with progressive movements in religion and education. None of his writings, which were largely sermons and aphorisms, were published during his lifetime. He died while on a visit to Cambridge at seventy-four.

PRINCIPAL WORKS: Some Select Notions, 1685; A Treatise of Devotion, 1697; Select Sermons, 1698; Several Discourses, 1701; The True Notion of Place in the Kingdom or Church of Christ, 1717; Moral and Religious Aphorisms, 1753.

ABOUT: Hunt, J. Religious Thought in England; Mullinger, J. B. History of the University of Cambridge; Salter, S. Biographical preface to Whichcote's Moral and Religious Aphorisms.

WHITE, GILBERT (July 18, 1720-June 26, 1793), naturalist, was born and died in the place that will always be inseparable from his name, Selborne, Hampshire. His paternal grandfather was the vicar there; his mother, Anne Holt, was a clergyman's daughter. His father, John White, was a barrister. Gilbert was the oldest of eleven children. He was sent to Basingstoke Grammar School, where he met Joseph and Thomas Warton, whose father was headmaster. In 1740 he entered Oriel College, Oxford, of which he was a fellow for nearly fifty years, from 1744 to his death. He graduated B.A. in 1743, M.A. 1746, and was ordained deacon in 1747. Even before he was ordained priest he took over his first curacy, under an uncle; thereafter he served as curate in several Hampshire towns, constantly trying to get back to his beloved Selborne.

In 1752 he was made junior proctor and dean of his college, and had every right to expect the provostship, but someone else was appointed over his head. It is the only occasion known on which White was seriously offended. As a sort of revenge, he insisted on being given the nonresident living of Moreton-Pinckney, Northamptonshire, which was in the gift of Oriel. In 1763 his uncle died, and left him The Wakes, the house in which he had been born; his income, however, was small and he was able to prove to the college that he still needed his fellowship. By this time he was at last curate in his

GILBERT WHITE

own village, having refused all preferment in the church that would take him farther away.

With the exception of frequent horseback journeys about England, and an annual visit to London, the rest of White's life was spent in The Wakes. It was far from an eventful life, outwardly. He never married, and he was a kindly uncle to a succession of nephews. The little man—he was only five feet three inches and very spare, but remarkably erect in posture—was greatly beloved by those who knew him. Sweet natured, generous with what little he had, deaf during his last years but still carrying on his clerical duties out of a sense of obligation, his real self was entirely absorbed in natural history, which had been his passion from childhood.

White began his famous book—"the solitary classic of natural history in English literature"—as a sort of garden calendar, as early in 1751. The book itself took shape in a series of letters, between 1767 and 1787, to Thomas Pennant and Daines Barrington. Long before it was published, both his correspondents had urged that a book be made of it, but White was diffident and it took him a long time to get around to facing the publishers. Pennant has been condemned for insufficient appreciation of White and for not mentioning him in his own *British Zoology*, but as White himself edited the fourth edition, apparently he felt no neglect.

In his youth White had been an ardent sportsman, but very soon he began to prefer studying animals to killing them. He was, indeed, as he has been called, "a prince among observers." This alone would not have been enough to make his book a classic; what did that was the unconscious revelation of himself, the record of his simple days, the humor that brings a smile rather than a laugh —*vide* the passages about Timothy, the famous tortoise—and the grace and charm of his style. The *Natural History of Selborne* was popular from the first, among both naturalists and laymen, and it has been the pleasure of many scientists since his time to work on editions of it. His manuscripts are among the treasures of the British Museum. All he lamented was the lack of a like-minded companion in his studies.

PRINCIPAL WORKS: Natural History and Antiquities of Selborne, 1789; A Naturalist's Calendar (J. Aikin, ed.) 1795; The Works in Natural History of the late Rev. Gilbert White (J. White, [nephew] ed.) 1802.

ABOUT: Holt-White, R. (great-grandnephew) The Life and Letters of Gilbert White of Selborne; Johnson, W. Gilbert White, Pioneer, Poet, and Stylist; Martin, E. A. Bibliography of Gilbert White; Scott, W. S. White of Selborne and his Times.

WHITEFIELD, GEORGE (December 1714-September 30, 1770), missionary to America, author of hymns, sermons, and autobiographical works, was born in Gloucester. His favorite subject at St. Mary de Crypt School was dramatics, at which he excelled. He left school at fourteen to work in a public house, but his mother persuaded him to work his way through Oxford, where he met and was converted to Methodism by the Wesley brothers. He received his B.A. in 1736, was ordained the same year, and followed the Wesleys to Georgia in 1738.

On the seven trips he made to America, Whitefield preached throughout New England, in Philadelphia, and in the South. He projected and in some instances established institutions of reform and education, his principal interest being the Bethesda orphanage at Savannah, which he later helped convert to Bethesda College. In England, he was mainly concerned with raising funds to continue his missionary work in America. He early broke with the Wesleys on doctrinal grounds, veering toward Calvinism, although his personal friendship with them survived.

He was the greatest popular orator of the eighteenth century. This was apparently due largely to his dramatic ability and to his remarkably beautiful and powerful voice, since his written works show no distinction of composition, no intellectual depth, and a commonplace style. Thomas Carlyle relates that in Scotland, when Whitefield pleaded for money for the Indians, his auditors ran home to bring more money, food and blankets. Benjamin Franklin testified to his almost hypnotic power to draw money out of the pockets of even reluctant hearers. A contemporary quotes an "ignorant man" as saying that Whitefield "preached like a lion."

Forced by the opposition of the church to preach in the open air, in dissenting meeting houses, or in public halls, Whitefield nevertheless had enormous personal popularity and influence. He died during his seventh visit to the United States, at Exeter, New Hampshire, having preached twice on the day before his death.

His extensive journals were published over a period of several years during his lifetime. Of the eighteen thousand sermons he preached, only eighty-one were ever printed, many of these from inadequate stenographic notes.

PRINCIPAL WORKS: Journals, 1738-1741; Christian History, 1740-1747; Full Account, 1747; Further Account, 1747.

ABOUT: Gillies, J. Memoirs of the Life of the Rev. George Whitefield; Gledstone, J. P. Life and Travels of George Whitefield; Nicholas, E. Hours and the Ages; Philip, R. Life of the Rev. George Whitefield; Tyerman, L. The Life of the Rev. George Whitefield.

WHITEHEAD, WILLIAM (February 1715-April 14, 1785), dramatist, poet, poet laureate, was born in Cambridge, the son of a baker, an extravagant and rather eccentric man who died while his son was still a boy. From 1729 to 1735, through the influence of Lord Montfort, who was interested in the talented youth, he attended Winchester College. There, after he won a prize for a poem, Pope, who was the judge, employed him to turn the first epistle of the *Essay on Man* into Latin verse. He entered Clare Hall, Cambridge, as a sizar in 1735, soon winning a scholarship for orphan sons of Cambridge tradesmen. He graduated B.A. in 1739, M.A.

After R. Wilson
WILLIAM WHITEHEAD

in 1743, and in 1742 became a fellow of his college. In 1745 he was appointed tutor to the sons of the Earl of Jersey and Earl Harcourt, and thenceforth lived for the most part in the city or country homes of his two patrons, the whole family becoming his intimate friends. He resigned his fellowship, so as not to have to take orders. With his pupils he traveled in Germany and Italy from 1754 to 1756.

Whitehead's whole career depended on the patronage of his social superiors, but though he was amiable he was never servile. He was an unambitious man, who accepted things as they came, but never strove for them—first the post of secretary and registrar of the Order of the Bath, in 1755, then the laureateship in 1757. He succeeded Colley Cibber as laureate, after Gray had refused the honor. It was not a good thing for his literary reputation; his forte was light verse, and the pompous official odes he had to write as laureate caused Dr. Johnson, for one, to allude to his work contemptuously as "grand nonsense."

He was a close friend of David Garrick, and for years was Garrick's reader of play manuscripts at Drury Lane. It was under Garrick's influence that he wrote his plays—two "classic" tragedies, a comedy which skirted dangerously near the sentimental, and

a farce. He left several unfinished plays and fragments of plays at his death.

In poetry, Whitehead was a disciple of Pope. He had all Pope's elegance, but little of his wit; on the credit side, he had a modesty quite alien to his master, and was keenly aware of his own limitations. His most attractive work is his tales in verse, which are often quite charming. He knew as well as anyone how pretentious and stodgy were his official poems as laureate, and he never resented the ridicule they aroused. His tragedies were more or less paraphrases, in one case of Corneille, in the other of Euripides. He had some comic verve and energy, but as a playwright he was negligible. He was by no means the worst poet to become laureate, but he certainly added no particular luster to the office.

Whitehead never married. After the death of the Earl of Jersey and the succession to the title of the ex-pupil, he took lodgings of his own in London, and died there at seventy.

PRINCIPAL WORKS: *Plays*: The Roman Father, 1750; Creusa, Queen of Athens, 1754; The School for Lovers, 1762; A Trip to Scotland, 1770; Plays and Poems, 1774. *Poems*: On the Danger of Writing in Verse, 1741; Ridicule, 1743; Hymn to the Nymph of Bristol Spring, 1751; A Charge to the Poets, 1762; Poems (W. Mason, ed.) 1788.

ABOUT: Mason, W. Memoir *in* Poems; Ward, A. W. A History of English Dramatic Literature to the Death of Queen Anne.

WIAT, Sir THOMAS. See WYATT, Sir THOMAS

WICLIF, JOHN. See WYCLIFFE, JOHN

WILKES, JOHN (October 17, 1727-December 26, 1797), journalist, miscellaneous writer, was born in London, the son of a prosperous malt distiller, Israel Wilkes, and of Sarah Heaton. His older brother went to America in his youth and was the grandfather of Admiral Charles W. Wilkes, explorer and Civil War figure.

The mother was a dissenter (the father was Anglican), and John was sent to study with a Presbyterian minister, in Aylesbury, Buckinghamshire, and then under his supervision to the University of Leyden, in 1744. It was there that he met d'Holbach, the French encyclopedist. He returned at twenty, to find himself forced by his father into a loveless marriage with Mary Mead, an Aylesbury heiress almost twice his age. She and her mother were fanatical dissenters, and the marriage could not endure, though they did have one daughter—Wilkes' only legitimate child; he also had an illegitimate daughter and son. He and his wife were separated after a financial settlement, and Wilkes soon became notorious as a rake and profligate, a member of the scandalous Hellfire Club.

Already, however, he had begun his political career. In 1754 he was high sheriff of Buckinghamshire, and in 1757 he practically bought a seat in Parliament, sitting for Aylesbury. He was a convinced and sincere Whig, a disciple of Pitt and of Lord Temple, though in later years he broke with both. In 1762, the same year he became colonel of the Buckinghamshire militia, he founded the *North Briton*, which under the guise of a Scottish Tory periodical attacked the prime minister, Lord Bute, and satirized the government. It was really more of a weekly political essay than a newspaper. In 1763 the famous No. 45 as good as called George III a liar. The Tories were quick to act. On a general warrant (with no names, an equivalent of the French *lettre de cachet*) Wilkes and forty-seven others were arrested and thrown into the Tower. This was an invasion of Wilkes' Parliamentary immunity. It took him until 1769 to get £4000 damages from Lord Halifax, the secretary of state, and thereby to end general warrants forever. Meanwhile, Lord Temple had got him out of the Tower on a writ of habeas corpus. He was soon arrested again, this time for seditious libel, in connection with an "obscene and blasphemous" burlesque of the *Essay on Man*, called *Essay on Woman*, probably not of his authorship but printed on his private press. Fearing life imprisonment, he fled to Paris, and when he did not stand trial was outlawed. He was at this time invalided as the result of a duel, but his excuse was not accepted.

Wilkes stayed in Paris, the intimate of d'Holbach and Diderot (or traveled about with his Italian mistress) from 1764 to 1768. He then returned to England and after being elected to Parliament for Middlesex, surrendered as an outlaw. He was the popular idol, "Wilkes and Liberty" the popular slogan. There were mobs and massacres, and

R. Earlom

JOHN WILKES

he had actually to escape from his friends to go to the Tower and carry out the test case. His sentence was comparatively light, and he appealed it. He had been expelled from Parliament, was re-elected and expelled again, and finally took his seat in 1774. Meanwhile he had been elected alderman of Farringdon Without, sheriff of London and Middlesex (1771), and, in 1774, Lord Mayor. In Parliament he fought hard for parliamentary reform and was the constant friend of the American rebels. By 1782 he succeeded in having the verdict of his "incapacity to serve in Parliament" expunged from the record. Though he remained in Parliament until 1790, he was increasingly inactive; his last political office in London itself was as city chamberlain in 1779.

Wilkes has been called a demagogue, and to some extent he was—he himself said he was "never a Wilkite." This ugly, squinting man made no secret of his cynicism, his violence and brutality, his complete disregard for conventional morals. But he was unswervingly honest, courageous, naturally good humored, full of charm and graceful manners, given to what has been called "selfish kindness." The fact that he was a freethinker naturally made him anathema in his time. He was extravagant, always in debt, and died insolvent. His adoration by the workers came to an abrupt end when as city

563

chamberlain he jailed his own followers in the Gordon riots; but he hated religious bigotry and never flinched from doing his duty.

He was something of a scholar, edited Catullus and Theophrastus, and was a noted wit; his political pamphlets are full of quotable—and often quoted—passages. He was purely a dilettante as a writer, but one of talent approaching genius.

PRINCIPAL WORKS: Observations on the Papers relative to the Rupture with Spain, 1762; The North Briton (collected) 1763-772; A Letter to Earl Temple, 1763; A Letter to the Duke of Grafton, 1767; A Letter on the Publick Conduct of Mr. Wilkes, 1768; An Introduction to the History of England, from the Revolution to the Accession of the Brunswick Line, 1768; A Letter to Mr. Grenville in answer to his Speech, 1769; Letter to Samuel Johnson, LL.D., 1770; Controversial Letters, 1771; Speeches in the House of Commons, 1777, 1786; Letters . . . addressed to his daughter, 1804; Correspondence, 1805; Epigrams and Miscellaneous Poems, 1871; John Wilkes, Patriot: an Unfinished Autobiography (W. F. Taylor, ed.) 1888.

ABOUT: Bleackley, H. W. Life of John Wilkes; Postgate, R. W. That Devil Wilkes; Quennell, P. Four Portraits; Rae, W. F. Wilkes, Sheridan, Fox; Sherard, O. A. A Life of John Wilkes; Wilkes, J. John Wilkes, Patriot.

WILKINS, JOHN (1614-November 19, 1672), bishop of Chester, author of astronomical, mathematical, and philosophical works, was the son of a goldsmith. He was born at the home of his maternal grandfather, John Dod, who, following his father's death, supervised his early education. He entered Oxford at thirteen, graduated from Magdalen Hall with a B.A. at seventeen, received his M.A. three years later, and was the vicar of Farnsley at twenty-three.

While serving as private chaplain to three successive noble houses, he became one of a group of distinguished men interested in the new fields of "experimental philosophy," as the enlarging world of science was called. Holding weekly meetings, this group became known as the "Invisible College." When, in 1648, Wilkins became Warden of Wadham College, Oxford, an even more brilliant branch of the "Invisible" met at his home, including Seth Ward, Robert Boyle, Robert Hooke, and Christopher Wren.

Appointed master of Trinity College by Parliament, Wilkins was dismissed following the Restoration. He soon came into royal favor, however, and rose rapidly until, in 1668, he was appointed bishop of Chester.

Meanwhile, in 1662, the Invisible College had, with much credit due to Wilkins, become the Royal Society, of which Wilkins was the first secretary. He died at the age of fifty-eight, leaving much of his estate to Wadham College and the Royal Society.

Wilkins was almost universally loved and honored, and received the highest tributes as a warm friend, a writer of clear, simple and eloquent prose, and an indefatigable worker in the cause of science. He married Cromwell's sister, Robina French. His stepdaughter married the great preacher, John Tillotson, and Wilkins' influence on Tillotson had much to do with the latter's reputation as one of the greatest of the early English prose writers.

Wilkins' first book, published anonymously when he was twenty-four, explored the possibility of life on the moon, and feasible methods of getting there; his second posited the idea that the earth was a planet. His most important work was a scheme and dictionary for a universal language, a project carried out for the Royal Society.

PRINCIPAL WORKS: Discovery of a World in the Moon, 1638; Discourse Concerning a New Planet, 1640; Mercury, or the Secret and Swift Messenger, 1641; Ecclesiastes, or a Discourse Concerning the Gift of Preaching, 1646; Essay Toward a Real Character and a Philosophical Language, and Dictionary, 1668; Principles and Duties of a Natural Religion, 1678; Sermons, 1682.

ABOUT: Aubrey, J. Brief Lives; Burnet, G. History of My Own Time; Evelyn, J. Diary; Pepys, S. Diary; Wood, A. à, Athenae Oxonienses.

WILLIAM of MALMESBURY (d. 1143?), historian, was born (he said) on November 30, somewhere between 1090 and 1096, and probably in Somerset. He was of mixed Saxon and Norman descent. At an early age (some time before 1105) he entered Malmesbury Abbey, where most of his life was spent. With the eager encouragement of his father—of whom nothing else is known —he studied medicine, logic, and ethics, but above all, history, to which he was attracted from early youth. By 1125, when Earl Robert of Gloucester became his patron, he had already completed his histories of the kings and the bishops of England. He was librarian of the monastery, perhaps precentor as well, and said that he could twice have been elected abbot had he so desired. Later, in the 1130's, he seems to have had some dispute with the ruling abbot, and he may have been temporarily a resident at Glastonbury Abbey. His last public appearance was at the Council of Winchester, in 1140; his "modern history" stops at 1142, and nothing is known of him beyond that date. He had traveled much throughout England, he had a knowledge of the world and was free of monkish prejudices, and he spoke both English and Norman French, while always writing in Latin.

William's confessed master was Bede, and his aim was to restore to English history the standing which Bede had given it, and to "fill up the chasm of 223 years" (his own words) after Bede's time, neglected by Eadmer in his *Historia Novorum*. Besides his two English histories and his history of the bishops, he wrote a history of Glastonbury and lives of four saints connected with that monastery. He lived, of course, before the invention of printing, and his manuscripts were first printed in 1596.

William was a born historian, who made vast collections (both Malmesbury and Glastonbury were treasure-houses) and used material wherever he could find it, though with discrimination. Milton considered him, "both for style and judgment, by far the best" of the twelfth century chroniclers. He was sometimes careless about dates, and arbitrary in his arrangement of events, but from the Norman Conquest at least he is still a reliable authority for the period up to the middle of the twelfth century. He was accused of time-serving, but actually, though he was perhaps not so impartial as he believed himself to be, he gave no unfair advantage to his patron or his patron's party. He was credulous, and repeated supernatural marvels as true if they were vouched for by respectable "eye-witnesses."

What gives him a special place among the chroniclers, and keeps him good reading even today, is the fact that he was, besides being a born historian, a born story-teller as well. His many anecdotes, reminiscences, and personal comments may be irrelevant, but they are highly interesting. He made use of the old English ballad literature, and he had a gift for graphic, colorful, imaginative writing. A very lively book could be made from selections from his histories, chosen for their tales and vivid descriptions.

PRINCIPAL WORKS: De Gestis Regum Anglorum (concerning the deeds of the English kings) (448-1128) 1596; Historia Novella (modern history) (1125-1142) 1596 (J. A. Giles, tr. 1847; W. Stubbs, ed. 1887-89); Gesta Pontificum Anglorum (deeds of the English bishops) 1596 (N. E. S. A. Hamilton, ed. 1870); Vita S. Wulfstani (life of St. Wulfstan) (H. Wharton, ed.) 1691; Vita S. Dunstani (life of St Dunstan) (W. Stubbs, ed.) 1874.

ABOUT: Birch, DeG. Life and Writings of William of Malmesbury; Norgate, K. England under the Angevin Kings; Stubbs, W. Historical Introduction, Historia Novella, 1887-89 ed.

WILLIAM of NEWBURGH (1136?-1198?), historian, was born in Yorkshire, near Bridlington. He was connected with the monastery of Newburgh from childhood. It was near the end of his life, probably about 1199, that he was asked by Ernauld, abbot of Reviaulx, to write a history of England. In his preface to his one great work, *History of English Affairs*, he says, "For in our times such great and memorable events have happened that the negligence of us moderns were justly to be reprehended, should they fail to be handed down to eternal memory in literary monuments."

Unlike the chroniclers and romancers of his time, William of Newburgh had high standards of veracity and a critical and rational approach to the material of history. His preface includes a scathing denunciation of the earlier chronicler, Geoffrey of Monmouth, who certainly included legends and myths as facts in his *History of the Britons,* and whose work William calls "a tissue of lies." His own work began with a scanty and relatively unimportant review of Anglican history from Gildas and Bede to the year of his own birth, for which his chief authority was Henry of Huntingdon. Thereafter his sources were largely first hand, and for much of the period of his own lifetime, notably the first twenty years of the reign of Henry II, he is one of the main sources of information upon which we can rely. Not always accurate as to date and detail, he is nevertheless scrupulously exact in reporting only what seemed to him authenticated facts. And in contrast to other historians of the twelfth century, he saw these facts in perspective, made independent political and social judgments, related causes to effects, and was rationally sceptical of miracles and legends.

There is some evidence that he may, when a young man, have lived in the world for about twenty years, married a woman named Emma de Peri, and had a son, whose descendants were named Fitz Ellis (from William's supposed patronymic of Elias), before he re-entered the monastery of Newburgh. This story has been given credence by some because such a worldly experience could account for his sophisticated approach to history. Conversely, it is possible that the very remoteness of Newburgh from the court and society may have added to his objectivity and impartiality. Certainly his work is the best of its kind of his day.

PRINCIPAL WORK: History of English Affairs, prob. 1199-1201.

ABOUT: Gairdner, J. England; Hardy, T. D. Descriptive Catalogue; Howlett, R. Chroniclers of the Reigns of Stephen, Henry II, and Richard I; Salter, H. E. English Historical Review, 1907.

WILMOT, JOHN, Second Earl of Rochester (April 10, 1647-July 26, 1680), poet, satirist, was born at Ditchley, near Woodstock, Oxfordshire, the son of Henry Wilmot, the first earl, who was one of Charles II's closest associates during the civil wars, and his second wife. The father died, and the son succeeded, in 1659, when John Wilmot was only twelve. He was an exceedingly precocious boy, who after some schooling in Burford, Oxfordshire, entered Wadham College, Oxford, at thirteen and was given his M.A. degree the following year. After a tour of France and Italy, he appeared at the court, young, handsome, and brilliant, at seventeen, and immediately became a gentleman of the bedchamber, Charles' petted and pampered favorite (he was unbelievably impudent to the king), and a sort of "chartered libertine," the intimate of all the profligates and noble ruffians of the court—all much his senior, but all his inferiors in debauchery and vice. He was rebuked and exiled continually, then called back, thanks to his charm; during these exiles, he engaged in incredible escapades—he set up once in disguise as a tavern keeper, once as an astrologer and he finally capped the climax by abducting a beautiful heiress, Elizabeth Malet, in 1665. She was rescued and he was sent briefly to the Tower, but in 1667 he married her. There was no pretense at fidelity, but on the whole he showed her some tenderness and respect, and she seems to have made the best of it—at least to the extent of a son and three daugh-

W. Wissing

JOHN WILMOT, 2ND EARL
OF ROCHESTER

ters. (He also had a daughter by Elizabeth Barry, whom he trained as an actress.) In 1665 Rochester served as a naval volunteer, and in 1674 Charles made him keeper of Woodstock Park, with a house which became his chief residence and in which he died.

The fact that Rochester was seldom sober, and that he shocked his contemporaries even more by his cynicism, his irreligion, and his materialistic views learned from Hobbes than by his obscene verse or his promiscuity, completes the standard picture of "the wicked Earl." But it is far from exact; Rochester was, besides, loyal to his friends, kind and generous, and usually courageous. The most discreditable action of his life was his hiring of thugs to beat up Dryden when the poet transferred his dedications from Rochester to the latter's enemy the Earl of Mulgrave, and then boasting unrepentantly of the deed. He was not an admirable man—though in his last weeks, when, worn out by debauchery, he was dying at thirty-two, he astonished his friends by becoming serious about both politics and religion, and sending for Bishop Burnet to help him toward an "edifying end."

But, admirable or not, he was indisputably an extremely talented writer. Marvell, no mean judge, called him "the only man in England who has the true vein" of satire. His brutal exposures of the king and the court are evidence that however he ran with the pack he was intellectually not one of them. Moreover, he was capable of lyrics which, when they are not imitations of Cowley, display real and exquisite feeling. His was a complex and subtle nature, and he was obviously a victim of his environment.

When not blinded by resentment (as in the case of Dryden), he was a shrewd critic —witness *The Session of the Poets*. He had vigor, originality, wit, and passion. He was the model for Etherege's *Man of Mode*, and he had "theater sense," though his own plays are poor—*Valentinian* is only a bad revision of Beaumont and Fletcher; *Sodom*, aimed at Charles, is a piece of shameless pornography. But he will live for his epigrams, for a few of his lyrics, and for his bold satires. The best of them is *A Satyr against Mankind*, which, though imitated from Boileau, is far indeed from its sources. Carelessly willing to help his critics build up the worst possible picture of his character and life, Rochester was indeed his own worst enemy.

PRINCIPAL WORKS: A Satyr against Mankind, 1675; The Enjoyment, 1679; Poems . . . on Several Occasions, with Valentinian: a Tragedy, 1680; A Pastoral Dialogue between Alexis and Strephon, written at the Bath, 1682; Sodom, 1684; Familiar Letters (T. Brown, ed.) 1686; The Miscellaneous Works of the . . . late Earls of Rochester and Roscommon, 1707; Poem upon Nothing, 1711; Works (including Letters) 1714; Poetical Works, 1731-32.

ABOUT: Burnet, G. Some Passages of the Life and Death of John, Earl of Rochester; Johnson, S. Lives of the English Poets; Murdock, K. B. The Sun at Noon: Three Biographical Sketches; Pepys, S. Diary; Pinto, V. de S. Rochester: Portrait of a Restoration Poet; Prinz, J. John Wilmot, Earl of Rochester, His Life and Writings [including Correspondence and Bibliography]; Saintsbury, G. History of English Prosody; Williams, C. Rochester.

WILMOT, ROBERT (fl. 1568-1608), dramatist, was a clergyman who at one time was a member of, or associated with, the Inner Temple. In 1582 he became rector of North Ockendon, and three years later was vicar of nearby Horndon-on-the-Hill. Of a play *Syrophenisia, or the Canaanitish Woman; Conflicts at Horndon-on-the-Hill in Essex County*, which he wrote in 1598, no copy remains.

He is chiefly known as the co-author and editor of a play, *Gismond of Salerne*, which in 1565 was performed before an audience that included Queen Elizabeth. Five members of the Inner Temple wrote it, each writing one act. The basic story is from Boccaccio, a tale of desperate and tragic passion of great dramatic intensity. Overcome by moral scruples, the authors twisted the story into a more conventional shape and bolstered their emasculated material with characters and situations from Seneca, *Phaedra*, and Dolce's tragedy *Dido*. They then appended an epilogue assuring the audience that they did not intend to attribute such illicit and uncontrolled passion as Gismond's to the "virtuous and chaste" ladies of Britain, who were

worthy to live where fury never came
where love can see, and bears no deadly bow.

Twenty-six years later, Wilmot, although expressing doubts of the propriety of such occupation for a clergyman, re-wrote and published the play putting its originally rhymed quatrains into the more popular form of blank verse, with a pantomime presaging the action at the beginning of each act, and a summarizing chorus at each curtain. The published play has literary merit, in spite of its patchwork source, and is an interesting example of the school of drama which presented plays of classic tragedy and horror with such moralistic reservations as Wilmot attributed to the authors of *Gismond:* "Herein they all agree, commending virtue, detesting vice, and lively deciphering their overthrow that suppress not their unruly affections."

PRINCIPAL WORK: The Tragedy of Tancred and Gismond, pub. 1591.

ABOUT: Collier, J. P. History of Dramatic Poetry; Fleay, F. History of the Stage; Hallam, H. Literature of Europe; Ward, Sir A. W. A History of English Dramatic Literature.

WILSON, JOHN (1627?-1696?), dramatist, was the son of Aaron Wilson, an Irish clergyman with strong royalist sympathies. He was born in London. He attended Exeter College, but did not graduate, entering Lincoln's Inn in 1646 and becoming a member of the bar in 1649.

In the period between 1662 and 1665 he wrote three plays. The first, *The Cheats*, was produced in Clare Market in 1663 and won enormous popularity, but was "so scandalous it was forbidden." It is a broad satire which frankly imitates Ben Jonson in form, but has a vigorous, racy originality of treatment. The second play was *Andronicus Commenius,* a tragedy in blank verse, based on a story from Peter Heylyn's *Cosmography,* which also shows an inventive and original use of classic material. The third, *The Projectors,* is again a Jonsonian comedy, adapted from the *Aulularia* of Plautus, which was also the source for Molière's *L'Avare.* The characters of the loan shark Suckdry and his servant Leanchops, and of their victim Sir Gudgeon Credulous, are excellently drawn. The two latter plays were apparently never produced.

Wilson's reputation was now high, and, with his inherited royalist tendencies, he attracted the attention of the court. He became secretary to the Duke of York, and in 1681, through the Duke of Ormonde, Lord Lieutenant of Ireland, was given the office of Recorder of Londonderry. His literary output for the next few years was dedicated to his royal sponsors, and consisted of a poem addressed to Ormonde, a discourse dealing with the succession of the Duke of York, a panegyric on the occasion of the coronation of James II, and a dissertation on royal prerogatives in legal matters.

He remained in Ireland following the revolution, but returned to London in 1690. That year his last play was produced at Dorset Garden, a detailed and rather dull tragicomedy from an Italian story told by Machiavelli, titled *Belphegor, or the Marriage of the Devil.* The exact date of his death is not known.

PRINCIPAL WORKS: The Cheats, 1662; Andronicus Commenius, 1664; The Projectors, 1665; Poem, 1682; A Discourse of Monarchy, 1684; A Pindaric to Their Sacred Majesties James II and His Royal Consort Queen Mary on Their Coronation, 1685; The King's Supreme Power in Dispensing with Penal Statutes, 1688; Belphegor, or the Marriage of the Devil, 1691.

ABOUT: Bibliographia Britannica; Genest, J. History of the English Stage; Halliwell-Phillips, I. Dictionary of Old English Plays; Langbaine, G. English Dramatic Poets; Ward, Sir A. W. A History of English Dramatic Literature.

WILSON, THOMAS (1525-June 16, 1581) rhetorician, man of letters, was the son of Thomas and Anne Wilson of Strubly, Lincolnshire. He attended Eton and King's College, Cambridge, graduating B.A. in 1546 and receiving his M.A. in 1549.

He spent a few years in writing, under the patronage of John Dudley, Earl of Warwick, son of Northumberland. Upon the latter's fall from power, Wilson went into exile in Italy, first at Padua and later at Rome. Here he was involved in intrigue at the papal court, for which he was ordered back to England to stand trial. Ignoring the summons, he was charged by the Inquisition at Rome with heretical writings, was tortured and imprisoned, but escaped in 1559 when indignant mobs opened the jails. Returning to England after Elizabeth's accession, he found favor with the court, became a court advocate, Master of St. Catherine's Hospital, and Master of Requests. The rest of his life was spent in political and diplomatic circles; he was a Member of Parliament, went on embassies to Portugal and the Netherlands, and in 1577 was appointed Secretary of State. The year before his death, Elizabeth made him lay dean of Durham. He died at fifty-six. He had been married twice, and had two daughters and one son.

Running concurrently with his political career was an equally active intellectual life. At Cambridge he had come under the influence of the group of scholars interested in the revival of Greek learning, particularly of his friend Roger Ascham. His most important work was a treatise on rhetoric, in which he analyzed elements of literary style and of elocution. It has been called the first English work of criticism, and while Wilson applied the classical rules of form of Aristotle, Cicero, and Quintilian, his greatest contribution is in his elevation of the native vernacular of England to the respectable status of a language to which scholarly standards should be applied. His pride in the English language, and his confidence in its resources, did a great deal to purify literature of the use of foreign phrases which were then in vogue. He made the first English translation of Demosthenes, adding a remarkable comparison of the states of Athens and England, which was as important for its political significance as for its high standard of scholarship.

PRINCIPAL WORKS: The Rule of Reason, 1551; Art of Rhetoric, 1553; The Three Orations of Demosthenes, 1570; Discourse Upon Usury, 1572; A Discourse Touching upon the Kingdom's Perils with Their Remedies, 1578.

ABOUT: Collins, A. Letters and Memorials of State; Fuller, T. History of Cambridge; Fuller, T. Worthies of England; Ritson, J. Bibliographia Anglo-Poetica.

WINCHILSEA, ANNE FINCH, Countess of (April 1661-August 5, 1720), writer of occasional verse, was born Anne Kingsmill, daughter of Sir William Kingsmill, at Sidmonton, near Southampton. As with most girls of her era, what education she had was received at home. She became maid of honor to Mary of Modena, Duchess of York, and in 1684 left the court to marry Colonel Heneage Finch, who in 1712 became fifth Earl of Winchilsea. (The name is sometimes spelled Winchelsea.) They had no children.

In 1690 she moved to Eastwell, Kent, and it was from this country residence that she drew her fondness for nature, which later caused Wordsworth to admire her verses and make up an anthology of them. She was a friend of Anne Killigrew and an admirer of "the matchless Orinda" (Katherine Philips), and like them she circulated her poems among her acquaintances, and what little she published appeared anonymously. Her pen name was "Ardelia."

The chief influences on her work were Cowley, Prior and La Fontaine; she also wrote blank verse dramas (*Aristomenes* was the best known) in imitation of "Orinda." She was not a salonist as were most of the "female wits," but she was acquainted with many of the litterateurs of her day. Pope even wrote verses in her honor.

Her forte was gay light verse, especially occasional verse, though in her own time she was most celebrated for her Pindaric ode, *Spleen* (meaning melancholy). This and her other odes, which were much admired, have been called by a later critic "unbearable." In addition to her original writing, she did some translations from French and Italian.

After Wordsworth "discovered" her, the Countess of Winchilsea became a cult among a few nineteenth century writers, principally Dowden and Gosse. She was, it was true, a good observer and sincere lover of natural beauty, but her talent for describing it was very slight. It was ridiculous for Wordsworth to call her "a wood lark among the town sparrows." Actually her nature poems are few and slender. She had some gift for rhyme, and she had a certain freshness of sentiment, but she was the most minor of minor versifiers.

Very little is known of her personality or her uneventful private life. She died in her London house at sixty-one. Most of her poems remained in manuscript, where Wordsworth found some of them and Dowden discovered more; these have not been published, but apparently they are in no way superior to those which have been. *The Spleen* appeared first as part of Gildon's *Miscellany*, and *Aristomenes* was included in her volume of poems issued in 1713.

PRINCIPAL WORKS: The Spleen, a Pindarique Ode, with a Prospect of Death, a Pindarique Essay, 1709; Miscellany Poems Written by a Lady, 1713; Poems (M. Reynolds, ed.) 1903; Poems (J. M. Murry, ed.) 1928.

ABOUT: Dowden, E. Essays, Modern and Elizabethan; Gosse, E. Gossip in a Library; Murry, J. M. Introduction, Poems, 1928 ed.; Reynolds, M. The Treatment of Nature in English Poetry between Pope and Wordsworth; Walpole, H. Catalogue of Royal and Noble Authors.

WIREKER, NIGEL (fl. 1190), satirist, was a monk of the priory of Christ Church, Canterbury. He was probably a kinsman of William Longchamp, who was both Bishop of Ely and Chancellor of England.

Wireker's known works include several Latin poems, a prose treatise, and a satire in elegiac verse. The poems are on traditional religious themes, except for one, which may not be Wireker's, which describes in some detail life in a twelfth century monastery. The treatise, *Contra Curiales et Officiales Clericos*, written about 1193, was directed to Longchamp and deals with his holding of the bishopric and the chancellorship at the same time. Wireker's purpose was to attack those members of the clergy who neglected their religious duties for more worldly occupations.

It is the satire, *Speculum Stultorum*, by which his name is remembered. It was extremely popular for three centuries, and Chaucer refers to it as a well known story. The leading character is Burnellus, an ass, whom Wireker in a prose introduction identifies as the typical ambitious and discontented monk. Burnellus, who desires a longer tail, is sent by Galen to Salerno with a prescription. Returning, he is attacked and robbed not only of his goods and the potion which was to give him a longer tail, but also of one half the tail he has. Ashamed to return home, he studies liberal arts for seven years at the University of Paris, studies theology at each of the monastic orders in England, and determines to found his own order. In the end he meets his old master, and is ordered to resume his life as an ordinary monk. The satire is sharp and witty, and is directed not only at the religious orders of Wireker's day, but at the vice and corruption of society as well.

PRINCIPAL WORKS: Miracula S. Mariae Virginis; Passio S. Laurentii; Vita Pauli Primi Eremitae; Contra Curiales et Officiales Clericos, c. 1193 (pub. 1872); Speculum Stultorum, before 1180 (pub. 1872).

ABOUT: Wright, T. Anglo-Latin Satirical Poets; Wright, T. Biographia Britannica Literaria.

WITHER, GEORGE (June 11, 1588-May 2, 1667), poet, author of hymns and miscellaneous works, was born in Bentworth, near Alton, Hampshire, the son of George Wither and Anne Serle. After being tutored by John Greaves, the neighboring vicar, he entered Magdalen College, Oxford, in 1604. Two years later his father called him home to the farm. Farming was not his forte, however, and by 1610 he had escaped to London, where after being enrolled in one of the minor Inns of Court, he entered Lincoln's Inn in 1615. Apparently he had no intention of becoming a lawyer, and he was never called to the bar. Instead, in 1612, he was introduced at the Court, where his elegies on Prince Henry (oldest son of James II) and his nuptial poems for Princess Elizabeth (afterwards Elizabeth of Bohemia) had already attracted attention.

The next year this favor was withdrawn when he published his *Abuses Stript and Whipt*, which earned him several months in Marshalsea Prison—just why, it is difficult to understand, since the satire was mild and general. It was in prison that he wrote his pastoral, *Shepherds Hunting*, in imitation of his friend William Browne. *Wither's Motto* ("nec habeo, nec careo, nec curio"—I have nothing, I lack nothing, I don't care) landed him in the Marshalsea again, and again incomprehensibly, but this time the libel charge was dismissed without a trial. John Taylor, the "Water Poet," satirized this poem in his rough style.

With 1625 or thereabouts, Wither's first period as a poet ends—the period of his lighthearted lyrics and pastorals and his genial satire. He became increasingly puritanical in belief, and though an occasional poetic gleam lights up his hymns and devotional verses, the greater part of his output

—nearly a hundred volumes in all—was in topical pamphlets in prose and verse. *Faire-Virtue* was his last purely literary production; the rest was religious or political propaganda. In consequence, his early reputation as a lyric poet died long before he did; he became known as a hack rhymester, Pope's "wretched Withers" (the name was sometimes so spelled), who, according to Dryden, "rhymed and rattled." He was rediscovered by Percy and his later reputation—based entirely on his early poems—was founded on the admiration of Lamb, Coleridge, and Southey.

Meanwhile, the civil wars had broken out. In spite of his religious convictions, Wither actually took part in them first on the side of the king, as captain of horse against the Scottish Covenanters in 1639. By the next year he was an officer (eventually a major) in the Parliamentary Army. He seems to have had very little military ability. When he commanded the garrison of Farnham Castle, in Surrey, he abandoned it and marched toward London, leaving it to be retaken by another officer. In consequence he was captured by the Royalists, and released—he was in danger of hanging—only by the intervention of Sir John Denham, who humorously begged his life so that he himself might not be "the worst poet in England" (another proof of how soon Wither's exquisite early poems had been forgotten). Wither, incidentally, far from feeling gratitude, never forgave Denham for the slur.

Though he was later made major general of all the horse and foot in Surrey, and justice of the peace as well, the Farnham Castle episode boomeranged. He wrote his *Justiarius Justificatus*, in which he justified his action by blaming Sir Richard Onslow. Onslow retorted by suing him, he was fined, the book was burned publicly, and he was deprived of both his military and civil offices. He had become wealthy by means of land sequestered from the Royalists (including Denham's house), but the pension and annuity promised him by the government in exchange for this property was never paid in full. (He had offended the younger Cromwell by some plainspoken criticism.) Worse, with the Restoration he was immediately arrested and thrown into the Tower. Though he was acquitted of libel, he spent

After J. Payne

GEORGE WITHER

three years, from 1663 to 1667, in Newgate. After his release he lived quietly in London until his death at nearly seventy-nine.

Wither married Elizabeth Emerson or Emerton, who also wrote verses and was known as a wit. They had six children, though only one son and one daughter and his wife survived him. The daughter later edited his *Divine Poems.* He remained the lifelong friend both of Browne and of Michael Drayton until the latter's death. Indeed, he was in general a Puritan without Puritanism—he was never dour, he never lost his taste for humor or his fundamental joy of living.

Wither's *Workes* were surreptitiously printed, without authorization, in 1620. Two years later he himself brought out most of the same poems, sardonically labeling the new volume *Juvenilia.* Unfortunately, the joke, from a literary standpoint, was on him; nearly everything he had had to say as a pure poet was now behind him.

One other episode from his early days must be recounted. In 1624 he secured from James · II a patent of monopoly for his *Hymnes and Songs of the Church,* requiring that they be inserted in every authorized Psalter. As may be imagined, the booksellers and publishers of other collections of hymns were furious, and for years he and the printers waged a wordy battle. Among the enemies he made was Ben Jonson, who

caricatured Wither as "Chronomastix" in *Time Vindicated.*

Lamb remarked that it was "left to Wither to discover that poetry was a present possession as well as a rich reversion." In his earlier period at least poetry was to him a joyful thing. He had little depth at any time, but he had grace and lyric freshness. His later works, mostly in verse, became increasingly pieces of doggerel, didactic, garrulous, and smug. The best that can be said for them is that they are sincere, and that in small doses they have quaintness and unmistakable individuality.

PRINCIPAL WORKS: Prince Henrie's Obsequies, 1612; Epithalamia, or Nuptiall Poems, 1612; Abuses Stript and Whipt, 1613; Fidelia, 1615; The Shepherds Hunting, 1615; Workes, 1620; Withers Motto, 1621?; Faire-Virtue, the Mistresse of Phil'arete, 1622; Juvenilia, 1622; The Hymnes and Songs of the Church, 1624; The Schollers Purgatory, 1625?; Britain's Remembrancer, 1628; The Psalmes of David Paraphrased, 1632; A Collection of Emblemes [verses for pictures] 1634-35; The Nature of Man (prose tr. Nemesius) 1636; Hallelujah, or Britain's Second Remembrancer, 1641; Mercurius Rusticus, or the Rustic Messenger, 1643; Campo-Musae, or Field-Musings, 1644; Withers Prophecie of the Downfall of Antichrist, 1644; Vox Pacifica, 1645; Justitiarius Justificatus, 1646; Opobalsum Anglicanum, or the British Herb, 1646; Carmen Eucharisticon: a Private Thank-Oblation, 1649; British Appeals, with God's Mercifull Replies, on the Behalfe of the Commonwealth of England, 1651; The Dark Lantern, 1653; Three Private Meditations (prose) 1659; The Petition, 1659; Fides-Anglicana, Or, a Plea for the Publick-Faith of These Nations (prose) 1660; Speculum Speculationum, 1660; Tudor-Poeticus, A Poetick-Phrensie, 1660; Parallelogrammaticon, An Epistle to . . . England, Ireland, Scotland (prose) 1662; Echoes from the Sixth Trumpet, 1666 (as Nul Ultra; or, the Last Workes of Captain G. W., 1668); Divine Poems (E. Barry [daughter] ed.) 1688; Poems (H. Maley, ed.) 1891; The Poetry of George Wither (F. Sidgwick, ed.) 1902.

ABOUT: Aubrey, J. Brief Lives; Lamb C. Essays; Sidgwick, F. Introduction, Poetry; Wood, A. à, Athenae Oxonienses.

WODROW, ROBERT (1679-March 21, 1734), ecclesiastical historian, was born in Glasgow. He attended the University of Glasgow, where his father, James Wodrow, was professor of divinity. For four years after receiving his M.A. he served as librarian of the university, and then went to live with Lord Pollock, a relative. In 1703 he was licensed to preach, and was presented by Pollock with the living at Eastwood, where he remained for the rest of his life. In 1708 he married Margaret Warner, by whom he had sixteen children. A popular preacher and an active figure in church politics, he carried on a voluminous correspondence, some of the twenty-four manuscript volumes being published posthumously.

Most of his writings were unpublished at his death. Among these were *Analecta, or Materials for a History of Remarkable Providences*, a collection of anecdotes about Scottish ministers, and *Memoirs of Reformers and Ministers of the Church of Scotland*, both of which, with his correspondence, were published more than a century after his death by the Wodrow Society, an association formed in 1841 in Edinburgh for the purpose of publishing historical writings of the Scottish church. His biography of his father was published in 1828.

His most important work, stemming from his interest in antiquarian and historical studies, was a history of the persecution of the Scottish church from the Restoration to the Revolution. A pioneer work in this field, it required a tremendous amount of research, and Wodrow achieved remarkable accuracy considering the size of his task. The manuscript was approved by the general assembly of the church, and was published in 1721-22. Wodrow died at Eastwood at the age of fifty-five.

PRINCIPAL WORKS: The Oath of Abnegation, 1712; The History of the Sufferings of the Church of Scotland, 1721-22; Life of James Wodrow, pub. 1828; Memoirs of Reformers and Ministers of the Church of Scotland, pub. 1834-45, 1890; Analecta, pub. 1842-43; Correspondence, pub. 1842-43.

ABOUT: Irving, D. Lives of Scottish Writers; Lippe, R. ed. Selections From Wodrow's Biographical Collections; Scott, H. Fasti Ecclesiae Scoticanae; Wodrow, R. History of the Sufferings of the Church of Scotland (see biographical preface by R. Burns, ed. 1808).

WOLCOT, JOHN ("PETER PINDAR")
(May 1738-January 14, 1819), satirist, poet, was born in Dodbrooke, Devonshire (he was not a Cornishman as has been claimed), the son of Alexander Wolcot, a surgeon, and Mary Ryder. When he was thirteen his father died and he was reared by his uncle, also a surgeon. He attended schools in Kingsbridge, Liskeard, and Bodmin, and was then sent to France for a year to learn the language. He went to London in 1762 to study medicine, and in 1764 became his uncle's assistant at Fowey, Cornwall. He received his M.D. degree from Aberdeen University in 1767.

In 1769 he went to Jamaica as physician to the governor, Sir William Trelawny, a distant relative. In the expectation of a good living to become vacant on the island, he took orders, but was disappointed of the living, though he was given a smaller one at Vere, Jamaica. He soon abandoned the clergy and returned to medicine, becoming physician-general to the British horse and foot. Sir William died and he returned to England with Lady Trelawny; the expectation was that they were to be married, but she died soon after their return, and he remained a bachelor.

He went back to the practice of medicine, successively at Truro, Helstone, and Exeter. Then he met the painter John Opie, at the beginning of his career, and took him to London on an arrangement by which he was to bring Opie to public attention and receive half his profits from painting. They soon quarreled, though not before Wolcot, a good art critic, had begun his series of satirical poems attacking the Royal Academy, and Benjamin West in particular. All Wolcot's satires were published under the name of "Peter Pindar," and he claimed to be a "distant cousin" of the ancient Theban poet.

From art he turned to politics, and the numerous verse satires on the private life of George III and his Tory ministers. The Prince of Wales enjoyed his work (later as

W. S. Lethridge

JOHN WOLCOT

Regent he turned against him), but he was threatened with legal action, and for two or three years he aimed his shafts at lesser fry. His verse was a sort of blackmail, and he came near to receiving a pension to stop his mouth. When this hope proved vain, he returned to the assault on the king, Pitt, and Canning. He met his match when William Gifford not only attacked him in verse but gave him a sound beating. In any case, his powers had waned, and his last work was very bad. In his last years he was blind, a misfortune he met with cheerful stoicism. He was a good musician, and in general lived on the edges of Bohemia. His knowledge of art was good enough for him to edit Pilkington's *Dictionary of Painters*. He was of course anathema to the Tories, who agreed with Gifford that he was "this disgustful subject, the profligate reviler of his sovereign and impious blasphemer of his God." Actually, though Wolcot was undeniably vulgar, coarse, and malicious, he was personally not a bad fellow, and his friends praised his "kind and hearty disposition." His mock-heroic *Lousiad* was very popular, but is unbearably long and tedious, as are most of his "rambling drolleries." He was in fact more of a caricaturist than a true satirist. His serious poems are dull, though occasionally they show an unexpected vein of tenderness and sentiment.

Wolcot lived well on a shrewd sale of his copyrights, and survived to the age of eighty-one. He died in London and was buried in St. Paul's, with his coffin, at his request, touching that of the satirist Samuel Butler.

PRINCIPAL WORKS: Poetical Epistle to Reviewers, 1778; Poems on Various Subjects, 1778; Lyric Odes to the Royal Academicians, 1782, 1783, 1785; The Lousiad, 1785; Farewell Odes to Academicians, 1786; Bozzy and Piozzi, or the British Biographers, 1786; Ode upon Ode, or a Peep at St. James's, 1787; Instructions to a Celebrated Laureat (*sic*) 1787; Expostulatory Odes to a Great Duke and a Little Lord, 1789; A Rowland for an Oliver, 1790; Ode to Mr. Paine, Author of "Rights of Man," 1791; One Thousand Seven Hundred and Ninety-Six: A Satire, 1797; Out at Last! or the Fallen Minister, 1801; Tristia, or the Sorrows of Peter, 1806; One More Peep at the Royal Academy, 1808; Carlton House Fete, or the Disappointed Bard, 1811; Works, 1812; A Most Solemn Epistle to the Emperor of China, 1817.

ABOUT: Courthope, W. J. History of English Poetry; Hazlitt, W. Essays; Redding, C. Past Celebrities.

WOLLSTONECRAFT, MARY. See GODWIN, Mrs. MARY WOLLSTONECRAFT

WOOD, ANTHONY or ANTHONY à (December 17, 1632-November 29, 1695), antiquary, historian, was born in Oxford, lived there all his life, and died in the house in which he was born. His father was Thomas Wood, a lawyer who did not practice but lived on his rents, his mother was Mary Petty, a second wife. He was educated at New College School, then, though his family wanted him to enter business, matriculated at Merton College in 1644. Though he was but a dull pupil, he graduated B.A. in 1652, M.A. in 1655. From boyhood he was interested in antiquities, made antiquarian notes, and counted the day he first saw the Bodleian Library "the happiest of his life."

In 1669 he edited the sermons of his older brother, but already he was at work on his history of the university. Finally in 1669 the newly founded university press agreed to publish it, but only if it were translated into Latin, "for the honour of the university in forreigne countries." The liberties taken with his work aroused all his easily excited resentment, and he was aggrieved especially at Dr. John Fell, dean of Christ Church, who was his firmest supporter. The original English version did not appear until almost a century after Wood's death. From this book grew, first, the study of the antiquities of the city of Oxford, never really completed, published in a garbled version in 1773 and finally printed fully in 1888, and—more important, and Wood's chief claim to fame—the *Athenae Oxonienses*, a series of biographies of Oxford graduates. In this, monumental work that it is, Wood gave free rein to his spite, arrogance, and ill temper, with the result that he was sued for libel by the son of the first Earl of Clarendon, and in consequence was expelled from the university and the offending pages were publicly burned. He died, unmarried, in the garret-study which had been his hermit's cell for many years. From 1667 to 1670 he was much in London, looking up authorities, but for his last twenty years he had gravitated only between his house, the bookshops, the Bodleian, and the neighboring inns.

573

Aubrey, who like others gave him much help and received no gratitude, said that Wood "never spake well of any man." He was universally disliked for his pettishness, meanness, and surliness, and his utter lack of either humor or kindliness. He was enormously industrious, and he did love scholarship. Deaf from middle age, in his youth he was fond of music and played the violin.

Wood was inspired first by Dugdale's history of Warwickshire, and he was extremely indebted to the records kept by Brian Twyne—though he never mentioned Twyne's name. He was no stylist, but he is eminently readable—largely because of the outspokenness and malice which earned him so much hatred. His autobiography, which he left in manuscript with his diaries, contains more minute and intimate details than any in print except perhaps that of Pepys. If it is not so celebrated, it is because he possessed none of the warmth, humaneness, and interest in others so characteristic of that great diarist. In later years Wood pedantically dubbed himself "à Wood."

PRINCIPAL WORKS: Historia et antiquitates Universitatis Oxoniensis (Latin tr. by R. Peers, and R. Reeve) 1674 (as The History and Antiquities of the Colleges and Halls in the University of Oxford, 1786); Athenae Oxonienses, An exact history of all the writers and bishops who have had their education in the University of Oxford from 1500 to 1690: to which are added the Fasti or Annals of the said University, 1691-92; Modius Salium, a collection of such pieces of humour as prevail'd at Oxford in the time of Mr. Anthony à Wood, 1751; The Antient and Present state of the City of Oxford (J. Peshall, ed.) 1773 (as Survey of the Antiquities of the City of Oxford [A. Clark, ed.] 1888-89); The Life and Times of Anthony Wood, Antiquary of Oxford, Described by Himself (W. Huddesford, ed.) 1777 (A. Clark, ed. 1891-1900; abridged, L. Powys, ed. 1932).

ABOUT: Aubrey, J. Lives of Eminent Men; Clark, A. Introduction, Life and Times, 1891 ed.; Granger, T. Biographical History of England; Nichol, J. Literary Anecdotes; Wood, A. Life and Times.

WOOLSTON, THOMAS (1670-January 1733), author of controversial religious tracts, was born at Northampton. He graduated from Sidney-Sussex College, Cambridge, receiving a B.A. in 1689, an M.A. in 1692, and a B.D. in 1699. He was elected a fellow of the college in 1691, took holy orders, and was appointed ecclesiastical lecturer in 1697. For a few years his career was that of an estimable and popular preacher of a scholarly turn of mind. Devoted to the study of the early church fathers, he was so impressed by the works of Origen, the ancient patristic writer of Alexandria, that he adopted the thesis that the stories of the Old Testament were allegorical rather than historical.

This interpretation of Biblical history was embodied in his first important work, *The Old Apology for the Christian Religion Against the Jews and the Gentiles Revived.* His career at this point took a sharp turn. He left Cambridge and began publishing a series of pamphlets and letters which shocked the country not only because of their heretical content, but also because of their peculiarly coarse and irreverent style. His sanity began to be doubted. Deprived of his Cambridge fellowship, he was supported by his brother and a few faithful friends. There was startling contrast between his sound and able B.D. thesis, written in 1699 and published in 1722, and his series of pamphlets attacking the clergy, written from 1722 to 1725. When he extended his allegorical method to the New Testament and applied it to the stories of the virgin birth and the resurrection, he was indicted for blasphemy. Following the publication of six *Discourses* on the same subject, of which 30,000 copies were sold, he was tried, found guilty, and sentenced to one year imprisonment and a fine of £100. Unable to raise the amount of the fine, he remained in prison for the next four years, until his death.

In spite of the almost universal disapprobation of his work, there were "queer gleams of distorted sense, and even of literary power, in the midst of his buffoonry," and his writings are said to have had some influence on Voltaire.

PRINCIPAL WORKS: The Old Apology for the Christian Religion Revived, 1705; A Free-Gift to the Clergy, 1722; The Exact Fitness of the Time in Which Christ was Manifested, 1722; A Moderator between an Infidel and an Apostate, 1725; A Defense of the Miracle of the Thundering Legion, 1726; Discourse on the Miracles of Our Savior, 1727; Defense, 1729.

ABOUT: Biographia Britannica; Cairns, J. Unbelief in the 18th Century; Hunt, J. Religious Thought in England; Stackhouse, T. A Fair Statement of the Controversy Between Mr. Woolston and his Adversaries.

WOTTON, Sir HENRY (1568-December 1639), poet, miscellaneous writer, was born at Boughton Malherbe, Kent, the son of Thomas Wotton and his second wife.

Eleanor (Finch) Morton. He was educated at Winchester and in 1584 matriculated at New College, Oxford. Two years later he went to Queen's College, and secured his B.A. in 1588. At the university he met Donne and Sir Edward Dyer, who became his close friends. At this period he wrote a play, *Tancredo*, based on Tasso, but it has been lost. His chief interest was in science; he studied optics and corresponded later with Francis Bacon on this subject.

His father died in 1587, and as soon as he had graduated B.A. he left for the Continent, staying until 1594. In Geneva he resided with the scholar Casaubon—and left owing Casaubon a good deal of money, which the latter had trouble in collecting. During his time abroad Wotton had frequently corresponded on political matters with Elizabeth's courtiers, principally with Essex, and on his return he became Essex's secretary and agent. When Essex fell, though he was not involved, he fled immediately, and never dared return to England while Elizabeth lived. From Florence, he was sent by Duke Ferdinand of Tuscany to warn James VI of Scotland of a plot discovered against his life; he traveled through Norway and stayed three months in Scotland as one "Ottavio Baldi," an Italian, only the king knowing his identity. As soon as James became James I of England, he sent for Wotton, knighted him, and offered him the ambassadorial post at Madrid or Venice. He took the last, as being the least expensive. He was ambassador from 1604 to 1612, from 1616 to 1619, and from 1621 to 1624.

Unfortunately, he lost James' personal friendship; one Caspar Schoppe, an enemy of Wotton's, quoted his indiscreet remark that an ambassador is "an honest man sent to lie abroad for the good of his country." He regained the king's good will only by abject subservience to his tyrannical usurpation of power. In 1624 Wotton was made provost of Eton, a post he held to his death, though he served twice in Parliament. He was a good provost, though otherwise lazy and idle—his greatest joy was to fish with his friend Izaak Walton. He was constantly hard up, once even arrested for debt, until Charles I increased his pension in exchange for a history of Henry VIII which Wotton never wrote. Other plans—lives of Luther

SIR HENRY WOTTON

and Donne, a history of Venice—also went undone or were unfinished. He had been exempted from the necessity of taking orders on becoming provost, but was ordained deacon in 1627, thereafter appealing in vain for preferment.

As a writer, Wotton was on the whole an amiable dilettante. He wrote two beautiful poems—"The Character of a Happy Life" and "To his Mistress, the Queen of Bohemia." He was a master of witty table talk, and his official and personal letters are among the finest of their kind, but in spite of his fresh and graceful style, his genial humor, and the nobility of his ideals, he never emerged as a writer of genuine standing, but remained a diplomat and courtier who occasionally wrote as an avocation.

Wotton was never married. He died and was buried in Eton, leaving a curious Latin epitaph which did not mention his name.

PRINCIPAL WORKS: The Elements of Architecture (from Vitruvius) 1624; Ad Regem e Scotia reducem [to the king on his return from Scotland] (verse) 1633; A Parallell betweene Robert, late Earle of Essex, and George, late [first] Duke of Buckingham, 1641; A Short View of the Life of George Villiers, Duke of Buckingham, 1642; Reliquiae Wottonianae [remains of Wotton: but work by others included] 1651; The State of Christendom, 1657; Letters and Despatches, 1850.

ABOUT: More, P. E. Shelburne Essays; Smith, L. P. The Life and Letters of Sir Henry Wotton; Walton, I. Life of Sir Henry Wotton; Ward, A. W. Sir Henry Wotton, a Biographical Sketch; Wood, A. à, Athenae Oxonienses.

WULFSTAN (d. May 28, 1023), writer of homilies, was a member of a "good family" of which nothing further is known except that his mother died at his birth. He entered the monastery of Ely, became an abbot, and sometime before 1003 was made Bishop of Worcester. In that year he became Archbishop of York, still retaining his office at Worcester. He was as busy with worldly matters as with those of the church, often being consulted on affairs of state. In 1014 he assisted King Aethelred the Unready in formulating the laws of the land.

His lifetime saw the most disastrous wars and destruction in England, and in a famous homily Wulfstan recounted these disasters, and took to task the people of England for those sins for which God had thus punished them. He was not a poet in a creative sense, but occasionally there are short poetic passages, which may have been borrowed from folk ballads, on the subject of the hardships of the time.

Wulfstan, intensely patriotic and moralistic, painted a vivid picture of the dreadful results of the invasions in which the English had come off so badly, and in rousing terms exhorted the people to repent and reform. There are traces of his legalistic language in the writing, and the style is the balanced, rhythmic, vehement one of the rhetorician. The homily ends on a gentle note of pleading, "Let us order rightly our words and our deeds, and keep faith with one another without guile."

Many other homilies have been ascribed to Wulfstan, but only five are certainly his work. Two deal with Biblical history, one with the Catholic church, and another is entitled *Address to the English*. He died at York in 1023, and was buried at Ely.

PRINCIPAL WORK: Homilies, pub. 1880.

ABOUT: Kinard, J. P. A Study of Wulfstan's Homilies; Napier, A. Wulfstan's Homilies.

WYATT (WYAT or WIAT), Sir THOMAS (1503?-October 11, 1542), poet, was born near Maidstone, Kent, the son of Sir Henry Wyatt, joint constable with Anne Boleyn's father at Norwich Castle, and of Anne Skinner. He was educated at St. John's College, Cambridge, graduating B.A. in 1518, M.A. in 1522; there is a legend that he attended Oxford also, but no proof of it.

By 1516 he was a "server extraordinary" at court, and by 1524 clerk of the king's jewels.

His diplomatic career began in 1525, when he was sent on a mission to France, and the next year to the papal court. On this occasion he visited a number of the Italian cities. On his return he was captured by the imperial army and held for ransom, but escaped. In 1529 and 1530 he was high marshal of Calais.

Wyatt had been reared with Anne Boleyn, and it was generally believed, and probably true, that he was her first lover. What is probably not true is that he told this to Henry VIII when the king was considering marrying her. In view of Henry's touchy and jealous nature, it is quite unlikely that in that event Wyatt would have remained in the king's favor, as he did. At Henry's marriage to Anne, Wyatt was the chief ewerer. True, when Anne was condemned, in 1536, Wyatt was thrown into the Tower, but only for a month, and apparently merely as a witness.

He was knighted in 1537, and from that date to 1539 he was ambassador to the emperor, for the most part in Spain. Edmund Bonner, his co-ambassador, intrigued against him and accused him of misfeasance; Wyatt was recalled, but Cardinal Cromwell undertook his defense and he was sent to the emperor again, in Flanders and Paris, until 1540. Then, however, Cromwell himself fell, Bonner renewed his allegations, this time adding treason to the charges and Wyatt once more found himself in the Tower.

This time it was Catherine Howard, the current queen, who rescued him. Wyatt had been married, in 1520, at only seventeen or so, to Elizabeth Brooke, daughter of Lord Cobham. The marriage was a failure, and for fifteen years the two had lived apart. Now Wyatt was pardoned, on condition first that he would confess to the Bonner charges (which probably were not true), and secondly that he would take his wife back and never again be unfaithful to her. He swallowed both hard conditions, though there is no evidence that the marriage was any happier than before. The couple had one son, who was executed as a conspirator during the reign of Mary; their great-grandson was Sir Francis Wyat, governor of Virginia.

After H. Holbein

SIR THOMAS WYATT

After his death his widow married Sir Edward Warner.

After his release from the Tower, Wyatt retired to his estate in Allington, Kent. There he wrote his epigrams, his three fine satires, and his paraphrase of the penitential Psalms. In 1542 he was knight of shire for Kent, and represented the county in Parliament. He was sent on a mission to conduct the imperial ambassador to London, caught a fever (he had been in ill health when he started the journey), and died on the road, at Sherborne, Dorset.

Wyatt is usually thought and spoken of in connection with Henry Howard, Earl of Surrey [qv]; the two are considered the writers of the first true English sonnets, modeled on those of Petrarch. Actually, though their sonnets were published together after Wyatt's death, Surrey was much his junior and was his disciple. It was Wyatt who first "drew ideas out of Italy for the rejuvenation of English poetry." He found chaos and confusion—the grammar, rhythm, and accent of Chaucer had long been forgotten or debased —and he brought about order and seemliness. Sidney and Spenser followed him and Surrey, and the way was prepared for the great Elizabethan age.

Wyatt's sonnets, though Petrarchan in form, were a modification, for he almost always ended the octet with a couplet, which the Italian poet never did. He was the first also to introduce the personal note into English poetry, to write of his own sufferings from the cruelty of his mistress—almost his only theme in the sonnets and lyrics. Often these were paraphrases of Petrarch, but often also they were genuinely subjective.

What he called epigrams were not witty sayings, but organized conceits or paradoxes in verse, in an ababbcc rhyme scheme. His satires, also in verse, stem from Horace though they are in *terza rima*; they deal with the evils of court life as contrasted with the virtues of the country. In this particular form of satire Wyatt was also a pioneer. The fact that he returned to court as soon as he felt welcome there, and that his whole life was that of a courtier, does not invalidate the sincerity of the satires, however temporary the sentiment may have been.

Indeed, Wyatt would have been a better known poet had not his primary interests been in diplomacy and in the court. As it was, he had scant leisure for poetry except in periods of misfortune and retirement, and his output was very small. Though he was immensely influenced by Italian literature (his epigrams came from Serafino, as his sonnets from Petrarch), and to a slighter extent by Latin, he had his own individual voice, a voice of fervor, manly virtue, and sensitivity. His paraphrases of the Psalms are so far from translations that they take the original merely as a point of departure. His forthright standing up to his unkind love in some of his lyrics is more to modern taste than the abjectness of his sonnets—a legacy from medieval "courts of love" which was the fashion in Italian poetry in his day and which Wyatt—whom one pictures in vain as an impassioned lover, with his long black beard and bald head—made for a while the fashion in English poetry as well.

PRINCIPAL WORKS: Certayne Psalmes, etc., 1549; Songs and Sonettes (with Surrey) (Tottel's Miscellany) 1557; Works (G. F. Nott, ed.) 1816; Poetical Works (R. Bell, ed.) 1854 (G. Gilfillan, ed. 1858; G. Yeowell, ed. 1904).

ABOUT: Arber, E. The Surrey and Wyatt Anthology; Carpenter, F. I. English Lyric Poetry, 1500-1700; Foxwell, A. K. Study of Wyat's Poems; Gilfillan, G. Memoir *in* Poetical Works, 1858 ed.; Hangen, E. C. A Concordance to the Complete Poetical Works of Sir Thomas Wyatt; Simonds, W. E. Sir Thomas Wyatt and His Poems; Yeowell, G. Memoir *in* Poetical Works, 1904 ed.

WYCHERLEY, WILLIAM (1640?-January 1, 1716), dramatist, poet, was born at Clive, near Shrewsbury, Shropshire, the son of Daniel Wycherley—then teller to the exchequer, later chief steward of the Marquis of Winchester (and in that post suspected of peculation)—and of Bethia Shrimpton. His childhood being coeval with the civil wars, he was sent for his education to the west of France. There he became a protégé of the famous Madame de Montausier, who promptly converted "the little Huguenot" to the Roman Catholic faith. His father brought him back and entered him in Queen's College, Oxford, where he became an Anglican again. (Wycherley's various conversions and reconversions seem to have been more a matter of adapting himself to his environment than to have been caused by any deep religious convictions.) He left the university without a degree, and indeed seems never to have formally matriculated.

He had been entered in Lincoln's Inn since 1659, and now went into residence there, but the law received very little of his attention. The fashionable and profligate court of Charles II contained all he desired, and he soon became a favorite of the king's mistress, the Duchess of Cleveland. It was to her that he dedicated his first play, and the handsome young man with accommodating manners was a member of her inner circle. Some time during this period he spent a few months at sea, fighting the Dutch—not that he had any naval experience, but "all gentlemen must pack to sea." In 1674 he was made a captain in the Duke of Buckingham's regiment, but resigned his commission within a week. In 1678, his health being poor after a fever, he went to Montpelier for a while to recuperate, and Charles gave him £500 for his expenses. His four plays, which were all performed between 1671 and 1677, kept him in the public eye; only the second was a comparative failure. Finally Charles offered him a munificent position—he was to become tutor of the king's son, the Duke of Richmond, at a salary of £1500 a year—quite a recompense for a tutor even today—with a pension to follow when his charge no longer needed him.

All this Wycherley rashly threw away by a foolish marriage—and not a marriage justi-

Sir P. Lely

WILLIAM WYCHERLEY

fied by love or even passion, but a purely commercial gesture. In a bookshop he heard a young lady inquire for a copy of his *Plain Dealer*. He promptly introduced himself. She was the young and recent widow of the Earl of Drogheda, Laetitia Isabella, daughter of the Earl of Radnor; and she was an heiress. They were married about 1680, soon after they met, but the marriage was a secret one, so as not to jeopardize his position at court, where bachelorhood was expected of the favorites. Of course the secret came out. Wycherley never got his tutorship; he was banished in disgrace, and neither Charles nor the Duchess of Cleveland ever forgave him.

In exchange he got a wife who was ill tempered, accustomed to having her own way, dominating, and pathologically jealous. The only place he was allowed to go without her was to a tavern across the street from their home, and then he must keep the window open so she could be sure no women were in the party. She died a year later—and all she left him was debts. Her estate was tied up in litigation, and in the end Wycherley found himself in Fleet Prison as a debtor. He stayed there for seven years. Then James II ascended the throne, and oddly enough believed himself pictured as "Manly" in *The Plain Dealer* and was flattered—though few persons would have been. He got Wycherley out of prison, gave him a pension of £200, and offered to pay his debts. But Wycherley was ashamed to tell the king how very large they were, so the amount given him was quite inadequate. Finally his father, very reluctantly, paid off the remainder. By way of recompense to the king, Wycherley once more became a Roman Catholic, and remained in that church to the end; his father died soon after.

Wycherley never wrote another play. He did write a great deal of verse, which displayed none of the brilliant talent he had shown as a dramatist. One strange episode of his later years was his friendship (by correspondence) with Alexander Pope, who when it began was a boy of sixteen, fifty years Wycherley's junior. By way of showing off, Wycherley claimed that he too had written his first play, *Love in a Wood*, at nineteen, and all the others before he was twenty-five. It was pure boasting; there may have been rough early drafts of the plays, but their content reveals their later date— the influence of Etherege, for example. The friendship was ruffled, first by Pope's merciless revision of his friend's verses, then by his malicious reference to him in *An Essay on Criticism*, but they were reconciled eventually.

The other strange event of Wycherley's old age was his marriage to a young girl, Elizabeth Jackson, eleven days before he died at about seventy-six. He did this deliberately, to spite his nephew and heir, who he felt had ill treated him. The jointure the girl brought him let him die out of debt, and her inheritance from him left his nephew with a barren legacy on his hands. Wycherley made her promise she would never again marry an old man, and she obeyed; she married his young cousin, Thomas Shrimpton. Wycherley died in London, and was buried in St. Paul's, Covent Garden.

Gay and frivolous in his youth, self-seeking and cynical in his old age, Wycherley nevertheless had many virtues. He hated deceit and injustice, and he had a "tenderness of temper" which made his friends love him. And he was, in his last play at least, a true moralist, who castigated savagely the vices of his time. As Congreve put it: "Since the Plain-Dealer's scenes of manly rage, Not one has dared to lash this crying age." If he depicted heartless brutes, he showed that they were made so by the vice and hypocrisy of their age. He was indubitably coarse— *The Country-Wife* is one of the smuttiest plays ever written—but he was also witty, inventive, a skilful craftsman, and a master of brilliant and colloquial dialogue. His characters, particularly his minor characters, are full of life. He was a child of his era, a profligate old roué, and the fashion of the moment was his god; but Dryden loved him, Congreve admired him, and even Pope respected him. He belongs with Congreve and Vanbrugh in the front rank of Restoration drama.

PRINCIPAL WORKS: *Plays*: Love in a Wood or St. James's Park, 1671; The Gentleman Dancing-Master, 1673; The Country-Wife, 1675; The Plain Dealer, 1677; Dramatic Works (with Congreve, Farquhar, Vanbrugh) (L. Hunt, ed.) 1840; Plays (W. C. Ward, ed.) 1888. *Miscellaneous*: Poetical Epistles to the King and Duke, 1683; Miscellany Poems, 1704; Posthumous Works in Prose and Verse (R. Pack, ed.) 1728; Complete Works (M. Summer, ed.) 1924.

ABOUT: Cibber, C. Lives of the Poets; Connely, W. Brawny Wycherley, First Master in English Modern Comedy; Hazlitt, W. Lectures on the English Comic Writers; Klette, J. Wycherleys Leben und Dramatische Werke; Langbaine, G. An Account of the English Dramatic Poets; Pack, R. Memoir *in* Posthumous Works; Pepys, S. Diary; Perromat, C. William Wycherley, sa Vie et son Oeuvre; Perry, H. T. E. The Comic Spirit in Restoration Drama; Ward, A. W. History of English Dramatic Literature.

WYCLIFFE (Wiclif, Wyclif, Wiklif), JOHN (1320?-December 31, 1384), religious reformer, philosopher, author of religious works, was born in Ipreswel or Hipswell, near Richmond, Yorkshire. He may possibly (though probably not) have belonged to a branch of the ancient family of the lords of Wycliffe-on-the-Tees. They, in any event, had close connections with Balliol College, Oxford, and it was in this college that Wycliffe spent most of his life. He studied arts first, graduating B.A. and M.A., and received his doctorate of divinity in 1372. At some time after 1356 he had become master or warden of Balliol. This office he resigned when he was named prebend of Aust, in the collegiate church of Westbury-on-Trym, Worcestershire, in 1361. He was made vicar of Fillingham, Lincolnshire, in 1361. He resigned when he was given the living of Ludgershall, Buckinghamshire in 1368, which he exchanged for Lutterworth, Leicestershire in 1374. All these livings were more or less nonresident, and he remained

JOHN WYCLIFFE

at Oxford until he was forced to leave in 1382; he was all this time a fellow of Balliol, but was obliged to depend on church preferment for his livelihood.

Wycliffe's first writing was philosophical, an outgrowth of his lectures at Oxford. He was the last of the Platonic "realist" Schoolmen, opposed to the Aristotelian nominalists, and holding that general ideas have real being. In the list of Schoolmen he is known as "Doctor Evangelicus." There was no hint of his heresy or opposition to the papal power until he had been freed by his theological doctorate to preach and lecture on religion. Then in 1376 he lectured at Oxford on "civil dominion."

The actuating cause was the long dispute in England (with John of Gaunt as leader of the anti-papal party) about taxation by the church. At the Council of Bruges, in 1374, Wycliffe was one of the English delegates. In 1376 he was called before a convocation of bishops in London, and five papal bulls were issued against him. The support of Richard II saved him from further censure, but in 1378, at Lambeth, he was ordered no longer to preach the doctrines charged against him. Actually, up to this time, his heresies had been minor ones. He had long been engaged in controversy against the endowed orders of monks, though at first he was sympathetic with the mendicant friars. From about 1377 on, he had

trained and sent out as evangelists his "poor priests," mostly university men, but with some laymen among them, who preached in the vernacular. The usual result of such a movement was the establishment of still another monastic order, but the "poor priests" remained secular. As time went on, extremists and even fanatics appeared among them, who translated into action what Wycliffe had advanced as theory. It is in this sense that Wycliffe is the founder of the Lollards; actually, he himself was "no Wyclifite," and though he sympathized with the Peasants' Revolt in 1381, he had too exalted a regard for the king and the state to have countenanced all its objectives. The Lollards were primitive Communists, and he was not. John Ball, the Peasants' Revolt leader, claimed to be a disciple of Wycliffe, but actually he had been excommunicated while Wycliffe was still orthodox.

Wycliffe did, however, become more and more at odds with the church as time went on. This was the period of the papal schism, and when the Pope in Rome called a crusade against the Pope in Avignon, Wycliffe was outraged. From 1383 on, his former moderation and reserve left him, and he regarded the Pope as literally anti-Christ. Moreover, beginning in 1381 he had been attacking the doctrine of transubstantiation, until he denied altogether that the wine and wafer became the body and blood of Christ, calling it "a deceit and a blasphemous folly." The only reason he was not condemned as a heretic was that his opponents knew well his immense influence, and that it would only spread his ideas to make a martyr of him. But even John of Gaunt ordered him now to be silent.

The Bible itself, as with the later Lutherans, became the final test. Wycliffe had written impartially in Latin and English; now his supporters began their famous translation of the Bible from the Vulgate into English. It is far from true that this is the first English Bible, though it is the first complete one. There are two versions, quite unlike each other in style, and Wycliffe himself translated only the Gospels and perhaps some other portions of the New Testament. In England, the Lollards who claimed him as their master were finally crushed; but in Bohemia his pure doctrine became the creed of Huss, and through the Hussite influence on Luther and Calvin, Wycliffe may be called the grandfather of the Protestant Reformation.

He himself was to his last day a Roman Catholic priest. In 1382, at the "Earthquake Council," he was suspended from his scholastic duties at Oxford and his teachings, especially on transubstantiation, were formally condemned. There were riots, and there were heated protests from Oxford, but Wycliffe left the university and retired to Lutterworth, where he devoted himself to writing. There in 1382 he suffered a paralytic stroke, followed by another, nearly two years later, while he was celebrating mass. His death followed a few days after. He was buried at Lutterworth, but in 1415 the Council of Nice ordered his body disinterred and burned. It was not until 1428 that this order was carried out, and his ashes were thrown into the nearby River Swift.

Under the cumbersome weight of scholastic dryness, with its continuous citing of authorities, Wycliffe's writing reveals a strong mind and a potent personality. Little is known of him as a person, except that he was hot-tempered but knew how to discipline his temper, and that he was so spare as to embarrass him, since his leanness was thought to result from asceticism, and that was one of the monkish practices he condemned. He had no purely literary aspirations, and his style is simple. It is highly individual, however, and unmistakably his own; this is not true of the Wycliffe Bible, because he actually translated so little of it. Even his Latin is English in form and spirit, and he ended by writing in English altogether. (His work, of course, was all in manuscript; none of it was printed until 1525.) He owed much to William of Ockham (though Ockham was a nominalist), and even more to Grosseteste and to Richard Fitz Ralph. He knew no Greek; but he had studied natural science in so far as it existed in his day. He is in a way, as a writer as well as in theology, a bridge between the Middle Ages and the Modern Age, an anticipation of the Renaissance.

PRINCIPAL WORKS: Trialogus, 1525 (G. V. Lechler, ed. 1869); Wyclif's Wicket, 1546; The Wycliffite Versions of the Holy Bible (J. For-

shall and F. Madden, eds.) 1850; Select English Works (T. Arnold, ed.) 1869-71; English Works of Wycliffe hitherto unprinted (F. D. Matthew, ed.) 1880; Polemical Tracts (R. Buddensieg, ed.) 1883; Latin Works (R. L. Poole et al. eds.) 1885-1905.

ABOUT: Bale, J. Scriptorum Illustrium Majoris Britannia Catalogus; Buddensieg, R. Johann Wiclif und Seine Zeit; Cadman, S. P. The Three Religious Leaders of Oxford and Their Works; Carrick, J. C. Wycliffe and the Lollards; Foxe, J. Acts and Monuments; Innis, G. F. Wycliffe: the Morning Star; Lechler, G. V. John Wiclif and His English Precursors; Lewis, J. Life and Sufferings of J. Wiclif; Loserth, J. Wiclif and Hus; Morley, J. English Writers; Poole, R. L. Wycliffe and the Movements for Reform; Rogers, J. E. T. Historical Gleanings; Russell, B. History of Western Philosophy; Sergeant, L. John Wycliffe, Last of the Schoolmen and First of the English Reformers; Vaughan, R. John de Wycliffe; Workman, H. B. John Wycliffe, a Study of the English Mediaeval Church.

WYNTOUN, ANDREW of (1350?-1420?), Scottish chronicler, was a canon regular of St. Andrews, where, in 1413, the first Scottish university was established. He was elected prior of St. Serf's Inch in Loch Leven, a monastery related to St. Andrews.

About 1422, at the request of Sir John of Wemyss, he began work on a metrical chronicle of Scots history, beginning before creation with a history of angels, and therefore called the *Original Chronicle*. The work is in nine books, ending with the beginning of the reign of James I in 1406. The material of the earlier part is neither accurate nor important, but commencing with his own period, Wyntoun's industrious gathering of facts and anecdotes, his interest in detail, and his accuracy, give his chronicle great historical importance.

He was not an inventive nor creative poet, but his style is fresh and animated, his language pure, and his versification smooth. Occasionally he indulged in a poetic description of a scene, and it was said that he described battle scenes so vividly that if you stood on the battleground with his chronicle in hand, you could reconstruct the scene in detail. Among the legends he related, that of Macbeth and the three weird sisters is especially well told.

Wyntoun's chronicle has great philological value as one of the two extant examples of the vernacular known as "Early Scots," the literary language of Teutonic Scotland. The other example is the chronicle of John of Fordun, and these two writers have been called the "fathers of Scottish history."

PRINCIPAL WORK: Original Chronicle, c. 1422.

ABOUT: Amours, F. J. Biographical preface to Original Chronicle of Andrew of Wyntoun; Laing, D. Series of Scottish Historians; Scottish Review, 1897.

YOUNG, ARTHUR (September 11, 1741-April 20, 1820), agricultural theorist, travel writer, was born in London, the son of Arthur Young, rector of Bradfield, Suffolk, and of Anna Coussemaker. He was educated at a school in Lavenham, and was a markedly precocious youth. His father, however, apprenticed him in 1758 to a mercantile firm in Lynn, with a view to making a bookkeeper of him. He spent more time in social enjoyment than he did in business, and to finance his pleasures he wrote political pamphlets and four forgotten novels. His father died opportunely and he rushed back to London, where he established a monthly magazine, the *Universal Museum*, which, as Dr. Johnson warned him it would do, lasted only a few months. He was obliged to return to Bradfield, where his mother gave him one of her farms to work. From 1763 to almost the end of his life he was a farmer, constantly seeking more lucrative farms, experimenting, writing (too soon, he acknowledged) on agricultural theory. After his mother's death in 1785 he lived on and worked the home farm in Bradfield which had been her dowry. All his journeys before this, except in Ireland, were undertaken to find a better farm; he worked himself to death but he was always in debt, and frequently thought of emigrating to America. But from his hardships came the finest English writing on agriculture, which did for farming what the industrial revolution had done for industry.

In 1765 Young married Martha Allen, and they were unhappy from the beginning. They quarreled until she died in 1815. But he loved his son and his three daughters. He adored his youngest daughter, who died at thirteen, and (like his mother before him, when his sister died) he spent the rest of his life in grief and mourning, ending as a religious fanatic. Until the end, however, he kept up his public duties. To eke out a living, he had reported debates in Parliament for the *Morning Post* in 1773; in 1777 he went to Ireland as agent for Lord Kingsborough in County Cork, but returned in two years because of dissension with his employer's family; and in 1793 Pitt made him secretary of the newly organized Board of Agriculture. This post he kept (spending week-ends on his farm) until he went blind from cataracts; an operation failed when a description of the plight of agriculture caused him to weep. He died in London, of stone, and was buried in Bradfield.

Young was widely recognized for his pioneer work; he corresponded with Washington and Lafayette, became a Fellow of the Royal Society in 1774, and was an honorary member of numerous foreign academies. His books were translated into French, German, and Russian. Catherine the Great decorated him, and George III ("Farmer George") made a pet of him, and even contributed (under his gardener's name) to the *Annals of Agriculture*, which Young edited from 1784 to 1809.

As a political theorist he was negligible (he was an isolationist and "little Englander"), but he was a shrewd observer, and he had the inestimable advantage of being in France, with a keen eye to note what happened, just before and at the beginning of the Revolution. With the exception of the *Tour in Ireland* (for which his notes were lost), his books are alive with vivid

G. Dance, 1794

ARTHUR YOUNG

vignettes, and he wrote in the racy, forthright style that might have been expected of a restless, high-spirited, and emotional man gifted with a sharp intelligence.

PRINCIPAL WORKS: The Theatre of the Present War in North America, 1758; Reflections on the Present State of Affairs at Home and Abroad, 1759; A Farmer's Letters to the People of England, 1767; A Six Weeks' Tour Through the Southern Counties of England and Wales, 1768; Letters Concerning the Present State of the French Nation, 1769; A Course of Experimental Agriculture, 1770; The Farmer's Tour Through the East of England, 1770-71; A Six Weeks' Tour Through the North of England, 1771; Political Essays Concerning the Present State of the British Empire, 1772; Political Arithmetic, 1774; Tour in Ireland, 1780; The Example of France a Warning to England, 1793; Travels . . . with a View of Ascertaining the Cultivation, Wealth, Resources, and National Prosperity of . . . France, 1794; An Idea of the Present State of France, 1795; Enquiry into the State of the Public Mind Amongst the Lower Classes of England, 1798; Baxteriana, 1815; Oweniana, 1817; The Autobiography of Arthur Young, with Selections from His Correspondence (M. Betham-Edwards, ed.) 1898.

ABOUT: Martinengo-Cesaresco, E. L. H. Lombard Studies; Stephen, L. Studies of a Biographer; Young, A. Autobiography.

YOUNG, EDWARD (June, 1683-April 5, 1765), poet, dramatist, satirist, was born in Upham, near Winchester, the son of Edward Young, rector of Upham, later dean of Salisbury and chaplain to William and Mary. He was educated at Winchester, then in 1702 entered New College, Oxford, soon migrating to Corpus Christi, and in 1708 to All Souls, where he obtained a law fellowship. He received a B.C.L. degree in 1714, D.C.L. in 1719.

Young's whole life was a search for patrons and preferment, and fame and wealth came to him only when it was too late. He was not above using devious means or soliciting and accepting the favors of profligate men of wealth and station. In a sense, all his writing stems from the disappointments of his life, and he was given to complaint and lamentation to an extent that wearies the modern reader. Yet his disappointments were real, and though it is hard to see why he felt himself *entitled* to preferment and benefactions, that was a common attitude among men of talent in his day. There was one rather unsavory lawsuit, in 1749, in which he claimed large annuities from the Duke of Wharton, and gained a partial victory. As Pope said, Young had "more genius than common sense," and

After J. Highmore
EDWARD YOUNG

"passed a foolish youth, the sport of peers and poets." Fielding and Swift (whom he met in Ireland in 1717) both ridiculed him unmercifully. But Richardson and Colley Cibber were both his faithful and admiring friends, and Dr. Johnson with his rough kindness remarked that "with all his defects he was a man of genius and a poet."

Some time in his forties—the exact date is not known—Young, despairing of worldly success, took holy orders. In 1728 he was chaplain to George II—his adulation of royalty is among his least pleasant traits— and in 1730 he received the living of Welwyn, Oxfordshire, in the gift of All Souls. Welwyn was thenceforth his home. In 1731, at forty-eight, he married Lady Elizabeth Lee, a widow with one daughter, herself the daughter of the Earl of Lichfield. In 1736 he went to the Riviera with his stepdaughter, who had tuberculosis. She died in France, her husband soon followed her, and in 1741 Young's wife died. His natural melancholy became settled gloom. The end-result was *The Complaint*, usually known as *Night Thoughts*.

It is difficult to understand why this dreary didactic poem swept Europe, why Robespierre slept with it under his pillow, Klopstock thought it finer than anything of Milton's, Diderot and Mme. de Stael worshiped its author. But so it was, and Young now had all the money he wanted and universal fame.

But nature had formed him for sorrow; his beloved wife was dead (it is said that he never smiled after her death), and he was estranged from their only son, whom he forgave only on his deathbed. He spent his last quarter century in "dignified retirement" at Welwyn, but not entirely out of the world, for he entertained his friends and continued to write. In 1761 he succeeded Stephen Hales as "clerk of the closet" to the Princess Dowager—a sinecure office which probably superseded the royal pension he had received from 1726. A grim spinster named Hallows kept house for him, and alienated his friends by her extreme influence over the old man. He died in Welwyn at almost eighty-two.

In his younger days Young had had two tragedies—mixtures of bombast and artificial sententiousness—produced at Drury Lane. *The Revenge*, on an Othello-like theme, had some success. After *Night Thoughts* had made him the idol of the devout, he had a third tragedy produced, but feeling that it was a bit unbecoming to his clerical position and his established reputation for piety, he gave all the profits to the Society for the Propagation of the Gospel.

Young's satires often have bite, though as often they are labored and heavy. He was probably the worst craftsman among recognized poets; his rhyme, his metrics, and his phraseology all were bad. As George Saintsbury said, he was "most singularly lacking in art." Yet—besides exactly touching the spirit of his time—he had a real gift for epigram, which emerged occasionally amid the sentimentalism and the platitudinousness. Some of his phrases are worthy of Pope—and have sometimes been ascribed to him. He admired Pope as an artist, but disagreed heartily with his philosophy.

Young, who was overwhelmingly popular in his lifetime, is practically unreadable now. Yet something has survived—"procrastination is the thief of time," "tired nature's sweet restorer," "how blessings brighten as they take their flight," "man wants but little, nor that little long," "death loves a shining mark"—these, and others, are all from Young.

His extravagant odes to the great whom he was courting—Whig and Tory alike, even when he was an intimate of the Whig circle around Addison—are so dripping with flattery that they are more absurd than they are disgusting; they reveal only too plainly the seeker after patronage, maladroitly advertising himself, and lamenting loudly when the effects were little or none. Just what he expected as his just deserts it is hard to say —a deanery, someone has suggested; perhaps even the laureateship. He stood for Parliament, and was beaten. He failed, for the most part, as a dramatist. His satires, though sometimes apt, were too obviously grounded in disgruntlement. By the time he received all and more than he had dreamed of, the habit of gloom was too strong to break—and besides, he was old and alone. One cannot help feeling that the true pathos of his life was that he did not study and cultivate his undeniable gift, instead of expending most of his energy in trying to pull strings.

PRINCIPAL WORKS: Epistle . . . to Lord Lansdoune, 1713; A Poem on the Last Day, 1714; The Force of Religion, or Vanquish'd Love, 1714; On the late Queen's Death, and His Majesty's Accession, 1714; A Paraphrase on Part of the Book of Job, 1719; Busiris, King of Egypt (tragedy) 1719; A Letter to Mr. Tickell [on] the Death of Addison, 1719; The Revenge (tragedy) 1721; The Universal Passion, 1725 (as The Love of Fame, *in* Seven Satires, 1728); The Instalment, 1726; Cynthio, 1727; Ocean: an Ode, 1728; A Vindication of Providence, 1728; Imperium Pelagi, A Naval Lyrick, 1730; Two Epistles to Mr. Pope Concerning the Authors of the Age, 1730; The Foreign Address . . . . in the Character of a Sailor, 1734; Works, 1741; The Complaint, or Night Thoughts on Life, Death, and Immortality, 1742-45; Reflections on the Public Situation of the Kingdom, 1745; The Brothers (tragedy) 1753; The Centaur Not Fabulous (prose) 1754; Conjectures on Original Composition (prose) 1759; Resignation, 1762; Works, 1757-78; Poetical Works (J. Mitford, ed.) 1834.

ABOUT: Eliot, G. (Cross, M. E.) Essays; Kind, J. L. Edward Young in Germany; Mitford, J. Life, *in* Poetical Works; Saintsbury, G. History of English Prosody; Shelley, H. C. The Life and Letters of Edward Young; Thomas, W. Le Poète Edward Young.